Watergate:

CHRONOLOGY OF A CRISIS

Volume 2

June 1974

CONGRESSIONAL QUARTERLY

1414 22nd STREET, N.W., WASHINGTON, D.C.

Congressional Quarterly Inc.

Congressional Quarterly Inc., an editorial research service and publishing company, serves clients in the fields of news, education, business and government. It combines specific coverage of Congress, government and politics by Congressional Quarterly with the more general subject range of an affiliated service, Editorial Research Reports.

Congressional Quarterly was founded in 1945 by Henrietta and Nelson Poynter. Its basic periodical publication was and still is the CQ *Weekly Report,* mailed to clients every Saturday. A cumulative index is published quarterly.

The CQ *Almanac,* a compendium of legislation for one session of Congress, is published every spring. *Congress and the Nation* is published every four years as a record of government for one presidential term.

Congressional Quarterly also publishes paperback books on public affairs. These include the twice-yearly *Guide to Current American Government* and such recent titles as *Impeachment and the U.S. Congress* and *The Middle East—U.S. Policy, Israel, Oil and the Arabs.*

CQ Direct Research is a consulting service which performs contract research and maintains a reference library and query desk for the convenience of clients.

Editorial Research Reports covers subjects beyond the specialized scope of Congressional Quarterly. It publishes reference material on foreign affairs, business, education, cultural affairs, national security, science and other topics of news interest. Service to clients includes a 6,000-word report four times a month, bound and indexed semi-annually. Editorial Research Reports publishes paperback books in its fields of coverage. Founded in 1923, the service merged with Congressional Quarterly in 1956.

Political Editor: Mercer Cross
Watergate: Chronology of a Crisis, Volume II, **was compiled by Janice L. Goldstein.**
Contributors: Susan A. Bischoff, F. Rhodes Cook, Mary Cohn, Prudence Crewdson, Bruce F. Freed, Mary Link, Carolyn Mathiasen, John L. Moore, Warden Moxley, Peg O'Hara, Daniel Rapoport, Pat Ruck, Donald Smith, Margaret Thompson, Jane Wales, Elder Witt.
Index: Diane Huffman, Janice L. Goldstein
Cover design: Howard Chapman, art director. Cover photos: Wide World, Newsweek, White House. Production Supervisor: Richard C. Young. Assistant Production Supervisor: Richard Butler.

Library of Congress
Cataloging in Publication Data

Congressional Quarterly Inc.
    Watergate: Chronology of a Crisis.

    1. Watergate Affair, 1972-   I. Diamond Robert A., ed.
II. Title.
E859.C62 1973   364.1'32'0973   73-12792
ISBN 0-87187-059-2

Table of Contents

Each chapter includes the entire Congressional Quarterly *Weekly Report* coverage of a single week's Watergate developments. The dates appearing in the table of contents and at the beginning of each chapter represent the publication date of each *Weekly Report*. A detailed *Index* is at the back of the book to further isolate facts, names and incidents.

PREFACE

In his first inaugural address Richard M. Nixon told a troubled American people, who had experienced a rising tide of violence in 1968 capped by the senseless assassinations of Martin Luther King and Robert Kennedy, that they were a people "rich in goods, but ragged in spirit.... To a crisis of the spirit," he offered "an answer of the spirit."

The great irony and tragedy of the Nixon presidency is that the man who had pitched his appeal to a call for "law and order," who had called for moral rectitude and had offered as a credential the solid and simple virtues of his middle-western mother, has presided over an administration that has been implicated in an unparalleled series of crimes and misconduct in public office.

The President's role in the Watergate scandal was unclear and yet to be tested in the historic impeachment proceedings which commenced in the House Judiciary Committee in the second week of May. But regardless of the judgment Congress returned on Nixon, or whether he resigned his high office to end the national ordeal, it was clear that his presidency presented a moral and political crisis unprecedented in American history.

Watergate poses an issue much broader than the question repeatedly asked by Sen. Howard H. Baker Jr. (R Tenn.) during the Senate Watergate hearings in the summer of 1973. It is not simply what Richard Nixon knew and when he knew it. It extends to public confidence in the American political system. For at the very time that the President plummeted to record lows in the public opinion polls, the surveys have demonstrated an equally alarming decline in the people's trust in other elected officials and in other institutions of government.

Watergate was therefore, not merely "a cancer growing around the presidency," as John Dean described it to Nixon; it was a disease that afflicted the entire body politic. Watergate posed the two key questions a democratic people must be able to answer affirmatively for democracy to survive: can its leaders be trusted and does the system work?

About This Book

In August 1973, Congressional Quarterly published *Watergate: Chronology of a Crisis, Vol. I.* That book detailed the initial unfolding of the Watergate scandal and focused on the activities of the Senate Select Committee on Presidential Campaign Activities. A major portion of the book was devoted to the hearings conducted by that committee before a nationwide television audience during the summer of 1973. It was during those hearings that the nation first learned of the existence of White House tapes. On July 16, 1973, former White House aide Alexander P. Butterfield told the committee that a taping system had had been installed which recorded conversations in the President's White House oval office, as well as in the President's separate office in the adjacent Executive Office Building. *(Vol. I, p. 194; this volume, p. xi)*

One week after Butterfield's testimony, the committee and the Office of the Special Prosecutor initiated proceedings to obtain certain White House tapes. *(Vol. I, p. 208; see p. 337 of this volume for a chronology of the ensuing and continuing battle to obtain White House tapes.)*

Volume I concluded with the completion in early August of the first round of Senate committee hearings and President Nixon's Aug. 15, 1973, speech responding to damaging testimony presented during the hearings.

Volume II. This book continues the format set in Volume I. Each week's Watergate developments constitute a separate chapter and are based entirely on Congressional Quarterly's *Weekly Report* coverage. The dates appearing in boldface type in the table of contents and at the beginning of each chapter represent the publication date of each *Weekly Report* since Aug. 25, 1973. For reference convenience within each chapter appears a separate "Week's Watergate Chronology." *(See, for example, pp. 15, 20, 27)*

An Overview. A comprehensive analysis of the events of the past ten months leading up to publication of the transcripts appears in the accompanying introduction *(p. x-xvi)*. The introduction examines these important themes: the continued erosion of political support for the President and his efforts to stem the tide, the shift in the focus of congressional activity from the Senate Watergate Committee to the impeachment inquiry by the House Judiciary Committee, the controversy over the tapes and the role of the Office of Special Prosecutor under Archibald Cox and Leon Jaworski. A chronology of key events appears on pages xii-xiii.

Transcripts. The appendix contains summaries and excerpts from the White House transcripts covering the following topics: the administration and Congress *(p. 345)*, Nixon's knowledge of Watergate *(p. 348)*, "Hush Money" and clemency *(p. 354)*, the relationship between Assistant Attorney General Henry E. Petersen and the White House *(p. 361)*, John Dean's downfall *(p. 367)* and the President's press relations *(p. 375)*.

The full texts of three transcripts are included: Sept. 15, 1972 *(p. 380)*; March 13, 1973 *(p. 384)* and March 21, 1973 *(p. 394)*. In addition, the full texts of the White House summary of the transcripts and the President's April 29, 1974, speech are included. *(p. 412, 408)* A directory of persons mentioned in the transcripts appears on page 394.

Robert A. Diamond
Book Service Editor
June 1974

INTRODUCTION: TEN MONTHS OF SETBACKS FOR NIXON

During the period from the late summer of 1973 through the spring of 1974—the time span covered in this book—Richard M. Nixon was losing his hold on the presidency. Repeatedly, he appealed to the public to "put Watergate behind us" and turn toward the more constructive business of government. But it was too late. Watergate, and all the word had come to imply, had engulfed the Nixon administration by the late spring of 1974. There seemed to be no way to put it behind.

At stake by mid-May was Nixon's presidency itself. For the first time in 106 years, an American President was going through formal impeachment proceedings.

Apart from the constitutional formalities of impeachment, Nixon was under intensifying pressure to resign. Public-opinion polls showed his popularity to be the lowest of any president's since Harry Truman's 23 years earlier, during the Korean war. More and more former supporters in Nixon's Republican Party, both on and off Capitol Hill, were demanding his resignation or impeachment. The editorial clamor of a previously loyal press was rising.

Faithful to his traditions, the President defied his opponents in this latest and most important of all the crises that had periodically beset him throughout his remarkable 28-year political career. He made clear time and again that he had no intention of resigning. He did intend, he said, to fight impeachment through the House of Representatives and, if necessary, through the Senate, no matter how many members deserted him.

Whether Nixon could succeed in the end was problematical. If he did not, there would be irony in his failure, because his own voluntary actions would contribute to his removal from office. He had made public his tax records and intimate details of his private financial affairs. He had released transcripts of tape-recorded conversations with his White House assistants. He had made speech after speech in his own defense.

But all his efforts to restore confidence in his presidency seemed to boomerang. The President who had made so much of his historic overtures for world peace was threatened with the ignominious distinction of becoming the first President to be impeached and convicted.

The Transcripts. Nixon's final, fatal miscalculation might have been his decision to make public on April 30, 1974, more than 1,200 pages of edited transcripts of 46 tape-recorded conversations about Watergate involving him and his staff. "The materials I make public tomorrow," said Nixon in a nationally televised speech April 29, "will provide all the additional evidence needed to get Watergate behind us, and to get it behind us now."

What the President apparently did not anticipate was the overwhelmingly negative response that would greet the transcripts' release. "I realize these transcripts will provide grist for many sensational stories in the press," he said. "Parts will seem to be contradictory with one another, and parts will be in conflict with some of the testimony given in the Senate Watergate committee hearings."

He was right. Careful reading of the transcripts revealed many contradictions and raised many questions. Moreover, the submission of the transcripts to the House Judiciary Committee failed to satisfy committee members who had sought the actual tapes.

As important as the actual contents of the transcripts, however, were the insights they gave the American people into the man they had put in the White House for a second term and the manner in which their President conducted himself in private. The transcripts, even as edited by Nixon, gave a revealing portrait of a man willing to bargain for his political survival, conferring with his advisers in an atmosphere of suspicion and hostility toward real or imagined enemies. The conversations were sprinkled liberally with profanity and obscenity, much of it deleted from the transcripts. And the frequent notations of "unintelligible" often left enigmas about the true meaning of the conversations.

No one could accurately predict the course of events after the transcripts had become instant paperback best-sellers. But then no one could have predicted, either, that an event described by the White House as a "second-rate burglary" almost two years earlier would bring a presidency to the threshold of collapse.

One certainty was that events would have taken a different course if the existence of the White House taping system had not been brought to light inadvertently by a former member of Nixon's staff. The revelation by Alexander P. Butterfield to the Senate select Waterate committee in July 1973 opened up the scandal to a scrutiny that otherwise might not have been possible. *(Box, next page)*

The Senate Investigation

Even before the existence of the tapes became known, however, the complex tangle labeled as Watergate had enveloped all three branches of the American government. The name, as every newspaper reader and television watcher had long since learned, came from the office-hotel complex in Washington, D.C., that housed the Democratic National Committee headquarters burglarized on June 17, 1972.

Eleven months to the day later, on May 17, 1973, the Senate Select Committee on Presidential Campaign Activities opened its public hearings into Watergate. North Carolina Democrat Sam J. Ervin Jr., the committee chairman, and the six other members of the committee became familiar faces on the nation's television screens. So did the parade of witnesses who came before the committee—and the cameras—throughout the summer to answer questions about their roles in the break-in and its coverup.

The summer's most important witness was a smooth-faced, flat-voiced young man named John W. Dean III. He had been Nixon's White House counsel. At the committee hearings, he became the President's chief adversary, accusing him of complicity in covering up the break-in. Nearly a year after Dean's testimony, the accuracy of his damning statements remained one of the great riddles of Watergate. *(Vol. I, p. 151)*

Like other episodes in the unfolding Watergate drama, the electronically transmitted activities of the Senate committee had a limited life. The hearings were recessed early in August, when Congress went on vacation. Much

Discovery of the Tapes

The existence of President Nixon's tapes relating to the Watergate scandal became known through circumstances that, taken individually, were relatively minor at the time.

In his opening 245-page statement to the Senate Watergate committee on June 25, 1973, former presidential counsel John W. Dean III publicly aired his suspicions that at least some of his conversations with Nixon had been recorded.

Describing an April 15 meeting with the President, Dean said that "the President almost from the outset began asking me a number of leading questions, which made me think the conversation was being taped and that a record was being made to protect himself."

Later in this meeting, Dean said, "The most interesting thing that happened during the conversation was, very near the end, he got up out of his chair, went behind his chair to the corner of the Executive Office Building office and in a barely audible tone said to me, he was probably foolish to have discussed (Watergate conspirator E. Howard) Hunt's clemency with (former presidential special counsel Charles W.) Colson."

But it was not until 18 days later—on Friday, July 13, 1973—that four committee staff members obtained the dramatic confirmation that there was, indeed, a White House recording system.

Donald G. Sanders, deputy minority counsel, asked the question that elicited the information from Federal Aviation Administrator Alexander P. Butterfield, former deputy assistant to the President.

Sanders told Congressional Quarterly that this was the question as he recalled it: "John Dean has testified that at the end of one conversation with the President he was taken to the side of the office and addressed by the President in a very low voice. Do you know of any basis for the implications in Dean's testimony that conversations in the President's office are recorded?"

Butterfield remained calm but was clearly troubled, Sanders said. "I was hoping you fellows wouldn't ask me that," he quoted Butterfield as saying. But Butterfield went on to disclose that Nixon had the taping system installed "for historical purposes" in 1970.

Sanders asked the question after Butterfield had been interrogated for three hours by Scott Armstrong, a committee investigator, about Nixon's office routine. At one point, Armstrong showed Butterfield a log by presidential counsel J. Fred Buzhardt Jr. containing detailed summaries of the Nixon-Dean conversations.

"I felt a growing certainty during the interview that Buzhardt's summaries were much more specific than if they were merely recollections," Sanders recalled.

Called as the next committee witness, Butterfield publicly told of the tapes on July 16. But the conversation that triggered the tapes' discovery apparently was not recorded. In response to subpoenas, the White House later said that the tape ran out in that office prior to the April 15 Nixon-Dean meeting.

work, public and otherwise, remained to be done by the committee. Still to be investigated were two other aspects of Watergate: sabotage and espionage—the "dirty tricks" of the scandal—and the financing of the 1972 presidential campaign.

When Congress returned in September 1973, the hearings reopened before a waning audience. Saboteur Donald H. Segretti and others who testified about dirty tricks lacked the drawing power of earlier witnesses, and much of what they said had been published earlier.

The work of the Senate committee's investigative staff nevertheless went on, mostly outside the public view. Testimony continued to be taken, and staff members formulated legislative recommendations, as prescribed by the legislation establishing the committee. Originally, the deadline for submission of the committee's final report was Feb. 28, 1974. That date was extended three months, to May 28, and there was talk of waiting even longer to turn in the final report to the Senate.

Differences arose within the committee and its staff early in 1974 over the feasibility of resuming public hearings. The idea was discarded when members agreed that further hearings might interfere with court trials of former administration officials and with the impeachment investigation of the House Judiciary Committee.

From Ervin to Rodino

The House committee and its previously little-known chairman, Peter W. Rodino Jr., a New Jersey Democrat, assumed new importance after the shattering events known as the "Saturday night massacre" focused attention on impeachment. The date of those events was Oct. 20, 1973. The reverberations that followed them included a surge of demands for Nixon's resignation or impeachment. The House is, under the Constitution, the body that takes the lead in impeachment proceedings. (Box p. xvi)

Since Butterfield's disclosure of the White House tapes, the Senate Watergate committee and the presidentially appointed Watergate special prosecutor, Archibald Cox, had been trying to get their hands on the tapes. The White House had resisted. Two levels of federal courts had supported the special prosecutor's demands, and the matter appeared to be headed toward a showdown before the Supreme Court.

It did not go that far. Instead of forcing a showdown, the President and his lawyers offered Cox what they described as a compromise. Their arguments up to that time had been based on the principle of presidential confidentiality, the right of a chief executive to keep his private conversations to himself. Faced with an adverse appeals court decision, Nixon decided to turn over written summaries of the tapes to Sen. John C. Stennis (D Miss.), who would verify them against the actual tapes and then give the summaries to both the special prosecutor and the Ervin committee.

As part of the compromise, Nixon ordered Cox to cease further judicial attempts to obtain data on presidential conversations. Cox rejected what he considered a limitation on his investigative authority.

His defiance cost him his job and ignited what a leading presidential adviser described as a "firestorm." When Cox spurned the compromise, Nixon ordered Attorney General Elliot L. Richardson to fire him. Richardson

(Continued on p. xiv)

Chronology of Major Watergate Developments ...

Aug. 22, 1973. In his first press conference in five months, President Nixon repeated his refusal to give up the tapes of White House conversations sought by the Senate Watergate investigating committee and the Watergate special prosecutor. *(p. 1)*

Nixon's attorney, Charles Alan Wright, and Special Prosecutor Archibald Cox presented arguments before U.S. District Judge John J. Sirica on Cox's subpoena of nine White House tapes. *(p. 9)*

Aug. 29. Sirica ordered Nixon to turn the tapes over to him for a decision on their use by the Watergate grand jury. White House spokesmen said the President would refuse. *(p. 13)*

Sept. 4. A Los Angeles, Calif., grand jury indicted John D. Ehrlichman, Egil Krogh Jr., David R. Young and G. Gordon Liddy for the 1971 break-in at the office of Dr. Lewis Fielding, Daniel Ellsberg's psychiatrist. *(p. 20, 30)*

Sept. 6. White House lawyers appealed Sirica's tapes ruling to the U.S. Court of Appeals. *(p. 20)*

Sept. 26. The second phase of public hearings before the Senate Watergate committee, on political sabotage, opened after a congressional recess. *(p. 40)*

Oct. 12. The U.S. Court of Appeals upheld Sirica's ruling that Nixon should surrender the Watergate tapes. *(p. 57)*

Oct. 17. Sirica rejected the Senate Watergate committee's suit for access to White House tapes on grounds that the court lacked jurisdiction. *(p. 60)*

Oct. 19. Nixon proposed a compromise on the tapes issue: He would give Sirica a statement of the tapes' contents prepared under the supervision of Sen. John C. Stennis (D Miss.). Cox, who was ordered by Nixon to seek no further presidential tapes or documents as part of the bargain, said he could not comply. *(p. 75)*

Oct. 20. Attorney General Elliot L. Richardson and Deputy Attorney General William D. Ruckelshaus resigned rather than fire Cox for rejecting Nixon's proposal. Solicitor General Robert H. Bork became acting attorney general and fired Cox. *(p. 69)*

Oct. 23. White House attorney Wright announced in court that Nixon would comply with the tapes subpoena. *(p. 75)*

Oct. 26. Nixon pledged at a news conference that Bork would appoint a new special prosecutor who would have "total cooperation" from the executive branch. He attacked press coverage of the Watergate scandals as "outrageous, vicious, distorted." *(p. 112)*

Oct. 31. White House attorney J. Fred Buzhardt revealed in court that two of the nine subpoenaed tapes did not exist. *(p. 92)*

Nov. 1. Nixon appointed Leon Jaworski to succeed Cox as Watergate special prosecutor. *(p. 111)*

Nov. 7. The Senate Watergate committee began the third and final phase of its inquiry, on campaign financing. *(p. 119)*

Nov. 9. Judge Sirica sentenced six of the seven original Watergate defendants to terms of 2½ to eight years in prison. *(p. 117)*

Nov. 12. Nixon submitted a statement to Sirica explaining why two of the subpoenaed tapes did not exist and offering to provide the court with his own handwritten notes of the two conversations. *(p. 139)*

Nov. 17. Nixon vigorously asserted his innocence of wrongdoing during an hour-long televised question-and-answer session with members of the Associated Press Managing Editors Association near Orlando, Fla. *(p. 148)*

Nov. 21. White House counsel Buzhardt announced in court that one of the subpoenaed tapes contained an 18½-minute gap. *(p. 141)*

Nov. 26. The White House turned over to Judge Sirica the existing subpoenaed tapes and related materials, along with a list of claims of executive privilege over portions of the materials. *(p. 161)*

Nixon's personal secretary, Rose Mary Woods, testified that she had accidently caused the 18½-minute gap while transcribing the tapes on Oct. 1. The next day she modified her testimony to say she could have been responsible for no more than five minutes of the gap. *(p. 160)*

Nov. 27. The Senate Watergate committee voted to suspend its hearings on campaign financing until early 1974. *(p. 162)*

Nov. 29. Dwight L. Chapin, Nixon's former appointments secretary, was indicted for lying about his alleged knowledge of 1972 political sabotage activities. He pleaded not guilty Dec. 7. *(p. 160)*

Nov. 30. Egil Krogh Jr., former head of the White House investigative unit called the "plumbers," pleaded guilty to federal charges for his role in the 1971 burglary of the office of Daniel Ellsberg's psychiatrist. The California charges and a federal perjury charge were dropped as a result. *(p. 160)*

Dec. 8. Nixon released a series of documents on his personal finances, including income tax returns for 1969-72. He asked the Joint Committee on Internal Revenue Taxation to rule on his claimed deductions for donation of personal papers and his failure to pay capital gains tax on a land sale. *(p. 181)*

Dec. 11. Senate Democratic leaders decided to delay action indefinitely on a bill to grant the courts power to appoint a special Watergate prosecutor. *(p. 176)*

Dec. 12. The Joint Committee on Internal Revenue Taxation decided to investigate all aspects of Nixon's tax returns, not just the matters he named. *(p. 180)*

Dec. 19. The Senate Watergate investigating committee issued three subpoenas covering more than 500 tapes and documents relating to a wide range of administrative activities on the White House. *(p. 183)*

Dec. 20. John M. Doar was appointed as the House Judiciary Committee's chief counsel for its impeachment inquiry. *(p. 183)*

Jan. 4, 1974. Nixon wrote Sen. Sam J. Ervin Jr. (D N.C.), chairman of the Senate Watergate committee, refusing to comply with the Dec. 19 subpoenas. *(p. 190)*

...from August 1973 to May 1974

The White House announced that Buzhardt would be replaced as head of the White House Watergate legal team by Boston attorney James D. St. Clair. *(p. 192)*

Jan. 7. Albert E. Jenner, a Chicago trial lawyer, was appointed chief minority counsel for the House Judiciary Committee's impeachment inquiry. *(p. 193)*

Jan. 15. The 18½-minute gap on the White House tapes was the result of five separate erasures and re-recordings, according to a panel of six technical experts appointed by Judge Sirica. *(p. 201)*

Jan. 18. Ending a four-day hearing into gaps in the Watergate tapes, Sirica recommended a grand jury investigation into "the possibility of unlawful destruction of evidence and related offenses" and said that "a distinct possibility of unlawful conduct on the part of one or more persons exists." *(p. 124)*

Jan. 30. Calling for an end to the Watergate probes, Nixon vowed in his State of the Union message that he had "no intention whatever" of leaving office. *(p. 228)*

Feb. 3. Rebutting the President's claim, Special Prosecutor Jaworski said the White House had not turned over to him all the tapes and documents he had requested.

Feb. 4. St. Clair, Nixon's lawyer, said that John Dean's sworn statement implicating the President was not supported by the White House tapes.

Feb. 6. With only four dissenting votes, the House approved requests of the Judiciary Committee for broad power to conduct its impeachment inquiry. *(p. 233)*

Feb. 19. By unanimous vote, the Senate Watergate Committee ended public hearings. *(p. 248)*

The trial of former cabinet secretaries John N. Mitchell and Maurice H. Stans on charges of perjury, conspiracy and obstruction of justice opened in New York. *(p. 248)*

Feb. 20. Lawyers for the House Judiciary Committee's impeachment inquiry said that grave offenses not in the public interest, which were not legal crimes, were sufficient grounds to impeach and convict a President. *(p. 245)*

Feb. 22. The Jaworski list of White House materials amassed during his investigation, including more than 700 pages of documents and 17 tapes, was given to House Judiciary Committee lawyer Doar. *(p. 257)*

March 1. Seven former Nixon aides—Mitchell, H.R. Haldeman, John D. Ehrlichman, Charles W. Colson, Robert C. Mardian, and Kenneth W. Parkinson and Gordon Strachan—indicted by a federal grand jury in Washington for conspiring to hinder the investigation of the Watergate burglary. *(p. 251)*

March 6. Nixon said the tape of his March 21, 1973, conversations with Haldeman and Dean might imply that he considered promises of clemency for Watergate defendants or authorized the payment of hush money to them. But he denied any such actions. *(p. 268)*

March 7. A grand jury in Washington indicted six men for violating the civil rights of the burglarized psychiatrist of Daniel Ellsberg: Ehrlichman, Colson,

G. Gordon Liddy, Bernard L. Barker, Eugenio R. Martinez and Felipe De Diego. *(p. 217)*

March 18. Sirica ruled that the House Judiciary Committee could obtain the Watergate grand jury report and any related material dealing with the President's possible involvement in Watergate matters. *(p. 283)*

March 21. Sirica's decision to turn over the grand jury's secret report to the House impeachment inquiry was upheld on a 5-1 vote by the U.S. Court of Appeals for the District of Columbia. *(p. 283)*

March 26. Sirica turned over to the Judiciary Committee a briefcase full of Watergate evidence that had been given to the court March 1 at the time of the coverup indictments. *(p. 293)*

April 3. The staff of the Joint Committee on Internal Revenue Taxation found that Nixon owed $476,431, including interest, on back taxes for 1969 through 1972.

Five hours later, Nixon said he would pay $467,-000 in back taxes and interest, in compliance with an Internal Revenue Service report. *(p. 298)*

April 5. Chapin, Nixon's former appointments secretary, was convicted on two counts of perjury. *(p. 301)*

April 11. The House Judiciary Committee voted to subpoena the tapes of more than 40 presidential conversations and set April 25 as the deadline for compliance. *(p. 319)*

April 16. Jaworski petitioned Judge Sirica to subpoena tapes and documents of 64 presidential conversations with Dean, Ehrlichman, Haldeman and Colson. *(p. 317)*

April 18. House Judiciary Committee Chairman Peter W. Rodino Jr. (D N.J.) rejected a White House proposal that the relevance of tapes to the impeachment inquiry be determined unilaterally by White House lawyers. *(p. 322)*

April 28. Mitchell and Stans were acquitted on all 15 counts in their criminal conspiracy case. *(p. 333)*

April 29. In a nationally televised speech, Nixon responded to the House Judiciary Committee's request for 42 tapes by announcing he would make public the edited transcripts of White House Watergate conversations. Rodino said the tapes recordings were "necessary and relevant" to the impeachment inquiry and that the transcripts would not suffice. *(327, 408)*

April 30. The White House released a 1,308-page document containing the edited transcripts. *(p. 327, 380)*

St. Clair said the President would refuse to yield tapes and documents sought by Jaworski. *(p. 336)*

May 1. The Judiciary Committee sent a letter to the President formally notifying him that he had failed to comply with the committee's subpoena. *(p. 327)*

St. Clair said that Nixon would resist the Judiciary Committee's request for additional materials. *(p. 336)*

May 2. The Judiciary Committee voted to give St. Clair wide latitude in questioning witnesses at the impeachment inquiry and to permit live television coverage of the hearings.

May 9. The House Judiciary Committee formally opened its impeachment hearings.

resigned rather than do so. His deputy, William D. Ruckelshaus, followed suit. Cox finally was fired by U.S. Solicitor General Robert H. Bork, whom Nixon had abruptly appointed acting attorney general and ordered to get rid of Cox.

Negative Response. It was, as the White House later acknowledged, a miscalculation. Public and congressional response was immediately and decisively negative. Four days after the "massacre," Chairman Rodino announced plans for the Judiciary Committee to "proceed full steam ahead" with an impeachment investigation.

Judiciary Committees of both houses set to work almost immediately on legislation to create the position of another special prosecutor, this time to be independent of the executive branch. But by Nov. 1, Nixon had appointed a replacement for Cox and had pledged him greater independence than his predecessor had had. The new prosecutor was Leon Jaworski, a wealthy Texas lawyer. The same day he appointed Jaworski, Nixon named Republican Sen. William B. Saxbe of Ohio as his new attorney general.

By early January 1974, New York lawyer John M. Doar, an assistant attorney general in the Kennedy and Johnson administrations, had been appointed by Rodino as special counsel to direct the Judiciary Committee's impeachment investigation. Republicans on the 38-member committee had chosen as their counsel a well-known trial lawyer from Chicago, Albert E. Jenner. Another famous trial lawyer, James D. St. Clair of Boston, had been appointed to head Nixon's legal team.

With only four dissenting votes, the House gave the Judiciary Committee the authority to issue subpoenas for administration records in its impeachment inquiry. Attempting to appear fair and bipartisan, the committee agreed, after initial Democratic resistance, to permit St. Clair to participate in the inquiry and to ask questions of witnesses. In recognition of the historic nature of the proceedings, the committee voted to open its investigation to the public and to allow television cameras in the hearing room.

More often than not, the committee was able to maintain at least a surface appearance of bipartisanship. One basic point of disagreement, and one remaining to be resolved, was the definition of an impeachable offense. Committee Democrats took the view that an impeachable offense need not be equated with an indictable crime. Committee Republicans took the narrower position that a president must be accused of a crime to be impeached.

The committee's immediate response to being given transcripts and tapes April 30 was a general consensus that the transcripts were inadequate. Only the wording of the letter informing Nixon he had not complied with the committee subpoena resulted in a party-line vote.

The actual impeachment hearings began May 9—in closed session. The Judiciary Committee voted, after a brief public session, to shut its doors temporarily while evidence was presented concerning Nixon's possible involvement in the Watergate break-in and coverup.

The Tapes Controversy

The focal point in the long and often confusing controversy over who was entitled to listen to which White House tapes was U.S. District Court in Washington, D.C.

The battle for the tapes began in July 1973, immediately after their existence had been disclosed at the Senate hearings. On Aug. 22, at his first televised news conference in 14 months, Nixon explained his concept of presidential confidentiality. He said that it "either exists or it doesn't exist. And once it is compromised, once it is known that a conversation that is held with a president can be subject to a subpoena by a Senate committee, by a grand jury, by a prosecutor, and be listened to by anyone, the principle of confidentiality is thereby irreparably damaged."

Earlier that same day, Special Prosecutor Cox and Charles Alan Wright, then an attorney for Nixon, faced off before District Judge John J. Sirica. "There are times when other national interests are more important even than the fullest administration of criminal justice," said Wright. He argued that no court had ever been asked to enforce a subpoena against a president.

"There is strong reason to believe that the integrity of the executive offices has been corrupted," said Cox. "Public confidence in our institutions is at stake."

A week later, Sirica ordered the White House to turn over to him, for his private inspection, nine tapes subpoenaed by a federal grand jury investigating the Watergate break-in.

The White House rejected the order and appealed Sirica's ruling. Nixon's lawyers wrote in their petition that the judge's order was "clearly erroneous and beyond the power of the judicial branch in that it purports to subject the President of the United States to compulsory process for acts performed in his official capacity."

The next step was the federal appeals court in Washington. Wright and Cox filed briefs Sept. 10 and argued their cases the next day. On Sept. 20, they wrote identical letters to the court admitting their failure to arrive at a court-suggested compromise on the taped conversations.

Oct. 12 was the date of the appeals court ruling upholding Sirica's order and setting the stage for the "massacre" eight days later. "Sovereignty remains at all times with the people, and they do not forfeit through elections the right to have the law construed against and applied to every citizen," the opinion stated.

At about the same time the White House suffered a court setback on the tapes, so did the Senate Watergate committee. Sirica Oct. 17 dismissed the committee's case asking him to enforce its subpoenas of tapes. His court, he ruled, lacked jurisdiction over the matter.

The Senate later passed a bill giving the court jurisdiction. The Watergate investigating committee tried again to obtain access to more than 500 tapes and documents that it previously had been denied. By the time the House Judiciary Committee had begun its impeachment investigation, the Watergate committee still had no tapes; with its report deadline in sight, prospects for obtaining the tapes appeared dim.

Disappearances and Gaps. On Oct. 23, 1973, three days after the firing of the first special prosecutor, Nixon's lawyer, Wright, stood before Sirica and said, "The President does not defy the law, and he has authorized me to say he will comply in full with the orders of the court." Wright promised to turn over the nine subpoenaed tapes "as expeditiously as possible."

But the tapes controversy, it turned out, was only beginning. What came later did even more damage to the credibility of the Nixon administration.

Two of the nine tapes did not exist, a White House lawyer told Sirica Oct. 31. Moreover, a White House aide testified Nov. 2, the President had discovered that the tapes did not exist nearly a month before the White House publicly acknowledged their non-existence. "I have passed the point of reacting," said House Speaker Carl Albert (D Okla.) in a fairly typical response from Congress.

The next uproar over tapes arose in late November, when White House spokesmen disclosed that an 18½-minute gap had been discovered in an important conversation between Nixon and his former chief of staff, H. R. Haldeman, on June 20, 1972, three days after the Watergate break-in. Rose Mary Woods, the President's personal secretary, changed her earlier story and said she might have caused the gap accidentally. A six-man panel of court-appointed electronics experts examined the tape and reported that the gap apparently was no accident.

The Judiciary Committee and the Tapes. By early March 1974, the battle for the tapes and other White House materials had shifted from grand juries to the Judiciary Committee's impeachment inquiry. And another confrontation seemed to be in the making.

It began with the indictment March 1 of seven men by a Watergate grand jury for their alleged roles in the coverup. Along with the indictment came a sealed envelope and a locked briefcase containing tapes and documents. Counsel Doar and Jenner of the Judiciary Committee appeared before Sirica March 6 seeking the materials. The judge granted the request March 18.

The White House transcripts given to the Judiciary Committee April 30 were a response to an April 11 subpoena of 42 tapes. The committee originally had asked for the tapes Feb. 25.

Submission of the transcripts appeared to end, at least temporarily, White House cooperation on subpoenas. The Judiciary Committee April 19 had asked for 76 additional tapes related to the coverup. The special prosecutor had subpoenaed 64 additional tapes April 16.

"As far as Watergate is concerned, the President has concluded...that that full story is now out," said counsel St. Clair May 7 about the Judiciary Committee request. "I think the President feels he has given them everything he thinks they need," St. Clair said on national television May 6.

But committee counsel Doar said, "Definitely not," when asked if the Judiciary Committee had sufficient evidence. "The committee will be adamant in seeking this material," said Rodino.

The First Family's Finances

Not helpful in any way to Nixon's position—particularly with the tax-paying public—was the disclosure in the fall of 1973 that the country's elected leader had paid only nominal federal income taxes several years during his first term.

The first report on the President's tax situation appeared in October in *The Providence* (R.I.) *Evening Bulletin.* The story said he had paid only $792 in federal income taxes in 1970 and $878 in 1971.

A question about Nixon's taxes was asked at a televised meeting of the President with Associated Press managing editors Nov. 17 at Disney World, Florida. The President distributed an audit that had been conducted earlier on his personal finances in response to questions about his homes in San Clemente, Calif., and Key Biscayne, Fla.

Nixon acknowledged the payment of nominal taxes in the two years in question. His payments were small, he explained, because of a tax deduction related to his donation of vice presidential papers to the National Archives. The papers, he said, were donated under a law that was changed in 1969.

What got Nixon in trouble was the persistent question of whether he had violated the new law by not meeting the deadline for donations of papers. "No question has been raised by the Internal Revenue (Service) about it," Nixon told the editors, "but if they do, let me tell you this: I will be glad to have the papers back, and I will pay the tax, because I think they are worth more than that."

It was at the Florida session that Nixon made one of the most-quoted remarks of his presidency: "I am not a crook."

On Dec. 8, Nixon made an unprecedented public disclosure of his personal finances, releasing 50 documents and permitting the press to compare summaries of his tax returns with copies of the returns themselves. The President asked the Joint Committee on Internal Revenue Taxation to rule on two items and pledged to pay whatever additional taxes the committee recommended. The two items, already allowed by the IRS, were a capital gains tax on a land sale at San Clemente and a $576,000 deduction on his vice presidential papers.

The committee's staff report, released April 3, 1974, was bad news for Nixon: he owed $476,531 in back taxes and interest. Similar findings were contained in an IRS report issued April 2 but not made public. Nixon said April 3 that he would pay some $467,000 in taxes and interest that the IRS said he owed.

The White House statement on the President's agreement to settle up was somewhat defensive. "It should be noted that the report by the Internal Revenue Service rebuts any suggestion of fraud on the part of the President," said the statement. "The committee's staff report offers no facts which would support any such charge." Any errors on the returns, the statement continued, "were made without his knowledge and without his approval."

Exit Vice President Agnew

Also contributing to Nixon's multiplying woes in 1973 was one not related directly to Watergate but nevertheless reflecting on the President's judgment of men: Vice President Spiro T. Agnew.

Early in August, newspaper reports said Agnew was under investigation in connection with a probe of corruption in Baltimore County. Agnew called the allegations "damned lies." The investigation, it developed, was being conducted by the U.S. attorney in Baltimore.

Over the next two months, Agnew was linked with charges of corruption during his years as Baltimore County executive, governor of Maryland and Vice President. He continued to protest his innocence and to deny any plans to resign.

By Oct. 1, the White House acknowledged that Agnew's lawyers were plea bargaining with attorneys for the Justice Department. Agnew formally resigned as Vice

President Oct. 10. Then he pleaded "no contest," in U.S. District Court in Baltimore, to a single charge of income tax evasion. He was sentenced to three years of unsupervised probation and fined $10,000. Federal prosecution for alleged bribery and extortion was dropped as Elliot L. Richardson, then the attorney general, asked for leniency in the sentencing.

Nixon praised Agnew's performance as Vice President and said he was "deeply saddened by this whole course of events."

Enter Ford. Nixon wasted no time in finding a replacement for Agnew, but his choice remained a well-kept secret until the announcement was made. House Republican Leader Gerald R. Ford of Michigan, a representative for 25 years, was his choice. The nomination was announced at a gala, nationally televised ceremony at the White House Oct. 12. A jovial, smiling President, making no reference to Agnew, said that "it is vital that we turn away from the obsessions of the past...this is a time for a new beginning for America."

After an investigation that may have been the most thorough ever conducted of a vice presidential nominee, Ford was confirmed easily by the Senate and was sworn in Dec. 6. His filling of the vacancy was a relief to some members of Congress, who had been reluctant to pursue impeachment without a vice president in office.

Key Aides Involved

Spiro Agnew was not by any means the only former close associate of the besieged President to fall afoul of the law. The roster of indicted or convicted persons who had worked either in the White House or for the Nixon re-election committee was long, and growing longer. Federal grand juries were at work in May 1974.

• Seven men were indicted March 1 in the Watergate coverup. Four of them were men who had been among the President's closest advisers: John N. Mitchell, H. R. Haldeman, John D. Ehrlichman and Charles W. Colson. Their trial was to begin in September.

• Six men were indicted March 7 for the 1971 break-in at the office of Dr. Lewis J. Fielding, psychiatrist to Pentagon Papers defendant Daniel Ellsberg. Colson and Ehrlichman were among them. Trial was scheduled for June.

• The most important trial of former administration leaders through April to that time was the criminal conspiracy trial of former Attorney General John N. Mitchell and former Commerce Secretary Maurice H. Stans. Mitchell and Stans, accused of attempting to impede a Securities and Exchange Commission investigation in return for a $200,000 contribution to the Nixon re-election campaign, were acquitted on all counts April 28.

Impeachment Defined

Impeachment is the process by which the House of Representatives by majority vote formally brings charges against a federal official, thereby impeaching him. He is then tried by the Senate on those charges. If found guilty by a two-thirds voe of the senators present, the officer is removed from office and may be disqualified from holding any future federal office.

• Dwight L. Chapin, Nixon's former appointments secretary, was convicted April 5 of two counts of perjury for his testimony about campaign sabotage. His accomplice, saboteur Donald Segretti, had been convicted earlier and served most of a six-month prison term.

• Herbert W. Kalmbach, Nixon's former personal attorney and fund-raiser, pleaded guilty Feb. 25 to two criminal charges related to his 1970 fund-raising activities.

• Lt. Gov. Ed Reinecke of California, a candidate for the Republican gubernatorial nomination, was indicted April 3 on three counts of lying to the Senate Judiciary Committee about his dealings with International Telephone and Telegraph Corporation (ITT) in connection with the 1972 Republican national convension.

And there were many others, either convicted earlier or still free and awaiting sentencing after plea bargaining. In the second category were three former officials who had been involved in the coverup: John W. Dean III, Frederick C. LaRue and Jeb Stuart Magruder.

Areas of Exploration. Besides the still undecided future of many of his former assistants, Nixon continued to face queries about a number of unresolved matters. Although the White House had issued position papers on two of the matters—1972 campaign contributions from milk producers and administration involvement in an antitrust suit against ITT—Nixon had not released taped conversations related to either. It was not clear whether the White House decision not to comply with requests for other subpoenaed tapes and documents would apply to the milk money and ITT cases.

Also unresolved were some details of a $100,000 cash contribution from billionaire Howard Hughes to Charles G. Rebozo, a close friend of Nixon, in 1969 and 1970, and the extent and purpose of the administration's use of wiretaps on newsmen and others for "security reasons."

Nixon Reaction. Throughout his Watergate ordeal, Nixon had fluctuated between accessibility and privacy in his efforts to get his side of the story across to the American public. His dramatic 35-minute television speech April 29, 1974, was an appeal to the public for support.

Startled by the unexpectedly negative reaction to the Cox firing in October 1973, Nixon had embarked on a series of travels that the press labeled "Operation Candor." A few months later, this campaign was abandoned. As his standing in the polls remained low and his policies continued to come under attack, he began appearing before carefully selected, friendly audiences, usually in the South. His relations with the press, always cool, deteriorated on a few occasions to rank bitterness. In his April 29 speech, he referred to his "political and journalistic opponents."

He made clear that he was going straight to the public. "In giving you these records—blemishes and all—I am placing my trust in the basic fairness of the American people," he said.

And he concluded with a quotation from a man whose words he often quoted, Abraham Lincoln: "I do the very best I know how—the very best I can; and I mean to keep doing so until the end. If the end brings me out all right, what is said against me won't amount to anything. If the end brings me out wrong, 10 angels swearing I was right would make no difference."

Mercer Cross
Political Editor

NIXON MEETS THE PRESS, INTERROGATED ON WATERGATE

President Nixon Aug. 22 held his first news conference since March 15—the only press conference since the Watergate scandal bloomed and the first televised meeting with the press in 14 months.

The President revealed that Secretary of State William P. Rogers would resign, and that national security adviser Henry A. Kissinger had been appointed to replace him—an announcement that normally would have raised enough questions to dominate a news conference. *(Text, p. 3)*

But for a White House press corps starved for presidential answers to questions about the Watergate

scandal, Nixon might just as well have announced a minor postmaster appointment.

As it had for weeks, Watergate virtually dominated the news Aug. 18-24, only receiving competition in the headlines with another potential scandal —Vice President Spiro T. Agnew's problems with an investigation of charges that he may have received kickbacks from four Maryland contractors while serving in public office in that state.

After opening the news conference with the Rogers-Kissinger announcement, the President's responses to questions made these points regarding Watergate:

• While his capacity to govern had been hampered by the scandal, he never had considered resigning and would not consider it.

• Watergate was "water under the bridge" and it was time to move forward with "the business of the people."

• He was still adamant in his refusal to hand over his tape recordings of crucial White House conversations to the Senate Watergate committee, the special prosecutor or even an independent intermediary.

• He accepted all the blame for the "climate" at the White House and re-election committee that resulted in the "abuses" of Watergate.

• H. R. Haldeman and John D. Ehrlichman, his former top aides who were deeply implicated in the scandal, were still, in his opinion, "two of the finest public servants" he had ever known, and he predicted that they would be exonerated by the courts.

• Wiretapping and burglaries for national security purposes occurred in previous administrations. There was more wiretapping when Robert F. Kennedy was attorney general from 1961 to 1964 than in the Nixon years.

He was asked whether he ever considered resigning and whether his capacity to govern had been affected by

Nixon's Mood

When they turned up at all, clues to Richard Nixon's state of mind during the Senate Watergate committee hearings were generally unreassuring. Some congressional leaders and others who saw the 60-year-old President described him as appearing increasingly haggard and tense. Presidential Counselor Melvin R. Laird told a *Washington Post* reporter after Nixon's nationally televised Watergate speech Aug. 15 that "it might have been better if the President had taken a long rest" after his bout with pneumonia in July.

Speculation about Nixon's mood quickened after a rare public display of temper in New Orleans Aug. 20. As the presidential entourage was about to enter a convention hall for a speech before the Veterans of Foreign Wars, Nixon, in full view of television cameras, suddenly grabbed Press Secretary Ronald L. Ziegler by the shoulders and issued a sharp order. The President then spun his assistant around and gave him a neck-popping shove toward the astonished press corps. According to nearby reporters, Nixon was irritated because some members of the press pool were following him into the hall instead of using the door that had been designated for them. "I don't want the press near me," a reporter overheard him tell Ziegler. "You take care of it."

In a briefing a few hours later, Deputy Press Secretary Gerald L. Warren responded to questions about the incident by acknowledging that "the past few months have been periods of pressure on the President." But he passed the episode off as a minor flare-up, maintaining that Nixon's relationship with Ziegler was "excellent."

Warren offered a further explanation for the President's testiness. On the same day, a reported plot to assassinate Nixon had caused the Secret Service to re-route the President's motorcade through the city. Though Nixon agreed to the diversion, he reportedly was "very upset" that the motorcade had to avoid the crowds.

the scandal. (Nixon's daughter, Julie Eisenhower, twice had reported that her father had talked about resigning.) But Nixon said he had never considered resigning and never would.

Asked what degree of blame he accepted "for the climate at the White House and at the re-election committee for the abuses of Watergate," Nixon responded tersely, "I accept it all."

At one point he was questioned about a 1970 intelligence plan he had approved, but later rescinded, call-

Key Questions: Nixon Press Conference Adds Few Details

Many questions left unanswered by the President in his Aug. 15 Watergate statement were asked a week later by reporters at the presidential press conference Aug. 22. The press conference responses added few new details to the President's earlier Watergate statements.

Nixon's answers coincided with those given the Senate select Watergate committee by his former top aides, H.R. Haldeman and John D. Ehrlichman. *(Ehrlichman testimony, Vol. I, p. 212, Haldeman Vol. I p. 231)*

Following are some of the key questions remaining after Nixon's Aug. 15 address, and his Aug. 22 responses:

Gray Warning. L. Patrick Gray, former acting director of the FBI, testified that he warned Nixon July 6, 1972, three weeks after the Watergate break-in, that persons on his staff were trying to "mortally wound" him by involving the CIA in the FBI's investigation. The President was asked why he did not ask who those persons were.

Nixon said that "whether the term was 'mortally wounding' or not, I don't know. That's irrelevant." He went on to say that the "main point" was that he asked Gray whether he had contacted the deputy CIA director, Gen. Vernon Walters, to make sure the CIA did not become involved in the bureau's investigation. When assured by Gray that contact with Walters had been made, and that Walters wanted the investigation pursued, Nixon said he ordered Gray to press forward with his investigation.

"It seemed to me," Nixon said, "that with that kind of a directive to Mr. Gray, that was adequate for the purpose of carrying out the responsibilities. As far as the individuals were concerned, I assume that the individuals that he was referring to involved this operation with the CIA. That's why I asked him the Walters question."

Clemency and Payoffs. Former presidential counsel John W. Dean III, Nixon's chief accuser at the hearings, testified that the President discussed executive clemency and silence money for Watergate defendants with him at meetings March 13 and 21, 1972, which, Dean said, indicated the President's knowledge of the coverup. The President was asked about the March 21 meeting.

Nixon, like Haldeman, revealed no knowledge of a March 13 meeting with Dean. The President said he and Dean did discuss silence money and clemency March 21, but in the context that both would be wrong and illegal.

The President said that when Dean raised the issue of silence money, Nixon said even if it were paid, the seven defendants would not "sit there in jail for four years; they're going to have clemency. Isn't that correct?' He said, 'Yes.' I said, 'We can't give clemency.' He agreed."

Nixon added he told Dean that while the $1-million Dean was suggesting was needed could be raised, he told him, "It's wrong. It won't work."

Who Got Orders. The President, in his April 30 Watergate statement, said that on March 21 he personally assumed responsibility for coordinating new inquiries into Watergate and ordered those conducting the investigation to report back to him. Gray, Attorney General Richard G. Kleindienst, and Assistant Attorney General Henry E. Petersen told the Senate committee that they received no such orders from the President. Nixon was asked exactly who he talked to March 21.

The President did not answer the question directly prefacing his answer by saying, "Now in terms of after March 21...." Nixon said Dean first was given the responsibility of writing a report on the affair. Dean failed to write the report, Nixon said, so he contacted Kleindienst March 27 and told him to report anything he found back to the oval office. The President then said he ordered Ehrlichman March 29 to continue the White House probe in place of Dean.

Mitchell Testimony. John N. Mitchell, former attorney general and re-election committee director, testified that he never told Nixon what he knew about Watergate because the President never asked him. If he had told him, Mitchell said, Nixon would have "lowered the boom" on his aides and possibly lost the election. In view of Nixon's assertions that he discussed Watergate with Mitchell and others March 22, and "kept pressing" to get the full story out, the President was asked if Mitchell had lied to the committee in saying he would have told Nixon what he knew if asked.

The President said he would not question Mitchell's veracity before the committee, but added that "I would have expected Mr. Mitchell to tell me in the event that he was involved or that anybody else was." Nixon said he did not blame Mitchell for not telling him because "I would have blown my stack, just as I did at (press secretary Ronald L.) Ziegler the other day."

ing for burglaries, wiretaps and mail inspections of suspected subversives. Pointing out that the President had sworn to uphold the Constitution and the laws of the United States, the reporter asked whether, if Nixon were serving in Congress, he would consider impeachment proceedings against an elected official who had violated his oath of office. "I would if I had violated the oath of office," the President replied.

With some anger in his voice, he added, "I should also point out to you that in the three Kennedy years and

the three Johnson years through 1966, when burglarizing of this type did take place, when it was authorized on a very large scale, there was no talk of impeachment...."

"I should also point out that when you ladies and gentlemen indicate your great interest in wiretaps, and I understand that, that the height of the wiretaps was when Robert Kennedy was attorney general in 1963. I don't criticize it, however. He had over 250 in 1963, and of course the average in the Eisenhower administration and the Nixon administration was 110."

TEXT OF PRESIDENT NIXON'S AUG. 22 NEWS CONFERENCE

Following is an unofficial text of President Nixon's Aug. 22 news conference at San Clemente, Calif.:

Opening Statement

First, gentlemen, I have an announcement before going to your questions.

It is with the deep sense of not only official regret but personal regret that I announce the resignation of Secretary of State William Rogers, effective Sept. 3.

A letter which will be released to the press after this conference will indicate my appraisal of his work as Secretary of State.

I will simply say at this time that he wanted to leave at the conclusion of the first four years.

He agreed to stay on because we had some enormously important problems coming up including the negotiations which resulted in the end of the war in Vietnam, the Soviet summit, the European Security Conference as well as in other areas, Latin America and in Asia where the Secretary of State as you know has been quite busy over these past eight months.

As he returns to private life we will not only miss him in terms of his official service but I shall particularly miss him because of his having been through the years a very close personal friend and adviser. That personal friendship and advice, however, I hope still to have the benefit of and I know that I will.

As his successor I shall nominate and send to the Senate for confirmation the name of Dr. Henry Kissinger.

Dr. Kissinger will become Secretary of State, assume the duties of the office after he is confirmed by the Senate.

I trust the Senate will move expeditiously on the confirmation hearings because there are a number of matters of very great importance that are coming up. There are, for example, some matters that might even involve some foreign travel by Dr. Kissinger that will have to be delayed in the event that the Senate hearings are delayed.

Dr. Kissinger's qualifications for this post I think are well known by all of you ladies and gentlemen as well as those looking to us and listening to us on television and radio.

He will retain the position, after he becomes Secretary of State, of assistant to the President for national security affairs. In other words he will have somewhat a parallel relationship to the White House which George Shultz has. George Shultz as you know is Secretary of the Treasury but is also an assistant to the President in the field of economic affairs.

The purpose of this arrangement is to have a closer coordination between the White House and the departments and in this case between the White House and the National Security Affairs, the N.S.C. and the State Department, which carries a major load in this area.

And also another purpose is to get the work out in the departments where it belongs and I believe that this change in this respect of Dr. Kissinger moving in as Secretary of State and still retaining the position as Assistant to the President for National Security Affairs will serve the interest not only of coordination but also of the interests of an effective foreign policy.

I will simply say finally with regard to Secretary Rogers that he can look back on what I think and I suppose it is a self-serving statement, but I will say it about him rather than about myself at the moment, one of the most successful eras of foreign policy in any Administration in history, an era in which we ended a war, the longest war in America's history, an era in addition in which we began to build a structure of peace, particularly involving the two great powers, the People's Republic of China and the Soviet Union, where before there had been nothing but ugly and at sometimes very, very difficult confrontation.

We still have a long way to go. There are trouble spots in the area of the Mideast, others, Southeast Asia which we could go into in detail. But as Secretary Rogers looks back on his years, four and a half years of service as Secretary of State, he can be very proud that he was one of the major architects of what I think was a very successful foreign policy.

And now we'll go to the question. I think, A.P.

Questions

WHITE HOUSE TAPES

Nixon: A.P., Miss Lewin, has the first question.

Q. On Watergate you have said that disclosure of the tapes could jeopardize and cripple the posture of the presidency. Question. If disclosure carries such a risk, why did you make the tapes in the first place and what is your reaction to surveys that show three out of four Americans believe you were wrong to make the tapes?

A. Well, with regard to the questions as to why Americans feel we were wrong to make the tapes, that is not particularly surprising. I think that most Americans do not like the idea of the taping of conversations and, frankly, it is not something that particularly appeals to me. As a matter of fact that is why when I arrived in the White House and saw this rather complex situation set up where there was a taping capacity not only in the President's office, the room outside of his office, but also in the Cabinet room and at Camp David and in other areas, that I had the entire system dismantled.

It was put into place again in June of 1970 because my advisers felt it was important in terms particularly of national security affairs to have a record for future years that would be an accurate one, but a record which would only be disclosed at the discretion of the President, or according to directives that he would set forth.

As you know, of course, this kind of capability not only existed during the Johnson administration, it also existed in the Kennedy Administration, and I can see why both President Johnson and President Kennedy did have the capability because, not because they wanted to infringe upon the privacy of anybody but because they felt that they had some obligation particularly in the field of foreign policy and some domestic areas to have a record that would be accurate.

As far as I'm concerned, we now do not have that capability and I am just as happy that we don't. As a matter of fact, I have a practice whenever I'm not too tired at night, of dictating my own recollections of the day. I think that perhaps will be the more accurate record of history in the end. I think we'll go to the U.P. now and then we'll come to the television....

GRAY WARNING

Q. On July 6, 1972 you were warned by Patrick Gray you were being mortally wounded by some of your top aides. Can you explain why you didn't ask who they were, and why, what was going on?

A. Well, in the telephone conversation that you refer to that has been, of course, quite widely reported in the press as well as on television, Mr. Gray said that he was concerned that as far as the investigation that he had responsibility for, that some of my top aides were not cooperating. Whether the term used was "mortally wounded" or not, I do not know. Some believe that it was. Some believe that it wasn't. That is irrelevant. He could have said that.

The main point, however, I asked him whether or not he had discussed this matter with General Walters because I knew that there had been meetings between General Walters repre-

3

senting the C.I.A. to be sure that the C.I.A. did not become involved in the investigation and between the director of the F.B.I. He said that he had. He told me that General Walters agreed that the investigation should be pursued and I told him to go forward with a full press on the investigation, to which he has so testified. It seemed to me that with that kind of directive to Mr. Gray that was adequate for the purpose of carrying out the responsibilities. As far as the individuals were concerned, I assume that the individuals that he was referring to involved this operation with the C.I.A.

That's why I asked him the Walters question. When he cleared that up, he went forward with the investigation and he must have thought that it was a very good investigation because when I sent his name down to the Senate for confirmation the next year, I asked him about his investigation and he said he was very proud of it and he said it was the most thorough investigation that had ever taken place since the assassination of President Kennedy, that he could defend it with enthusiasm and that under the circumstances, therefore, he had carried out the directive that I had given him on July 6. So there was no question about Mr. Gray having direct orders from the President to carry out an investigation that was thorough.

Mr. Jarriel.

HALDEMAN'S ACCESS

Q. Assistant Attorney General Henry Petersen has testified that on April 15th of this year he met with you and warned you at that time there might be enough evidence to warrant indictments against three of your top aides, Messrs. Ehrlichman, Haldeman, and Dean. You accepted their resignations on April 30 calling Mr. Haldeman and Mr. Ehrlichman two of the finest public servants you have known. After that you permitted Mr. Haldeman after he had left the White House to hear confidential tapes of conversations you had had in your office with Mr. Dean. My question is why did you permit a man who you knew might be indicted to hear those tapes which you now will not permit the American public or the Federal prosecutors handling the case to listen to.

A. The only tape that has been referred to, that Mr. Haldeman has listened to, he listened to at my request and he listened to that tape that was the one on Sept. 15th, because he had been present and was there. I asked him to listen to it in order to be sure that as far as any allegations that had been made by Mr. Dean with regard to that conversation, I wanted to be sure that we were absolutely correct in our response.

That's all he listened to. He did not listen to any tapes in which only Mr. Dean and I had participated. He listened only to the tape on Sept. 15, this is after he left office, in which he had participated in the conversation throughout.

FIRM ON TAPES

Q. Mr. President, one of the lingering doubts about your denial of any involvement in (Watergate), is concerning your failure to make the tapes available, either to the Senate committee or the special prosecutor. You've made it perfectly clear you don't intend to release those tapes.

A. Perfectly clear?

Q. Perfectly clear, but is there any way that you could have some group listen to tapes and give a report so that that might satisfy the public mind?

A. I don't believe first that it would satisfy the public mind, and it shouldn't. The second point is that as Mr. Wright, who argued the case, I understand, very well before Judge Sirica this morning, has indicated to have the tapes listened to—he indicated this also in his brief—either by a prosecutor or by a judge or *in camera* or in any way would violate the principle of confidentiality, and I believe he is correct.

That is why we are standing firm on the proposition that we will not agree to the Senate committee's desires to have, for

example, its chief investigator listen to the tapes or the special prosecutor's desire to hear the tapes, and also why we will oppose, as Mr. Wright did in this argument this morning, any compromise of the principle of confidentiality. Let me explain very carefully that the principle of confidentiality either exists or it doesn't exist. And once it is compromised, once it is known that a conversation that is held with the President can be subject to a subpoena by a Senate committee, by a grand jury, by a prosecutor, and be listened to by anyone, the principle of confidentiality is thereby irreparably damaged.

Incidentally, let me say that now that tapes are no longer being made I suppose it could be argued what difference does it make now, now that these tapes are also in the past. What is involved is not only the tapes, what is involved, as you ladies and gentlemen well know, is the request on the part of the Senate committee and the special prosecutor as well, that we turn over Presidential papers, in other words, the record of conversations with the President made by his associates. Those papers and the tapes as well cannot be turned over without breaching the principle of confidentiality. It was President Truman that made that argument very effectively in his letter to a Senate committee for his response to a Congressional committee, a House committee, it was, in 1953 when they asked him to turn over his papers. So whether it is a paper or whether it's a tape, what we have to bear in mind is that for a President to conduct the affairs of this office and conduct effectively, he must be able to do so with the principle of confidentiality intact.

Otherwise, the individuals who come to talk to him, whether it's his advisers or whether it's a visitor in the domestic field or whether it's someone in a foreign field, will always be speaking in a eunuch-like way, rather than laying it on the line. It has to be laid on the line if you're going to have the creative kind of discussions that we have often had and have been responsible for some of our successes in the foreign policy period, particularly in the past few years.

MAGRUDER AND MacGREGOR

Q. Mr. President, could you tell us who you personally talked to in directing that investigations be made both in June of '72 after the Watergate incident and last March 21, when you got new evidence and ordered a more intensive investigation?

A. Certainly. In June I of course talked to Mr. MacGregor first of all who was the new chairman of the committee. He told me that he would conduct a thorough investigation as far as his entire committee staff was concerned. Apparently that investigation was very effective except for Mr. Magruder who stayed on, but Mr. MacGregor does not have to assume responsibility for that, I say not responsibility for it because basically what happened there was that he believed Mr. Magruder and many others had believed him, too. He proved, however, to be wrong.

In the White House, the investigation's responsibility were given to Mr. Ehrlichman at the highest level and, in turn, he delegated them to Mr. Dean, the White House counsel, something of which I was aware of and of which I approved. Mr. Dean, as White House counsel, therefore sat in on the F.B.I. interrogations of the members of the White House staff because what I wanted to know was whether any member of the White House staff was in any way involved. If he was involved, he would be fired.

And when we met on Sept. 15 and again throughout our discussions in the month of March, Mr. Dean insisted there was not—and I used his words—a "scintilla of evidence" indicating that anyone on the White House staff was involved in the planning of the Watergate break-in.

Now in terms of after March 21st, Mr. Dean first was given the responsibility to write his own report but I did not rest it there—I also had a contact made with the Attorney General himself, and Attorney General Kleindienst told him—this was on the 27th of March—to report to me directly anything that he found in this particular area, and I gave the responsibility to Mr. Ehrlichman on the 29th of March to continue the investigation that Mr. Dean was unable to conclude, having spent a week at Camp David and unable to finish the report.

Mr. Ehrlichman questioned a number of people in that period at my direction, including Mr. Mitchell, and I should also point out that as far as my own activities were concerned I was not leaving it just to them.

I met at great length with Mr. Ehrlichman, Mr. Haldeman, Mr. Dean, Mr. Mitchell on the 22nd. I discussed the whole matter with them. I kept pressing for the view that I had had throughout, that we must get this story out, get the truth out, whatever and whoever it's going to hurt, and it was there that Mr. Mitchell suggested that all the individuals involved in the White House appear in an executive session before the Ervin committee.

We never got that far. But at least that was, that's an indication of the extent of my own investigation.

I think we'll go to Mr. Lisagor now.

MITCHELL TESTIMONY

Q. Mr. President, you have said repeatedly that you tried to get all facts and just now you mentioned a March 22nd meeting. Yet former Attorney General John Mitchell said that if you had ever asked him at any time about the Watergate matter he would have told you the whole story chapter and verse. Was Mr. Mitchell not speaking the truth when he said that before the committee?

A. Now Mr. Lisagor, I'm not going to question Mr. Mitchell's veracity. And I will only say that throughout I had confidence in Mr. Mitchell. Mr. Mitchell, in a telephone call that I had with him immediately after it occurred, expressed great chagrin that he had not run a tight enough shop and that some of the boys, as he called them, got involved in this kind of activity, which he knew to be very, very embarrassing to—apart from its illegality—to the campaign.

Throughout I was expecting Mr. Mitchell to tell me, in the event that he was involved or that anybody else was. He did not tell me. I don't blame him for not telling me. He's given his reasons for not telling me. I regret that he did not; because he's exactly right—had he told me I would have blown my stack. Just as I did at Ziegler the other day.

We'll get you next, Mr. Rather.

RESPONSIBILITY

Q. Mr. President. How much personal blame do you accept for the climate in the White House and of the re-election committee for the abuses of Watergate?

A. I accept it all.

JUDGE BYRNE

Q. Mr. President, I want to state this question with due respect to your office but also as directly as....

A. That would be unusual.

Q. I'd like to think not. It concerns....

A. Only...you're always respectful, Mr. Rather.

Q. It concerns the events surrounding Mr. Ehrlichman's contact and on one occasion your own contact with the judge in the Pentagon paper case, Judge Byrne. As I understand your own explanation of events in putting together your statement with Mr. Ehrlichman's testimony and what is currently said, what happened here is sometime late in March, on March 17, I believe he said, you first found out about the break-in at the psychiatrist's office of Mr. Ellsberg, that you asked to have that looked into and that you later, I think in late April, talked with Attorney General Kleindienst to inform the judge. Now, my question is this, that while the Pentagon papers trial was going on, Mr. Ehrlichman secretly met once with the judge in that case, you secretly met another time the judge with Mr. Ehrlichman, now,

you're a lawyer and given the state of the situation and what you did, could you give us some reason why the American people shouldn't believe that that was at least a subtle attempt to bribe the judge in that case and it gave at least the appearance of a lack of moral leadership?

A. Well I would say the only part of your statement that is perhaps accurate is that I'm a lawyer. Now, beyond that, Mr. Rather, let me say with regard to the secret meeting that we had with the judge that as he said, I met the judge briefly—after all, I had appointed him to the position—I met him for perhaps one minute outside my door here in full view of the whole White House staff and everybody who wanted to see.

I asked him how he liked his job. We did not discuss the case. And he went on with his meeting with Mr. Ehrlichman. Now why did the meeting with Mr. Ehrlichman take place. Because we had determined that Mr. Gray could not be confirmed, as you will recall. We were on a search for a director of the F.B.I. Mr. Kleindienst had been here, and I asked him what he would recommend with regard to a director and I laid down certain qualifications.

I said I wanted a man preferably with F.B.I. experience and preferably with prosecutor's experience. And preferably, if possible, a Democrat, so that we would have no problem on confirmation. He said the man for the job is Byrne. He says he's the best man. I said, are you, would you recommend him? He said, yes. Under those circumstances, then, Mr. Ehrlichman called Mr. Byrne. He said under no circumstances will we talk to you, he, Ehrlichman will talk to you, unless if he felt that it would in any way compromise his handling of the Ellsberg case.

Judge Byrne made the decision that he would talk to Mr. Ehrlichman, and he did talk to him privately, here. And on that occasion he talked to him privately. The case was not discussed at all. Only the question of whether or not at the conclusion of this case Mr. Byrne would like to be considered as director of the F.B.I.

I understand, incidentally, that he told Mr. Ehrlichman that he would be interested. Of course, the way the things broke, eventually we found another name with somewhat the same qualifications, although in this case, not a judge, in this case, a chief of police with former F.B.I. experience.

Now, with regard to the Ellsberg break-in, let me explain that in terms of that I discussed that on the telephone with Mr. Henry Petersen on the 18th of April. It was on the 18th of April that I learned that the grand jury was going away from some of its Watergate investigation and moving into national security areas.

I told Mr. Petersen at that time about my concern about the security areas and particularly about the break-in as far as the Ellsberg case was concerned. And then he asked me a very critical question, which you as a nonlawyer will now understand, and lawyers probably will too. He said, was any evidence developed out of this investigation, out of this break-in, and I said, no, it was a dry hole. He said, good. Now what he meant by that was that in view of the fact that no evidence was developed as the result of the break-in, which is incidentally, illegal, unauthorized as far as I was concerned, and completely deplorable, but since no evidence was developed, there was no requirement that it be presented to the jury that was hearing the case.

That was why Mr. Petersen, a man of impeccable credentials in the law enforcement field, did not at that time, on the 18th, at a time when I told him about, that I had known about the Ellsberg break-in, say, 'Let's present it then to the grand jury' because nothing had been accomplished, nothing had been obtained that would taint the case.

It was approximately 10 days later that Mr. Kleindienst came in and said that after a review of the situation in the prosecutor's office in Washington in which Mr. Petersen had also participated that they believed that it was best that we bend over backwards in this case and send this record of the Ellsberg break-in even though there was no evidence obtained from it that could have affected the jury one way or another, send it to the judge.

When they made that recommendation to me I directed that it be done instantly. It was done. Incidentally, the prosecutor argued this case just the way that I've argued it to you, and whether or not it had an effect on the eventual outcome, I do not know. At least as far as we know, Mr. Ellsberg went free, this being one of the factors, but that is the explanation of what happened, and obviously you in your commentary tonight can attach anything you want to it. I hope you will be just as fair and objective as I try to be in giving you the answer. But I know you will be, sir.

CONFIDENCE IN AGNEW

Q. Mr. President, what is the state of your confidence in your Vice President at this point in time?

A. I noted some press speculation to the effect that I have not expressed confidence in the Vice President and therefore I welcome this question, because I want to set the record straight.

I had confidence in the integrity of the Vice President when I selected him as Vice President when very few knew him, as you may recall, back in 1968, knew him nationally.

My confidence in his integrity has not been shaken, and in fact it has been strengthened by his courageous conduct and his ability even though he's controversial at times, as I am, over the past four and a half years and so I have confidence in the integrity of the Vice President and particularly in the performance of the duties that he has had as Vice President, and as a candidate for Vice President.

Now obviously the question arises as to charges that have been made about activities that occurred before he became Vice President.

He would consider it improper, I would consider it improper for me to comment on those charges and I shall not do so. But I will make a comment on another subject that I think needs to be commented upon and that is the outrageous leak in information from either the grand jury or the prosecutors or the Department of Justice or all three—and incidentally I'm not going to put the responsibility on all three till I have heard from the Attorney General who at my request is making a full investigation of this at the present time.

I'm not going to put the responsibility—but the leak of information with regard to charges that have been made against the Vice President and leaking them all in the press, convicting an individual, not only trying him but convicting him in the headlines and on television before he's had a chance to present his case in court is completely contrary to the American tradition. Even a Vice President has a right to some, shall I say consideration in this respect, let alone the ordinary individual.

And I will say this, and the Attorney General I know has taken note of this fact, any individual in the Justice Department or in the prosecutor's office who is in the employ of the United States, who has leaked information in this case, to the press or to anybody else, will be summarily dismissed from Government service. That's how strongly I feel about it and I feel that way because I would make this ruling whether it was the Vice President or any individual.

We have to remember that a hearing before a grand jury and that determination in the American process is one that is supposed to be in confidence, because all kinds of charges are made which will not stand up in open court, and it's only when the case gets to open court that the press and the TV have a right to cover it. Well, they have a right to cover it, but I mean, have a right, it seems to me to give such broad coverage to the charges.

RESIGNATION POSSIBILITY

Q. Mr. President, did at any time during the Watergate crisis have you ever considered resigning? Would you consider resigning if you felt that your capacity to govern had been seriously weakened? And in that connection, how much do you think your capacity to govern has been weakened?

A. The answer to the first two questions is no. The answer to the third question is that it is true that as far as the capacity to govern is concerned, that to be under a constant barrage—12 to 15 minutes a night on each of the three major networks for four months—tends to raise some questions in the people's minds with regard to the President; and it may raise some questions with regard to the capacity to govern.

But I also know this: I was elected to do a job. Watergate is an episode that I deeply deplore; and, had I been running the campaign—other than trying to run the country, and particularly the foreign policy of this country at this time—it would never have happened. But that's water under the bridge. Let's go on now.

The point that I make now is, that we are proceeding as best we know how to get all those guilty brought to justice in Watergate. But now we must move on from Watergate to the business of the people—the business of the people is continuing with initiatives we began in the first Administration.

WATERGATE OBSESSION

Q. Mr. President— —

A. Just a moment. We've had 30 minutes of this press conference. I have yet to have, for example, one question on the business of the people. Which shows you are—how we're consumed with it.

I'm not criticizing the members of the press; because you naturally are very interested in this issue. But let me tell you, years from now people are going to perhaps be interested in what happened in terms of the efforts of the United States to build a structure of peace in the world. They are perhaps going to be interested in the efforts of this Administration to have a kind of prosperity that we haven't had since 1955—that is, prosperity without war and without inflation.

Because, throughout the Kennedy years and throughout the Johnson years, whatever prosperity we had was at the cost of either inflation or war, or both.

I don't say that critically of them. I'm simply saying, we've got to do better than that.

Now our goal is to move forward then—to move forward to build a structure of peace. And when you say, have I—do I consider resigning: the answer is no. I shall not resign. I have three and a half years to go, or almost three and a half years, and I'm going to use every day of those three and a half years trying to get the people of the United States to recognize that whatever mistakes we have made that in the long run this Administration, by making this world safer for their children, and this Administration, by making their lives better at home for themselves and their children, deserves high marks rather than low marks.

IMPEACHMENT

Q. Mr. President, as long as we're on the subject of the American tradition and following up Mr. Rather's questions, what was authorized even if the burglary of Dr. Fielding's office wasn't, what was authorized was the 1970 plan which by your own description permitted illegal acts, illegal breaking and entering, mail surveillance and the like. Now, under the Constitution you swore an oath to execute the laws of the United States faithfully. If you were serving in Congress, would you not be considering impeachment proceedings and discussing impeachment possibility against an elected public official who had violated his oath of office?

A. I would if I had violated the oath of office. I would also, however, refer you to the recent decision of the Supreme Court or at least an opinion that even last year which indicates inherent power in the Presidency to protect the national security in cases like this. I should also point to you that in the three Kennedy years and the three Johnson years through 1966 when burglarizing of this type did take place, when it was authorized, on a very large sacle there was no talk of impeachment and it was quite well known.

I should also like to point out that when you ladies and gentlemen indicate your great interest in wiretaps and I understand that the heights of the wiretaps was when Robert Kennedy was Attorney General in 1963. I don't criticize him, however. He had over 250 in 1963 and of course the average in the Eisenhower Administration and the Nixon Administration is about 110.

But if he had had 10 more and as a result of wiretaps had been able to discover the Oswald plan it would have been worth it.

So, I will go to another question.

EHRLICHMAN AND HALDEMAN

Q. Mr. President, do you consider Haldeman and Ehrlichman two of the finest public servants you have ever known?

A. I certainly do. I look upon public servants as men who've got to be judged by their entire record—not by simply parts of it. Mr. Ehrlichman, Mr. Haldeman for four and a half years served with great distinction, with great dedication and, like everybody in this deplorable Watergate business, at great personal sacrifice and with no personal gain.

We admit the scandalous conduct. Thank God, there's been no personal gain involved. That would be going much too far, I suppose.

But the point that I make with regard to Mr. Haldeman and Mr. Ehrlichman is that I think, too, that if all the facts come out, that—and when they have an opportunity to have their case heard in court, not simply to be tried before a committee, and tried in the press and tried in television—they will be exonerated.

CONVERSATION WITH DEAN

Q. Mr. President, could you tell us your recollection of what you told John Dean on March 21 on the subject of raising funds for the Watergate defendants?

A. Certainly. Mr. Haldeman has testified to that, and his statement is accurate.

Basically, what Mr. Dean was concerned about on March 21 was not so much the raising of money for the defendants but the raising of money for the defendants for the purpose of keeping them still. In other words so-called hush money.

The one would be legal, in other words raising the defense funds for any group, any individual, as you know is perfectly legal and is done all the time. But you raise funds for the purpose of keeping an individual from talking, that's obstruction of justice.

Mr. Dean said also, on March 21, that there was an attempt to, as he put it, to blackmail the White House, to blackmail the White House by one of the defendants; incidentally, that defendant has denied it, but at least this is what Mr. Dean declared, and that unless certain amounts of money were paid, I think it was $120,000 for attorneys' fees and other support, that this particular defendant would make a statement, not with regard to Watergate but with regard to some national security matters in which Mr. Ehrlichman had particular responsibility.

My reaction very briefly was this: I said as you look at this, I said isn't it quite obvious, first, that if it is going to have any chance to succeed, that these individuals aren't going to sit there in jail for four years, they're going to have clemency. Isn't that correct?

He said yes.

I said we can't give clemency.

He agreed.

Then I went to another point. The second point is that isn't it also quite obvious, as far as this is concerned, that while we could raise the money, and he indicated in answer to my question that it would probably take a million dollars over four years to take care of this defendant and others on this kind of a basis, the problem was, how do you get the money to them. And also,

how do you get around the problem of clemency because they're not going to stay in jail simply because their families are being taken care of.

And so that was why I concluded, as Mr. Haldeman recalls, perhaps, and did testify very effectively, when I said "John, it's wrong, it won't work, we can't give clemency, and we've got to get this story out. And therefore I direct you and I direct Haldeman and I direct Ehrlichman and I direct Mitchell to get together tomorrow and then meet with me as to how we get this story out."

And that's how the meeting on the 22d took place.

COORDINATING DEFENSE

Q. Mr. President, earlier in the news conference you said that you gave Mr. Haldeman the right to listen to one tape because you wanted to be sure "that we are correct." And I think I'm quoting you correctly. Now, you have indicated that you still feel that Mr. Haldeman and Mr. Ehrlichman are two of the finest public servants that you've ever know. You have met with their lawyer at least twice that we know of. Are you and Mr. Haldeman and Mr. Ehrlichman coordinating their and your defense and if so why.

A. No, no. As far as my defense is concerned, I make it myself. As far as their defense is concerned, their lawyer demonstrated very well before the committee that he can handle it very well without any assistance from me.

AGNEW RESIGNATION

Q. Mr. President, a follow-up question on the Agnew situation. You have said in the past that any White House official who was indicted would be suspended and that anyone convicted would be dismissed. Should Vice President Agnew be indicted, would you expect him to resign or somehow otherwise stand down temporarily until cleared?

A. Well Mr. Theis, a perfectly natural question and one that any good newsman as you are would ask. But as you know it's one that would be most inappropriate for me to comment upon. The Vice President has not been indicted. Charges have been thrown out by innuendo and otherwise, which he has denied to me personally and which he has denied publicly. And the talk about indictment and the talk about resignation even now. I'm not questioning your right to ask the question, understand. But for me to talk about it would be totally inappropriate that I make no comment in answer to that question.

CHECK ON PRESIDENT

Q. Mr. President.

A. I'll take the big man.

Q. Thank you, Mr. President.

A. I know my troubles if I don't take him—or if I do.

Q. Looking to the future on executive privilege, there are a couple of questions that come to mind.

A. I thought we just passed the point.

Q. Well we speak here of the future.

A. All right.

Q. Where is the check on authoritarianism by the executive that the President is to be the sole judge of what the executive branch makes available and suppresses? And would you obey a Supreme Court order if you are asked and directed to produce the tapes or other documents for the Senate committee or for the special prosecutor? And if this is not enough, is there any limitation on the President, short of impeachment to compel the production of evidence of a criminal nature?

A. Is there anything else?

Q. No. I think that will be enough.

A. No, I was not being facetious; but I realize it's a complicated question. The answer to the first question is that there's a limitation on the President in almost all fields like this.

There's, of course, the limitation of public opinion; and, of course, congressional and other pressures that may arise.

As far as executive privilege is concerned in the Watergate matter—and I must say the I.T.T. file, etc.—that this Administration has, I think, gone further in terms of waiving executive privilege than any Administration in my memory. Certainly a lot further than Mr. Truman was willing to go when I was on the other side, as you recall, urging that he waive executive privilege.

Now, with regard to what the Supreme Court will do, or say —the White House press secretary, assistant secretary—Mr. Warren—has responded to that already. I won't go beyond that. And particularly I won't make any statement on that matter at this time, while the matter is still being considered by Judge Sirica.

I understand his decision will come down on Wednesday, and then we will make a comment. As far as the statement that Mr. Warren has made with regard to the President's position of complying with a definitive order of the Supreme Court is concerned, that statement stands.

EXPLOITERS OF WATERGATE

Q. Mr. President, sir, last week in your speech you referred to those who would exploit Watergate to keep you from doing your job. Could you specifically detail who those are?

A. I would suggest that where the shoe fits, people should wear it. I would think that some political figures, some members of the press perhaps, some members of the television, perhaps, would exploit it. I don't impute, interestingly enough, motives, however, that are improper interests, because here's what is involved.

There are a great number of people in this country that would prefer that I do resign. There are a great number of people in this country that didn't accept the mandate of 1972. After all, I know that most of the members of the press corps were not enthusiastic. And I understand that about either my election in '68 or '72. That's not unusual. Frankly, if I had always followed what the press predicted or the polls predicted, I would have never been elected President.

But what I am saying is this. People who did not accept the mandate of '72, who do not want the strong America that I want to build, who do not want to give, who do not want to cut down the size of this Government bureaucracy that burdens us so greatly and to give more of our Government back to the people, people who do not want these things naturally would exploit any issues. If it weren't Watergate, anything else in order to keep the President from doing his job.

And so I say I have no improper motives to them. I think they would prefer that I failed. On the other hand, I'm not going to fail. I'm here to do a job, and I'm going to do the best I can, and I'm sure the fair-minded members of this press corps, and that's most of you, will report when I do well, and I'm sure you'll report when I do badly.

WIRETAPS

Q. Mr. President, you recently suggested that if the late Robert Kennedy had initiated 10 more wiretaps, he would have been able to discover the Oswald plan, as you described it, and thereby presumably prevent the assassination of President Kennedy.

A. Let me correct you, sir. I want to be sure that the assumption is correct. I said if 10 more wiretaps could have found the conspiracy, if it was a conspiracy, or the individual, then it would have been worth it. As far as I'm concerned, I'm no more of an expert on that assassination than anybody else, but my point is that wiretaps in the national security area were very high in the Kennedy Administration for a very good reason.

Because there were many threats on the President's life, because there were national security problems, and that is why that in that period of 1961 to '63 there were wiretaps on news organizations, on news people, on civil rights leaders and on other people. And I think they were perfectly justified and I'm sure that President Kennedy and his brother, Robert Kennedy, would never authorize them, unless he thought they were in the national interest.

Q. Do you think, then, that threats to assassinate the President merit more national security, wiretaps particularly?

A. No, no, as far as I'm concerned, I was only suggesting that in terms of those times that to have the Oswald thing happen just seemed so unbelievable that it—with his record, with his record, that it, with everything that everybody had on him, that that fellow could have been where he was in a position to shoot the President of the United States seems to me to be, to have been a terrible breakdown in our protective security areas. I would like to say, however, that as far as protection generally is concerned, I don't like it. And my family doesn't like it. Both of my daughters would prefer to have no Secret Service. I discussed it with the Secret Service. They say they have too many threats and they have to have it. My wife doesn't want to have Secret Service. And I would prefer and I recommended this just three days ago, to cut my detail by one third because I noticed there were criticisms of how much the Secret Service is spending.

Let me say, that we always are going to have threats against the President. But I frankly think that one man, probably, is as good against a threat as a hundred, and that's my view, but my view doesn't happen to be in a majority there and it doesn't happen to agree with the Congress, so I will still have a great number of Secret Service around me, more than I want, more than my family wants.

Q. Mr. President, during March and April you received from your staff, on several occasions, information about criminal wrongdoing and some indication that members of your staff might have been involved. The question, sir, is why didn't you turn this information over immediately to the prosecutors, instead of having your own staff continue to make these investigations?

A. Well, for the very obvious reason that in March, for example, the man that was in constant contact with the prosecutors was my counsel, Mr. Dean. Mr. Dean was talking to Mr. Petersen. I assumed that anything he was telling me, he was telling the prosecutors.

And in April, after Mr. Dean left the investigation, Mr. Ehrlichman was in charge. I would assume—and, incidentally, Mr. Ehrlichman did talk to Mr. Kleindienst—that is why it was done that way.

The President doesn't pick up the phone and call the Attorney General every time something comes up on a matter. He depends on his counsel, or whoever he's done the job to—or, given that assignment to—to do the job. And that is what I expected in this instance.

Q. Following on that, Mr. President— **A.** You've had one now, you don't—you've had three. Go ahead.

Q. Mr. President, in your Cambodian invasion—in your Cambodian invasion speech of April, 1970, you reported to the American people that the United States had been strictly observing the neutrality of Cambodia. I'm wondering if you, in light of what we now know, that there were 15 months of bombing of Cambodia previous to your statement, whether you owe an apology to the American people?

A. Certainly not, and certainly not to the Cambodian people. Because, as far as this area is concerned, the area of approximately 10 miles—which was bombed during this period— no Cambodians had been in it for years. It was totally occupied by the North Vietnamese Communists. They were using this area for the purpose of attacking and killing American marines and soldiers by the thousands.

The bombing was taking—took place against those North Vietnamese forces in enemy-occupied territory.

And as far as the American people are concerned, I think the American people are very thankful that the President ordered what was necessary to save the lives of their men and shorten this war—which he found when he got here, and which he ended.

COX, WRIGHT FACE OFF IN COURT ON TAPES SUBPOENA

After weeks of dueling with legal memoranda, Watergate Special Prosecutor Archibald Cox faced the President's attorney, Charles Alan Wright, across a courtroom on Aug. 22.

Before John J. Sirica, chief judge of the federal district court for the District of Columbia, the two law professors argued whether or not Sirica should attempt to enforce the grand jury subpoena served on President Nixon seeking evidence in the grand jury Watergate investigation.

"Is it true that no instance can be cited when a court has attempted to enforce a subpoena on a President?" Sirica asked.

"It is true," replied Cox, admitting the depths of the uncharted constitutional waters into which he was asking Sirica to venture.

Sirica listened intently to two hours of arguments by Cox and Wright. He then told the courtroom that he hoped to announce his decision in the matter a week later on Aug. 29. *(Subpoena, Vol. I, p. 208; Nixon reply, Vol. I, p. 255; Cox brief, Vol. I, p. 273; Nixon reply, p. 10)*

Wright: Not for the Court

Arguing first, Wright, a University of Texas law professor, cited the "simple fact of history": no court has ever attempted to do what Cox asked. Courts do not have this power, he argued, and only the "hydraulic force" of Watergate has changed legal minds on this matter.

"There are times when other national interests are more important even than the fullest administration of criminal justice," he asserted. This weighing of interests is a matter for the executive, not the courts.

"This is not a unique case," Wright argued, countering Cox's claim that the decision would be a narrow one. The decision to require the President to produce the tapes would set a precedent, he said, for claims before all the 400 federal district judges in the country. "The breach in presidential privacy would not be small; it would not be contained in Watergate, but would be exposed to a very wide extent."

"If there are doubts concerning the good judgment of the President," said Wright, "there are other forums to resolve that issue."

"What is the public interest served in the withholding of these tapes?" asked Sirica, the heavy-browed, tight-lipped judge who presided over the trial of the original Watergate defendants.

"The public interest in having the President able to talk in confidence with his closest advisers," responded Wright.

"The President is the sole judge of the public interest, then?" continued Sirica.

"That has been the law," replied Wright.

"The President, then, is the sole judge of executive privilege?" pressed Sirica.

"Yes," responded Wright.

"There is potential for grave abuse then, it appears to me," said Sirica, noting that such absolute power appeared "contrary to the system of checks and balances."

The framers created a remedy for such abuse, noted Wright: impeachment, then formal criminal charges and a trial. "But so long as he is President, he is the judge" of executive privilege. The essence of executive privilege is that it is the executive's decision "to decide what can be given, when it can be given, and to whom it can be given."

Cox: A Matter of Public Confidence

"There is strong reason to believe that the integrity of the executive offices has been corrupted.... Public confidence in our institutions is at stake," declared the bespectacled Cox, rising to present his argument.

Not only can the court overrule the claim of executive privilege which threatens to impede the complete investigation of Watergate, stated Cox, but it has ample powers to enforce the subpoena if it chooses to do so.

Executive privilege cannot protect specific evidence needed by a grand jury investigating criminal matters, continued Cox. It is a question "not of person but of duty." The public has the right to every man's evidence: principle and precedent require that this subpoena be enforced.

Wright's claims of a broad and dangerous effect of a decision to enforce the subpoena were "exaggerated," said Cox. This case is unique, he argued, expressing the belief that discussions involving criminal activity—and thereby not protected by executive privilege—were relatively infrequent in the presidential offices. "If more frequent discussions of crime occur in presidential offices, what we need is not more privilege" anyway, he concluded.

Whatever power the executive has to terminate a prosecution—as claimed in the Aug. 17 reply brief—Cox said, the executive does not have the power to limit or terminate a grand jury investigation. "If this matter is to be left to the courts," Cox added, alluding to Nixon's Aug. 15 statement, "then it should be done with a willingness to proceed under the settled rules of law...not while bringing in by the back door the matter of the executive's ultimate power of dismissal." *(Nixon statement, Vol. I, p. 272)*

In conclusion, Cox cited the statement of Justice Robert H. Jackson that "with all its defects...men have discovered no technique for long preserving free government except that the executive be under the law."

Rebuttal. Rising to reply to Cox, Wright spoke briefly. In response to questions from Sirica, he said that the President would not be willing to produce the tapes for Sirica to examine in private in order that the national security-threatening and other irrelevant parts might be excised and the remaining recorded information presented to the grand jury. Under a 1969 Supreme Court ruling, he said, a judge did not have that power.

"We do not contend for one moment," Wright concluded, "that Richard M. Nixon is above the law. But the presidency has many unique aspects under our constitutional system which limit the extent to which the law can make its force felt against the man who holds that position."

Nixon Reply to Cox Argument for Tapes

Following are excerpts from President Nixon's Aug. 17 reply brief responding to Watergate Special Prosecutor Archibald Cox's Aug. 13 memorandum in support of his suit to compel Nixon to turn over to the grand jury the recordings of nine conversations related to the Watergate case.

In a prefatory paragraph to the 16-page reply brief, the President's lawyers stated that "we do not wish to reply at length to the 68-page submission of the special prosecutor nor to burden the court by restating the arguments set out in our initial brief.... Thus we content ourselves with calling the court's attention to a few key points that must be borne in mind in appraising the (special prosecutor's) brief." (Cox brief in summary, Vol. I p. 273; Nixon brief, p. 255)

I

The Special Prosecutor asserts that the grand jury will not be able to function as effectively as he would like unless it has access to the tapes in question. The President...has asserted that he, and his successors, will not be able to function effectively if the tapes are disclosed. The principal theme of the (special prosecutor's) brief...is that this conflict may appropriately be resolved by the Judiciary and that it is more important that a grand jury have access to every possible bit of evidence and that indictments against wrongdoers contain every possible count than that the confidentiality that the President regards as indispensable to the performance of his Constitutional duites be preserved....

This notion that the extraction of the last ounce of flesh by the criminal process is the highest and most important purpose of government, and that courts have the power to impose this goal on the Chief Executive though he believes that to pursue it will harm other important government interests, is not the law.

...The court may tell the Executive that it is to produce, but if the Executive chooses not to do so, it is free to make that choice and the only power in the court is to dismiss the prosecution....

These are merely special applications of the general principle that it is exclusively for the Executive Branch, and not for the courts, to decide whether other governmental interests outweigh the interest in a particular criminal prosecution....

The (special prosecutor's) brief suggests that it is "a false conflict to see the present controversy as a struggle between the powers of the Judiciary and the prerogatives of the President," and indicates that the authority of the grand jury is derived from the people themselves, rather than from a court.... The short answer is that this is not true.

A grand jury is an arm of the court, and it does not have power, any more than does the court that convenes it, to decide that it is more important that a particular prosecution go forward than that other important governmental interests be protected.

Surely the Special Prosecutor is being unduly gloomy when he suggests that his failure to obtain the tapes might require "termination of this grand jury investigation."

...the controlling fact is that there is no power in the Judicial Branch to decide that the public interest requires a particular criminal investigation or prosecution to continue if the Executive Branch has determined that other governmental interests dictate to the contrary.... An important part of the "executive power * * * vested in a President of the United States of America" is the power to decide whether he will sacrifice the confidentiality he deems essential to the proper functioning of that office in order to make possible a particular criminal prosecution. This is a power that resides in the Executive alone. No court has any power to make the choice that the (special prosecutor's) brief...asks.

II

...(W)e have not suggested and do not contend in any way that the President is above the law. What we have undertaken to assert and support is the proposition that the Office of the Presidency is treated differently under the law, that the Presidency has certain unique attributes, few in number but indispensable to its character and effective operations, and among these, perhaps more important than any other, is Presidential privacy—the right, indeed the absolute need, to be able to speak freely, to encourage others to speak freely, and thereby encourage confidence that the President and he alone has the absolute power to decide what may be disclosed to others.

The tapes at issue here are of conversations between the President and his close advisers. The tapes are subject to his sole control.... It is a simple fact of history that no President has ever been compelled to produce information if he thought the public interest would be harmed by doing so, and, as we have pointed out before, consistent practice has its own weighty claims in construing the Constitution....

Against all of this the decision of the circuit court in *United States* v. *Burr*...is a slim foundation for the proposition that the President "has an enforceable legal duty not to withhold material evidence from a grand jury." ...The court confined its inquiry to whether the subpoena should issue and not to whether the court could or would compel compliance....

Though it is consoling to be given the assurance that "compliance with the subpoena will not interfere with or burden in any direct or material way the proper performance of the duties and responsibilities of the President or the Executive Office," ...the President, who has occupied that great office for 4½ years, has reached a very different judgment. He has solemnly represented, both to this Court and to the country, that the confidentiality of his conversations in connection with his official duties is absolutely essential to the effective performance of his duties.

III

...The (special prosecutor's) brief is at pains to minimize the effect of a decision in this case. It presents "only a minimal threat" to the confidentiality of the Presidency "for surely there will be few occasions" in which there will be similar cause to call for Presidential papers....

Any suggestion that this case is unique because high Presidential advisers are being investigated for possible criminal acts flies in the face of history....

Of course it is true that in the vast majority of Presidential conversations there would never be anything said that could arguably be material evidence in a criminal investigation. But the inhibiting effect comes from the difficulty of a particular participant in a particular conversation being sure that this is true, unless he is certain that he knows the motivations of all of the other participants. Thus the deterrence of a ruling that courts can compel disclosure of Presidential conversations would be very extensive even though the actual instances in which disclosure would be ordered would be less frequent, though still hardly unique.

Week's Watergate Chronology

Following is a day-to-day chronology of the week's events in the week ending Aug. 25 (*Earlier events, Vol. I, p. 262*):

AUG. 16

Agent Resigns. The Secret Service announced that agent James C. Bolton Jr., who helped guard Sen. George McGovern (D S.D.) during the 1972 election campaign, had resigned after an agency probe revealed campaign information Bolton acquired was passed to the White House. According to reports, Bolton gave information about a McGovern meeting with an alleged subversive to his father, an aide to Rep. Glenn R. Davis (R Wis.). Bolton senior then passed it to the White House. The Secret Service said the "matter was an isolated incident."

Weicker Prison Visit. Sen. Lowell P. Weicker Jr. (R Conn.), a member of the select Watergate committee, held a six-hour meeting with four convicted Watergate burglars at the Danbury, Conn., federal prison Aug. 13. A spokesman for the senator said the four prisoners—Bernard L. Barker, Frank A. Sturgis, Virgilio R. Gonzalez and Eugenio R. Martinez—sought Weicker's aid and advice.

Bittman Withdrawal. William O. Bittman, a defense lawyer for E. Howard Hunt Jr., a convicted Watergate conspirator, withdrew as Hunt's attorney. A motion approved by Federal District Court Judge John J. Sirica gave no reason for the withdrawal, but said that Hunt had approved it. Austin Miller, Bittman's associate, also withdrew from the case. Bittman had been identified during the Watergate hearings as a recipient of secret funds for Hunt and other defendants.

AUG. 17

Nixon Response. President Nixon's lawyers filed his response to special Watergate prosecutor Archibald Cox's brief of Aug. 13 calling on the President to give up tapes of Watergate-related conversations. Nixon's attorneys, in their rebuttal brief, claimed the President had "the absolute power" to maintain the secrecy of his conversations. If the tapes were vital to the successful prosecution of some Watergate defendants, the Nixon brief stated, the courts would have no choice but to dismiss the cases. (*Story, p. 9*)

Kalmbach Deposition. Herbert W. Kalmbach, in a deposition released Aug. 17, said former White House aide John D. Ehrlichman lied to the Senate select Watergate committee when he said he never assured Kalmbach that raising secret funds for the Watergate defendants was legal and proper. Kalmbach, the President's personal lawyer, said in his deposition and at the Senate hearings that Ehrlichman gave him those assurances at a meeting July 26, 1972. The deposition was given July 31, 1973, in connection with the Democratic National Committee's civil suit against the Committee for the Re-Election of the President for invasion of privacy stemming from the Watergate burglary.

AUG. 18

Y.A.F. Resolution. The politically conservative Young Americans for Freedom approved a resolution at its annual convention in Washington, D.C., demanding that the President "bring about full disclosure of the truth or falsity of his alleged involvement in Watergate and/or the coverup."

Illegal Contribution. The Minnesota Mining and Manufacturing Co. acknowledged an illegal contribution of $30,000 to President Nixon's re-election finance committee. The disclosure brought to six the number of corporations admitting to having made illegal contributions to the President's re-election effort. Others were American Airlines ($55,000), Phillips Petroleum Co. ($100,000), Ashland Oil, Inc. ($100,000), Gulf Oil Corp. ($100,000), and Goodyear Tire and Rubber Co. ($40,000).

AUG. 19

Campaign Spying. Lucianne Cummings Goldberg, a New York City free-lance journalist, admitted to the Washington *Star-News* that she had been hired by Murray M. Chotiner, a long-time Nixon political adviser, to spy on McGovern's presidential campaign. She said she had been paid $1,000 a week plus expenses for her assignment, which lasted from Labor Day 1972 to election day.

Impeachment. McGovern, appearing on CBS-TV's "Face the Nation," said Congress would have to consider impeachment of the President if he defies a possible court ruling to release tapes of Watergate-related conversations.

AUG. 20

Political Spying. Chotiner said there was another journalist, in addition to Mrs. Goldberg, who spied on McGovern's campaign. Mrs. Goldberg admitted Aug. 19 that she had been hired by Chotiner to spy on McGovern's election campaign. Chotiner, who did not identify the second journalist, insisted there was nothing illegal about the arrangements. He said the second journalist, a man, worked for him from early 1971 to Labor Day 1972.

Sullivan Memo. A document alleging that Presidents Roosevelt and Johnson used federal investigators against their political opponents will not be disclosed by the Senate select Watergate committee, deputy counsel Rufus L. Edmisten stated. Edmisten said the memo, written by former FBI associate director William C. Sullivan, was "far too personal" and undocumented. The memo was turned over to the committee by former presidential counsel John W. Dean III, who received it from Sullivan. Dean told the committee that when President Nixon learned the FBI had conducted political intelligence operations in Democratic administrations, he ordered Dean to get examples from Sullivan.

Bank Subpoena. The Senate select Watergate committee announced it had issued subpoenas for an officer and certain records of the Key Biscayne (Fla.) Bank and Trust Co. headed by President Nixon's close friend, Charles G. (Bebe) Rebozo. The purpose of the subpoenas was to see whether improper campaign contributions moved through the bank. The official under committee subpoena was identified as Franklin S. DeBoer.

AUG. 21

Laird. Presidential Counselor Melvin R. Laird said Nixon's legislative programs had been harmed by the Watergate hearings.

AUG. 22

Nixon Press Conference. In his first press conference in five months and the first to be televised live in more than a year, President Nixon said that he had never considered resigning because of the Watergate scandal and that he intended to remain in office until his term expired. He also reiterated his stand against providing the Senate select Watergate committee or the special Watergate prosecutor the tapes of his conversations with White House aides. Nixon also announced the resignation of William P. Rogers as secretary of state and appointment of foreign policy adviser Henry A. Kissinger as a replacement. *(News conference story, p. 1; text, p. 3)*

Court Fight. Meanwhile, White House lawyer Charles Alan Wright appeared before United States District Court Judge John J. Sirica in Washington to argue the President's legal case against releasing the tapes. After hearing the arguments from both Wright and special prosecutor Archibald Cox, Sirica said he would hand down his ruling on the release of the White House tapes by Aug. 29. *(Story, p. 9)*

AUG. 23

Clark, Katzenbach. Two former attorneys general in the Kennedy and Johnson administrations denied ever having authorized burglaries in the interest of national security. President Nixon said during his press conference Aug. 22 that burglaries had occured "on a very large scale" during the Kennedy-Johnson years. Nixon said the existence of the burglaries "was quite well known."

But Nicholas deB. Katzenbach and Ramsey Clark, who served as attorneys general during the two administrations, denied the charge. Clark said he had never authorized the burglaries nor did he know of anyone who had. Katzenbach, Clark's predecessor at the Justice Department, echoed the denial.

"If the President is going to say things like that he ought to say who authorized it and who knew about it," Katzenbach told the *Washington Post*.

The White House declined to elaborate on the President's allegation, citing the "sensitivity" of the matters involved. Deputy Press Secretary Gerald L. Warren said the President made the charge "because it was a fact." But when Warren was pressed by reporters to reveal more information on the subject, he refused to detail the alleged burglaries.

"I'm not going to go beyond what the President has said," Warren said. The Justice Department also declined to provide any information on the activities of the department during the Kennedy-Johnson years.

Ervin Response. The chairman of the Senate select committee investigating Watergate, Sam J. Ervin Jr. (D N.C.), blasted Nixon's charge while attending a political rally in his home state. Ervin accused the President of trying to justify abuses in his administration by citing alleged abuses in preceeding administrations.

"Murder and theft have been committed since the earliest history of mankind," Ervin said, "but that fact has not made murder meritorius or larceny legal." Ervin added that he had never heard of any burglaries in either the Kennedy or Johnson administrations.

Poll Report

Although President Nixon's popularity recovered slightly following his televised speech Aug. 15, two major polls showed that a majority of Americans still had doubts about his role in the Watergate affair.

Results of the Gallup poll, conducted Aug. 17-19 and published Aug. 22, showed that 38 per cent of those interviewed approved of the way the President was handling his job. Public approval of the President had dipped to 31 per cent—the lowest of his administration—in ratings published Aug. 14. *(Previous poll reports, Vol. I, p. 274, p. 262, p. 218)*

The gain in popularity was expected, according to Gallup, since approval generally rises following a nationwide television address.

Gallup interviewers asked 1,452 adults, "Do you approve or disapprove of the way Nixon is handling his job as President?" The results:

	Latest	Aug. 3-6
Approve	38	31
Disapprove	54	57
No Opinion	8	12

A Harris poll, however, showed that nearly two-thirds of those interviewed, 66 per cent, felt the President had not dispelled doubts about his involvement in Watergate.

In the Harris survey, published Aug. 21, individuals interviewed in 1,536 homes Aug. 18-19 were asked, "Do you tend to agree or disagree with critics of President Nixon who feel he has yet to answer the serious doubts about his involvement in Watergate which have come out of the Senate hearings?" The results:

Agree, not answered doubts	66%
Disagree, answered doubts	25%
Not sure	9%

Harris also found that 71 per cent felt the President had withheld "important information" about Watergate and had not been "frank and honest."

The Gallup poll had similar findings, with 58 per cent of those who had seen or heard the speech saying they were dissatisfied with Nixon's explanation regarding Watergate while 34 per cent said they were satisfied.

Both polls showed, however, that despite public skepticism over the President's explanations, most Americans did not favor his resignation or impeachment.

Harris found that a plurality of 49-44 per cent felt the President should not resign even if it were proved he knew about the concealment of White House involvement in Watergate and that 63 per cent were opposed to his resignation over the Watergate issue. The number of those favoring resignation, 28 per cent, had doubled from 14 per cent in May.

Only 23 per cent of those interviewed by Gallup said they favored impeachment, while 70 per cent were opposed to the President's removal from office.

NIXON ORDERED TO PRODUCE TAPES FOR COURT REVIEW

"It was the system that has brought the facts to light and that will bring those guilty to justice—a system that in this case has included...a courageous judge, John Sirica...."

—Richard M. Nixon
April 30, 1973

Four months after praising his performance as presiding judge at the Watergate trial, President Nixon found himself on opposite sides of 69-year-old U.S. District Court Judge John J. Sirica in what seemed the beginning of a historic, and to some frightening, confrontation between the executive and judicial branches of government. On Aug. 29, Sirica ordered the President to turn over tapes of nine conversations relating to the Watergate scandal for a private judicial review. Sirica himself, he said, should decide whether the tapes were protected by the doctrine of executive privilege or whether they should be turned over to Watergate special prosecutor Archibald Cox. *(Text, p. 17)*

The White House immediately rejected the order. In their first reaction, Nixon lawyers Charles Alan Wright and J. Fred Buzhardt hinted that they might carry the question directly to the Supreme Court. Another possibility was simply to ignore Sirica's decision, thus risking a contempt citation.

However, after an hour-long meeting Aug. 30 in San Clemente between Nixon and the two lawyers, the White House announced that it would take the fight to the U.S. Court of Appeals in the District of Columbia. Thus, the President seemed to opt for a prolonged legal duel which, assuming neither side backed down, could end in nothing short of a landmark decision by the U.S. Supreme Court.

Even then, the possibility of a deadlock between the two branches loomed. Nixon had stated earlier that he would only comply with a "definitive" decision by the high court; and apparently he reserved for himself the option of determining the court's definitiveness.

The day before Sirica issued his order, White House officials had described President Nixon as being convinced that the worst of Watergate was behind him. "They think we've turned the corner on Watergate," presidential counselor Anne Armstrong, the administration's liaison with state Republican organizations, told a *Washington Post* reporter. However, the same aides expressed fears about the nation's continued inflation headaches.

A Congressional Quarterly survey of 60 members of Congress, taken as they were preparing to return to Washington after a month-long recess, gave evidence that inflation far outweighed Watergate as a pressing public concern. Almost without exception, the legislators said their constituents had been besieging them with complaints about the cost of living, asking what

the government could do about it, and then turning to Watergate almost as an afterthought.

The President faced another problem as Congress returned: though much legislative work remained to be completed, the administration's goals on Capitol Hill were foundering.

COURT ORDER

"Ordered that...President Richard M. Nixon...is hereby commanded to produce forthwith for the court's examination in camera, the subpoenaed documents or objects which have not heretofore been produced to the grand jury...."

With those words Federal District Judge John J. Sirica "attempted to walk the middle ground" between the positions argued Aug. 22 by Charles Alan Wright, attorney for President Nixon, and Archibald Cox, the Watergate special prosecutor. *(p. 9)*

Sirica Aug. 29 issued the order directing Nixon to turn over to him—for his private *(in camera)* inspection —the nine tape recordings of presidential conversations subpoenaed July 23 by the original grand jury investigating the Watergate break-in.

After listening to the tapes in his chambers, Sirica would determine whether or not Nixon had properly claimed that they were protected by executive privilege from disclosure to the grand jury. If, said Sirica, he found that any portion of the tapes were not properly covered by the claimed privilege, he would turn them over to the grand jury.

During the Aug. 22 arguments, Sirica had asked Wright what the President's reaction would be to an order directing surrender of the tapes to Sirica himself for this sort of private examination. Wright had said that the President felt such an order would not be appropriate.

Sirica delayed the date that the order would take effect for five business days, until Sept. 6, so that the President might appeal it. On Aug. 30 the White House announced that the President would appeal the ruling by that date to the court of appeals, District of Columbia circuit. The Sirica ruling then would not become effective until all appeals had been acted upon.

Three Questions, Two Answers

Central to the legal arguments concerning enforcement of a subpoena on a president were three questions:
• Does a court have the authority to decide whether a claim of executive privilege is properly raised to block grand jury access to certain material?
• Does a court have authority to enforce a subpoena against the President with an order for private inspection of the material by the judge?

• Were the tapes in fact covered by executive privilege and thus protected from the subpoena?

Reserving judgment on the third question, Sirica answered the first two with a firm "yes."

Privilege in Disfavor. Although a search of the Constitution and its history revealed "a general disfavor of government privileges," courts had held that executive privilege did protect—and allow the withholding of—evidence sought in a civil case concerning military secrets, Sirica noted.

"There can be executive privileges that will bar the production of evidence," said Sirica. "The court is willing here to recognize and give effect to an evidentiary privilege based on the need to protect presidential privacy."

But it was not up to the President alone to decide when executive privilege was properly asserted, continued Sirica. When that decision affected the availability of evidence, it fell also within the province of the courts. "Executive fiat is not the mode" for resolving such problems, he said.

A Private Look. "In all candor, the court fails to perceive any reason for suspending the power of the courts to get evidence and rule on questions of privilege in criminal matters simply because it is the President of the United States who holds the evidence," declared Sirica.

Judge John J. Sirica

The court had the right to avail itself of a private examination of the documents or tapes, held Sirica. "To call for the tapes *in camera* is thus tantamount to fully enforcing the subpoena as to any unprivileged matter." He had concluded, he said, that the court had the authority to order a President to obey the command of a grand jury subpoena as it related to unprivileged evidence in his possession.

It was up to the President, he continued, "to define exactly what it is about his office that court process commanding the production of evidence (a subpoena) cannot reach there.... What distinctive quality of the Presidency permits its incumbent to withhold evidence?"

Separation of Powers

Sirica found unpersuasive the arguments that the need for presidential privacy and respect for the separation of powers justified withholding of evidence: "the special prosecutor has correctly noted that the framers' intention to lodge the powers of government in separate bodies also included a plan for interaction between departments."

"A 'watertight' division of different functions was never their design. The legislative branch may organize the judiciary and dictate the procedures by which it transacts business. The judiciary may pass upon the constitutionality of legislative enactments and in some instances define the bounds of congressional investigations. The executive may veto legislative enactments, and the legislature may override the veto.

The executive appoints judges and justices and may bind judicial decisions by lawful executive orders. The judiciary may pass on the constitutionality of executive acts."

It is immaterial whether the court has the physical power to enforce an order against the President, continued Sirica. "Regardless of its physical power...the court has a duty to issue appropriate orders." Agreeing with the special prosecutor's argument concerning grand jury powers, Sirica stated: "The grand jury derives its authority directly from the people, and when that group, independent in its sphere, acts according to its mandate, the court cannot justifiably withhold its assistance, nor can anyone, regardless of his station, withhold from it evidence not privileged."

The Claim of Privilege

The eventual decision on the width of the protection of executive privilege as applied to the tapes would be heavily influenced, Sirica indicated, by the well documented and imposing need for the tapes as evidence.

"This is a criminal investigation. Rather than money damages at stake, we deal here in matters of reputation and liberty. Based on this indisputably forceful showing of necessity by the grand jury, the claim of privilege cannot be accepted lightly."

"The special prosecutor cites a substantial possibility, based on the sworn testimony of participants, that the privilege is improperly invoked as a cloak for serious criminal wrong-doing." Should that be the case, said Sirica—"if the interest served by a privilege is abused or subverted—the claim of privilege is invalid.

But Sirica found himself unable, under the circumstances of Aug. 29, to rule that the present claim of privilege by Nixon was invalid. "The court...is extremely reluctant to finally stand against a declaration of the President of the United States on any but the strongest possible evidence. Need for the evidence requires that a claim not be rejected lightly. The court is simply unable to decide...without inspecting the tapes."

He admitted that if the tapes were indeed protected by executive privilege, even his private inspection of them would compromise that privilege. But "it would be an extremely limited infraction and in this case an unavoidable one.... The court is unable to design a more cautious approach.... The court has attempted to walk the middle ground between a failure to decide the question of privilege...and a wholesale delivery of tapes to the grand jury at the other. The one would be a breach of duty; the other an inexcusable course of conduct."

"If it be apparent that the tapes are irrelevant to the investigation, or that for state reasons they cannot be introduced into the case, the subpoena *duces tecum* would be useless. But if this be not apparent, if they *may* be important in the investigation, if they *may* be safely heard by the grand jury, if only in part, would it not be a blot on the page which records the judicial proceedings of this country, if, in a case of such serious import as this, the court did not at least call for an inspection of the evidence in chambers?"   √

Week's Watergate Chronology

Following is a day-to-day chronology of the week's events in the week ending Aug. 25. *(Earlier Aug. 23 events, p. 11)*:

AUG. 23

GAO Report. The General Accounting Office (GAO) released its most comprehensive campaign financing report to date. The four-volume, 21-pound document listed the names of about 70,000 persons who contributed or loaned money to all candidates in the 1972 presidential campaign. A total of $63.6-million was given outright, while $15.5-million was loaned to candidates. The GAO pointed out that the figures cover only the period after April 7, 1972, when the new election financing law took effect.

Illegal Contribution. Braniff Airways, Inc. released a statement in Dallas, Texas, saying it had contributed $40,000 in corporate funds to the Finance Committee to Re-elect the President, in violation of federal election law. It was the seventh voluntary public disclosure of corporate contributions to Nixon's 1972 campaign. *(Earlier disclosures, p. 11)*

AUG. 24

Burglary History. *The New York Times* quoted informed sources as saying that the FBI had conducted illegal burglaries over a 30-year period beginning with the administration of Franklin D. Roosevelt and ending in 1966, when Director J. Edgar Hoover decided the practice was too risky. The sources said the burglaries, carried out in connection with national security investigations and criminal cases, were unknown to any of the attorneys general who served during the period, or to anyone else outside the FBI.

In his press conference of Aug. 22, Nixon said burglarizing similar to the Ellsberg break-in was authorized and took place on "a very large scale" during the Kennedy and Johnson years and was "quite well known." But the *Times* article described the practice as one of the best-kept secrets within the FBI. *(Earlier response, p. 12)*

Illegal Contributions. *The New York Times* reported that, according to its sources, lawyers for about 20 companies had approached the special prosecutor's office about the possibility of disclosing illegal contributions to Nixon's 1972 campaign. The companies in question, along with the seven which had already admitted publicly to such contributions, were reportedly represented on a master list of 2,000 Nixon contributors that was obtained in June by Common Cause, the "citizens' lobby," and later by Senate and special prosecution investigators. The investigators believed 15 or 20 names on the list indicated illegal corporate contributions, the Times said.

AUG. 25

Wiretaps. *The New York Times* identified three high-ranking foreign service officers whose telephones were tapped under Nixon's authority between 1969 and 1971. They were: William H. Sullivan, ambassador to the Philippines and former State Department liaison at the Paris peace talks; Richard F. Pedersen, ambassador to Hungary and former State Department counselor; and Richard L. Sneider, deputy assistant secretary of state for East Asian affairs.

In his May 22 statement on Watergate, the President said he authorized the two-year wiretap effort to halt news leaks that were jeopardizing sensitive foreign policy matters. He said the individuals tapped were chosen by his national security adviser, Henry A. Kissinger, Attorney General John Mitchell and FBI Director J. Edgar Hoover. Secretary of State-designate Kissinger was expected to face questioning on the taps during his upcoming confirmation hearings before the Senate Foreign Relations Committee. *(Nixon statement, Vol. I, p. 79)*

Rogers Reaction. Outgoing Secretary of State William P. Rogers responded to the wiretap report through acting State Department spokesman Paul J. Hare. Rogers "had no knowledge of these wiretaps and did not approve them and would not have approved them," Hare said.

Martha Mitchell Disclosure. Mrs. Martha Mitchell, wife of former Attorney General John Mitchell, told United Press International that the Senate Watergate Committee should call her to testify because she had seen a campaign strategy book for 1972 written by Nixon and his former staff director, H. R. Haldeman. "It included the whole procedures of everything that has happened," she said. Mrs. Mitchell also disputed Nixon's contention that Mitchell never informed him of the Watergate coverup, saying: "Why did they go out on the Sequoia (the presidential yacht) every night last summer during the re-election campaign?"

AUG. 28

Haldeman Tapes. Sen. Daniel K. Inouye (D Hawaii), a member of the Senate Watergate investigating committee, said the committee had received information that "supports my doubts" about whether the tapes of presidential conversations could be used as evidence at a trial. Inouye cited an Aug. 10 letter to committee Chairman Ervin from Frank Strickler, an attorney for H. R. Haldeman, which corrected some details of Haldeman's testimony about his handling of the tapes.

Haldeman told the committee during his testimony July 30 and 31 that he had listened to two tape recordings of conversations Nixon held with former White House counsel John W. Dean III on Sept. 15, 1972, and March 21, 1973. Haldeman said he received the tapes from White House aide Stephen Bull in the Executive Office Building during early July. Strickler's letter said Haldeman later recalled he had received some of the material from Bull while at the home of another White House aide, Lawrence Higby. *(Haldeman testimony, Vol. I, p. 231)*

Inouye said he had "no reason to doubt the veracity of Mr. Haldeman and no evidence that the tapes were doctored," but he added that the new information raised serious questions about their reliability.

Senate Hearings. Rufus L. Edmisten, deputy counsel to the Senate Watergate committee, told reporters that Chairman Ervin wanted to end the hearings by Nov. 1 "or shortly thereafter." Edmisten said the committee would meet Sept. 11 to take stock of what had been accomplished and what remained to be done when the hearings resumed Sept. 17. *(Committee plans, Vol. I, p. 274)*

AUG. 29

Tapes Ruling. U.S. District Judge John J. Sirica ordered President Nixon to make tape recordings of White House conversations involving the Watergate case available to him for a decision on their use by the Watergate grand jury. Sirica had heard arguments in the tapes dispute from Nixon's lawyer, Charles Alan Wright, and Watergate special prosecutor Archibald Cox on Aug. 22.

Sirica ruled that inspecting the tapes himself was the only way for him to decide the validity of Nixon's argument that they contained privileged information. "In all candor," he said, "the court fails to perceive any reason for suspending the power of courts to get evidence and rule on questions of privilege in criminal matters simply because it is the President of the United States who holds the evidence." Nixon was given five days to appeal the ruling. *(Details, p. 14)*

Response. A spokesman for the special prosecution expressed satisfaction with the ruling and said his office would do everything possible to expedite the case if an appeal was sought. From the western White House in San Clemente, officials announced that the President would not comply with the court order on grounds that inspection of the tapes by a judge would be "inconsistent with the President's position relating to the question of separation of powers as provided by the Constitution, and the necessity of maintaining precedents of confidentiality of private presidential conversations...." The White House statement said Nixon's lawyers were considering an appeal "or how otherwise to sustain" the President's legal position.

Senate Tapes Dispute. There also were new developments in the Senate Watergate investigating committee's suit seeking access to the presidential tapes. White House lawyers filed a four-page brief in federal district court in Washington rejecting the committee's demand mainly on procedural, rather than substantive, grounds. They argued that the committee had conducted a "criminal investigation and trial" that exceeded the authority granted to Congress by the Constitution, and that the court had no jurisdiction over their client, either as an individual or as President.

In a legal countermove, the committee filed with the court a motion for summary judgment in the case, asking that the court enforce two subpoenas served on the President without further delay.

Mitchell-Stans Ruling. Judge Lee P. Gagliardi of the federal district court in New York City rejected a defense motion to dismiss or delay the trial of former Attorney General John N. Mitchell and former Commerce Secretary Maurice Stans on charges of conspiracy, obstruction of justice and perjury in connection with a Securities and Exchange Commission investigation of financier Robert L. Vesco. The trial was scheduled to begin Sept. 11. Defense lawyers had asked for dismissal of the indictments against the two men because "massive prejudicial publicity" had made a fair trial impossible.

Political Spying. A General Accounting Office (GAO) official said its auditors were investigating the apparent failure of the Nixon re-election campaign to report properly $1,000 weekly salaries paid to two correspondents hired to report to long-time Nixon adviser Murray M. Chotiner on the activities of Democrats. They were Lucianne Goldberg, a journalist who admitted she was hired by Chotiner to report on the McGovern campaign, and Seymour Freidin, who reported to Choitner on Democratic presidential primary candidates. The GAO official, Phillip S. Hughes, said a finding on the question could come within two weeks. *(Previous developments, p. 11)*

AUG. 30

Dole Threat. Sen. Robert Dole (R Kan.), former chairman of the Republican National Committee, said he was considering introducing a resolution in the Senate to halt the Watergate committee hearings. "I think people have had enough of watching the seven senators try Richard Nixon on television," Dole said.

Greenspun Subpoena. H.M. "Hank" Greenspun, publisher of *The Las Vegas Sun*, announced that he would comply with a subpoena to appear before the Senate investigating committee but that he would not produce his paper's records. The subpoena was thought to be a result of testimony to the committee by convicted Watergate conspirator James W. McCord Jr. that the White House "plumbers" group once considered burglarizing the safe in Greenspun's office because it contained documents damaging to a Democratic presidential contender. ✓

TEXT OF JUDGE SIRICA'S ORDER AND OPINION ON TAPES

Following is the complete text of District Court Chief Judge John J. Sirica's Aug. 29 order requiring President Nixon to produce tapes of presidential conversations for his examination:

This matter having come before the Court on motion of the Watergate Special Prosecutor made on behalf of the June, 1972 grand jury of this district for an order to show cause, and the Court being advised in the premises, it is by the Court this 29th day of August, 1973, for the reasons stated in the attached opinion,

ORDERED that respondent, President Richard M. Nixon, or any subordinate officer, official or employee with custody or control of the documents or objects listed in the grand jury subpoena *duces tecum* of July 23, 1973, served on respondent in this district, is hereby commanded to produce forthwith for the Court's examination *in camera,* the subpoenaed documents or objects which have not heretofore been produced to the grand jury; and it is

FURTHER ORDERED that the ruling herein be stayed for a period of five days in which time respondent may perfect an appeal from the ruling; and it is

FURTHER ORDERED that should respondent appeal from the ruling herein, the above stay will be extended indefinitely pending the completion of such appeal or appeals.

Sirica's Opinion

Following are excerpts from Sirica's Aug. 29 opinion on the presidential tapes:

The parties to the controversy have briefed and argued several issues including the Court's jurisdiction in the matter of compulsory process, the existence and scope of "executive privilege" generally, applicability of "executive privilege" to the tape recordings subpoenaed, and waiver of privilege. The Court has found it necessary to adjudicate but two questions for the present: (1) whether the Court has jurisdiction to decide the issue of privilege, and (2) whether the Court has authority to enforce the subpoena *duces tecum* by way of an order requiring production for inspection *in camera.* A third question, whether the materials are in fact privileged as against the grand jury, either in whole or in part, is left for subsequent adjudication. For the reasons outlined below, the Court concludes that both of the questions considered must be answered in the affirmative.

I

A search of the Constitution and the history of its creation reveals a general disfavor of government privileges, or at least uncontrolled privileges. Early in the Convention of 1787, the delegates cautioned each other concerning the dangers of lodging immoderate power in the executive department. This attitude persisted throughout the Convention, and executive powers became a major topic in the subsequent ratification debates. The Framers regarded the legislative department superior in power and importance to the other two and felt the necessity of investing it with some privileges and immunities, but even here an attitude of restraint, as expressed by James Madison, prevailed.... The upshot...regarding a definition of executive privileges was that none were deemed necessary, or at least that the Constitution need not record any.

...Are there, then, any rights or privileges consistent with, though not mentioned in, the Constitution which are necessary to the Executive? One answer may be found in the Supreme Court decision, *United States v. Reynolds,* 346 U.S. 1 (1953). The Court recognized an executive privilege, evidentiary

in nature, for military secrets. *Reynolds* held that when a court finds the privilege is properly invoked under the appropriate circumstances, it will, in a civil case at least, suppress the evidence. Thus, it must be recognized that there can be executive privileges that will bar the production of evidence. The Court is willing here to recognize and give effect to an evidentiary privilege based on the need to protect Presidential privacy.

The Court, however, cannot agree with Respondent that it is the Executive that finally determines whether its privilege is properly invoked. The availability of evidence including the validity and scope of privileges, is a judicial decision.... In all the numerous litigations where claims of executive privilege have been interposed, the courts have not hesitated to pass judgment. Executive fiat is not the mode of resolution....

The measures a court should adopt in ruling on claims of executive privilege are discussed under Part III herein.

II

If after judicial examination *in camera,* any portion of the tapes is ruled not subject to privilege, that portion will be forwarded to the grand jury at the appropriate time. To call for the tapes *in camera* is thus tantamount to fully enforcing the subpoena as to any unprivileged matter. Therefore, before the Court can call for production *in camera,* it must have concluded that it has authority to order a President to obey the command of a grand jury subpoena as it relates to unprivileged evidence in his possession. The Court has concluded that it possesses such authority.

Analysis of the question must begin on the well established premises that the grand jury has a right to every man's evidence and that for purposes of gathering evidence, process may issue to anyone.... The important factors are the relevance and materiality of the evidence.... The burden here then, is on the President to define exactly what it is about his office that court process commanding the production of evidence cannot reach there. To be accurate, court process in the form of a subpoena *duces tecum* has already issued to the President, and he acknowledges that...courts possess authority to direct such subpoenas to him. A distinction is drawn, however, between authority to issue a subpoena and authority to command obedience to it. It is this second compulsory process that the President contends may not reach him. The burden yet remains with the President, however, to explain why this must be so. What distinctive quality of the Presidency permits its incumbent to withhold evidence? To argue that the need for Presidential privacy justifies it, is not persuasive. On the occasions when such need justifies suppression, the courts will sustain a privilege. The fact that this is a judicial decision has already been discussed at length, but the opinion of Chief Justice Marshall (*United States v. Burr,* 25 Fed. Cas. 30, 1807) on the topic deserves notice here. When deciding that a subpoena should issue to the President, the Chief Justice made it clear that if certain portions should be excised, it being appropriate to sustain a privilege, the Court would make such a decision upon return of the subpoena....

To argue that it is the constitutional separation of powers that bars compulsory court process from the White House, is also unpersuasive. Such a contention overlooks history. Although courts generally, and this Court in particular, have avoided any interference with the discretionary acts of coordinate branches, they have not hesitated to rule on non-discretionary acts when necessary. Respondent points out that these and other precedents refer to officials other than the President, and that this distinction renders the precedents inapplicable. Such an argument tends to set the White House apart as a fourth branch of government. It is true that *Mississippi v. John-*

son, 4 Wall. 475 (1866) left open the question whether the President can be required by court process to perform a purely ministerial act, but to persist in the opinion, after 1952, that he cannot would seem to exalt the form of the *Youngstown Sheet & Tube Co.* (343 U.S. 579) case over its substance. Though the Court's order there went to the Secretary of Commerce, it was the direct order of President Truman that was reversed.

The Special Prosecutor has correctly noted that the Framer's intention to lodge the powers of government in separate bodies also included a plan for interaction between departments. A "watertight" division of different functions was never their design. The legislative branch may organize the judiciary and dictate the procedures by which it transacts business. The judiciary may pass upon the constitutionality of legislative enactments—and in some instances define the bounds of Congressional investigations. The executive may veto legislative enactments, and the legislature may override the veto. The executive appoints judges and justices and may bind judicial decisions by lawful executive orders. The judiciary may pass on the constitutionality of executive acts....

That the Court has not the physical power to enforce its order to the President is immaterial to a resolution of the issues. Regardless of its physical power to enforce them, the Court has a duty to issue appropriate orders. The Court cannot say that the Executive's persistence in withholding the tape recordings would "tarnish its reputation," but must admit that it would tarnish the Court's reputation to fail to do what it could in pursuit of justice. In any case, the courts have always enjoyed the good faith of the Executive Branch, even in such dire circumstances as those presented by *Youngstown Sheet & Tube Co.* v. *Sawyer,* 343 U.S. 579 (1952), and there is no reason to suppose that the courts in this instance cannot again rely on that same good faith. Indeed, the President himself has publicly so stated.

It is important also to note here the role of the grand jury. Chief Justice Marshall, in considering whether a subpoena might issue to the President of the United States observed:

> In the provisions of the constitution, and of the statute, which give to the accused a right to the compulsory process of the court, there is no exception whatever. *(United States.* v. *Burr, 25 Fed. Cas. 20, 1807)*

Aaron Burr, it will be remembered, stood before the court accused though not yet indicted. The Chief Justice's statement regarding the accused is equally true with regard to a grand jury: "there is no exception whatever" in its right to the compulsory process of the courts. The Court, while in a position to lend its process in assistance to the grand jury, is thereby in a position to assist justice.

The grand jury is well known to Anglo-American criminal justice as the people's guardian of fairness.... (It) has been.... a shield for the innocent and a sword against the guilty. Among the Bill of Rights enacted by the First Congress was the Fifth Amendment which reads in part: "No person shall be held to answer for a capital or otherwise infamous crime, unless on a presentment or indictment of a grand jury." The grand jury derives its authority directly from the people, and when that group, independent in its sphere, acts according to its mandate, the court cannot justifiably withhold its assistance, nor can anyone, regardless of his station, withhold from it evidence not privileged. Marshall concluded that, contrary to the English practice regarding the King, the laws of evidence do not excuse anyone because of the office he holds....

In all candor, the Court fails to perceive any reason for suspending the power of courts to get evidence and rule on questions of privilege in criminal matters simply because it is the President of the United States who holds the evidence. The Burr decision left for another occasion a ruling on whether compulsory process might issue to the President in situations such as this. In the words of counsel, this is a new question," with little in the way of precedent to guide the Court. But Chief Justice Marshall clearly distinguished the amenability of the King to appear and give testimony under court process and that of this nation's chief magistrate. The conclusion reached here cannot be inconsistent with the view of that great Chief Justice nor with the spirit of the Constitution.

III

In deciding whether these tape recordings or portions thereof are properly the objects of a privilege, the Court must accommodate two competing policies. On the one hand, as has been noted earlier, is the need to disfavor privileges and narrow their application as far as possible. On the other hand, lies a need to favor the privacy of Presidential deliberations; to indulge a presumption in favor of the President. To the Court, respect for the President, the Presidency, and the duties of the office, gives the advantage to this second policy. This respect, however, does not decide the controversy. Such a resolution on the Court's part, as Chief Justice Marshall observed, "would deserve some other appellation than the term respect." Nevertheless, it does no hurt for the courts to remind themselves often that the authority vested in them to delimit the scope and application of privileges, particularly the privileges and immunities of government, is a trust. And as with every trust, an abuse can reap the most dire consequences. This Court, then, enters upon its present task with care and with a determination to exercise that judicial restraint that characterizes the conduct of courts.

The teaching of *Reynolds* is that a Court should attempt to satisfy itself whether or not a privilege is properly invoked without unnecessarily probing into the material claimed to be privileged. A decision on how far to go will be dictated in part by need for the evidence....

The grand jury's showing of need here is well documented and imposing. The Special Prosecutor has specifically identified by date, time and place each of the eight meetings and the one telephone call involved. Due to the unusual circumstances of having access to sworn public testimony of participants to these conversations, the Special Prosecutor has been able to provide the Court with the conflicting accounts of what transpired. He thus identifies the topics discussed in each instance, the areas of critical conflict in the testimony, and the resolution it is anticipated the tape recordings may render possible. The relative importance of the issues in doubt is revealed....

The point is raised that, as in *Reynolds,* the sworn statements of witnesses should suffice and remove the need for access to documents deemed privileged. Though this might often be the case, here, unfortunately, the witnesses differ, sometimes completely, on the precise matters likely to be of greatest moment to the grand jury. Ironically, need for the taped evidence derives in part from the fact that witnesses *have* testified regarding the subject matter, creating important issues of fact for the grand jury to resolve. It will be noted as well in contradistinction to *Reynolds,* that this is a criminal investigation. Rather than money damages at stake, we deal here in matters of reputation and liberty. Based on this indisputably forceful showing of necessity by the grand jury, the claim of privilege cannot be accepted lightly.

In his Brief in Support, the Special Prosecutor outlines the grand jury's view regarding the validity of the Respondent's claim of privilege. Its opinion is that the right of confidentiality is improperly asserted here. Principally, the Special Prosecutor cites a substantial possibility, based on the sworn testimony of participants, that the privilege is improperly invoked as a cloak for serious criminal wrongdoing....

If the interest served by a privilege is abused or subverted, the claim of privilege fails. Such a case is well described in *Clark* v. *United States,* 289 U.S. 1 (1933), a decision involving the privilege of secrecy enjoyed by jurors....

These principles are, of course, fully applicable throughout government. A court would expect that if the privacy of its deliberations, for example, were ever used to foster criminal conduct or to develop evidence of criminal wrongdoings, any privilege might be barred and privacy breached. So it is that evidentiary privileges asserted against the grand jury may be ruled inapplicable if the interest served by the privilege is subverted.

Nevertheless, without discrediting the strength of the grand jury's position, the Court cannot, as matters now stand, rule that the present claim of privilege is invalid. The President contends that the recorded conversations occurred pursuant to an exercise of his duty to "take care that the laws be faithfully executed." Although the Court is not bound by that conclusion, it is extremely reluctant to finally stand against a declaration of the President of the United States on any but the strongest possible evidence. Need for the evidence requires that a claim not be rejected lightly. The Court is simply unable to decide the question of privilege without inspecting the tapes.

It is true that if material produced is properly the subject of privilege, even an inspection *in camera* may constitute a compromise of privilege. Nevertheless, it would be an extremely limited infraction and in this case an unavoidable one. If privileged and unprivileged evidence are intermingled, privileged portions may be excised so that only unprivileged matter goes before the grand jury (which also meets in secret proceedings). If privileged and unprivileged evidence are so inextricably connected that separation becomes impossible, the whole must be privileged and no disclosure made to the grand jury.

It should be observed as well that given the circumstances in this case, there is every reason to suppose an *in camera* examination will materially aid the Court in its decision. The fact that extensive accounts of the recorded conversations given under oath by participants are available, will enable the Court to make an intelligent and informed analysis of the evidence.

The Court is unable to design a more cautious approach consistent with both the demonstrated critical need for the evidence and the serious questions raised concerning the applicability of the privilege asserted. The Court has attempted to walk the middle ground between a failure to decide the question of privilege at one extreme, and a wholesale delivery of tapes to the grand jury at the other. The one would be a breach of duty; the other an inexcusable course of conduct. The approach comports with precedent in this district, and honors the injunction of *Reynolds* and *Burr* to pursue fairness and protect essential privacy.

To paraphrase Chief Justice Marshall, if it be apparent that the tapes are irrelevant to the investigation, or that for state reasons they cannot be introduced into the case, the subpoena *duces tecum* would be useless. But if this be not apparent, if they *may* be important in the investigation, if they *may* be safely heard by the grand jury, if only in part, would it not be a blot on the page which records the judicial proceedings of this country, if, in a case of such serious import as this, the Court did not at least call for an inspection of the evidence in chambers?

THE PRESIDENT FILES AN APPEAL ON DISPUTED TAPES

As the Senate Watergate committee prepared to go back to work, the most important developments in the case were occurring in the courts. During the week ended Sept. 8:

• President Nixon's lawyers filed a petition in U.S. District Court in Washington, D.C., to prevent Chief Judge John J. Sirica from listening to several tape-recorded conversations of the President. Sirica had ordered Nixon to turn over the tapes of nine conversations. *(p. 13)*

• A Los Angeles, Calif., grand jury indicted four former White House aides for their parts in the 1971 burglary of the office of the former psychiatrist of Pentagon Papers defendant Daniel Ellsberg. The four were John D. Ehrlichman, Nixon's former chief domestic affairs adviser; Egil (Bud) Krogh Jr., Ehrlichman's former assistant who later was in charge of the White House special investigative unit, the "plumbers"; David R. Young, Krogh's former assistant, and convicted Watergate conspirator G. Gordon Liddy. Krogh, the first to be arraigned, pleaded innocent.

• Although the bribery and conspiracy trial of former Attorney General John N. Mitchell and former Commerce Secretary Maurice H. Stans was scheduled to begin Sept. 11 in U.S. District Court in New York City, a motion for postponement was scheduled the same day in federal appeals court.

Nixon Appeal. In their petition for a writ of mandamus to reverse Sirica's Aug. 29 order for the tapes, Nixon's lawyers labeled the order "clearly erroneous and beyond the power of the judicial branch in that it purports to subject the President of the United States to compulsory process for acts performed in his official capacity."

The case, "of grave importance," according to the Nixon brief, raised the question of Sirica's authority to hear the tapes in his chambers, as he sought to do, "in the face of a formal and valid claim of presidential privilege."

Besides Sirica, special Watergate prosecutor Archibald Cox was named in the petition as an interested party. Filed with the petition was a suggestion for a hearing before the full nine-member U.S. Court of Appeals for the District of Columbia circuit. The request was granted, and the hearing was scheduled for Sept. 11.

Committee Motion. On Sept. 6, the same day the President's petition was filed, attorneys for the Senate investigating committee failed in their efforts to speed up the legal processes involved in obtaining the tapes. Judge Sirica granted Nixon's lawyers a two-week delay in filing a response to the committee's latest motion.

Samuel Dash, chief counsel for the committee, argued that Nov. 1 had been set as the target date for completion of the committee's hearings. Granting the delay,

he said, would have the effect of "ruling the Senate really out of court."

Sirica rejected Dash's plea. "The court believes this is a very important case," he said, "and it is determined not to be pushed into a half-baked job."

Senate Action. With a few more witnesses to be heard in the first phase of its hearings—on the Watergate bugging and its coverup—the Senate committee was to meet on Sept. 11. Still to be resolved were details about investigation of the two other phases, campaign espionage and sabotage and campaign financing.

Sen. Majority Leader Mike Mansfield (D Mont.) suggested that the tapes dispute be settled by a meeting of Nixon and committee members. Sen. Robert Dole (R Kan.) introduced a resolution to close further hearings to the public and the news media.

News Conference. At a news conference Sept. 5, the President expressed confidence that his position would be upheld by the appellate courts, despite his setback in U.S. District Court Aug. 29. Once again he argued for the need to protect the principle of "confidentiality which is so essential and indispensable for the proper conduct of the presidency."

But, in response to another question, Nixon refused to spell out what he meant by a "definitive ruling" of the Supreme Court. He had said earlier that he would abide by such a ruling on the tapes.

Week's Watergate Chronology

Following is a day-to-day chronology of the week's events in the week ending Sept. 8 *(Earlier Aug. 30 events, p. 16)*:

AUG. 30

White House Appeal. Nixon met with his Watergate attorneys in San Clemente, Calif., and decided to appeal the Aug. 29 ruling of U.S. District Judge John J. Sirica that the President should turn over to the judge disputed tape recordings of White House conversations. *(p. 13)*

Senate Tapes Dispute. Sirica refused to rule simultaneously on the parallel lawsuits brought against Nixon for release of White House tape recordings by the special prosecution and by the Senate Watergate investigating committee. The committee had requested the joint ruling in an Aug. 22 letter to the judge.

Without issuing an opinion, Sirica accepted the requests of special prosecutor Archibald Cox and White House attorneys that the suits be kept separate. Cox argued that joining the suits would delay a final decision on his demand for access to the tapes—and consequently delay the handing down of indictments by the Watergate grand jury. The White House lawyers opposed the committee's move on grounds that it would not have given them enough time to prepare their response to the suit.

AUG. 31

Florida Prosecution. Dade County, Florida, States Attorney Richard Gerstein said that he had agreed, after meeting with Justice Department officials, to call off his planned prosecution of several figures in the Watergate case at least until the term of the Washington, D.C., Watergate grand jury expired Dec. 5. Gerstein claimed jurisdiction in the case after Jeb Stuart Magruder, the former deputy director of the President's re-election campaign, testified before the Senate investigating committee June 14 that former Attorney General John N. Mitchell approved the Watergate break-in at a meeting held in Key Biscayne, Fla. *(Magruder testimony, Vol. I, p. 136)*

Wiretaps. *The New York Times* identified three more government officials whose telephones were tapped between 1969 and 1971 in an effort described by Nixon as aimed at stopping leaks of sensitive foreign policy information. They were James W. McLane, deputy director of the Cost of Living Council and former staff member of the White House Domestic Council; John P. Sears, former deputy White House counsel and a former Nixon law partner, and Lt. Gen. Robert E. Pursley, commander of American forces in Japan and former military assistant to former Secretary of Defense Melvin R. Laird. *(Earlier references, p. 15; Vol. I, p. 79, 69)*

SEPT. 1

Meany Charge. George Meany, president of the AFL-CIO, said in his Labor Day remarks that working people were horrified by the Watergate scandal. They viewed it, he said, as "an attack on the whole democratic structure—it was an attempt, really, to pervert the whole structure." On the subject of contributions to Nixon's 1972 campaign, Meany said, "What was going on was not campaign collection—what these people were doing was extortion."

SEPT. 3

Nixon Strategy. *Newsweek* magazine (Sept. 10) reported it had learned from White House sources that Nixon was planning a "tough it out" strategy for dealing with the Watergate crisis. According to the magazine, the President's decision to appeal Sirica's tapes ruling was the beginning of "a protracted strategy of delay" designed to prevent a final decision in the Supreme Court until he could rebuild domestic support. When the final ruling did come, Nixon reportedly was prepared to defy anything but a unanimous or near-unanimous decision on grounds that it was not the "definitive decision" he had promised to obey. At that point the President might even be willing to fire Attorney General Elliot L. Richardson and special prosecutor Archibald Cox if either of them opposed him, *Newsweek* added.

SEPT. 4

Tapes Dispute. Chief Judge David L. Bazelon of the U.S. Court of Appeals for the District of Columbia

circuit ordered a speeded-up schedule for appeals of Sirica's order that Nixon surrender White House tapes for judicial inspection. The move was aimed at getting the case to the Supreme Court as soon as possible after the Court convened Oct. 1, in the hope that the high court would rule on the tapes dispute in time for the Watergate grand jury to complete its work before its mandate expired Dec. 5.

With appeals yet to be filed, Bazelon advised White House attorneys and the special prosecutor that the Appeals Court would receive briefs Sept. 10 and hear oral arguments the next day. Both sides would have until Sept. 14 to file any further papers, and a decision most likely would come the following week, Bazelon said.

California Indictments. A grand jury in Los Angeles, Calif., heard its final day of testimony in its investigation of the 1971 break-in at the office of the psychiatrist of Pentagon Papers defendant Daniel Ellsberg, and returned secret indictments against unnamed defendants. The burglary at the office of Dr. Lewis Fielding was planned by members of the White House "plumbers" group assigned to stop national security leaks after the Pentagon Papers were published. Superior Court Judge James G. Kolts, who received the indictments, said the names of the accused and nature of the charges would not be revealed until one of the defendants was in custody.

Agnew Case. Samuel Dash, chief counsel of the Senate Watergate investigating committee, said the committee had turned up no evidence to warrant its own investigation of Vice President Agnew, who was under federal investigation for possible involvement in an alleged kickback scheme involving Maryland contractors.

Weicker, Mansfield. At a press conference in Hartford, Conn., Sen. Lowell P. Weicker Jr. (R Conn.), a member of the Senate investigating committee, said the committee should press ahead with its hearings. "If we keep saying 'forget about what happened, we really don't want to know, we're tired, etc.,' then all of a sudden this matter is going to come to the Republican bosom when it wasn't there to begin with," he said.

In an interview in Washington, D.C., Senate Majority Leader Mike Mansfield (D Mont.) offered a proposal for ending the tapes dispute between Nixon and the committee. "I would hope the President will invite the full committee, or at least its chairman and vice chairman, to meet with him" in order to work out a reasonable solution to the dispute, Mansfield said. He suggested the President turn the tapes over to the committee for a private hearing.

SEPT. 5

California Indictments. John D. Ehrlichman, Nixon's former domestic affairs adviser, and three other former White House aides were identified in news reports as the defendants in the secret indictments handed down the previous day by a Los Angeles grand jury that had been investigating the burglary of the office of Daniel Ellsberg's former psychiatrist. The others were said to be Egil Krogh Jr., former aide to Ehrlichman; David R. Young Jr., a former aide to Henry A. Kissinger, and G. Gordon Liddy, a convicted Watergate conspirator.

Nixon News Conference. Nixon refused during a White House news conference to comment on the kind of

Supreme Court decision on the tapes dispute that he would consider "definitive" and thus one he would honor. "We believe—my counsel believes—that we will prevail in the appellate courts," the President said. Nixon defended what he called his "hard line" on the dispute as necessary to preserve the constitutional prerogatives of the presidency. He also repeated his contention that the tapes in question contained "nothing whatever" that would contradict any of his previous statements on Watergate. *(Text, this page)*

Magruder, McCord Ruling. U.S. District Judge John J. Sirica ordered convicted Watergate conspirator James W. McCord Jr. and confessed conspirator Jeb Stuart Magruder, former deputy director of the Nixon re-election committee, to refrain from making public addresses or granting interviews if they wanted to remain free pending sentencing. The judge said it would be a "disgrace" for the two men to profit by their wrong-doing and that speeches might endanger the rights of others involved in the case.

Mitchell, Stans Trial. Lawyers for former Attorney General John N. Mitchell and former Commerce Secretary Maurice H. Stans had a preliminary success in their efforts to delay their clients' trial on bribery and conspiracy charges, scheduled to begin Sept. 11 in Federal District Court in New York City. Judge Henry J. Friendly of the U.S. Court of Appeals for the 2nd Circuit scheduled a hearing for the morning of Sept. 11 on the defense attorneys' request for a postponement of the trial in order to allow more time for preparation. *(Previous development, p. 16)*

Dole Resolution. Sen. Robert Dole (R Kan.) introduced a resolution providing that if the Senate Watergate investigating committee continued its hearings, they should be closed to the public and to the news media.

SEPT. 6

Nixon Appeal. White House attorneys asked the U.S. Court of Appeals for an immediate judicial review of Judge Sirica's order that Nixon turn over his Watergate tapes for judicial inspection. In an additional petition, the attorneys asked that the court hear the motion *en banc*—with a full bench of nine judges rather than the usual three-judge panel.

Donald Nixon Wiretap. Citing "four highly reliable sources," *The Washington Post* reported that President Nixon ordered the Secret Service to tap the phone of his brother, Donald, for more than a year during the President's first term. The tap was said to be aimed at monitoring Donald Nixon's business activities to prevent possible embarrassment to the administration. Two of the sources said the tap was only one of several conducted by the Secret Service on behalf of the President.

Responding to the report, deputy White House press secretary Gerald L. Warren said that any monitoring, if it took place, would have been related to "the protective function of the Secret Service."

NEWS CONFERENCE TEXT

Following are excerpts dealing with Watergate from President Nixon's Sept. 5 news conference in the East Room of the White House:

Poll Report

A majority of persons interviewed for a Gallup Poll published Sept. 2 responded positively to questions about the Senate Watergate hearings but negatively to a question about President Nixon's performance. The survey was conducted Aug. 17-19, when Congress was in recess, among 1,502 adults nationwide. *(Earlier poll report, p. 12)*

The question and answers:

"In general, do you think the Watergate hearings are a good thing for the country or a bad thing?"

Good	52%
Bad	41
No opinion	7

"Some of the people who have testified at the Watergate hearings may in the future be brought to trial. Do you think the news coverage given the hearings will make it less likely for these men to get a fair trial, or don't you think it will make any difference?"

Less likely	36%
Not much difference	56
No opinion	8

"Do you think the Senate Watergate committee is more interested in trying to discredit the Nixon administration, or more interested in getting at the facts surrounding the Watergate situation?"

Discredit	28%
Get facts	57
Both	9
No opinion	6

"Do you approve or disapprove of the way Mr. Nixon is handling his job as President?"

Strong approval	19%
Mild approval	19
No opinion	8
Mild disapproval	17
Strong disapproval	37

TAX AUDIT

Q. Mr. President, there have been some conflicting reports about your real estate dealings in California, and I would like to ask about that. Several different versions have been released by the White House, both as to your own personal financial involvement and as to the Government's expenditures in San Clemente and Key Biscayne, and your auditors, I understand from news reports, say that the entire audit has not been released on your financial dealings out there.

I would like to ask you why we have had so many conflicting reports to start with, and second, one of the questions that is raised by the only partial release of the audit is have you paid the taxes on the gain realized from the sale of the land to Mr. Rebozo and Mr. Abplanalp at San Clemente?

A. Of course, whatever a President does in the field of his property is public knowledge, and questions of that sort I

(Continued on p. 24)

Excerpts of Committee Memo, Presidential Answer

Attorneys for the Senate Select Committee on Presidential Campaign Activities filed a motion in U.S. District Court in Washington, D.C., on Aug. 29 for summary judgment in the committee suit seeking access to certain tape-recorded conversations of President Nixon. The committee's memorandum asked the court to enforce, without further delay, two subpoenas served on the President.

In a related development the same day, Nixon's lawyers filed with the court the President's response to the committee's case.

Excerpts from the committee memorandum and the presidential reply:

COMMITTEE MEMORANDUM

We will dispute...the proposition that executive privilege covers the communications of an innocent President with guilty aides about their criminal activities, but our arguments in this regard should not obscure a critical circumstance: Unfortunately, the involvement or noninvolvement of the President himself in that congeries of criminal activities falling under the general rubric of "Watergate" is very much an integral part of the present investigation.... John Wesley Dean, III, in his sworn testimony before the Select Committee, has accused the President of complicity in serious crimes. If Dean be believed, the President may be guilty of several crimes, including obstruction of a criminal investigation, misprision of a felony, conspiracy to commit an offense or to defraud the United States, and unlawfully influencing a witness. And Dean's charges are consistent with other evidence in the record that bears on the question of presidential involvement (there is, of course, also evidence in the record that would exonerate the defendant President of such charges). In such circumstances, the Committee would be derelict if it did not proceed to further examination of the President's complicity or lack thereof, no matter how distasteful that task may be....

The mere fact that the issue of privilege comes to the Court by way of suit by the Committee, rather than in a suit by the subpoena's recipient or his defense to a criminal prosecution, cannot affect the Court's authority to resolve that issue. Nor is this suit precluded because it is directed at the President and asks the Court to resolve conflicting claims of executive and legislative power under the Constitution. Indeed, in the circumstances presented here, it is the responsibility of the judiciary, as the neutral third branch of government, to discharge its role "as the ultimate interpreter of the Constitution,"...and mark the respective bounds of executive and legislative power....

...the conduct of the President is no more immune from judicial review than is that of any other executive officer. It is, to be sure, the normal practice in litigation to name a subordinate officer as the party defendant, even if the conduct sought to be reviewed is in reality the President's. But that course was precluded in this case by the defendant President's unexplained action in taking personal possession of the evidence sought by the Committee. Where, as here, effective relief can only be had against the President, he may be named as a party. Moreover, since the only relief now sought by plaintiffs in this action is a declaratory judgment, the question of judicial power to enforce a command against the chief executive is not before the court....

Congress' "informing function" is a necessary component of lawmaking power because it generates needed public support for legislation. Moreover, legislative scrutiny serves as a potent deterrent to official wrongdoing. As Louis D. Brandeis observed, "Sunshine is said to be the best of disinfectants; electric light the most efficient policeman." And when evidence of such wrongdoing is unearthed in circumstances that generate doubts as to the executive's capacity to cleanse its own house, a thorough, public investigation by Congress can play a vital role in restoring public confidence in the self-corrective processes of government....

The above principles are most relevant to the work of the Select Committee. Created by unanimous vote of the Senate, the committee is invested with a broad mandate to get to the bottom of widespread but incompletely substantiated suspicions of serious wrongdoing at the highest executive levels in connection with the 1972 presidential campaign and election and to consider the need for corrective legislation. We believe that the Committee's work to date (together with the work of this Court and of the press) has achieved partial success.... But the Committee's task is unfinished, and the evidence which the Committee seeks from defendant President is vital to the completion of its work.

...The very fact that the defendant President has secretly taped the conversations without notifying the participants is a breach of the confidence that the defendant President purports to protect. He has, in addition, permitted his aides to testify concerning these conversations whose confidentiality he now claims to be of critical importance. He has also permitted at least one private citizen, H. R. Haldeman, to review tapes of conversations to which he was not a party in preparation for Mr. Haldeman's Select Committee testimony. And the defendant President has given out his own version of so much of those conversations as he has deemed in his own interest. For the defendant President now to assert a claim of privilege on the basis of a supposed need for inviolate confidentiality is, we respectfully submit, totally unpersuasive....

NIXON'S ANSWER

Richard M. Nixon...states as follows:

1. ...denies that plaintiffs acted within their authority in issuing the subpoenas duces tecum to the President of the United States and thereafter in instituting this action....

3. ...denies that plaintiffs are entitled to investigate criminal conduct; and further denies that plaintiffs are empowered to bring suit against the President of the United States.

4. ...denies that the members of the Senate Select Committee are empowered to bring suit in their official capacities as members of that Committee.

5. ...denies that the President of the United States can be sued in his official capacity; and further denies that he can be sued individually for acts performed in his official capacity....

7. ...denies that plaintiffs are empowered to subpoena materials from the President of the United States....

9. ...denies that any court has jurisdiction to quash, modify, or narrow a subpoena issued by a Committee of Congress....

11. ...denies that he has conceded the relevancy of any "tapes" to plaintiffs' investigation....

do not resent at all. I do resent, I might say, the implications, however, first, that whether at Key Biscayne or in San Clemente my private property was enriched because of what the Government did.

As a matter of fact, what the Government did in San Clemente reduced the value of the property. If you see three Secret Service gazebos and if you see some of the other fences that block out the rather beautiful view to the hills and the mountains that I like, you would realize that what I say is quite true, it reduces its value as far as a residential property is concerned.

The second point is this: At rather considerable expense, and a great deal of time on my part, I ordered an audit, an audit by a firm highly respected, Coopers and Lybrand of New York. That audit has been completed. It covered at my request not simply the last year, but it covered the years 1969, 1970, 1971 and 1972.

The audit has been completed, and the audit gave the lie to the reports that were carried usually in eight-column heads in most of the papers of this country—and incidentally the retractions ended up back with the corset ads for the most part—but on the other hand, it gave the lie to the charge that there was $1 million worth of campaign funds, that that is how I acquired the property in San Clemente.

It also gave the lie to any other charges that as far as my acquisitions in Florida are concerned, or in California, that there was any money there except my own.

Now, I would make two or three other points briefly about it that I think all laymen could understand. I borrowed the money to acquire the property, and I still owe it. I own no stocks and no bonds—I think I am the first President in this office since Harry Truman. I don't own a stock or a bond. I sold everything before I came into office.

All that I have are the two pieces of property in Florida which adjoin each other, the piece of property in San Clemente with which you are familiar, and a house on Whittier Boulevard in which my mother once lived. I have no other property, and I owe money on all of them.

Third, as far as the capital gain matter, which is a technical matter that you have mentioned, I should point out—and maybe this is good news for people who wonder if Presidents are exempt from what the IRS does—the IRS has had a full field review or audit of my income tax returns for 1971 and 1972, and included in its audit is the transaction which you refer to, in which some argue there was a capital gain and some argue that there was not. It is a matter of difference between accountants.

The IRS, after its audit, did not order any change. If it had, I would have paid the tax. It did not order a change.

Now, with regard to the audit itself is concerned, the results of that audit insofar as the acquisition of the property have been put out. That is all that is going to be put out because I think that is a full disclosure.

I would simply say finally that in this particular case I realize that naturally there is a suspicion that a President, because he has the great power of this office and because he has the benefit of the Secret Service and GSA and all the rest to protect him, that he some way or other is going to profit from all of that security that is provided for him.

As I pointed out in my press conference two weeks ago, I'd far less rather have the security than have my privacy, but that just can't be done.

TAPES: DEFINITIVE RULING

Q. Mr. President?

A. Mr. Jarriel?

Q. Mr. President, in association with the legal dispute going on over possession of the Presidential tapes relating to Watergate conversations in your office, you and your attorneys have said you would abide only by a definitive ruling of the Supreme Court in this case. As it moves along, the definitive ruling, an interpretation of definitive ruling takes on great importance. Would you elaborate for us what you mean by a "definitive ruling"?

A. No, Mr. Jarriel, that would not be appropriate. I discussed this with White House Counsel, and, as you know, the matter is now on appeal and the appellate procedure will now go to the Circuit Court of Appeals in the District of Columbia and, if necessary, further on. The matter of definitive ruling is one that will be discussed in the appeal procedure and for me, in advance of the discussion, the briefs, the oral arguments, to discuss that would be inappropriate.

I think it should come to Mr. Rather now.

TAPES: ABOVE THE LAW

Q. Mr. President, if I may follow on to my colleague Tom Jarriel's question, while I can understand—

A. It shows the two networks working together.

Q. No, not always, Mr. President.

A. Thank heaven you are competitors.

Q. This is a question that we find a lot of people ask us.

A. Surely.

Q. As you know, President Lincoln said, "No man is above the law." Now, for most, if not every other American, any Supreme Court decision is final, whether the person, in terms of the decision, finds it definitive or not. Would you explain to us why you feel that you are in a different category? Why, as it applies to you, that you will abide only by what you call a definitive decision and that you won't even define "definitive"?

A. Well, Mr. Rather, with all due deference to your comment with regard to President Lincoln, he was a very strong President and, as you may recall, he indicated several times during his presidency that he would move in the national interest in a way that many thought was perhaps in violation of law, the suspension of the writ of *habeas corpus*, for example, during the Civil War for 15,000 people, and other items, to mention only one.

As far as I am concerned, I am simply suggesting—saying that the President of the United States, under our Constitution, has a responsibility to this office to maintain the separation of power and also maintain the ability of not only this President but future Presidents to conduct the office in the interests of the people.

Now, in order to do that, it is essential that the confidentiality of discussions that the President has with his advisers, with members of Congress, with visitors from abroad, with others who come in, that those discussions be uninhibted, that they be candid, they be free-wheeling.

Now, in the event that Presidential papers, or in the event that Presidential conversations as recorded on tapes, in my opinion, were made available to a court, to a judge *in camera*, or to a committee of Congress, that principle would be so seriously jeopardized that it would probably destroy that principle—the confidentiality which is so essential and indispensable for the proper conduct of the presidency.

That is why I have taken the hard line that I have taken with regard to complying with the lower court's order.

Now, when we come to the Supreme Court, the key there is what kind of an order is the Supreme Court going to issue, if any. And as I have said, in answer to Mr. Jarriel, it would not be appropriate for me to comment on whether an order would be definitive or not. I will simply say that as far as I am concerned, we are going to fight the tape issue. We believe, my Counsel believe, that we will prevail in the appellate courts.

And so, consequently, I will not respond to your question until we go through the appellate procedure.

MARCH 21 INVESTIGATION

Q. Mr. President, to follow up on that Watergate question, you have referred repeatedly to having ordered a new Watergate investigation on the 21st of March of this year. Several high officials of your Administration, Mr. Petersen, Mr. Gray and Mr. Kleindienst, have testified before the Senate committee that they didn't know anything about it, this investigation that you referred to. And I wonder if you could explain how it is that they apparently didn't know anything about this new investigation?

A. Well, because I had ordered the investigation from within the White House itself. The investigation, up to that time, had been conducted by Mr. Dean, and I thought by him, working as he had been in close communication with the Justice Department.

I turned the investigation—asked Mr. Dean to continue his investigation as I, as you remember, said last week, two weeks ago, in answer to a similar question. When he was unable to write a report, I turned to Mr. Ehrlichman. Mr. Ehrlichman did talk to the Attorney General, I should remind you, on the 27th of March, I think it was the 27th of March. The Attorney General was quite aware of that and Mr. Ehrlichman, in addition, questioned all of the major figures involved and reported to me on the 14th of April; and then, at my suggestion, direction, turned over his report to the Attorney General on the 15th of April. An investigation was conducted in the most thorough way.

REBUILDING CONFIDENCE

Q. Mr. President, you listed several areas of domestic concern—

A. Now we have the three networks.

Q. You listed several areas of domestic concern in the message you are going to send to Congress, but it has also been written that one of the major problems facing your Administration now is rebuilding confidence in your leadership.

Do you share that view and, if so, how do you plan to cope with it?

A. Mr. Valeriani, that is a problem, it is true. It is rather difficult to have the President of the United States on prime time television—not prime time, although I would suppose the newscasters would say the news programs are really the prime time—but for four months to have the President of the United States by innuendo, by leak, by, frankly, leers and sneers of commentators, which is their perfect right, attacked in every way without having some of that confidence being worn away.

Now, how is it restored? Well, it is restored by the President not allowing his own confidence to be destroyed; that is to begin. And, second, it is restored by doing something. We have tried to do things. The country hasn't paid a great deal of attention to it, and I may say the media hasn't paid a great deal of attention to it because your attention, quite understandably, is in the more fascinating area of Watergate.

Perhaps that will now change. Perhaps as we move in the foreign policy initiatives now, having ended one war, to build a structure of peace, moving not only with the Soviet Union and with the PRC where Dr. Kissinger incidentally will go, after he is confirmed by the Senate, which I hope will be soon, but as we move in those areas and as we move on the domestic front, the people will be concerned about what the President does, and I think that that will restore the confidence. What the President says will not restore it, and what you ladies and gentlemen say will certainly not restore it.

TAPES: NOTHING INCONSISTENT

Q. Mr. President, to follow up on the tapes question, earlier you have told us that your reasons are based on principle—separation of powers, Executive privilege, things of this sort. Can you assure us that the tapes do not reflect unfavorably on your Watergate position, that there is nothing in the tapes that would reflect favorably?

A. There is nothing whatever. As a matter of fact, the only time I listened to the tapes, to certain tapes—and I didn't listen to all of them, of course—was on June the 4th. There is nothing whatever in the tapes that is inconsistent with the statement that I made on May 22 or of the statement that I made to you ladies and gentlemen in answer to several questions, rather searching questions I might say, and very polite questions two weeks ago, for the most part, and finally nothing that differs whatever from the statement that I made on the 15th of August. That is not my concern.

My concern is the one that I have expressed and it just does not cover tapes, it covers the appearance of a President before a Congressional Committee which Mr. Truman very properly turned down in 1953 although some of us at that time thought he should have appeared. This was after he had left the Presidency but it had to do with matters while he was President. It covers papers of the President written for him and communications with him and it covers conversations with the President that are recorded on tape. Confidentiality once destroyed cannot in my opinion be restored.

TAPES: DISPELLING DOUBTS

Q. Mr. President, could I ask you one more question about the tapes. If you win the case in the Supreme Court—

A. That's the fifth one.

Q. —and establish the right of confidentiality for Presidents, then would you be willing voluntarily to disclose the tapes to dispel the doubt about their content?

A.: Well, again I would like to respond to that question in a categorical way but I shall not due to the fact that when the matter as it is at the present time is actually in the appeal process, White House counsel advise that it would not be appropriate to comment in any way about what is going to happen during that process. You put that question to me a little later, I will be glad to respond to it.

THE PRESS. Thank you, Mr. President.   ✓

COMMITTEE AIMING FOR END OF HEARINGS BY NOV. 1

The Senate select Watergate committee voted Sept. 12 to delay its hearings a week longer than expected and to abbreviate sharply the remaining public sessions.

The committee, in a closed 75-minute meeting, decided to resume public hearings Sept. 24, limit them to three a week and attempt to end them by Nov. 1. There was also a possibility, according to committee sources, that Charles W. Colson, a former White House aide and the expected lead-off witness when the committee resumed its hearings, would not appear.

In other Watergate-related developments the week ended Sept. 14:

• Special prosecutor Archibald Cox and presidential Attorney Charles A. Wright filed briefs Sept. 10 in the U.S. appellate court for the District of Columbia asking that Judge John J. Sirica's Aug. 29 decision be modified in Cox's case and overturned in Wright's case. The two lawyers argued their cases orally Sept. 11. *(Excerpts from briefs, p. 29)*

• The trial of former Attorney General John N. Mitchell and former Secretary of Commerce Maurice H. Stans for obstruction of justice was delayed indefinitely Sept. 11 by New York Federal District Court Judge Lee P. Gagliardi.

Senate Committee

Sam J. Ervin Jr. (D N.C.), chairman of the Senate Select Committee on Presidential Campaign Activities, and Howard H. Baker Jr. (R Tenn.), the ranking Republican, denied that the committee was limiting its hearings in the face of White House and public pressures. Ervin told reporters the seven-member committee was concerned that extended hearings would bring out so much detail "that we won't be able to see the forest for the bushes and trees." He said the hearings would focus on "key witnesses," and "salient points."

The new schedule meant the committee would have only 18 days to complete phases two and three—on sabotage and campaign financing—of its hearings. This was exactly half the number of days the committee met on phase one—the Watergate affair.

Phase one, in fact, had not been completed. Seven witnesses, including Colson, remained on the witness list when the committee recessed Aug. 7. Committee sources said Colson's lawyer informed the committee that Colson might be indicted by a federal grand jury investigating the September 1971 break-in at the office of Daniel Ellsberg's psychiatrist. The lawyer, David Shapiro, reportedly asked the committee to delay Colson's appearance pending the return of indictments by the grand jury.

If indicted, Colson presumably would refuse to testify before the Senate committee. The indictments, if any, were expected in one to two weeks.

Already indicted for the Ellsberg break-in by a state grand jury in Los Angeles, Calif., were two other men on the committee's witness list for phase one. They were Egil Krogh Jr. and David Young, two leaders of the White House "plumbers," the group responsible for the Ellsberg break-in. They were not expected to give Senate testimony.

Those remaining on the phase one list were E. Howard Hunt Jr., one of the seven convicted Watergate burglars; Paul O'Brien and Kenneth Parkinson, lawyers for the Committee for the Re-Election of the President, who allegedly were involved in the distribution of money to Watergate defendants, and William O. Bittman, Hunt's lawyer, who, according to Senate testimony, received and distributed money for the defendants and their lawyers. Hunt, too, was expected to testify.

The hearings had been scheduled to resume Sept. 18. Ervin and Baker attributed the delay in their resumption to a need by the committee's staff for more time to prepare for the hearings.

Ervin, asked how the committee could do a thorough job on phases two and three in only half the time it devoted to phase one, said the committee saw its function in the last two phases as revealing only "the broad outlines" of what occurred. "You could carry this on forever, you know, until the last lingering echo of Gabriel's horn trembled into ultimate silence," he said.

The committee appeared to be agreeable to continued television coverage of its hearings. Thus the matter rested with the networks as to whether and how coverage would be handled. Network spokesmen said no decisions had been made on television coverage of the remaining hearings.

The committee's determination to obtain certain tape recordings on Watergate-related presidential conversations had not flagged. Ervin said the tapes were "crucial" to the committee's investigation, because they would confirm or deny former White House counsel John W. Dean III's testimony that Nixon was aware of the Watergate coverup. Baker said the committee would write its report, due Feb. 28, 1973, regardless of whether it received the tapes, but that the tapes would "greatly enhance" the committee's efforts to learn the truth about Watergate. The committee had sued the President to obtain tapes and other documents.

Cox-Wright Arguments

Meanwhile, the historic legal battle over the tapes took another step toward judicial resolution as Cox and Wright argued their respective cases before the U.S. appellate court in Washington Sept. 11.

More than 250 persons listened as Wright asked that Sirica's ruling be overturned because it would cause grave damage to the presidency to give up confidential tapes to the Watergate grand jury. Cox, who was in charge of the grand jury probe, said the search for truth depended on access to the tapes. Also arguing before the court were lawyers for Judge Sirica.

Sirica technically was being sued by Cox and Wright over his Aug. 29 decision. The judge ruled that the President had to turn over to him—for his *in camera* (private) inspection—nine tape recordings of presidential conversations subpoenaed July 23 by the Watergate grand jury. Sirica said he would then determine whether any parts of the tapes were covered by executive privilege and should be withheld from the grand jury.

Wright objected to the decision, because he said it infringed on what he believed was the President's right to determine how evidence in his possession should be used. Cox objected to Sirica's "middle ground" approach between allowing the President to keep the tapes, as Wright wanted, and yielding them unconditionally to the grand jury, as Cox wanted.

The case was argued before only seven members of the nine-man court. Two judges, both considered members of the court's conservative wing, disqualified themselves. Judge Roger Robb, a Nixon appointee, withdrew from the case, according to court officials, because he and Kenneth Parkinson, a scheduled witness before the Senate Watergate committee, once were members of the same law firm. Judge Edward A. Tamm, a Johnson appointee, gave no reason for disqualifying himself.

Liddy Contempt Citation

The House Sept. 10 voted, 334-11, to cite Watergate conspirator G. Gordon Liddy for contempt of Congress. The case was turned over to the U.S. attorney in the District of Columbia for presentation to a grand jury.

Liddy, a former member of the "plumbers" special investigative unit at the White House, was cited for his refusal to be sworn in to testify before the House Armed Services Committee's Special Intelligence Subcommittee July 20. The subcommittee and then the full committee approved the resolution (H Res 536) citing him for contempt.

Ordinarily, witnesses reluctant to testify before congressional committees take the oath and then refuse to testify on constitutional grounds such as the Fifth Amendment. Liddy, already serving an eight-month contempt of court sentence in the District of Columbia jail for refusing to testify before a federal grand jury, was summoned before the subcommittee in connection with the 1971 burglary of the office of Pentagon Papers defendant Daniel Ellsberg's former psychiatrist. He was one of four men indicted for the burglary by a California grand jury. *(Box, p. 30)*

Besides the eight-month contempt sentence, Liddy was sentenced to six to 20 years for his part in planning the June 17, 1972, break-in at Democratic national headquarters in the Watergate building. He was counsel to the Nixon re-election finance committee at that time.

The maximum penalty, if Liddy were convicted, would add a $1,000 fine and a one-year jail sentence to his earlier sentence.

Wright told the court that there were no circumstances under which the President could be forced to give up the tapes. He urged that the judges avoid an "aura of confrontation" that would result from a judicial order for Nixon to release the recordings. He proposed that the court merely "suggest what it feels should be done" and rely on the President's good judgment to do what is right.

The President had said he would obey a "definitive" Supreme Court ruling to turn over the tapes, but he had not spelled out what he meant by definitive. Thus, Wright was asking the appellate court to pass the issue up to the Supreme Court.

Wright said "great damage to the presidency" would result from an order upholding Sirica's decision. There would then be no limit for Nixon or future presidents "on the extent to which presidential privacy can be invaded," he maintained. The lawyer, a constitutional expert from the University of Texas, said that release even of parts of the tapes to the Watergate grand jury would entitle any defendants indicted on the basis of that information to demand the complete recordings.

Cox disagreed sharply, arguing that if any defendant demanded the full tapes, he would require some showing that the portions kept from the grand jury would help the defense.

But the special prosecutor's main argument was that Sirica's ruling should be stiffened so that the tapes, if obtained by the court, would go directly to the grand jury. The need to protect the confidentiality of the President's conversations was far outweighed, he said, by the need for the truth and the preservation of the integrity of the White House.

Alternately, Cox asked the court at least to modify the Sirica ruling so that he and his assistants could be permitted to listen to the tapes with the judge in order to identify relevant parts. He suggested that any national security information on the tapes could be deleted by the White House on submission of an affidavit setting out the need for the deletion.

Sirica's lawyers asked the judges to uphold Sirica's Aug. 29 ruling, although they invited the appellate court to add any guidelines it saw fit.

Week's Watergate Chronology

Following is a day-to-day chronology of the week's events in the week ending Sept. 8. *(Earlier Sept. 6 events, p. 22):*

SEPT. 6

Committee Suit. U.S. District Judge John J. Sirica gave White House lawyers until Sept. 24 to respond to the Senate Watergate investigating committee's suit seeking access to nine tape-recorded conversations of President Nixon. *(Committee motion, p. 24)*

Krogh Plea. Egil Krogh Jr., a former White House aide, pleaded not guilty in Los Angeles, Calif., Superior Court to charges stemming from his alleged involvement in the planning of the 1971 burglary of the office of Daniel Ellsberg's psychiatrist. *(Box, p. 30)*

SEPT. 7

Cox Appeal. Special prosecutor Archibald Cox asked the U.S. Court of Appeals to grant the Watergate grand jury direct access to the disputed presidential tapes, bypassing Judge Sirica's ruling that he should review the tapes in private to determine if any of the information contained in them should be withheld from the grand jury because of its privileged nature. If the court upheld Sirica's review, Cox asked that it establish guidelines for the judge to use in assessing the tapes.

Ehrlichman Plea. John D. Ehrlichman, Nixon's former domestic affairs adviser, and David R. Young, a former White House aide, were arraigned in Los Angeles Superior Court on charges connected with the 1971 burglary of Ellsberg's psychiatrist. Both pleaded not guilty and were released. *(Box, p. 30)*

Colson-Hunt Tape. *The Washington Star-News* printed excerpts of the transcript of a July 1, 1971, telephone conversation between Charles W. Colson, former special White House counsel, and E. Howard Hunt, a convicted Watergate conspirator. According to the transcript, obtained from Senate investigators, the two men agreed that it would be politically advantageous to the administration to "go to the line to nail" Pentagon Papers defendant Daniel Ellsberg. "It's going to take some resourceful engineering," Colson said.

SEPT. 8

Agnew on Watergate. Vice President Agnew assured listeners at a Republican Party rally in St. Charles, Ill., that the party had weathered the Watergate scandal and emerged healthy. But he warned that some "embittered critics" would continue their "morbid preoccupation with Watergate that threatens the ability of a government to concentrate on problems it was elected to solve."

SEPT. 9

Nixon Tapes. *The New York Times* reported that the Senate Watergate investigating committee had received new information on the handling of the disputed White House tapes during an interview with Stephen Bull, a White House aide. Bull reportedly said Nixon on several occasions had asked aides to play tapes of his conversations with former White House counsel John W. Dean III and to brief him on their content. The incidents were said to have taken place at the time of Dean's testimony before the committee in June, before the existence of the tapes became publicly known. *(Earlier charge, p. 16)*

Inouye Remarks. Sen. Daniel K. Inouye (D Hawaii) of the Senate investigating committee said on NBC-TV's "Meet the Press" that it was not the business of the committee to decide the guilt or innocence of anyone, and therefore, "We can proceed and file an adequate report without the tapes."

SEPT. 10

Briefs Filed. President Nixon's lawyers submitted a 95-page brief in the U.S. Court of Appeals for the District of Columbia, asking that the Court nullify Sirica's

Poll Report

The latest Harris Survey found that a majority of the 1,536 adults interviewed in mid-August felt that the press was overplaying the Watergate story. This was a reversal of the public's attitude in a July poll. But the August survey also found that a two-thirds majority credited the press with exposing the scandal. *(Earlier poll report, p. 22)*

These were the results of the Harris Survey, published Sept. 8:

"If it had not been for the press exposés, the whole Watergate mess would never have been found out."

	August	July
Agree	66%	56%
Disagree	22	18
Not sure	12	26

"If Watergate hadn't been exposed, the free press in this country would have been threatened with censorship next."

	August	July
Agree	40%	38%
Disagree	39	33
Not sure	21	29

"The press and television have given more attention to Watergate than it deserves."

	August	July
Agree	50%	40%
Disagree	44	46
Not sure	6	14

"The press is just out to get President Nixon on Watergate."

	August	July
Agree	24%	17%
Disagree	66	61
Not sure	10	22

"Do you think the Watergate episode is a very serious question involving the honesty of the White House, or do you think it is mostly politics?"

	August	July
Serious question	49%	46%
Mostly politics	46	47
Not sure	5	7

Aug. 29 ruling that the President must surrender certain tape recordings for Sirica's private review. Archibald Cox, Watergate special prosecutor, filed a 46-page brief requesting the court to order the tapes delivered directly to the grand jury without Sirica's prior inspection, or to establish guidelines for that inspection. Both of the actions were directed against Judge Sirica, so his lawyers in turn filed papers with the appeals court defending the Aug. 29 ruling. *(Details, p. 32)*

Liddy Citation. The House voted 334 to 11 to cite convicted Watergate conspirator G. Gordon Liddy for contempt of Congress for refusing to take an oath as a witness at a July 20 hearing of the House Armed Services Special Subcommittee on Intelligence. The panel was investigating possible CIA involvement in the Watergate scandal. *(Details, box, p. 27; subcommittee citation, Vol. I p. 218)*

Connally Speech. Commenting on the presidential tapes dispute, former Texas Gov. John B. Connally said: "We're leading ourselves into believing the Supreme Court is the ultimate arbiter of all disputes, and I don't believe it. I think there are times when the President of the United States would be right in not obeying a decision of the Supreme Court." Connally made the remarks to reporters at a reception for members of the Republican National Committee in Washington.

SEPT. 11

Tapes Appeal. Nixon attorney Charles Alan Wright, special prosecutor Archibald Cox and two attorneys for Judge Sirica argued Sirica's Aug. 29 ruling on presidential tapes before the U.S. Court of Appeals. The seven-judge panel—two members of the court disqualified themselves—questioned the attorneys for three hours. *(Details, p. 26)*

Mitchell-Stans Trial. Judge Lee P. Gagliardi of U.S. District Court in New York City agreed to postpone for at least a month the trial of former Attorney General John N. Mitchell and former Commerce Secretary Maurice H. Stans on charges arising from the Vesco case. An appeals court had urged the postponement in order to give the defense more time to prepare its case. The trial had been scheduled to begin Sept. 11.

SEPT. 12

Committee Plans. After conferring at a private meeting, members of the Senate Watergate investigating committee announced that they would resume hearings on Sept. 24, a week later than expected, and would aim at a completion date of Nov. 1. *(Details, p. 26)*

Wiretap Policy. Attorney General Elliot L. Richardson commented on the Justice Department's national security wiretap policy in a letter to Senate Foreign Relations Committee Chairman J. W. Fulbright (D Ark.). Richardson said he would not order wiretaps without court warrants unless a "genuine national security interest" was at stake. The administration would continue the practice "in a limited number of cautiously and meticulously reviewed instances," he said. The letter, made public by the Justice Department, came in response to an inquiry by the committee in connection with its confirmation hearings for Secretary of State-designate Henry A. Kissinger. The committee had been questioning Kissinger on his possible involvement in wiretaps on officials and newsmen undertaken by the administration between 1969 and 1971.

ITT Case. The Justice Department had decided not to reopen its antitrust case against International

Telephone and Telegraph Corporation (ITT), Attorney General Richardson said in a letter read aloud at a Senate Judiciary Committee hearing by Sen. John V. Tunney (D Calif.). Tunney had asked for a review of the 1971 out-of-court settlement after new evidence of possible wrong-doing in the case came to light during the Senate Watergate hearings. The Judiciary Committee, which was considering confirmation of William D. Ruckelshaus as deputy attorney general, indicated it would not immediately contest Richardson's decision. *(Hearings, Vol. I, p. 235)*

Ruckelshaus assured the committee that documents relating to the ITT and Watergate investigations had been turned over to special prosecutor Archibald Cox, who would decide whether the committee could examine them.

Excerpts from Legal Briefs

Following are excerpts from briefs submitted Sept. 10 to the U.S. Court of Appeals for the District of Columbia by special Watergate prosecutor Archibald Cox, presidential attorney Charles A. Wright and John J. Sirica, U.S. District Court Chief Judge.

Cox and Wright were appealing Sirica's ruling of Aug. 29 that the President turn over to the judge tape recordings of nine Watergate-related conversations. Cox argued that the tapes should go directly to the grand jury, rather than be inspected first by Sirica. Wright's position was that the judge had no power to order release of the tapes.

Sirica's brief, written by George D. Horning Jr. and Anthony C. Morella of American University Law School, argued the correctness of this decision. (Aug. 29 decision, p. 13)

COX BRIEF

On August 29, 1973, respondent (Sirica) filed his opinion... and order.... Respondent ruled, in accordance with the position urged by the Special Prosecutor, that the court has jurisdiction to decide the issue of executive privilege, even when asserted by the President in connection with evidence relating to his activities and conversations, and that the courts have the power and authority to issue a legally binding order enforcing a subpoena addressed to the President. On those constitutional issues, we believe respondent was correct, and thus the President's petition for a writ of mandamus should be denied.

Two aspects of the respondent Chief Judge's decision are we believe, clearly erroneous and warrant immediate intervention by this Court on our petition for a writ of mandamus. first, respondent abstained from ruling whether the subpoenaed evidence is covered by a privilege. Instead, he apparently concluded that it will be necessary to examine the tapes *in camera* in order to resolve that question. We submit that this approach, while perhaps reasonable in other cases, is fundamentally erroneous here where it has been shown that, as a matter of law, the evidence is not covered by a valid privilege. Second, respondent failed to articulate the standards he considers proper for determining what evidence will be ordered produced to the grand jury, and what evidence, if any, will be kept secret. In light of the importance of those standards and of the need for expeditious action, there is a pressing need for the authoritative intervention of this Court.

....In the district court, counsel for the President claimed only a general privilege or immunity applicable to all the tapes and papers covered by the subpoena. Since the only privilege claimed is unavailable as a matter of law under the circum-

Los Angeles Indictments: 4 White House 'Plumbers'

Four members of the "plumbers"—a secret White House investigative team set up at President Nixon's direction in 1971 to plug security leaks—were indicted Sept. 4 by a Los Angeles, Calif., grand jury for their role in the burglary of the office of Dr. Lewis Fielding, a psychiatrist who treated former Pentagon Papers defendant Daniel Ellsberg. (*Ellsberg case, Vol. I, p. 46*)

Named in the indictments were John D. Ehrlichman, Nixon's former domestic affairs adviser; Egil (Bud) Krogh Jr., former deputy assistant to the President; David R. Young, another former White House aide, and convicted Watergate conspirator G. Gordon Liddy. Four other men were listed as co-conspirators in the plot but were not indicted. They were E. Howard Hunt Jr., Bernard L. Barker and Eugenio Martinez—all convicted for the Watergate break-in—and Felipe DeDiego, a Cuban national.

The district attorney did not announce the names of the defendants or the charges against them until Sept. 6, when the first of them surrendered for arraignment. But the information leaked out almost immediately.

All were charged with one state count of burglary and one count of conspiracy to commit burglary. In addition, Ehrlichman was charged with one count of perjury and Krogh with one count of solicitation to commit burglary. Each count carries a possible sentence of one to 14 years in state prison, with the exception of solicitation, which has a five-year maximum.

Krogh was the first to surrender. He was arraigned Sept. 6 in Los Angeles Superior Court, pleaded not guilty and was released on his own recognizance. Ehrlichman and Young followed the same procedure the next day, also pleading not guilty.

Arrangements for Liddy's appearance were being made in Washington, D.C., where he was serving a contempt of court sentence for refusing to answer questions put to him by a Watergate grand jury there. Presiding Judge James G. Kolts of Los Angeles Superior Court set a pretrial hearing for Sept. 20.

Plot Outlined. The indictments charged that Krogh and Young, acting on Ehrlichman's authority, directed Liddy, Hunt and other co-conspirators to burglarize the psychiatrist's office to find Ellsberg's records. Krogh said after his arraignment that he believed the burglary to be lawful because it was done in the interests of national security.

Perjury Charge. Ehrlichman's July 8 testimony before the Los Angeles grand jury, in which he denied having advance knowledge of the burglary, was cited in his indictment for perjury. A tape recording of his July 24 testimony before the Senate Watergate committee, when he admitted having approved a "covert operation" to obtain Ellsberg's psychiatric records but insisted he did not intend to approve a burglary, was to be introduced as evidence against Ehrlichman at the trial. (*Senate testimony, Vol. I, p. 212*)

The grand jurors reportedly also based their perjury charge on two memos written by Krogh and Young indicating that Ehrlichman had advance knowledge of the burglary plan.

Federal Investigation. According to press reports, the Los Angeles indictments had been held up for several months at the request of the Justice Department's special Watergate prosecutor, Archibald Cox, so that the Washington, D.C., grand jury investigating Watergate could question Ehrlichman further on the Ellsberg burglary. "In our view," Cox told reporters Sept. 7, "the federal interest in dealing with any possible illegal activities by White House employees is clearly predominant." He expressed confidence that federal and California authorities could work cooperatively on the overlapping prosecutions.

Ehrlichman appeared Sept. 11 before a federal grand jury in Washington, D.C., to answer questions on the 1971 Ellsberg break-in and other subjects, after losing a bid to have his subpoena quashed on grounds that any further questioning would constitute harassment. His attorney, John J. Wilson, conceded that Ehrlichman could, "as a matter of law," be indicted twice for his role in the break-in.

stances of the present case, the present record reveals no need for *in camera* inspection. Therefore, the provision of *in camera* inspection should be deleted from the order of the district court.

Inspection *in camera* is not required automatically whenever there is a claim of executive privilege. The procedure often has been used to separate producible material from nonproducible material.... In such cases the court already has determined that at least some of the evidence is privileged—that is, memoranda containing state secrets or reflecting deliberative processes and policy decisions—and the task *in camera* is merely the excision of the privileged evidence from the unprivileged. In some instances such a procedure might even be useful in ruling upon the claim of privilege itself if "the balance between competing needs for confidentiality and disclosure cannot be made without analysis of the disputed data." ... Nevertheless, "(i)n camera inspection is not an end in itself, but only a method that in given instances may be indispensable to the decision of that question."

In the present case, as we have shown, the generalized claim of privilege—the only claim presented—fails as a matter of law upon the present record, leaving no occasion for requiring *in camera* inspection rather than direct submission to the Special Prosecutor for presentation of relevant portions to the grand jury.

Bare supposition that the tapes and papers may include discrete segments that would be privileged as containing state secrets or wholly irrelevant information is not enough to justify the provision for *in camera* inspection. Nor is speculation that the tapes may contain utterly irrelevant and thus still privileged communications. Contrary to respondent's suggestion below, the Special Prosecutor never has sought "wholesale delivery of tapes to the grand jury."

Indeed, the Special Prosecutor concedes that separable matters clearly irrelevant to the grand jury's investigation retain their privileged status and should not be presented to the grand jury. If some of the recordings or other memoranda should include wholly irrelevant and separable material, those portions will not be presented to the grand jury. The Special Prosecutor is well aware of his duty as an Executive officer to protect executive privilege where appropriate and to winnow out any irrelevant evidence in order to save time and avoid unnecessary embarrassment or prejudice to those affected. The procedure of excising any irrelevant material undoubtedly can be accomplished through cooperation and agreement between the Special Prosecutor, an officer of the Executive Branch, and counsel for the President.

On the present record, the President has not made a sufficient showing that the tapes contain irrelevant—and thus still privileged—information to warrant *in camera* screening even under ordinary principles. Nor should the court speculate that parts of the recordings or documents identified in the subpoena may be subject to some particularized claim of privilege. There must be a formal claim of privilege lodged with the court. At a minimum it must include an affidavit based upon personal knowledge stating that particularly identified subjects and portions are protected by privilege....

....Although both logic and sound procedure dictate vacating the portion of the district court's order providing for *in camera* inspection, we recognize that the need for extraordinary care and sensitivity in dealing with Presidential conversations might be thought to require closer judicial supervision under the established principles of substantive law. On this view, it would be proper to order the tapes and other items described in the subpoena delivered to the district court for it to determine any timely claims of particularized privilege applicable to specific portions of a recording or papers, and also to withhold any separable portions clearly irrelevant to any inquiry proper to the grand jury. Because the two functions require different standards and procedure, we consider them *seriatim*.

1. "State Secrets." Under settled law there is an absolute privilege for certain state secrets—that is, information relating to military or, possibly, diplomatic affairs that must be kept secret in the interest of national security.... There has never been a formal claim in this proceeding that the conversations identified in the subpoena contain state secrets, although counsel for the President suggested for the first time in his rebuttal at the hearing below that one of the recordings—which he did not specify—contains matter relating to the "national security." Counsel did not elaborate on how the portion of that one unspecified recording involves the "national security" and indeed disclaimed any personal knowledge of the basis for the contention. If a sufficient showing were to be made that one of the recordings in fact contains state secrets, properly defined, those portions of that recording should be excised....

The appropriated procedure is described in (a case cited in the brief). *In camera* inspection would not necessarily be required. If the President were to make a sufficient showing by affidavit that described portions of the tape contain state secrets, the court could permit the President to arrange for deletion of those portions.... If any *in camera* inspection were considered necessary upon this narrow issue, the Special Prosecutor need not be present.

2. Irrelevant, Separable Material. Normally, claims of privilege arise in the course of litigation where the judge has become generally familiar with the issues and has heard the evidence already introduced. The instant case presents the distinct situation of a claim of executive privilege during a grand jury investigation. In such a situation the court has little basis for judging what is relevant. Although there is substantial and far-reaching public testimony concerning the break-in and alleged subsequent cover-up, the court cannot know either the full extent and scope of the grand jury investigation or how particular pieces of evidence tie together. In the unique circumstances of this case, therefore, we submit that any determinations of irrelevance must be made with the Special Prosecutor present to advise and aid the court in determining what matters are pertinent to the grand jury's investigations....

WRIGHT BRIEF

The District Court, in a decision utterly without precedent, has held that it is for it, and not for the President, to decide whether the public interest requires that private Presidential conversations be kept confidential, and it has held that it may, by compulsory process, order the President to produce recordings of these conversations if the Court determines to do so.

As recently as a year ago such a ruling would have been unthinkable. The change in the climate of legal and popular opinion that has made a ruling such as that of the District Court possible is the result of Watergate. The hydraulic force arising out of that sordid and unhappy episode has led men of great distinction to suppose that the Constitution means something different today than it meant throughout all of our history and to contend that the need to exhaust every avenue of factual inquiry concerning Watergate ranks so high in our national priorities that it must be served, even if the cost is to impair markedly the ability of every President of the United States from this time forward to perform the Constitutional duties vested in him....

With all respect, the (Sirica) decision below did not harmlessly walk the "middle ground" between an overbroad claim of privilege and an excessive demand for discovery. We do not doubt at all but that this was the well-intentioned aim of the distinguished judge of the court below. But in result, the ruling below, in decisive terms, came down squarely on the side of breaching the wall of confidentiality of Presidential communications. If sustained, that decision will alter the nature of the American Presidency profoundly and irreparably. If sustained, it will alter, equally irreparably, the delicate balance that has existed between three heretofore separate and co-equal branches of government.

The issue on this appeal is whether the District Court had the power to do this....

The reasons for preserving Presidential privacy...apply with special force when recordings or notes of Presidential conversations are sought. Recordings are the raw material of life. By their very nature they contain spontaneous, informal, tentative, and frequently pungent comments on a variety of subjects inextricably intertwined into one conversation. Disclosure of information allegedly relevant to this inquiry would mean disclosure as well of other information of a highly confidential nature relating to a wide range of matters not relevant to this inquiry. Some of these matters deal with sensitive issues of national security. Others go to the exercise by the President of his Constitutional duties on matters other than Watergate. The nature of informal, private conversations is such that it is not practicable to separate what is arguably relevant from what is clearly irrelevant. Once the totality of the confidential nature of the recordings is destroyed, no person could ever be assured that his own frank and candid comments to the President would not eventually be made public. No government can function if its internal operations are to be subject to that kind of open scrutiny....

There are intimations in the Opinion of the District Court,...that the usual rules of executive privilege and of Presidential privacy are inapplicable here because the subpoena is from a grand jury seeking evidence relevant to a criminal case.

This point was made more explicitly by the Special Prosecutor in his submission to the District Court. He asserted repeatedly that the grand jury will not be able to function as effectively as he would like unless it has access to the tapes in question. The President of the United States had argued, as he does here, that he, and his successors, will not be able to function effectively if the tapes are disclosed. The principal theme of the Brief in Support was that a conflict of this kind may appropriately be resolved by the judiciary that that is more important that a grand jury have access to every possible bit of evidence and that indictments against wrongdoers contain every possible count than that the confidentiality that the President regards as indispensable to the performance of his Constitutional duties be preserved.

Yet no case has ever held, and no suggestion has ever been made in legal literature, that an otherwise valid claim of executive privilege must give way because a grand jury is looking into charges of criminal conduct. Only last year the Supreme Court recognized that ordinarily a grand jury has the right to every man's evidence, but immediately qualified that statement by adding "except for those persons protected by a constitutional, common-law, or statutory privilege."...

It may well be that statements made by other persons to the President at the meetings that are the subjects of the recordings were made by them pursuant to a conspiracy to obstruct justice, or that some of those other persons may subsequently have perjured themselves by their testimony about what occurred at the meetings. Executive privilege cannot be claimed to shield executive officers from prosecution for crime....

It is precisely with that consideration in mind, and with a strong desire that the truth about Watergate be brought out, that the President has not asserted executive privilege with regard to testimony about possible criminal conduct or discussions of possible criminal conduct. But testimony can be confined to the relevant portions of the conversations and can be limited to matters that do not endanger national security. Recordings cannot be so confined and limited, and thus the President has concluded that to produce recordings would do serious damage to Presidential privacy and to the ability of that office to function.

Although remarks made by others in conversations with the President may be relevant evidence of crimes on their part, the President's participation in these conversations was in accordance with his Constitutional duty to see that the laws are faithfully executed. It is the President, not those who may be subject to indictment by the grand jury, who is claiming executive privilege. He is doing so, not to protect those others, but to protect the right of himself and his successors to preserve the confidentiality of discussions in which they participate in the course of their Constitutional duties, and thus ultimately to protect the right of the American people to informed and vigorous leadership from their President of a sort for which confidentiality is an essential prerequisite.

It will not do to argue, as is done (in the Sirica opinion), that if the interest served by a privilege is abused or subverted, the claim of privilege fails. The privilege is the President's. That others may have abused his trust by criminal acts in their conversations with him or by subsequent perjury in testimony about those conversations is not an abuse or subversion of the interest in allowing privacy to the President and does not defeat the privilege....

The right of Presidential confidentiality is not a mystical prerogative. It is, rather, the raw essence of the Presidential process, the institutionalized recognition of the crucial role played by human personality in the negotiation, manipulation, and disposition of human affairs.

Were it to be held, on whatever ground, that there is any circumstance under which the President can be compelled to produce recordings or notes of his private conversations, from that moment on it would be simply impossible for any President of the United States to function. The creative interplay of open and spontaneous discussion is essential in making wise choices on grave and important issues. A President would be helpless if he and his advisers could not talk freely, if they were required always to guard their words against the possibility that next month or next year those words might be made public. The issue in this case is nothing less than the continued existence of the Presidency as a functioning institution.

It is tempting to give way to the forces that have been set in motion by Watergate, to issue orders of a kind entirely without precedent in our history, and to alter settled principles of Constitutional government. A decision that it is for the Judiciary, rather than for the President, to decide how the Presidency is to function might be popular with those who do not count the long-term consequences. That cannot be a concern of this Court....

SIRICA BRIEF

Exhaustive briefs on this question (of jurisdiction) were submitted to Respondent (Sirica) by counsel for Petitioner (Wright) and the Party in Interest (Cox). Oral argument was had thereupon. After mature deliberation and consideration of the authorities cited by respective counsel and their oral arguments thereon, the Respondent rendered an Opinion accompanying his order and in Part I thereof concluded, for the reasons therein stated, that the availability of evidence including the validity and scope of privilege is a judicial decision.

In support of this conclusion reliance was placed upon the celebrated case of *Marbury v. Madison*,... holding that it is emphatically the province and duty of the judicial department to determine the law. Reliance was furthermore placed upon *U.S. v. Reynolds*,... and the decision of this Honorable Court in *Committee for Nuclear Responsibility, Inc. v. Seaborg*.... It is respectfully submitted that *Reynolds* is authoritative and controlling in that therein the Court described the resolution of questions of privilege as a judicial role which cannot be abdicated. Petititoner's assertion of an unqualified right to personally declare a privilege not reviewable by any Court contravenes this vital principle....

The grand jury has a right to every person's evidence, and for the purpose of gathering evidence, judicial process may issue to anyone, including Petitioner.... Petitioner conceded that the trial court possessed authority to direct a subpoena to him but asserted a lack of authority to command obedience thereto. In support of such contention he merely asserts a formal claim of executive privilege predicated upon his conception of the public interest. Respondent agreed with Petitioner that such presidential privacy in and of itself has no merit....

Accordingly, Respondent held that the need for presidential privacy was not persuasive on the issue of submission of the materials described in the subpoena duces tecum....

Respondent was confronted with an extremely difficult decision. He correctly concluded that, as matters stood, he was unable to decide the question of privilege without inspecting the tapes in issue.... In fairness to the interests asserted by Petitioner and Party in Interest, Respondent attempted to walk a middle ground required because of his inability to determine the validity of the asserted privilege without access to further facts contained within the tapes in question. In utter fairness, he concluded that when the material subpoenaed was submitted and reviewed by him and determined to be privileged, those portions deemed privileged would be excised. This accords with prevailing practice in other comparable situations. *In camera* examination would materially aid the Respondent in his decision and without it he is simply unable to decide the issue presented....

The Petition for Writ of Mandamus was predicated upon the all writs statute, 28 U.S.C. 1651(a).... No basis for recourse to this section appears inasmuch as the Petition presents as issues the same questions raised in the Court below. Obviously, the jurisdiction of this Honorable Court is in no wise threatened and usual and normal appeal from Respondent's order is the preferred course. Respondent's order of August 29, 1973, was a final and appealable order and was intended as such. In paragraph 3 thereof the ruling was specifically stayed for a period of five days "in which time respondent (Petitioner herein) may perfect an appeal from the ruling" and was, in the final paragraph thereof, stayed indefinitely pending the completion of such appeal.

It seems therefore that this Petition for Writ of Mandamus is being employed erroneously in lieu of a direct appeal from said order. The authorities cited in the Petition for Writ of Mandamus do not support the necessity for recourse to this extraordinary writ. It is deemed by Respondent, however, that if this Honorable Court so determines, it may view this Petition as a direct appeal and proceed to a hearing of the cause on the merits under its inherent and supervisory powers. ✓

NIXON-COX FAILURE TO AGREE ON CONTROVERSIAL TAPES

President Nixon's lawyer and special Watergate prosecutor Archibald Cox announced Sept. 20 that they had failed to reach a compromise agreement on access by Cox to the tape recordings of Watergate-related presidential conversations. In virtually identical letters to the U.S. Court of Appeals for the District of Columbia, both sides said they had met three times since the court suggested in a Sept. 13 memorandum that they try to reach an out-of-court settlement on the tapes issue. But the three meetings—Sept. 17, 18 and 20—"were not fruitful," Cox and Charles A. Wright, Nixon's attorney, informed the court. *(Box, next column)*

The tapes in dispute concerned conversations in the White House and Executive Office Building among the President and some of his aides. They related to the June 1972 break-in at the Democratic National Committee offices in the Watergate building and to subsequent efforts by high government and re-election committee officials to cover up the crime.

The failure to compromise brought the issue of the tapes a step closer to its expected resolution by the Supreme Court. The appeals court was expected to issue its ruling in one to two weeks, with an appeal to the high court by either party almost a certainty. The Supreme Court was to convene Oct. 1.

The outcome of the Cox-Wright discussion was not a surprise. The President's lawyer had stated repeatedly in legal briefs and courtroom arguments that the tapes were covered by executive privilege and that no court could order their removal from the White House. *(Excerpts from Wright appeal brief, p. 31)*

In a reply brief filed Sept. 19 in the appellate court, a day before the letter on the tapes was delivered, Wright repeated his hard-line stand on the tapes: "To tear down the office of the American presidency is too high a price to pay, even for Watergate," he argued. The President, he said, "has not delegated to the special prosecutor, and will not abrogate, his constitutional duties and prerogatives. That would move beyond accommodation to irresponsibility."

In other Watergate developments during the week ended Sept. 21:

• Former presidential counsel Charles W. Colson was excused Sept. 19 from testifying before the Senate select Watergate committee after invoking the Fifth Amendment in a private meeting with the committee.

• Donald H. Segretti, a political operator hired by White House aides during the 1972 presidential primary campaign, agreed in Washington, D.C., Sept. 17 to plead guilty to a four-count indictment involving political sabotage in the Florida primary. He also agreed to cooperate with Cox's investigation of Nixon's re-election campaign.

• E. Howard Hunt, one of seven convicted Watergate conspirators, asked U.S. District Court Chief Judge John J. Sirica to allow him to withdraw his guilty plea in

---

Text of Cox, Wright Letters

Following is the text of a Sept. 20 letter from President Nixon's attorney, Charles A. Wright, to the U.S. Court of Appeals for the District of Columbia, telling the court that Wright and special Watergate prosecutor Archibald Cox had failed to reach a compromise on the tapes issue. A letter from Cox to the court, dated the same day, was identical except for the order of names of the persons involved. (Excerpts from court's Sept. 13 compromise proposal, box, p. 35)

This is to advise you that counsel in the above entitled matter have had lengthy meetings pursuant to the suggestion in the court's memorandum of Sept. 13.

Mr. Cox and Mr. (J. Fred) Buzhardt met on Sept. 17 and 18 and today Mr. Cox and Mr. (Philip A.) Lacavara of his office met with Mr. Buzhardt, Mr. (Leonard) Garment and myself. I regret to advise the court that these sincere efforts were not fruitful.

All participants in these conversations have agreed that we shall say nothing about them except to make this report to the court. I understand that Mr. Cox will similarly advise you of these meetings and of their unsuccessful outcome.

---

the case and to dismiss charges against him. Hunt said he had acted in the belief that White House officials had approved the burglary.

• Four other men convicted with Hunt asked Sirica for a new trial on grounds that they had entered guilty pleas under pressure from Hunt and high government officials.

Committee Actions

Colson's invocation of his Fifth Amendment right against self-incrimination was not a surprise. His lawyer and law partner, David Shapiro, earlier had informed the committee that his client was a target of a federal grand jury investigating the 1971 break-in at the office of Daniel Ellsberg's psychiatrist. The committee denied Shapiro's request that Colson's appearance be delayed until after the grand jury had handed down indictments. Shapiro reportedly had informed the committee that if Colson were indicted, or if he were compelled to testify before the indictments were handed down, Colson would invoke the Fifth Amendment. *(p. 26)*

Committee Chairman Sam J. Ervin Jr. (D N.C.) told reporters after the 2½-hour committee meeting with Colson and Shapiro that the former White House aide would not be called to testify as long as he continued to invoke the Fifth Amendment.

The committee voted to compel Colson's testimony despite urgings by Senators Howard H. Baker Jr. (R Tenn.)

and Edward J. Gurney (R Fla.) that Colson be granted a 10-day postponement. According to one newspaper account, Shapiro asked that the committee not force Colson's testimony because his client might feel stigmatized if he felt it necessary to invoke the Fifth Amendment. But the committee rejected the plea. Ervin said afterward, "I must note that a man is entitled to plead the Fifth Amendment even if he is not guilty of any offense."

Other Witnesses. In other action Sept. 18, the committee released a list of further witnesses for its hearings, which were to resume Sept. 24. The one surprise on the list was the name of Patrick J. Buchanan, a special consultant to President Nixon.

Buchanan had not been mentioned previously in the Watergate affair, but according to committee sources quoted by *The Washington Post,* the committee had memos indicating that Buchanan had advocated influencing the 1972 Democratic presidential primaries so that the Democrats would endorse a weak candidate. According to one Post source, Buchanan advocated "infiltrating the opposition" during the campaign. Queried by the press, Buchanan admitted having written political campaign strategy memos but denied suggesting that infiltration be used.

Others on the list were Hunt, John J. Caulfield, a former White House aide who conducted secret investigations on orders of superiors, and John J. Ragan, an electronic surveillance expert once employed by the FBI. Hunt was expected to be questioned about his role in the Ellsberg and Watergate burglaries and other activities while a member of the White House special investigations unit known as the "plumbers."

Court Actions

The appellate court's memorandum to President Nixon and special Watergate prosecutor Cox was an attempt to have the two disputants resolve the issue of the tapes without a constitutional showdown. It suggested that they might be able to agree on what portions of the tapes the Watergate grand jury could listen to. *(Memo excerpts, box p. 35)*

"If the President and the special prosecutor agree as to the material needed for the grand jury's functioning, the national interest will be served," said the court in unanimously approving the memorandum. "At the same time, neither the President nor the special prosecutor would in any way have surrendered or subverted the principles for which they have contended."

Cox jumped at the chance, but White House officials said nothing publicly about the meetings until Sept. 20, the court's deadline for answering its memo. Said Cox in a statement issued Sept. 13: "I shall, of course, be more than glad to meet with the President or his delegate or any of his attorneys in a sincere effort to pursue the Court of Appeals' suggestion to a mutually satisfactory conclusion."

Segretti Indictment. Segretti, 32, a lawyer, was reportedly recruited for political intelligence activities by Dwight L. Chapin, the President's former appointments secretary, and paid out of funds controlled by Herbert W. Kalmbach, Nixon's personal attorney. The new Segretti indictment reportedly replaced one handed

down in May 1973 in Tampa, Fla. He had pleaded innocent to the two-count Tampa indictment. The new indictment included one count of conspiracy and three counts of illegally distributing campaign literature without identifying who was responsible for it. Each count carried a maximum penalty of a year in prison and $1,000 fine.

The new indictment, secretly handed down in Tampa Aug. 24, accused Segretti of participating in the mailing of posters in Tampa reading "Help Muskie Support Busing Our Children Now" and listing "Mothers for Busing" as the sponsor. The indictment also accused him of conspiring to distribute cards at a rally for Alabama Gov. George C. Wallace during the Florida primary that said, "If you like Hitler, you'll love Wallace...Vote for Muskie."

Wallace won the Florida primary. Sen. Edmund S. Muskie (D Maine) finished a poor fourth.

The indictment also repeated earlier charges against Segretti that he fabricated and distributed two letters on Citizens for Muskie stationery. One accused Senators Henry M. Jackson (D Wash.) and Hubert H. Humphrey (D Minn.), two other primary candidates, of sexual misconduct. The other alleged that Muskie's headquarters was using personnel and equipment of Rep. Sam Gibbons (D Fla.).

Also named in the new indictment—as co-conspirators but not as defendants—were Robert M. Benz, 25, a former president of the Tampa Young Republicans, and George A. Hearing, 40, a Tampa accountant. Hearing had pleaded guilty to the first indictment and was sentenced to a year in prison. Benz was not indicted in the case. *(Vol. I, p. 69, 8)*

Hunt Motion. Hunt told Judge Sirica that he helped plan and participate in the Watergate burglary because he was led to believe the mission was approved by the White House "pursuant to the President's power to protect the national security." He specifically accused his codefendant, G. Gordon Liddy, of misleading him into believing the break-in was a lawful act.

"Defendant was led by Mr. Liddy to believe that the program was required by the Attorney General John N. Mitchell, and that it was approved also by Messrs. Liddy; Jeb Stuart Magruder, a former White House aide; John W. Dean III, counsel to the President; and Charles W. Colson, special counsel to the President," the motion said.

Liddy was convicted for his role in the break-in, along with Hunt and five others, and refused to discuss his role in the affair. Magruder pleaded guilty to obstruction of justice in the coverup. Mitchell, Dean and Colson faced possible indictment for their alleged roles in the affair. Hunt, a former agent of the Central Intelligence Agency, had pleaded guilty to charges of conspiracy, burglary and wiretapping during the Watergate break-in trial in January 1973.

Hunt's lawyers claimed two defenses for their client in their motion to Judge Sirica: "The first is that his acts were lawful because they were performed pursuant to the President's power to protect the national security. The second, assuming (for the sake of argument) that the acts were not lawful, is that he was justified in believing they were lawful."

Hunt, the motion maintained, was "coerced into abandoning these defenses" because the government "unconstitutionally deprived him of evidence to support them." The motion mentioned specifically the failure of the White House to disclose the existence of taped conversations; the destruction of documents from Hunt's office by L. Patrick Gray III, the former acting FBI director, and instances of perjury by government officials before the original Watergate grand jury and at Hunt's trial.

Four Men's Motion. The four men seeking a jury trial for the break-in were Bernard L. Barker, Frank Sturgis, Eugenio R. Martinez and Virgilio R. Gonzalez. All had pleaded guilty at the original Watergate trial to charges of conspiracy, burglary and illegal wiretapping and eavesdropping. Each was given a provisional sentence by Judge Sirica of a maximum of 40 years in prison and a $50,000 fine.

They told the judge that they had participated in the break-in because they had been told it was a legitimate government intelligence-gathering operation and had entered their guilty pleas out of a concern for "national security." In a motion filed by attorney Daniel E. Schultz, the four Miamians claimed their guilty pleas "were false and involuntarily entered under the force and compulsion of a belief that the necessity to protect national security interests precluded them from asserting the defenses they had.... The pleas were premised on the false assumptions which had been fostered on them by others, including codefendant E. Howard Hunt and ultimately, high officials in the executive branch of the government."

Schultz said their participation in the break-in was "the product of blind and ignorant loyalty fostered in these defendants' minds by deceptions practiced on them by others who purported to act under color of a higher law." Since it later was shown that the break-in was "purely political in nature," the motion said, the defendants were "the victims of a cruel fraud inititially perpetrated on them to obtain their participation in the activities (and) perpetrated in order to safeguard against these defendants disclosing what little information they did know...."

With the motions by Hunt and the four Miamians, only Liddy among the seven defendants had not asked for a new trial or that his conviction be set aside. The seventh defendant, James W. McCord, asked June 8 that he be granted a new trial on the grounds that he was enticed into the operation by high government officials and that a "massive obstruction of justice" denied him a defense at his trial. McCord was the only defendant who had not been sentenced. Cox opposed McCord's motion. *(Motion, Vol. I, p. 137)*

Week's Watergate Chronology

Following is a day-to-day chronology of the week's events in the week ending Sept. 15:

SEPT. 13

Appeals Court Compromise. The seven U.S. Court of Appeals judges who heard the arguments in the White House tapes case issued a unanimous memorandum urging the President and special prosecutor Archibald Cox to settle their dispute over the tapes out of court and thus avoid a constitutional ruling in the case. The court asked both sides to respond to the memorandum by Sept. 20.

Appeals Court Memorandum

Following are excerpts from a memorandum issued Sept. 13 by the U.S. Court of Appeals for the District of Columbia to President Nixon, Chief Judge John J. Sirica of U.S. District Court and special Watergate prosecutor Archibald Cox:

...The doctrine under which courts seek resolution of a controversy without a constitutional ruling is particularly applicable here. The possibility of a resolution of this controversy without the need for a constitutional ruling is enhanced by the stature and character of the two counsels charged with representation of each side in this cause, and by the circumstances that each was selected for his position, directly or indirectly, by the Chief Executive himself.

Whereas Judge Sirica contemplated an *in camera* examination of the subpoenaed tapes, which would have necessitated the presence of the judiciary, we contemplate an examination of the tapes by the Chief Executive or his delegate, assisted by both his own counsel, Professor Wright, and the special prosecutor, Professor Cox.

We say this without intimating a decision on any question of jurisdiction or privilege advanced by any party. Apart from noting that the likelihood of successful settlement along the lines indicated contemplates a voluntary submission of such portions of the tapes to the two counsels as satisfies them, we do not presume to prescribe the details of how the Chief Executive will work with the two counsels.

This procedure may permit the different approaches of the parties to converge. The President has maintained that he alone should decide what is necessarily privileged and should not be furnished the grand jury. The special prosecutor has maintained that he should have the opportunity of examining the material and asserting its relevance and importance to the grand jury investigation. If the President and the special prosecutor agree as to the material needed for the grand jury's functioning, the national interest will be served. At the same time, neither the President nor the special prosecutor would in any way have surrendered or subverted the principles for which they have contended....

Mitchell, Stans Tapes Bid. New demands on White House documents came to light as the government moved to quash a subpoena issued Aug. 31 by lawyers for former Attorney General John N. Mitchell and former Commerce Secretary Maurice H. Stans, who were nearing trial in New York City on obstruction of justice and perjury charges. The subpoena called on the President to release "all books, records, telephone toll records, tape recordings, notes and memoranda" relating to financier Robert L. Vesco and his secret $200,000 contribution to the Nixon campaign.

Kennedy on Impeachment. "If President Nixon defied a Supreme Court order to turn over the tapes, a responsible Congress would be left with no recourse but to exercise its power of impeachment," Sen. Edward M. Kennedy (D Mass.) declared in a speech on the Senate floor. "The President has no argument from history for such defiance. The only argument he has is the law of the jungle, the law of raw and naked power."

SEPT. 14

Plea Changes. Four of the original seven Watergate defendants filed a petition with U.S. District Court Judge John J. Sirica asking that they be allowed to change their original pleas of guilty to not guilty and be granted a new trial. The men—Bernard L. Barker, Frank A. Sturgis, Virgilio R. Gonzalez and Eugenio R. Martinez—said they had been pressured by co-conspirator E. Howard Hunt Jr. and "high officials of the executive branch" into pleading guilty to keep from exposing national security operations they had participated in. They said they took part in the break-in with the understanding that it was a legitimate government intelligence operation. Judge Sirica had sentenced the men provisionally to the maximum terms pending review.

Class Action Suit. The National Citizens' Committee for Fairness to the Presidency Inc. filed a class action suit in U.S. District Court in Washington, D.C., asking that the Senate Watergate investigating committee's hearings be ended because the committee had "deliberately and inequitably disrupted the domestic tranquility of the country by undermining the confidence of citizens in the government."

SEPT. 17

Hunt Plea. Attorneys for convicted Watergate conspirator E. Howard Hunt Jr. submitted to Judge Sirica a motion to allow Hunt to withdraw his guilty plea and to dismiss charges against him. The prosecution of Hunt for his participation in the Watergate break-in was "replete with deliberate obstruction of justice, destruction and withholding of evidence, perjury or subornation of perjury," Hunt's attorneys argued.

Segretti Plea. Donald H. Segretti, who was hired to play tricks on the Democrats during the 1972 presidential campaign, appeared before a U.S. magistrate in Washington, D.C., and agreed to plead guilty to an expanded four-count indictment charging campaign law violations. He also agreed to cooperate with the special prosecutor.

Secret Service Wiretaps. Sen. Joseph M. Montoya (D N.M.), a member of the Senate Watergate investigating committee and chairman of the Senate Appropriations subcommittee that oversees the Secret Service, reported that the Treasury Department had refused to say whether the President had instructed the Secret Service to tap the phone of his brother, Donald Nixon. "I personally am assuming there was a wiretap on the President's brother's phone" that was in violation of federal law, Montoya said after meeting with two Treasury Department officials who would not deny or confirm the report of the tap. *(p. 22)*

Mondale Resolution. Sen. Walter F. Mondale (D Minn.) introduced a resolution calling for establishment of a commission on the presidency "to examine what has happened to the office, why it has happened and what can be done to ensure that the presidency remains open and accountable to the American people and the Congress."

SEPT. 18

Committee Suit. Sen. Sam J. Ervin (D N.C.), chairman, and lawyers for the Senate Watergate investigating committee filed a series of papers with Judge Sirica ask-

ing for a favorable summary judgment in the committee's suit seeking access to presidential tapes. "We submit that the public interest in determining the extent of malfeasance in the executive branch and the need for corrective legislation is of greater moment to the nation than the indictment of a few guilty individuals," the lawyers argued. *(Earlier action, p. 20, 16)*

Committee Plans. The Senate investigating committee announced that it would call convicted Watergate conspirator E. Howard Hunt Jr. to the witness table when the hearings resumed Sept. 24. Hunt was to be followed by Patrick J. Buchanan, a White House speech writer and political strategist.

SEPT. 19

Tapes Dispute. President Nixon's lawyers, in a strong hint that they would reject a proposed out-of-court settlement of the White House tapes dispute, declared in a brief filed with the U.S. Court of Appeals that Nixon would not delegate "his constitutional duties and prerogatives" to the special prosecutor. But it was revealed that White House lawyers and special prosecutor Archibald Cox had been meeting in an attempt to negotiate an agreement.

Colson Refusal. Charles W. Colson, a former White House special counsel and key political adviser during Nixon's first term, appeared with his attorney at a closed session of the Senate Watergate investigating committee and invoked the Fifth Amendment against self-incrimination. Colson told the committee he would not answer questions while he was a target of a federal grand jury investigation into the burglary of the office of Daniel Ellsberg's psychiatrist. The senators unanimously rejected Colson's request for a grant of immunity for his testimony before the committee.

SEPT. 20

Liddy Plea, Dismissal Motion. In arraignment procedures in Los Angeles Superior Court, Watergate conspirator G. Gordon Liddy pleaded not guilty to charges connected with the 1971 break-in at the office of Daniel Ellsberg's psychiatrist.

After Liddy's arraignment, an attorney for John D. Ehrlichman introduced a motion to dismiss the indictments in the Ellsberg case on grounds of insufficient evidence. He was joined by lawyers representing the three other defendants in the case—Liddy, Egil Krogh Jr. and David R. Young. *(Indictments, p. 30)*

Kraft Surveillance. According to a *New York Times* report, the late FBI Director J. Edgar Hoover ordered one of his top deputies, William C. Sullivan, to follow syndicated columnist Joseph Kraft to Paris in 1969 and to arrange with French authorities to have Kraft kept under electronic and physical surveillance. The administration reportedly was concerned about Kraft's contacts with North Vietnamese officials. One of the Times' sources said the information gathered was passed on to John D. Ehrlichman, former White House domestic affairs adviser. *(Vol. I, p. 151)*   √

TESTIMONY: SHARP CONTRAST BETWEEN HUNT, BUCHANAN

The reconvened Watergate hearings were a study in contrasts. First there was the mild-mannered former spy, E. Howard Hunt Jr., testifying in a sometimes almost inaudible voice, anxious to shorten his sentence for the crimes he had been convicted of. Then there was the self-assured Patrick J. Buchanan, a speechwriter and consultant for President Nixon, whose aggressive responses kept his questioners on the defensive much of the time.

The hearings before the Senate Select Committee on Presidential Campaign Activities, which had adjourned early in August, were once again the center of attention in the Watergate scandal. Temporarily shelved, as the U.S. Court of Appeals in Washington weighed the arguments, was the dispute over several tape-recorded conversations of the President. *(p. 33)*

Of far more public interest than Watergate, in the week ended Sept. 29, was the shift in scandal from the presidency to the vice presidency. Spiro T. Agnew's troubles overshadowed, for the time being, at least, those of Nixon.

But even without the distractions of the Agnew matter, Watergate was no longer the hot item it had been before the August recess. It was clear that the remaining witnesses to be heard in the second phase of the committee's investigation—the campaign "dirty tricks" of 1972—did not have the public appeal of those who appeared during the first round, on the break-in and its coverup.

A measure of the subsiding news value of the hearings was the decision of the three major television networks to discontinue live coverage. And there was talk among the committee staff of cutting even shorter the phase-three investigation of campaign spending practices.

Hearings Sept. 24

The Senate Watergate committee resumed its hearings Sept. 24 after a seven-week recess with testimony from convicted Watergate conspirator E. Howard Hunt Jr. *(Previous testimony, Vol. I, p. 254)*

Hunt, 55, testified that Charles W. Colson, former special counsel to President Nixon, knew of the intelligence plan that led to the Watergate break-in. He also said Colson assigned him to collect information on Pentagon Papers defendant Daniel Ellsberg, a process that resulted in the burglarizing of Ellsberg's psychiatrist's office.

Hunt was under a provisional 35-year prison sentence for his part in the Watergate break-in on June 17, 1972. He had pleaded guilty at his trial in January,

E. Howard Hunt Jr.

but on Sept. 17 asked that his plea be withdrawn and the charges against him dismissed. *(p. 33)*

While testifying that his friend Colson was aware as early as January 1972 of a large-scale political espionage plan that included electronic surveillance, Hunt said that he could not be sure Colson had prior knowledge of the Watergate break-in. The over-all plan was code-named "Gemstone." Colson, who on Sept. 19 invoked the Fifth Amendment to keep from testifying before the committee, repeatedly had denied any knowledge of the Watergate and Ellsberg break-ins. *(p. 33)*

Asked if Colson knew about Gemstone, Hunt replied that he did, although he noted that Colson never had used the code name in conversations with him. Hunt said he told Colson in a late January 1972 meeting that he could no longer devote most of his time to the special investigations unit in the White House—the job for which Colson had recruited him—because he (Hunt) was working on a large-scale intelligence plan for then Attorney General John N. Mitchell and the President's re-election committee.

Hunt said Colson answered that he was aware of the plan and even suggested that Hunt should have been its chief, rather than G. Gordon Liddy. Liddy also was convicted for his role in the Watergate break-in. Since there was only one plan in existence at the time that called for surveillance of Democrats and alleged radicals, Hunt testified, he and Colson must have been referring to the same one—Gemstone.

"Your testimony is that while Mr. Colson was aware of the over-all Gemstone plan, he was not aware of the Watergate break-in?" asked minority counsel Fred D. Thompson. "Yes," replied Hunt.

Questioned earlier by majority counsel Samuel Dash, Hunt gave further evidence of Colson's knowledge of the over-all intelligence plan. He said he had been present at a February 1972 meeting with Colson and Liddy which Liddy had initiated in order to help the plan move alone.

Hunt said he was out of earshot of Liddy and Colson during part of the meeting, but that Colson made some telephone calls and Liddy said afterward, "I think I may have done us some good." One of the calls Colson made, according to Hunt, was to Jeb Stuart Magruder, deputy director of the Nixon re-election campaign. Magruder had testified that he received a call in February from Colson urging him to approve the budget for Liddy's plan. *(Magruder testimony, Vol. I, p. 136)*

Early Planning. Hunt testified that he first learned about the Gemstone plan in November 1971 from Liddy, its creator, but that the scheme to break into Democratic headquarters in the Watergate building did not materialize until April 1972. According to Hunt, Liddy told him then that he had learned from government sources that

Cuba was financing Democratic candidates and that the Watergate break-in was aimed at seeking proof of the allegation.

Hunt said he took Liddy's word that Mitchell approved the break-in. After taking orders for 21 years in the CIA, Hunt said, "it never occurred to me...to question the legality or propriety of orders from the attorney general of the United States."

Mitchell testified in July that he rejected Liddy's surveillance plans on three different occasions because they were too extreme. He testified that he merely wanted a plan developed to counter expected anti-Nixon demonstrations at the Republican convention.

Hunt went to work as a $100-a-day White House security consultant in July 1971. At the same time, he was a vice president of a Washington public relations firm, Robert R. Mullen Company. He had retired from the CIA in 1970. *(Opening statement text, p. 41)*

Target: Ellsberg. Hunt joined the special investigations unit—or "plumbers," as they later became known —but his primary assignment involved Daniel Ellsberg rather than plugging security leaks, the job for which the plumbers were created. Hunt testified that his assignment from Colson was to develop derogatory information on Ellsberg, who had leaked the Pentagon Papers to the press, in an effort to discredit Ellsberg. One of his sources of data on Ellsberg was the FBI, but he also used materials from the State and Defense Departments and from newspaper stories, Hunt said.

Dash introduced a July 28, 1971, memorandum from Hunt to Colson, which Hunt acknowledged writing, entitled, "Neutralization of Ellsberg." In it, Hunt proposed obtaining Ellsberg's files from the psychiatrist's office. No one understood why Ellsberg released the Pentagon Papers, Hunt told the committee. He wanted, he said, "to plumb Dr. Ellsberg's mind. We had no idea what type of animal we were dealing with."

Another memo, to Colson from John D. Ehrlichman, a former top presidential assistant, also was introduced by Dash. This one, dated Aug. 27, 1971, asked for a "game plan" on the "Hunt-Liddy special project No. 1." This was a reference to the Sept. 3, 1971 break-in at the Los Angeles, Calif., office of Ellsberg's psychiatrist, Dr. Lewis J. Fielding. Ehrlichman denied during his testimony before the committee in July that he had prior knowledge of the break-in. *(Vol. I, p. 210)*

Hunt testified that Ellsberg's psychiatric file never was found by the burglars, but that photographs were taken of the invaded office. When he tried to show Colson the photos, Colson refused to look at them, saying he did not want to know anything about the break-in, Hunt told the committee.

Other Activities. At Colson's urging, Hunt said, he faked several diplomatic cables in order to implicate President Kennedy in the 1963 assassination of President Diem of South Vietnam. According to Hunt, Colson wanted to leak the cables to the press to show that a Catholic American President conspired in the death of the Catholic President of South Vietnam, thereby costing Democrats Catholic votes in 1972. The cables were shown to a *Life* magazine reporter, William Lambert, but nothing came of the story, Hunt testified.

In the summer of 1971, Hunt said, he went to New England under a disguise to interview a man named Clifton DeMotte, who was believed to have information about the 1969 auto accident of Sen. Edward M. Kennedy (D Mass.) at Chappaquiddick, Mass. But Hunt said he learned nothing from DeMotte.

Another time, Hunt related, there was a plan to rifle the safe of a Las Vegas, Nev., newspaper publisher, Hank Greenspun, who supposedly had some derogatory information on Sen. Edmund S. Muskie (D Maine), then a leading prospect for the presidential nomination. But the plan was not carried out because Muskie's campaign faded in the Democratic primaries and he no longer presented a challenge to Nixon, said Hunt.

Hunt also told of several Washington street corner meetings with a man he knew only as "Fat Jack." The man handed him photographs of Muskie campaign documents in exchange for cash, Hunt testified.

After the Break-in. He related for the first time publicly what happened after the five Watergate burglars were caught on June 17, 1972. He said he was in room 214 of the Watergate hotel when he learned of the arrests. He said he grabbed the briefcase of one of the burglars, James W. McCord Jr., which contained some electronic equipment, and went to his office in the Executive Office Building. He put the briefcase in his safe, which also contained the Diem cables, Gemstone materials and a transcript of his talk with DeMotte, he said.

Hunt said he took $10,000 from the safe, money Liddy had given him for "contingency purposes," and delivered it to the apartment of C. Douglas Caddy, a lawyer who originally represented the five arrested burglars.

Returning to his office on June 19, Hunt said, he informed Colson's secretary, Joan Hall, of the contents of his safe. "I just want you to know that that safe is loaded," he said he told her. Hunt testified that he divulged its contents to her because he knew she had the combination to the safe.

The same day, Hunt went on, he met Liddy and was told that "they wanted me to get out of town." Hunt said he did not know who "they" were, but that he immediately left for California, where he stayed with a lawyer, Morton Jackson. Liddy visited him at Jackson's home June 22 and gave him $1,000 to give to Jackson, Hunt told the committee. Hunt said Jackson referred him to two Washington attorneys, one of whom was William O. Bittman, whom Hunt hired when he returned to Washington July 3.

Hunt said Liddy told him his legal fees and personal expenses would be taken care of just as with the "company," a slang term meaning the CIA. He said he received thousands of dollars from anonymous sources until three days before his sentencing on March 23, 1973. A final cash payment of $75,000 was given to him after he mentioned to a Colson associate that he had engaged in many other "seamy" activities for the White House besides Watergate, he said. But Hunt insisted that he did not mean the remark to be a threat. John Dean, a former White House counsel, testified that Hunt was trying to blackmail the White House and Nixon re-election committee into giving him more money. *(Dean testimony, Vol. I, p. 125)*

No U.S. Support. Hunt appeared tired and ill at ease during his four hours of testimony. Twice, his new lawyer, Sidney S. Sachs, asked that the committee recess early—once for lunch and once at the end of the day—because his client was fatigued. The committee agreed each time.

In his opening statement, Hunt said he had been attacked and robbed while in jail and had suffered a stroke. His greatest disappointment over the affair appeared to be the lack of government support for his actions.

Hearings Sept. 25

Hunt suggested to the committee that Alfred C. Baldwin III, a participant in the Watergate burglary, may have been a double agent hired by the Democrats to sabotage the Watergate break-in. Baldwin, a former FBI agent, was granted immunity from prosecution at the Watergate trial in exchange for his cooperation with the prosecution.

The possibility of a double agent was raised by Sen. Edward J. Gurney (R Fla.). Hunt replied that he had been thinking the matter over for some months and had come to believe that the police had been tipped off about the 1972 burglary.

Asked to explain why, Hunt said Baldwin had "rather intimate" ties to the Democratic Party. He said Baldwin was the nephew of a Democratic judge in Connecticut and had a girl friend employed by the Democratic National Committee. Also, said Hunt, District of Columbia police remained in the vicinity of Watergate for hours after the end of their normal shift and Baldwin, who was staked out across the street from the Watergate office building, failed to warn the burglars of the police presence.

Sen. Lowell P. Weicker Jr. (R Conn.), clearly disagreeing with the double agent theory, told Hunt that Baldwin's uncle, Raymond Baldwin, was a Republican and former governor and state supreme court justice in Connecticut. In fact, said Weicker, he was known in Connecticut as "Mr. Republican."

In other testimony Sept. 25, Hunt told the committee that government officials destroyed notebooks in his White House safe which contained the names of persons who had authorized the Gemstone plan, that Liddy had told him Mitchell ordered the ill-fated Watergate burglary and that he never was promised executive clemency for pleading guilty in his trial.

Notebooks. Hunt said his safe contained two notebooks that, in effect, gave the "parameters" of the Gemstone espionage plan. He said he did not know what happened to the notebooks but assumed they had been destroyed by high White House officials.

The committee earlier had heard testimony from Dean and others that some of the contents of Hunt's safe were turned over to authorities. But other items, such as the fake Diem assassination cables, were handed to former acting FBI Director L. Patrick Gray III, who destroyed them. *(Gray testimony, Vol. I, p. 255)*

Hunt described one notebook as a list-finder of CIA names and telephone numbers, and the other as an address book listing all the names and pseudonyms of everyone he had come in contact with concerning the Gemstone plan. The second book, he said, contained the names of the four Cuban-Americans convicted with him in the Watergate break-in, plus those of Liddy, CIA technical personnel, Gen. Robert E. Cushman, former deputy director of the CIA, and the number of a "sterile" (untraceable) White House telephone he could call when necessary.

Asked why the two books might have been removed from his safe and destroyed, Hunt replied: "They would provide a ready handbook that any investigator with any resources whatsoever could readily use to determine the parameters of the Gemstone operation and other operations I was involved in."

First Burglary. The Watergate break-in at which the five men were caught was actually their second burglary of the Democratic offices. An earlier, undetected burglary took place May 27, 1972. Hunt was asked who ordered the second break-in, in view of the fact that the first burglary failed to provide any information embarrassing to the Democrats.

Liddy, he answered, "indicated to me in the strongest terms that it was Mr. Mitchell who was insisting on it." Hunt added that he argued against the June 17 break-in, but that once the order was given, he obeyed like a good soldier.

Clemency. Asked by Gurney whether he ever had been promised executive clemency by anyone and whether such a promise might have influenced his guilty plea, Hunt replied, "No sir." At another point, he was asked by Sen. Joseph M. Montoya (D N.M.) whether he had ever had any conversations with anyone at the White House or the re-election committee about clemency, and he again replied no. This contradicted testimony by Dean, who said Hunt had been promised executive clemency by Colson through William Bittman, then Hunt's lawyer.

Hunt said his guilty plea was predicated solely on the belief that the government was withholding pertinent evidence and that such a plea might cause the court to show him mercy. He added that he made no attempt to influence the pleas of the four Cuban-Americans, who also pleaded guilty.

ITT Meetings. Hunt revealed some of the details of his secret 1972 meetings with Dita Beard, a former lobbyist for the International Telephone and Telegraph Corporation (ITT). Justice department officials had been linked in a memorandum, allegedly written by Beard, to the settlement of a federal antitrust suit against the giant conglomerate in exchange for a contribution to the 1972 Republican convention.

Hunt said he was dispatched by Colson to Denver, Colo., where Beard was hospitalized. He said he called himself "Mr. Warren" and told her he represented "high levels of the (Nixon) administration" who were interested in her welfare.

He said Colson had given him two basic questions to ask her: Why had she secretly left Washington, where she was being sought, and was the memo a fraud? She did not answer the second question, Hunt told the committee. "To the best of my recollection, she left it up in the air," he said.

Beard initially was suspicious of him and was reluctant to answer his questions, Hunt stated. Beard's doctor, he said, would come in periodically to administer oxygen to his patient, and he seized such opportunities to run to a pay telephone to call Colson and explain what the situation was and ask for further instructions.

Bremer Burglary. Hunt said Colson told him to burgle the Milwaukee, Wis., apartment of Arthur Bremer, the man convicted of attempting to kill Alabama Gov. George C. Wallace, shortly after Bremer's arrest in 1972. According to Hunt, Colson "suggested that I review the contents of Mr. Bremer's apartment." He did not explain why Colson gave such an order, but stated that he argued against it. Sometime later, said Hunt, Colson's secretary called him and told him the job no longer was required.

'Fat Jack.' At another point in the hearing, Hunt identified a photograph handed to him by Weicker as "Fat Jack," the man who, he testified on Sept. 24, had given him campaign documents from the office of Sen. Muskie of Maine. Weicker said the man's name was John Buckley, but Hunt said he never had heard of him. Sen. Herman E. Talmadge (D Ga.) later said Buckley was a former employee of the Office of Economic Opportunity.

Hearings Sept. 26

White House speechwriter Patrick J. Buchanan acknowledged authorship of several memorandums urging strong partisan attacks on the 1971-72 presidential campaign of Sen. Edmund S. Muskie (D Maine), but denied any responsibility for so-called "dirty tricks" against Muskie or other Democrats. Buchanan, 35, a special consultant to the President, lived up to his reputation as a tough, conservative, combative political adviser in his day-long appearance before the committee.

He admitted suggesting that the Nixon campaign force attack Muskie during the Democratic primaries. At one time, Muskie, who was the Democratic front-runner for the nomination, led Nixon in the polls and appeared to have the best chance of uniting the various factions of his party, Buchanan explained. It was Buchanan's hope, he said, that by concentrating their attacks on Muskie, the Republicans might open up the Democratic primaries and prevent a closed convention. "There was nothing—and is nothing—in my judgment, illicit or unethical or improper or unprecedented in recommending or adopting such a political strategy," he told the committee in a prepared statement.

In other testimony, Buchanan denied any advance knowledge of the Ellsberg break-in, the creation of the "plumbers" or their operations, Segretti's campaign sabotage activities or the spying by agents of the re-election committee. He said that at one point he recommended hiring a political prankster to harass the Democrats, but urged that those activities be kept on a small scale. But he said he had not heard of Segretti until reading about him in the press.

Buchanan repeatedly upstaged committee majority counsel Dash and other Democrats by his witty replies and unashamed acknowledgement of writing several memos. When Dash asked the witness how far he would have gone to ensure Nixon's re-election in 1972, Buchanan said he would have done "anything not immoral, unethical, illegal or unprecedented in previous Democratic campaigns."

One of his main lines of defense for many of the suggestions contained in his memos was that they were "not unprecedented" or that "the line was probably breached in both campaigns in '72."

Committee Vice Chairman Howard H. Baker Jr. (R Tenn.) appeared to support this defense in some of his questions. Referring to political spying in general, he asked whether it fell into the scope of what both parties did. "It appears to be routine," answered Buchanan. What about political monitoring? asked Baker. There has "always been tracking of the opposition," replied the witness.

Specific Acts. Sen. Daniel K. Inouye (D Hawaii), however, asked Buchanan a series of questions pertaining to specific acts of espionage or sabotage attributed to the Republicans. Was it ethical or proper, he asked, to transfer $400,000 in presidential campaign funds to the 1970 gubernatorial campaign opponent of Gov. George C. Wallace (D Ala.)? Buchanan said he did not know the law on that issue.

Is it all right, asked Inouye, to infiltrate another's campaign organization? Buchanan said he would not do it himself, but declined to rule it out for others. What about campaign sabotage? asked Inouye. Buchanan said that depended on whether it was a prank. For example, he said, there was nothing wrong with drafting a letter or an advertisement for some individual or committee to sign. That was the same as ghost-writing a speech, he maintained. But something such as the "Canuck letter," which was purported to have injured Muskie's New Hampshire primary campaign, was "unethical" and "a dirty trick," he said.

Foundations. Buchanan admitted writing a March 3, 1970, memo to the President urging the administration to wage war on liberal tax-exempt foundations "that succor the Democratic Party." In the memo he recommended that such foundations be cut off from administration discretionary grants and that conservative foundations be aided through such grants.

Buchanan told the committee that many of the tax-exempt foundations, such as the Ford Foundation and the Brookings Institution, "unbalance the political process" by their ability to influence public policy. He labeled the Brookings Institution a "government in exile for the Democratic Party."

He said he advocated using the Internal Revenue Service (IRS) against "leftist" institutions and foundations. "The tax-exempt division of the IRS had been biased" against conservative foundations, Buchanan stated, adding that the Nixon administration tried to fill jobs in that division with persons politically loyal to Nixon.

Attack on Committee. The memos used in the questioning of Buchanan were subpoenaed from the re-election committee or provided by the office of special Watergate prosecutor Archibald Cox, Dash stated. Buchanan said he did not accede to the committee's request that he bring other political strategy memos he had written, because White House laywers advised him they were covered by executive privilege.

Buchanan began his appearance with a harsh attack on the committee and its staff. He said the committee had lacked the "elementary courtesy" to inform him of his upcoming appearance before telling the press, and that "character assassins" on the staff had "maligned" his reputation by leaking information on him to the press.

Patrick J. Buchanan

Week's Watergate Chronology

Following is a day-to-day chronology of the week's events in the week ending Sept. 29 (*Earlier Sept. 20 events, p. 36*):

SEPT. 20

Tapes Dispute. President Nixon's attorney, Charles A. Wright, and special Watergate prosecutor Archibald Cox announced that they had failed to reach a compromise agreement on access by Cox to the tape recordings of Watergate-related presidential conversations. (*Details, p. 33*)

Wiretap Report. The Senate Foreign Relations Committee, in its report recommending Senate confirmation of Henry A. Kissinger as secretary of state, said that "very little, if any, justification, was presented in most instances" for White House-sanctioned wiretapping of the phones of 13 officials and four newsmen from 1969 to 1971. Kissinger had told the committee his role in the effort had been to provide names of people with access to information which had been leaked to the press.

SEPT. 21

Class Action Suit. U.S. District Judge June J. Green dismissed a class action suit brought in Washington, D.C., by the Rhode Island-based National Citizens Committee for Fairness to the Presidency Inc., seeking to halt the Senate Watergate hearings. An attorney for the group argued that the hearings represented a "de facto impeachment" of the President, but the judge said the organization had no basis for suing the Senate. (*Earlier story, p. 36*)

SEPT. 23

Hunt Leaks. *The Washington Post* quoted from a summary of private interviews conducted by the Senate Watergate investigating committee staff with convicted conspirator E. Howard Hunt Jr., who was scheduled to testify when the hearings reopened the next day. The Post said Hunt told Senate investigators that he believed former special White House counsel Charles W. Colson knew of plans to burglarize the office of Daniel Ellsberg's psychiatrist and that Colson also had prior knowledge of plans to conduct a surreptitious intelligence operation against the Democrats.

Dash Remarks. In an interview quoted in *The New York Times*, the Watergate committee's chief counsel, Samuel Dash, said the committee's second round of hearings would focus on whether political dirty tricks by Nixon supporters in the 1972 campaign differed "in kind or in degree" from past political practices. There would be time only to "define the key problem" in the committee's third area of inquiry, campaign spending, he said. Dash added that the committee might bypass the U.S. Court of Appeals in its suit for access to certain presidential tapes, so that its case could reach the Supreme Court along with a similar lawsuit being pursued by special prosecutor Archibald Cox.

SEPT. 24

Hunt Testimony. Hunt, the former CIA agent convicted for his role in the Watergate break-in, was the lead-off witness as the Senate Watergate investigating committee resumed its hearings. Interest focused on Hunt's allegation that Charles W. Colson, a former special White House counsel, had been aware in early 1972 of a large-scale intelligence plan that led to the June 17 break-in. (*Testimony, p. 37*)

Committee Suit. In a 71-page motion filed with U.S. District Judge John J. Sirica, Nixon's lawyers asked the court to reject the Senate investigating committee's request for a summary judgment forcing Nixon to release to the committee certain tape recordings. They argued that the court had no jurisdiction in the matter and that the committee's suit exceeded constitutional limits and its own mandate. (*Previous action, p. 36*)

SEPT. 25

Hunt Testimony. Howard Hunt returned for a second and final day of testimony before the Senate investigating committee. He answered questions on the Ellsberg burglary, Watergate break-in and numerous other undercover activities during the 10-hour session. Hunt surprised but did not convince the panel with a suggestion that the Watergate burglars had been betrayed by a double agent, Alfred C. Baldwin—the lookout stationed across the street from the Watergate complex during the June 17 break-in. (*Testimony, p. 39*)

SEPT. 26

Buchanan Testimony. White House speechwriter and political strategist Patrick J. Buchanan was the first witness in the Senate Watergate investigating committee's second phase of hearings covering alleged political sabotage by Nixon backers in the 1972 presidential election. The committee questioned Buchanan on a series of internal memos he had written proposing campaign tactics to undercut Democrats in the election—proposals he defended as legal, ethical and consistent with the past practices of both political parties. (*Testimony, p. 40*)

Hearings Coverage. Representatives of the three commercial television networks, which had been covering the Senate Watergate hearings live on a rotating basis, met in New York City and voted to discontinue their coverage when the hearings resumed Oct. 2. CBS President Richard Salant said he had favored continued coverage but was overruled by NBC and ABC. The noncommercial educational TV network planned to continue its complete filmed coverage in the evening.

HUNT'S OPENING STATEMENT

Following are excerpts from the opening statement of E. Howard Hunt Jr. before the Senate Watergate investigating committee on Sept. 24:

...In 1949, I joined the Central Intelligence Agency, from which I retired on May 1, 1970, having earned two commendations for outstanding contributions to operations ordered by the National Security Council.

During the 21 years I spent with CIA, I was engaged in intelligence, covert action, and counter-intelligence operations. I was trained in the techniques of physical and electronic surveillance, photography, document forgery and surreptitious entries into guarded premises for photography and installation of electronic devices. I participated in and had the responsibility for a number of such entries, and I had knowledge of many others.

To put it unmistakably, I was an intelligence officer—a spy —for the government of the United States.

There have been occasions, as one might expect, when covert operations by the United States or other nations have been exposed. Such episodes have not been uncommon. When such mishaps have occurred, it has been universally the practice for the operation to be disavowed and "covered up." Usually, this has been done by official intervention with law enforcement authorities. In addition, the employing governments have paid legal defense fees. Salaries and family living expenses have been continued. Former CIA Director Helms has testified before this committee in regard to some aspects of this practice.

After retiring from CIA, I was employed by a firm whose officials maintained a relationship with CIA. Some months after I joined the firm, I was approached by Charles W. Colson, special counsel to the President, to become a consultant to the executive office of the President. Mr. Colson told me the White House had need for the kind of intelligence background which he knew I possessed. This was the basic reason for my employment, which I understood at the time was approved by John D. Ehrlichman, and now understand was approved also by H.R. Haldeman, both assistants to the President of the United States.

From the time I began working at the White House until June 17, 1972, the day of the second Watergate entry, I engaged in essentially the same kind of work as I had performed for CIA. I became a member of the special investigations unit, later known as the plumbers, which the President had created to undertake specific national security tasks for which the traditional investigative agencies were deemed by the President to be inadequate. In this connection, I was involved in tracing leaks of highly classified information.

These investigations led to an entry by the plumbers into the office of Dr. Lewis Fielding, Dr. Daniel Ellsberg's psychiatrist. The entry was authorized by Mr. Egil Krogh, deputy to John Ehrlichman. It was considered necessary because of the belief that Dr. Ellsberg or his associates were providing classified information to the Soviet Union. The operation was carried out with my assistance, under the direction of G. Gordon Liddy, a lawyer, former FBI agent and member of the plumbers unit.

The Fielding entry occurred in September 1971. In late November, I was told by Mr. Liddy that Attorney General John N. Mitchell proposed the establishment of a large-scale intelligence and counter-intelligence program, with Mr. Liddy as its chief. Mr. Liddy and I designed a budget for categories of activities to be carried out in this program, which came to be known as Gemstone. It was my understanding that the program had been approved by Messrs. Jeb Stuart Magruder, a former White House aide, and John W. Dean III, counsel to the President. Later I learned that Charles W. Colson, special counsel to the President, had approved it, too.

In April 1972, Mr. Liddy told me that we would be undertaking the Watergate operation as part of the Gemstone program. He said that he had information, the source of which I understood to be a government agency, that the Cuban government was supplying funds to the Democratic Party campaign. To investigate this report, a surreptitious entry of Democratic national headquarters at the Watergate was made on May 27, 1972, and a second entry on June 17th. The second entry was accomplished by a group, two of whose members had been among those who accomplished the Fielding entry. I was indicted for my part in the Watergate entry.

Following indictment and prior to my guilty plea, the court ordered the government to produce all material taken from my White House safe, and other evidence. Some material was produced, but significant material was withheld or destroyed. Because the government had withheld evidence, I knew there was no chance of proving my defenses. In addition, my wife had been killed in an accident in December and I was deeply depressed and anxious to devote myself as quickly as possible to the welfare of my children. Accordingly, I had no alternative but to concede that I was legally wrong, and so I pleaded guilty, hoping for merciful treatment by the court.

Instead, on March 23 of this year, I was provisionally sentenced to prison for more than 30 years. The court stated that my cooperation with the grand jury and with this committee would be considered in determining my final sentence.

Since being sentenced, I have been questioned under oath on more than 25 occasions, often for many hours, sometimes for an entire day. I have answered thousands of questions by innumerable investigators, prosecutors, grand jurors and staff members of this committee. I am informed that such intensive and repeated interrogation is a most extraordinary procedure and of dubious legality. Even so, urged by the court to cooperate fully, I have not contested the procedure. In fact, I have answered all questions, even those which involved confidential communications between my attorneys and myself.

After my plea, I learned of obstruction of justice by government officials. I learned of willful destruction and withholding of evidence, and perjury and subornation of perjury before the Watergate grand jury. This official misconduct deprived me of evidence which would have supported my position that (a) my participation in the Watergate was an activity authorized within the power of the President of the United States, and (b) if my participation was not so authorized, I justifiably believed that it was.

Within the past few days, therefore, I have asked the court to permit me to withdraw my plea of guilty and to dismiss the proceedings against me. I believe the charges should be dismissed because, based on revelations made public since my plea, evidence is now available to prove that my participation was not unlawful, and because, to quote Judge Byrne when he dismissed charges in the Ellsberg case: "The totality of the circumstances of this case...offend a 'sense of justice.' The bizarre events have incurably infected the prosecution of this case."

It has been alleged that I demanded clemency and money for my family and for those who helped in the Watergate entry. I did not ask for clemency. Mr. Liddy assured me that, in accordance with the established practice in such cases, funds would be made available. I did seek such funds, but I made no threats.

Now I find myself confined under a sentence which may keep me in prison for the rest of my life. I have been incarcerated for six months. For a time I was in solitary confinement. I have been physically attacked and robbed in jail. I have been transferred from place to place, manacled and chained, hand and foot. I am isolated from my motherless children. I have suffered a stroke. The funds provided me and others who participated in the break-in have long since been exhausted. I am faced with an enormous financial burden in defending myself against criminal charges and numerous civil suits. Beyond all this, I am crushed by the failure of my government to protect me and my family as in the past it has always done for its clandestine agents.

In conclusion, I want to emphasize that at the time of the Watergate operation, I considered my participation as a duty to my country. I thought it was an unwise operation, but I viewed it as lawful. I hope the court will sustain my view, but whatever that outcome, I deeply regret that I had any part in this affair. I think it was an unfortunate use of executive power, and I am sorry that I did not have the wisdom to withdraw. At the same time, I cannot escape feeling that the country I have served for my entire life and which directed me to carry out the Watergate entry is punishing me for doing the very things it trained and directed me to do.... √

SABOTAGE: A BIG BAG OF ANTI-MUSKIE CAMPAIGN TRICKS

Three young men filled a Capitol hearing room with imagination-staggering tales of campaign dirty tricks as the Senate Select Committee on Presidential Campaign Activities continued its hearings on political sabotage and espionage in 1972.

The witnesses, two of them contrite and one of them defiant, spilled out stories of fake campaign literature, scurrilous letters, disrupted rallies and lesser pranks, all designed to create confusion and dissension among Democratic presidential contenders. The senators on the committee listened with interest, their reactions varying from indignation to occasional amusement.

Perhaps the most significant testimony during the week ended Oct. 6 involved the relationship of the chief prankster, Donald H. Segretti, with Dwight L. Chapin, President Nixon's former appointments secretary and the man who hired Segretti. Chapin had been scheduled as the week's lead-off witness, but his appearance was canceled after he said he would plead the Fifth Amendment. Segretti testified that Chapin had been his boss while the dirty tricks were being carried out. This contradicted what Chapin reportedly had said earlier.

Hearings Oct. 3

Admitted political saboteur Donald H. Segretti testified before the Senate select Watergate committee Oct. 3 as the committee continued its investigation of 1972 campaign "dirty tricks." Segretti, a short, boyish-looking, 32-year-old lawyer from California, had pleaded guilty Oct. 1 to three counts of political sabotage connected with the 1972 Democratic presidential primary in Florida. He was cooperating with special Watergate prosecutor Archibald Cox and testified before the committee under a grant of immunity.

There was little new or surprising in Segretti's day-long testimony, although he did provide added details about some of his activities in Florida. In his prepared statement, Segretti confirmed that he had been hired in the summer of 1971 by two former University of Southern California classmates, Dwight L. Chapin and Gordon Strachan, then high White House aides. Segretti said his two friends told him he was "to perform certain political functions" for the re-election of the President, which Segretti said he considered "to be similar to college pranks which had

Donald H. Segretti

occurred at U.S.C. The impression was given to me that these so-called pranks were performed by both parties in presidential campaigns and that there was nothing improper or illegal in such traditional activities," he said. *(Excerpts of opening statement, p. 47)*

At a later meeting, near Nixon's San Clemente, Calif., home, Segretti said Chapin, President Nixon's appointments secretary, told him his "duties would consist of various activities tending to foster a split between the various Democratic hopefuls and to prevent the Democratic Party from uniting behind one candidate." Chapin instructed him, Segretti said, never to use the names of any White House or Republican Party personnel when making contacts and never to use his own name in order not to embarrass the President or his campaign supporters.

Code names Segretti said he used were Don Morris, Bob Morse and Don Simmons. He said he used the name Mr. Chapman to refer to Chapin on several occasions. Segretti said he received $45,000 in expense money from Herbert W. Kalmbach, Nixon's personal attorney, during the period of September 1971 to March 1972, and bi-weekly salary payments of $667 during the same period.

Undercover Action. Segretti said his 1971 activities included preparing a list of embarrassing questions to be asked of Sen. Edmund S. Muskie (D Maine) during a California campaign appearance; arranging for persons to picket a Democratic meeting in San Francisco with "Kennedy for President" signs and having Muskie followed for two days in Los Angeles. He said his Florida activities were carried out with the help of Martin D. Kelly and Robert M. Benz. Benz, 25, a former president of the Tampa, Fla., Young Republicans, was named as an unindicted co-conspirator with Segretti. Kelly, 22, a former state president of the Florida Young Republicans, was not indicted, although he had testified before a federal grand jury.

Segretti said he and Benz began their activities in January 1972 by sending a letter on Muskie's stationery falsely alleging unauthorized use of government typewriters by the senator's staff. They also hired two persons to carry "Muskie for President" signs at a rally for Sen. Henry M. Jackson (D Wash.), made posters indicating Muskie supported busing (then a volatile issue in Florida), placed stink bombs in Muskie's headquarters and sent a letter on Muskie stationery accusing Senators Jackson and Hubert H. Humphrey (D Minn.) of sexual misconduct.

In addition, Segretti said, Kelly helped him place ads harmful to Muskie in Florida newspapers and on radio stations, and went with him to Washington, D.C., to disrupt a Muskie dinner by placing false orders for food and beverages. The witness said his last political activity of the 1972 campaign was to hire a plane to fly over the Democratic convention center with a trailer reading, "Peace, pot, promiscuity. Vote McGovern."

Segretti apologized for his actions, saying they "were wrong and have no place in the American political system," but he insisted that they had been blown out of proportion by the news media. "I cannot help but feel that I have been abused by rumor, character assassination, innuendo and a complete disregard for the privacy of myself, my friends and family," he said.

Chapin Relationship. The extent of Segretti's direction by Chapin was unclear from his testimony. He said many of his actions resulted from his own ideas "thought up over a beer," but that some were suggested by Chapin. For example, Segretti testified, in answer to a question, that Chapin ordered him to concentrate his efforts on Muskie, and even showed him how to position anti-Muskie picketers at rallies so that their signs would be in the view of television cameras. Chapin also gave him a list of 1968 Nixon campaign advance men as a source of agents, he said. All his activities were reported to Chapin at the White House, Segretti said. He acknowledged that Chapin was his "boss."

His testimony conflicted with the reported statements of Chapin on this issue. Chapin, who left the White House in January to become a United Air Lines executive, had pleaded the Fifth Amendment in refusing to testify before the Senate Watergate committee. But he had told FBI interviewers that he had had little to do with Segretti after hiring him.

The number of agents Segretti recruited also was in dispute. Segretti estimated it at 11, but committee majority counsel Samuel Dash said Segretti's subpoenaed expense records showed he paid a total of 22 persons and that his agents paid another six, for a total of 28.

Denials. The witness denied that he was responsible for the so-called "Canuck letter" that damaged Muskie's New Hampshire primary campaign, or that he ever undertook any sabotage activities in New Hampshire. Segretti said he went to New Hampshire but made

the mistake of revealing his real name, and Chapin ordered him to leave the state.

Segretti also denied published reports that he ran a "spy school" for Republican agents and that he got a look at secret FBI reports in preparation for his grand jury testimony.

In answer to other questions, Segretti said he did not realize at the time he committed the various acts of campaign sabotage that they were illegal. He said he knew some of them might have been improper, but that he "got caught up on the zeal of...the campaign. These things were done without a great deal of foresight."

Limited Inquiry. Segretti told the committee he had come to believe, after appearing before the Watergate grand jury in the summer of 1972, that "there was something going on behind the scenes" among federal prosecutors, who were not probing him deeply in their investigation of campaign sabotage. John W. Dean III, then Nixon's counsel, told him at that time that Dean "might be able to put parameters" on the grand jury investigation, Segretti testified.

Hearings Oct. 4

Kelly and Benz spent half a day apiece telling the committee about their activities. They agreed that the campaign sabotage and espionage they helped perpetrate probably had little effect on the final outcome of the 1972 Florida presidential primary, but that they did succeed in their goal—making the candidates angry at each other.

What Kelly said he did was not aimed at influencing voters, he explained, but rather at dividing the candidates so that they would be so embittered at each other that they would be unable to unite behind a single candidate after the Democratic convention. Most of their work was concentrated against Muskie, they said, because Muskie was the Democratic front-runner at the time, although Wallace was expected to win the Florida primary. Kelly said he believed the Segretti-directed campaign "certainly angered Muskie" and indirectly may have had a "slight effect" on causing him to finish fourth in the primary.

No Remorse. While Kelly expressed contrition over what he did, Benz showed little remorse. Benz admitted that what he did was neither right nor proper, but said, "I felt I did the things I should do."

He expressed the belief that his activities might help in the long run to clean up the American political system "by causing a deterrent to actions of this type." Benz's motive, he said, was revenge for what he claimed were "dirty tricks" perpetrated against Republicans he had supported in prior elections. He said he felt that "if the Democrats got a little bit of a dose of their own type of activities, they'd be reluctant to do it to us again."

When Committee Chairman Sam J. Ervin Jr. (D N.C.) lectured him that two wrongs do not make a right, Benz, a husky dock worker, shot back that the members of the committee probably knew of illegal acts in their own past campaigns and therefore were in no position to sit in judgment on the 1972 elections. "Where were you in 1960 when an election was stolen" from Richard M. Nixon? he demanded of Ervin.

Watergate Bomb Scare

A series of telephoned bomb threats temporarily interrupted the public hearings of the Senate select Watergate committee Oct. 3 when Capitol police cleared the caucus room for a search.

The room was evacuated and sealed off shortly after 11 a.m., after Capitol telephone operators had received three calls. "I'm only attempting to warn you," said a man's voice. "It's scheduled to go off in 45 minutes." The last call came in at 10:30.

Rufus Edmisten, deputy counsel to the committee, arranged for the members to be summoned to the Senate floor for a quorum call. This was the reason Chairman Sam J. Ervin Jr. (D N.C.) stated publicly as the reason for the recess.

A similar bomb threat was made for the House caucus room, which also was cleared and searched. No bombs were found in either room. The Watergate hearings resumed at 1 p.m.

In an unusual postscript the next morning, a tear gas canister was discovered in a wastebasket in a restroom on the Senate side of the Capitol.

Kelly, on the other hand, said he deeply regretted the political and personal damage he helped cause Senators Muskie, Humphrey and Jackson. Several times he told the committee, "I'm not here defending my position. I don't have any position to defend."

Pattern of Skulduggery. Describing the genesis of his operations, Kelly said he first met Segretti in December 1971. Segretti asked his thoughts on "negative campaigning," Kelly said, adding, "I had no idea what he meant." But he said the $150-a-month salary offer was attractive, and the private hope that his work might lead to a job in Washington caused him to accept.

Kelly said he worked for Segretti until April or May 1972, with most of their activities directed against Muskie. He said Segretti told him "Muskie had a short fuse" and that if enough pressure were put on him week after week, "he might blow it."

Enumerating '' activities, Kelly said he placed ads in newspapers and on radio stations, usually under Jackson's or Humphrey's names, implying Muskie insults of Cuban-Americans; sent bogus invitations to Muskie picnics; falsely ordered chicken, pizza and liquor for the Muskie headquarters, and even hired a woman for $20 to walk naked in front of a hotel Muskie was staying at, shouting, "Muskie, I love you."

On one occasion, he said, he released a finch at a Muskie press conference, and the bird flew around the room and distracted the participants. At the same time he released two white mice trailing signs saying, "Muskie Is a Rat Fink." Kelly described going to Washington, D.C., to harass a Muskie dinner party in the Washington-Hilton hotel. This included issuing fake invitations to African diplomats. "The result was regrettable," Kelly said, "but it was embarrassing for Muskie and the Democrats."

Records Destroyed. Fake invitations and press releases as well as picketing also were employed against Humphrey and Jackson, Kelly said. He said he destroyed all his records, receipts and other possibly incriminating evidence in the fall of 1972 when Segretti's name began appearing in newspapers as the alleged head of the sabotage operation. Kelly denied ever personally infiltrating a campaign or participating in violent acts against Democrats.

Asked if he had had any misgivings about his work, he said he was not sure he realized exactly what he was doing at the time. He said he began to feel remorse when he had stopped his activities and had time to think about them. He attributed his actions to immaturity and ambition.

Like Benz, Kelly said Segretti never told him whom he was working for. But Kelly said he suspected it was the Nixon re-election committee or the Republican National Committee, because, he said, Segretti always had a lot of money and did much traveling.

Taciturn Witness. Benz's manner was in sharp contrast to that of Kelly and Segretti. Whereas the others provided expansive answers to questions and seldom had to be prodded for more detail, Benz was tight-lipped. He often gave one-word answers that require follow-up questions to pry details from him.

Benz said he, too, was contacted by Segretti in December 1971 for what Segretti at first called a "voter research project." Later, said Benz, Segretti asked him to take part in disrupting the Democratic prim-

---

Poll Report

Watergate and inflation were credited with President Nixon's low ratings in the latest Gallup Poll. His approval score, in interviews conducted Sept. 7-10 and published Sept. 23, was three percentage points lower than it was in the poll conducted just after his Aug. 15 Watergate speech. But it was four points above his low point in early August. *(Earlier polls, p. 28)*

These were the questions and results in the nationwide sample of 1,463 adults:

"Do you approve or disapprove of the way Nixon is handling his job as President?"

	Latest	Aug. 17-19
Approve	35%	38%
Disapprove	55	54
No opinion	10	8

"Which one (of the following statements) comes closest to your own point of view? (A) Nixon planned the Watergate bugging from the beginning. (B) Nixon did not plan the bugging but knew about it before it took place. (C) Nixon found out about the bugging after it occurred, but tried to cover it up. (D) Nixon had no knowledge of the bugging and spoke up as soon as he learned about it."

	Latest	Aug. 17-20
Planned	11%	9%
Knew about	28	24
Covered up	33	40
Had no knowledge	18	23
No opinion	10	4

"President Nixon has said he will not turn over to Chief U.S. District Judge John Sirica tapes of his conversations with advisers involved in the Watergate affair. Do you think he should or should not give Sirica the tapes?"

Should	61%
Should not	32
No opinion	7

---

ary in Florida. Benz said his salary was $150 a month plus expenses.

The witness described his first task as infiltrating the Muskie, Jackson and Humphrey camps. He said he hired a woman, whom he named as Patricia Griffin, to get a job in Muskie's headquarters by having her say she was a Republican who had gone sour on Nixon. Similar methods were used to infiltrate the other campaign headquarters, Benz related, and the spies provided him with campaign stationery, schedules and names of contributors. This information and materials were forwarded to Segretti, he said.

Some of the actions Benz said he participated in were hiring pickets to parade in front of Jackson's headquarters with signs saying, "Muskie Country"; distributing literature at a Wallace rally saying, "If you liked Hitler, you'll love Wallace," and urging people to vote for Muskie; distributing a fake Muskie handbill indicating the senator favored more busing, and having distributed on Muskie stationery allegations of sexual improprieties by Jackson and Humphrey.

George Hearing, whom Benz said he had recruited, was serving a year in jail for distributing the allegations about Humphrey and Jackson. Benz was granted immunity in order to testify against Segretti and Hearing. Hearing, however, pleaded guilty.

Benz said he traveled to Milwaukee, Wis., where he harassed Muskie headquarters by sending out fake press releases announcing a free dinner. He said he was sent by Segretti to Pittsburgh, Pa., to set up an organization similar to that in Florida, but neither senators nor committee staff members asked him about it.

The witness said he, too, destroyed all his records and other materials related to the spying and sabotage activities when he learned Segretti was under investigation.

Week's Watergate Chronology

Following is a day-to-day chronology of the week's events in the week ending Sept. 29. (Earlier Sept. 26 events, p. 41):

SEPT. 26

Kissinger Denial. Secretary of State Henry A. Kissinger denied allegations in an affidavit released Sept. 25 by the Senate Watergate investigating committee. The document, submitted by Dr. Bernard M. Malloy, a staff psychiatrist for the Central Intelligence Agency, quoted David M. Young Jr., a former White House official who once worked in Kissinger's office, as having told Malloy that Kissinger authorized the request for a psychiatric profile of Daniel Ellsberg in 1971. Kissinger denied all knowledge of the profile at a press conference in New York City. (Hunt testimony, p. 38)

SEPT. 28

Committee Suit. Lawyers for the Senate Watergate investigating committee filed a 27-page brief in U.S. District Court in Washington, D.C., in support of the committee's Aug. 29 motion for a summary judgment that would force Nixon to turn over White House tape recordings. The brief argued that Nixon had no right to withhold evidence of his own possible wrong-doing and that there was "sufficient evidence to establish a prima facie case that the President was engaged in criminal conduct." (Previous action, p. 41)

SEPT. 30

Hearings Delayed. Chief counsel Samuel Dash of the Senate Watergate committee announced that the committee's hearings would resume Oct. 3, a day later than scheduled, because two of its planned witnesses had been dropped after threatening to plead the Fifth Amendment in response to questions. They were Dwight L. Chapin, Nixon's former appointments secretary, and

John R. (Fat Jack) Buckley, an alleged campaign spy for the Republicans in 1972. (Hearings, p. 40, 38)

OCT. 1

Sirica on Sentencing. Chief Judge John J. Sirica of U.S. District Court in Washington called five of the convicted Watergate conspirators to his chambers to assure them he did not plan to give them maximum sentences. The men—E. Howard Hunt Jr., Bernard L. Barker, Eugenio R. Martinez, Frank A. Sturgis and Virgilio Gonzalez—had been given provisional maximum sentences while the court attempted to gather more information on which to base final sentences. Sirica described the maximum sentences of up to 60 years as "unwarranted." All five had filed appeals seeking to set aside their guilty pleas and asking for new trials. (p. 36, 35)

Segretti Plea. Donald H. Segretti, the California lawyer allegedly hired by Nixon aides to sabotage Democratic presidential candidates in 1972, appeared before Federal District Judge Gerhard A. Gesell in Washington and pleaded guilty to three misdemeanor charges for his actions in the 1972 Florida Democratic primary. Segretti appeared later before Judge Sirica, who signed orders granting him limited immunity from prosecution for testimony before the Watergate federal grand jury and the Senate Watergate investigating committee. (p. 36)

Ellsberg Break-In. Release of the transcript of the Los Angeles, Calif., grand jury investigation into the 1971 break-in at the office of Daniel Ellsberg's psychiatrist brought to light a contention by John D. Ehrlichman, Nixon's former domestic affairs adviser, that the President played an active role in organizing and supervising the "plumbers" unit responsible for the burglary. Ehrlichman testified that Nixon specifically authorized the use of covert tactics to gather information about Ellsberg. Both Nixon and Ehrlichman had denied specific advance knowledge of the break-in. (Ellsberg case, p. 36)

OCT. 3

Segretti Testimony. Donald H. Segretti, the California lawyer who had pleaded guilty to illegal activities involving the 1972 presidential primary in Florida, told the Senate Watergate committee about "dirty tricks" he performed during the primaries in an attempt to confuse Democratic presidential candidates. Segretti testified that he had reported regularly throughout the campaign to Nixon's former appointments secretary, Dwight L. Chapin. (Testimony, p. 43)

OCT. 4

Jackson on Segretti. Sen. Henry M. Jackson (D Wash.), a defeated candidate for the Democratic presidential nomination in 1972, charged that Segretti had "engaged in filth, muck and slime," and said he was not satisfied with Segretti's public apology for such acts as sending out bogus letters accusing Jackson and Sen. Hubert H. Humphrey (D Minn.) of sexual misconduct.

Hearings. The Senate Watergate investigating committee heard testimony from two men employed by Segretti in 1972. They were Martin D. Kelly of Miami, Fla., and Robert Benz of Tampa, Fla., both former leaders in the state Young Republican organization. *(Testimony, p. 44)*

SEGRETTI'S OPENING STATEMENT

Following are excerpts from the opening statement of Donald H. Segretti before the Senate Watergate investigating committee on Oct. 3:

...After my graduation from U.S.C. I maintained infrequent social contact with two college friends, Dwight Chapin and Gordon Strachan; so, it did not seem unusual when I was contacted in early 1971 by these two friends about the possibility of doing some work for them after my release from active duty. I indicated interest although I had no concept of what they had in mind.

In the summer of 1971 I flew to Washington, D.C., and met with Mr. Chapin and Mr. Strachan. It was explained to me that I would be employed to perform certain political functions for the re-election of President Nixon. At that time I was aware that both men were employed at the White House. I considered the political functions we discussed to be similar to college pranks which had occurred at U.S.C. The impression was given to me that these so-called pranks were performed by both parties in presidential campaigns and that there was nothing improper or illegal in such traditional activities.

Subsequently, I was told to contact Mr. Herbert Kalmbach in Newport Beach, Calif., for the purpose of finalizing my employment. I met with Mr. Kalmbach in August 1971 and was offered a salary of $16,000 per annum plus expenses for my activities. Mr. Kalmbach and I did not discuss the specifics of my employment, and I myself had no concrete ideas as to what work I was to perform. It was not even clear to me whether or not I would be working for Mr. Kalmbach, Mr. Chapin or others. However, I was happy to accept employment from people who held prominent positions in and out of the government.

After meeting with Mr. Kalmbach I met with Mr. Chapin not far from the Western White House in Sam Clemente, Calif. During this meeting, Mr. Chapin gave me a list of cities in which I was to acquire acquaintances to assist me in my future endeavors. Mr. Chapin stressed the secrecy of my duties and stated that he would be my contact at the White House. He further explained that my duties would consist of various activities tending to foster a split between the various Democratic hopefuls and to prevent the Democratic Party from uniting behind one candidate. I was told that this was a common campaign strategy....

Early Duties. From September 1971 to the end of the year, I traveled to various parts of the United States attempting to line up political associates. Mr. Chapin had instructed me not to use the names of any persons at the White House or the name of any person associated with the Republican Party when making my contacts. I was also told not to use my real name so that I would never prove an embarrassment to the President or his campaign supporters. It was therefore difficult for me to explain to people exactly what I was doing, who I was working for, or what we would be doing together. During the initial period of my employment, I myself had no specific idea as to what I was doing or how I was to do it. I did indicate to people I "recruited" that their tasks would be to picket various Democratic candidates under the guise of working for a rival Democratic candidate, to ask difficult questions at news conferences and, if possible, get someone to work in a candidate's headquarters. The purpose of planting so-called "spies" was primarily to obtain candidates' traveling schedules to assist in the plan-

ning of picketing activities. During this period I received $5,000 traveling expenses from Mr. Kalmbach and the sum of $667 every two weeks as salary.

Apart from the above, I did the following during 1971:

• 1. I prepared a list of questions to ask Senator Muskie when he appeared at Whittier College. The questions were passed out among the audience, and I believe one of the questions was asked.

• 2. I contacted an individual in California who provided three or four persons in San Francisco who picketed a meeting of various Democrats with signs saying, "Kennedy for President."

• 3. I had Senator Muskie followed for two days while he was in Los Angeles, Calif. This was the one and only time that I ever had any candidate followed, and it was done pursuant to an earlier suggestion from Mr. Chapin that I have a familiarity with how presidential candidates traveled. To the best of my recollection, those are the only activities I performed in 1971.

> *"I deeply regret that I initiated this incident and wish to apologize publicly for this stupid act. I can only hope that this apology will in some way rectify the harm done to these senators and their families."*

'Switch to Green.' In January of 1972, I received a second sum of $5,000 from Mr. Kalmbach. This sum was paid following my request for additional monies to cover my travel expenses. On or about Jan. 15, 1972, I received my last biweekly check in the sum of $667 from a trust account apparently maintained by Mr. Kalmbach. At about this time Mr. Kalmbach explained to me that rather than receiving further monies by check he preferred that we "switch to green." On or about March 1, 1972, I received the sum of $5,000 in cash from Mr. Kalmbach's secretary, and on or about March 23, 1972, I received the sum of $25,000 in cash from Mr. Kalmbach. This latter payment was made upon my request for the sum of $5,000 which I anticipated was needed to cover my traveling and salary expenses. It was my impression at the time that the extra $20,000 was given to me so that I would not have to contact Mr. Kalmbach on a frequent basis. I now believe that the new campaign law regarding the reporting of income had something to do with this payment. The funds referred to herein are the only monies that I have received. I did not at any time discuss with Mr. Kalmbach any of the specifics of my political activity, and I have no personal knowledge as to whether or not he spoke with others about what I was doing.

All of the monies received were spent for traveling and living expenses. A complete accounting, to the best of my ability, has been provided to this committee and to the special prosecutor's office.

Florida Campaign. In December of 1971, I traveled to the state of Florida for the purpose of seeking additional contacts. During my visit I met a Mr. Robert Benz in Tampa, Fla., and a Mr. Douglas Kelly in Miami, Fla.

Mr. Benz and Mr. Kelly seemed very knowledgeable as to the inner workings of a political campaign and expressed a willingness to assist me in my endeavors. In fact, both young men seemed to know much more about how political campaigns operated than I did. Therefore, I gave to each a modest sum and asked that they make contact with other persons who would be of future assistance. The intention was, as previously indicated, to line up pickets, recruit persons to ask hard questions at news conferences and to obtain the travel schedules of the various Democratic candidates.

In early January 1972, I returned to Florida. At this time Mr. Benz had obtained two students to picket the opening of Senator Jackson's headquarters in Tampa..., carrying "Muskie for President" signs. He also had recruited approximately 10 persons to picket a Muskie rally with signs relating to Muskie's reluctance to consider a black American as a running mate. These activities of Mr. Benz were done pursuant to my suggestions. I also understand that Mr. Benz, on his own initiative, added a sentence to a Muskie press release, which announced the sending of 10,000 invitations for a Muskie rally to be followed by a $1,000-a-plate dinner. This press release was sent to one or two newspapers.

In addition to the above, Mr. Benz and I collaborated in one way or another on the following matters:

• 1. A letter on Senator Muskie's stationery alleging unauthorized use of government typewriters by his staff. This letter was sent to various persons whom I do not recall at this time.

• 2. The placing of posters stating, "Help Muskie In Busing More Children Now." The poster bore the legend "Mothers Backing Muskie Committee." Approximately 100 to 150 such posters were distributed or posted by me.

• 3. The placing of stink bombs at a Muskie picnic and at the Muskie headquarters.

• 4. The sending of a letter on Muskie stationery accusing Senators Jackson and Humphrey of sexual improprieties. I would like to make clear that this letter was my idea and was not suggested by any other person. I assume full responsibility for its contents. Each and every allegation in the letter was untrue and without any basis in fact. It was not my desire to have anyone believe the letter, but instead it was intended to create confusion among the various candidates. It is my belief that from 20 to 40 such letters were sent out, mainly to Sen. Jackson's supporters. I deeply regret that I initiated this incident and wish to apologize publicly for this stupid act. I can only hope that this apology will in some way rectify the harm done to these senators and their families....

At this time, it is my best recollection that I paid Mr. Kelly and Mr. Benz a total of approximately $5,500.

Warren/Hunt. In February of 1972, a man called me, identifying himself as Ed Warren. From a prior conversation with Mr. Chapin, I had been informed that a person would call me who would give me assistance. In Miami...I met with Mr. Warren and another individual who was introduced to me as George Leonard. I now recognize Ed Warren as being Mr. E. Howard Hunt. I have been unable to identify Mr. George Leonard; however, it is my understanding that he was probably G. Gordon Liddy. Mr. Warren provided me with the name of a printer in Miami whom I subsequently used for various purposes. I recall meeting Mr. Warren a second time in June 1972 at the Four Ambassadors hotel in Miami.... During this meeting, Mr. Warren suggested that I put together a group of peaceful demonstrators to picket the Doral hotel during the Democratic convention, at which time another group of pickets was to join in the demonstration and act in an unruly manner. It was explained to me that the bad conduct of the crowd would be blamed on Sen. McGovern. It was never my intention to create, nor did I ever participate in, any kind of physical violence, and Mr. Warren's plan was something in which I did not want to get involved. As fate would have it, the Watergate burglary preceded these plans and they were never carried out.

At this point I would like to state to the committee that at no time did I have any knowledge of, nor did I participate in, the Watergate burglary or any activity involving electronic surveillance....

Free Lunch. On April 1, 1972...in Milwaukee, Wis., Mr. Benz and I distributed a flier advertising a free all-you-can-eat lunch with drinks at Hubert Humphrey's headquarters. I have given the committee and the special prosecutor's office a copy of the flier. There was, of course, no such party.

Also in April of 1972, in response to a telephone call from Mr. Warren, I flew to Washington, D.C. I had Mr. Kelly meet me there. Sen. Muskie was to have a fund-raising dinner at the Washington Hilton hotel, and Mr. Kelly and I, ostensibly acting for the Muskie organizers, ordered flowers, pizzas and liquor for the campaign workers. In addition, we invited certain foreign guests and provided for their delivery to the dinner by chauffeured limousine. A magician was also hired to attend the dinner and to entertain. We also made inquiries about renting an elephant, but were unable to make the necessary arrangements. The purpose of all this was to cause confusion at the Muskie dinner. Mr. Kelly and I also distributed a flier stating, "Come. Protest the fat cats with signs." This was in reference to the Muskie dinner. Mr. Kelly and I constructed various protest signs, but no one showed up to protest.

During 1972, I performed activities of a similar, but less extensive and significant, nature in other states. I have given a full statement to this committee's staff regarding these events. I believe my activities in these other states produced little if any commotion, and do not need to be elaborated on in this statement....

In July of 1972, Mr. Kelly and I made arrangements for a small plane to fly over the Democratic convention center with a trailer reading: "Peace, pot, promiscuity. Vote McGovern." This was my last political activity of the 1972 campaign.

> *"We also made inquiries about renting an elephant, but were unable to make the necessary arrangements."*

Dean's Counsel. After news stories began mentioning my name, I sought legal counsel from Mr. John W. Dean. I met Mr. Dean through Mr. Chapin and Mr. Strachan. Over a period of months Mr. Dean acted as my lawyer, and I confided in him in this capacity. At Mr. Dean's request, I made a tape recording explaining my activities in 1971 and 1972 and gave it to him. I also prepared a written statement and gave it, along with many documents, to an attorney in Los Angeles...who was suggested as counsel by Mr. Dean. It is my understanding that this attorney sent to Mr. Dean copies of the material left with him and that Mr. Dean subsequently turned over said material, which was obviously intended to be confidential and part of the attorney-client privilege, to this committee. Although I feel that Mr. Dean betrayed my confidence, I do wish to state that at no time did he tell me to be anything but honest and truthful with the Federal Bureau of Investigation and the United States attorney's office.

This general statement was prepared with the advice and assistance of my present counsel, Victor Sherman, and was not intended by us to be a complete statement of all my activities during the months in question. I am sure that this committee is now aware that my activities have been blown out of all proportion by the news media.

I accept the fact that most of my present problems are the direct result of my own conduct. However, I cannot help but feel that I have been abused by rumor, character assassination, innuendo and a complete disregard for the privacy of myself, my friends and my family. I have literally had to avoid the onslaught of the media during the past year, and their attempts to get a story at all costs. I understand that under various guises, some of the news media illegally obtained my telephone, bank account and credit card records, and generally conducted their investigations without any concern for my rights. Nonetheless, this in no way lessens my sincere belief that my activities were wrong and have no place in the American political system. To the extent my activities have harmed other persons and the political process, I have the deepest regrets. I am now ready to answer the questions of this committee.   √

EXCERPTS FROM NIXON'S OCT. 3 NEWS CONFERENCE

President Nixon's news conference was dominated by questions about Vice President Agnew and the possibility of a vice presidential resignation.

Nixon announced that Secretary of State Kissinger would travel to Peking and Japan as part of a "continuing dialogue" between China and the United States.

Other questions asked concerned U.S. relations with Japan, inflation, the plight of Russian emigrants and foreign travel by the President.

Following are questions dealing with Watergate:

San Clemente

Q: Mr. President, at your last press conference you said that some of the government work done at San Clemente had diminished the value of the property for use as a home. I would like to ask about two items that are in the GSA reports on it.

First, do you think that the $13,500 electrical heating system that was installed diminished its value? And, second, do you thank when the GSA hired a local landscape architect to redesign the flower beds on the west side of the residence four times a year, that they were spending the taxpayer's money wisely?

A: Well, I can plow that ground again, I guess. If any of you have lived in California, you will know that gas heat costs less than electric heat. I preferred the first, gas heat. For security reasons, apparently, they decided it presented a fire hazard which could not be tolerated. And so that decision was made.

With regard to the other matters that have been brought up, I think full statements have been made over and over again on this, and I really think anything I would say in answer to your question, in view of the way you have already presented it as a statement, would not convince you or anybody else.

Watergate Tapes

Q: Sir, there is at least the possibility that if you don't give up the Watergate tapes, some of the cases or potential cases against your former aides might be aborted. I wonder if you are concerned about this, and further, whether you might see some room for compromise in the Appellate Court suggestion?

A: Well, since the Appellate Court is still considering the matter, it would be inappropriate for me to talk about what should be done with regard to compromise. As you know, discussions, extended discussions, took place between Mr. Buzhardt and the Special Prosecutor in this respect, and they agreed to disagree.

As far as the tapes are concerned, I have stated my position, and I restate it again today. The position is that the confidentiality of Presidential discussions must be maintained and whether it is a Presidential paper, a memorandum of conversation prepared by a member of his staff after meeting with the President, or whether it is a tape of a conversation, it is the responsibility of the President, with regard to the separation of powers principle, to defend the integrity of those conversations so that Presidents in the future will be able to conduct

1807 Subpoena Precedent

During the 1973 debate over the propriety of issuing and enforcing a subpoena against the President of the United States, lawyers on both sides of the issue dusted off an 1807 case involving President Thomas Jefferson and one of the nation's more famous Vice Presidents, Aaron Burr. *(Sirica decision p. 17; appeals court p. 62)*

Burr, no longer vice president at the time, was on trial in Richmond, Va. on charges of treason. In the third week of his trial he announced, to the surprise of those in the court, that he intended to ask the court to issue a subpoena to President Jefferson requiring him to produce as evidence a letter dated Oct. 21, 1806, to Jefferson from General James Wilkinson. Then—as 166 years later—an immediate controversy arose over the propriety of issuing a subpoena to the nation's chief executive.

Chief Justice John Marshall, sitting on circuit as a trial judge, heard four days of arguments on the subpoena issue. Then, on June 13, 1807, he ruled: the President was subject to a subpoena just like any other citizen. Marshall wrote that if there was any principle because of which the President was exempted from this requirement, "it would be because his duties as chief magistrate demand his whole time for national objectives."

"But it is apparent that this demand is not unremitting," Marshall wrote, "and, if it should exist at the time when his attendance on a court is required, it would rather constitute a reason for not obeying the process of the court than a reason against its being issued."

The day before Marshall had ruled, however, President Jefferson in Washington had written the federal attorney in the case to say that he had sent all the relevant papers to Richmond, including the subpoenaed letter. Jefferson told George Hay, the attorney, that he did not remember the precise and entire contents of that letter and that would like Hay to exercise his discretion in withholding any part of the letter which was not relevant to the case.

Several days later, the President sent additional papers to Hay, saying that if questions still remained concerning the object of the subpoena, he would give sworn testimony in a deposition, taken in Washington, but that he could not travel to Richmond to appear at the trial. To do so, he argued, would set a precedent which might require him to travel all over the country to respond to subpoenas in trials in various places: "To comply with such calls would leave the nation without an executive branch, whose agency ...is understood to be so constantly necessary, that it is the sole branch which the Constitution requires to be always in function."

free-wheeling, extended conversations with no holds barred with foreign visitors and, of course, with those who come to see him from the United States.

WASHINGTON, D.C., INDICTMENT OF 'PLUMBERS' CHIEF KROGH

Special Watergate prosecutor Archibald Cox obtained his first indictment the week ended Oct. 13 in what was expected eventually to be a long list of indicted former Nixon administration officials. The Senate's Watergate hearings, meanwhile, continued with three days of testimony about Republican "dirty tricks."

Indictment. Former White House aide Egil (Bud) Krogh Jr. was indicted Oct. 11 by a federal grand jury in Washington, D.C., for lying during the initial Watergate investigation in 1972. Krogh, former head of the White House special investigations unit, nicknamed the "plumbers," also was under indictment in Los Angeles, Calif., with three other persons, for his part in the September 1971 burglary of the office of Daniel Ellsberg's psychiatrist. *(p. 20)*

The Washington indictment charged Krogh with two counts of making false statements concerning the burglary while giving a deposition Aug. 28, 1972, to the government's former Watergate prosecutor, Earl Silbert. According to the indictment, Krogh denied knowledge of any trip to California by E. Howard Hunt Jr. and G. Gordon Liddy. But Krogh had admitted in a May 7, 1973, affidavit during Ellsberg's trial that he had sent Hunt and Liddy to Los Angeles for the burglary.

Krogh's lawyer, Stephen N. Shulman, said Krogh would plead innocent to the Washington indictment on the grounds that he was under White House secrecy orders when he gave the deposition.

Hearings. There were few revelations as the Watergate committee continued its investigation of campaign sabotage. Perhaps that fact, plus the lack of television coverage, resulted in slackened attendance by the seven-member committee. During an appearance Oct. 11 by Frank Mankiewicz, a top aide to Sen. George McGovern (D S.D.) during the 1972 presidential campaign, only two senators stayed for the full testimony.

Ervin Subpoenas. In a committee-related development Oct. 10, Chairman Sam J. Ervin Jr. (D N.C.) announced he had been subpoenaed to appear and provide evidence in federal court in New York City at the upcoming trial of former Commerce Secretary Maurice H. Stans and former Attorney General John N. Mitchell. They were charged with perjury in connection with campaign contributions by financier Robert L. Vesco. The Senate swiftly approved a resolution authorizing Ervin to comply with the subpoenas. *(Indictments, Vol. I, p. 63)*

Hearings Oct. 9

John R. Buckley, a former Office of Economic Opportunity (OEO) official, told the Senate select Watergate committee that he photographed dozens of documents from the office of Sen. Edmund S. Muskie's (D Maine) presidential campaign and forwarded them to the President's re-election committee. Buckley, 53, identified in earlier hearings by convicted Watergate conspirator E. Howard Hunt Jr. as "Fat Jack," said he operated under Kenneth S. Rietz, the re-election committee's youth director. *(Hunt testimony, p. 37)*

Buckley, a portly, moon-faced man, described how he enlisted a semi-retired taxi driver to work in Muskie's campaign as a messenger and to bring political documents to an office Buckley had rented. Buckley said he photographed the documents he thought were important, took the film home for developing and then passed the photos to Rietz.

John R. Buckley

While admitting he had engaged in political espionage, Buckley, a lawyer, strongly denied that his actions were illegal. He also denied that he had violated the Hatch Act, which bars political activity by government employees. Buckley was director of OEO's inspections division at the time he worked for Rietz. Buckley contended that the Hatch Act provides that government employees conduct political activity in their "official capacity" in order to come under the law. He said, however, that he always did his political work on his lunch hour or otherwise on his own time. The act, he said, is silent in this regard.

Committee Reaction. The committee seemed disturbed by Buckley's assertion that his actions were legal and proper. Each member questioned him on his interpretation of laws and ethics. Asked, for example, if what he did came under the heading of theft or larceny, he replied that it did not. "Senator, I think it's political espionage,... something that occurs in every major election," he said.

Nor were his actions unethical "in terms of an election year," he said. "It goes on all the time.... I don't think I invented it." Was it his theory, he was asked, that one evil justified another? No, he answered, adding, "My theory is that a candidate has a right...to gather intelligence on his opponent."

Buckley retired from government service in June. Before working for OEO, he spent 13½ years with the FBI and four years as an investigator for the Republican staff of the House Education and Labor Committee. He said that he met Rietz while both were working on Capitol Hill.

Rietz, he said, contacted him in the summer of 1971, asking his help in determining the operations of the Muskie campaign. Rietz wanted to know where Muskie's headquarters was located and the Muskie campaign's plans and strategies, Buckley said.

Photographed Documents. Buckley said he hired an acquaintance, Elmer Wyatt, a semi-retired taxi driver, to volunteer as a part-time driver for the Muskie campaign. One of Wyatt's regular assignments was to carry messages and papers from the Muskie headquarters in downtown Washington to the senator's Capitol office, Buckley told the committee.

Wyatt would call him when he left the headquarters, Buckley said, telling him what papers he had and arranging a meeting. At first Wyatt would pick him up at his office and drive around while Buckley photographed the documents in the back seat of the taxi, Buckley said. But this proved unsuccessful because of the poor light, so Buckley said he rented an office near OEO headquarters.

Buckley said he never tampered with sealed envelopes. The meetings lasted 30 to 40 minutes and always took place during his lunch hour, Buckley related. He said he photographed as many as four documents a day, for a total of two to three dozen.

The witness said he was paid $1,000 a month from September 1971 to April 1972, but never took any money for himself. He said he paid Wyatt $150 a week at first, later raising that to $175. The office rental was $100 a month, said Buckley, and he paid $413 for photographic materials and equipment, including an enlarger.

Rietz Meetings. Buckley said he called Rietz every nine or 10 days and arranged meetings, usually near re-election committee headquarters. He testified that he had no idea what use Rietz made of the photographed documents, but believed that one of them turned up in the syndicated newspaper column of Rowland Evans and Robert Novak. Buckley said he was angered by this and threatened to quit if it happened again.

Another thing that almost resulted in his quitting, Buckley told the committee, was Rietz's tardiness for their meetings. When Buckley complained about this, he said, Rietz arranged for him to give the photographs to a man named "Ed Warren." This was actually ex-CIA agent E. Howard Hunt. Hunt testified that the man he met was known to him as "Fat Jack," an alias Buckley said he had never heard of. Buckley said he called himself "Jack Kent."

Buckley said he was well satisfied with the change, because "Warren" always was punctual for their eight to 12 meetings over four months. Buckley said he and Warren never talked—they just exchanged envelopes.

Buckley said that his work for the re-election committee ended with the demise of Muskie's candidacy in April 1972 and that he never was asked to spy on anyone else. Buckley became an investigator for a law firm headed by Jerris Leonard, a former assistant attorney general. He testified under a grant of limited immunity from the committee, having first invoked in private testimony his constitutional right against self-incrimination.

Hearings Oct. 10

Michael W. McMinoway, a spy for the President's re-election committee, testified that he infiltrated the primary campaigns of three Democratic contenders and eventually rose to serve as a security man for one of them, Sen. George McGovern (S.D.). McMinoway, who was given the code name of Sedan Chair II by re-election committee officials, also said that prostitutes frequented McGovern's Miami Beach, Fla., hotel headquarters, and he described how he once acted as a driver for a Democratic convention delegate and two women who engaged in immoral activities.

A private detective from Louisville, Ky., McMinoway, 27, said he was paid $5,808 from February to July 1972 to spy on McGovern and Senators Hubert H. Humphrey (D Minn.) and Edmund S. Muskie (D Maine). He testified that he was hired by a man who identified himself as "Jason Rainier," but who he later learned was Roger Stone, an aide to re-election committee official Herbert L. Porter. Porter, according to testimony by Robert Reisner, a former committee official, was McMinoway's paymaster *(Reisner testimony, Vol. I, p. 110)*

McMinoway told the Senate committee that he communicated with "Rainier" originally through a

Michael W. McMinoway

Washington, D.C., post office box, but later began telephoning him daily reports. While admitting that he took documents from the headquarters of the various candidates he worked for, and sent some of them to Washington, he insisted that he had done nothing illegal, unethical or improper. He justified his actions by saying that any materials he sent to "Rainier" had been given to him by campaign officials in his position as a volunteer and that they would have been made public later anyway. His objective, he said, "was to get the information before the newspapers had printed it."

Throughout his half day of testimony, McMinoway denied that his work as a volunteer for the candidates amounted to deception or fraud, even though, in addition to being paid to spy by re-election committee officials, he sometimes identified himself falsely as "Michael Snow."

McMinoway declined to characterize his work as political espionage, preferring instead to call it intelligence-gathering. He said activities such as his went on in all campaigns.

Triple Infiltration. The witness testified that he infiltrated successively the Muskie headquarters in Milwaukee, Wis., the Humphrey campaigns in Philadelphia, Pa. and Los Angeles, Calif., and the McGovern suite in the Doral hotel in Miami Beach. He was so close to McGovern as a security man, he said, that one evening he watched television with McGovern before his nomination.

McMinoway said the hotel's hospitality suite usually was loaded with prostitutes and women of "low moral standards." It was while working in the McGovern security force, he related, that he came to act as a driver for the two women and the delegate. Under further questioning, McMinoway admitted that he never heard McGovern or any member of his staff suggest or discuss the use of women to influence delegate votes.

Describing his work with the Humphrey campaign in Philadelphia, he said he quickly was put in charge of the telephone bank and block captains. He hesitated to admit that he disrupted Humphrey's campaign, but under pressure from committee majority counsel Samuel Dash said, "I didn't help the situation any." He acknowledged that he shuffled supporters' cards so that the night shift on the telephone bank would re-call the same persons contacted by the day shift. He said the result was that some of the supporters quit because of the repeated phone calls. On another occasion, he said he used the phones to urge Humphrey supporters to vote for Sen. Henry M. Jackson (D Wash.).

"This is more than just intelligence-gathering, isn't it?" asked Dash. "Yes, sir," McMinoway replied.

As with some previous witnesses, McMinoway insisted that his activities were similar to those carried out by the Democrats. He said that while working for Muskie in Milwaukee, he learned that McGovern supporters were planning to heckle the Maine senator and that in other states one candidate's supporters often tore down the placards or signs of another candidate. He said the youth coordinator for McGovern's campaign, a man he identified as Tom Southwick, once told him of plans by McGovern people to demonstrate against Muskie. The witness also testified to seeing campaign documents of one candidate in another candidate's headquarters—evidence, he said, of infiltration by one campaign of another.

Other Witnesses. McMinoway, who testified under subpoena without immunity, was followed to the witness table by Frederick J. Taugher of Sacramento, Calif., the chief administrative officer of the California Senate. Taugher formerly was southern California campaign coordinator for McGovern.

He was asked to testify about an anti-war demonstration outside the Century Plaza Hotel in Los Angeles during a Nixon speech Sept. 27, 1972. H. R. Haldeman, Nixon's former top aide, had testified earlier before the committee that the demonstration was supported by McGovern's people and that it was violent. *(Haldeman testimony, Vol. I, p. 231)*

Taugher denied that the McGovern headquarters backed the demonstration, but acknowledged that the coalition which sponsored it was allowed to use a bank of 10 to 12 McGovern telephones to notify sympathizers and that handbills announcing the rally were placed in some of McGovern's precinct headquarters.

He said he approved the use of the phones at a meeting Sept. 21, 1972, because he was told that "responsible individuals" would run the demonstration and that care had been taken to ensure it would be orderly. He emphasized, however, that the anti-war coalition manned the phones and used their own, rather than McGovern's, lists for their calls. He added that McGovern workers were not allowed to make signs or placards for the demonstration.

The police and hotel were notified in advance of the demonstration, and it was peaceful, he said. Lt. Kenneth Hickman of the Los Angeles Police Department, who followed Taugher to the witness table, confirmed that the demonstration was non-violent.

Hearings Oct. 11

Two top McGovern campaign officials appeared before the committee. Rick Stearns, who held a variety of jobs in the campaign, including chief of political intelligence, denied that he authorized the use of McGovern telephones to drum up support for an anti-war demonstration in Los Angeles Sept. 27, 1972. Frank Mankiewicz, McGovern's national political coordinator, said Republi-

can "dirty tricks" successfully damaged Democratic unity. *(Mankiewicz opening statement, p. 54; Stearns statement, p. 55)*

Stearns, 29, a law student at Harvard, contradicted testimony Oct. 10 by Frederick J. Taugher that Stearns had attended a meeting at which the use of the McGovern phone bank was discussed and that he had seconded Taugher's approval of the demonstrators' use of the phones. Taugher said the meeting took place Sept. 21, 1972, and that the phone bank ultimately was used by anti-war coalition personnel.

Frank Mankiewicz

Stearns told the committee he did not recall the meeting and did not learn what use had been made of the phone bank until the next month. "As a general policy we discouraged" help to anti-war demonstrators because the Nixon re-election committee was portraying McGovern supporters as violence-prone and he did not want to reinforce that false impression, he said. He denied that his testimony was conflicted materially with Taugher's, saying it was just a difference in recollection.

Asked what he would have done if he had known of Taugher's decision to approve the demonstrators' request, he refused to answer, claiming he would not respond to hypothetical questions. He denied that he ever advocated violent demonstrations or use of obscene signs against McGovern's opponents or that he was aware of anyone in the McGovern camp who did.

Attack on Committee. Stearns was an aggressive, combative witness. In his prepared statement, he charged that his appearance was requested for partisan political purposes "to absolve the outrages of the most corrupt presidential campaign in American history by finding something, anything, no matter how insubstantial," in order to lay blame on the Democrats.

Stearn's criticism prompted a tongue-lashing by minority counsel Fred Thompson, who told him to read the committee's authorizing resolution, which directed it to probe the activities of both parties in the 1972 election. Vice Chairman Baker, also clearly affronted by Stearns' charge of partisanship, said he had sat through much criticism of Republicans since the hearings began in May and added: "I think you screamed before you were stuck."

Stearns also drew the wrath of Sen. Edward J. Gurney (R Fla.) over his allegation that DeVan L. Shumway, a publicist for the re-election committee, had smeared Stearns by spreading a rumor during the campaign that he had been a leader of Al Fatah, an Arab terrorist group. Stearns' signature on a 1967 advertisement that was interpreted by Jewish voters as anti-Israel was believed to have hurt McGovern among that religious group. The witness stated that by 1972 his views coincided with those of McGovern, which were pro-Israel, but that Shumway and other re-election committee officials tried to capitalize on his 1967 position.

Gurney announced that he had talked to Shumway after Stearns made his reference to Shumway, and that

Shumway denied he had tried to spread such a rumor. Gurney then asked Stearns where he had heard it. Stearns replied that he had learned it from a German reporter who had telephoned him to ask him to recount some of his exploits.

When Stearns said he could not recall the name of the reporter or his newspaper, Gurney angrily replied that Stearns was relying on unidentified sources to hide information from the committee. "The 'Source' family must be the biggest family in the United States," shouted Gurney. Every reporter quotes a source for his story, he said.

Mankiewicz Testimony. In his prepared testimony, Mankiewicz, who described himself as an "inside man" for McGovern with responsibilities for campaign financing, contributions, media relations and strategy, said the 1972 campaign of dirty tricks against Democrats "would appear to have been successful."

Their purpose, he said, "seems to have been not to influence the result of any single primary election, but to create within the Democratic Party a strong sense of resentment among the candidates and their followers as to make unity of the party impossible once a nominee was selected."

Discussing the results of the tricks, he said he thought it a "reasonable question" whether Humphrey would have attempted to challenge McGovern's primary victory in California had he not been convinced that McGovern had attacked him unfairly. Later, in answer to questions, he said Muskie's delay in endorsing McGovern after dropping out of the campaign may have been caused by tricks Muskie thought had been perpetrated by McGovern workers.

Mankiewicz told the committee that pro-Nixon witnesses before the committee were trying to leave the false impression that "dirty tricks" were standard in political campaigns and that those actions connected to the re-election committee were not unusual for either party. If that is believed, he said, "the final Watergate dirty trick will have been played—on all of us."

Week's Watergate Chronology

Following is a day-to-day chronology of the week's events in the week ending Oct. 6. *(Earlier Oct. 4 events, p. 46):*

OCT. 4

Senate Committee Suit. Samuel Dash, chief counsel to the Senate Watergate investigating committee, and Nixon attorney Charles A. Wright presented arguments on the committee's suit for access to White House tapes in a two-hour hearing before Chief U.S. District Judge John J. Sirica. Dash said the President had no right to claim executive privilege over the documents "as a shield for self-protection" in possible criminal matters. Wright countered that Dash's argument was evidence of the Senate committee's undue preoccupation with extra-legislative matters that should be left to grand juries. *(Previous action, p. 46)*

Liddy Motion. G. Gordon Liddy became the last of the seven original Watergate defendants convicted for the break-in to ask for a new trial. In a brief filed with the U.S. Court of Appeals in Washington, D.C., his attorneys contended that Judge Sirica, who presided over the original trial, had violated Liddy's constitutional rights during the proceedings. *(Other motions, p. 35; trial, Vol. I, p. 136, p. 8)*

ACLU Impeachment Call. Edward J. Ennis, chairman of the American Civil Liberties Union, announced that the organization's board of directors had voted 10-1 to call on the House of Representatives to initiate impeachment proceedings against President Nixon. At a news conference in New York City, Ennis enumerated six grounds for the move: "specific proved violations of the rights of political dissent; usurpation of congressional war-making powers; establishment of a personal secret police which committed crimes; attempted interference in the trial of Daniel Ellsberg; distortion of the system of justice, and perversion of other federal agencies."

Democratic Convention Bugging. Richard M. Gerstein, the state's attorney in Dade County, Florida, revealed that his investigators were looking into the possibility that Republican espionage agents bugged rooms and tapped phones of Democrats at their 1972 convention in Miami Beach—less than a month after the Watergate break-in arrests. NBC News quoted Gerstein as saying the information came from an interrogation of conspirator James W. McCord Jr. and that Gerstein believed the alleged operation was part of conspirator G. Gordon Liddy's "Gemstone" espionage plan.

The New York Times, in an Oct. 6 article further detailing the Florida investigation, reported that the investigators had found no evidence to support Gerstein's conclusion that illegal bugging had occurred. "We're convinced it happened, but we're still seeking proof of it," Gerstein said. *(Gerstein-Cox conflict, p. 20)*

ABA Purge. Chesterfield Smith, president of the American Bar Association, announced that he had asked the Senate Watergate investigating committee for a computer hookup in order to gather information on possible wrong-doing by lawyers connected with the scandal. "We want to purge from our profession any crooks who are unworthy of our high profession," Smith said at a news conference in Cincinnati, Ohio.

OCT. 8

Buckley-Ervin Exchange. Sen. James L. Buckley (Cons.-R N.Y.) released the text of a letter he had received Oct. 4 from Sam J. Ervin Jr. (D N.C.), chairman of the Senate Watergate committee, in reply to Buckley's suggestion that the committee's staff be questioned under oath about whether it had leaked information to the news media in violation of the committee's rules of procedure. Ervin listed four reasons for rejecting the proposal, including the argument that such an investigation would damage staff morale without uncovering any guilty parties.

Buckley's proposal was prompted by charges made Sept. 26 by witness Patrick J. Buchanan, a White House speechwriter, that "character assassins" on the committee staff had "maligned" his reputation by leaking information on him to the press. *(Buchanan testimony, p. 40)*

OCT. 9

Senate Hearings. The Senate Watergate investigating committee heard testimony from John R. (Fat Jack) Buckley, a retired FBI agent who worked in the Office of Economic Opportunity (OEO) until June 1973. Buckley said he had been paid $1,000 a month in late 1971 and early 1972 by Kenneth S. Reitz, then youth director of the Nixon re-election committee, to gather inside information on the campaign operations of Sen. Edmund S. Muskie (D Maine). *(Testimony, p. 50)*

'Think Tank' Charge. The committee made public an affidavit submitted by Mitchell Rogovin, attorney for the Institute for Policy Studies, a public affairs "think tank," stating he had evidence that the institute's Washington, D.C., headquarters had been illegally infiltrated, wiretapped and burglarized by federal and local agents. He also asserted that the institute was in danger of losing its tax-exempt status because of political differences with the Nixon administration. The affidavit was made in response to testimony Sept. 26 by White House speechwriter Patrick J. Buchanan on a proposed strategy for administration sanctions against liberal tax-exempt foundations. *(Testimony, p. 40)*

OCT. 10

Senate Hearings. Michael W. McMinoway, a political spy who was known at the Nixon re-election committee as Sedan Chair II, told the Senate Watergate investigating committee of infiltrating 1972 presidential campaigns of Senators Edmund S. Muskie (D Maine), Hubert H. Humphrey (D Minn.) and George McGovern (D S.D.) to gather information that went to Nixon re-election campaign officials. McMinoway was followed by Frederick J. Taugher, a legislative analyst for the California State Legislature, who served as southern California coordinator for McGovern's 1972 campaign. *(Testimony, p. 51)*

Hughes-Rebozo Transaction. *The Washington Post* and other newspapers carried reports that a staff member of the Senate Watergate committee had interviewed Nixon's close friend, Charles G. Rebozo, on Oct. 8 about allegations that he had collected a $100,000 cash campaign contribution to Nixon from billionaire Howard R. Hughes, possibly in exchange for government approval of certain business deals. The Post said it had learned that Rebozo had been keeping the cash in a safe deposit box for nearly three years but had returned it sometime in the summer of 1973 because he feared it might prove embarrassing.

Dairy Money. Political contributions from the dairy industry to Nixon's re-election campaign were used to repay a loan that had covered the expenses of the men who burglarized the office of Daniel Ellsberg's psychiatrist in 1971, *The Washington Star-News* reported. The money for the loan, which was said to have been arranged by former White House special counsel Charles W. Colson, reportedly came from the Trust for Agricultural Political Education (TAPE).

OCT. 11

Senate Hearings. Two top officials of the McGovern campaign, Rick Stearns and Frank Mankiewicz, appeared before the Senate Watergate investigating committee and countered the theory, propounded by several other witnesses, that Democrats had engaged in "dirty tricks" as often as Republicans did in the 1972 presidential campaign. *(Testimony, p. 52)*

Krogh Indictment. A federal grand jury in Washington, D. C., indicted Egil (Bud) Krogh Jr. on two counts of perjury. Krogh was the former chief of the White House special investigative unit, or "plumbers."

MANKIEWICZ' OPENING STATEMENT

Following are excerpts from the text of the opening statement made by Frank Mankiewicz, national political coordinator for George McGovern, the 1972 Democratic presidential nominee, before the Senate Watergate committee on Oct. 11:

...We have all heard, thanks to these hearings and other investigations, both public and private, of a wide variety of "dirty tricks," of sabotage and of espionage and of an unprecedented assault on the integrity of the political process itself. I should like to take this opportunity to describe what is in my view one of the most serious of these assaults—one of the most dangerous of all the attempts to cover up what was done by the Nixon campaign in 1972.

I refer...to the systematic attempt by administration witnesses before this committee, either presently in the White House, recently in the White House, or controlled either by the White House or the Nixon campaign, to convey to the American people the idea that the actions of which they were admittedly or proved guilty are somehow acts common to American politics and political campaigns.

I think it important for someone to state, clearly and firmly, that these "dirty tricks" are not politics as usual—that American politics does not include any history of or tolerance for sabotage, espionage, perjury, forgery or burglary. The political process does not, and has not, countenanced firebombing of government institutions or the slandering of an opponent by accusing him of sexual misconduct—nor, to be sure, slandering the memory of a slain president by the use of a forgery which accuses him of murder. American "politics as usual" does not include stealing documents from an opponent in order to photograph and pass them on to favored journalists, nor plotting to kidnap those with whom you may disagree—nor does it traditionally include wiretapping or bugging, the throwing of stink bombs or hiring people to create disturbances or riots in the name of your opponent. And it has certainly never included—at the presidential level—using agencies of government to harass and punish your "enemies" nor the use of special White House gumshoes to count the bottles in a senator's trash.

There is grave danger in all this. I think we are strong enough as a nation to survive Watergate and the crimes with which that word is now forever associated; I doubt if we are strong enough to survive for very long the widespread belief that those actions are the normal things to expect in the practice of electoral politics. And yet we have seen——over the past months— one witness after another proclaim the notion that "both sides do it," that "this is typical politics," or that somehow the Nixon people's activities were justified because "the other side" had done the same things. This steady stream can have been no accident. And if it is believed, then the already lowered esteem which many now have for our political system will sink even lower, and the final Watergate dirty trick will have been played —on all of us.

Haldeman Example. Let me cite only one example. In his prepared testimony, H. R. Haldeman listed the following: "Violent demonstrations and disruption, heckling or shouting down speakers, burning or bombing campaign headquarters, physical damage or trashing of headquarters and other buildings, harassment of candidates' wives and families by obscenities, disruption of the national convention by splattering dinner guests with eggs and tomatoes, indecent exposure, rock throwing, assaults on delegates, slashing bus tires, smashing windows, setting trash fires under the gas tank of a bus, knocking policemen from their motorcycles."

He then went on to charge that these were "all activities which took place in 1972—against the campaign of the President of the United States by his opponents. Some of them took place...with the clear knowledge and consent of agents of the opposing candidate in the last election; others were acts of people who were clearly unsympathetic to the President but may not have had direct orders from the opposing camp."

Now that statement is false in whole and in each part. There is no activity listed there which had the knowledge and consent of any agent of the McGovern campaign, and no evidence of any kind has been presented—or ever will be presented, for none exists—to the contrary. Furthermore, we now know, from testimony before this committee, that some of those acts were in fact committed by agents of the Nixon campaign—*agents provocateurs*, hired for that purpose.

And from Mr. Haldeman's written expression that some prospective violence at a Nixon rally was both "good" and "great" we can only conclude that more of that kind of activity was actually promoted by the Nixon campaign.

But...Mr. Haldeman did more. He attempted, on more than one occasion—according to memoranda in evidence here—to "leak" to favored newsmen the story that the McGovern campaign was financing these activities—this violence—and that it was itself financed by sinister foreign sources. Now when he made those statements, Mr. Haldeman knew them to be false—but they are widely believed nevertheless.

What I am trying to express here is that this kind of activity, and all of the illegal and unethical activity we have heard described here, is not typical of American politics at all. None of it was done in the Democratic campaign of 1972. In the campaign with which I am most familiar—that of Senator McGovern—I can state categorically that it was wholly free of each and all of the dirty tricks, the crimes, the deceits and the coverups the nation has now learned were committed in behalf of his opponent.

Furthermore, I am prepared to state, based on my own knowledge as well as extensive research, that it was also not "politics as usual" in the other Democratic campaigns of 1972—such as those of Sen. Humphrey, Sen. Muskie, Sen. Jackson and Mayor Lindsay—and that this kind of politics has not been present in other Democratic or Republican presidential campaigns. This kind of activity may well be politics as usual for Nixon campaigns, but not for any other Democratic or Republican presidential campaign of which I have any knowledge. And I believe it to be the gravest disservice to the republic to suggest that it is.

Effects on Campaign. As to the effect on the 1972 campaign of the so-called "dirty tricks," it would appear to have been successful. The purpose of it all—the slimy letters, the forged press releases, the fake leaflets—seems to have been not to influence the result of any single primary election, but to create within the Democratic Party such a strong sense of resentment among the candidates and their followers as to make unity of the party impossible once a nominee was selected. At that, the effort seems to have been most successful.

Workers in Sen. Muskie's campaign have told me that they believed the "dirty tricks" played on Sen. Muskie in New Hampshire to have been the work of the McGovern campaign. Certainly there must have been those Humphrey and Jackson partisans who, seeing the filthy letter about the candidates in Florida, forged so as to appear to be from the Muskie campaign, must have turned their anger on the senator from Maine.

This was, I believe, particularly true in the later stages of the primary campaign. Deliberately false statements about Sen. McGovern's positions on such matters as the legalization of

marijuana, amnesty, abortion, and even the legalization of prostitution were put out in Ohio, Nebraska and California, and they were made to seem the work of the campaigns—or even the statements of the candidates themselves—of Senators Jackson and Humphrey. In California, leaflets deliberately distorting the record and maligning the character of Senators Humphrey and McGovern were issued in the name of the other, rival candidate. Thus both Sen. McGovern and Sen. Humphrey were led to believe that the other was involved in a vicious campaign of distortion and vilification, and any reuniting of factions—normally the course in a Democratic campaign after the primaries—became far more difficult. I think it is a reasonable question whether Sen. Humphrey would have lent himself to the so-called "California challenge" in June and July of 1972 had he not become convinced—because of the Nixon campaign's planned sabotage—that Sen. McGovern's campaign had attacked him unfairly in May.

We know that an insulting telephone call was placed to AFL-CIO President George Meany in June by someone masquerading as the McGovern campaign manager, Gary Hart. How much of Mr. Meany's hostility to Sen. McGovern's campaign can be attributed to this or other such incidents is difficult to measure. So, for that matter, is the impact of numerous similar fake telephone calls to local union and party officials during the fall campaign, all of an insulting nature and all from people purporting to be McGovern campaign officials.

In short, what was created by the sabotage effort was an unparalleled atmosphere of rancor and discord within the Democratic Party. And, as Mr. Segretti perhaps unwittingly revealed before this committee, that was the aim—and the only aim—of

> *"I think it important for someone to state, clearly and firmly, that these 'dirty tricks' are not politics as usual—that American politics does not include any history of or tolerance for sabotage, espionage, perjury, forgery or burglary."*
>
> —Frank Mankiewicz

the campaign of illegal and unethical acts which he largely executed, but which had been carefully conceived by the various assistants, counsels, special assistants and special counsels to the President of the United States.

STEARNS' OPENING STATEMENT

Following is the text of the opening statement made by Rick Stearns, political intelligence chief for the 1972 McGovern campaign, before the Senate Watergate committee on Oct. 11:

I would have appreciated the elementary courtesy of reasonable notice in advance of this appearance, because I would have preferred to prepare a comprehensive statement for the committee. The subject you have been charged to examine is critical, and it deserves the best reflection and insight any witness can offer. Mr. Buchanan complained that this was difficult, despite having all the resources of the White House at his disposal, because he was given only six days to prepare. But as at least some of you are aware, I was notified of this request to appear less than 24 hours ago, in the course of an oral presentation to one of the classes at Harvard Law School, where I am a student.

In recent weeks, the press has reported that some of the committee staff has been engaged in a fishing expedition for a partisan purpose—to absolve the outrages of the most corrupt presidential campaign in American history by finding something, anything, no matter how insubstantial, in order to place blame on a Democratic campaign which sought honestly and decently to provide a different kind of national leadership. It is perhaps revealing that no one on this committee had to strain at figuring out who among the Nixon campaign to subpoena, or what questions to ask them. The scandal there was pervasive. The abuses screamed for attention and correction. Nothing could any longer conceal the crimes and the coverups. The problem was not whether there was an excuse to start an investigation, but whether there was any way to end it.

Now some of those who have been forced at last to face the beam in one party's eye are searching to find a mite in the other party's eye.

'Disservice.' This is not the appropriate exercise of a power that was supposed to reach beyond partiansanship in order to renew the principles we all profess. More than that, it is a profound disservice.

First, it is a disservice to the facts. The McGovern campaign was founded not on dirty tricks, but on the truth. In 1972, we made mistakes, but we did not commit crimes. Let me list some of the things we did not do. We did not tap any telephones. We did not burgle any offices. We did not hire any demonstrators. We did not employ any spies. We did not refuse—indeed, we welcomed the opportunity—to disclose the sources of our financing. We never solicited, we never took—and we never expected—

"We were beaten, but we were not dishonored. And the attempt to find fault where there is none, to lay blame where it does not belong, to whitewash the guilty by blackening the innocent is a pathetic piece of political gamesmanship."

—Rick Stearns

---

an illegal corporate contribution. We never committed perjury, or asked anyone to commit perjury for us. We never manipulated or debased the FBI, the CIA, the Secret Service or the Justice Department. We never considered a firebombing or the enlistment of prostitutes to compromise the opposition—or even kidnaping those who saw the world differently than we did. We were beaten, but we were not dishonored. And the attempt to find fault where there is none, to lay blame where it does not belong, to whitewash the guilty by blackening the innocent is a pathetic piece of political gamesmanship.

And let me tell you some of the things we did do. We were honest about who was paying for our campaign and the principles and programs for which we stood. We were open and frank with the press and the American people. We invited the scrutiny of everyone, at times to our disadvantage—and I welcome such scrutiny now, but not the innuendoes and slanders which are the last refuge of those who cannot acquit themselves except by accusing others. I believe that when this committee's work is done, when the last witness has been heard and the final recommendations are written, you will call for the kind of honest and decent politics George McGovern practiced in 1972.

Second, unfounded attacks on Democratic integrity are a disservice to the Republican Party. It is not necessary for Republicans to prove that Democrats are just as bad. For the truth is that most people in both parties have held to high standards of conduct. Republicans and Democrats alike have waged fair fights in most campaigns at every level. Indeed, most of those who thought last year the President's re-election was right did nothing in that cause which any of us would regard as wrong. They voted to reelect the President, not to bug the Democratic National Committee.

Finally, it is a disservice to the nation to imply that all politics is as bad as a few men made it in 1972. I have not been long in politics—only five years; but I have met so many people and politicians from the grass roots to the Senate, in both parties, whom I proudly call my friends and who give constant witness to the ideals of the American system. This committee at its best exemplifies politics at its best. And the worst disservice now would be to convince the nation that this cannot be—that the political process is inevitably degraded and unworthy. For that does not save Republicans or the administration. It not only slanders Democrats; instead, it unjustifiably strains the faith of the American people in the American system.

Fact and Fiction....in these last months, you have heard—and all of us have seen—a record of sabotage and slander unprecedented in American history. I experienced personally some of that slander last year. The facts are different from the fiction which was widely promoted.

In 1967, I signed a newspaper appeal which endorsed the Middle East policy that was subsequently supported by the United States and adopted by the United Nations. At that time, I favored what the Nixon administration once hailed as an even-handed policy in the Middle East. I consistently advocated that policy—in a responsible way—until the outbreak of Arab terrorism and the escalation of Soviet intervention convinced me that I was wrong. My earlier position was no secret. It was publicly expressed at the time, as was my current position during the 1972 campaign.

Despite that, the most outlandish and outrageous smears were spawned and perpetuated by the Committee to Re-Elect the President. For example, the committee's publicist, Mr. DeVan L. Shumway, spread a rumor among the press that I had been a guerrilla leader in Al Fatah. It hardly merited the denial it deserved, but it was dangerous and vicious slander. Finally I called my friend Pat Buchanan, and Mr. Shumway, at least, was apparently restrained.

Yet what I resented most was not the unfounded attack on me, but the implication that views I never held, in years already past, were the views of George McGovern in 1972. Certainly Senator McGovern's position was well and widely stated. Yet CREEP wanted to take the views they had created for me and make them his. By the same logic, we could conclude that Mr. Colson's alleged plan for bombing the Brookings Institution proved that President Nixon was the new mad bomber.

I think we have experienced too much of such logic. We have heard too many unscrupulous smears. We have seen too often men who should have served their country but shamed it instead.

We need no more forged cables, no more inoperative coverups, no more smears against good and decent citizens, among them an assassinated President, who seek only to do what they believe is right for their country—whether they are Democrats like Senator Humphrey, who was accused of sexual misconduct, or Republicans like Senator Weicker, who was accused of campaign financing abuses.

In my view, we need instead to remember the words of Edmund Burke: "I am aware that our age is not everything we wish it to be, but I am convinced that the only means of checking its degeneracy is to concur heartily in whatever is best in our times."

For me, in 1972, George McGovern represented what was best for our times. Not all of you agreed, and obviously millions of voters disagreed. But at least I am confident of this much—that the McGovern campaign kept faith with what is best in the American political tradition. √

NIXON'S APPEAL REJECTED; COMMITTEE LOSES IN D.C. COURT

On Oct. 12 the U.S. Court of Appeals for the District of Columbia upheld District Judge John J. Sirica's Aug. 29 decision directing President Nixon to turn over the tapes to Sirica for inspection. The ruling had come in the suit filed by the Justice Department's special prosecutor, Archibald Cox. The White House was expected to appeal that decision to the Supreme Court.

Five days later, Oct. 17, Sirica ruled on the Senate Watergate investigating committee's request for the same tapes of presidential conversations. In this decision the district judge ruled that he had no jurisdiction to consider the Senate committee's effort to force Nixon to give up tapes of conversations recorded in the White House. In dismissing the case, the judge said Congress had never enacted any law giving federal courts jurisdiction in such a case. The committee was expected to appeal Sirica's decision to the U.S. Court of Appeals for the District of Columbia.

Appeals Court Decision

"Sovereignty remains at all times with the people, and they do not forfeit through elections the right to have the law construed against and applied to every citizen," stated the court of appeals, District of Columbia circuit, Oct. 12. That afternoon, by a 5-2 vote, the court upheld the order of Federal District Judge John J. Sirica directing President Nixon to turn over to Sirica the nine tapes of presidential conversations sought by the original grand jury investigating the Watergate break-in and coverup.

A view of their decision as limited in its impact— and of executive privilege as a qualified privilege to be weighed by courts against competing public interests— emerged from the unsigned *(per curiam)* 44-page majority opinion. Joining in that opinion were Chief Judge David L. Bazelon and Judges J. Skelly Wright, Carl McGowan, Harold Leventhal and Spottswood W. Robinson III. All five were appointed by Democratic presidents: Bazelon by Truman, Wright and McGowan by Kennedy, Leventhal and Robinson by Johnson.

On the other hand, the far-reaching impact of their decision—and a view of executive privilege as absolute and exercised at the sole discretion of the President— marked the two lengthy dissenting opinions written by Judges George E. MacKinnon and Malcolm R. Wilkey, both Nixon appointees. Not participating in the consideration or decision of the matter were two other members of the appeals court—Edward Allen Tamm, appointed by Johnson, and Roger Robb, another Nixon appointee.

Background. The grand jury investigating the Watergate coverup—and possible perjury by White House aides —on July 23 subpoenaed nine tapes of conversations between Nixon and John D. Ehrlichman, H.R. Halde-

man, John N. Mitchell and John W. Dean III. Asserting that executive privilege protected the tapes from disclosure, Nixon July 25 declined to produce them. To do so, he said, would be "inconsistent with the public interest and with the constitutional position of the presidency."

The next day, special Watergate prosecutor Archibald Cox—for the grand jury—asked Sirica to order Nixon to comply with the subpoena. *(Vol. I, p. 208)*

After more than a month, the exchange of many legal documents and oral arguments between Cox and Charles Alan Wright, counsel for the President, Sirica Aug. 29 took a middle road: he ordered Nixon to surrender the tapes to him so that Sirica might examine them in his chambers *(in camera)* and decide whether or not Nixon had properly asserted his claim of executive privilege. *(p. 13, 10, 9, Vol. I, p. 273, 255)*

The White House and the special prosecutor both appealed this order to the court of appeals. Arguments were made before the full seven-member court on Sept. 11. *(p. 29, 20)*

Two days after the court of appeals heard arguments, it issued a memorandum urging the President and the special prosecutor to reach a settlement and resolve the constitutional controversy without a ruling by the court. A week later, Wright and Cox informed the court that they had failed to reach any agreement. *(p. 35, 33)*

It was then up to the appeals court to decide the issue it had hoped to avoid.

What Comes Next?

The President was given five business days, until Oct. 19, to appeal the decision to the Supreme Court. However, the President did not appeal. *(p. 69)*

If usual procedures were followed, the Supreme Court would allow a certain period of time after the White House petition for review of the decision was filed for special prosecutor Cox to file papers telling the court why it should not review the lower courts' rulings.

Then, probably at a regular Friday conference— or possibly at a specially called conference—the court would discuss the matter and vote whether or not to accept the case for argument. Four of the nine justices must vote in order for the court to set arguments on the case. If fewer than four voted to hear it, review would be denied, leaving in effect Sirica's original order.

The Supreme Court was scheduled to recess Oct. 23 until Nov. 5. If this schedule were followed, the court's next regular Friday conference after Oct. 19 would not be held until Nov. 9.

LIMITED NATURE OF RULING

Before addressing the questions raised on appeal, the majority emphasized the limited nature of the case and, consequently, of their ruling:

"We deem it essential to emphasize the narrow contours of the problem that compels the court to address the issues raised by this case. The central question before us is, in essence, whether the President may, in his sole discretion, withhold from a grand jury evidence in his possession that is relevant to the grand jury's investigations. It is our duty to respond to this question, but we limit our decision strictly to that required by the precise and entirely unique circumstances of the case."

The grand jury's need for the tapes was clearly shown: it is "a need that the District Court...correctly termed 'well-documented and imposing.'" Continuing, the opinion stated: "The strength and particularity of this showing were made possible by a unique intermeshing of events unlikely soon, if ever, to recur."

Because Nixon had allowed his present and former aides to testify before the Senate committee on the Watergate affair, because their testimony had revealed a strong possibility that a high-level conspiracy had existed, important evidence of which was contained in statements made during conversations of those aides with Nixon, there was a clear need for the taped records to clear up questions about exactly what was said during those conversations, the court stated.

"Most importantly...significant inconsistencies in the sworn testimony of these advisers relating to the content of the conversations raised a distinct possibility that perjury had been committed," the opinion said. And so the special prosecutor could make his case that the tapes contained "evidence critical to the grand jury's decisions as to whether and whom to indict."

TWO REJECTED ASSUMPTIONS

The President's appeal of Sirica's order rested on two primary assumptions:

• An incumbent president is absolutely immune from judicial orders enforcing subpoenas.

• Executive privilege over presidential communications is absolute: only the president may decide when and what to disclose.

Both points were rejected by the appeals court majority.

Courts have frequently ordered officials of the executive branch to produce evidence, the opinion noted. It then pointed out the signal instance of the steel seizure case in which the Supreme Court directed the secretary of commerce not to follow President Truman's order to assume control of the nation's steel mills.

It made no difference that in the case at hand Nixon personally assumed possession of the tapes and therefore was personally the object of the court order: "The practice of judicial review would be rendered capricious—and very likely impotent—if jurisdiction vanished whenever the President personally denoted an executive action or omission as his own."

In Chief Justice John Marshall's comments in the Burr case—in which he issued a subpoena to President Thomas Jefferson—the appeals court majority saw "the

clear implication...that the President's special interests may warrant a careful judicial screening of subpoenas after the President interposes an objection but that some subpoenas will nevertheless be properly sustained by judicial orders of compliance."

Thus the court ruled that the President then is not immune from such orders: "The Constitution makes no mention of special presidential immunities," although it does give explicit immunity and privilege of a limited nature to members of the legislature. Yet lacking this support, the President's counsel asked the court to "infer immunity from the President's political mandate, or from his vulnerability to impeachment, or from his broad discretionary powers. These are invitations to refashion the Constitution and we reject them.

"Though the President is elected by nationwide ballot and is often said to represent all the people, he does not embody the nation's sovereignty. He is not above the law's commands. 'With all its defects, delays and inconveniences, men have discovered no technique for long preserving free government except that the executive be under the law....' Sovereignty remains at all times with the people, and they do not forfeit through elections the right to have the law construed against and applied to every citizen."

NO ABSOLUTE PRIVILEGE

Essential to the President's case was the argument that once he invoked executive privilege to protect evidence, a court could not inquire as to whether he had properly claimed that privilege.

On the contrary, the court majority held, "whenever a privilege is asserted...it is the courts that determine the validity of the assertion and the scope of the privilege." In no case had a court accepted the mere assertion of privilege as sufficient to withhold subpoenaed evidence.

But, Wright argued for the President, separation of powers dictated that this executive privilege be absolute, asserted without question by the President alone. Such a claim, the majority held, misconstrued the purpose and the operation of separated powers: "To leave the proper scope and application of executive privilege to the President's sole discretion would represent a mixing, rather than a separation, of executive and judicial functions."

Such an absolute privilege is unnecessary for workable government, the court held: "Wholesale public access to executive deliberations and documents would cripple the executive as a co-equal branch. But this is an argument for recognizing executive privilege and for according it great weight, not for making the executive the judge of its own privilege.

"If the claim of absolute privilege was recognized, its mere invocation by the President or his surrogates could deny access to all documents in all the executive departments to all citizens and their representatives, including Congress, the courts as well as grand juries, state governments, state officials and all state subdivisions. The Freedom of Information Act could become nothing more than a legislative statement of unenforceable rights. Support for this kind of mischief simply cannot be spun from incantation of the doctrine of separation of powers."

In a footnote, the majority added that the reason separation of powers was adopted by the founding fathers as the basic form of American government was not to promote efficiency but "to preclude the exercise of arbitrary power. The purpose was not to avoid friction, but, by means of the inevitable friction incident to the distribution of governmental power among three departments, to save the people from autocracy."

Weighing of Interests. If the privilege is not absolute, the instances of its proper application depend upon a balancing, in each case, of "the public interest protected by the privilege against the public interests that would be served by disclosure." In this case the interest in confidentiality of White House conversations fails to outweigh the grand jury's—and the public's—need for this evidence, the court held.

Nixon's May 22 statement that he would not invoke executive privilege as to any testimony concerning possible criminal conduct reflected his judgment that public interest in disclosure outweighed the interest in confidentiality, the court said. And public testimony given after May 22 left those conversations no longer confidential.

Therefore, "the district court may order disclosure of all portions of the tapes relevant to matters within the proper scope of the grand jury's investigations, unless the court judges that the public interest served by nondisclosure of particular statements or information outweighs the need for that information demonstrated by the grand jury."

Inspection by Sirica. Expressing the hope that their decision would be followed by "maximum cooperation" between the President and the special prosecutor as to what might be handed over to the grand jury, the majority held that if such cooperation did not resolve the matter, it approved Sirica's private inspection of the tapes. Then the President could present more particular claims of privilege—for parts of the tapes—if he provided analytical background for those claims.

If the President claimed certain information should not be disclosed because it related to national defense or foreign relations, he could decline to send that part of the material to Sirica and ask Sirica to reconsider whether inspection of that material was necessary. The special prosecutor could see the claim, the evidence behind it, and could argue to the judge, against that claim.

The President should provide the court all other items covered in the subpoena, specifying which segments he felt could be disclosed and which could not. At the request of either side, the judge should privately hear arguments—and then inspect the disputed items.

Sirica could allow special prosecutor Cox to inspect the tapes in order to help the judge determine their relevance to the grand jury investigation. But if he decided to do this, he should allow time for the White House to contest the decision.

After his inspection, Sirica could, in regard to particular tapes or segments, 1) allow them to be withheld by the President under the claim of privilege; 2) order disclosure to the grand jury of all or part of the tapes; or, if possible, 3) write a complete statement for the grand jury of those parts of a tape that relate to possible criminality. In any case, the court should allow the White House an opportunity to appeal the decision.

Conclusion. "We end, as we began, by emphasizing the extraordinary nature of this case," the majority stated, saying that they had attempted to deal with no more

than the precise problem before them. "The order represents an unusual and limited requirement that the President produce material evidence. We think this is required by law and by the rule that even the Chief Executive is subject to the mandate of the law when he has no valid claim of privilege."

IN DISSENT: AN ABSOLUTE PRIVILEGE

"The ultimate issue is the effect that our decision will have upon the constitutional independence of the presidency for all time," MacKinnon wrote in his 65-page dissenting opinion. "The preservation of the confidentiality of the presidential decision-making process is of overwhelming importance to the effective functioning of our three branches of government. Therefore, I would recognize an absolute privilege for confidential presidential communications."

Established usage and custom supported this view, MacKinnon wrote, and included a list of instances since 1796 when presidents had refused Congress papers or information. "A president need not produce information which he considers would be contrary to the public interest," he concluded.

Confidentiality is as essential to protect presidential communications as to protect military secrets, MacKinnon continued. "Confidentiality (is) essential to insure thorough and unfettered discussion between a president and his advisers.... To allow the courts to breach presidential confidentiality whenever one of 400 federal trial judges considers that the circumstances...demonstrate a compelling need...would frustrate the privilege's underlying policy.... The lessons of legal history teach that it will be impossible to contain this breach of presidential confidentiality if numerous federal judges may rummage through presidential papers."

Contrary to the majority view, MacKinnon did see support for the claim of absolute privilege in the separation of powers: "This doctrine...prohibits intrusion in any form by one branch into the decisional processes of an equal and coordinate branch."

"The greatest vice of the decision...is that it would establish a precedent that would subject every presidential conference to the hazard of eventually being publicly exposed.... It is this precedential effect that transforms this case from one solely related to the recordings sought here, to one which decides whether this President, and all future presidents, shall continue to enjoy the independency of executive action contemplated by the Constitution and fully exercised by all their predecessors."

In MacKinnon's view, only a minimal role existed for the courts. Once executive privilege is invoked, "the only inquiry is whether the...invocation...promotes the policy which the privilege was designed to protect." If the majority would adopt his reasoning, he said, Nixon would then be free voluntarily to type up a transcript of the sought-after tapes and to present it to the grand jury, with his explanation of any deleted material.

Who Decides? It is for the executive, not the courts, to decide when and to what extent executive privilege may be properly asserted, Wilkey said in his 79-page dissent. Any weighing of competing public interests should be done by the president, not the courts, he held.

This view was based by Wilkey on the dual origin of executive privilege—in the constitutional separation of powers as well as in common sense and common law. Without the constitutional base for the privilege, it would be possible for courts to balance other interests against it and thus determine if the privilege were properly invoked.

Because of the constitutional origin of this privilege, it "is no more subject to weighing and balancing" than the constitutional privilege not to provide testimony incriminating oneself. "If the constitutional privilege has been asserted," Wilkey stated, "then no court has the right to determine what the President will or will not produce.

"It was and is the President's right to make that decision initially, and it is the American people who will be the judge as to whether the President has made the right decision.... If the decision is not visibly on sound grounds of national public interest, in political terms the decision may be ruinous for the President, but it is his to make. The grand design has worked; the separate independent branch remains in charge of and responsible for its own papers, processes and decisions, not to a second or third branch, but it remains responsible to the American people."

Inherent in the system of separated powers, conceded Wilkey, is the possibility of irreconcilable conflict. But this did not appear necessarily bad to the founding fathers "because above all this would guarantee that the national government could never become an efficient instrument of oppression of the people."

"Leaving the three branches in an equilibrium of tension was just one of their devices to guard against oppression," Wilkey stated. "This healthy equilibrium of tension will be destroyed if the result reached by (the majority opinion) is allowed to stand. My colleagues cannot confine the effect of their decision to Richard M. Nixon. The precedent set will inevitably have far-reaching implications on the vulnerability of any chief executive to judicial process.... The courts will have been enlisted on one side of...a political question."

The Committee's Suit

Derailing—at least for a time—the Senate Watergate committee's effort to subpoena certain tapes of presidential conversations from President Nixon, Judge Sirica Oct. 17 dismissed the committee's case asking him to enforce its subpoenas. Sirica said he could find no basis for his court having jurisdiction over the matter.

In an 18-page opinion, Sirica discussed each of the four reasons that the committee attorneys had argued as the basis for federal court jurisdiction over their civil suit for enforcement of the subpoenas. Each was dismissed by the judge as insufficient. Because he dismissed the case on the threshold question of whether the case should be in his court at all, Sirica did not consider the other basic questions raised by the case.

The subpoenas in question were served on the President July 23, after informal efforts by the committee to secure the desired tapes were unsuccessful. Nixon responded with a letter to Chairman Sam J. Ervin Jr. (D N.C.) saying that he would not comply with the subpoenas. The committee then rejected the alternatives of a contempt proceeding against the President or sending the sergeant at arms to bring the President to the com-

mittee as "inappropriate and unseemly"—and filed the civil suit. It asked Sirica to declare the subpoenas lawful and to order the President to comply. Arguments were held Oct. 4. *(p. 23, Vol. I, p. 220, 211, 209)*

A Matter of Jurisdiction. The only question which Sirica considered was whether the federal court had jurisdiction over the matter. He concluded that it did not.

In civil suits, he explained, "jurisdiction is a threshold issue.... For the federal courts, jurisdiction is not automatic and cannot be presumed. Thus, the presumption in each instance is that a federal court lacks jurisdiction until it can be shown that a specific grant of jurisdiction applies. Federal courts may exercise only that judicial power provided by the Constitution in Article III and conferred by Congress. All other judicial power or jurisdiction is reserved to the states.... When it comes to jurisdiction of the federal courts, truly, to paraphrase the scripture, the Congress giveth, and the Congress taketh away...(and) jurisdictional requirements cannot be waived."

Sirica then considered the four bases which the committee claimed gave the court jurisdiction:

• Federal law providing that federal courts have jurisdiction over "all civil actions, suits or proceedings commenced by the United States." But, Sirica said, other provisions of the law make clear that the attorney general and the Justice Department are the only ones who can qualify to litigate as the United States under that law.

• Federal law granting the federal courts jurisdiction over any effort to get an order to compel an official of the United States to perform a duty owed to a citizen. Sirica found that the President had no official duty to comply with the committee's subpoenas "regardless of whatever duty...(he) may owe the select committee as a citizen."

• The Administrative Procedure Act, which Sirica held did not confer jurisdiction when a suit would not otherwise be properly before the federal courts.

• Federal law providing that federal courts have jurisdiction over all civil cases involving "a matter in controversy" of more than $10,000. In this case, Sirica found no "matter in controversy...capable of valuation in dollars and cents." The tapes and documents were not worth that much; access to that information could not be considered as worth that amount; the rights and responsibilities of legislators were not measurable in dollars and cents; nor was Nixon's interest in keeping the tapes secret.

"No jurisdictional statute known to the court," Sirica concluded, "warrants an assumption of jurisdiction, and the court is therefore left with no alternative here but to dismiss the action....

"The court has here been requested to invoke a jurisdiction which only Congress can grant but which Congress has heretofore withheld. Whether such jurisdiction ought to be conferred is the prerogative of the Congress. Plaintiffs...are free to pursue whatever remedy they now deem appropriate, but the court cannot, consistent with law and the constitutional principles that reserve to Congress the conferral of jurisdiction, validate the present course."

Week's Watergate Chronology

Following is a day-to-day chronology of the week's events in the week ending Oct. 13. *(Earlier Oct. 11 events, p. 56)*

OCT. 11

Grand Jury Extension. Attorney General Elliot L. Richardson, acting for special Watergate prosecutor Archibald Cox, submitted to Congress a bill to extend the life of the Watergate grand jury for as long as one year. The mandate of the grand jury, empaneled June 5, 1972, was due to expire Dec. 4, 1973—too early for it to consider evidence contained in the White House tapes Cox was seeking, Richardson argued. A Supreme Court decision on the tapes case "cannot reasonably be expected before mid-November," he said. White House spokesmen offered no objections to the bill, but reiterated Nixon's stand against relinquishing the tapes.

Mitchell-Stans Tapes Dispute. Federal prosecutors fought off a defense bid for White House tapes and documents at a pretrial hearing in New York City on the government's perjury-obstruction of justice case against former Attorney General John N. Mitchell and former Commerce Secretary Maurice H. Stans. The prosecution contended that the materials had been subpoenaed by the defense as a ploy to force the President to invoke executive privilege on constitutional grounds and thus force dismissal of the charges. A similar attempt to obtain White House tapes and documents was being made by the defense in the pending Los Angeles, Calif., trial of four former White House aides, including John D. Ehrlichman, on charges related to the burglary of the office of Daniel Ellsberg's psychiatrist. *(Earlier development, p. 35)*

OCT. 12

Appellate Court Ruling. In a 5-2 decision, the U.S. Circuit Court of Appeals upheld Chief U.S. District Judge John J. Sirica's Aug. 29 ruling that President Nixon should surrender to the court tape recordings relevant to the Watergate case. *(Details, p. 57)*

OCT. 14

Nixon Finance Probe. *The Washington Post* reported that the Senate Watergate investigating committee had started an investigation of President Nixon's personal finances. The Post's sources said committee investigators were planning to question the President's personal secretary, Rose Mary Woods, and to subpoena bank records and documents Nixon submitted to an accounting firm that audited the purchase of his California and Florida homes.

The investigation reportedly was sparked by conflicting testimony the committee had received on the purpose and use of a $100,000 contribution given to Nixon's close friend, Charles G. Rebozo, by billionaire Howard R. Hughes. Several Republicans on the committee told the Post the probe was a "fishing expedition" aimed at putting the committee back in the limelight. *(Hughes-Rebozo transaction, p. 54)*

OCT. 16

Bail Denied. Judge Sirica denied bail to five of the original Watergate defendants who had pleaded guilty in January but later filed motions to change their pleas and be retried. The men—E. Howard Hunt Jr., Bernard L. Barker, Frank A. Sturgis, Eugenio R. Martinez and Virgilio R. Gonzalez—had asked to be released from jail until they were sentenced. *(Sentencing issue, p. 46)*

Impeachment Possibility. Nixon's chief domestic affairs adviser, Melvin R. Laird, told reporters he had warned Nixon to expect an impeachment attempt in Congress if he defied a Supreme Court ruling on the tapes dispute. Laird said he had predicted the attempt would fail. It was the first time since the Watergate case broke that a high White House official had discussed publicly the possibility that impeachment proceedings might be started. *(Earlier Laird advice, Vol. I, p. 239-240)*

OCT. 17

Committee Suit. Chief Judge John J. Sirica ruled that the U.S. District Court lacked jurisdiction to entertain a congressional civil lawsuit against the President, thus rejecting the Senate Watergate investigating committee's suit to obtain certain White House recordings. "The court has here been requested to invoke a jurisdiction which only Congress can grant, but which Congress has heretofore withheld," Sirica wrote in his 18-page decision. *(Details, p. 60)*

White House on Rebozo. White House spokesman Gerald L. Warren said Nixon was "confident" that his close associate Charles G. Rebozo "did not act in any improper way" by keeping a $100,000 gift from billionaire Howard Hughes for more than three years before returning it. Rebozo reportedly had told the Senate investigating committee that the money was a campaign contribution for Nixon. The day before, Warren had told reporters that Nixon became aware of the Hughes contribution, allegedly made in two installments in 1969 and 1970, after the 1972 election. *(p. 54)*

Corporate Contributions. Three corporations, American Airlines, Goodyear Tire and Rubber Company and Minnesota Mining and Manufacturing Company (3M) pleaded guilty to making illegal coporate contributions to Nixon's 1972 re-election campaign. The board chairmen of Goodyear and 3M also pleaded guilty under a policy, announced by special Watergate prosecutor Archibald Cox, that the "responsible corporate officer" would be charged along with the company in such cases. George A. Spater, the former chairman of American Airlines who was the first to disclose voluntarily an illegal corporate contribution, was not charged. Cox said similar charges against other corporations and officers could be expected. *(p. 11, Vol. I, p. 187)*

OCT. 18

Krogh Plea. Egil Krogh Jr., a former presidential aide who headed the White House "plumbers" group, pleaded innocent to two counts of giving false testimony before the Watergate grand jury. *(Indictment, p. 50)* √

EXCERPTS FROM APPEALS COURT DECISION ON TAPES

Following are excerpts from the District of Columbia Circuit Court of Appeals decision Oct. 12 affirming Judge Sirica's Aug. 29 order and from the dissenting opinions of Judges George E. MacKinnon and Malcolm R. Wilkey:

Per Curiam: This controversy concerns an order of the District Court for the District of Columbia entered on August 29, 1973, by Chief Judge John J. Sirica as a means of enforcing a grand jury subpoena *duces tecum* issued to and served on President Richard M. Nixon. The order commands the President, or any subordinate official, to produce certain items identified in the subpoena so that the Court can determine, by *in camera* inspection, whether the items are exempted from disclosure by evidentiary privilege.

Both the President and Special Prosecutor Archibald Cox, acting on behalf of the grand jury empanelled by the District Court in June, 1972, challenge the legality of this order. All members of this Court agree that the District Court had, and this Court has, jurisdiction to consider the President's claim of privilege. The majority of the Court approves the District Court's order, as clarified and modified in part, and otherwise denies the relief requested.

I

We deem it essential to emphasize the narrow contours of the problem that compels the Court to address the issues raised by this case. The central question before us is, in essence, whether the President may, in his sole discretion, withhold from a grand jury evidence in his possession that is relevant to the grand jury's investigations. It is our duty to respond to this question, but we limit our decision strictly to that required by the precise and entirely unique circumstances of the case.

On July 23 of this year, Special Prosecutor Cox caused to be issued a subpoena *duces tecum* directed to the President. The subpoena called upon the President to produce before the grand jury certain documents and objects in his possession.... In a letter dated July 25, 1973, addressed to the Chief Judge of the District Court, the President declined to produce the subpoenaed recordings. The President informed the Court that he had concluded "that it would be inconsistent with the public interest and with the Constitutional position of the Presidency to make available recordings of meetings and telephone conversations in which (he) was a participant...."

On July 26, at the instruction of the grand jury, the Special Prosecutor applied to the District Court for an order requiring production of the evidence. Having determined by poll in open court the grand jury's desire for the evidence, the District Judge ordered the President, or any appropriate subordinate official, to show cause "why the documents and objects described in (the subpoena) should not be produced...." On August 7, in answer to the order, the President filed a Special Appearance and Brief in Opposition, stating that the letter of July 25 constituted a "valid and formal claim of executive privilege" and that therefore the District Court "lack(ed) jurisdiction to enter an enforceable order compelling compliance with the subpoena...."

The District Court then allowed the Special Prosecutor to submit a memorandum in response to that of the President and in support of the Court's order. This memorandum contains a particularized showing of the grand jury's need for each of the several subpoenaed tapes—a need that the District Court subsequently and, we think, correctly termed "well-documented and imposing."

The strength and particularity of this showing were made possible by a unique intermeshing of events unlikely soon, if ever, to recur. The President had previously declared his intention to decline to assert any privilege with respect to testimony by his present and former aides, whether before the grand jury or the Select Committee of the Senate on Presidential Campaign Activities, concerning what has come to be known as the "Watergate" affair. As a result, detailed testimony by these aides before the Senate Committee enabled the Special Prosecutor to show a significant likelihood that there existed conspiracies among persons other than those already convicted of the Watergate break-in and wiretapping, not only to commit those offenses, but to conceal the identities of the persons involved. Moreover, the Special Prosecutor was able to show from the public testimony that important evidence relevant to the existence and scope of the purported conspiracy was contained in statements made by the President's advisers during certain conversations that took place in his office. Most importantly, perhaps, significant inconsistencies in the sworn testimony of these advisers relating to the content of the conversations raised a distinct possibility that perjury had been committed before the Committee and, perhaps, before the grand jury itself.

Thus, the Special Prosecutor was able to show that the tape recordings of the disputed conversations—conversations specifically identified as to time, place, and content—were each directly relevant to the grand jury's task. Indeed, the Memorandum demonstrates, particularly with respect to the possible perjury offenses, that the subpoenaed recordings contain evidence critical to the grand jury's decisions as to whether and whom to indict.

On August 29th, the Chief Judge of the District Court entered the order at issue in this case. In the accompanying opinion, he rejected the President's challenge to the Court's jurisdiction and to its authority to enter orders necessary to the enforcement of the subpoena. The President, petitioner in No. 73-1962, asks this Court for a writ of mandamus commanding the District Court to vacate its August 29th order....

For the reasons stated herein, we decline to command the District Court to vacate its order....

II

In their petitions for relief, both the President and the Special Prosecutor, invoke this court's statutory authority to issue "all writs necessary or appropriate in aide of" its jurisdiction....

From the viewpoint of mandamus, however, the central question that the President raises—whether the District Court exceeded its authority in ordering an *in camera* inspection of the tapes—is essentially jurisdictional. It is, too, a jurisdictional problem of "first impression" involving a "basic, undecided question." And if indeed the only avenue of direct appellate review open to the President requires that he first disobey the court's order, appeal seems to be "a clearly inadequate remedy." These circumstances, we think, warrant the exercise, at the instance of the President, of our review power under the All Writs Act, particularly in light of the great public interest in prompt resolution of the issues that his petition presents....

III

We turn, then, to the merits of the President's petition. Counsel for the President contend on two grounds that Judge Sirica lacked jurisdiction to order submission of the tapes for inspection. Counsel argue, first, that, so long as he remains in office, the President is absolutely immune from the compulsory process of a court; and, second, that Executive privilege is absolute with respect to presidential communications, so that disclosure is at the sole discretion of the President. This immunity and this absolute privilege are said to arise from the doctrine of separation of powers and by implication from the Constitution itself. It is conceded that neither the immunity nor the privilege is express in the Constitution.

A.

It is clear that the want of physical power to enforce its judgments does not prevent a court from deciding an otherwise justiciable case. Nevertheless, if it is true that the President is legally immune from court process, this case is at an end. The judiciary will not, indeed cannot, indulge in rendering an opinion to which the President has no legal duty to conform. We must, therefore, determine whether the President is *legally* bound to comply with an order enforcing a subpoena.

We note first that courts have assumed that they have the power to enter mandatory orders to Executive officials to compel production of evidence.

The courts' assumption of legal power to compel production of evidence within the possession of the Executive surely stands on firm footing. *Youngstown Sheet & Tube v. Sawyer,* in which an injunction running against the Secretary of Commerce was affirmed, is only the most celebrated instance of the issuance of compulsory process against Executive officials.... If *Youngstown* still stands, it must stand for the case where the President has himself taken possession and control of the property unconstitutionally seized, and the injunction would be framed accordingly. The practice of judicial review would be rendered capricious—and very likely impotent—if jurisdiction vanished whenever the President personally denoted an Executive action or omission as his own. This is not to say that the President should lightly be named as a party defendant.... Here, unfortunately, the court's order must run directly to the President, because he has taken the unusual step of assuming personal custody of the Government property sought by the subpoena.

The President also attempts to distinguish *United States v. Burr,* in which Chief Justice Marshall squarely ruled that a subpoena may be directed to the President. It is true that *Burr* recognized a distinction between the issuance of a subpoena and the ordering of compliance with that subpoena, but the distinction did not concern judicial power or jurisdiction. A subpoena *duces tecum* is an order to produce documents or to show cause why they need not be produced. An order to comply does not make the subpoena more compulsory; it simply maintains its original force....

The clear implication is that the President's special interests may warrant a careful judicial screening of subpoenas after the President interposes an objection, but that some subpoenas will nevertheless be properly sustained by judicial orders of compliance.....

The Constitution makes no mention of special presidential immunities. Indeed, the Executive Branch generally is afforded none. This silence cannot be ascribed to oversight. James Madison raised the question of Executive privileges during the Constitutional Convention, and Senators and Representatives enjoy an express, if limited, immunity from arrest, and an express privilege from inquiry concerning "Speech and Debate" on the floors of Congress. Lacking textual support, counsel for the President nonetheless would have us infer immunity from the President's political mandate, or from his vulnerability to impeachment, or from his broad discretionary powers. These are invitations to refashion the Constitution, and we reject them.

Though the President is elected by nationwide ballot, and is often said to represent all the people, he does not embody the nation's sovereignty. He is not above the law's commands: "With all its defects, delays and inconveniences men have discovered no technique for long preserving free government except that the Executive be under the law...." Sovereignty remains at all times with the people, and they do not forfeit through elections the right to have the law construed against and applied to every citizen.

Nor does the Impeachment Clause imply immunity from routine court process. While the President argues that the Clause means that impeachability precludes criminal prosecution of an incumbent, we see no need to explore this question except to note its irrelevance to the case before us.... By contemplating the possibility of post-impeachment trials for violations of law committed in office, the Impeachment Clause itself reveals that incumbency does not relieve the President of the routine legal obligations that confine all citizens.... (Because impeachment is available against all "civil Officers of the United States," not merely against the President...it is difficult to understand how any immunities peculiar to the President can emanate by implication from the fact of impeachability.) The legality of judicial orders should not be confused with the legal consequences of their breach: for the courts in this country always assume that their orders will be obeyed, especially when addressed to responsible government officials....

B.

There is, as the Supreme Court has said, a "longstanding principle" that the grand jury "has a right to every man's evidence" except that "protected by a constitutional, common law, or statutory privilege." The President concedes the validity of this principle. He concedes that he, like every other citizen, is under a legal duty to produce relevant, non-privileged evidence when called upon to do so. The President contends, however, that whenever, in response to a grand jury subpoena, he interposes a formal claim of privilege, that claim without more disables the courts from inquiring by any means into whether the privilege is applicable to the subpoenaed evidence. The President agrees that, in theory, the privilege attached to his office has limits.... Nonetheless, he argues that it is his responsibility, and his alone, to determine whether particular information falls beyond the scope of the privilege. In effect, then, the President claims that, at least with respect to conversations with his advisers, the privilege is absolute, since he, rather than the courts, has final authority to decide whether it applies in the circumstances.

We of course acknowledge, the longstanding judicial recognition of Executive privilege.... The Judiciary has been sensitive to the considerations upon which the President seems to rest his claim of absolute privilege: the candor of Executive aides and functionaries would be impaired if they were persistently worried that their advice and deliberations were later to be made public. However, counsel for the President can point to no case in which a court has accepted the Executive's mere assertion of privilege as sufficient to overcome the need of the party subpoenaing the documents. To the contrary, the courts have repeatedly asserted that the applicability of the privilege is in the end for them and not the Executive to decide....

To do otherwise would be effectively to ignore the clear words of *Marbury v. Madison*, that "(i)t is emphatically the province and duty of the judicial department to say what the law is."... Whenever a privilege is asserted, even one expressed in the Constitution, such as the Speech and Debate privilege, it is the courts that determine the validity of the assertion and the scope of the privilege. To leave the proper scope and application of Executive privilege to the President's sole discretion would represent a mixing, rather than a separation, of Executive and Judicial functions.... The Constitution mentions no Executive privileges, much less any absolute Executive privileges. Nor is an absolute privilege required for workable government. We acknowledge that wholesale public access to Executive deliberations and documents would cripple the Executive as a co-equal branch. But this is an argument for recognizing Executive privilege and for according it great weight, not for making the Executive the judge of its own privilege.

If the claim of absolute privilege was recognized, its mere invocation by the President or his surrogates could deny access to all documents in all the Executive departments to all citizens and their representatives, including Congress, the courts as well as grand juries, state governments, state officials and all state subdivisions. The Freedom of Information Act could become nothing more than a legislative statement of unenforceable rights. Support for this kind of mischief simply cannot be spun from incantation of the doctrine of separation of powers. (The doctrine of separation of powers was adopted by the Convention of 1787, not to promote efficiency but to preclude the exercise of arbitrary power.)

IV

The President's privilege cannot, therefore, be deemed absolute. We think the *Burr* case makes clear that application of Executive privilege depends on a weighing of the public interest protected by the privilege against the public interests that would be served by disclosure in a particular case. We direct our attention, however, solely to the circumstances here. With the possible exception of material on one tape, the President does not assert that the subpoenaed items involve military or state secrets; nor is the asserted privilege directed to the particular kinds of information that the tapes contain. Instead, the President asserts that the tapes should be deemed privileged because of the great public interest in maintaining the confidentiality of conversations that take place in the President's performance of his official duties....

We recognize this great public interest, and agree with the District Court that such conversations are presumptively privileged. But we think that this presumption of privilege premised on the public interest in confidentiality must fail in the face of the uniquely powerful showing made by the Special Prosecutor in this case...the Special Prosecutor has made a strong showing that the subpoenaed tapes contain evidence peculiarly necessary to the carrying out of this vital function—evidence for which no effective substitute is available.... The grand jury seeks evidence that may well be conclusive to its decisions in on-going investigations that are entirely within the proper scope of its authority....

Our conclusion that the general confidentiality privilege must recede before the grand jury's showing of need, is established by the unique circumstances that made this showing possible. In his public statement of May 22, 1973, the President said: "Executive privilege will not be invoked as to any testimony concerning possible criminal conduct or discussions of possible criminal conduct, in the matters presently under investigation, including the Watergate affair and the alleged cover-up." We think that this statement and its consequences may properly be considered as at least one factor in striking the balance in this case. Indeed, it affects the weight we give to factors on both sides of the scale. On the one hand, the President's action presumably reflects a judgment by him that the interest in the confidentiality of White House discussions in general is outweighed by such matters as the public interest, stressed by the Special Prosecutor, in the integrity of the level of the Executive Branch closest to the President, and the public interest in the integrity of the electoral process... it supports our estimation of the great public interest that attaches to the effective functioning of the present grand jury....

At the same time, the public testimony given consequent to the President's decision substantially disminishes the interest in maintaining the confidentiality of conversations pertinent to Watergate. The simple fact is that the conversations are no longer confidential.... (w)e see no justification, on confidentiality grounds, for depriving the grand jury of the best evidence of the conversations available....

Nonetheless, we hold that the District Court may order disclosure of all portions of the tapes relevant to matters within the proper scope of the grand jury's investigations, unless the Court judges that the public interest served by nondisclosure of *particular* statements or information outweighs the need for that information demonstrated by the grand jury.

V

The question remains whether, in the circumstances of this case, the District Court was correct in ordering the tapes produced for *in camera* inspection, so that it could determine whether and to what extent the privilege was properly claimed.... It is our hope that our action in providing what has become an unavoidable constitutional ruling, and in approving, as modified, the order of the District Court, will be followed by maximum cooperation among the parties. Perhaps the President will find it possible to reach some agreement with the Special Prosecutor as to what portions of the subpoenaed evidence are necessary to the grand jury's task.

Should our hope prove unavailing, we think that *in camera* inspection is a necessary and appropriate method of protecting the grand jury's interest in securing relevant evidence. The exception that we have delineated to the President's confidentiality privilege depends entirely on the grand jury's showing that the evidence is directly relevant to its decisions. The residual problem of this case derives from the possibility that there are elements of the subpoenaed recordings that do not lie within the range of the exception that we have defined....

VI

With the rejection of this all-embracing claim of prerogative, the President will have an opportunity to present more particular claims of privilege, if accompanied by an analysis in manageable segments....

1. In so far as the President makes a claim that certain material may not be disclosed because the subject matter relates to national defense or foreign relations, he may decline to transmit that portion of the material and ask the District Court to reconsider whether *in camera* inspection of the material is necessary. The Special Prosecutor is entitled to inspect the claim and showing and may be heard thereon, in chambers. If the judge sustains the privilege, the text of the government's statement will be preserved in the Court's record under seal.

2. The President will present to the District Court all other items covered by the order, with specification of which segments he believes may be disclosed and which not. This can be accomplished by itemizing and indexing the material, and correlating indexed items with particular claims of privilege. On request of either counsel, the District Court shall hold a hearing in chambers on the claims. Thereafter the Court shall itself inspect the disputed items.

Given the nature of the inquiry that this inspection involves, the District Court may gave the Special Prosecutor access to the material for the limited purpose of aiding the Court in determining the relevance of the material to the grand jury's investigations.... And, here, any concern over confidentiality is minimized by the Attorney General's designation of a distinguished and reflective counsel as Special Prosecutor. If, however, the Court decides to allow access to the Special Prosecutor, it should, upon request, stay its action in order to allow sufficient time for application for a stay to this Court.

Following the *in camera* hearing and inspection, the District Court may determine as to any items (a) to allow the particular claim of privilege in full; (b) to order disclosure to the grand jury of all or a segment of the item or items; or, when segmentation is impossible; (c) to fashion a complete statement for the grand jury of those portions of an item that bear on possible criminality. The District Court shall provide a reasonable stay to allow the President an opportunity to appeal. In case of an appeal to this Court of an order either allowing or refusing disclosure, this Court will provide for sealed records and confidentiality in presentation.

VII

We end, as we began, by emphasizing the extraordinary nature of this case. We have attempted to decide no more than the problem before us—a problem that takes its unique shape from the grand jury's compelling showing of need. The procedures we have provided require thorough deliberation by the District Court before even this need may be satisfied. Opportunity for appeals, on a sealed record, is assured.

We cannot, therefore, agree with the assertion of the President that the District Court's order threatens "the continued existence of the Presidency as a functioning institution." As we view the case, the order represents an unusual and limited requirement that the President produce material evidence. We think this required by law, and by the rule that even the Chief Executive is subject to the mandate of the law when he has no valid claim of privilege.

Dissenting Opinions

MacKINNON, *Circuit Judge,* concurring in part and dissenting in part: I concur in the decision on the jurisdiction of this court as expressed in part II of the Per Curiam opinion, but I respectfully dissent from its conclusion on the principal issue....

I. INTRODUCTION

This case presents for consideration an important constitutional question which has not confronted the courts in the 186 years since the Constitution was written. While the issues involved have arisen many times in the relations between the Congress and the President, there are no controlling judicial precedents. The immediate issue involves the requested disclosure of confidential discussions between the President and his close advisers, but the ultimate issue is the effect that our decision will have upon the constitutional independence of the Presidency for all time....

....It is my view that a constitutional decision in this case is unavoidable. It is my opinion that the preservation of the confidentiality of the Presidential decision-making process is of overwhelming importance to the effective functioning of our three branches of government. Therefore, I would recognize an absolute privilege for confidential Presidential communications....

II. THE HISTORICAL PERSPECTIVE

The established usage and custom between the executive, legislative and judicial branches warrant the most respectful consideration....

A. Presidential Refusals to Comply with

Congressional Subpoenas

In each of these (17) instances the Congress sought information from the President or the executive branch in order to enable it to legislate upon subjects within its constitutional power, and in each instance cited the request was refused by the President, who determined that to furnish the information would be an unconstitutional intrusion into the functioning of the executive branch and contrary to the public interest. The numerous confrontations between Congress and prior Presidents over the confidentiality of presidential information firmly establish a custom and usage that a President need not produce information which he considers would be contrary to the public interest.

B. The Similarity Between Congressional

and Judicial Subpoenas

The Special Prosecutor contends that custom and usage between the executive and legislative branches are not con-

trolling because the subpoena in this case was not issued by Congress, but by a federal court pursuant to a grand jury investigation. However, a congressional subpoena issued for the purpose of obtaining facts upon which to legislate carries at least as much weight as a judicial subpoena issued for the purpose of obtain evidence of criminal offenses....

...(A) judicial subpoena cannot be exalted over a Congressional subpoena, and the historic precedents involving congressional requests to the executive department are persuasive authority in the present dispute over a judicial subpoena to a President....

C. Congressional Privilege

Congress has asserted a privilege with respect to subpoenas addressed to members of Congress for documents in its possession and for the testimony of its employees. The practice which has been consistently followed is that no documents can be taken from the possession of either House except by the express consent of such House....

D. Judicial Privilege

The judicial branch of our government claims a similar privilege, grounded on an assertion of independence from the other branches. Express authorities sustaining this position are minimal, undoubtedly because its existence and validity has been so universally recognized....

...(T)he judiciary, as well as the Congress and past Presidents, believes that a protected independence is vital to the proper performance of its specified constitutional duties. It is my conclusion that the deliberative functions of the President's office should be afforded the same essential protection that has been recognized for, and asserted and enjoyed by, the legislative and judicial branches of our government since 1787.

III. THE PRESIDENTIAL COMMUNICATIONS

PRIVILEGE

A. The Importance of Confidentiality

By recognizing an absolute privilege, my opinion places the presidential communications privilege on an equal footing with that recognized for military or state secrets.... Military or state secrets are never subject to disclosure regardless of the weight of countervailing interests.

The rationale underlying the absolute privilege for military or state secrets is the policy judgment that the nation's interest in keeping this information secret always outweighs any particularized need for disclosure. A similar policy judgment supports an absolute privilege for communications between a President and his advisers on matters of official concern.

The interest supporting an absolute privilege for presidential communications is the confidentiality essential to insure thorough and unfettered discussion between a President and his advisers....

To allow the courts to breach presidential confidentiality whenever one of 400 federal trial judges considers that the circumstances of the moment demonstrate a compelling need for disclosure would frustrate the privilege's underlying policy of encouraging frank and candid presidential deliberations....

The lessons of legal history teach that it will be impossible to contain this breach of presidential confidentiality if numerous federal judges may rummage through presidential papers to determine whether a President's or a litigant's contentions should prevail in a particular case. Furthermore, the decision in this case inevitably will be precedent for assaults on the presently asserted absolute privileges of Congress and the Judiciary.....

C. Presidential Privilege Against a Grand Jury

...The presidential communications privilege, as here outlined, does not immunize executive officers from criminal prosecution. This evidentiary privilege, which protects the presidential deliberative process by preventing disclosure of the exact details of that process, is not premised on any notions of immunity from civil or criminal liability....

The possibility that an occasional criminal prosecution may be hampered by the privilege does not justify abandoning the compelling long-range necessity for presidential confidentiality. The inability of a prosecutor or grand jury to obtain specific privileged information will seldom prevent a successful criminal prosecution....

D. Constitutional Dimensions of the Privilege

...The privilege also has constitutional dimensions which derive both from the separation of powers doctrine and from the logical principle that inherent in any constitutional right are the means requisite to its effective discharge.

The doctrine of separation of powers...requires that each branch's "proceedings, and the motives, views, and principles, which produce those proceedings, should be free from the remotest influence, direct or indirect, of either of the other two powers." This doctrine, then, prohibits intrusion in any form by one branch into the decisional processes of an equal and coordinate branch....

...The greatest vice of the decision sought by the Special Prosecutor is that it would establish a precedent that would subject every presidential conference to the hazard of eventually being publicly exposed at the behest of some trial judge trying a civil or criminal case. It is this precedential effect which transforms this case from one solely related to the recordings sought here, to one which decides whether this President, and all future Presidents, shall continue to enjoy the independency of executive action contemplated by the Constitution and fully exercised by all their predecessors.

IV. THE PRIVILEGE IN THIS CASE

A. The Privilege Was Properly Invoked

After the President has claimed the privilege, the court must satisfy itself that "the circumstances are appropriate for the claim of privilege." In determining whether the privilege is appropriate in a particular case, the only inquiry is whether there is a "reasonable danger" that disclosure of the evidence would expose matters which the privilege is designed to protect. Since the presidential communications privilege is an absolute rather than a qualified privilege, there is no occasion to balance the particularized need for the evidence against the governmental interest in confidentiality. The balance between these competing interests was examined and resolved when the absolute presidential communications privilege was formulated. Having concluded that the privilege is available, the only inquiry is whether the President's invocation of the privilege promotes the policy which the privilege was designed to protect....

Yet the court must make this determination without forcing disclosure of the very communication which the privilege protects. Thus an *in camera* inspection is proper only if the court cannot otherwise satisfy itself that the privilege should be sustained. In the present case, we are satisfied that appropriate circumstances do exist and, therefore, would hold that even *in camera* inspection is improper.

B. Privilege Not Destroyed by Possibility of Criminal Conspiracy by Advisers

The Special Prosecutor also argues that the privilege disappears upon a *prima facie* showing that the conversations occurred as part of a criminal conspiracy by certain of the Presi-

dent's advisers. He strenuously argues that abuse of the privileged relationship vitiates any otherwise valid privilege possessed by the President. The argument is fatally defective, however, since the President alone holds the privilege which is designed to ensure the integrity of his decisional processes. The possibility that those close to him may have perverted the relationship cannot destroy the privilege held in the public interest exclusively by the President....

D. Prior Testimony by Presidential Advisers Does Not Require Disclosure of the Tape Recordings

...The privilege has not be waived at least as to any matters not already testified to by his advisers. The confidentiality surrounding as yet undisclosed conversations has not been impaired. As to those portions of the tape recordings that have been the subject of testimony before the Senate Investigating Committee, the resolution of the waiver issue is more complex, but the answer appears equally clear. There has been no waiver. This conclusion rests upon three factors: the strict standards applied to privileges of this nature to determine waiver; the distinction between oral testimony and tape recordings; and, most important, considerations of public policy that argue persuasively for a privilege that permits the Chief Executive to disclose information on topics of national concern without decimating entirely his right and duty to withhold that which properly ought to be withheld in the public interest....

V. CONCLUSION

For the reasons above stated it is my conclusion that the presidential communications privilege may be exercised to decline to produce the recordings, and that this privilege has not been waived. I would thus enter judgment accordingly in all cases.

If this rule were recognized, the President would then be free voluntarily to type up a transcript of the recordings that are the subject of this litigation and present it to the grand jury with the material deleted that he considers confidential. He could explain the deleted matter. As to the deleted material the President's action would be submitted to the test of public opinion and eventually, when the tapes are released for posterity, to the test of history.

WILKEY, *Circuit Judge,* dissenting. The critical issue on which I part company with my five colleagues is, in the shortest terms, *Who Decides?*

There is no issue as to the existence of Executive Branch privilege, and questions as to its scope and applicability to a given set of facts will be relatively easy to determine once the principal question is settled. The basic issue is *who decides* the scope and applicability of the Executive Branch privilege, the Judicial Branch or Executive Branch?

Throughout the *Per Curiam* this issue appears obfuscated; there is an effort to slide away from the square confrontation produced by the Judicial Branch ordering the Executive Branch to turn over records of private conversations in the Chief Executive's own office....

The *Per Curiam* here never confronts the fundamental Constitutional question of separation of powers, but instead prefers to treat the case as if all were involved was a weighing and balancing of conflicting public interests. There are conflicting public interests involved, they must be carefully weighed, balanced, and appraised; the President says he has done just that. Therefore, the most fundamental, necessarily decisive issue is, Who does the weighing and balancing of conflicting public interests? The District Judge or the President?....

I. The Dual Origin of the Privilege Asserted

I respectfully submit that the errors in the *Per Curiam's* analysis stem from a frequent source of confusion, the failure to recognize and separate the two origins of the Executive Branch privilege: on one hand, the common sense-common law privilege of confidentiality necessary in government administration, which has been partly codified in statutes such as the Freedom of Information Act; on the other hand, the origin of the privilege in the Constitutional principle of separation of powers....

In theory, if only the ancient customary Governmental confidentiality privilege is involved, whether the Chief Executive should disclose the information should be decided no differently from the case of any other Government official.... It would be permissible for the courts to talk in terms of balancing the public interest of those seeking disclosure versus the public interest of the President in retaining confidentiality....

As a practical matter, as history shows, the theory breaks down. Not only is the grist of the Presidential mill of a higher quality than that processed by the average bureaucrat, but the institutions or individuals daring to confront the Chief Executive directly have been of a character and power to invoke immediately the other source of the Chief Executive's privilege, the Constitutional doctrine of separation of powers.... If the Chief Executive can be "coerced" by the Judicial Branch into furnishing records hitherto throughout our history resting within the exclusive control of the Executive, then the Chief Executive is no longer "master in his own house."

This is not a matter of "coercing" the Executive to "obey the law"; there has never before in 184 years been any such law that the Executive could be compelled by the Judiciary to surrender Executive records to the Judiciary. This is an assertion of privilege by the Executive, not a refusal to obey a court's interpretation of the law. This the Executive has *always* done, even when the Executive's interpretation of the law was different.... But also, the Executive has *always* been the one who decided whether the Executive Branch privilege of confidentiality of its records should be asserted, and to what extent, when confronted with demand of another Branch for such records.... Never in 184 years, until Senator Ervin's committee filed the pending action in Judge Sirica's court for these same Watergate tapes, has the Congress desired to take the Constitutional separation of powers issue to a court for adjudication. The reasons are obvious: (1) if the Constitutional principle of separation of powers was valid and effective as a barrier, Congress would lose; (2) acutely aware of its own assertions of privilege, even if Congress won and established that the separation of powers was no barrier to a demand of one Branch for the papers of another, on a reciprocal basis Congress would have to abandon its equally time-honored practice of refusing the demands of the Judicial Branch for its papers; and (3) submitting a dispute between two co-equal Branches to the third Branch would recognize that the Judiciary is "more equal" than the other two....

...(W)here the privilege of the Chief Executive is derived from the *Constitutional principle* of separation of powers, it is no more subject to weighing and balancing than any other Constitutional privilege can be weighed and balanced by extraneous third parties....

We all know that when a Constitutional privilege under the Fifth Amendment is asserted by the humblest individual, the court does not weigh and balance the public interest in having the individual's testimony. All the court can do is make a preliminary inquiry as to a prima facie justification for the assertion of the privilege.... If the Constitutional privilege has been asserted, then no court has the right to determine what the President will or will not produce....

II. Development of the Tripartite Privilege with Reference to Executive Documents

Throughout this nation's 184-year Constitutional history, Congress and the Executive have succeeded in avoiding any near-fatal confrontation over attempts by Congress to procure documents in the Executive's possession. In recognition of the delicate balance created by the doctrine of separation of powers,

the two Branches have generally succeeded in fashioning a *modus vivendi* through mutual deference and cooperation....

Congressional demands for Executive papers are as numerous as autumn leaves, and frequently fall due to a frost between the two ends of Pennsylvania Avenue. In contrast, Judicial demands for Executive documents can be summarized in the drama and legal intricacies of one *cause celebre,* the two trials of Aaron Burr in 1807, the major historical example of the issuance by a federal court of a subpoena *duces tecum* directing the President to produce documents. Although the United States Circuit Court for Virginia, per Chief Justice Marshall, issued the subpoena *duces tecum* to President Jefferson, the court never directly decided the question of the scope of the President's asserted privilege to withhold documents or portions thereof, nor did it determine who should decide the scope of the privilege....

If we go on *what was actually done,* the Burr Trials prove that the final "weighing of the public interest" is done by the Chief Executive. If we go on what was *said* by Marshall, the *Burr* trials leave the ultimate issue of Who finally decides the public interest completely undecided, for Marshall never faced up, even verbally, to a confrontation with the President himself with the issue drawn on the question of separation of powers.

These two great Constitutional and political antagonists— Marshall and Jefferson, Chief Justice and President—had circled each other warily, each maintaining his position, each, out of respect for the other and for the delicate fabric of the Constitution, not forcing the ultimate issue. Who *should* decide the scope and applicability of the Chief Executive's privilege? The portions of the letter determined by the President to be confidential remained confidential; the full letter was never produced to the court....

IV. Amenability of the President to Judicial Process— An Illusory Issue in the Instant Case

It can hardly be questioned that in any direct confrontation between the Judiciary and the Executive, the latter must prevail. Therefore, the "issue" of whether the President is amenable to court process is an illusory one. No one questions that the court can issue to the President a piece of paper captioned "Subpoena" and that the President owes some obligation at least to inform the court of how he intends to respond....

...(T)he real issue...is whether it is appropriate for the court to determine the legal validity of a claim of privilege by the President, or whether the Constitutional principle of separation of powers requires the court to yield to the President's judgment as to where the public interest lies. My answer would be the latter.

V. Application of the Constitutional Tripartite Privilege

...(T)he best (and historically only) answer is that judgment on the proper exercise of the Executive and Judical powers ultimately rests, and was intended to rest, with the American people. Having created three co-equal separate Branches, the Constitutional Convention did not foul up the grand design by providing that one Branch was to be superior and prevail over another, nor did the grand scheme entrust the decision between two conflicting Branches to the third Branch. This was graphically demonstrated by the Constitutional theory on which Washington and his cabinet first acted, that the Executive himself should determine what papers in the public interst could be furnished to another Branch.

It was and is the President's right to make that decision initially, and it is the American people who will be the judge as to whether the President has made the right decision, *i.e.,* whether it is or is not in the public interest that the papers (tapes) in question be furnished or retained. If his decision is made on visibly sound grounds, the people will approve the action of the Executive as being in the public interest. If the decision is not visibly on sound grounds of national public interest, in political terms the decision may be ruinous for the President, but it is his to make. The grand design has worked; the separate, independent Branch remains in charge of and responsible for its own papers, processes and decisions, not to a second or third Branch, but it remains *responsible* to the American people.

This may seemingly frustrate the role of the Special Prosecutor in part of his work, it may frustrate what a Congressional investigative committee conceives to be its role, but in my judgment this was the way the Constitution was intended to work. The Constitution was not designed as an all-powerful efficient instrument of government. The primary concern in the minds of the Founding Fathers of 1787 was to devise a reasonably efficient method of government that above all did not have the in-built capacity to become oppressive. And to that end they first designed the separation of powers, making each Branch independent, and then left inherent in the structure they had designed the possiblity of irreconcilable conflict. But in their view, the possibility of irreconcilable conflict was not necessarily bad, because above all this would guarantee that the National Government could never become an efficient instrument of oppression of the people.

The Founding Fathers were not looking for the *most efficient* government design. After all, they had been subject to and rebelled against one of the most efficient governments then existing. What the Founding Fathers designed was *not efficiency, but protection against oppression.* Leaving the three Branches in an equilibrium of tension was just one of their devices to guard against oppression.

This healthy equilibrium of tension will be destroyed if the result reached by the *Per Curiam* is allowed to stand. My colleagues cannot confine the effect of their decision to Richard M. Nixon.

The precedent set will inevitably have far-reaching implications on the vulnerability of any Chief Executive to judicial process, not merely at the behest of the Special Prosecutor in the extraordinary circumstances of Watergate, but at the behest of Congress. Congress may have equally plausible needs for similar information. The fact that Congress is usually or frequently locked in political battle with the Chief Executive cannot mean that Congress' need or right to information in the hands of the Chief Executive is any less than it otherwise would be.

The courts will have been enlisted on one side of what would be even more undeniably and fundamentally a political question....

To put the theoretical situation and possibilities in terms of "absolute" privilege sounds somewhat terrifying—*until one realizes that this is exactly the way matters have been for 184 years of our history,* and the Republic still stands. The practical capacity of the three independent Branches to adjust to each other, their sensitivity to the approval or disapproval of the American people, have been sufficient guides to responsible action, without imposing the authority of one co-equal Branch over another.

The American Constitutional design may look like sloppy craftsmanship, it may upset tidy theoreticians, but it has worked —a lot better than other more symmetrical models.

At the least, this is a point in favor of its continuance unchanged; at the most, this may be all the answer we need.

CONGRESS EXAMINES PRESIDENTIAL IMPEACHMENT

Responding to an enormous outpouring of public rage over the firing of special prosecutor Archibald Cox, Congress moved for the first time in more than a century toward consideration of the impeachment of a president.

Rep. Peter W. Rodino Jr. (D N.J.), chairman of the House Judiciary Committee, told reporters Oct. 24 the committee would "proceed full steam ahead" with an impeachment investigation. He said the panel would investigate any allegation of "impeachable offenses," a phrase which other committee sources said included the secret bombing of Cambodia in 1970, an aborted administration plan for burglary and wiretapping of suspected subversives and President Nixon's refusal to spend funds appropriated by Congress.

The Democratic majority on the committee, Rodino said, had decided to hire a separate chief counsel and staff to investigate any charges that might bear on the President's impeachment. This group also would seek authority for Rodino to subpoena, without a vote of the full committee, any documents, tapes or other materials bearing on the investigation.

Archibald Cox

It was apparent that Nixon, despite a dramatic admission of defeat on the question of court access to secret White House tape recordings, had failed to stem the determination of many Democrats in the House to push forward with, at the least, an impeachment inquiry. Some Republican members of the Judiciary Committee said they opposed the procedures announced by Rodino.

Public Outcry. Public pressure to impeach the President struck Congress with tornado-like velocity after the President, on Oct. 20, ordered the firing of special prosecutor Cox, a Harvard law professor who until his discharge had almost unlimited, independent authority to investigate charges of illegal acts by any member of the administration—including the President and his staff. Attorney General Elliot L. Richardson and Deputy Attorney General William D. Ruckelshaus resigned rather than carry out Nixon's order to fire Cox. The prosecutor was then fired—and the office of special prosecutor was abolished—by Solicitor General Robert H. Bork, who had become acting attorney general.

"Whether we shall continue to be a government of laws and not of men is now for Congress and ultimately the American people to decide," said Cox.

In This Chapter

Cox-Richardson drama, below; CQ House poll, p. 71; Andrew Johnson's impeachment, p. 72; presidential disability, p. 74; Nixon's reversal on tapes, Rodino profile, p. 77; impeachment resolution, p. 76; Bork profile, p. 77; congressional action, p. 78; Petersen profile, Senate Watergate committee, p. 79; fired and resigned administration officials, p. 80; Albert profile, p. 81; interest groups' plans, p. 82; week's chronology, Dean guilty plea, p. 83; document texts, p. 85.

Public response to the President's action was overwhelmingly negative. A Congressional Quarterly poll of House members showed telephone calls, telegrams and mail received by most Democratic representatives to be heavily in favor of impeachment. Most Republican representatives said their constituents strongly opposed Nixon's action but generally stopped short of calling for impeachment.

Congressional Reaction. On the first two days after Congress returned from its Veterans Day recess, 84 representatives introduced legislation calling for impeachment of the President or an investigation of impeachment procedures.

In addition, 98 representatives—including four Republicans—sponsored legislation to establish a special prosecutor's office that would be independent of administration restrictions. A number of House and Senate Republicans urged the President to appoint a new special prosecutor to forestall passage of such legislation.

Protection of Records. Assistant Attorney General Henry E. Petersen, to whom the task of investigating Watergate and other cases had reverted, Oct. 26 petitioned U.S. District Court Chief Judge John J. Sirica to declare all investigative records the property of the court. The petition noted that "within a few minutes" of Cox's ouster, "agents of the FBI acting of direct instructions of the White House 'sealed' the offices of the Watergate Special Prosecution Force, as well as of the former Attorney General and deputy attorney general."

The Cox-Richardson Drama

Nixon's confrontation with Congress first surfaced to public view at 8:25 p.m. Oct. 20 when presidential spokesman Ronald L. Ziegler announced the firing of Cox and the departure of Richardson and Ruckelshaus. Nixon also ordered all investigations of Cox's office returned to the jurisdiction of the Justice Department.

It was the greatest administration upheaval since April 30, when White House aides H. R. Haldeman, John D. Ehrlichman, John W. Dean III and Attorney General

Richard G. Kleindienst resigned in the wake of the broadening Watergate scandal.

The issue was, as Richardson told a news conference Oct. 23, "presidential authority versus the independence and public accountability of the special prosecutor"—a historic confrontation between the principle of executive privilege, or presidential confidentiality, as stated by President Nixon, and the right of other parties to investigate the executive branch when there is apparent evidence of wrongdoing by members of that branch.

Order to Cox. The "firestorm," as Nixon's chief of staff, Alexander M. Haig Jr., described it, began the evening of Oct. 19.

Nixon, who had been ordered by the U.S. Circuit Court of Appeals to turn over nine tape recordings of White House conversations to the special Watergate prosecutor, let the deadline expire for an appeal to the Supreme Court. Then he offered a compromise.

Rather than giving Cox the tapes, the President said, he would prepare summaries of their contents and then permit Sen. John C. Stennis (D Miss.) to listen to the tapes to verify the President's account. He would do so "with the greatest reluctance," he said, because he considered even this offer a violation of the principle of the presidential confidentiality he had vowed to uphold.

Nixon also ordered Cox "as an employee of the executive branch to make no further attempts by the judicial process to obtain tapes, notes or memoranda of presidential conversations." It was understood that the President was prepared to fire Cox if he did not acquiesce.

The President decided on his proposal Monday afternoon, Oct. 15, Richardson said, and negotiations proceeded throughout the week. The chairman and vice chairman of the Senate select Watergate committee, Senators Sam J. Ervin Jr. (D N.C.) and Howard H. Baker Jr. (R Tenn.), reportedly agreed to the tapes plan, although they later disagreed on their interpretation of its exact details. Cox, however, had questions about it, and refused to accept the limitation on his future investigative efforts. Richardson sided with Cox, and was not informed in advance of the President's decision to order Cox to cease and desist.

Cox's Statement. Cox held a televised Saturday afternoon news conference Oct. 20. He denied he was "looking for a confrontation," and said he was "certainly not out to get the President of the United States." But, he said, he could not accept the President's proposal and would go back into court for a decision on Nixon's apparent noncompliance with the court's order—a decision which could have resulted in a contempt of court citation against the President.

"I think it is my duty as the special prosecutor, as an officer of the court and as the representative of the grand jury, to bring to the court's attention what seems to me to be noncompliance," Cox said.

To accept Nixon's proposal would create "insuperable difficulties" for him as prosecutor, Cox said. He doubted summaries of the tapes would be admissible as evidence in court, and said barring him from seeking further White House tapes and documents would prevent him from conducting his investigation. He complained of "repeated frustration" in his attempts to get information from the White House about Watergate, the alleged coverup, the "White House plumbers" activities and related matters.

Cox contended Nixon's instructions were "inconsistent with pledges that were made to the United States Senate and through the Senate to the American people before I was appointed and before Attorney General Richardson's nomination was confirmed"—pledges to appoint and guarantee the independence of a special Watergate prosecutor.

Richardson's Position. Richardson agreed. He wrote the President Oct. 20 that while he considered the Stennis part of the proposal to be reasonable and constructive and hoped U.S. District Court Judge John J. Sirica would accept it, he could not accept the ban on any future attempts by Cox to obtain records from the White House.

"As you point out, this instruction does intrude on the independence you promised me with regard to Watergate when you announced my appointment," Richardson wrote. *(Nixon, Richardson letters, p. 85)*

The two men talked. The President was "very deliberate, very restrained in tone...but he was absolutely firm on the course he had determined upon," Richardson later told a news conference.

"When, therefore, Mr. Cox rejected that position, and gave his objections to the Stennis proposal, as well as his reasons for insisting on assured access to other tapes and memoranda, the issue of presidential authority versus the independence and public accountability of the special prosecutor was squarely joined," Richardson said.

"The President, at that point, thought he had no choice but to direct the attorney general to discharge Mr. Cox. And I, given my role in guaranteeing the independence of the special prosecutor, as well as my belief in the public interest embodied in that role, felt equally clear that I could not discharge him. And so I resigned," Richardson said.

Elliot L. Richardson

"At stake, in the final analysis, is the very integrity of the governmental processes I came to the Department of Justice (in May) to help restore," Richardson noted. He did not dispute the President's right to change the rules of the game, but said he could not abide by the change.

After Richardson offered his resignation, Deputy Attorney General Ruckelshaus was called by Haig and asked to fire Cox. "I simply could not do it," Ruckelshaus told *The New York Times*. And so he wrote out a letter of resignation. The White House did not wait to receive it before announcing that Ruckelshaus had been fired for refusing to obey the President's orders.

Solicitor General Robert H. Bork then was informed that under the law he was acting attorney general and must fire Cox. He did so.

At 8:25 p.m. Oct. 20, in an unusual Saturday night news conference, White House press secretary Ronald L. Ziegler stunned newsmen with the announcements of the firing of Cox and abolition of his special prosecutor's office, the resignation of Richardson and the firing of Ruckelshaus.

Ziegler also announced that Bork had ordered the FBI to seal off the special prosecutor's offices to prevent the removal of any files. This act, with the firings, set off cries of outrage across the country, and protests began to mount immediately, along with cries for impeachment of the President.

Some critics doubted that the issue of confidentiality was as important to the President as getting rid of Cox, and Nixon's capitulation on the tapes issue Oct. 23 heightened those feelings. Some felt the entire tapes issue had been contrived as a means of forcing an issue on which to fire Cox.

Cox himself said he had the impression he was being deliberately "confronted with things that were drawn in such a way that I could not accept them." Richardson said the possibility of firing Cox was first raised with him by presidential aides earlier in the week as "one way of mooting the (tapes) case, and thereby in effect resolving the constitutional impasse." Richardson said he rejected the suggestion as "totally unacceptable."

The Washington Post reported the President had wanted to abolish the special prosecutor's office since last June because Cox's investigation was "hitting too close to the President and his friends and former aides, and was probing too deeply into every aspect of White House activity going back to 1969."

Cox acknowledged in a CBS television interview Oct. 24 that at the time he was fired, his staff was looking into large political contributions, chiefly in cash, raised by White House aides in 1970, and "possible abuses" of national security and other government agencies, including the Internal Revenue Service. Cox declined to say whether he had evidence sufficient to compel Congress to impeach the President.

Richardson News Conference. Richardson acknowledged that there had been "continuing arguments" with the President's lawyers on the scope of Cox's investigation, but denied any attempts had been made to head off the investigation. He defended Cox against charges that he was conducting a "witch hunt" or was trying to "get Nixon," but conceded that "many people" in the Republican Party, on the Hill and on the President's staff felt there was partisanship because Cox and some of his top aides are Democrats and formerly served in Democratic administrations. Cox was solicitor general in the Kennedy administration. He also was a law professor of Richardson's at Harvard Law School, and was picked by Richardson for the special prosecutor's job.

Richardson spoke at a packed news conference in the Great Hall of the Department of Justice Oct. 23. He had asked Acting Attorney General Bork for use of the room. He had praise for the Nixon administration and said he strongly believed in its general purposes and priorities, but "I have been compelled to conclude that I could better serve my country by resigning my public office than by continuing in it."

Both Richardson and Ruckelshaus stressed their belief that an independent special prosecutor was necessary in the Watergate investigation. They praised the integrity of Assistant Attorney General Henry Petersen, chief of the criminal division, who will now take charge of the investigation, but, Richardson said, "I think the situation is fraught with great difficulty for him, and I think that whoever is attorney general and Mr. Petersen would both

(Continued on p. 74)

CQ House Poll

President Nixon's decision to release secret White House tapes to the courts failed to dampen sentiment among House Democrats to appoint an independent special prosecutor to handle all Watergate-related cases, according to a survey made by Congressional Quarterly Oct. 23.

The informal poll of House members—made just hours before and hours after the decision was announced—also documented enormous public pressure on Democratic House members to begin impeachment proceedings against the President. Most Democrats interviewed said their constituents were overwhelmingly in favor of impeachment; most Republicans said their constituents strongly opposed Nixon's actions but stopped short of calling for impeachment.

House members of both parties agreed with relatively few exceptions that the firing of special prosecutor Archibald Cox and the resignations of Attorney General Elliot L. Richardson and Deputy Attorney General William D. Ruckelshaus would delay action on the nomination of House Minority Leader Gerald R. Ford (R Mich.) to become vice president.

Poll Technique. CQ staff members polled all members of the House on the first day Congress was in session after the ouster of Cox and the resignations of Richardson and Ruckelshaus. A total of 132 responded before it was announced that the President would release the Watergate tapes to U.S. District Judge John J. Sirica; 108 answered after the announcement.

Representatives who had indicated they favored impeachment or a study of impeachment before the announcement were re-polled to see if their views had changed. The happenstance of timing provided an unusual opportunity to measure the impact of a major political development on House attitudes.

Special Prosecutor. Asked—prior to the announcement that the tapes would be released—what action Congress should take next, 31 Democrats and six Republicans volunteered the opinion that Congress should establish an independent prosecutor's office to handle cases Cox had been investigating. Not one of these representatives said his view had been changed when he was re-polled, but not all could be reached. An additional 36 Democrats and seven Republicans said after the announcement that they favored a special prosecutor.

Constituent Reaction. Fifty Democrats and 19 Republicans said mail, telegrams and telephone calls were overwhelmingly in favor of impeachment of the President. An additional 32 Democrats and 27 Republicans said their constituents were strongly opposed to the President's action.

Ford Nomination. More than 80 per cent—95 of the 116 representatives who offered an opinion—said the President's action would delay consideration of Ford's nomination to become vice president. Sixteen representatives said this would have no effect and three Republicans said the nomination would be speeded up.

President Andrew Johnson's Impeachment in 1868: . . .

The impeachment and trial of President Andrew Johnson in 1868, the only presidential impeachment in American history, was based on the charge of his violation of a federal statute, the Tenure of Office Act. But in addition, the procedure was a profoundly political struggle between irreconcilable forces.

Questions such as control of the Republican Party, how to deal with the South, in a state of chaos following the Civil War, and monetary and economic policy all had an effect on the process.

Johnson as President was an anomaly. Lincoln's running mate in 1864, he was a southerner at a time when the South was out of the union; a Jacksonian Democrat who believed in states' rights, hard money, and minimal federal government activity running with an administration pursuing a policy of expansion both in the money supply and the role of government; a man who had little regard for the Negro in the midst of a party many of whose members were actively seeking to guarantee the rights of the newly freed slaves.

In these contradictions lay the basis for an inevitable conflict. The interplay of personalities and policies decreed that the conflict would result in an impeachment process.

Johnson had been the only member of the U.S. Senate from a seceding southern state (Tennessee) to remain loyal to the Union in 1861. Lincoln later made him military governor of Tennessee and chose him as his running mate in 1864 as a southerner and Democrat who was also a loyalist and in favor of prosecuting the war.

Sources

Michael Les Benedict, *The Impeachment and Trial of Andrew Johnson,* W. W. Norton and Company Inc., New York, 1973.

Raoul Berger, *Impeachment: The Constitutional Problems,* Harvard University Press, Cambridge, 1973.

James G. Blaine, *Twenty Years of Congress, 1861-1881,* The Henry Hill Publishing Company, Norwich, Conn., 1886.

On Lincoln's death in 1865, this outsider without allies or connections in the Republican Party succeeded to the presidency. Johnson's ideas on what should have been done to reconstruct and readmit the southern states to representation clashed with the wishes of a majority of Congress, overwhelmingly controlled by the Republicans.

Among the latter, there was a strong desire to secure the Negroes in their rights. Some had selfish motives: black votes and support were necessary for the Republicans to maintain their political hegemony. Others were more idealistic: the ex-slaves were helpless and had to be protected by the federal government, or they would quickly lose their new freedom.

Congress was divided into roughly three groups. The small minority of Democrats supported the President. About half the Republicans were known as "radicals," because they favored strong action to revolutionize southern society, by harsh military means if necessary. The other half of the Republicans were more conservative; while unwilling to go as far as the radicals, they wanted to make sure the South did not return to the unquestioned control of those who ruled it before the Civil War.

Over the years 1866-69, the conservative Republicans were repeatedly thrown into coalition with the radicals, often against their wishes. The radicals always counted on Johnson to help them out by behaving aggressively and uncompromisingly. They were usually confirmed in their expectations.

Upon taking office, Johnson began to pursue Lincoln's mild and tolerant reconstruction plans. The new President felt that a few basics were all that needed to be secured: abolition of slavery; ratification of the 13th Amendment, which abolished slavery in all states; repudiation of all state debts contracted by the Confederate governments; nullification of secession. When the southern states had done these things, Johnson felt they should be readmitted.

But Republicans wanted more: a Freedmen's Bureau, to protect and provide services for the ex-slaves; a civil rights bill, guaranteeing the Negroes their rights, and an over-all plan of reconstruction providing for temporary military governments in the South.

Throughout 1866, Johnson and Congress battled over these issues. In February, the President vetoed the Freedmen's Bureau bill. The Senate failed to override, but this was the last Johnson veto to be sustained. For the rest of the year, bill after bill was passed over Johnson's veto, including a second Freedmen's Bureau bill, a civil rights bill and, in early 1867, a reconstruction bill and the Tenure of Office Act.

The Tenure of Office Act, the violation of which was to be the legal basis for Johnson's impeachment, was passed over his veto March 2, 1867. The act forbade the President to remove civil officers (appointed with the consent of the Senate) without the approval of the Senate. Its purpose was to protect incumbent Republican officeholders from executive retaliation if they did not support the President. Johnson had made wholesale removals from rank-and-file federal offices both during and after the election campaign of 1866.

UNSUCCESSFUL ASHLEY RESOLUTION

About the time the Tenure of Office Act was being debated, the first moves toward impeachment began. On Jan. 7, 1867, two Missouri representatives, Benjamin F. Loan (R Mo. 1863-69) and John R. Kelso (R Mo. 1865-67), attempted in turn to introduce resolutions in the House proposing impeachment, but each was prevented by parliamentary maneuver.

But later the same day, Rep. James M. Ashley (R Ohio 1859-69) rose on a question of privilege and formally charged the President with high crimes and misdemeanors. (Ashley was the great-grandfather of Rep. Thomas L. Ashley (D Ohio), who was elected in 1954 in the same district as his ancestor.)

... An Inevitable Clash with an Unpopular President

Ashley made general charges, and no specific violations of law were mentioned. Most members recognized the charges as basically political grievances rather than illegal acts. The matter was referred to the House Judiciary Committee, which reported on March 2, 1867, two days before the expiration of the 39th Congress, that the committee had reached no conclusion. Its members recommended that the matter be given further study by the next Congress.

On March 7, 1867, the third day of the 40th Congress, Ashley again introduced his resolution, and it was referred to the Judiciary Committee for further investigation. The committee studied the matter throughout the year and issued a report on Nov. 25, 1867. A majority of the committee reported an impeachment resolution. When the House voted on the matter Dec. 7, the radicals suffered a crushing defeat. The resolution calling for impeachment was turned down, 57 to 108.

SUCCESSFUL SECOND TRY

Johnson appeared to have won. But, observed James G. Blaine in his memoirs, "Those best acquainted with the earnestness of purpose and the determination of the leading men who had persuaded themselves that the safety of the Republic depended upon the destruction of Johnson's official power, knew that the closest watch would be kept upon every action of the President, and if an apparently justifying cause could be found the project of his removal would be vigorously renewed." Within a month, the radicals found their issue.

Johnson had long wanted to rid himself of Secretary of War Edwin M. Stanton. Stanton was a close ally of the radical Republicans. After repeatedly trying to get him to resign, Johnson suspended him on Dec. 12, 1867. On Jan. 13, 1868, the Senate refused to concur, thus, under the terms of the Tenure of Office Act, reinstating Stanton.

Apparently flushed by his recent victory on the impeachment issue in the House, Johnson decided to force the issue. He dismissed Stanton on Feb. 21, citing the power and authority vested in him by the Constitution. In effect, he was declaring the Tenure of Office Act unconstitutional and refusing to abide by it.

This action enraged Congress, driving conservative Republicans into alliance with the radicals on impeachment. A House resolution on impeachment was immediately offered and was referred to the Committee on Reconstruction, headed by Rep. Thaddeus Stevens (R Pa. 1859-68; Whig 1849-53), one of the radical Republican leaders. The next day, Feb. 22, the committee reported a resolution favoring impeachment. The House vote, taken two days later, was 126 to 47 in favor, on a strict party-line basis.

TRIAL IN THE SENATE

The House took the next step of drawing up the specific articles of impeachment and appointing managers to present and argue the charges before the Senate. There were 11 articles in all, the main one concerning Johnson's removal of Stanton in contravention of the Tenure of Office Act.

Between the time of the House action and the beginning of the trial in the Senate, the conservative Republicans had time to reflect. One of the main objects of their reflection was fiery Ben Wade of Ohio. Wade was president pro tem of the Senate and, under the succession law then in effect, was next in line for the presidency. He was also one of the most radical of the radical Republicans, a hard-liner on southern reconstruction and a monetary expansionist—anathema to conservatives.

Another concern of both factions of Republicans was the upcoming national convention and presidential election. Conservatives were in favor of nominating Gen. Ulysses S. Grant, a hero in the North after the Civil War. They viewed him as the most likely candidate to win and were confident they could control him and keep him from adopting radical policies. Radicals were anxious to gain control of the presidency to prevent Grant's nomination and dictate the party's platform.

The trial started March 30, when one of the House managers made the opening argument. Although other charges were presented against the President, the House managers relied mainly on Johnson's removal of Stanton as a direct violation of the Tenure of Office Act. One of the House managers revealed the bitter emotions prevailing at the time when he said, "The world in after times will read the history of the administration of Andrew Johnson as an illustration of the depth to which political and official perfidy can descend."

By May 11, the Senate was ready to ballot. The first vote was taken on the 11th article, which was a summary of many of the charges set forth in some of the preceding articles. The result was 35 guilty, 19 not guilty. If one vote had switched, the necessary two-thirds would have been reached. Seven Republican senators joined the 12 Democrats in supporting the President.

After the first vote, the Senate adjourned as a court of impeachment until May 26. When they reconvened on that date, two more ballots were taken, on the second and third articles of impeachment. The results were the same as on the first ballot, 35 to 19. The Senate then abandoned the remaining articles and adjourned as a court of impeachment.

UNCONSTITUTIONAL GROUNDS

The Tenure of Office Act was virtually repealed early in Grant's administration, once the Republicans had control of the appointing power, and was entirely repealed in 1887. And in 1926, the Supreme Court declared, "The power to remove...executive officers... is an incident of the power to appoint them, and is in its nature an executive power." (Myers vs. United States) The opinion, written by Chief Justice William Howard Taft, himself a former president, referred to the Tenure of Office Act and declared that it had been unconstitutional.

(Continued from p. 71)

Presidential Disability

In the crush of Watergate and Middle East events, the problem was hardly noticed. But a handful of legislative experts on Capitol Hill began quietly worrying about a particularly disturbing aspect of the vacancy in the vice presidency and the pressures President Nixon had been under.

The question: What would happen if Nixon were to become physically or mentally incapable of continuing his duties as President before Congress confirmed vice presidential nominee Gerald R. Ford? The answer, these experts said, was clear: until Ford was confirmed, there was no provision in the Constitution for removing the President from office on grounds of disability—even if he were to suffer a clearly disabling heart attack, stroke or other catastrophe.

"It could very easily be a hairy situation," said Karl O'Lessker, Sen. Birch Bayh's (D Ind.) legislative assistant. Bayh is chairman of the Senate Judiciary Constitutional Amendments Subcommittee, which helped draft the 25th Amendment dealing with presidential disability.

The chief counsel of the subcommittee, William J. Heckman, told Congressional Quarterly that the disability part of the amendment is "inoperative" in the absence of a vice president to take over as acting president. "Nothing could be done about it," Heckman said. "Essentially I suppose somebody at the White House would still issue instructions in (Nixon's) name."

The 25th Amendment was designed to make clear the mechanics of who could declare a president disabled. Once the determination had been made, the vice president would become the "acting president" until the period of disability ended. However, if there is no vice president to take over the job, the amendment cannot be invoked, Heckman said.

Would Speaker of the House Carl Albert (D Okla.), who under the laws of succession was next in line after the vice president for the presidency, step into the job? Not so long as the President remained alive, said Heckman—no matter what the degree of his disability. "It is clear in the legislative history (of the amendment) and in the Succession Act that Albert is not eligible to become the acting president," he said.

A dissenting view on this point came from Nicholas deB. Katzenbach, who was the acting attorney general when the 25th Amendment was being debated in Congress in 1965. Katzenbach said he believed that, in the absence of a vice president, the procedure would revert to the Succession Act and that Albert could become president in the event Nixon became disabled.

Katzenbach agreed that a less clear-cut case of presidential disability, in which a president refused to allow himself to be removed, could lead to a constitutional crisis that could dwarf those threatened by Watergate.

be in a better position if a new special prosecutor were appointed."

"The problem really is not, in my view, the problem of the real integrity or the courage or the determination of Mr. Petersen and those working with him to do this job," Richardson said. "The problem is one of public perception and public confidence.... These were the reasons why, in the first place, I believed that the special prosecutor should be appointed. And certainly I think that both problems remain and therefore point again to the same result."

There was no indication the White House would name a special prosecutor, but there were demands in Congress that one be appointed, either by Congress or by the courts.

Bork and Petersen pledged a vigorous, swift investigation. Bork said Oct. 24 that the White House had agreed on "regularized procedures" for turnover of evidence. He stopped short of saying he would go to court if necessary to get information, but said he would "go wherever we need to get the evidence."

Members of the special prosecutor's staff, now Justice Department employees, indicated they would resign in protest if real efforts did not continue to seek out all necessary information.

Ruckelshaus News Conference. Ruckelshaus said that since he was picked by Richardson to be his deputy, he felt bound by the same agreement regarding the special prosecutor, and when he was asked to violate it, he had no choice but to refuse. "These were not heroic acts" by Richardson and himself, he added. Since Bork

was not a party to the agreement, Ruckelshaus said, he urged Bork that "if he could find it in himself to comply (and fire Cox), it would probably be a good thing."

However, Ruckelshaus reiterated his belief that a special prosecutor is needed. He spoke at a news conference Oct. 23 at the National Press Club.

Like Richardson, Ruckelshaus said that in Cox's shoes, he would have done the same thing Cox did, and, also like Richardson, he declined to give his own judgment of whether Nixon should be impeached. That judgment was up to the American people, Ruckelshaus said.

William D. Ruckelshaus

On hearing just before the end of the news conference that the President had decided to comply with the court decision on the tapes, Ruckelshaus said, "I am very glad he has complied. I certainly applaud his action. It remains to be seen to what extent the investigation can be carried forward."

Cox's Reaction. Cox, on hearing of Nixon's actions Oct. 20, said: "Whether we shall continue to be a government of laws and not of men is now for Congress and ultimately the American people to decide." He appeared at the special prosecutor's office Oct. 23 for a farewell party given by his staff. On hearing of the President's decision to turn over the tapes, Cox said: "I know that all citizens will be as happy as I am that the President wisely chose to respect the rule of law."

References. *Impeachment background, Vol. I, p. 55; Drinan's impeachment resolution, Vol. I, p. 242; ACLU call for impeachment, p. 53; Cox biography, Vol. I, p. 96; tapes controversy, p. 57.*

Nixon's Reversal on Tapes

The dramatic announcement came quietly. "I am... authorized to say that the President of the United States would comply in all respects with the order of Aug. 29 as modified by the order of the court of appeals," said Charles Alan Wright, special White House counsel, standing stiffly before Judge John J. Sirica. That crisis had passed: no longer did the President stand in direct conflict with the federal courts.

That Aug. 29 order, issued by Sirica to President Nixon, directed that the taped recordings of specific presidential conversations—subpoenaed by the original grand jury investigating Watergate—be surrendered to Sirica. In order to ascertain whether the tapes were properly protected from disclosure to the grand jury by the President's claim of executive privilege, Sirica then would privately examine them. On Oct. 12, the court of appeals, District of Columbia circuit, upheld Sirica's order with modifications allowing the President to withhold any portions of the tapes which related to national security—and to have those specific claims of executive privilege examined individually. *(p. 57, 13)*

The effect of the order was delayed by the court of appeals until Oct. 19 in order that Nixon—who had repeatedly made clear his determination not to release the tapes—might appeal the ruling to the Supreme Court.

The week passed, and late on Friday evening, Oct. 19, no appeal had been filed. The Sirica order thus became effective. The President then announced his compromise—he would release to the grand jury and to the Senate Watergate Committee summaries of the tapes, validated and certified by Sen. John C. Stennis (D Miss.) as accurate and complete. Special Watergate prosecutor Archibald Cox rejected this compromise and was fired; his firing was followed by the resignations of Attorney General Elliot L. Richardson and Deputy Attorney General William Ruckelshaus. Public reaction to these weekend events was strongly hostile.

On Monday, Oct. 22, a summary of the compromise proposal was delivered to Sirica's court in preparation for a hearing during which Wright would try to convince Sirica to accept this as a satisfactory response to his order. A hearing was set for the following day.

Grand Jury Session. On the morning of Oct. 23 Sirica met in public session with the original Watergate grand jury and the newly convened additional grand jury investigating Watergate-related matters. He spoke to them, he said, in an effort to alleviate the anxiety concerning their role which might have developed as a result of the weekend's events.

"You are advised first," he said, "that the grand juries of which you serve remain operative and intact.... You are not dismissed and will not be dismissed except as provided by law upon the completion of your work or the conclusion of your term.... You may rely on the court to safeguard your rights and to preserve the integrity of your proceedings," he concluded.

Rodino's Career Highlights

Seniority is the force that suddenly put Rep. Peter W. Rodino Jr. (D N.J.) at the center of national attention and gave him a decisive role he had not played in 24 years of House service.

Rodino, a 63-year-old Newark lawyer, became chairman of the House Judiciary Committee in January 1973, succeeding Emanuel Celler (D N.Y. 1923-73), the Brooklyn Democrat who had chaired the committee for more than 20 years.

Rodino had not been personally associated with many major pieces of legislation, but he participated in most of the historic work done by Celler's Judiciary Committee over two decades. He was a key supporter of civil rights bills in 1957, 1964 and 1965, and floor manager of a 1966 bill. Rodino's speciality, however, was immigration. He chaired the subcommittee that deals largely with that topic, and he was at the center of the successful drive to liberalize immigration quotas in 1965.

Rep. Peter W. Rodino Jr.

Concern with immigration and with civil rights makes good political sense for Rodino, who has to win re-election in a district dominated by blacks and ethnics. An Italian-American, Rodino won the seat when members of his ethnic group were beginning to achieve political power in the area for the first time.

But Rodino's ethnic heritage and background in the ward politics of Newark led to frequent rumors of connection with organized crime. The late Angelo (Gyp) DeCarlo, a convicted extortionist, mentioned Rodino in a taped telephone conversation as a source of favors for DeCarlo and his friends. Rodino insisted he never knew DeCarlo. Herbert Stern, U.S. attorney for New Jersey and prosecutor of numerous gangland figures, said Rodino is "an honest man and a fine public servant."

Rodino's consistent support for civil rights legislation is also good politics in a district now more than 50 per cent black. But the growing black population of Newark has become a threat to his career, as each new election raises the possibility that a single black challenger and a unified black community could defeat him in a Democratic primary. Black opposition was split in 1972, and Rodino was renominated handily. Rodino has had little trouble in the heavily Democratic district since he was first elected in 1948.

Rodino was born June 7, 1909, in Newark. He graduated from Rutgers University Law School and ran for the House on his return from military service in 1946, nearly unseating Fred W. Hartley Jr. (R N.J. 1929-49). Hartley retired in 1949, and Rodino narrowly defeated another Italian-American for the seat.

Nixon's Change. The rusty machinery of impeachment, shaken loose by a surge of grassroots sentiment in favor of congressional action against the President, was beginning to move on Capitol Hill early in the afternoon of Oct. 23 even as Sirica's courtroom at the foot of that hill was filling with spectators. Law students, members of the press and interested citizens overflowed the room, expecting to hear Wright's arguments that the compromise was a satisfactory response to Sirica's order.

Without drama, the bespectacled Sirica began to read to the courtroom the pertinent documents: the Oct. 12 appeals court order; his original Aug. 29 order—already in effect—and the relevant sections of the appeals court opinion outlining the procedure which that court had approved.

When he completed the reading, Sirica asked: "Are counsel for the President prepared at this time to file with the court the response of the President to the modified order of the court?"

Rising from his chair and walking slowly to the podium facing Sirica, Wright began to speak. But instead of launching into an expected explanation of the President's compromise proposal, he said in a low voice: "I am not prepared at this time to file a response.

"I am, however, authorized," he continued, "to say that the President of the United States would comply in all respects with the order.... It will require some time... to put those materials together, to do the indexing, itemizing as the court of appeals calls for."

As if fearful that he had not heard correctly, Sirica asked: "As I understand your statement, that will be delivered to this court?"

"To the court *in camera* (in chambers)," replied Wright.

"You will follow the decisions or statements delineated by me," repeated Sirica.

Impeachment Resolutions

Of the 44 Watergate-related bills and resolutions introduced in the House Oct. 23 and 24, when Congress returned from the Veterans Day weekend, 22 called for the impeachment of the President or for an investigation of impeachment procedures.

Eighty-four representatives cosponsored legislation dealing with impeachment. All but one were Democrats. The one exception was Paul N. McCloskey Jr. (R Calif.).

Twelve bills and resolutions were introduced calling for the appointment of a special prosecutor. This legislation was sponsored by 94 Democratic representatives and four Republicans, Margaret M. Heckler (Mass.), Edward G. Biester Jr. (Pa.), Joseph M. McDade (Pa.) and H. John Heinz III (Pa.).

Earlier in 1973, before the Watergate tape recordings became an issue, four resolutions were introduced by 20 representatives calling for investigation or impeachment.

In the Senate Oct. 23, two bills were introduced dealing with the Watergate investigation, one by Sen. Lawton Chiles (D Fla.) and the other by Sen. Adlai E. Stevenson III (D Ill.).

"Will comply in all respects with what your honor has just read," said Wright. The previous day, he noted, the White House had filed a response "along different lines, along the lines indicated in the statement to the country on Friday. That statement...is now withdrawn."

Explaining the sudden decision to surrender the tapes and scuttle the compromise, Wright continued: "The President's statement on Friday was what we hoped would be a satisfactory method of accommodating the needs that led your honor and the court of appeals to rule as they did while minimizing the danger to confidentiality. We had hoped that that kind of solution would end a constitutional crisis." (Wright later told newsmen that he had left Washington on Saturday after the compromise was announced, thinking that his work for the White House was over.)

Referring to the public uproar arising from the President's decision to fire Cox, Wright continued: "The events of the weekend, I think, have made it very apparent that it would not (end the constitutional crisis). Even if I had been successful, as I hoped I would be in persuading you, Mr. Chief Judge, that this did adequately satisfy the spirit of the court of appeals ruling, there would be those who would have said that the President is defying the law.

"This President does not defy the law, and he has authorized me to say he will comply in full with the orders of the court."

"The court is very happy that the President has reached this decision," Sirica responded, asking for an approximate idea of the time when the tapes might actually be delivered to the court. Wright replied that he did not know the timetable, except to say that it would be done "as expeditiously as possible."

After thanking Wright, Sirica adjourned the hearing.

White House Briefing

The President's dramatic reversal of position on the Watergate tapes was the outgrowth of a miscalculation on the part of Nixon and his top advisers, two presidential aides told the press Oct. 23. According to Alexander M. Haig, the President's chief of staff, and Charles A. Wright, his special counsel, no one in the White House expected that the President's compromise on the tapes would lead to the dismissal of special prosecutor Archibald Cox and the resignations of Attorney General Elliot L. Richardson and Deputy Attorney General William Ruckelshaus, or to the "firestorm" of protest and demands for the President's impeachment.

"We all miscalculated Friday night (Oct. 19)," Wright said at a White House press conference two hours after he had announced in court that Nixon would comply with the judicial order to turn over the Watergate tapes. He said his own mood had been one of "euphoria" that the President apparently had averted a constitutional crisis with an "extraordinarily generous proposal" to turn over summaries of the tapes to the Senate Watergate committee after they were checked by Sen. John C. Stennis (D Miss.). As to the Justice Department shake-up, Haig said "it was not preplanned, not desired and probably not too well visualized on Friday morning by all of the participants."

Asked if the talk of impeachment in Congress had caused Nixon to change his mind about the tapes, Haig replied that it did not stem solely from the threat of impeachment, but from the "whole milieu" of concerns that arose over the weekend. The nation could not continue to be torn by the disruptive events of the last few days, he said, adding that he did not believe Congress would have impeached Nixon if he had not given in. When the confusion of the people, press and Congress had been cleared away and the truth had emerged, he said, impeachment would have died as an issue. Haig added that the President never considered resigning over the latest series of events.

Haig denied reports that the President's intent all along was to fire Cox because the special prosecutor's investigation was getting too broad. He admitted, however, that there was concern in the White House about the "political alignment" of Cox's staff and because it appeared to be "roaming" outside the special prosecutor's purview. While he specifically exempted Cox from criticism, he said there had been "occasions where we haven't been especially pleased" with the investigation.

Pending Investigations. Haig also said that the President would allow Cox's investigations of the ITT affair and the Howard Hughes-Charles (Bebe) Rebozo campaign contribution to continue under Justice Department auspices, but he declined to say whether Nixon would resist attempts to get presidential documents relating to those circumstances. The ITT matter concerned allegations that the Justice Department made a favorable antitrust settlement with International Telephone and Telegraph Corporation in exchange for a corporate contribution to the 1972 Republican national convention.

The Hughes-Rebozo matter concerned a reported $100,000 cash contribution after the 1968 campaign from millionaire industrialist Hughes which Rebozo, a close friend of the President, admitted keeping in a safe deposit box for three years before returning the money to Hughes. *(Story, p. 61)*

In answer to other questions, Haig said it was he who ordered FBI agents to seal Cox's offices after his firing. Haig explained that he had been given reports that some of Cox's staff were removing materials from their offices. Wright, asked why it was necessary to abolish Cox's office in addition to firing the special prosecutor, said "it made much more sense" to move the Watergate investigation into the institutional framework of the Justice Department.

Wright also was asked how people could believe in the President's assurances of a continued impartial investigation now that three highly respected legal officials had left in protest. "I don't see what the departures have to do with the credibility of the President," he replied.

The press conference began with Haig giving the White House's side of the events that led to the crisis weekend of Oct. 20-21. *(Richardson's and Cox's versions, p. 70)*

Unfolding Drama. Haig said the President decided on the weekend of Oct. 13 to make a "herculean effort" to resolve the tapes controversy. At that time the President had a choice of turning over the tapes to U.S. District Court Chief Judge John J. Sirica by midnight Oct. 19 or appealing an appellate court's decision upholding Sirica to the Supreme Court. *(Story, p. 57)*

Acting Attorney General Bork

Red-bearded Robert H. Bork does not look like a conservative member of the Nixon cabinet. He looks instead like the law professor he was until being tapped late in 1972 for the post of solicitor general, the third-ranking official in the Justice Department. From that spot, he rose Oct. 20 to become acting attorney general, the fourth man to head the Justice Department during the Nixon administration.

President Nixon chose Bork from the faculty of the Yale Law School to succeed Erwin N. Griswold, who retired as the nation's chief courtroom attorney at the end of the 1972-73 Supreme Court term. Bork assumed his new post late in June 1973, taking charge of all the cases which the government decides to

Robert H. Bork

appeal to the Supreme Court. Bork or members of his staff argue the government's cases before that court. Only three weeks before he moved up to head the department, Bork was formally introduced to the Supreme Court by then-Attorney General Elliot L. Richardson.

Bork's entry into government service marked the beginning of a third phase of his legal career. A graduate of the University of Chicago and that university's law school, Bork, a native of Pittsburgh, practiced law for eight years—until 1962. The last seven of those years were spent with one of Chicago's most well-known firms—Kirkland & Ellis—where he became a partner and enjoyed the benefits of a lucrative law practice.

At 35, however, Bork left the practice of law to accept a post on the Yale law faculty; three years later, in 1965, he became a full professor. His speciality was constitutional and antitrust law. After 10 years in that position, he received the President's nomination and moved on again, this time into government service. Bork had advised the Nixon administration earlier on its anti-busing policy and is generally considered a likely candidate for appointment to the Supreme Court, should another vacancy occur during the Nixon administration.

A skillful writer, Bork often expressed his opinions through articles published in various national magazines. Some of his strongest criticism has been directed at judicial activism—as evidenced in the work of the Supreme Court under the leadership of former Chief Justice Earl Warren: "We have also damaged law, and created disrespect for it, through our failure to observe the distinction, essential to a democracy, between judges and legislators. The era of the Warren Court was, in my opinion, deeply harmful to the prestige of law.... If that court did indeed inspire the young, it taught them to confuse the desirability of ends with the legitimacy of means, perhaps to confuse the idea of law and the fact of power," Bork wrote in late 1971.

Two factors led to Nixon's decision to resolve the issue, Haig related. One was the domestic "storm of controversy" that surrounded the issue and which would have "polarized the body politic" if the case had been appealed to the Supreme Court, he said. The other was "international implications of some gravity." He explained that any foreign leader, friend or foe, would note the disunity in America and make his calculations based on his perceptions of the strength and permanency of the Nixon administration.

"For these two reasons and no others" the President acted, Haig said.

Stennis was chosen as the go-between for four reasons, Haig said: he was a Democrat and a former judge, he had an impeccable reputation and no one was more highly qualified to assess the national security implications of the tapes. After getting Stennis' consent, Richardson was instructed to get Cox's agreement.

Haig said Richardson spent Oct. 15-18 trying to get Cox to agree to the compromise, but that it became apparent by the evening of Oct. 18 that Cox would not comply. Haig cited Cox's "strong desire" for access to documents and memorandums covering "private conversations of the President," in addition to the tapes.

That was not the kind of cooperation the White House expected from Cox, Haig stated, so efforts were made the evening of Oct. 19 to get the approval of Chairman Sam J. Ervin Jr. (D N.C.) of the Senate Watergate committee and Vice Chairman Howard H. Baker Jr. (R Tenn.). When Ervin and Baker agreed, "we set in train the chain of events that brought us to Saturday's firestorm," Haig said.

The President believed he was making an important concession in the national interest, Haig said, and he instructed Richardson to inform Cox that he was going through with his plan.

"We all assumed" Cox had three options, Haig said. He could have accepted the fact that he was receiving the information he wanted, he could have delayed his decision or resigned, or he could have rebutted and challenged the President.

When he took the latter course in a televised news conference Oct. 20, the President had no choice but to fire him, Haig stated.

Both Haig and Wright said they had not heard the tapes, but felt certain they would support the President's position that he knew nothing about the Watergate break-in or coverup.

Congressional Action

By the time most members of Congress returned Oct. 23 from their Veterans Day weekend holiday, the impeachment process had begun. Shortly before noon that day, House Speaker Carl Albert (D Okla.) told a crowded press briefing that he would refer all impeachment resolutions to the Judiciary Committee, headed by Peter W. Rodino Jr. (D N.J.).

Albert urged that the unity of the nation be kept in mind. "For the Congress to act in a reckless or hasty manner," he said, "would further engender disunity." Rodino, standing next to him at the briefing, promised that the impeachment controversy would not delay action on the nomination of Gerald R. Ford as vice president, which the Judiciary Committee was also considering.

Three hours later, the mood of Congress was changed somewhat by the announcement of the President's decision to surrender the tapes. But the plans to go ahead with a study of impeachment remained intact. A spokesman for Rodino's committee said the committee would be "basically unaffected" by the President's reversal.

On Oct. 24, Albert followed up on his call for action on the Ford nomination by telling reporters that the Judiciary Committee should handle that first, before working on presidential impeachment. Committee leaders were saying, meanwhile, that if necessary it could do both at once.

For Albert, the issue of Ford's nomination was of more than casual significance. Without a vice president, the speaker was next in line for the presidency. If he pushed hard for impeachment, critics would charge that he was acting more out of ambition than out of principle.

Republican Reaction. Within minutes of Albert's Oct. 24 briefing, some Republicans were already talking of impeachment as a partisan power grab. "What they couldn't win by election, they're trying to do by other means," said Rep. Samuel L. Devine (R Ohio). "They're trying to create a Democratic government."

Those closer to Albert insisted, however, that the presidency was the last thing on the 65-year-old speaker's mind. There were reports that Albert had been so reluctant to appear ambitious that he refused even to send the impeachment resolutions to committee until other members of the leadership convinced him that national feeling required it.

"The speaker is conscious that he might by some remote degree become president," explained Rep. John J. McFall (D Calif.), the majority whip. "He wants it to be clear that he doesn't want to undermine or destroy anybody." McFall had urged Albert to press on with the impeachment study.

Another member of the leadership, Democratic caucus chairman Olin E. Teague (Texas), said that the Judiciary Committee would have to handle the Ford nomination carefully to avoid a negative reaction. "If we go too fast on Ford," Teague told Congressional Quarterly, "we'll be accused of rubber-stamping a colleague. If we go too slow, we'll be accused of trying to keep Carl Albert in succession. We want to do it right."

Senate Role. For the time being, the House was the focus of the fight. The Senate, ultimate jury in an impeachment case, had no constitutional role to play at the outset of the impeachment process. But there was some action.

The Senate Judiciary Committee met in closed session Oct. 24 and agreed to begin a public investigation of the firing of Cox. The former prosecutor himself was scheduled to appear before the committee in its first day of hearings, expected Oct. 28. The committee rejected arguments by Sen. Edward M. Kennedy (D Mass.) and other liberal Democrats to begin the hearings immediately. Action also was delayed on a resolution calling on the President to reinstate Cox. Republican leaders of the Senate urged the President Oct. 24 to appoint a new special prosecutor.

Justice's Petersen: Return of Veteran Investigator

With the abolition of the office of special prosecutor, supervision of the federal government' Watergate investigation reverted—at least temporarily—to Henry E. Petersen, the outspoken, frank and intense assistant attorney general in charge of the Justice Department's criminal division.

Petersen, a veteran of 22 years with the department, was in charge of the Watergate probe from the break-in June 17, 1972, until special prosecutor Archibald Cox was appointed in May 1973, an appointment that Petersen admittedly resented. Petersen's conduct of the investigation became the subject of controversy, however, when allegations surfaced that the investigation had been less than adequate. Petersen heatedly denied the charges in an appearance before the Senate Watergate panel Aug. 7. *(Vol. I, p. 261)*

Agnew Investigation. Barely two months later, Petersen's investigatory activities again became embroiled in a dramatic controversy—this time over the Justice Department's probe of alleged misconduct by then Vice President Spiro T. Agnew when Agnew was governor of Maryland. In an emotional speech Sept. 29, Agnew accused top Justice officials of attempting to destroy him with "malicious and outrageous" news leaks, and he charged that Petersen was attempting to rescue through an Agnew prosecution a reputation lost through "ineptness and blunder" in the Watergate and other cases.

Immediately thereafter, Attorney General Elliot L. Richardson countered with a statement praising Petersen as "a distinguished government lawyer who has had more than two decades of prosecutorial experience and

Henry E. Petersen

is greatly respected by his colleagues in law enforcement." And at a news conference Oct. 3, the President said he supported Petersen's handling of the investigation. *(p. 49)*

Tough Reputation. Before the Watergate scandal, Petersen had established a reputation with many of his colleagues as a courageous and tough criminal investigator. His appointment as assistant attorney general in charge of the criminal division in 1972 capped a long but steady climb up the bureaucratic ladder at the Justice Department.

Born March 26, 1921, in Philadelphia, Petersen served in the U.S. Marine Corps from 1942 to 1945. He attended Georgetown University from 1946 to 1947 and received his law degree from Columbus (now Catholic) University Law School, Washington, D.C., in 1951.

While still a student, Petersen was employed in 1947 as a clerk at the Federal Bureau of Investigation. He joined the Justice Department in 1951 as an attorney in the antitrust division, and in 1952 he joined the criminal division, where he served as chief of the organized crime and racketeering section from 1966 to 1969. During that period, he played a major role in creating the organized-crime strike forces, coordinating the efforts of various federal agencies to investigate organized crime.

When John N. Mitchell became attorney general in 1969, Petersen—although a Democrat—was promoted to positions normally reserved as political rewards. In rapid succession, Petersen was named deputy assistant attorney general, then acting assistant attorney general, then assistant attorney general in charge of the criminal division. Like Mitchell, Petersen was known to take a hard line on law-and-order issues. He once described Mitchell as "a man of high integrity and a tough prosecutor—he's such a refreshing breath of air after Ramsey Clark (former attorney general)."

As chief Watergate investigator, Petersen reported to then Attorney General Richard G. Kleindienst until Kleindienst disqualified himself from the case April 19.

The Senate hearings were expected to include testimony by Richardson and Ruckelshaus. James O. Eastland (D Miss.), the Judiciary Committee chairman, said he would favor calling both as witnesses.

Senate Watergate Committee

For the Senate select Watergate committee, the week was like a ride on a roller coaster. The committee's investigatory hopes rose to a peak Oct. 19 with a White House promise of access to summaries and transcripts of Watergate-related presidential tapes. But these hopes hit bottom Oct. 23 when the senators learned they would get nothing at all.

While the committee was disappointed that it would not receive the transcripts or summaries, the seven members appeared to be in agreement that the President had made a wise decision in obeying a court order to

release the tapes to the Watergate grand jury. As a result of the events, the committee canceled a scheduled meeting for Oct. 25, at which it would have voted on the President's offer. It was to meet instead on Oct. 29 or 30 to discuss future courses of action.

One route, according to Deputy Chief Counsel Rufus L. Edmisten, was for the committee to call for the testimony of the three officials who left the government in the wake of the tapes controversy: special prosecutor Archibald Cox, Attorney General Elliot L. Richardson and Deputy Attorney General William D. Ruckelshaus. This had been proposed by Committee Vice Chairman Howard H. Baker Jr. (R Tenn.) and was being considered by the staff, Edmisten told Congressional Quarterly. Another proposal reportedly being considered by the staff was to subpoena millionaire industrialist Howard Hughes and Charles G. (Bebe) Rebozo, a close friend of the President. Rebozo was reported to have accepted a cash contribution of $100,000 from Hughes in 1969 and 1970, and to have kept

(Continued on p. 81)

Administration Officials Who Have Quit or Been Fired

Archibald Cox, Elliot L. Richardson and William D. Ruckelshaus joined the list of Watergate-related departures from the Nixon administration on Oct. 20, when special prosecutor Cox was fired by President Nixon and Attorney General Richardson and his deputy, Ruckelshaus, resigned over the dismissal. At least five of Richardson's aides and four of Ruckelshaus' assistants resigned or announced they would do so, and more Justice Department officials were expected to step down as a result of Nixon's abolition of the special prosecutor's office.

Before the dramatic weekend events, at least 12 persons had resigned or been fired from government posts because of the Watergate scandals. They were, in chronological order in 1973:

• Dwight L. Chapin, Nixon's appointments secretary since 1969, resigned Feb. 28 to join United Air Lines as an executive after being named in press reports as a link to political saboteur Donald H. Segretti. In Senate testimony Oct. 3, Segretti confirmed that Chapin had hired him to play dirty tricks on Democrats in the 1972 presidential campaign. *(Segretti testimony, p. 43; Chapin profile, Vol. I, p. 38-39)*

• Jeb Stuart Magruder, who had served as deputy director of the Nixon re-election campaign, resigned as director of policy development in the Commerce Department on April 26. Testifying before the Senate Watergate committee June 14, Magruder admitted his involvement in the Watergate break-in and coverup and implicated other administration officials. He pleaded guilty Aug. 16 to a reduced one-count charge and promised to testify against others allegedly involved in the scandal. *(Senate testimony, p. 10)*

• L. Patrick Gray III resigned as acting FBI director April 27 after it was reported that he had destroyed documents belonging to convicted Watergate conspirator E. Howard Hunt at the orders of presidential aides. Gray confirmed the reports during his Aug. 3 and 6 testimony before the Senate Watergate committee. *(Testimony, Vol. I, p. 264, p. 22)*

• John W. Dean III resigned under fire as presidential counsel on April 30, saying he would not become a "scapegoat" in the Watergate case. Dean, who pleaded guilty Oct. 19 to one conspiracy count for his role in the coverup, was the only administration official to accuse President Nixon of involvement in the scandal. *(Box, p. 83)*

• John D. Ehrlichman, the President's chief domestic affairs adviser, resigned April 30. Ehrlichman denied any wrong-doing in testimony before the Senate committee July 24-27, but he was indicted Sept. 4 in connection with the 1971 burglary of the office of Daniel Ellsberg's psychiatrist. *(Indictment, p. 30; testimony, Vol. I, p. 212)*

• H. R. Haldeman, White House chief of staff who also resigned April 30, denied during Senate testimony July 30-Aug. 1, Dean's charges that he participated in the coverup. *(Testimony, Vol. I, p. 229; resignation, Vol. I, p. 24)*

• Richard G. Kleindienst, whose resignation as attorney general was announced by Nixon April 30 along with those of Dean, Ehrlichman and Haldeman, cited "close personal and professional associations" with others implicated in the scandal as his reason for leaving. *(Senate testimony, Vol. I, p. 254)*

• David R. Young, who had first joined the White House as an assistant on Henry A. Kissinger's National Security Council staff and later was transferred to the domestic council, resigned April 30. He was indicted Sept. 4 in connection with the Ellsberg break-in. *(Indictment, p. 30; profile, Vol. I, p. 52)*

• Gordon C. Strachan, former staff assistant to Haldeman, resigned April 30 as general counsel of the United States Information Agency. He told the Senate committee July 20 and 23 of his duties as liaison between Haldeman and the re-election committee. *(Testimony, Vol. I, p. 210; profile, Vol. I, p. 38)*

• Robert C. Odle Jr., former director of administration for the re-election committee, was fired from his consultant's job at the Agriculture Department May 7. He had been named by the General Accounting Office as one of several persons who handled "unrecorded" campaign funds. *(Senate testimony, Vol. I, p. 57)*

• Egil (Bud) Krogh Jr., who joined the White House staff in 1969 and became transportation under secretary in 1973, resigned May 9, taking "full responsibility" for the Ellsberg break-in. Krogh was indicted Sept. 4 for his role in that incident and again on Oct. 11 for lying during the initial Watergate investigation in 1972. *(Indictments, p. 50, 30; profile, Vol. I, p. 52)*

• John J. Caulfield, a retired New York City undercover policeman who had worked at the White House, resigned May 24 as assistant director for criminal enforcement in the Treasury Department's Bureau of Alcohol, Tobacco and Firearms. He told the Senate investigating committee May 22-23 that he had relayed an offer of executive clemency to conspirator James W. McCord Jr., under instructions from Dean.

• In addition to the government departures, Kenneth Rietz, director of the Republican National Committee's "new majority" campaign for the 1974 elections, resigned unexpectedly on April 24 to join a private business. News reports had linked Rietz with an effort to recruit campaign spies while he was running the Nixon youth campaign in 1972.

it in a safe deposit box for three years before returning the money to Hughes.

Committee Chief Counsel Samuel Dash told Congressional Quarterly the up and down events of the week changed nothing as far as the committee was concerned. The hearings would continue as scheduled. He added, however, that the committee might delve more deeply into the Watergate break-in and coverup because "I don't really have confidence that the Department of Justice can act independently under the President." He said the committee "felt comfortable" with Cox in charge of the government's investigation. The White House said Cox's probe would be carried on by the Justice Department.

At week's end, the committee was scheduled to resume its hearings Oct. 30 with further testimony into campaign "dirty tricks." (Previous testimony, p. 50)

Tape Disclosure Reaction. Baker and Committee Chairman Sam J. Ervin Jr. (D N.C.) expressed pleasure at the President's Oct. 23 decision to yield the tapes to the grand jury, even though it meant the deal with the committee was off. Baker said Nixon made "a tough decision that will spare the nation the agony and grief of a constitutional confrontation." At the same time he asked the White House to work out an arrangement that would allow "pertinent information" on the tapes to be given to the committee. According to a spokesman for the senator, Baker was, in effect, asking for the resurrection of the President's Oct. 19 offer.

Sen. Herman E. Talmadge (D Ga.) said the President's decision "should remove the cloud of doubt, suspicion and uncertainty" that hovered over his head for the last several months. Sen. Daniel K. Inouye (D Hawaii) said he hoped Nixon would follow up his latest tapes decision with the rehiring of Cox, Richardson and Ruckelshaus.

Inouye, speaking to the AFL-CIO convention Oct. 22, had called for Nixon's resignation. "Like many of you," he told the delegates, "I have sadly concluded that President Nixon can no longer effectively lead our nation." He added that Congress should consider impeaching the President if he refused to resign. Inouye, responding through a spokesman Oct. 25, told Congressional Quarterly he would retract his call for the resignation or impeachment of the President only if Nixon rehired Cox, Richardson and Ruckelshaus.

Sen. Lowell P. Weicker Jr. (R Conn.), who angrily rejected the President's original deal with the committee, told Congressional Quarterly after Nixon reversed himself on the tapes issue that he was "delighted the President has put himself on the same footing as all the rest of us" by obeying the court order. "It wouldn't have happened without the firings and resignations and the U.S. people's protests. They tried to float one out of the White House and it just didn't work," he said in reference to the Oct. 19 tapes proposal.

Court Action. On the legal front, the committee was continuing its court battle to get the tapes on its own. The committee filed a motion Oct. 23 in the U.S. Court of Appeals in Washington asking for an expedited appeal of the decision by U.S. District Court Chief Judge John J. Sirica rejecting the committee's subpoena to obtain the tapes. Sirica ruled Oct. 17 that he lacked jurisdiction to order the President to hand over the tapes to the committee. (Decision, p. 57)

Albert's Career Highlights

Rep. Carl Albert (D Okla.) has had a career of unbroken success in politics, but the presidency is one office he has made no effort to attain. With the vice presidency vacant and the President threatened with impeachment or forced resignation, his ascendency became a possibility—even if a remote one.

When Albert became speaker of the House in 1971, after the retirement of John W. McCormack (D Mass. 1928-71), it was the climax of 24 years in the House, not the prelude to anything. He won the speakership, as have most men in recent times, through patient service as majority whip and majority leader. When McCormack stepped down at age 79, there was little argument over the choice of Albert to succeed him.

Elected in 1946 to represent a southern-style farm district in southeastern Oklahoma, Albert worked hard during most of his early career to go along with national Democrats when possible but to pay his respects to the more conservative sentiments of the peanut farmers and coal miners of his district.

Albert's constituency adjoined the Texas district of the late Speaker Sam Rayburn (D Texas 1913-61), and Albert made his way in the House as

Rep. Carl Albert

a Rayburn protege. In 1954, Rayburn selected the Oklahoman for majority whip, thus beginning the climb up the leadership escalator.

As his seniority in Congress and his security in the district grew, Albert began to take more liberal positions. He voted against civil rights bills in 1956 and 1957, but for them in 1960 and 1964. He went along with the Taft-Hartley labor bill in 1947, but opposed the Landrum-Griffin bill of 1959.

The one field in which his views clashed with liberal Democratic thinking during the 1960s was foreign policy. Albert consistently supported Johnson administration Indochina policy. Not until 1972 did the speaker break with the Nixon administration to call for American withdrawal.

At the start of the 93rd Congress in 1973, Albert lent his support to efforts at reforming procedure in the House, and was largely responsible for the success of moves to modify the seniority system, limit secrecy in House committees and make major legislation easier to amend on the floor.

Albert was born May 10, 1908, on a farm near McAlester, Oklahoma. He went to the University of Oklahoma, won a Rhodes Scholarship, took a law degree in England and returned home to practice. Shortly after returning home from military service in 1946, he took advantage of an incumbent's retirement to win the first of 13 House terms.

Edmisten told CQ that an unfavorable ruling by the appellate court would result in the committee introducing legislation establishing its jurisdiction for the tapes. The President probably would veto it, he said, but he expressed confidence Congress would override the veto.

The President's Oct. 19 proposal to turn over summaries and transcripts of the tapes to the committee and the grand jury came as a complete surprise to Ervin and Baker. Each was out of town and had to return to Washington to meet with Nixon. There was speculation that the senators had been "used" by the President to fire Cox, the theory being that their acceptance of the proposal while Cox had rejected it made it easier for Nixon to isolate the special prosecutor and dismiss him.

But Edmisten, who is very close to Ervin, denied this. He said Ervin "felt he'd won a victory for the committee and the country." In any case, he added, Ervin and Baker had nothing to lose. The committee still could appeal Sirica's decision and had a chance to get the tapes themselves rather than White House summaries.

Dash, however, had a different view. He told CQ there probably was "never a good faith offer in the first place. After flying in Senators Baker and Ervin to the Oval Office it now appears to have been a basis of an offer to Cox, and Cox was fired," he said.

Weicker was the only member of the committee who publicly rejected the tapes offer outright. He issued a statement Oct. 20 calling it a compromise of investigative procedure. "Rather than appearing wise and honorable," he said, "last night's compromise looks like what it is—a deal between an evasive President and an easily diverted Congress. I am glad the special prosecutor had no part of it. I will have no part of it."

Interest Groups' Plans

Despite President Nixon's surprise decision to hand over the secret Watergate tape recordings to Judge John J. Sirica, a roster of influential pressure groups, which before Oct. 23 had called for the President's impeachment or condemned him for obstructing investigation of administration problems, stood steadfast on their public resolutions and statements.

Before the Oct. 23 tapes announcement, delegates attending the AFL-CIO's national convention in Florida voted to ask the President to resign, and to demand his impeachment if he did not, "in the interest of restoring a fully functioning government."

"Essentially the action of the convention will stand," an AFL-CIO official told Congressional Quarterly Oct. 24. The presidents of two other unions, the United Auto Workers and the United Mine Workers, renewed their appeals for Nixon to step aside.

On another crucial front, the president of the American Bar Association, who on Oct. 22 had urged Congress to re-establish the office of special prosecutor in the Watergate case, stated on the NBC "Today Show" Oct. 24 that the "people of America will never be satisfied with the Watergate investigation until there is an independent prosecutor."

And the board of directors of the American Civil Liberties Union stood behind an Oct. 4 resolution, adopted 10-1, demanding that the House begin impeachment proceedings.

Labor. Standing and cheering, delegates at the convention of the AFL-CIO, the nation's most powerful labor union, Oct. 22 approved a bluntly worded resolution calling for the President's resignation or impeachment.

Citing the dismissal of special prosecutor Archibald Cox, the resignations of Elliot L. Richardson and William D. Ruckelshaus, and the President's intransigence on the tape issue, the resolution asserted: "We believe the American people have had enough. More than enough."

The resolution, read by AFL-CIO President George Meany, who during the 1972 presidential campaign steered the union into a position of neutrality, called upon the President to resign "in the interest of restoring a fully functioning government, which this administration is too deeply in disarray to provide."

According to union officials, the resolution was to be distributed to every member of Congress, followed by the AFL-CIO's army of legislative lobbyists. "We don't just adopt these things just to hear the sound of our own voice," one AFL-CIO official was quoted as saying. "Our people will be up there on the Hill."

After the news broke on the tapes decision, Meany again called for the President's resignation or impeachment on the basis that Nixon suffered from "dangerous, emotional instability."

Jerry Wurf, president of the AFL-CIO affiliate the American Federation of State, County and Municipal Employees, said after the tape announcement that the President still must resign or be impeached. Nixon's action, he said, was one more illustration of the "frightening irresponsibility of this man."

United Mine Workers President Arnold Miller noted that Nixon should not be allowed to trade nine tape recordings for an end to the Watergate investigation. "He has lost the moral authority to lead the nation (and) should resign...." Miller said.

The Lawyers. In contrast to its usual cautious approach on public controversies, the American Bar Association (ABA) Oct. 22 urged Congress to re-establish the office of special prosecutor in the Watergate case and make him "absolutely independent of the direction and control of those whom he is investigating."

The ABA Oct. 24 stood by its plea that was endorsed by the group's 22-member board of governors. "The people of this country will never believe that justice has been done in the Watergate affair until an independent prosecutor is permitted to go into all aspects of the affair," ABA President Chesterfield Smith stated.

In the ABA's Oct. 22 statement, a strongly worded document, Smith charged: "By declaring an intention, and by taking overt action to abort the established processes of government," the President "has now instituted an intolerable assault upon the courts, our first line of defense against tyranny and arbitrary power."

Deans of 17 law schools signed a petition, to be sent to Congress as soon as other deans could be reached and their signatures obtained, asking Congress to create an independent Watergate prosecution office and to "consider the necessity" of impeaching President Nixon.

ACLU. The day after President Nixon decided to release the Watergate tapes, the American Civil Liberties

Union (ACLU), with a national membership of 200,000, ran a full-page ad in *The Washington Post* that was headlined: "Why it is necessary to impeach President Nixon. And how it can be done."

Unlike other pressure groups calling for the President to resign because of the tapes controversy and the dismissal of Cox, the ACLU listed six reasons "affecting civil liberties" that it said mandated impeachment. They were: "specific proved violations of the rights of political dissent, usurpation of congressional war-making powers, establishment of a personal secret police which committed crimes, attempted interference in the trial of Daniel Ellsberg, distortion of the system of justice and perversion of other federal agencies."

The organization planned to press for the President's resignation or impeachment by asking its members to lobby their representatives and by using the ACLU's Washington lobby apparatus to bring pressure on Congress. "We're putting all out for impeachment," an ACLU spokesman told CQ. "We're backpedaling on everything else."

Ripon Society. Calling for Congress to determine whether the President should be removed from office, the Ripon Society, a liberal Republican organization, stated that "more is at stake than the disposition of the President's tapes...." In April, the group said it urged President Nixon "to affirm the principle that the 'President is fully within the reach of the law and is bound by the Constitution and its underlying ethical precepts just as every other citizen.'" Congress, the Ripon Society urged, "must act now if that principle is to have any meaning."

Nader. Consumer advocate Ralph Nader and his Public Citizen Inc. filed suit in federal district court Oct. 23 challenging Cox's dismissal. The suit charged that Cox could not legally be fired by anyone but an attorney general confirmed by the Senate. Cox was dismissed by Solicitor General Robert H. Bork who was called in to serve as acting attorney general after Richardson and Ruckelshaus resigned.

Announcing the suit at an Oct. 22 news conference, Nader said that "what this most decisive obstruction of justice by Richard Nixon means is that every citizen in this land must strive to reclaim the rule of law which this tyrant has been destroying month by month, strand by strand."

Week's Watergate Chronology

Following is a day-to-day chronology of the week's events in the week ending Oct. 27. *(Earlier Oct. 18 events, p. 61):*

OCT. 18

White House Tapes. One day before the deadline for the White House to appeal the Oct. 12 ruling of the U.S. Court of Appeals that the President should turn over nine tape recordings to Judge Sirica, a White House spokesman revealed that Attorney General Richardson and Nixon's lawyers had been meeting to discuss the case. Justice Department sources reported that Richardson also had met twice during the week with special Watergate prosecutor Cox.

Dean Pleads Guilty

John W. Dean III, the former Nixon counsel who had become the only high administration official to accuse the President of complicity in the Watergate coverup, Oct. 19 ended a protracted struggle to escape prosecution. He pleaded guilty to a single felony count of conspiracy to obstruct justice and defraud the United States in connection with his own role in attempting to hide the truth about Watergate. *(Senate testimony, Vol. I, p. 151)*

The plea was part of a bargain struck with special prosecutor Archibald Cox, who was fired Oct. 20. Dean also agreed to testify for the prosecution in future trials of other White House officials who allegedly were involved in the scandal. For his part, Cox promised not to prosecute Dean for any other Watergate-related crimes. He reserved the right to prosecute for any future perjury.

In a statement released after his appearance before Chief U.S. District Court Judge John J. Sirica in Washington, D.C., Dean explained that he had abandoned attempts to win immunity from prosecution because he no longer feared becoming "the Watergate scapegoat." He had "excellent technical and procedural potentials of obtaining a dismissal or an acquittal," Dean said, "but given the nature of the coverup conspiracy and the importance of restoring public confidence in our governmental process, to have defeated the government on legal technicalities would have, indeed, been a shallow victory."

Dean was thought to be a potential key witness against such former administration leaders as John N. Mitchell, H. R. Haldeman and John D. Ehrlichman, and against the President himself, if criminal proceedings were ever brought against him.

Judge Sirica delayed sentencing until after Dean had held up his end of the agreement by testifying at trials. When sentenced, he would face a maximum of five years in prison and a $10,000 fine. The six overt acts cited in the charges against him indicated that Dean could have faced much more serious charges.

The six were subornation of perjury, giving and concealing evidence in a trial, offering clemency to defendants, paying to keep arrested men silent, asking for confidential FBI information and attempting to involve the CIA in obstruction of justice.

In his statement, Dean expressed his hope that "others involved will also come forward and accept responsibility for their complicity."

Two former Nixon re-election campaign officials, Jeb Stuart Magruder and Frederick C. LaRue, also had pleaded guilty to reduced charges and agreed to testify for the prosecution in future Watergate trials.

Mitchell-Stans Tapes Dispute. U.S. District Judge Lee P. Gagliardi, presiding over the impending trial of former Attorney General John N. Mitchell and former Commerce Secretary Maurice H. Stans in New York City on obstruction of justice and perjury charges, quashed a defense subpoena of White House tapes and documents, calling it "a fishing expedition." But the judge told government prosecutors they would have to provide the defense with any relevant information on their witnesses or risk dismissal of those witnesses. The ruling prompted speculation that former White House counsel John W. Dean III, who was to be an important prosecution witness at the trial, might be barred from testifying if the President refused to release certain tapes. *(Dean guilty plea, box, p. 83; earlier development, p. 61)*

Hughes-Rebozo Transaction. The $100,000 given to Nixon friend Charles G. Rebozo by billionaire Howard Hughes in 1969 and 1970 was collected for campaign purposes, White House spokesman Gerald L. Warren told reporters. Warren refused to say for which campaign the money was intended or whether Rebozo had been authorized to collect campaign funds. Rebozo reportedly told the Senate Watergate investigating committee that he had returned the money to Hughes in 1973. *(Earlier Warren statement, p. 61)*

Abplanalp Case. Special prosecutor Cox informed Rep. Bertram L. Podell (D N.Y.) that investigators had found "no evidence of improper conduct" in the Justice Department's veto of an antitrust investigation of the Precision Valve Corporation, a company owned by Nixon friend and contributor Robert H. Abplanalp. Podell had charged July 8 that the decision was a result of political pressure. He himself was indicted shortly afterward on conspiracy, perjury and bribery charges. *(Abplanalp loan, Vol. I, p. 271)*

OCT. 19

Nixon Tapes Proposal. Nixon released a statement saying he would not seek Supreme Court review of the Appeals Court ruling ordering him to release the disputed tapes. Instead, he offered to supply Judge Sirica and the Senate investigating committee with a statement of the contents of the Watergate-related tapes, which he would prepare. Sen. John C. Stennis (D Miss.) would be given full access to the tapes in order to verify the accuracy of the statement. The special prosecutor was to make "no further attempt...to subpoena still more tapes or other presidential papers of a similar nature."

Nixon said his proposal "would comply with the spirit" of the appeals court decision and would give Cox "the information he claims he needs for use in the grand jury." Cox explained in a response statement that he could not comply with the proposal because it would "defeat the fair administration of justice." *(Details, p. 69)*

Dean Plea. John W. Dean III, the former Nixon counsel whose Senate testimony implicated the President in the Watergate coverup, pleaded guilty to one count of conspiracy to obstruct justice for his role in the coverup. Dean agreed to testify for the prosecution at future trials of other alleged participants in the coverup. In return, Cox promised not to prosecute him for any other Watergate-related crimes.

Andreas Violation. Cox filed charges in U.S. District Court in Minneapolis, Minn., against the First Interoceanic Corporation and its chairman, Dwayne O. Andreas, for illegally contributing $100,000 in corporate funds to Sen. Hubert H. Humphrey's 1968 presidential campaign. The special prosecution had been authorized to investigate only 1972 campaigns, but Attorney General Richardson made an exception in the case because the relevant statute of limitations was about to expire. *(Previous corporate violations, p. 61)*

OCT. 20

Cox Press Conference. Cox, at an afternoon press conference to explain his refusal to comply with Nixon's tapes proposal, said he had no intention of resigning and emphasized that only Richardson was authorized to fire him.

Dismissals, Resignation. White House press secretary Ronald L. Ziegler announced that Nixon had ordered Elliot L. Richardson to dismiss special prosecutor Archibald Cox, that Richardson had resigned rather than comply and that Nixon then had fired Deputy Attorney General William D. Ruckelshaus, who also refused the order. (Ruckelshaus said later he had resigned before being fired.) Ziegler explained that Solicitor General Robert H. Bork, next in line of authority at the Justice Department, had become acting attorney general and had fired Cox. *(Details, p. 70)*

Special Prosecution Office. Several hours after Ziegler's announcement, FBI agents sealed off the offices and files of the special prosecution team headed by Cox, as well as those of Richardson and Ruckelshaus. U.S. marshals replaced the FBI agents at the special prosecution offices the next day, and the guards were removed from the Justice Department offices.

OCT. 21

Laird, White House Position. Speaking on NBC-TV's "Meet the Press," presidential counselor Melvin R. Laird described Nixon's tapes proposal as a "very substantial" compromise and portrayed Cox as inflexible for refusing to agree to it. "You cannot set one individual up supreme to the Congress...or supreme to the executive branch," Laird said, referring to Cox. He said he thought Congress would reject attempts to impeach the President or to establish an independent special prosecutor to replace Cox—two ideas that had been suggested.

Special Prosecutor. After a day of speculation on the status of former special prosecutor Cox's 80-member staff, spokesman James S. Doyle announced that while they had no formal notification of their status, they intended to stay on the job if the Justice Department would allow them to.

OCT. 22

AFL-CIO Reaction. Nearly 900 delegates to the biennial convention of the AFL-CIO, meeting in Bal Harbour, Fla., approved a resolution of their executive council calling on President Nixon to resign and asking the House to begin impeachment proceedings if he refused to step down. *(Details, p. 82)*

Lawyers' Reaction. Chesterfield Smith, president of the American Bar Association, attacked Nixon's weekend actions as attempts to "abort the established processes of justice" and called on Congress to take "appropriate action" to counter them. The deans of 17 law schools signed a petition asking Congress to create a committee to "consider the necessity" of impeaching Nixon and to establish an independent special prosecutor to carry on the Watergate investigation. *(p. 82)*

Congressional Reaction. House Democratic leaders met in the office of Speaker Carl Albert (Okla.) and tentatively agreed to have the House Judiciary Committee begin an inquiry into the grounds for impeaching Nixon.

Watergate Prosecution. Acting Attorney General Bork announced that Henry E. Petersen, assistant attorney general in charge of the criminal division, would replace Cox as head of the Watergate investigation. *(Bork profile, box, p. 77; Petersen profile, box, p. 79)*

OCT. 23

Tapes Reversal. White House attorney Charles Alan Wright announced at a tense, crowded hearing in U.S. District Court that because of "the events of the weekend," Nixon had decided to abide by an appeals court ruling that he must turn over to the lower court tapes and other documents relating to the Watergate case. *(Details, p. 75)*

Committee Suit. Before the announcement of Nixon's reversal, the Senate Watergate investigating committee had filed a brief with the U.S. Court of Appeals asking for early action on its appeal of the district court ruling that the committee had no authority to sue for the White House tapes. After the tapes reversal was revealed, a White House spokesman announced cancellation of Nixon's agreement with the committee to hand over a statement of the tapes' contents as verified by Sen. John C. Stennis (D Miss.). *(Details, p. 79)*

News Conferences. Former Attorney General Richardson, holding a farewell news conference before an auditorium full of Justice Department employees, said he supported Cox's refusal to obey the President's order on the tapes dispute—and would have done the same thing himself. Former Deputy Attorney General Ruckelshaus also held a news conference to explain his reasons for refusing to fire Cox. *(Details, p. 71)*

Mitchell-Stans Trial. The trial of former Attorney General Mitchell and former Commerce Secretary Stans on perjury and obstruction of justice charges was postponed until Jan. 7, 1974, in order to give the prosecution time to resolve legal difficulties over certain White House tapes bearing on the case. According to a pretrial ruling, the trial could be dismissed if the prosecution could not give defense attorneys tapes and other documents relating to key prosecution witnesses.

Dairy Letter. A letter to Nixon promising a $2-million 1972 campaign contribution from a dairy industry group in return for action to curb dairy imports was leaked to the press. Signed by a representative of Associated Milk Producers Inc. of San Antonio, Texas, the letter was dated Dec. 16, 1970. Two weeks after that, Nixon imposed quotas on certain dairy products. The letter reportedly had fallen into the hands of Archibald Cox shortly before he was fired as special prosecutor. The dairy industry's financial support of Nixon's campaign had been linked previously to a 1971 increase in milk price supports.

Nixon Fund. ABC News reported that the Senate investigating committee and the Internal Revenue Service were looking into a report of a "private investment portfolio" set up for Nixon and administered by the bank owned by his friend Charles G. Rebozo. According to the network's sources, the fund was being probed to determine if it included political contributions for Nixon's personal use and if taxes were paid on it. Cox was said to have been informed about the fund hours before he was fired as special prosecutor.

OCT. 24

Bork Comments. In his first news conference since taking over the Justice Department, Acting Attorney General Robert H. Bork said he was prepared to take any necessary steps, including judicial action, to obtain any evidence he needed from the White House in prosecuting the Watergate case.

Congressional Reaction. Senate Republican Leader Hugh Scott (Pa.) relayed to the White House an appeal by Senate Republican leaders that Nixon restore public confidence in the Watergate investigation by naming a new special prosecutor. The leaders urged Assistant Attorney General Henry E. Petersen, who inherited the case, to press for quick indictments to assure the public that the investigation had not stopped. Rep. Peter W. Rodino Jr. (D N.J.), chairman of the House Judiciary Committee, announced that, in spite of the tapes reversal, the committee would proceed "full steam ahead" with an investigation of the grounds for impeaching Nixon.

Nixon Address. President Nixon canceled a scheduled television address to explain his actions in the White House tapes controversy and announced instead a news conference for the following night. That too was postponed the next day because of the Middle East crisis.

NIXON ORDER, RICHARDSON REPLY

Following are the texts of letters exchanged between President Nixon and Attorney General Elliot L. Richardson on Oct. 19 and 20 and released by Richardson on Oct. 23. In his letter Nixon instructs Richardson to direct the Watergate special prosecutor to cease all attempts to obtain presidential documents or tapes by the judicial process. Richardson responds that he cannot carry out the order. (Richardson resignation text, p. 87)

NIXON INSTRUCTION

October 19, 1973

Dear Elliot:

You are aware of the actions I am taking today to bring to an end the controversy over the so-called Watergate tapes and that I have reluctantly agreed to a limited breach of Presidential confidentiality in order that our country may be spared the agony of further indecision and litigation about those tapes at a time when we are confronted with other issues of much greater moment to the country and the world.

As a part of these actions, I am instructing you to direct special prosecutor Archibald Cox of the Watergate Special Prosecution Force that he is to make no further attempts by judicial process to obtain tapes, notes, or memoranda of Presidential conversations. I regret the necessity of intruding, to this very limited extent, on the independence that I promised you with regard to Watergate when I announced your appointment. This would not have been necessary if the Special Prosecutor had agreed to the very reasonable proposal you made to him this week.

Sincerely,

RICHARD NIXON

RICHARDSON RESPONSE

Dear Mr. President:

Thank you for your letter of October 19, 1973, instructing me to direct Mr. Cox that he is to make no further attempts by judicial process to obtain tapes, notes or memoranda of Presidential conversations.

As you point out, this instruction does intrude on the independence you promised me with regard to Watergate when you announced my appointment. And, of course, you have every right as President to withdraw or modify any understanding on which I hold office under you. The situation stands on a different footing, however, with respect to the role of the special prosecutor.

Acting on your instruction that if I should consider it appropriate, I would have the authority to name a special prosecutor, I announced a few days before my confirmation hearing began that I would, if confirmed, "appoint a special prosecutor and give him all the independence, authority, and staff support needed to carry out the tasks entrusted to him."

I added, "Although he will be in the Department of Justice and report to me—and only to me—he will be aware that his ultimate accountability is to the American people."

At many points throughout the nomination hearings, I reaffirmed my intention to assure the independence of the special prosecutor, and in my statement of his duties and responsibilities I specified that he would have "full authority" for "determining whether or not to contest the assertion of 'executive privilege' or any other testimonial privilege."

And while the special prosecutor can be removed from office for "extraordinary improprieties," his charter specifically states that "the Attorney General will not countermand or interfere with the special prosecutor's decisions or actions."

Quite obviously, therefore, the instruction contained in your letter of October 19 gives me serious difficulty. As you know, I regarded as reasonable and constructive the proposal to rely on Senator Stennis to prepare a verified record of the so-called Watergate tapes and I did my best to persuade Mr. Cox of the desirability of this solution of that issue.

I did not believe, however, that the price of access to the tapes in this manner should be the renunciation of any further attempt by him to resort to judicial process, and the proposal I submitted to him did not purport to deal with other tapes, notes, or memoranda of Presidential conversations.

In the circumstances I would hope that some further accommodation could be found along the following lines:

First, that an effort to be made to persuade Judge Sirica to accept for purposes of the grand jury the record of the Watergate tapes verified by Senator Stennis. In that event, Mr. Cox would, as he has, abide by Judge Sirica's decision.

Second, agreement should be sought with Mr. Cox not to press any outstanding subpoenas which are directed merely to notes or memoranda covering the same conversations that would have been furnished in full through the verified record.

Third, any future situation where Mr. Cox seeks judicial process to obtain the record of Presidential conversations would be approached on the basis of the precedent established with respect to the Watergate tapes. This would leave to be handled in this way only situations where a showing of compelling necessity comparable to that made with respect to the Watergate tapes had been made.

If you feel it would be useful to do so, I would welcome the opportunity to discuss this matter with you.

Respectfully,

ELLIOT L. RICHARDSON

RICHARDSON STATEMENT

Following is the text of a statement read by former Attorney General Elliot L. Richardson at the start of a news conference Oct. 23:

There can be no greater privilege and there is no greater satisfaction than the opportunity to serve one's country. I shall always be grateful to President Nixon for giving me that opportunity in several demanding positions.

Although I strongly believe in the general purposes and priorities of his administration, I have been compelled to conclude that I could better serve my country by resigning from public office than by continuing in it. This is true for two reasons:

(1) Because to continue would have forced me to refuse to carry out a direct order of the President.

(2) Because I did not agree with the decisions which brought about the necessity for the issuance of that order.

In order to make clear how this dilemma came about, I wish to set forth as plainly as I can the facts of the unfolding drama which came to a climax last Saturday afternoon. To begin, I shall go back to Monday of last week. Two courts—the District Court and the Court of Appeals of the District of Columbia—had ruled that the privilege protecting presidential communications must give way to the criminal process, but only to the extent that a compelling necessity had been shown. The President had a right of further review in the Supreme Court of the United States; he had a right, in other words, to try to persuade the Supreme Court that the long-term public interest in maintaining the confidentiality of presidential communications is more important than the public interest in the prosecution of a particular criminal case, especially where other evidence is available. Had he insisted on exercising that right, however, the issue would have been subject to continuing litigation and controversy for a prolonged additional period, and this at a time of acute international crisis.

Against this background, the President decided on Monday afternoon to make a new effort to resolve the impasse. He would ask Sen. John Stennis, a man of impeccable reputation for truthfulness and integrity, to listen to the tapes and verify the completeness and accuracy of a record of all pertinent portions. This record would then be available to the grand jury and for any other purpose for which it was needed. Believing, however, that only the issue of his own involvement justified any breach of the principle of confidentiality and wishing to avoid continuing litigation, he made it a condition of the offer to provide a verified record of the subpoenaed tapes that access to any other tapes or records would be barred.

I regarded the proposal to rely on Sen. Stennis for a verified record (for the sake of brevity I will call it "the Stennis proposal") as reasonable, but I did not think it should be tied to the foreclosure of the right of the special prosecutor to invoke judicial process in future cases. Accordingly, I outlined the Stennis proposal to Mr. Cox later on Monday afternoon and proposed that the question of other tapes and documents be deferred. Mr. Cox and I discussed the Stennis proposal again on Tuesday morning.

On Wednesday afternoon, responding to Mr. Cox's suggestion that he could deal more concretely with the proposal if he had something on paper, I sent him the document captioned "A Proposal," which he released in his Saturday press conference. On the afternoon of the next day he sent me his comments on the proposal, including the requirement that he have assured access to other tapes and documents. The President's lawyers regarded Mr. Cox's comments as amounting to a rejection of the Stennis proposal, and there followed the break-off of negotiations reflected in the correspondence with Charles Alan Wright released by Mr. Cox.

My position at that time was that Sen. Stennis' verified record of the tapes should nevertheless be presented to the district court for the court's determination of its adequacy to satisfy the subpoenas, still leaving other questions to be dealt with as they arose. That was still my view when at 8 p.m. Friday evening the President issued his statement directing Mr. Cox to make no further attempts by judicial process to obtain tapes, notes or memoranda of presidential conversations.

A half hour before this statement was issued, I received a letter from the President instructing me to give Mr. Cox this order. I did not act on the instruction, but instead, shortly after noon on Saturday, sent the President a letter restating my position. The President, however, decided to hold fast to the position announced the night before. When, therefore, Mr. Cox rejected that position and gave his objections to the Stennis proposal, as well as his reasons for insisting on assured access to other tapes and memoranda, the issue of presidential authority versus the independence and public accountability of the special prosecutor was squarely joined.

The President at that point thought he had no choice but to direct the attorney general to discharge Mr. Cox. And I, given my role in guaranteeing the independence of the special prosecutor, as well as my belief in the public interests embodied in that role, felt equally clear that I could not discharge him. And so I resigned.

At stake in the final analysis is the very integrity of the governmental processes I came to the Department of Justice to help restore. My own single most important commitment to this objective was my commitment to the independence of the special prosecutor. I could not be faithful to this commitment and also acquiesce in the curtailment of his authority. To say this, however, is not to charge the President with a failure to respect the claims of the investigative process: given the importance he attached to the principle of presidential confidentiality, he believed that his willingness to allow Sen. Stennis to verify the subpoenaed tapes fully met these claims.

The rest is for the American people to judge. On the fairness with which you do so may well rest the future well-being and security of our beloved country.   √

TEXTS OF OCT. 20 RESIGNATION STATEMENTS, LETTERS

Following are the White House text of press secretary Ronald L. Ziegler on Oct. 20 announcing the resignation or dismissal of Attorney General Eliot L. Richardson, Deputy Attorney General William D. Ruckelshaus and Watergate special prosecutor Archibald Cox and the texts of letters from Richardson to Nixon, Nixon to Richardson, Ruckelshaus to Nixon, Nixon to acting Attorney General Robert H. Bork and Bork to Cox. (Story, p. 69)

ZIEGLER STATEMENT

I know many of you are on deadline. I have a brief statement to give at this time, and following the reading of the statement we will have an exchange of a series of letters relating to action which President Nixon has taken tonight.

President Nixon has tonight discharged Archibald Cox, the Special Prosecutor in the Watergate case. The President took this action because of Mr. Cox's refusal to comply with instructions given Friday night through Attorney General Richardson that he was not to seek to invoke the judicial process further to compel production of recordings, notes or memoranda regarding private Presidential conversations.

Further, the office of the Watergate special prosecution force has been abolished as of approximately 8:00 p.m. tonight. Its function to investigate and prosecute those involved in the Watergate matter will be transferred back into the institutional framework of the Department of Justice, where it will be carried out with thoroughness and vigor.

In his statement Friday night, and in his decision not to seek Supreme Court review of the Court of Appeals decision with regard to the Watergate tapes, the President sought to avoid a constitutional confrontation by an action that would give the Grand Jury what it needs to proceed with its work with the least possible intrusion of Presidential privacy. That action taken by the President in the spirit of accommodation that has marked American constitutional history was accepted by responsible leaders in Congress and the country. Mr. Cox's refusal to proceed in the same spirit of accommodation, complete with his announced intention to defy instructions from the President and press for further confrontation at a time of serious world crisis, made it necessary for the President to discharge Mr. Cox and to return to the Department of Justice the task of prosecuting those who broke the law in connection with Watergate.

Before taking this action, the President met this evening with Attorney General Richardson. He met with Attorney General Richardson at about 4:45 today for about thirty minutes.

The Attorney General, on hearing of the President's decision, felt obliged to resign, since he believed the discharge of Professor Cox to be inconsistent with the conditions of his confirmation by the Senate.

As Deputy Attorney General, Mr. William Ruckelshaus, refused to carry out the President's explicit directive to discharge Mr. Cox. He, like Mr. Cox, has been discharged of further duties effective immediately.

We have available for you now the exchange of letters between Attorney General Richardson and the President and the other correspondence.

RICHARDSON RESIGNATION

October 20, 1973

The President
The White House

Dear Mr. President:

It is with deep regret that I have been obliged to conclude that circumstances leave me no alternative to the submission of my resignation as Attorney General of the United States.

At the time you appointed me, you gave me the authority to name a special prosecutor if I should consider it appropriate. A few days before my confirmation hearing began, I announced that I would, if confirmed, "appoint a special prosecutor and give him all the independence, authority, and staff support needed to carry out the tasks entrusted to him." I added, "Although he will be in the Department of Justice and report to me—and only to me—he will be aware that his ultimate accountability is to the American people."

At many points throughout the nomination hearings, I reaffirmed my intention to assure the independence of the special prosecutor, and in my statement of his duties and responsibilities, I specified that he would have "full authority" for "determining whether or not to contest the assertion of 'Executive Privilege' or any other testimonial privilege." And while the special prosecutor can be removed from office for "extraordinary improprieties," I also pledged that "The Attorney General will not countermand or interfere with the Special Prosecutor's decisions or actions."

While I fully respect the reasons that have led you to conclude that the Special Prosecutor must be discharged, I trust that you understand that I could not in the light of these firm and repeated commitments carry out your direction that this be done. In the circumstances, therefore, I feel that I have no choice but to resign.

In leaving your Administration, I take with me lasting gratitude for the opportunities you have given me to serve under your leadership in a number of important posts. It has been a privilege to share in your efforts to make the structure of world peace more stable and the structure of our own government more responsive. I believe profoundly in the rightness and importance of those efforts, and I trust that they will meet with increasing success in the remaining years of your Presidency.

Respectfully,

ELLIOT L. RICHARDSON

NIXON TO RICHARDSON

October 20, 1973

Dear Elliot:

It is with the deepest regret and with an understanding of the circumstances which brought you to your decision that I accept your resignation.

Sinerely,

RICHARD NIXON

Honorable Elliot L. Richardson
The Attorney General
Justice Department
Washington, D.C.

RUCKELSHAUS TO NIXON

Dear Mr. President,

It is with deep regret that I tender my resignation. During your Administration, you have honored me with four appointments—first in the Justice Department's Civil Division, then as administrator of the Environmental Protection Agency, next as acting director of the Federal Bureau of Investigation, and finally as Deputy Attorney General. I have found the challenge of working in the high levels of American Government an unforgettable and rewarding experience.

I shall always be grateful for your having given me the opportunity to serve the American people in this fashion.

I am, of course, sorry that my conscience will not permit me to carry out your instruction to discharge Archibald Cox. My disagreement with that action at this time is too fundamental to permit me to act otherwise.

I wish you every success during the remainder of your Administration.

Respectfully,
William D. Ruckelshaus

NIXON TO BORK

October 20, 1973

Dear Mr. Bork:

I have today accepted the resignations of Attorney General Richardson and Deputy Attorney General Ruckelshaus. In accordance with Title 28, Section 508(b) of the United States Code and of Title 28, Section 0.132(a) of the Code of Federal Regulations, it is now incumbent upon you to perform both the duties as Solicitor General, and duties of and act as Attorney General.

In his press conference today Special Prosecutor Archibald Cox made it apparent that he will not comply with the instruction I issued to him, through Attorney General Richardson, yesterday. Clearly the Government of the United States cannot function if employees of the Executive Branch are free to ignore in this fashion the instructions of the President. Accordingly, in your capacity of Acting Attorney General, I direct you to discharge Mr. Cox immediately and to take all steps necessary to return to the Department of Justice the functions now being performed by the Watergate Special Prosecution Force.

It is my expectation that the Department of Justice will continue with full vigor the investigations and prosecutions that had been entrusted to the Watergate Special Prosecution Force.

Sincerely,

RICHARD NIXON

Honorable Robert H. Bork
The Acting Attorney General
Justice Department
Washington, D.C.

BORK TO COX

October 20, 1973

Dear Mr. Cox:

As provided by Title 28, Section 508(b) of the United States Code and Title 28, Section 0.132(a) of the Code of Federal Regulations, I have today assumed the duties of Acting Attorney General.

In that capacity I am, as instructed by the President, discharging you, effective at once, from your position as Special Prosecutor, Watergate Special Prosecution Force.

Very truly yours,

ROBERT H. BORK
Acting Attorney General

Honorable Archibald Cox
Special Prosecutor
Watergate Special Prosecution Force
1425 K Street, N.W.
Washington, D.C.

TEXT OF NIXON'S OCT. 19 WATERGATE TAPES COMPROMISE

Following is the White House text of President Nixons's Oct. 19 statement announcing his decision not to appeal the Watergate tapes decision of the U.S. Court of Appeals and his compromise plan for revealing a summary of the tapes' contents:

For a number of months, there has been a strain imposed on the American people by the aftermath of Watergate, and the inquires into and court suits arising out of that incident. Increasing apprehension over the possibility of a constitutional confrontation in the tapes cases has become especially damaging.

Our Government, like our Nation, must remain strong and effective. What matters most, in this critical hour, is our ability to act—and to act in a way that enables us to control events, not to be paralyzed and overwhelmed by them. At home, the Watergate issue has taken on overtones of a partisan political contest. Concurrently, there are those in the international community who may be tempted by our Watergate-related difficulties at home to misread America's unity and resolve in meeting the challenges we confront abroad.

I have concluded that it is necessary to take decisive actions that will avoid any possibility of a constitutional crisis and that lay the groundwork upon which we can assure unity of purpose at home and end the temptation abroad to test our resolve.

It is with this awareness that I have considered the decision of the Court of Appeals for the District of Columbia. I am confident that the dissenting opinions, which are in accord with what until now has always been regarded as the law, would be sustained upon review by the Supreme Court. I have concluded, however, that it is not in the national interest to leave this matter unresolved for the period that might be required for a review by the highest court.

Throughout this week, the Attorney General, Elliot Richardson at my insistence, has been holding discussions with Special Prosecutor Archibald Cox, looking to the possibility of a compromise that would avoid the necessity of Supreme Court review. With the greatest reluctance, I have concluded that in this one instance I must permit a breach in the confidentiality that is so necessary to the conduct of the Presidency. Accordingly, the Attorney General made what he regarded as a reasonable proposal for compromise, and one that goes beyond what any President in history has offered. It was a proposal that would comply with the spirit of the decision of the Court of Appeals. It would have allowed justice to proceed undiverted, while maintaining the principle of an independent Executive Branch. It would have given the Special Prosecutor the information he claims he needs for use in the grand jury. It would also have resolved any lingering thought that the President himself might have been involved in a Watergate cover-up.

STENNIS CHOICE

The proposal was that, as quickly as the materials could be prepared, there would be submitted to Judge Sirica, through a statement prepared by me personally from the subpoenaed tapes, a full disclosure of everything contained in those tapes that has any bearing on Watergate. The authenticity of this summary would be assured by giving unlimited access to the tapes to a very distinguished man, highly respected by all elements in American life for his integrity, his fairness, and his patriotism, so that that man could satisfy himself that the statement prepared by me did indeed include fairly and accurately anything on the tapes that might be regarded as related to Watergate. In return, so that the constitutional tensions of Watergate would not be continued, it would be understood that there would be no further attempt by the Special Prosecutor to subpoena still more tapes or other Presidential papers of a similar nature.

I am pleased to be able to say that Chairman Sam Ervin and Vice Chairman Howard Baker of the Senate Select Committee have agreed to this procedure and that at their request, and mine, Senator John Stennis has consented to listen to every requested tape and verify that the statement I am preparing is full and accurate. Some may ask why, if I am willing to let Senator Stennis hear the tapes for this purpose, I am not willing merely to submit them to the court for inspection in private. I do so out of no lack of respect for Judge Sirica, in whose discretion and integrity I have the utmost confidence, but because to allow the tapes to be heard by one judge would create a precedent that would be available to 400 district judges. Further, it would create a precedent that Presidents are required to submit to judicial demands that purport to override Presidential determinations on requirements for confidentiality.

SPECIAL PROSECUTOR

To my regret, the Special Prosecutor rejected this proposal. Nevertheless, it is my judgment that in the present circumstances and existing international environment, it is in the overriding national interest that a constitutional confrontation on this issue be avoided. I have, therefore, instructed White House counsel not to seek Supreme Court review from the decision of the Court of Appeals. At the same time, I will voluntarily make available to Judge Sirica—and also to the Senate Select Committee—a statement of the Watergate-related portions of the tapes, prepared and authenticated in the fashion I have described.

I want to repeat that I have taken this step with the greatest reluctance, only to bring the issue of Watergate tapes to an end and to assure our full attention to more pressing business affecting the very security of the nation. Accordingly, though I have not wished to intrude upon the independence of the Special Prosecutor, I have felt it necessary to direct him, as an employee of the Executive Branch, to make no further attempts by judicial process to obtain tapes, notes, or memoranda of Presidential conversations. I believe that with the statement that will be provided to the court, any legitimate need of the Special Prosecutor is fully satisfied and that he can proceed to obtain indictments against those who may have committed any crimes. And I believe that by these actions I have taken today America will be spared the anguish of further indecision and litigation about tapes.

Our constitutional history reflects not only the language and inferences of that great document, but also the choices of clash and accommodation made by responsible leaders at critical moments. Under the Constitution it is the duty of the President to see that the laws of the Nation are faithfully executed. My actions today are in accordance with that duty, and in that spirit of accommodation. ✓

COX RESPONSE

Following is the Oct. 19 statement of Watergate special prosecutor Archibald Cox in response to President Nixon's compromise plan on the Watergate tapes:

In my judgment, the President is refusing to comply with the court decrees. A summary of the context of the tapes lacks the evidentiary value of the tapes themselves. No steps are being taken to turn over the important notes, memoranda and other documents that the court orders require. I shall bring these points to the attention of the court and abide by its decision.

The President's directions to make no further attempts by the judicial process to obtain tapes, notes or memoranda of presidential conversations will apply to all such matters in the future.

These directions would apply not only to the so-called Watergate investigation but all matters within my jurisdiction.

The instructions are in violation of the promises which the Attorney General made to the Senate when his nomination was confirmed. For me to comply to those instructions would violate my solemn pledge to the Senate and the country to invoke judicial process to challenge exaggerated claims of executive privilege. I shall not violate my promise.

Acceptance of these directions would also defeat the fair administration of criminal justice. It would deprive prosecutors of admissible evidence in prosecuting wrongdoers who abused high government office. It would also enable defendants to go free, by withholding material a judge ruled necessary to a fair trial. The President's action already threatens this result in the New York prosecution of John Mitchell and Maurice Stans. I cannot be a party to such an arrangement.

I shall have a more complete statement in the near future. ✓

TEXTS OF RICHARDSON COMPROMISE MEMORANDA

Following are texts of Oct. 17-19 memoranda exchanged between Attorney General Elliot L. Richardson, Watergate special prosecutor Archibald Cox and presidential attorney Charles Alan Wright concerning a possible compromise on access to the White House tapes. (Story, p. 69)

OCT. 17 RICHARDSON PROPOSAL

The Objective

The objective of this proposal is to provide a means of furnishing to the court and the grand jury a complete and accurate account of the content of the tapes subpoenaed by the special prosecutor insofar as the conversations recorded in those tapes in any way relate to the Watergate break-in and the cover-up of the break-in, to knowledge thereof on the part of anyone, and to perjury or the subornation of perjury with regard thereto.

The Means

The President would select an individual, the verifier, whose wide experience, strong character, and established reputation for veracity would provide a firm basis for the confidence that he would put above any other consideration his responsibility for the completeness and accuracy of the record.

Procedure

The subpoenaed tapes would be made available to the verifier for as long as he considered necessary. He would also be provided with a preliminary record consisting of a verbatim transcript of the tapes except (a) that it would omit continuous portions of substantial duration which clearly and in their entirety were not pertinent and (b) that it would be in the third person. Omissions would be indicated by a bracketed reference to their subject matter.

With the preliminary record in hand, the verifier would listen to the entire tapes, replay portions thereof as often as necessary, and, as he saw fit, make additions to the preliminary record. The verifier would be empowered to paraphrase language whose use in its original form would in his judgment be embarrassing to the President and to paraphrase or omit references to national defense or foreign relations matters whose disclosure he believed would do real harm. The verifier would take pains in any case where paraphrased language was used to make sure that the paraphrase did not alter the sense or emphasis of the recorded conversation. Where, despite repeated replaying and adjustments of volume, the verifier could not understand the recording, he would so indicate.

Having by this process converted the preliminary record into his own verified record, the verifier would attach to it a certificate attesting to its completeness and accuracy and to his faithful observance of the procedure set forth above.

Court Approval

Court approval of the proposed procedure would be sought at two stages: (a) In general terms when or soon after the verifier began his task, but without identifying him by name, and (b) when the verified record was delivered to the court with the verifier's certificate. At the second stage, the special prosecutor and counsel for the President would join in urging the court to accept the verified record as a full and accurate record of all pertinent portions of the tapes for all purposes for which access to those tapes might thereafter be sought by or on behalf of any person having standing to obtain such access.

Assurance Against Tampering

Submission of the verified record to the court would be accompanied by such affidavits with respect to the care and custody of the tapes as would help to establish that the tapes listened to by the verifier had not at any time been altered or abbreviated.

OCT. 18 COX RESPONSE TO RICHARDSON MEMO

The essential idea of establishing impartial but non-judicial means for providing the special prosecutor and grand jury with an accurate record of the content of the tapes without his participation is not unacceptable. A courtroom "victory" has no value per se. There should be no avoidable confrontation with the President, and I have not the slightest desire to embarrass him. Consequently, I am glad to sit down with anyone in order to work out a solution along this line if we can.

I set forth below brief notes on a number of points that strike me as highly important.

1. The public cannot be fairly asked to confide so difficult and responsible a task to any one man operating in secrecy, consulting only with the White House. Nor should we be put in the position of accepting any choice made unilaterally.

2. Your idea of tying a solution into court machinery is a good one. I would carry it farther so that any persons entrusted with this responsibility were named "special masters" at the beginning. This would involve publicity but I do not see how the necessary public confidence can be achieved without open announcement of any agreement and of the names of the special masters.

3. The stated objective of the proposal is too narrow. It should include providing evidence that in any way relates to other possible criminal activity under the jurisdiction of this office.

4. I do not understand the implications of saying that the "verbatim transcript...would be in the third person." I do assume that the names of all speakers, of all persons addressed by name or tone, and of all persons mentioned would be included. (The last is too broad. I mean to refer only to persons somehow under investigation.)

5. The three standards for omission probably have acceptable objectives, but they must be defined more narrowly and with greater particularity.

6. A "transcript" prepared in the manner projected might be enough for investigation by the special prosecutor and grand jury. If we accept such a "transcript" we would try to get it accepted by the courts (as you suggest). There must also be assurance, however, that if indictments are returned, if evidence concerning any of the nine conversations would, in our judgment, be important at the trial, and if the court will not accept our "transcript" then the evidence will be furnished to the prosecution in whatever form the trial court rules is necessary for admissibility (including as much of the original tape as the court requires). Similarly, if the court rules that a tape or any portion must be furnished a defendant or the case will be dismissed, then the tape must be supplied.

7. I am glad to see some provision for verifying the integrity of the tapes even though I reject all suggestions of tampering. Should we not go further to dispel cynicism and make provision for skilled electronic assistance in verifying the integrity of the tapes and to render intelligible, if at all possible, portions that appear inaudible or garbled?

8. We ought to have a chance to brief the special masters on our investigations, etc., so as to give them an adequate background. The special masters should be encouraged to ask the prosecutor for any relevant information. What about a request for reconsideration in the case of an evident mistake?

9. The narrow scope of the proposal is a grave defect, because it would not serve the function of a court decision in establishing the special prosecutor's entitlement to other evidence. We have long pending requests for many specific documents. The proposal also leaves half a lawsuit hanging (i.e., the subpoenaed papers). Some method of resolving these problems is required.

10. I am puzzled about the practical and political links between (a) our agreeing upon a proposal and (b) the demands of the Ervin committee.

11. The Watergate special prosecution force was established because of a widely felt need to create an independent office that would objectively and forthrightly pursue the prima facie showing of criminality by high Government officials. You appointed me, and I pledged that I would not be turned aside. Any solution I can accept must be such as to command conviction that I am adhering to that pledge.   A.C.

OCT. 18 LETTER FROM WRIGHT TO COX

Dear Mr. Cox:

This will confirm our telephone conversation of a few minutes ago.

The fundamental purpose of the very reasonable proposal that the Attorney General put to you, at the insistence of the President, was to provide a mechanism by which the President could voluntarily make available to you, in a form the integrity of which could not be challenged, the information that you have represented you needed to proceed with the grand jury in connection with nine specified meetings and telephone calls. This would have also put to rest any possible thought that the President might himself have been involved in the Watergate break-in or cover-up. The President was willing to permit this unprecedented intrusion into the confidentiality of his office in order that the country might be spared the anguish of further months of litigation and indecision about private Presidential papers and meetings.

We continue to believe that the proposal as put to you by the Attorney General is a reasonable one and that its acceptance in full would serve the national interest. Some of your comments go to matters of detail that we could talk about, but your comments 1, 2, 6 and 9, in particular depart so far from that proposal and the purpose for which it was made that we could not accede to them in any form.

If you think that there is any purpose in our talking further, my associates and I stand ready to do so. If not, we will have to follow the course of action that we think in the best interest of the country. I will call you at 10 A.M. to ascertain your views.

Sincerely,
Charles Alan Wright

OCT. 19 LETTER FROM COX TO WRIGHT

Dear Charlie:

Thank you for your letter confirming our telephone conversation last evening.

Your second paragraph referring to my comments 1, 2, 6, and 9 requires a little fleshing out although the meaning is clear in the light of our telephone conversation. You stated that there was no use in continuing conversations in an effort to reach a reasonable out-of-court accommodation unless I would agree categorically to four points.

Point One was that the tapes must be submitted to only one man operating in secrecy, and the President has already selected the only person in the country who would be acceptable to him.

Point Two was that the person named to provide an edited transcript of the tapes could not be named special master under a court order.

Point Three was that no portion of the tapes would be provided under any circumstances. This means that even if the edited transcript contained evidence of criminality important in convicting wrongdoers and even if the court were to rule that only the relevant portion of the original tapes would be admitted in evidence, still the portion would be withheld. It is also clear that, under your Point Three, the tapes would be withheld even if it meant dismissal of prosecutions against former Government officials who have betrayed the public trust.

Point Four was that I must categorically agree not to subpoena any other White House tape, paper, or document. This would mean that my ability to secure evidence bearing upon criminal wrongdoing by high White House officials would be left to the discretion of White House counsel. Judging from the difficulties we have had in the past receiving documents, memoranda, and other papers, we would have little hope of getting evidence in the future.

These points should be borne in mind in considering whether the proposal put before me is "very reasonable."

I have a strong desire to avoid any form of confrontation, but I could not conscientiously agree to your stipulations without unfaithfulness to the pledges which I gave the Senate prior to my appointment. It is enough to point out that the fourth stipulation would require me to forgo further legal challenge to claims of executive privilege. I categorically assured the Senate Judiciary Committee that I would challenge such claims so far as the law permitted. The Attorney General was confirmed on the strength of that assurance. I cannot break my promise now.

Sincerely,
Archibald Cox
Special Prosecutor

OCT. 19 LETTER FROM WRIGHT TO COX

Dear Archie:

This is in response to your letter of this date. It is my conclusion from that letter that further discussions between us seeking to resolve this matter by compromise would be futile, and that we will be forced to take the actions that the President deems appropriate in these circumstances. I do wish to clear up two points, however.

On what is referred to in your letter today as Point Three, that no portion of the tapes would be provided under any circumstances, the proposal of the Attorney General was simply silent. That would have been an issue for future negotiation when and if the occasion arose. Your comments of the 18th, however, would have required an advance commitment from us that we cannot make on an issue that we think would never arise.

In what you list as Point Four you describe my position as being that you "must categorically agree not to subpoena any other White House tape, paper, or document." When I indicated that the ninth of your comments of the 18th was unacceptable, I had in mind only what I referred to in my letter as "private Presidential papers and meetings," a category that I regard as much, much smaller than the great mass of White House documents with which the President has not personally been involved.

I note these points only in the interest of historical accuracy, in the unhappy event that our correspondence should see the light of day. As I read your comments of the 18th and your letter of the 19th, the differences between us remain so great that no purpose would be served by further discussion of what I continue to think was a "very reasonable"—indeed an unprecedentedly generous—proposal that the Attorney General put to you in an effort, in the national interest, to resolve our disputes by mutual agreement at a time when the country would be particularly well served by such agreement.

Sincerely,
Charles Alan Wright   ✓

APPOINTMENTS AND HEARINGS; TWO TAPES DO NOT EXIST

Congress, as if numbed by exposure to too many major, unexpected developments that could affect the course of the nation, appeared to look to the people for guidance on how far to assert itself to resolve a continuing crisis of confidence in the nation's leadership.

"I have passed the point of reacting," said House Speaker Carl Albert of the week's events. Other members of Congress said the situation boiled down to what the people of the country believed.

It was a week in which the administration attempted to repair damage to its Justice Department by filling two important vacancies but saw its credibility challenged when it reported two secret White House tape recordings did not exist. It also was a week in which Congress moved toward confirmation of a new vice president but saw its efforts to establish a special prosecutor's office slowed by wrangling. The major events:

• Senate and House Judiciary Committees began hearings on legislation to establish a special prosecutor with complete independence from the President and power to investigate and prosecute charges against the President, his staff and former aides. *(Senate hearings, p. 93, House hearings, p. 97)*

• Attorneys for the President announced that two of the nine tape recordings sought by ousted special prosecutor Archibald Cox and the U.S. District Court did not exist. *(this page)*

• President Nixon announced the nomination of Sen. William B. Saxbe (R Ohio) to become attorney general, succeeding Elliot L. Richardson, who resigned rather than fire Cox. *(Saxbe nomination and background, p. 109)*

• Acting Attorney General Robert H. Bork announced the selection of Texas attorney Leon Jaworski to become special prosecutor. *(p. 111)*

• The Senate Rules Committee began hearings on the vice presidential nomination of Gerald R. Ford.

• After a 20-day recess, the Senate Watergate Committee resumed its hearings with testimony from Democratic and Republican campaigners. *(p. 103)*

The Missing Tapes

Two of the long-sought tapes of presidential conversations related to the Watergate case did not exist, J. Fred Buzhardt, special White House counsel, told Judge John J. Sirica Oct. 31.

The two conversations which Buzhardt said were never recorded at all were the President's first conversation with Attorney General John N. Mitchell after the Watergate break-in and his meeting with John W. Dean III in which Dean said the subject of executive clemency for E. Howard Hunt was discussed.

The first conversation was by telephone on June 20, 1972; Buzhardt said that the President was using a telephone extension not connected to the automatic recording system, and hence the conversation was not recorded.

The meeting with Dean took place in the President's office in the Executive Office Building next door to the White House on April 15, 1973; Buzhardt said at first that this conversation was not recorded due to a malfunctioning of the system. On Nov. 1, the explanation was revised to say that a six-hour tape had run out before the conversation began.

Sirica had announced Oct. 30: "The White House will prepare as soon as possible an analysis of the materials which will be transmitted to the court together with the tapes and documents themselves." The announcement followed a lengthy meeting between Sirica, Buzhardt and two members of the Watergate prosecution force, Henry S. Ruth Jr. and Philip A. Lacovara.

All parties, Sirica said, agreed to procedures for submitting the tapes for him to examine privately and determine whether any part of them was protected from disclosure to the Watergate grand jury by the claim of executive privilege. The procedures were developed within the guidelines set forth by the appeals court ruling backing Sirica's initial order. *(p. 75, 57, 13)*

Sirica said that, before he examined the materials, he would hear arguments in a closed session on the various claims of privilege relevant to particular parts of the tapes. Then, he said, he would examine the tapes and other material and decide individually on each portion for which executive privilege was claimed. His rulings would be handed down one at a time, he said.

Another meeting was set by Sirica with Buzhardt, Ruth and Lacovara for the afternoon of Nov. 2. At that time, he indicated, a timetable for turning over the materials and for hearing arguments would be set up.

TESTIMONY

The early testimony focused on the April 15 conversation between Nixon and Dean. The tape was considered to be of vital importance in establishing the truth of Dean's charges at the Senate Watergate hearings that Nixon was personally aware of efforts to give executive clemency to Hunt, one of the seven men convicted in connection with the Watergate burglary. *(Contents of tapes, box, p. 96)*

Technical Malfunction. The first witness, Raymond C. Zumwalt, a security specialist with the Secret Service who oversaw the day-to-day operations of the taping system until mid-1972, suggested that a six-hour reel of tape had run out before Nixon and Dean met late on April 15, a Sunday. A possible reason, in Zumwalt's opinion, was the failure of a timer that was automatically supposed to start another reel of tape when the first reel ran out.

On Nov. 1, Buzhardt, however, gave a different version of what had happened when he said that no Secret Service agent had turned on the machinery to switch the tape to another reel. The reason, he suggested, was that

Shuffling 'Presidential Papers'

White House officials often hindered his investigation by switching documents from one file to another and then contending they were "presidential papers" covered by executive privilege, former special prosecutor Archibald Cox told the Senate Judiciary Committee Oct. 29.

He said this was one of the reasons he refused to agree not to press claims against executive privilege, one of the factors in the firing of Cox as special prosecutor. In some instances, Cox said, presidential papers turned out to be "papers taken from one file and put into another to make them harder to get."

As one example, Cox read a section of a memorandum of an interview with "a member of the White House staff" whom he declined to identify.

"X also explained that immediately after Y testified before the Senate Watergate Committee, Y indicated to X that the Senate was going to subpoena Y's political files. X consulted with Mr. Buzhardt, who determined, to avoid subpoena problems, all of Y's political files should be deposited in the President's files. That day X combed his files and deposited the relevant material in the President's files."

Cox did not identify either X or Y. J. Fred Buzhardt Jr. is a special counsel to the President on loan to the White House from the Defense Department to assist in Watergate-related matters.

Cox also told the senators that files of Egil Krogh Jr., a former under secretary of transportation and, before that, head of the secret White House "plumbers" unit, had been taken from the files of that department and transferred to the White House.

they had not anticipated there would be so much conversation in the taped offices during a weekend.

Other questioning raised the possibility that there might have been another segment of the April 15 tape. Richard Ben-Veniste, assistant public prosecutor, showed Zumwalt a box of tape, covering the April 13-16 period, that was marked "Part 1." He asked him if such a marking did not indicate that there must have been a "Part 2." Zumwalt gave no explanation for the marking.

Zumwalt testified that his assistant, James Baker, had advised him of several malfunctions of the taping system, but that neither he nor Baker had knowledge of the April 15 breakdown. Zumwalt conceded he could not "directly recall" any other malfunction. He said the equipment had been checked daily, Monday through Friday.

Zumwalt, who answered questions with much deliberation and volunteered little information, testified that a tape covering the period between April 11 to April 16, 1973, had been checked out of a heavily guarded storage room in the Executive Office Building July 11 to Stephen B. Bull, a presidential assistant. The tape was returned July 12.

Bull, testifying in district court on Nov. 2, made a new disclosure: Nixon had discovered, Bull said, that the two tapes were missing on Sept. 29, nearly a month before the White House publicly said they did not exist.

On Oct. 23, 25 days after Nixon's reported discovery, the President's attorneys had appeared before Sirica and agreed to make available the nine recordings that had been denied previously. *(p. 75)*

Other Tapes Removed. Zumwalt's logs showed that 22 tapes, covering a period in late February and March of 1973, had been given to Bull April 25 and returned the same day. Bull checked out the same 22 tapes the following day and returned them May 2, 1973. Twenty-six tapes were checked out by Bull June 4 and returned at some unrecorded date, Zumwalt said.

On June 25, Zumwalt testified, he personally delivered tapes of telephone conversations between Feb. 28 and March 22, 1973, to Buzhardt. He said his recollection was hazy, but that, while he was present, he heard a discussion between Nixon and Dean on the tapes. On July 11, Bull received six tapes, including the controversial April 15 tape.

CONGRESSIONAL REACTION

Members of Congress reacted skeptically to Buzhardt's revelation about the two tapes.

Rep. Harley O. Staggers (D W.Va.), asked, "Who's going to believe that?"

Rep. John E. Moss (D Calif.) said, "Coincidences, coincidences, coincidences. It may be true, but it is regrettable that one even has to question a president's statement."

Rep. John B. Anderson (R Ill.), chairman of the House Republican Conference, said, "My deepest concern is with the credibility of the White House reduced to a minimum level, the American public might not accept this explanation."

Rep. Philip E. Ruppe (R Mich.) had a milder reaction. "It has to depend on whether Judge Sirica is willing to accept the explanation," he said. "If he refuses to accept the explanation, the whole question of the President's credibility comes back again. If he accepts it, that should cut the damage and be the end of it."

Sen. James L. Buckley (Cons-R N.Y.), stated, "As of this moment, President Nixon has the clear burden of satisfying the American people that he has been speaking the truth. If he fails in this, then we are faced with a political crisis of the most profoundly disturbing proportions."

Sen. Mark O. Hatfield (R Ore.) said the revelation that "the very tapes that have been fought over to the brink of a constitutional confrontation" don't exist "dramatically escalates the problem of this administration's credibility."

Sen. Hubert H. Humphrey (D Minn.) called the development incredible and said, "Surely, the President and his counsel must have known the situation on these tapes during all of the discussions with the court and with the Senate committee. The public is fed up with this sort of business."

Senate Minority Leader Hugh Scott (R Pa.) gave the President kinder treatment. "This machine age isn't always perfect," he said.

Senate Judiciary Hearings

Strong support in the Senate to establish a special prosecutor's office with complete independence from the President was sidetracked—at least temporarily—

by charges and countercharges over the improper leaking of confidential information to newspapers. Harvard Law Professor Archibald Cox, fired as special prosecutor after he refused to desist from additional attempts to secure documents from the White House, told the Senate Judiciary Committee that the "only complete assurance" of independence would be through guarantees written into law.

Cox recommended that Congress pass legislation authorizing the 15-member U.S. District Court for the District of Columbia to appoint a prosecutor to handle all cases his office had been investigating. This approach varied only slightly from a bill cosponsored by a majority of the Senate.

Some Republican members of the committee attacked Cox as partisan, noting his work for Democrats and his anti-administration statements made before his appointment as prosecutor. Cox's position and that of his supporters was weakened by his admission that he had made what he called an "inexcusable" error in revealing to two Democratic senators information told him in confidence. The information was published by *The New York Times*. One of the two senators, Edward M. Kennedy (D Mass.), countered that the information also had been made available to the Justice Department and might have been leaked there.

LEGISLATION

Three bills were introduced in the Senate to establish an independent prosecutor's office.

The major one (S 2611) was cosponsored by 55 senators—47 Democrats and eight Republicans—led by Birch Bayh (D Ind.). Eight members of the 16-man Senate Judiciary Committee were among the sponsors.

The bill would direct the chief judge of the U.S. District Court for the District of Columbia to appoint a special prosecutor and deputy special prosecutor. The prosecutor would have the exclusive authority to investigate and prosecute:

• Offenses arising out of the entry into the Democratic National Committee offices at the Watergate building in June 1972.

• Other offenses arising out of the 1972 presidential election.

• Offenses alleged to have been committed by the President, presidential appointees or members of the White House staff.

• All other matters delegated to Cox by former Attorney General Elliot L. Richardson before Richardson resigned and Cox was fired.

The bill would give the special prosecutor power "to review all documentary evidence available from any source" and "to determine whether or not to contest the assertion of executive privilege or any other testimonial privilege."

The prosecutor would "receive appropriate national security clearance and review all evidence sought to be withheld on grounds of national security and if necessary contest in court, including where appropriate through participation in *in camera* (closed) proceedings, any claim of privilege or attempt to withhold evidence on grounds of national security."

Thurmond-Bayh Exchange

Normally the Senate and Senate committee hearings are models of courtesy and decorum, but occasionally senators display their feelings.

Such an event occurred Oct. 31 during a hearing of the Senate Judiciary Committee. Sen. Strom Thurmond (R S.C.) had finished some sharp cross-examination of former special prosecutor Archibald Cox; Sen. Birch Bayh (D Ind.) began his questioning with a reference to browbeating of witnesses.

"Is the senator saying I browbeat this witness?" demanded Thurmond.

"Yes," said Bayh with a small smile.

"The senator is making a very false, malicious statement," shot back Thurmond.

"But the senator (Thurmond) is within his rights; he can do anything he wishes," said Bayh.

"If you are impugning my motives, you have gotten below a snake and don't deserve to be a senator," said Thurmond, angrily.

"This is not the time and I hope the time never comes when the senator from Indiana responds in kind," said Bayh.

The hearing continued.

The prosecutor could be dismissed only by the chief judge of the U.S. District Court and only on grounds that he violated provisions of the act "or committed extraordinary improprieties.

"Neither the chief judge nor the President of the United States shall have any authority to direct, countermand, or interfere with any action taken by the special prosecutor...," the bill declared. "Neither the President of the United States, nor any other officer of the United States, shall have any authority to remove the special prosecutor from office."

Another bill (S 2603), introduced by Sen. Adlai E. Stevenson (D Ill.), contained many of the same provisions but would permit removal of the prosecutor only by impeachment.

A third bill was to be introduced by Sen. Robert Taft Jr. (R Ohio).

COX STATEMENT

Referring only to hand-written notes, Cox Oct. 29 gave the Senate Judiciary Committee his version of the events surrounding his hiring and firing as special prosecutor. When he accepted the post in May, Cox said, "there had been charges that high offices in the executive branch had been perverted" and used for illegal acts.

He said he took the job during a period of distrust in government "to prove if I could that the cynics were wrong and our institutions would work." There were four items of agreement under which he took the post, Cox said: (1) the special prosecutor would be independent of the President, his cabinet, the attorney general and his advisers; (2) the prosecutor would be "not only free to contest claims of executive privilege, but I pledged myself that I would press those claims"; (3) the prosecutor's office would be used "to establish innocence as well as guilt" because "I emphasized that charges were not proof"; (4) the prosecutor's responsibility would, as the guidelines made clear, not be limited "to Watergate and what has been called the coverup." The guidelines, he said, included investigation of evidence regarding charges against the President and his staff.

Characterizing the progress of each of three major phases of the inquiry, Cox said the Watergate investigation had been "pretty much complete three weeks ago" except for the guilty plea of former presidential attorney John W. Dean III, the examination of nine presidential tapes under subpoena and investigation of a memo "that seemed to contradict everything" an important figure had said. Cox did not identify the "important figure."

Also uncompleted, he said, were investigations into money said to have been paid by industrialist Howard Hughes to Charles G. Rebozo, a close friend of Nixon, and reports of what seemed to be large money-raising activities in 1969. In addition, Cox said, his office was investigating evidence of attempts to use the Internal Revenue Service for improper purposes, "the question of whether bugging was conducted for purposes of harassment," and various aspects of the settlement of an antitrust suit against the International Telephone and Telegraph Corporation.

Cox said he was dismissed because the President was apparently unwilling to allow him to pursue claims of executive privilege regarding White House tape records and documents and because he was unwilling to surrender the independence of the special prosecutor's office. On the first point, Cox said: "The tapes case had become sort of a test, and there were hanging fire many additional demands." On the second point, Cox said he considered White House demands that he not pursue access to some evidence "serious political interference" and that agreeing to the proposed "compromise" on the tapes and documents "would have had the aspects of a coverup."

He said a congressionally mandated special prosecutor's office should have "responsibilities and powers at least as great as that in the past," with "independent power to decide what matters to investigate and what matters not to investigate," and "the power to determine how far to pursue an investigation."

Independence was needed, he said, "to avoid divided loyalties," and so "witnesses will be assured that they will be protected." One of the reasons Dean decided to plead guilty, Cox said, was that Dean became convinced that the prosecutor's office would continue to press its investigations forward and not make him a scapegoat.

Cox said he had impressions that a number of people at the White House thought they could call Attorney General Richardson and Richardson would call Cox. But Cox said Richardson never put any improper pressure on him.

Another reason for independence, he said, was that "much of the evidence was in the White House." He disputed a statement by Alexander M. Haig Jr., the President's chief of staff, that the White House had furnished Cox with a full array of evidence. Cox

detailed requests for logs of conversations between the President and former administration officials and between various other officials. "For the most part, it seemed to me our efforts were very unsuccessful," he said. He noted that records regarding campaign contributions by milk producers were in the hands of the civil division of the Justice Department and said he had asked Richardson for them. He said Richardson claimed he saw no reason why the records should not be made available to Cox but needed to inform the White House of the request. "When he did tell them, he was forbidden to turn them over," Cox said.

Answers to Questions. Answering a question put to him by Sen. John L. McClellan (D Ark.), Cox said the "single most important factor by far that I understood (for his dismissal) was that I was being asked to forego judicial process to obtain evidence from the White House files."

He said he had no evidence to support "any of the rumors that I have seen in the papers" that he was on the trail of some new information that would be embarrassing to the President.

Under sharp questioning by Sen. Strom Thurmond (R S.C.), Cox conceded he might have said he had strong philosophical and ideological differences with the Nixon administration and would not take a position in the Justice Department under Nixon. He said he took part in President Kennedy's 1962 campaign, served as solicitor general during the Kennedy administration and was on the Muskie slate of delegates for the 1972 Democratic convention. "I was defeated," he said of the last effort. Cox denied participation in any anti-Nixon demonstration.

Responding to friendly questions from Sen. Edward M. Kennedy (D Mass.), Cox said that "most difficult decisions remained to be taken" in the investigations. Some phases of the campaign contribution investigations were "in difficult and critical stages" and some new information was just beginning to come to light, he said. The ITT investigation was three-fourths finished, but "very central questions remain of how far to pursue it, who should be indicted and what charges should be brought," Cox said. "It is clear that the job is nowhere near done."

ITT STORY

Cox's testimony on Oct. 30 was overshadowed by publication on the same day of a story in *The New York Times* about the ITT investigation. Quoting "sources close to the case," the Times said former Attorney General Richard G. Kleindienst had told the Watergate prosecution that Nixon personally ordered him not to press a series of antitrust actions against ITT. *(Kleindienst role, box, p. 100)*

The newspaper said Kleindienst received a telephone call in 1971 from John D. Ehrlichman, then the President's domestic affairs adviser, who asked that the Justice Department stop its appeal on the ITT case. Kleindienst, the story continued, told Ehrlichman he could not do this, because the appeal had been recommended by Richard W. McLaren, then head of the department's antitrust division, and approved by then Solicitor General Erwin N. Griswold. Ehrlichman hung up, and a short time later President Nixon called, and after calling Kleindienst a vulgar name, ordered that the appeal be halted, according to the paper's account.

(Continued on p. 97)

White House Tapes: What Cox Thought They Contained

President Nixon's surprise agreement to relinquish to the court nine tape recordings that had been sought by former special Watergate prosecutor Archibald Cox, compounded by the White House announcement Oct. 31 that two of the tapes—for June 20, 1972, and April 15, 1973—did not exist, refocused interest on what was thought to be on the tapes. Cox provided a summary of the conversations, along with his assessment of their importance to his case, in a memorandum filed in U.S. District Court in Washington Aug. 13. The memo supported his suit to compel the President to turn over the tapes to the Watergate grand jury. (Summary, Vol. I p. 273)

Following is a synopsis of the contents of the tapes, based on Cox's memo:

June 20, 1972, meeting of Nixon, H.R. Haldeman and John D. Ehrlichman. Three days after James W. McCord Jr. and his espionage team were apprehended inside the Watergate complex, the President met for over two hours with his two top assistants. Earlier in the day, Ehrlichman and Haldeman had met with John N. Mitchell, White House counsel John W. Dean III and Attorney General Richard G. Kleindienst at the White House.

The tape of the conversation "should show the extent of the knowledge of the illegal activity by the participants" at the meeting," or any effort to conceal the truth" from the President, the Cox memo said.

June 20, 1972, phone conversation between Nixon and Mitchell. Nixon talked with Mitchell, who was then his campaign manager, for four minutes in the evening after his meeting with Haldeman and Ehrlichman. According to Mitchell's Senate testimony, all he told Nixon was that the five men arrested were the only ones involved in the break-in. Nixon asked no questions and he volunteered nothing, Mitchell said.

"Evidence of this conversation with a man who had no public office at the time and was concerned solely with (the President's) political interests will either tend to confirm Mitchell's version or show a more candid report" to Nixon, the Cox memo said.

White House attorney J. Fred Buzhardt told U.S. District Judge John J. Sirica Oct. 31 that a few days earlier it had been discovered that no tape of this conversation existed because the phone used had not been hooked up to the White House recording system.

June 30, 1972, meeting of Nixon, Haldeman and Mitchell. One day before Mitchell announced his departure from the re-election committee for personal reasons, he met for an hour and 15 minutes with Nixon and Haldeman in the Executive Office Building. Mitchell testified that they discussed his impending resignation.

It "strains credibility to suppose that Watergate and how Watergate affected Mitchell and the campaign were not topics of conversation," Cox wrote.

Sept. 15, 1972, meeting of Nixon, Dean and Haldeman. The session took place in the Oval Office late on the day seven men were indicted for their roles in the Watergate break-in. According to Dean's version,

Nixon congratulated him on the "good job" he had done in keeping the investigation in bounds. Dean said he left the meeting "with the impression that the President was well aware" of the coverup operation.

Haldeman testified that Nixon never congratulated Dean on the coverup. "Resolution of this conflict between two of the three persons present and an accurate knowledge of plans or admissions made on this occasion would be of obvious aid to the grand jury's investigation," said the Cox memo.

March 13, 1973, meeting between Nixon and Dean, attended for a short time by Haldeman. The White House told the Senate investigating committee this meeting was concerned primarily with Watergate, and that Nixon had asked Dean for a report on possible involvement in the scandal of Haldeman and other White House officials. But Dean told the Senate committee that Nixon said he had approved an offer of executive clemency for break-in defendant E. Howard Hunt Jr. and that there would be "no problem" raising $1-million to keep the defendants silent.

"Confirmation of Dean's testimony would aid the grand jury in determining the existence, membership and scope of a coverup conspiracy," Cox concluded.

March 21, 1973, meeting of Nixon, Dean and Haldeman. All accounts agree that Dean, referring to the coverup, warned Nixon of a "cancer growing on the presidency."

March 21, 1973, second meeting of Nixon, Ehrlichman, Haldeman, Dean and White House press secretary Ronald L. Ziegler. Watergate-related matters were again discussed. Dean said he was sure after the meeting that his warnings about the coverup would not be heeded. Evidence of the meeting would help determine "the existence of a coverup, its thrust, and its membership," Cox wrote.

March 22, 1973, meeting of Nixon, Dean, Ehrlichman, Haldeman and Mitchell. The four former Nixon aides all testified that this conversation involved Watergate issues, such as how to handle the upcoming Senate hearings. Dean described it as a coverup strategy session.

"This meeting was apparently concerned, at least in major part, with political assessments and operations, not exclusively with establishing 'government' policy, and is likely to reveal the knowledge and motives of the participants," the Cox memo said.

April 15, 1973, meeting between Nixon and Dean. By the time this evening encounter between the President and his counsel took place, Dean had concluded that his colleagues at the White House were attempting to set him up as the Watergate "scapegoat." According to his version of the meeting, Dean informed Nixon that he had gone to the U.S. attorney to tell what he knew of the coverup.

On Oct. 31, White House counsel Buzhardt announced that the discussion had not been recorded because the machine had malfunctioned.

Conflicting Court Opinions

As usual in any debate between lawyers, both sides in the discussion of whether it was appropriate for Congress to authorize Federal District Judge John J. Sirica to appoint a special Watergate prosecutor cited Supreme Court decisions to back up their points.

Former special prosecutor Archibald Cox told the Senate Judiciary Committee that he had become convinced that such a measure would be appropriate after reading a 93-year-old decision, *Ex Parte Siebold.* In that case, the Supreme Court upheld a federal law that made it a crime to interfere with supervisors appointed by federal courts to oversee state elections. Speaking of the power of Congress to oversee state law enforcement, the court said: "Content to leave the laws as they are, it (Congress) is not content with the means provided for their enforcement. It provides additional means for that purpose; and we think it is entirely within its constitutional power to do so."

Cox said that if the Supreme Court had upheld the appointment of federal election supervisors, it seemed to him that it would also uphold the court's appointment of a special prosecutor, since the prosecutor would perform much more of a judicial function than election supervisors. Some state constitutions, he noted, authorized the state supreme court to appoint the state attorney general.

On the other side, arguing for the President's unfettered right to hire and fire executive branch employees, Sen. Hugh Scott (R Pa.) cited the 1926 ruling of the Supreme Court *(Myers v. United States)* that it was unconstitutional for Congress to limit the right of the President to remove any executive official from office. The Tenure of Office Act, enacted in 1867, forbade the President to remove any civil officers appointed with the consent of the Senate without the approval of the Senate. In the 1926 majority opinion, Chief Justice William Howard Taft, who had himself served as president, declared that the act was unconstitutional and that "the power to remove...executive officers...is an incident of the power to appoint them, and is in its nature an executive power."

(Continued from p. 95)

Cox, in opening his testimony, said he had been "greatly upset" upon learning the previous afternoon that the Times planned to run the story and began speculating about where the information had come from. "When I woke up this morning I had this image in my mind that at times during the past few weeks I have spoken more freely than I had wished to my friends," Cox said. He said he placed a telephone call and confirmed that he told Senators Kennedy and Philip A. Hart (D Mich.) and two of their aides of the Kleindienst conversation. "In fact, I did break Attorney General Kleindienst's confidence," Cox said. "I feel very badly this morning."

Later testimony revealed that Cox had visited Kennedy's home in McLean, Va., Oct. 23 at the invitation of Hart.

The White House issued a statement Oct. 29 calling *The New York Times* story "an inexcusable breach of confidence" on the part of the staff of the former prosecutor.

The President's direction to Mr. Kleindienst was based on his belief that the...case represented a policy of the Justice Department with which he strongly disagreed, namely, that bigness per se was unlawful," the statement continued. "When the specific facts of the appeal were subsequently explained in greater detail, the President withdrew his objection and the appeal was prosecuted in exactly the form originally proposed."

In response to a question by Sen. James O. Eastland (D Miss.), Cox said he thought terms of the ITT settlement were "a perfectly good bargain from the government's point of view, and that's the opinion I get from most antitrust lawyers." Cox told reporters later that this judgment referred only to the "substantive" terms of the agreement. The two answers left open the possibility of prosecutions regarding events before the agreement or sworn statements made afterward.

Sen. Hugh Scott (R Pa.), who said he did not approve of the firing of Cox, said he was concerned with the innuendo connected with the story. He complained of stories that "...each day with clockwork regularity appear that have called for replies from the White House...since your staff remained and you departed."

Kennedy, Hart and their aides denied leaking the story to the Times.

In testimony Oct. 29, Cox—in response to questions by Kennedy—said he understood that his staff had briefed the Justice Department on the Kleindienst story and other aspects of the investigation Oct. 26. "So," said Kennedy, "the long trunk may lead to the Justice Department itself."

The Justice Department denied that it had leaked the story. The effect of the leaking dispute was to delay committee consideration of substantive issues regarding the establishment of a special prosecutor's office. The committee decided in executive session that it would take testimony from members of Cox's staff. Also scheduled to testify were Richardson and various legal authorities with views on the constitutionality of proposed legislation.

TESTIMONY ON BILLS NOV. 1

Senators Stevenson and Taft testified in favor of their special prosecution legislation. Taft's plan called for the attorney general to nominate an independent special prosecutor and deputy with the advice and consent of the Senate. The prosecutors could be removed from office by the attorney general, but there would be a 30-day period before the dismissal was final. Taft said this would give the President, the Congress and the people a 30-day period to consider or reconsider such action.

House Judiciary Hearings

Members of a House Judiciary subcommittee generally split along party lines in questioning witnesses during hearings Oct. 31 and Nov. 1 on legislation to establish a court-appointed Watergate special prosecutor who would be completely independent of the executive branch.

(Continued on p. 99)

Nixon and Richardson on Special Prosecutor's Role

The following excerpts from statements of President Nixon and former Attorney General Elliot Richardson show the evolution of Nixon's publicly stated concept of the special Watergate prosecutor's role.

April 30. In announcing Richardson's appointment in his April 30 televised address to the nation, Nixon said, "I have given him (Richardson) absolute authority to make all decisions bearing upon the prosecution of the Watergate case and related matters. I have instructed him that if he should consider it appropriate, he has the authority to name a special supervising prosecutor for matters arising out of the case.... I know that as attorney general, Elliot Richardson will be both fair and he will be fearless in pursuing this case wherever it leads. I am confident that with him in charge, justice will be done."

May 14. In testimony during his confirmation hearings May 14 before the Senate Judiciary Committee, Richardson said:

"...I think that the end to be sought is clear. That is that the special prosecutor must have a degree of authority and responsibility and independence, and staff resources that can, taken together, give confidence that he is going to be in a position to do this job (of investigating Watergate)....

"The special prosecutor would be my appointee, in this case an appointee who, although not technically confirmed by the Senate, would still have been the subject of full opportunity for the Senate to satisfy itself as to his qualifications. And if I were directed to fire him and I refused, and I would refuse in the absence of some overwhelming evidence of cause, then the President's only recourse would be to replace me.

"Now, again, these are things that in the present circumstances are so remotely possible as to be practically inconceivable."

May 18-19. Richardson named Archibald Cox special prosecutor on May 18 and, on May 19, issued guidelines for Cox's authority:

"...In exercising this authority, the special prosecutor will have the greatest degree of independence that is consistent with the attorney general's statutory accountability for all matters falling within the jurisdiction of the Department of Justice. The attorney general will not countermand or interfere with the special prosecutor's decisions or actions. The special prosecutor will determine whether and to what extent he will inform or consult with the attorney general about the conduct of his duties and responsibilities. The special prosecutor will not be removed from his duties except for extraordinary improprieties on his part."

May 22. On May 22, Nixon issued a 4,000-word statement denying any personal complicity in Watergate. *(Vol. I p. 79)*

In the conclusion of the statement, Nixon said: "With his (Richardson's) selection of Archibald Cox—who served both President Kennedy and President Johnson as solicitor general—as the special supervisory prosecutor for matters related to the case, Attorney General-designate Richardson has demonstrated his own determination to see the truth brought out. In this effort he has my full support.

"Considering the number of persons involved in this case whose testimony might be subject to a claim of executive privilege, I recognize that a clear definition of that claim has become central to the effort to arrive at the truth. Accordingly, executive privilege will not be invoked as to any testimony concerning possible criminal conduct or discussions of possible criminal conduct, in the matters presently under investigation, including the Watergate affair and the alleged coverup."

Oct. 19. But by the time Nixon reached what he termed a compromise on the release of the tapes Oct. 19, he had this to say: "Accordingly, though I have not wished to intrude upon the independence of the special prosecutor, I have felt it necessary to direct him, as an employee of the executive branch, to make no further attempts by judicial process to obtain tapes, notes or memoranda of presidential conversations." *(p. 89)*

That was the day Cox rejected the proposal.

Oct. 20. The following day, Oct. 20, Cox was fired and Richardson resigned.

In ordering the dismissal of Cox, Nixon said: "Clearly the government of the United States cannot function if employees of the executive branch are free to ignore in this fashion the instructions of the president." *(p. 88)*

Oct. 23. At a news conference, Oct. 23, Richardson said "...the issue of presidential authority versus the independence and public accountability of the special prosecutor was squarely joined." *(p. 87)*

Oct. 26. At his televised news conference Oct. 26, Nixon reviewed the events leading to his eventual decision to give the tapes to the court: "...we worked out what we thought was an acceptable compromise.... Under the circumstances, when he (Cox) rejected it and indicated that despite the approval of the attorney general, and, of course, of the President and and of the two major senators on the Ervin Committee, when he rejected the proposal, I had no choice but to dismiss him." *(p. 112)*

As for a successor to Cox, Nixon said: "The special prosecutor will have independence. He will have total cooperation from the executive branch, and he will have as a primary responsibility to bring this matter, which has so long concerned the American people, bring it to an expeditious conclusion, because we have to remember that under our Constitution it has always been held that justice delayed is justice denied...."

A few minutes later, he said:

"We will not provide presidential documents to a special prosecutor. We will provide, as we have in great numbers, all kinds of documents from the White House, but if it is a document involving a conversation with the President, I would have to stand on the principle of confidentiality."

Republicans sharply questioned the constitutionality of the proposal and the wisdom of moving too hastily in an area that lacked definitive legal precedents. Democrats acknowledged the constitutional questions the bill raised. But they almost uniformly stressed the importance of quick action on the bill in order to restore public confidence in the investigation of Watergate.

Members of both political parties on the Select Subcommittee on Reform of Criminal Laws agreed, however, that a new special prosecutor needed a higher degree of independence from the White House than that afforded the fired former Watergate special prosecutor, Archibald Cox.

"My hunch would be that something would be reported out," Rep. David W. Dennis (R Ind.) told Congressional Quarterly. "How soon is anyone's guess." Dennis acknowledged that the hearings seemed to be pointing toward a partisan test.

The Democrats would win a purely partisan vote, 5-4. The full Judiciary Committee had already split along party lines, 21-17, in two procedural votes Oct. 30 on subpoenaing documents and witnesses for both the impeachment inquiry of President Nixon and committee consideration of House Minority Leader Gerald R. Ford to be vice president.

CULVER BILL

Partisanship flared early in the hearings on the bill, H J Res 784, introduced Oct. 23 by Rep. John C. Culver (D Iowa) with 111 cosponsors, including four Republicans. More than 25 pieces of legislation dealing with authorizing a new special prosecutor had been introduced since Cox was fired, including a bill similar to Culver's introduced in the Senate by Birch Bayh (D Ind.). *(Senate hearings, p. 93)*

Rep. Wiley Mayne (R Iowa) told Culver, who was the first witness, that the speed with which his bill had been drawn up was "remarkable" and noted that the Democratic Study Group had helped Culver draft the bill. Mayne also pointedly questioned the political background of a legal expert who accompanied Culver at the witness table. "I think the country is entitled to know a little more about him," Mayne said, beyond the fact mentioned by Culver that at one time he had been a law clerk to the late Supreme Court Justice Felix Frankfurter.

Culver responded that his co-witness, Roland S. Homet Jr., had been a classmate of his in college and law school. Homet added that he was practicing law in the District of Columbia and acting as a legal consultant to Culver, and that he had served in various positions under both Democratic and Republican administrations—including the Nixon administration.

Observers took the polite but prickly exchange as a signal that subcommittee Republicans were alert for evidence of steamroller tactics on the part of the Democrats.

As originally introduced, Culver's bill would allow U.S. District Court Chief Judge John J. Sirica to appoint a special Watergate prosecutor who would not be subject to removal by the White House. However, during his testimony Culver said he would favor a slightly different approach to ensure that Sirica would not feel it necessary to disqualify himself from hearing Watergate cases on the basis of conflict of interest because of having appointed the prosecutor. Under the new approach endorsed by Culver, Sirica would be empowered to convene a three-judge panel, which would appoint the prosecutor.

Constitutionality Questioned. Republican members of the subcommittee questioned the constitutionality of allowing a court to appoint a prosecutor—who, they pointed out, would be an officer of the executive branch. Such legislation could violate the separation of powers doctrine, they said, and also raise the possibility that indictments or convictions obtained by the prosecutor might be overturned on those grounds. "If we come up with some scheme that is thrown out by the court, the average citizen is going to think we're a bunch of jackasses," Dennis said at one point.

A string of witnesses, including three law professors and Chesterfield Smith, president of the American Bar Association (ABA), asserted that the Constitution is flexible enough to allow the approach the bill would take.

Restoration of Confidence. "...Public confidence has been sapped" by Nixon's firing of Cox, Culver said, and it was up to Congress to step in and restore credibility in the government's investigation of Watergate. "It would be the clear preference of us all, I'm sure, not to legislate in this field, but rather to rely on a unity of purpose among the three branches of government. All of us who have approached the task before us are well aware that there are no absolutely settled constitutional dogmas or perfect precedents for the situation before us. But there has also never been such aroused, widespread expression of public concern that justice be done, or so powerful and spontaneous a public reaffirmation of commitment to our constitutional system of law."

Culver argued that the new special prosecutor should be "totally independent and free from control by the President, which further dictates an immunity from the President's removal power."

Legal Precedents. In his testimony and in a separate memorandum, Culver cited legal precedents calling for prosecutors to exercise independent discretion in their investigations and in their decisions whether or not to prosecute. The discretion should not be "one guided by political concerns and certainly not one controlled by or in the interests of a potential defendant," Culver said. He thereby became the first of several witnesses who raised the possibility that Nixon himself could eventually become the subject of criminal proceedings.

Another precedent Culver cited was the practice in a number of states of allowing court-appointed prosecutors. "...The supreme court of my state, Iowa, has said that it would be a 'burlesque upon the law' if crimes went unpunished for lack of power in the courts to appoint a special prosecutor," Culver said.

Still another precedent was an opinion by Supreme Court Justice Oliver Wendell Holmes in 1926, holding that Congress could "at any time take the appointment of even postmasters away from the President and 'transfer the power to other hands.'" In any case, Culver argued, the Constitution gave Congress the authority to create offices and to define their powers and functions.

Culver discounted an alternative to his bill that would allow the President to appoint a special prosecu-

(Continued on p. 101)

Nixon's Intercession in 1971 ITT Antitrust Ruling

An Oct. 30 *New York Times* article on the 1971 out-of-court settlement of an antitrust suit against the International Telephone and Telegraph Corporation (ITT), and White House reaction to the report, raised questions about previous administration explanations of the controversial case. The article quoted sources close to the Watergate prosecution team as saying that former Attorney General Richard G. Kleindienst had told prosecutors that in 1971 President Nixon personally ordered him to halt a Justice Department appeal of an antitrust ruling favorable to ITT. Kleindienst was then deputy attorney general.

The White House statement on the story acknowledged for the first time that the President had talked with Kleindienst about the suit, but denied that there was an attempt to obstruct it for political or other reasons. Kleindienst had told the Senate in 1972 that he was involved in the settlement, but was never pressured by the White House on how to conduct it.

Kleindienst, who resigned as attorney general April 30 because of what he described as "close personal and professional associations" with administration figures implicated in the Watergate scandal, testified about the ITT case during his lengthy confirmation hearings before the Senate Judiciary Committee in the spring of 1972.

The hearings explored allegations that the settlement, announced July 31, 1971, and considered favorable to the company was the result of a pledge made by ITT officials to contribute as much as $400,000 to help finance the Republican national convention, then scheduled for San Diego, Calif.

Throughout the hearings, Kleindienst denied suggestions that he had been pressured to come to terms with ITT. Responding to Sen. Birch Bayh on March 2, 1972, he said: "For me to say that no one in the White House with whom I might have talked would not have raised the ITT question, I would not be prepared to say that. So far as discussing with anybody on the staff of the White House what I was doing, what do you think I ought to do, what do you feel about it, what are your recommendations—no."

Again on March 8, Kleindienst insisted he had not been "interfered with by anybody at the White House" in his conduct of the case. "I was not importuned; I was not pressured; I was not directed," he said. Asked about the White House role once more on April 27, the day the committee voted to confirm him, Kleindienst said: "I would have had a vivid recollection if someone at the White House had called me up and said, 'Look, Kleindienst, this is the way we are going to handle that case.'...No such conversation occurred."

According to the Times account, however, Kleindienst told Watergate prosecutors he had received a call in 1971 from John D. Ehrlichman, then White House domestic affairs adviser, asking him to call off the Justice Department's appeal of the ITT case. Kleindienst refused. A short time later, the Times reported, he received a call from Nixon, informing him in blunt language that Ehrlichman's request was an order.

White House Response. In response to the story, the White House issued a reply confirming that Nixon had called Kleindienst to request that he hold off on appealing the ITT case to the Supreme Court, but putting the call in a different context. "The President's direction to Mr. Kleindienst was based on his belief that the Grinnell case (one of the companies in a proposed ITT merger plan) represented a policy of the Justice Department with which he strongly disagreed, namely, that bigness per se was unlawful. When the specific facts of the appeal were subsequently explained in greater detail, the President withdrew his objection and the appeal was prosecuted in exactly the form originally proposed," the statement said. (An appeal was filed May 17, 1971, after a month's delay. The settlement was announced in July.)

Kleindienst issued a statement Oct. 31 saying, "I did not perjure myself or give false information to the Senate Judiciary Committee" on the subject of White House pressure concerning the ITT case. But he acknowledged receiving the calls from Ehrlichman and Nixon ordering him to drop the government's appeal. "I sent word to the President that if he persisted in that direction, I would be compelled to submit my resignation," Kleindienst said.

Perjury Fear. The Times reported Nov. 1 that Kleindienst had told the special prosecutor of Nixon's call to him on the ITT case because he feared indictment on perjury charges. The Senate hearings on his nomination had ended inconclusively, and the Judiciary Committee voted to refer the hearing record to the Justice Department to determine whether any witness had committed perjury. On June 8, then Attorney General Elliot L. Richardson turned the investigation over to then special prosecutor Archibald Cox. Sen. Birch Bayh (D Ind.), a member of the Senate Judiciary Committee, asked Acting Attorney General Robert H. Bork Oct. 31 to expedite the inquiry into possible perjury by Kleindienst.

Colson Memo. The possibility that Nixon was personally involved in the ITT settlement was raised by a memorandum written March 30, 1972, by Charles W. Colson, then a special counsel to the President, to H.R. Haldeman, former White House chief of staff. The memo, made public Aug. 1 by the Senate Watergate investigating committee, discussed political strategies for dealing with the Kleindienst nomination hearings and warned of the existence of documents that could "directly involve the President" in the case. (*Memo text; Vol. I, p. 162*)

Nader Efforts. The Colson memo had prompted consumer advocate Ralph Nader and his associate, Reuben Robertson, to resume their effort, begun in 1971, to get the U.S. District Court in Hartford, Conn., to investigate possible criminal actions related to the ITT merger settlement. On Oct. 19 they filed a memorandum with the court asking the judge to look into "a pattern of massive and grossly improper political intrusions" in the settlement, which resulted in ITT's merger with the Hartford Fire Insurance Company.

tor and require that the choice be confirmed by the Senate, agreeing with Nixon that "it is inappropriate to have 'a suit filed by a special prosecutor within the executive branch against the President of the United States.'"

The remedy, Culver said, "is to take the special prosecutor out of the executive branch." Culver also referred to a position taken by Bayh in introducing his bill in the Senate: that "senatorial participation in the appointment and or removal process would 'have the unfortunate effect of injecting politics into an area which must be totally void of partisan consideration.'"

"I entirely agree with this observation," Culver told the subcommittee. "...Again, the answer is to take appointment functions away from the Senate."

Culver acknowledged that his bill might be challenged on constitutional grounds; but he maintained that it could withstand such challenges and urged that the subcommittee work closely with its Senate counterpart "to the end that we can not only report a bill out speedily but so that conference with the other body will be either unnecessary or very brief." He added, "Sometimes there is fear that Congress may merely respond to a transient mood, or hysteria, or a passing burst of public controversy. But in this instance we are asked to meet a much more fundamental and permanent constitutional responsibility."

"If you are not right (about the constitutionality of the bill), then we have a flawed system," Robert W. Kastenmeier (D Wis.) told Culver.

Hogan's Questioning. Some of the bluntest questioning of Culver came from Rep. Lawrence J. Hogan (R Md.). "I think we are in the possibly perilous situation of (being asked to) respond too quickly" to a heated issue, Hogan said. "And I share the fear...of setting up a fourth branch of government" in an independent prosecutor.

Hogan urged instead that the subcommittee look into reforming the grand jury system so that federal grand juries could hand down indictments without the approval of the prosecutor. Homet countered that it was only through Judge Sirica's action in the original Watergate trial, when he delayed sentencing of the defendants in order to encourage them to testify, that information about the Watergate break-in started to flow.

Hogan argued that a prosecutor working through normal Justice Department channels and with department resources would have a better chance of success in investigating Watergate. He also complained that he had not been given time to study the legal memorandum submitted by Culver. Culver jokingly observed that it was unusual for him to be criticized for acting too speedily. He said the memorandum had been prepared for the guidance of the subcommittee.

Precedence Question. In answer to a question posed by Subcommittee Chairman William L. Hungate (D Mo.), Culver said he thought a special prosecutor appointed under a congressional mandate would supersede a presidential appointment. ABA President Smith later noted that if the court, acting under a congressional mandate, were to appoint the same person the President appointed, the question of who would take precedence might be avoided.

Bayh Testimony. During his testimony, Bayh stressed the similarities between his bill and Culver's

and said there should be no problem in working out minor differences. "Any inference that (the proposal) is an attempt to take advantage of public opinion and shoot from the hip is wrong," Bayh said. He also cited endorsements of the proposal by law professors and several state bar associations, as well as that of the American Bar Association.

Bayh said Nixon had betrayed the assurances of former Attorney General Richardson during his Senate confirmation hearings that the White House would not intervene in Cox's activities. "Mr. Richardson was specifically asked whether the President would ever dismiss the special prosecutor, and he replied, 'It just will not happen,'" Bayh said. *(Nixon and Richardson statements, box, p. 98)*

"But it did happen," Bayh continued, "and we must learn from this experience. We cannot vest authority for investigating and prosecuting offenses in the executive branch in an individual or individuals who are agents of the executive branch and subject to dismissal by the President."

Bayh and most of the other witnesses emphasized that the new prosecutor should operate under a system that not only guaranteed justice, but also the appearance of justice, to restore public confidence. "It seems to me we are faced with a dilemma," Dennis told Bayh. "The prosecution of criminal laws is an executive function. Under this approach we would hand over an executive function to the judicial branch...." Dennis asserted that if, on the other hand, a system whereby a prosecutor would be appointed and confirmed by the senate did not work, the constitutional problem could be avoided and Congress could then resort to impeachment.

Bayh countered that Dennis should "read the agreements (set forth by Nixon and Richardson in the appointment of Cox) and then see what the average constituent is going to think about going down this same track again and again." If Congress did not pass the Culver-Bayh legislation, and if it thus acquiesced in the appointment of another special prosecutor subject to the President's dismissal, Bayh asserted, "it will be the fifth time that the Congress has permitted the executive branch to investigate itself on Watergate and related cases.

"In two of those instances, the persons charged with directing the investigations—Mr. Dean and Mr. Cox—were fired by the President. In the other two cases the persons charged with directing the investigations—Mr. Ehrlichman and Mr. Kleindienst—resigned. How, then, I ask, can we possibly expect to get speedy, thorough and unbiased administration of justice by going to this dry well one more time?"

Bayh referred to Cox's contention that evidence withheld from the prosecutor because of presidential claims of executive privilege could cause some Watergate defendants and potential defendants to go free because of lack of evidence. "...Without legislation such as that which you are considering, it is entirely possible that justice will never be achieved in the Watergate and a number of other cases," Bayh argued.

Smith Testimony. ABA President Smith, testifying Nov. 1, praised Nixon's appointment of Leon Jaworski as Cox's replacement. Jaworski served in 1971 and 1972 as president of the ABA. However, Smith said, the appointment of a qualified person to the job did not remove the basic problem of the independence of the office of special prosecutor. *(Jaworski profile, p. 111)*

Smith urged Congress to "create by legislation an independent office of special prosecutor," as called for in a resolution passed during an emergency meeting of the ABA board of governors in Chicago Oct. 27. "The President, in my judgment, violated basic principles of justice" by ordering Cox not to continue to seek White House documents, Smith said. He added that Nixon's actions "constituted a clear and present danger to our national way of life.... I reiterate my personal opinion that the gravity of the situation demands resolute action on the part of the Congress.... The President is not above the law.... I submit that our people will never feel that justice has been done in Watergate until such time as an independent prosecutor is permitted to go into all aspects of the matter without limitations imposed on him by those whom he is to investigate."

GRAND JURY EXTENSION

An extraordinary measure authorizing two six-month extensions of the life of the original Watergate grand jury was approved Oct. 30 by the House Judiciary Committee. The Criminal Justice Subcommittee had approved the bill (HR 10937) Oct. 29 after hearing testimony in its support from Henry S. Ruth and Philip A. Lacovara, members of the Watergate prosecution force.

The grand jury, convened on June 5, 1972, and assigned to the Watergate matter after its occurrence 12 days later, would, if it had had a normal life of no more than 18 months, have expired Dec. 4, 1973. The bill approved by the committee would allow the district court to extend the life of the grand jury for a six-month period after Dec. 4 and for another six-month period if the court found that the grand jury had not been able to complete its work during the first extension. The life of the grand jury was not to exceed 30 months.

The language of the bill was based on a title of the Organized Crime Control Act of 1970, an administration-backed bill, which authorized the creation of special grand juries with possible lives of up to 36 months.

The grand jury itself had requested this extension, said Lacovara when queried about the hardship which the extended term might inflict on the lives of the 23 grand jurors. "The jurors do not want to leave this work unfinished," he said. The extension was requested in mid-October by then Attorney General Elliot Richardson, and the bill was introduced by Judiciary Committee Chairman Peter W. Rodino Jr. (D N.J.).

The extension was necessary, Lacovara noted, "because of the time being consumed in litigating important constitutional issues involving the grand jury's subpoenaing of White House tapes and documents which the grand jury believes are highly important in its investigation." Surrender of the tapes did not remove the need for the extension, he said, because the examination of the tapes by Sirica under the procedures outlined by the appeals court could be quite time-consuming, delaying the date when the evidence would go to the grand jury.

Ruth told the committee that the special prosecution force, reconstituted in the Justice Department's criminal division, was intact, that there had been no resignations

Counteracting the Media

President Nixon asked his top aides 21 times in one month in 1969 to counter what he regarded as unfavorable press coverage, according to an internal White House memo made public Oct. 31. Senate Watergate committee member Lowell P. Weicker Jr. (R Conn.) said he was releasing the document to show "the type of thinking that was going on at the White House."

The memo, written by former presidential aide Jeb Stuart Magruder, argued that a "shotgunning" approach was not the best way "to get the media." Magruder recommended harassment of unfriendly news organizations by the Internal Revenue Service and the antitrust division of the Justice Department.

News of a concerted White House effort in late 1969 to offset media coverage followed a strong attack on the television networks by the President at his Oct. 26 news conference. "I have never heard such outrageous, vicious, distorted reporting in 27 years of public life," the President said. *(Text, p. 112)*

A log of presidential requests for action against the media from mid-September to mid-October 1969 was attached to the memo. During that period, the President asked aides to register complaints about coverage by all three commercial television networks, *Times, Newsweek* and *Life* magazines and political columnist Jack Anderson.

According to the log, some of the requests were general and others were directed toward particular reporters. In one request, the President asked Herbert G. Klein, then White House communications director, to "take appropriate action to counter the biased TV coverage of the Adm. (administration) over the summer."

But in another entry in the log, Nixon suggested that aides "take action to counter" a specific report by Dan Rather, CBS White House correspondent. Klein also was asked in one case to generate letters to *Newsweek* "mentioning the President's tremendous reception in Miss. (Mississippi) and (at) last Sat. Miami Dolphin football game."

According to a *New York Times* account of the content of the log entries, the President did not suggest any specific actions against individual reporters or news organizations. Weicker added that there was "no way to know" if Magruder's proposals for an alternate strategy were accepted.

or firings since that of Cox and that a "full, fair, and thorough" investigation was continuing.

Nixon on Watergate

During a sometimes stormy news conference Oct. 26, President Nixon lashed the press—particularly the television networks—for its coverage of his firing of Archibald Cox. Some observers said it was his bitterest attack on the news media since 1962, when, at his famous "last press conference," he assailed reporters covering his losing race for the California governorship.

Nixon characterized coverage of the Cox firing as "frantic, hysterical," and likened it to the reporting of his 1972 decision to bomb North Vietnam. "I have never heard or seen such outrageous, vicious, distorted reporting in 27 years of public life," Nixon complained to the newsmen and to a nationwide television audience. *(Other story, p. 112)*

At another point, a CBS reporter asked Nixon, "What is it about the television coverage of you in the past weeks and months that has so aroused your anger?" Smiling icily, Nixon replied, "Don't get the impression that you arouse my anger." After a moment of uncertain laughter among the reporters, Nixon added, "You see, one can only be angry with those he respects."

He returned to the question a few moments later, saying he was criticizing commentators but not reporters. Nixon answered one more question and then abruptly walked out, leaving some correspondents still on their feet and shouting for recognition.

New Prosecutor. Nixon defended his firing of Cox and announced that Acting Attorney General Robert H. Bork would appoint a replacement. However, the President said the new prosecutor would not be allowed to go to court to obtain evidence from Nixon's files.

"I would anticipate that that would not be necessary," the President said. "We will provide, as we have in great numbers, all kinds of documents from the White House, but if it is a document involving a conversation with the President, I would have to stand on the principle of confidentiality." But Nixon said he would provide summaries of information from such documents, as he had offered in the case of the White House Watergate tapes. Cox's refusal to accept this approach led to his firing on Oct. 20. *(p. 69)*

Nixon said he hoped the appointment of a new prosecutor would halt proceedings in Congress to establish a prosecutor's office by legislation. "The special prosecutor will have independence," he said. "He will have total cooperation from the executive branch. And he will have as his primary responsibility to bring this matter, which has so long concerned the American people—bring it to an expeditious conclusion.... It's time for those who are guilty to be prosecuted, and for those who are innocent to be cleared."

Cox Firing. Nixon outlined the compromise proposal under which the White House would have released summaries of the tapes, to be verified by Sen. John C. Stennis (D Miss.). "Under the circumstances, when (Cox) rejected (the proposal) and indicated that, despite the approval of the attorney general, and of course of the President, and of the two major senators from the Ervin Committee, when he rejected the proposal, I had no choice but to dismiss him," Nixon said. He added that the White House had cooperated with Cox and had "tried to work out in a cooperative way this matter of the production of the tapes. He seemed to be more interested in the issue than he was in the settlement."

The compromise proposal, Nixon said, was "a proper solution to a very aggravating and difficult problem."

Nixon praised former Attorney General Elliot L. Richardson and former Deputy Attorney General William D. Ruckelshaus, who both resigned as a result of the impasse, as "two fine public servants" and said he regretted losing them.

Rebozo. Nixon endorsed the handling by his long-time friend, C. G. (Bebe) Rebozo, of a $100,000 cash contribution from an emissary of billionaire Howard Hughes, saying Rebozo had exercised "very good judgment in doing what he did." The contribution, which was made in two parts during 1969 and 1970 and returned to Hughes in 1973, was being investigated by the Senate Watergate Committee and by Cox's special prosecution team before Nixon dissolved the team and fired Cox. In his first detailed public explanation of Rebozo's involvement, Nixon said Rebozo had received the money as a Nixon campaign contribution. Rebozo was prepared to turn it over to the 1972 campaign's finance chairman as soon as one was appointed, Nixon declared.

"In that interlude, after (Rebozo) received the contribution, and before the finance chairman was appointed, the Hughes company, as you all know, had an internal fight of massive proportions, and he felt that such a contribution to the campaign might prove embarrassing," the President said. He added that Rebozo's return of the entire amount intact after such a long time was "a pretty good indication that (Rebozo) is a totally honest man, which he is."

Nixon also complained that a network television commentator, later identified in the press as CBS' Walter Cronkite, had alluded during a broadcast to an unverified report that Rebozo was the administrator of a secret, private $1-million investment portfolio, without mentioning that the White House had denied the story. "....When a commentator takes a bit of news and then, with knowledge of what the facts are, distorts it viciously, I have no respect for that individual," Nixon said.

Watergate Witnesses Oct. 31

Berl Bernhard, Sen. Edmund S. Muskie's (D Maine) presidential campaign manager in 1972, testified before the Senate Watergate investigating committee Oct. 31 that Republican dirty tricks disrupted the senator's campaign strategy, created tensions within Muskie's staff and among the Democratic contenders and made it difficult for Muskie to raise money for his campaign. While emphasizing that the dirty tricks alone did not defeat Muskie in his bid for the Democratic nomination, Bernhard said they "took a toll." Bernhard, a lawyer, was the primary witness as the committee resumed hearings after a 20-day layoff. *(Earlier testimony, p. 50)*

He accused the Committee for the Re-election of the President, whose operatives admitted in earlier testimony that they helped sabotage the Democratic contenders, principally Muskie, through dirty tricks, of behaving like "cunning barbarians." *(Opening statement summary, p. 104)*

Muskie, Bernhard said, was an experienced politician who knew that "politics is a body-contact sport. What he did not expect was that it would be a sport where he and his Democratic competitors would play by certain elementary rules, while outsiders to the primaries would behave like cunning barbarians. Their lack of political ethics was matched only by their fear of a fair contest, and by the money at their disposal. The term 'dirty tricks' doesn't do justice to the slimy deceptions that characterized the CREP campaign."

Excerpts of Bernhard's Statement

Following are excerpts from the summary of the opening statement made by Berl Bernhard, presidential campaign manager for Sen. Edmund S. Muskie (D Maine) in 1972, before the Senate Watergate investigating committee on Oct. 31:

...You will have to appraise the impact. I have tried to give my view of that impact on our campaign. In my judgment, the unceasing events to unhorse Sen. Muskie took a toll. They took a toll in the form of diverting our resources, changing our schedules, altering our political approaches, and being thrown on the defensive.

They generated suspicion and animosity between the staffs of Democratic contenders. Internally, they resulted in demoralizing distrust, in erroneous accusations by me of my own staff members for what I believed were their indiscretions and even their treachery. This impeded a coordinated effort because, not knowing whom one could trust, fewer and fewer people were taken into the councils when it came to making decisions. These events certainly helped to undermine the image of Sen. Muskie by making him appear unable to adequately manage a staff which had been made to appear as sieve-like amateurs who couldn't keep a confidence. It also made him appear as a man who at times would not hesitate to take unfair advantage of his opponents.

Lastly, these events did not advance our ability to survive financially. Contributors raised questions about the loyalty of the staff and its apparent indiscretions and fumbling. No contributor wanted to see his money frittered away. So time and energy were consumed not only in securing funds to campaign, but also in explaining defensively our efforts to maintain security and efficiency.

There is a momentum in politics, and when it is with you, nothing is wrong. When it begins to ebb, everything goes wrong. If things were going wrong for perfectly legitimate political reasons, our problems were magnified by the efforts not of other Democrats but of members of the Republican Party who had no place in the Democratic primaries at all.

I would point out that there is nothing in the resolution establishing your committee that says this conduct is reprehensible only if it has decisive significance. It speaks rather of whether the object was "to disrupt, hinder, impede or sabotage" the campaign. Does anyone here doubt that this was the objective of the dirty tricks? If they were not successful, that's a comment on the ineptitude of the perpetrators, not their moral fibre. I am troubled by the moral viewpoint implicit in offering that line of reasoning as a defense. The doctrine that the end justifies the means is pernicious enough. The doctrine that the failure to attain the end justifies—or at least excuses—the means is terrifying....

One of the worst pieces of sabotage against Muskie, Bernhard testified, was the photocopying of major campaign advance and scheduling proposals for 1971-72. He said this was the "most vital document" of the campaign, and that therefore only two copies were made. But within a few days, he said, one copy disappeared. It was later found on the campaign copying machine, its staples removed apparently for easier copying, he said. "It takes little expertise to realize the importance of this document," Bernhard said. "It reflected our entire political strategy."

Berl Bernhard

Disruption of Muskie's campaign would have been facilitated with a copy of the schedule, he said, because "it stated where the senator was going, for what purposes (and) what states or conventions we might choose to consider lightly." In addition, he said the lifting of the document created internal staff suspicion that a spy was loose in the campaign and cost much time in trying to learn who the spy was.

Bernhard said that raw polling data disappeared twice from the desk of the campaign polling expert. In answer to questioning, Bernhard said that because of those and other leaks, "we began to run something in the nature of a police state" within the campaign. He said he felt he could not take chances with large, daily meetings. People on the staff resented that, he said. "I found it disruptive; it was unpleasant" to imply a lack of trust in people.

Sabotage Examples. Bernhard reviewed a number of examples of campaign sabotage directed at Muskie for which Donald H. Segretti, a California lawyer turned political saboteur, had accepted credit. Segretti pleaded guilty Oct. 1 to three counts of political sabotage. *(Segretti testimony, p. 43)*

Referring to posters that misstated Muskie's position on busing, a volatile issue in the Florida primary, Bernhard said that campaign workers tried to remove such posters, but it was "difficult to try to clarify and to explain his true position." Bernhard said a letter printed on Citizens for Muskie stationery accusing his opponents, Senators Henry M. Jackson (D Wash.) and Hubert H. Humphrey (D Minn.), of sexual misconduct, antagonized admirers of the two senators and fair-minded people in general. "We did seek to inform the press immediately that it was a fraud," Bernhard said, but "our denials never caught up with the lie."

Another event he cited occurred at the Washington (D.C.) Hilton hotel during a Muskie fund-raising dinner April 17, 1972. He said Segretti, in a "gross insensitivity to the national interest and to the individual victims," invited six or more African diplomats and their wives to the affair. Bernhard said it was to have been his job to introduce Muskie to the contributors in attendance, but instead he spent his time apologizing to the diplomats and trying to make them comfortable.

Asked for an example of changed political strategy as a result of the tricks, Bernhard cited a Whittier (Calif.) College appearance by Muskie on Nov. 8, 1971. He said the senator's original plan anticipated more time for question-and-answer sessions than for speeches, because it was felt that Muskie handled himself well on an impromptu basis. But at Whittier, he said, persons kept interrupting Muskie's answers with repeated questions about abortion, amnesty, gay liberation and race. Similar questions kept coming up at other rallies, Bernhard said, and finally it was decided to cut back on the time allotted to questions so that the senator would have enough time to put forth his positions on other issues.

Bernhard offered several solutions for reform of presidential campaigns, the "most urgently needed" of which was public financing of elections, he said. Bernhard added that he did not offer the suggestion because Muskie had run out of money, but because candidates were forced to devote too much time to fund-raising. "America deserves candidates who have enough time to consider the issues...and to compete equally on the merits," he said, rather than candidates who are the best fund-raisers.

Lackritz Testimony. Another witness Oct. 31 was Mark Lackritz, an investigator for the Senate committee, who testified that at least $110,000 was spent by the Nixon re-election committee to hire 22 political spies and saboteurs to infiltrate Democratic campaigns in 1972. He also said that $10,000 was spent in a California re-registration drive run in part by members of the American Nazi Party. Its purpose was to prevent the Democratic presidential primary candidacy of Alabama Gov. George C. Wallace, he said.

Witness Nov. 1

Clark MacGregor, President Nixon's re-election campaign manager, disputed earlier statements of Nixon, former presidential aide John D. Ehrlichman and former acting FBI Director L. Patrick Gray III. In addition, MacGregor told the Senate Watergate committee he had been used during the campaign by former White House and re-election committee officials to cover up the Watergate break-in.

MacGregor, a vice president of United Aircraft Corporation, served as Nixon's campaign manager from July 1, 1972, to election day. He succeeded John N. Mitchell, who quit June 30, two weeks after the break-in, explaining that his wife wanted him out of politics. MacGregor had been a member of the House (R Minn. 1961-1971) and a counsel to the President for congressional relations in 1971 and 1972.

MacGregor contradicted sworn testimony by Gray and Ehrlichman that he had urged the President to call Gray July 6, 1972, after Gray had warned MacGregor that persons on the President's staff were trying to hurt the President by covering up the Watergate break-in. Ehrlichman, in testimony released Oct. 30 by the House Armed Services Special Subcommittee on Intelligence, said in May that Nixon had called Gray as a result of MacGregor's having strongly urged Nixon to do so. *(Box on subcommittee report, p. 107)*

Gray, in testimony before the Watergate committee Aug. 6, said he talked to the President July 6, 1972, over the telephone, warning him that some of his top aides were trying to "mortally wound" him by involving the CIA in the FBI's Watergate investigation. Gray said his call from the President came 37 minutes after he had called MacGregor, telling him that the activities of certain White House aides "could be wounding" to Nixon. *(Gray testimony, Vol I, p. 264)*

Nixon, in an Aug. 22 press conference, said he did not recall the warning from Gray, but conceded that Gray could have been trying to warn him. *(Text of press conference, p. 3)*

MacGregor, however, denied that he had asked Nixon to call Gray or that Gray had used the term "wound" in talking to him before Gray's conversation with the President. MacGregor said he received a long distance call from Gray about 11 p.m. July 5, while he was in Newport Beach, Calif., near the President's San Clemente home. He testified that there was nothing unusual about the call, saying Gray merely wanted to congratulate him on his new job as campaign manager.

MacGregor said Gray expressed some concern to him about the Watergate break-in and its impact on Nixon's campaign, and that he agreed with Gray that this was serious. Gray also said, according to MacGregor, that "either it will damage him (the President) more seriously than you know or than you realize." MacGregor said he interpreted this as referring to the campaign, not the President personally. He said he did not recall Gray using the word "wound" in their conversation and that Gray did not mention FBI, CIA, or White House aides.

Clark MacGregor

Asked by Sen. Lowell P. Weicker Jr. (R Conn.) whether Gray had asked him to convey his thoughts to the President, MacGregor said he had not, and "I did not speak to the President about this. I guess our testimony is at some variance." Under further questioning by Weicker, MacGregor said he thought it was unlikely that someone had heard about his conversation with Gray and had relayed it to Nixon. MacGregor insisted that the President's log of telephone calls, which he termed "rigidly accurate," would prove that he did not call Nixon July 6 about the Gray conversation.

The sequence of events regarding the Gray talks with MacGregor and the President was important because some observers felt the talks indicated an early warning to Nixon and his campaign manager of a possible Watergate coverup. Nixon had never mentioned receiving a request from MacGregor to call Gray. MacGregor also testified that on Oct. 11, 1973, as he went through a White House reception line, Nixon told him that he and MacGregor never had discussed Gray on July 6, 1972.

Investigation. MacGregor also disputed press conference statements by the President that MacGregor was conducting a thorough investigation of the Watergate break-in for Nixon within the re-election committee. The press conferences took place Aug. 29, 1972, and Aug. 22, 1973.

In testimony before the committee, however, MacGregor said he merely conducted a "limited inquiry" of re-election committee personnel, asking them face-to-face whether they had been involved in the break-in. He said he always received assurances of non-involvement. Asked if Nixon had asked him to conduct such an investigation, MacGregor said he did not think he had. The witness said that in addition to his own inquiries, he felt reassured by the denials emanating from the White House and from John N. Mitchell, his predecessor, and from the Justice Department's promise of an exhaustive investigation of the break-in.

'Used' by Others. But in view of subsequent events, MacGregor said he felt he had been used by White House and re-election committee personnel. He singled out John W. Dean III, the former presidential counsel, and Jeb Stuart Magruder, the deputy campaign manager. MacGregor said that all the while Magruder was denying to him any involvement in the coverup, Magruder and Dean where rehearsing false testimony Magruder would give to the Watergate grand jury.

MacGregor said he repeatedly released press statements denying re-election committee or White House knowledge of or involvement in the break-in and coverup. This was done, he said, at the urging of people such as Ehrlichman and others he did not name. *(MacGregor deposition on Ehrlichman, Vol. I, p. 236)*

"It doesn't make one happy to subsequently learn that one has been used," he told the committee. "The year 1973 was a very sad year," because he learned his trust had been misplaced, he said. MacGregor specifically excluded Nixon from criticism, saying the President had always dealt honestly with him.

MacGregor was asked if he had been used by Mitchell, because Mitchell knew that G. Gordon Liddy, one of seven persons convicted in the Watergate break-in, had proposed a plan, while working for the re-election committee, that encompassed electronic surveillance. MacGregor said he felt Mitchell should have told him about the plan and added that he disagreed with Mitchell's testimony before the committee that such a disclosure would have prevented Nixon's re-election. *(Mitchell testimony, Vol. I, p. 179-188)*

Disputed Testimony. In other testimony, MacGregor denied he told Robert Mardian, another re-election committee official, that he did not want to hear about the involvement of committee personnel in the break-in. Mardian testified July 19 that he warned MacGregor at the Republican convention in 1972 not to make any more categorical denials of involvement by committee personnel in the break-in and that MacGregor answered, "I do not want to hear any more about it." *(Mardian testimony, Vol. I, p. 200)*

MacGregor also disputed testimony by Robert Reisner, a re-election committee official, that he had been informed about the Gemstone file. The file was reported to have contained copies of Democratic campaign documents and logs of wiretapped Democratic conversations. *(Reisner testimony, Vol. I, p. 112)*

MacGregor said he had no knowledge of campaign spying by the re-election committee or the White House and pointed out that virtually all spying had ended by the time he took over as campaign manager.   √

Week's Watergate Chronology

Following is a day-to-day chronology of the week's events in the Watergate case:

OCT. 25

Ford on Impeachment. Vice President-designate Ford told reporters he thought the House Judiciary Committee should continue its investigation of the grounds for impeaching Nixon. He said he would agree to the appointment of a new Watergate special prosecutor to replace

Succession Order at Justice

When Attorney General Elliot L. Richardson and his deputy, William D. Ruckelshaus, both quit their jobs rather than fire special Watergate prosecutor Archibald Cox at President Nixon's order Oct. 20, Solicitor General Robert H. Bork was the only man left in the Justice Department line of succession. This was one of the reasons he decided to obey the President and fire Cox, he said later. He knew that after him, no one was in charge, and he feared mass resignations and chaos in the department if he were to resign too.

On Oct. 23, his first regular business day in the office of acting attorney general, Bork moved to remedy the situation. He issued an order designating officials to act as attorney general in the event of resignations, firings or other causes of vacancy or inability or disqualification to act.

Under the new order, if the offices of attorney general, deputy attorney general and solicitor general were vacant, the assistant attorneys general would succeed to the office of acting attorney general in this order:

• Chief of the criminal division, Henry E. Petersen. Petersen was in charge of the department's Watergate investigation before Cox's appointment and headed it again during the interim before the selection of a new special prosecutor.

• Antitrust division, Thomas E. Kauper.

• Civil rights division, J. Stanley Pottinger.

• Office of legal counsel, Robert G. Dixon Jr.

• Tax division, Scott P. Crampton.

• Land and natural resources division, Wallace H. Johnson Jr.

Archibald Cox and that the appointee "probably ought to be brought before the Senate and his views and his guidelines be properly brought out."

Republicans on Prosecutor. Members of the House Republican Conference met with top Nixon aides and urged that the President name a new special prosecutor and make public the contents of the secret Watergate tapes. *(Senate Republican reaction, p. 85)*

Prosecution Files. Assistant Attorney General Henry E. Petersen and members of the Watergate special prosecution force asked Chief District Court Judge Sirica to take protective custody over the force's investigative records to resolve uncertainty over who was responsible for their security. *(FBI action, p. 84)*

Crisis Rumors. House Majority Leader Thomas P. O'Neill Jr. (D Mass.) spoke out on the House floor to reassure his colleagues that there was "absolutely nothing political" about the President's ordering of a military alert that morning because of the Middle East situation. O'Neill was responding to widespread rumors that Nixon had taken the action to distract attention from his Watergate problems.

Special Election Proposal. Mayor Kevin White of Boston proposed at a news conference in Philadelphia that Congress pass a law providing for a special election to replace Nixon. He cited as precedent the Succession

Subcommittee Report on CIA

Top Central Intelligence Agency (CIA) officials were "unwitting dupes for purely domestic White House staff endeavors" in the Watergate and Daniel Ellsberg matters, a House subcommittee reported Oct. 30 after a 12-week investigation. The Special Intelligence Subcommittee concluded unanimously:

• White House aides H. R. Haldeman, John D. Ehrlichman and John W. Dean III tried to "deflect" the FBI investigation into the Watergate break-in by getting the CIA to claim that covert national security operations would be endangered by an investigation. Dean made "almost unbelievable attempts to involve CIA in Watergate as a brazen cover for those actually involved," to get the CIA to pay bail money and salaries for the Watergate burglars and to stifle the FBI investigation into the Mexican money-laundering operation, said Subcommittee Chairman Lucien N. Nedzi (D Mich.).

• The CIA believed the three officials spoke for the President, and considered their requests as orders.

• The White House aides avoided CIA Director Richard Helms and dealt instead with his deputies, Gen. Robert E. Cushman Jr. and later Gen. Vernon A. Walters, career military officers from whom they apparently expected unquestioning compliance.

• The CIA improperly provided equipment to E. Howard Hunt Jr. in 1971 on White House request—equipment later used in the break-ins at Democratic national headquarters and the office of Daniel Ellsberg's psychiatrist. White House demands for a psychiatric profile on Ellsberg were another "abuse of CIA facilities." The CIA is forbidden, under the National Security Act of 1947, to engage in any domestic intelligence operations.

• The CIA did not know it was being used for improper purposes and resisted later White House efforts to involve it in such activities.

The subcommittee report raised questions about President Nixon's version of a phone call he made to L. Patrick Gray III, then acting head of the FBI, on July 6, 1972. The President said that he called Gray "to congratulate him" on the handling of a plane hijacking the day before and that the two then discussed the progress of the Watergate investigation. However, testimony before the subcommittee by Ehrlichman supported Gray's version—that Nixon called Gray in response to Gray's complaints about White House pressures on him to stifle the investigation. (*Nixon's statement, Vol. I, p. 91; White House pressures, p. 66; Gray's testimony, p. 264*)

The subcommittee proposed three legislative remedies for some of the abuses: prohibiting any CIA deviation from the National Security Act without personal approval of the President; tightening the act regarding protection of intelligence sources and methods by the director, and prohibiting transactions between former CIA employees and the agency beyond purely administrative matters.

Act of 1792, which provided for a special election if there were vacancies in the presidency, vice presidency, House speakership and presidency pro tem of the Senate. The act was nullified by the Succession Act of 1886.

OCT. 26

Nixon Press Conference. President Nixon announced at a nationally televised news conference that Acting Attorney General Robert H. Bork would appoint a special Watergate prosecutor who would have "total cooperation from the executive branch." But Nixon added that he would not provide the new prosecutor with documents involving presidential conversations. He did not intend to resign, the President said, despite the public outcry over his firing of special prosecutor Cox or the congressional impeachment investigation. (*Details, p. 102, text, p. 112*)

Special Prosecutor Bill. Sen. Birch Bayh (D Ind.) introduced a bill with 52 cosponsors authorizing Judge Sirica to appoint a new special prosecutor who would be independent of the executive branch and who could be fired only by Sirica.

Democratic Resolution. The Democratic National Committee, meeting in Louisville, Ky., adopted a resolution calling on Congress to "take all necessary action, including impeachment...if warranted" against the President.

Butz Investigation. *The Washington Star-News* reported that Secretary of Agriculture Earl L. Butz was under investigation by the Watergate special prosecution staff for allegedly attempting to block, for political purposes, a possible Federal Trade Commission action against a California wine distributor. Butz denied any wrongdoing in the case and branded the investigation "another evidence of how far afield the Cox investigation has gone from the commission to investigate Watergate."

OCT. 27

Press Attack Reaction. Executives of the three major television networks issued statements rebutting the President's press conference characterization of reporting on the Watergate case, particularly by the networks, as "outrageous, vicious, distorted." Vice President-designate Ford told a reporter that Nixon, "on second thought, probably wished he hadn't attacked the press so violently."

Congressional Reaction. Senate Majority Leader Mike Mansfield (D Mont.) and House Majority Leader O'Neill said Congress would not accept the President's plan to appoint a new special prosecutor in the executive branch.

Bar Association Position. The American Bar Association's 22-member board of governors adopted a resolution rejecting Nixon's proposed prosecutor and calling on Congress to pass legislation requiring the judges of the federal bench in the District of Columbia to name a special prosecutor answerable to them. (*Earlier story on bar, p. 82*)

OCT. 28

Cox, Haig Statements. Former special prosecutor Cox, speaking on NBC-TV's "Meet the Press," said he favored a bill that would provide for a special prosecutor responsible to the courts, but added that he was unsure of the constitutionality of such an arrangement. Appearing on CBS-TV's "Face the Nation," White House chief of staff Alexander M. Haig said the new prosecutor would not "have to make a pledge of any kind" not to seek White House documents.

OCT. 29

Cox Testimony. Cox testified before the Senate Judiciary Committee on the events surrounding his dismissal Oct. 20. He said the Watergate prosecution was "nowhere near done" and described instances of White House refusals to release documents pertaining to the investigation. *(Details, p. 94)*

Time, Newsweek Reports. *Time* magazine reported that Cox was fired after the White House challenged his pursuit of four sensitive areas of investigation: wiretaps on government officials and newsmen rationalized on national security grounds, a 1970 operation that raised $4-million for congressional and gubernatorial candidates, the handling of anti-Nixon demonstrators during the 1972 presidential campaign and the activities of the White House "plumbers" special investigations unit.

A report in *Newsweek* said federal and congressional investigators were looking into possible "corruption at the highest levels of the Nixon administration" and had been focusing on the personal finances of the President himself.

OCT. 30

ITT Settlement. *The New York Times* reported that, according to sources close to the Watergate prosecution team, former Attorney General Richard G. Kleindienst had told prosecutors that in 1971, President Nixon personally ordered him to halt a Justice Department appeal of an antitrust ruling favorable to the International Telephone and Telegraph Corporation (ITT). Kleindienst had told the Senate Judiciary Committee in 1972 that there were no White House attempts to influence the case, which was settled out of court. In a response statement, the White House acknowledged that the President had asked Kleindienst to hold off on the appeal, but denied any attempt to obstruct the case for political purposes. *(Box, p. 100)*

Cox Testimony. Testifying before the Senate Judiciary Committee on his dismissal as special Watergate prosecutor, Archibald Cox admitted having told two Democratic senators and some members of their staffs about a confidential conversation he had with Kleindienst about the ITT affair. "It's quite clear that I broke former Attorney General Kleindienst's confidence. It was, as the White House said, inexcusable," Cox said.

CIA Study. The House Armed Services Subcommittee on Intelligence issued a report on its 12-week investigation of Central Intelligence Agency involvement in the Watergate scandal. It concluded that the agency had been used by top White House officials to obstruct an FBI investigation of the Watergate break-in, and detailed contradictions in statements by Nixon and his top aides. *(Box, p. 107)*

Impeachment Inquiry. The House Judiciary Committee held its first meeting to discuss procedures for investigating whether Nixon should be impeached, and voted to grant Chairman Peter W. Rodino Jr. (D N.J.) power to issue subpoenas to obtain witnesses and documents both for the impeachment inquiry and for the committee's consideration of Vice President-designate Gerald R. Ford.

Senate on Special Prosecutor. The Senate Democratic caucus overwhelmingly approved a resolution calling for an independent special prosecutor to pursue the Watergate case. Majority Leader Mike Mansfield (D Mont.) said the Senate should consider extending the mandate of the Watergate investigating committee, with authorization to follow up on "all the matters which were under consideration by the special prosecutor's office in the Justice Department at the time of the summary dismissal of Mr. Archibald Cox."

Tunney On Resignation. Sen. John V. Tunney (D Calif.) became the second senator (Daniel K. Inouye (D Hawaii) was first) to call for Nixon's resignation. "He must leave office for the common good," Tunney said. "The people do not believe him, and he has shamed them." *(Inouye statement, p. 81)*

OCT. 31

Nonexistent Tapes. J. Fred Buzhardt Jr., a White House attorney, told Federal District Judge John J. Sirica at a special hearing that two of the nine tape recordings the President had been ordered to turn over to the court did not exist. He said that one conversation in question, between Nixon and his former campaign manager, John N. Mitchell, had been conducted on a phone that was not hooked into the White House recording system. The other, between Nixon and his counsel, John W. Dean III, had not been recorded because of a malfunctioning machine. *(Details, p. 92)*

Senate Watergate Committee. The Senate Watergate investigating committee resumed its hearings on political sabotage in the 1972 presidential election, with testimony from Berl I. Bernhard, who was presidential campaign manager for Sen. Edmund S. Muskie (D Maine). Bernhard said dirty tricks sponsored by Republicans demoralized the Muskie staff and caused dissension among Democratic candidates for the nomination. *(Details, p. 103)*

Nixon Press Memo. Sen. Lowell P. Weicker Jr. (R Conn.) of the Senate investigating committee, in a television interview, made public a memo written by former White House aide Jeb Stuart Magruder indicating that during a one-month period in 1969, Nixon made 21 separate requests to his top aides to counter what he saw as unfavorable news coverage. The memo suggested use of the Internal Revenue Service and the antitrust division of the Justice Department to "get the media."

Gurney Investigation. Sen. Edward J. Gurney (R Fla.) of the Senate investigating committee revealed that he was under investigation by the Justice Department because of allegations that Florida builders secretly contributed large sums of money to him and expected preferential treatment by the Federal Housing Administration in return. √

SAXBE: NIXON'S SECOND SELECTION FROM CONGRESS

For a man who has repeatedly expressed his disillusionment with Washington politics and who had decided to go back to Ohio to practice law, Sen. William B. Saxbe (R Ohio) has suddenly been thrust into the center of the national Watergate-stained political arena. Barely three weeks after he announced that he would not be a candidate for a second Senate term in 1974, Saxbe Nov. 1 was selected by President Nixon as his nominee for attorney general.

Known in the Senate for his outspokenness and unpredictability, Saxbe is no stranger to controversy. When he entered the Senate in 1969, it was widely expected that Saxbe would tread a stalwart Republican, pro-administration path. In many cases he did; but in others, he deviated sharply from the White House position.

When Nixon resumed massive bombing of Vietnam in December 1972, for example, Saxbe remarked that the President appeared "to have left his senses.... The bombing order exhibited arrogance and irresponsibility.... Resumption of the bombing appears like pettiness caused by failure to negotiate a satisfactory peace agreement with Hanoi." But after the peace agreement was signed, he said, "The nation owes a debt of gratitude to the President for his steadfastness in pursuit of an honorable peace agreement."

Although Saxbe was named one of President Nixon's surrogate campaigners in the 1972 campaign, he did not refrain from criticizing the administration's policies on occasion. He was critical of Nixon's statements on taxation and spending and also remarked that the President had passed up a chance to end U.S. involvement in Vietnam when he entered office in 1969.

Saxbe's reputation as a maverick provoked the Cleveland *Plain Dealer* to editorialize (June 8, 1973): "Saxbe's stances are much as Cleveland's weather. If a person doesn't like today's offering, don't panic. Something new will come along in a few hours."

Although he is outspoken, Saxbe apparently has no future political aspirations; he had planned to return home to practice law in Mechanicsburg, Ohio, and had said he had expected to be happier there than in the Senate. The fact that he has no political ambitions is one of several factors that could facilitate his confirmation.

Another is the fact that a Democratic governor, John J. Gilligan, would appoint a successor to fill Saxbe's seat, thus giving the Democrats another vote in the Senate. A third is the fact that Saxbe is a senator, and, as such, his nomination would receive the "senatorial courtesy" usually afforded to a colleague. Nonetheless, a staff member of the Judiciary Committee predicted that action on the nomination would be postponed until Congress votes on a vice president and special prosecutor and that, given the controversial circumstances surrounding the position of attorney general, quick approval of a nominee —however acceptable—is unlikely.

Background and Early Career. In considering Saxbe as his nominee for attorney general, the President chose a man with 26 years' experience in Ohio politics, including eight years as attorney general at the state level.

Saxbe first entered politics when he ran successfully for the Ohio House of Representatives in 1946. He then

Saxbe's Background

Profession: Attorney.
Born: June 24, 1916, Mechanicsburg, Ohio.
Home: Mechanicsburg.
Religion: Episcopalian.

Education: Ohio State University, A.B., 1940; LLB., 1948.

Offices: State representative, 1947-55 (majority leader 1951-53; speaker of the House, 1953-55); state attorney general, 1957-59; 1963-69; U.S. Senate, 1969 to date.

Military: Enlisted in Ohio National Guard, 1937; active duty 1940-45; 1951-52.

Memberships: American and Ohio Bar Associations, American Judicature Society, American Legion, AMVETS, War Veterans Republican Club, Elks, Lions, Moose, Ohio Farm Bureau, Ohio Grange.

Family: Married Ardath (Dolly) Kleinhans in 1940; three children.

Committees: Armed Services Committee and Government Operations Committee since 1971; Post Office and Civil Service Committee since 1973; Special Committee on Aging since 1969; Aeronautical and Space Sciences Committee and Labor and Public Welfare Committee, 1969-71; Select Small Business Committee 1971-73.

Career Highlights: Saxbe was first elected to the Ohio House of Representatives in 1946, at the age of 29. He was elected House majority leader at 34 and speaker of the House at 37.

He first ran for the Senate in 1954, challenging the party organization candidate, George H. Bender (House 1939-49; 1951-54; Senate 1954-57) in the Republican primary. Saxbe gathered 42 per cent of the vote in his losing effort.

In 1956, he was elected to a two-year term as attorney general, defeating Democrat Stephen M. Young (House 1933-37, 1941-43, 1949-51; Senate 1959-71).

Saxbe lost his bid for re-election in 1958, but was elected to four-year terms as attorney general in 1962 and 1966, and served in that office longer than any other person in the state's history.

went on to win three additional two-year terms. In 1951, he was selected majority leader and in 1953 he was elevated to speaker of the House.

Saxbe first ran for the Senate in 1954, losing in the primary to George H. Bender (U.S. Rep. 1939-49, 1951-54;

Senate 1954-57), the party organization candidate. In 1956, Saxbe won a two-year term as attorney general, but lost a bid for re-election in 1958 when Democrats won landslide victories in the state because of their opposition to right-to-work laws. Saxbe was one of the most prominent Republicans to also oppose right-to-work laws. In 1962, Saxbe ran successfully for attorney general —by then a four-year term—and won re-election in 1966.

In 1968, Saxbe again ran for the Senate, this time with success. He faced former Rep. John J. Gilligan (D 1965-67) in the general election, whom he defeated by 114,812 votes out of a total 3,743,121 cast (51.5% to 48.5%). Gilligan went on to win election as governor of the state in 1970; it is he who would name Saxbe's successor in the Senate for the remainder of the term.

Throughout the 1968 Senate race, Saxbe—who served as chairman of the Ohio Crime Commission and the Interim Ohio Law Enforcement Advisory Commission—made crime and law and order the predominant themes of his campaign. Saying that civil disorders must be stopped, Saxbe also urged restraint in law enforcement procedures, arguing, "What we've got to do is to be firm but fair."

Voting Record in the Senate

Given his background as a staunch member of the Ohio Republican Party organization and his generally conservative reputation, many observers expected that Saxbe would become a loyal member of the "conservative coalition" on entering the Senate. Instead, he became a major figure in the informal Wednesday Club, a group of moderate and liberal Republican senators who meet regularly to plan strategy and develop alternatives to the views of the conservative majority of their party in the Senate.

Almost from the start, Saxbe fashioned himself into somewhat of a maverick among his Republican colleagues, supporting the Nixon administration on some crucial votes and sharply deviating from the White House position on others. Early in 1969, he lobbied vigorously against deployment of an antiballistic missile (ABM) system, and when the crucial vote came in August, after lengthy and hard-fought debate, he joined the opposition in its unsuccessful attempt to slash funds for the administration's Safeguard ABM program. Saxbe also voted against confirming the President's nominee, Clement F. Haynsworth Jr., as an associate justice of the Supreme Court, and he opposed an extension of the 10 per cent surcharge sought by the administration.

During 1970, Saxbe's presidential support and party unity scores dipped even lower, but his ability to frustrate attempts to label him a "liberal" or "conservative" remained solid.

He broke with Senate liberals by voting to retain the controversial administration-backed "no-knock" search warrant provision in the 1970 crime control bill, but he joined a majority of liberal Democrats in their successful move to increase funds for the food stamp program for the poor. He joined a bipartisan coalition of liberals to pass the "Cooper-Church" amendment barring funds for U.S. military operations in Cambodia, but he voted against the McGovern-Hatfield "end-the-war" amendment, which was vigorously opposed by the administration.

In 1971, Saxbe appeared to move closer to the administration's position on a number of issues. He voted against both a Mike Mansfield (D Mont.) Indochina withdrawal amendment and a Cooper-Church funds cut-off for U.S. operations in Vietnam. He supported the President's nomination of William H. Rehnquist to the Supreme Court, and he voted to uphold Nixon's veto of a $6.3-billion bill extending the Office of Economic Opportunity for two years and establishing a comprehensive child care program. At the same time, however, Saxbe deserted the administration's side on two crucial votes: he joined a majority to slash funds for the supersonic transport (SST) project, and he voted against the $250-million Lockheed loan guarantee.

During 1972, Saxbe continued his drift back to the Republican fold, joining a majority in his party to vote for confirmation of Richard G. Kleindienst as attorney general, for a Republican substitute reducing a proposed minimum-wage increase and against a Vietnam war funds cut-off.

The Establishment. Within months after entering the Senate, Saxbe began criticizing the exclusive club of legislators that he had joined. By August of 1969, he was reportedly so disappointed and discouraged that some Ohio newspapers were speculating he might not return to Washington after the summer recess. "The first six months in the Senate you wonder how you got there. The next six months you wonder how the rest of them got here," he remarked that November.

One year later, Saxbe had apparently not modified his critical appraisal of congressional practices and procedures: "Instead of the great debates of the past, I find no attempt by the present leadership in either party or senior members to try to change procedure down here."

In December 1970, Saxbe joined several other senators in offering a series of proposals to streamline and reform Senate practices. And in early 1973, he was among a group of Republican liberals voting to reform committee selection practices and to limit the seniority system.

Watergate. Soon after the Senate Watergate committee opened its public hearings, Saxbe lambasted the panel as a "kangaroo court" and "rump court," terming the hearings a "Roman holiday." In an interview June 5, Saxbe suggested the hearings were a publicity-seeking device that Chairman Sam Ervin Jr. (D N.C.) was using for political purposes. Saxbe expressed the fear that, as a result, the nation was "being brought to the brink of financial catastrophe just to embarrass the President or a few jerks he had around him."

The Ohio Republican said he agreed with former special prosecutor Archibald Cox that the hearings should be suspended on the ground that continuation would hinder prosecutions. "I want to find the truth, too," he said. "The best way to get it is through a grand jury."

On April 15, 1972, however, Saxbe had said he thought the White House had known all along what was going on, commenting, "It's like the guy playing piano downstairs in a bawdy house saying he doesn't know what's going on upstairs."

Following the resignations of presidential advisers H. R. Haldeman and John D. Ehrlichman, Saxbe said, "I have long felt they have not served the President as he should have been served." Previously, Saxbe had reportedly called Haldeman and Ehrlichman "Nazis" in the way they ran the White House. √

PROFILE: LEON JAWORSKI, THE NEW SPECIAL PROSECUTOR

The search for a new special prosecutor to replace ousted Archibald Cox officially ended Nov. 1, with the announcement that a well-known Texas trial lawyer had been asked and had agreed to take over the beleaguered post. The announcement of the selection of Leon Jaworski, 68, as the new Watergate special prosecutor was coupled with the nomination of Sen. William B. Saxbe (R Ohio) to succeed Elliot L. Richardson as attorney general. *(Story, p. 92)*

Appearing briefly before newsmen to announce the Saxbe nomination, President Nixon did not mention Jaworski by name, but said Acting General Robert H. Bork had selected a man who is "the best we could get for this very important position." A highly successful trial lawyer, Jaworski has been president of the American Bar Association (1971-72), a special assistant to the U.S. attorney general (1962-65), a member of two presidential commissions and a close friend of President Lyndon B. Johnson. He is a Democrat.

Immediately following the President's appearance, acting Attorney General Bork said Jaworski would have the same broad mandate and independence which had been given Cox. He said Jaworski had been "promised the full cooperation of the executive branch," and, should he decide that he needs presidential documents, "there will be no restrictions placed on his freedom...."

In addition, Bork said, Nixon had given his personal assurance that he would not fire Jaworski without the agreement of a "substantial majority" of an eight-member congressional group: majority and minority leaders of the House and Senate, chairmen and ranking minority members of the Judiciary Committees of both houses. It was Nixon's dismissal of Cox Oct. 20 that had triggered an outburst of criticism, demands for impeachment, and calls for a new prosecutor independent of the executive branch.

Leon Jaworski

Bork said he did not expect that court battles over access to White House tapes and documents would continue. "I anticipate reasonableness on both sides," he said. It will be up to Jaworski, Bork added, to decide whether to pursue such investigations as the reported probe of presidential friend C. G. "Bebe" Rebozo's handling of a $100,000 campaign contribution from billionaire Howard Hughes—a matter that Cox had been investigating.

Speaking to newsmen in Houston Nov. 1, Jaworski confirmed that "there are no restraints on what I'll be permitted to do." He said he was first approached about the job before the appointment of Cox in May, but he turned it down because "I did not think at the time the independence was there that is there now." Jaworski said he was accepting the position since "it was put on the basis of duty to one's country which I felt I must perform."

Congressional Reaction. Initial congressional reaction to the Jaworski appointment was mixed. Despite assurances of independence, skepticism persisted that the office of special prosecutor could only be truly independent if it were not tied to the executive branch.

Career Highlights

The son of a rural Baptist minister, Jaworski was born in Waco, Texas, Sept. 19, 1905. After graduating from high school at age 15, he went on to Baylor University, where he received an LL.B. at age 19. He then went to George Washington University, where he received a master of laws degree—also working part-time for Rep. Thomas (Tom) Connally (D Texas, 1917-29).

Jaworski made his courtroom debut at age 20, defending a man accused of moonshining in Waco. He won an acquittal for his client, even though the trial took place in a bone-dry Baptist county during Prohibition.

Following World War II, he served as a colonel in the war crimes section of the Judge Advocate General's department of the Army, prosecuting major war criminals in Nuremberg. In 1961, he published a book, "After Fifteen Years," describing his experiences as a war-crimes prosecutor. The late President Johnson wrote the introduction to the book, referring to Jaworski as "my friend and counselor." Jaworski had represented Johnson in 1960, defending him successfully in two suits filed by Republicans who sought to enjoin Johnson from running simultaneously for senator and vice president.

In 1962, at Johnson's suggestion, Attorney General Robert F. Kennedy appointed Jaworski to serve as special prosecutor in the contempt case against Gov. Ross R. Barnett of Mississippi for Barnett's attempt to prevent the registration of black student James H. Meredith at the University of Mississippi. One year later, he was named special state counsel in a Texas court of inquiry into the assassination of President Kennedy. Later, he was retained as special counsel by the Warren Commission investigating the assassination.

Jaworski was a member of the President's Commission on the Causes and Prevention of Violence (1968-69), established after the assassinations of the Rev. Martin Luther King Jr. and Robert F. Kennedy. He also served on President Johnson's Commission on Law Enforcement and the Administration of Justice, and in 1967 joined four other commission members in partial dissent from the final commission report, arguing that the Supreme Court had gone too far in some of its decisions regarding defendants' rights.

In 1969, Jaworski said the violence commission's report should have taken a stronger stand against campus disorders.

Since 1951, Jaworski has been a senior partner in the Houston-based law firm of Fulbright, Crooker and Jaworski. The firm, which employs more than 150 lawyers, also has offices in Washington, D.C., and Mexico City.

Jaworski has long been associated with leading Texas Decmorats, among them former Gov. John B. Connally (1963-69). Married in 1931 to Jeannette Adam, Jaworski has three children and several grandchildren. ✓

NIXON: 'OUTRAGEOUS, VICIOUS, DISTORTED REPORTING'

In his first press conference since firing special Watergate prosecutor Archibald Cox, President Nixon Oct. 26 portrayed himself as a strong, decisive leader in his efforts to help settle the Middle East crisis. He characterized press coverage of the Cox firing as "frantic" and "hysterical," and declared, "I have never heard or seen such outrageous, vicious, distorted reporting in 27 years of public life." *(Story, p. 92)*

However, Nixon said, public and congressional reaction to Cox's firing and demands that he resign or be impeached had not affected his Middle East performance.

"I have a quality which is—I guess I must have inherited it from my Midwestern mother and father—which is that the tougher it gets the cooler I get," Nixon said. At another point he asserted, "...even in this week, when many thought that the President was shell-shocked, unable to act, the President acted decisively in the interest of peace, in the interest of the country, and I can assure you that whatever shocks gentlemen of the press may have or others—political people—these shocks will not affect me in doing my job."

The press conference lasted 38 minutes, including an eight-minute opening statement. The President had postponed planned television appearances twice during the week. The first had been billed as an address to the people, but that was cancelled in favor of a press conference the following day. That press conference was postponed, however, because of the Middle East crisis.

Watergate. Concerning Watergate, the President defended his firing of Cox and announced that Acting Attorney General Robert H. Bork would appoint a replacement. But Nixon added that the new prosecutor would not be allowed to go to court to obtain evidence from his own files.

The President also endorsed the handling by his long-time friend, C. G. (Bebe) Rebozo, of a $100,000 cash contribution from an emissary of billionaire Howard Hughes, saying Rebozo had exercised "very good judgment in doing what he did." *(Details on Nixon remarks on Watergate, p. 102)*

Middle East. In an opening statement, Nixon outlined the chronology of negotiations between the United States and the Soviet Union for enforcing the settlement of the Israeli-Arab war.

A "very significant and potentially explosive crisis developed" on Oct. 24, Nixon said. "We obtained information which led us to believe that the Soviet Union was planning to send a very substantial force into the Mideast —a military force."

As a result, the President continued, he ordered a "precautionary" world-wide military alert for American forces shortly after midnight to signal to the Soviets that the United States "could not accept any unilateral move on their part to move military forces into the Mideast." Shortly thereafter, Nixon sent Soviet Communist Party Leader Leonid I. Brezhnev "an urgent message" asking him not to send troops, and urging instead that the Soviets join the United States in supporting a United Nations resolution that would exclude major powers from participating in a peacekeeping force.

During the "several exchanges" that followed, Nixon said, "we reached the conclusion that we would jointly support the resolution, which was adopted in the United Nations."

Criticism from the press "has been my lot throughout my political life, and I suppose because I have been through so much, that may be one of the reasons that when I have to face an international crisis, I have what it takes."

The "outlook for a permanent peace is the best that it has been in 20 years" as a result of the two powers having agreed to "participate in trying to expedite the talks between the parties involved," Nixon said. He added that he was optimistic for a permanent settlement, since "what the developments of this week should indicate to all of us is that the United States and the Soviet Union, who admittedly have very different objectives in the Mideast, have now agreed that it is not in their interests to have a confrontation there—a confrontation which might lead to a nuclear confrontation."

In response to questions, Nixon denied inferences that he had orchestrated the crisis to take attention away from public and congressional criticism of his firing of Cox. "It was a real crisis," he said. "It was the most difficult crisis we've had since the Cuban confrontation in 1962."

NEWS CONFERENCE TEXT

Following is the White House text of President Nixon's Oct. 26 news conference.

THE PRESIDENT: Will you be seated, please?

Ladies and gentlemen, before going to your questions, I have a statement with regard to the Mideast which I think will anticipate some of the questions, because this will update the information which is breaking rather fast in that area, as you know, for the past two days.

The cease-fire is holding. There have been some violations, but generally speaking it can be said that it is holding at this time. As you know, as a result of the U.N. resolution which was agreed to yesterday by a vote of 14 to 0, a peacekeeping force will go to the Mideast, and this force, however, will not include any forces from the major powers, including, of course, the United States and the Soviet Union.

The question, however, has arisen as to whether observers from major powers could go to the Mideast. My up-to-the-minute report on that, and I just talked to Dr. Kissinger five minutes before coming down, is this: We will send observers to the Mideast if requested by the Secretary General of the United Nations, and we have reason to expect that we will receive such a request.

With regard to the peacekeeping force, I think it is important for all of you ladies and gentlemen, and particularly for those listening on radio and television, to know why the United States has insisted that major powers not be part of the peace-keeping force, and that major powers not introduce military forces into the Mideast. A very significant and potentially explosive crisis developed on Wednesday of this week. We obtained information which led us to believe that the Soviet Union was planning to send a very substantial force into the Mideast, a military force.

When I received that information, I ordered, shortly after midnight on Thursday morning, an alert for all American forces around the world. This was a precautionary alert. The purpose of that was to indicate to the Soviet Union that we could not accept any unilateral move on their part to move military forces into the Mideast. At the same time, in the early morning hours, I also proceeded on the diplomatic front. In a message to Mr. Brezhnev, an urgent message, I indicated to him our reasoning and I urged that we not proceed along that course, and that, instead, that we join in the United Nations in supporting a resolution which would exclude any major powers from participating in a peacekeeping force.

As a result of that communication, and the return that I received from Mr. Brezhnev—we had several exchanges, I should say—we reached the conclusion that we would jointly support the resolution which was adopted in the United Nations.

We now come, of course, to the critical time in terms of the future of the Mideast. And here, the outlook is far more hopeful than what we have been through this past week. I think I could safely say that the chances for not just a cease-fire, which we presently have and which, of course, we have had in the Mideast for some time, but the outlook for a permanent peace is the best that it has been in 20 years.

The reason for this is that the two major powers, the Soviet Union and the United States, have agreed—this was one of the results of Dr. Kissinger's trip to Moscow—have agreed that we would participate in trying to expedite the talks between the parties involved. That does not mean that the two major powers will impose a settlement. It does mean, however, that we will use our influence with the nations in the area to expedite a settlement.

The reason we feel this is important is that first, from the standpoint of the nations in the Mideast, none of them, Israel, Egypt, Syria, none of them can or should go through the agony of another war.

The losses in this war on both sides have been very, very high. And the tragedy must not occur again. There have been four of these wars, as you ladies and gentlemen know, over the past 20 years. But beyond that, it is vitally important to the peace of the world that this potential troublespot, which is really one of the most potentially explosive areas in the world, that it not become an area in which the major powers come together in confrontation.

What the developments of this week should indicate to all of us is that the United States and the Soviet Union, who admittedly have very different objectives in the Mideast, have now agreed that it is not in their interest to have a confrontation there, a confrontation which might lead to a nuclear confrontation and neither of the two major powers wants that.

We have agreed, also, that if we are to avoid that, it is necessary for us to use our influence more than we have in the past, to get the negotiating track moving again, but this time, moving to a conclusion. Not simply a temporary truce, but a permanent peace.

I do not mean to suggest that it is going to come quickly because the parties involved are still rather far apart. But I do say that now there are greater incentives within the area to find a peaceful solution and there are enormous incentives as far as the United States is concerned, and the Soviet Union and other major powers, to find such a solution.

Turning now to the subject of our attempts to get a cease-fire on the home front, that is a bit more difficult.

Today White House Counsel contacted Judge Sirica. We tried yesterday but he was in Boston, as you know, and arrangements were made to meet with Judge Sirica on Tuesday to work out the delivery of the tapes to Judge Sirica.

Also, in consultations that we have had in the White House today, we have decided that next week the Acting Attorney General, Mr. Bork, will appoint a new special prosecutor for what is called the Watergate matter. The special prosecutor will have independence. He will have total cooperation from the Executive Branch, and he will have as a primary responsibility to bring this matter which has so long concerned the American people, bring it to an expeditious conclusion, because we have to remember that under our Constitution it has always been held that justice delayed is justice denied. It is time for those who are guilty to be prosecuted, and for those who are innocent to be cleared. I can assure you ladies and gentlemen, all of our listeners tonight, that I have no greater interest than to see that the new special prosecutor has the cooperation from the Executive Branch and the independence that he needs to bring about that conclusion.

And now I will go to Mr. Cormier.

Role of New Prosecutor

Q: Mr. President, would the new special prosecutor have your go-ahead to go to court if necessary to obtain evidence from your files that he felt were vital?

A: Mr. Cormier, I would anticipate that that would not be necessary. I believe that as we look at the events which led to the dismissal of Mr. Cox, we find that these are matters that can be worked out and should be worked out in cooperation and not by having a suit filed by a special prosecutor within the Executive Branch against the President of the United States.

This, incidentally, is not a new attitude on the part of a President. Every President since George Washington has tried to protect the confidentiality of Presidential conversations and you remember the famous case involving Thomas Jefferson where Chief Justice Marshall, then sitting as a trial judge, subpoenaed the letter which Jefferson had written which Marshall thought or felt was necessary evidence in the trial of Aaron Burr. Jefferson refused to do so but it did not result in a suit. What happened was, of course, a compromise in which a summary of the contents of the letter which was relevant to the trial was produced by Jefferson and the Chief Justice of the United States, acting in his capacity as Chief Justice, accepted that.

That is exactly, of course, what we tried to do in this instant case.

I think it would be well if I could take just a moment, Mr. Cormier, in answering your question to point out what we tried to do and why we feel it was the proper solution to a very aggravating and difficult problem.

The matter of the tapes has been one that has concerned me because of my feeling that I have a Constitutional responsibility to defend the Office of the Presidency from any encroachments on confidentiality which might affect future Presidents in their abilities to conduct the kind of conversations and discussions they need to conduct to carry on the responsibilities of this Office. And, of course, the special prosecutor felt that he needed the tapes for the purpose of his prosecution.

That was why, working with the Attorney General, we worked out what we thought was an acceptable compromise, one in which Judge Stennis, now Senator Stennis, would hear the tapes and would provide a complete and full disclosure, not only to Judge Sirica, but also to the Senate Committee.

Attorney General Richardson approved of this proposition. Senator Baker, Senator Ervin approved of the proposition. Mr. Cox was the only one that rejected it.

Under the circumstances, when he rejected it and indicated that despite the approval of the Attorney General, and, of course, of the President and of the two major Senators on the Ervin Committee, when he rejected the proposal, I had no choice but to dismiss him.

Under those circumstances, Mr. Richardson, Mr. Ruckelshaus felt that because of the nature of their confirmation that their commitment to Mr. Cox had to take precedence over any commitment they might have to carry out an order from the President.

Under those circumstances, I accepted with regret the resignations of two fine public servants.

Now we come to a new special prosecutor. We will cooperate with him, and I do not anticipate that we will come to the time when he would consider it necessary to take the President to court. I think our cooperation will be adequate.

Prosecutor and Presidential Documents

Q: This is another way of asking Frank's question, but if the special prosecutor considers that information contained in Presidential documents is needed to prosecute the Watergate case, will you give him the documents, beyond the nine tapes which you have already turned over?

A: I have answered that question before. We will not provide Presidential documents to a special prosecutor. We will provide, as we have in great numbers, all kinds of documents from the White House, but if it is a document involving a conversation with the President, I would have to stand on the principle of confidentiality. However, information that is needed from such documents would be provided. That is what we have been trying to do.

Congressionally Mandated Prosecutor

Q: Mr. President, you know in the Congress there is a great deal of suspicion over any arrangement which will permit the Executive branch to investigate itself or which will establish a special prosecutor which you may fire again. As 53 Senators, a majority, have now co-sponsored a resolution which would permit Judge Sirica to establish and name an independent prosecutor, separate and apart from the White House Executive branch, do you believe this arrangement would be constitutional and would you go along with it?

A: I would suggest that the action that we are going to take of appointing a special prosecutor would be satisfactory to the Congress, and that they would not proceed with that particular matter.

Response to Impeachment Talk

Q: Mr. President, I wonder if you could share with us your thoughts and tell us what goes through your mind when you hear people who love this country, and people who believe in you, say reluctantly that perhaps you should resign or be impeached.

A: Well, I am glad we don't take the vote of this room, let me say. And I understand the feelings of people with regard to impeachment and resignation. As a matter of fact, Mr. Rather, you may remember when I made the rather difficult decision, I thought the most difficult decision of my first term on December 18th, the bombing by B-52s of North Vietnam, that exactly the same words were used on the networks—I don't mean by you, but they were quoted on the networks—that are used now: tyrant, dictator, he has lost his senses, he should resign, he should be impeached.

But I stuck it out, and as a result of that, we not only got our prisoners of war home, as I have often said, on their feet rather than on their knees, but we brought peace to Vietnam, something we haven't had and didn't for over 12 years.

It was a hard decision, and it was one that many of my friends in the press who had consistently supported me on the war up to that time disagreed with. Now, in this instance I realize there are people who feel that the actions that I have taken with regard to the dismissal of Mr. Cox are grounds for impeachment.

I would respectfully suggest that even Mr. Cox and Mr. Richardson have agreed that the President had the right, constitutional right, to dismiss anybody in the Federal Government; and second, I should also point out that as far as the tapes are concerned, rather than being in defiance of the law, I am in compliance with the law.

As far as what goes through my mind, I would simply say that I intend to continue to carry out, to the best of my ability, the responsibilities I was elected to carry out last November. The events of this past week—I know, for example, in your head office in New York, some thought that it was simply a blown-up exercise; there wasn't a real crisis. I wish it had been that. It was a real crisis. It was the most difficult crisis we have had since the Cuban confrontation of 1962.

But because we had had our initiative with the Soviet Union, because I had a basis of communication with Mr. Brezhnev, we not only avoided a confrontation, but we moved a great step forward toward real peace in the Mideast.

Now, as long as I can carry out that kind of responsibility, I am going to continue to do this job.

Cox Motives

Q: Mr. President.

A: Mr. Lisagor.

Q: There have been reports that you felt that Mr. Cox was somehow out to get you. I would like to ask you if you did feel that, and if so, what evidence did you have?

A: Mr. Lisagor, I understand Mr. Cox is going to testify next week under oath before the Judiciary Committee, and I would suggest that he perhaps would be better qualified to answer that question.

As far as I am concerned, we had cooperated with the Special Prosecutor. We tried to work out in a cooperative way this matter of the production of the tapes. He seemed to be more interested in the issue than he was in a settlement, and under the circumstances, I had no choice but to dismiss him. But I am not going to question his motives as to whether or not he was out to get me. Perhaps the Senators would like to ask that question.

'Vicious, Distorted Reporting'

Q: Mr. President, in 1968, before you were elected, you wrote that too many shocks can drain a nation of its energy and even cause a rebellion against creative change and progress. Do you think America is at that point now?

A: I think that many would speculate. I have noted a lot on the networks particularly and sometimes even in the newspapers. But this is a very strong country, and the American people, I think, can ride through the shocks they have.

The difference now from what it was in the days of shocks, even when Mr. Lisagor and I first met 25 years ago, is the electronic media. I have never heard or seen such outrageous, vicious, distorted reporting in 27 years of public life. I am not blaming anybody for that. Perhaps what happened is what we did brought it about, and therefore, the media decided that they would have to take that particular line.

But when people are pounded night after night with that kind of frantic, hysterical reporting, it naturally shakes their confidence. And yet, I should point out that even in this week, when many thought that the President was shell-shocked, unable to act, the President acted decisively in the interest of peace, in the interest of the country, and I can assure you that whatever shocks gentlemen of the press may have, or others, political people, these shocks will not affect me in my doing my job.

Mideast Alert

Q: Mr. President, getting back to the Middle East crisis for a moment, do you consider that the crisis is over now and how much longer will the American forces be kept on alert around the world?

A: With regard to the alert, the alert has already been discontinued with regard to NORAD, that is the North American Command, and with regard to SAC. As far as other forces are concerned, they are being maintained in a state of readiness and obviously, Soviet Union forces are being maintained in a state of readiness.

Now, as far as the crisis in the Mideast is concerned, I don't want to leave any impression that we aren't going to continue to have problems with regard to the cease-fire. There will be outbreaks because of the proximity of the antagonistic forces and there will be some very, very tough negotiating in attempting to reach a diplomatic settlement. But I think now that all parties are going to approach this problem of trying to reach a settlement with a more sober and a more determined attitude than ever before, because the Mideast can't afford, Israel can't afford, Egypt can't afford, Syria can't afford another war. The world cannot afford a war in that part of the world, and because the Soviet Union and the United States have potentially conflicting interests there, we both now realize that we cannot allow our differences in the Mideast to jeopardize even greater interests that we have, for example, in continuing a detente in Europe, in continuing the negotiations which can lead to a limitation of nuclear arms and eventually reducing the burden of nuclear arms, and in continuing in other ways that can contribute to the peace of the world.

As a matter of fact, I would suggest that with all of the criticism of detente, that without detente, we might have had a major conflict in the Middle East. With detente, we avoided it.

Mideast Oil

Q: Mr. President, the question from the electronic medium related to the Middle East—

A: Radio.

Q: —radio. I have heard there was a meeting at the State Department this afternoon of major oil company executives on the fuel shortage.

Whether or not you confirm that, has this confrontation in the Middle East caused a still more severe oil problem and is there any thinking now of gasoline rationing?

A: Well, we have contingency plans for gasoline rationing and so forth which I hope never have to be put into place.

But, with regard to the oil shortage, which you referred to, one of the major factors which gave enormous urgency to our efforts to settle this particular crisis was the potential of an oil cut-off.

Let me say that I have also noted that in the State Department or from the State Department today a statement raised a little difficulty in Europe to the effect that our European friends hadn't been as cooperative as they might have been in attempting to help us work out the Middle East settlement or at least the settlement to the extent that we have worked it out as of the resolution of yesterday.

I can only say on that score that Europe which gets 80 percent of its oil from the Mideast would have frozen to death this winter unless there had been a settlement and Japan, of course, is in that same position.

The United States, of course, gets only approximately 10 percent of its oil from the Mideast.

What I am simply suggesting is this: That with regard to the fuel shortage potentially in the United States and in the world, it is indispensable at this time that we avoid any further Mideast crisis so that the flow of oil to Europe, to Japan and to the United States can continue.

Mideast Brezhnev Message

Q: Mr. President, against this background of detente, Mr. Brezhnev's note to you has been described as rough or perhaps brutal by one Senator. Can you characterize it for us and for history in any way you can mention?

A: Yes, I could characterize it, but, Mr. Theis, it wouldn't be in the national interest to do so. My notes to him he might characterize as being rather rough. However, I would rather—perhaps it would be best to characterize it. Rather than saying, Mr. Theis, that his note to me was rough and brutal, I would say that it was very firm and it left very little to the imagination as to what he intended.

And my response was also very firm and left little to the imagination of how we would react. And it is because he and I know each other and it is because we have had this personal contact, that notes exchanged in that way result in a settlement rather than a confrontation.

Rebozo-Hughes Contribution

Q: Mr. President.

A: Yes, Mr. Deakin.

Q: Is it credible, can the American people believe that your close friend, Mr. Rebozo, for three years, during which time you saw him weekly sometimes, kept from you the fact that he had $100,000 in cash from Mr. Howard Hughes?

Is that credible, is it credible that your personal attorney, Mr. Kalmbach, knew about this money for at least a year and never told you about it?

And, if this was a campaign contribution, as your press secretaries say, who authorized Mr. Rebozo to collect campaign contributions for your reelection or for the Republican Party?

What campaign committee was he an official of?

A: Well, it is obviously not credible to you, and I suppose that it would sound incredible to many people who did not know how I operate. In terms of campaign contributions, I have had a rule, Mr. Deakin, which Mr. Stans and Mr. Kalmbach and Mr. Rebozo and every contributor will agree has been the rule—I have refused always to accept contributions myself. I have refused to have any discussion of contributions. As a matter of fact, my orders to Mr. Stans were that after the campaign was over, I would then send notes of appreciation to those that contributed, but before the election, I did not want to have any information from anybody with regard to campaign contributions.

Now, with regard to Mr. Rebozo, let me say that he showed, I think, very good judgment in doing what he did. He received a contribution. He was prepared to turn it over to the Finance Chairman when the Finance Chairman was appointed. But in that interlude, after he received the contribution, and before the Finance Chairman was appointed, the Hughes company, as you all know, had an internal fight of massive proportions, and he felt that such a contribution to the campaign might prove to be embarrassing.

At the conclusion of the campaign, he decided that it would be in the best interests of everybody concerned rather than to turn the money over then, to be used in the '74 campaigns, to return it intact. And I would say that any individual, and particularly a banker who would have a contribution of $100,000 and not touch it—because it was turned back in exactly the form it was received—I think that is a pretty good indication that he is a totally honest man, which he is.

Tapes: No Public Disclosure

Q: Mr. President, after the tapes are presented to Judge Sirica and they are processed under the procedure outlined by the U.S. Court of Appeals, will you make those tapes public?

A: No, that is not the procedure that the court has ordered, and it would not be proper. Judge Sirica, under the Circuit Court's order, is to listen to the tapes, and then is to present to the Grand Jury the pertinent evidence with regard to its investigation. Publication of the tapes has not been ordered by the Circuit Court of Appeals, and Judge Sirica, of course, would not do anything that would be in contravention of what the Circuit Court of Appeals has ordered.

Bearing Up Under Stress

Q: Mr. President—

A: Mr. ter Horst.

Q: Mr. President, Harry Truman used to talk about the heat in the kitchen—

A: I know what he meant. (Laughter)

Q: —and a lot of people have been wondering how you are bearing up emotionally under the stress of recent events. Can you discuss that?

A: Those who saw me during the Middle East crisis thought I bore up rather well, and, Mr. ter Horst, I have a quality which is—I guess I must have inherited it from my Midwestern mother and father—which is that the tougher it gets, the cooler I get. Of course, it isn't pleasant to get criticism. Some of it is justified, of course. It isn't pleasant to find, for example, that, speaking of my friend Mr. Rebozo, that despite the fact that those who printed it, and those who said it, knew it was untrue—said that he had a million-dollar trust fund for me that he was handling—it was nevertheless put on one of the networks, knowing it was untrue. It isn't pleasant, for example, to hear or read that a million dollars in campaign funds went into my San Clemente property, and even after we had a complete audit, to have it repeated.

Those are things which, of course, do tend to get under the skin of the man who holds this office. But as far as I am concerned, I have learned to expect it. It has been my lot throughout my political life, and I suppose because I have been through so much, that may be one of the reasons that when I have to face an international crisis, I have what it takes.

Watergate and Mideast

Q: Mr. President, I would like to ask you a question about the Mideast. To what extent do you think your Watergate troubles influenced Soviet thinking about your ability to respond in the Mideast, and did your Watergate problems convince you that the U.S. needed a strong response in the Mideast to convince other nations that you have not been weakened?

A: Well, I have noted speculation to the effect that the Watergate problems may have led the Soviet Union to miscalculate. I tend to disagree with that, however.

I think Mr. Brezhnev probably can't quite understand how the President of the United States wouldn't be able to handle the Watergate problems. He would be able to handle it all right, if he had them. (Laughter) But I think what happens is that what Mr. Brezhnev does understand is the power of the United States. What he does know is the President of the United States.

What he also knows is that the President of the United States, when he was under unmerciful assault at the time of Cambodia, at the time of May 8, when I ordered the bombing and the mining of North Vietnam at the time of December 18, still went ahead and did what he thought was right; the fact that Mr. Brezhnev knew that regardless of the pressures at home, regardless of what people see and hear on television night after night, he would do what was right. That is what made Mr. Brezhnev act as he did.

Television Anger

Q: Mr. President, you have lambasted the television networks pretty well. Could I ask you, at the risk of reopening an obvious wound, you say after you have put on a lot of heat that you don't blame anyone. I find that a little puzzling. What is it about the television coverage of you in these past weeks and months that has so aroused your anger?

A: Don't get the impression that you arouse my anger. (Laughter)

Q: I'm afraid, sir, that I have that impression. (Laughter)

A: You see, one can only be angry with those he respects.

Regaining Confidence

Q: Mr. President, businessmen are increasingly saying that many chief executive officers of corporations do not get the latitude you have had, if they have the personnel problems that you have had, to stay in the job and correct them. You have said you are going to stay. Do you have any plan set out to regain confidence of people across the country, and these businessmen who are beginning to talk about this matter? Do you have any plans, besides the special prosecutor, which looks backward, do you have any plan that looks forward for regaining the confidence of the people?

A: I certainly have. First, to move forward in building a structure of peace in the world, in which we have made enormous progress in the past and which we are going to make more progress in in the future: our European initiative, our continued initiative with the Soviet Union, with the People's Republic of China. That will be the major legacy of this Administration.

Moving forward at home in our continuing battle against the high cost of living, in which we are now finally beginning to make some progress, and moving forward also on the matters that you referred to, it is true that what happened in Watergate, the campaign abuses, were deplorable. They have been very damaging to this Administration; they have been damaging certainly to the country as well.

Let me say, too, I didn't want to leave an impression with my good friend from CBS over here that I don't respect the reporters. What I was simply saying was this: That when a commentator takes a bit of news and then, with knowledge of what the facts are, distorts it, viciously, I have no respect for that individual.

Executive Privilege

Q: Mr. President—

A: You are so loud, I will have to take you.

Q: I have to be, because you happen to dodge my questions all of the time.

A: You had three last time.

Q: Last May you went before the American People and you said, "Executive privilege will not be invoked as to any testimony concerning possible criminal conduct or discussing of possible criminal conduct, including the Watergate affair and the alleged cover-up."

If you have revised or modified this position, as you seem to have done, could you explain the rationale of a law-and order Administration covering up evidence, prima facie evidence, of high crimes and misdemeanors?

A: I should point out that perhaps all of the other reporters in the room are aware of the fact that we have waived Executive privilege on all individuals in the Administration. It has been the greatest waiver of Executive privilege in the whole history of this Nation.

And as far as any other matters are concerned, the matters of the tapes, the matters of Presidential conversations, those are matters in which the President has a responsibility to defend this office, which I shall continue to do.

THE PRESS: Thank you, Mr. President. ✓

CONGRESS CONTINUES HEARINGS ON TAPES, PROSECUTOR

Editorial and congressional demands for President Nixon's resignation rose dramatically after reports of two missing White House tape recordings. But a determined Nixon ended a television speech on the energy crisis Nov. 7 with a firm statement that "I have no intention whatever of walking away from the job I was elected to do.

"As long as I am physically able," he said, "I am going to continue to work 16 to 18 hours a day for the cause of a real peace abroad, and for the cause of prosperity without inflation and without war at home. And in the months ahead, I shall do everything that I can to see that any doubts as to the integrity of the man who occupies the highest office in this land, to remove those doubts where they exist."

While the public debate continued over whether or not the President should remain in office, three congressional committees and a federal court heard testimony that would have some impact on Nixon's survival in office.

• The Senate Judiciary Committee and a House Judiciary subcommittee listened to witnesses argue the pros and cons of a special Watergate prosecutor appointed either by the courts or by the executive branch. Meanwhile, Leon Jaworski, the new special prosecutor appointed by Acting Attorney General Robert H. Bork, was pursuing the investigation.

• The Senate Watergate investigating committee finished its hearings on dirty tricks and entered the third and final phase of hearings, on campaign financing.

• Chief Judge John J. Sirica of U.S. District Court in Washington, D.C., heard high-ranking present and former members of the Nixon administration try to untangle the riddles of the presidential tapes.

Special Prosecutor Legislation

Despite warnings of a floor fight, a presidential veto and the prospect of a protracted legal battle if the veto were overridden, a House Judiciary subcommittee Nov. 8 began its final action on legislation to create a new, independent office of Watergate special prosecutor. The bill that appeared likely to emerge would leave the appointment of the prosecutor up to a panel of judges, thus removing the office from the control of the executive branch. (Earlier House Judiciary hearings, p. 124)

After four days of lively debate, the five Democrats on the Select Subcommittee on Reform of Criminal Laws seemed to favor a court-appointed prosecutor. The four Republican members opposed the measure. The full Judiciary Committee was to take up the proposal Nov. 13.

Republican subcommittee members favored a different approach: allowing the newly appointed special prosecutor, Jaworski, to continue his work as an executive branch appointee but adding statutory guarantees that he could not be removed by the President except for "gross

Sentencing of Conspirators

Six of the seven original Watergate conspirators were sentenced to prison terms Nov. 9 by U.S. District Court Judge John J. Sirica in Washington, D.C. Sirica sentenced E. Howard Hunt, a former White House consultant, to 2½ to eight years in prison and a $10,000 fine; Bernard L. Barker, 1½ to six years; James W. McCord Jr., one to five years; Eugenio R. Martinez, Frank A. Sturgis and Virgilio R. Gonzalez, one to four years.

The men were sentenced on six to eight counts of conspiracy, burglary, electronic eavesdropping and wiretapping, but the sentences were to run concurrently. The conspirators could have received 35- to 45-year terms. They would be eligible for parole after serving the minimum term. All except McCord already had served nearly a year on provisional sentences imposed by Sirica March 23. (Vol. I, p. 9, 10, 137)

The seventh conspirator, G. Gordon Liddy, former counsel to the Finance Committee to Re-elect the President and a leader of the Watergate conspiracy, pleaded not guilty and was sentenced to six years and eight months to 20 years in prison. He appealed that, but was serving an 18-month term for refusing to testify before a grand jury.

Sentencing of McCord had been delayed while he testified before the Senate Watergate committee and grand juries. He was the first of the conspirators to implicate high officials in the White House in the Watergate case, and apparently received a lighter sentence because of his cooperation with government prosecutors.

improprieties." The Republicans argued that a court-appointed prosecutor was both unconstitutional and impractical. But the Democrats maintained that their approach was the only way to ensure a completely independent and thorough investigation of the Watergate scandals. (Court decisions, previous hearings, p. 97)

Opponents also argued that if the measure were enacted, it could snarl the Watergate investigations by inviting constitutional challenges to any indictments or convictions a court-appointed prosecutor might obtain. These court tests could last for months, they noted. Advocates answered that the legislation could include requirements for a prompt judicial decision as to its constitutionality, and that in the meantime the investigations could continue.

The practical issue was whether the constitutional risks of such a course were worth taking if it were true, as some witnesses maintained, that Nixon would not dare fire a second special prosecutor. Witnesses with this view noted Nixon's assurances that he would not dismiss Jaworski, as he had dismissed Archibald Cox, the first special prosecutor, without the consensus of congressional leaders. They also cited Jaworski's own integrity and his public pledges that he would accept nothing less than full cooperation from the White House. *(Jaworski appointment, p. 111)*

Nixon would invite impeachment if he violated these assurances of independence, opponents of the bill argued. Advocates of the legislation asserted that Nixon had withdrawn his guarantees of independence once before in firing Cox, and that Jaworski could, unless he were totally independent, be subjected to subtle interference or pressures from the White House to limit the investigation.

Legislation. More than 25 pieces of legislation dealing with guaranteeing the independence of the special prosecutor had been introduced since Cox was fired. The major bill under consideration by the subcommittee was H J Res 784, introduced Oct. 23 by Rep. John C. Culver (D Iowa) with 111 cosponsors. A similar bill (S 2611) was introduced in the Senate by Birch Bayh (D Ind.) with 55 cosponsors. Both measures called for judicial appointment.

A compromise bill was introduced in the House by five Republican members of the Judiciary Committee Nov. 6. The measure, HR 11263, would allow authority for the appointment of a special prosecutor to remain in the executive branch but would limit the conditions under which he could be dismissed. Still another compromise bill (HR 11264) introduced Nov. 6 by two Republicans would set up a new office of special prosecutor and would limit the conditions of his removal, but would still keep the office within the executive branch.

Jaworski Testimony. During testimony Nov. 8, Jaworski refused to take a stand on the legality of the various proposals, saying only that his interest was in proceeding with the Watergate investigation "with all dispatch." Debates and possible judicial proceedings over the constitutionality of a court-appointed prosecutor, he said, "could well stall the effective labors of the special prosecutor's office for an extended period of time." He also argued that the "continuity" of the special prosecutor force "has now been restored."

Jaworski said he had received assurances from President Nixon through Nixon's chief of staff, Alexander M. Haig Jr., that he would have complete cooperation and would be able to test presidential claims of executive privilege by going to court.

Richardson Testimony

As the House committee prepared to come forth with a bill, the Senate Judiciary Committee continued its hearings on a special prosecutor. Former Attorney General Elliot L. Richardson testified before the committee Nov. 6, and he returned Nov. 8 to provide additional details about White House concern over the Cox investigation. *(Earlier Senate Judiciary hearings, p. 120)*

The former attorney general lost his characteristically composed demeanor only once, when Sen. Edward M. Kennedy (D Mass.) asserted that White House "pressures" had been exerted on Richardson to curb Cox.

Raising his voice in anger, Richardson denied that White House complaints had constituted pressures. "There were not any pressures," he said. "Cox was not going to be subject to pressures. I was not going to be the instrument for pressures. The White House was not going to exert pressures."

Richardson, who characterized his role as that of a middle man between the White House and Cox, insisted that the White House complaints were not an "attempt to do anything in an improper way." He attributed the complaints to "chronic unhappiness" with Cox's probe, as it was perceived in the White House. A "chronic sense of strain" erupted from time to time, he said.

White House Complaints. On Nov. 8, however, Richardson dated White House interest in firing Cox even earlier than he had in his testimony Nov. 6. On July 23, he said, he was told by Alexander M. Haig Jr., White House chief of staff, that Nixon was "very uptight about Cox." Haig, described by Richardson as troubled by a planned probe by Cox into possible unauthorized wiretapping by the Secret Service or the Central Intelligence Agency (CIA), was quoted by Richardson as saying he wanted a "tight line drawn" around Cox. The chief of staff suggested that if Cox did not restrain his investigations, "We will have to get rid of Cox, with all the problems that would entail," according to Richardson.

Cox later conceded that his plan to investigate such activities of the Secret Service and the CIA had been too broad.

Consulting handwritten notes, Richardson testified that he had been contacted by the White House staff about the scope of Cox's investigation twice in June, three times in July, once in August, four times in September and several more times between Oct. 15 and 20, immediately before Cox was fired and Richardson resigned.

On Oct. 18, Richardson said, Haig called him to complain that the investigation of Nixon's friend, Charles G. Rebozo, was outside the charter of Cox's prosecution force.

Question of Tapes' Quality

The quality of the recordings of White House conversations was a subject of disagreement between two of President Nixon's closest aides, both of whom testified before Judge Sirica Nov. 8. *(Earlier Court hearings, p. 120)*

Nixon's longtime personal secretary and executive assistant, Rose Mary Woods, told the court of her month-long struggle to get the "gist" of the subpoenaed conversations down in type for the President's review. She described the job as very difficult, at times almost impossible, due to the location of the microphones and of the persons speaking, the acoustic qualities of the rooms in which the recordings were made and the intervening noise. "Sometimes the President puts his feet up on the desk," she said. "Then you hear a noise (on the tape) like a bomb. Boom!"

H. R. Haldeman, Nixon's former chief of staff until his resignation under fire on April 30, agreed that intervening noise was somewhat of a problem. Noting that the microphones in one of the presidential offices were buried in the top of the desk, he warned Sirica that when china coffee cups were set down on the desk, it was "ear-splitting" for the person listening to the tapes. The tapes were not "great," he continued, but he said he had no particular trouble understanding them. They were of "fair" quality, he said, "a quite adequate record of the conversations" they were designed to preserve.

Hard Listening. Woods, who has worked with Nixon since 1951, said that she had "no knowledge whatsoever" about the existence of the White House recording system until former White House aide Alexander Butterfield disclosed it to the Senate Watergate committee in mid-July. She said she first saw one of the tapes on Sept. 29, when, at the request of the President, she went to Camp David, Md., to try to listen to the subpoenaed tapes and write down what was audible. *(Butterfield testimony, Vol. I, p. 192)*

Her work on the initial eight tapes she was given continued during the first week in October, the weekend of Oct. 4-7 at Key Biscayne, Fla., and subsequent weeks in Washington, being completed only on Oct. 23-24, she said. The original (and only) typed record of the tapes was given to the President, she said.

Woods said that the eight tapes were still in her office safe and that she alone possessed the combination to the safe. In addition, she said, in that safe were six tapes she had been given Nov. 5. Explaining the "gap" which she reportedly had found in one of those tapes on which she had worked most recently, Woods said that she had been searching for a conversation on April 16 between Nixon and former presidential counsel John W. Dean III —and that the tape she had been using apparently began after the time of that conversation—so she feared a gap. She said she found a tape containing that conversation Nov. 8.

Wong Testimony. Following Woods, Alfred Wong, deputy assistant director of the Secret Service and former chief of the White House technical security unit, continued his testimony, begun Nov. 7. Wong said that it should be possible for the exact equipment used in making each set of tapes to be located and identified. Sirica asked him to do so, in case such knowledge might be helpful in evaluating the tapes.

A Memory Problem. Haldeman, the first witness to appear at the hearings at the behest of the special prosecution force, appeared under subpoena. Until he himself received tapes to listen to on April 25-26, Haldeman said, he was not aware that anyone else had heard the tapes—apart from one time that Butterfield had checked to ascertain that the system was operating.

The first tapes that he received were related to the March 21 meeting of Dean, Nixon and himself, he said. He listened to them twice at the request of the President. Haldeman could not recall any explanation for the fact that 22 tapes were provided to him in order for him to find that specific conversation. Nor could he remember why Secret Service records showed that the tapes, after their second delivery to him, were not returned to their vault until May 2, after his departure from the White House staff. Also lost from Haldeman's memory, he said, was the origin of the idea of his listening in mid-July to several more tapes, particularly that of the Sept. 15, 1972, meeting of Dean, Nixon and himself. *(Haldeman testimony, Vol. I, p. 229)*

Fund-Raising Dispute

A Nixon fund-raiser, in testimony before the Senate Watergate committee Nov. 8, denied prior testimony that

Nixon on Resigning

Following is the statement President Nixon made Nov. 7 at the conclusion of his televised statement on the energy crisis:

As a result of the deplorable Watergate matter, great numbers of Americans have had doubts raised as to the integrity of the President of the United States. I've even noted that some publications have called on me to resign the office of President of the United States.

Tonight I would like to give my answer to those who have suggested that I resign.

I have no intention whatever of walking away from the job I was elected to do.

As long as I am physically able, I am going to continue to work 16 to 18 hours a day for the cause of a real peace abroad and for the cause of prosperity, without inflation and without war, at home.

And in the months ahead, I shall do everything that I can to see that any doubts as to the integrity of the man who occupies the highest office in this land—to remove those doubts where they exist.

And I am confident that in those months ahead, the American people will come to realize that I have not violated the trust that they placed in me when they elected me as President of the United States in the past.

And I pledge to you tonight that I shall always do everything that I can to be worthy of that trust in the future.

he offered to have former Commerce Secretary Maurice H. Stans intercede in a government legal matter for a potential contributor in exchange for a $100,000 donation to the President's re-election campaign. Benjamin Fernandez, who headed the Hispanic Finance Committee to Re-elect the President, rejected the charges made against him Nov. 7 by John J. Priestes, a Florida builder and the potential contributor. *(Priestes testimony, p. 127)*

Fernandez, an economist from Chatsworth, Calif., branded Priestes' accusations "onerous" and a misstatement of the facts. "I am appalled, shocked and disgusted with the tenor" of Priestes' testimony, Fernandez told the committee. Fernandez said that virtually every statement by Priestes was "totally false." The only thing they agreed on was Priestes' testimony that the two of them met in a Washington, D.C., hotel on March 12, 1972.

Specifically, Fernandez denied Priestes' testimony that he had asked Priestes for a $100,000 contribution in exchange for a promise to solve his problems with the Federal Housing Administration (FHA), that the donation was to be in cash and that Priestes had asked Stans to call the secretary of housing and urban development (HUD) about his troubles with the FHA.

Fernandez said he learned of Priestes from someone in the Spanish-speaking community in Florida, who told him of a "dynamic millionaire" who wanted to give $50,000 to the Nixon campaign. Fernandez said that when he met Priestes, he was offered $25,000, not $50,000. Despite the reduction, Fernandez said he was happy to get the money and did not complain.

Business Problems. But after they agreed on the $25,000 contribution, Fernandez told the committee, Priestes said, "Now, Mr. Fernandez, I have a problem to discuss with you." Priestes said he was a "victim of a bad press" that was harassing him about his business dealings, and wanted assurances the FHA would give him a fair hearing, Fernandez related.

Fernandez said he told Priestes he could not do anything about his problem, but when Priestes persisted about getting a fair shake from the government, Fernandez offered to let him plead his case personally with Stans, he said.

Stans' Meeting. Fernandez' recollection of the March 13 meeting in Stans' office differed markedly from that of Priestes. According to Fernandez, after Stans accepted the $25,000 check from Priestes, the builder said he wanted to discuss the problem of press harassment with Stans. Fernandez said Stans looked at a collection of Priestes' newspaper clips for only 10 to 15 seconds, but at no time did Priestes ask Stans to call George Romney, then secretary of housing and urban development.

Fernandez said Priestes mentioned having some "minor technical difficulties" with the government. Stans replied that he would look into Priestes' background and, if he were found to be in serious trouble, the finance committee would have nothing to do with him, Fernandez recalled. Priestes answered, "Fine," Fernandez said. Fernandez then told the committee that Stans gave him Priestes' check and said, "Don't deposit this until you hear from me."

Ten days later, Fernandez said, Stans called him to say that Priestes "was in serious trouble," that the check should be returned and that contact should be broken off with him.

According to Fernandez, he never discussed a $100,-000 contribution with Priestes and cash never was mentioned in their meetings.

The Missing Tapes

In hearings Nov. 6-8 before Judge Sirica on the accessibility and integrity of tapes of White House conversations—and the reason for the non-existence of two tapes—it became clear that the tapes were well-traveled. *(Earlier story, p. 92)*

White House Special Assistant Stephen Bull told the court that he had received a dozen of the subpoenaed tapes from John C. Bennett, deputy assistant to the President. On Sept. 28, Bull said, he and Rose Mary Woods had taken the tapes to Camp David, Md., that weekend, where the President, with their assistance, had reviewed the contents of the tapes. Bull, who refused to say that Woods was making a transcript of the tapes, said only that she was listening to the tapes and typing. Bull said he returned five of the tapes to Bennett the next Monday and that the other tapes remained, as far as he knew, in Woods' possession. He said that the tapes had gone to Key Biscayne, Fla., the weekend of Oct. 5-8, where the review had continued.

Bull testified that during the weekend at Camp David in September, he realized that the April 15 tape, recorded in the President's Executive Office Building office, "trailed off in mid-sentence" before providing any record of the subpoenaed conversation with John W. Dean III. He said he called Bennett, who brought another tape which might have contained the conversation,

to Camp David, but that the second tape did not pick up where the other one trailed off. Bull said that he so informed Woods and Alexander Haig, White House chief of staff, of the absence of the specific April 15 recording and that he assumed Haig had conveyed this information to Nixon.

Incomplete Records. Bennett's testimony made clear that the records kept of the whereabouts and precise contents of the more than 900 tapes made between early 1971 and mid-1973 were incomplete and occasionally inaccurate. He and Bull admitted that the same tape reel often was identified in a variety of ways, creating ambiguity about which tape went where.

Woods, Bennett revealed in his testimony Nov. 6, had been given six additional tapes on Nov. 5, tapes containing conversations recorded on April 16 and soon thereafter. Furthermore, he said Nov. 7, Woods had informed him—after he returned to his office from testifying the previous day—that there were "gaps" in the conversations recorded on those tapes. Bennett said he did not know which conversations were involved, but he assumed that they were conversations between Dean and Nixon. Woods also had told him early the morning of Nov. 7, Bennett said, that "transcribe" was not the proper word to describe what she had been doing to the tapes.

The only person on the "access list" for the vault in which the tapes were stored after the system was dismantled July 18 was Nixon, Bennett said. He admitted, however, that any close aide to the President probably would not be challenged if he tried to enter the vault. Bennett said that he himself had been into the vault on at least eight occasions since July 18.

Secret Service agent Randy Nelson, who had installed the taping systems, explained the way in which they functioned and in which they were checked twice daily during the week, but not usually on weekends. Nelson explained that the appropriate tape recorder was activated through the functioning of a locator system which indicated where the President was and turned on the appropriate equipment. He admitted that, given limitations in the design and equipment of the system, it was not likely that all conversations would be recorded.

Senate Judiciary Hearings

Former Attorney General Elliot L. Richardson told the Senate Judiciary Committee Nov. 6 that he favored presidential appointment of a Watergate special prosecutor—this time with a personal guarantee of independence from the President "on the dotted line."

Making his first appearance before a congressional committee since the firing of special prosecutor Archibald Cox and his own resignation as attorney general Oct. 20, Richardson recommended that Congress make the special prosecutor subject to Senate confirmation.

The Senate then should exact a written promise from the President to waive executive privilege on all Watergate-related matters as the price for confirming both the special prosecutor and the nominee for attorney general, Sen. William B. Saxbe (R Ohio), Richardson said.

As additional guarantees for independence, he said Congress might pass a law assuring the special prosecutor of the right to challenge presidential claims of executive privilege in the courts and forbidding dismissal except for "extraordinary impropriety."

(Continued on p. 122)

Congressional Reaction to Nixon on Missing Tapes

In the wake of the surprise announcement Oct. 31 that two of the nine White House tape recordings ordered turned over to a federal district court did not exist, two senators asked President Nixon to resign. Several congressional leaders urged Nixon to restore public confidence in his leadership by publicly disclosing all information regarding his role in the Watergate scandals. *(Editorial demands for resignation, box, p. 123; Nixon statement, box, p. 119)*

Resignation Requests. Sen. Edward W. Brooke (R Mass.) became the first Republican senator to ask the President to step down. Appearing Nov. 4 on ABC's "Issues and Answers," Brooke was asked if he had come to believe that Nixon should resign. "I have reluctantly come to that conclusion," Brooke replied. "I don't think that the country can stand the trauma that it has been going through for the past few months. It has been like a nightmare, and I know that he doesn't want to hurt the country, and I certainly don't want to prejudge the case. He might not be guilty of any impeachable offense.

"On the other hand, there is no question that President Nixon has lost his effectiveness as the leader of this country, primarily because he has lost the confidence of the people of the country, and I think therefore that in the interests of this nation that he loves that he should step down, should tender his resignation." Brooke actively campaigned for Nixon in 1968 and 1972.

Later in the day on Oct. 31, White House deputy press secretary Gerald L. Warren said Nixon had "absolutely no intention of resigning.... The President intends to pursue his objectives in foreign policy, national policy and in clearing up the Watergate matter."

Walter F. Mondale (D Minn.) became the second senator within the week to urge Nixon to resign. Mondale, who was considering running for the presidency in 1976, said Nov. 6 that Nixon's moral credibility was gone and the chances that he could restore it were "pretty remote."

Mondale and Brooke both urged Congress to confirm Gerald R. Ford as vice president, although Mondale said he was "not particularly impressed" by Ford.

Two other senators had called for Nixon's resignation before the announcement that the two tapes did not exist—John V. Tunney (D Calif.) and Daniel K. Inouye (D Hawaii), a member of the Senate Watergate committee. *(Tunney statement, p. 107; Inouye statement, p. 81)*

Aiken Advice. The Senate's senior Republican, George D. Aiken of Vermont, passed along to Congress some advice he had received from a constituent: "Either impeach him or get off his back." Aiken, in a Senate speech Nov. 7, said it was the duty of the House to "set a deadline, of weeks or months, in which to come up with an impeachment charge." It was, he said, "the President's duty to his country not to resign," although resignation would relieve Congress of its duty.

Disclosure Demands. Pressure on the President to make public all his knowledge related to the Water-

gate incidents came from three Republicans and one Democrat who had generally supported the President. In a statement Nov. 1, Sen. Barry Goldwater (R Ariz.) said that Nixon's credibility had "reached an all-time low from which he may not be able to recover" and urged the President to appear before the Senate select Watergate committee to answer questions. "I feel now more than ever that this may offer the only way out," Goldwater said.

"As one schooled in electronics," Goldwater said, he could understand the circumstances under which the two tapes were not made, "but as a practical person in close touch with the American people, I doubt that they will accept this." *(Missing presidential tapes, p. 92)*

The strongest statement came from Sen. Peter H. Dominick (R Colo.) in a speech to the Denver Bar Association Nov. 5. Declaring that there was a "crisis of confidence in our leadership," Dominick urged the President to release all tapes, documents, papers, files and memorandums requested by the Senate Watergate committee and the special prosecutor's office. Nixon should also "make available voluntarily all other information within his control—whether in or out of the executive branch—which he feels will have a strong bearing on the issues that have been raised," Dominick continued. "The breadth of this disclosure should be limited only by constraints imposed by the national interest."

Dominick, who was chairman of the Republican Senate Campaign Committee in 1972 and who himself would be up for re-election in 1974, also advised Republicans to "follow a more independent course from here on. I think a good place to start would be for the Republican Party to take the leadership in resolving the crisis of confidence in our government."

Senate Minority Leader Hugh Scott (R Pa.) Nov. 5 also urged Nixon to "give the people all the information and let them judge.... A forum has to be found to make the information available."

Similar sentiments were expressed by Sen. Henry M. Jackson (D Wash.) in a Nov. 4 interview on CBS's "Meet the Press." "I believe we have reached the point where the President must appear before an appropriate forum and lay his cards on the table," he said. He added that the Senate Watergate committee would be an appropriate forum. Jackson, who had usually supported the President on questions of national security and defense, said that if the President did not divulge the information, he would face "an unchallengeable demand for impeachment or the possibility of a direct request for resignation, and I think the push will come from the Republican leadership, not just from Democrats."

While reiterating his belief that Nixon was innocent of any wrong-doing, Vice President-designate Ford (R Mich.) told the Senate Rules Committee Nov. 5 that he thought the President should produce all documents necessary to clear up questions of his involvement in Watergate.

The way in which a special prosecutor was appointed would be secondary if such conditions were imposed, Richardson stated.

Like Acting Attorney General Robert H. Bork, Richardson expressed doubts about the constitutionality of a court-appointed prosecutor. Fifty-five senators cosponsored a bill to authorize U.S. District Court Judge John J. Sirica to name a special prosecutor. About 100 House members introduced similar bills.

Practical Reasons. Practical reasons, as well as the constitutional issue, determined Richardson's preference for presidential appointment. A court test of constitutionality could delay Watergate prosecutions, he said. He also doubted that a court-appointed prosecutor could receive backup assistance from the Justice Department and the FBI.

Richardson was reminded by Birch Bayh (D Ind.) that, at confirmation hearings in May 1973, Richardson had assured the committee that Cox would be free from presidential interference and removal.

Bayh: "You said that will just not happen."

Richardson: "Yes, I remember that."

Bayh said the "Maginot Line" protecting the special prosecutor from presidential interference had been destroyed Oct. 20.

Richardson said public opinion would not permit a second dismissal. The President "could not afford to fire the new special prosecutor," he declared.

"We didn't think he could afford to do it the last time," Bayh said.

First Agreement. The agreement on the independence of Cox came apart because of a lack of personal commitment by Nixon, Richardson testified.

"The President was not personally committed to the terms of the charter. He approved it, at least he acquiesced in it, but he was not consulted while the guidelines were being drawn."

Another weakness in the agreement, according to Richardson, was a misunderstanding about access to presidential documents. He said that he had interpreted a statement by Nixon on May 22, 1973, to mean that he would waive executive privilege on presidential documents in addition to testimony from White House aides. In fact, the waiver covered only testimony and was limited to the case of the Watergate burglary.

Committee Chairman James O. Eastland (D Miss.) asked if reports were true that Cox was fired because he was on the verge of discovering "sensational stuff."

"Yes, in a general way," Richardson replied. He said the President had been upset by reported investigations of improvements to his private residences in Key Biscayne, Fla., and San Clemente, Calif. Nixon telephoned Richardson from Key Biscayne July 3 and requested a public statement from Cox that his San Clemente home improvements were not under investigation. Richardson checked with Cox, who told him that he was not conducting such an investigation.

The White House, according to Richardson, also had been irritated by reports that Cox was investigating the President's close friends, Charles G. Rebozo and Robert Abplanalp, and his secretary, Rose Mary Woods.

The White House staff looked upon Cox's office as a "ravenous beast with an insatiable appetite," Richardson said.

Nixon talked with Richardson in September or early October about "getting rid of Cox," Richardson stated.

Even if all of Cox's investigations had led to indictments, there would have been "no very shattering impacts," the former attorney general said.

At this point, the only way for Nixon to reassure Congress and the American people that the special prosecutor can get to the "bottom of all these matters" is to drop all claims of executive privilege, Richardson asserted.

Hiram L. Fong (R Hawaii) asked whether the scope of the prosecution should go "all over the place."

Richardson replied that there should be some showing of materiality to protect the President against "fishing expeditions."

President's Health. Edward M. Kennedy (D Mass.) asked about published reports that Richardson had been worried about the President's psychological health.

The President showed "a considerable sense of strain" from around early July, Richardson replied. But he added that in later meetings with the President, "he certainly seemed very restrained and deliberate."

Chiles Testimony. Sen. Lawton Chiles (D Fla.), who introduced one of the first bills to create an independent special prosecutor to be appointed by Sirica, told the committee Nov. 5 that credibility in government cannot be restored by the "executive branch investigating itself."

In reply to a question by Charles McC. Mathias (R Md.), Chiles said that the Constitution makes clear that impeachment by the House does not preclude criminal prosecution.

The two procedures are "not mutually exclusive," Mathias agreed. "The Constitution says nothing about the order of procedure as to whether one or the other should come first."

American Bar Association. Jack G. Day, chairman of the criminal justice section of the American Bar Association (ABA), testified Nov. 5 that "the country will lose confidence in a judicial system which has no machinery to deal with the investigation of the claimed illegal conduct of the chief magistrate, his associates or appointees."

The Constitution was not intended to mask official misconduct through the doctrine of separation of powers, especially because that doctrine was intended to establish checks and balances, Day declared.

The system was saved Oct. 20, Day said, because of the courageous action of three men who put integrity above place and position. But he argued that the system should be "arranged by law so that men of ordinary bravery can operate within it with the sure knowledge that duty can be done with impunity."

The ABA's position, according to Davis, was based on four propositions:

• The rule of law applies to all citizens without exception.

• The rule of law requires complete severance and independence between the subject of the investigation and the investigator.

• Independence means neither the appointment nor tenure of persons conducting the investigation shall be controlled in any way by the subject under investigation.

• If a controversy relating to the scope or propriety of a procedure of investigative objectives arises, the resolution of the issues is for the courts.

(Continued on p. 124)

Excerpts of Media Demands for Nixon's Resignation

Following are excerpts from several editorials demanding or suggesting that President Nixon resign:

TIME MAGAZINE NOV. 12

Richard Nixon and the nation have passed a tragic point of no return. It now seems likely that the President will have to give up his office: he has irredeemably lost his moral authority, the confidence of most of the country, and therefore his ability to govern effectively....

The editors of Time Inc., speaking on the editorial pages of *Time's* sister publication *Life*, have endorsed Nixon for President three times, in 1960, 1968 and 1972.... Thus we come with deep reluctance to our conclusion that he must leave office. We consider the situation so unprecedented, the issue so crucial to the country, that we publish this first editorial in *Time's* 50-year history.

In two centuries, no American President has been removed from office other than by death or the voters' will. Once the spell is broken, would it become too easy for political opponents of any future president to oust him? We think not. Watergate is unique. In fact, the really dangerous precedent would be the opposite: to allow a President with Nixon's record to continue in office. This would be a terrible circumstance to lodge in our history, a terrible thing to explain to our children and their children....

A President's "big decisions" cannot be put into a compartment separate from his other actions, his total behavior. His integrity and trustworthiness are perhaps the most important facts about him to his country and to the world. And these Nixon has destroyed. The nightmare of uncertainty must be ended.

THE NEW YORK TIMES NOV. 4

The visible disintegration of President Nixon's moral and political authority, of his capacity to act as chief executive, of his claim to leadership and to credibility leads us to the reluctant conclusion that Mr. Nixon would be performing his ultimate service to the American people—and to himself—by resigning his office before this nation is forced to go through the traumatic and divisive process of impeachment....

The gravity of the case against him rests...on his deliberate violations of the letter and the spirit of the Constitution and, flowing out of this, the collapse of public confidence in the integrity of the man who only one year ago was elected to the presidency by the largest popular majority in history....

The one last great service that Mr. Nixon can now perform for his country is to resign. He has been trying to "tough it out" for too long at too great a cost to the nation. As long as he clings to office, he keeps the presidency swamped in a sea of scandal and the American public in a morass of concern and confusion. The state of the union requires nothing less than a change in the sorry state of the presidency.

THE DETROIT NEWS NOV. 4

After Rep. Gerald Ford has been confirmed as vice president, President Richard Nixon should resign.... This newspaper has been one of Mr. Nixon's strongest supporters. Watergate aside, we still agree with many of his basic policies....

However, unless the present crisis of authority is resolved... the country must endure 38 more months of the doubts, charges and recriminations which have destroyed the President's ability to lead....

The White House's assertion that two key Watergate tapes never existed and can't be delivered sinks President Nixon's credibility to an all-time low. Someone in the White House is guilty of either unbelievable stupidity or outright lies. In either case, public confidence in this administration suffers the final shattering blow....

We hope Mr. Nixon will see this suggestion (to resign) as a wise one for himself and as a necessary one for the national welfare. If he does not see it that way, the next step in the unfolding tragedy of Richard Nixon may be impeachment. Distressing as that procedure might be, it would be less distressing than three more years of political vendetta. Enough is enough.

THE DENVER POST NOV. 4

Ironically, it was just a year ago this Sunday that The Post wrote its final editorial supporting Mr. Nixon for the presidency because among other reasons we believed he was the better man to produce effective national unity....

But in a time of national crisis, such as the recent alerting of our military forces in the Middle Eastern situation, the people must be able to trust automatically the President's integrity. And on simpler matters, it is intolerable that on a question of whether or not the tapes were really lost, a great number of people simply don't take the word of their President....

When the vice presidency is filled, the Republican party must live up to its responsibilities.... The Republican party should try to persuade the President to resign.... History would think well of a Nixon decision to step down, not as an admission of guilt, but as a recognition that the needed trust essential to the conduct of his office has been lost....

If, however, resignation is not in the cards, then this newspaper has come to the reluctant conclusion that only an impeachment proceeding will heal our hemorrhaging of national confidence in the presidency.

NATIONAL REVIEW NOV. 9

Richard Nixon is still the legal head of government, but is he, in the meaning proper to a constitutional, republican society, still a legitimate ruler? ...Perhaps the surrender on the tapes will prove a turning point but...if the public distrust and rejection of Mr. Nixon persists, deepens further, and hardens, the country will be facing the crippling and possibly catastrophic prospect of three years without—a legitimate government....

The one way and the only way to close out that crisis would be by Richard Nixon's departure.... If Mr. Nixon becomes convinced—and by a few more months at most it will be sure, one way or another—that he has irretrievably lost the support and trust of a solid majority of the people, it will then be his duty to resign his office as the only act able to heal the grievous wound.

This would be, under the circumstances, the highest act of loyalty and patriotism on his part, and we therefore feel that Richard Nixon, facing the reality, would see resignation as his duty; and if he did not, it would become the duty of his closest friends and associates to persuade him so to see it.

But if, by the New Year say, no charge of criminal conduct against the President takes unequivocal and public form...it will then be time for his critics, and especially his critics in Congress, to put up or shut up.

House Judiciary Hearings

The House Judiciary subcommittee Nov. 5 heard opposing testimony from Acting Attorney General Bork during the morning session and from Archibald Cox—the man Bork had fired as special prosecutor—that afternoon. The two lawyers disagreed on the constitutionality of a court-appointed prosecutor and the practical need for such legislation.

Resignation Threatened. Bork made it clear he would resign if the White House interfered with the new special prosecutor's investigation. "I do not expect that there will be any further trouble with regard to the special prosecutor," Bork said in response to a question. "But should these investigations or prosecutions be compromised, I would regard my position as morally untenable."

Bork added that both he and Leon Jaworski, Cox's replacement as special prosecutor, had understood from White House aides that Jaworski would be allowed to try to obtain White House documents through the courts. Cox's refusal to obey President Nixon's order that he not go to court to force the release of presidential documents led to Cox's dismissal.

"I envision a great deal of cooperation from the White House," Bork said. "Should there come a point at which the President feels that the confidentiality of a certain piece of paper is important and he ought not to turn it over, I understand, and it's clear to me, that Mr. Jaworski can go to court and test out that claim."

"Then what you're telling us, Mr. Bork, is that the executive department has turned over a new leaf insofar as Watergate is concerned, that they really are very much interested now in getting to the bottom of this," Rep. Don Edwards (D Calif.) interjected at one point. "Is that correct?"

Not having been involved in the events that led up to Cox's dismissal, Bork replied, "I could certainly not agree that somebody has turned over a new leaf. All I know is the leaf I'm looking at. And the leaf I'm looking at is one of freedom for the special prosecutor and power to use the judicial process."

"Well, as Adam said to Eve in the garden of Eden, there seems to be a leaf missing somewhere," quipped Subcommittee Chairman Rep. William L. Hungate (D Mo.).

Dubious Constitutionality. Aside from the dubious constitutionality of a court-appointed special prosecutor, Bork said such legislation would create a precedent "that has great potential danger" for abuse. He argued that if the late Sen. Joseph R. McCarthy (R Wis. 1947-57) had been able to get a special prosecutor to hunt subversives in government, "it would have just been a terrible situation.... It would always be better if an investigator and a prosecutor were separated from whoever might turn up as the subject of his investigation. I think, however, we have a Constitution we have to live with.... There are a number of times when this kind of distrust of the executive branch exists, and a special prosecutor could be appointed. I think (it) would be a very tough precedent."

At another point, Bork argued, "The question is whether congressional legislation appointing a special prosecutor outside the executive branch or empowering courts to do so would be constitutionally valid and wheth-

er it would provide significant advantages that make it worth taking a constitutionally risky course. I am persuaded that such a course would almost certainly not be valid and would, in any event, pose more problems than it would solve." However, Bork said he did not believe legislation guaranteeing the independence of the special prosecutor without taking the office out of the executive branch would be unconstitutional.

Cox Opening Statement. During a lengthy opening statement delivered from hand-written notes, Cox repeated much of what he had said during his Senate committee appearance in support of a court-appointed prosecutor. He urged passage of the legislation for four reasons: to avoid any conflict of interest—or the appearance of one—that might arise from allowing the executive branch to investigate itself; to assure informants and potential witnesses that their confidentiality would be protected; to assure that the prosecutor would be able to "resist direct and indirect White House pressure to limit the investigation," and to give the prosecutor and his staff "the legal standing and the will to use all forms of legal process to obtain information from other parts of the executive branch of government." *(Senate appearance, p. 93)*

Cox cited instances of what he characterized as noncooperation and attempted interference by the White House during his own tenure as special prosecutor. He appealed to "the ancient principle of equal justice under the law," that "those guilty of wrong-doing in high office are subject to the same laws as those whose station in life may not be as high. The kind of investigation required and the essential public confidence in its integrity can be commanded, I believe, only by an independent prosecution force outside the normal hierarchy of the executive branch, with statutory powers and duties, resting upon a statutory base."

Partisan Questions. The pattern of political partisanship that had surfaced early in the hearings continued during the appearances of Cox and Bork, particularly in the openly hostile questioning of Cox by one of the Republican members. Rep. Lawrence J. Hogan (R Md.) at one point cited the past Democratic affiliations of Cox and a string of top-ranking former staff members, and asked, "Couldn't a reasonable man assume, on the basis of the things that I have said about your staff and your former involvement in Democratic politics, that someone might suspect" that the special prosecution team was politically motivated toward embarrassing a Republican administration?

"I think that it is wholly possible, and I certainly pray that it would be wholly possible, for people to engage in law enforcement, the administration of justice in this country, without their political affiliations having any part to play, or being suspected of having any part to play," Cox responded. *(Composition of Cox team, Vol. I, p. 198)*

A short time later, Hogan brought up Cox's admission during his Senate appearance that Cox had made an "inexcusable" error in revealing to two Democratic senators information that had been told to him in confidence while he headed the prosecution team. The information was published by *The New York Times*. *(Senate hearings, p. 93)*

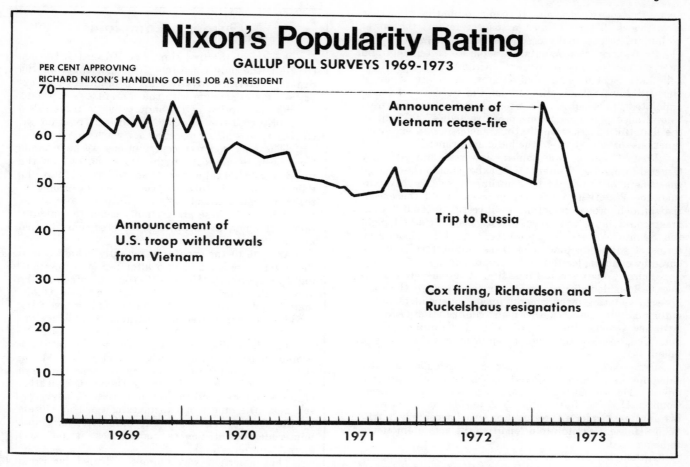

Nixon's Popularity Rating
GALLUP POLL SURVEYS 1969-1973

PER CENT APPROVING
RICHARD NIXON'S HANDLING OF HIS JOB AS PRESIDENT

Announcement of
Vietnam cease-fire

Announcement of
U.S. troop withdrawals
from Vietnam

Trip to Russia

Cox firing, Richardson and
Ruckelshaus resignations

1969   1970   1971   1972   1973

PUBLIC ENTHUSIASM FOR PRESIDENT DROPPED TO LOW OF 27 PER CENT

"I'm concerned about other possible news leaks...(a) whole series of leaks that could only have come from your office," Hogan said. He then listed several stories about Cox investigations that had appeared in *The Washington Post*, *The Washington Star-News* and the Times. "You're aware, I'm sure...that the rules of grand jury prohibit disclosure of matters that are under investigation, and I wonder if maybe this doesn't cast some aspersion on the professionalism...of your staff," Hogan said.

"I would be obliged to dispute...your statement that that information could have come only from the Watergate special prosecution force," Cox replied, his voice cracking. "...In many instances I have seen things attributed to sources in my office (that) I knew with virtual moral certainty did not emanate from my office."

Another Republican member of the panel, Rep. Wiley Mayne (Iowa), questioned the reversal of the opinion Cox had voiced during an Oct. 28 television appearance, that there would be "severe constitutional problems" in allowing a court to appoint a special prosecutor. "I'm profoundly impressed today, Mr. Cox, just as I was Oct. 28, that a man with your long experience and knowledge would express these serious reservations about the approach which is taken in some of this legislation," Mayne said. He then asked Cox if it would be "inappropriate for me to inquire" who had referred Cox to the legal precedents that Cox said had changed his mind.

"It was one of my colleagues at the Harvard Law School, and I don't...whichever was the one who called me, I couldn't tell you which one," Cox replied hesitantly.

"Well, now, that satisfies me, Mr. Cox," Mayne said.

Whalen Testimony. The debate over the constitutionality of the legislation and the practical need for it continued Nov. 7 as the subcommittee heard from Rep. Charles W. Whalen Jr. (R Ohio), sponsor of one of the bills calling for a court-appointed special prosecutor, and from two law professors. Whalen's bill, HR 11135, called for U.S. District Court Chief Judge John J. Sirica to appoint a special prosecutor. However, Whalen said he would not object to another version, which would allow a panel of judges to choose the prosecutor and thereby avoid having Sirica remove himself from the case on grounds of conflict of interest because of having chosen the prosecutor.

"I have no pride of authorship," Whalen said. But, he added, "I do not believe (members of the executive branch) can be expected to investigate themselves. Therefore the responsibility must be placed elsewhere, outside of the executive branch.... All Americans must be convinced beyond any doubt that the Watergate investigation has been absolutely thorough."

On the constitutionality of a court-appointed prosecutor, Whalen said he rested his case on "the simple proposition that the role of the courts in our society is to assure that justice prevails. It seems to me that the cause of justice is ill served when a suspect retains the power both to investigate and prosecute himself."

Professors' Statements. In separate statements and later in joint testimony, Roger C. Cramton, dean of Cornell Law School, and Paul Bator, associate dean of Harvard Law School, differed on the need for a court-appointed prosecutor. Cramton urged that Congress "simultaneously pursue four other remedies" in light of the doubtful constitutionality of transferring an executive function—prosecution—to the judiciary branch.

First, Cramton maintained, Jaworski and Attorney General-designate William B. Saxbe should be "given the benefit of the doubt for the time being" as they pursued the Watergate investigation. Second, "if the executive branch proves reluctant to investigate itself," Congress could launch its own investigation to supplement the Senate Watergate committee. "Any deficiencies in terms of subpoena powers of these committees could be cured by enabling legislation," Cramton said.

Third, Congress could pass a joint resolution "censuring the President for the breach of faith toward the Congress in violating arrangements for an independent prosecutor made in connection with the confirmation of former Attorney General Richardson." Finally, Cramton pointed out, Congress could resort to impeachment if all else failed.

Cramton's testimony carried particular weight, since he had recently served as Nixon's constitutional adviser. He was head of the Justice Department's Legal Counsel Division from July 1972 to March 1973, when his routine tender of resignation was accepted by the White House. Cramton told reporters the action amounted to being fired.

Although Cramton opposed the court-appointed prosecutor proposal, Rep. Robert W. Kastenmeier (D Wis.) remarked, "I take it from your concluding remarks that you do not come here today as an apologist for the President." Cramton said he was testifying as a private citizen and was not representing any special interest. A few moments later he told Kastenmeier, "If you ask me to explain the...fits and starts of presidential decision-making over the past few months, I cannot. I view them as irrational...."

Bator, who like Cox had first said the proposal might be unconstitutional, said he also had changed his mind after studying legal precedents. "...Though the matter is not entirely free from doubt...the more persuasive authority under the law" holds the measure to be constitutional, he said. He disagreed with Cramton that Congress should not legislate at all. "I think it's quite ironic that the country should be told by the Congress that it can't help them," he said.

Watergate Witnesses Nov. 6

In a renewed effort at obtaining presidential testimony on the Watergate affair, the Senate select Watergate committee decided Nov. 6 to have its staff explore with the President's lawyers the possibility of a meeting of the senators with Nixon.

Chairman Sam J. Ervin Jr. (D N.C.) made the announcement to reporters at the noon recess of committee hearings. The committee had decided on the move at an early-morning executive session, and it reportedly was

---

Gurney's Complaint

It was not the first time Sen. Edward J. Gurney (R Fla.), the only consistent Nixon defender on the Senate Watergate investigating committee, had expressed dissatisfaction with the committee's methods. But his description of the inquiry as "a travesty"— in a private letter to Gov. Meldrim Thomson Jr. (R N.H.)—was his strongest attack yet.

"The only concrete contributions we have made have been to force down the stock market, up the price of gold, devalue the American dollar, hurt the economy, and destroy the confidence of people in the American political system," Gurney wrote in the Oct. 5 letter. "These are certainly concrete contributions but about as useful as a block of concrete tied around a swimmer's neck."

An aide to the senator reluctantly acknowledged the letter's existence Nov. 5 after repeated questioning by reporters. "He was letting off steam," the aide said. Thomson had wired Committee Chairman Sam J. Ervin Jr. (D N.C.) to complain about the activities of committee investigators in New Hampshire.

The immediate object of Gurney's wrath appeared to be the committee's contact with a Miami construction contractor, John Priestes, who had been giving evidence in connection with an investigation of the senator's fund-raising activities. "I have myself been the object of two investigations in Florida by the staff of our very own committee, an action unprecedented in Senate committees as far as I know," Gurney wrote.

That assertion was promptly denied by Ervin and chief counsel Samuel Dash. Testifying at the open hearings Nov. 7, Priestes told of a 1972 offer by Nixon's former chief fund-raiser, Maurice H. Stans, of favorable government treatment in exchange for a $100,000 contribution. "We did not get to him because of any investigation having anything to do with Sen. Gurney," Dash insisted. *(Hearings, p. 127)*

Gurney revealed Oct. 31 that he was under investigation by the Justice Department because of allegations that he received secret contributions from Florida builders in exchange for his influence in their behalf with the Federal Housing Administration.

---

a result of a motion by Sen. Lowell P. Weicker Jr. (R Conn.). The Weicker proposal did not request Nixon to testify under oath, but it was believed to call for a full transcript of the session and the quick release of that transcript to the public. Committee members repeatedly had expressed a desire to meet with the President at any time or place, but this was the first concrete step toward such an arrangement.

The seven-member committee, meanwhile, concluded its probe into so-called dirty tricks during the 1972 presidential election with testimony from five witnesses requested by the Republican committee minority.

Campbell Testimony. The leadoff witness was Truman Campbell, a Republican Party official from

Fresno, Calif. Campbell said a Nixon rally he had organized for Republican women at a Fresno shopping center Oct. 30, 1972, was disrupted by demonstrators who indicated their support for Democratic nominee George McGovern. He said the demonstrators were "unruly and loud" and that they struck one woman who subsequently required medical attention.

Campbell identified members of United Farm Workers (UFW) as predominant among the demonstrators, based on the banners they carried and their slogans, but he conceded that he could not say for sure whether they were in fact UFW people or impostors. He added that he had no information that the demonstrators were supported by the McGovern campaign.

Heller Testimony. Another witness was Michael Heller, 19, a college student from Gresham, Ore., who headed a Democrats for Nixon office in West Los Angeles, Calif. Heller said he saw several pieces of "scurrilous" literature attacking Nixon in one of McGovern's campaign offices.

He identified one flyer headed, "Nixon is treyf." "Treyf" is a Yiddish word meaning not kosher, or unclean. The flyer was distributed by McGovern volunteers, he said, and included this sentence: "Thanks to modern technology, Nixon brings the ovens to the people rather than bringing the people to the ovens." This, he testified, was a reference to the use of napalm in Vietnam and was intended to anger Jewish voters by drawing a parallel between Nixon's war policies and Nazi crematoria in World War II.

Brindze Testimony. Following Heller to the witness table was Paul Brindze, a law student at the University of California at Los Angeles. Brindze said he had been responsible for three McGovern offices in West Los Angeles and conceded that he had allowed a stranger to use his office equipment to print 1,500 to 3,000 of the "Nixon is treyf" flyers.

Watergate Committee Subpoenas

The Senate Nov. 7 adopted a resolution (S Res 194) stating the sense of Congress than the Senate Select Committee on Presidential Campaign Activities—the Watergate committee—had the authority to subpoena President Nixon. The resolution was agreed to by voice vote and without debate.

S Res 194 stated that a provision of the resolution which established the investigating committee (S Res 60) gave the committee the power to subpoena the President. The provision authorized the committee to issue subpoenas to any officer of the United States.

In addition, S Res 194 endorsed the committee's actions in subpoenaing the President on July 27 and in pursuing litigation to achieve compliance with the subpoenas. The resolution stated that the information sought was vital to the performance of the committee's functions.

The committee's civil suit to obtain several subpoenaed tapes had been dismissed Oct. 17 by U.S. District Judge John J. Sirica on the grounds that he could find no basis for his court's having jurisdiction over the matter. *(p. 60)*

Brindze said he did so without reading the copy on the flyer comparing Nixon to the Nazis. He apologized for it, adding that he would not have allowed use of his machines to print extra copies had he read the entire flyer. Brindze said he had acted on his own, rather than for the McGovern campaign, out of his deep anti-war convictions.

Carter Testimony. Another witness was Rep. Tim Lee Carter (R Ky.), who described demonstrators outside his hotel in Miami Beach, Fla., during the 1972 Republican convention. Carter said he and his wife were on their way to dinner Aug. 20, 1972, when a "fanatical" group of demonstrators began shouting obscenities and assaulting them. He described them as "inhuman," "whirling dervishes" and "revolutionaries."

Carter said that when one demonstrator called him a "murderer," he lost his composure and struck him, knocking the man down. Another demonstration witnessed by Carter took place Aug. 23 outside the Kentucky delegation's hotel. Carter said mobs of demonstrators set trash fires, broke windows, struck a member of his delegation and disabled a bus to prevent it from taking the delegates to the convention site.

He declined, however, to attribute the actions of the demonstrators to any one candidate. He said they appeared to have been organized, but that he did not know who organized them or whether they had been paid.

Sullivan Testimony. The last witness was Jeremiah P. Sullivan, a police official from Boston, who described a demonstration outside the Commonwealth Armory Oct. 31, 1972, while the President's wife was inside. He said only strong police precautions prevented some of the crowd of 7,500 from storming the armory. Nine policemen were injured during a melee outside the building, Sullivan said. There was no evidence, he said, that the demonstration violence was preplanned. "Much of it seemed spontaneous," he said.

Affidavits. The dirty tricks phase of the hearings ended with Vice Chairman Howard H. Baker Jr. (R Tenn.) placing in the committee's record sworn affidavits from about 30 persons claiming Nixon's re-election committees around the country were harassed by demonstrations, property damage, obscene signs, break-ins and threats of violence.

Witnesses Nov. 7

A Florida home builder testified that officials of the President's re-election finance committee promised to solve his problems with the Federal Housing Administration (FHA) in return for a $100,000 contribution to the Nixon re-election campaign.

John J. Priestes of Coral Gables said he discussed the deal with former Commerce Secretary Maurice H. Stans, but that it fell through when Stans was unable to help him. At the time of their meeting, Stans was chairman of the Finance Committee to Re-elect the President and Priestes was on the FHA's suspensions list for registering under a false corporate name. Inclusion on the list had an adverse effect on Priestes' business.

In a statement from Stans read into the committee record by Baker, Stans denied arranging any favors for

Watergate Grand Jury

With only one dissenting vote, the House Nov. 6 approved and sent to the Senate Judiciary Committee a bill (HR 10937) extending for six months the life of the original federal grand jury investigating the Watergate break-in and coverup. Without congressional approval of such a measure, the term of the grand jury would expire Dec. 4, 1973.

As passed under suspension of the rules by a roll-call vote of 378-1, HR 10937 legislatively extended the term of the grand jury to June 4, 1974, and allowed still another six-month extension of its term by the federal district court for the District of Columbia, if the grand jury so requested. If the court failed to grant the requested extension, the bill allowed the grand jury to apply for that extension to the chief judge of the court of appeals, District of Columbia circuit.

Upon request of the grand jury in October, then Attorney General Elliot L. Richardson requested that Congress approve the extension. As originally drafted, the bill would have left the decision on extension up to the federal district court; the House committee amended the bill to make the first extension congressional action, leaving the second to judicial discretion. *(Committee action, p. 102)*

The grand jury would not be able to complete its work by the Dec. 4 expiration date, said William L. Hungate, chairman of the House Judiciary subcommittee that initially considered the bill. "If we do not extend the term," Hungate continued, "it will then be necessary to impanel a new grand jury.... (which) will then have to receive all of the evidence and testimony (already once) presented to the June 5, 1972, grand jury."

The lone dissenting vote was cast by Earl F. Landgrebe (R Ind.).

Priestes and said all contacts with him were dropped when he learned Priestes was in trouble with the FHA.

An earlier witness Nov. 7, William H. Marumoto, described how the White House tried to get political mileage out of government programs for Spanish-speaking citizens.

Prison Term. When he testified, Priestes was one week away from the start of a one-year prison sentence for filing a false tax return. He testified under committee subpoena, but without immunity from further prosecution.

Priestes was a spectacularly successful south Florida home builder, mainly through FHA programs boosting construction for low-income home purchasers. In one year he went from 19th to 2nd among south Florida builders, mainly through his contacts with the Miami FHA administrator, William Pelski, it was reported.

He said he was contacted Feb. 26, 1972, by Benjamin Fernandez, who identified himself as head of a Nixon fund-raising group, the National Hispanic Finance Committee to Re-elect the President. Fernandez, Priestes testified, told him he could help with his FHA problem in exchange for a $100,000 contribution to the finance committee. Priestes said Fernandez promised that Stans would personally intercede for him with the FHA in exchange for the contribution in cash or cashier's checks.

According to Priestes, Fernandez said the contribution would have to be made in three steps. First, a $25,000 contribution would allow Priestes to meet Stans and Stans would personally call George Romney, then secretary of housing and urban development (HUD), to plead Priestes' cause. A second $25,000 payment would be due after the Stans call to Romney, and a third payment of $50,000 would be due when Priestes was removed from the suspensions list.

The witness said he checked out the offer with his friend, Pelski, before accepting it, and that Pelski told him to go through with it. Priestes said Pelski never told him whom he contacted to confirm the arrangement.

Priestes said a Florida land investor, Martin Woolin, loaned him the first payment of $25,000 in the form of a personal check made out to the Republican National Committee. Woolin refused to give him cash or write out the check to the finance committee because he had never heard of the fund-raising arm of the Nixon re-election effort, Priestes said.

A meeting with Fernandez took place March 12, 1972, in a Washington hotel, Priestes said. He told the committee that he was upset because he had read in the papers that the International Telephone and Telegraph Corp. (ITT) had promised $200,000 to the Nixon campaign. Priestes said he felt it was unfair for Fernandez to demand $100,000 from him, half the amount a huge corporation like ITT was reportedly contributing.

Meeting with Stans. Fernandez answered, according to Priestes, that ITT actually was giving $400,000, but that Priestes could halve his required contribution to $50,000. The meeting with Stans took place the next day, March 13. Priestes said he took along a scrapbook of news stories detailing his troubles with the FHA at Fernandez' request.

Priestes said Stans looked over the news clippings for about 15 minutes while he explained his problems. Fernandez had promised him, Priestes said, that as soon as he had handed over the check, Stans would call Romney. But, Priestes said, when he gave Stans the check, Stans did not reach for the telephone.

"I said wait a minute," Priestes related. "What about the call to Romney?

"Stans said he'd make the call later, and if he couldn't do any good he'd give me back the money," the witness said. According to Priestes, Stans noted that the check was made out to the wrong committee and urged him to get all the money in before April 7, when a new law requiring public disclosure of campaign contributors was to go into effect. Fernandez, Priestes added, suggested that Priestes get the rest of the money in cash or in checks of smaller denominations signed by persons with Spanish surnames.

Priestes said he heard virtually nothing from Fernandez after that meeting, but two weeks later a man identifying himself as from the finance committee came to his home with the check Priestes had given Stans. Priestes said the man told him the situation was "serious," and demanded $25,000 in cash to settle the deal. Priestes refused and the stranger gave him back the check.

Priestes said he called Fernandez, who told him, "We can't do anything for you." Fernandez then asked for a $5,000 cash contribution, Priestes related. "What would I get for the $5,000?" Priestes said he asked Fernandez. When Priestes said he was told he would get nothing in return, he declined to make a contribution and returned the check to Woolin.

Stans' Statement. Stans' unsworn statement then was read into the record by Baker. The statement, in the form of a letter to the committee, confirmed much of Priestes' testimony, including the meeting in Stans' office. But despite his admitting to having read the scrapbook about Priestes' troubles with the FHA, Stans insisted he did not know Priestes was on the suspensions list until informed later by a HUD official.

Stans said he did tell Priestes he would check with HUD on his problem and confirmed that he told him the check was made out incorrectly. But he said that when he learned Priestes was on the FHA suspensions list, he ordered the check returned and future contact with him broken. Stans insisted he never intended to put pressure on the FHA for Priestes in return for the contribution.

Asked to comment on Stans' statement, Priestes called it "basically true." He declined to term the deal he had arranged with Fernandez a bribe. It was a political favor, he explained. "It's the way things are done."

Gurney Link. Priestes also had been linked to Sen. Edward J. Gurney (R Fla.), a member of the Senate Watergate committee. Priestes reportedly made secret cash payments over the last two years to Larry E. Williams, a former FHA Miami director, who had been described as a Gurney fund raiser. Gurney, who did not hear Priestes' testimony, had denied that Williams was a fund-raiser for him. *(Gurney blast at committee investigation, p. 126)*

Minority Politics. Marumoto was the committee's first witness in the third and final phase of its hearings, campaign contributions. He had worked in the White House from 1970-73 on liaison with Spanish-speaking communities. Marumoto operated in conjunction with Fernandez, who, he said, raised about $400,000 from Spanish-speaking communities for Nixon's re-election campaign.

Marumoto conceded that federal grants, particularly from the Commerce Department's Office of Minority Business Enterprise, were run through a political screen and judged on how well they might promote Nixon's re-election. "When an organization (seeking a federal grant) was totally anti-administration," he said, "there would be a neutralizing effect" on its proposal.

The witness, who was of Japanese-American descent, said Alexander Armendaris, a re-election committee official, would "sign off" (approve) on all grants before they were awarded to the Spanish-speaking grantee. Asked by committee counsel Samuel Dash whether that meant a "political signing off" was required for grants to the Spanish-speaking community, Marumoto replied, "Yes, sir."

But he insisted that the administration's intent at all times was to help the Spanish-speaking people advance economically. He said that federal grants always went to qualified awardees, but conceded that the more supportive they were of the administration the better their chances for a grant. Marumoto said he never asked for a campaign contribution from any awardee in ex-

change for a federal grant. He said he was proud of what Nixon and he had done to help Spanish-speaking Americans.

Marumoto's testimony drew a scathing retort from Sen. Joseph M. Montoya (D N.M.), who called it an "incredible insult" to Spanish-speaking people and "a blatant attempt to buy" their votes.

But Sen. Lowell P. Weicker Jr. (R Conn.), who had been the most critical of the committee Republican members toward the administration, came to its defense. He said there was nothing unusual or illegal in what Marumoto or the administration had done. Such things had gone on for years, Weicker said, and was one of the reasons why the Democratic Party was the majority party and the Republicans were in the minority. This was an attempt to get the Spanish-speaking people into the Republican Party, he said.

Week's Watergate Chronology

Following is a day-to-day chronology of the week's events in the Watergate case for the week ending Nov. 3 *(Earlier Oct. 31 events, p. 108):*

OCT. 31

Krogh Tapes. In a series of motions filed in U.S. District Court in Washington, D.C., attorneys for Egil Krogh Jr. asked for access to presidential tapes and files related to the White House "plumbers" investigation unit Krogh headed. He had been indicted for his role in the 1971 break-in at the office of Daniel Ellsberg's psychiatrist and for making false statements to a federal prosecutor. The tapes and files would show, the lawyers said, that Krogh had been protecting "classified information from unauthorized disclosure" when he allegedly committed perjury. President Nixon was present at all four of the meetings recorded by the tapes in question. *(Krogh indictment, p. 92)*

NOV. 1

Tapes Hearing. Presidential counsel J. Fred Buzhardt Jr. and two White House Secret Service agents testified before U.S. District Judge Sirica on the circumstances surrounding the nonexistence of two of the nine subpoenaed White House tapes. Clarifying an earlier explanation, Buzhardt said there was no record of a conversation between Nixon and his former counsel, John W. Dean III, on the evening of April 15, 1973, because the recorder had run out of tape earlier that day. One of the agents said that a presidential assistant, Stephen B. Bull, had removed 26 tapes from their storage safe on June 4 but had never checked them back in. *(Details, p. 92)*

Saxbe, Jaworski Appointments. Nixon appointed a prominent Houston lawyer, Leon Jaworski, to replace Watergate special prosecutor Archibald Cox. At the same time, he nominated Sen. William B. Saxbe (R Ohio), who had criticized the President sharply on a number of issues, to succeed Elliot L. Richardson as attorney general. *(Details, p. 111, 109)*

Senate Hearings. The Senate Watergate investigating committee heard testimony from Clark Mac-

Gregor, who replaced John N. Mitchell in July 1972 as Nixon's campaign manager. MacGregor, who said he believed he had been duped by White House and re-election committee employees, disputed earlier statements of Nixon, former presidential aide John D. Ehrlichman and former acting FBI Director L. Patrick Gray III. *(Details, p. 105)*

Goldwater Statement. In a prepared statement, Sen. Barry M. Goldwater (R Ariz.) said he thought Nixon's credibility had "reached an all-time low from which he may never be able to recover." Goldwater urged the President to go before the Senate Watergate investigating committee to explain the nonexistent tapes and other Watergate matters. *(Congressional reaction, box, p. 121)*

NOV. 2

Nixon Resignation. Gerald L. Warren, deputy White House press secretary, told reporters that Nixon was "not giving any thought" to resigning. Warren spoke at a briefing near Key Biscayne, Fla., where Nixon had flown suddenly the day before without the usual retinue of reporters and photographers.

Tapes Hearing. Judge Sirica's hearing on the handling of the White House tapes continued to create confusion. Stephen B. Bull, a presidential aide, said he had arranged for Nixon to hear some of the tapes Sept. 29 and that the President had informed him then that two of the nine tapes were missing.

Another witness, a White House Secret Service agent, said that White House attorney J. Fred Buzhardt had been aware as early as Oct. 22 that two of the critical conversations had not been recorded. Buzhardt had testified that he got the news the weekend of Oct. 27-28. Sirica said he wanted to establish "the chain of possession" of the tapes and "the technical reasons why the conversations weren't recorded."

Accounting Funds. *The Washington Post* reported that federal prosecutors in New York City were investigating a possible attempt by Nixon fund-raisers to solicit at least $100,000 from partners in the nation's largest firm of certified public accountants, Peat Marwick Mitchell & Company. The firm's general counsel was quoted as saying that former Nixon finance chairman Maurice H. Stans had pressed for the contribution despite the fact that the company was a government contractor.

NOV. 4

Resignation Calls. Edward W. Brooke (R Mass.) became the first Republican senator to publicly advocate Nixon's resignation, as calls for the President to step down multiplied. Brooke, in an interview on ABC-TV's "Issues and Answers," said he had reached his position reluctantly. Sen. Henry M. Jackson (D Wash.), speaking on NBC-TV's "Meet the Press," did not call for resignation, but said Nixon should appear before the Senate Watergate committee to "lay his cards on the table."

Time magazine, in its first editorial in 50 years of publication, said Nixon had lost his ability to govern effectively and should resign. A number of newspapers, including *The New York Times, The Detroit News* and *The Denver Post*, echoed the call. A White House spokes-

man repeated that Nixon had "absolutely no intention of resigning." *(Box, p. 121)*

NOV. 5

Dominick Remarks. Sen. Peter H. Dominick (R Colo.), a longtime Nixon supporter, called on the President to restore the people's confidence by making "a complete disclosure of all information" about the Watergate case. His strongly worded remarks were made in an address to the Denver Bar Association.

Special Prosecutor. Leon Jaworski was sworn in as the new Watergate special prosecutor. Acting Attorney General Robert H. Bork sought to reassure a House Judiciary subcommittee that Jaworski would have a "free hand" in prosecuting the cases. *(Hearings, p. 124)*

Segretti Sentence. Donald H. Segretti, who had pleaded guilty to violations of federal election law for his activities as a political saboteur for the Republicans in 1972, appeared in U.S. District Court in Washington, D.C., and was sentenced to six months in prison and three years of probation. *(Plea, p. 46; Senate testimony, p. 43)*

Dean Admission. During a U.S. District Court hearing on motions by five of the seven convicted Watergate conspirators to withdraw their guilty pleas, a prosecutor revealed that Nixon's former counsel, John W. Dean III, had admitted destroying two notebooks that had been taken from the White House safe of conspirator E. Howard Hunt Jr. two days after the Watergate break-in. Dean told prosecutors he found the notebooks, which contained names and addresses of people connected with the scandal, while going through Nixon's personal financial file in January. Hunt's attorney argued that evidence vital to his client's defense had been destroyed.

NOV. 6

Tapes Hearing. White House aide Stephen B. Bull testified before Judge Sirica that Rose Mary Woods, Nixon's personal secretary, had heard and summarized all the disputed White House tapes in late September. Another White House aide, John C. Bennett, said Woods had 14 recordings of presidential conversations in her desk, eight of which she had been keeping for more than a month. Sirica announced he would subpoena Woods to give her version of the handling of the tapes. *(Details, p. 120)*

Richardson Testimony. Former Attorney General Elliot L. Richardson, testifying before the Senate Judiciary Committee on the question of establishing an independent special prosecutor, said the President should drop all claims of executive privilege in relation to the Watergate investigations. Under questioning, he revealed that Nixon had mentioned to him "getting rid of" former special prosecutor Cox sometime in September or early October. Richardson said he did not take the remark seriously. *(Hearings, p. 120)*

Senate Watergate Committee. The Senate Watergate investigating committee agreed at a private session to contact the White House about a possible meeting with the President at which committee members could ask Nixon questions relating to their investigation. The committee heard testimony from four witnesses called by the minority to discuss "dirty tricks" in the 1972 campaign. A fifth witness, called by the majority, had worked for Democratic presidential candidate George McGovern. *(Hearings, p. 119)*

NOV. 7

Nixon Speech. Nixon ended a nationally televised address on the energy crisis by vowing he would not resign. "I shall do everything that I can to see that any doubts as to the integrity of the man who occupies the highest office in this land" are removed, he said. *(Box, p. 121)*

Aiken on Impeachment. The 81-year-old dean of Senate Republicans, George D. Aiken (Vt.), spoke out on the Senate floor against the mounting calls for Nixon's resignation, which he described as "the politics of righteous indignation." Aiken said it was the duty of the President to remain in office, while it was the "clear duty" of Congress to initiate impeachment proceedings against him. *(p. 121)*

Tapes Hearing. The possibility that a third important presidential conversation had not been recorded was raised by White House aide John C. Bennett in testimony on the tapes before Judge Sirica. Bennett said that Rose Mary Woods, Nixon's personal secretary, had reported a "gap" in one of the White House tapes—believed to be a conversation between the President and John W. Dean III. *(Details, p. 120)*

Senate Watergate Committee. The Senate Watergate investigating committee started the third and final phase of its inquiry, on campaign financing. A former White House official, William H. Marumoto, testified that political considerations were important in determining which Spanish-speaking Americans received government contracts. A second witness, Miami homebuilder John J. Priestes, reported that Nixon's chief fund-raiser, Maurice H. Stans, promised to intercede for him with a government agency in exchange for a $100,000 contribution. *(Hearings, p. 127)*

Motions Rejected. Judge Sirica rejected motions by six of the original Watergate defendants for either new trials or permission to withdraw guilty pleas. He set Nov. 9 for final sentencing of James W. McCord Jr., E. Howard Hunt Jr., Eugenio R. Martinez, Virgilio R. Gonzalez, Bernard L. Barker and Frank A. Sturgis.

NOV. 8

Tapes Condition. *The Washington Post* quoted White House sources as saying that parts of the seven White House tapes Nixon had agreed to turn over to the court probably would not qualify as evidence of Nixon's role in the Watergate affair because they were inaudible. White House press secretary Ronald L. Ziegler responded to the report, saying he was "confident there have not been any erasures" on the tapes.

New Prosecutor. Leon Jaworski, the new Watergate special prosecutor, told a Senate Judiciary subcommittee that he had "all of the freedom of action that could be expected of a special prosecutor appointed under any other procedure" and that he was "already actively involved in the continued conduct of the investigations initiated by the special prosecution force." *(Hearings, p. 118)*

NIXON GOES PUBLIC, PLEDGES DISCLOSURE, COOPERATION

An embattled Richard Nixon, fighting to preserve his presidency and restore his credibility, took his case to Congress, to his party and to the American public during the week ended Nov. 17.

His drive to regain the initiative began the previous week. He met with Republican congressional leaders Nov. 9 and pledged his full cooperation with federal courts and with the Watergate prosecution force.

Starting Nov. 13 and continuing the rest of the week, Nixon held a series of meetings at the White House. He met with all 234 Republican members of Congress. He met with a selected group of moderate and conservative southern Democratic members. He met with the Republican Coordinating Committee, a newly reactivated policy group. *(Box, p. 135)*

His performance received mixed reviews. Adjectives frequently heard from participants who came out of the private sessions were "frank, candid and free-wheeling." But there was general agreement among the participants that Nixon still had a long way to go.

At the meetings, the President reportedly reaffirmed his intention not to resign and said he would not submit voluntarily to impeachment proceedings, as one senator suggested.

Statement on Tapes. In addition to the meetings, Nixon issued a statement Nov. 12 that offered tape recordings and other materials not among those already subpoenaed to the federal court considering the President's taped conversations. In particular, he offered material related to conversations with former Attorney General John N. Mitchell and former presidential counsel John W. Dean III. But the statement acknowledged that a dictated memo, besides the two tapes previously reported, was missing. *(Statement text, p. 139)*

In other Watergate-related activities:

• Chief U.S. District Court Judge John J. Sirica issued a memorandum permitting Nixon to make public the subpoenaed tapes and related materials. Whether or how the President would go about this was not immediately clear. *(Court actions, below)*

• The Senate Watergate investigating committee asked for a meeting of the full committee with the President, who turned down the idea but said he would meet with the chairman and vice chairman. The committee spent the week listening to corporate executives describe how they made illegal contributions to the 1972 Nixon campaign. *(p. 137, 136, 133)*

• Congressional action on appointment of a court-appointed special prosecutor was delayed. *(p. 135)*

Court Actions

Two federal courtrooms in Washington were the scenes of these Watergate-related developments:

• A third relevant White House tape did not exist, special White House counsel J. Fred Buzhardt told Judge Sirica Nov. 12.

• Federal District Judge Gerhard A. Gesell Nov. 15 refused to dismiss charges of lying under oath against Egil Krogh Jr., the former White House aide who had headed the "plumbers" investigation. Krogh's attorney had argued for dismissal earlier in the week, basing his case on the claim that Krogh was acting under presidential orders to maintain the secrecy of the "plumbers" unit at all costs—even perjury.

• It was illegal for Acting Attorney General Robert H. Bork to carry out Nixon's orders to fire special Watergate prosecutor Archibald Cox, Gesell ruled Nov. 14. He cited a Justice Department regulation which specified that Cox would be dismissed only for extraordinary improprieties. Gesell did not order Cox reinstated.

• Nixon could make public any material he wished from tapes or other documents in his possession, Sirica stated Nov. 14, refusing Nixon's offer of Nov. 12 to supply Sirica with additional unsubpoenaed tapes and materials in place of the subpoenaed and apparently non-existent tapes of the Dean conversation and the June 20, 1972, Mitchell telephone conversation.

Another Non-Existent Tape. By the time Sirica recessed the fact-finding hearings on the tapes Nov. 12, uncertainty appeared to be their primary product—uncertainty concerning the fidelity of the recording system, the quality of the tapes, their whereabouts since early 1973, the records kept of persons with access to them and their reliability as evidence. *(Earlier stories, p. 120, 118)*

Buzhardt's testimony, intended to resolve inconsistencies in the accounts of previous witnesses, instead added new questions. On Nov. 9, questioning revealed that in June, Cox had requested access to a tape related to the April 15 conversation between Nixon and Dean. Buzhardt had replied to the request by stating that "the tape to which the President referred...was a tape on which the President dictated his own recollections of that conversation." The special prosecutor was denied access to that tape.

Buzhardt said Nov. 12 that he could not recall whether he had been told in June that no actual tape of the April 15 meeting existed, but he said he was told that a dictation belt recording of the President's recollection of the meeting did exist. Under questioning, Buzhardt then admitted that no such recording could be found. Minutes later, the White House issued Nixon's statement offering Sirica the additional material.

Sirica, recessing the hearings Nov. 12, announced that tapes and other subpoenaed materials would be copied and then delivered to him by Nov. 20. Then, he said, a panel of court-appointed experts would examine the materials. On Nov. 30, he would meet in closed session with the prosecutors and White House counsel to discuss specific claims of executive privilege.

Two days later, Sirica issued a memorandum rejecting Nixon's offer of additional unsubpoenaed material, saying that the court's function was simply to enforce the grand jury subpoena and to determine possible justification for the White House claim that two of the subpoenaed tapes did not exist. If Nixon wished the grand jury to have the additional material, Sirica said, he should provide it to the jury through the special prosecutor.

In response to news reports that Nixon wished to make public certain information from the tapes but hesitated to do so so long as the matter was under consideration by Sirica, the judge stated that in his opinion the President was free to make such information public at any time.

Cox Firing. Little of practical consequence was accomplished by the Gesell ruling on the firing of Cox, beyond placing the stamp of illegality upon the action for purposes of precedent and public opinion. The ruling was made in an action filed by Sen. Frank E. Moss (D Utah), Rep. Bella S. Abzug (D N.Y.) and Rep. Jerome R. Waldie (D Calif.). Cox said he would not use the ruling to regain his former post.

Illegal Corporate Contributions

Braniff Airways and its board chairman pleaded guilty Nov. 12 to criminal misdemeanor charges for making an illegal corporate contribution of $40,000 to President Nixon's re-election campaign. The next day, Gulf Oil Corporation and Ashland Oil Company, and a top official of each, pleaded guilty to similar charges for illegally giving $100,000 apiece to the 1972 Nixon campaign. The pleas brought to six the number of large corporations to confess in court to such charges, brought by the Watergate special prosecution with the understanding that voluntary disclosure would result in reduced penalties.

Each of the three companies was fined the maximum of $5,000, and the executives were ordered to pay maximum fines of $1,000. Braniff Chairman Harding L. Lawrence and Gulf Vice President Claude C. Wild Jr. entered their pleas in U.S. District Court in Washington, D.C. Ashland's board chairman, Orin E. Atkins, appeared before a federal judge near his company's headquarters in Catlettsburg, Ky.

Gulf also pleaded guilty to making illegal contributions of $15,000 to Rep. Wilbur D. Mills (D Ark.) and $10,000 to Sen. Henry M. Jackson (D Wash.). Mills and Jackson were unsuccessful candidates for the Democratic presidential nomination in 1972.

Lawrence said the Braniff contribution was made shortly before April 7, 1972, when a new federal election law that requires disclosure of political contributors took effect. "We consider it a very serious mistake," he told Judge George L. Hart Jr. A defense attorney pleaded for leniency on grounds that Lawrence had been "under some pressure to make this contribution" by Nixon campaign officials, but he refused to name them. *(Previous pleas, p. 61)*

Bills under consideration in Congress to authorize the courts to appoint a new Watergate prosecutor were "most unfortunate," Gesell wrote in his opinion: "Congress has it within its own power to enact appropriate and legally enforceable protections against any effort to thwart the Watergate inquiry.... The courts must remain neutral. Their duties are not prosecutorial." *(Bills, p. 135)*

Krogh Case. In rejecting Krogh's motion for dismissal of the charges against him, Gesell stated that no instructions "given the defendant in the guise of national security can make an otherwise false statement under oath legal." Gesell also refused a request from Krogh that certain presidential tapes and documents be subpoenaed.

Watergate Witnesses Nov. 15

George A. Spater, former president and board chairman of American Airlines, told the Senate select committee Nov. 15 that he made an illegal corporate contribution of $55,000 to the Nixon re-election campaign because he was afraid of the consequences if he did not.

Spater said he was approached in late 1971 by Herbert Kalmbach, Nixon's lawyer and fund-raiser, who asked him for $100,000, saying such contributors would "be considered in a special class." At the time, Spater said, he knew Kalmbach was Nixon's personal attorney and that Kalmbach's firm handled legal matters for United Airlines, an American Airlines competitor. Also, American was trying to merge with Western Airlines, a move United opposed, Spater said.

George A. Spater

"I think I was motivated by a host of fears," he said. "You just don't know what's going to happen to you...sometimes the fear of the unknown is greater than the fear of what you know." Spater said the merger needed the President's approval, and he had been hearing rumors that the White House opposed it. The merger was disapproved in June 1973.

Spater, who resigned from the corporation in September shortly after voluntarily disclosing the contribution, said he also gave $20,000 in personal funds to the Nixon campaign, for a total contribution of $75,000. The $20,000, he said, came from a friend of his whom he did not identify.

The $75,000 was contributed in four cash installments, said Spater. But he added that cash had not been requested by Kalmbach and no "quid pro quo" was involved. The money, he said, was provided through a Lebanese businessman who was associated with American Airlines.

Spater said the existing system of campaign financing caused "unfair pressures" to be exerted on businessmen who had to deal with the government. He suggested that legislation be enacted making it illegal for a cabinet officer or an associate of a high administration official to solicit campaign contributions. To his knowledge, he

Poll Report: Persistent Low Ratings for Nixon

President Nixon's popularity apparently bottomed out at 32 per cent for the third month in a row, according to a Harris Survey published Nov. 12. But a Gallup Poll published Nov. 13 found that a majority opposed impeaching Nixon. Another Gallup Poll, published Nov. 11, learned that support for Republicans in the House had sunk to its lowest level in 38 years.

Nixon Popularity. In a special telephone poll of 1,007 households, Harris interviewers asked, "How would you rate the job President Nixon is doing as President—excellent, pretty good, only fair, or poor?"

	Latest	September
Excellent-good	32%	32%
Fair-poor	64	65
Not sure	4	3

The Harris poll reflected some credit to Nixon for his handling of the Middle East crisis. A Gallup Poll on presidential popularity, reflecting public reaction to the President's handling of the Watergate tapes situation, showed him at his all-time low of 27 per cent. *(Graph, p. 125)*

Watergate. Gallup noted an increase in support for impeachment after Nixon's firing of Watergate special prosecutor Archibald Cox and the disclosure that tapes were missing late in October. Interviewers asked 1,498 adults Nov. 2-5: "Do you think President Nixon should be impeached and compelled to leave the presidency or not?"

	Latest	Oct. 19-22
Yes	37%	33%
No	54	52
No opinion	9	15

The sample also was asked which of the following statements came closest to their views: "Nixon planned the Watergate bugging from the beginning; Nixon did not plan the bugging but knew about it before it took place; Nixon found out about the bugging after it occurred, but tried to cover it up; Nixon had no knowledge of the bugging and spoke up as soon as he learned about it."

	Latest	Sept. 7-10
Planned	10%	11%
Knew about	32	28
Covered up	34	33
No knowledge	15	18
No opinion	9	10

Congressional Support. Gallup, after finding support for Republicans in the House at a low ebb, commented: "If the indicated seat losses are reflected in next year's congressional elections, President Nixon could be deprived of the veto power which he has successfully exercised on several occasions during the current year." This would be the likely division of the vote for representatives if the election were held at the time of the surveys, Gallup reported:

Democrats	58%
Republicans	30
Undecided/other	12

Gallup's results were only a few percentage points different from those in a similar Harris Survey a few weeks earlier.

---

added, the laws against corporate contributions had never been enforced until the Watergate scandal broke.

DeYoung Testimony. Another witness, Russell DeYoung, board chairman of Goodyear Tire and Rubber Company, denied that his corporation made its illegal $40,000 contribution under pressure. "It was made solely because we thought the re-election of the President was in the best interest of the country," he told the committee in a prepared statement. "It was not made with a view to obtaining government favors. Nor was I pressured in any way into making it." DeYoung admitted under questioning that Goodyear's contribution was made in cash for concealment purposes.

He told the committee that former Commerce Secretary Maurice H. Stans had asked him in February 1972 for a contribution of unspecified size. DeYoung said he decided to give $20,000, but when the money was presented to Stans on March 9 by Arden Firestone, a Goodyear vice president, Stans told Firestone he had been hoping for $50,000. DeYoung said he decided to donate another $20,000.

As had previous corporate witnesses, DeYoung said he had not been asked to donate corporate funds. The money came from amounts transferred to the United States before 1967 from a Swiss account, he said. DeYoung said he and his wife also gave a total of $5,000 in personal checks to the Nixon re-election campaign.

American Airlines and Goodyear pleaded guilty Oct. 17 to making illegal campaign contributions. Each company was fined $5,000. DeYoung was given a personal fine of $1,000, but Spater was not charged because he was the first corporate executive to volunteer information to government investigators. *(Box, p. 133, p. 61)*

Braniff Testimony. Other witnesses Nov. 15 were Camilo Favrega, head of the Panamanian office of Braniff Airways, and Neal Robinson, assistant treasurer of Braniff. They discussed the financial arrangements whereby Braniff was able secure $40,000 in cash for another illegal contribution to the Nixon re-election effort. The corporation and its president, Harding L. Lawrence, pleaded guilty Nov. 11 to making illegal contributions.

Court-Appointed Prosecutor

The drive to create a court-appointed Watergate special prosecutor appeared to be suspended, at least temporarily, with the House Judiciary Committee Nov. 13 voting in favor of the idea but the Senate Judiciary Committee postponing a vote. Members of the Senate committee appeared to be divided evenly on the issue, 8-8. The full House was not scheduled to act until after the Thanksgiving recess.

Advocates of the legislation suffered a setback Nov. 14 when U.S. District Court Judge Gerhard A. Gesell criticized the principle of a court-appointed prosecutor, saying such legislation would impair the neutrality of the court. *(Details, p. 132)*

Gesell thus seemed to provide ammunition to opponents of the legislation on the two Judiciary Committees. They had said during hearings that creation of such an office would trigger a drawn-out court battle over its constitutionality, even if a predicted presidential veto were overridden. *(Earlier hearings, p. 124, 120)*

House Judiciary Action. The Special Prosecutor Act of 1973 (HR 11401) was introduced Nov. 12 by House Judiciary Subcommittee Chairman William L. Hungate (D Mo.) after four days of hearings. The bill was an outgrowth of a similar bill, H J Res 784, introduced three days after Cox's firing by Rep. John C. Culver (D Iowa).

Under the Hungate bill, the 15-member U.S. District Court of the District of Columbia would appoint a three-judge panel, which would then appoint the special prosecutor. The prosecutor could be removed only by the three judges for gross impropriety, gross dereliction of duty or mental or physical incapacity. To avoid any conflict of interest, members of the judicial panel would be disqualified from hearing any cases brought by the prosecutor. A defendant would have 15 days in which to contest the constitutionality of legal action taken by the special prosecutor.

The subcommittee adopted the Hungate bill Nov. 12 by a five-to-four party-line vote, with Republicans opposed. The full Judiciary Committee then adopted the bill Nov. 13 on a voice vote.

The key vote in the full committee came on a compromise measure, HR 11369, introduced Nov. 12 by subcommittee member David W. Dennis (R Ind.). The Dennis bill sought to avoid constitutional challenges by leaving the special prosecutor's office in the executive branch. However, to prevent arbitrary dismissal, the bill would have limited the conditions under which the prosecutor could be fired. The substitute failed, 17-21. Rep. Walter Flowers (D Ala.) was the only Democrat voting for it, and Rep. Harold V. Froehlich (R Wis.) was the only Republican voting against it.

The committee adopted, 26-12, an amendment submitted by Rep. Tom Railsback (R Ill.) which would require the special prosecutor to report monthly to the House Judiciary Committee chairman and ranking minority member "such information pertinent to the question of whether impeachable offenses have been committed by the President."

Seven Republicans and 19 Democrats voted for the amendment, with two Democrats and 10 Republicans opposing it.

Republican Coordinating Committee

A rejuvenated Republican Coordinating Committee, a 28-member organization made up of governors, members of Congress and party leaders, passed a resolution Nov. 12 urging President Nixon to make "full disclosure of all facts arising from the so-called Watergate affair."

Such disclosure had been pledged by the President two days earlier in a meeting with congressional leaders. He repeated his willingness to cooperate with Watergate investigators at a breakfast meeting with the coordinating committee Nov. 12 at which he spoke for 40 minutes.

But the comments of the leaders who were interviewed after the meeting reflected considerable skepticism over Nixon's ability to win back the confidence of the country. Some members of the committee, chaired by Republican National Chairman George Bush, expressed the feeling that the group should establish an identity of its own, separate from the White House, before the 1974 election campaign.

A similar coordinating committee was formed after the crushing defeat of Barry Goldwater for the presidency in 1964. The committee met occasionally from 1965 through 1968, offering alternative policies to those of the Johnson administration, but ceased to exist when Nixon became President.

According to press accounts of the Nov. 12 meeting, comments of those who met with the President were mixed. Sen. Bill Brock (Tenn.), chairman of the Republican Senatorial Campaign Committee, was asked if Nixon were "out of the woods."

"By no means," answered Brock. "But he's opened the door to cleaning things up."

Sen. Hugh Scott (R Pa.), Senate minority leader, told reporters that he expected Nixon's compliance with a federal court order to produce tapes and other records would lead to making the material available to the public.

Rep. John B. Anderson (Ill.), chairman of the House Republican Conference, was asked about impeachment proceedings. "I want to be very careful," he said. "This is a time when mere words will not suffice. But this will give him an opportunity to make his case before we rush headlong into action."

One of the least optimistic committee members to emerge from the private breakfast meeting was Gov. Francis W. Sargent (R Mass.). "I indicated that we shouldn't have some sort of pablum resolution that will blindly ignore the problems we have," he said.

Another Republican governor, Iowa's Robert Ray, said of the President's announcement of full cooperation: "I think that most of us wish it happened a long time ago."

An unidentified committee member described the meeting with Nixon as "very frank and at times quite critical of the President's past actions on Watergate."

Senate Judiciary Hearings. Senate Judiciary Committee hearings on special prosecutor legislation continued Nov. 14 with an argument by Sen. Charles

H. Percy (R Ill.) in behalf of his bill, S 2616, which he introduced along with Senators Howard H. Baker Jr. (R Tenn.), Bill Brock (R Tenn.) and Marlow W. Cook (R Ky.). The bill, with amendments Percy recommended, would require Senate confirmation of a presidentially appointed prosecutor, would limit the conditions of his removal and would allow the Senate to override removal by a majority-vote "resolution of disapproval."

Passage of his bill, Percy argued, would avoid the constitutional test that would come to a court-appointed prosecutor and would allow Jaworski to sue for reinstatement if he were fired.

The committee also heard from Acting Attorney General Robert H. Bork Nov. 14 and 15. As he had during House hearings, Bork criticized the court-appointed prosecutor idea on constitutional and practical grounds.

Watergate Witnesses Nov. 13

The Senate Watergate committee voted five to one, in an early-morning executive session Nov. 13, for a resolution requesting a meeting with the President to question him on the Watergate case. The resolution also included a request that the President hand over all tape recordings and documents relevant to the committee's inquiry.

The move was more formal than a step taken by the committee Nov. 6. At that time, the committee, without taking a formal vote, ordered its counsels to explore with Nixon's lawyers the possibility of a meeting between the President and the seven committee members. *(p. 126)*

Sen. Lowell P. Weicker Jr. (R Conn.) introduced the Nov. 13 resolution proposing the meeting. Committee sources said Sen. Edward J. Gurney (R Fla.) opposed the action and Herman E. Talmadge (D Ga.) was absent.

Weicker's resolution called for a meeting between the committee and the President in the White House at Nixon's earliest convenience. The resolution also specified that the President not be required to answer questions under oath, that counsels for the President and the committee would attend and that a complete transcript of the meeting would be made public immediately afterward.

Shipbuilding Witnesses. The committee, meanwhile, continued its probe of campaign financing in the 1972 election with testimony from two officials of the American Shipbuilding Company of Cleveland, Ohio. Matthew E. Clark Jr., director of purchasing for the company, and Robert E. Bartlome, company secretary, told how they made illegal contributions to Nixon's re-election finance committee. *(Previous testimony, p. 126, 119)*

Clark, the first witness, told of being awarded a $5,000 "bonus" in 1972, from which he said Bartlome ordered him to write two checks to fronts for the re-election finance committee, one for $3,000 and the other for $100. The rest of the $5,000 was returned to the company, Clark said.

Under questioning by committee chief counsel Samuel Dash, Clark said he lied under oath to the FBI when agents questioned him about the contributions, telling them the donations were voluntary and that he had gone to Bartlome with the idea for the contributions because the Nixon administration had been helpful to the shipbuilding industry. Asked by Dash whether he knew it was illegal for corporations to contribute to political campaigns, Clark said he did not at the time.

Bartlome confirmed Clark's version, adding that a total of eight company employees had received the "bonuses" and were ordered by him to donate a total of $25,000 to various fronts for the re-election finance committee. The idea for the contributions, said Bartlome, came from company President George M. Steinbrenner III. He said Steinbrenner told him he was under some kind of pressure to contribute to the Nixon re-election ef-

---

The Committee and the Court

To overcome the obstacle which resulted in Federal Judge John J. Sirica's dismissal of the Senate Watergate committee's suit asking enforcement of its subpoenas of White House tapes, the Senate by voice vote Nov. 9 approved a bill (S 2641) specifically granting the federal district court in the District of Columbia jurisdiction over any such suit. Sirica had dismissed the committee's suit Oct. 17 because he said he could find no basis for his court's having jurisdiction over such a suit. *(p. 60)*

S 2641 gave the federal district court jurisdiction, "without regard to the sum or value of the matter in controversy," over any civil action "heretofore or hereafter" brought by the Senate Select Committee on Presidential Campaign Activities to enforce—or secure a ruling on the validity of—any subpoena or order issued by the committee to the President or any other federal official for information or materials relevant to the committee's investigation. The bill also stated that the committee was authorized to prosecute in its own name or in the name of the United States in any such case seeking enforcement of a subpoena or an order declaring a subpoena valid. Without such a provision, only the Justice Department is ordinarily authorized to litigate in the name of the United States.

The version of S 2641 approved was substantially narrower than the original version, introduced and placed on the calendar Nov. 2. Before passage on Nov. 9, Sen. Sam J. Ervin Jr. (D N.C.), chairman of the Watergate committee, proposed a substitute version as an amendment, approved by the Watergate committee. Roman L. Hruska (R Neb.) had suggested that the original bill—which gave the district court jurisdiction over any such cases brought by any congressional committee to enforce its subpoenas—was too broad, Ervin said. As a result Ervin proposed, and the Senate approved by voice vote, a substitute limiting the effect of the bill to cases brought by the Watergate committee alone.

Hruska found, however, that even the modified bill flew "in the face of the role of the courts in our constitutional system of government." The bill would not solve the problem, he said, but would instead "cast (the) judicial branch in the role of umpire or referee between Congress and the executive in disputes over the production of documents and information."

fort, but Bartlome said he never learned who was pressuring Steinbrenner.

Bartlome said that Steinbrenner gave himself a "bonus" of $75,000, which also was donated in separate checks of $3,000 each to affiliates of the re-election finance committee, for a total of $100,000 from the company. The checks were delivered, Bartlome said, to Herbert W. Kalmbach, Nixon's personal attorney and an unofficial campaign fund-raiser.

To cover for the "bonuses," Bartlome said, he directed that the employees make out false expense reports. Both Bartlome and Clark were granted immunity from prosecution by former Watergate special prosecutor Archibald Cox in exchange for their testimony before the Watergate grand jury. Steinbrenner had refused to cooperate with the grand jury and the Watergate committee, Dash said.

Witnesses Nov. 14

Two corporation executives testified Nov. 14 that Nixon's campaign finance chairman, former Commerce Secretary Maurice H. Stans, pressured them into making contributions to Nixon's 1972 re-election effort. The contributions were illegal, because they came from corporate funds, and the two men and their companies later were convicted and fined.

Orin E. Atkins, board chairman of Ashland Oil Company, and Claude C. Wild Jr., vice president for governmental affairs of Gulf Oil Corporation, told the committee that while Stans never asked specifically for corporate funds, there was no doubt in their minds that only their company treasuries could afford the $100,000 requested of each of them.

Atkins, Wild and their companies cooperated with former special Watergate prosecutor Archibald Cox in his investigation of campaign finances. In court action Nov. 13, Atkins and Wild each drew $1,000 fines, and their companies were fined $5,000 each. Ashland's fine was aimed at Ashland Petroleum Gabon, a subsidiary. *(Box, p. 133)*

Asked to describe the nature of the pressure put on him for the contributions, Wild said, "I considered it considerable." He noted that both Stans and former Attorney General John N. Mitchell were aware of the requests for money. "That's different from it (a request) coming from the Boy Scouts," he said.

Ashland Contribution. Atkins said he was solicited by Stans in March 1972. He described Stans' telephone call as brief—no more than three or four minutes long—with Stans telling him what a good job Nixon had done as President and suggesting a contribution of $100,000 to the re-election finance committee and the purchase of an advertisement in the Republican convention program at a cost of $10,000.

Atkins said he talked over Stans' request with three officers of the company, and they decided to make the donation even though they knew it was illegal. He explained that the illegality was viewed as somewhat analogous to prohibition laws which were seldom observed, and that he was more concerned with the tax aspects of the contribution than with whether it broke the law. "I guess we had our priorities in the wrong sequence," he said. Atkins also told the committee that it

Grand Jury Extension

The Senate Judiciary Committee, by voice vote Nov. 13, ordered reported two bills that would provide different formulas for extending the original federal grand jury investigating the Watergate break-in and coverup. The committee proposed letting the Senate take its pick between HR 10937, passed by the House Nov. 6, and S 2585, introduced by Sen. James O. Eastland (D Miss.), chairman of the Judiciary Committee.

The House bill would extend the grand jury for six months by law and would permit the jury to seek a further six-month extension from the U.S. District Court for the District of Columbia. *(House action, p. 128)*

Eastland's bill would leave the initiative with the grand jury for seeking both a first and second six-month extension from the district court.

was felt the contribution would assure Ashland of "a forum" within the administration if the company had problems.

The Ashland subsidiary in Gabon was decided on as the source for the money, because the $100,000 could easily be hidden by that company as an investment in land, Atkins said. Stans never specified what form the contribution should take, Atkins went on, but it was delivered to him in cash by a company officer on April 3, 1972, four days before a new contributions disclosure law went into effect.

Gulf Contribution. Wild told a somewhat different story, saying he first was solicited in February 1971 by Lee Nunn, a re-election committee official, who told him the committee was "hopeful" for a $100,000 contribution from Gulf. He said he had not heard of Nunn or the committee at that time, so he checked with Mitchell, then the attorney general, who assured him that Nunn and the committee were legitimate.

Wild said he gave Nunn $50,000 in cash, instead of $100,000. He said he had received the money from an official of a Gulf subsidiary, Bahamas Exploration Ltd. The money was charged to a miscellaneous expense account. The subsidiary was liquidated in 1972, he said.

Wild said he had an idea that he would hear from Nunn again, and did in fact hear from him in January 1972. Nunn asked for another $50,000, Wild said, telling him that a "quota" of $100,000 from all large corporations was expected by the finance committee. Wild said Stans made a similar request on Feb. 4, 1972. The Gulf official said he secured the additional $50,000 in the same manner as before. Again there was no request for cash, but that was the easiest form for the donation to take, Wild told the committee.

Asked why he agreed to make the contributions, Wild said he feared Gulf would find itself on an administration "blacklist" or at the "bottom of the totem pole" if it refused a donation. He said he knew that other corporations would be giving money.

Wild conceded that he also donated $15,000 of corporate money to the presidential primary campaign of Rep. Wilbur D. Mills (D Ark.) and $10,000 to the campaign of Sen. Henry M. Jackson (D Wash.). In each case, the money came from the same Bahamas subsidiary, he said.

In the cases of both Gulf and Ashland, the contributions were returned by the re-election finance committee. Jackson's and Mills' offices said similar arrangements would be made.

Week's Watergate Chronology

Following is a day-to-day chronology of the week's events in the Watergate case *(Earlier Nov. 8 events, p. 129):*

NOV. 8

Tapes Hearing. Rose Mary Woods, Nixon's personal secretary, testified at a U.S. District Court hearing that she had been unable to prepare a full transcript of the tapes subpoenaed by the Watergate prosecutors because parts of the recordings were inaudible or hard to understand. Woods denied an earlier report that there was a gap in the tape of an April 16 conversation between the President and his former counsel, John W. Dean III. H.R. Haldeman, Nixon's former chief of staff, testified that tapes he had listened to were "quite adequate for getting a report of the conversations," despite flaws. *(p. 118)*

Senate Watergate Committee. Benjamin Fernandez, who headed the National Hispanic Finance Committee for the Re-election of the President, denied before the Senate investigating committee that he had solicited a contribution from a Miami, Fla., builder with the promise of favorable government treatment.

AFL Impeachment Drive. The AFL-CIO opened a nationwide drive for Nixon's impeachment, mailing out 500,000 copies of a pamphlet listing 19 charges against the President. "The federation's action is ill-conceived and can only result in harming the nation at home and abroad," said White House spokesman Ken W. Clawson. *(Previous action, p. 82)*

Richardson, Ruckelshaus Comments. Former Attorney General Elliot L. Richardson, who resigned rather than fire former special prosecutor Archibald Cox, said on NBC-TV that he was convinced the President had told the "whole truth" about his knowledge of the Watergate bugging and coverup. Richardson said his trust in the President was based in part on conversations he had had with White House officials who "have some awareness" of the contents of the presidential tapes.

Former Deputy Attorney General William D. Ruckelshaus, who resigned the same day as Richardson, told reporters he thought Nixon should make public all documents relevant to the Watergate case in order to regain public confidence.

NOV. 9

Defendants Sentenced. U.S. District Judge John J. Sirica sentenced six of the seven original Watergate conspirators to prison terms. E. Howard Hunt Jr. received 2½ to eight years in prison and a $10,000 fine; Bernard L. Barker, 1½ to six years; James W. McCord Jr., one to five years; Eugenio R. Martinez, Frank A. Sturgis and Virgilio R. Gonzalez, one to four years. *(Details, p. 117)*

Tapes Hearing. Sirica recessed hearings on the White House tapes during testimony by White House counsel J. Fred Buzhardt in order to consider whether or not Buzhardt would be required to tell the prosecution if the President knew in June that a crucial recording did not exist.

Nixon-Republican Meeting. President Nixon met at the White House with a group of Republican congressional leaders on the Watergate situation. The President "indicated he is going to be totally cooperative with Sirica, the court and the special prosecutor and that he will devote a good deal of time to assuring the American people he was not involved in the Watergate burglary or coverup," Rep. John B. Anderson (R Ill.) told reporters. Anderson said the efforts would include making public the White House tapes and other Watergate documents after they were submitted to the grand jury.

NOV. 11

Nixon-Republican Meetings. Sen. Charles H. Percy (R Ill.) announced on NBC-TV's "Meet the Press" that Nixon was planning a series of informal meetings at the White House that would give every member of Congress a chance to ask him questions about the Watergate scandal. A White House spokesman acknowledged that six meetings on Watergate would be held the next week but would be limited to Republican members.

NOV. 12

Tapes Hearing. Nixon submitted a statement to Judge Sirica promising to provide the court with his own handwritten notes sought by prosecutors on two conversations that were not recorded, as originally thought. Nixon said that contrary to a White House statement of a week before, he had no dictation belt recording of his summary of one of the conversations. *(Text, p. 139)*

Sirica announced details of an agreement between the White House and Watergate prosecutors designed to expedite the transferral of evidence from the tapes to the grand jury. *(Details, p. 132)*

Braniff Contribution. Braniff Airways and its board chairman pleaded guilty in U.S. District Court in Washington, D.C., to making an illegal $40,000 corporate contribution to Nixon's 1972 campaign. *(Box, p. 133)*

Jaworski on National Security. "In the recent past, national security has become a kind of talisman, invoked by officials at widely disparate levels of government service to justify a wide range of apparently illegal activities," the new Watergate special prosecutor, Leon Jaworski, argued in a brief filed in U.S. District Court in opposition to a motion by Egil Krogh Jr. for dismissal of perjury charges against him. Krogh, who headed the White House investigation unit that broke into the office of Daniel Ellsberg's psychiatrist in 1971, was indicted for allegedly lying to the Watergate grand jury in Washington, and had argued that he did so to protect national security matters.

Cox Remarks. Former special prosecutor Cox told the New York City Bar Association that he met administration resistance whenever he attempted to investigate matters other than the Watergate break-in. The President's lawyers prevented him from seeing files on a suspect dairy industry contribution and Nixon told him to "keep the hell out" of the 1971 burglary of Ellsberg's psychiatrist, Cox said.

NOV. 13

Nixon Meetings. With only Sen. Edward J. Gurney (R Fla.) dissenting, the Senate Watergate investigating committee voted to formally request a private meeting of its members with Nixon, saying "such a procedure must take precedence over other nonpublic opportunities for discussion afforded by the President to individual members of the committee." *(Details, p. 136)*

Senate Watergate Committee. Two officials of the American Shipbuilding Company testified before the Senate investigating committee about their participation in a kickback scheme through which their company made illegal contributions to Nixon's 1972 campaign. *(Details, p. 136)*

Illegal Oil Contributions. Gulf Oil Corporation and Ashland Oil Company, and a top official of each, pleaded guilty to illegally contributing $100,000 apiece to the 1972 Nixon campaign. *(Box, p. 133)*

NOV. 14

Cox Ruling. U.S. District Court Judge Gerhard A. Gesell of Washington, D.C., ruled that in dismissing Archibald Cox as special Watergate prosecutor, Acting Attorney General Robert H. Bork had violated a Justice Department regulation prohibiting such an action "except for extraordinary improprieties." *(Details, p. 132)*

Sirica Memorandum. Judge Sirica issued a memorandum stating that he would reject Nixon's offer to make available to the court several recordings of Watergate-related conversations not subpoenaed by the prosecution. But Sirica said Nixon was free to "waive any privilege and make tapes or other materials public...at any time." *(Details, p. 132)*

Senate Watergate Committee. Officials of Ashland Oil Company and Gulf Oil Corporation explained to the Senate Watergate investigating committee the circumstances surrounding illegal contributions their companies made to Nixon's 1972 campaign. *(Testimony, p. 133)*

Plumbers' Tapes. Special prosecutor Leon Jaworski filed a memorandum in U.S. District Court in Washington, D.C., reporting that he would have access to White House tapes and other documents requested by attorneys for Egil Krogh Jr., who was facing trial on perjury charges relating to his activities on a secret White House investigation unit known as the "plumbers." The White House earlier had refused to release the materials on national security grounds.

NIXON STATEMENT ON TAPES

Following is the text of a Nov. 12 statement by President Nixon on tape recordings and other materials related to White House conversations:

As a consequence of the public disclosure, two weeks ago, that two conversations of the President were not recorded on the White House recording system, doubts have arisen about just

what happened to these conversations and why they were not recorded. The purpose of this statement is to help dispel those doubts and to spell out certain steps I will take to offer information to the Court that will help determine the substance of all nine conversations subpoenaed by the Court.

First, there are no missing tapes. There are two conversations requested by the Courts which were not recorded. The first is a four-minute conversation with the former Attorney General, John Mitchell, on June 20, 1972. The second is a meeting of 55 minutes with John Dean, late in the evening of Sunday, April 15, 1973.

There is no question in my mind but that the open Court hearing, now being conducted, will demonstrate to the Court's satisfaction the truth of our statements that these two conversations were never recorded. In fact there is no affirmative evidence to the contrary. I believe that when the Court concludes its evaluation of the testimony and documentary evidence, public doubt on this issue will be completely and satisfactorily removed.

In the meantime, I believe it important to make a statement about this proceeding so that misconceptions about this matter do not persist simply because certain basic facts are not presented to the American public.

No Committee Subpoena. First, the Senate Select Committee did not subpoena the substance of the two unrecorded conversations. That material was requested only by the Special Prosecutor, and the Court, who believed the substance of nine presidential conversations was necessary for completion of the Watergate investigation.

We are complying fully with the Federal Court decision. In seven of nine instances, the actual recording of the conversation is being submitted; this includes 5 conversations in which John Dean participated—September 15, 1972, March 13, 1973, two on March 31, 1973, one on March 22, 1973. For all nine conversations covered by the subpoena, such contemporaneous notes and memoranda as were made of the conversations are being provided in accordance with the Court order.

Chronological Perspective. Before discussing these matters, the issue of when and why the recorded conversations were listened to by me, and by others on my behalf, should be placed in chronological perspective.

On June 4, 1973, I listened to the tape recordings of a number of conversations I had with John Dean in order to refresh my memory of those discussions. All of the conversations to which I listened that day had taken place prior to March 21, 1973. My purpose in reviewing the recordings of my conversations with Mr. Dean was to confirm my recollection that he had not reported certain facts to me prior to March 21, 1973. In late April, 1973, I asked H. R. Haldeman to listen and report on the conversation of March 21, 1973, in which he had been present for a substantial portion of time. My primary purpose in having Mr. Haldeman listen to this tape was to confirm my recollection that March 21, 1973, was the date on which John Dean had first reported certain facts to me.

There had been rumors and reports to the contrary—one of them suggesting that John Dean and I had met 30 to 40 times to discuss Watergate—and I wanted to refresh my recollection as to what was the precise and entire truth.

On September 29, 1973, I began a review of the tape recordings subpoenaed by the Special Prosecutor for the grand jury and by the Senate Select Committee. The reason was it had been my deliberate intention to litigate the matter up to the Supreme Court, if necessary, to protect the right of confidentiality and the related principle of separation of powers. By late September, however, I had come to the conclusion that the national interest would be better served by a reasonable compromise.

Thus, in late September, I began to consider various approaches which led to what has come to be known as the "Stennis Compromise"—turning over to both the Senate Committee and the Court the full substance of the relevant recorded conversations, leaving the verification of the precision and accuracy of that substance to Senator Stennis. That compromise offer, accepted by the Senate Committee Chairman and Vice Chairman, proved unacceptable to the Special Prosecutor.

Unrecorded Conversations. It was during this process that I first became aware of the possibility that two of the ten conversations in question had not been recorded.

I proceeded with a review of the eight recorded conversations and subsequently ordered a further search for recordings of the two conversations in question and an investigation into the circumstances which caused the conversations not to be recorded. The search and investigation were not finally completed until October 27.

One of the conversations for which no recording could be found was a four-minute telephone call I made to John Mitchell on the evening of June 20, 1972. The only telephone calls which were recorded in the residence of the White House were those made in the Lincoln Sitting Room which I use as an office. Telephone conversations in the family quarters have never been recorded during this Administration. The telephone call with John Mitchell was one that I made on the telephone in the family quarters just before going in to dinner, and consequently it was not recorded.

My conversation with John Dean on Sunday evening, April 15, 1973, was not recorded because the tape on the recording machine for my Executive Office Building office was used up and ran out earlier in the day. The tape which was on the operating recorder on Sunday, April 15, 1973, contains recordings of the conversations in my Executive Office Building office on Saturday, April 14, 1973. It also contains a portion of the first conversation I had in that office on Sunday, April 15, 1973, which was with Attorney General Kleindienst. During that conversation the tape ran out. Normally, I see very few people in my Executive Office Building office on the weekends. However, on the weekend of April 14 and 15, the activity in my Executive Office Building office was unusual and unanticipated. Certain reports made to me by my staff early in the morning of April 14, 1973, led me to have lengthy discussions with staff members during the day in my office in the Executive Office Building. In addition, international developments required a lengthy meeting with my Assistant for National Security Affairs late that morning.

On Sunday, April 15, 1973, I began another series of meetings in my Executive Office Building office at about one o'clock, p.m. The first meeting was with Attorney General Kleindienst. Thereafter the meetings continued until late in the evening with the exception of a break of about two hours for dinner. I did not meet with John Dean until approximately nine o'clock that evening. Since the tape on the recorder for my Executive Office Building office had run out during my afternoon meeting with Attorney General Kleindienst, the Dean meeting was not recorded.

Search for Records. It should be pointed out that the Court order calls for evidentiary materials such as notes and memoranda in addition to recordings of specified conversations. The Court order spells out a detailed procedure for turning materials over for Judge Sirica's private review. In recent days, in an effort to locate materials for the Court, a diligent search has been made for materials that might shed further light on the substance of the conversations in question, including the unrecorded conversations with John Mitchell on June 20, 1972, and with John Dean, on the evening of April 15, 1973.

Since I have been in office, I have maintained a personal diary file which consists of notes which I have personally taken during meetings and of dictation belts on which I record recollections. The dictation belts and notes are placed in my personal diary file by my secretary. They are sealed under specific instructions that they not be transcribed.

In the course of searching my personal diary files, I have located a dictation belt that I dictated at 8:30 p.m. on June 20, 1972, on which, among other activities of the day, I referred to a telephone call with John Mitchell. The portion of the belt relating to the conversation with John Mitchell will be submitted to the Court.

We have also located the dictation belt of my recollections of the conversations in question for March 21, 1973; and the relevant portions of these recollections, together with the actual recordings of the conversations, of course, will also be submitted to the Court in compliance with its order.

No Dictation Belt. Over the weekend of November 4 and 5, 1973, upon checking my personal diary file for April 15, 1973, to locate information to be produced in accordance with the Court's order, I found that my file for that day consists of personal notes of the conversation held with John Dean the evening of April 15, 1973, but not a dictation belt. My original handwritten notes, made during my meeting with John Dean on the evening of April 15, 1973, will be submitted to the Court.

On June 11, 1973, the Special Prosecutor requested a tape of a conversation I had with John Dean on April 15, 1973, (which I had previously offered to let Assistant Attorney General Petersen hear).

As has been pointed out, my personal diary file consists of notes of conversations and dictation belts of recollections, and I believed in June that I had dictated my recollections of April 15, 1973, of conversations which occurred on that day. The response to the Special Prosecutor made on June 16, 1973, referred to such a dictation belt. At that time, however, I did not review my file to confirm that it contained the belt.

April 16 Dean Meeting. I have made a diligent search for other evidentiary materials that might shed light on the substance of my conversation with John Dean on the evening of April 15, 1973. Other than my contemporaneous notes of that meeting mentioned above, I have found no such evidence. However, I did meet with John Dean on Monday, April 16, 1973, on two occasions. The first was in the morning in the Oval Office; the second was in the afternoon in the Executive Office Building office. This was my final meeting with Mr. Dean before he left the White House staff. Both of these conversations were recorded on the White House recording system. I recently reviewed the recordings of these conversations. A comparison of my notes of the April 15, 1973 meeting and the recording of the conversation with Mr. Dean on the morning of April 16, 1973, shows both conversations covered much the same subject matter. There are references throughout the conversation on the morning of April 16 to the conversation held the evening before.

I shall voluntarily submit to the Court, under the procedures applicable to recordings of conversations already covered by the Court order, these recordings of my two conversations with John Dean on April 16, 1973.

Other Records. In addition, as stated above and consistent with the Court order, the Court will be provided with:

(1) The portion of the dictation belt containing my recollection of the June 20, 1973 conversation with Mr. Mitchell.

(2) The portion of the dictation belt of my recollections of the meetings with Mr. Dean on March 21, 1973.

(3) Contemporaneous notes from the April 15, 1973 conversation with Mr. Dean.

(4) All other materials covered by the Court order.

I have also authorized my Counsel to make available to the Court certain tape recordings not covered by the Court order to assist the Court in verifying that the two conversations in question were not recorded. The additional tape recordings to be provided are (a) the full reel of telephone recordings covering the period of June 20, 1972, and (b) the two reels of tape which were on the recorders for my Executive Office Building office on April 15, 1973. This will permit the Court to check the sequence of the conversations against my daily logs of meetings and telephone conversations already provided to the Court, and thus further demonstrate that the Mitchell and Dean conversations in question were not recorded.

Expert Examination. I have also agreed that a group of Court-approved independent experts employing the most advanced technological methods shall examine all tapes in question for any evidence of alterations to the tapes.

It is my hope that these steps will clear up this aspect of the Watergate matter once and for all.   √

WATERGATE: VITAL WORK AHEAD FOR SENATE COMMITTEE

"I have an idea the greatest crisis the country faced has passed on Watergate."
—Sen. Howard H. Baker Jr., Sept. 10, 1973

"It is entirely possible that Watergate will not be over any time soon."
—Sen. Baker, Nov. 19, 1973

The contrast between Senator Baker's two observations was understandable. Ten weeks is a relatively short time, but Watergate disclosures came so quickly in the fall of 1973 that politicians and pundits alike found themselves eating their words.

In September, the Senate Watergate committee was in recess after hearing from key witnesses: John W. Dean III, John N. Mitchell, John D. Ehrlichman and H. R. Haldeman. Meanwhile, the criminal investigation was in the hands of special prosecutor Archibald Cox and the country seemed confident that justice would be done. So what more could be expected of a dramatic nature?

But Watergate had a life of its own. Like a snowball rolling downhill, it continued to grow until it created one constitutional and cabinet crisis after another—and ultimately the presidency itself was endangered. First there was the court battle over the President's refusal to hand over the tapes. Then came the firing of Cox and the resignations of Attorney General Elliot L. Richardson and his deputy, William D. Ruckelshaus. Then the President reversed himself and agreed to release the tapes. Then it was learned that two of the nine tapes never existed, and it developed that the seven remaining tapes were not distinct. And from it all emerged the threat of presidential impeachment.

Submerged in all the mind-boggling events were the hearings of the seven-member Senate Select Committee on Presidential Campaign Activities—the Watergate committee. Its witnesses since September were relatively unknown dirty tricksters and political contributors. They lacked the glamour and impact of their predecessors, so for many Americans the hearings became only a small part of the Watergate story. *(Major events of hearings, box, p. 144)*

But while the committee no longer remained in the limelight of Watergate events, some observers believed that its most important work lay ahead: the report and recommendations it was required to make to the Senate—and thus to the American people—on how to prevent another Watergate.

What corrective legislation would the members recommend? What had the hearings proved, if anything? What would the senators have done differently if they had it to do all over again? Why could not the entire matter have been left in the hands of the special prosecutor?

Tape Missing 18 Minutes

The Nov. 21 revelation that 18 minutes of a subpoenaed presidential Watergate tape was blank caused Federal District Judge John J. Sirica to order the remaining subpoenaed tapes to be turned over to the U.S. court for safekeeping.

The 18-minute blank occurred in the middle of a taped conservation between President Nixon and former presidential adviser H.R. Haldeman, recorded June 20, 1972, just three days after the Watergate break-in. In subpoenaing the tape, former special prosecutor Archibald Cox said "there is every reason to infer that the meeting included discussion of the Watergate incident."

These and other questions were put to five of the seven committee members, top committee staffers and Senate leaders by Congressional Quarterly before the committee recessed for Thanksgiving. Senators Edward J. Gurney (R Fla.) and Daniel K. Inouye (D Hawaii) were not available for interviews.

Legislative Recommendations

While a wide variety of remedies were suggested, almost all those interviewed agreed that some controls would have to be put on the use of cash in future campaigns. Free-flowing cash—hundreds of thousands of dollars of it—was at the heart of the Watergate scandal, it was believed. Cash in large, untraceable quantities bought the Watergate burglars and paid for the coverup.

There was a secret $350,000 cash fund in the White House that helped get things going and, according to testimony by Frederick C. LaRue, a Nixon re-election committee official, and Anthony T. Ulasewicz, a money courier, $449,000 was raised on quick order to maintain the burglars and pay their lawyers' fees. Herbert W. Kalmbach, a Nixon lawyer and fund-raiser, told the committee of getting $75,000 in $100 bills from a California businessman by telling him it was for a "special assignment." *(Testimony, Vol. I, p. 192)*

Cash and Corruption. Chairman Sam J. Ervin Jr. (D N.C.), Vice Chairman Baker (R Tenn.) and Sen. Joseph M. Montoya (D N.M.) said they wanted to see tight limits placed on cash contributions and disbursements. Checks or some other traceable notes were what Ervin had in mind. "Big amounts (of cash) tend to breed corruption, and Watergate was part of that," said Montoya. According to Ervin, there was only one reason for the use of cash: "Funds are received and disbursed in cash to conceal transactions," he said. Congress, he

Phase I of Committee Hearings: Unanswered Questions

After the first phase of the Senate investigating committee's hearings—the phase dealing with the Watergate break-in and coverup—there were enough conflicts of testimony to keep students of Watergate busy for months. These were some key questions raised by the witnesses:

When did President Nixon learn about the Watergate coverup—and what, if anything, was his role in it?

No witness directly disputed Nixon's May 22 statement that "the burglary and bugging of the Democratic National Committee headquarters came as a complete surprise to me." But former Acting FBI Director L. Patrick Gray III said he had warned the President during a phone conversation July 6, 1972, that "people on your staff are trying to mortally wound you" by interfering with the bureau's Watergate investigation. Asked if he thought a reasonable person would have inferred that his staff was engaging in illegal conduct, Gray replied: "I do...."

Nixon's two former top assistants, John D. Ehrlichman and H. R. Haldeman, and former Attorney General John N. Mitchell, all insisted on the President's innocence of the coverup. Against them stood John W. Dean III, former presidential counsel, who testified that Nixon knew of the coverup as early as Sept. 15, 1972.

Nixon set out his version of the meeting in an Aug. 15 television address. He said Dean gave him "no reason ...to believe any others were involved. Not only was I unaware of any coverup, but at that time, and until March 21, I was unaware that there was anything to cover up."

Did former Attorney General John N. Mitchell approve the bugging plan in advance?

Jeb Stuart Magruder, former deputy director of the Nixon re-election committee, said Mitchell approved the plan at a meeting in Key Biscayne, Fla., on March 30, 1972. Mitchell said he rejected it. Frederick C. LaRue, another committee official, said Mitchell had been vague, neither rejecting nor approving the plan. Magruder also testified that he had shown Mitchell reports on the first wiretaps on the Democratic headquarters—an allegation Mitchell described as "a palpable, damnable lie."

What was the involvement, if any, of Haldeman and Ehrlichman in the break-in or coverup?

Both denied any participation or early awareness. But Gordon C. Strachan, Haldeman's former assistant, testified that Haldeman told him to "make sure our files are clean" shortly after the break-in. Dean said Ehrlichman told him to shred documents taken from Hunt's White House safe after the break-in. Nixon's former personal attorney, Herbert W. Kalmbach, testified that Ehrlichman assured him in July 1972 that making payments to the Watergate defendants was a proper and approved activity.

One week after the break-in, on June 23, 1972, Haldeman and Ehrlichman met with then CIA Director Richard M. Helms and then CIA Deputy Director Vernon A. Walters. According to Helms and Walters, Haldeman told Walters to talk to Acting FBI Director Gray about limiting his agency's Watergate probe. "Mr. Haldeman said there was a lot of flak about the Watergate burglary, that the opposition was capitalizing on it," Helms related.

Sen. Sam J. Ervin Jr.

asserted, "should outlaw any substantial contribution of cash and disbursement of cash" in future campaigns.

While agreeing that a ban or limit on the use of cash in campaigns was desirable, Sen. Lowell P. Weicker Jr. (R Conn.) said a law along those lines would be difficult to enforce. Such a law might be a deterrent, he noted, but "if enforcement is difficult, it's not that much of a deterrent."

Public Funding. Public financing of federal elections was an issue that had been around for a while and could get the boost it needed to succeed if backed by the committee. But no member seemed interested in that route. None volunteered any thoughts along those lines, and Rufus L. Edmisten, the committee's deputy chief counsel, said he detected "no movement on the part of anyone on the committee" for public campaign financing. All the members supported a motion on the Senate floor July 26 that tabled a public campaign financing amendment.

Baker, who had steadfastly opposed public campaign financing, said only that he was keeping an "open mind" on the subject.

Nevertheless, several witnesses—all Democrats—had urged such legislation. Berl Bernhard, Sen. Edmund S. Muskie's (D Maine) presidential campaign manager in 1972, said that was one reform most urgently needed, because candidates were being forced to devote too much time to "passing the hat. America deserves candidates who have enough time to consider the issues, enough funds to present their views to the voters and to compete equally on the merits, not men who make the best fund-raisers because they appeal to a particular interest group or because they are in a position to put pressure on people with money." *(p. 105)*

Election Commission. Another legislative idea, boosted by Ervin and Senate Minority Leader Hugh Scott (R Pa.), was an independent commission to supervise federal elections. Ervin said the commission should have the power to obtain injunctions against certain activities and to prosecute law violators. He said he believed it should be composed of equal numbers of Republicans and Democrats—serving staggered terms by presidential or congressional appointment—and be given most of the Justice Department's legal responsibilities regarding elections.

The committee chairman noted that campaign contributions from corporations had been illegal for about half a century, but that the laws never had been enforced until Archibald Cox acted against several corporations in 1973.

Cabinet Officials. Ervin also said that he would like to see laws barring cabinet officers or recent cabinet officers from soliciting political contributions. The penalties against corporations for making illegal contributions should be "substantially increased," he suggested. It was brought out during committee testimony that former Commerce Secretary Maurice H. Stans asked for contributions from corporations while he was in the cabinet. Most of the corporations got off with $5,000 fines, and their presidents or board chairmen were sentenced to $1,000 fines. *(Testimony, box 137, 136, 133)*

Other Ideas. Also under discussion by the committee and its staff were suggestions for shortening the length of campaigns, requiring public disclosure of all contributions and expenditures two weeks before an election and strengthening provisions of the Hatch Act against political activity by government employees.

Yet the committee was aware that not all the abuses of Watergate could be solved by legislation. "Human decency and morality must take up the slack somewhere," said Fred D. Thompson, the chief minority counsel. "There is so much where the adage, 'You can't legislate morality,' applies."

Value of the Hearings

Not surprisingly, there was almost universal agreement that the hearings had been a worthwhile undertaking. Such sentiments would be expected not only from the members themselves, who had put so much time and effort into their work, but from the Senate as a whole, which voted 77-0 to authorize the committee.

But the reasons cited for this view were not necessarily the predictable ones—that no other group could have done the job or that the legislature is best-suited to investigate the executive branch. The members spoke instead of a reaffirmation of the American governmental system, of education and of deterrence.

The Senate probe, which reached high into the executive branch, threatened the delicate system of government checks and balances, some people said they believed. The hearings showed not only that Congress had the courage to undertake such an investigation in a highly charged political atmosphere, but that the system was strong enough to withstand it, said Baker. To Thompson, the hearings gave added proof of the essential strength of the governmental system: "We've proven to ourselves that we can go through this trauma, deliberately inflicting pain on ourselves...as no other country in the world could."

Sen. Howard H. Baker Jr.

Weicker and Montoya, their parties' two junior members of the committee, said the hearings informed the public of governmental excesses. "The exposure of perjury, the arrogant use of power as a means to hide wrong-doing or truth, the perversion of government agencies for political uses, the use of power for the sake of the retention of power—all these things are understood clearly today," said Montoya in a speech before the Center for the Study of the Presidency in Nashville, Tenn., Oct. 22.

Baker spoke of the hearings as a deterrent force. He related a conversation he had with Ervin in which Ervin said, "Howard, we can't pass legislation on some of these things." Baker replied, "Well, it'll be 10 years 'til someone tries it (election wrong-doing) again."

Sen. Inouye of Hawaii spoke in a similar vein on NBC-TV's "Meet the Press" Sept. 9 when he said, "I think the public has in its mind established a very severe code of ethics, a code of political ethics, moral ethics, and I think politicians would have to bear this in mind from now on, that if they don't walk the narrow path, that it can be legal, but if it is not quite ethical, that they might suffer the consequences."

The public appeared to agree with the senators' views. A Gallup Poll in September found that 52 per cent of Americans felt the hearings were a "good thing for the country."

Committee Criticized. The committee's severest criticism came from former Vice President Spiro T. Agnew and one of its members, Sen. Edward J. Gurney (R Fla.). Gurney called the hearings a "travesty" in an Oct. 5 letter to Republican Gov. Meldrim Thomson Jr. of New Hampshire. *(p. 126)*

"The only concrete contributions we have made have been to force down the stock market, up the price of gold, devalue the American dollar, hurt the economy, and destroy the confidence of people in the American political system," wrote Gurney. "These are certainly concrete contributions, but about as useful as a block of concrete tied around a swimmer's neck."

Sen. Joseph M. Montoya

Gurney apparently was incensed over what he alleged to be a committee probe into his own campaign finances. This was denied by Ervin, who pointed out that the committee's mandate authorized it to investigate only the 1972 presidential campaign. The committee as a whole remained mute to Gurney's critical blast.

Special Prosecutor's Role

One of the criticisms most often hurled at the committee, particularly before Cox was fired, was that it duplicated the special prosecutor's inquiry and therefore was interested in exposure for exposure's sake. Although the committee agreed that one of its purposes was exposure, the members said it was done for educational purposes, not for sensationalism. And the committee's

(Continued on p. 145)

Highlights of Senate Watergate Hearings, Feb. 7-Nov. 15

Feb. 7: The Senate unanimously approved S Res 60, establishing a select committee "to conduct an investigation and study of the extent, if any, to which illegal, improper, or unethical activities were engaged in by any persons, acting individually or in combination with others, in the presidential election of 1972, or any campaign, canvass, or other activity related to it." *(Vol. I, p. 3)*

May 17: The committee opened its hearings with testimony from Robert C. Odle Jr., a former office manager at the Nixon re-election committee. *(Vol. I, p. 63)*

May 18: Convicted conspirator James W. McCord Jr. testified that he had been offered executive clemency in exchange for his silence, on Nixon's authority. But the man who made the offer, John J. Caulfield, later testified he had no proof that Nixon had approved it. *(Vol. I, p. 163)*

June 13: Chairman Sam J. Ervin's questioning of Nixon's chief 1972 fund-raiser, Maurice H. Stans, led to the first open conflict among committee members, as Sen. Edward J. Gurney (R Fla.) charged Ervin with harassing the witness. *(Vol. I, p. 132)*

June 14: Jeb Stuart Magruder, former deputy director of the re-election committee, gave the first inside look at events leading up to and following the Watergate break-in. He said former Attorney General John N. Mitchell approved the break-in plans and participated in the coverup along with Stans and other high administration officials. Mitchell and Stans denied the allegations. *(Vol. I, p. 135)*

June 15: Nixon's former counsel, John W. Dean III, began five days of explosive testimony. He read for six hours from a 245-page statement, which included allegations that Nixon knew of the coverup as early as Sept. 15, 1972, and had discussed hush money for Watergate defendants. *(Vol. I, p. 151)*

June 27: Dean revealed the names on a secret White House political "enemies list." *(Vol. I, p. 153)*

July 6: Nixon wrote to Ervin refusing to appear in person before the committee or to provide it with any presidential files. *(Vol. I, p. 189)*

July 10: Former Attorney General Mitchell testified that he had rejected the break-in plan, but deliberately kept Nixon ignorant of its true dimensions later in order to ensure the President's re-election.

July 16: Surprise witness Alexander P. Butterfield, a former White House aide who had become head of the Federal Aviation Administration, disclosed that an automatic recording system had been taping presidential conversations at the White House and Executive Office Building since the spring of 1971. The next day, the committee asked for access to some of the tapes in an effort to clear up conflicts in testimony. *(Vol. I, p. 192)*

July 23: After receiving a written refusal from Nixon, the committee voted unanimously to subpoena tapes and other White House documents in his posses-

sion—making him the first president since Thomas Jefferson to be subpoenaed. *(Vol. I, p. 225)*

July 24: Former White House domestic affairs adviser John D. Ehrlichman testified he had approved a "covert operation" that led to the 1971 attempted burglary of the office of Daniel Ellsberg's psychiatrist—but had not approved the burglary. *(Vol. I, p. 212)*

July 30: H. R. Haldeman, Nixon's former chief of staff, testified that the President had authorized him in July to take some of the crucial White House tapes home for a private listening. Haldeman echoed Ehrlichman's denials of involvement in the break-in or coverup. *(Vol. I, p. 229)*

Aug. 3: Former Acting FBI Director L. Patrick Gray III testified that he had warned Nixon July 6, 1972, that "people on your staff are trying to mortally wound you" by using the FBI and CIA in a coverup. Gray acknowledged having lied about Watergate-related documents he destroyed, at what he thought was the bidding of Ehrlichman and Dean. *(Vol. I, p. 255)*

Sept. 24: When the hearings resumed after a seven-week recess, conspirator E. Howard Hunt Jr. testified that former special White House counsel Charles W. Colson knew of the plan that led to the Watergate break-in. *(p. 37)*

Sept. 26: The committee began its second phase of hearings, on political sabotage, with witness Patrick J. Buchanan, a White House speechwriter who vigorously defended Nixon and attacked the committee staff as "character assassins." *(p. 40)*

Oct. 3: Donald H. Segretti, who conducted a political sabotage program against Democrats in 1972, said he reported frequently on his activities to former White House appointments secretary Dwight L. Chapin. *(p. 62)*

Oct. 17: U.S. District Judge John J. Sirica rejected the committee's suit for access to White House tapes on grounds that the court lacked jurisdiction. *(p. 62)*

Nov. 7: The committee began its third and final phase of hearings, exploring campaign financing. John J. Priestes, a Miami homebuilder, testified that officials of Nixon's re-election finance committee promised to help solve his problems with the Federal Housing Administration (FHA) in exchange for a $100,000 contribution—a deal that eventually fell through. *(p. 127)*

Nov. 13: The committee adopted a resolution calling on the President to meet with all seven members to answer questions about the Watergate case. *(p. 136)*

Nov. 13-15: Executives for several large corporations testified that Nixon fund-raiser Stans had pressured them into making illegal corporate contributions in 1972. The men and the companies had pleaded guilty and been fined for violating a federal law prohibiting corporate contributions to political campaigns. *(p. 137)*

counsels saw their probe as complementing, not duplicating, the work of the special prosecutor and his staff.

Thompson, the minority counsel, pointed out that the committee's investigation was essentially public, because it was not concerned with punishment, but the Cox probe, being prosecutorial, had to be done in secret. And the committee, being interested in improper or questionable acts in addition to illegal ones, did not need proof before presenting evidence in public testimony, he said. "Our essential function," Thompson said of the committee, "was to elicit facts from which the public could make up its own mind."

The tapes controversy ultimately played a part in Nixon's dismissal of Cox and the resignations of Richardson and Ruckelshaus, in what became known as the Saturday Night Massacre (Oct. 20). Cox later was replaced by Leon Jaworski, and Sen. William B. Saxbe (R Ohio) was nominated to replace Richardson as attorney general.

Resignation Requested. The events of Oct. 20 resulted in many calls for the President's impeachment or resignation. But among committee members, only Inouye joined those demanding Nixon's removal. In a speech to the AFL-CIO convention Oct. 22, the day before Nixon reversed himself and agreed to give up the tapes to a federal judge, Inouye called for Nixon's resignation or, failing that, his impeachment. After the Nixon tapes reversal, Inouye said he would retract his demand only if Nixon reappointed Cox, Richardson and Ruckelshaus.

Sen. Daniel K. Inouye

Three other senators called for Nixon's removal: John V. Tunney (D Calif.), Edward W. Brooke (R Mass.) and Philip A. Hart (D Mich.). Others, however, urged the President to undertake various courses of action to alleviate the crisis of his government, such as yielding the tapes to the committee or appearing before the committee in public or private session. Nixon declined a meeting with the full committee but said he would meet with Ervin and Baker. Ervin insisted on involving all committee members.

Ervin blamed Nixon for part of the tense Watergate atmosphere. "The great tragedy is the failure of Mr. Nixon to make available information in his possession," said Ervin. "It's a tragedy for him as well as for the country."

Doing Things Differently

Without apologizing for anything they or the committee as a whole had done, most of the members and counsels said they felt, in retrospect, that things might have been handled differently. None, however, said he viewed these second guesses as involving major areas of the investigation.

Weicker and Edmisten, for example, said they felt the committee should not have taken an August-September recess. Both mentioned this in connection with testimony the committee wanted, but had not received, from

former White House aide Charles W. Colson. According to Edmisten, Colson "was begging to come" before the committee. But by the time the committee got around to interviewing him Sept. 19, Colson said he was under investigation by a federal grand jury, so he invoked his constitutional right against self-incrimination in a private committee interview. The committee regularly declined to call any witness who said he would invoke his Fifth Amendment rights. *(p. 33)*

"The committee was so anxious to go home—they were so tired—they let a golden opportunity (to question Colson) go by," said Edmisten.

Baker rejected the idea that the summer recess was wrong. He said on CBS' "Face the Nation" July 29, about a week before the recess, that he, the committee and the staff were tired. "I would even be so bold as to say the country's tired," he added.

Baker agreed with many of the other members, however, about the need for quicker, tighter questioning of witnesses. Throughout most of the hearings there was a time limit—usually 10 minutes—for each senator, with unlimited rounds of questioning, but it seldom was observed. "There was too much pontificating and moralizing" by the senators, said committee member Herman E. Talmadge (D Ga.), who declined to name names.

Talmadge favored speeding up the hearings by dividing the committee into two subcommittees after the summer recess to investigate dirty tricks and campaign contributions separately. But the committee's staff did not have enough time to prepare for two phases during the recess, he said.

Shortly after the hearings began in May, Gurney complained that the committee was wasting too much time on "minor witnesses" who shed little light on the extent of presidential involvement, if any, in Watergate. He proposed that witnesses such as Dean, Haldeman and Mitchell, who ultimately did not testify until late June and July, be called right away. But the committee majority rejected this, insisting that a foundation had to be laid for their testimony.

Montoya, who was criticized by some who followed the hearings as the least effective of the committee's interrogators, complained that resumes of witness staff interviews usually got to him only the night before the public testimony, so that he did not have enough time to prepare.

Sen. Herman E. Talmadge

Edmisten said the committee might have been better prepared earlier if he could have had more staff and office space from the beginning, in February 1973. "The Senate moves in slow and mysterious ways," he said half jokingly, adding that he and chief counsel Samuel Dash doubled up in his office at the start and that he could not get an adequate staff for a month and a half. The staff eventually reached 70 persons with a budget of $1-million.

None of the committee members interviewed admitted that he personally would have done anything differently. Weicker, for example, offered no apologies for what many people considered his harsh questioning of Haldeman and Ehrlichman. That was a "hard bunch we were up against," he said. *(Testimony, Vol. I, p. 212, 229)*

Baker was viewed as trying to walk a narrow line between not alienating the administration on the one hand and asking tough questions of the mostly Republican witnesses on the other. He replied, as he always had, that he did not try to strike a balance in his questioning. "I try to dig for the facts—following them wherever they lead—and be as fair and impartial as I know how," he said.

Gurney was perceived to be the panel member most friendly to the administration. He questioned the President's chief accuser, John Dean, particularly hard. Ehrlichman, Dean testified, told him that Gurney alone among the committee members could be counted on to defend the President. *(Dean testimony, Vol. I, p. 151)*

Gurney said on ABC's "Issues and Answers" July 8 about the pro-administration allegation, that "nothing could be further from the truth." He said there had been no attempt by anyone in the White House to contact him or his staff. Referring to his questioning of Dean, he said, that "because I question hard, then I think perhaps I am cast in a role of being the administration defender, but I believe...that a man is innocent until he is proven guilty, and I want to get all the facts out."

Television and Its Effects

Television cameras, which made national personalities out of the members and insomniacs out of late-night re-run viewers, in September departed the marble-columned Senate caucus room, where the hearings were held, to cover the more exciting aspects of the Watergate story elsewhere.

While the networks maintained live coverage, there were a few calls for removal of the cameras, mostly from outside the committee membership. Sen. Robert Dole (R Kan.) introduced a resolution Sept. 5 to "turn off the TV lights. It is time to move the Watergate investigation from the living rooms of America and put it where it belongs" in the courts and behind the closed doors of the committee, he said. Watergate "has come to stand for the longest running day and night time telethon in history." The resolution went nowhere.

"I can't think of anything the committee should have done differently, except perhaps that it should have ended the televising of the hearings sooner than it did," said Sen. Robert C. Byrd (D W.Va.), the assistant majority leader. Even Inouye questioned the use of television, explaining that if he were a defense attorney, his client would have a better chance in a courtroom.

But the issue became moot when the networks removed their cameras shortly after the committee returned from its recess in late September. With the end of live coverage, there was a noticeable drop in attendance by senators. Whether this was attributable to the lack of cameras or to the witnesses' lack of star quality was in dispute.

Asked whether the television cutoff resulted in lowered member interest, Weicker laughed and cited the testimony by Frank Mankiewicz, national political coordinator for the 1972 McGovern campaign, Oct. 11,

Dirty Tricks

Dirty tricks, political sabotage, negative campaigning, black advance, pranks—those were some of the terms used to describe activities examined in the Senate investigating committee's second phase of hearings. The key witness was Donald H. Segretti, a 32-year-old California lawyer who said he was hired in 1971 by former White House aides Dwight L. Chapin and Gordon C. Strachan to coordinate "activities tending to foster a split between the various Democratic hopefuls and to prevent the Democratic Party from uniting behind one candidate." *(Testimony, p. 43)*

At one time or another during the campaign, Segretti said, he had a total of 28 agents working either directly or indirectly for him in 12 states. His testimony centered on the "tricks" he and his collaborators played during the 1972 Florida and California primaries. These ranged from sophomoric but disruptive stunts—such as setting off stink bombs at political events—to clearly illegal acts such as distributing phony campaign literature.

Three of Segretti's Florida tricks brought him a six-month prison sentence for violation of federal election laws. Working with two others, he:

• Mailed out letters on the stationery of Sen. Edmund S. Muskie (D Maine), falsely accusing Senators Henry M. Jackson (D Wash.) and Hubert H. Humphrey (D Minn.) of sexual improprieties and excessive drinking.

• Distributed flyers at a rally for Gov. George C. Wallace (D Ala.) that said: "If you liked Hitler, you'll love Wallace—Vote for Muskie."

• Printed and put up posters, attributed to a fictitious "Mothers for Busing" committee, that said: "Help Muskie Support Busing More Children Now."

Segretti's California activities, as he outlined them for the committee, were similar. One was a phony press release sent out on Humphrey stationery saying that another candidate, Rep. Shirley Chisholm (D N.Y.), had once been a patient in a mental institution.

Despite the serious implications of Segretti's sabotage operation, which he ruefully admitted, some of his tales evoked smiles in the hearing room. At one point, the poker-faced witness described how he and another agent, posing as organizers of a planned Muskie fund-raising dinner in Washington, D.C., arranged for a number of uninvited African diplomats to be delivered to the gala in rented limousines. Segretti said he and his associates ordered large quantities of pizza, flowers and liquor for the real organizers of the event, and hired a magician who showed up to entertain. "We also made inquiries about renting an elephant, but were unable to make the necessary arrangements," Segretti added.

His final act of the 1972 political campaign, Segretti said, was to hire a small plane to fly over the Miami Beach, Fla., convention center during the Democratic national convention in July, trailing a sign that read: "Peace, pot, promiscuity. Vote McGovern."

attended only by himself and Montoya. "That's the best answer to that," he said.

Edmisten and Thompson, however, saw the slackened attendance as stemming from the different type of witness appearing before the committee. The members

are human beings, Edmisten said, and "no witness could be as interesting as a Dean, Haldeman or Mitchell." The later subjects of the committee's inquiry were not as interesting as the Watergate break-in itself, explained Thompson. This, he said, caused a "psychological winding down" of the members from the hectic pre-recess days.

Sen. Lowell P. Weicker Jr.

Network Costs. Televising the hearings had mixed results for the networks. It cost them all substantial revenues from normal daytime programming, but they scored points by performing a public service, network spokesmen said. While none would say how much money his network lost because of its coverage, the CBS spokesman called it "considerable." The spokesmen agreed that the network that covered the hearings on any particular day—coverage was rotated among the three—scored highest in audience ratings for that time period. The hearings at first were covered simultaneously by all networks, then by rotating coverage after about two weeks.

Public Broadcasting. The big winner among television broadcasters was the Public Broadcasting System, a non-commercial network that showed the complete hearings on tape each evening. The hearings "put the public broadcast stations on the map," said a PBS spokesman. The individual stations captured a greater share of their localities' evening audiences and acquired new funding in the form of memberships. An average of 216, or 90 per cent, of the PBS stations carried the hearings, the spokesman said.

Political Partisanship

Despite an outburst now and then, the committee has been remarkably free of the partisanship and public rancor that have characterized many other sensitive congressional investigations.

All the members, in their interviews with Congressional Quarterly, cited the Army-McCarthy hearings of 1954 as an example of the kind of political divisiveness they had avoided. Those hearings, involving Sen. Joseph R. McCarthy (R Wis. 1947-57), included innuendo, name-calling, and character assassination. The unanimous Senate vote authorizing the Watergate committee, the personalities of its members and its ground rules

Sen. Edward J. Gurney

were cited as reasons for the lack of partisanship.

But Senate Minority Leader Scott disagreed, saying the committee's early stance of nonpartisanship "has

moved in recent months heavily toward partisanship." Although he gave no specifics, an aide to Scott explained that the "dirty tricks" phase of the committee's investigation saw an unusually large number of persons who worked for the President's re-election being called to testify, but relatively few Democrats. The committee finally located five witnesses to testify about 'dirty tricks' against the President, but not one could put any blame on a Democratic candidate. *(Box, p. 146; testimony, p. 126)*

Countering charges of partisanship, Edmisten said there never had been a straight party-line vote among the members. He said all their ballots had been unanimous, except for 6-to-1 votes granting partial immunity to Dean and delaying the hearings for a week during the visit of Soviet Communist leader Leonid I. Brezhnev in June. *(Vol. I, p. 145)*

Backing up Edmisten and committee views of nonpartisanship was a September Gallup Poll, which found that 57 per cent of the nation felt the committee was more interested in gathering facts about Watergate than in discrediting the President. Only 28 per cent viewed discrediting Nixon as the committee's goal, but 52 per cent said they thought the committee was more interested in getting at the facts. And 52 per cent said they thought the hearings were good for the country.

Unanswered Questions

Many important questions about the Watergate affair were not answered with any finality, due primarily to conflicting testimony. "What did the President know and when did he know it?" was Baker's oft-repeated question early in the hearings. Did Mitchell order the break-in, and if not, who did? *(Major unanswered questions, box, p. 142)*

The committee took some heat over its inability to find the answers to these and other important questions, but the members responded that this was not their main responsibility. They saw their job as laying the facts on the table and letting the American public judge for itself. They pointed to the special prosecutor as the man responsible for collecting the facts and developing the proof about who actually did what to whom and who might have helped out.

"While the committee's evidence may leave the exact degree of complicity of some individuals in question, it did show what happened," said Ervin. Exposure and education were the only roles the committee could perform, he said.

Wrapped up in the contradictory testimony was the matter of perjury. Perjury is difficult to prove, because intent must be shown. Most of the witnesses protected themselves by prefacing their answers with, "To the best of my recollection...." Ervin also noted that contradictory testimony about conversations did not necessarily mean perjury had been committed, because one party might not have expressed himself clearly or the other might not have heard correctly.

In any case, perjury was a matter for the special prosecutor, not the committee, to deal with, members said. They conceded, however, that they would have to make informed judgments about who was telling the truth in preparing their report.

NIXON COUNTERATTACKS: 'I HAVE EARNED EVERY CENT'

"I am not a crook." The remark by Nixon before an Associated Press Managing Editors press conference Nov. 17 was an extraordinary comment from a President, but it came at an extraordinary time, when allegations of impropriety and illegality against him were rampant.

With Nixon's popularity at a record low, he sought to bring himself and his case before the public during the week ended Nov. 23 with speeches and visits to former Rep. Carl Vinson (D Ga. 1914-65) in Macon, Ga., and the Republican Governors' Conference in Memphis, Tenn., in addition to the press conference in Orlando, Fla. "Operation Candor," the White House was calling it. The President had spent the previous week in private meetings with members of Congress, explaining his actions and urging their support. *(p. 132)*

But Watergate did not recede as a presidential problem. And Nixon was being buffeted by criticism over his handling of his personal income taxes, a 1971 case involving milk price supports, the energy crisis and White House charges that former Attorney General Elliot L. Richardson lied before the Senate Judiciary Committee in explaining his motives for resigning. All these matters except the Richardson episode came up at the press conference. *(Text of press conference, p. 152; Richardson case, box, p. 151)*

Tax Payments. The televised, hour-long press conference was held at Walt Disney World near Orlando, with about 400 Associated Press managing editors in attendance. The "I am not a crook" remark came in answer to a question about Nixon's personal finances and tax payments. Press reports had noted that Nixon paid only $1,670 in income taxes in 1970 and 1971 on income of $400,000. In his answer, Nixon did not confirm or deny the figures, stating only that he paid "nominal amounts" in taxes for those years.

He said this situation resulted from the $500,000 worth of income deductions he claimed by donating his vice presidential papers to the government. This decision, he said, had been recommended to him by former President Johnson and had not been questioned by the Internal Revenue Service.

The President then detailed some of his personal finances, saying he left the office of vice president in 1961 with a $47,000 net worth, but during the next eight years earned between $100,000 and $250,000 annually from his law practice and from a book he wrote.

"I made my mistakes," the President went on, "but in all my years of public life, I have never profited, never profited from public service. I have earned every cent.... Well, I am not a crook. I have earned everything I have got."

Watergate Questions. Half of the 20 questions at the press conference concerned Watergate and related events. The President repeated his innocence of any wrong-doing and promised to supply more evidence to prove his case. While conceding he had made a mistake in not more closely supervising his 1972 campaign, he refused to blame subordinates.

Asked if he still considered former White House aides John D. Ehrlichman and H. R. Haldeman the "finest public servants" he had ever known, as he had characterized them when they quit under fire in April, Nixon replied that they were "dedicated, fine public servants" who eventually would be proven innocent of any wrong-doing.

The President was questioned about two of nine tape recordings of his conversations that were not turned over to the Watergate grand jury under a court order. The White House had explained Oct. 31 that the tapes never existed. *(p. 94)*

Nixon repeated the reasons for the missing June 20, 1972, conversation with former Attorney General John N. Mitchell and an April 15, 1973, talk with former presidential counsel John W. Dean III. The Mitchell telephone conversation was held on a phone that was not hooked up to the automatic recording device, and the Dean conversation took place after the recording machine had run out of tape, Nixon stated.

He said he was first informed on Sept. 29 or 30 that the tapes might not exist, but that this was not confirmed to him until about Oct. 27. Nixon repeated, however, that he would provide the grand jury with a Dictabelt recording that contained references to the Mitchell conversation and his notes on the Dean meeting.

As additional explanation for the missing tapes, Nixon characterized the recording devices as unsophisticated. He called one "a little Sony" with "little lapel mikes" in his desk, and said the system cost about $2,500. This was a contradiction of testimony before the Senate Watergate committee by Alexander P. Butterfield, a former White House aide, who told of an elaborate arrangement of tapes, microphones and triggering devices in Nixon's offices and telephones. *(Vol. I, p. 192)*

Milk Prices. None of his interrogators asked Nixon about the milk price supports case, so the President

---

Grand Jury Extension

The Senate Nov. 19 cleared for the President a bill (HR 10937—S Rept 93-527) that would extend the original federal grand jury investigating the Watergate break-in and coverup. Approval was by voice vote.

The Senate Judiciary Committee Nov. 13 gave the Senate a choice between HR 10937, which had been approved by the House Nov. 6, and a different version (S 2885), which had been proposed by the committee chairman, Sen. James O. Eastland (D Miss.). *(Senate committee action, p. 137; House action, p. 128)*

The Senate leadership scheduled the House-passed bill for consideration by the Senate. It was passed without debate.

HR 10937 would extend the grand jury, which was created June 5, 1972, for six months by law and would permit the jury to seek a further six-month extension from the U.S. District Court for the District of Columbia.

brought up the subject himself. It had been alleged that in exchange for a $422,500 donation to the Nixon re-election campaign from the dairy industry, former Secretary of Agriculture Clifford Hardin reversed himself in March 1971 and ordered increased price supports for milk producers. The increase was estimated to add $500-million to $700-million in income for dairy farmers.

Nothing of the sort occurred, said the President. He related that he had accepted Hardin's original recommendation not to raise price supports, but that three weeks later, "Congress put a gun to our head." He agreed to an increase when his legislative advisers told him that members of Congress, mostly Democrats, he said, wanted the increase and could override his veto if he tried to prevent it.

Donald Nixon Wiretap. Nixon was questioned about reports that the Secret Service had tapped the telephone of his brother, F. Donald. He confirmed that the tap took place, but gave no details as to time or place. Nixon said the tap was put on Donald Nixon for "security reasons," not national security reasons, but did not explain what he meant by the former description. He said his brother was aware of the tap and approved it.

"The surveillance involved not what he was doing. The surveillance involved what others who were trying to get him, perhaps to use improper influence and support, might be doing, and particularly anybody who might be in a foreign country," he said.

Other Appearances. The press conference was sandwiched between other public appearances, starting with a speech before the National Association of Realtors Nov. 15 in Washington, D.C. Most of the President's remarks there dealt with energy matters, but he drew his lustiest cheers when he told the audience he was "not going to walk away" from the presidency. Standing before a huge replica of the American flag in colored light bulbs, Nixon asserted, "As far as the President of the United States is concerned, he has not violated his trust, and he isn't going to violate his trust now."

But Nixon drew a mixed reaction Nov. 18 in Macon, Ga., where he went to help celebrate Vinson's 90th birthday and the 100th anniversary of Mercer University's law school. A crowd estimated at more than 5,000 persons greeted him when his plane landed at Robins Air Force Base, and others greeted him along his motorcade route to the campus.

But at the campus itself, hundreds of students and faculty members met him with hostile signs calling on him to resign and denouncing his role in the Watergate affair.

Nixon did not dwell on his problems in his speech, which was given inside the college chapel. He announced that the nation's third nuclear aircraft carrier would be named after Vinson, the former chairman of the House Armed Services Committee.

Nixon's pre-Thanksgiving travels ended with a private appearance Nov. 20 before the Republican governors in Memphis.

The governors gave Nixon a warm welcome, seemed convinced by his protestations of innocence and reassured by his pledge to clear up doubts about his actions, according to news reports. White House deputy press secretary Gerald L. Warren told reporters afterward that Nixon

Poll Report

The founder and chairman of the Gallup Poll warned the nation's Republican governors Nov. 19 that their party could expect to feel the effects of the Watergate scandal in the 1974 elections.

Anyone with doubts on that score should study the results of the state and local elections of 1973, said George Gallup Sr. at the governors' convention in Memphis, Tenn. "While many dismiss the elections of this month throughout the nation as being mixed, the fact is they point unmistakably to serious problems which the Republicans must face in 1974," he said.

Gallup cited state elections in New Jersey and local elections in Connecticut as reflecting frustration among voters, who he said vented their feelings on the Republicans. Many Republicans stayed home on election day, he said. And he referred to one of his organization's polls that showed voter support for Republican congressional candidates at its lowest ebb since he started polling in 1935. *(P. 134)*

Nixon Popularity. The latest Gallup Poll, published Nov. 15, found that President Nixon's popularity rating had leveled off at its all-time low point of 27 per cent approval. A similar leveling off had been noted in an earlier Harris Survey. *(Harris, p. 134, earlier Gallup, p. 125)*

Gallup interviewers asked 1,550 adults nationwide Nov. 2-5: "Do you approve or disapprove of the way Nixon is handling his job as President?"

	Latest	Oct. 19-22
Approve	27%	27%
Disapprove	63	60
No opinion	10	13

Republican Support. A Harris Survey published Nov. 20 found that the number of Americans who called themselves Republicans had declined to its lowest point in the decade the poll had been conducted. As in other surveys in recent months, the results also showed an increase of independent voters at the expense of both parties.

In October interviews among 1,598 households, Harris asked: "Regardless of how you may vote, what do you usually consider yourself—a Republican, a Democrat, or what?"

	Latest	August 1973
Republican	25%	27%
Democrat	47	48
Independent	28	25

had not said anything new to the governors, "but he said it to them."

Oregon Gov. Tom McCall, who warned his colleagues against "knee jerk reactions" in favor of the President when the conference began three days earlier, said after the meeting that he was "relieved both as a citizen and as a politician." Iowa Gov. Robert D. Ray, another who had been critical of the President, praised Nixon after the meeting.

During the nearly four-hour meeting, the President reportedly was questioned about all the matters that came up at the Orlando press conference. When asked if "other bombs" were about to explode, Nixon's response, according to Tennessee Gov. Winfield Dunn, was, "If there are, he was not aware of them."

Jaworski's Committee Testimony

Special Watergate prosecutor Leon Jaworski told the Senate Judiciary Committee Nov. 20 that he would not allow White House claims of national security stand in the way of his Watergate investigation. However, he added that he did not expect he would have to review White House tapes or see documents relating to national security, which he said White House aides had offered.

During committee questioning about special prosecutor legislation, Jaworski acknowledged that presidential assistants the preceding week had brought a "national security" problem involving the "plumbers" team to his attention. He assured the committee that "my analysis was I could proceed, and I told them I expected to proceed."

"What assurances do you have that the veil of national security won't be drawn over the matter?" Sen. Edward M. Kennedy (D Mass.) asked.

"One, much as I respect the issue of national security, I'm not going to be blinded by it," Jaworski replied, "and two, there was no resistance (from White House special counsel J. Fred Buzhardt and chief of staff Alexander M. Haig Jr.) when I said I thought some indictments could be brought, and I was going to pursue them."

The "plumbers" unit, set up in 1971 to plug news leaks of national security information, was in charge of the break-in of the office of Pentagon Papers figure Daniel Ellsberg's psychiatrist.

In earlier testimony, former Attorney General Elliot L. Richardson told the committee that Buzhardt had informed him during the summer of 1973 of a "very significant national security problem" involving the break-in case. Depending on "how it is handled," Richardson said, the problem could be a serious impediment to Jaworski's efforts to bring federal indictments. *(p. 120, 118)*

New Regulation. On the same day that Jaworski testified, his boss, Acting Attorney General Robert H. Bork, issued a departmental regulation designed to strengthen Jaworski's independence. The regulation ordered that the special prosecutor's jurisdiction would not be limited without approval of eight congressional leaders. An earlier regulation had required the consensus of the eight leaders before President Nixon could fire Jaworski. The leaders included majority and minority leaders of the House and Senate and the chairmen and ranking minority members of the House and Senate Judiciary Committees.

Week's Watergate Chronology

Following is a day-to-day chronology of the week's events in the Watergate case: *(For week ending Nov. 17)*

NOV. 15

Impeachment Conflicts. In a floor speech, House Majority Leader Thomas P. O'Neill Jr. (D Mass.) denounced the President's meetings with members of Congress on the Watergate case as an "unbecoming, if not improper" attempt to influence the outcome of the impeachment investigation. His attack provoked a partisan debate over a resolution granting the Judiciary Committee $1-million for the investigation. It was adopted by a 367-51 vote. *(Details, box, p. 152)*

Richardson-White House Clash. Several Republican senators who had met with Nixon the previous evening told reporters the President had accused former Attorney General Elliot L. Richardson of giving the Senate Judiciary Committee misleading information about his role in the dismissal of former special prosecutor Archibald Cox. White House spokesman Kenneth W. Clawson denied that Nixon had accused Richardson of lying. *(Box, p. 151)*

Sirica on Special Prosecutor. U.S. District Judge John J. Sirica, who was presiding over the Watergate tapes case, said he agreed with the Nov. 14 opinion of U.S. District Judge Gerhard A. Gesell that bills to create a court-appointed Watergate special prosecutor were unconstitutional. "I don't know of any judge who thinks it's a good idea," Sirica said *(Gesell opinion, p. 135)*

Guild on Impeachment. The 16-member International Executive Board of the American Newspaper Guild adopted a resolution calling on Congress to initiate impeachment proceedings against Nixon because of "improper, unconstitutional and illegal conduct involving both the President and his closest associates." Some union members objected that the action compromised their objective stance as reporters.

Senate Hearings. Executives for several large corporations testified before the Senate Watergate investigating committee on why their companies made illegal corporate contributions to Nixon's 1972 campaign. *(Testimony, p. 133)*

Nixon Speech. Nixon assured a friendly audience at the National Association of Realtors convention in Washington, D.C., that he would not resign and had "not violated his trust."

NOV. 16

CIA Watergate Involvement. The CIA's involvement in the Watergate burglary was brought up at a closed session of the Senate Armed Services Committee, where freelance writer Andrew St. George testified that the agency was given advance information about the operation by one of its participants, Eugenio R. Martinez. CIA Director William E. Colby and former CIA Director Richard Helms submitted statements denying the charges. But Colby acknowledged that Martinez, working for the CIA on a contract basis, had informed the agency that E. Howard Hunt Jr., a leader of the burglary, was in Miami in late 1971 and early 1972.

Dairy Contributions. Release of a deposition given by Jake Jacobsen, a former lawyer for the Associated Milk

What Did Richardson Say About Compromise on Tapes?

President Nixon's hectic round of meetings with Republican members of Congress during the week of Nov. 12-16 was intended to clear up confusions and doubts about all aspects of the Watergate case. In at least one area, the effect was exactly the opposite.

The new conflict involved the circumstances of Nixon's Oct. 20 dismissal of former special prosecutor Archibald Cox. It surfaced Nov. 15, when several Republican senators who had met with the President the night before reported that Nixon told them former Attorney General Elliot L. Richardson had agreed to a White House compromise plan on the tapes dispute that would have prevented Cox from seeking any further documentary evidence from White House files.

Under oath before the Senate Judiciary Committee Nov. 6, Richardson said he had never approved such attempts to limit Cox. The White House plan, announced Oct. 19, provided for review of the subpoenaed tapes by Sen. John C. Stennis (D Miss.) before handing them over to the court. The next day, Cox was fired for refusing to comply with the plan, and Richardson resigned rather than do the firing. *(Richardson testimony, p. 120; firing, p. 71)*

White House spokesman Kenneth W. Clawson issued a statement Nov. 15 denying that Nixon had accused Richardson of lying. The President had referred to "several versions of the events" surrounding Cox's dismissal and that was all, Clawson explained. But the incident did not end there.

Rep. Charles W. Whalen Jr. (R Ohio) took notes during the last Watergate meeting Nov. 16. He quoted Nixon as saying that Cox had agreed to the White House tapes compromise plan until the night of Oct. 19, when he suddenly decided Stennis was not trustworthy.

Denying that report, Cox pointed out that he had written a memo to Richardson Oct. 18 citing his substantial objections to the so-called "Stennis plan"—and that he and White House attorney Charles Alan Wright had exchanged letters about those objections during the day of Oct. 19.

Senators who were later questioned by reporters about the Nov. 13-14 Watergate sessions agreed that Nixon and his chief of staff, Alexander M. Haig Jr., had implied that Richardson—contrary to his Senate testimony—voiced no objection to the firing of Cox until after the fact.

Sen. Charles McC. Mathias Jr. (R Md.) said Haig, who sat in on the Nov. 14 meeting, asserted that Richardson was the one who first suggested that Cox's power to seek White House documents be removed. "I have read Elliot's testimony, and it is not true," Mathias quoted Haig as saying.

Mathias, a member of the Judiciary Committee, said Nov. 19 that the charges of lying under oath to a congressional committee were serious enough to warrant calling on Haig, Wright and other White House insiders to testify on the issue. He made a motion to that effect during a closed meeting of the committee Nov. 20, but a final decision on the matter was delayed until Nov. 27.

The Washington Post reported Nov. 18 that documents given to the Senate Judiciary Committee by Richardson appeared to support Richardson's version of the disputed events. Richardson himself made no formal statement on the controversy, but said he was "incredulous" that the White House would accuse him of misrepresenting the truth.

Asked about the allegation at the Republican Governors Conference in Memphis, Tenn., on Nov. 20, President Nixon insisted that he had not accused Richardson of lying but said there was a "difference of recollection" between Richardson and three White House attorneys. The governors reportedly did not question Nixon on which version of the events he accepted.

Producers Inc., brought to light an apparent conflict with the Senate testimony of Herbert W. Kalmbach, Nixon's former personal attorney and campaign fund-raiser. Jacobsen said the dairy organization secretly paid Kalmbach $100,000 in cash in 1969 "to get a more sympathetic understanding" from the Nixon administration. Kalmbach told the Senate Watergate investigating committee July 16 that he did not start soliciting funds for Nixon until November 1970.

Watergate Indictments. *The Washington Post* reported that, according to informed sources, White House attorney J. Fred Buzhardt had been trying to block the possible indictment of former presidential aides John D. Ehrlichman, Charles W. Colson and Egil Krogh Jr. on grounds that certain national security-related activities would come to light during prosecution of the cases. Former Attorney General Richardson later denied that Buzhardt had acted improperly.

NOV. 17

Nixon Appearance. President Nixon vigorously asserted his innocence of wrong-doing in the Watergate and related cases during an hour-long televised question-and-answer session with participants in the Associated Press Managing Editors Association convention in Orlando, Fla. "People have got to know whether or not their President is a crook. Well, I'm not a crook," he said. *(Details, p. 148)*

NOV. 18

Impeachment Call. *The Hartford (Conn.) Courant* switched its editorial stand and called for the impeachment of the President. "The miasma enveloping the nation and the presidency has got to be cleared up now without being allowed to drag its weary length any further," the paper said.

NOV. 19

Agnew Committee Plea. The Salute to Ted Agnew Committee, which held a fund-raising dinner for former Vice President Agnew on May 19, 1972, pleaded guilty in Annapolis, Md., to four counts of violating state election laws in connection with the event. The seven-

Impeachment Investigation

Over sometimes bitter opposition from Republicans, the House Nov. 15 appropriated $1-million for the House Judiciary Committee's staff investigation into whether President Nixon should be impeached.

Republicans opposed passage of the funding bill, H Res 702, without written guarantees that Republican members of the Judiciary Committee could have a say in choosing staff members for the inquiry. Committee Chairman Peter W. Rodino Jr. (D N.J.) promised that Republicans would have a chance to choose some of the staff—but he declined to say exactly how many.

The bill, which required no further action before taking effect, was adopted, 367-51, on a recorded teller vote.

However, the key vote came in an earlier effort by Rep. William L. Dickinson (R Ala.) to recommit the bill to the Committee on House Administration with instructions to report back an amended bill providing that at least one-third of the investigation be under the control of Republicans, and that the funds not become available until the Judiciary Committee had "defined the nature and scope" of the staff's work. Dickinson's motion was rejected on an almost straight party-line recorded teller vote, 190-227, with Democrats opposed.

Three other votes were taken:

• A motion by Administration Committee Chairman Wayne L. Hays (D Ohio) ordering the previous question on a committee amendment to reduce the recommended funding from $1.5-million to $1-million was adopted on a recorded vote, 230-182. The heavily party-line vote, with Republicans opposed, had the effect of cutting off further amendments to the amendment and limiting debate.

The amendment was then adopted by voice vote.

• A motion by Hays ordering the previous question on the resolution was adopted on a recorded vote, 233-186, with most Republicans voting against. The vote, which came after nearly an hour of debate on the resolution, cut off further discussion.

Early Staff Work. Before the House acted, 19 staff members were already at work investigating impeachment charges. They included five people from the General Accounting Office. Republican members complained that all were operating under the direction of the Democratic Judiciary Committee chairman, Rodino, and that Republican members of the committee had not been kept informed of their progress.

"In other words, the minority has been kept in the dark while 19 majority staff members have been busily at work for impeachment," said Rep. Wiley Mayne (R Iowa), a member of the Judiciary Committee. "We in the minority have been given no real opportunity to participate or be informed."

member committee was fined $2,000 for filing an election report that falsely described a $49,900 loan from the Nixon re-election committee as contributions from 32 individual donors.

Watergate Investigator. Samuel Dash, chief counsel of the Senate investigating committee, suspended one of his staff investigators, Scott Armstrong, for one month. Armstrong was accused of being the source of some sharp criticism of the committee's top staff quoted in the Nov. 22 issue of a biweekly newspaper, *Rolling Stone.*

Hughes-Rebozo Funds. A *New York Times* report brought up the possibility that there were differing versions of Charles G. Rebozo's handling of a secret $100,000 contribution to Nixon from billionaire Howard Hughes that Rebozo eventually returned. Nixon told a group of Republican senators Nov. 14 that Rebozo had the money he returned checked by an FBI agent to verify that it was the same money he received. The Times said the agent in question, Kenneth Whitaker, had told his superiors in Miami, Fla., that Rebozo had shown him the money but that he had not been able to check it out, as Nixon said.

NOV. 20

Jaworski Investigation. Leon Jaworski, the new Watergate special prosecutor, testified before the Senate Judiciary Committee that national security problems raised by the White House would not prevent him from investigating cases thoroughly and pressing for indictments. Jaworski was questioned about a particularly sensitive national security matter connected with the White House "plumbers" investigation unit which had been mentioned by former Attorney General Richardson as a possible impediment to a full investigation of the unit's activities. *(Box, p. 150)*

Nixon-Governors Meeting. Nixon assured the Republican Governors' Conference, meeting in Memphis, Tenn., that he would clear up public doubts by releasing detailed information to answer scandal charges against his administration.

ADA Letter. Americans for Democratic Action (ADA) sent a letter to all members of Congress listing 73 charges against Nixon. "These 73 allegations make it clear that there is a prima facie case of criminality on the part of Richard Nixon which must be fully investigated," said Rep. Donald M. Fraser (D Minn.), ADA chairman. "Nixon himself was involved in some of these acts; others involved men under his direction."

QUESTION-AND-ANSWER TEXT

Following is the White House text of President Nixon's question-and-answer session Nov. 17 at a conference of the Associated Press Managing Editors Association in Walt Disney World, near Orlando, Fla. The session was nationally televised.

THE PRESIDENT: President Quinn and ladies and gentlemen: When Jack Horner, who has been a correspondent in Washington and other places around the world, retired after 40 years, he once told me that if I thought the White House Press Corps answered (asked) tough questions, he (I) should hear the kind of questions the managing editors asked him. Consequently, I welcome this opportunity tonight to meet with the managing editors of the nation's newspapers.

I will not have an opening statement because I know, with 400 of you, it will be hard to get through all of the questions you have, and I understand the president has a prerogative of asking the first question.

Mr. Quinn.

Q: This morning, Gov. Askew of Florida addressed this group and recalled the words of Benjamin Franklin. When leaving the constitutional convention he was asked, "What have you given us, sir, a monarchy or a republic?" Franklin answered, "A republic, sir, if you can keep it."

Mr. President, in the prevailing pessimism of the larger matter we call Watergate, can we keep that republic, and how?

A: Mr. Quinn, I would certainly not be standing here answering these questions unless I had a firm belief that we could keep the republic; that we must keep it, not only for ourselves, but for the whole world. I recognize that because of mistakes that were made, and I must take responsibility for those mistakes, whether in the campaign or during the course of an administration, that there are those who wonder whether this republic can survive. But I also know that the hopes of the whole world for peace, not only now, but in the years to come, rests on the United States of America. I can assure you that as long as I am physically able to handle the position to which I was elected, and then re-elected last November, I am going to work for the cause of peace in the world, for the cause of prosperity without war and without inflation at home, and also to the best of my ability to restore confidence in the White House and in the President. It is a big job, but I think it can be done, and I intend to do it.

DELAYS ON NON-EXISTENT TAPES

Q: Mr. President, I am George Gill of the *Louisville Courier-Journal.* Would you please tell us, sir, when did you personally discover that two of the nine subpoenaed White House tapes did not exist, and why did you apparently delay for a matter of weeks disclosing this matter to the federal court and to the public?

A: Well, the first time that the fact that there were no recordings of the two conversations to which you referred—that they did not exist—came to my attention on approximately Sept. 29 or Sept. 30.

At that time, I was informed only that they might not exist because a search was not made because seven of the nine recordings requested did exist, and my secretary, listening to them for me and making notes for me, proceeded to go through those seven tapes.

I should point out, incidentally, that the two which did not exist, which there were no tape recordings of the conversations, were not ones which were requested by the Senate committee and consequently, we felt we should go forward with the ones requested, both by the Senate committees and the others.

When we finally determined that they could not be in existence was on Oct. 26 of this year. And we learned it then when I directed the White House counsel, Mr. Buzhardt, to question the Secret Service operatives as to what had happened to make sure there might not be a possibility, due to the fact that the mechanism was not operating properly, that we might find them in some other place.

He questioned them for two days and reported on the 27th that he could not find them. He then, having had a date made—and he asked for the date sooner with Judge Sirica, he asked for the date on Thursday; you may recall I pointed that out in the press conference on the 26th—Judge Sirica saw him on Tuesday *in camera.* The White House counsel reported to Judge Sirica that the two tapes did not exist and gave him the reasons for it.

The judge decided, and I think quite properly, that the reasons for the tape not existing should be made public and those involved with access to the tapes and those who operated the machines should be questioned so that there would be no question of the White House, somebody around the President or even the President, himself, having destroyed evidence that was important, even though the Senate committee had not, as I have

already pointed out, subpoenaed either of these two tapes. And since we are on this subject, and I do not want to be taking all of the time on it except I know there is going to be enormous interest in it, not only among this audience here, but among our television viewers, let me point this out.

I have done everything I possibly can to provide the evidence that would have existed had we found the tapes.

June 20 Tape. First, with regard to the tape of June 20, as you may recall, it was a five-minute telephone conversation with the former attorney general, John Mitchell, who had just left as campaign manager or was planning to leave as campaign manager at that time.

I have a practice of keeping a personal diary. I can assure you not every day. Some times you are too tired at the end of a day to either make notes or dictate it into a dictabelt.

On that particular day I happened to have dictated a dictabelt and on the dictabelt for June 20, which I found, I found that I had referred to the conversation to John Mitchell, and I think it is fair to disclose to this audience what was there, because it will be disclosed to the court. It has already been offered to the court and eventually I assume will be made public.

It said, first, that I called John Mitchell to cheer him up because I knew he was terribly disheartened by what had happened to the so-called Watergate matter. Second, he expressed chagrin to me that the organization over which he had control could have gotten out of hand in this way. That was what was on that tape.

Turning now to the one on April 15, I thought that I might have a Dictabelt of that conversation as well. Let me tell you first why the telephone conversation was not recorded, not because of any deliberate attempt to keep the recording from the public, but because the only telephones in the residence of the White House which are recorded, the only telephone, there is only one, the one that is in the office, the Little Lincoln sitting room right off the Lincoln bedroom. The call I made to John Mitchell was made at the end of the day at about 6:30 just before going in to dinner from the family quarters, and no telephones in the family quarters ever were recorded. That is why the recording did not exist.

April 15 Tape. Turning to April 15, the conversation referred to there was at the end of the process in which Mr. Dean came in to tell me what he had told U.S. attorneys that day. He saw me at 9 o'clock at night, Sunday night. There should have been a record. Everybody thought there probably was a recording. The reason there was not a recording is that the tape machines over the weekend only can carry six hours of conversation, and usually that is more than enough, because I do not use the EOB office, that is the Executive Office Building office rather than the Oval Office over the weekend to that extent.

But that weekend I was in the EOB for a long conversation with Dr. Kissinger on foreign policy matters. I was there for two other hours, or two or three other hours, and the tape ran out in the middle of a conversation with Mr. Kleindienst in the middle of the afternoon, Sunday afternoon.

A later conversation I had, the rest of Kleindienst's conversation, a later conversation I had also with Mr. Petersen, and the conversation at 8 o'clock at night with Mr. Dean was not there.

So I tried to find whatever recording whatever record that would help the prosecutor in this instance to reconstruct the evidence, because it was the evidence that I was after and not just this tape.

What I found was not a Dictabelt. What I found was my handwritten notes made at the time of the conversation. I have turned those over to or authorized my counsel to turn those notes over to the judge, so that he can have them checked for authenticity, and I understand there are ways that he can tell that they were written at that time.

Those handwritten notes are available, and then I did one other thing which I think will also be helpful. The next day I had a conversation with Mr. Dean in the morning at 10 o'clock. That conversation was recorded, and in that conversation there are repeated references to what was said the night before, and when compared with my handwritten notes it is clear that we are discussing the same subjects.

That entire tape, as well as the conversation I had with Mr. Dean for about 20 minutes will be made available to the court even though the court has not subpoenaed it.

Inadequate Recording System. I would just simply say in conclusion you can be very sure that this kind of a subject is one that is a difficult one to explain. It appears that it is impossible that when we have an Apollo system that we could have two missing tapes when the White House is concerned. Let me explain for one moment what the system was. This is no Apollo system. I found that it cost—I just learned this—$2,500. I found that instead of having the kind of equipment that was there when President Johnson was there, which was incidentally much better equipment, but I found—and I am not saying that critically—but I found that in this instance it was a Sony, a little Sony that they had, and that what they had are these little lapel mikes in my desk, and as a result the conversation in the Oval Office, the conversation in the cabinet room, and particularly those in the EOB, those are the three rooms only, only those three rooms where they recorded. For example, the Western White House has no recording equipment, and my houses in Key Biscayne and San Clemente had none, but as far as those particular recordings are concerned, the reason that you have heard that there are difficulties in hearing them is that the system itself was not a sophisticated system.

Points to be Proven. I do not mean to suggest by that that the judge, by listening to them, will not be able to get the facts, and I would simply conclude by saying this: I think I know what is on these tapes from having listened to some, those before March 21, and also from having seen from my secretary's notes the highlights of others. I can assure you that those tapes, when they are presented to the judge, and I hope eventually to the grand jury, and I trust in some way we can find a way at least to get the substance to the American people, they will prove these things without question:

One, that I had no knowledge whatever of the Watergate break-in before it occurred. Two, that I never authorized the offer of clemency to anybody and, as a matter of fact, turned it down whenever it was suggested. It was not recommended by any member of my staff but it was, on occasion, suggested as a result of news reports that clemency might become a factor. Third, as far as any knowledge with regard to the payment of blackmail money, which you recall was the charge that was made that Mr. Hunt's attorney had asked for $120,000 in money to be paid to him or he would tell things about members of the White House staff, not about Watergate, that might be embarrassing.

Testimony had been given before the Senate committee that I was told that before the 21st of March, actually told it on the 13th of March. I know I heard it for the first time the 21st of March, and I will reveal this much of the conversation. I am sure the judge wouldn't mind.

I recall very well Mr. Dean, after the conversation began, telling me, "Mr. President, there are some things about this I haven't told you. I think you should know them."

And then he proceeded then for the first time to tell me about that money. Now, I realize that some will wonder about the truth of these particular statements that I have made. I am going to hand out later—I won't hand them out, but I will have one of your executives hand out my May 21 statement, my Aug. 15 statement and one with regard to these two tapes, you can believe them if you want.

I can tell you it is the truth, because I have listened to or have knowledge of, from someone I have confidence in, as to what is in the tapes.

PERSONAL, POLITICAL REACTION

Q: Mr. President, Richard Tuttle, *Democrat and Chronicle,* Rochester, N.Y. Could you tell us your personal reaction and your political reaction—within that word I mean your credibility

with the American people—your reaction to the discovery that the Dean and Mitchell tapes do not exist?

A: Well, my personal reaction was one of great disappointment, because I wanted the evidence out, and I knew that when there was any indication that something didn't exist, immediately there would be the impression that some way, either the President, or more likely, perhaps somebody on the President's staff, knew there was something on those tapes that it wouldn't be wise to get out. But let me point out again, while I was disappointed, let me say I would have been a lot more disappointed if the tapes that had been considered important by both Mr. Cox, the special prosecutor and the Ervin committee, if any one of those had been missing, because I should point out that the tape of Sept. 15 which, as you recall, has been testified that I was first informed there was a cover-up—that, of course, is there.

The tape of March 13, where is has been testified, as I pointed out in the answer to *the Louisville Courier-Journal*, where it has been testified that I was informed then of the demands for money for purposes of blackmail, that is available. And the tape of March 21, where we discussed this in great detail, as well as three other tapes in which Mr. Dean participated, three other conversations, are all available.

But as far as these two tapes are concerned, even though they were not considered by the Ervin committee to be an indispensable part of their investigation, the fact that they were not there was a great disappointment, and I just wish we had had a better system.

I frankly wish we hadn't had a system at all. Then maybe I wouldn't have to answer this question.

ELLSBERG CASE

Q: Mr. President, when did you decide to stay out of the Ellsberg case and if you did, why, and do you think that the new special prosecutor should be kept from investigating the Ellsberg case?

A: I have never spoken to Mr. Cox at all, as a matter of fact; however, I did talk to Mr. Petersen about it, before Mr. Cox took over.

I told Mr. Petersen that the job that he had, and I would have said the same thing to Mr. Cox, was to investigate the Watergate matter, that national security matters were not matters that should be investigated, because there were some very highly sensitive matters involved, not only in Ellsberg but also another matter so sensitive that even Sen. Ervin and Sen. Baker have decided that they should not delve further into them.

I don't mean by that that we are going to throw the cloak of national security over something because we are guilty of something. I am simply saying that where the national security would be disserved by having an investigation, the President has the responsibility to protect it, and I am going to do so.

PLANS TO INFORM PEOPLE

Q: Albert L. Abbott from *The Detroit News*. Are you personally satisfied, sir, that the investigation of the Watergate matter is complete, to your satisfaction, and if so, could you tell us what your plans are to tell the American people about the facts of the case with regard, again, to your credibility on this matter?

A: First, with regard to whether the investigation is complete, as you know, there is now a new special prosecutor, Mr. Jaworski. He is a Democrat. He has always supported the Democratic ticket. He is a highly respected lawyer, former president of the ABA in the year 1971. I may have met him. I have never talked to him personally and certainly never talked to him about this matter. I refuse to, because I want him to be completely independent.

He cannot be removed unless there is a consensus of the top leadership Of the House and Senate, Democrat and Republican. The speaker and majority and minority leaders of the House and the president pro tem, the majority and minority leaders of the

Senate and the ranking two members of the Judiciary Committees of both the House and Senate, which, incidentally, gives you, as you can see, a very substantial majority, as far as the Democrats are concerned.

The second point, and the point I am trying to make is, one, he is qualified; two, he is independent, and will have cooperation; and three, he will not be removed unless the Congress, particularly the leaders of the Congress, and particularly the Democratic leaders who have a strong majority of this group I have named, agree that he should be removed, and I do not expect that that time will come.

As to what I can tell the American people, this is one forum, and there may be others. As to what the situation is as to when it can be done, it is of course, necessary to let the grand jury proceed as quickly as possible to a conclusion and I should point out to you, as you may recall, Mr. Petersen testified before the Ervin committee when he was removed from his position—you recall he was removed in April and a special prosecutor was put in—that the case was 90 per cent ready. For six months, under the special prosecutor then appointed, the case has not been brought to a conclusion.

And I think that now, after six months of delay, it is time that the case be brought to a conclusion. If it was 90 per cent finished in April, they ought to be able to finish it now.

Those who are guilty, or presumed to be guilty, should be indicted. Those who are not guilty at least should get some evidence of being cleared, because in the meantime, the reputations of men, some maybe who are not guilty, have been probably irreparably damaged by what has happened in the hearings they have appeared before publicly. They have already been convicted and they may never recover. That isn't our system of government.

The place to try a man or woman for a crime is in the court and not to convict them either in the newspaper or on television before has a fair trial in the courts.

ATTITUDE TOWARD HALDEMAN, EHRLICHMAN

Q: Bob Haiman from *The St. Petersburg Times* in St. Petersburg, Fla. When Mr. Ehrlichman and Mr. Haldeman left your administration, you said they were guiltless in the Watergate affair, and you referred to them as two of the finest public servants you have ever known. After what has transpired and been revealed since then, do you still feel the same way about both men and both statements?

A: First, I hold that both men and others who have been charged are guilty until we have evidence that they are not guilty, and I know every newspaper man and newspaper women in this whole audience would agree with that statement. That is our American system. Second, Mr. Haldeman and Mr. Ehrlichman had been and were dedicated fine public servants, and I believe, it is my belief based on what I know now, that when these proceedings are completed that they will come out all right.

On the other hand, they have appeared before the grand jury before, they will be appearing again, and as I pointed out in answer to an earlier question, it probably does not make any difference, unfortunately, whether the grand jury indicts them or not, whether they are tried or not, because unfortunately they have already been convicted in the minds of millions of Americans by what happened before a Senate committee.

ROLE IN ELLSBERG BREAK-IN

Q: Mr. President, this is Ed Heins from *The Des Moines Register and Tribune*. At the time you gave Egil Krogh approval for the Dr. Ellsberg project, was there any discussion of surreptitious entry to any premises and was there any discussion of legality or illegality in that situation?

A: I think, sir, that you have made an assumption that Mr. Krogh and others have not testified to, but I am not saying that critically. But I think I do remember what the evidence is. I don't think Mr. Krogh has said, or Mr. Ehrlichman or anybody

else, that I specifically approved or ordered the entrance into Dr. Ellsberg's psychiatrist's office. As a matter of fact, on the other hand, I learned of that for the first time on the 17th of March, which I have stated in my Aug. 15 statement, which will be available to the members of the press when this meeting is concluded.

Second, with regard to such activities, I personally thought it was a stupid thing to do, apart from being an illegal thing to do, and third, I should also point out that in this particular matter, the reason Mr. Krogh and others were engaged in what we call the "plumbers" operation was because of our concern at that time about leaks out of our government, the Pentagon Papers, which as you recall is what Ellsberg was all about, as well as other leaks which were seriously damaging to the national security, including one that I have pointed out—that was so serious that even Sen. Ervin and Sen. Baker agreed it should not be disclosed. That is what they were working on.

NIXON'S TAX PAYMENTS

Q: Joe Ungar of *The Providence Evening Bulletin.*

The Providence Evening Bulletin and *The Journal* on Oct. 3 reported that you paid $792 in federal income tax in 1970 and $878 in 1971. Are these figures accurate, and would you tell us your views on whether elected officials should disclose their personal finances?

A: Well, the answer to the second question is I have disclosed my personal finances, and an audit of my personal finances will be made available at the end of this meeting, because obviously you are all so busy that when these things come across your desk, maybe you don't see them. I can simply point out that that audit I paid for—I have not gotten the bill yet but I know it is several thousand dollars, and I think that that audit is one that is a pretty good one. That audit, however, deals with the acquisition of my property and knocks down some of the ideas that have been around. But since this question has been raised, let me, sir, try to respond to it as fully as I can.

I paid $79,000 in income tax in 1969. In the next two years, I paid nominal amounts. Whether those amounts are correct or not, I do not know, because I have not looked at my returns, and obviously *The Providence Journal* has much better sources than I have to find such returns. I congratulate you, sir, for having such a lively staff.

Now, why did I pay this amount? It was not because of the deductions for, shall we say, a cattle ranch or interest or all of these gimmicks that you have got where you can deduct from, which most of you know about, or if you don't, your publishers do. But the reason was this. Lyndon Johnson came in to see me shortly after I became President, and he told me that he had given his presidential papers, or at least most of them, to the government, and he told me that under the law, up until 1969, presidential or vice presidential papers given to the government were a deduction, and should be taken, and could be taken as a deduction from the tax.

And he said, "You, Mr. President, ought to do the same thing." I said, "I don't have any presidential papers." He said, "You have got your vice presidential papers."

I thought of that a moment and said, "All right, I will turn them over to the tax people." I turned them over. They appraised them at $500,000. I suppose some wonder how could the Vice President's papers be worth that. Well, I was, shall we say, a rather active Vice President. All of my personal notes, including matters that have not been covered in my book—which I don't advise other people to write, but in any event I wrote one and I will stand by it—all of my papers on the Hiss case, on the famous fund controversy in 1952, on President Eisenhower's heart attack, on President Eisenhower's stroke, on my visit to Caracas when I had a few problems in 1968, and on my visit with Khrushchev, all of those papers, all of my notes, were valued, many believed conservatively, at that amount.

So the tax people who prepared it, prepared the returns, and took that as a deduction. No question has been raised by the

Internal Revenue about it but if they do, let me tell you this: I will be glad to have the papers back, and I will pay the tax, because I think they are worth more than that.

I can only say we did what we were told was the right thing to do and, of course, what President Johnson had done before and that doesn't prove, certainly, that it was wrong, because he had done exactly what the law required.

Since 1969, of course, I should point out, presidents can't do that. So I am stuck with a lot of papers now that I have got to find a way to give away, or otherwise my heirs will have a terrible time trying to pay the taxes on things people aren't going to want to buy.

Q: Mr. President, may I suggest you may have misspoke yourself when you said that you assumed Haldeman and Ehrlichman are considered guilty until proven not guilty.

A: Yes, I certainly did, if I said that. Thank you for correcting me.

SHARING PRESIDENTIAL RESPONSIBILITIES

Q: Richard Smyser, *The Oak Ridge,* Oak Ridge, Tenn. Sen. Mark Hatfield said recently that we demand so much of a president, we ask him to play so many roles, that no man can hold that kind of responsibility without having to share that responsibility with all Americans. To what extent do you think that this explains possibly how something like Watergate can occur?

A: I could stand here before this audience and make all kinds of excuses, and most of you probably would understand because you are busy also. Seventy-two was a very busy year for me. It was a year when we had the visit to China, it was a year when we had the visit to Moscow and the first limited nuclear ban on defensive weapons, you recall, as well as some other very significant events.

It was a year, too, when we had the very difficult decisions on May 8, the bombing and mining of Haiphong and then the negotiations and then in December, of course, the very, very difficult—perhaps the most difficult—decision I made of the December bombing, which did lead to the break-through and the uneasy peace, but it is peace with all of the Americans home, all of our POWs home, and peace at least for a while in that period.

Now, during that period of time, frankly, I didn't manage the campaign. I didn't run the campaign. People around me didn't bring things to me that they probably should have, because I was frankly just too busy trying to do the nation's business to run the politics.

My advice to all new politicians, incidentally, is always run your own campaigns. I used to run mine and I was always criticized for it, because you know whenever you lose you are always criticized for running your own campaign, but my point is Sen. Hatfield is correct, whether you are a senator or a congressman, you are sometimes very busy, you don't watch these things. When you are president, you don't watch them as closely as you might. On that, I say if mistakes are made, however, I am not blaming the people down below. The man at the top has got to take the heat for all of them.

Let me just respond, if I could, sir, before going to your question—I will turn left and then come back to the right; I don't want to tilt either way at the moment, as you can be sure (laughter)—since the question was raised a moment ago about my tax payments, I noted in some editorials and perhaps in some commentaries on television, a very reasonable question.

Property Investments. They said, you know, how is it that President Nixon could have a very heavy investment in a fine piece of property in San Clemente and a big investment in a piece of property in Florida, in which I have two houses, one which I primarily use as an office and the other as a resident and also an investment in what was my mother's home, not very much of a place, but I do own it, those three pieces of property.

I want to say first, that is all I have. I am the first President since Harry Truman who hasn't owned any stock since ever I have been President. I am the first one who has not had a blind

trust since Harry Truman. That doesn't mean those who owned stocks or had blind trusts did anything wrong, but I felt that in the presidency it was important to have no question about the President's personal finances, and I thought real estate was the best place to put it.

But then the question was raised by good editorial writers—and I want to respond to it because some of you might be too polite to ask such an embarrassing question—they said, "Now, Mr. President, you earned $800,000 when you were President. Obviously, you paid at least half that much or could have paid half that much in taxes or a great deal of it. How could you possibly have had the money? Where did you get it?"

Then, of course, overriding all of that is the story to the effect that I had a million dollars in campaign funds which was broadly printed throughout this country with retractions not quite getting quite as much play as the printing of the first, and particularly not on television. The newspapers did much better than television in that respect, I should point out.

And second, they said, how is it that as far as this money is concerned, how is it possible for you to have this kind of investment when all you earned was $800,000 as President?

Personal Finances. Well, I should point out I wasn't a pauper when I became President. I wasn't very rich as presidents go. But you see, in the eight years that I was out of office—first, just to put it all out, and I will give you a paper on this, we will send it around to you, and these figures I would like you to have, not today, but I will have it in a few days—when I left office after four years as a congressman, two years as a senator and eight years at $45,000 a year as Vice President, and after stories had been written, particularly in *The Washington Post,* to the effect that the President had purchased a mansion in Wesley Heights and people wondered where the money came from, you know what my net worth was? It was $47,000 total, after 14 years of government service, and a 1958 Oldsmobile that needed an overhaul.

Now, I have no complaints. In the next eight years, I made a lot of money. I made $250,000 from a book—and the serial rights which many of you were good enough to purchase—also, in the practice of law—and I am not claiming I was worth it, but apparently the former vice presidents or presidents are worth a great deal to the law firms—and I did work pretty hard.

But also in that period, I earned between $100,000 and $250,000 every year. So that when in 1968, I decided to become a candidate for president, I decided to clean the decks and to put everything in real estate. I sold all my stock for $300,000. That is all I owned. I sold my apartment in New York for $300,000 —I am using rough figures here. And I had $100,000 coming to me from the law firm.

So that is where the money came from. Let me just say this: I want to say this to the television audience—I made my mistakes, but in all of my years of public life, I have never profited, never profited from public service. I have earned every cent. And in all of my years of public life, I have never obstructed justice. And I think, too, that I could say that in my years of public life, that I welcome this kind of examination, because people have got to know whether or not their President is a crook. Well, I am not a crook. I have earned everything I have got.

TAP ON DONALD NIXON'S PHONE

Q: Mr. President, Harry Rosenfeld of *The Washington Post.* Sir, there have been reports that the Secret Service was asked, at your direction or authorization, to tap the telephone of your brother, Donald Nixon. Is this true, sir, and if so, why?

A: That, of course, is a question that has been commented upon before. It will not take long to respond to it.

The Secret Service did maintain a surveillance. They did so for security reasons, and I will not go beyond that. They were very good reasons, and my brother was aware of it.

And may I say, too, to my friend from *The Washington Post,* I like your sports page. And make sure that Shirley Povich doesn't get paid too much for what I said there. (Laughter)

Q: Edward D. Miller, *Call-Chronicle Newspapers,* Allentown, Pa. Was your brother aware before or after the fact of the surveillance?

A: He was aware during the fact, because he asked about it, and he was told about it. And he approved of it. He knew why it was done.

Q: Excuse me. Does it make any sense to conduct surveillance when somebody knows about it?

A: Does it make any sense? Certainly. The surveillance involved not what he was doing. The surveillance involved what others who were trying to get him, perhaps, to use improper influence and support might be doing, and particularly anybody who might be in a foreign country.

Q: Is some of this full story that you can't state today because of national security? Have you told that to congressmen or anyone else? Will this story come out in the next few weeks, as you present more of the facts?

A: Yes, as a matter of fact, I should tell all of the editors—and I don't want to leave any implication that you have not tried to publish as much as you could—you have just got so much room in your newspapers, but I do want you to know that—well, since you haven't raised some of these subjects, I will raise them myself—ITT; how did we raise the price of milk—I wish someone would ask me that one; and who else wanted it raised?

What about the situation with regard to the $1-million secret stock portfolio that you have; a few of those things. I think all of those things need to be answered, and answered effectively, and I think the best way to answer them is twofold:

One, obviously through the medium of a televised conference like this; but two, through sending to the editors of the nation's newspapers, all 10,000 of them, the facts. I trust that you will use them. If you don't believe them, I don't mean—what I mean, I am not suggesting that you wouldn't believe them, but if you feel you need more information, write to me and I will give it to you. I want the facts out, because the facts will prove that the President is telling the truth.

SHIELD LAW FOR THE PRESS

Q: Mr. President, John Finnegan, *St. Paul Dispatch-Pioneer Press.* I know the Watergate situation has raised questions of executive privilege, and a recent Gallup Poll indicated that 62 per cent of the American people favor a confidential news source law if adopted by Congress. There is a two-tiered law before the Judiciary Committee which would provide an absolute privilege in case of investigative or grand jury hearings, and a qualified shield in case of a civil or criminal case. If such a law were passed, would you sign it or veto it?

A: Well, you are talking about shield laws in general, are you not?

Q: Yes.

A: Well, my attitude toward the shield laws briefly is this: First, I share the objective. I believe that reporters, if you are going to have a free press, ought to have some kind of a shield, except, of course, if they are involved in criminal activities, and then I don't think the shield law that any of you have suggested would cover those. As I understand, if there are criminal activities involved in by a reporter, obviously a shield law can't protect them.

The second point has to do with the particular legislation and how it reaches my desk, and I will have to take a look at it when it gets there to see if it is proper. If it is proper, I will sign it. But I think that a shield law which would have the effect of providing to reporters what the general public felt after they had a chance to consider it all, provide for them privileges that went beyond what the general public thought was in the national interest, then I would have to take a second look.

Incidentally, I should point out, too, that I followed your editorials—not yours in just the *St. Paul Pioneer Press,* but by

others around the country—and the newspapers of the country are not united on this. So on the shield law I am not trying to duck the question. It is an open question.

But I will answer one thing that I think is important. The new attorney general, Mr. Saxbe, under my direction, will follow this practice: Any federal case involving a reporter will not be brought unless it comes expressly to the attorney general and he approves it, and in that way, that is a pretty good shield, I think.

EXECUTIVE PRIVILEGE

Q: May I ask one other question, sir?
A: Sure.
Q: Do you feel that the executive privilege is absolute?
A: I, of course, do not. I have waived executive privilege with regard to all of the members of my staff who have any knowledge of or who have had any charges made against them in the Watergate matter. I, of course, voluntarily waived privilege with regard to turning over the tapes, and so forth.

Let me point out it was voluntary on my part, and deliberately so to avoid a precedent that might destroy the principle of confidentiality for future presidents, which is terribly important.

If it had gone to the Supreme Court—and I know many of my friends argued, "Why not carry it to the Supreme Court and let them decide it?"—that would, first, have had a confrontation with the Supreme Court, between the Supreme Court and the President. And second, it would have established very possibly a precedent, a precedent breaking down constitutionality that would plague future presidencies, not just this President.

I can say in that respect, too, that I have referred to what I called the Jefferson Rule. It is the rule that I think we should generally follow, a President should follow with the courts when they want information, and a President should also follow with committees of Congress, even when they want information from his personal files. Jefferson, as you know, in that very, very famous case, had correspondence which it was felt might bear upon the guilt or innocence of Aaron Burr. Chief Justice Marshall, sitting as a trial judge, said that Jefferson, as President, had to turn over the correspondence. Jefferson refused.

What he did was to turn over a summary of the correspondence, all that he considered was proper to be turned over for the purposes of the trial.

Then Marshall, sitting as chief justice, ruled for the President.

Now, why did Jefferson do that? Jefferson didn't do that to protect Jefferson. He did that to protect the presidency. That is exactly what I will do in these cases. It isn't for the purpose of protecting the President; it is for the purpose of seeing that the presidency, where great decisions have to be made, and great decisions cannot be made unless there is very free flow of conversation, and that means confidentiality, I have a responsibility to protect that presidency.

At the same time, I will do everything I can to cooperate where there is a need for presidential participation.

THE PRESIDENT: I will go to you next.

GASOLINE RATIONING

Q: Murray Light, *Buffalo Evening News.* The American people, sir, are very interested in one subject other than Watergate. Is gas rationing imminent?

THE PRESIDENT: Really? (Laughter) I didn't hear the last, I am sorry.

Q: Is gas rationing imminent?

A: I will tell you a little about my career that I didn't put in my campaign folders when I ran for Congress in 1946. I was once in OPA and I was in tire rationing. I suppose they put me in tire rationing—this is just before I went into the service. I was waiting for my service call—because I had worked in a service station, but I didn't know anything about tire rationing, and neither did the man above me, who I don't think had ever been in a service station, but we put out the rationing regulations on tires, and we were as fair as we could be. But also I found that if you get a bunch of government bureaucrats—and in order to have rationing you would have to have thousands of them—making decisions with regard to who is going to get this much, this much, this much in rationing, if you are going to try to do that in peacetime when you do not have what we had in wartime, you know, support, for, you know—"Don't use a C ration card when you are only entitled to an A"—then you are sort of disloyal or something, or unpatriotic. If you do not have that behind it, I can assure you that a rationing system in peacetime, run by a group of well-intentioned but being bureaucrats that they are, gaining and feeling their power, would be something that the American people would resent very, very much.

Now, what we have asked the Congress for is for a contingency plan in the event that rationing becomes necessary, but in the meantime let me tell you, our goal is to make it not necessary. I am not going to pledge to this audience and I am not going to pledge to the television audience that rationing may never come. If you have another war in the Mideast, if you have a complete cut-off and not a resumption of the flow of oil from the Mideast or some other disaster occurs, rationing may come, but if on the other hand the things that I recommended in my message of a week ago for immediate action, if the voluntary cooperation of keeping the speed down to 50 miles an hour—and I am going to talk to the governors about that on Tuesday in Memphis, urging that every state do exactly the same thing—if we cut back on the aircraft flights, and we have done that—and, for example, I came down here in a plane today, Air Force One. I asked them if I couldn't take the Jetstar. They said, "No, it doesn't have communication." So I had to take the big plane. But we did one thing that saved half the cost: We didn't have the back-up plane. The Secret Service didn't like it, Communication didn't like it, but I don't need a back-up plane. If this one goes down, it goes down, and then they don't have to impeach. (laughter)

RELATIONS WITH MITCHELL

Q: Mr. President, Larry Allison from *The Long Beach* (Calif.) *Independent Press-Telegram.* Back to Watergate. Former Attorney General John Mitchell has testified the reason he did not give you details on the Watergate problems was that you did not ask him. Now, I realize that you were very busy at that time, as you said, but there were reports in newspapers that linked people very high in your staff with Watergate problems. Could you tell us, sir, why you did not ask Mr. Mitchell what he knew?

A: For the very simple reason that when I talked to Mr. Mitchell—and I saw him often in that period—that I had every reason to believe that if he were involved, if he had any information to convey, he would tell me. I thought that he would. As a matter of fact, when I called him on the telephone, what did he say—he expressed chagrin that anything like that could have happened in his organization.

Looking back, maybe I should have cross-examined him and said, "John, did you do it?" I probably should have asked him, but the reason I didn't is that I expected him to tell me, and he had every opportunity to do so and decided he wouldn't apparently. At least—now, that doesn't mean to tell me that he was involved, because you understand that is still a matter that is open. The question is whether he could have told me about other people that might be involved where he had information where members of my staff did not have information.

Yes, sir.

ANTICIPATING THE ENERGY CRISIS

Q: I am Joe Shoquist, *Milwaukee Journal.* Why didn't the administration anticipate the energy crisis several years ago, formulate a positive action plan to do something about it?

A: You walked into one there. And that is a great paper, incidentally, as is *The Milwaukee Sentinel,* but, anyway, seriously, you see what happened was that I sent the first energy message ever sent to the Congress. I sent it to the Congress over two years ago. I saw this thing coming, and you know why I saw it coming? Not because of the Mideast or the Alaska pipeline and the rest, but because this world with all of its problems is getting richer. Oh, I don't mean there aren't a lot of hungry people, not only in America, too many here, but if you want to see hungry people, go to India or go to some of the countries in Latin America or upper Brazil, et cetera, et cetera. Generally, as the world gets richer, there is more air conditioning, there is more need for power and there is more need for energy. That is why I sent the message two years ago and asked at that time that the Congress consider a program so that the United States should become self-sufficient in energy. All right, I followed that up this year in April before we even knew there might be or had any idea of the Mideast crisis, which made a serious problem, a serious crisis. I asked them for seven pieces of legislation to deal with energy. One has reached my desk, the Alaska pipeline. I signed it. The other six I hope they act before they go home for Christmas.

Now, I am not saying here the Congress is to blame. The President should have done something. What I do say is that the President warned about it and the Congress did not act even though he warned them two years ago. The President warned in April; the Congress did not act; and now, it is time for the Congress to getaway from some of these other diversions if they have time and get on to this energy crisis.

Let me—since that question has come up, I would like to point out, though, how we should react, because the question about rationing is one that your average reader is going to be interested in.

I am interested in it, too, because I remember how we all went through it, the car pools and all that sort of thing. There are a few of you here old enough to remember a car pool, I am sure. Taxicabs in Washington: you couldn't get one unless five of you rode in one, you remember.

We don't want that. But if we look at this energy crisis as simply the crisis of this year, we could not make a greater mistake. If there never had been a Mideast war, there would have been an energy crisis eventually. That is why I have set as a goal for the American people, and I trust all of you will subscribe to it, what I call Project Independence 1980.

Why 1980, and why not 1976? Because, in checking with the experts, I find it will not be possible doing everything that we can do to become self-sufficient in energy until 1980. But if the Congress cooperates, if the nation cooperates, this nation in 1980 can have all of the energy we need.

Areas of Cooperation. Let us just briefly tell you what areas of cooperation are needed.

One, coal. We have half of the coal in the world, and yet we have conversions from coal to oil. Why? Because coal is not a clean fuel. Coal can be made a clean fuel. Coal can be mined in a way that does not despoil the landscape. It will be argumentative, I am sure. Some of the environmentalists—and I am an environmentalist along with anybody who cares about the landscape for our children—but we have got to get that coal out of the ground and we have to develop the shale oil, for example, that exists in Colorado and some of our western states. That will solve part of the problem.

And second, you have to deregulate natural gas. Some protection for the consumer, yes, but you have got wells in Louisiana, and other places, that are shut down and many that are not being explored, because the price is held at a price too low to make the explorer a profit. Therefore, he isn't going to do it. And natural gas, as you know, is one of the cleanest fuels we can possibly have.

And then, third, the most exciting of all, nuclear power. Now, don't write an editorial on that—you are really going to catch it from your readers if you do, because it scares people.

Nuclear power—they think of the bomb. They think of the possibility that one of them is going to blow up. My house in San Clemente is just 12 miles from the Southern California Edison Company's nuclear power plant. It is safe. It produces good power. It is clean power. And the United States, which first found the secret of the atom, is behind where it ought to be in the development of nuclear power.

If we go all out in developing our coal resources, our natural gas resources, as well as of course our oil from Alaska, which will provide one-third—I said incorrectly the other day in talking to a group not one-third of all of our oil needs, but one-third of all of our oil imports—and if we add to that nuclear power, the United States in 1980 can be self-sufficient. Just closing that off, let me tell you why that is so terribly important. The Arabs, they say, "Well, the Arabs, maybe they are irrational and we shouldn't depend on them anyway."

Need for Independence. Let me tell you, when you are in trouble, don't depend on anybody but yourself. Venezuela. What is going to happen in Venezuela? They send us a lot of oil, but they could change their minds under a radical government, and they could get one some day. I don't think so, but they could.

What about Canada, our great friend to the north? A lot of Canadians are listening here, but I can tell you, your present minister of the interior, or whoever is in charge of oil, he is a tough guy, and they drive hard bargains, and I guess we would, too, if we were Canadians.

My point is, the United States of America, as the greatest industrial power of the world, with 7 per cent of the world's people, and using 30 per cent of the world's energy, shouldn't have to depend on any other country for energy that provides our jobs and transportation and our light and our heat. We can become self-sufficient. This is a great project, and I am going to push it.

POST-PRESIDENCY PLANS

Q: Mr. President, I am John Chandley of *The Kansas City Times*. Not being a member of the Washington press corps, I am not going to ask when you are going to retire, but I am going to ask you when you do leave the White House, what do you plan to do?

A: I think it depends on when I leave. (Laughter)

No, seriously, I know that this group has asked very good questions and very appropriate ones. I was hoping you would ask me about the milk. Would you mind asking me about the milk?

Q: I don't know anything about the milk.

A: I will answer this, and then I will go to the milk, and then I will go to the man in the back.

As far as retirement, at that time I understand I will be 63 years of age, and I am relatively healthy at present. I don't know how healthy I will be then.

Among these I will not do: I will not practice law. I won't go on any board of directors. I will tell you, after being president, you never want to sit at any other end of the table, and being on a board of directors, it pays well, but it is rather boring. That is what I found when I was Vice President, and not out of any conceit or anything, it is just a fact that boards of directors are fine, but not for former presidents.

What I will try to do is do a little writing. I will not do any speaking. I have made enough speeches in a year to last most people for a lifetime, particularly my audiences.

And so, under the circumstances, what I will probably do is some writing, and perhaps contribute to bettering the political process. Let me say this: Neither party is without fault in the campaign of 1972. There was quite a bit of violence on the other side, and I never spoke anyplace without getting a pretty good working over.

Neither party was without fault with regard to the financing. They raised $36-million and some of that, like some of ours,

came from corporate sources and was illegal, because the law had been changed, and apparently people didn't know it.

As far as congressmen and senators are concerned, they will all tell you with the new laws and so forth, there ought to be some changes.

I think if we can't get the Congress to act on the proposal I gave to them six months ago to provide a commission to set up new rules for campaign procedures, then after I leave office, I am going to work for that, because I don't want to be remembered as the man who maybe brought peace for the first time in 12 years, who opened to China, who opened to Russia, maybe avoided a war in the Mideast, maybe if we can continue it, cut unemployment down for the first time in 18 years, for the first time in peacetime it is down to 4½ per cent. It was never at that level, never below 5 per cent in the '60s, any time in the '60s, neither the Kennedy or Johnson administration except during the war years.

I want to be remembered, I would trust, as a President that did his best to bring peace, and also did his best to bring a degree of prosperity, perhaps a contribution in the energy field, in the environmental field, but also one who did his best, when his own campaign got out of hand, to do everything possible to see that other campaigns didn't get out of hand in the future.

MILK PRICE SUPPORTS

Now we will go to the milk case.

Q: Mr. President, APME would like to ask you about the milk, but our 60-minute commitment of time has run out. APME appreciates your appearance—

A: I will take the time. Television, keep me on just a minute. (Laughter)

Q: Thank you.

A: It is a lousy movie anyway tonight. (Laughter)

The reason the milk case question—and this will be the last one I will take—ought to be asked is that just some awful nice people are getting a bad rap about it. And I am not referring about myself. I am referring about people in the administration. They have had John Connally down. They have run him around the track. I guess they are going to have Cliff Hardin down, and Pete Peterson and all the rest.

The whole charge is basically this: That this administration, in 1971, raised the support price for milk as a quid pro quo for a promise by the milk producers that they would contribute substantial amounts, anywhere from $100,000 to $2-million to $10-million, to our campaign.

Now that is just not true. I will tell you how it happened. I was there. Cliff Hardin, in the spring of that year, came in and said, "The milk support prices are high enough." I said, "All right, Cliff, that is your recommendation, the Department of Agriculture?" He said, "Yes." Within three weeks after he had made that announcement, Congress put a gun to our head.

Let me tell you what it was. Republicans? Uh-uh. One hundred and two members of Congress signed a petition demanding not 85 per cent of parity, but a 90 per cent support price, and 28 members of the Senate, most of them Democrats, including Sen. McGovern, signed a petition demanding—a petition, or signed a bill, which would have made the milk support price between 85 and 90 per cent.

So I talked to my legislative leaders and I said, "Look here, what I am concerned about, what I am concerned about is what people pay for that milk, and I don't want to have that price jigged up here if we can keep it and get the supply with the present support price." You know what I was told. They said, "With the kind of heat that we are getting from the Congress, there is no way that you are not going to get on your desk a bill—and they will be able to override your veto—that will raise he support price probably to 90 per cent." So we said 85 per cent.

And that is why it was done, and that is the truth.

Thank you very much, gentlemen. I guess that is the end. ✓

COURTS: CHAPIN INDICTMENT, KROGH GUILTY PLEA

In separate federal court actions during the week ended Dec. 1, President Nixon's former appointments secretary was indicted on four counts of perjury, and the former chief of the White House "plumbers" unit pleaded guilty to a one-count civil rights violation.

Chapin Indictment. The indictment of Dwight L. Chapin, 32, who resigned in January to become a United Air Lines executive in Chicago, was the first indictment since Leon Jaworski became special Watergate prosecutor. A federal grand jury in Washington, D.C., returned the indictment to Chief U.S. District Judge John J. Sirica on Nov. 29.

All four counts of alleged lying in testimony before the Watergate grand jury in April were related to Chapin's association with convicted campaign saboteur Donald H. Segretti. Segretti was sentenced Nov. 5 to six months in federal prison. *(Sentencing p. 30; Chapin background, p. 38, 39)*

The maximum sentence on each of the four perjury charges was five years in prison and a $10,000 fine.

Presidential press secretary Ronald L. Ziegler said the indictment "in no way undercuts a presumption of innocence."

Krogh Plea. The guilty plea, to a civil rights violation in the 1971 break-in at the office of Pentagon Papers defendant Daniel Ellsberg's psychiatrist, was made by Egil Krogh Jr. Nov. 30 in U.S. District Court in Washington. At the time of the break-in, Krogh was in charge of the White House special investigative unit, nicknamed the "plumbers," that had been formed to plug security leaks to the press.

Krogh, 34, had pleaded not guilty to two counts of perjury in the break-in. Under an agreement worked out with Jaworski, in return for his plea of guilty to the civil rights violation, he did not face further federal charges related to the break-in. Indictments in the case also had been returned by a Los Angeles County, California, grand jury. *(Krogh's not guilty plea, p. 61; indictment, p. 50; Los Angeles indictment, p. 30)*

The Tapes and the Gaps

Disclosure of further gaps in recorded conversations on the subpoenaed White House tapes brought Nixon's personal secretary and his special counsel back to the witness stand in U.S. District Court in Washington, D.C.

Rose Mary Woods, the secretary, testified for three days about an 18-minute gap in a recorded conversation between Nixon and aide H. R. Haldeman on June 20, 1972, three days after the Watergate break-in. She said she apparently had made a mistake while working with the tape by pressing the "record" button when she meant to push the "stop" button.

Special counsel J. Fred Buzhardt testified Nov. 28 that there were yet other gaps on the subpoenaed tapes. This was discovered by the experts who duplicated the tapes Nov. 13-14, he said.

Claims of Privilege. For safekeeping, the tapes were turned over to Judge Sirica on the afternoon of Nov. 26. They were accompanied by an analysis and index prepared by the White House and by several claims of executive privilege. *(p. 161)*

The new special prosecutor, Leon Jaworski, Nov. 29 asked Sirica to deny the claims of executive privilege and to turn over all the tapes to the grand jury. He also asked the judge to order that the White House give to the court the summaries of the tapes typed by Woods for Nixon.

Sirica scheduled a hearing in his chambers Nov. 30 on the claims of privilege asserted to cover three of the subpoenaed conversations and a portion of a fourth. Sirica said he would later rule on the validity of the claims.

Woods Testimony. Woods, who in her first appearance before Sirica Nov. 8 had reacted angrily to suggestions that she might have accidentally altered or erased any of the conversation on the tapes she was making transcripts from, returned Nov. 26 with a different attitude. *(Previous testimony, box, p. 162)*

There were two new principals in the courtroom Nov. 26: Jaworski and Charles S. Rhyne, former American Bar Association president. The questioning of Woods was conducted by Jaworski's assistant, Jill Volner. Woods had retained Rhyne as her attorney Nov. 22 after presidential assistant Alexander M. Haig Jr. had informed her that none of the White House lawyers would come to the courtroom with her.

Explaining what she said "must" have happened to cause the gap in the June 20 tape, Woods related: "I had been working all those hours at Camp David (the weekend of Sept. 29-30) on the Ehrlichman tape. I got back to my office (Oct. 1) and still had several hours to go on it, plus all the other work that had piled up over the weekend.... The telephone rang, and I must have pushed the record button which is right next to the stop button (on the recording machine)." Woods said she apparently kept her foot on a pedal she was using to run the machine during her telephone conversation, which, she said, lasted no longer than five minutes. When it ended, she saw the "record" button was down, played the tape back and heard about five minutes of only a hum, she said. She immediately went to tell the President of what she termed her "terrible mistake," she added.

Nixon asked which taped conversation was affected, and, when she told him it was the conversation with Haldeman after the Ehrlichman conversation on the morning of June 20, he told her not to worry, because only the Ehrlichman conversation was subpoenaed, Woods testified. She said she told no one else about the gap.

Under questioning Nov. 27 and 28, Woods made clear that she did not feel responsible for the entire 18-minute gap on the tape. She was not on the telephone that long, she insisted. Furthermore, she said, she had never heard that portion of the tape before the time when her telephone rang, and to her knowledge there was no conversation on it to begin with. Therefore, she resisted the prosecutor's description of the 18-minute period as an erasure and referred to it instead as a gap.

Volner read into the court record Haldeman's notes of the conversation, which indicated that the part of the conversation now missing related to Watergate, specifically to instructions from President Nixon about a public relations offensive to divert public attention from the Watergate matter.

Sirica, visibly perturbed, asked Woods if she had mentioned this gap during her previous testimony. She said she had not because she did not think it relevant, because she thought the tape concerned was not under subpoena and because she was "petrified" by her first appearance in court. Sirica asked Volner to read relevant portions of Woods' Nov. 8 testimony. Volner did, including a section in which Woods testily replied that she had "used her head" to avoid any inadvertent erasures.

The tape recorders Woods used were introduced into evidence, and one was used Nov. 27 to play the tape which included the hum to the crowded courtroom. Questions about her actual physical moves in picking up the telephone, pushing the record button and pressing the foot pedal were followed by a trip by Volner and Woods to Wood's office, where photographs were taken of Woods re-enacting the sequence of moves.

Buzhardt Testimony. Under questioning Nov. 29, Buzhardt admitted that when he first discovered the 18-minute gap on the June 20 tape, he did not think that there was any innocent explanation for it.

But, in admitting that there were other spots on the tapes without conversation, he de-emphasized their importance. He said that noise other than voices, such as a heavy vehicle passing by or the air conditioning machinery beginning to operate, could have been sufficient to keep the machine recording.

In further testimony, Buzhardt said that on the evening of Nov. 21—after disclosing the fact of the gap to Sirica—he had gone to Woods' office and reproduced the same hum on a blank tape by punching the "start" and "record" buttons and letting them run with both Woods' electric typewriter and her high-intensity lamp on. This had satisfied him, he later told reporters, "that there are innocent ways in which it could have occurred." After this testimony, Jaworski suggested that all the original White House tapes be placed in Sirica's custody "so that there couldn't be anything happening to them." Ronald L. Ziegler described the suggestion as "nonsense."

White House Tapes Analysis

Almost exactly four months from the date they were subpoenaed by the Watergate grand jury, seven presidential tapes were submitted to Judge Sirica on Nov. 26. They were accompanied by an analysis and index of their contents and by several claims of executive privilege by which the President sought to protect certain conversations from disclosure to the grand jury.

Privilege Claims. Three conversations and part of a fourth were the subject of claims of privilege:

• The conversation between John D. Ehrlichman and the President on June 20, 1972. According to the White House analysis:

"This conversation relates primarily to the Higher Education Bill then under consideration by the Congress. Other subjects discussed include school busing, the Supreme Court decision (*U.S. v. U.S. District Court*) on national security wiretapping, press conferences and press conference formats, legislative action on proposals for welfare reform and the Stockholm Conference on environment....

"There is no discussion or comment which relates, either directly or indirectly, to the incident at the Democratic National Committee offices at Watergate which occurred a few days prior to the conversation....

"The conversation recorded on this tape consists of advice to the President by his then senior assistant for domestic affairs on official policy decisions then pending before the President, and the conveyance to the President by his assistant of the advice of other identified persons within the administration on the same matters. Nothing in the conversation relates to Watergate or anything connected therewith.

"The President believes that the conversation is subject in its entirety to a claim of Executive Privilege in order to protect the confidentiality of advice given to the President. There is nothing in this conversation concerning possible criminal conduct or discussions of possible criminal conduct as to testimony concerning which the President announced he would not invoke Executive Privilege on May 22, 1973.

(Ehrlichman's notes of this conversation were also submitted to Sirica, and the President claimed the protection of executive privilege for them also.)

• The conversation between H. R. Haldeman and the President on June 20, 1972. This was the conversation—on the same tape as the preceding conversation with Ehrlichman—during which the hum occurred. According to the White House analysis:

"This conversation relates primarily to scheduling and travel. For a portion of this recording, in lieu of any audible conversation there is a constant hum....

"It is believed that the hum which occurs approximately 3 minutes and 40 seconds from the beginning of this conversation between President Nixon and H. R. Haldeman, and which continues for approximately 18 minutes and 15 seconds was caused by the depression of a record button during the process of reviewing the tape, possibly while the recorder was in the proximity of an electric typewriter and a high intensity lamp.

"The incident was detected and reported when made to the President, and shortly thereafter to White House counsel, J. Fred Buzhardt, as having occurred on a portion of the tape recording subsequent to that of the meeting between the President and John Ehrlichman, which at that time and until November 14, 1973, was believed to be the only part of that recording subpoenaed. The incident was therefore believed to be inconsequential.

"The delay in discovering that the incident affected a portion of the tape containing a subpoenaed conversation was due to the ambiguity of the language of the subpoena...." (which led White House counsel to think that only the Ehrlichman conversation of June 20 was subpoenaed).

"It was not until the evening of Wednesday, November 14, 1973...that all materials remotely relating to the subpoenaed conversations were reviewed.... Among the materials then reviewed was the opinion of the United States Court of Appeals for the District of Columbia, *Nixon* v. *Sirica*, decided October 12, 1973. Appendix II...is a memorandum filed by the Special Prosecutor with this court on August 13, 1973....

"Only the most careful reading of even this memorandum discloses that the Special Prosecutor seeks a recording of more than one meeting on June 20, 1972...."

"White House Special Counsel J. Fred Buzhardt received an inquiry on September 28, 1973, as to the conversation covered by the first item of the subpoena, to which he replied that the conversation at the meeting with Ehrlichman was what was involved, and that the Special Prosecutor must have been mistaken in assuming that Haldeman also was in the meeting. This response was relayed to the President and to Mr. Steve Bull....

"The conversation on the tape recording of the meeting between H. R. Haldeman and the President consists of advice to the President by a senior advisor on official decisions then pending before the President. None of the conversation recorded relates to Watergate.

"The President believes that the conversation is subject in its entirety to a claim of Executive Privilege in order to protect the confidentiality of advice given to the President. There is nothing in this conversation concerning possible criminal conduct as to the testimony concerning which the President announced he would not invoke Executive Privilege on May 22, 1973."

(Part of the notes taken by Haldeman on this meeting, which reflected "that the President gave instructions to Mr. Haldeman to take certain actions of a public relations character which related to the Watergate incident," were also the subject of the claim of executive privilege. The claim included the portions unrelated to Watergate and reflecting confidential matters.)

• The conversation of June 30, 1972, among the President, John N. Mitchell and Haldeman just before Mitchell announced his resignation as chairman of the Committee for the Re-election of the President. According to the White House analysis:

"The conversation related primarily to the reasons for, the timing of, and the procedures for, Mitchell's announcement of his resignation, and the choice and announcement of his successor. There are a few passing and collateral references to Watergate which are not substantive....

"The conversation recorded consists of advice to the President by his senior staff assistant and his former Attorney General relating to matters which had a direct bearing on the President's ability to operate his office and conduct his official business at that time. The conversation includes discussions of highly personal matters. The President believes that the conversation is subject in its entirety to a valid claim of Executive Privilege in order to protect the confidentiality of the matters discussed. There is nothing in this conversation 'concerning possible criminal conduct or discussions of possible criminal conduct' as to testimony concerning which the President announced he would not invoke Executive Privilege on May 22, 1973....

(Haldeman's notes of this meeting were also, the White House claimed, protected by executive privilege from disclosure to the grand jury.)

• The conversation of Sept. 15, 1972, among the President, John W. Dean III and Haldeman. According to the White House analysis:

"For the first approximately 33 minutes and 9 seconds after Dean entered the Oval Office, the conversation involves subjects directly or indirectly related to the Watergate matter. Included are discussions of the indictments, the time of the pending trials, the civil cases connected with the incident and potential Congressional committee inquiries into the matter, as well as press coverage of the matter. After the first approximately 33 minutes and 9 seconds of the conversation, the conversation turns to other subjects within the President's official cognizance not directly or indirectly related to the Watergate matter....

'I Used My Head....'

During her first appearance as a witness at the fact-finding court hearings concerning the White House tapes, presidential secretary Rose Mary Woods was questioned about the precautions she had taken to avoid accidentally erasing the tapes while listening to them in September and October. *(p. 118)*

Q (from Jill Volner, assistant to the special prosecutor): "Were any precautions taken to assure you that you did not accidentally hit the 'erase' button?"

A: "Everybody said 'be terribly careful'—which I am. I don't want this to sound like I am bragging, but I don't believe I am so stupid that they had to go over and over it. I was told 'if you push the button, it will erase,' and I do know, even on a small machine, you can dictate over something and that removes it. I think I used every possible precaution to not do that."

Q: "What precautions specifically did you take to avoid either recording over it and thereby getting rid of what was already there?"

A: "What precautions? I used my head. It's the only one I had to use."

"No particularized claim of Executive Privilege is asserted to the conversation recorded on the first approximately 33 minutes 9 seconds of playing time of the tape....

"The conversation recorded subsequent to that point on the tape consists of discussions with and advice from the President's senior Assistant and his counsel on matters relating to the President's conduct of his official duties and are unrelated to Watergate matters.

"The President believes that the conversation recorded... following the first 33 minutes 9 seconds of playing time is subject to a claim of Executive Privilege, in order to protect the confidentiality of the advice and counsel provided to the President.

(The first and last parts of Haldeman's notes of this meeting were also protected by executive privilege, said the White House.)

Watergate Committee Postponement

Acknowledging that its investigation of election campaign financing had been stymied, the Senate Watergate committee decided Nov. 27 to postpone further hearings until after Congress returned from its Christmas recess in January 1974. Chairman Sam J. Ervin Jr. (D N.C.) and Vice Chairman Howard H. Baker Jr. (R Tenn.) blamed the delay on witnesses who failed to honor committee subpoenas, lack of White House cooperation on turning over documents requested by the committee and the resultant inability of the committee staff to proceed.

The two senators left open the possibility that the hearings might never resume. While both said they anticipated more hearings, Baker said the staff needed more time to develop "hard facts" in the campaign-financing phase of its investigation. If those facts were not forthcoming, he added, "We won't have any hearings."

Speaking to reporters after the committee met in executive session, the two senators insisted that the committee would complete its report on Watergate and related 1972 campaign scandals by its Senate-imposed deadline of Feb. 28, 1974, even if the hearings ran into late January. The staff already was working on its report of the Watergate break-in and coverup, Ervin said.

The committee was to have ended its hearings Dec. 7, leaving almost three months to complete its report and recommendations to the Senate. When it recessed Nov. 15, it had heard from 63 witnesses in 52 days of testimony since opening hearings May 17. *(Latest witnesses, p. 133)*

The vote by the seven-member committee to postpone the hearings was unanimous, Ervin said, but he acknowledged that there was disagreement on when to resume them. Sen. Lowell P. Weicker Jr. (R Conn.) reportedly objected to a resolution, passed by the committee, leaving the date of resumption up to Ervin. Weicker, the outspoken junior member of the committee, wanted the hearings to resume the first week in January.

More Money. Baker said the committee planned to ask for another $500,000 to complete its investigation, and would begin to trim some of its staff. The committee was working on a budget of $1-million and had a staff of 70.

There were four areas of inquiry remaining before the committee, Baker said. He identified them as a $100,000 contribution to the Nixon campaign from billionaire Howard Hughes; allegations of administration favoritism toward milk producers in exchange for large contributions to Nixon's re-election; charges that the Democrats had prior knowledge of the Watergate break-in, and the question of Central Intelligence Agency involvement in the coverup.

Ervin announced that the committee was prepared to seek contempt of Congress citations against six or seven Hughes Tool Company employees for refusing to honor subpoenas for their testimony. Ervin said the employees, whom he declined to name, insisted that their testimony be given only in public session. The committee's practice was to interview prospective witnesses under oath in private sessions before bringing them before the public. "My judgment is that ultimately they (the Hughes employees) will comply" with the subpoenas, Baker said.

More Tapes, Documents. Ervin also announced that the committee had given its staff authority to subpoena more tapes and documents from the White House. He said the committee wanted all nine presidential tapes requested by the Watergate special prosecutor—the committee had subpoenaed only five—and other materials it considered relevant to its investigations. The White House materials were believed to relate to the milk industry contributions. Ervin said subpoenas for the materials would be issued if negotiations with White House officials failed to release them.

Baker and Ervin soft-pedaled criticism of the White House while at the same time leaving no doubt that they were dissatisfied with its response to committee requests for materials. "By and large," Baker said, the White House had given the committee all it had asked for, with only a "narrow range" of documents withheld.

Court-Appointed Prosecutor

In a move aimed at assuring a special Watergate prosecutor shielded from influence by the President, the House Judiciary Committee Nov. 26 reported a bill (HR 11401—H Rept 93-660) calling for a court-appointed prosecutor.

Background. The action stemmed from the firing Oct. 20 of former special Watergate prosecutor Archibald Cox by the acting attorney general, Robert H. Bork, on orders from the President. The former attorney general, Elliot L. Richardson, and his deputy, William D. Ruckelshaus, resigned the same day rather than carry out the President's order to fire Cox. Leon Jaworski was named Nov. 1 to replace Cox. *(Cox affair, Jaworski appointment, p. 69, 111)*

Richardson, during his Senate confirmation hearings, had promised that the special prosecutor would have "the greatest degree of independence," that he would not countermand or interfere with the prosecutor's decisions or actions and that the prosecutor would not be fired except for "extraordinary improprieties."

The response to Cox's dismissal was one of shock and outrage. About 140 House members reacted by cosponsoring bills providing for a court-appointed special prosecutor, as did 55 senators.

In reporting HR 11401, the committee said it was "convinced that the only way to assure that the American people will have complete trust and confidence in the aggressiveness and independence of the special prosecutor is to make him truly independent of the executive, give him tenure and legislate limited grounds for his removal."

Provisions. As reported, the bill provided for the U.S. District Court for the District of Columbia to appoint a three-member panel which, in turn, would make the appointment. The three-judge panel also could remove the prosecutor, but only for "gross dereliction of duty, gross impropriety or physical or mental inability" to carry out his duties.

The special prosecutor would have duties similar to those of Cox and Jaworski: Investigation and prosecution of offenses arising out of the 1972 presidential election, including the Watergate break-in and coverup, campaign financing and other alleged improprieties. The prosecutor would have a three-year term and would be required to make annual reports on his activities to the three-judge panel, the attorney general and Congress.

The bill as reported included an amendment offered by Rep. Tom Railsback (R Ill.). It required the special prosecutor to report each month to the chairman and ranking minority member of the House Judiciary Committee such information relevant to the question of whether the President had committed impeachable offenses. The amendment also called on the prosecutor to provide, on request of the committee, information, documents or other evidence "as may be necessary to enable the Committee to conduct an investigation or inquiry into whether grounds exist for impeachment of the President."

The amendment was approved by the full committee on a 26-12 vote.

Dennis Substitute. During its deliberations, the committee rejected a substitute bill (HR 11467) offered by David W. Dennis (R Ind.) by a 17-21 vote, with all Democrats but one voting against the substitute and all Republicans but one favoring it. Under the Dennis substitute, Jaworski would have been kept in office, and similar powers concerning the special prosecutor that were granted to the three-judge panel in the committee-reported bill would have been given to the attorney general.

The Dennis substitute, expected to be offered as a floor amendment when the House debated HR 11401 Dec. 4, provided that the attorney general could fire the special prosecutor only for gross misconduct, dereliction of duty, impropriety or physical incapacity, and that any replacement named by the attorney general would require Senate approval.

Dissenting Views. House Judiciary Committee opponents of HR 11401, led by Dennis, noted in their dissenting views that the bill raised "grave and unnecessary constitutional questions" by vesting in the judicial branch the appointment of an individual to investigate the executive. This violated the principal of separation of powers, they maintained.

Opponents also said enactment of the bill would create practical problems, because it could result in two special prosecutors getting in each other's way while the validity of HR 11401 was being tested in the courts. "Instead of prosecuting the guilty we may be engaged in a time-consuming and unproductive struggle over jurisdiction between prosecutorial rivals," they said.

Week's Watergate Chronology

Following is a day-to-day chronology of the week's events in the Watergate case:

NOV. 21

Tape Defect. White House special counsel J. Fred Buzhardt told U.S. District Judge John J. Sirica that an 18-minute section of the tape of a June 20, 1972, conversation between Nixon and his former staff chief, H. R. Haldeman, consisted of "an audible tone and no conversation." The President had been told of the defect in the subpoenaed tapes shortly after White House attorneys discovered it Nov. 14, Buzhardt said. To ensure the safety of the remaining subpoenaed tapes, Sirica ordered the White House to turn them over to the court by Nov. 26. *(p. 141)*

NOV. 22

Tapes Reaction. Gov. Winfield Dunn (Tenn.), chairman of the Republican Governors' Association, expressed disappointment that Nixon had not mentioned the 18-minute gap in the tape at a meeting the President had with Republican governors in Memphis, Tenn., on Nov. 20. "I came out of there assured that we've bottomed out, and now I'm not sure that we have...this revelation does call for some further explanation," Dunn said. Nixon had been quoted as 'having assured the governors that all the crucial tapes were intact and audible, and that he knew of no further "bombshells" in the Watergate case. *(p. 149)*

NOV. 23

Andreas Plea. Dwayne O. Andreas entered a plea of not guilty in U.S. District Court in Minneapolis, Minn., to misdemeanor charges that he illegally contributed

Poll Report

Confidence in President Nixon continued to erode as Watergate developments unfolded, according to the latest Harris Survey. Interviewing of 1,459 households for the poll, published Nov. 26, was conducted Nov. 12-15. *(Earlier poll report, p. 149)*

These were the questions and answers:

"When all of the investigations and crises have finished, do you think that President Nixon will be found to have violated the law, as was true of Vice President Agnew, or don't you think this will happen?"

	Latest	October
Violated law	44%	39%
Won't happen	34	36
Not sure	22	25

"Do you tend to agree or disagree that President Nixon is a man of high integrity?"

	Latest	October	September 1972
Agree	39%	39%	76%
Disagree	46	44	13
Not sure	15	17	11

"Do you tend to agree or disagree that President Nixon does not inspire confidence as a president should?"

	Latest	October	September 1972
Agree	65%	58%	49%
Disagree	29	30	40
Not sure	6	12	11

Democrats on Presidency. For a Gallup Poll published Nov. 25, 627 persons who call themselves Democrats (in a total sample of 1,550 adults), in interviews Nov. 2-5, were shown a list of 11 men and asked: "Which one would you like to see nominated as the Democratic candidate for president in 1976?"

Sen. Edward M. Kennedy (Mass.)	41%
Gov. George C. Wallace (Ala.)	15
Sen. Edmund S. Muskie (Maine)	9
Sen. Henry M. Jackson (Wash.)	6
Sen. George McGovern (S.D.)	6
Sen. Adlai E. Stevenson III (Ill.)	4
Sen. Birch Bayh (Ind.)	3
Sen. Walter F. Mondale (Minn.)	2
Sen. William Proxmire (Wis.)	2
Sen. Robert C. Byrd (W.Va.)	1
Sen. John V. Tunney (Calif.)	1
Undecided	10

$100,000 in corporate funds to the 1968 presidential campaign of Sen. Hubert H. Humphrey (D Minn.). The charges were filed Oct. 19 by former special prosecutor Archibald Cox, under an exception to the requirement that the prosecution deal only with the 1972 campaign. Andreas was the first of several executives cited for illegal corporate contributions to plead not guilty. *(Other pleas, p. 133; Andreas charge, p. 84)*

ITT Investigation. Rep. J. J. Pickle (D Texas), a member of the House Interstate and Foreign Commerce Investigating Subcommittee, said in Austin, Texas, that neither Watergate special prosecutor Leon Jaworski nor Acting Attorney General Robert H. Bork would assume responsibility for investigating allegations that the White House interceded improperly in a 1971 settlement of an antitrust suit against the International Telephone and Telegraph Corporation (ITT). "Both IRS (Internal Revenue Service) and SEC (Securities and Exchange Commission) failed to follow up apparent violations" connected with the case, he added. Pickle said he had written to Bork, Jaworski and the two agencies to ask for an explanation. *(ITT case, p. 102)*

Vesco Watergate Connection. *The New York Times* reported that the Senate Watergate investigating committee and the special prosecution force were interested in questioning indicted financier Robert L. Vesco about his relationship with President Nixon and his brothers, and with "certain government aides"—as well as about his dealings with the SEC.

NOV. 24

IRS Investigation. Donald C. Alexander, Commissioner of the Internal Revenue Service since May, said in an interview with the Associated Press that he had found no evidence that his agency had been put to political use by the Nixon administration. But he said he could speak only for his term of office at the agency. Former White House counsel John W. Dean III told the Senate investigating committee in June that administration officials discussed using tax audits to punish people they perceived as enemies. The Joint Committee on Internal Revenue Taxation responded to the charges by initiating an investigation of possible political use of the IRS. *(Dean testimony, Vol. I, p. 161)*

Nixon Charges. A Washington, D.C., public interest law firm headed by William A. Dobrovir issued a report citing 28 counts of criminal violations allegedly committed by President Nixon or his associates in connection with the Watergate scandal, campaign financing, violation of civil liberties, use of federal funds for personal gain and income tax evasion. The firm cited a 1938 case against racketeer Charles (Lucky) Luciano as precedent for holding the head of an organization criminally responsible for the illegal acts of his subordinates.

Donald Nixon Surveillance. *The Washington Post* reported that an informed source said that former White House aide John J. Caulfield had told the staff of the Senate investigating committee that the Secret Service appeared to have conducted a physical surveillance of F. Donald Nixon, the President's brother. Nixon acknowledged in his Nov. 17 press briefing that his brother's phone had been tapped for "security reasons." Caulfield reportedly said former White House aide John D. Ehrlichman had asked him to monitor the surveillance project in 1970. *(Nixon statement, p. 149)*

Vesco Allegations. *The New York Times* reported that the Senate Government Operations Permanent In-

vestigations Subcommittee had been looking into allegations that federal agents halted a narcotics investigation after an undercover worker brought up the name of financier Robert L. Vesco as a backer of a heroin operation.

NOV. 25

Executive Privilege Study. Rep. Joshua Eilberg (D Pa.) said a study by the Library of Congress disputed President Nixon's version of an executive privilege case that involved President Thomas Jefferson. Nixon had referred to the case, in which Jefferson was ordered to produce evidence in the murder trial of Vice President Aaron Burr, as precedent for his own actions in withholding the Watergate tapes and other documents sought by investigators. The report cited errors of fact and interpretation in Nixon's version of the case. *(Jefferson subpoena, Vol. I, p. 209)*

Kissinger Wiretap. Citing an unnamed "former White House associate," *The New York Times* reported that Secretary of State Henry A. Kissinger had said privately that he was convinced his phone had been tapped at some time during his tenure in the Nixon administration. *(Kissinger wiretap involvement, Vol. I, p. 213)*

NOV. 26

Tapes Turnover. Complying with Judge Sirica's request, the White House turned over to the court the existing subpoenaed tapes and related materials. Included was a 22-page "index and analysis" of the tapes, which listed claims of executive privilege for portions of the evidence. *(Details, p. 161)*

Woods Testimony. The President's personal secretary, Rose Mary Woods, testified before Judge Sirica that she had accidently caused an 18-minute erasure while transcribing a June 20, 1972, tape for Nixon's personal use on Oct. 1. She said that she told the President of the mistake the same day and that he replied that it was not crucial because "that's not one of the subpoenaed tapes." *(Details, p. 160)*

Hearing Delay. Samuel Dash, chief counsel of the Senate investigating committee, announced after meeting with committee staff and members that hearings would be suspended until late January, in part because investigators had encountered White House resistance to their requests for documents and some key witnesses had refused to appear.

Seafarers Contribution. *Time* magazine reported that investigators from the Watergate special prosecution force were looking into the circumstances of a $100,000 contribution from the Seafarers International Union to Nixon's 1972 campaign. The article said the union borrowed $100,000 from the Chemical Bank of New York on the same day it made the contribution and that the Nixon committee failed to report the funds for three months.

Prosecution Leaks. The *Time* report was one of two instances cited by deputy White House press secretary Gerald L. Warren as examples of improper news leaks by the Watergate special prosecution team. The other was an article by syndicated columnists Rowland Evans and Robert Novak that said two White House attorneys had personally asked prosecutors to delay for several days the revelation about the 18-minute erasure on a subpoenaed White House tape.

Chapin-Hunt Link. *The New York Times* reported that Dwight L. Chapin, a former White House aide who hired convicted political saboteur Donald H. Segretti, had alerted Segretti to a call he would receive from E. Howard Hunt Jr., a former White House consultant and CIA agent who was convicted for the Watergate break-in. Chapin, who resigned in February to work for United Airlines in Chicago, had publicly denied knowing Hunt. *(Segretti testimony, p. 43)*

NOV. 27

Tapes Hearing. Nixon's personal secretary, Rose Mary Woods, played the subpoenaed June 20, 1972, White House tape, containing an 18-minute blank, during an open court hearing before Judge Sirica. Woods testified that she accidently erased five minutes of the tape while transcribing it, but she could not account for the rest of the gap. The recording was of poor quality and often inaudible to the audience. *(Details, p. 160)*

Senate Hearings Suspension. The Senate Watergate investigating committee voted to suspend its hearings on campaign financing until Chairman Sam J. Ervin Jr. (D N.C.) reconvened them, probably in late January. Ervin and Vice Chairman Howard H. Baker Jr. (R Tenn.) told reporters the action was taken to give the staff more time to complete several investigations in progress. The committee also voted to subpoena unspecified additional White House tapes and documents that might bear on its investigation of campaign financing. *(Details, p. 162)*

Hughes Subpoena. Chester C. Davis, an attorney for billionaire Howard Hughes, and other aides to Hughes asked U.S. District Judge Sirica to order the Senate investigating committee to allow them to testify in public hearings without first undergoing private questioning by committee staff. The committee was seeking testimony about a $100,000 contribution Hughes gave Nixon which was returned after three years. Davis and the other Hughes aides argued that news organizations had been given "incomplete, distorted and speculative accounts" of what was said during committee interviews.

ITT Investigation. Responding to inquiries by Rep. J. J. Pickle (D Texas), special prosecutor Leon Jaworski promised to pursue vigorously allegations of illegal White House interference in a 1971 settlement of an antitrust suit against International Telephone and Telegraph Corp. (ITT). Jaworski said his office would take responsibility for investigating "allegations of federal criminal offenses by executives, including alleged misconduct in the relationship between ITT and any federal agency or official."

Vesco Drug Charges. Deputy White House press secretary Gerald L. Warren denied allegations, contained in news reports, that White House officials sought to limit an investigation of a heroin smuggling operation after federal investigators were told by an informant that financier Robert L. Vesco was involved. Vesco issued a statement from the Bahamas denying any involvement in or knowledge of the operation.

ABA President on Impeachment. Chesterfield Smith, president of the American Bar Association, strongly advocated impeachment proceedings against Nixon as the only proper way to determine his guilt or innocence. "It is my personal position that there can be no matter more important to us on the domestic scene, nor more detrimental to our foreign relations, than a continuation of this political never-never land where a majority of our citizens do not believe the President and suspect his motives and every move he makes," Smith said. He spoke before the American Life Insurance Association convention in Washington, D.C. *(ABA position, p. 82)*

SBA Hearings. The House Banking and Currency Subcommittee on Small Business opened public hearings into allegations that the White House had used the Small Business Administration for political purposes and that the agency had been criminally mismanaged.

NOV. 28

Tapes Hearing. White House attorney J. Fred Buzhardt testified before Judge Sirica that each of the subpoenaed tapes included "a number of blank spots lasting several minutes each." He and other White House spokesmen said the blanks were insignificant, but prosecutors at the hearing disagreed. *(Details, p. 160)*

Richardson Remarks. Former Attorney General Elliot L. Richardson said he did not think there was a White House campaign to discredit him by charging that he had given an incorrect version of the firing of former special prosecutor Archibald Cox. But he conceded that there was "an impulse" at the White House to challenge the credibility of many people, himself included. Richardson spoke to reporters after testifying before the Senate Special Committee on Termination of the National Emergency on ways to limit the emergency powers of the president. *(Richardson-White House dispute, p. 151)*

Vesco Drug Charges. Frank Peroff, a former undercover agent for the Drug Enforcement Administration, reportedly told the Senate Government Operations Permanent Investigations Subcommittee that, despite White House denials, he spoke to several White House aides in July about the halting of a narcotics investigation after it led to financier Robert L. Vesco. Peroff reportedly said he told White House counsel J. Fred Buzhardt about the affair. Buzhardt denied ever having talked to the agent.

Nixon Finances. Deputy White House press secretary Gerald L. Warren announced that Nixon would release a series of papers providing "complete information" on the President's personal finances.

McGovern on Impeachment. Sen. George McGovern (D S.D.), Nixon's opponent in the 1972 election, called for impeachment of the President as the "only honorable way" to restore a sense of justice in the country. McGovern spoke to an audience at the University of North Carolina.

NOV. 29

Chapin Indictment. Dwight L. Chapin, Nixon's former appointments secretary, was indicted on four counts of lying to the original Watergate grand jury in Washington, D.C. The charges involved Chapin's alleged knowledge of the 1972 political sabotage activities of Donald H. Segretti, whom he hired. Chapin resigned from the White House in February to become an executive at United Airlines. √

POSSIBLY A 'SINISTER FORCE' BLANKED OUT THE TAPE

An exotic new brand of electronic demonology was offered as a possible explanation for the inexplicably missing segment of 18 minutes and 15 seconds from a tape recording of a Watergate-related presidential conversation.

A "devil theory" was the description given by Alexander M. Haig Jr., the White House chief of staff. Haig testified Dec. 6 at a hearing on the erased tape before Chief Judge John J. Sirica in U.S. District Court in Washington, D.C.

Alexander M. Haig

The tape he referred to was one of those subpoenaed by the court. It was made on June 20, 1972, three days after the break-in at Democratic national headquarters in Washington's Watergate complex. The blank segment contained a conversation, sought by investigators of the Watergate scandal, between President Nixon and his former chief of staff, H.R. Haldeman. For two weeks, the court had been trying to determine what caused the mysterious 18-minute hum, preceded and followed by other conversations, in the tape. *(Earlier testimony, next page)*

One possible explanation was that Rose Mary Woods, Nixon's personal secretary, had accidentally erased all or part of the 18 minutes by pushing the wrong button on the recorder while she took a phone call. White House lawyers had expressed skepticism about an accidental erasure of the tape.

Haig told the court that attorneys assigned to the case had informed him on Nov. 20 that they had been unable to recreate the buzz that had replaced conversation during the gap in the tape. That evening, he recounted, he learned of two tones in the prolonged hum—a lower-volume tone starting about five minutes into the segment.

He and the lawyers, Haig said, discussed the possibility that "perhaps there had been one tone applied by Miss Woods" and that perhaps later, "some sinister force had come in and applied the other energy source and taken care of the information on the tape."

Sirica asked Haig if he knew who the "sinister force" might be. Haig replied that he did not. According to White House records, only Woods, presidential assistant Stephen Bull and the President had access to the tape.

After the court hearing, reporters asked Haig if he had ever asked Nixon if he could have erased anything on the tape. Woods had testified earlier that the President had "pushed some buttons back and forth" while listening to excerpts of the tape as she was making a summary of its contents the weekend of Sept. 29 at Camp David, Maryland. Haig shook his head in the negative in response to the question.

Listening and Testing

Four months after the Watergate grand jury subpoenaed certain presidential tapes, four of those tapes were cleared for presentation to that body. John J. Sirica, chief U.S. District Court judge in Washington, D.C., Nov. 30 agreed with a motion by special prosecutor Leon Jaworski that the four tapes, to which no particular claim of executive privilege had been raised, could be turned over to the grand jury. *(p. 161)*

On Dec. 3, Sirica began listening to the other tapes in a heavily guarded jury room. He was listening to the conversations for which executive privilege had been claimed, and he would decide whether or not those tapes should also go to the grand jury.

Meanwhile, in New York City, the June 20, 1972, tape containing the mysterious 18-minute hum was undergoing intensive examination by a panel of experts selected jointly by the White House and the special prosecutor's office. The tape was carried to New York by armed federal marshals the night of Nov. 29 along with the machines related to its production and, perhaps, to the origin of the hum. Experts were seeking the cause of the hum and were working to discover if the original signals of the conversation first recorded there—and covered or erased by the hum—could be electronically enhanced and thus recovered.

The examination and testing were taking place in Manhattan at the Federal Scientific Corporation Laboratory, whose vice president for acoustics research, Mark R. Weiss, was one of the agreed-upon panel of experts. The panel also included Richard H. Bolt of Cambridge, Mass.; Franklin Cooper, professor of linguistics at the University of Connecticut; James L. Flanagan, a digital coding expert from Bell Laboratories; Thomas G. Stockham Jr., professor of computer sciences at the University of Utah, and John G. McKnight, an audio systems consultant.

White House lawyers said they discovered the 18-minute gap on Nov. 14. Haig said he told Nixon about it the next day. The court was notified of the erasure on Nov. 21.

Haig said in his testimony Dec. 6 that the White House had been reluctant to make public the new discrepancy in the tapes because of the earlier disclosure that two tapes did not exist. "We had just had two non-recordings, which was fairly traumatic from our perspective, and it was important we not have a repeat of that kind of thing, which led to perceptions by the American people which I don't think were justified by the facts," he testified.

Other Tapes

White House lawyers and aides took turns during the week that ended Dec. 8 testifying about the 18-minute gap on one of the subpoenaed Watergate tapes before Judge John J. Sirica. While that drama drew most of the attention, the Justice Department announced Dec. 4 that a White House tape and documents related to another potential scandal for the Nixon administration would be handed over to the Watergate special prosecutor and to a federal judge.

The other tape contained a conversation President Nixon and his top aides held March 23, 1971, reportedly about the issue of milk price support payments. Earlier the same day, they had met with representatives of the dairy industry. On March 25, the administration reversed its policy and announced a large increase in milk price supports.

The tape, with 69 related documents, was to be turned over to U.S. District Judge William B. Jones in Washington, D.C. He was hearing a civil suit brought by consumer advocate Ralph Nader charging the government with preferential treatment of the dairy industry in exchange for campaign contributions.

President Nixon denied any "quid pro quo" arrangement behind the decision to raise the price supports during his Nov. 17 appearance before a group of newspaper editors near Orlando, Fla. He said a petition signed by 102 members of Congress demanding the increase forced him to act. *(Text, p. 159)*

As with portions of the nine subpoenaed Watergate tapes, the White House claimed executive privilege over the milk tape and documents. Judge Jones was to review their contents in private and rule on the validity of the claim. Justice Department spokesmen left open the possibility that the White House could appeal an unfavorable decision on the claim.

ITT Tape. Watergate special prosecutor Leon Jaworski also was to be granted access to the milk tape, the Justice Department said. *The Washington Post* reported Dec. 4 that Jaworski had requested a tape related to yet another potential administration scandal.

This one concerned a phone call from Nixon to then Attorney General Richard G. Kleindienst on April 19, 1971, in which the President ordered Kleindienst to drop, or at least delay, a Justice Department antitrust action against International Telephone and Telegraph Company (ITT). The White House acknowledged the call Oct. 30 after *The New York Times* revealed it.

ITT and the Justice Department reached an out-of-court settlement of the antitrust suit in July 1971. Former special prosecutor Archibald Cox had been attempting to obtain the ITT tape when he was fired Oct. 20. *(ITT call, p. 102)*

After the introduction of the new conspiratorial element in the already cloudy issue of the tapes, Sirica announced that a panel of experts scrutinizing the partially blank tape in New York City were expected to report to the court the next week. If necessary, Sirica said, he then would resume the hearings. *(Box, p. 167)*

Haldeman Influence. In earlier court testimony, the inference was left by another witness that former staff chief Haldeman continued to exert considerable influence on White House policy. Haldeman resigned April 30 as a result of pressure from Watergate. *(Earlier testimony, p. 170)*

Haig tersely dismissed such speculation. "Mr. Haldeman does not influence what we do in the White House," he said.

Ford and Nixon. A few hours after the court recessed on Dec. 6, Gerald R. Ford was sworn in as Vice President before a joint session of Congress.

Ford's accession to the vice presidency immediately opened up a new round of speculation on Capitol Hill about the survivability of Nixon as President. With the vice presidency no longer vacant, some Republican members of Congress were speaking more candidly than before about impeachment or resignation of the scandal-damaged President.

One Republican senator, Jacob K. Javits of New York, spoke out publicly Dec. 5, the day before Ford's confirmation and swearing in. When Ford was sworn in, said Javits, "there will exist a new situation concerning any call on the President to resign in the interest of the country.... I and others will have to give every thoughtful consideration to that possibility."

Other Republicans on the Hill disagreed with Javits, or were more circumspect. But even some Nixon loyalists were anxious for the President to make a full report on his personal finances, as he had promised to do as part of his "Operation Candor." *(Box, p. 169)*

Continuing Tapes Riddles

Presidential secretary Woods made her fourth appearance in Sirica's court on Dec. 5. She had testified previously that she might have caused part of the 18-minute hum through an accident while she was working on the tapes Oct. 1. She told the President immediately, but no one else. The President was not concerned, because at the time, reportedly, he did not believe the hum to be in a subpoenaed tape. *(p. 160)*

Special White House counsel J. Fred Buzhardt Jr., appearing before Sirica Nov. 30, said that he had first learned of the full extent and import of the missing conversation on Nov. 14, six weeks after Woods had informed the President of her mistake and a week before Sirica was informed of the gap. He said that the official White House explanation, included in the documents given to Sirica with the tapes themselves on Nov. 26—that the hum was produced by the current of a high-intensity lamp and an electric typewriter—was "just a possibility," not a certainty. *(p. 161)*

Buzhardt said that the day after he learned of the gap, he and White House attorney Samuel J. Powers met with Woods. But to his recollection, he added, he did not ask her how her mistake, during a five-minute telephone call, could have created a gap more than three times as long in the recorded conversations.

A week later, on Nov. 22, Buzhardt discovered that Woods had nine other original presidential tapes in her possession, the lawyer testified. These tapes covered the period Jan. 3-4, 1973, and special prosecutor Leon Jaworski had requested some of them from the White House Nov. 15. The tapes included conversations of the Presi-

(Continued on p. 170)

Nixon's Finances: Questions Still To Be Answered

Portions of a promised report on President Nixon's personal finances were leaked to the press Dec. 2, and more information from the report surfaced after Republican congressional leaders met with Nixon and his tax lawyers Dec. 4. White House spokesmen insisted that the report, to be released the week ended Dec. 8, would lay to rest all questions raised by the fragmentary and sometimes contradictory information that had come to light previously.

Income Taxes. The Associated Press reported Dec. 2 that Nixon paid a total of $78,651 in federal income taxes for the years 1969-1972—$72,686 for 1969, $789 for 1970, $878 for 1971 and $4,298 for 1972. The unusually small sums for 1970 and 1971 were the result of deductions, primarily $570,000 which Nixon claimed for donating his vice presidential papers to the government.

White House spokesmen were noncommittal when the President's 1970 and 1971 payments were first revealed Oct. 3 in *The Providence (R.I.) Journal.* But in his Nov. 17 press conference at the Associated Press Managing Editors convention in Orlando, Fla., Nixon admitted that he paid "nominal amounts" in those years. He said he did not know the exact figures, but promised to release them in the future. *(Press conference text, p. 155)*

The propriety, if not the legality, of Nixon's deduction for the papers had been widely questioned because of the legal circumstances of the transaction. The law that allowed public officials to take tax deductions for donating their papers to the government was repealed in December 1969 and was retroactive to July 25, 1969.

The White House had said Nixon gave the papers to the National Archives in March 1969. Questions had been raised about whether a proper deed existed for the transaction—the archives reportedly did not receive the document until April 1970.

Some congressional leaders who attended the Dec. 4 meeting reported that Nixon's lawyers were amenable to the idea of allowing the Joint Committee on Internal Revenue Taxation, chaired by Rep. Wilbur D. Mills (D Ark.), to investigate the deductions and rule on their legality and propriety.

Real Estate. Another issue the committee might be asked to look into, it was said, was whether the President took proper tax deductions on his home in San Clemente, Calif., and on the resale of some adjoining property to industrialist Robert Abplanalp, who financed the purchase of the home.

During the Nov. 17 press conference, Nixon said his income tax payments had not been the result of "deductions for, shall we say, a cattle ranch or interest or all of these gimmicks...." But a partial audit of financial transactions relating to Nixon's personal property, released Aug. 27, showed a number of interest payments he made which apparently would have qualified as legal tax deductions.

Although the President told the managing editors that he bought his California and Florida homes with his personal savings, the Aug. 27 audit and other financial statements released by the White House showed that most of the funds used to purchase the homes were borrowed.

The wire service report on the expected Nixon financial report said the President was planning to will his San Clemente estate to the government. That prompted speculation on what tax deductions Nixon might be able to claim, but did not appear likely to end criticism about the large sums of government money spent on the properties since 1969—supposedly for the President's security.

Net Worth. Some of the participants in the Dec. 4 White House meeting reported that they were told the President's net worth had tripled since he took office—from about $300,000 at the beginning of 1969 to about $988,000 by May 31, 1972. Those net worth figures did not coincide exactly with figures given in earlier financial statements the President had released while campaigning.

Bank Account. Because "it was important to have no question about the President's personal finances," Nixon said Nov. 17, he decided in 1968 "to clean the decks and to put everything in real estate." But the Republicans who attended the Dec. 4 meeting were told that the President had $250,000 in certificates of deposit at the Key Biscayne Bank and Trust Company, owned by his close friend Charles G. Rebozo.

Part of that money was the subject of an investigation by Dade County State Attorney Richard Gerstein, who revealed Dec. 1 that he had learned Nixon bought a $100,000 certificate of deposit at the bank in the fall of 1970. The bank agreed Dec. 5 to give Gerstein its records on Nixon, and a spokesmen said the White House had approved the turnover.

Gerstein refused to say why he wanted the records, but there was speculation that his interest was related to the disclosure that Rebozo had received the second installment of a $100,000 campaign contribution from billionaire Howard Hughes shortly before Nixon purchased the certificate. Rebozo and Nixon had contended that the money was returned, unused, after Rebozo had kept it for three years in a safe deposit box at his bank. *(Committee testimony, p. 173)*

Tax Returns. "I have disclosed my personal finances," Nixon told the newspaper executives Nov. 17. But he promised to provide more information, "because obviously you are all so busy that when these things come across your desk, maybe you don't see them."

Rumors circulated in the following weeks about whether or not the promised report would include complete copies of the President's income tax returns or only summaries. The Republicans who met with Nixon Dec. 4 urged him to make complete returns public, but White House spokesmen remained unclear Dec. 5 on what form the disclosure would take. *(p. 132)*

dent with John D. Ehrlichman and former White House special counsel Charles W. Colson. Former White House counsel John W. Dean III had testified before the Senate Watergate committee in June that Ehrlichman had told him Jan. 4 that discussions were under way concerning the possibility of executive clemency for Watergate defendant E. Howard Hunt Jr.

Woods obtained the nine additional tapes on Nov. 19, according to records kept by deputy presidential assistant John C. Bennett. As soon as he realized that Woods was working with the original tapes, Buzhardt said, he had copies made for her that she could use to compile a digest of the conversations included. The nine tapes were returned to Bennett on the morning of Nov. 26.

Untangling Subpoena Confusion

"He told me not to worry, because that was not one of the subpoenaed tapes," said Rose Mary Woods Nov. 28. She was relating to U.S. District Judge John J. Sirica what President Nixon's reaction had been on Oct. 1 when she had informed him that she feared she had mistakenly erased some conversation on the June 20, 1972, tape.

But, as it turned out, that conversation between Nixon and H. R. Haldeman was indeed one of those sought by the grand jury in its subpoena of July 23, 1973. Testimony from various White House lawyers attributed their confusion over the specific conversations of June 20 included in the subpoena to its ambiguous language.

The subpoena sought: "All tapes and other electronic and/or mechanical recordings or re-productions, and any memoranda, papers, transcripts and other writings relating to (the) meeting of June 20, 1972, in the President's Executive Office Building office involving Richard Nixon, John Ehrlichman and H. R. Haldeman from 10:30 a.m. to noon (time approximate.)"

White House lawyers said that there was no three-way meeting of Nixon, Ehrlichman and Haldeman on the morning of June 20, but instead two consecutive meetings, one with Ehrlichman from 10:25 to 11:30 and then one with Haldeman from 11:26 to 12:45. Because the first meeting occurred at times closer to those mentioned in the subpoena, White House attorneys assumed that was the only conversation desired, they said.

More precise language, contained in a memorandum filed by former special prosecutor Archibald Cox with Sirica Aug. 13, resulted, when read by the White House attorneys in November, in the realization that both conversations were desired. The memorandum described the meeting as follows:

"Respondent (Nixon) met with John D. Ehrlichman and H. R. Haldeman in his old Executive Office Building office, on June 20, 1972, from 10:30 a.m. until approximately 12:45.... Early on the morning of June 20, Haldeman, Ehrlichman, Mitchell, Dean and Attorney General Kleindienst met in the White House. This was their first opportunity for full discussion of how to handle the Watergate incident.... From there, Ehrlichman and then Haldeman went to see the President...."

Haldeman Role. Haldeman's continuing role in White House activities, more than six months after his departure April 30 as chief of staff, was further detailed in testimony Dec. 4 before Sirica. Lawrence M. Higby, an official in the Office of Management and Budget and Haldeman's former deputy, said that he learned Nov. 14 or 15, in a telephone call from his former boss, that Haldeman was already aware of the 18-minute gap in the June 20 tape.

During the conversation, Higby said, he received the clear impression that someone at the White House had asked Haldeman for his handwritten notes taken during the conversation the hum eliminated. Haig said Dec. 5 that he had telephoned Haldeman. Buzhardt said that when he told the President Nov. 14 about the long gap, Nixon suggested that Haldeman's notes of that meeting be obtained. The notes indicated that the missing portion of the conversation between Haldeman and Nixon dealt with Watergate. *(p. 161)*

Those notes and other files that Haldeman had left at the Executive Office Building were in a locked file cabinet, and only Haldeman knew the combination to the lock, Higby said. On Nov. 15, Haldeman gave Higby precise instructions about how to find and remove the notes, making clear that any deviation from the instructions should be reported to him, according to Higby. Higby said that he read the notes to Haldeman over the telephone before handing them over, with Haldeman's acquiescence, to Buzhardt.

Repeat Performance. Rose Mary Woods made a surprise repeat performance Dec. 5 in court, upstaging the star witness of the day, Alexander Haig. Judge Sirica recalled Woods to "get to the bottom" of complaints by her attorney, Charles S. Rhyne, that White House lawyers had placed the President's interests ahead of hers. *(Previous Woods testimony, p. 160, 118)*

Woods said that she had the impression before her first court appearance Nov. 8 that Leonard Garment, Buzhardt and Samuel J. Powers of the White House legal staff were her lawyers. However, she testified that the three had counseled her not to volunteer information and to answer questions "yes" or "no," without otherwise coaching her.

Haig recommended that she obtain her own lawyer late Thanksgiving Day, Woods said. Haig telephoned Rhyne, when she suggested him, and he accepted her as a client the next day.

Sirica Skepticism. Woods said that she had been "terribly worried" that she might have accidentally caused a 4½-minute hum in the June 20 taped conversation between Nixon and Haldeman. But she added that she "could see no way at all I could have caused an 18-minute gap." Buzhardt had informed Sirica Nov. 21 of an 18-minute blank in the recording.

Sirica expressed skepticism about Woods' earlier explanation of the erasure. "I'm not saying I don't believe you," he said. "I haven't made up my mind." The judge assured her that she was not on trial and that the hearing gave her the "greatest forum you'll ever have to speak in" to provide information about what might have caused the hum.

Woods replied that she was on trial by the press, although "I'm not supposed to say that.... If I could offer any idea, any proof, any knowledge of how that 18-minute

Box Score of Watergate Indictments and Convictions

By the first week of December, 18 men had been indicted for or pleaded guilty to criminal offenses related to the Watergate scandal. Eight had been convicted and sentenced.

The first indictment since Leon Jaworski was named Watergate special prosecutor in October was returned on Nov. 29, when Dwight L. Chapin, President Nixon's former appointments secretary, was accused of lying to a federal grand jury. *(p. 160)*

Jaworski was quoted by the Dec. 10 *U.S. News & World Report* magazine as saying that he expected more indictments in the first few weeks of 1974. "I would be very disappointed if the trials themselves were not completed within a year's period of time," he said.

These were the indictments and convictions in the Watergate and related cases—not including campaign contribution violations:

Watergate Break-In. Seven men were indicted Sept. 15, 1972, for the June 17, 1972, break-in at the Watergate complex. They were E. Howard Hunt Jr., G. Gordon Liddy, James W. McCord Jr., Bernard L. Barker, Eugenio R. Martinez, Virgilio R. Gonzalez and Frank A. Sturgis.

Liddy and McCord were the only ones to plead not guilty and stand trial—U.S. District Judge John J. Sirica convicted them Jan. 30, 1973, of conspiracy, burglary and wiretapping violations. Sirica sentenced all but Liddy on Nov. 9; Liddy was serving an 18-month sentence for refusing to testify before a grand jury while appealing his break-in conviction. *(Sentences, p. 117)*

Watergate Coverup. Three men who participated in the attempt to keep the lid on the Watergate scandal agreed to cooperate with prosecutors in exchange for reduced charges for their coverup roles. None had been sentenced by Dec. 8.

• Frederick C. LaRue, once an aide to former Attorney General John N. Mitchell and an official of the Nixon re-election committee, pleaded guilty June 27 in U.S. District Court in Washington, D.C., to charges of conspiracy to obstruct justice. *(Vol. I, p. 161)*

• Jeb Stuart Magruder, a former White House aide who became deputy director of the Nixon re-election committee in late 1971, pleaded guilty Aug. 16 to a charge of conspiracy to obstruct justice, unlawfully intercept wire and oral communications and defraud the United States.

• John W. Dean III, Nixon's chief counsel until he was dismissed April 30, pleaded guilty Oct. 19 to a single felony count of conspiracy to obstruct justice and defraud the United States. *(p. 83)*

Plumbers Break-In. Four former members of the secret White House investigations unit known as the "plumbers" were indicted Sept. 4 by a Los Angeles, Calif., county grand jury for their roles in the 1971 break-in at the office of Dr. Lewis Fielding, a psychiatrist who had treated Pentagon Papers defendant Daniel Ellsberg. *(Indictments, p. 21)*

They were John D. Ehrlichman, Nixon's former domestic affairs adviser; David R. Young, a former White House aide; G. Gordon Liddy, former counsel to the Nixon re-election finance committee and convicted Watergate conspirator, and Egil Krogh Jr., former White House aide and leader of the plumbers.

All four were charged with state counts of burglary and conspiracy. Ehrlichman was also cited for perjury because of conflicts in his testimony before the Senate Watergate investigating committee and the California grand jury. All four pleaded not guilty. The California charges against Krogh were dropped Dec. 3, after he pleaded guilty Nov. 30 in U.S. District Court in Washington, D.C., to violating Fielding's civil rights. An Oct. 11 federal indictment brought against Krogh for allegedly lying about his role in the burglary also was dropped in light of his plea. *(p. 160)*

Political Sabotage. In addition to Dwight Chapin, two men were charged in connection with a 1972 political sabotage campaign directed against the Democrats.

• Donald H. Segretti, a California lawyer, pleaded guilty Oct. 1 in U.S. District Court in Washington to three misdemeanor charges for his political activities in the Florida primary. An earlier federal indictment in Tampa, Fla., to which Segretti had pleaded not guilty, was dropped. He was sentenced Nov. 5 to six months in prison. *(p. 46)*

• George Hearing, who worked for Segretti in Florida, was indicted May 4 by a federal grand jury in Tampa. He pleaded guilty to one count of violation of campaign laws for distributing a phony campaign letter and was sentenced to a maximum prison term of one year.

Vesco Case. Former Attorney General John N. Mitchell and former Commerce Secretary Maurice H. Stans were indicted May 10 by a federal grand jury in New York City on obstruction of justice and perjury charges. They allegedly attempted to block a government investigation of the activities of financier Robert L. Vesco in exchange for a $200,000 contribution to the Nixon campaign. Their trial was scheduled to begin Jan. 7, 1974. *(Vol. I, p. 46)*

---

gap happened, there is no one on earth who would rather. I'm doing the very best I can."

Woods said that the President or Haig had first informed her that a full 18 minutes of the conversation consisted of the hum.

Jill Volner, assistant Watergate prosecutor, asked, "Do you have any knowledge, direct or indirect, of anyone tampering or obliterating any of the tapes?"

"No, ma'am, I have not," Woods replied.

Fact Witness. Powers, who preceded Woods to the witness stand, testified that she had been brought to court Nov. 8 by the White House legal team not as a client but as a "fact witness."

Richard Ben-Veniste, assistant Watergate prosecutor, asked Powers whether "anyone at any time" had told

Woods to delete anything from her testimony. "No," Powers replied.

Woods had said nothing in court Nov. 8 about her accident, although the mistake had occurred Oct. 1. She testified that in October, "I was not aware that this was going to be any great huge problem."

Conflicting Testimony. On one point, Woods contradicted testimony by Powers on Dec. 5 and Buzhardt on Nov. 29. The two lawyers said that on Nov. 14, Woods had brought her tape-recording machine into a White House room, where they were monitoring the June 20, 1972, conversation. She wanted to demonstrate how she might have pressed a wrong button, the attorneys said.

Woods denied carrying the machine into the office. She testified that all Powers and Buzhardt had told her on that occasion was that the 18-minute gap had been discovered by "a meter of some sort." She said that she had been in the room only two or three minutes and had not even sat down.

Haig's Testimony. Haig, following Woods to the witness stand, testified that Nixon told him of the erasure the day it happened. The President said that Woods had inadvertently pushed a wrong button in transcribing the tape, according to Haig. Nixon mentioned a gap of four or five minutes, Haig testified.

Nixon, according to Haig, instructed him to find out whether the erased conversation was part of nine tapes subpoenaed by the special prosecutor. Haig asked Buzhardt, who told him it was not a subpoenaed conversation.

Six weeks later, on Nov. 14, Buzhardt told Haig that he had discovered that the conversation was subpoenaed after all, Haig testified. Buzhardt had described the subpoena itself as ambiguous, according to Haig. *(Box, p. 170)*

Haig said that he did not inform Nixon about the new problem Nov. 14, so as not to upset him when he was busy with Middle East negotiations, the energy crisis and meetings with members of Congress about Watergate. He waited until Nixon had finished speaking to the National Association of Realtors convention Nov. 15 before telling him.

Concern, Not Chagrin. The President was "very, very disturbed" about the news that the gap had occurred on a subpoenaed conversation, Haig testified. "He expressed concern, not chagrin. He himself could not recall what had been said in the conversation."

Haig said that he looked for Haldeman's notes on the conversation, only to find they were stored in a safe for which Haldeman had the combination. He telephoned Haldeman in California and got the combination. Buzhardt and Lawrence M. Higby opened the safe and found the notes, Haig said.

Nixon told him to do whatever was technically feasible to reconstitute the tape, Haig testified. Experts advised Haig that the possibility of "reclamation" was "very slim indeed," he said.

Haig said that Buzhardt, who had been working with the tape recorders, "couldn't find any confirmation that the machine itself could have caused the hum (in the erased portion of the tape). This was a shocking piece of news. I was very disturbed about it...it suggested a very serious turn in an already serious situation."

Under questioning by Ben-Veniste, Haig confirmed that for some time after the Oct. 1 accident, Woods had had several original tapes in her possession as "part of a continuing process" of transcribing them for the President.

Tapes for Haldeman. Under cross-examination, Haig admitted that he had not known that several tapes were released to Haldeman in July until "well after the fact."

Stephen Bull, a presidential assistant, had given the tapes to Haldeman, because the President requested Haldeman to review their contents and report to him, Haig said. Haig testified that he told Bull, "I don't want anything like that to happen again without my knowing about it."

Haig said that he never learned of the substance of Haldeman's report to Nixon on the tapes. "I stayed very clear of this situation."

Haig testified that he had terminated the voice-actuated White House recording system on his own authority July 18, while the President was hospitalized with pneumonia. Nixon approved the action later, he said.

Haig did not know about the automatic White House recording system until he took over Haldeman's job as

---

Reorganized Legal Team

Presidential unhappiness with the performance of his Watergate lawyers and with the special prosecutor's staff was clear by the first week of December.

Reorganization of the White House counsel's office was announced Nov. 29 by White House press secretary Ronald L. Ziegler, who conceded that the existing legal team, headed by J. Fred Buzhardt, had made some mistakes. Buzhardt would continue to work on the Watergate defense, however, Ziegler said. Joining the staff, he said, would be Illinois Judge John J. Sullivan, former Under Secretary of the Treasury H. Chapman Rose and former Internal Revenue Service counsel Kenneth W. Gemmill. The latter two had volunteered their services, Ziegler said.

But by Dec. 4, at least one of the proposed recruits had dropped out. Sullivan expressed his intention to decline the job of heading the defense team, saying that he could not get a clear delineation of responsibility between himself and Buzhardt.

The White House Nov. 30 listed the members of the White House counsel staff: Leonard Garment, acting counsel, who would return from the Watergate matter to general legal work for the White House; Buzhardt, special counsel; Fred F. Fielding, deputy counsel, and staff assistants Dudley Chapman, Douglas M. Parker, Robert Andrews, Richard Alan Hauser, Kenneth Gregory Haynes and George Paul Williams. Consultants to the staff were Charles Alan Wright, Samuel J. Powers Jr. and Thomas P. Marinis Jr.

Irritation with the staff of the special prosecutor's office was expressed by Ziegler Nov. 29. Jaworski, said Ziegler, was a "very responsible and fair man," but members of his staff, inherited from Archibald Cox, displayed "ingrained suspicion and visceral dislike for this President and this administration."

---

chief of staff in May, he testified. The President told him about it in late May, and even then he had only a "general knowledge" of it, he said.

The former general testified that, on July 18, the tapes were transferred from the Secret Service to the personal custody of the President. That meant that Haig had the keys and safe combination to the well-guarded tape storage room in the Executive Office Building. Only he and John C. Bennett, his deputy, could authorize access, he said. Bull had entered with Bennett's approval.

Haig never personally touched or had access to the tapes, he said. He had not "focused" on tape mishaps until close to the time public revelations were made, he testified.

After listening to several tapes in June, Nixon told Haig that they did not reveal much information, according to Haig.

Senate Watergate Committee

The fortunes of the Senate select Watergate committee were on the upswing the week ended Dec. 8, as the Senate approved an additional $500,000 for its operations and some important witnesses who had been refusing to testify in private sessions relented after being threatened with contempt citations.

The initial refusal of 12 employees of billionaire industrialist Howard Hughes to submit to questioning by the committee staff had been a factor in the committee's Nov. 27 decision to postpone its public hearings for at least a month. *(p. 162)*

The breakthrough for the committee came Dec. 3, when the first of the Hughes employees appeared for questioning. Led by Chester C. Davis, an attorney for the Hughes organization, they had filed suit Nov. 27 in federal court in Washington, D.C., asking that they be required to testify only in public session. *(p. 166)*

Davis argued that inaccurate information from committee interviews would be leaked to the press. The committee suspected he was stalling until its report was due in February 1974, so it openly prepared for a meeting to vote on citing the subpoenaed Hughes aides for contempt of Congress. That brought the reluctant witnesses around, and chief counsel Samuel Dash said Dec. 3 that he was "pleasantly surprised."

Hughes' $100,000 Gift. The committee was after information about a $100,000 cash gift to Nixon which Hughes gave to the President's close friend, Charles G. Rebozo, in two $50,000 installments in 1969 and 1970. Nixon and Rebozo had said the money was intended for the 1972 presidential campaign, but that Rebozo returned it after three years because of the eruption of an internal dispute at the Hughes organization that might have made such a gift embarrassing to acknowledge. Rebozo said he returned the cash, which he had been keeping in a safe deposit box, to attorney Davis.

Senators Sam J. Ervin Jr. (D N.C.), the committee chairman, and Lowell P. Weicker Jr. (R Conn.) and senior committee staffers interrogated Davis Dec. 4. Davis brought with him two manila envelopes containing 1,000 $100 bills—the refunded contribution the committee had subpoenaed several weeks earlier. Davis reportedly dumped the cash on a table in front of Ervin and announced: "Here it is...do what you want with it."

The Committee and the Court

With only brief discussion, the House by voice vote Dec. 3 cleared for the President's signature a bill (S 2641) giving the U.S. District Court for the District of Columbia jurisdiction over any civil suit brought in the future by the Senate Watergate investigating committee to enforce a subpoena against the President or any other executive branch official. The bill was approved under suspension of the rules. The Senate had approved the bill Nov. 9. *(p. 136)*

Passage of the measure came in direct response to Judge John J. Sirica's decision to dismiss the Senate committee's suit seeking validation and enforcement of its subpoenas for White House tapes. Sirica had found that Congress had never granted the federal courts jurisdiction over such a case. *(p. 60)*

The committee wanted to check the serial numbers on the bills to see if they were printed before the dates Rebozo received them. The results would confirm or explode Nixon's Oct. 26 assertion that the cash was "turned back in exactly the form it was received." The money was photocopied and returned to Davis. *(Nixon press conference, p. 112)*

Nixon's Deposit. The mystery surrounding the Hughes contribution deepened Nov. 30 with the revelation that Dade County, Florida, State Attorney Richard Gerstein had been told that Nixon purchased a $100,000 certificate of deposit at a bank headed by Rebozo not long after Rebozo received the second half of the Hughes contribution. An official of the Key Biscayne Bank and Trust Company, the Rebozo Bank, confirmed the report but denied that the deposit had anything to do with the Hughes contribution.

Gerstein said he had subpoenaed bank "certificates of deposit, trust accounts and other records" on 10 individuals. Those named reportedly included Nixon, his brother, Donald, and his two former top aides, John D. Ehrlichman and H. R. Haldeman. Gerstein also was said to have subpoenaed records relating to an account opened at the bank by the Nixon re-election committee in April 1972, just before a federal campaign finance law requiring disclosure of large contributions took effect.

An attorney for the Key Biscayne bank announced Dec. 5 that Nixon's records and other materials would be turned over to Gerstein promptly. He said the White House had approved the transaction.

There were also reports that a Miami FBI agent who was a friend of Rebozo had attempted to check the Hughes cash to prove it was the original money, but had failed. *(p. 152)*

Ervin predicted Dec. 4 that Rebozo would be called to testify when the committee resumed its public hearings, probably in late January. He was expected to be asked about his contention that the Hughes contribution was to be used for the 1972 campaign. Two former Hughes aides had submitted court depositions with conflicting versions, including an allegation that part of the money was given in exchange for Justice Department approval of a proposed Hughes acquisition.

The Senate Dec. 4 agreed on a voice vote to S Res 209, granting the committee $500,000 in additional funds to complete its investigation and prepare its report. Sen. Carl T. Curtis (R Neb.) objected that the request had not been reviewed by the Rules and Administration Committee and that the investigating committee had filed no report on the dispensation of its original $1-million appropriation. Ervin said no such report was required and invited Curtis to inspect the committee's financial records.

Week's Watergate Chronology

Following is a day-to-day chronology of the week's events in the Watergate case *(earlier Nov. 29 events, p. 116)*:

NOV. 29

Jaworski Tapes Response. Watergate special prosecutor Leon Jaworski submitted to U.S. District Judge John J. Sirica a written response to the White House claims of executive privilege over certain tapes and documents submitted to the court. He asked the judge to review the materials and decide for himself what parts of the evidence should go to the grand jury. Jaworski also asked Sirica to order the White House to turn over to the court transcripts and summaries of subpoenaed presidential tapes. *(White House claims, p. 161)*

Buzhardt Testimony. White House attorney J. Fred Buzhardt, under questioning by prosecutors at a hearing on the subpoenaed tapes before Judge Sirica, conceded that his original explanation of an 18-minute erasure on one of the tapes was "just a possibility." Buzhardt had told the court the entire erasure was mistakenly caused by Nixon's personal secretary, Rose Mary Woods, but she took responsibility for only five minutes of the gap. *(p. 161)*

Buzhardt Controversy. White House press secretary Ronald L. Ziegler said at a briefing that the White House legal team, which Buzhardt headed, had made some mistakes in handling the Watergate case. At the next day's briefing, deputy press secretary Gerald L. Warren announced changes in the White House counsel's office but confirmed, after receiving a hand-delivered note, that Buzhardt was still in charge.

Ziegler on Prosecutors. At the same briefing where he cited legal mistakes, Ziegler charged that members of the Watergate prosecution team had shown an "ingrained suspicion and visceral dislike for this President and this administration." He exempted Jaworski, whom he described as "a very respected man, a very fair man."

Laird Departure. Melvin R. Laird, who had replaced John D. Ehrlichman as Nixon's domestic affairs adviser on June 6, told reporters he would resign as soon as Vice President-designate Gerald R. Ford was confirmed.

National Security Secret. News reports based on informed sources said that White House attorneys had told federal investigators that the life of a Central Intelligence Agency (CIA) spy in the Soviet Union would be endangered if a secret operation of the White House "plumbers" investigating team were disclosed. The operation reportedly related to the stifling of news stores that would reveal CIA eavesdropping on Russian leaders inside the Kremlin. White House officials had referred to the need to protect a sensitive national security operation in refusing to release documents on the plumbers' activities.

NOV. 30

Krogh Plea. Egil Krogh Jr., who headed the White House plumbers unit, pleaded guilty in U.S. District Court in Washington, D.C., to violating the civil rights of Dr. Lewis Fielding, a former psychiatrist of Daniel Ellsberg, for his role in the 1971 break-in at Fielding's office. "I cannot in conscience assert national security as a defense," Krogh said in a brief statement. He asked to be sentenced before agreeing to testify for the prosecution at other trials, in order not to influence the length of the sentence. Federal perjury charges against Krogh were dropped the same day, and California burglary charges brought against Krogh earlier were to be dropped. *(Earlier story, p. 160)*

Tapes Examination. In an electronics factory in New York City, a panel of electronics experts appointed by Judge Sirica began studying the subpoenaed July 20, 1972, White House tape with the 18-minute gap. They also had on hand for examination the tape recorder, foot pedal, earphones, electric typewriter and high-intensity lamp that Rose Mary Woods testified she was using when at least part of the gap was made.

Nixon Bank Deposit. State Attorney Richard Gerstein of Dade County, Florida, was quoted in news reports as saying that a former official of a Key Biscayne bank headed by Charles G. Rebozo had testified that Nixon purchased a $100,000 certificate of deposit at the bank in the fall of 1970. A bank official confirmed the report the next day, but said it was unrelated to a cash contribution in the same amount given to Nixon at about the same time, which Rebozo said he had kept in a strongbox for three years and then returned. Gerstein said the testimony had led him to subpoena bank documents relating to 10 individuals, reportedly including Nixon, as "part of an investigation to determine whether there can be a Watergate prosecution in Miami."

Scott on Credibility. Senate Republican Leader Hugh Scott (Pa.) called on Nixon to make "a complete, all-out disclosure" on the Watergate case, and complained that he was having "a terribly difficult job trying to strike a balance as party leader and at the same time trying to hold the confidence of people that I'm telling the truth" about Watergate. Scott made the remarks in a television interview prepared for his constituents.

DEC. 1

Minority Business Investigation. Sen. Alan Cranston (D Calif.), chairman of the Senate Banking, Housing and Urban Affairs Subcommittee on Small Business, said the Senate Watergate investigating committee would reopen its investigation of possible extortion of Nixon campaign support from minority businessmen who received federal contracts and loans.

DEC. 3

Krogh Charges Dismissal. A Los Angeles Superior Court judge dismissed charges of burglary and conspiracy to commit burglary brought Sept. 4 against Egil Krogh Jr. for his role in the 1971 burglary of the office of Daniel Ellsberg's psychiatrist. *(Indictment, p. 30)*

Tapes Review. Judge Sirica began his private review of the subpoenaed White House tapes to determine which portions of them could be passed on to the grand jury. Sirica's law clerk, Todd Christofferson, was the only other person present.

Hughes Employees. Employees of billionaire Howard Hughes began testifying in private to the staff of the Senate Watergate investigating committee, after the committee threatened to cite them for contempt for refusing to appear. The panel was interested in a $100,-000 cash payment Hughes made to Nixon's friend Rebozo. *(Details, p. 172; earlier development, p. 166)*

Woods' Complaint. *Newsweek* magazine reported that Nixon's personal secretary, Rose Mary Woods, and her attorney, Charles S. Rhyne, were upset about the way White House lawyers had been handling the matter of the 18-minute tapes erasure. Rhyne was quoted as telling a friend the lawyers were "throwing (Woods) to the wolves." Rhyne had indicated his displeasure with White House counsel J. Fred Buzhardt during court hearings the previous week.

Committee Tapes Suit. Congress cleared legislation giving the U.S. District Court in Washington, D.C., jurisdiction over the Senate Watergate investigating committee's subpoena of White House tapes. Judge John J. Sirica dismissed a committee suit for access to certain tapes on Oct. 17, saying he lacked jurisdiction. *(Box, p. 173)*

DEC. 4

Tapes Hearing. Lawrence M. Higby, who served in the White House under former chief of staff H. R. Haldeman, testified at the court hearing on the subpoenaed tapes that Haldeman had instructed him by telephone Nov. 15 to take Haldeman's notes for June 20, 1972, out of a White House file and summarize them for White House lawyers. The Haldeman notes covered an 18-minute conversation with Nixon, touching on the Watergate break-in, which had been erased from the tape. Higby said Haldeman was aware of the erasure at the time of the call. *(Details, p. 170)*

Phillips Petroleum Plea. The Phillips Petroleum Company and its board chairman, William W. Keeler, pleaded guilty in U.S. District Court in Washington, to making an illegal $100,000 contribution to Nixon's 1972 campaign. The company was fined $5,000, as had been the case with six other companies that had admitted similar illegal Nixon donations. Keeler, like five other executives, was fined $1,000. *(Previous convictions, p. 133)*

Hughes-Rebozo Money. Chester C. Davis, a lawyer employed by billionaire Howard Hughes, was questioned in executive session by the Senate Watergate investigating committee. He brought with him $100,000 in cash—a campaign contribution to Nixon from Hughes that had been returned after three years. The committee staff made photocopies of the bills and returned them. *(Details, p. 173)*

Milk Decision Tape. Justice Department officials revealed that they had obtained a White House tape of a March 23, 1971, conversation between Nixon and his top aides at which price supports for the milk industry reportedly were discussed. The officials said they would turn the tape and 69 related documents over to U.S. District Court Judge William B. Jones, who was hearing arguments in a civil suit brought by consumer advocate Ralph Nader accusing the government of granting favors to the dairy industry in return for campaign contributions. The judge was to rule on the validity of White House claims of executive privilege over the tape and documents. The officials said special prosecutor Leon Jaworski also would be given access to the tape.

DEC. 5

Tapes Hearing. Alexander M. Haig, the President's chief of staff, testified at a court hearing on the subpoenaed White House tapes that Nixon was "almost incredulous" when he was told Nov. 15 of the 18-minute erasure in one of the tapes. Rose Mary Woods, the President's personal secretary, returned to the witness stand to answer more questions on her involvement in the erasure. *(Details, p. 172; earlier Woods testimony, p. 162)*

Haldeman Influence. White House deputy press secretary Gerald L. Warren was asked whether H. R. Haldeman, Nixon's chief of staff until April 30, still retained any influence at the White House. Warren said Nixon had talked on the phone to Haldeman "very rarely" and that press secretary Ronald L. Ziegler had talked with him "four or five times." But Warren refused to say who controlled Haldeman's White House files.

Stennis on Tapes. *The Washington Post* reported that Sen. John C. Stennis (D Miss.) said he never had agreed to the unsuccessful White House tapes proposal announced Oct. 19, in which he was to participate. Nixon had said Stennis consented to prepare a summary of the subpoenaed tapes, and that the summary would be submitted to the Senate investigating committee and the court. But the Post quoted Stennis as saying that "there was never any mention" of submitting the material to the court and that he thought he was to provide a verbatim transcript, not a summary, of all the Watergate-related conversations on the tapes.

Hughes Employee. Hughes attorney Chester C. Davis lost a bid in federal district court to have the Senate investigating committee question him in public instead of private immediately, but the judge scheduled a hearing Dec. 10 on Davis' claim that the committee should not be allowed to question him in private because of the threat of news leaks.

Nixon Bank Records. An official of the Key Biscayne, Fla., bank headed by Nixon friend Charles G. Rebozo said the bank would turn over Nixon's bank records to Dade County State Attorney Richard Gerstein. The official said the White House had approved the transaction. √

WATERGATE: AN INCONCLUSIVE REPORT ON GAP IN TAPE

It was a week of inconclusive action on the Watergate scandal. Congress set aside legislation for a court-appointed special prosecutor. A preliminary report on a taped presidential conversation produced no solid explanation of what might have caused an 18-minute gap in the tape.

Chief Judge John J. Sirica of U.S. District Court in Washington, D.C., announced from the bench the initial findings of a six-man panel of experts who had been examining the tape. These, he said, were the questions the court wanted the panel to answer:

• "Is this tape the original one that was recorded on June 20, 1972? Does it contain erasures or splices? Or is it a copy that has been edited by operations such as cutting and splicing before re-recording?

• "How was the 18-minute section of buzzing sounds produced? Was all the buzzing produced continuously at one time?

• "Can speech be detected under the buzzing? If so, to what extent can the speech be recaptured and made intelligible?"

It was feared that voices recorded during the missing segment might be beyond retrieval. A final report, Sirica said, would not be made until early in 1974.

Among the other Watergate developments during the week ended Dec. 15:

• President Nixon's "Operation Candor" seemed to be paying off with improved ratings in public-opinion polls. *(Box, p. 180)*

• As part of that operation, the President made an unprecedented, comprehensive disclosure of his personal finances. *(p. 181)*

• Watergate special prosecutor Leon Jaworski said the White House had given him "significant" numbers of unsubpoenaed tapes. And the White House said it hoped to release several reports on related matters before Christmas. *(p. 177)*

Experts' Report on Tape

Contrary to White House assumptions, neither the lamp nor the electric typewriter on Rose Mary Woods' desk appeared, to expert ears, to have caused the 18-minute hum on the crucial White House tape recording. This was the conclusion of the interim report delivered to Sirica Dec. 13 by the panel of experts who had spent two weeks studying the tape on which the gap occurred during a conversation between Nixon and his former chief of staff, H. R. Haldeman. *(p. 167)*

Earlier in December, during hearings before Sirica, Woods, Nixon's long-time secretary, testified that she might have caused the hum, or part of it, by pressing the wrong button on the tape machine when a telephone call interrupted her work with the tapes. Special White House counsel J. Fred Buzhardt later told the court that he had nearly duplicated the hum found on the tape by pressing the "record" button on the machine while the high-

intensity lamp and the electric typewriter on Woods' desk were both turned on. The lamp, the machine and the typewriter had been taken to New York for use by the expert panel in their examination of the tape. *(p. 168, 160)*

The experts reported that tests conducted with sophisticated instruments had failed to produce the conclusion that either the light or the typewriter, or both, were the source of the hum. They said that they had not yet ruled out the possibility that the recorder itself might have caused the gap and the hum. If so, they said, it probably would be impossible to recover the conversation through "signal enhancement," a method usable if a conversation has merely been covered up by another sound.

Special Prosecutor Legislation

With confidence growing in Watergate special prosecutor Leon Jaworski's performance, leaders in both the House and the Senate postponed until 1974 floor action on bills to establish a special prosecutor independent of the executive branch. In case Jaworski's freedom from White House interference with his Watergate-related investigations subsequently was threatened, the measures were kept on the House and Senate calendars, ready for prompt action.

In postponing the measures, the leaders made clear they would act promptly to head off a repeat of President Nixon's Oct. 20 firing of former prosecutor Archibald Cox. After that action—which caused the resignation of former Attorney General Elliot L. Richardson and the dismissal of his deputy, William D. Ruckelshaus—Acting Attorney General Robert H. Bork appointed Jaworski as special prosecutor on Nov. 1. *(Cox dismissal, p. 69; Jaworski appointment, p. 111)*

With the special prosecutor bills on the calendar, Senate Majority Leader Mike Mansfield (D Mont.) maintained, Jaworski's independence "will be protected as Richardson attempted to protect Cox.... If there is another Saturday night massacre, the Senate has at its disposal a number of resolutions that can be taken up immediately." If necessary, Mansfield said, he would call the Senate back from adjournment to take up the issue.

Mansfield and Senate Minority Leader Hugh Scott (R Pa.) Dec. 11 announced their decision to postpone floor action that had been scheduled for Dec. 12 on a Judiciary Committee bill (S 2611) providing for a court-appointed special prosecutor. The House also canceled plans for a Dec. 12 debate on its Judiciary Committee bill (HR 11401) also calling for a court-appointed prosecutor. *(House committee action, p. 163)*

In the Senate, floor action on the special prosecutor bill was replaced by a three-hour debate Dec. 12 in which sponsors of alternative measures providing independence for the Watergate prosecution team protested the decision to delay. Terming the leadership's decision "a mistake," Birch Bayh (D Ind.), a sponsor of S 2611, said he had hoped the Senate would act on the bill "as an ounce of prevention."

Charles H. Percy (R Ill.), a sponsor of legislation (S 2616) allowing Congress to veto removal of a special prosecutor appointed by the President, argued that the Senate "at the very least should make clear where we are on this matter." Asked by Percy for assurances that the Judiciary Committee would protect the integrity of the Watergate investigation, Mansfield replied that "the Senate itself, collectively, should consider itself as the oversight committee" for Jaworski and his staff.

At Percy's prompting, Mansfield said that the Judiciary Committee in confirmation hearings would ask Sen. William B. Saxbe (R Ohio), the attorney general-designate, for assurances that he would consult the Senate before limiting the special prosecutor's authority or tenure. Mansfield also agreed with Percy's demand for assurances from Saxbe that "the cloak of national security will not be used to deprive the special prosecutor of having access to certain documents."

Percy invited the sponsors of other special prosecutor measures to discuss a possible compromise version that could be introduced Dec. 17. A last-minute compromise, however, seemed unlikely, because Mansfield insisted that no time to take it up remained before Congress adjourned.

Week's Watergate Chronology

Following is a day-to-day chronology of the week's events in the Watergate case:

DEC. 6

Tapes Hearing. Alexander M. Haig Jr., the President's chief of staff, told U.S. District Judge John J. Sirica that White House lawyers had considered the possibility that "some sinister force" had caused an 18-minute gap in a subpoenaed Watergate tape. Judge Sirica recessed his hearings on the handling of the tapes until a panel of electronics experts completed its examination of the one with the gap. *(p. 167)*

Gurney Defense. In a news conference televised throughout Florida, Sen. Edward J. Gurney (R Fla.), a member of the Senate Watergate investigating committee, defended himself against news reports that he authorized his aides to collect campaign contributions from real estate developers and home builders by promising to intercede in their favor with the Federal Housing Administration. Gurney conceded that he had been "careless and unobservant" in not discovering that one of his aides had collected a $100,000 fund in his name, but he denied that he knew of the collection or personally received any of the funds. Federal grand juries in Jacksonville and Miami were investigating the charges. *(Earlier statement, p. 126)*

Vesco Tape. Federal prosecutors announced that the White House had agreed to turn over to a federal judge a tape of a Feb. 28, 1973, conversation between Nixon and his former counsel, John W. Dean III. The tape had been requested by attorneys for former Attorney General John N. Mitchell and former Commerce Secretary Maurice H. Stans. The former Nixon officials

were scheduled to go on trial Jan. 9, 1974, in New York City on charges of perjury and obstruction of justice in connection with a $200,000 campaign contribution from financier Robert L. Vesco. Dean testified before the Senate Watergate investigating committee that he and Nixon discussed Vesco's affairs on Feb. 28. The judge was to examine the tape in private to determine whether it could be used as evidence for the defense.

DEC. 7

Chapin Plea. Nixon's former appointments secretary, Dwight L. Chapin, appeared in U.S. District Court in Washington, D.C., and pleaded not guilty to four counts of making false statements before a grand jury about his knowledge of political sabotage activities carried out against Democrats in 1972. *(Indictment, p. 160)*

Vesco Extradition. A court in Nassau, Bahamas, rejected a Justice Department attempt to extradite financier Robert L. Vesco to the United States, where he would face criminal charges in a number of cases. Watergate prosecutors and Senate committee investigators also reportedly were interested in questioning Vesco. *(Details, p. 165)*

Proxmire vs. Bork. Sen. William Proxmire (D Wis.) filed suit in U.S. District Court in Washington, D.C., challenging the legality of Robert H. Bork's continuance as acting attorney general beyond the 30 days legally allowed for temporary heads of executive departments. The Justice Department claimed it was exempt from the 30-day rule. Bork became acting attorney general Oct. 20. *(p. 69; Bork profile, p. 77)*

DEC. 8

Nixon Financial Report. Nixon made public a series of documents on his personal financial dealings, including his federal income tax returns for 1969-1972. He asked the Joint Committee on Internal Revenue Taxation to rule on whether he owed additional taxes and promised to abide by the committee's judgement. *(Details, p. 181)*

DEC. 10

White House Tapes. Special prosecutor Leon Jaworski issued a statement saying he had received from the White House a "significant" number of unsubpoenaed tapes. They were thought to concern the Watergate case as well as political contributions from dairy interests and the settlement of an antitrust suit against the International Telephone and Telegraph Corporation (ITT). Jaworski also received from Judge Sirica two of the seven subpoenaed Watergate tapes, covering conversations among Nixon, Dean and other aides on March 13 and 22. *(Details, p. 168)*

More Reports. Deputy White House press secretary Gerald L. Warren said the President hoped to make public before Christmas a series of reports on the ITT case, dairy contributions and the "plumbers" operation.

New Break-in Theory. A transcript of a Dec. 4 executive session of the Senate Watergate investigating committee, filed in U.S. District Court in Washington,

(Continued on p. 180)

'Operation Candor': Still Considerable Confusion...

"Operation Candor," President Nixon's campaign to clear up confusion about his role in the Watergate and other alleged scandals, had raised new questions and left many of the old ones unanswered one month after its initiation in early November.

Tapes

In a television appearance Nov. 17, Nixon told a group of newspaper editors that he hoped there would be some way to make public "the substance" of the subpoenaed White House tapes. That, he said, would prove he did not know about the Watergate break-in or coverup.

But nothing seemed to be preventing the President from releasing his transcripts of the taped conversations, as his remark implied. U.S. District Judge John J. Sirica, who had jurisdiction over the tapes, said Nov. 14 that Nixon was free to "waive any privilege and make tapes or other materials public" whenever he wished. *(p. 132)*

Also at the Nov. 17 question-and-answer session at Disney World, Fla., Nixon said he "voluntarily waived privilege with regard to turning over the tapes." He had not surrendered the tapes, however, until two federal courts ordered him to do so.

Nonexistent Tapes. Why, the President was asked during the session, did his spokesmen wait so long to tell Judge Sirica that two of the nine tapes subpoenaed by the special prosecutor might not exist? Nixon replied that he was informed of the possibility on Sept. 29 or 30 and that the tapes' absence was definitely determined Oct. 26 after a thorough search.

Nixon did not explain why his legal adviser, Charles Alan Wright, who told Sirica Oct. 23 that the President would "comply in all respects" with the subpoena, had not been kept informed of those developments. Wright later said he did not learn that the two tapes could not be found until Oct. 31, when it was announced in open court.

Tape Gap. The 18-minute gap discovered in one of the subpoenaed tapes, and conflicting explanations of it offered by White House aides and attorneys in Sirica's court, were other murky areas.

White House counsel J. Fred Buzhardt publicly announced Nov. 21 that a gap existed in a subpoenaed June 20, 1972, tape. The revelation came only a day after Nixon had assured a group of Republican governors in Memphis, Tenn., that he knew of no "bombshells" still to explode in the Watergate case.

The part of the tape obliterated by a humming sound covered a discussion on Watergate between Nixon and his then chief of staff, H.R. Haldeman. According to Haldeman's notes of the talk, Nixon instructed him to begin a public relations effort to offset the effects of the Watergate break-in three days earlier. It was the only discussion on the tape that touched on the Watergate case.

White House attorneys suggested, in a statement filed with the court Nov. 26, that the gap had been caused accidentally by Rose Mary Woods, the President's personal secretary, while she was transcribing the tape on Oct. 1. In testimony the same day, Woods apologized to Judge Sirica for not mentioning her "terrible mistake" Nov. 8, when she first testified on the handling of the tapes. *(p. 162)*

Woods later modified her testimony to say that she might have caused only about five minutes of the gap while taking a phone call. Buzhardt conceded Nov. 29 that his original Nov. 26 explanation for the erasure was "not a certainty at all," but "just a possibility."

Alexander M. Haig Jr., the President's chief of staff, told Sirica Dec. 6 that he and others at the White House had theorized that the gap might have been created by some mysterious "sinister forces." Outside the court, Haig suggested the more mundane possibility that Woods had misjudged the length of her phone call. *(p. 167)*

When the hearings recessed Dec. 7 to await the judgment of technical experts examining the tape, the White House had come up with no explanation for the 18-minute gap. A preliminary report by the experts to Sirica Dec. 13 indicated that the gap probably was not caused by Woods.

Woods testified that she told the President of her Oct. 1 mistake on the tape immediately, and that he shrugged it off, saying the Haldeman conversation was not included in the subpoena. The White House statement of Nov. 26 said Buzhardt was informed of the erasure "shortly thereafter."

Buzhardt said he and another White House attorney played the tape Nov. 14 and realized for the first time that the gap lasted 18 and not five minutes. It was also then, he said, that he realized for the first time that the subpoena did cover the partially obliterated conversation. Buzhardt said Nixon was informed of this new information right away. The next day, when Haldeman's notes mentioning the public relations offensive turned up, the President was told of them also, Buzhardt testified.

The puzzle remained: Why did Buzhardt wait for more than a month to assess the extent of damage supposedly done to the tape by Woods on Oct. 1 and to inform the court about it? And why were he and Nixon unclear in October on the details of a subpoena issued by the special prosecutor in July? *(Subpoena details, p. 170)*

Campaign Financing

In the 1972 presidential election, Nixon told the newspaper editors, "Neither party was without fault with regard to the financing. They (the Democrats) raised $36-million, and some of that, like some of ours, came from corporate sources and was illegal, because the law had been changed, and apparently people didn't know it."

By the time Nixon said that, six corporations had been fined in federal court for making illegal contributions to his campaign. In contrast, the special prosecutor had disclosed no such illegal contributions to the McGovern campaign. A law prohibiting corporate gifts in federal campaigns was first passed in 1907, and the restriction had never been lifted.

Milk Deal. Throughout the first month of "Operation Candor," Nixon did not defuse charges that his 1972 campaign officials and others had solicited illegal corporate contributions with the promise of favorable government treatment or the threat to withhold favors. One of the most publicized cases was the alleged "milk deal," in which the administration had been accused of receiving more than $400,000 in contributions from three milk cooperatives in return for raising price supports paid to milk producers.

Nixon and some of his top aides met with representatives of the dairy industry on March 23, 1971. They reportedly discussed the price support issue at another meeting among themselves later the same day. Two days later, the administration reversed its policy and announced a large increase in milk price supports.

In his Nov. 17 briefing, Nixon denied that the decision represented a "quid pro quo" for a campaign contribution. The real reason behind it, he said, was that "Congress put a gun to our head" in the form of a petition demanding the increase, signed by 102 members, mostly Democrats.

Nixon said his advisers warned him that if he did not act, Congress would pass legislation raising the support payments even higher, and that Congress would override a veto. Some Senators expressed skepticism that the President would capitulate so readily on that matter, when his usual policy had been to veto, with little fear of an override, any legislation he thought inflationary.

ITT Case. Another alleged case of quid pro quo involved a favorable out-of-court settlement of an antitrust suit against the International Telephone and Telegraph Corporation (ITT), reportedly arranged after the company pledged at least $100,000 to the Nixon re-election campaign.

A White House statement confirmed Oct. 30 that Nixon had ordered then Deputy Attorney General Richard G. Kleindienst in April 1971 to delay appealing the suit—but denied that the action was politically motivated. Kleindienst never mentioned the call from Nixon during extensive questioning on the matter by the Senate Judiciary Committee in 1972, and the call was not acknowledged by the White House until a newspaper wrote about it in October. (Details, p. 102)

Nixon's role in the ITT settlement was also brought into question by an internal White House memo, released Aug. 1 by the Senate Watergate committee, warning of the existence of documents that could "directly involve the President" in the case. (Memo text, Vol. I, p. 168; Dairy and ITT tapes, p. 168)

Hughes-Rebozo Transaction. Nixon's close friend, Charles G. Rebozo, received $100,000 in cash from billionaire Howard Hughes in two installments in 1969 and 1970. The money was returned in June 1973. Nixon and Rebozo said it was intended as a 1972 campaign contribution but eventually was returned because of an internal dispute at the Hughes company that might have made the gift embarrassing to acknowledge.

Two former Hughes aides had submitted court depositions with differing versions of the contribution, one of them alleging that part of it was given in exchange for Justice Department approval of a proposed Hughes acquisition.

"If this was a campaign contribution," Nixon was asked at a press conference Oct. 26, "who authorized Mr. Rebozo to collect campaign contributions for your re-election or for the Republican Party?" Nixon answered that a finance chairman for his campaign had not been appointed when Rebozo first received the gift, and that the internal dispute had erupted by the time the chairman took office.

Nixon said Rebozo showed "very good judgment" in the matter, but did not explain why his friend kept the cash in a strongbox so long before returning it to Hughes. (News conference, p. 112; Hughes employees' testimony, p. 173)

National Security Issue

The President's definition of national security—a doctrine he had invoked to justify a number of his actions—remained unclear. His former top aides, H. R. Haldeman and John D. Ehrlichman, had testified before the Senate Watergate committee that the President was justified in ordering illegal activities to protect national security.

Nixon did not answer a Nov. 17 question on whether he had discussed the legality or illegality of plans by the White House "plumbers" unit to gather information on Pentagon Papers defendant Daniel Ellsberg. He said only that he had not authorized the 1971 break-in at the office of Ellsberg's psychiatrist—and that the plumbers were set up to prevent "leaks which were seriously damaging to the national security." Nixon also said he had blocked an earlier investigation of the plumbers because it might have jeopardized sensitive national security matters.

Wire Taps. Nixon confirmed Nov. 17 that the Secret Service had maintained a surveillance of his brother, F. Donald Nixon, "for security reasons." He did not explain those reasons, beyond indicating there was concern that people "who might be in a foreign country" might attempt "to use improper influence." Nixon did not say what legal authority the Secret Service acted on in conducting the surveillance.

There were also unanswered questions about wiretaps of 13 government officials and four newsmen conducted by the administration from 1969 to 1971, supposedly in order to find the sources of national security news leaks.

D.C., in connection with a law suit by employees of billionaire Howard Hughes to prohibit the committee from questioning them in closed sessions, revealed a new theory on the motivation for the Watergate break-in. The transcript, inadvertently released to reporters, indicted that the committee was considering the possibility that the burglars were seeking information on what former Democratic National Chairman Lawrence F. O'Brien, who was once a partner in an advertising agency that represented the Hughes Tool Company, knew about Hughes' relationship with Nixon and his brothers. Chief counsel Samuel Dash insisted the idea was just "one of a number of theories" about the break-in. O'Brien issued a statement saying he had no information that the burglars would have wanted.

DEC. 11

Tax Ruling. U.S. District Judge Charles R. Richey, ruling that the Center for Corporate Responsibility should be granted tax-exempt status which it had been denied earlier, declared that four White House documents related to the case "demonstrated that the White House staff did in fact consider using the Internal Revenue Service (IRS) against their enemies." Although he found no specific evidence of political pressure in the case, Richey expressed concern with "the creation of a political atmosphere generated by the White House in the Internal Revenue Service which may have affected the objectivity of their participation in the ruling in the plaintiff's case." *(Earlier development, p. 165)*

Special Prosecutor Bill. Senate Democratic leaders decided to delay indefinitely action on a bill to grant the courts power to appoint a special Watergate prosecutor. The move was viewed as an expression of confidence in Leon Jaworski, the special prosecutor appointed by the President. The bill was to be placed on the calendar, ready to be called up in case the President began interfering with Jaworski's actions. *(Details, p. 176)*

Weicker on Nixon Taxes. Sen. Lowell P. Weicker Jr. (R Conn.) held a news conference to present a detailed statement questioning whether Nixon was legally entitled to deduct from his income taxes the value of his vice presidential papers. *(Details, p. 182)*

DEC. 12

White House Documents. Watergate special prosecutor Leon Jaworski disclosed that the White House had agreed to allow his investigators to search its files for documents pertaining to their investigations. The arrangement, confirmed by a White House spokesman, had been denied to former special prosecutor Archibald Cox, who was fired Oct. 20. Jaworski also received from Judge Sirica two more of the seven subpoenaed Watergate tapes.

Saxbe on Special Prosecutor. Attorney General-designate William B. Saxbe assured the Senate Judiciary Committee during hearings on his confirmation that he would "vigorously support" the special prosecutor's efforts to determine if any "high crimes and misdemeanors" were committed by the President.

Nixon Tax Investigation. The Joint Committee on Internal Revenue Taxation met for two hours in executive session and decided that it would not limit its investigation of Nixon's tax returns to the two areas on which he had asked for a ruling, but would examine every aspect of his returns for 1969-1972. *(Box on committee, p. 181)*

Ford on Impeachment. At a breakfast with reporters, Vice President Gerald R. Ford urged the House Judiciary Committee to expedite its investigation of possible impeachment charges against the President and bring the matter to a vote "in three to four months at the most." Committee Chairman Peter W. Rodino (D N.J.) said later that he doubted it would be possible to meet Ford's April target date, but denied that Democrats on the panel were delaying the proceedings for partisan advantage.

Mitchell Dairy Case. News reports said the Senate Watergate investigating committee and a Senate Judiciary subcommittee were looking into allegations from the Justice Department that former Attorney General John N. Mitchell had blocked a criminal antitrust investigation of a dairy cooperative that donated $202,000 to Nixon's re-election campaign. Mitchell's lawyer said his client could not recall the case.

DEC. 13

Tapes Experts Report. Electronics experts who had been examining the June 20, 1972, subpoenaed White House tape containing the 18-minute gap gave Judge Sirica a preliminary report on their findings. They concluded that it was unlikely that Rose Mary Woods, Nixon's personal secretary, had caused the gap while transcribing the tape, and also that the gap was "probably not retrievable." *(Details, p. 176)* √

Poll Report

President Nixon's popularity gained several percentage points in both the Gallup Poll and the Harris Survey, at least partly as a result of his counter-attack on his critics in the Watergate scandal. Both polls were published Dec. 13. *(Earlier poll report, p. 164)*

It was the first time since February that Nixon's ratings had climbed in the two polls.

Gallup. Interviewing of 1,550 adults for the Gallup Poll was done Nov. 30-Dec. 3, after disclosures of two nonexistent tape recordings and an 18-minute gap in one subpoenaed tape. The question was, "Do you approve or disapprove of the way Nixon is handling the job as President?"

	Latest	Nov. 2-5
Approve	31%	27%
Disapprove	59	63
No opinion	10	10

Harris. The Harris Survey was conducted Nov. 13-16, after reports of the missing tapes but before the gap was discovered. Of those questioned, 37 per cent rated the President's performance as "good" or "excellent," compared with 32 per cent in October.

NIXON'S FINANCES: TRIPLED ASSETS DURING FIRST TERM

In a financial disclosure apparently without historical precedent, the White House Dec. 8 released 50 documents revealing details of President Nixon's personal finances during his term in office. Release of the information, along with a pledge that Nixon would give his San Clemente, Calif., home to the government after he and Mrs. Nixon died, was the latest move in the President's campaign to restore credibility in his administration. *(Earlier story, p. 169)*

The papers, including summaries of Nixon's tax returns for 1969 through 1972, showed that Nixon's net assets had increased from $307,141 on Jan. 1, 1969, to $988,522 on May 31, 1973. They also revealed that the President paid $78,651.10 in federal income taxes during the four-year period—$72,682.09 in 1969; $792.81 in 1970; $878.03 in 1971, and $4,298.17 in 1972. Reporters were allowed to verify the summaries of Nixon's tax returns against copies of the actual returns.

Committee Verification. The President asked the Joint Committee on Internal Revenue Taxation to rule on two tax items that the Internal Revenue Service already had allowed. The committee was to decide whether Nixon should pay a capital gains tax on the sale of land adjoining San Clemente and whether Nixon had acted properly in claiming a $576,000 deduction for the gift of his vice presidential papers to the United States.

Nixon promised to follow the committee's recommendations and to pay whatever amount in additional taxes it called for. Officials estimated that the President could be subject to as much as $299,000, excluding interest, in extra taxes.

Meeting in closed session Dec. 12, the committee formally agreed to review Nixon's tax returns, but not to limit the review to the two issues the President designated.

"We think it perhaps was intended by him to look at all aspects," committee chairman Rep. Wilbur D. Mills (D Ark.) told reporters. "He probably listed the two because they were mentioned prominently by the news media."

Mills directed the staff of the committee to begin work immediately to review Nixon's returns for 1969 through 1972. He said a decision whether or not to have public hearings could not yet be made.

Release of the documents came after 3-1/2 weeks of intensive preparation by a team of two tax lawyers, four White House aides and an accountant. Nixon had declared his innocence of fiscal wrongdoing during his Nov. 17 appearance at a conference of the Associated Press Managing Editors Association in Florida. *(Text, p. 150)*

Highlights of the disclosures included:

Real Estate Transactions

Nixon reported proceeds of $771,396 from three sales of real estate.

Fisher's Island Inc. The President sold 185,891 shares of stock in Fisher's Island, a Biscayne Bay, Fla., development firm, on May 22, 1969, for $371,782. His 1969 federal income tax return showed a capital gain from that sale of $184,891 and tax paid on that amount.

Weicker Charges on Nixon Papers

The Internal Revenue Service (IRS) should take a fresh look at irregularities in President Nixon's large income tax deductions for a gift of pre-presidential papers to the government in 1969, Sen. Lowell P. Weicker Jr. (R Conn.) said Dec. 11. The papers, involving $576,000 in deductions saved Nixon $235,000 in taxes during his first term.

Weicker, a member of the Senate Watergate committee, wrote IRS Commissioner Donald C. Alexander that he questioned the thoroughness of the agency's review of Nixon's 1971 and 1972 tax returns. His own investigation revealed, Weicker said, that neither the General Services Administration, recipient of the gift for the National Archives, nor the appraiser of the gift, Ralph Newman of Chicago, had ever been contacted about the matter.

Nixon, in his financial disclosure statement Dec. 8, conceded that experts disagreed on the deduction's validity and suggested that the matter be examined by the Joint Congressional Committee on Internal Revenue Taxation.

Weicker said that the IRS should decide the issue.

Key Questions. For the deduction to be valid, Weicker said that Nixon would have had to donate the papers before July 25, 1969, the date a 1969 law repealed such gifts as deductible items.

The senator suggested in an 11-page brief that no gift existed legally before the deadline, because the papers to be donated had no separate identity. On March 26 and 27, 1969, Nixon transferred 1,217 cubic feet of papers to the National Archives. Only 392 cubic feet of papers eventually constituted the gift, a determination not made until December 1969—several months after the deadline.

Contradictions. In his disclosure statement, Nixon said Newman had designated the papers to be donated in April 1969. However, according to Weicker, Newman told him that he did nothing then but look at many boxes of papers for about 10 minutes and place a "ballpark" appraisal of $500,-000 on them.

Questions About Deed. A deed transferring the papers to the government was not valid, Weicker asserted, because it was never delivered, never executed by Nixon and never accepted by the General Services Administration or the National Archives.

Frank DeMarco, the President's tax attorney, had stamped his notary seal on the deed certifying that it had been prepared by Edward L. Morgan, a presidential lawyer, on March 27, 1969, an important date in establishing that the gift was made before the July 25 deadline. However, there was no proof of the date DeMarco notarized the document. The deed was not delivered to the National Archives until April 10, 1970.

Apartment. Nixon sold his New York City apartment on May 31, 1969, for $312,500, for a profit of $142,912. Capital gains tax was deferred because of Nixon's subsequent purchase of his house in California.

Florida Land. In a joint venture with his daughter, Tricia, who had received funds from a trust set up for her as a child by a family friend, Nixon on Dec. 28, 1972, sold two undeveloped lots in Florida for $150,000. The total profit was $111,270. The White House said the documents disputed claims that Nixon tried to shield his daughter from income taxes she owed on this sale.

Key Biscayne Houses. Nixon bought two neighboring houses in Key Biscayne on Dec. 19, 1968, for a total of $253,455. After a refinancing of the mortgages and as a result of monthly payments, Nixon had by May 31, 1973, reduced the total balance of his mortgages on both properties to about $161,000. He had also paid $76,421 from his personal funds for improvements, including furniture and remodeling.

San Clemente. Although the Nixons wanted to buy only 5.9 acres of a 26-acre tract for their California residence, the sellers insisted that they buy the entire parcel of land. Nixon set up a trust and borrowed $450,000 from his friend, Robert Abplanalp, the owner of the Precision Valve Company of Yonkers, N.Y., to finance the down payment. The trust bought the property July 15, 1969, for $1,400,100. Abplanalp made a second loan to Nixon of $175,000 to finance the initial mortgage payment. The Nixons sold all but the 5.9 acres they had originally wanted to Abplanalp and another close Nixon friend, Charles G. Rebozo, on Dec. 15, 1970, for $1,249,000.

Taxes

Local Income Taxes. The Nixons did not pay California income tax, because California tax officials had ruled that Nixon's principal residence was in Washington, press secretary Ronald L. Ziegler said at a news briefing Dec. 8. White House lawyer Kenneth Gemmill added that Nixon did not have to pay taxes in the District of Columbia, either, since D.C. law excludes from taxation all elected federal officials.

Tax Preparation. The President retained the law firm of Kalmbach, DeMarco, Knapp & Chillingworth of Los Angeles and Newport Beach, Calif., for tax advice. The firm in turn hired Arthur Blech & Company, certified public accountants in Los Angeles, to maintain Nixon's financial books and records and to help prepare his tax returns. In 1973, the Internal Revenue Service (IRS) audited the Nixons' returns for 1971 and 1972, including a review of his 1970 San Clemente sale and the gift of his vice presidential papers in 1969. In a letter to Nixon on June 1, 1973, the IRS district director in Baltimore wrote, "Our examination of your income tax returns for the years 1971 and 1972 revealed that they are correct. Accordingly, these returns are accepted as filed...."

Papers Gift. The White House claimed that the President on March 27, 1969, had crates containing papers and memorabilia of his career, including his vice presidential papers, delivered to the National Archives as a gift to the American people. Documents appraiser Ralph Newman appraised the fair market value of the papers at $576,000, part of which Nixon had deducted from his income tax returns for 1969 through 1972.

Although the statement released by the White House did not mention it, critics of the papers gift said Newman's final valuation of the papers did not come until Dec. 8, 1969—more than four months after the date Congress had set for repeal of the law permitting a tax deduction for a donation of private papers.

San Clemente Tax. According to tax accountant Blech, Nixon realized no profit from his 1970 sale of most of his San Clemente property to Rebozo and Abplanalp, and thus he paid no capital gains tax. However, the White House statement noted, another accounting firm, Coopers & Lybrand, which audited the transaction, concluded that Nixon had gained $117,370 from the sale and thus was subject to tax.

According to the White House, even if a $117,370 gain had been reported on Nixon's 1970 tax return, no tax would have been payable that year, because the President's declared deductions exceeded his income by $44,239, and he could have taken more of a deduction for his papers gift than he did that year. ✓

THREAT OF RENEWED LEGAL DISPUTE OVER SUBPOENAS

A bill became law against President Nixon's wishes, enabling the Senate Watergate investigating committee to subpoena hundreds of White House documents and raising anew the prospects of a legal dispute over executive privilege.

The much-argued executive privilege doctrine received a boost in U.S. District Court in Washington, D.C., when Chief Judge John J. Sirica ruled that the Watergate grand jury had no business listening to most of three tapes of presidential conversations. *(Details, below)*

A target date of April 1974 was approved for completion of a House Judiciary Committee investigation of

presidential impeachment. A special counsel was appointed to direct the investigation. *(Box, this page)*

Subpoenas. The President on Dec. 17 allowed S 2641, a bill giving Sirica's court jurisdiction over Watergate subpoenas, to become law without his signature. Sirica, arguing that his court lacked jurisdiction in the case, on Oct. 17 had dismissed the committee's request for him to enforce its subpoenas of presidential records. *(p. 60)*

Nixon, explaining that a veto under the circumstances would be misunderstood by the public, called the bill bad legislation. "The intent of this legislation is to circumvent the established judicial processes by making the court a vehicle for congressional actions not envisaged in the Constitution," he said.

At issue when the tapes and other materials were sought was the doctrine of executive privilege, which the White House claimed in its arguments before the court. Although this position had been reversed Oct. 23 when the White House agreed to give certain tapes to the Watergate special prosecutor, there was no assurance that the doctrine would not again become an issue in relation to Watergate committee access to presidential documents.

On Dec. 18, the Senate select committee voted unanimously to subpoena the materials. The next day, subpoenas for nearly 500 tape recordings and other documents were served on J. Fred Buzhardt Jr., the White House attorney in charge of the Watergate legal team. Whether or not the White House would comply with the subpoenas was not immediately known.

Executive Privilege Ruling

Judge Sirica Dec. 19 upheld White House claims of executive privilege for most of three presidential tapes, agreeing with the White House analysis that most of the recorded conversations on the subpoenaed tapes were not relevant to the Watergate inquiry. The tapes would not, therefore, be turned over to the Watergate grand jury. Sirica made this determination after listening to the tapes.

The White House had surrendered the tapes and the claims of privilege to Sirica Nov. 26. In his Dec. 19 ruling, Sirica held:

• That all of the June 20, 1972, conversations between the President and John D. Ehrlichman, and later between the President and H.R. Haldeman, were properly covered by the claim of privilege, except the 39-minute segment that included the 18-minute hum. *(p. 160)*

• That most of the long luncheon conversation of June 30, 1972, among Nixon, Haldeman and John N. Mitchell was not relevant and was properly protected by executive privilege, except for two brief segments of the conversation that should be turned over to the special prosecutor for possible presentation to the grand jury.

Impeachment Investigation Counsel

Former Assistant Attorney General John M. Doar, who served in the Justice Department during the Eisenhower, Kennedy and Johnson administrations, was named Dec. 20 as special counsel to the House Judiciary Committee. Doar's assignment was to direct the staff investigating and assembling evidence concerning possible charges of impeachment against President Nixon.

Doar's appointment was announced at a press conference by Judiciary Committee Chairman Peter W. Rodino Jr. (D N.J.), who had selected the counsel. Rodino said that he, exercising the traditional powers of the chairman to hire staff, had selected Doar without seeking approval from the committee. He did say that he had advised the ranking minority member of the committee, Edward Hutchinson (R Mich.), of his choice on Dec. 19. Rodino emphasized that he expected Doar to serve the committee, not only its majority members.

Doar, 52, a graduate of Princeton University and the University of California Law School, came to Washington in 1960 as assistant to the assistant attorney general for civil rights. He continued in that post until 1965, when he became assistant attorney general for civil rights.

After his departure from government service in 1967, Doar served as president of the Bedford Stuyvesant Development and Services Corporation, a nonprofit organization devoted to rebuilding part of central Brooklyn, N.Y. He had served as president of the New York City School Board in 1968-69.

Doar said that his background was Republican, but that he had been registered as an independent in New York during his work with Bedford-Stuyvesant, an organization which received large amounts of federal funds. Doar resigned his post with the corporation the week before he accepted the post of special counsel.

• That the final 17 minutes of the Sept. 15, 1972, conversation among Nixon, John W. Dean III and Haldeman were not relevant and were properly covered by the claim of privilege, but that the intial 33 minutes were relevant and should be turned over to the grand jury. *(p. 161)*

Week's Watergate Chronology

DEC. 14

Ervin, Weicker Tax Returns. Senators Sam J. Ervin Jr. (D N.C.) and Lowell P. Weicker Jr. (R Conn.) of the Senate Watergate investigating committee submitted their 1972 federal income tax returns for publication in the *Congressional Record.* Speaking on the Senate floor, they said they were acting in response to a news report that some White House aides were urging the President to counterattack on the finances issue by demanding Ervin and Weicker to make financial disclosures. *(Nixon tax details, p. 181)*

DEC. 17

Committee Suit. Nixon allowed a bill granting U.S. District Court in Washington, D.C., jurisdiction over a Senate Watergate investigating committee subpoena of White House tapes and documents to become law at midnight Dec. 17 without his signature. *(Details, p. 183; bill passage, p. 173)*

Goldwater on Nixon. In an interview published in *The Christian Science Monitor,* Sen. Barry Goldwater (R Ariz.), said he thought "only time is going to tell" whether Nixon would recover from the Watergate scandal. *(Box, next column)*

Papers Donations. Scripps-Howard news service reported that, based on a General Services Administration list of public officials who had contributed their personal papers to the government in the last 10 years, "a surprisingly large number of prominent and even middle-echelon officials in the last five administrations donated their papers on which they could have claimed tax deductions from 1963 through the first six months of 1969 when the law was changed." *(Nixon papers issue, p. 182)*

DEC. 18

Senate Committee Subpoenas. The Senate Watergate investigating committee voted unanimously to serve subpoenas on White House attorneys calling for tapes relating to the Watergate break-in and coverup and documents on campaign financing matters. The subpoenas covered materials never before requested by the committee. The committee was planning to seek enforcement of its original July 23 subpoena of tapes and documents, which was rejected Oct. 17 on grounds that the court lacked jurisdiction. *(Details, p. 183)*

DEC. 19

Tapes Ruling. Judge Sirica ruled that nearly all of two subpoenaed White House tapes and part of

Goldwater on Nixon

President Nixon missed his chance to set the record straight with the American people, leaving doubts about his honesty and ability to govern, Sen. Barry Goldwater (R Ariz.) said in an interview published in *The Christian Science Monitor* Dec. 17.

Goldwater, his party's presidential candidate in 1964 and a leading spokesmen for Republican conservatives, said he had advised the President in April to cooperate fully with the Senate Watergate investigating committee. "I think Watergate would have been history by now and Mr. Nixon would be way back up on the popularity poll by now, but he didn't do that," said Goldwater. "He chose to dibble and dabble and argue on very nebulous grounds like executive privilege and confidentiality, when all the American people wanted to know was the truth.

"....I think that only time is going to tell whether or not Mr. Nixon can climb back up that ladder. And I would say that he can't say this morning whether or not he's even started back up it."

Goldwater was asked if Watergate would impede Nixon in governing the nation for the next three years. "I don't think it's Watergate, frankly, as much as it's just a question in people's minds of just how honest is this man," he answered. "I hate to think of the adage, 'Would you buy a used car from Dick Nixon?' But that's what people are asking around the country."

Goldwater made these remarks on other aspects of the Nixon presidency:

Nixon's advisers: ".... I've never known a man to be such a loner in any field...business, profession, politics, or what...I can't sit here and tell you who his advisers are. I know that Mel Laird has quit mainly because the President won't listen to him. Bryce Harlow is reportedly quitting for the same reason.... Now I can't believe...that Nixon would listen to Gen. Haig on political matters when Gen. Haig doesn't know anything about political matters.... I just can't believe he would listen to Ziegler. That, in my opinion, would be something disastrous. Again, there is nothing personal, but Ziegler doesn't understand politics."

Impeachment: ".... I think the people who are yelling for impeachment should shut up or put up, one of the two. Let's stop talking about it.... I think it's incumbent on the leadership of the House to get it done. They're not playing around with the Republican Party and the Democratic Party— they're playing around with the American people."

"Operation Candor": "....I think it started to work, but I think that 18-minute lapse in the tape knocked it all out. Now if I were the President, I would quit making speeches, but have a weekly press conference and iron the whole thing out, not just on Watergate or his tax problems and all that. But he should get on to the problems that face the American people."

a third would not be turned over to the special Watergate prosecutor, because they contained nothing related to Watergate. The ruling sustained, with a few exceptions, the description of the tapes and claims of executive privilege Nixon's attorneys had filed with the court Nov. 26. The Watergate special prosecution force released a statement agreeing to the judge's findings. *(White House tapes analysis, p. 161)*

Committee Subpoenas. Attorneys for the Senate Watergate investigating committee delivered to the White House three subpoenas covering almost 500 presidential tape recordings and other documents related to a broad range of administration activities.

Milk Tape. U.S. District Judge William B. Jones agreed to a Justice Department request to temporarily seal all subpoenaed documents and tapes related to a civil suit brought by consumer advocate Ralph Nader against the Nixon administration for alleged favors to the milk industry. Jones acted after a Nader attorney, William A. Dobrovir, admitted in court that he had played one of the tapes at a party. Dobrovir apologized for what he called the "very foolish mistake." The tape he played contained a March 31, 1971, conversation between Nixon and dairy industry representatives, which White House attorneys had turned over in response to a subpoena. *(Milk case, p. 179)*

Rebozo Interview. Interviewed on CBS television, news, Nixon's close friend, Charles G. Rebozo, insisted that "there was no quid pro quo involved whatsoever" in a $100,000 contribution he accepted for Nixon's re-election campaign from a representative of billionaire Howard Hughes. *(Hughes money, p. 179)*

Ervin Retirement. Sen. Ervin announced that he would not seek re-election in 1974.

Carnation Donation. The Carnation Company and its board chairman, H. Everett Olson, pleaded guilty in U.S. District Court in Washington, D.C., to making illegal corporate contributions of $8,900 to 1972 Republican presidential and congressional campaigns. The company was fined $5,000, and Olson was fined $1,000. Carnation was the eighth corporation to be cited by the Watergate special prosecution force for making illegal contributions. *(Previous convictions, p. 179, 133)*

Impeachment Target Date. After meeting with an ad hoc subcommittee of the House Judiciary Committee, Chairman Peter W. Rodino Jr. (D N.J.) announced that he had set a target date of April for a completion of the committee's presidential impeachment inquiry. Republicans on the panel, who had been pressing for early resolution of the matter, approved of the plan.

Ziegler Testimony. White House press secretary Ronald L. Ziegler invoked executive privilege several times during secret testimony in the $6.4-million civil suit filed by the Democratic National Committee against Nixon and some of his campaign officials over the Watergate break-in. White House attorney J. Fred Buzhardt issued a statement saying that Nixon's May 22 pledge not to invoke executive privilege on matters of criminal conduct relating to the Watergate break-in or coverup applied to "official investigations into the Watergate matter," but not to the civil suit.

Poll Report

A minority of the persons questioned by the Gallup Poll said they thought President Nixon should be forced out of the White House. But a plurality in the Harris Survey said they would respect Nixon more if he resigned. *(Earlier poll report, p. 180)*

Gallup. For the Gallup Poll published Dec. 16, interviewers asked 1,550 adults Nov. 30-Dec. 3: "Do you think President Nixon should be impeached and compelled to leave the presidency, or not?"

	Latest	Nov. 2-5	June 22-25
Should	35%	37%	19%
Should not	54	54	69
No opinion	11	9	12

Gallup found that strong approval for the President had declined 11 percentage points between April and December, from 27 to 16. The question: "How strongly would you say you approve (disapprove)—very strongly or not so strongly?"

Strong approval	16%
Mild approval	15
No opinion	10
Mild disapproval	18
Strong disapproval	41

Harris. Harris interviewers surveyed 1,493 households Nov. 13-16 for a poll published Dec. 17, asking: "Would you respect President Nixon more or less if he resigned from the office of president to allow Gerald Ford to take over as president in an act of national unity?"

More	45%
Less	31
Not sure	24

DEC. 20

Impeachment Counsel. Rep. Peter W. Rodino Jr. (D N.J.), chairman of the House Judiciary Committee, announced the appointment of John M. Doar, a Republican civil rights lawyer, as chief counsel in the committee's investigation of impeachment charges against President Nixon. *(Details, box, p. 183)*

Goldwater Spying. *The Washington Post* reported it had learned that Watergate conspirator E. Howard Hunt Jr. had told Watergate committee investigators that he conducted surveillance of Sen. Barry Goldwater (R Ariz.) during Goldwater's 1964 presidential campaign on orders from Johnson.

Nixon Taxes. The Post reported that Nixon apparently underpaid his federal income taxes for 1969-1972 by more than $13,000 "because his returns were prepared in a manner described by the Internal Revenue Service and other tax authorities as improper under the law." √

WATERGATE: DENIALS OF EXTORTION OF MILK PRODUCERS

Following is a day-to-day chronology of the week's events in the Watergate case: *(Earlier Dec. 20 events, p. 185)*

DEC. 20

Tax Report. The Joint Committee on Internal Revenue Taxation released a report that included a list of 490 names given to the Internal Revenue Service (IRS) by former presidential counsel John W. Dean III with a request that the agency "see what type of information could be developed" about those named. But the committee said it found no evidence that any of the people on the list actually were harassed by the IRS. The 490 names were an addition to the original, 216-name "enemies list" Dean described to the Senate Watergate investigating committee in June. *(Vol. I, p. 151)*

DEC. 21

Goldwater Spying. Clarifying its story of the previous day, *The Washington Post* reported that the surveillance that Watergate conspirator and former CIA agent E. Howard Hunt Jr. had carried out against Sen. Barry Goldwater (R Ariz.) during his 1964 presidential campaign consisted of having a secretary pick up press releases, speeches and similar public material at Republican Party headquarters. *(Previous story, p. 185)*

Watergate Documents. U.S. District Judge John J. Sirica turned over to special prosecutor Leon Jaworski the remaining Watergate-related portions of the subpoenaed White House tapes and documents *(Earlier action, p. 183)*

Committee Subpoenas. Deputy White House press secretary Gerald L. Warren described the three subpoenas served on the White House Dec. 19 by the Senate Watergate committee as "incredible" and "extraordinary." Warren refused to predict the President's response to the committee's request for more than 500 tapes and documents related to Watergate and other administration activities. *(Subpoenas, p. 183)*

DEC. 26

Milk Suit. Two affidavits filed in U.S. District Court in San Antonio, Texas, in relation to the government's civil suit against the Associated Milk Producers Inc. were released. One, by Richard W. McLaren, former assistant attorney general in charge of the antitrust division, rebutted the cooperative's claim that government officials threatened it with an antitrust action in order to extort campaign contributions.

McLaren also disclosed that in 1971, then Attorney General John N. Mitchell twice rejected his recommendations that a federal grand jury be empaneled to investigate possible criminal antitrust actions by the dairy co-

Poll Report

A Harris Survey of public attitudes toward President Nixon uncovered a mixture of skepticism and confidence. The poll of 1,493 households was conducted Nov. 13-16 and published Dec. 24. *(Earlier poll report, p. 185)*

The sample agreed, 73 to 21 per cent, with the statement that Nixon "has lost so much credibility that it will be hard for him to be accepted as president again."

Forty-five per cent rejected the statement that Nixon "has reached the point where he can no longer be an effective president and should resign for the good of the country." But 44 per cent accepted the statement.

A large majority, 82 per cent, agreed that the President "is not afraid to take decisive action, as in his trips to Peking and Moscow and in his recent handling of the Middle East war." Twelve per cent disagreed.

operative, favoring instead a civil action. The other affidavit, filed by assistant Watergate special prosecutor Jon A. Sale, asserted that none of the documents and tapes obtained by his office and a federal grand jury supported the cooperative's claim of government extortion. Sale also disclosed that the special prosecution force was investigating possible criminal conduct by the cooperative. *(Scandal charges, p. 179)*

Gurney Role. An aide to Sen. Edward J. Gurney (R Fla.) said the senator was not planning to resign from the Senate Watergate investigating committee or "slack off" on his work there, despite a Dec. 25 *Washington Post* report that Gurney had missed the committee's last eight public sessions and numerous private sessions. The aide denied that Gurney's absences were related to a Justice Department investigation into allegations that Gurney accepted secret donations from Florida builders in exchange for promised favors. *(Investigation, p. 177; Gurney attack on committee, p. 117)*

Gray on Wiretaps. *The New York Times* reported that according to a confidential FBI report, the agency's former acting director, L. Patrick Gray III, knew about the secret 1969-71 administration program of domestic "national security" wiretaps in advance of his testimony before the Senate Judiciary Committee in March 1973 that he was unaware of such a program. The existence of the wiretaps of four newsmen and 13 government officials, uncovered in 1973, was acknowledged by the President in his May 22 statement on Watergate. *(Statement Vol. I, p. 264; Gray testimony, Vol. I, p. 255)*

PROSECUTION PREDICTS MORE INDICTMENTS EARLY IN YEAR

In a year-end report on its activities, the Watergate special prosecution force took credit for bringing about 19 guilty pleas and one no contest plea in 1973 and promised more indictments early in 1974.

Special Prosecutor Leon Jaworski said in a statement accompanying the Dec. 31 report: "Although investigations in various areas within the special prosecutor's jurisdiction are continuing, including the review of White House files, the presentation of evidence to the grand juries has progressed to the point that in January and February these bodies will be prepared to consider the matter of returning indictments in a substantial number of major involvements." The statement did not elaborate.

The report listed 12 persons who had pleaded guilty or no contest as a result of the prosecution force's investigations, which began in late May 1973 under the direction of Archibald Cox. Jaworski replaced Cox after President Nixon had Cox fired on Oct. 20. *(Cox approval, Vol. I, p. 96; firing, p. 69; Jaworski appointment, p. 111)*

Also listed were eight corporations that pleaded guilty to charges of making illegal campaign contributions. Not included were the seven men convicted for the Watergate break-in June 17, 1972. *(Box score of indictments and convictions, p. 171)*

Administration, Campaign Officials. These were the five White House or Nixon re-election campaign officials who pleaded guilty:

- Frederick C. LaRue, a former re-election committee official, pleaded guilty June 28 to a charge of conspiracy to obstruct justice. Sentencing was deferred.
- Jeb Stuart Magruder, former deputy director of the re-election committee, pleaded guilty Aug. 16 to charges of conspiracy to obstruct justice and defraud the United States. Sentencing was deferred.
- Donald H. Segretti, a paid campaign *provocateur*, pleaded guilty Oct. 1 to one count of conspiracy and three counts of distributing illegal campaign literature. He was sentenced on Nov. 6 to six months in prison.
- Egil Krogh Jr., former head of the White House "plumbers" unit, pleaded guilty Nov. 30 to a charge of conspiracy against the rights of citizens. Two counts of perjury were dropped. Sentencing was scheduled for early 1974.
- John W. Dean III, former counsel to the President, pleaded guilty Oct. 19 to one count of conspiracy to obstruct justice and defraud the United States. Sentencing was deferred.

In addition, Dwight L. Chapin, Nixon's former appointments secretary, was indicted on Nov. 29 on four counts of perjury. His trial was scheduled for Feb. 19.

Executives, Corporations. Six corporate executives pleaded guilty or no contest and were fined $1,000 each for making illlegal contributions to the Nixon campaign. A

Mitchell, Stans Trial Delay

Trial of two former Nixon cabinet officers, Attorney General John N. Mitchell and Commerce Secretary Maurice H. Stans, was delayed for the third time Jan. 2 in U.S. District Court in New York City. "This is the last false start that we are going to have in this case," said Judge Lee P. Gagliardi.

Mitchell, who left the Justice Department to become President Nixon's campaign director in 1972, and Stans, finance director of the re-election campaign, were indicted in May 1973 on charges of obstructing an investigation of financier Robert L. Vesco, who fled to the Caribbean to avoid extradition. Vesco had contributed $200,000 to the Nixon campaign. *(Indictments, Vol. I p. 46)*

Gagliardi granted the defense lawyers' motion for a delay because of their involvement in another trial that could keep them occupied until sometime in February.

The Mitchell-Stans trail had been scheduled to begin Jan. 9. No new date was set for it.

seventh, Harry Heltzer, board chairman of Minnesota Mining and Manufacturing Company, was fined $500 after pleading guilty. Those fined $1,000 were:

- Russell DeYoung, board chairman, Goodyear Tire and Rubber Company, guilty.
- Harding L. Lawrence, board chairman, Braniff Airways, guilty.
- Claude C. Wild Jr., vice president, Gulf Oil Corporation, guilty.
- Orin E. Atkins, board chairman, Ashland Oil Inc., no contest.
- William W. Keeler, board chairman, Phillips Petroleum Company, guilty.
- H. Everett Olson, board chairman, the Carnation Company, guilty.

Minnesota Mining and Manufacturing was fined $3,000 for making an illegal campaign contribution. The other six corporations were fined $5,000 each. All seven pleaded guilty.

An eighth corporation, American Airlines, also was fined $5,000. But its former board chairman, George A. Spater, was not fined along with the other executives, because he had been the first to disclose an illegal corporate contribution voluntarily.

Dwayne O. Andreas, board chairman of the First Interoceanic Corporation, was charged on Oct. 19 with four counts of making illegal contributions. First Interoceanic also was charged. Both Andreas and the corporation pleaded not guilty.

Baker on 'Grave Matter'

Sen. Howard H. Baker Jr. (R Tenn.), vice chairman of the Senate Watergate investigating committee, said Dec. 30 that he had strongly urged President Nixon to disclose a matter of "grave national importance" related to the Watergate case and perhaps touching on national security. "The odds are probably better that it would be helpful to the President than hurtful," Baker said, and the new information might "justify or at least explain some of the conduct that appears otherwise unexplainable."

Baker said he was referring to a matter Nixon described in his Nov. 17 Orlando, Fla., appearance before newspaper editors as "so sensitive that even Sen. Ervin (Sam J. Ervin Jr., the committee chairman) and Sen. Baker have decided that they could not delve further" into it. News reports had speculated that it involved Nixon's concern that investigations into the activities of the White House "plumbers" unit might reveal the name—and thus endanger the life—of a Soviet agent operating as an American spy. *(Nixon statement, p. 154)*

Baker made his remarks on ABC-TV's "Issues and Answers." Asked if he thought there were any more Watergate bombshells waiting to explode, he said, "There are animals crashing around in the forest. I can hear them, but I can't see them." Some of those undisclosed things did involve national security, Baker conceded, but he said "there must be a balance at some point, a value judgment...on whether the requirements of national security are greater than the requirements of domestic tranquility."

Operation Candor. Baker, who had refrained from open approval or condemnation of the Nixon administration since the Watergate scandals broke, said he thought "Operation Candor" so far had failed to restore public confidence in the President. In urging disclosure of all tapes and documents, Baker stressed the importance of good appearances because "the level of concern and disquiet in the country is so great that we can't stand on narrow technicalities...."

Committee Subpoenas. Baker also was asked about activities of the Senate investigating committee. While exempting Chairman Ervin from blame, he questioned both the procedure and substance of the committee's Dec. 19 subpoenas of more than 500 White House tapes and documents. Baker said that he had not been notified of the subpoenas before they were served and that the committee had not requested the materials first and given the White House time to respond, as was the usual practice.

An aide to Baker said the senator was not present when the committee voted Dec. 18 to issue the subpoenas, and did not know about them until they were served. Baker said the committee should reconsider the subpoenas when it met in January. *(Committee subpoenas, p. 183)*

Ervin said Dec. 31 that he would have no objection to reopening the subpoena issue when he reconvened the committee in late January. But he said he thought the substance of the requests was justified.

Week's Watergate Chronology

Following is a day-to-day chronology of the week's events in the Watergate case:

DEC. 27

Hughes Indictment. Billionaire Howard Hughes was indicted by a federal grand jury in Las Vegas, Nev., on charges of stock manipulation and conspiracy in connection with his acquisition of Air West airlines in 1968. The Senate Watergate investigating committee was looking into a possible connection between Nixon's approval of the merger and the $100,000 campaign contribution Hughes gave to Nixon's close friend, Charles G. Rebozo, in 1969 and 1970. *(Hughes gift, p, 179)*

Dairy Suit. The Justice Department filed a civil antitrust suit in U.S. District Court in Kansas City, Mo., against Mid-America Dairymen Inc., one of three dairy cooperatives under investigation for contributions of $427,000 to Nixon's 1972 campaign. Suits already had been brought against the other two companies, Associated Milk Producers Inc. and Dairymen Inc. *(Suit development, p. 186)*

DEC. 28

Operation Candor. According to White House sources quoted by *The Washington Post*, Nixon and his top advisers had decided not to release transcripts or summaries of presidential tapes bearing on the Watergate case—as previously promised—because they would indicate "at a minimum" that Nixon had knowledge of the coverup several days before March 21, 1973, when he had said he learned of it. The Post's sources said the new strategy was "aimed less at regaining public support than avoiding the impeachment or forced resignation of the President."

White House Response. Gerald L. Warren, deputy White House press secretary, acknowledged at a press briefing near San Clemente, Calif., that the question of whether to release summaries of the White House tapes was being "re-evaluated" by Nixon's advisers. Warren said they had been forced to reconsider by the Senate Watergate investigating committee's subpoena of more than 500 tapes and documents and by the Dec. 17 incident in which a Washington lawyer played a White House tape at a cocktail party. *(Committee subpoena and tape incident, p. 185)*

Hunt, Barker Release. The U.S. Court of Appeals in Washington, D.C., ordered convicted Watergate conspirators E. Howard Hunt Jr. and Bernard L. Barker released from prison without bail while the court considered their appeals of sentences handed down Nov. 9 by U.S. District Judge John J. Sirica. Sirica had rejected requests by the two men for permission to change their pleas of not guilty and stand trial for their roles in the Watergate break-in. *(Sentences, p. 117)*

Senate Committee Suit. The Appeals Court also ordered Judge Sirica to reconsider his Oct. 17 ruling that denied the Senate Watergate investigating committee access to Watergate tapes and documents, in light of new legislation specifically granting Sirica's court jurisdiction over the case. *(New law, p. 183)*

Nixon Papers Suit. Robert M. Brandon, director of the Tax Reform Research Group, an affiliate of Ralph Nader's Public Citizen Inc., filed suit in U.S. District Court in Washington for access to the vice presidential papers Nixon donated to the National Archives. Brandon argued that the General Services Administration should not honor the restrictions placed by Nixon on release of the papers, because the documents should be considered public property. Even if the papers were Nixon's to donate, Brandon said, the gift was invalidated, because the deed was not properly signed and contained so many limitations on their use that the gift was really just a transferal of custody. Nixon's Dec. 8 financial statement said the papers had been valued at $576,000 and that he was deducting the amount from his federal income taxes over a period of years. *(Nixon statement, p. 181; papers controversy, p. 182)*

DEC. 30

Baker Remarks. Speaking on ABC-TV's "Issues and Answers," Howard H. Baker Jr. (R Tenn.), vice chairman of the Senate investigating committee, said he had urged Nixon to disclose a "matter of grave national importance" that he said might explain some of the covert Watergate activities. He would not reveal details. *(Box, p. 188)*

Schorr Investigation. Citing a personal memorandum from former FBI Director J. Edgar Hoover and other Justice Department documents, *The New York Times* reported that H. R. Haldeman, Nixon's former chief of staff, requested the FBI and the White House to give a false explanation of an agency investigation of Daniel Schorr, a reporter for CBS News, after the investigation became public knowledge in November of 1971. Both the FBI and White House said that Schorr was being checked out because he was under consideration for an important government job, but Haldeman admitted in Senate testimony Aug. 1 that Schorr had never been considered for a post. He testified he had requested an FBI background check on the reporter, but could not recall why. The Times said the bureau apparently had initiated a full-scale investigation, but it was called off by the White House. *(Haldeman testimony, Vol. I, p. 229)*

DEC. 31

Jaworski Report. In a year-end summary of his official activities, Watergate special prosecutor Leon Jaworski reported that "although investigations in various areas within the special prosecutor's jurisdiction are continuing, including the review of White House files, the presentation of evidence to the grand juries has progressed to the point that in January and February these bodies will be prepared to consider the matter of returning indictments in a substantial number of major involvements." *(Details, p. 187; indictments and convictions status, p. 171)*

Nixon Foundation. *The Los Angeles Times* reported that the Richard Nixon Foundation, a tax-exempt corporation formed by the President's friends to build a presidential library, had paid at least $21,000 in consulting fees to Nixon's brother, Edward. Leonard G. Firestone, president of the foundation, said Edward Nixon was paid to look into possible sites for the planned library, although no site had yet been chosen.

Sirica Award. *Time* magazine chose Judge Sirica as its "man of the year" for his handling of the original Watergate break-in trial in January and his insistence that the President abide by the special prosecutor's demand for court evidence in the form of the White House tapes.

JAN. 1

Nixon Oil Contributions. Rep. Les Aspin (D Wis.) released a report on oil company and oil executive contributions to Nixon's 1972 campaign, showing that officials and principal stockholders of 178 oil and gas companies contributed a total of almost $5-million. Aspin said the report, compiled from contributor lists of the General Accounting Office and a private citizens' group, Common Cause, demonstrated that "President Nixon's hands are tied, preventing him from dealing effectively with the current energy crisis." *(Illegal oil company contributions, p. 133)*

JAN. 2

Nixon Tax Audit. The Internal Revenue Service announced that it would re-examine President Nixon's recent income tax returns, but did not specify for which years. In a statement, the agency said it was conducting the audit because of "questions raised in the press as to the relationship of the consideration of the President's tax returns by the Joint Committee on Internal Revenue Taxation and any consideration of the returns by the Internal Revenue Service." *(Nixon tax statement, p. 181)*

Nixon California Taxes. The President's California tax lawyer, Dean S. Butler, said in Sacramento that all details of Nixon's California taxes would be disclosed publicly, after the California State Franchise Tax Board had time to review the issue of whether the President was liable for California state taxes while he was in office. Nixon's Dec. 8 financial statement said he had paid no California taxes since becoming President.

Mitchell-Stans Trial. Judge Lee P. Gagliardi of U.S. District Court in New York City postponed for the third time the trial of former administration officials John N. Mitchell and Maurice H. Stans on charges of obstructing an investigation of financier Robert L. Vesco in return for a $200,000 contribution to the 1972 Nixon campaign. The trial, scheduled to start on Jan. 9, was held up to allow a defense lawyer to finish another case. *(Box, p. 188; earlier development, p. 85)*

Hunt Release. Convicted Watergate conspirator E. Howard Hunt Jr. was released from the federal prison at Allenwood, Pa., and driven to Washington, D.C., where he was released without bail to await a decision by the U.S. Court of Appeals on his conviction for the Watergate break-in. √

HINTS OF PRESIDENTIAL PROMISE ON SUBPOENAED TAPES

Although the week began with a firm refusal by President Nixon to hand over hundreds of subpoenaed tapes and documents to the Senate select committee investigating Watergate, it appeared possible by week's end that a compromise might be worked out.

A committee staff member announced that public hearings would resume late in January. But press reports indicated that most members of the committee were undecided about the need to hold more hearings.

On Jan. 8, the White House released lengthy statements explaining its role in two events under investigation by the Senate committee: increased milk price supports and the government's antitrust suit against International Telephone and Telegraph Corporation (ITT).

The White House also announced a shake-up in its Watergate legal staff, with a new lawyer brought in to head the team. And House Judiciary Committee Republicans named a well-known Chicago attorney as minority counsel for the committee's impeachment investigations.

Committee Subpoenas

The President's Jan. 4 refusal to turn over about 500 Watergate-related tapes and documents subpoenaed by the Senate Watergate committee had softened into a possible compromise by Jan. 8.

Two days after Vice President Gerald R. Ford suggested that a compromise might be possible, the White House hinted Jan. 8 that the President might be willing to consider a more limited request from the committee. Committee Chairman Sam J. Ervin Jr. (D N.C.) indicated the same day that the committee might settle first for the five tapes it had subpoenaed initially in 1973.

Nixon Refusal. In an unyielding letter to Ervin, the President refused Jan. 4 to turn over the materials subpoenaed by the committee Dec. 19. He condemned the subpoena "as an overt attempt to intrude into the executive to a degree that constitutes an unconstitutional usurpation of power." (Subpoenas issued, p. 183)

The President again defended the need for a president and his staff to be able to communicate among themselves candidly and confidentially. "To produce the material you now seek would unquestionably destroy any vestige of confidentiality of presidential communications...," the President asserted.

Committee Reaction. Ervin immediately issued a statement acknowledging that the committee had not expected the President to comply with the subpoena. But, Ervin added, "There is nothing in the Constitution of the United States that gives the President the power to withhold information concerning political activities or information concerning illegal activities."

Other committee members were more blunt. Herman E. Talmadge (D Ga.) charged that Nixon's refusal made people think "he has something to hide."

"Candor has been a word, it has not been a deed, in the White House for a considerable period of time," said Lowell P. Weicker Jr. (R Conn.).

But Howard H. Baker Jr. (R Tenn.), committee vice chairman, said the committee had made a mistake in attempting to subpoena so many documents. He urged the committee to reconsider the matter in order to avoid "a fishing expedition."

Renewed Suit. While delaying any decision on a court battle over materials covered by the rejected subpoena, the committee Jan. 7 renewed its original suit in the U.S. District Court in Washington, D.C., for five presidential tapes.

Chief Judge John J. Sirica had dismissed the committee's original suit on Oct. 17, ruling that his court did not have jurisdiction over the case. After the decision, Congress approved legislation (S 2641—PL 93-190) giving the district court jurisdiction over Watergate subpoenas issued by Congress. The President allowed the bill to become law against his wishes Dec. 18. (p. 183)

The Court of Appeals, District of Columbia circuit, which had been considering the case on appeal by the committee, returned the suit to District Judge Gerhard A. Gesell after enactment of PL 93-190.

The President had 10 days to reply to the new suit. The White House confirmed Jan. 8 that constitutional expert Charles Alan Wright had returned on a part-time basis to represent the President in the suit. Wright, who returned to the University of Texas law faculty in late 1973, was to work with the President's new top lawyer, James D. St. Clair. (p. 192)

Lawyers for the Senate committee said that no new suits would be filed until Gesell had ruled on the initial case.

Ford Compromise Plan. Appearing on NBC-TV's "Meet the Press," Vice President Ford suggested Jan. 6 that the committee and the President might be able to reach a compromise on the subpoena issue. Ford said he agreed with the President's decision to ignore the subpoena because of its "scattergun approach."

But if the committee were willing to scale down its demands, the Vice President said, "There may be—and I underline may be—some area of compromise." Ford made it clear that he had not discussed the matter in any depth with the President, and the next day the White House confirmed that Ford was speaking on his own initiative.

In response to Ford's statement, Ervin said Jan. 7 that he would welcome a compromise, but pointed out the need for its careful delineation. "The agreement should be written so there could be no misunderstanding," he said. Some administration officials said privately that it would be "premature" for the President to express a desire to compromise until he knew how the committee would cut down its requests.

Milk Price Supports

Political and national economic considerations, but not campaign financial needs, guided the administration's decision to approve higher milk price supports in March 1971, the White House contended in a Jan. 8 background paper. The paper denied any connection between the milk support decision and the fact that dairy industry groups contributed $427,500 to the Nixon campaign in 1972. *(Excerpts, p. 195)*

The White House, however, acknowledged that Nixon knew as early as September 1970 that dairy groups planned to contribute large sums to his 1972 campaign. According to the White House, the President was informed in a 1970 memo of a $2-million campaign pledge from the Associated Milk Producers Inc., the largest dairy cooperative. But at no time, the statement added, did Nixon discuss the contributions with the dairy industry.

The White House also noted that the dairy contributions fell far short of the expected total, made up less than 1 per cent of total contributions to Nixon and represented only a fraction of dairy gifts to congressional candidates.

Economic Consequences. The White House defended the milk support decision on the grounds that its economic consequences had been "beneficial to the entire country." Specifically, the document said the decision had kept increases in the price of milk to the consumer low and had not cost the federal government any additional money.

Congressional Pressure. The statement detailed the President's Nov. 17, 1973, contention that "Congress put a gun to our head" on the milk support issue. After concluding that Congress would pass legislation increasing the support, which he could not veto for political reasons, the President approved the increase, according to the statement. *(Previous Nixon statement, p. 148)*

After former Agriculture Secretary Clifford Hardin's initial decision on March 8, 1971, that price supports would not go up, the White House noted that 29 senators and more than 100 representatives began a push to boost price supports. Vetoing such a bill, the statement argued, would be "politically disastrous in some of the Midwestern states."

Political Repercussions. The White House made it clear that it feared the financial influence of the dairy groups in the 1972 congressional campaigns. This fear and the possibility of alienating the farm vote influenced the President's decision to approve the increase, the White House acknowledged. The statement termed farmers "an essential part" of the President's political constituency.

The paper also revealed that the White House had hoped that the Democratic congressional leadership, which had joined the drive for higher supports, would back some of the administration's domestic legislation if the White House played up their role in reversing Hardin's decision.

March Meeting. Dairy group representatives met with the President to urge higher supports on March 23, 1971, the same day the decision to approve the increase was reached. But there was "no mention whatsoever of campaign contributions" during the meeting, the White House statement said.

Poll Report

President Nixon's popularity rating in the Gallup Poll at the end of 1973 was only two percentage points above its lowest level. A plurality in a Harris Survey favored a special presidential election in 1974. A Roper Poll found that nearly four of five persons questioned believed one or more serious charges against the President. *(Earlier poll report, p. 186)*

Gallup. In interviews Dec. 7-10 for the Gallup Poll published Jan. 6, 1,536 adults were asked: "Do you approve or disapprove of the way Nixon is handling his job as president?"

	Latest	Nov. 30-Dec. 3
Approve	29%	31%
Dissapprove	60	59
No opinion	11	10

During the year, Nixon's popularity sank 39 percentage points. Its high mark of 68 per cent was in January, just after the Vietnam peace agreement. Its low, 27 per cent, was in October and November.

Harris. For the Harris Survey published Jan. 7, persons in 1,496 households were presented with this question: "It has been suggested that it might be proper under the Constitution for Congress to call an election for President in 1974. The person elected would serve until the regular election in 1976. If the U.S. Supreme Court found it was constitutional to have a special election for president in 1974, would you favor or oppose such a step?

Favor	50%
Oppose	36
Not sure	14

Roper. The Roper Poll was conducted for 51 subscribers and made available to *The New York Times*, which published it Jan. 6. A sample of 2,020 persons was interviewed in early November.

Roper found that 79 per cent believed that one or more of 13 charges against the President were serious and probably involved him. But a plurality of 45 to 44 per cent opposed impeachment.

The White House explanation that the President himself made the decision conflicted with statements by Hardin that the agriculture secretary had decided to reverse his first position on his own initiative.

ITT Antitrust Suit

A promise from an ITT subsidiary to help defray the costs of the 1972 Republican national convention had nothing to do with the President's attempt to block a 1971 Justice Department appeal of an antitrust suit against ITT, according to a Jan. 8 White House statement. *(Excepts, p. 199)*

Rather, the White House said, the President "had concluded that the ITT litigation was inconsistent with his own views of antitrust policy" because it was an attack on "bigness" more than an attempt to ensure cor-

New White House Lawyer

The White House Jan. 5 announced the appointment of James D. St. Clair, a Boston trial lawyer, to head President Nixon's Watergate legal team. The appointment came after high-level criticism within the administration over the way J. Fred Buzhardt, who had headed Nixon's Watergate defense since May 10, 1973, had handled the issue of the Watergate tapes.

Deputy White House press secretary Gerald L. Warren also announced that Buzhardt had been promoted to the position of White House counsel, a job last held by John W. Dean III, whom Nixon fired during the early stages of the Watergate disclosures.

Nixon's other principal Watergate lawyer, Leonard Garment, returned to his former post as assistant to the President. Garment was to advise Nixon on domestic affairs and a wide range of other areas. He had advised Nixon chiefly on cultural, education and civil rights matters before his appointment as acting counsel May 10.

St. Clair, 53, was a staff member to Joseph N. Welch, the special Army counsel whose televised clashes with the late Sen. Joseph R. McCarthy (R Wis. 1947-57) helped end the so-called McCarthy era. St. Clair sat alongside Welch during McCarthy's 1954 Senate subcommittee hearings investigating alleged Communist influence in the Army.

Although St. Clair was a registered Republican, his defense clients had included Yale Chaplain William Sloane Coffin Jr., who was tried in 1968 for his part in an anti-war demonstration. In 1958, St. Clair defended a Harvard University professor accused of contempt for refusing to name colleagues who allegedly sympathized with Communists. St. Clair also took part in school desegregation cases in Boston, where he worked before joining the White House staff.

The President's new special counsel had a reputation as a painstakingly thorough lawyer in the preparation of his cases and as a brilliant courtroom tactician with an uncanny recall of details.

Born in Akron, Ohio, April 4, 1920, St. Clair was graduated from the University of Illinois in 1941. After Navy service aboard a patrol boat based at San Pedro, Calif., he received a law degree from Harvard in 1947 and joined the Boston firm of Hale & Dorr. Welch was one of his partners in the firm. St. Clair resigned Jan. 2 to take the White House post.

porate competition. When it appeared that former U.S. Solicitor General Erwin N. Griswold might quit in protest, the statement added, Nixon was dissuaded from pursuing his order to drop the appeal.

The White House branded charges that Nixon had ordered the case dropped in return for a convention contribution pledge from Sheraton Hotel Corporation, an ITT subsidiary, "totally without foundation." The document claimed that Nixon did not know about any financial commitment from Sheraton at the time of his order.

Justice Department Suit. The Justice Department suit sought to divest ITT of three companies it had acquired. The lower court decision on the first divestiture case went against the department, but the department expressed confidence that it could win on appeal. After the President's intercession, the case was settled out of court.

Sequence of Events. According to the White House version of events leading to the settlement, the President ordered then Deputy Attorney General Richard G. Kleindienst not to file the appeal on April 19, 1971. Kleindienst's role in the ITT case was the subject of lengthy hearings in 1972 on his confirmation as attorney general, a position he resigned on April 30, 1973.

On April 21, 1971, according to the White House account, former Attorney General John N. Mitchell advised the President against ordering that the appeal be dropped. Mitchell told Nixon that Griswold was prepared to resign if there were no appeal, according to the White House. The statement added that Mitchell "feared legislative repercussions if the matter were dropped entirely."

At that point, the White House said, Nixon withdrew his April 19 order and authorized the Justice Department to proceed with the case as it wished. ITT and the department reached their settlement in July 1971.

The statement expanded on the admission by the White House in October 1973 that the President had talked with Kleindienst about stopping the suit. At that time, the White House also issued denials that the President had tried to obstruct the case for political reasons. *(p. 102)*

Contradictions. The White House statement left several major questions about the ITT controversy unanswered and raised the possibility that either Kleindienst or Mitchell could face perjury charges for 1972 testimony before the Senate Judiciary Committee.

During his confirmation hearings, Kleindienst maintained that no one in the White House had pressured him to dispose of the suit in any particular way. But on Oct. 31, 1973, Kleindienst acknowledged that the President had ordered him to drop the suit and contended that his threat to resign forced the President to withdraw the order.

Mitchell testified during the Kleindienst hearings that he never had talked to the President about the ITT antitrust case and that he was not informed about the progress of litigation against ITT.

Judiciary Advisory Group Meeting

Staffing, security, subpoenas and schedules for the impeachment inquiry were some of the items discussed Jan. 7 by the advisory group composed of senior members of the House Judiciary Committee. Eleven of the 15 senior members, many interrupting their between-sessions vacation, met in Washington to receive a progress report from special counsel John M. Doar. The advisory group had been created in mid-December by Committee Chairman Peter W. Rodino Jr. (D N.J.).

Doar said that his staff was not completed but that he expected it eventually to include about 30 lawyers. He told the advisory group that he had directed members of his staff not to communicate with the press and that he was concerned about security arrangements for the staff offices on the second floor of a congressional annex in a converted hotel.

After the meeting, Rodino said that the advisory group discussed the advisability of asking the House to grant the committee subpoena power for the impeachment inquiry in order to preclude any possible challenge to the exercise of that power by the committee, whose jurisdiction did not explicitly include impeachment. He said that he still hoped the committee could complete its work and report to the House on its findings by the end of April. He added that he did not know whether there would be hearings, but that, if there were, he would not expect them before March.

Doar stated that he had had no contact with the White House, that he had met twice with Special Prosecutor Leon Jaworski to discuss arrangements for conveying information from Jaworski's office to the committee but that no agreement had been reached. He also said Watergate committee counsel Samuel Dash had assured him that material from that committee's files would be available to Doar's staff.

Week's Watergate Chronology

Following is a day-to-day chronology of the week's events in the Watergate case:

JAN. 3

Saxbe Remarks. The day before his swearing in as Nixon's fourth attorney general, William B. Saxbe dismissed as "a fishing expedition" the Senate Watergate investigating committee's Dec. 19 subpoenas of more than 500 White House tapes and documents. "To keep in business, the committee has to have grist for its mill," he said. "If they can keep dredging stuff up, they'll go on forever." Saxbe also repeated his pledge not to interfere with the work of special Watergate prosecutor Leon Jaworski. *(Saxbe confirmation, p. 111)*

JAN. 4

Committee Subpoenas. In a strongly worded letter to Chairman Sam J. Ervin Jr. (D N.C.) of the Senate investigating committee, President Nixon refused to comply with the committee's Dec. 19 subpoenas. To do so, he said, "would unquestionably destroy any vestige of confidentiality of presidential communications...."

Ervin wrote back that the President had no constitutional power "to withhold information concerning political activities or information concerning illegal activities." Samuel Dash, the committee's chief counsel, said the panel would not seek enforcement of the subpoenas until a decision was reached on the committee's earlier subpoena of five presidential tapes. *(Details, p. 190)*

Nixon Attorneys. A White House spokesman announced in San Clemente, Calif., that J. Fred Buzhardt Jr. would be replaced as head of the White House Watergate legal team by Boston attorney James D. St. Clair. Buzhardt was named counsel to the President, a post previously held by John W. Dean III. Leonard Garment,

Minority Impeachment Counsel

Albert E. Jenner, a well-known trial lawyer from Chicago, was named Jan. 7 as chief minority counsel for the House Judiciary Committee's inquiry into charges of impeachment against President Nixon.

Jenner, 66, was senior counsel to the Warren Commission, which investigated President Kennedy's assassination. He was a member of the National Commission on the Causes and Prevention of Violence (the Kerner Commission).

Jenner's appointment was announced by Rep. Edward Hutchinson (Mich.), the ranking Republican on the committee. Jenner and the attorneys working with him and responsible to the minority members of the committee would, Hutchinson said, cooperate fully with special counsel John M. Doar in "ensuring that the inquiry is conducted in a fair, thorough and expeditious manner."

Jenner himself praised Doar as "a very able and conscientious lawyer" and said that the staff inquiry would be a "joint effort.... There is no controversy on the professional staff."

A graduate of the University of Illinois Law School and a senior partner in the Chicago law firm of Jenner and Block, Jenner had served in a variety of important posts within the legal profession. Most recently, he headed the Supreme Court's advisory committee on rules of evidence for federal courts, whose work led to legislation pending in the 93rd Congress. From 1960 to 1970, he served as a member of a similar advisory committee on federal rules of civil procedure.

Jenner was formerly president of the American Judicature Society, the American College of Trial Lawyers, the National Conference of Bar Association Presidents, the National Conference on Uniform State Laws and the Illinois Bar Association.

He had been a member of the American Bar Association (ABA) House of Delegates since 1948 and also served as chairman of the ABA's committee on the federal judiciary. In that post, he led the association's fight against confirmation of Francis X. Morrissey, a friend of the Kennedy family, as a federal district judge. The nomination was shelved at the request of Sen. Edward M. Kennedy (D Mass.).

who had been acting counsel since Dean's departure on April 30, 1973, became an assistant to the President. *(Box, p. 192)*

Barker Release. Bernard L. Barker, one of seven men convicted in January 1973 for their roles in the Watergate break-in, was released from the federal prison camp at Eglin Air Force Base, Florida, to await the outcome of his appeal. *(Release order, p. 188)*

JAN. 5

Subpoena Reaction. Sen. Herman E. Talmadge (D Ga.) of the Senate investigating committee said the President was "making a great mistake" by refusing to honor the committee's wide-ranging subpoenas. "It indicates to the public he has something to hide," Talmadge added.

"It doesn't come as any surprise," commented another committee member, Sen. Lowell P. Weicker Jr. (R Conn.). "The President and/or his aides continue to duck the hard one." Nixon's new Watergate counsel, St. Clair, said at a Boston news conference that he had advised the President to turn down the subpoenas. *(Baker comment, p. 188)*

JAN. 6

Ford on Tapes. Vice President Gerald R. Ford suggested on NBC-TV's "Meet the Press" that if the Senate investigating committee was "willing to make some refinements" in its demands for White House tapes and documents, "there may be—and I underline may be —some area of compromise." White House deputy press secretary Gerald L. Warren said the next day that Ford was speaking for himself only and that the President still stood on his Jan. 4 letter to Committee Chairman Ervin, firmly refusing all the committee's demands.

Committee Schedule. The Senate Watergate committee would resume public hearings Jan. 28 and continue throughout February, according to deputy committee counsel Rufus Edmisten, quoted in *The Washington Post.* Edmisten said the first topic to be taken up would be campaign contributions to Nixon from the milk industry, followed by the issue of a $100,000 contribution given to Nixon's friend, Charles G. Rebozo, by billionaire Howard Hughes. The committee's final report, due Feb. 28, would have to be delayed, Edmisten said. *(Milk case, p. 191; Hughes case, p. 179)*

Cox Firing. *The New York Times* reported that, according to "well-informed sources," one factor in Nixon's Oct. 20 firing of special prosecutor Archibald Cox was the fear that a grand jury would name the President as an unindicted co-conspirator in the Watergate coverup. Cox confirmed that former Attorney General Elliot L. Richardson had inquired about the matter shortly before Oct. 20, and that he told Richardson it was an unfounded rumor. Gerald L. Warren, deputy White House press secretary, described the reported interpretation of Cox's firing as "totally false." *(Earlier Cox firing dispute, p. 151)*

JAN. 7

Committee Suit. The Senate investigating committee filed a brief in U.S. District Court asking Judge John J. Sirica to reconsider its original subpoena of five presidential tapes in light of a new law granting the court jurisdiction over such a suit. Sirica, who had rejected the first suit Oct. 17 on grounds that his court lacked jurisdiction, referred the case to U.S. District Judge Gerhard A. Gesell. *(Box, next column)*

Impeachment Inquiry. An ad hoc advisory committee on impeachment, composed of the 15 senior members of the House Judiciary Committee, met to receive a progress report from chief counsel John Doar. At a news conference afterward, Republican members announced the appointment of Albert E. Jenner, a Chicago trial lawyer, as chief minority counsel for the inquiry. Chairman Peter W. Rodino Jr. (D N.J.) said the committee did not have subpoena power in impeachment proceedings and

would ask the House to grant such authority. *(Details, p. 192; Jenner biography, p. 193)*

Conspirators' Parole. The U.S. Board of Parole granted parole, effective March 7, to three of the seven convicted Watergate conspirators—Frank A. Sturgis,

---

Possible Campaign Reform

The Senate Watergate investigating committee revealed Jan. 7 that it might recommend limiting presidential tenure to one term if abuses in the 1972 Nixon re-election campaign proved serious enough. But before considering such "far-reaching legislative remedies," the committee said in legal papers renewing its suit for five White House tapes, it needed more evidence.

Without supplying any additional details, the committee added that other possible proposals included a "radically new campaign financing system that would severely curtail the amount of private monies that could be contributed." Again without amplification, the committee also said it was considering limiting the participation of a president in a campaign to choose his own successor. *(Committee members' views on proposals, p. 141)*

The select committee made it clear that the possible recommendations hinged on the availability of further evidence. "It would be folly," the committee said in its legal memorandum, "to proceed to the enactment of such far-reaching legislation without knowing if the abuse has been great enough to warrant it."

Revealing the extent of executive wrongdoing, the committee added, would be critical to generating wide public support for its legislative proposals. Changing the limit on presidential tenure, for example, would require approval of a constitutional amendment by a two-thirds majority of each house.

New Hearings. Rufus L. Edmisten, the committee's deputy chief counsel, announced Jan. 5 that the committee would resume open hearings on Jan. 28 to investigate campaign contributions to Nixon. The hearings probably would continue through February, Edmisten added, delaying the committee's final report until late March or early April. But, according to a *Washington Post* report Jan. 10, most of the committee's seven members had not decided whether or not hearings should resume.

If resumed, the hearings would explore the circumstances around $427,500 in contributions to the 1972 Nixon campaign from dairy groups, which coincided with an administration decision to increase milk support prices. The contributions were the subject of document released Jan. 8 by the President which denied any connection between the two events. *(p. 57)*

The committee also would look into a cash gift of $100,000 in 1970 from billionaire-recluse Howard Hughes to C.G. (Bebe) Rebozo, the President's close friend. Rebozo had said the gift was intended as a campaign contribution to Nixon, but that he did nothing with the money before returning it to a Hughes associate in June 1973.

Virgilio R. Gonzalez and Eugenio R. Martinez. Three others, Bernard L. Barker, E. Howard Hunt Jr. and James W. McCord Jr., had been released from prison to await judgment on appeals of their convictions. The seventh, G. Gordon Liddy, in jail in California awaiting trial for his role in the Ellsberg break-in, still faced a minimum sentence of six years and eight months for the Watergate break-in. *(Hunt release, p. 189; release order, p. 188)*

JAN. 8

ITT and Milk Statements. The White House released two lengthy papers detailing the President's rebuttal of charges that he granted favors to the dairy industry and to the International Telephone and Telegraph Corporation (ITT) in exchange for large campaign contributions. The papers showed the allegations to be "utterly false," said a statement accompanying them. *(Excerpts, this page)*

JAN. 9

Hughes Contribution. U.S. District Judge Charles R. Richey ordered unsealed a deposition made May 11, 1973, by Sally Harmony, a former secretary to convicted Watergate conspirator G. Gordon Liddy, in connection with a civil suit brought by Democrats against Republicans. Harmony said that while working for Liddy at the Nixon re-election finance committee, she had received several blank checks signed by Robert Bennett, a Washington representative of billionaire Howard Hughes. Harmony said she filled in amounts on the checks but could not recall the exact figures.

Chapin Motion. Attorneys for Dwight L. Chapin, Nixon's former appointments secretary, filed motions in U.S. District Court in Washington, D.C., asking that their client's April 1 trial be moved somewhere with a more favorable political climate. The attorneys also filed a motion asking for dismissal of the perjury charges because of prejudicial publicity. *(Chapin plea, p. 177)*

JAN. 10

Senate Committee Plans. Most members of the Senate Watergate investigating committee, including Chairman Ervin, remained undecided about whether to resume public hearings when Congress reconvened, *The Washington Post* reported. Senators Weicker and Edward J. Gurney (R Fla.) were said to be convinced the hearings should not continue. √

EXCERPTS OF PAPERS ON MILK SUPPORTS, ITT DECISION

Milk Support Price Decision

Following are excerpts from the White House text of a background paper released Jan. 8 on the administration decision to raise price supports on some dairy products in March 1971:

During the spring of 1971, Secretary of Agriculture Clifford Hardin announced that certain dairy products would be supported by the Federal Government at 80 percent of parity during the 1971-72 marketing season. Subsequently, under heavy pressure from the Congress to increase supports and after consultation with his senior advisers, the President reconsidered and requested the Secretary to raise the price support level for the coming year to 85 percent of parity.

Because the President also met with dairy leaders during this same period and because campaign contributions were given to his re-election effort during 1971, there have been charges in the media and elsewhere that the President's actions on price supports were the result of promises from the dairy industry to contribute to the 1972 Republican Presidential campaign. These allegations are unsupported by evidence and are totally false.

I. THE DECISIONS OF MARCH 1971

The decision announced each year by the Secretary of Agriculture of the price at which the Government will support milk prices has a significant impact on the Nation's dairy farmers. In 1970, Secretary Hardin had announced that for the marketing year running from April 1, 1970 through March 31, 1971, the Government would support manufacturing milk at $4.66 per 100 pounds, or at 85 percent of parity. This figure represented an increase of 38 cents and an increase of 2 percent of the parity rate over the year before (1969-1970).

As the 1971-72 marketing season approached, the question within the Government was whether to continue supporting the milk price at $4.66 per 100 pounds or to raise the price. Because a grain shortage and other factors had increased the costs of production for dairy farmers, a continuation of the $4.66 price meant that the parity rate would actually fall to approximately 80 percent. To the farmers, a drop in parity rate would result in a possible loss of income which in turn could deter production. The farmers therefore advocated an increase in the price support to $5.21 per 100 pounds, or 90 percent of parity; at the very least, they argued, the Government should raise the price to $4.92 per 100 pounds and thereby maintain the current parity rate of 85 percent. At the Department of Agriculture, it was feared that such price increases might encourage excess production on the farms, raise the prices of dairy products for consumers, and ultimately force the Government to purchase the surplus products.

The dairy industry, which had become highly organized in the 1960s, moved to exert maximum, direct pressure on the Secretary of Agriculture in early 1971. In a few weeks, over 13,000 letters from milk producers were received by the Department of Agriculture.

At the same time, the dairy industry worked to achieve its objectives indirectly through Members of the Congress who agreed with industry views. The upper Midwestern affiliate of the Associated Milk Producers, Inc. (AMPI) estimated that its members alone sent some 50,000 letters to Congressmen on the subject of milk supports. Between February 23 and March 12, 1971, some 25 Senators and 65 Congressmen wrote the Secretary of Agriculture to urge that the $4.66 support price be increased. Some twenty Senators and 53 Representatives indicated that they wanted to see the price raised to a full 90 percent of parity ($5.21 per cwt.). Four Senators and eight Representatives adopted a more restrained position, asking that the price be raised to at least 85 percent of parity ($4.92).

Some of the letters openly referred to the fact that spokesmen for the dairy cooperatives—AMPI, Dairymen, Inc., or their affiliates—had written or called upon the Congressmen to ask for support. A number of letters were apparently drafted by lobbying groups.

Many of the Members also took to the floor of the House and Senate to express their concern....

While their colleagues were marshalling support in open floor speeches, senior Democratic leaders in the Congress were expressing their concerns privately to representatives of the Administration. On February 10, the Chairman of the House Ways and Means Committee, Wilbur Mills (D. Ark.), arranged a meeting in the office of Speaker Carl Albert (D. Okla.) to discuss the dairy issue. Representatives of the dairy industry had apparently asked for the meeting to plead their case. In attendance were Harold Nelson and David Parr from AMPI; Congressmen Mills, Albert and John Byrnes (R Wis.); William Galbraith, head of congressional liaison for the Department of Agriculture; and Clark MacGregor, then Counsel to the President for Congressional Relations.

The Congressional leaders continued to make their views known in several private conversations thereafter. According to Mr. MacGregor's records, Congressman Mills urged him on at least six occasions in late February and early March to urge the President to raise the support price. Congressman Mills and Speaker Albert also telephoned the Director of the Office of Management and Budget, George Shultz, with the same request. Mr. Shultz sent a memorandum to John Ehrlichman at the White House indicating the substance of the Mills request for a rise in the support level.

Nevertheless, on March 12, Secretary Hardin announced that the price support for the coming year would be approximately 80 percent of parity—not 90 percent as the dairy industry wanted. The Secretary's announcement acknowledged that some dairymen believed that the support price should be increased. But, he said, higher support prices might lead to excessive supplies and large surpluses. Mr. Hardin believed his action was "in the long-term best interests of the dairy producers."

Immediately following the Agriculture Department announcement of March 12, 1971, a campaign was initiated on Capitol Hill by both Democrats and Republicans for mandatory legislation to increase the parity level to 85 or 90 percent. *Thirty separate bills* were introduced in the House of Representatives between March 16th and March 25th with this specific goal in mind. *One hundred and twenty-five Members of the House of Representatives* introduced or co-sponsored legislation to support the price of manufacturing milk at a level of not more than 90 percent nor less than 85 percent. In other words, 85 percent would be an absolute floor for price supports. Of these Representatives, 29 were Republicans and 96 were Democrats. Two Congressmen, one from each side of the aisle, also introduced legislation for a mandatory level of 90 percent of parity.

In the Senate, 28 Senators, led by Democratic Senator Gaylord Nelson of Wisconsin, introduced legislation on March 16, 1971, that would have required support levels at a minimum of 85 percent of parity. Of the Nelson bill sponsors, one was a Republican (Senator Cook of Kentucky) and 27 were Democrats (Senators Allen, Bayh, Burdick, Bentsen, Cranston, Eastland, Eagleton, Fulbright, Gravel, Hart, Harris, Hollings, Hartke, Hughes, Inouye, Long, Mondale, McGee, McGovern, Muskie, Moss, Nelson, Proxmire, Sparkman, Stevenson, Symington, Tunney). Three days later, Senator Hubert Humphrey sponsored his own bill seeking higher parity.

Philosophically, the Nixon Administration had hoped to gradually move away from Federal policies which provide massive subsidies to agriculture. These subsidies had initially been instituted during the Depression years when the Government undertook a variety of measures to ease the plight of the farmers and to give them some degree of economic stability and continuing purchasing power. During the ensuing decades, when these support policies might have been phased out, they instead became political footballs, tossed about in the Congress, aided and abetted by well-organized farm lobbying groups....

With 29 Senators and more than 100 Congressmen actively spearheading the effort to achieve an increased parity rate for the dairy industry, it thus became increasingly clear that mandatory legislation would be enacted and, further, that a Presidential veto of such legislation could well be overridden. Moreover, if the President were to try to force his will in this matter (i.e., to push parity down to 80 percent) it could be politically disastrous in some of the Midwestern States, and, in the light of known Congressional intentions, would be both foolish and futile....

With the pressures from Capitol Hill mounting rapidly, President Nixon during the afternoon of March 23rd met with seven of his senior advisers to explore the situation with regard to milk price supports. This was the President's second meeting of the day concerning dairy matters. As will be discussed below, the President and other Administration officials met that morning with dairy representatives in response to a long-standing appointment. Meeting with the President that afternoon were John Connally, then Secretary of the Treasury; Clifford Hardin, then Secretary of Agriculture; Under Secretary of Agriculture, J. Phil Campbell; George Shultz, then Director of the Office of Management and Budget; John D. Ehrlichman, then Assistant to the President for Domestic Affairs; John Whitaker, then Deputy Assistant to the President for Domestic Affairs; and Donald Rice, then Associate Director of the Office of Management and Budget. The discussion was frank and wideranging. It included an appraisal of the support which the milk price legislation had on Capitol Hill and the fact that the legislation had the support of two of the most powerful legislators in the country—Speaker of the House of Representatives Carl Albert and the Chairman of the House Ways and Means Committee, Wilbur Mills.

The political power of the dairy industry lobby was also brought to the President's attention in the March 23rd meeting. Secretary Connally said that their votes would be important in several Midwestern States and he noted that the industry had political funds which would be distributed among House and Senate candidates in the coming election year—although neither the Secretary nor anyone else discussed possible contributions to the President's campaign. Mr. Connally argued that the milk industry's case also had merit on strictly economic grounds, and rising costs for dairy producers were mentioned.

The President himself concluded that the final decision came down to the fact that the Congress was going to pass the higher support legislation, and he could not veto it without alienating the farmers—an essential part of his political constituency. It was also believed that by raising the support level in 1971, similar action in 1972 could be precluded—thus holding the price line for two years.

The fundamental themes running through this March 23rd meeting were two: (1) the unique and very heavy pressures being placed upon the President by the Democratic majority leadership in the Congress and (2) the political advantages and disadvantages of making a decision regarding a vital political constituency.

After the President announced his decision there was discussion of the great power of the House Democratic leadership (which was then pressing for the milk price support increase) and how that power might be enlisted in support of certain of the President's key domestic legislation if the Administration acknowledged the key role these leaders played in securing the reversal of Secretary Hardin's March 12 decision. The meeting concluded with a discussion of the manner in which the decision would be announced and implemented.

Two days later, on March 25, Secretary Hardin officially announced the decision to raise the support level to approximately 85 percent of parity for the 1971-72 marketing season....

II. THE DAIRY INDUSTRY CONTRIBUTIONS AND LOBBYING ACTIVITIES

The discussion in the foregoing section shows that overwhelming Congressional pressure—and the political consequences of ignoring it—was the reason for the milk price support decision reached on March 23rd.

The lobbying and contribution activities of the dairy industry followed a separate track. Not unexpectedly the industry undertook to cover every available base. But there was no arrangement or understanding between the industry and the President as has been so widely and falsely alleged.

The very nature of the Governmental process—with decisions frequently being made within the executive branch on the administration of critical dairy programs and with dairy legislation constantly under review in the Congress—encouraged the dairy farmers to organize and become a potent political force in recent years. There are now three major dairy cooperatives in the United States: AMPI, Mid-America Dairies (Mid Am) and Dairymen, Inc. (DI). Together these cooperatives have over 66,000 members and account for about 25 percent of all the milk produced in the United States.

These dairy organizations not only represent in Washington the interests of their members, they also exert influence through the ballot box and through political contributions. Their activity is not unlike the fundraising and contributing activities of a number of special interest groups such as the Committee on Political Education (COPE) of the AFL-CIO.

The record shows the following lobbying and contribution activities by the dairy industry representatives between 1969 and 1971:

1969-1970

President Nixon had no direct contact with any of the members of these dairy organizations until 1970 when AMPI officials invited him to address their annual convention in Chicago in September. The President was unable to accept the invitation, and Secretary Hardin spoke in his place.

Although he could not attend the convention, the President —as he frequently does—placed a courtesy phone call on September 4, 1970 to the General Manager of AMPI, Mr. Harold Nelson. He also spoke with Secretary Hardin, who was with Mr. Nelson. During that conversation, the President invited the dairy leaders to meet with him in Washington and to arrange a meeting with a larger delegation of dairy leaders at a later date.

Accepting the President's invitation, Mr. Nelson and his special assistant, David Parr, paid a brief courtesy call on the President on September 9, 1970.

The meeting, which was publicly announced to the press, occurred in the Oval Office, and, according to the President's diary, lasted approximately nine minutes. Most of that time was consumed with introductions, photographs and the distribution of Presidential souvenirs.

The context of the meeting was a greeting during a Presidential "Open Hour"—a session frequently arranged for short courtesy calls from diverse groups and individuals. During the "Open Hour" of September 9, the visit from the AMPI representatives was fitted in between the visits of 25 other people, including a group to encourage military servicemen to exercise their votes, a group of concerned citizens from the State of South Dakota and a contingent of Gold Star Mothers.

Mr. Parr has stated in a sworn deposition that it was essentially a social visit. He and Mr. Nelson invited the President to address the next AMPI convention in 1971 and also expressed a hope that he would meet with other dairy industry leaders. Mr. Parr also remembers that the men spoke about the economic plight of the dairy farmer.

Although money was not discussed in the meeting between AMPI representatives and the President in September of 1970, it is evident that raising and making political contributions to both Democrats and Republicans were important, continuous and conspicuous activities of the dairymen during 1970, 1971 and 1972.

During the late 1960's each of the three major dairy cooperatives established a trust fund in order to raise and distribute money to political candidates. AMPI established the Trust for Agricultural Political Education (TAPE), Mid-America Dairies established the Agriculture and Dairy Educational and Political Trust (ADEPT), and Dairymen, Inc. created the Trust for Special Agricultural Community Education (SPACE).

In August of 1969, an attorney for AMPI delivered to Mr. Herbert Kalmbach the sum of $100,000. Mr. Kalmbach deposited the funds in a trustee account he maintained at the Security Pacific National Bank in Newport Beach, California. The account contained political contributions remaining from the 1968 election campaign. The President had no knowledge of this contribution.

Reports on file with the Clerk of the House of Representatives showed that contributions to Congressional candidates in 1969 and 1970 by TAPE, SPACE, and ADEPT totaled over $500,-000. The bulk of the money was earmarked for Democratic candidates. Representatives of the dairy co-ops have indicated in an Associated Press account of December 17, 1973 that Republican candidates received approximately $135,000, or less than 30 percent of the funds.

Some members of the White House staff knew that the dairymen were giving financial support to Republican and Democratic candidates in Senate elections in 1970. One member of the staff, Charles W. Colson, asserted in a memorandum to the President that AMPI had pledged $2 million to the 1972 campaign. (Whether any such pledge was actually made is unknown, but the total amount given to the President's 1972 campaign was $437,000. As noted below, AMPI's campaign contributions to other candidates during this period were even more generous.) That memorandum was attached to a Presidential briefing paper for the courtesy meeting between the President and the AMPI representatives in September of 1970. It was suggested in the memorandum that the President acknowledge AMPI's support. No suggestion was made that any commitment whatsoever be made to do any substantive act. There was also no mention of the asserted pledge during the meeting.

Another reference to fundraising was in a letter addressed to the President on December 16, 1970 from Patrick J. Hillings, a former Congressman who had succeeded Mr. Nixon in his Congressional seat after the latter had been elected to the Senate. At that time, Mr. Hillings was a member of a Washington, D.C. law firm that represented the dairymen in the Nation's Capital. In his letter, Mr. Hillings asked for the immediate imposition of revised dairy import quotas in accordance with recommendations recently presented to the President by the Tariff Commission. President Nixon did not see the letter.

Since the President had already been informed of the fundraising efforts by the dairy industry, the only possible relevance of the Hillings letter would lie in what action was taken on the Tariff Commission recommendations that Mr. Hillings asked the President to accept.

The fact is that the action taken by the President on import quotas was less favorable to the dairy industry than the steps recommended by the Tariff Commission. The Commission, a body of impartial experts, had recommended on economic grounds and pursuant to statutory requirements that imports be closed off entirely for three dairy products (ice cream, certain chocolate products, and animal feeds containing milk derivatives) and that much lower import quotas be set for a fourth item, low-fat cheese. Rather than closing off imports—an action that would have been more favorable to the dairy industry—the President instead reduced the import quotas on each item, permitting all four goods to continue their competition with American dairy products.

1971

The President next met with dairy representatives at 10:30 a.m. on March 23, 1971, in the Cabinet Room of the White House. Included in the meeting were a delegation from the dairy cooperatives as well as several Administration officials, including OMB Director, George Shultz; Assistant to the President, John Ehrlichman; Deputy Assistants to the President, Henry Cashen and John Whitaker; and Donald Rice, Associate Director of OMB. From the Department of Agriculture were Secretary Hardin; Under Secretary Phil Campbell; Assistant Secretaries Clarence Palmby and Richard Lyng; and Deputy Assistant Secretary William Galbraith.

Contrary to allegations which have since been made, the meeting had been scheduled more than three weeks *before* the

March 12 announcement on price supports by Secretary Hardin. As noted above, the meeting stemmed from an invitation first extended on September 4, 1970 when the President spoke by telephone to Harold Nelson of AMPI. In January of 1971, Secretary Hardin recommended to the White House that the meeting be placed on the President's schedule. Thereafter, in February, the White House arranged the March meeting.

The President opened the meeting by thanking the dairy leaders for the support they had given to Administration policies and praised them for their activism in pursuing goals which were important to them. The remainder of the meeting was taken up with the dairy leaders pleading their case for higher supports and with other Administration officials expressing concerns about overproduction and higher retail prices. There was no mention whatsoever of campaign contributions. Nor were any conclusions regarding dairy supports reached at the meeting, as the President pressed the attendees as to whether or not they could control overproduction. Much was said by the dairy representatives of the higher costs of their doing business.

Prior to this meeting, a staff memorandum was prepared as a briefing paper for the President. That paper briefly noted that the dairy lobby—like organized labor—had decided to spend political money and that Pat Hillings and Murray Chotiner were involved. There was no suggestion that the President should give special treatment to the dairymen. In fact, that same paper discussed in much more detail the pressure which was coming from the Congress for higher supports; that the Congress was acting at Speaker Albert's instigation; that the Democratic leadership wanted to embarrass the President; and that a bill for higher supports would probably be passed, thus presenting the President with a very tough veto situation.

There were no other discussions between the President and the dairy industry representatives prior to the President's decision on the afternoon of March 23, 1971.

There are a number of mistaken notions with regard to these lobbying efforts of the dairy industry. One is that they had a substantial influence upon the President's decisions. That is untrue. Another is that the dairy contributions represented a substantial portion of the total funding of the President's re-election effort. The truth is that the contributions from the dairymen amounting to some $427,000, constituted less than one percent of the total....

III. CONSEQUENCE OF PRESIDENT'S DECISION

Although the President's decision of March 23rd was based largely on political realities, unrelated to campaign contributions, it also proved to be sound economics. Here, in brief, were the economic results:

Milk Production: One of the continuing concerns of the Department of Agriculture is to assure that milk supplies are adequate but not excessive. In the mid-1960's, there was a downward trend in the production of milk from 126.9 billion pounds in 1964-65 to 116.5 billion pounds in 1969-70. Supplies had become sufficiently low by the late 1960's that Secretary Hardin's decision to raise the milk support level in 1970 was based in large part upon his desire to increase production. The support increase of 38 cents per hundredweight for that year helped to end the decline in production as some 117.4 billion pounds of milk were produced in the 1970-71 marketing year. The additional increase in the support price to $4.93 as a result of the March 25th announcement provided still further assurances against the resumption of a downward trend in production. For the marketing year 1971-1972, the total milk production was 119.4 billion pounds.

Cost of Milk to the Consumer: The average retail price per half gallon of milk has been rising steadily since 1965, as shown by this chart:

1965	47.3 ¢
1966	49.8
1967	51.7
1968	53.7
1969	55.1
1970	57.4
1971	58.9
1972	59.8

(Yearly average retail price per half gallon of milk in leading cities of the United States; U.S. Department of Agriculture)

From the view of the consumer, it can be seen that prices continued to rise, but that the 1971-72 increase was the smallest of all the years shown on the chart—and was considerably less than the rate of general inflation. These reductions in the rate of milk inflation in 1971 and 1972 are directly related to the President's decision of March 23 because the announcement of March 25 encouraged the production of milk to a level higher than it otherwise would have been. Thus, because supplies increased, market price increases have been less than they otherwise would have been.

Cost of the Milk Support Program to the Government: Net expenditures for the dairy price support program and related costs (butter, cheese, dried milk and similar products) were as follows for the recent fiscal years (Commodity Credit Corporation Net Expenditures):

Fiscal Year 1970—$ 87.2 million
Fiscal Year 1971— 214.3 million
Fiscal Year 1972— 174.2 million
Fiscal Year 1973— 116.6 million

As can be seen, the cost during the fiscal year in question—1972 —was considerably lower than the year before. It dropped again the following year.

Government Inventories of Dairy Products: One of the concerns of the Secretary of Agriculture is to ensure that his Department has reasonable supplies of dairy products to meet the goals of its family feeding and child nutrition programs. At the same time, the Secretary wants to avoid excessive production which would tend to overload the Department's stocks. The aim is thus to achieve a balance in the Commodity Credit Corporation (CCC) stockpiles. As of January, 1971, there was some concern that the stocks might fall too low if production of milk were reduced. As it turned out, the butter, processed cheese and nonfat dry milk stocks in the CCC dipped between a high of 257.9 million pounds to a low of 62.7 million pounds during 1971, even with increased production of milk, but it is a virtual certainty they would have been even lower if the decision had not been made to raise the parity level to 85 percent. Here are the figures for the CCC's uncommitted inventory as of January 31 of each year: (in millions of pounds)

Marketing Year	Butter	Cheese	Nonfat Dry Milk
1968	124.7	67.9	208.4
1969	73.0	23.1	221.1
1970	35.2	—	116.5
1971	61.8	6.6	18.7
1972	37.1	1.9	1.4

IV. CONCLUSIONS

The information contained in this discussion can be summarized as follows:

• Immediately after the Agriculture Department first announced on March 12 that milk would be supported at approximately 80 percent of parity, pressures developed on Capitol Hill for mandatory legislation to increase the parity level to 85-90 percent. Several of the President's advisers believed that the legislation would be enacted and that a Presidential veto of such legislation would be politically disastrous for Mr. Nixon in several States.

• Except for the fear that a rise in supports would create problems of overproduction, several advisers believed the dairymen's case to be meritorious due to the rising costs of fuel, feed, and labor for those producing dairy products. In fact, the corn blight of 1970 considerably reduced many supplies of feed grain for the 1971 marketing year.

• With the Congress putting "a gun to our head" and with his senior advisers supporting him, the President decided that the parity level should be increased to 85 percent.

• Economically, the President's decision to raise the support level proved to be sound and beneficial for the Nation.

• While the President had been advised that the dairymen had decided to make contributions towards the re-election effort of 1972, this did not influence the President's decision to raise the level of supports.

ITT Antitrust Decision

Following are excerpts from the White House text of a background paper released Jan. 8 on the administration's actions in an antitrust case against International Telephone and Telegraph Corporation (ITT):

In the thousands of pages of testimony and analysis regarding the ITT case since 1971, the only major charge that has been publicly made against President Nixon is that in return for a promise of a political contribution from a subsidiary of ITT, the President directed the Justice Department to settle antitrust suits against the corporation. That charge is totally without foundation:

• The President originally acted in the case because he wanted to avoid a Supreme Court ruling that would permit antitrust suits to be brought against large American companies simply on the basis of their size. He did not direct the settlement or participate in the settlement negotiations directly or indirectly. The only action taken by the President was a telephoned instruction on April 19, 1971 to drop a pending appeal in one of the ITT cases. He rescinded that instruction two days later.

• The actual settlement of the ITT case, while avoiding a Supreme Court ruling, caused the corporation to undertake the largest single divestiture in corporate history. The company was forced to divest itself of subsidiaries with some $1 billion in annual sales, and its acquisitions were restricted for a period of 10 years.

• The President was unaware of any commitment by ITT to make a contribution toward expenses of the Republican National Convention at the time he took action on the antitrust case. In fact, the President's antitrust actions took place entirely in April of 1971—several weeks before the ITT pledge was even made.

I. PRESIDENT'S INTEREST IN ANTI-TRUST POLICY

Mr. Nixon made it clear during his 1968 campaign for the Presidency that he stood for an antitrust policy which would balance the goals of free competition in the marketplace against the avoidance of unnecessary government interference with free enterprise. One of Mr. Nixon's major antitrust concerns in that campaign was the Government's treatment of conglomerate mergers. Conglomerates had become an important factor in the American economy during the 1960's, and despite public fears that they were threatening free competition in the marketplace, the administrations of those years—in Mr. Nixon's opinion—had not been clear in their attitude toward them....

A second major concern of the President and his advisors was their fear that the ability of U.S. companies to compete in the world market might be threatened by antitrust actions against conglomerates. The United States faced a shrinking balance of trade surplus and the President and many of his advisors felt that U.S. multi-national companies could play an important role in improving the balance.

The President feared that antitrust action against those companies which was based upon something other than a clear restraint of trade would render them less able to compete with the government-sheltered and sponsored industrial giants of Europe and Asia. The President and his advisors were keenly aware that the large industrial entities of foreign countries did not operate under the kind of antitrust pressure faced by American companies, and they believed that the absence of such pressure enabled those countries to compete more successfully in world markets....

The President and his advisors, (but not Attorney General Mitchell, who had disqualified himself on matters related to ITT) were thus seriously concerned about two aspects of antitrust policy which would eventually bear on the ITT matter: 1) the policy of attacking bigness *per se* and whether such policy had any economic justification, and 2) the need to prevent misguided antitrust attacks upon U.S. companies in competition with large foreign industrial entities.

II. BACKGROUND ON THE ITT LITIGATION

The Justice Department in 1969 initiated civil litigation against the International Telephone and Telegraph Co., a major "conglomerate," for alleged violations of the antitrust laws. The allegations involved acquisitions by ITT of the Grinnell Corporation, the Hartford Fire Insurance Company, and the Canteen Corporation. These were only the latest and among the largest of a series of acquisitions made by ITT in the years since 1963, a period in which favorable tax laws, among other things, made acquisitions popular.

Under Assistant Attorney General McLaren, the Antitrust Division of the Justice Department was concerned with the implementation of an antitrust policy which attacked the general merger trend not only because the effect of the corporate growth "may be substantially to lessen competition," conduct clearly proscribed by the antitrust laws, but also because of the economic concentration itself.

Other experts, including many of the President's advisors, did not see the role of antitrust law in such all-encompassing terms. They believed that to use the law of antitrust to achieve political and economic aims beyond prevention of restraint of trade was unsound. If there were dangers such as Mr. McLaren and his colleagues feared from conglomerates, President Nixon and his advisors, along with other experts, preferred solving them through legislation.

Executives of ITT were also concerned about the Justice Department action, and talked with various administration officials to learn their views. The chief executive officer of ITT, Harold Geneen, was sufficiently concerned that he attempted to talk to the President personally about these issues in the summer of 1969. The President's advisors thought that such a meeting was not appropriate, and the meeting was not held.

Other White House officials, however, did talk to various representatives of ITT about antitrust policy. Those discussions invariably focused on the legal and economic issues of whether antitrust suits should be pursued simply because companies are large or rather because they are actually restraining trade in a tangible way. Papers relating to those conversations have been voluntarily turned over to the Special Prosecutor.

III. MAKING THE ITT CASES CONSISTENT WITH ADMINISTRATION POLICY ON ANTITRUST

During the latter part of 1970, there was a question among White House advisors about whether the antitrust actions against the ITT were consistent with the notion of keeping hands off companies unless they had committed some clear restraint of trade rather than simply becoming large in size, and generally whether the ITT suits were consistent with administration policy on antitrust.

While these discussions were taking place, the Justice Department lawsuits against ITT were continuing. The Justice Department's action against ITT to enjoin the acquisitions of the Grinnell Corporation and Hartford Fire Insurance Company were presented to the United States District Court for the District of Connecticut on September 17, 1969. The court (Chief Judge Timbers, presiding) issued a Memorandum of Decision on October 21, 1969, denying the Government's motion for a preliminary injunction to enjoin the proposed acquisitions by ITT, but directing that "hold separate" orders be entered to preserve the status quo, pending a trial and a decision on the merits.

Subsequently, a trial of the Grinnell case on the merits was held on September 15, 1970 and concluded on October 30, 1970. The court again refused to find that ITT had violated the antitrust laws....

As a result of this litigation and pending a determination to appeal the adverse judgment to the Supreme Court of the United States, Assistant Attorney General McLaren discussed a compromise settlement with ITT during 1970. He indicated he would recommend that ITT be allowed to keep the Grinnell Corporation, but divest itself of the Canteen Corporation and not proceed with its pending acquisition of the Hartford Fire Insurance Company.

By the Spring of 1971, the President, based on the information and advice he had received, had concluded that the ITT litigation was inconsistent with his own views on anti-trust policy. The Department of Justice and some of the President's advisors continued to maintain, however, that the cases were not an attack on bigness and were based on clear anti-competitive effects of the acquisitions.

On April 19, 1971, in a meeting with John Ehrlichman and George Shultz, then Director of the Office of Management and Budget, the President was told by Mr. Ehrlichman that the Justice Department had filed an appeal with the Supreme Court in the Grinnell case which Mr. Ehrlichman described as an "attack on a conglomerate." Mr. Ehrlichman further told the President that he believed that prosecution of the case was contrary to the President's antitrust policy and that, as a result, he had tried to persuade the Justice Department not to file a jurisdictional statement (due the following day) so as to terminate the appeal. He indicated, however, that he had been unsuccessful with the Justice Department.

The President expressed irritation with the failure of the head of the Antitrust Division, Mr. McLaren, to follow his policy. He then placed a telephone call to Deputy Attorney General Kleindienst and ordered that the appeal not be filed. The meeting continued with a further discussion of antitrust policy during which Mr. Shultz expressed the view that conglomerates had been unfairly criticized.

The Justice Department, on April 20, 1971, requested and was granted a delay in filing the appeal which was due that day. On the following day, April 21, 1971, Mr. John N. Mitchell, the Attorney General, advised the President that in his judgment it was inadvisable for the President to order no appeal to the Supreme Court in the Grinnell case. The Attorney General reasoned that, as a personal matter, Mr. Erwin N. Griswold, Solicitor General of the United States, had prepared his brief for appeal and would resign were the appeal not to proceed. The Attorney General further feared legislative repercussions if the matter were dropped entirely. Based upon the Attorney General's recommendations, the President reversed his decision of April 19, 1971, and authorized the Department of Justice to proceed with the case in accordance with its own determinations. He said that he did not care about ITT as such, but that he wanted the Attorney General to see that his antitrust policy was carried out.

At the end of the same month, April 1971, the President approved a proposal for creating a central clearing house for information about government antitrust policy within the White House, to ensure that the President's views on the subject could be made known to all the operating agencies.

On April 29, 1971, a meeting of ITT representatives, Department of Justice and Department of Treasury officials was held at the Department of Justice wherein ITT made a presentation concerning the financial ramifications of the proposed divestiture actions. Following the meeting, the Department of Justice requested that the Treasury Department and an outside consultant specializing in financial analysis evaluate the ITT claims. These evaluations were made in addition to the Justice Department's own analysis of competitive effect.

Based on the completed assessment, Assistant Attorney General McLaren, on June 17, 1971, sent a memorandum to the Deputy Attorney General outlining a proposed settlement. This proposal was subsequently communicated to ITT representatives and after further negotiations a final settlement, extremely similar to Mr. McLaren's June 17 proposal, was agreed upon in principle on July 31, 1971, and final consent judgments were entered by the United States District Courts on September 24, 1971. On the first trading day after the settlement was announced the common stock of ITT fell 11 per cent, from 62 to 55 on investor reaction to the terms of the settlement....

IV. SELECTION OF SAN DIEGO FOR REPUBLICAN NATIONAL CONVENTION

The separate and unrelated process of decision-making regarding the Republican National Convention began in 1971, when the Site Selection Committee started to examine prospective sites.

In the 1971 selection process, six cities were seriously considered for the 1972 convention, and were being considered seriously by the site selection committee. Working with the Republican National Committee were White House staffers who were concerned for the security, logistics and effective functioning of the Presidency in any given location.

On June 29, 1971, the San Diego City Council adopted a resolution authorizing the mayor of the City of San Diego to submit a bid on the Republican National Convention to be held in San Diego, and to offer financial support of $1,500,000. Of this amount, $600,000 was to be used for city services, such as police and fire protection, extra public works responsibilities and other service requirements connected with a convention.

The remaining $900,000 to be used for facilities, rents and other convention requirements was conditioned upon contributions in cash and services by other State and local governmental agencies, individuals, corporations and organizations.

A large part of the cash portion of the bid was committed by the Sheraton Hotel Corporation, a subsidiary of ITT, about June 1, 1971, and subsequently confirmed on July 21, 1971. A new Sheraton hotel was under construction in San Diego, and Sheraton apparently felt that television publicity for the hotel and the chain would be a worthwhile business investment The exact provisions of the donation were and are unclear. Apparently ITT-Sheraton offered $200,000 with some requirement of matching by other San Diego businessmen as to one-half of the commitment. In any event, a payment of $100,000 to the San Diego Convention and Visitors' Bureau was returned when the convention site was changed.

The White House Staff report to Chief of Staff H. R. Haldeman on possible convention sites made no mention of ITT. Rather, it recommended San Diego because of California's Republican Governor, San Diego's Republican Congressman, its proximity to the Western White House, its outstanding climate, its relatively large bid in money and services, the importance of California in the electoral tally, the attractive outdoors atmosphere of the town, and the excellent security which could be offered.

The President, himself, informed Senator Robert Dole, Chairman of the Republican National Committee, that whatever Senator Dole and the Site Selection Committee decided was agreeable to him. Subsequently, the President approved the selection of San Diego by the Site Selection Committee. √

WATERGATE: INDICATIONS OF DELIBERATE TAPE ERASURES

The long-awaited results of a study by experts of what caused the celebrated 18½-minute gap in a tape recording of a Watergate-related presidential conversation were made public the week ending Jan. 19. They were bad news for President Nixon.

The six-man panel of electronics specialists reported on Jan. 15 that the hum on the June 20, 1972, tape had been caused by at least five separate, manual erasures. The missing segment contained a conversation between the President and H. R. Haldeman, then the White House chief of staff. It was considered crucial evidence in proving whether or not Nixon knew of or participated in the Watergate coverup. He denied that he did.

The experts made their report to Chief Judge John J. Sirica of U.S. District Court in Washington, D.C. Sirica started four days of hearings the day he received the report. At the conclusion of the hearings, Sirica announced that he would send the case to a federal grand jury for action.

But the bad news for Nixon did not end with the disclosures about the June 20 tape. On Jan. 18, it was brought out that two other tapes of presidential conversations also contained gaps.

One was a 57-second blank space in a cassette recording of the President's recollection of a March 21, 1973, meeting with John W. Dean III, then the White House counsel and later the man who first alleged White House involvement in the Watergate coverup.

The other was a 38-second blank in Nixon's taped recollection of a telephone conversation with former Attorney General John N. Mitchell on June 20, 1972, three days after the Watergate break-in and the same day as the conversation containing the 18½-minute gap.

Experts' Report. The possibility that the Nixon-Haldeman conversation was deliberately erased was raised after the court-appointed panel of technical experts reported that the gap resulted from a manual process of repeated erasures and re-recording. *(Report excerpts, p. 203)*

The experts said the gap could not possibly have been caused accidentally by Nixon's personal secretary, Rose Mary Woods, in the process of transcribing the tapes, as she had testified "must have" happened. Woods also said, however, that she could not have caused more than four or five minutes of the gap.

The panel's report shook the nation, already shocked by previous disclosures of missing or inaudible White House tapes. *(p. 118, 94)*

The report and succeeding days of conflicting court testimony by White House aides and Secret Service agents set off a quick chain of reactions:

• The FBI entered the case of the Watergate tapes for the first time, at the request of Watergate Special Prosecutor Leon Jaworski. The White House said Jan. 17 that it would cooperate with the investigation, but would

not say what would happen if agents tried to interview the President on the subject. FBI Director Clarence M. Kelley did not rule out the possibility that this would be necessary. Kelley said that only Jaworski would receive the results of the FBI inquiry.

• Congressional reaction was quick and almost unanimous in the belief that the latest disclosures represented a damaging blow to the President. Any evidence of his involvement in the Watergate coverup or tampering with tapes would make impeachment almost inevitable, some members said. *(Reaction, p. 206)*

Rep. Jerome R. Waldie (D Calif.), a member of the House Judiciary Committee, which was considering impeachment, said that if Nixon refused to turn over materials needed by the committee, he would demand an immediate House vote on impeachment.

• The disclosures probably helped give a new lease on life to the Senate select Watergate committee and its hearings, which some committee members reportedly had wanted to end. The committee was to decide after the opening of Congress Jan. 21 whether or not to continue public hearings into Watergate-related matters, including campaign contributions made to Nixon by the milk producers and by billionaire Howard Hughes.

• The White House denied Jan. 16 that Nixon himself had erased the tapes, either accidentally or deliberately, and said any "premature judgments" about the report of erasures on the tapes were "unwarranted." Gerald L. Warren, the deputy White House press secretary, refused to answer any other questions about the reports.

• Vice President Gerald R. Ford said Jan. 17 that it would be "premature to jump in on the testimony of six witnesses, who may or may not be upheld, and call for impeachment."

• Sen. Barry Goldwater (R Ariz.) also defended the President, saying the technical experts' report "doesn't mean a thing." But most of the reaction to the news was grim and indicated serious damage to the President, who already was at the lowest point of his career in public opinion polls. *(Goldwater, Ford speeches, p. 204; poll report, p. 202)*

District Court Hearings

Scarcely had the implication of the technical experts' report sunk in—that the June 20 taped conversation had been obliterated deliberately—than further questions began to be raised. In the hearing Jan. 15-18 before Judge Sirica, most of the questions centered on who had access to the tape with the 18½-minute gap and the Uher 5000 recorder on which the erasures were made.

However, on Jan. 18 a new question was introduced when Richard Ben-Veniste, Watergate assistant special prosecutor, disclosed the two new tape gaps, raising the question of whether other possibly incriminating tapes had been erased. Ben-Veniste told Congressional Quarterly that the technical experts had not yet studied those tapes, so no determination had been made that there were erasures.

Presidential Counsel J. Fred Buzhardt, appearing as a witness, confirmed that the gaps existed but said they could be accounted for by the President's shutting off the machine when interrupted while dictating his recollections of conversations, then resuming dictation before turning the recorder back on—a common occurrence, he said.

Poll Report

President Nixon's popularity sank to its all-time low in the Harris Survey published Jan. 17. *(Earlier poll report, p. 191)*

In interviews Jan. 7-10 of 1,460 households nationwide, Harris asked: "How would you rate the job Nixon is doing as president—excellent, pretty good, only fair, or poor?"

Excellent-good	30%
Fair-poor	68
Not sure	2

The favorable rating represented a 7 per cent drop from the 37 per cent in the previous poll, conducted in November 1973. *(p. 180)*

Another question in the survey: "Do you tend to agree or disagree with the statement that President Nixon has reached the point where he no longer can be an effective president and should resign for the good of the country?"

	Latest	November 1973
Agree	47%	44%
Disagree	42	45
Not sure	11	11

Nixon also dropped to his all-time low in Harris ratings on "inspiring confidence personally in the White House."

	Latest	February 1973
Positive	17%	48%
Negative	78	41
Not sure	5	11

The latest Harris Survey was conducted near the conclusion of "Operation Candor," the White House effort to restore confidence in Nixon by releasing information about the President's role in Watergate-related matters. But 73 per cent of those questioned agreed that Nixon "has withheld important information about his involvement in the Watergate affair." Only 18 per cent disagreed.

"Thus," Harris concluded, "the issue of Watergate and its spreading implications about presidential integrity has not gone away, and President Nixon is in worse shape than ever before with American public opinion. The public is still deeply interested in the issue, and, with the passage of time, Mr. Nixon appears to be in more, rather than less, trouble."

"Is it also possible the dictation was gone over with an erase button?" asked Ben-Veniste.

"No," said Buzhardt. However, he later said he could only give his own opinion on that.

Buzhardt said that he did not specifically recall any gaps in the tapes when he first listened to them in order to prepare an index and analysis of them at the court's request. But the gaps were there when the tapes were turned over to the court Nov. 26.

The 18½-minute gap on the June 20 tape was disclosed to the prosecutors and the court Nov. 21. Buzhardt said at that time that the gap did not appear to be accidental and that "at its worst, it looks like a very serious thing," according to a previously sealed transcript of a court meeting at the time the gap was disclosed. Buzhardt also suggested that the matter be taken before the grand jury for investigation, the transcript showed.

Sirica permitted Woods' defense counsel, Charles S. Rhyne, to read the 30-page transcript aloud in court Jan. 18. Rhyne attempted to show that Woods was not informed of White House actions on the tapes, that other persons unknown to her had access to her office at night when she was not present and that she was not properly represented by White House counsel.

"These lawyers for Miss Woods came down here and pleaded her guilty before this proceeding ever started," said Rhyne, a law school classmate of Nixon at Duke University. Both Rhyne and the White House denied a report in *The Washington Post* Jan. 17 that Nixon had asked Woods to take the blame for the 18½-minute erasure, which the experts' report indicated was made after Oct. 1.

Woods and Stephen B. Bull, a White House aide, had custody of the tapes during that period. Bull said he was the only one who could open the safe in which they were kept, but denied he was responsible for the erasures.

Bull said Jan. 18 that he did not recall many details about who might have had access to the tapes. Nor did he recall, he said, most of his conversations with Woods, orders given him by the President or two post-midnight visits to a safe with the tapes in Key Biscayne, Fla., on Oct. 4, 1973, as recorded in Secret Service logs.

Bull also described how he carried a brown manila envelope from Woods' villa to the President's study about midnight one night during the Oct. 4-7 weekend at Key Biscayne, but said he recalled nothing else about the incident.

Technicians' Findings on Tapes

The latest bombshell in the case of the Watergate tapes exploded Jan. 15 when the panel of court-appointed technical experts delivered its unanimous report to Judge Sirica, the special Watergate prosecutor and the White House Watergate defense counsel. The six experts had been approved by both sides. Sirica called them to testify about their report at a hearing the same day. *(Text of report, p. 203; panel members, p. 168; interim report p. 176)*

Contents of Tape. The tape with the well-publicized 18½-minute hum presumably contained a conversation between Nixon and his former chief of staff, H. R. Haldeman. According to Haldeman's notes on the June 20 meeting, the two men talked about the Watergate

Experts' Report to Court on 18-Minute Hum in Tape

Following are excerpts of the report made to Chief Judge John J. Sirica Jan. 15 by the advisory panel of electronics specialists that studied the June 20, 1972, presidential tape containing an 18½-minute gap:

In response to your request we have made a comprehensive technical study of the White House tape of June 20, 1972, with special attention to a section of buzzing sounds that lasts approximately 18.5 minutes. Paragraphs that follow summarize our findings and indicate the kinds of tests and evidence on which we base the findings.

Magnetic signatures that we have measured directly on the tape show that the buzzing sounds were put on the tape in the process of erasing and re-recording at least five, and perhaps as many as nine, separate and contiguous segments. Hand operation of keyboard controls on the Uher 5000 recorder was involved in starting and again in stopping the recording of each segment. The magnetic signatures observed on the tape show conclusively that the 18.5-minute section could not have been produced by any single, continuous operation. Further, whether the footpedal was used or not, the recording controls must have been operated by hand in the making of each segment.

The erasing and recording operations that produced the buzzing section were done directly on the tape we received for study. We have found that this tape is 1814.5 feet long, which lies within a normal range for tapes sold as 1800 feet in length. We have examined the entire tape for physical splices and have found none. Other tests that we have made thus far are consistent with the assumption that the tape is an original and not a re-recording.

A Uher 5000 recorder, almost surely the one designated as Government Exhibit #60, was used in producing the 18.5-minute section. Support for this conclusion includes recorder operating characteristics that we measured and found to correspond to signal characteristics observed on the evidence tape.

The buzzing sounds themselves originated in noise picked up from the electrical power line to which the recorder was connected. Measurements of the frequency spectrum of the buzz showed that it is made up of a 60 cycles per second fundamental tone, plus a large number of harmonic tones at multiples of 60. Especially strong are the third harmonic at 180 and the fifth harmonic at 300 cycles per second. As many as forty harmonics are present in the buzz and create its "raucous" quality. Variations in the strength of the buzz, which during most of the 18.5-minute section is either "loud" or "soft," probably arose from several causes including variations in the noise on the power line, erratic functioning of the recorder, and changes in the position of

the operator's hand while running the recorder. The variations do not appear to be caused by normal machine operations.

Can speech sounds be detected under the buzzing? We think so. At three locations in the 18.5-minute section, we have observed a fragment of speech-like sound lasting less than one second. Each of the fragments lies exactly at a place on the tape that was missed by the erase head during the series of operations in which the several segments of erasure and buzz were put on the tape. Further, the frequency spectra of the sounds in these fragments bear a reasonable resemblance to the spectra of speech sounds.

Can the speech be recovered? We think not. We know of no technique that could recover intelligible speech from the buzz section. Even the fragments that we have observed are so heavily obscured that we cannot tell what was said....

In developing the technical evidence on which we have based the findings reported here, we have used laboratory facilities, measuring instruments, and techniques of several kinds, including: digital computers located in three different laboratories, specialized instruments for measuring frequency spectra and waveforms, techniques for "developing" magnetic marks that can be seen and measured directly on the tape, techniques for measuring the performance characteristics of recorders and voice-operated switches, and statistical methods for analyzing experimental results.

In summary we have reached complete agreement on the following conclusions:

1. The erasing and recording operations that produced the buzz section were done directly on the evidence tape.

2. The Uher 5000 recorder designated Government Exhibit #60 probably produced the entire buzz section.

3. The erasures and buzz recordings were done in at least five, and perhaps as many as nine, separate and contiguous segments.

4. Erasure and recording of each segment required hand operation of keyboard controls on the Uher 5000 machine.

5. Erased portions of the tape probably contained speech originally.

6. Recovery of the speech is not possible by any method known to us.

7. The evidence tape, in so far as we have determined, is an original and not a copy.

Respectfully submitted,
Richard H. Bolt
Franklin S. Cooper
James L. Flanagan
John G. (Jay) McKnight
Thomas G. Stockham, Jr.
Mark R. Weiss

break-in three days before and about Nixon's instructions to mount a public relations offensive to divert public attention from the affair. *(p. 161)*

The taped conversation could have given evidence of whether and when the President had knowledge of the Watergate break-in and subsequent cover-up—a subject of intense concern to the Senate select Watergate committee and the House Judiciary Committee, which was investigating whether to impeach Nixon.

How Erasures Occurred. The panel of experts, after two months of exhaustive tests in laboratories

around the country, agreed that the 18½-minute gap in the tape resulted from the repeated manual activation of the "erase head" of the Uher 5000 tape recorder used by Nixon's personal secretary, Woods. Distinctive marks, or "quartet signatures," which show up only under magnetic fluid, proved that there were at least five, and perhaps as many as nine, separate and contiguous erasures, the panel said.

None of the erasures, the experts said, could have resulted from the accidental touching of the "record" key while keeping a foot on the machine's foot pedal, as Woods testified "must have" happened while she was transcribing the tape Oct. 1. *(Woods' testimony, p. 168, 160, 118)*

The President's new Watergate defense attorney, James D. St. Clair, making his first court appearance in the case, objected repeatedly to attempts by the prosecution to have the expert witnesses characterize the erasures as either accidental or deliberate. However, Dr. Richard H. Bolt, unofficial chairman of the panel, did confirm, under questioning by Richard Ben-Veniste, the assistant Watergate special prosecutor, that if the erasures were caused by accident, "it would have to be an accident that was repeated at least five times."

Although the panel of experts was agreed on jointly by the White House and the Watergate prosecutors, St. Clair made it clear that he would seek to discredit their report by bringing in "his own experts" when the hearing resumed Jan. 17.

Tests indicated the erased tape originally had contained speech, the panel said, but "recovery of the speech is not possible by any method known to us."

The buzzing sound on the 18½-minute portion of the 70-minute tape resulted from amplification of noise picked up from the power source to which the recorder was connected, and was due to a faulty part (the bridge rectifier) in the machine, the panel said. The experts did not believe the buzzing was caused by Woods' electric typewriter or high-intensity lamp, as White House Counsel J. Fred Buzhardt suggested Nov. 29, panel member Mark R. Weiss testified. *(Buzhardt testimony, p. 161)*

The buzzing itself, and its source, were not relevant to the issue of the erasures, Bolt added.

Secret Service Testimony. Called to testify Jan. 16 before Judge Sirica were Bull and the two Secret Service agents who purchased the Uher tape recorder Oct. 1 and delivered it to Bull. Bull subsequently delivered it to Woods to use in transcribing the White House tapes. Ben-Veniste said previous attempts to get the two agents to testify apparently had been blocked by White House counsel.

The testimony of Bull and Louis Sims, chief of the technical security division of the Secret Service, conflicted with several statements made by Woods in her testimony and raised new doubts about her story.

Sims said he did not deliver the tape recorder to Bull until about 1:15 p.m. Oct. 1. Woods had testified that she used the machine for two or two and one-half hours that day before the accidental erasure occurred, a "terrible mistake" she immediately reported to Nixon—at 2:08 p.m., according to White House logs. Woods also said that Oct. 1 was the only day she worked on that tape.

The contradictions in testimony raised questions as to how long Woods actually used the Uher machine, what other persons may have had access to it, and when. Since the panel said the erasures "almost surely" were produced by that particular machine, they must have occurred between Oct. 1, when it was purchased, and Nov. 21, when the tape gap was first reported to the court. However, Sims said the machine was modified so it could not erase between Nov. 12 and Nov. 20.

Sims said he was unable to supply documentary evidence on who used the tape recorder, because such records were destroyed as soon as the machine was returned to Secret Service custody. Bull testified that in

(Continued on p. 206)

Defenders of the President

Two Republican leaders, Vice President Gerald R. Ford and Arizona Sen. Barry Goldwater, coupled strong defenses of President Nixon with harsh attacks on his critics.

Ford. On Jan. 15, two hours before new information damaging to the administration was disclosed in a Washington, D.C., court hearing, Ford told the American Farm Bureau Federation in Atlantic City, N.J., that "powerful pressure organizations" were engaged in "an all-out attack" on the President and his policies.

Ford declined to comment later in the day on the report of technical experts that an 18½-minute gap in the crucial spot on one of the subpoenaed White House tapes was caused by erasing and re-recording at least five segments of the tape. But an aide said the Vice President had no information about the report before he spoke. *(Tapes report, p. 202)*

Two of the groups Ford cited were the AFL-CIO and Americans for Democratic Action (ADA), both of which had been lobbying publicly for Nixon's impeachment. "If they can crush the President and his philosophy, they are convinced that they can then dominate the Congress and, through it, the nation," he said.

Ford lashed out at "the relatively small group of activists who are out to impeach the President." If they cannot succeed immediately, he said, "they will try to stretch out the ordeal, to cripple the President by dragging out the preliminaries to impeachment for as long as they can, and to use the whole affair for maximum political advantage."

The uncharacteristically combative tone of Ford's speech led to speculation that it had been written by White House speech writers. *The Washington Star-News* printed such a report Jan. 16, and Ford acknowledged that White House writers had worked with him to draft the speech, because he had not yet hired writers of his own. But he insisted that he initiated and approved its substance.

Goldwater. Barry Goldwater, who earlier had emerged as a leading Republican critic of Nixon's handling of the Watergate scandals, echoed Ford's attacks on administration critics during a party fund-raising dinner Jan. 15. Speaking in Hunt Valley, Md., he charged that "liberal Democrats do not have what it takes either in evidence or guts" to impeach Nixon. *(Earlier Goldwater comments, p. 184)*

Goldwater said he would not lead a delegation of Republicans to ask Nixon to resign, as some rumors had suggested. But he repeated his earlier characterization of Watergate affair as "one of the most scandalous and stupid in the history of this country." Goldwater had first changed direction on the issue in a Jan. 13 appearance on "Meet the Press," where he defended the President and attacked his critics.

Asked about the technical experts' report on the Watergate tape, Goldwater said the new information "doesn't mean a thing to me."

Conflicting Reports on White House Security Leaks

News reports that military "spies" copied and leaked secret information on U.S. diplomatic plans in 1971 brought demands for investigations during the week ending Jan. 19.

The reports also said the military "spying" was the "national security" matter cited by President Nixon as the reason he sought to suppress investigations into activities of the White House "plumbers"—the secret investigative unit later found to have been involved in the Watergate break-in and other illegal activities. The "plumbers," while investigating a news leak to columnist Jack Anderson in 1971, reportedly uncovered a military "spy ring" in the White House, which forwarded secret plans of Henry A. Kissinger and information from National Security Council (NSC) meetings to high Pentagon officials and occasionally leaked them to the press.

The week's escalating news stories on the unauthorized passing of diplomatic secrets brought about these developments:

• Sen. John C. Stennis (D Miss.), chairman of the Senate Armed Services Committee, said he would begin an informal inquiry into the matter at once and would consult the committee the next week before deciding whether to call for hearings and a full investigation.

• Rep. William S. Cohen (R Maine) compared the incident to the celebrated Pentagon Papers case and asked Attorney General William B. Saxbe to investigate for possible law violations.

• Secretary of Defense James Schlesinger launched his own informal investigation into the matter.

The Pentagon already had tentatively decided, however, that the "spying" amounted to no more than "over-zealous improprieties" by several staff members of the joint chiefs of staff, Pentagon spokesman William Beecher said Jan. 16. High White House officials also sought to minimize the significance of the "spying" by characterizing as "ludicrous" a 1972 report on it by David R. Young Jr., then codirector of the plumbers. White House sources said Young's portrayal of an organized spy ring was terribly overdrawn, according to *The New York Times*. The sources pinned the blame on a young Navy yeoman who "was told to keep his eyes open and who went ape."

Nixon Concern. This view seemed to contradict Nixon's version of the case as a national security matter so serious that it justified his preventing a Justice Department investigation of the plumbers. Nixon alluded in a Nov. 17 press conference to a "matter so sensitive that even Sen. Ervin and Sen. Baker (the chairman and vice chairman of the Senate select Watergate committee) have decided that they should not delve further into it." *(p. 154)*

Young's Report. Young, an aide to Kissinger before he served with Egil Krogh Jr. as codirector of the White House plumbers, reported to Nixon in 1972 that the Pentagon had been receiving National Security Council documents taken from Kissinger's office. Kissinger, later appointed secretary of state, was then Nixon's national security adviser.

Young reportedly said that at least six military men were involved in purloining the papers and that stolen documents were received by Adm. Thomas H. Moorer, chairman of the joint chiefs of staff, as well as by columnist Anderson, according to *The New York Times* reports.

Two military aides who had access to the secret papers were transferred, but not disciplined, when Kissinger discovered that information about his top-secret diplomatic negotiations with China, Russia and other countries was being leaked, *The Washington Post* reported Jan. 12. The aides were identified as Yeoman First Class Charles E. Radford and his superior, Rear Adm. Robert O. Welander, then the Navy's liaison officer to the National Security Council.

Welander, who later became assistant chief of naval operations in the Pentagon, was transferred to a sea command after the alleged spying came to light. Radford, 30, was transferred to naval reserve duty in Oregon. Although he said he knew Jack Anderson, Radford denied he was the source of leaks and said the Navy had ordered him not to discuss the case. Pentagon sources indicated that if there was "spying," it was done only to keep defense officials up to date on Kissinger's secretive negotiations, not with any sinister intent.

An earlier investigation by then Defense Secretary Melvin R. Laird cleared Moorer of any involvement in the spying episode, Pentagon sources said. They cited his reappointment as chairman of the joint chiefs as proof of Nixon's continued faith in him. Pentagon spokesman Jerry W. Friedheim said Jan. 15 that Moorer had denied any involvement and that so far Schlesinger had found "nothing that would impair his confidence in (Moorer's) professional capabilities" or in his "personal dedication and honesty."

Critics of Nixon said it appeared that he had made unwarranted use of the term "national security" in trying to contain the investigation of the plumbers. They said neither the "spy ring" matter nor other matters previously reported justified "coverups" on grounds of national security.

The Times had reported earlier that Nixon was concerned about the possible exposure of a Soviet spy working for the United States, a CIA informant in India and some nuclear targeting information, if the plumbers unit were to be investigated. White House Counsel J. Fred Buzhardt also attempted to discourage criminal indictments of former presidential aides John D. Ehrlichman, Charles W. Colson and Krogh on grounds they might disclose national security matters as part of their defense, the Post reported.

The Times reported that during his investigation of the leaks, Young was ordered to report periodically to Gen. Alexander M. Haig Jr., then Kissinger's deputy in the National Security Council. It was the first indication that Young maintained a professional relationship with the council while serving with the plumbers, the Times said. Kissinger repeatedly had denied any knowledge of the plumbers' activities.

(Continued from p. 204)

addition to himself and Woods, persons who might have had access to the Uher machine and the June 20 tape between Oct. 1 and Nov. 21 included Gen. John C. Bennett, a presidential aide officially responsible for the tapes during that period; Buzhardt; possibly several Secret Service agents, and the President.

Possible Grand Jury Action

Sirica said during the Jan. 16 hearing that he would decide "in due course" whether to recommend a grand jury investigation into the tape erasures matter. Such a recommendation, legal sources said, would amount to a finding that a crime or crimes probably had been committed, either in the erasing of the tape or in the testimony about it.

If the grand jury found evidence to support criminal charges, it could issue indictments on such charges as obstruction of justice, tampering with evidence or perjury. Long legal battles were forecast if the grand jury should attempt to call the President as a witness or to indict him on a criminal charge.

Jaworski Moves. In addition to Sirica, the Watergate special prosecutor had the power to bring the case of the erased tape to the grand jury, and Jaworski's request for FBI assistance in gathering evidence was regarded as an indication that he might be planning to do so.

Earlier in the week, Jaworski told newspaper interviewers that he regarded criminal indictments and trials resulting from the Watergate affair as his first responsibility. He said that he would not share tapes or other evidence, given to him by the White House on a confidential basis, with the House Judiciary Committee for its impeachment investigation. Rules regarding the secrecy of grand jury proceedings precluded him from doing so, he said.

Jaworski told *The Washington Post* the White House "never once volunteered anything," but had turned over since mid-December a substantial number of tapes and documents under threat of subpoena. He said he expected indictments in Watergate-related matters to be handed down by the end of February, and trials to begin by March.

Congressional Reaction

Reaction on Capitol Hill was quick and almost unanimously unfavorable to the President when the tape experts' report became public.

Rep. Robert Kastenmeier (D Wis.), a senior member of the House Judiciary Committee, said any reasonable man would have to conclude the White House tapes "have been tampered with," probably because the evidence on them "affects the President himself."

"This is the most serious single bit of evidence to date," said Rep. John B. Anderson (R Ill.), chairman of the House Republican Conference. The "deliberate doctoring" of the tape "is the penultimate link in the chain of evidence that has steadily been forged to show that there has been a conscious, deliberate effort to obstruct justice," Anderson added. "One has the feeling of approaching the final denouement in this drama. I fail to see how this can do anything but accelerate the tempo of the impeachment process."

'Departmental Responsiveness'

The Senate Watergate investigating committee had obtained internal White House documents that revealed a plan to award millions of dollars in federal contracts to 1972 campaign supporters of President Nixon, *The St. Louis Post-Dispatch* reported Jan. 14. The two memos, outlining the plan and reporting on its progress, were prepared by Fred V. Malek, a former White House aide who later became deputy director of the Office of Management and Budget. They were addressed to Nixon's former chief of staff, H. R. Haldeman.

In a cover letter attached to the first memo, dated March 17, 1972, Malek described the proposal as a "program for improving departmental responsiveness in support of the President's re-election." He provided a list of funds available for various programs administered by the federal government and added: "Even if only five per cent of this amount can be rechanneled to impact more directly on target groups or geographic areas, it would be a substantial increase over the current efforts."

Malek wrote that special precautions would be taken to keep the plans from being leaked to the press and to disassociate the White House from the program if it were discovered. But when questioned by the Post-Dispatch, he portrayed the program as a legitimate political activity.

The second memo, dated June 7, 1972, and also prepared under Malek's supervision, was a progress report on the plan. It claimed credit for switching, at the request of Sen. John G. Tower (R Texas), a grant for Texas migrant workers from an anti-administration group to one that was considered favorable to the Nixon campaign.

Another action said to be taken at Tower's request was the quashing of a suit charging the University of Texas with discrimination in hiring. And in a move described by Malek as "very helpful to the administration" with blue-collar voters, a federal investigation was canceled and subpoenaed books were returned to a Philadelphia local of the Dock and Wharf Builders Union.

Malek told the Post-Dispatch that Haldeman had pressed him for the progress report. "It was just, frankly, fluffed up a little bit to assure Bob (Haldeman) that things were okay," he said.

The original memo said the proposal had been "reviewed and concurred in" by William Gifford, who was than a special assistant to the President for congressional affairs. Gifford told *The Washington Post* that he did not take the plan seriously and that the memos "were not in fact related to what was done."

William H. Marumoto, a former White House liaison with Spanish-speaking communities, testified before the Senate Watergate committee Nov. 7, 1973, that federal grants, particularly from the Commerce Department's Office of Minority Business Enterprise, were judged on how well they might promote Nixon's re-election. *(Testimony, p. 129)*

The new House Republican leader, John J. Rhodes of Arizona, admitted that the new development "didn't help" Nixon supporters in their arguments against impeachment.

The experts' report "shifts the burden back to the President to substantiate the original story or explain that something happened of which he had no knowledge," said Rep. Tom Railsback (R Ill.), a member of the House Judiciary Committee. Sen. Henry M. Jackson (D Wash.) agreed.

Vice President Ford said that "even if you take the worst side" of the erased tape disclosure, "it doesn't justify impeachment."

Rep. Barber B. Conable Jr. (R N.Y.), chairman of the House Republican Policy Committee, said that every new disclosure "is part of a downward spiral of confidence the public can feel in government."

Week's Watergate Chronology

Following is a day-to-day chronology of the week's events in the Watergate case (*Previous Jan. 10 events, p. 195*):

JAN. 10

Ford on Compromise. Vice President Gerald R. Ford told the Associated Press he thought top White House officials were willing to "release tapes and other material on a selected basis" to the Senate Watergate investigating committee instead of refusing the committee's subpoenas of more than 500 tapes and documents. (*Earlier Ford remark, p. 194*)

JAN. 11

Milk Case. Lawyers associated with consumer advocate Ralph Nader filed a motion in U.S. District Court in Washington, D.C., asking for access to more White House tapes and documents relating to their suit charging that the Nixon administration based a 1971 decision to raise milk price supports on political considerations, including campaign contributions from milk industry groups. The brief included a quotation from a White House recording of a March 23, 1971, discussion between Nixon and industry representatives, which the attorneys said brought into question Nixon's contention that he did not refer to campaign contributions during the meeting. According to the brief, Nixon said: "And I must say a lot of businessmen and others I get around this table, they yammer and talk a lot but they don't do anything about it. But you and I appreciate that. I don't need to spell it out." (*Nixon milk statement, p. 191*)

Saxbe on Impeachment. In his first press conference as attorney general, William B. Saxbe said he thought Nixon should be impeached only for indictable offenses. The Justice Department would not participate in the President's defense should he be impeached and tried for such offenses, Saxbe added, although it might defend Nixon in the pretrial stages if he were being accused on "obviously political grounds." The attorney

general said Watergate Special Prosecutor Leon Jaworski should provide the House Judiciary Committee with information he might develop on criminal activity by the President.

Pentagon Spying. *The Chicago Tribune* reported that military liaison aides to the National Security Council (NSC) in 1971 secretly passed NSC documents to high Pentagon officials who were concerned about the changes in U.S. foreign policy being pursued by Henry A. Kissinger, then the President's national security adviser. The unauthorized dissemination of the materials reportedly was discovered by the White House "plumbers" group after Kissinger ordered them to investigate the publication in late 1971 by columnist Jack Anderson of secret information on U.S. policy in the India-Pakistan war. It was identified by some sources quoted in later reports as the national security matter Nixon had cited repeatedly as the cause of his opposition to investigation of the plumbers' activities. A White House statement on the reports said the source of the leaks was "a low-level employee" and that the matter was "inappropriate for public disclosure" for the time being. (*Box, p. 205*)

JAN. 12

Senate Committee Plans. Sen. Sam J. Ervin Jr. (D N.C.), chairman of the Senate Watergate investigating committee, said in a North Carolina television interview that if Nixon surrendered to the committee the five tapes it had originally demanded, "I'd be inclined to say that we'd bring the hearings to a very speedy end." But Samuel Dash, the committee's chief counsel, insisted that he and Ervin were agreed that the five tapes "would not be enough" to conclude the panel's investigation. (*Previous development, p. 194*)

JAN. 13

Jaworski on Judiciary. Special Prosecutor Jaworski was quoted as saying he would not make the mass of material collected by his office available to the House Judiciary Committee for its impeachment inquiry, because such a transfer would violate the legal restrictions under which the material was gathered. Jaworski said he had not reached a decision on whether the President could be indicted before being impeached and convicted, but he indicated that he might submit the matter to the court.

Jenner Remarks. Albert Jenner, the newly appointed minority counsel for the Judiciary Committee's impeachment inquiry, said he thought the President should be held responsible for some of the actions of his aides, even if Nixon did not know about them in advance. Break-ins and wiretapping by the plumbers were instances where the President should be held responsible, Jenner said in a Chicago television interview. (*Jenner profile, p. 193*)

Goldwater Remarks. Sen. Barry Goldwater (R Ariz.), speaking on NBC-TV's "Meet the Press," backed off from his earlier criticisms of Nixon's handling of the Watergate scandals. "We have much greater problems in this country and in this world than Watergate....Let's get other things solved, and unless there is something more unusual about the President and Watergate than has come out, let's get off his back," Goldwater said. *(Box, p. 204)*

JAN. 14

Pentagon Spying. *The New York Times* reported that David R. Young, a leader of the White House plumbers unit, had reported to Nixon in early 1972 that Adm. Thomas H. Moorer, chairman of the Joint Chiefs of Staff, had received secret National Security Council documents taken from Henry A. Kissinger's White House office. Sen. John C. Stennis (D Miss), chairman of the Armed Services Committee, said he would begin an informal investigation of the spying allegations. *(Box, p. 205)*

Senate Committee Plans. The Senate Watergate investigating committee's chief counsel, Samuel Dash, said he would recommend that the committee resume public hearings to air "important new information" it had developed. He said the committee would be willing to negotiate a compromise with the White House on its subpoenas of tapes and documents.

White House Memos. *The St. Louis Post Dispatch* printed excerpts from internal White House memos obtained by the Senate Watergate committee showing that White House aides drew up and executed a plan to use government departments and agencies for Nixon's political benefit in the 1972 campaign. The memos were prepared under the supervision of Fred V. Malek, a former White House aide who later became deputy director of the Office of Management and Budget, and were addressed to former White House chief of staff H. R. Haldeman. Malek admitted that he drafted and monitored the plan, but insisted it was not improper. *(Box, p. 206)*

JAN. 15

Tapes Report. A panel of six technical experts, appointed by Judge John J. Sirica to examine one of the subpoenaed White House tapes, reported to Sirica that an 18½-minute gap on the tape was caused by at least five separate erasures and re-recordings, not by a single accidental pressing of the wrong button on the tape recorder, as White House attorneys had suggested. *(Details, p. 201)*

Ford Speech. Vice President Ford attacked what he called "a small group of political activists" who he said would attempt "to cripple the President by dragging out the preliminaries to impeachment." He spoke to the American Farm Bureau Federation in Atlantic City, N.J. *(Box, p. 201)*

Hughes Gift. News reports said that Richard G. Danner, an employee of the Howard Hughes organization, had told the Senate Watergate investigating committee that Nixon personally suggested to him before the election in 1968 that he attempt to solicit a campaign contribution from Hughes. Both Nixon and his friend, Charles G. Rebozo, had insisted that Nixon was unaware before the 1972 election of a $100,000 contribution given to Rebozo by Hughes in two installments in 1970. *(p. 179)*

Jenner Remarks. Rep. Charles E. Wiggins (R Calif.), a senior Republican on the House Judiciary Committee, said he had written to minority counsel Jenner to reprimand him for remarks made in a televised interview about presidential responsibility for the actions of his aides. Wiggins said he did not think "any member of the staff should be making pronouncements" on the committee's impeachment investigation, and asked Jenner to withdraw his comments.

Attorney General Saxbe told reporters he thought Jenner's contention that Nixon should be held accountable for some of his aides' actions was "a rather bizarre theory of American law."

Ehrlichman Remarks. John D. Ehrlichman, Nixon's former domestic affairs adviser, was quoted by the Associated Press as saying he had lost his earlier optimism about the President's chances of regaining public confidence. "I think there have been some intervening and superseding events that have made it more difficult. But I still think it can be done," Ehrlichman said.

He denied a report in *The Los Angeles Times* that, while he was in Washington, D.C., the previous week, special prosecutor Jaworski had offered him a deal in return for cooperation in testifying against others in future Watergate trials.

JAN. 16

Tapes Erasure. U.S. District Judge John J. Sirica held further hearings on the 18½-minute erasure on a subpoenaed White House tape, taking testimony from White House aide Stephen B. Bull, who had access to the tapes before they were turned over to the court. Sirica said he was considering recommending a grand jury investigation of the erasure in light of the report of technical experts that at least five erasures and re-recordings were found on the tape. A spokesman for the FBI said Watergate special prosecutor Leon Jaworski had asked the bureau to "investigate the whole matter of the tapes." *(Details, p. 204)*

White House Denial. The White House press office issued a statement saying that further discussion of the erasure would be improper while the matter was still in court. But reporters pressed deputy White House press secretary Gerald L. Warren into denying that Nixon himself had erased part of the tape, either accidentally or intentionally. *(Details, p. 201)*

Waldie on Impeachment. Rep. Jerome R. Waldie (D Calif.), a member of the House Judiciary Committee, sent a letter to its chairman, Rep. Peter W. Rodino Jr. (D N.J.), warning that if Nixon refused to give the committee any materials it requested for its impeachment investigation, he would demand an impeachment vote without further investigation. Waldie asked Rodino to have the staff research the question of whether a president could invoke executive privilege in an impeachment investigation.

Hughes Gift. Deputy White House press secretary Warren denied news reports that Nixon had asked Richard G. Danner, an aide to billionaire Howard Hughes, to solicit a contribution from Hughes in 1968. Danner also denied the reports, which were said to be based on secret testimony Danner gave to the Senate Watergate committee. √

SIX MONTHS IN PRISON FOR 'PLUMBER' EGIL KROGH

As the first major White House staff alumnus was sentenced to prison for Watergate-related activities, President Nixon made it perfectly clear in the week ending Jan. 26 that he would not resign and would "fight like hell" against impeachment.

That word came as Congress reconvened after its month-long recess with new suggestions that Nixon resign.

Nixon's "hard line" also included a refusal, for the third time, to meet with the Senate select Watergate committee, which voted to resume hearings Jan. 29. *(Box, p. 132)*

Senior members of the House Judiciary Committee also met, on Jan. 24, and decided to ask the full House to formally ratify the committee's impeachment investigation and to grant subpoena powers to its chairman and vice chairman. The full committee was to act on the resolution Jan. 31, and Chairman Peter W. Rodino Jr. (D N.J.) said he hoped the House would approve it Feb. 5.

Krogh Sentencing

The former codirector of the secret White House investigative unit known as the "plumbers," Egil Krogh Jr., was sentenced Jan. 24 to six months in prison for approving the burglary of the office of Pentagon Papers defendant Daniel Ellsberg's psychiatrist Sept. 3, 1971. The charge was conspiracy to violate the rights of a citizen. The sentence was two to six years, but U.S. District

Egil Krogh Jr.

Judge Gerhard A. Gesell ordered Krogh to serve only six months, with another 18 months of unsupervised probation.

Krogh, 34, expressed contrition for what he said he had come to consider "repulsive conduct." But, he added, at the time he believed covert efforts to investigate and discredit Ellsberg were justified in the name of national security.

Although a friend, former Assistant Treasury Secretary Edward L. Morgan, had said he expected Krogh to "spill his guts" and implicate Nixon in the plumbers' illegal activities, Krogh said he "received no specific instruction or authority whatsoever regarding the break-in from the President, directly or indirectly." *(Morgan comments, p. 211, 213)*

Krogh did say that in July 1971, John D. Ehrlichman, then Nixon's chief domestic aide, told him "the President wanted me to perform an urgent assignment" in response to the Pentagon Papers disclosure. Ehrlich-

man told him to set up a special top-secret unit to investigate Ellsberg, Krogh said, and gave the unit authority to engage in covert activity.

A week later, Krogh said in a 12-page statement, Nixon personally directed him to expand the work of the unit to cover another "intolerable" news leak, and to conduct extensive lie detector tests to do it. Nixon "made clear that the protection of national security information must outweigh any individual reluctance to be polygraphed," Krogh said. The intensity of the President's concern for national security "fired up and overshadowed every aspect" of the plumbers' work, he said.

"It was in this context" that the break-in into psychiatrist Lewis F. Fielding's office took place, and "doubtless this explains why John Dean has reported that I told him that instructions for the break-in had come directly from the Oval Office (Nixon's office)," Krogh said.

After the break-in, Krogh said, he "immediately felt that a mistake had been made" and recommended to Ehrlichman that no such actions be undertaken in the future. Ehrlichman agreed and said he felt the break-in had been "in excess of his authorization," Krogh said.

He said he made "inconsistent" statements to Watergate investigators because he thought in 1972 that the President wanted the unit's work kept secret, but that in 1973 Nixon authorized him to tell the truth. Krogh was indicted Oct. 11, 1973, on two counts of lying to Watergate investigators in 1972. He also was indicted in California for his role in the break-in. Those charges were dismissed after he pleaded guilty Nov. 30 to the conspiracy charge. *(p. 175, 174)*

President's Position

Nixon's firm intention to remain in office was made increasingly clear during the week, after a rash of resignation requests starting Jan. 18.

Although the week began with a defense of the President by Senate Minority Leader Hugh Scott (R Pa.) and Vice President Gerald R. Ford, the defense turned into an offense as the week wore on. The President met with three groups from Congress and told them all he was prepared to wage a fight to the finish to remain in office. Nixon's press secretary, Ronald L. Ziegler, Jan. 24 confirmed reports on the meetings.

Scott, Ford. Scott said Jan. 20 that he had seen evidence which could prove the President was innocent of "specific items" in the Watergate affair and which indicated no impeachable offenses on the part of the President. He said he had urged Nixon to release the information, which reportedly consisted of a summary of tape-recorded conversations with former presidential counsel John W. Dean III. The evidence would show, Scott said, that Nixon had no knowledge of the Watergate break-in and coverup before March 21, 1973, contrary to what Dean had said.

Resumed Senate Hearings

On a four-to-three party-line vote, the Senate select Watergate committee voted Jan. 23 to hold six more days of hearings into two new matters, starting Jan. 29.

Republican members argued that the committee should finish its work and leave further investigations of Watergate-related matters to the House Judiciary Committee, which was considering whether or not to impeach President Nixon. But the Democrats backed Chairman Sam J. Ervin Jr. (D N.C.), who said it was "essential" that evidence gathered by the committee staff in the two new matters be presented. The two areas were:

• The $100,000 given by billionaire Howard Hughes to Nixon's friend, Charles G. (Bebe) Rebozo, in 1969 and 1970. *(p. 173, 179)*

• The $427,500 in contributions to the Nixon re-election campaign by milk producers in 1971, at the same time Nixon raised dairy price supports. *(p. 195)*

In other action, the committee agreed unanimously to ask again for a meeting with President Nixon. Like the two previous requests, this one was rejected by the White House Jan. 24.

The committee also agreed to submit a report, although probably not a final report, to the Senate by Feb. 28, the date on which the committee was scheduled to go out of existence.

Ervin said he would ask · for an extension of time, if necessary, to pursue the committee's court suit to gain access to various White House tapes and documents.

Among the witnesses recommended by the committee staff to testify the first week were Rebozo; Thomas Wakefield, an official of Rebozo's bank; Robert A. Maheu, a key figure in Hughes' gambling and hotel empire; Richard Danner, who delivered the Hughes money to Rebozo, and William Griffin, a lawyer for another Nixon friend, industrialist Robert Abplanalp.

Ford said on Jan. 22 that the President had assured him he (Nixon) was innocent of wrongdoing and had evidence to prove it. However, Ford said he had not had time to listen to or read the evidence.

President's Views. Ziegler Jan. 22 announced that the President was determined to finish out his term and did not want to be "consumed another year by Watergate."

Nixon met with members of Congress Jan. 22, 23 and 24. Rep. Peter H. B. Frelinghuysen (R N.J.) said he wrote down Nixon's words Jan. 22: "There is a time to be timid. There is a time to be conciliatory. There is a time to fly and there is a time to fight. And I'm going to fight like hell" against congressional efforts to impeach him. That meeting was with 18 Republican members of Congress.

Meeting Jan. 23 with southern Democratic members, Nixon said it was "unthinkable" that he resign and that he would fight impeachment "right down to the wire," according to Rep. G. V. (Sonny) Montgomery (D Miss.).

Senate Majority Leader Mike Mansfield (D Mont.) said Nixon made similar statements at a private meeting Jan. 23. Mansfield had said Jan. 22 that he did not favor resignation. A number of other persons also indicated that they felt an impeachment proceeding would "clear the air" better than a resignation.

Congressional Statements

Rep. Wilbur D. Mills (D Ark.) said Jan. 18 that he would advise Nixon to resign rather than permit a bitter impeachment struggle in the House.

House Majority Leader Thomas P. O'Neill Jr. (D Mass.) said Jan. 21 that resignation would be "in the best interest of the nation." That sentiment was echoed by Democratic Representatives B. F. Sisk (Calif.), Wayne Hays (Ohio) and Jack Brooks (Texas). However, House Speaker Carl Albert (D Okla.) and Democratic Whip John J. McFall (Calif.) said Jan. 21 that they were not ready to suggest that Nixon resign.

Republican Representatives John B. Anderson (Ill.) and Silvio O. Conte (Mass.) and former Attorney General Elliot L. Richardson all said impeachment was the proper course. Sen. Barry Goldwater (R Ariz.) said he had not seen enough evidence to favor either resignation or impeachment.

Week's Watergate Chronology

Following is a day-to-day chronology of the week's events in the Watergate case:

JAN. 17

Tapes Hearing. The White House became concerned about its secret tape recordings immediately after the public warning by John W. Dean III, then the presidential counsel, in April 1973 that he would not be a "scapegoat" in the Watergate affair, a Secret Service agent indicated at a U.S. District Court hearing in Washington, D.C. The agent in charge of the taping system, Louis B. Sims, said he assured Nixon's appointments secretary, Stephen B. Bull, that Dean did not know about the tapes. *(Other testimony, p. 201; Dean warning, Vol. I, p. 105)*

Cooperation Pledged. The White House promised to cooperate fully with an FBI investigation into the 18½-minute erasure on a key Watergate tape, but declined to say whether Nixon himself would agree to be interviewed.

Secretary's Role. Neither Nixon nor his attorneys asked Rose Mary Woods, the President's personal secretary, a "single question" about the 18½-minute tape erasure, Woods' attorney, Charles S. Rhyne, said. Rhyne was critical of White House treatment of his client, but he and the White House both denied a *Washington Post* story that Nixon had asked her to take the blame for the tape gap. *(p. 202)*

Suit Dismissal Sought. Attorneys for the President asked for dismissal of a suit by the Senate select Watergate committee to gain access to five Watergate tapes. In a 52-page brief filed in U.S. District Court, Nixon's lawyers said the President had the "power to withhold information from Congress...(that) he determines to be contrary to the public interest." The committee was exceeding its investigative authority, the White House lawyers argued, calling the matter a "political question... clearly inappropriate for judicial resolution."

Nixon Subpoenaed. The citizen action organization, Common Cause, subpoenaed Nixon and several aides and ordered them to produce documents Jan. 31 relating to fund-raising and expenditures in the 1972 re-election campaign.

Tax Returns Audited. Nixon's accountant, Arthur Blech of Los Angeles, disclosed that the Internal Revenue Service was auditing the tax returns of the Richard Nixon Foundation as well as the President's personal tax returns. Blech, also the accountant for the foundation, defended apparent errors or omissions in the foundation's report.

JAN. 18

Grand Jury Referral. U.S. District Court Judge John J. Sirica ended a four-day hearing into gaps in the Watergate tapes and recommended that a grand jury investigate "the possibility of unlawful destruction of evidence and related offenses." Sirica said it was his "considered opinion that a distinct possibility of unlawful conduct on the part of one or more persons exists." The White House issued a statement stressing that the decision was "not a conviction...nor even an indictment." *(Texts, p. 214; earlier story, p. 201)*

Plea-Bargaining. Watergate Special Prosecutor Leon Jaworski confirmed on the NBC-TV "Today" show that his office was plea-bargaining with several figures in the Watergate investigation. He did not name them.

Resignation Urged. Rep. Wilbur D. Mills (D Ark.) said President Nixon should resign "in the near future" rather than subject the nation to a bitter impeachment struggle in the House. Mills headed the Joint Committee on Internal Revenue Taxation, which was investigating Nixon's tax deductions.

Morgan Resignation. Assistant Secretary of the Treasury Edward L. Morgan resigned from the government, in part, he said, because his handling of the President's gift of papers to the National Archives for a $576,000 tax deduction had caused Nixon "another problem." Morgan was deputy White House counsel when he signed the deed turning Nixon's papers over to the government. *Newsweek* magazine Jan. 28 reported that Morgan and California lawyer Frank DeMarco had admitted to government investigators that they back-dated the deed by more than a year, making it appear that the gift was made before the law was changed to bar such deductions.

IRS Resignation. The Internal Revenue Service confirmed that the employee accused of leaking information about Nixon's income tax returns in the fall of 1973 had resigned under threat of being fired. The IRS would not identify the employee and said the Justice Department had decided not to prosecute.

Sturgis Freed. The U.S. Court of Appeals in Washington, D.C., ordered Frank A. Sturgis, one of the original Watergate defendants, freed pending his appeal to withdraw his guilty plea in the case.

JAN. 19

Impeachment Plan. Fugitive financier Robert L. Vesco said in an ABC-TV interview that at least six

---

Porter Charged with Lying

Herbert L. Porter, a former official of the Committee to Re-elect the President, was charged Jan. 21 with lying to FBI agents investigating the Watergate break-in in 1972. Porter had admitted, in testimony before the Senate select Watergate committee in June 1973, that he had lied to the Watergate grand jury, at the original Watergate trial and to FBI agents who interviewed him July 19, 1972. *(Vol. I p. 121)*

He indicated that he would plead guilty, but U.S. District Judge William B. Bryant was ill and the case was delayed. Assistant Watergate Special Prosecutor Richard Ben-Veniste presented the one-count charge to Chief Judge John J. Sirica in Washington, D.C., Jan. 21. Porter waived a formal indictment by a grand jury.

The charge carries a maximum penalty of five years in prison and a $10,000 fine.

Porter, director of scheduling Nixon's "surrogate" candidates in 1972, was the third official of President Nixon's re-election committee to be charged in connection with covering up the Watergate break-in. Jeb Stuart Magruder, deputy director of the committee, and Frederick C. LaRue, political coordinator, pleaded guilty to conspiracy to obstruct justice. They had not been sentenced. *(LaRue plea, Vol. I p. 163)*

Porter testified June 7 that Magruder had asked him to tell a false story about what happened to $100,000 in cash given to convicted Watergate conspirator G. Gordon Liddy. Porter swore that Liddy was allocated $100,000 to gather intelligence legally on possible violence against Nixon's surrogate candidates in the 1972 primaries, when the money actually was used for bugging the Watergate and other "dirty tricks." Porter said he agreed to the lie because he felt a "deep sense of loyalty" to Nixon and wanted to be considered a good "team player."

Porter could have been charged with perjury, but Watergate Special Prosecutor Leon Jaworski apparently agreed not to bring that charge if Porter would agree to plead to the false-statement charge. Both charges carry the same penalty.

---

months before the Watergate scandal became public, he was approached to take part in "a well-calculated plan" for impeachment of President Nixon. He said he refused.

JAN. 20

Scott on Nixon. Senate Minority Leader Hugh Scott (R Pa.) said he had seen some unpublished White House information that he believed would prove Nixon innocent of specific items in the Watergate affair. Scott said he did not see any impeachable offenses by the President.

McGovern Opinion. Sen. George McGovern (D S.D.), Nixon's opponent in 1972, said he thought there were ample grounds for the House to vote a bill of impeachment of Nixon.

Presidential Immunity?

Unique questions were raised by the suggestion that Congress might immunize President Nixon from criminal prosecution should he resign.

Apparently originated by former Supreme Court Justice Abe Fortas—who described it as "plea bargaining in advance"—the idea was picked up and backed by two prominent House Democrats. Ways and Means Committee Chairman Wilbur D. Mills (D Ark.) and Majority Leader Thomas P. O'Neill Jr. (D Mass.) said that they would sponsor such a bill, if it was necessary to persuade Nixon to resign. By late January, however, these appeared to be little more than off-the-cuff remarks. No research into the matter was going on in either Mills' or O'Neill's offices on the matter.

Fortas told *The New York Times* Jan. 12 that he had suggested such an action, but "not very seriously." However, a bill granting presidents immunity in the event they resigned could be carefully drafted to avoid constitutional problems, he said. For one thing, he said, the measure could not apply to Nixon alone, but must apply to all future presidents. Otherwise, it could be challenged as in violation of the guarantee of equal protection of the law.

Not only would such a grant of immunity be a unique action by Congress. It could also be argued that it would run directly counter to the intent of the men who took pains to put in the Constitution language specifying that an impeached, convicted and removed official "shall nevertheless be liable and subject to indictment, trial, judgment and punishment, according to law."

Furthermore, the Constitution makes impeachment the only offense for which the President cannot grant a reprieve or a pardon.

Fortas' suggestion certainly raised "very difficult and sticky questions," said one constitutional expert. "It is the other side of the coin from a bill of attainder," he noted, pointing out that the Constitution forbids Congress to pass that sort of bill, which punishes a particular person or group without a trial.

JAN. 21

Calls for Resignation. House Majority Leader Thomas P. O'Neill (D Mass.) called for President Nixon's resignation as the 93rd Congress reconvened. Similar opinions were expressed by Democratic Representatives B. F. Sisk (Calif.), Wayne Hays (Ohio) and Jack Brooks (Texas). *(Details, p. 210)*

Grand Jury Probe. A federal grand jury began studying whether indictments should be issued in the Watergate tapes case.

Porter Charged. Herbert L. Porter, a former Nixon re-election committee official, was charged in U.S. District Court with making false statements to the FBI. *(Box, p. 211)*

Ford Warned. Vice President Gerald R. Ford's hometown newspaper, *The Grand Rapids* (Mich.) *Press*, urged him to "put some distance between himself and Nixon on Watergate." Ford had defended Nixon. *(p. 204)*

JAN. 22

Ziegler on Resignation. Nixon was determined to serve out his term and not to be "consumed another year by Watergate," presidential press secretary Ronald L. Ziegler said. *(Details, p. 209)*

Ford Defense. Vice President Ford said Nixon had assured him personally that he was innocent of complicity in the Watergate case and had evidence to prove it. *(Details, p. 209)*

Goldwater Warning. Sen. Barry Goldwater (R Ariz.) said polls showed that Watergate would cost every Republican candidate for office 10 per cent of the vote in 1974. He suggested that candidates would try to disassociate themselves from Nixon, but stopped short of calling for the President's resignation.

Impeachment Preferred. Former Attorney General Elliot L. Richardson said a House vote for Nixon's impeachment was likely to be easier than a vote against it. He said impeachment would better serve the public interest than resignation, which could set a "dangerous precedent."

Aid to IRS. Special Prosecutor Jaworski asked the U.S. District Court for permission to turn over to the Internal Revenue Service information he obtained on possible illegal corporate campaign contributions.

Labor Contributions. The Republican National Committee published a survey showing that organized labor gave $189,195 in 1972 campaign contributions to 19 Democrats on the House Judiciary Committee and $2,100 to two Republican members. The committee was considering impeaching President Nixon, and the AFL-CIO favored impeachment. The figures were compiled by Americans for Constitutional Action.

Kissinger Role. Secretary of State Henry A. Kissinger admitted listening to one tape recording of a White House "plumbers" investigation into an alleged military spy ring in the White House, but denied he knew anything about the group's illegal activities or the role of his former personal assistant, David R. Young Jr., as its leader. *(Earlier story, p. 205)*

JAN. 23

More Hearings. The Senate select Watergate committee voted four to three along party lines to hold six days of additional hearings into the $100,000 given by billionaire Howard Hughes to Nixon's friend, Charles G. (Bebe) Rebozo, and the $427,500 given to the Nixon campaign in 1971 by milk producers. *(Details, p. 210)*

Nixon Attitude. Rep. Peter H. B. Frelinghuysen (R N.J.) said President Nixon told a group of Republican House members Jan. 22 that he would "fight like hell" against impeachment.

Dean Testimony. Watergate Special Prosecutor Jaworski confirmed that he would call former White House counsel John W. Dean III as a witness in the trial of Dwight L. Chapin, Nixon's former appointments secretary, and other staff members.

Poll Report: More Low Ratings for the President

President Nixon's continued low standing with the American public was again reflected by the latest public-opinion polls. *(Earlier poll report, p. 202)*

Gallup. A Gallup Poll published Jan. 20 found that Nixon's approval rating had returned to 27 per cent, where it had been late in 1973 before improving slightly as a result of "Operation Candor." Gallup's interviewing of 1,504 adults was done Jan. 4-7, before a panel of experts reported that an 18½-minute segment on a White House tape might have been deliberately erased.

The question: "Do you approve or disapprove of the way Nixon is handling his job as president?"

	Latest	Dec. 7-10, 1973
Approve	27%	29%
Disapprove	63	60
No opinion	10	11

Gallup compared Nixon's high and low ratings with those of the past four presidents:

	High	Low
Nixon	68%	27%
Johnson	80	35
Kennedy	83	57
Eisenhower	79	49
Truman	87	23

The same sample was asked, for a poll published Jan. 21: "Do you think President Nixon should resign from the presidency, or not?"

Should	46%
Should not	46
No opinion	8

And this question was asked by Gallup: "Do you think President Nixon should be impeached and compelled to leave the presidency, or not?"

	Latest	Nov. 30-Dec. 3, 1973
Should	37%	35%
Should not	53	54
No opinion	10	11

Harris. A Harris Survey, conducted Jan. 7-10 and published Jan. 21, asked a nationwide sample if it thought Nixon "knew about the attempt to cover up White House involvement in Watergate while it was going on."

Yes	67%
No	21
Not sure	12

The sample was asked if it believed the missing taped segment "were erased by mistake by the President's secretary, Rose Mary Woods."

Yes	21%
No	60
Not sure	19

Another question was whether or not the sample felt the 18½ minutes "were deliberately erased because they would have proven Mr. Nixon's involvement in the coverup."

Yes	59%
No	22
Not sure	19

Finally, Harris asked persons interviewed if they thought Nixon "should be impeached if Judge Sirica were to decide that the President was negligent in the care he took of the Watergate tapes."

Yes	48%
No	40
Not sure	12

Nixon's Taxes. Sen. Russell B. Long (D La.), chairman of the Joint Committee on Internal Revenue Taxation, said Nixon almost certainly would be asked to pay back taxes, because evidence indicated he was not entitled to the $576,000 deduction he claimed on the donation of his vice presidential papers to the National Archives.

Morgan Comments. Edward L. Morgan, who signed the deed turning Nixon's papers over to the Archives, predicted in *The Wall Street Journal* that former presidential aide Egil Krogh Jr. would "spill his guts" about the White House plumbers operation, and that Krogh's confession, plus the Watergate tapes' erasures, would "probably do the President in."

Dairy Funds. H. R. Haldeman, former White House chief of staff, was advised by a deputy in 1971 that dairy industry officials were expected to pay $90,-000 a month to Nixon's re-election campaign, according to a memo made public in a lawsuit filed against dairy interests by consumer advocate Ralph Nader. The memo from Gordon C. Strachan was written six months after Nixon had raised dairy price supports. It indicated that only half of the "commitment" had been paid.

JAN. 24

Krogh Sentencing. Egil Krogh Jr., the former White House plumbers' chief, was sentenced to six months in prison by U.S. District Judge Gerhard Gesell in Washington, D.C. *(Details, p. 209)*

Nixon Meets Democrats. Nixon told 18 southern Democratic members of Congress he would not resign and would fight impeachment "right down to the wire," Rep. G. V. (Sonny) Montgomery (D Miss.) reported.

Spending Suit. Representatives Bella S. Abzug (D N.Y.) and Louis Stokes (D Ohio) filed a lawsuit against Nixon to make him pay back to the Treasury the cost of government improvements to his homes in San Clemente, Calif., and Key Biscayne, Fla. The amount could exceed $3-million, Abzug said.   √

SIRICA, WHITE HOUSE TEXTS

Following are the texts of a memorandum issued Jan. 18 by Chief Judge John J. Sirica of U.S. District Court in Washington, D.C., recommending a grand jury investigation of erasures on White House tapes, and of a White House statement responding to the memorandum:

SIRICA MEMORANDUM

These proceedings, commenced on Oct. 31, 1973, have to date produced approximately 2,800 pages of testimony by 23 separate witnesses, and nearly 200 exhibits of every description. The objective throughout has been to determine whether anyone has attempted by unlawful means to resist the grand jury subpoena *duces tecum* of July 23, 1973, issued to the President.

The grand jury subpoena has been ruled valid and binding on the President to an extent defined in the opinion of this Court and that of the Court of Appeals for this circuit. The President on Oct. 23, 1973, stated through counsel that the subpoena would be honored as requested.

Since that time, in three instances known to the Court, there has been a failure to comply: the tape recording of a June 20, 1972, telephone conversation, the tape recording of an April 15, 1973, conversation, and an 1,100-second portion of conversation on a June 20, 1972, tape recording (sought under Parts 1.B., 1.1., and 1.A. of the subpoena respectively) have not been produced for *in camera* examination.

As in any case where a party is required to honor a subpoena and full compliance is not forthcoming, the failure to produce may or may not be justified. Where such a question arises, the Court generally pursues an investigation into the matter to determine responsibility and justification.

In pursuing this central issue here, the testimony has principally concerned what might be called three component issues: (1) The chain of custody of subpoenaed materials, (2) the record of access to those materials, and (3) the physical or technical integrity of the subpoenaed matter. As suggested above, the investigation has been both lengthy and involved, and in the Court's opinion, not yet conclusive.

The proceedings have now arrived at a point where the Court has essentially three choices regarding their future. The Court might elect to terminate the hearings entirely without additional testimony of any sort. As a second choice, the Court could suspend the proceedings and recommend to the special prosecutor that he conduct a grand jury investigation of the entire matter. Thirdly, the Court might proceed with additional evidence-gathering in the hope of one day being able to finally resolve the compliance issue.

Of these alternatives, the Court has elected to follow the second as the preferred course.

Analyzing the evidence now before it, the Court would consider it a dereliction of duty to terminate the present inquiry without further action of any sort. Substantial questions remain unanswered. It would be inappropriate to thus abruptly terminate a proceeding of this kind in any case, but particularly so in a case possessing the significance of this one.

At the same time, the subject matter of these proceedings does not appear capable of a simple or swift resolution. There remain to be delivered reports on the technical analysis of nine tape recordings and possibly other materials as well. It appears also that, lacking extensive out-of-court investigation at this juncture, continued in-court hearings can accomplish little. In short, we have reached a point where the present fact-gathering process is no longer an efficient one.

The final alternative, a referral to the special prosecutor for grand jury action, has affirmative characteristics to recommend it. The grand jury, able to enlist the aid of court process, assisted directly by the special prosecutor, and assisted indirectly by other agencies, is uniquely equipped to conduct the sort of investigation now required. Where allegations of wrongdoing arise, the grand jury is the traditional institution charged with determining whether criminal charges are warranted.

It is the Court's considered opinion that a distinct possibility of unlawful conduct on the part of one or more persons exists here. A grand jury should now determine whether indictments are appropriate.

These statements can not be construed as identifying any particular wrongdoer or unlawful act. The Court refrains absolutely from accusing any person or persons, and refrains as well from a final conclusion that any illegal conduct has occurred. Rather, the Court has concluded from the evidence now before it that the possibility of unlawful tampering with or suppression of evidence is sufficiently strong to merit grand jury scrutiny.

In view of the foregoing, then, the Court hereby strongly recommends to the special prosecutor that he give immediate and serious consideration to opening a grand jury investigation into the possibility of unlawful destruction of evidence and any related offenses. It is suggested that the special prosecutor and grand jury consider the entire record of these proceedings, and that they give attention as well to future reports of the panel of experts treating additional materials produced under the July 23 subpoena.

The special prosecutor is free, of course, to incorporate within the investigation any suggestion of tampering that related to evidence in his possession obtained independently of the instant subpoena. Should the special prosecutor choose to initiate an investigation as recommended, the Court sees no need to continue these proceedings, at least for the present, and they would therefore be suspended.

The Court also takes this occasion to instruct the panel of six experts, jointly selected by White House counsel and the special prosecutor and appointed by the Court, to continue their analysis of the nine remaining tape recordings and any other subpoenaed items that may be submitted to them for testing. Their work is to continue subject to the same restrictions and procedures that have applied heretofore. They will report from time to time, as they deem appropriate, to the Court, White House counsel and the special prosecutor in joint conference.

The Court and counsel express their appreciation to all members of the panel for their diligence, and urge them to conclude their work at the earliest practicable time.

These proceedings are now declared recessed, and will be deemed suspended indefinitely should the special prosecutor commence the recommended grand jury investigation.

WHITE HOUSE STATEMENT

The decision of Judge John Sirica to refer the matter of the 18-minute gap to the Federal grand jury is not a conviction of any individual, nor is it even an indictment. And it would be wrong to conclude on the basis of Judge Sirica's decision that any individual in the White House is guilty of impropriety or wrongdoing in the handling of the Watergate case.

Further, the American people should bear in mind that the focus of the investigation by the Federal grand jury is primarily how the tape may have been erased, not what the tape contained.

Forgotten in the rhetoric about the lost 18 minutes is the fact that: hand-written notes do exist concerning the conversation between the President and Mr. Haldeman. Those notes, written contemporaneously by Mr. Haldeman, now in the possession of the special prosecutor, clearly indicate that Presidential conversation and concern in the 18-minute segment were directed solely to the negative public relations impact of the Watergate break-in on the campaign of 1972.   √

ANATOMY OF A COMMITTEE: IMPEACHMENT INQUIRY BEGINS

"A well-constituted court for the trial of impeachments is an object not more to be desired than difficult to be obtained in a government wholly elective. The subjects of its jurisdiction are those offenses which proceed from the misconduct of public men...from the abuse or violation of some public trust...which may with peculiar propriety be denominated POLITICAL.... The prosecution of them...will seldom fail to agitate the passions of the whole community, and to divide it into parties more or less friendly or inimical to the accused. In many cases it will connect itself with the pre-existing factions, and will enlist all their animosities, partialities, influence and interest on one side or the other; and in such cases there will always be the greatest danger that the decision will be regulated more by the comparative strength of the parties than by the real demonstrations of innocence or guilt."

—Alexander Hamilton in *The Federalist Papers,*
No. 65

Peter Rodino, New Jersey Democrat, hoped to prove Alexander Hamilton, founding father, wrong in 1974.

In 1787, 56 years before the first presidential impeachment attempt, Hamilton warned that an impeachment would invariably erupt in partisan dispute. Rodino, on the other hand, repeatedly warned that it would be a national disaster if the impeachment inquiry currently underway in the House Judiciary Committee, which he heads, becomes a partisan matter. *(Box p. 218)*

But since Oct. 23, 1973, when the committee was formally granted jurisdiction over the inquiry into charges against President Nixon, the grim prospect of impeachment threatened the committee's traditional nonpartisan comity. As 1974 began, few persons were more aware of the dangers which Alexander Hamilton had predicted than the 38 lawyers who compose the committee.

'The Judicious Committee'

"The Judiciary Committee likes to think of itself as the judicious committee," said Edward Hutchinson (R Mich.), the committee's ranking Republican. But that judiciousness has been jeopardized already by the actions which led committee member David W. Dennis (R Ind.) to note that "the chairman has been running this inquiry pretty much out of his hat."

"We in the minority have been given no real opportunity to participate or be informed," protested Wiley Mayne (R Ind.) in November, as he and other Republicans moved to postpone House approval of $1-million to fund the committee inquiry.

Acutely sensitized to the effect their part in presidential impeachment might have on their own political fortunes, Republican committee members were anxious to be kept informed about what was going on—and to have some role in deciding what should be done. "What is at issue," said freshman Republican Harold V. Froehlich (R Wis.), "is letting the minority participate.... Let us know what is what, and let us know what is going on."

"All we can do is complain," conceded Robert McClory (R Ill.), second-ranking Republican on the committee. "We don't have the votes to override whatever the majority decides to do."

And complain was what McClory did, leading 10 of the other Republican committee members for an hour Dec. 18, 1973, from the floor of the House.

" 'Consultation' according to the chairman," lamented McClory, "seems to mean reporting to the committee members decisions which the chairman has already made. That really is not consultation."

The following day, Dec. 19, Rodino assembled the seven senior members of both parties on the committee and informed them that they were an advisory group for the inquiry. Alluding vaguely to their 'supervisory' role, Rodino left their responsibilities undefined.

Doar Appointment. Creation of—and their inclusion in—the advisory group encouraged the committee Republicans, but their feelings were still somewhat ruffled as the session ended just before Christmas. Rodino had singlehandedly selected John M. Doar, a former as-

---

An Impeachable Offense Is....

✓ ..."treason, bribery, or other high crimes and misdemeanors."—*The Constitution*

✓ ..."one in its nature or consequences subversive of some fundamental or essential principle of government, or highly prejudicial to the public interest...a violation of the Constitution, of law, of an official oath, or of duty, by an act committed or omitted, or, without violating a positive law, by the abuse of discretionary powers from improper motives, or for any improper motives, or for any improper purpose."—*Benjamin F. Butler* (R Mass.), one of the House managers of the impeachment case against Andrew Johnson, March 30, 1868

✓ ..."of such a character to commend itself at once to the minds of all right thinking men, as beyond all question, an adequate cause (for impeachment). It should...leave no reasonable ground of suspicion upon the motives of those who inflict the penalty...." —*William Pitt Fessenden* (Whig Maine), one of the seven "Republicans" in the Senate who voted against the conviction of Andrew Johnson

✓ ...actions "as an individual and such judge.... (which brought) his court into scandal and disrepute, to the prejudice of said court and public confidence in the administration of justice therein, and to the prejudice of public respect and confidence in the federal judiciary and to render him unfit to serve as such judge."—*Articles of Impeachment against Federal District Judge Halsted Ritter,* 1936

✓ ..."whatever a majority of the House of Representatives considers it to be at a given moment in history; conviction results from whatever offenses two-thirds of the other body considers to be sufficiently serious to require removal of the accused from office.... There are few fixed principles among the handful of precedents."—*Rep. Gerald R. Ford,* speech on the House floor, April 15, 1970

sistant attorney general for civil rights under the Kennedy and Johnson administrations, as the committee's special impeachment counsel. No other committee members were informed of Rodino's choice before the public announcement, except for Hutchinson, to whom Rodino introduced Doar the previous afternoon.

"There are some Democrats on the committee who would vote to impeach Nixon today. And there are a few Republicans who wouldn't vote to impeach Nixon if he were caught in a bank vault at midnight."

—William L. Hungate (D Mo.)

Despite Doar's background as a Republican, Hutchinson and McClory made it clear that his ties to the Kennedy family were of concern to them. At the Dec. 20 press conference announcing Doar's appointment, Hutchinson, at the request of one of Rodino's aides, sat at the small table with Rodino and Doar. But he moved his chair down to one end, out of camera range, and turned to the side, making clear that he was an onlooker, not a participant in the announcement.

Equal Footing. But a two-hour meeting early in January of the advisory group with Doar, who presented his first progress report, and the naming of Albert E. Jenner, a distinguished trial attorney, as minority counsel for the inquiry, bolstered the confidence of Republican members.

Now, they indicated, they felt themselves on a more equal footing with their Democratic colleagues on the slippery subject of impeaching the President.

And yet committee comity faced severe strains in the early months of 1974. A number of questions demanding committee attention were certain to arouse partisan suspicions and tensions anew. These included: the committee's relationship to the special prosecutor, the proper manner of exercising subpoena power in the inquiry, the limitations of the areas of the inquiry, the timetable for the inquiry, and the definition of an impeachable offense.

A Reputation to Preserve

The committee's reputation as one of the least partisan in the House was a matter of quiet pride for most of its members, virtually all of whom indicated a desire to preserve that reputation through the impeachment inquiry, and beyond. When questioned concerning the committee and the inquiry, most members chose their words carefully to avoid any aggravation of the already building tension.

"We're all lawyers," Dennis and several other members pointed out, noting one major factor which has worked to create this reputation for nonpartisanship. The

shared professional background, members noted, would hopefully encourage a "lawyer-like" approach to the inquiry.

"There are some Democrats on the committee who would vote to impeach Nixon today," admitted William L. Hungate (D Mo.). "And there are a few Republicans who wouldn't vote to impeach Nixon if he were caught in a bank vault at midnight. But the majority (of the members) will, I hope, decide the matter on the basis of the evidence presented."

Past Leadership. Another element in the committee's reputation was the legacy of a unique leadership team—Emanuel Celler (D N.Y. 1923-1973) and William M. McCulloch (R Ohio 1947-1973), who served as chairman and ranking minority member together from 1959 until both left the House at the end of 1972. They saw eye-to-eye on many of the issues which came before the committee during those years, a coincidence of views which contributed to bipartisan support of most measures emerging from the committee, and one which left dissenting Republicans on the committee out in the cold, and leaderless.

Legal Matters. Still a third influence was the subject matter which generally fell within the committee's jurisdiction. As Charles E. Wiggins (R Calif.) reflected: "The jurisdiction of the committee has tended to shield it from partisan controversy." If disagreement arises over bankruptcy, civil liberties, constitutional amendments, federal courts and judges, immigration, prisons or patents, it is more likely to reflect philosophical rather than party differences.

Hutchinson agreed: "In the ordinary course of committee work, the great bulk of the matters coming before the committee are more legal than political.... There have been extremely few issues that end up being partisanly political."

Philosophical Gap. The philosophical cleavage in the committee appeared to be widening, however. As Walter Flowers (D Ala.), one of the more conservative Democrats on the committee, described it: "The committee make-up doesn't really reflect the make-up of the House: the Democrats are more liberal than the Democrats in the House as a whole, the (committee) leadership in particular, and the Republicans are more conservative than the Republicans in the House as a whole."

Voting studies by Congressional Quarterly supported his observation: in 1973 the average House Democrat supported President Nixon on 35 per cent of the votes—while the average Democrat on the committee supported him less frequently, on only 31 per cent of the votes. The same year, the average Republican on the committee supported the President on 64 per cent of the votes, more often than the average Republican in the House, whose record was 62 per cent.

Democrats held 21 of the 38 seats on the committee. As the 1974 session began, there was a vacancy in one of the 17 Republican seats, left by the resignation of William J. Keating (R Ohio 1971-1974) in January. The Republican Committee on Committees selected Delbert L. Latta (Ohio) as his replacement on the committee on Feb. 13.

The 38 members represented districts in 21 states, from Maine to California. Three were black; two were women. Six were in their thirties; half were younger than 50, and five were older than 60.

A Year of Changes

The 1972 election returns contained drastic changes for the House Judiciary Committee. The departure of the Celler-McCulloch team moved into leadership posts two men little known outside the House and untried as leaders. As power, released from Celler's tight grasp, was diffused, some of the more junior committee members began to emerge as influential figures.

Also, 11 freshmen were added to the committee in 1973. Including the six members who first had been elected in 1970, the committee wound up with almost half its members elected for the first time within the last four years.

The Leaders. Caution marked Rodino's move to the chair occupied for decades by one of the House's strongest committee leaders, caution which drew criticism. Late in 1973 a freshman Republican complained of the committee's lack of direction; another member remarked, with a resigned air, of Rodino's ability to be "firmly indecisive." Others attributed this characteristic to Rodino's effort to accommodate a range of individual views on the Democratic side—from conservative members like Flowers and James R. Mann (D S.C.) to vociferous liberals like John Conyers Jr. (D Mich.) and Robert Drinan (D Mass.). "I don't think that he can control his troops as well as he might," one Republican remarked.

"Pete is trying very hard to conduct this (impeachment inquiry) right," another one said later, "but he is riding a real bucking horse on his side, and the Republicans are not making things any easier, I guess."

"Peter is not an institution; Celler was," noted a Democrat, adding that he and others had been pleasantly surprised by the leadership ability Rodino had shown in his first year as chairman.

Most members felt that they had more input into committee decisions under Rodino's more democratic rule, although one senior Democrat warned that the change might be more of style than of substance: "Rodino gives the appearance of softer leadership, but in fact he exercises a strong hand," he said, noting that Rodino had acted alone in the selection of special counsel Doar.

Hutchinson, a quiet man with a ponderous manner, also was criticized by some of his more activist colleagues who saw his low profile as evidence of distaste for his leadership post. Advising against any underestimation of the man, a committee Democrat recalled that, when Hutchinson served in the Michigan legislature before coming to the House, "he practically ran the state.... He knows what he is doing." And McClory praised Hutchinson for his leadership of the committee's Republicans: under him the Republicans on the committee were more cohesive than they had been in a decade, he said.

Hutchinson viewed his role as a coordinator of equals, not a director of strategy. He attempted "to work with the minority to formulate or ascertain what the minority views are on major legislation. And in that role, my policy has been to meet with Republican members very fre-

---

Potential Prosecutors

One little-known fact was likely to make even the most vigorous supporter of impeachment on the House Judiciary Committee carefully examine the evidence assembled to support impeachment charges against President Nixon: any member could end up prosecuting that case for impeachment before the Senate, and the nation. And—as ranking committee Republican Edward Hutchinson (R Mich.) told Congressional Quarterly— "if the first phase (the staff investigation) is not done well, the managers of impeachment in the Senate will find themselves left up the creek without a paddle."

After the impeachment is announced to the Senate, the case against the president traditionally has been presented and 'prosecuted' by House members. After the House votes to impeach, these "managers of impeachment" are selected—by ballot, by resolution, or by the speaker. In the past, the number selected has varied from five to 11—members from both parties who voted for impeachment. Once selected, they choose their own chairman.

The managers present the Senate the articles of impeachment. The chairman then impeaches the person to be tried, by accusing him orally before the Senate of the charges. Then the trial begins, and the House managers act as prosecutors of the impeachment case, examining witnesses and presenting evidence.

---

quently, sometimes as often as once a week—not as a caucus so much as a forum for finding out what each other is thinking."

Next in Line. The House Judiciary Committee in 1973 was no longer under the close control of the finely honed working relationship between Celler and McCulloch. As Rodino and Hutchinson, vastly different men with dissimilar styles, began learning to work together in their new roles, power spread beyond them into the ranks of the committee.

During the year several of the other committee members in both parties gained stature as significant figures, whose contributions were influential in committee deliberations. Among those on the Democratic side were Jack Brooks of Texas, Robert W. Kastenmeier of Wisconsin and Hungate; on the Republican side—McClory, Tom Railsback of Illinois, Wiggins and Dennis. All were included as members of the impeachment advisory group.

Brooks, 51, a blunt and outspoken liberal with 22 years of service in the House, was considered talented and forceful by his colleagues. He played a lesser role than he might in Judiciary Committee deliberations as a whole, devoting more time to the Government Operations Subcommittee which he chairs and which in 1973 investigated federal spending on Nixon's homes at San Clemente and Key Biscayne.

Kastenmeier, at 49, a veteran of 15 years' service in the House, was a liberal who headed the Judiciary Subcommittee on Courts, Civil Liberties, and the Administration of Justice. Hungate, 51, a moderate midwesterner, won his colleagues' praise in 1973 for the hard work his subcommittee put in on the complex federal rules of evidence, and on the special prosecutor measures.

On the Republican side, McClory, of equal seniority with Hutchinson and, except for the luck of the draw, ranking minority member himself, spoke out more and more often for the minority. Railsback, a moderate young member also from Illinois and fifth ranking on the committee, also was heard and seen more frequently voicing Republican members' concerns. Reports of friction between the two, and of McClory's resentment of Railback's assertiveness, were said by other committee members to be exaggerated.

Less outspoken but highly respected was Wiggins of California, considered by many the best legal mind on the committee. And Dennis of Indiana was praised by members on both sides for his "feisty" independence.

The Freshmen. Frustration about his role as a freshman member of the committee was voiced by Trent Lott (R Miss.), but most of the new members agreed with Elizabeth Holtzman's (D N.Y.) description of the committee leadership as "very open, receptive and fair" in dealing with the freshmen. Acknowledged stand-outs in their first year on the committee were Holtzman and Barbara Jordan (Texas) on the Democratic side and William S. Cohen of Maine among the Republicans.

A Time of Tension

Events conspired late in 1973 to place two historic tasks before this unpracticed committee.

In early October Vice President Spiro T. Agnew resigned; two days later, his successor—Rep. Gerald R. Ford (R Mich.)—was nominated. The House Judiciary Committee was designated to investigate the nomination, the first made under the Twenty-Fifth Amendment.

But before the hearings could begin, the Watergate tapes crisis had culminated in the firing of special prosecutor Archibald Cox and the introduction of more than 20 measures calling for an impeachment investigation. On Oct. 23, House Speaker Carl Albert (D Okla.) said he would refer all impeachment bills to the House Judiciary Committee. Referral to that committee was not automatic; impeachment is not listed in the House Rules as falling within the jurisdiction of that or any other committee.

"This cannot be a partisan effort," said Rodino Oct. 29, referring to the impeachment inquiry. But the following day, when the committee first met to discuss procedures for the inquiry regarding the Ford nomination and impeachment, partisan sensitivities flared.

One-Man Subpoena Power. The first skirmish came on Rodino's request that the committee delegate to him alone the power to subpoena witnesses and documents for these two inquiries. This would prevent delay, he said, by precluding the necessity of his calling the full committee together to approve each subpoena.

Wary of the potential of "one-man subpoena power," the Republicans countered with a suggestion that this power be exercised jointly by Rodino and Hutchinson. Cohen urged adoption of this alternative: com-

---

Tyler Impeachment Attempt

John Tyler, one of the most unpopular presidents in history, was the target of the first attempt to impeach a president. Ostracized by both major parties after moving up to the presidency on the death of William Henry Harrison, Tyler was saved from impeachment when the House Jan. 10, 1843, rejected a resolution proposing an investigation into his possible impeachment.

---

pared to questions down the road this was an easy matter, and if the subpoenas were issued jointly, they would be less vulnerable to partisan attack, he contended. Approval of the alternative, he later said, would have been basically symbolic. Hutchinson's objection to a subpoena always could have been overridden by the full committee.

But Rodino opposed the suggestion, apparently viewing it as a challenge to his leadership. The Republican move was rejected on a straight party-line vote, 17-21; Rodino's request then was granted by another party vote, 21-17. Rodino said he would consult fully with Hutchinson on each subpoena, a promise which satisfied Cohen and some of the other Republicans. But the partisan animus aroused by the matter remained alive.

As Wiggins later commented: "The chairman states unequivocally that he wants to be fair. But as soon as the minority tries to require fair treatment in terms of the staff or subpoena power, the majority rises up, and by a staright party-line vote, rebuffs that effort."

Ford and the Prosecutor. That concern was not allayed by the partisan divisions which surfaced on the Ford confirmation vote in the House, and on the matter of authorizing a court-appointed special prosecutor.

Although there were Republican complaints of footdragging before the House hearings on the Ford nomination began, Rodino's conduct of the hearings once they were underway won high praise for their fairness. But when the House confirmed Ford Dec. 6, nine of the 35 negative votes were cast by Democrats on the Judiciary Committee.

Most surprising of these votes was Rodino's, which he explained on the floor as a response to the needs of his district. Republicans criticized the vote as partisan and strictly political, dictated by the political insecurity of a white man who represented a predominantly black constituency.

On the matter of a special prosecutor, the full committee rejected a Republican measure which would have left the prosecutor within the executive branch by a vote of 17-21—down party lines except that one Democrat (Flowers) and one Republican (Froehlich) switched sides.

One Million Dollars. 1973, as the committee began the Ford hearings Nov. 15, a resolution was introduced on the House floor granting the committee an additional $1-million to finance the impeachment inquiry. Anxious for answers to some preliminary questions about the inquiry, Republican members sought a delay of House action on the matter.

"Do the members realize," asked Wiggins, "that the committee...has not had its first meeting on the subject of impeachment? We have not yet decided what we are going to do, what is impeachable, what is not, and what instructions are to be given this staff?....Would it not be more fair and judicious and prudent for the committee to decide itself what we are going to do before we run to the House administration for money?"

McClory urged that the resolution be postponed until the Judiciary Committee could be called together to discuss plans for the inquiry.

Rodino protested that the Republicans were creating partisan feeling by their complaints. "Only yesterday, in addressing myself to a query...as to what might happen if this were not a bipartisan effort," Rodino noted, "I said it would be disastrous for the country."

A motion to kill the resolution by recommitting it failed by only 37 votes; the only Republicans on the committee who opposed recommittal were Cohen and Railsback. The House then approved the $1-million.

Problems of Procedure

Aware that the rules governing and limiting the impeachment inquiry would have substantial impact on its outcome, Republican members began pressing in December, 1973, for decisions on a variety of procedural matters. After one informal committee meeting and an hour of voicing their concerns from the House floor, they had, by Dec. 22, won establishment of the advisory group and a general target date of April for the end of the committee's work.

But a variety of unresolved procedural matters were certain to provoke intense discussion when the committee resumed its work after Jan. 21.

Even the procedural matters divided the committee along party lines. As Wiggins reflected: "It is the desire and the political interest of the majority to not have rules, so that there can be the broadest possible range for the investigation. But the interest of the law and the minority are served by deciding the rules first."

The Timetable. The need for some time limit was one of the first matters broached by the Republicans. Ralph Nader, not known to be a Republican ally in this matter, already had criticized the committee for dilly-dallying. Rodino was "suffering a crisis of a lack of self-confidence," he said, warning that "if the House does not vote impeachment by March, there will be none."

Nevertheless, Rodino Dec. 11 rebuffed Republican suggestions that the committee continue work in January during the recess in order to expedite its decision.

But Republicans persisted, interpreting Democratic resistance as calculated to delay a final decision on impeachment until election season. If there was no vote by April, Vice President Ford said Dec. 13, "then you can say it's partisan." And committee member Hamilton Fish Jr. (R N.Y.) warned a few days later: "The closer we get to the 1974 elections, and the further...from the events which generated this in-

quiry, the more likely whatever we do will be described as partisan."

Although a number of committee Democrats found March a reasonable target date, Rodino just before adjournment in December agreed that the committee should be finished by April. He made it clear that this was a hope more than a promise, and by Jan. 7, the target date had become "the latter part of April."

A Select Group. Concerned also about supervision of the staff working on the inquiry, Republicans pressed Rodino to appoint a select subcommittee to conduct certain phases of the investigation. Such a body had been created in 1970 to investigate impeachment charges against Supreme Court Justice William O. Douglas.

"All we can do is complain. We don't have the votes to override whatever the majority decides to do."

—Robert McClory (R Ill.)

"The full committee is too large a body to direct any project," said Hutchinson, who advocated that the Nixon impeachment charges also be handled by a small subcommittee. On Dec. 11, committee members apparently agreed on the need for a subcommittee, but failed to reach consensus on what precisely the subcommittee should do.

Railsback, one of the subcommittee proposal's chief proponents, would have the subcommittee, composed of an equal number of members from each party, "formulate procedural rules...set up a timetable...determine the admissibility of evidence...decide what standard of proof should be required...(and) narrow the issues by screening the evidence."

Although a number of Democrats opposed the subcommittee idea, reluctant to delegate too much of the grand jury function of the committee in an impeachment inquiry, Ray Thornton (D Ark.), a freshman, backed the idea of a small bipartisan panel "to accept evidence and conduct hearings."

Creation of the advisory group by Rodino took the steam out of the drive for a select committee, although it could be revived since there was little indication that the advisory body would perform as anything more than a steering committee.

An Impeachable Offense? Ultimately, it would be for each member of the committee—and possibly the House—to decide the definition of an impeachable offense. That debate had begun with the Constitution, and recurred with each impeachment attempt. Traditionally, those more reluctant to see impeachment of the accused official defined an impeachable offense more narrowly than those who were supporting impeachment. Rodino agreed that the problem was "something we're going to have to reason with."

And practical reasons militated for a committee determination—at least of what was not likely to be an impeachable offense. Initially, the staff investigation was divided into the areas of President Nixon's personal finances, his campaign finances, Watergate, and possible abuse of presidential authority in matters such as impoundment and secret bombing.

In order not to waste Judiciary Committee staff time and energy, the committee should "decide what of the charges shows promise of being an impeachable offense," and then "give the rest" away to committees who might write legislation to prevent further such misconduct, Wiggins told Congressional Quarterly. He distinguished between a legally impeachable offense and a politically impeachable offense. Political popularity, he noted, can offset a technically impeachable offense: "There will be no votes to impeach a president if the people condone what he has done."

Expressing the need for some definition in a different—and more partisan—context, Lott advised: "What needs to be done is for the Democrats to draw a line and say, 'At least this much must be proved for us to go on to impeachment,' and for the Republicans to do the same, and say, 'If this much is proved, then we will have an impeachable offense.' "

The advisory group agreed Jan. 24 to hold open committee hearings in February on the definition of an impeachable offense. Doar said that that definition was one of the first matters for the committee to resolve.

Access to Information. Ironically, despite hours of investigation by all three branches of the government, and the news media, one of the problems facing the House Judiciary Committee was its access to information and evidence to confirm or refute the charges brought against Nixon.

Early in the inquiry, Rodino said the committee would look to other committees which already had inquired into some of these matters for their evidence. Chief among these was the Senate Watergate Committee. Doar said Jan. 7 that he had received no material yet from the committee but that he did have assurances that such was forthcoming.

"It is the desire and the political interest of the majority to not have rules, so that there can be the broadest possible range for the investigation. But the interest of the law and the minority are served by deciding the rules first."

—Charles E. Wiggins (R Calif.)

A major problem arose in mid-January, however, when special prosecutor Leon Jaworski, after at least two meetings with Doar, said that he would not make available to the Judiciary Committee the material he had received from the White House. All of that, he said, "we have insisted upon as part of our investigation, and when we received the material it was accompanied by the stated understanding that it was made available to us under an agreement of confidentiality."

Earlier that week White House Counsel J. Fred Buzhardt, terming the impeachment inquiry a basically political matter, had said that the White House would resist the committee's demands for presidential documents and tapes.

"The Committee on the Judiciary will have to seek subpoena power from the House" for the impeachment inquiry, Rodino announced Jan. 7. The purpose of this move was to perfect the committee's right to this power and so to ensure against any challenge of its subpoenas.

As granted to many standing committees by the Rules of the House, the power of subpoena generally was seen as intended for use in regard to matters within the committee's jurisdiction. As of January 1974, impeachment was not specifically included within the jurisdiction of the House Judiciary Committee, an omission which could raise questions about the propriety of its use of its usual subpoena power in regard to an impeachment inquiry. A clear grant of subpoena power from the House to the committee for this inquiry would scotch such questions.

This new subpoena matter raised questions on which partisan lines threatened to form again. The key, Railsback said Jan. 7, was whether Rodino would share this power. The answer came soon. The advisory group Jan. 24 agreed on a resolution by which the House granted this special power to the committee, to be exercised by Rodino and Hutchinson together, with any disagreements settled by the full committee.

Rodino said Jan. 24 that the committee had received a letter from Jaworski indicating a willingness to work out procedures for cooperation on evidence.

Outlook: Cloudy

"All of us...are aware," said Rodino Jan. 8, "that partisanship may crop up from time to time...but this (inquiry) must be conducted in a bipartisan manner." Hutchinson, a few days earlier, also had forecast the committee's working relationship during the inquiry in fairly optimistic terms: "I expect to see outcroppings of more partisanship in regard to impeachment than in regard to general legislative matters...but I know that every attempt will be made to keep political partisanship at its lowest level."

"It would, however, be unrealistic to expect this to be devoid of partisanship," he added.

More pessimistic forecasts were voiced by two other committee members. "I just can't see this turning out nonpartisan," says Flowers, whose hometown newspaper already had labeled him one of the "swing" votes on the matter. "But I hope it does," he added.

"It has all been decided," lamented Lott, one of the more conservative Republicans on the committee. "We are just going through an exercise. Right now I doubt whether it will be expeditious or fair.... All we can do is try to see that what is done is done fairly."

A more measured reaction came from Cohen: "It's easy now to say that everything should be done in a nonpartisan manner, but there are some tough questions down the road.... We are anxious to protect our part, our voice in the proceedings."

"So far," he continued, "the things which may have created negative feelings in this regard have not colored the entire process; they are not yet strong enough to skew it all."

PROFILES OF THE 38 JUDICIARY COMMITTEE MEMBERS

Following are profiles of all 38 members of the House Judicary Committee—21 Democrats and 17 Republicans. Included are district descriptions, presidential support scores for 1973 and any comments each member may have made concerning the impeachment investigation.

THE DEMOCRATS

Peter W. Rodino Jr., 64, represents New Jersey's 10th district (Newark), which was in 1974 about 52 per cent black. A member of the House since 1949 and chairman of the committee since 1973, he faces the possibility of a strong primary challenge from a black candidate in 1974. A liberal, he supported Nixon on 28 per cent of the votes on which the President took a position during 1973. He has commented: "I must say that the consideration of resolutions relating to the possible impeachment of the President is a task I would have preferred not to undertake."

Harold D. Donohue, 72, represents Massachusetts' heavily industrialized 3rd district (central, Worcester). First elected to the House in 1947, Donohue did not go on the Judiciary Committee until the early 1950s, after Rodino. A quiet man who heads the Subcommittee on Claims, Donohue has a liberal voting record, supporting Nixon on 28 per cent of the votes in 1973.

Jack Brooks, 51, represents Texas' industrial 9th district (Beaumont-Port Arthur, Galveston). Brooks was first elected to the House in 1952 at the age of 29. He is a tough and outspoken liberal, was close to Lyndon Johnson and active on civil rights issues. He chairs the government operations subcommittee which investigated federal spending on the presidential homes at San Clemente, Calif., and Key Biscayne, Fla. He supported Nixon on 34 per cent of the votes in 1973.

Robert W. Kastenmeier, 49, represents Wisconsin's 2nd district, which includes the University of Wisconsin at Madison (southern). He has been a member of the House since 1959, is a highly regarded, issue-oriented liberal, and serves as chairman of the Subcommittee on Courts, Civil Liberties, and the Administration of Justice. He supported Nixon on 26 per cent of the votes in 1973. Kastenmeier has not said that he favors impeachment, but commented that before the "Saturday night massacre" firing of Archibald Cox, impeachment was "really unthinkable in practical terms. That is no longer the case."

Don Edwards, 58, represents the blue-collar suburbs of California's 9th district (Oakland to San Jose). He has been a member of the House since 1963, is a former FBI agent and national chairman of the Americans for Democratic Action. Edwards has gained the reputation of a hard-working liberal and is chairman of the Subcommittee on Civil Rights and Constitutional Rights. In 1973, he supported Nixon on 21 per cent of the votes. "We plan to prepare through our staff the most honest hard-hitting bill of particulars we can get," he has said, "and then present it to the American people."

William L. Hungate, 51, represents the rural and small-town 9th district of Missouri (northeast, St. Charles). A moderately liberal member of the House since 1964, Hungate heads the hard-working Subcommittee on Reform of Federal Criminal Laws. He supported Nixon on 34 per cent of the votes during 1973.

John Conyers Jr., 44, represents Michigan's predominantly black 1st district (residential areas of Detroit). A member of the House since 1966 and a forceful proponent of civil rights measures, Conyers heads the Subcommittee on Crime. He supported Nixon on 20 per cent of the votes during 1973.

Chapman

Peter W. Rodino Jr.
(D N.J.)

Harold D. Donohue
(D Mass.)

Jack Brooks
(D Texas)

Robert W. Kastenmeier
(D Wis.)

Don Edwards
(D Calif.)

Joshua Eilberg, 52, represents Pennsylvania's middle-income residential 4th district (Philadelphia). He is a former majority leader in the state house of representatives, and was elected to the House in 1966. Liberal, quiet and hard-working, he heads the Subcommittee on Immigration, Citizenship, and International Law. He supported Nixon on 28 per cent of the votes in 1973. Eilberg has said that he would define an impeachable offense as a presidential action "which shocks the conscience," not necessarily a criminal action.

Jerome R. Waldie, 48, represents California's heavily industrial 14th district (most of Contra Costa County). Former majority leader of the state legislature, Waldie was elected to the House in 1966. He is regarded as very liberal and independent, and as one of the best lawyers on the committee. He is planning to run for governor of California in 1974. Waldie supported Nixon's position on 20 per cent of the votes during 1973. Sponsor of the first impeachment resolution introduced after the Cox firing, Waldie has said that "gross abuse of the office of the presidency, whether it is criminal or not, could be proper grounds for impeachment."

Walter Flowers, 40, represents the conservative Democratic 7th district of Alabama (west central, Tuscaloosa, Birmingham suburbs). He is a moderately conservative third-term member of the House, supporting Nixon's position 50 per cent of the time in 1973. Flowers has said that Congress has great latitude in defining an impeachable offense, but that it should not impeach a president simply because of "a lot of small things" or mere "distaste" for his actions.

James R. Mann, 53, represents the heavily industrialized 4th district of South Carolina (Greenville/Spartanburg). He is a former prosecutor, was elected to the House in 1969, and is regarded as one of the most conservative Democrats on the committee, supporting Nixon on 59 per cent of the votes in 1973. "Impeachment merely reveals the failure of the Judiciary Committee to exercise its oversight function" Mann has noted. "Congress is merely doing its duty to police executive power."

Paul S. Sarbanes, 40, represents the Baltimore suburbs of Maryland's 3rd district. Son of Greek immigrants, a Rhodes scholar and former state legislator, Sarbanes was elected to the House in 1970. He is a liberal with strong labor backing, and is respected by colleagues for his thoughtful intelligence. In 1973 he supported Nixon on 28 per cent of the votes.

John F. Seiberling, 55, represents Ohio's 14th district, which includes Akron and Kent State University. He is a decorated veteran of World War II, and was an attorney for the Goodyear Rubber Company—which his grandfather founded—before winning election to the House in 1970. Considered very liberal, he supported Nixon's position 25 per cent of the time in 1973.

George E. Danielson, 58, represents California's 29th district, which includes eastern Los Angeles. He is a former FBI agent and state legislator, and was elected to the House in 1970 with labor backing. Danielson has a tenuous hold on his seat because of recent redistricting, which placed him in the same district as Chet Holifield (D Calif.), chairman of the Government Operations

William L. Hungate
(D Mo.)

John Conyers Jr.
(D Mich.)

Joshua Eilberg
(D Pa.)

Jerome R. Waldie
(D Calif.)

Walter Flowers
(D Ala.)

| **James R. Mann**
(D S.C.) | **Paul S. Sarbanes**
(D Md.) | **John F. Seiberling**
(D Ohio) | **George E. Danielson**
(D Calif.) | **Robert F. Drinan**
(D Mass.) |

Committee. Danielson, a liberal, supported Nixon's position 22 per cent of the time in 1973. He has said that an impeachable offense should be defined narrowly as an indictable offense.

Robert F. Drinan, 53, represents Massachusetts' suburban and small-town 4th district (Boston suburbs, small industrial towns). Drinan is a Jesuit priest and former dean of Boston College Law School. He was elected to the House in 1970 and 1972 by narrow margins, has been highly critical of Nixon and was the first member of Congress (on July 31, 1973) to introduce an impeachment resolution. He has been a flamboyant spokesman for liberal causes, supporting Nixon on 33 per cent of the votes in 1973. "The first illusion we have to break is that you have to prove a criminal offense (to impeach the President). This is a political offense."

Charles B. Rangel, 43, represents New York's 19th district (Manhattan, Harlem). He is a former state legislator who defeated Adam Clayton Powell Jr. in a 1970 primary. In June 1973, he proposed that a special committee should be formed "to see if the President's role in the events surrounding the Watergate bugging and its subsequent coverup constituted grounds for impeachment." Rangel supported Nixon on 27 per cent of the votes in 1973.

Barbara C. Jordan, 36, represents Texas' primarily black 18th district (central Houston). She is a former state senator, was elected in 1972 as the first black woman to serve in Congress from the South and is an articulate and well respected member of the committee. She supported Nixon on 30 per cent of the votes in 1973.

Ray Thornton, 45, represents Arkansas' agricultural 4th district. A former state attorney general, he was elected to the House in 1972. He supported Nixon on 45 per cent of the votes in 1973 and has avoided making public statements concerning impeachment.

Elizabeth Holtzman, 32, represents New York's 16th district (Brooklyn) after upsetting former House dean and Judiciary Committee Chairman Emanuel Celler in the 1972 primary. She is a former state committeewoman, a liberal and is regarded as highly intelligent and hard-working. She supported Nixon's position 29 per cent of the time during 1973. She has commented: "We don't help to restore public confidence in the processes of government if we don't act expeditiously, with thoroughness, fairness and justice."

Wayne Owens, 36, represents Utah's 2nd district (Salt Lake City). A liberal who worked in the Robert F. Kennedy 1968 presidential primary campaign, Owens is expected to run for a Senate seat in 1974. He supported Nixon's position 32 per cent of the time in 1973.

Edward Mezvinsky, 36, was elected in 1972 over an incumbent Republican to represent Iowa's rural and rapidly growing industrial first district. He is a consumer advocate, a strong liberal, and a freshman spokesman in the House. He supported Nixon on 34 per cent of the votes in 1973.

| **Charles B. Rangel**
(D N.Y.) | **Barbara C. Jordan**
(D Texas) | **Ray Thornton**
(D Ark.) | **Elizabeth Holtzman**
(D N.Y.) | **Wayne Owens**
(D Utah) |

Edward Mezvinsky
(D Iowa)

Edward Hutchinson
(R Mich.)

Robert McClory
(R Ill.)

Henry P. Smith III
(R N.Y.)

Charles W. Sandman Jr.
(R N.J.)

THE REPUBLICANS

Edward Hutchinson, 59, represents Michigan's rural and small-town 4th district. He is a former state legislator who was elected to the House in 1963. He is conservative and quiet, preferring to stay out of the public eye. He supported Nixon's position 75 per cent of the time in 1973. "We've only got one president," he has said, "and impeachment of a president is something the country can't afford."

Robert McClory, 65, represents the outer Chicago suburbs of Illinois' 13th district. He has served in the House since 1963. Although he is of equal seniority as Hutchinson, he ranks second on the Republican side because of a draw for position. He has won reelection by wide margins in the past, but faces an energetic challenger for his seat in the March primary. He supported Nixon's position 67 per cent of the time in 1973. "There should be some kind of criminal offense (to justify impeachment)," he has said, "and there has to be direct evidence of (the President's) involvement."

Henry P. Smith III, 62, represents New York's 36th district (Niagara County). He is a conservative, elected to the House in 1964, and faces a strong Democratic challenger in 1974. In 1973, Smith supported Nixon on 68 per cent of the votes. He has not commented on impeachment.

Charles W. Sandman Jr., 52, represents the rural areas and resorts in the 2nd district of New Jersey. Former majority leader of the state senate and a member of the House since 1967, Sandman was soundly defeated in a 1973 race for governor. He is very conservative, supporting Nixon on 44 per cent of the votes in 1973. He missed a number of votes while campaigning for governor. He has said it is not proper for him as a member of the committee, to "prejudge" the impeachment case, and therefore has made no other public comment.

Tom Railsback, 41, represents Illinois' 19th district (western). He is a former state legislator and popular moderate conservative with labor support. He was first elected to the House in 1967 and is one of the more outspoken Republicans on the committee. He supported Nixon on 51 per cent of the votes in 1973. "You have an impeachment by the Democrats without any Republican participation," he has asserted, "and it's going to divide the country."

Charles E. Wiggins, 46, represents the primarily blue-collar suburbs of California's 25th district (eastern Los Angeles county), essentially the district Nixon once represented (1947-50). A thoughtful conservative considered by many the best legal mind on the committee, Wiggins was first elected to the House in 1967. He supported Nixon's position 64 per cent of the time in 1973. The President would be impeachable, he has said, for "conduct which, exposed to the light of day, produces moral outrage among the people that causes them to believe that he is no longer fit to serve."

David W. Dennis, 61, represents the industrial and agricultural 10th district of Indiana (Muncie and Richmond). Dennis is expected to face a tough fight for his seat in 1974. He supported Nixon on 76 per cent of the votes in 1973.

Tom Railsback
(R Ill.)

Charles E. Wiggins
(R Calif.)

David W. Dennis
(R Ind.)

Hamilton Fish Jr.
(R N.Y.)

Wiley Mayne
(R Iowa)

Lawrence J. Hogan
(R Md.)

M. Caldwell Butler
(R Va.)

William S. Cohen
(R Maine)

Trent Lott
(R Miss.)

Harold V. Froehlich
(R Wis.)

Hamilton Fish Jr., 47, represents the Hudson River communities of New York's 25th district (outer New York City suburbs, farms and small industrial towns). A moderate Republican first elected to the House in 1968, Fish supported Nixon on 49 per cent of the votes in 1973. He has said that an impeachable offense is not necessarily an indictable offense.

Wiley Mayne, 56, represents Iowa's agricultural 6th district (northwest). Elected to the House in 1966, he won with only 52 per cent of the vote in 1972, and is likely to face a strong challenge in the 1974 election. He supported Nixon on 70 per cent of the votes in 1973. Mayne feels that an impeachable offense must be a crime.

Lawrence J. Hogan, 45, represents the Washington, D.C., suburbs of Maryland's 5th district. A former FBI agent, elected to the House in 1968, Hogan is a strong conservative and supported Nixon on 67 per cent of the votes in 1973. He has stated: "We ought to disqualify those members from the grand jury (the House Judiciary Committee considering impeachment charges) who have said that the President ought to be impeached."

M. Caldwell Butler, 48, represents the traditionally Republican 6th district of Virginia (western, Roanoke). He is a former Republican leader in the state assembly and campaign manager for former Rep. Richard H. Poff (R 1952-72), who also was a Judiciary Committee member. Butler was elected in 1972 to fill Poff's seat. He supported Nixon's position 75 per cent of the time in 1973. "The time has come to impeach or cease-fire," he has said.

William S. Cohen, 33, represents Maine's 2nd district, which includes Bangor, a city of which he was formerly mayor. Elected in 1972 to his first House term after a walking campaign, he has been mentioned as a possible gubernatorial candidate. Cohen supported

Nixon on 53 per cent of the votes in 1973. In defining an impeachable offense, he has said: "It's like Robert Frost on love. It's indefinable and unmistakable—I know it when I see it."

Trent Lott, 32, represents the rapidly growing resort and industrial areas of Mississippi's 5th district (southeast). Formerly administrative assistant to now-retired Rep. William M. Colmer (D Miss. 1933-1973), Lott became a Republican and won Colmer's seat in 1972. A very conservative member, he supported Nixon's position 69 per cent of the time in 1973.

Harold V. Froehlich, 41, represents Wisconsin's rural 8th district (northeast). He was elected to the House by a narrow margin in 1972 and faces a hard contest in 1974 to hold his seat. He supported Nixon's position 60 per cent of the time in 1973.

Carlos J. Moorhead, 51, represents the conservative white-collar 20th district of California (Los Angeles). A former state assemblyman, he supported Nixon on 70 per cent of the votes during 1973. Impeachment should only come for criminal acts, he maintains. "The President has done a remarkable job considering Congress has spent $1-million to try to impeach him."

Joseph J. Maraziti, 61, represents the new rural 13th district in New Jersey (west). He is a former judge and state legislator. A moderate, he supported Nixon's position 61 per cent of the time in 1973.

Delbert L. Latta, 53, represents the largely agricultural 5th district of Ohio (northwest). Latta, a veteran Republican legislator, was first elected to the House in 1958. A conservative, Latta supported President Nixon's position 72 per cent of the time in 1973. Latta says "all impeachment proceedings must be defined within the confines of the Constitution, nothing more, nothing less."

Carlos J. Moorhead
(R Calif.)

Joseph J. Maraziti
(R N.J.)

Delbert L. Latta
(R Ohio)

CONGRESS: MIXED RESPONSE TO PLEDGE OF COOPERATION

President Nixon's pledge to cooperate with the House Judiciary Committee's impeachment investigation, on his terms, left Congress about where it was before—divided. Nixon, fighting to regain his political leadership as well as to retain his office, said in his state of the union message Jan. 30 that he would cooperate with the inquiry "in any way I consider consistent with my responsibility to the office of the presidency." *(Box, p. 229)*

Partisans of the President praised the statement as conciliatory and constructive. But some congressional Democrats interpreted it to mean that Nixon would attempt to withhold information from the impeachment panel on grounds of executive privilege, as he had from the Senate Watergate committee and the Watergate special prosecutor. The Senate committee's subpoenas of the President were still the subject of a court fight. *(p. 229)*

Other members of Congress in both parties, took a wait-and-see attitude. "We're glad to hear (Nixon) say he will cooperate," said House Judiciary Committee member Henry P. Smith III (R N.Y.). "The test is whether he will."

Judiciary Committee. The House Judiciary Committee made it clear Jan. 31 that it considered its impeachment role pre-eminent under the Constitution and that the President could not legally invoke executive privilege to keep information from it. The committee voted to seek special subpoena power from the House to get whatever information it considered necessary for its inquiry. Chairman Peter W. Rodino Jr. (D N.J.) told newsmen pointedly that once the power was granted, "no one is excluded from its authority."

The committee's action followed a rising tide of bipartisan congressional sentiment that Nixon had to give full cooperation to the inquiry if he were to survive the impeachment attempts against him. Such statements were made by Democratic Senators Robert C. Byrd (W. Va.) and Lloyd Bentsen (Texas), by the Republican leaders of both houses of Congress, Sen. Hugh Scott (Pa.) and Rep. John J. Rhodes (Ariz.), and by the ranking Republican on the Judiciary Committee, Rep. Edward Hutchinson (Mich.).

Hearings Postponed. As the Judiciary Committee's investigation of the President's role in the Watergate affair and related activities moved onto center stage, the Senate Watergate committee moved into the wings. On Jan. 26, just three days before the committee was scheduled to open new hearings into financial dealings connected with the 1972 Nixon presidential campaign, Chairman Sam J. Ervin Jr. (D N.C.) announced that the hearings would be postponed indefinitely, so as not to prejudice the Mitchell-Stans trial in New York. Some observers suspected the hearings might never resume. *(Earlier story, p. 210)*

The Senate committee's ranking Republican member, Howard H. Baker Jr. (Tenn.), summed up what seemed to be a fairly widespread attitude when he said Jan. 28 that the time had come for the committee to "shut down and to certify our findings to the House." The findings would be invaluable to the House impeachment inquiry, he said.

Chairman Ervin, commenting on Nixon's call to end the Watergate investigations, said, "If the President would not have spent time withholding information from our investigation, we could have ended it months ago." He said he expected hearings to resume as soon as the jury was chosen for the trial in New York City of former Attorney General John N. Mitchell and former Commerce Secretary Maurice H. Stans. The trial was to start on Feb. 19.

Special Prosecutor. In other Watergate developments, the special prosecutor's office told the U.S. District Court in Washington, D.C., that it had found no evidence to indicate that former White House counsel John W. Dean III had lied in his testimony linking the President to the Watergate coverup. Special Prosecutor Leon Jaworski also reportedly asked the Senate Watergate committee to delay issuing its report, due Feb. 28, to avoid endangering future trials.

Judiciary Committee Action

Girding itself with explicit authority and special powers to deal with the thorny matter of impeachment, the House Judiciary Committee Jan. 31 unanimously agreed to ask the full House to provide it with "appropriate power...to conduct an investigation of whether sufficient grounds exist to impeach Richard M. Nixon, President of the United States."

Under the resolution, which the House was expected to approve during the week of Feb. 4, the House would specifically authorize the committee to investigate and report on whether grounds for impeachment existed. In addition, the House would delegate to the committee special subpoena power to use in this inquiry. These subpoenas would be issued either by the full committee or subcommittee or by Chairman Rodino and the ranking Republican member, Hutchinson, acting jointly. Should either Rodino or Hutchinson decline to issue a particular subpoena which the other sought, either man could then take the dispute to the full committee for resolution.

This joint exercise of the subpoena power marked a deliberate move by Rodino to counter charges of partisanship; late in October 1973, the Republican members of the committee had been angered by a party-line vote delegating the committee's usual subpoena power to Rodino alone, for use in the inquiries concerning the nomination of Vice President Ford and the impeachment resolutions.

Nixon's California Subpoena

President Nixon, who had been fighting off sub-poenas from the Senate Watergate committee and the Watergate special prosecutor for months, was threatened with a subpoena from a new source Jan. 29. A California state judge ordered Nixon to appear Feb. 25 and April 15 as a material witness in the trial of of three former aides, John D. Ehrlichman, David R. Young Jr. and G. Gordon Liddy, for the burglary of Daniel Ellsberg's psychiatrist's office in 1971.

It apparently was the first time in history that a president had been subpoenaed by a state court. The White House said Jan. 30 that the President would refuse to testify personally, on constitutional grounds. Nixon's Watergate lawyer, James D. St. Clair, rec-ommended that the President "respectfully decline to appear," said Gerald L. Warren, deputy White House press secretary. Warren refused to say whether Nixon would answer written questions or submit to interrogation at the White House.

The subpoena was approved by Los Angeles Superior Court Judge Gordon Ringer. Nixon's ap-pearance was sought by Ehrlichman, apparently to support his claim that he was acting as a law en-forcement agent when he directed the activities of the White House "plumbers." If the claim were up-held, he would not be subject to prosecution for the plumbers' search of the psychiatrist's office.

As a state judge, Ringer actually had no power to issue a subpoena outside California. He said he would forward a certificate asking for the subpoena to be issued by the District of Columbia Superior Court under provisions of the Uniform Witness Act. A Washington judge then could schedule a hearing to determine whether the President was in fact a material witness, whether his appearance was neces-sary and whether appearing in California would im-pose an undue hardship on him.

Attorney General William B. Saxbe said Jan. 30 that the Justice Department was working to keep Nixon from being subpoenaed by "every court of the country" and that the department might intervene as a friend of the court in the California case be-cause of the importance of the presidential privilege question. It was "unrealistic," Saxbe said, to expect the President to "appear in every justice of the peace court at the whim of that justice of the peace."

While Nixon was the first president to be sub-poenaed in a state trial, Thomas Jefferson was sub-poenaed in the federal treason trial of Aaron Burr in 1807. *(Box, p. 230)*

Early in January, upon the recommendation of the staff, Rodino indicated that the committee would ask the House for special subpoena power for the impeachment inquiry in order to ensure against any challenge of this power. After Republican members made clear their determination to fight for a share in this power, Rodino indicated that he felt it should be exercised jointly by himself and Hutchinson. *(p. 215)*

Approval of the resolution concluded a three-hour meeting—the first, some members noted, by the full committee to discuss impeachment, which had been re-ferred to the committee Oct. 23. Discussion focused on several proposed amendments that would have set limits on the inquiry—and on an amendment designed to give the Republican minority the right to subpoena witnesses and evidence without the risk of a Democratic veto by the committee majority. All these amendments were re-jected.

A Deadline. Urging the need for a target date, and noting that Rodino himself had set a tentative dead-line of late April, Robert McClory (R Ill.) proposed that the committee write April 30 into the resolution as the date for its final report. McClory indicated his willing-ness to back an extension of that deadline, should events foreclose completion of the inquiry by that time.

Led by Rodino and Jack Brooks (D Texas,) com-mittee Democrats opposed the deadline. Describing the deadline effort as "erroneous and unrealistic," Brooks called it "an infringement on the reputation of this com-mittee and the chairman.... This is not a pregnancy, just the rabbit test." Rodino repeated his description of a deadline as "unwise and irresponsible," noting that committee special counsel John M. Doar and Albert E. Jenner Jr. both had expressed reluctance to set any such deadline.

Opposed by all committee Democrats and Republicans Charles E. Wiggins (Calif.) and M. Caldwell Butler (Va.), the McClory amendment was rejected, 14-23. The com-mittee then rejected, by a 7-29 vote, a proposal by Trent Lott (R Miss.), to set an expiration date of April 30 for the special subpoena power. And a third effort, by Wayne Owens (D Utah), to set April 30 as at least the date for an interim report, was rejected by a 12-24 vote.

Two Deficiencies. The grant of special subpoena power was "absolutely essential," but there were two deficiencies in the resolution granting it, said Wiggins. His efforts to amend the resolution to remedy those de-ficiencies were rebuffed by the committee.

Moving first to strike from the resolution the language that provided for settlement by the full committee of any disagreement between Rodino and Hutchinson on the issuance of a subpoena, Wiggins described the issue as "a matter of basic fairness." Should the minority have the right to subpoena witnesses? he asked, terming that the basic question posed by his motion.

If Rodino disagreed with a decision by Hutchin-son to subpoena a certain witness, Wiggins pointed out, and the matter were then referred to the full committee, the Democrats most likely would support Rodino, over-riding Hutchinson's decision. "The minority should possess no less right in this matter than the majority," said Wiggins. This amendment was rejected by a 16-21 vote, with Jerome R. Waldie (D Calif.), Robert F. Drinan (D Mass.) and Owens voting for the amendment along with all the Republicans except Hutchinson, McClory and Henry P. Smith III (N.Y.).

Wiggins' second amendment, which would have re-quired the committee to determine that certain testi-mony or material was relevant, as well as necessary, to the investigation before subpoenaing it, also was rejected. The vote was 15-22, with Drinan the only Democrat

'One Year Is Enough'

President Nixon used his state of the union message to Congress Jan. 30 to reiterate that he would not quit—but wished the Watergate investigators would.

"One year of Watergate is enough," said the President, in a postscript to his formal message, a postscript which to many applauding members of his congressional audience carried more drama and interest than anything else he said in his prepared text.

"I believe the time has come to bring that (Watergate) investigation and the other investigations of this matter to an end," Nixon said, and "for all of us to join together in devoting our full energies to these great issues that I have discussed tonight. As you know, I have provided to the special prosecutor voluntarily a great deal of material. I believe that I have provided all the material that he needs to conclude his investigations and to proceed to prosecute the guilty and to clear the innocent.

"I recognize that the House Judiciary Committee has a special responsibility in this area," Nixon went on, referring to the committee's impeachment investigation. The President said he would cooperate with the committee "in any way I consider consistent with my responsibilities to the office of the presidency of the United States. There is only one limitation. I will follow the precedent that has been followed by and defended by every president from George Washington to Lyndon B. Johnson of never doing anything that weakens the office of the president of the United States or impairs the ability of the presidents of the future to make the great decisions that are so essential to this nation and to the world."

Then Nixon added: "Like every member of the House and Senate assembled here tonight, I was elected to the office that I hold.... I was elected for the purpose of doing a job and doing it as well as I possibly can. And I want you to know that I have no intention whatever of ever walking away from the job that the people elected me to do for the people of the United States."

The President also said that "it would be an understatement if I were not to admit that the year 1973 was not a very easy year for me personally or for my family."

supporting the measure, and with Charles W. Sandman Jr. (R N.J.) and William S. Cohen (R Maine) opposing it with the Democrats.

Rodino accepted an amendment proposed by Butler which made clear that the subpoena power could only be exercised by a subcommittee specially constituted for the impeachment inquiry, and not simply by any of the standing subcommittees.

A Statutory Basis. Robert W. Kastenmeier (D Wis.), backed by Wiggins, asked Doar and Jenner to consider the possible need for a bill providing a statutory basis for the committee's subpoenas. Noting that the Senate Watergate committee had belatedly found such a measure necessary in order to win court enforcement of their subpoenas, Kastenmeier and Wiggins expressed concern that a similar situation could arise in regard to a challenge to one of the House Judiciary Committee's subpoenas.

Busy Week. The vote on the subpoena resolution capped a busy week for the Judiciary Committee.

On Jan. 28, the Republican members had met with Jenner, appointed as their counsel during the recess, for a discussion of the inquiry. During the meeting, Jenner explained and narrowed the implications of his earlier remark that a President, under investigation, could be held responsible for the acts of his subordinates. Some of the Republican members had criticized this remark.

Jenner indicated that he felt this responsibility extended only to those acts which the President had specifically authorized, whether or not he knew they had in fact taken place. Tom Railsback (R Ill.) and David W. Dennis (R Ind.) both indicated approval of this more limited reading of Jenner's remark.

At the same meeting, Republicans agreed on the need for some public hearing on impeachment, on the need for sharing of the special subpoena power between Hutchinson and Rodino and on their effort to write the April 30 deadline into the resolution.

That same day, House Speaker Carl Albert (D Okla.) said that he expected a House vote on impeachment in 1974, even if the Judiciary Committee did not report out a recommendation for impeachment. Noting that impeachment resolutions are highly privileged and may be called up for a vote by any member at any time, Albert said that he expected some member to take advantage of that privilege if an impeachment resolution did not arrive on the floor from the committee.

Executive Privilege. Hutchinson said Jan. 29 that he felt executive privilege could not be claimed by the President to protect any material or information from an impeachment inquiry. Wiggins, considered an expert in constitutional matters, said that he agreed, because he assumed Congress would win any impeachment case against the White House, since the Constitution clearly vests impeachment powers solely in the House and Senate. Political realities, however, Wiggins added, would probably preclude any White House refusal to cooperate with the committee.

These remarks on executive privilege followed a two-hour briefing of the full committee in closed session Jan. 29 by Doar and Jenner. During the briefing—and later in public—Doar indicated that by Feb. 20 the staff would have ready a report on impeachment issues, including the definition of an impeachable offense. He also said that the committee would receive a progress report on the staff's work by March 1.

Ruling on Committee Subpoenas

Six months and two days after the Senate Watergate Committee sent two subpoenas to the White House, one seeking tapes and the other seeking documents, a federal judge quashed one and directed Nixon to respond personally to the other.

On July 23, 1973, the committee subpoenaed the tapes of five meetings between Nixon and John W. Dean III, a former presidential counsel, and all records related to the possible involvement of some 25 persons in any alleged criminal acts concerning the 1972 presidential campaign. When Nixon refused to comply with the subpoenas, the committee went to court to seek enforcement.

The White House responded by pointing out that the federal district court did not have jurisdiction over such a suit. On Oct. 17, Chief Judge John J. Sirica accepted that argument and dismissed the committee's suit. *(p. 60, 57, 51, 36)*

Moving quickly to rectify the situation, Congress by Dec. 3 had sent to the White House legislation specifically granting the federal district court in the District of Columbia jurisdiction over suits brought by the Senate Watergate committee to enforce subpoenas. The bill became law (PL 93-190) without Nixon's signature. The Senate committee Dec. 19 approved new subpoenas for nearly 500 presidential tapes and documents; Nixon Jan. 4 refused to comply. *(p. 136, 127, 173, 183, 190)*

Deciding to seek enforcement of the original subpoenas before litigating Nixon's refusal to comply with the more recent demands, the committee Jan. 7 renewed its original suit and asked Sirica to reconsider it in light of PL 93-190. Sirica, busy with other matters concerning subpoenaed presidential tapes, referred the case to Federal District Judge Gerhard A. Gesell. Again the White House asked the court to dismiss the suit. *(p. 190)*

On Jan. 25 Gesell issued his ruling, quashing the July 23 subpoena for the documents involving the 25 persons and directing Nixon to respond more directly to the subpoena for the five tapes. The five meetings involved in that subpoena took place on Sept. 15, 1972; Feb. 28, 1973; March 13, 1973, and (two meetings) March 21, 1973.

All the tapes except that of the Feb. 28 meeting already had been examined by Sirica as part of his enforcement of the grand jury subpoena and had been turned over to the grand jury.

Gesell asked Nixon to provide a detailed statement by Feb. 6, explaining what parts of the subpoenaed tapes he considered covered by executive privilege and why. "This statement must be signed by the President," wrote Gesell, "for only he can invoke the (executive) privilege at issue." Nixon's first refusal to provide the tapes had been couched in sweeping claims of privileges, which Gesell indicated were no longer applicable after the intervening proceedings concerning the tapes subpoenaed by the grand jury.

In quashing the broader July 23 committee subpoena, Gesell described it as too broad and too vague, disregarding "the restraints of specificity and reasonableness which derive from the Fourth Amendment," which guarantees citizens protection against unreasonable search and seizure.

Gesell also asked special Watergate prosecutor Leon Jaworski to report to him on what effect he felt release of these tapes to the Senate committee would have on Jaworski's investigations and on forthcoming trials.

(Continued on p. 231)

Amnesty for Nixon?

Rep. Paul N. McCloskey Jr. (R Calif.) Jan. 28 proposed that Congress grant amnesty and a full pardon to President Nixon, should he resign, for any crimes he might have committed while in office. In a speech on the House floor, McCloskey made it clear that in his opinion, Nixon had committed "high crimes" (obstruction of justice) which would justify impeachment and criminal prosecution.

However, rather than tie up the functions of government in a lengthy impeachment trial, McCloskey said, Congress should consider an offer of full and unconditional amnesty in the event of resignation.

He said he was not asking Nixon to quit, although he hoped he would.

Two other members of Congress had suggested earlier that Congress grant Nixon immunity from prosecution should he resign, but they were not pursuing the matter. *(p. 212)*

McCloskey said he would introduce legislation, probably a joint resolution, as soon as he could draw it up. He told Congressional Quarterly that he did not consider his proposal a grant of immunity; Nixon was "not entitled to any immunity," McCloskey said. Amnesty, he said, would recognize that the President had committed a crime but would forgive him for it.

Under an amnesty act, the President still could be charged with crimes after he left office, and be convicted or plead guilty. But the new president, under the act, would have the power to pardon him, McCloskey said.

McCloskey, who opposed Nixon's Vietnam war policies and ran against him in the 1972 presidential primaries, told CQ that Nixon probably was "scared to death to resign because he knows he could go to jail. If I were his lawyer, I'd be urging him not to resign," McCloskey said. "The trouble is that there's nobody to plea-bargain with the President, as they did with (former) Vice President Agnew. The Justice Department can't do it; they work for him (Nixon)."

McCloskey's bill would state the sense of Congress that Nixon should be pardoned and forgiven, McCloskey said—not because he was above the law, but simply to get the government moving again. In his House speech, McCloskey said the government had been "almost paralyzed" for 10 months by "White House efforts to conceal the truth and by an accompanying malaise throughout the executive branches which look to the White House for decision and leadership."

In his House speech, McCloskey referred to the sentencing of former White House aide Egil Krogh Jr. Jan. 24 for his part in the burglary of the office of Daniel Ellsberg's psychiatrist. *(p. 209)*

"The President of the United States has publicly admitted that when he learned of Mr. Krogh's offense, he acted deliberately both to conceal that crime and to hinder the prosecution of those who committed it," McCloskey said. These actions constitute felonies under Sections 3 and 4 of Title 18 of the U.S. Criminal Code, he said.

Congressional Subpoena Power: Roots Deep in History

The Constitution grants Congress "all legislative powers." Among those, many of the first members assumed, was the authority to investigate, subpoena witnesses and documents and punish non-cooperators. The early members based this broad construction on the precedent of the British House of Commons, which had evolved for itself the power to conduct investigations in order to gather information for writing laws and monitoring the administrators of those laws.

Some "strict constructionists," in today's lexicon, thought congressional investigations should be confined to judicial functions such as election disputes and impeachment proceedings, but they were overruled in 1792, when the House authorized an inquiry into an Army disaster in Indian territory. The assumption that Congress had the constitutional authority to conduct investigations and enforce subpoenas was never seriously challenged after that.

Committee Power. From the beginning, Congress has delegated its investigative power to committees. Most of the early inquiries were conducted by special or select panels appointed for specific investigations and granted subpoena powers only for the duration of their work. The House first gave subpoena power to a standing committee—the House Committee on Manufactures—for an 1828 tariff investigation.

The Legislative Reorganization Act of 1946 extended permanent subpoena power to all standing committees of the Senate. House leaders, fearing their committees might use such an unlimited grant to indulge in sensational and partisan activities, succeeded in limiting the permanent subpoena power in their chamber to the Un-American Activities Committee. (When the committee was renamed Internal Security in 1969, the power was continued.) General subpoena power was granted in 1947 to what is now the Government Operations Committee and to the Appropriations Committee in 1953.

Specific Approval. Regular legislative committees must seek specific House approval for authority to compel testimony and documents. The House routinely grants these committees broad investigatory power at the beginning of each Congress. When the 93rd Congress opened in 1973, for example, the House on one day adopted resolutions authorizing eight standing committees to investigate subjects within their legislative jurisdictions and to issue subpoenas.

One of those committees was Banking and Currency, which issued more than 300 subpoenas between 1965 and 1974, according to staff counsel Benet D. Gellman. All subpoenas the committee issues must specify exactly what is requested and how the documents or testimony relate to the committee's jurisdictional mandate, Gellman explained. And because the investigative resolution grants authority to the committee as a whole and not just to its chairman, Gellman said, all members must approve a subpoena before the chairman signs it.

Gellman based what he described as his "conservative view" of the subpoena power on a 1967 Supreme Court decision—*Gojack v. U.S.* Gojack was convicted of contempt of Congress for refusing to answer certain questions while testifying before a subcommittee of the House Un-American Activities Committee in 1955. The court overturned his conviction on grounds that the committee did not follow its own rules by formally specifying the subject of the inquiry and authorizing the subcommittee to conduct it.

Watergate Subpoenas. The Senate Watergate investigating committee construed its subpoena power more broadly, many thought, when it sought a large but unspecified number of White House tapes and documents Dec. 18, 1973. *(p. 183)*

House Banking was the first congressional committee to attempt to use its subpoena power to investigate the Watergate break-in. On Oct. 3, 1972, the committee rejected, 20-15, a resolution, backed by Chairman Wright Patman (D Texas), to call 40 individuals and organizations to testify about possible violations of banking laws and irregularities in Republican campaign financing suggested by the break-in.

Impeachment Investigation. Subpoenas were issued in impeachment inquiries as early as the case of Sen. William Blount (Tenn. 1796-97), who was accused in 1797 of conspiring to help the British take over Louisiana and Spanish Florida. A special House committee, empowered to "send for persons, papers and records," conducted an investigation and recommended impeachment. The House, for the first time in its history, adopted the impeachment resolution, but later abandoned it when the Senate expelled Blount.

The House Judiciary Committee, responsible for conducting an inquiry into charges against President Nixon, was one of the standing committees granted general subpoena power by resolution at the beginning of the 93rd Congress in 1973. But the official list of subjects under the committee's jurisdiction does not include impeachment. Jurisdictional challenges would be avoided if the House adopted a resolution spelling out the committee's investigative authority in the matter of impeachment. *(Committee action, p. 227)*

Executive Resistance. If the Judiciary Committee decided to subpoena documents from Nixon, the country would be on uncharted ground. In the only precedent, the impeachment preceedings against President Andrew Johnson in 1867-68, Johnson himself was not subpoenaed. *(p. 72)*

Before President Nixon was served with subpoenas for tapes and documents July 23, 1973—two from the Senate Watergate investigating committee and one from the Watergate special prosecutor—the only president to be subpoenaed was Thomas Jefferson, who was asked to testify and produce a letter at the treason trial of Aaron Burr in 1807. He did not testify, but did turn over the letter.

Nixon eventually complied with the special prosecutor's subpoena but refused the Senate committee's requests. *(Vol. I, p. 225)*

Week's Watergate Chronology

Following is a day-to-day chronology of the week's events in the Watergate case: (*Previous Jan. 24 events, p. 213*)

JAN. 24

Nixon Attitude. White House press secretary Ronald L. Ziegler confirmed that President Nixon planned to fight to the finish to hold on to his office, and said Nixon would not agree to meet with the Senate select Watergate committee. (*p. 209*)

Nixon Comments. Rep. Edward J. Derwinski (R Ill.) was quoted in *The Washington Star-News* as saying Nixon told a group of Republican House members Jan. 22 that he hoped the House would "spare the Senate the heat" of an impeachment trial by voting down an impeachment resolution. However, if impeached, Nixon said, he would fight the charges "even if I am down to where I have just one senator on my side," Derwinski said.

Judiciary Committee. A 15-member subcommittee of the House Judiciary Committee agreed to ask the House to ratify the committee's impeachment investigation and grant subpoena powers to its chairman and vice chairman. (*p. 209*)

Military Spying. Secretary of Defense James R. Schlesinger said at a press conference that there were "improprieties" in the way secret White House documents were slipped to the Pentagon in 1971, but no evidence of illegalities or of a spy ring. (*Earlier story, p. 205*)

Grand Jury Leaks. An investigation ordered by the 15 judges of the U.S. District Court in Washington, D.C., into who gave Watergate grand jury transcripts to columnist Jack Anderson failed to uncover the source of the leaks. The judges urged a new law making publication of such leaks illegal. (*Earlier stories, Vol. I, p. 20, 22*)

JAN. 25

Nixon Tapes. U.S. District Court Judge Gerhard A. Gesell ordered Nixon to submit a signed statement by Feb. 6 giving specific reasons for refusing to turn over five subpoenaed tape recordings to the Senate select Watergate committee. Gesell said a general claim of executive privilege was too broad. He quashed another committee subpoena for all records involving 25 White House and campaign aids. (*Details, p. 228*)

Impeachment Information. The House Judiciary Committee went to court for the first time to obtain information for its impeachment inquiry—records of the Finance Committee to Re-elect the President, which already had been provided to the Senate Watergate committee. No opposition was expected to the motion filed in U.S. District Court in Washington, D.C.

Nixon-Danner Meeting. The White House confirmed that Nixon had met in May 1973 with Richard G. Danner, the man who delivered $100,000 in cash from billionaire Howard Hughes to Nixon's friend, Charles G. (Bebe) Rebozo, in 1970. However, Gerald L. Warren, deputy press secretary, said it was only a courtesy call by an old friend, not to discuss the money.

Ford Declines. Vice President Ford said he had decided not to examine evidence the White House claimed would clear Nixon of charges of involvement in the Watergate affair, *The New York Times* reported. "I don't want to be in the position of disclosing such evidence," he said. (*Earlier story, p. 209*)

Falsely Dated Deed. Thomas Quinn, California deputy secretary of state, said the April 21, 1969, date on the deed giving Nixon's vice presidential papers to the National Archives was "obviously false." The deed actually was signed April 10, 1970, his investigation disclosed, long after expiration of the law under which Nixon claimed $576,000 in tax deductions for the gift. (*Previous stories, p. 209, 213*)

Rhodes Statement. House Minority Leader John J. Rhodes (R Ariz.) called on three members of the House Judiciary Committee who had sponsored impeachment resolutions against Nixon to disqualify themselves from voting on the impeachment question. One of the three, Rep. Robert F. Drinan (D Mass.), called the suggestion "baloney." The other two were Representatives Jerome R. Waldie (D Calif.) and Charles B. Rangel (D N.Y.).

McCord Request. Convicted Watergate conspirator James W. McCord Jr. asked Chief U.S. District Judge John J. Sirica to hold a hearing to determine whether government agencies tapped his or his lawyer's telephones after McCord's arrest in the Watergate burglary. If they did, the case against him should be dropped, said his lawyer, Bernard Fensterwald. (*McCord sentencing, p. 117*)

JAN. 26

Hearings Postponed. The Senate select Watergate committee abruptly postponed indefinitely the hearings it had planned to open Jan. 29 into 1972 Nixon campaign financing. Chairman Sam J. Ervin Jr. (D N.C.) said he acted at the request of U.S. District Attorney Paul J. Curran of New York's southern district, who feared hearings might prejudice the trials of former Nixon cabinet members John N. Mitchell and Maurice H. Stans, scheduled to open there Feb. 19. (*Details, p. 226*)

Gift Defended. Frank DeMarco Jr., the California lawyer who handled Nixon's tax deduction claims for the gift of his vice presidential papers, said the process was legal because Nixon made his decision to give them and had them appraised before the law permitting such deductions expired, even though the final deed itself was not dated until April 1970.

JAN. 27

Krogh Comments. Former White House aide Egil Krogh Jr. said on CBS-TV that he had concluded President Nixon did not know of the Watergate coverup before March 21, 1973, because John W. Dean III, then White House counsel, told him March 20 that Nixon was being "badly served. He just doesn't know what's going on." Dean and Nixon met March 21.

Saxbe Interview. Attorney General William B. Saxbe said that he doubted the House of Representatives would impeach the President "on the basis of any evidence that's available to me today," and that it would be foolish to try. In an interview in the Feb. 4 *U.S. News & World Report*, Saxbe also said a "bitter, partisan impeachment, which it would have to be if no further crimes of a great nature are developed, would tear this country apart."

Calls to Resign. Two more senators, Abraham Ribicoff (D Conn.) and Claiborne Pell (D R.I.), called on Nixon to resign rather than subject the nation to impeachment.

Secret Trust Fund. Three separate investigations failed to turn up any evidence of a $1-million "secret trust fund" belonging to Nixon, a rumor which was widely publicized in October 1973, *The New York Times* reported. The report was investigated by the Senate select Watergate committee staff, the state's attorney in Miami, Fla., and the Times itself, the Times said. *(Previous story, p. 85)*

JAN. 28

Porter Plea. Herbert L. Porter, 35, former scheduling director for the Committee for the Re-election of the President, pleaded guilty in U.S. District Court in Washington, D.C., to a charge of lying to the FBI during its early investigation of the Watergate break-in on June 17, 1972. *(Earlier story, p. 211)*

Baker Comments. Sen. Howard H. Baker Jr. (R Tenn.), vice chairman of the Senate select Watergate committee, said in Atlanta, Ga., that the committee should "shut down and certify our findings to the House" for its impeachment investigation.

Access to Tapes. Deputy White House press secretary Warren refused to list the persons who had access to tape recordings or transcripts of Nixon's Watergate conversations. Warren said he was "not in a position to do that.... There are legal implications." *(Previous tapes story, p. 201)*

Amnesty for Nixon. Congress should grant President Nixon full and unconditional amnesty from prosecution if he resigned from office, Rep. Paul N. McCloskey Jr. (R Calif.) suggested in a speech on the House floor. *(Box, p. 229)*

Jenner Remarks. Albert E. Jenner, minority counsel for the House impeachment inquiry, said the President could be held responsible for actions of his subordinates only if he had specifically authorized them. Jenner had caused a stir Jan. 13 when he said he thought the President should be held responsible for acts of subordinates even if he did not know about them in advance. *(Earlier stories, 207, 208)*

Deadline Asked. The Dade County, Florida, state's attorney's office asked Watergate Special Prosecutor Leon Jaworski to set an early deadline for federal indictments in Florida Watergate offenses. If indictments were not returned by mid-March, the state would be forced to move on its own, because the two-year statute of limitations would soon expire, Florida officials said. They agreed to stall their own conspiracy investigation until March 1.

Grand Jury Probe. Stephen B. Bull, Nixon's appointments secretary, testified for more than four hours before a federal grand jury investigating missing and erased Watergate tapes. He told reporters that he did not make the 18½-minute erasures on the June 20, 1972, tape and had no idea who did. *(Earlier story, p. 201)*

JAN. 29

Nixon Testimony. A California state judge, Gordon Ringer of Los Angeles Superior Court, ordered Nixon to appear as a material witness in the trials of former White House aides John D. Ehrlichman, David R. Young Jr. and G. Gordon Liddy on Feb. 25 and April 15. *(Box, p. 227)*

Laird Prediction. Melvin R. Laird, in a farewell news conference before leaving his post as presidential counselor, predicted that the House would defeat, by 75 to 125 votes, a motion to impeach Nixon.

Scott's Wrath. Senate Minority Leader Hugh Scott (R Pa.) said his "wrath would be obvious and articulated" if he found the White House had misled him on what it called "proof" of Nixon's innocence in Watergate wrongdoing. Scott said if material he saw was inaccurate, it would be because of "tampering, forgery or some misuse of my confidence."

Rebozo Funds. Senate Watergate committee investigators had found Nixon's friend Rebozo might have converted some presidential campaign money to his own use, *The New York Times* reported.

Destroyed Tapes. The Central Intelligence Agency destroyed numerous tape recordings considered vital to the Watergate investigation, according to CBS News.

Offer Rejected. Democrats suing the Committee for the Re-election of the President for $6.4-million for bugging and breaking into their national committee offices rejected an offer to settle for $600,000, *The Washington Post* reported.

Silbert Nominated. Earl J. Silbert, 37, one of the three original Watergate prosecutors, was nominated by Nixon to be U.S. attorney for the District of Columbia. Silbert withdrew from the Watergate case June 29, 1973, a month after the first special prosecutor, Archibald Cox, was appointed. *(Vol. I, p. 177)*

JAN. 30

Nixon on Resigning. Nixon, in his state of the union message, said he had "no intention whatever" of resigning, and called for an end to the Senate Watergate investigation. *(Box, p. 228)*

Nixon Testimony. President Nixon would refuse, on constitutional grounds, to testify in the California trial of John D. Ehrlichman, the White House announced. *(Box, p. 227)*

Rebozo Reply. An attorney for Charles G. (Bebe) Rebozo asked the Senate Watergate committee to hold immediate public hearings to "rectify malicious, false and inaccurate leaks" of information about Rebozo and to suspend staff members responsible for the leaks. The lawyer, William S. Frates, referred to *The New York Times* report that Rebozo might have converted campaign funds to his own use.

Impeachment Campaign. The National Committee on the Presidency, seeking Nixon's impeachment, began a direct-mail campaign to reach six-million voters in 45 days.

Scott Statement. Senate Minority Leader Hugh Scott (R Pa.), saying he would not "be a patsy for anyone," said he had made new demands that Nixon make public tapes or transcripts of presidential conversations which allegedly could prove Nixon innocent of any involvement in the Watergate affair. √

APPROVAL OF SUBPOENA POWER FOR JUDICIARY COMMITTEE

With only four members voting "nay," the House Feb. 6 formally granted the Judiciary Committee power to investigate the conduct of President Nixon to determine whether there were grounds for his impeachment.

By a 410-4 vote, the House approved H Res 803, explicitly authorizing the committee to conduct the inquiry —already under way—and granting it special subpoena power during the inquiry. Voting against approval were four Republicans: Ben B. Blackburn of Georgia, Earl F. Landgrebe of Indiana, Carlos J. Moorhead of California, the only committee member of the four, and David C. Treen of Louisiana. *(Text of resolution, box, next page)*

Republican committee members tried to amend the resolution to add a deadline for the committee's action, to limit the scope of the subpoena power and to secure an equal right for the Republican minority to subpoena witnesses. All amendment efforts failed when the House, by a 342-70 vote, approved a procedural motion, offered by Peter W. Rodino Jr. (D N.J.), chairman of the committee, moving the resolution directly to a vote and thereby barring any amendments.

The committee had reported the resolution unanimously on Jan. 31. *(p. 227)*

Committee Views

"The committee's investigative authority is intended to be fully coextensive with the power of the House in an impeachment investigation—with respect to the persons who may be required to respond, the methods by which response may be required, and the types of information and materials required to be furnished and produced," stated the Judiciary Committee's report (H Rept 93-774) on H Res 803, filed Feb. 1.

Emphasizing the intention of the investigation to proceed "in all respects on a fair, impartial and bipartisan basis," the report emphasized the joint exercise of subpoena power by the chairman and ranking minority member to ensure maximum flexibility and bipartisanship.

Deadline Opposed. On the matter of a deadline, the report stated: "It is not now possible to predict the course and duration of its inquiry.... Establishment of dates would be unrealistic and thus misleading. The committee was anxious to avoid an arbitrary deadline that might ultimately operate as an unnecessary hindrance to an early and just conclusion to its inquiry."

In additional views, Robert McClory (R Ill.), Lawrence J. Hogan (R Md.) and Joseph J. Maraziti (R N.J.) explained the need for a deadline and expressed the hope that Rodino would yield for such an amendment.

Relevance of Inquiry. Setting forth his case for an amendment restricting to those which were relevant to the inquiry the materials and witnesses which the committee could compel, Charles E. Wiggins (R Calif.) said that without such an amendment the resolution would

authorize the committee "to engage in a politically motivated witch hunt.... It is not enough that good-faith disclaimers of any such intention have been repeatedly made by the chairman.... Rules must be fashioned which require the future performance which now is only promised."

In separate views, Moorhead (R Calif.) disapproved of "this overly broad grant of the subpoena power" which, he said, "can only precipitate a constitutional confrontation."

Fairness. David W. Dennis (R Ind.), Wiggins, Wiley Mayne (R Iowa), Hogan, M. Caldwell Butler (R Va.), Trent Lott (R Miss.), Maraziti and Robert F. Drinan (D Mass.) urged an amendment to allow either the chairman or the ranking minority member to exercise the subpoena power without fear of being overridden by the full committee.

Their amendment would have deleted language in H Res 803 authorizing the full committee to resolve any disagreement between the two men over a subpoena. If the amendment were not adopted, said its proponents, the inquiry would be launched "under ground rules which deliberately build in an inherent bias and inequity."

Floor Debate

"Whatever the result, we are going to be just and honorable and worthy of the public trust," said Committee Chairman Rodino in opening debate on the resolution. "We cannot turn away, out of partisanship or convenience, from problems that are now...our inescapable responsibility to consider. It would be a violation of our own public trust if we...chose not to inquire, not to consult, not even to deliberate, and then to pretend that we had not, by default, made choices."

After Rodino explained the contents and purpose of the resolution, he yielded small portions of the hour of debate under his control to various members on each side of the aisle "for the purposes of debate only." Because of the privileged nature of H Res 803, amendments could only be offered to it under two circumstances: if Rodino agreed to yield time for an amendment or if the House rejected the move to bring the resolution to an immediate vote.

"I will not join" in a subpoena of the President, announced ranking Republican committee member Edward Hutchinson (R Mich.). The question of such a subpoena was to be referred to the full committee for a decision, under an agreement previously reached between Hutchinson and Rodino. Furthermore, Hutchinson made clear that he would join in issuing subpoenas only if he knew exactly what they sought and if the information had been requested previously and sought by less coercive means.

Text of H Res 803

Following is the text of H Res 803, as approved by the House Feb. 6:

Resolved, That the Committee on the Judiciary, acting as a whole or by any subcommittee thereof appointed by the chairman for the purposes hereof and in accordance with the rules of the committee, is authorized and directed to investigate fully and completely whether sufficient grounds exist for the House of Representatives to exercise its constitutional power to impeach Richard M. Nixon, President of the United States of America. The committee shall report to the House of Representatives such resolutions, articles of impeachment, or other recommendations as it deems proper.

SEC. 2. (a) For the purpose of making such investigation, the committee is authorized to require—
(1) by subpena or otherwise—
(A) the attendance and testimony of any person (including at a taking of a deposition by counsel for the committee); and
(B) the production of such things; and
(2) by interrogatory, the furnishing of such information; as it deems necessary to such investigation.
(b) Such authority of the committee may be exercised—
(1) by the chairman and the ranking minority member acting jointly, or, if either declines to act, by the other acting alone, except that in the event either so declines, either shall have the right to refer to the committee for decision the question whether such authority shall be so exercised and the committee shall be convened promptly to render that decision; or
(2) by the committee acting as a whole or by subcommittee.
Subpenas and interrogatories so authorized may be issued over the signature of the chairman, or ranking minority member, or any member designated by either of them, and may be served by any person designated by the chairman, or ranking minority member, or any member designated by either of them. The chairman, or ranking minority member, or any member designated by either of them (or, with respect to any deposition, answer to interrogatory, or affidavit, any person authorized by law to administer oaths) may administer oaths to any witness. For the purpose of this section, "things" includes, without limitation, books, records, correspondence, logs, journals, memorandums, papers, documents, writings, drawings, graphs, charts, photographs, reproductions, recordings, tapes, transcripts, printouts, data compilations from which information can be obtained (translated if necessary, through detection devices into reasonably usable form), tangible objects, and other things of any kind.

SEC. 3. For the purpose of making such investigation, the committee, and any subcommittee thereof, are authorized to sit and act, without regard to clause 31 of rule XI of the Rules of the House of Representatives, during the present Congress at such times and places within or without the United States, whether the House is meeting, has recessed, or has adjourned, and to hold such hearings, as it deems necessary.

SEC. 4. Any funds made available to the Committee on the Judiciary under House Resolution 702 of the Ninety-third Congress, adopted November 15, 1973, or made available for the purpose hereafter, may be expended for the purpose of carrying out the investigation authorized and directed by this resolution.

"The majority of this committee is doing everything possible to avoid partisanship," said Walter Flowers (D Ala.). Jack Brooks (D Texas) admonished the Republicans to cooperate with the committee leadership, describing Rodino's sharing of the subpoena power with Hutchinson as "unprecedented" and indicating "bipartisan intent."

But Republicans still complained about the implementation of the inquiry and the subpoena power. McClory argued for inclusion of some deadline date in H Res 803. Wiggins described as "inherently unfair" the provisions allowing the full committee by majority vote to resolve any disputes between Hutchinson and Rodino over the issuance of a subpoena, an argument in which Drinan expressed support. Wiggins also pointed out the need for ensuring that all material subpoenaed was relevant to the inquiry and obtained from Rodino and Hutchinson assurances that relevance was implicit in the word "necessary" as used in H Res 803.

But Minority Leader John J. Rhodes (R Ariz.) stated that he would vote for Rodino's procedural motion and thus oppose any amendments, saying that the chairman's promise of a report by April 30 was sufficient for him. And committee Republican Tom Railsback (R Ill.) said he would not seek to amend the resolution: "We fought the procedural battle in committee, and we lost it. The amendments I supported then are not essential."

The House then adopted Rodino's motion on a 342-70 vote, and followed this vote with the 410-4 approval of H Res 803.

"This power authorizes the appearance of the President under compulsion if necessary," said Jerome R. Waldie (D Calif.), a committee member and sponsor of one of many impeachment resolutions. "No other forum can do so during his tenure.... Only through his appearance can he be required to disclose what he has so far refused to disclose; his appearance is essential."

Week's Watergate Chronology

Following is a day-to-day chronology of the week's events in the Watergate case: *(Previous Jan. 30 events, p. 232)*

JAN. 30

Nixon's Taxes. Nixon's tax attorney, Frank DeMarco Jr., said "some question" had arisen as to whether the appraiser of Nixon's vice presidential papers told him the truth about details of the appraisal. The legitimacy of Nixon's gift of the papers to the National Archives for a $576,000 income tax deduction was under study in the California secretary of state's office. *(Earlier stories, p. 231)*

Nixon Deposition. U.S. District Court Judge Joseph C. Waddy delayed proposed depositions of Nixon and former White House special counsel Charles W. Colson until after March 1. Waddy said he would rule then on a motion to dismiss a suit by Common Cause to obtain financial records of 1972 presidential campaign contributors before the April 7, 1972, campaign reporting law took effect. *(Earlier story, p. 211)*

Democratic Suit. Democratic National Chairman Robert S. Strauss said the party was willing to settle damage suits with the Republicans over the Watergate

Nixon's Refusal on Tapes: 'Not in National Interest'

President Nixon refused during the week ending Feb. 9 to turn over any more tapes to either the Watergate special prosecutor or the Senate Watergate committee.

Special Prosecutor. The battle continued between Nixon's lawyers and Special Prosecutor Leon Jaworski over whether Jaworski had all the evidence he needed to complete his Watergate investigation. Nixon said in his state of the union message Jan. 30 that he had. The President's special Watergate counsel, James D. St. Clair, hinted the next day that the time had come to halt the flow of White House material to the prosecutor.

Jaworski said Feb. 3 in a television interview that the White House had not turned over all the materials he had requested, and he indicated he would not hesitate to subpoena them if necessary. The White House responded with a lengthy communication, reportedly a refusal to turn over more material, but neither side would discuss the contents until a meeting between Jaworski and St. Clair had been held.

Watergate Committee. Nixon's refusal to give the Senate Watergate committee five tapes it sought was explained in a letter Feb. 6 from the President to U.S. District Judge Gerhard A. Gesell. Gesell on Jan. 25 had directed Nixon to explain personally why he had refused. *(p. 228)*

Nixon wrote that "out of respect for the court" he would answer, but reiterated his position that the courts had no power to force him to give up material he wanted to keep confidential. He said disclosure of the contents of the five tapes "would not be in the national interest."

The President said that giving the tapes to the Watergate committee would amount to giving them to "the world at large," violating the principle of confidentiality of presidential communications. He said the committee's request was a political question and "inappropriate for resolution by the judicial branch."

In addition, Nixon said, disclosing the contents of the tapes could have adverse effects on criminal proceedings in Watergate-related cases.

Jaworski, who was asked by the judge to comment on that question, said four of the tapes contained material to be used as evidence in forthcoming trials, but indicated their release would have only marginal effects on pretrial publicity. He suggested they could be turned over to the Watergate committee on the condition that they may not be made public.

Letter Text. The text of Nixon's letter follows:

I have been advised by special counsel to the President of the order issued by you on January 25, 1974, in which you solicited my personal response with reference to five specified taped conversations.

As indicated in the various briefs, pleadings and other papers filed in this proceeding, it is my belief that the issue before this court constitutes a nonjusticiable political question.

Nevertheless, out of respect for this court, but without in any way departing from my views that the issues presented here are inappropriate for resolution by the judicial branch, I have made a determination that the entirety of the five recordings of Presidential conversations described on the subpoena issued by the Senate Select Committee on Presidential Campaign Activities contains privileged communications, the disclosure of which would not be in the national interest.

I am taking this position for two primary reasons. First, the Senate select committee has made known its intention to make these materials public. Unlike the secret use of four out of five of these conversations before the grand jury, the publication of all of these tapes to the world at large would seriously infringe upon the principle of confidentiality, which is vital to the performance of my constitutional responsibilities as President.

Second, it is incumbent upon me to be sensitive to the possible adverse effects upon ongoing and forthcoming criminal proceedings should the contents of these subpoenaed conversations be made public at an inappropriate time. The dangers connected with excessive pretrial publicity are as well known to this court as they are to me. Consequently, my constitutional mandate to see that the laws are faithfully executed requires my prohibiting the disclosure of any of these materials at this time and in this forum.

---

break-in for $1.25-million but had rejected a Republican offer of $600,000. *(Earlier story, p. 232)*

JAN. 31

White House Files. Nixon's special Watergate counsel, James D. St. Clair, voiced reservations about continuing to supply Watergate prosecutors with evidence from White House files. *(Box, this page)*

Dean's Credibility. Assistant Watergate Special Prosecutor Richard J. Davis said in U.S. District Court in Washington that prosecutors had "no basis for believing" that former White House counsel John W. Dean III had lied under oath in any proceeding. The issue was raised by lawyers for Dwight L. Chapin, another former White House aide, who was scheduled to go on trial April 1 for lying to a grand jury.

Coxes' Defense. The President's son-in-law and daughter, Edward and Tricia Cox, denounced Watergate charges against Nixon as "one of the most vicious

witch hunts in American history." Cox also attacked Dean as a "coward" who didn't tell Nixon of the Watergate coverup and whose "whole object was to get immunity."

Richardson Opinion. Former Attorney General Elliot L. Richardson said in Austin, Texas, that Nixon could be held accountable for the Watergate break-in and coverup even if he was not aware of them, just as a corporation executive could be found culpable for acts of subordinates. However, he said he doubted there was a basis for impeaching the President.

FEB. 1

Watergate Questions. White House press secretary Ronald L. Ziegler told reporters he would stop answering Watergate-related questions, except when he felt a formal statement was necessary or Nixon's lawyers wished to provide "relevant answers."

Mansfield Statement. Senate Majority Leader Mike Mansfield (D Mont.), giving the Democrats' answer

Paying for Watergate

Watergate showed up in the 1975 budget in only one place, officially, but other hidden costs to the taxpayers could be detected in the fine print of the 1,059-page appendix to the budget.

Time magazine reported (Feb. 11) that the Watergate affair already had cost the country more than $8-million—most of it in public funds.

The only item in the President's budget was the $2.8-million request for the 80-member Watergate special prosecution force. Justice Department officials said Prosecutor Leon Jaworski received the full amount he requested. It was $47,000 less than the supplemental appropriation for the office for fiscal 1974, since $40,000 in original security costs and $7,000 for furniture and equipment were one-time expenses.

Other major Watergate expenses were included in the 1975 legislative, executive and judiciary branch budget requests, but not by name.

Congressional Committees. For example, the Senate select Watergate committee, which had received $1.5-million for its 63-member staff since it began operations Feb. 7, 1973, would be paid for from the Senate's $14.1-million fund for conducting investigations, if it continued to operate in fiscal 1975.

The House Judiciary Committee had received $1-million to conduct its impeachment inquiry. If necessary, in fiscal 1975 the impeachment staff of 45 would be paid along with other House committee employees from the $8.6-million appropriation requested for that purpose, up from $8.1-million in fiscal 1974.

Agencies. The General Services Administration had spent more than $100,000 investigating allegations that $10-million in government funds was spent to improve Nixon's homes in California and Florida, and the General Accounting Office spent an undetermined amount to audit Nixon campaign committees in all 50 states, according to *The Washington Post.*

Judiciary Expenses. The three Watergate grand juries already had cost the taxpayers more than $225,000, the U.S. District Court in Washington, D.C., reported. Grand jurors, 23 on each panel, were paid $20 a day for the first 30 days of service and $25 a day thereafter. Witnesses were paid $20 a day and travel expenses. Court reporting fees had run over $100,000 by November, the Post reported.

Executive Branch. In addition to financing the investigation and prosecution of Watergate crimes, the taxpayers were bearing the cost of Nixon's defense against charges that he was involved in Watergate activities. White House counsel J. Fred Buzhardt said Nixon's defense had cost $290,418 in the first six months of fiscal 1974, the Post reported Feb. 5. The White House also confirmed that 30 new jobs were included in the $16.5-million budget request of the President's office to enable Nixon to hire more lawyers for his Watergate and impeachment defenses.

to Nixon's state of the union message, said Congress and the courts must continue to investigate "the crimes of Watergate" for "however long may be necessary... whether it is months or years." Nixon had said Jan. 30 that "one year of Watergate is enough." *(p. 228)*

Report Delayed. The Senate Watergate committee would delay its scheduled Feb. 28 final report at the request of Watergate Special Prosecutor Leon Jaworski, so as not to prejudice potential jurors in forthcoming court trials, Mansfield announced.

Grand Jury Testimony. Rose Mary Woods, Nixon's personal secretary, testified before the Watergate grand jury on the 18½-minute erasures on one of the White House tapes. Her attorney, Charles S. Rhyne, denounced the experts who studied the tape erasures as "professors who don't know what they're doing," and he described their study as "a $100,000 boondoggle." *(Earlier story, p. 201)*

Nixon Aides. Nixon had maintained close ties with former aides H. R. Haldeman, John D. Ehrlichman and Charles W. Colson and had "built his public and legal defense in concert with them," *The Washington Post* reported. The Post said Secretary of State Henry A. Kissinger and White House chief of staff Alexander M. Haig had tried unsuccessfully for six months to persuade Nixon to disassociate himself from the three, all targets of the Watergate investigation.

Scott Statement. Senate Republican Leader Hugh Scott (Pa.) said at a White House news conference that he was "not backtracking one single inch" on his charge that John Dean had lied about Nixon's role in the Watergate coverup. Scott said he might have seen a tape the special Watergate prosecutor had not seen when he claimed the White House had evidence to disprove Dean's charges. *(Previous story, p. 232)*

Nixon Taxes. The California State Franchise Tax Board ruled that Nixon was not a California resident for tax purposes, but said he still might owe some state income taxes for the years 1969-73. White House sources had reported that Nixon appeared ready to pay California taxes, possibly in the course of amending his federal tax returns.

FEB. 3

White House Data. Special Prosecutor Jaworski said in a television interview that the White House had not turned over all the tapes and documents he had requested for his investigation. Nixon had said Jan. 30 that he had given the prosecutor everything he needed.

Donald Nixon Surveillance. The Secret Service was ordered to keep the President's brother, F. Donald Nixon, under surveillance during Nixon's first term in office because of concern that the brother's business dealings might embarrass the President and affect his chances of re-election in 1972, Senate Watergate committee sources told *The New York Times. (Earlier story, p. 165)*

FEB. 4

White House Statement. St. Clair issued a statement declaring "categorically" that White House tapes did not support John Dean's sworn statements implicating the President in the Watergate affair.

Nixon Subpoena. Los Angeles Superior Court Judge Gordon Ringer officially signed a subpoena requiring Nixon to appear as a material witness in the "plumbers" burglary trial there. *(Earlier story, p. 227)*

Krogh Imprisonment. Former presidential aide Egil Krogh Jr. surrendered to U.S. marshals in Washington, D.C., to begin serving a six-month prison sentence for his role in the break-in at the office of Daniel Ellsberg's psychiatrist. After questioning by Watergate prosecutors, Krogh was to be transferred to Allenwood prison farm near Lewisburg, Pa. *(Earlier story, p. 209)*

Hunt Plea Change. Convicted Watergate conspirator E. Howard Hunt Jr. asked the U.S. Court of Appeals in Washington to allow him to withdraw his guilty plea in the original Watergate break-in case. U.S. District Judge John J. Sirica had rejected his previous attempt. *(Hunt sentencing, p. 117)*

FEB. 5

Attack on Dean. The Feb. 4 White House attack on the credibility of John Dean was in acquiescence to the demands of Senate Minority Leader Hugh Scott (R Pa.), whose own credibility was at stake because of his continued insistence that he had seen evidence disproving Dean's charges, *The Washington Post* reported.

Nixon Travel Voucher. California Superior Court Judge Gordon Ringer sent Nixon a voucher for $790.48 for travel expenses to testify at the burglary trial of Erlichman and two former White House "plumbers." The voucher for Nixon's round-trip coach-class air fare was sent with the subpoena for his appearance.

Eisenhower Views. Nixon would not resign even if he were impeached by the House, his son-in-law, David Eisenhower, said at a news conference arranged by the White House communications director as part of a campaign to bolster Nixon's image by making family members and supporters available to the press.

FEB. 6

Nixon Refusal. Nixon explained in a letter to U.S. District Judge Gerhard A. Gesell that he would not give the Senate Watergate Committee five tapes it had subpoenaed because it would violate the principle of confidentiality and possibly have adverse effects on Watergate-related criminal trials. *(Box, p. 235)*

Impeachment Inquiry. The House voted 410-4 to give the Judiciary Committee broad powers to conduct its impeachment investigation of the President. *(Details, p. 233)*

Weicker Questions. Sen. Lowell P. Weicker Jr. (R Conn.), a member of the Senate Watergate committee, sent Nixon a list of 11 written questions about his conduct in the Watergate affair and subsequent statements about it. Weicker's questions suggested the President might have committed a criminal offense, misprision of felony, by failing to report what he knew about the Watergate break-in and coverup as soon as he learned of them.

Dean Disbarred. A three-judge state court in Alexandria, Va., disbarred former White House counsel John W. Dean III from the practice of law in Virginia, saying he was guilty of unprofessional conduct. Dean pleaded

---

Poll Report

Vice President Gerald R. Ford is the choice of a 14 per cent plurality of voters over President Nixon to serve the remaining three years of Nixon's term, according to a Gallup Poll published Feb. 4. *(Earlier poll report, p. 213)*

The question asked 1,592 adults Jan. 18-21: "Here is a question about President Richard Nixon and Vice President Gerald Ford: If you had a choice, which man would you rather have as president between now and the next presidential election in 1976—Nixon or Ford?"

Nixon	32%
Ford	46
Undecided, no opinion	22

Republicans nationwide supported the President over Ford, 57 to 28 per cent, with 15 per cent undecided or having no opinion. Democrats, on the other hand, favored Ford over Nixon, 55 to 18 per cent, with 27 per cent undecided or having no opinion.

Nixon Popularity. Another Gallup Poll, published Feb. 3, found that Nixon's ratings by the public had fallen another point to the all-time low of his administration. This question was asked the same persons surveyed Jan. 18-21, after experts had testified about erasures from White House tapes: "Do you approve or disapprove of the way Nixon is handling his job as president?"

	Latest	Jan. 4-7
Approve	26%	27%
Disapprove	64	63
No opinion	10	10

---

guilty Oct. 19 to a charge of conspiracy to obstruct justice and defraud the United States.

More Dairy Funds. Two dairy industry lobbying groups, whose pledges to Nixon's 1972 re-election campaign stirred lawsuits and investigations, reported that they had more than $1.5-million available for further political activity, *The New York Times* reported. The Associated Milk Producers reported $1.3-million and Mid-America Dairies, $250,000 in cash on hand. *(Nixon statement, p. 191)*

FEB. 7

Ford Statement. Vice President Gerald R. Ford said at a news conference that Nixon had told him release of key Watergate tapes and summaries was "being actively considered."

Campaign Donations. All three of the Senate Watergate committee members seeking re-election in 1974 received campaign contributions from individuals or groups that had been investigated by the committee, *The Washington Star-News* reported. The members were Edward J. Gurney (R Fla.), Daniel K. Inouye (D Hawaii) and Herman E. Talmadge (D Ga.). The contributions were not illegal or unusual, the senators said. √

WHITE HOUSE REFUSAL TO RELEASE DOCUMENTS

Watergate Special Prosecutor Leon Jaworski reported to the Senate Feb. 14 that President Nixon had refused to turn over any more presidential tapes or documents requested for investigations into Watergate-related matters.

Jaworski cited the impasse in a letter to Judiciary Committee Chairman James O. Eastland (D Miss.), who had requested Nov. 29 that the committee be kept informed of the status of White House cooperation. Two Judiciary Committee members, Edward M. Kennedy (D Mass.) and Birch Bayh (D Ind.), urged that Eastland call a meeting of the committee as soon as possible to hear Jaworski and consider, in Kennedy's words, "the ominous implications of Mr. Jaworski's letter." The committee was scheduled to meet Feb. 19 to consider a nomination.

Bayh indicated that he might revive his efforts to make the Watergate prosecutor independent of the executive branch. The proposal had been shelved in December after the White House pledged to cooperate with Jaworski. *(p. 176)*

Jaworski was appointed prosecutor Nov. 1 after Nixon ordered former prosecutor Archibald Cox fired Oct. 20 because Cox had persisted in trying to get access to White House tapes. *(p. 69, 111)*

Although Jaworski's letter was seen by some observers as setting the stage for a new public confrontation over the tapes, his press spokesman said its purpose was not to invite public hearings but merely to keep the Judiciary Committee informed, as promised.

The Letter. In his letter, Jaworski said he had requested in January 27 recordings of meetings between the President and aides believed to relate to the 1972 Watergate break-in and coverup and needed by the Watergate grand jury considering criminal indictments in the case. Six other requests for information, dating back to August 1973 and relating to 1972 dairy industry campaign contributions, activities of the White House "plumbers," the International Telephone and Telegraph Corporation case and other matters also were still outstanding, impeding the investigations into those areas, Jaworski said.

Nixon said in his state of the union message Jan. 30 that he had given the prosecutor all the material he needed to complete his investigations. Nixon's lawyers expressed concern that there would be "an endless stream" of requests for more material. *(p. 235)*

Jaworski said he assured Nixon's special Watergate counsel, James D. St. Clair, that if the requested material were turned over, he would make no further requests. But the President "refused to reconsider his earlier decision to terminate his cooperation with this investigation," St. Clair informed Jaworski in a letter delivered late Feb. 13. Jaworski immediately informed Eastland of the White House's final answer.

The President said that complying with Jaworski's requests "would be inconsistent with the public interest and the constitutional integrity of the office of the presidency," Jaworski wrote. Nixon did not base his refusal on claims that particular tapes requested were irrelevant to the prosecutor's investigations or subject to privilege, Jaworski added.

Jaworski said the White House refusal to cooperate would not block indictments, expected by the end of February, but would hamper collecting of evidence for future trials—indicating the possibility of new subpoenas.

Jaworski listed for the committee all the requests made for White House files, those which had been met and those denied. Most of the 13 recordings and copies of five others were turned over by court order. (On the tapes which had been turned over, more apparent gaps in "sensitive discussions" between the President and his aides had been discovered by audio experts, Westinghouse Broadcasting reported Feb. 14.)

House Judiciary Committee

Even as Jaworski and the Senate Watergate committee met frustration in their efforts to obtain more information from the White House, the House Judiciary Committee began negotiations with White House lawyers for material the committee required for its impeachment inquiry.

Agreement on the need for the House committee to adopt procedures to ensure the confidentiality of White House documents, tapes and logs appeared to be the primary product of a first meeting between White House defense chief St. Clair and special committee counsel John M. Doar and Albert E. Jenner Jr. Nixon had instructed St. Clair the first week in February to make himself available to consult with Doar and his staff. The first meeting took place in the impeachment staff's offices on Feb. 13; subsequent regular meetings—which would not be announced ahead of time to the public—were planned, Doar said later.

The meeting was cordial in tone and explanatory in nature, Doar and Jenner reported Feb. 14 after they had held a closed briefing for the full Judiciary Committee on the results of the meeting. "It was a meeting between several professional lawyers," said Jenner. "He related his problems; we told him ours. There was some sparring," as might be expected among three men accustomed to litigating cases and questions, Jenner noted. This was simply the first phase of negotiations at which "all the legal niceities" were observed, Jenner added. "We were all playing our cards close to our chest."

"St. Clair was basically interested in knowing...what procedures the committee would have for handling White House material," said Doar. "He was concerned that nothing be done which might jeopardize the fairness of later trials." The staff was already drafting such procedures, Doar said; they would be presented to the committee for approval and adoption, and then the committee could proceed to request specific materials.

"I didn't come out of the meeting," said Doar, "with any doubts whatsoever (about the White House intention to cooperate with the committee in furnishing information)...but St Clair was not in a position to give" any firm pledge on this matter. "There are a number of things which we discussed with St. Clair and with which we are now moving forward," Doar added. "We indicated the general nature of materials we were interested in...and it was clear that Mr. St. Clair understood."

There had been no progress in obtaining acess to the information provided by the White House to Jaworski, said Doar, expressing his continued hopefulness that some agreement could be worked out on this matter. Earlier, he had reported to the committee that he had requested from Jaworski a list of the materials the special prosecutor had sought from the White House and a second list of the materials actually obtained from the White House.

Doar also said that members of his staff had met with the staff of the Joint Committee on Internal Revenue Taxation, which is investigating the President's tax returns filed during his years in the White House.

Week's Watergate Chronology

Following is a day-to-day chronology of the week's events in the Watergate case (*Previous Feb. 7 events, p. 237*):

FEB. 7

Watergate Committee. The Senate Watergate committee agreed to postpone its final report to avoid interfering with forthcoming Watergate indictments; to ask the Senate to extend the committee's life three months, to May 28, and give it another $300,000 to complete its work, and to certify its complete investigative file to the House Judiciary Committee, which was considering the impeachment of Nixon.

FEB. 8

Reinecke Question. California Lt. Gov. Edward Reinecke wrote a letter asking Special Watergate Prosecutor Leon Jaworski if he was considering an indictment against him in the International Telephone and Telegraph Corporation case, *The Los Angeles Times* reported. If he were to be indicted, he would withdraw from the race for the Republican nomination for governor, Reinecke reportedly told Jaworski.

Nixon Taxes. Sen. Russell B. Long (D La.), chairman of the Joint Committee on Internal Revenue Taxation, indicated in a television interview that the committee would find that Nixon owed back taxes for claiming income tax deductions he was not entitled to. But Long said the President probably was not guilty of fraud, and declined to confirm or deny a report that the back taxes and interest would amount to $302,000.

Tape Experts' Tests. U.S. District Judge John J. Sirica said he had asked a panel of electronics experts to start testing other White House tapes for signs of tampering, despite protests from Nixon's lawyers, at the same time they finished their final report on the tape with the 18½-minute erasures.

No Tapes for Senate Committee

Chalking up another defeat in court, the Senate Watergate committee was rebuffed again Feb. 8 in its effort to convince a federal judge to enforce its subpoena of five presidential tapes. Federal District Judge Gerhard A. Gesell refused to require the White House to furnish the committee with the tapes, citing the risk that excessive publicity accompanying the committee's use of the tapes might make it difficult to obtain an unbiased jury for the trials arising out of the Watergate matter.

"The committee's role as a 'grand inquest' into governmental misconduct is limited," wrote Gesell. "It may only proceed in aid of Congress' legislative function. The committee has...ably served that function...but surely the time has come to question whether it is in the public interest for the criminal investigative aspects of its work to go forward in the blazing atmosphere of...publicity directed to issues that are immediately and intimately related to pending criminal proceedings."

Gesell Jan. 25 had directed Nixon to respond personally by Feb. 6 with his reasons for claiming that the five tapes were protected by executive privilege. On Feb. 6, Nixon sent Gesell a letter stating simply that disclosure of the tapes "would not be in the public interest." (*p. 229*)

Neither side had argued convincingly, wrote Gesell. "It has not been demonstrated to the court's satisfaction," he wrote, "that the committee has a pressing need for the subpoenaed tapes or that further public hearings before the committee concerning the contents of those tapes will at this time serve the public interest.

"Conversely, the court rejects the President's assertion that the public interest is best served by a blanket, unreviewable claim of confidentiality over all presidential communications, and the President's unwillingness...to particularize his claim...precludes judicial recognition of that privilege on confidentiality grounds."

Both the President and the special prosecutor had mentioned the risk of prejudice of pretrial publicity, said Gesell, and upon that he chose to base his order. "The President, the Congress, and the courts each have a mutual and concurrent obligation to preserve the integrity of the criminal trials arising out of Watergate," he wrote, and therefore "the public interest does not require that the President should be forced to provide evidence, already in the hands of an active and independent prosecution force, to a Senate committee...to furnish fuel for further hearings which cannot, by their very nature, provide the procedural safeguards and adversary format essential to fact finding in the criminal justice system."

However, Gesell added, with a glance to the future: "Congressional demands...for tapes in furtherance of the more juridical constitutional process of impeachment would present wholly different considerations."

CONTRIBUTIONS TO HOUSE JUDICIARY COMMITTEE MEMBERS

The 38 members of the House Judiciary Committee received a total of $680,460 in donations during the 1972 campaign from organizations contributing over $100 according to figures compiled by Common Cause. The 21 Democratic members received $352,647, while the 17 Republican members collected $327,613.

Nearly half of the contributions to Democratic representatives came from organized labor ($161,475), which was not a major source for the Republicans ($1,550). The bulk of labor contributions to Democratic committee members came from the AFL-CIO and its affiliated unions. Thirty-eight unions, two departments and the AFL-CIO's Committee on Political Education (COPE) contributed a combined total of $134,324 to the Democratic members of the committee.

The largest contribution went to Chairman Peter W. Rodino Jr. (D N.J.), who received $24,100 from the AFL-CIO. COPE alone contributed $13,000. In all, Rodino received $44,300 in campaign contributions from 46 different organizations, 25 of them labor unions.

Republican committee members received over half their 1972 contributions from Republican Party organizations ($200,167) at the national, state and local levels. Other major sources of support were state branches of the American Medical Association (AMA), $45,500, and the National Association of Manufacturers Business-Industry Political Action Committee (BIPAC), $22,000. The AMA affiliates contributed $10,000 each to the 1972 campaigns of Representatives David W. Dennis (R Ind.) and Carlos J. Moorhead (R Calif.) and amounts ranging from $500 to $5,500 to 11 other Republican members. BIPAC made contributions ranging from $1,000 to $4,000 to 11 Republican members.

Rep. Edward Hutchinson (Mich.), the ranking Republican member of the committee, received $6,200 in campaign donations from seven organizations. Four of the organizations, giving a total of $4,000, were affiliated with the Republican Party. The other contributions came from the Michigan Doctors Political Action Committee (Michigan branch, AMA), $1,000; the Associated General Contractors Committee for Action, $1,000; and the National Association of Life Underwriters Political Action Committee, $200.

The leading recipients of contributions among Judiciary Committee members were Wayne Owens (D Utah), $53,739; Edward Mezvinsky (D Iowa), $52,070; and Harold V. Froehlich (R Wis.), $50,395.

Following is a complete list of campaign contributions of over $100 made by organizations during the 1972 campaign to members of the committee.

Democrats

Peter W. Rodino Jr. (N.J.), chairman, $44,300: AFL-CIO Committee on Political Education (COPE), $13,000; AFL-CIO Industrial Union Department, $1,000; Amalgamated Clothing Workers Political Education Committee (AFL-CIO), $300; Amal-

gamated Meat Cutters and Butcher Workers of North America (AFL-CIO), $100; American Dairymen's Political Education, Mid America Dairymen (ADEPT), $2,000; American Federation of Musicians (AFL-CIO), $250; American Federation of State, County and Municipal Employees National People Commitee (AFL-CIO), $200; American Hotel and Motel Political Action Committee (AHMPAC), $300; Bankers Political Action Committee (BANKPAC), Washington area, $200; Carpenters Legislative Improvement Committee (AFL-CIO), $700; Certified Shorthand Reporters Association of New Jersey, $500; Committee of Automotive Retailers, $300; Committee for Thorough Agricultural Political Education (Associated Milk Producers, Inc.), $1,000; Communications Workers of America (AFL-CIO), $500; Democratic Congressional Campaign Committee, $6,700; DRIVE Political Fund (Teamsters), $1,000; Engineers Political Education Committee (AFL-CIO), $200; Gas Employees Political Election Committee, $200; Hotel, Restaurant Employees and Bartenders International Union (AFL-CIO), $250; International Association of Fire Fighters Committee on Political Education (AFL-CIO), $300; International Association of Machinists, District 47 (AFL-CIO), $1,000; International Brotherhood of Electrical Workers (AFL-CIO), $500; International Ladies Garment Workers Union (ILGWU), Eastern Region Campaign Committee (AFL-CIO), $500; Johnson and Johnson Employees Good Government Fund, $500; Machinists Non-Partisan Political League (AFL-CIO), $200; Maintenance of Way Political League (AFL-CIO), $300; Mortgage Bankers Political Action Committee (MORPAC), $200; National Association of Life Underwriters Political Action Committee, $200; National Cable TV Association (PACT), $1,200; New Jersey State Carpenters Non-Partisan Political Committee, $1,000; Railway Clerks Political League (AFL-CIO), $500; Railway Labor Executives Association Political League (AFL-CIO), $200; Real Estate Political Education Committee of New Jersey, $500; Recording Artists Political Action Committee, $300; Retail Clerks International Association, Active Ballot Club (AFL-CIO), $500; Retail Store Employees Union, Active Ballot Club, Local 1262 (AFL-CIO), $250; Seafarers Political Activity Donation (AFL-CIO), $1,500; Service Employees International Union Committee on Political Education (AFL-CIO), $200; Smith, Klein and French Voluntary Non-Partisan Political Fund, $150; Special Political Agricultural Community Education (SPACE Dairymen Inc.), $1,000; Textile Workers Union AFL-CIO), $750; Tobacco Peoples Public Affairs Committee, $200; Transportation Political Education League (United Transportation Union, AFL-CIO), $500; Truck Operators Non-Partisan Committee, $1,000; United Automobile Workers (UAW) Voluntary Community Action Program, Region 9, $750; United Steelworkers Political Action Fund (AFL-CIO), $500.

Harold O. Donohue (Mass.), $1,500: Amalgamated Meat Cutters and Butchers of North America (AFL-CIO), $300; American Insurance Men's Political Action Committee, $200; Democratic Congressional Campaign Committee, $1,000.

Jack Brooks (Texas), $22,950: Amalgamated Meat Cutters and Butchers (AFL-CIO), $300; Carpenters Legislative Improvement Committee (AFL-CIO), $500; Democratic Congressional Campaign Committee, $9,900; Engineers Political Education Committee (AFL-CIO), $250; National Maritime Union Fighting Fund, $500; National Rural Electric Cooperative Association Action Committee for Rural Electrification, $500; Political Committee for Design Professionals, $10,000; Seafarers Political Activity Donation (AFL-CIO),

$300; Transportation Political Education League (AFL-CIO), $500; UAW Voluntary Community Action Program, $200.

Robert W. Kastenmeier (Wis.), $14,642: Amalgamated Clothing Workers, Midwest Regional Joint Board Political Education Committee (AFL-CIO), $200; Amalgamated Meat Cutters and Butchers of America (AFL-CIO), $300; Carpenters Legislative Improvement Committee (AFL-CIO), $500; Committee for Thorough Agricultural Political Education, $2,650; Communications Workers of America (AFL-CIO), $600; D.C. Friends of Kastenmeier Committee, $624; Democratic Congressional Campaign Committee, $500; Democratic Party of Green County, $410; Democratic Party of Iowa County, $250; DRIVE Local 695 (Teamsters), $200; Machinists Non-Partisan Political League (AFL-CIO), $1,000; National Council of Farmer Cooperatives (PACE), $250; National Rural Electric Cooperative Association Action Committee for Rural Electrification, $500; National Rural Electric Cooperative Association, Wisconsin Action Committee for Rural Electrification, $200; Retail Clerks Active Ballot Club (AFL-CIO), $450; Sheet Metal Workers Political Action League (AFL-CIO), $500; Textile Workers Political Fund, $250; Transportation Political Education League (AFL-CIO), $500; UAW Voluntary Community Action Program, $500; United Steelworkers Political Action Fund (AFL-CIO), $1,500; Vote for Peace, $758; Wisconsin AFL-CIO COPE, $2,000.

Don Edwards (Calif.), $10,302: AFL-CIO COPE, $1,500; California National Nominees Fund, $500; United Brotherhood of Carpenters and Joiners Local 316 (AFL-CIO), $200; Democratic Congressional Campaign Committee, $3,055; Laborers Political League (AFL-CIO), $500; Machinists Non-Partisan League, District Local 93 (AFL-CIO), $200; Retail Clerks International Association, Local 428, Active Ballot Club (AFL-CIO), $450; Transportation Political Education League (AFL-CIO), $600; UAW Voluntary Community Action Program, $300; United Democratic Finance Committee, $740; United Steelworkers Political Action Fund, $1,000; Vote for Peace, $757; Wells Fargo Bank, Good Government Committee, $500.

William L. Hungate (Mo.), $11,490: Agriculture and Dairy Education Political Trust (American Dairymen, Inc.), $1,000; Amalgamated Meat Cutters and Butchers (AFL-CIO), $300; American Dairy Association Political Trust Fund, $300; Associated Dairymen (Associated Milk Producers, Inc.), $1000; Communications Workers of America (AFL-CIO), $250; Democratic Congressional Campaign Committee, $4,000; Democratic Study Group Campaign Fund, $1,000; DRIVE Political Fund, Joint Council 13 (Teamsters), $250; Hannibal Trades and Labor Council, $200; ILGWU Political Trust Fund (AFL-CIO), $140; Laborers Political League (AFL-CIO), $500; Machinists Non-Partisan League (AFL-CIO), $500; National Association of Life Underwriters Political Action Committee, $250; National Cable TV Association, $250; Retail Store Employees (AFL-CIO), $250; Seafarers Political Activity Donation (AFL-CIO), $300; UAW, Region 5, $500; United Steelworkers, St. Louis Political Action Committee (AFL-CIO), $500.

John Conyers Jr. (Mich.), $7,850: AFL-CIO, Metropolitan Detroit Council, $820; Democratic Congressional Campaign Committee, $250; DRIVE Political Fund (Teamsters), $1,000; Engineers Political Education Committee (AFL-CIO), $250; Laborers Political Action League (AFL-CIO), $500; National Rural Electric Cooperative Association, Action Committee for Rural Electrification, $300; Maintenance of Way Political League (AFL-CIO), $500; Transportation Political Education League (AFL-CIO), $300; United Automobile, Aerospace, and Agricultural Workers, Committee for Good Government, $200; UAW Voluntary Community Action Program, $685; Vote for Peace, $1795; Women in Community Service, $1,250.

Joshua Eilberg (Pa.), $20,150: AFL-CIO COPE, $2,500; Amalgamated Clothing Workers Political Education Committee of Philadelphia (AFL-CIO), $500; Amalgamated Meat Cutters and Butchers (AFL-CIO), $300; Building and Construction Trades Department, Political Education Fund (AFL-CIO), $500; Carpenters Legislative Improvement Committee (AFL-CIO),

$700; D.C. Committee of Businessmen to Assist Congressional Candidates, $500; Democratic Congressional Campaign Committee, $2,500; Firemen and Oilers Political League (AFL-CIO), $200; Fraternal Order of Police, Philadelphia Lodge #5, $200; International Brotherhood of Electrical Workers (AFL-CIO), $200; International Brotherhood of Printers and Allied Trades (AFL-CIO), $200; International Brotherhood of Pulp Sulphite and Paper Mill Workers (AFL-CIO), $1,000; ILGWU (AFL-CIO), $500; ILGWU, Knitgoods Local 190 (AFL-CIO), $500; Knitgoods Legislative Education Fund, $200; Labors' League for Political Education, Electrical Branch #98, $700; Laborers' Political Action League (AFL-CIO), $500; Machinists Non-Partisan Political League (AFL-CIO), $500; Maintenance of Way Political League (AFL-CIO), $500; National Life Underwriters Political Action Committee, $200; National Rural Electric Cooperative Association Action Committee for Rural Electrification, $250; Philadelphia Police, Fire and Park Police Federal Credit Union, $400; Railway Clerks Political League (AFL-CIO), $1,500; Retail Clerks International Association, Active Ballot Club (AFL-CIO), $250; Savings Association Public Affairs Committee, $300; Seafarers Political Activity Donation (AFL-CIO), $1,000; Sheet Metal Workers League for Political Education (AFL-CIO), $500; Shipwright Joiners, Local 1856, $200; Steam Fitters Union, Local 420, $500; Transportation Political Education League (AFL-CIO), $600; UAW, $500; United Brotherhood of Carpenters and Joiners (AFL-CIO), $250; United Steelworkers Political Action Committee Fund (AFL-CIO), $1,000.

Jerome R. Waldie (Calif.), $12,898: Alameda-Contra Costa Medical Association, $300; Amalgamated Meat Cutters and Butchers (AFL-CIO), $250; California Democratic National Nominees Fund, $500; California Medical Political Action Committee (California branch, American Medical Association), $1,000; Carpenters Legislative Improvement Committee (AFL-CIO), $800; Del Monte Corporation Voluntary Non-Partisan Good Government Fund, $300; Democratic Congressional Campaign Committee, $3,055; General Telephone Employees Good Government Club, $300; International Association of Fire Fighters (AFL-CIO), $500; International Union of Operating Engravers Voluntary Political Fund (AFL-CIO), $500; Laborers' Political League (AFL-CIO), $500; National Association of Life Underwriters Political Action Committee, $200; National Maritime Union Fighting Fund, $500; Transportation Political Education League (AFL-CIO), $200; UAW Voluntary Community Action Program, $500; United Democratic Finance Committee, $678; United Steelworkers of America Political Action Fund (AFL-CIO), $500; United Transportation Union, $300; Vote for Peace, $1,515; Wells Fargo Bank, Good Government Committee, $500.

Walter Flowers (Ala.), $5,249: Alabama Medical Association Political Action Committee, $3,000; Alabama Realtors Association, $500; Governors Committee to Elect Democrats, $1,749.

James R. Mann (S. C.), $4,625: Committee of 100 (Democratic Party organization), $500; Democratic Congressional Campaign Committee, $2,000; Democratic Party of Greenville County, $325; Savings Association Political Affairs Committee, $300; South Carolina Electric Co-operative Association, $500; South Carolina Political Action Committee, $1,000.

Paul S. Sarbanes (Md.), $10,125: AFL-CIO COPE, $2,300; Amalgamated Clothing Workers of America Political Education Committee, Baltimore Region Joint Board (AFL-CIO), $500; American Federation of State, County and Municipal Employees National People Committee (AFL-CIO), $1,000; Coolahan-Malene Committee, $250; Democratic Congressional Campaign Committee, $500; DRIVE Political Fund (Teamsters), Joint Council 62, $1,000; Laborers Political Action League (AFL-CIO), $500; National Maritime Union Fighting Fund, $250; Retail Clerks International Association, Active Ballot Club, Local 692, $1,250; Seafarers Political Activity Donation (AFL-CIO), $1,000; Transportation Political Education League (AFL-CIO), $300; UAW Voluntary Community Action Program, $1,275.

John F. Seiberling (Ohio), $11,400: AFL-CIO COPE, $2,000; Amalgamated Meat Cutters and Butchers (AFL-CIO), $400; American Federation of State, County and Municipal Employees,

National People Committee (AFL-CIO), $500; Communication Workers of America (AFL-CIO), $300; Democratic Congressional Campaign Committee, $500; Democratic Study Group Campaign Committee, $1,000; Hotel and Restaurant Employees and Bartenders International Union, Committee on Political Education (AFL-CIO), $250; International Brotherhood of Electrical Workers (AFL-CIO), $500; International Chemical Workers Union Voluntary Live Fund, $500; ILGWU Campaign Committee (AFL-CIO), $250; Laborer's Political League (AFL-CIO), $500; Machinists Non-Partisan Political League (AFL-CIO), $500; Ohio DRIVE Local, $200; Sheet Metal Workers' International Association Political Action League (AFL-CIO), $500; UAW Voluntary Community Action Program, $2,000; United Rubber Cork, Linoleum and Plastic Workers (AFL-CIO), $500; United Steelworkers, Akron Political Fund (AFL-CIO), $1,000.

George E. Danielson (Calif.), $11,097: AFL-CIO COPE, Los Angeles, $250; Amalgamated Meat Cutters and Butchers (AFL-CIO), $300; Democratic Congressional Campaign Committee, $5,305; Democratic State Central Committee of California, $642; Electrical Workers Political Education Committee (AFL-CIO), $300; General Telephone Employees Good Government Club, $800; Hotel and Restaurant Employees and Bartenders International Union (AFL-CIO), $300; Laborers' Political League (AFL-CIO), $1,000; Machinists Non-Partisan Political League (AFL-CIO), $500; Transportation Political Education League (AFL-CIO), $900; UAW Voluntary Community Action Program, $300; United Steelworkers Political Action Fund (AFL-CIO), $500.

Robert F. Drinan (Mass.), $20,314; AFL-CIO COPE, $3,000; AFL-CIO Industrial Union Department Voluntary Funds, $500; Amalgamated Clothing Workers, Boston (AFL-CIO), $300; Amalgamated Meat Cutters and Butchers (AFL-CIO), $300; American Federation of State, County and Municipal Employees (AFL-CIO), $300; Democratic Congressional Campaign Committee, $6,000; Democratic Study Group Campaign Fund, $2,000; International Brotherhood of Electrical Workers (AFL-CIO), $200; ILGWU Campaign Committee (AFL-CIO), $250; International Union of Electrical Workers (AFL-CIO), $1,000; Machinists Non-Partisan Political League (AFL-CIO), $1,000; National Committee for an Effective Congress, $1,000; O'Neill for Congress and the Election of All Democratic Candidates Committee, $500; Railway Labor Executives Association Political League (AFL-CIO), $200; Retail Clerks International Association, Active Ballot Club (AFL-CIO), $500; Sheet Metal Workers (AFL-CIO), $200; Transportation Political Education League (AFL-CIO), $300; UAW Voluntary Community Action Program, $1,000; Vote for Peace, $1,514.

Charles B. Rangel (N.Y.), $3,593: (American Federation of State, County, and Municipal Employees) Council 37, $243; Amalgamated Clothing Workers (AFL-CIO), $300; Brotherhood of Railway, Airline and Steamship Clerks (AFL-CIO), $200; Chefs, Cooks, Pastry Cooks and Assistants Union of New York, Local 89, $200; Laborers' Political League (AFL-CIO), $500; New York Republican County Committee, $500; Railway Labor Executives Association Political League (AFL-CIO), $200; Savings Association League of New York, $200; Seafarers Political Activity Donation (AFL-CIO), $1,000; UAW Local 259, $250.

Barbara C. Jordan (Texas), $26,676: Amalgamated Meat Cutters and Butchers (AFL-CIO), $300; Amalgamated Clothing Workers (AFL-CIO), $300; American Federation of State, County and Municipal Employees, National People Committee (AFL-CIO), $500; Citizens for Good Government, $500; Committee on Voter Education, $1,502; Democratic Congressional Campaign Committee, $1,000; Democratic Study Group Campaign Fund, $1,000; DRIVE Fund (Teamsters), Local 745, $2,000; Engineers Political Education Committee (AFL-CIO), $250; Fire Fighters Committee on Political Education (AFL-CIO), $200; Friends of Barbara Jordan, $500; Friends of Barbara Jordan Committee,

$2,980; Friends of Jordan for Congress Committee, $500; Houston Apartment Owners Association, $1,000; Houston Barristers Wives, $130; Houston Voters Association, $300; International Brotherhood of Electrical Workers (AFL-CIO), $200; ILGWU (AFL-CIO), $250; International Longshoremens Association, Local 872 (AFL-CIO), $331; Laborers Political Action Committee (AFL-CIO), $300; Lawyers Involved for Texas, $500; Machinists Non-Partisan Political League (AFL-CIO), $500; Ministers Wives Charity Union, $300; Ministers Wives Social Club, $500; National Education Association Political Action Committee, $500; Oil, Chemical and Atomic Workers (AFL-CIO), $200; Seafarers Political Activity Donation (AFL-CIO), $500; Southern Texas Communications Workers of America (AFL-CIO), $500; Texas AFL-CIO, $3,000; Texas DRIVE Fund (Teamsters), $3,500; TEXPAC (Texas branch, American Medical Association), $1,000; Texas State Beauty Culture League #47, $206; UAW Committee on Political Education, $750; West End Civic Club, $177; Volunteers for Hatcher, $500.

Ray Thornton (Ark.), $3,400: AFL-CIO COPE, $1,000; Business-Industry Political Action Committee (BIPAC, affiliated with National Association of Manufacturers), $1,000; Machinists Non-Partisan Political League (AFL-CIO), $500; UAW, $400; United Steelworkers of America (AFL-CIO), $500.

Elizabeth Holtzman (N.Y.), $4,765: Amalgamated Clothing Workers (AFL-CIO), $250; Committee for Judge Nanette Dembitz, $500; Democratic Congressional Campaign Fund, $1,500; Democratic Study Group Campaign Fund, $1,000; Vote for Peace, $1,515.

Wayne Owens (Utah), $53,739: AFL-CIO COPE, $3,100; AFL-CIO Industrial Union Department, $2,000; Agriculture and Dairy Education Political Trust (Dairymen, Inc.), $1,000; Amalgamated Meat Cutters and Butchers (AFL-CIO), $500; Amalgamated Clothing Workers (AFL-CIO), $450; American Federation of State, County and Municipal Employees, National People Committee (AFL-CIO), $250; American Federation of Teachers, Million Dollar Fund (AFL-CIO), $200; Carpenters Legislative Improvement Committee (AFL-CIO), $1,000; Christmas Tree Center, $690; Committee for Thorough Agricultural Political Education (Associated Milk Producers Inc.), $1,600; Committee for Twelve, $4,400; Communications Workers of America (AFL-CIO), $1,300; Democratic Congressional Campaign Committee, $7,000; Democratic State Committee, $528; Democratic Study Group Campaign Fund, $3,000; DRIVE Fund (Teamsters), $2,550; Fire Fighters Committee on Political Education (AFL-CIO), $300; Firemen and Oilers Political League (AFL-CIO), $200; International Brotherhood of Electrical Workers (AFL-CIO), $550; ILGWU Campaign Committee (AFL-CIO), $400; International Union of Electrical, Radio and Machine Workers (AFL-CIO), $500; Laborers Political League (AFL-CIO), $800; League of Conservation Voters, $3,000; Machinists Non-Partisan Political League (AFL-CIO), $450; National Committee for an Effective Congress, $3,200; National Education Association Political Action Committee, $1,000; National Maritime Union Fighting Fund (AFL-CIO), $500; National Rural Electric Cooperative Association Action Committee for Rural Electrification, $800; Oil, Chemical and Atomic Workers Union Political Education Account (AFL-CIO), $500; Railway Clerks Political League (AFL-CIO), $300; Research Industries Corporation, $210; Seafarers Political Activity Donation (AFL-CIO), $300; Sheet Metal Workers International Association Political Action League (AFL-CIO), $500; Textile Workers Union Political Fund (AFL-CIO), $250; Transportation Political Education League (AFL-CIO), $690; Union Pacific Railroad Fund for Effective Government, $200; UAW Political Fund, $1,016; United Rubber, Cork, Linoleum and Plastic Workers (AFL-CIO), $300; United Steelworkers Political Action Fund (AFL-CIO), $3,500; University of Utah, $500; Utah Council for Improvement of Education, $3,500; Utah Dental Political Action Committee (Utah branch, American Dental Association), $200; Utah Motor Transport Association, $505.

Edward Mezvinsky (Iowa), $52,070: AFL-CIO COPE, $6,000; AFL-CIO Industrial Union Department, $500; Agriculture and Dairy Education Political Trust, $2,000; Amalgamated Meat Cutters and Butchers (AFL-CIO), $1,000; Amalgamated Clothing Workers (AFL-CIO), $250; American Federation of State, County and Municipal Employees, National People Committee (AFL-CIO), $250; American Federation of Teachers, Million Dollar Fund (AFL-CIO), $150; Bricklayers Action Committee (AFL-CIO), $250; Brooklyn Longshoremen's Political Action and Education Fund, $500; Building Trades Department, AFL-CIO, $250; Chicago Joint Board Political Education Fund, $200; Committee for Thorough Agricultural Political Education, $1,000; Communications Workers of America (AFL-CIO), $500; Dairy Farmers Political League (ADEPT), $4,000; Democratic Campaign Committee, First District, $6,670; Democratic Central Committee of Johnson County, $200; Democratic Congressional Campaign Committee, $8,500; Democratic National Congressional Committee, $1,500; Democratic State Committee, $500; Democratic Study Group Campaign Fund, $3,000; Democratic Womens Club of North Lee County, $200; DRIVE Fund, $2,500; International Brotherhood of Electrical Workers (AFL-CIO), $400; International Brotherhood of Painters and Allied Trades (AFL-CIO), $150; International Brotherhood of Pulp, Sulphite and Paper Mill Workers (AFL-CIO), $500; ILGWU (AFL-CIO), $800; International Union of Operating Engineers (AFL-CIO), $250; Lithographers and Photoengravers Union, $200; Machinists Non-Partisan Political League (AFL-CIO), $1,500; National Committee for an Effective Congress, $1,000; National Rural Electric Cooperative Association Action Committee for Rural Electrification, $500; Oil, Chemical and Atomic Workers Union (AFL-CIO), $300; Railway Clerks Political League (AFL-CIO), $500; Retail Clerks International Association, Active Ballot Club (AFL-CIO), $250; Sheet Metal Workers Political Action League (AFL-CIO), $250; Special Political Agricultural Community Education (SPACE), $2,500; Transport Workers Union Political Fund (AFL-CIO), $250; Transportation Political Education League (AFL-CIO), $500; UAW Voluntary Community Action Program, $2,000; United Rubber, Cork, Linoleum and Plastic Workers (AFL-CIO), $300.

Republicans

Edward Hutchinson (Mich.), $6,200: Associated General Contractors Committee for Action, $1,000; Michigan Doctors Political Action Committee (Michigan branch, AMA), $1,000; National Association of Life Underwriters Political Action Committee, $200; National Republican Congressional Committee, $2,000; Republican Committee of Coloma, $300; Republican Committee of Lenawee County, $500; Three Hundred Club of Republican Party of Michigan, Hillsdale County Chapter, $1,200.

Robert McClory (Ill.), $4,394: AMSCO-Union 76 Political Awareness Fund, $300; Anderson for Congress Finance Committee, $329; Committee for Thorough Agricultural Political Education (Associated Milk Producers, Inc.), $500; Fox Valley Sheet Metal Employers Committee, $265; National Republican Congressional Committee, $1,000; United Republican Fund, $2,000.

Henry P. Smith III (N.Y.), $28,275: Donations from some Bell Aerospace Co. employees, $1,000; BIPAC (affiliated with NAM), $2,000; Congressional Victory Committee, $1,000; D.C. Businessmen, $500; Empire Dental Political Action Committee (New York branch, American Dental Association), $200; Food Processors Public Affairs Committee, $250; Frontier Republican Women's Committee, $300; Kushner and Kushner, attorneys, $250; National Association of Life Underwriters Political Action Committee, $250; New York Republican Congressional Campaign Committee, $2,500; Republican Committee of Niagara County, $4,000; Republican National Committee, $14,375; Republican Twelve Committee, $1,500; SeniorMeadows of Niagara, $150.

Charles W. Sandman Jr. (N.J.), $6,500: BIPAC, $2,000; JEMPAC (New Jersey branch, AMA), $1,000; Johnson and Johnson Good Government Fund, $500; National Republican Campaign Committee, $3,000.

Tom Railsback (Ill.), $5,388: Committee for Thorough Agricultural Political Education, $500; Kemper Campaign Fund,

$250; National Council of Farmer Cooperatives, Political Action for Cooperative Effectiveness, $250; National Republican Congressional Committee, $1,450; Republican National Committee, $138; Transportation Political Education League (AFL-CIO), $300; UAW Voluntary Community Action Program, $500; United Republican Fund of Illinois, $2,000.

Charles E. Wiggins (Calif.), $13,565: BIPAC, $2,000; California Medical Political Committee and AMPAC (California branch, AMA), $3,500; General Telephone and Electronics Good Government Club, $250; Hacienda Heights Women's Club, $120; Hughes Aircraft Company Active Citizenship Fund, $720; Lincoln Club of Orange County, $1,000; National Association of Life Underwriters Political Action Committee, $250; National Association of Real Estate Boards Political Action Committee, $500; National Republican Congressional Committee, $2,000; Orange County Finance Committee, $825; Republican Women's Club of Rancho La Habra, $200; Republican Women's Club of Whittier, $200; Union Oil Bipartisan Political Fund, $500; Wells Fargo Bank Good Government Committee, $500; Whittier Lincoln Club, $1,000.

David W. Dennis (Ind.), $27,100: American Conservative Union, $1,000; BIPAC, $3,000; Friends of Rural Electrification, $500; IMPAC (Indiana branch, AMA), $10,000; Indiana Republican State Central Committee, $1,000; Lincolnia Club of Jay County, $700; National Association of Life Underwriters Political Action Committee, $200; National Association of Real Estate Boards Political Action Committee, $500; National Republican Congressional Committee, $7,000; Republican Central Committee of Hancock County, $500; Republican Twelve, $1,750; Republican Committee of Union City, $500; Union Oil Company Political Awareness Fund, $300; Young America's Campaign Committee (Young Americans for Freedom), $150.

Hamilton Fish Jr. (N.Y.), $5,425: American Dental Association Political Action Committee, $500; National Association of Life Underwriters Political Action Committee, $300; National Republican Congressional Committee, $2,000; New York Republican Congressional Campaign Committee, $2,500; Republican Committee, Town of Washington, $125.

Wiley Mayne (Iowa), $14,377: BIPAC, $1,000; Dickinson County Central Committee, $400; Iowa Medical Political Action Committee (Iowa branch, AMA), $500; National Committee for Support of Free Broadcasting, $250; National Confectioners Association Government Improvement Group, $300; National Republican Congressional Committee, $3,700; National Rural Electric Cooperative Association Action Committee for Rural Electrification, $500; PACE (AFL-CIO), $250; Plymouth County Central Committee, $500; Republican Central Committee, Clay County, $943; Republican Central Committee, Humboldt County, $300; Republican Central Committee, Winnebago County, $884; Republican Finance Committee, Monona, $350; Republican Party of Iowa Fed. Elections Account, $900; Republican Party of Plymouth County, $800; Republican State Central Committee, $2,000; Republican Women, Buena Vista County, $150; Republican Women, Sixth District Federation, $650.

Lawrence J. Hogan (Md.), $14,949: American Apparel Manufacturers Association Committee for American Principles, $500; BIPAC, $1,000; D.C. Republican Committee, $1,000; Elephant Club of Prince Georges County, $1,340; Government Improvement Group in Maryland, $400; International Association of Fire Fighters Committee on Political Education (AFL-CIO), $500; Maryland Medical Political Action Committee (Maryland branch, AMA), $2,000; National Association of Real Estate Boards Political Education Committee, $700; National Republican Congressional Committee, $2,000; Neighbor to Neighbor Drive, Prince Georges County, $609; Republican Central Committee for Prince Georges County, $250; Republican Women's Club, Bethesda, $200; Republican Women's Club, Bowie, $200; Republican Women's Club, Rock Creek, $500; Republican Women's Club, University Park, $300; Salute to Ted Agnew Night Committee, $2,500; Truck Operators Non-Partisan Committee, $500; Young Republican Club, Prince Georges County, $450.

M. Caldwell Butler (Va.), $32,950: American Medical Association Political Action Committee (AMPAC), $3,000; BIPAC, $1,000; Butler-Robinson Dinner Committee, $869; Committee to Re-elect the President, $3,000; Dentists for Butler, $900; National Republican Congressional Committee, $500; Physicians for Butler, $1,000; Republican City Committee, Lynchburg, $1,293; Republican City Committee, Roanoke, $900; Republican City Committee, Waynesboro, $1,000; Republican Committee, Botecourt County, $900; Republican Committee, Radford, $200; Republican Committee, Sixth District, $1,060; Republican Committee, Waynesboro, $800; Republican Congressional Boosters, $10,000; Republican Party, Bath County, $250; Republican Women's Club, Roanoke, $168; Republican Women's Club, Roanoke Valley, $280; Sixth District Farmers for Butler, $330; SPACE Virginia Trust (Dairymen, Inc.), $1,000; VAMPAC (Virginia branch, AMA), $4,000; Virginia Licensing Home Association (VANHEPAC), $500.

William S. Cohen (Maine), $33,700: American Dental Association Political Action Committee, $500; BIPAC, $4,000; Maine Medical Political Action Committee (Maine branch, AMA), $4,000; Maine Republican Finance Committee, $14,000; National Republican Congressional Committee, $5,200; Republican Committee, Oxford County, $200; Republican Congressional Boosters Club, $5,000; Republican Town Committee, Hanover, $300; Ripon Society, $500.

Trent Lott (Miss.), $23,392: Associated General Contractors Construction Committee for Action, $500; Committee for Thorough Agricultural Political Education, $500; American Conservative Union Victory Fund, $5,500; Friends of Trent Lott Committee, $2,317; Mississippi Political Action Committee, $2,500; National Republican Congressional Committee, $500; Republican Committee, Pearl River County, $425; Republican National Boosters Club, $10,000; Republican Party, Jones County, $150; SPACE, $1,000.

Harold V. Froehlich (Wis.), $50,395: American Conservative Union Victory Fund, $5,700; Associated General Contractors Committee for Action, $750; BIPAC, $3,000; National Board of Life Underwriters Political Action Committee, $450; National Association of Real Estate Boards Political Action Committee, $1,100; Republican Congressional Boosters Club, $10,000; Republican Party, Marinette County, $200; Republican Party, Waupaca County, $995; Republican Party of Wisconsin, $20,200; Republican Voluntary Committee, Brown County, $2,500; WISPAC (Wisconsin branch, AMA), $5,500.

Carlos J. Moorhead (Calif.), $30,003: BIPAC, $1,000; California Medical Political Action Committee (California branch, AMA), $10,000; California Real Estate Association, 43rd District, $300; California Savings and Loan Association Century Club, $500; Fluor Construction Corporation Employees Political Fund, $500; General Telephone and Electronics Good Government Club, $300; Good Government Association, $300; National Association of Real Estate Boards Political Education Committee, $500; Republican Club, Sierra Madre, $550; Republican Congressional Boosters Club, $10,000; Republican Women's Club, Altadena, $350; Republican Women's Club, Arcadia, $250; Republican Women's Club, East Pasadena, Sierra Madre, $300; Republican Women's Study Club, Glendale, $452; Republican Women's Workshop, Glendale, $200; Republican Women's Club, La Canada Valley, $250; Republican Women's Club, Los Feliz, $800; Republican Women's Club, San Marino, $195; Union Bank Good Government Association, $200; Union Oil Political Awareness Fund, $250; Union Pacific Fund for Effective Government, $200; United Congressional Appeal, $1,500; United Republicans of California, Foothill Unit #23, $250; Wells Fargo Company Good Government Committee, $500; Young Republican Club, $356.

Joseph J. Maraziti (N.J.), $15,500: BIPAC, $2,000; JEMPAC (New Jersey branch, AMA), $2,500; Johnson and Johnson Good Government Fund, $500; National Association of Real Estate Boards Political Education Committee, $500; Republican Congressional Boosters Club, $10,000.

Delbert L. Latta (Ohio), $15,500: American Importers Association, American International Trade Political Affairs Committee (AITPAC), $200; National Republican Congressional Committee, $4,300; Ohio Contractors Political Action Committee, $500; Ohio Medical Political Action Committee (Ohio branch, AMA), $1,500; Republican State Central and Executive Committee, $9,000.

HOUSE JUDICIARY COMMITTEE MOVES TO CENTER STAGE

The center of attention in the Watergate scandal officially shifted during the week ending Feb. 23 as the Senate Select Committee on Presidential Campaign Activities yielded the public spotlight to the House Judiciary Committee.

The House committee began moving on its inquiry into the possible impeachment of President Nixon, receiving a staff report Feb. 21 on the constitutional grounds for presidential impeachment and then moving ahead to obtain information for its inquiry from the White House.

The Senate committee, which had gained national fame during its televised hearings in 1973, voted Feb. 19 to hold no further public hearings in order to avoid interfering with the impeachment inquiry and trials of Watergate-involved figures. *(p. 248)*

Even as the committee voted, John N. Mitchell and Maurice H. Stans went on trial in New York City on charges of obstruction of justice, perjury and conspiracy. Mitchell, formerly attorney general and chairman of the Committee for the Re-election of the President, and Stans, former secretary of commerce and chairman of the Finance Committee to Re-elect the President, were the first former cabinet members in 50 years to be tried on criminal charges. Both had testified before the Senate committee in the summer of 1973. *(Box, p. 248)*

'High Crimes and Misdemeanors'

"To limit impeachable conduct to criminal offenses would be incompatible with the evidence concerning the constitutional meaning of the phrase 'high crimes and misdemeanors' and would frustrate the purpose that the framers intended for impeachment," stated the report of the bipartisan impeachment inquiry staff to the House Judiciary Committee. Ranking Republican committee member Edward Hutchinson (Mich.) was quick to point out that this was a report to the committee, not a report of the committee.

Designed to illuminate the historical background and meaning of the phrase "high crimes and misdemeanors," the 49-page memorandum was prepared by the staff and was endorsed both by Special Counsel John M. Doar and by Special Minority Counsel Albert E. Jenner. Doar and Jenner had briefed Republican and Democratic committee members Feb. 20 on the contents of the memorandum, but the actual release of the report to the public and to committee members did not come until the next day. A Justice Department report on the law of impeachment was initially to be released the afternoon of Feb. 20. After the committee staff study was delayed, release of the Justice Department study was canceled.

No Public Hearing. Although a public committee discussion of the staff report had been scheduled for Feb. 21, it was canceled—and a press conference was held instead by the committee counsels and the senior members of the committee, led by Chairman Peter W. Rodino

Jr. (D N.J.) and Hutchinson. Doar had announced the week before that there would be a public hearing on the report, but committee Republicans privately conveyed to Rodino their distaste for the idea.

When asked why the idea of a public hearing had been dropped, Doar referred to the staff report, which stated: "Delicate issues of basic constitutional law are involved. Those issues cannot be defined in detail in advance of full investigation of the facts.... The House does not engage in abstract advisory or hypothetical debates about the precise nature of conduct that calls for the exercise of its constitutional powers; rather, it must await full development of the facts and understanding of the events to which those facts related."

Disagreement. But even without a full public committee discussion of the question of defining an impeachable offense, disagreement among senior committee members was apparent.

"It has been my view all along that grounds for impeachment need not arise out of criminal conduct," said Rodino, signaling his agreement with the staff report. But Hutchinson—although making clear that he would study the report, of which he and Rodino had received the final version only minutes before the press conference—disagreed with its basic conclusion. "There should be criminality involved" on the President's part, he said, stating that he would approach the study from that viewpoint, believing that the only grounds for impeachment of a president are his personal involvement in criminal activity.

Describing the report as a "useful document," Robert McClory (R Ill.) took a middle position between Rodino and Hutchinson, saying that he felt not every crime was an impeachable offense—using manslaughter as an example—and that some impeachable offenses might not be defined as crimes. The memorandum from the staff, he pointed out, was not the unanimous view—or even the consensus—of the staff but merely contained the points on which the staff could agree. McClory indicated that some items had been deleted from the report at the last moment in order that the report have the backing of Jenner as well as Doar.

Questioned about his definition of an impeachable offense, Jenner noted that the report described impeachable conduct as "constitutional wrongs that subvert the structure of government, or undermine the integrity of the office and even the Constitution itself," conduct close to criminality if not actually defined as criminal. Yet Jenner declined to limit his definition of impeachable conduct by confining it to criminal activity.

No Fixed Standards. "This memorandum offers no fixed standards for determining whether grounds for impeachment exist," the staff wrote. "The framers did not write a fixed standard. Instead they adopted from English history a standard sufficiently general and flexible to

(Continued on p. 247)

Impeachable Offense: Opinion of Inquiry Staff

Following are excerpts from a Feb. 20 memorandum prepared by the impeachment inquiry staff of the House Judiciary Committee:

The Historical Origins of the Impeachment Process

"The Constitution provides that the President '...shall be removed from Office on Impeachment for, and Conviction of, Treason, Bribery, or other high Crimes and Misdemeanors.' The framers could have written simply 'or other crimes'.... They did not do that .... They adopted instead a unique phrase used for centuries in English parliamentary impeachments....

"Two points emerge from the 400 years of English parliamentary experience with the phrase.... First, the particular allegations of misconduct, alleged damage to the state in such forms as misapplication of funds, abuse of official power, neglect of duty, encroachment on Parliament's prerogatives, corruption, and betrayal of trust. Second, the phrase...was confined to parliamentary impeachments; it had no roots in the ordinary criminal law, and the particular allegations of misconduct under that heading were not necessarily limited to common law or statutory derelictions or crimes.

"**The Intention of the Framers.** The debates on impeachment at the Constitutional Convention...focus principally on its applicability to the President.... Impeachment was to be one of the central elements of executive responsibility....

"The framers intended impeachment to be a constitutional safeguard of the public trust, the powers of government conferred upon the President...and the division of powers....

"**The American Impeachment Cases.** ...Does Article III, Section 1 of the Constitution, which states that judges 'shall hold their Offices during good Behavior,' limit the relevance of the ten impeachments of judges with respect to presidential impeachment standards as has been argued...? It does not....

"Each of the thirteen American impeachments involved charges of misconduct incompatible with the official position of the officeholder. This conduct falls into three broad categories: (1) exceeding the constitutional bounds of the powers of the office in derogation of the powers of another branch of government; (2) behaving in a manner grossly incompatible with the proper function and purpose of the office; and (3) employing the power of the office for an improper purpose or for personal gain....

"In drawing up articles of impeachment, the House has placed little emphasis on criminal conduct. Less than one-third of the eighty-three articles the House has adopted have explicitly charged the violation of a criminal statute or used the word 'criminal' or 'crime' to describe the conduct alleged....

"Much more common in the articles are allegations that the officer has violated his duties or his oath or seriously undermined public confidence in his ability to perform his official functions....

"All have involved charges of conduct incompatible with continued performance of the office; some have explicitly rested upon a 'course of conduct'.... Some of the individual articles seem to have alleged conduct that, taken alone, would not have been considered serious....

The Criminality Issue

"The central issue...is whether requiring an indictable offense as an essential element of impeachable conduct is consistent with the purposes and intent of the framers....

"Impeachment and the criminal law serve fundamentally different purposes. Impeachment is the first step in a remedial process.... The purpose...is not personal punishment; its function is primarily to maintain constitutional government....

"The general applicability of the criminal law also makes it inappropriate as the standard.... In an impeachment proceeding a President is called to account for abusing powers which only a President possesses.

"Impeachable conduct...may include the serious failure to discharge the affirmative duties imposed on the President by the Constitution. Unlike a criminal case, the cause for removal...may be based on his entire course of conduct in office.... It may be a course of conduct more than individual acts that has a tendency to subvert constitutional government.

"To confine impeachable conduct to indictable offenses may well be to set a standard so restrictive as not to reach conduct that might adversely affect the system of government. Some of the most grievous offenses against our constitutional form of government may not entail violations of the criminal law....

"To limit impeachable conduct to criminal offenses would be incompatible with the evidence...and would frustrate the purpose that the framers intended....

Conclusion

"In the English practice and in several of the American impeachments, the criminality issue was not raised at all. The emphasis has been on the significant effects of the conduct....Impeachment was evolved... to cope with both the inadequacy of criminal standards and the impotence of the courts to deal with the conduct of great public figures. It would be anomalous if the framers, having barred criminal sanctions from the impeachment remedy...intended to restrict the grounds for impeachment to conduct that was criminal.

"The longing for precise criteria is understandable.... However, where the issue is presidential compliance with the constitutional requirements and limitations on the presidency, the crucial factor is not the intrinsic quality of behavior but the significance of its effects upon our constitutional system or the functioning of our government."

(Continued from p. 245)

meet future circumstances and events, the nature and character of which they could not foresee.''

But to determine the meaning that ''high crimes and misdemeanors'' should properly have in the 1974 inquiry, the report, prepared by a group headed by Joseph A. Woods Jr., senior associate special counsel, took a long look at the English precedents for the use of impeachment: ''Two points emerge from the 400 years of English parliamentary experience with the phrase 'high crimes and misdemeanors.' First, the particular allegations of misconduct alleged damage to the state....

''Second, the phrase...was confined to parliamentary impeachments...the particular allegations of misconduct under that heading were not necessarily limited to... crimes.'' *(Excerpts, box, p. 246)*

Moving then to scrutinize the intention of the men who wrote those words into the Constitution, the staff report examined the debates at the Constitutional Convention and later at the state conventions called to ratify the new Constitution. This evidence, concluded the report, indicated that the framers intended impeachment to ''reach offenses against the government, and expecially abuses of constitutional duties.''

Impeachment in America. Looking then at the 13 American impeachments, 10 of which have been of federal judges, who are appointed to hold their jobs during ''good behavior,'' the report dismissed the argument that judicial impeachment was irrelevant to presidential impeachment because of that phrase—which implies that a judge may be impeached for bad behavior. ''The only impeachment provision...included in the Constitution...applies to all civil officers, including judges, and defines impeachment offenses as 'treason, bribery, and other high crimes and misdemeanors,' '' the report stated.

''Each of the thirteen American impeachments involved charges of misconduct incompatible with the official position of the officeholder. This conduct falls into three broad categories: exceeding the constitutional bounds of the powers of the office...; behaving in a manner grossly incompatible with the proper function and purpose of the office; and employing the power of the office for an improper purpose or for personal gain.''

In practice, the House in impeachment cases ''has placed little emphasis on criminal conduct. Less than one-third of the eighty-three articles (of impeachment) the House has adopted have explicitly charged the violation of a criminal statute.''

A pattern of conduct, rather than specific individual acts, often has been the primary charge against an impeachable official, stated the report. ''In the early impeachments the articles were not prepared until after impeachment had been voted by the House, and it seems probable that the decision to impeach was made on the basis of all the allegations viewed as a whole, rather than each separate charge.

''Unlike the Senate, which votes separately on each article after trial, and where conviction on but one article is required for removal from office, the House appears to have considered the individual offenses less significant than what they said together about the conduct of the official in the performance of his duties.''

The Criminality Issue. To restrict impeachable offenses to crimes would be to define the function of presi-

dential impeachment too narrowly, the staff memorandum concluded. The criminal law applies to all citizens; but impeachment of a President is the remedy for his abuse of powers that only he possesses. Criminal law is basically prohibitory—designed to prevent people from certain actions. ''Impeachable conduct, on the other hand, may include the serious failure to discharge the affirmative duties imposed on the President by the Constitution.

''To confine impeachable conduct to indictable offenses may well be to set a standard so restrictive as not to reach conduct that might adversely affect the system of government. Some of the most grievous offenses against our constitutional form of government may not entail violations of the criminal law....

''A requirement of criminality would be incompatible with the intent of the framers to provide a mechanism board enough to maintain the integrity of constitutional government. Impeachment is a constitutional safety valve.''

Committee Procedures

To allay the concern of Jaworski and St. Clair about the confidentiality of any information either the special prosecutor's office or the White House furnished to the 38-member House Judiciary Committee, the committee Feb. 22 adopted strict procedures to guard the secrecy of such documents or other material.

The previous day, at the committee's request, Jaworski had provided a list of all material his staff had received from the White House—some 700 documents and 17 tapes. With that list as a basis, letters were expected to go within a few days of the committee's action to the White House requesting materials necessary for the impeachment inquiry.

A letter from Doar to St. Clair was already written, Doar said Feb. 22, and a letter from Rodino to Nixon was still being drafted. Doar said that he intended to meet with Jaworski immediately after committee adoption of the confidentiality procedures in order to work toward obtaining the material in the possession of the special prosecutor's staff.

By unanimous voice vote, the committee adopted rules of procedure that would require each member personally to file his list of the materials made available to the committee. Under the strict rules, no committee member could discuss any of the material with any member of his personal staff, but only with other members of the committee and certain members of the impeachment inquiry staff.

Two sets of rules were adopted, one for the committee members and one for the staff. Under the committee rules, four men—Rodino, Hutchinson, Doar and Jenner—would at all times have access to and responsibility for all information received from any source in the impeachment inquiry. At the beginning of any presentation of that evidence to the committee, each member would be given a list of all the information obtained on a given subject.

Any member could examine any information in the staff's possession in a designated secure area. None of that information, or the list of information, could be copied or made public unless a majority of the committee agreed to release it. The committee would vote in executive session whether or not to hear certain testimony in open or closed session.

Mitchell-Stans Trial

The trial of two former members of President Nixon's cabinet opened in U.S. District Court in New York Feb. 19.

Former Attorney General John N. Mitchell and former Secretary of Commerce Maurice H. Stans were the first major Nixon administration officials to go on trial for involvement in the Watergate scandal. They were charged with conspiracy to obstruct justice, obstruction of justice and lying to a grand jury. They were the first cabinet officials to be tried on criminal charges since the 1920s, when members of the Harding administration were involved in the Teapot Done scandal.

Mitchell and Stans were accused of using their influence to impede a federal investigation into the affairs of fugitive financier Robert L. Vesco in return for a secret cash donation of $200,000 to Nixon's 1972 re-election campaign.

U.S. District Judge Lee P. Gagliardi told prospective jurors the trial probably would last four to five weeks, and that to avoid having jurors influenced by publicity about the case, they would be sequestered. More than half of the first panel of possible jurors examined were excused on grounds that being sequestered for that period would create hardships for them.

Defense attorneys unsuccessfully sought to have the charges dropped or the trial moved or postponed on grounds that extensive publicity about the case would prevent Mitchell and Stans from receiving a fair trial. "It is hard to know how any literate person in New York could be impartial as he approaches this trial," argued John P. Diuguid, a lawyer for Stans.

Senate Watergate Committee

The Senate select Watergate committee, which dominated the nation's television screens during the spring and summer of 1973, agreed unanimously Feb. 19 to hold no more public hearings. The committee would finish its remaining investigations in closed sessions, Chairman Sam J. Ervin (D N.C.) told the Senate, and then issue its final report and legislative recommendations.

It also would pursue an appeal of a U.S. District Court decision Feb. 8 dismissing its suit for five presidential tapes, Ervin said. *(p. 239)*

Ervin asked the Senate to give the committee a three-month extension, from Feb. 28 to May 28, to conclude its investigations and issue its report. The Senate by voice vote granted the extension.

Ervin said Watergate Special Prosecutor Leon Jaworski had requested the delay on grounds that a public report by Feb. 28 could hamper grand jury consideration of indictments in Watergate-related cases. Indictments were expected in late February or early March.

In addition, Ervin said, "the committee believes that it should be careful not to interfere unduly with the ongoing impeachment process of the House Judiciary Committee or the criminal cases which will soon be prosecuted by the special prosecutor, on which the attention of the country appears now to be focused."

A Graceful Exit. The progress of the Judiciary Committee and the special prosecutor's efforts convinced the Senate committee that it could safely step aside and leave further Watergate investigations in their hands, Ervin said. Or, as Majority Leader Mike Mansfield (D Mont.) said on the Senate floor, the other two efforts made it possible for the Watergate committee, "with good grace, to make an exit."

The committee's public hearings held the nation's attention for nearly three months in 1973, from May 17 to Aug. 7. Greater and lesser figures of the Nixon administration and the Committee for the Re-election of the President unfolded tales of big money, dirty tricks, taping of presidential conversations and possible law violations ranging from the original burglary of the Democratic National Committee headquarters in the Watergate building to illegal campaign contributions to perjury.

Declining Attention. Public attention fell off when the hearings resumed in the fall, and other developments took center stage— the fight over the President's tapes, gaps in the tapes, the firing of the first special prosecutor, Archibald Cox, and the ensuing "Saturday night massacre" and the beginning of the inquiry into possible impeachment of Nixon.

After the Christmas recess, the committee's reluctance to go back into public hearings was evident. It voted Jan. 23, on a four-three party-line vote, to resume, but for only two weeks. Democratic members admitted they were not eager to resume, but acceded to Chairman Ervin's wishes. Ervin, in turn, reportedly was acceding to the wishes of the committee staff, who felt there were facts still to be brought out.

Just three days later, on Jan. 26, at the request of New York prosecutors, the committee voted to postpone the opening of hearings until after a jury had been selected in the Mitchell-Stans trial there, so as not to prejudice prospective jurors. *(Box, this page)*

The principal matters still under investigation by the committee were the circumstances surrounding a $100,000 contribution given by agents of billionaire Howard Hughes to Nixon's friend, Charles G. (Bebe) Rebozo, and a $427,000 campaign contribution from the dairy industry. The committee vice chairman, Sen. Howard H. Baker Jr. (R Tenn.), also had expressed interest in investigating alleged "national security" and Central Intelligence Agency involvement in the Watergate case.

Committee chief counsel Samuel Dash said that "relevant portions" of the testimony given in the closed sessions would be made public. The decision to cancel further public hearings could be reversed, Ervin told the Senate, should some "unprecedented and novel evidence" be developed, but he said none was anticipated.

Judicial Warnings

In keeping with the traditional role of the courts as the preserver of order and fairness, two federal judges in Washington took the opportunity in mid-February to call for an end to public debate on two Watergate-related matters: the truthfulness of former White House counsel John W. Dean III and the integrity of the White House tapes.

Dean Debate. "Let's stop all this public debate" over Dean's veracity, said Judge Gerhard A. Gesell during a Feb. 15 hearing preceding the perjury trial of former White House appointments secretary Dwight L. Chapin. Vice President Gerald R. Ford and Senate Minority Leader Hugh Scott (R Pa.) both had voiced criticism of Dean's statements; Jaworski had responded with some public comments, including those on ABC-TV's "Issues and Answers" Feb. 3, making clear his confidence in Dean's testimony. *(p. 237, 235)*

"The court's control is over its own officers," said Gesell. "Obviously I cannot direct the President, the Vice President or Sen. Scott to cease doing what they are doing." He mentioned that he had received a letter from Nixon, expressing concern about pretrial publicity.

Speaking to Jaworski, Gesell warned that "any further lapse would have very serious consequences." Jaworski's "good sense" ought to keep him from appearing on television talk shows, the judge added.

Late Feb. 20, Gesell denied a motion by Chapin's attorney that Dean should not be allowed to testify against Chapin because a confidential attorney-client relationship had existed between them in the White House. Gesell said that Dean could testify, subject to a "single qualification" which he did not explain.

Tapes Tampering. Disturbed by continued public reports concerning possible tampering with the subpoenaed White House tapes, Judge John J. Sirica called Jaworski, White House defense counsel James D. St. Clair and Charles S. Rhyne, attorney for Rose Mary Woods, to a meeting in his chambers Feb. 19.

The Washington Post had reported Feb. 17 that the panel of experts, selected jointly by the special prosecutor and the White House to examine the subpoenaed tapes, had found evidence indicating that two of them had been tampered with. St. Clair and White House chief of staff Alexander M. Haig had denied the story angrily, and St. Clair had issued a statement that a White House technical investigation of the 18-minute gap in the June 20 tape "could well have been and probably...(was) caused by the admittedly defective recording machine" Woods used. The panel of experts had reported previously that marks found on the tape indicated that it had been deliberately erased. *(p. 203)*

At the Feb. 19 meeting, Sirica won agreement among the lawyers that "continued public comment on the grand jury's work (concerning the evidence of the tapes) by those who have any association with the investigation is inappropriate." Several precautionary measures had been agreed upon, Sirica said, to prevent disclosure "for the time being...of matters which ought... to remain confidential." Further public discussion of such matters, said his statement, "can do nothing but hinder that investigation."

Week's Watergate Chronology

Following is a day-to-day chronology of the week's events in the Watergate case:

FEB. 13

Telephone Records. The Internal Revenue Service (IRS) returned to a Washington, D.C., telephone com-

---

Jacobsen Indictment

A Texas lawyer, Jake Jacobsen, was indicted Feb. 21 for lying to a Watergate grand jury about an alleged $10,000 payoff from the dairy industry for help in bringing about a Nixon administration decision to raise milk price supports.

The indictment was the first resulting from the special Watergate prosecutor's investigation into the connection between the 1971 price support decision and large dairy industry contributions and pledges to President Nixon's 1972 re-election campaign.

Jacobsen, 54, was a White House aide in the Johnson administration, but became a Democrat for Nixon in 1972. He was a lawyer for the American Milk Producers Inc. at the time the industry was seeking the price support increase.

According to the indictment, Jacobsen testified in January that he received $10,000 from the milk producers' legislative director and put it in a safe deposit box, where it remained untouched until FBI agents inventoried it Nov. 27, 1973. That statement was the basis for the perjury charge.

The grand jury, investigating possible violations of bribery and conspiracy laws in connection with the price support increase, said it had evidence that the $10,000 was given to Jacobsen "to be paid to a public official for his assistance in connection with the price support decision." The indictment did not name the public official or claim that the official did in fact receive the money.

Jacobsen had testified in a civil suit previously that he enlisted the help of former Secretary of the Treasury John B. Connally in his efforts, but Connally denied he had accepted any money.

The White House had denied that its price support decision, a switch from its previous position, was in return for contributions. Nixon's campaign received $472,000 from dairy groups and reportedly had been promised $2-million. *(White House position, p. 179, 159)*

---

pany the records it had secretly subpoenaed of phone calls made from *The New York Times* Washington bureau from June 1973 to January 1974. An IRS spokesman said the agency was trying to determine the source of confidential IRS information leaked to the newspaper. But he declined to say whether the IRS also had subpoenaed the home telephone records of a Times reporter covering the Watergate investigation and working on a story about the possible criminal investigation of a large contributor to the 1972 Nixon campaign.

Reinecke Testimony. California Lt. Gov. Ed Reinecke told Watergate prosecutors he was willing to testify that former Attorney General Mitchell did not tell the truth when he denied knowing of an offer by International Telephone and Telegraph Corporation (ITT) to help finance the 1972 Republican national convention just before the Justice Department settled an anti-trust suit against ITT in 1971, according to *The Washington Post. (Earlier story, p. 240)*

FEB. 14

White House Refusal. Watergate Special Prosecutor Leon Jaworski informed Senate Judiciary Committee Chairman James O. Eastland (D Miss.) that the White House had refused to provide him with any further tapes or documents for his investigations. *(p. 238)*

FEB. 15

President's Position. The President wanted to avoid a confrontation with Jaworski, the White House said, and had instructed his lawyer, James D. St. Clair, to continue private conversations with the prosecutor. However, Nixon felt he had provided enough tapes and documents to enable the Watergate grand juries to issue indictments and would refuse on grounds of executive privilege to give up any more, St. Clair said.

Warning to Jaworski. U.S. District Judge Gerhard A. Gesell warned Jaworski to be more cautious with out-of-court statements about the Watergate case and urged an end to all "public debate" over the credibility of former White House counsel John W. Dean III. *(Details, p. 249)*

Dairy Contributions. At least $200,000 in dairy industry contributions for Republican congressional candidates was diverted in 1972 to the Finance Committee to Re-elect the President as part of an elaborate scheme to "launder" money promised by milk producers for Nixon's campaign, *The New York Times* reported.

ITT Investigation. The Joint Committee on Internal Revenue Taxation was looking into possible White House influence in a 1969 ruling by the IRS that made possible the takeover of the Hartford Fire Insurance Company by ITT and produced profits of nearly $6-million for ITT, *The New York Times* reported.

Reinecke Involvement. California Lt. Gov. Reinecke said after a three-day visit to Washington that Jaworski had refused to "clear his name" in the ITT investigation. He would run for governor and let the people of California decide whether he was worthy of trust, he said.

FEB. 17

Altered Tapes Report. Two of the originally subpoenaed Watergate tapes were suspected of being rerecordings, not originals, *The Washington Post* reported. The White House immediately denounced the story and said it would ask for an investigation of the sources of the information. *(Details, p. 249)*

FEB. 18

Tape Gap. The 18½-minute gap on a key Watergate tape could have been caused accidentally, due to a faulty part on Rose Mary Woods' tape recorder, Allan D. Bell Jr., president of Dektor Counterintelligence and Security Inc. of Springfield, Va., told *The New York Times*. Bell's report was contrary to the finding of a panel of experts that the gap was caused by at least five manual erasures. *(Previous tapes story, p. 201)*

AFL-CIO Position. Accusing Nixon of deliberately dragging out the Watergate investigations by refusing to provide evidence to Congress, the Watergate prosecutor and the public, the executive council of the AFL-CIO passed a new impeachment resolution, 31-1. Delegates to the AFL-CIO convention originally had called for Nixon's resignation or impeachment Oct. 22, 1973. *(p. 82)*.

FEB. 19

End to Hearings. The Senate Watergate committee agreed unanimously to hold no further public hearings in order not to jeopardize court cases by publicity and to let the House impeachment inquiry take center stage. *(Details, p. 248)*

End to Comments. U.S. District Judge John J. Sirica called all lawyers involved in the matter of the Watergate tapes to a closed meeting and obtained their agreement to cease all public comment about the tapes. *(Details, p. 249)*

Independent Prosecutor. Sen. Robert Taft Jr. (R Ohio) urged that the Senate revive measures to ensure the independence of the Watergate special prosecutor. *(Earlier story, p. 238)*

Mitchell-Stans Trial. The trial of former Attorney General John N. Mitchell and former Commerce Secretary Maurice H. Stans on charges of obstructing justice and conspiracy opened in New York. *(Box, p. 490)*

Hearing Scheduled. Washington, D.C., Superior Court Judge Harold H. Greene scheduled a hearing for March 15 on whether Nixon should be subpoenaed in the California trial of John D. Erlichman and two others for the 1971 burglary of the office of Daniel Ellsberg's psychiatrist, as requested by the California judge. The White House indicated that Nixon would reject a subpoena on grounds of executive privilege. *(Earlier story, p. 227)*

FEB. 20

Impeachable Offense. House Judiciary Committee lawyers briefed committee members on a staff study which concluded that a president could be impeached and removed from office for actions that were serious offenses against the public interest but not necessarily legal crimes. *(Details, p. 245)*

Trial Delayed. The California trial for the burglary of Ellsberg's psychiatrist's office was postponed a month, until March 25, to allow time for hearings on whether Nixon should be subpoenaed to testify.

Watergate Effects. Nixon reportedly conceded to Republican congressional leaders that Watergate was a factor in the Republican loss in the Michigan congressional election Feb. 18, but said the loss was not necessarily a harbinger of widespread party losses in November.

FEB. 21

Alteration of Documents. The FBI was investigating the possible alteration of some Watergate documents submitted by the White House to the special prosecutor, *The Washington Post* reported. Several documents appeared to have been cut with scissors, the Post said. *(Details, p. 249)*   √

SEVEN INDICTMENTS MAY ASSIST HOUSE INQUIRY

A major obstacle was cleared from the path of the House presidential impeachment investigation March 1 with the indictment of seven men by the Watergate grand jury.

Among the seven indicted for conspiring to impede the investigation of the June 1972 break-in at the Democratic national headquarters were three of President Nixon's closest advisers during his first term: former Attorney General John N. Mitchell and former presidential assistants H.R. Haldeman and John D. Ehrlichman.

All three were charged with conspiracy and obstruction of justice. Mitchell and Haldeman were charged with giving false testimony to the Senate Watergate investigating committee. Mitchell and Ehrlichman were also charged with lying to FBI agents and to the grand jury.

The House Judiciary Committee was conducting the inquiry into possible impeachment of the President. Earlier in the week, Watergate Special Prosecutor Leon Jaworski had indicated that issuance of indictments would make it easier for the Judiciary Committee to obtain information gathered by the prosecutor's staff from the White House.

Also indicted were four other former White House aides or officials of Nixon's re-election committee: Charles W. Colson, Robert C. Mardian, Kenneth W. Parkinson and Gordon Strachan.

After learning of the indictments, Rep. Robert McClory (Ill.), a senior Republican member of the Judiciary Committee, said he hoped their issuance would facilitate the release of material from Jaworski's office to the impeachment inquiry staff "so that we can wrap this thing up as soon as possible."

One of the grand jury's charges, that Haldeman had lied to the Senate Watergate committee, called into direct question the accuracy of a public statement by the President. *(Box, this page)*

Sealed Envelope. And further questions were raised concerning Nixon's involvement in the Watergate cover-up by a sealed envelope that the grand jury foreman handed to U.S. District Judge John J. Sirica along with the indictments. Sirica slit open the brown envelope with a letter opener, and, in front of the crowd assembled in the courtroom, silently read through the information on the top sheet.

Assistant Special Prosecutor Richard Ben-Veniste then stepped forward and handed a large briefcase to the judge. "The documents alluded to in the report you have just read are in this sealed briefcase," he said. "The key was sealed in the envelope with the report."

Sirica said he would seal the envelope again and hold it in his custody until he decided to issue a further order concerning it, an order that presumably could forward it to the House Judiciary Committee for its inquiry. Such an order appeared possible, in view of reports that Jaworski's office, after long study, had decided that any evid-

Haldeman, Nixon Statements

One count of perjury against H.R. Haldeman March 1 involved a key piece of testimony given by the Senate Watergate committee by Haldeman and later corroborated by President Nixon during a news conference.

In his appearance before the Senate committee in July 1973, Haldeman had testified under oath concerning his knowledge of a meeting March 21 between the President and former White House counsel John W. Dean III. Haldeman testified that he was present for the final 40 minutes of the Nixon meeting with Dean and had listened to a tape recording of the entire session. According to the transcript of Haldeman's testimony:

"He (Dean) also reported on a current Hunt blackmail threat. He said Hunt was demanding $120,000 or else he would tell about the seamy things he had done for Ehrlichman. The President pursued this in considerable detail, obviously trying to smoke out what was really going on. He led Dean on regarding the process and what he recommended doing. He asked such things as—'Well, this is the thing you would recommend? we ought to do this? is that right?' And he asked where the money would come from? how it would be delivered? and so on. He asked how much money would be involved over the years and Dean said 'probably a million dollars—but the problem is that it is hard to raise.' The President said 'there is no problem in raising a million dollars, we can do that, *but it would be wrong.*' " *(Vol. I, p. 231)*

According to the Watergate grand jury indictment, the underscored (italicized) portions of Haldeman's statement "were material to the said investigation and study and, as he then and there well knew, were false."

Nixon Statement. At his Aug. 22, 1973, press conference, the month after Haldeman's testimony on the subject, Nixon answered a question about the March 21 meeting with Dean. Nixon recalled Dean's mentioning a figure of $1-million. The President said he asked Dean "...how do you get around clemency because they're not going to stay in jail simply because their families are being taken care of?"

Then Nixon added: "And so that was why I concluded, as Mr. Haldeman recalls, perhaps, and did testify very effectively, when I said, 'John, it's wrong, it won't work, we can't give clemency and we've got to get this story out.' " *(Text, p. 3)*

From Burglary to Impeachment

Few would have guessed on June 17, 1972, when five men were arrested inside Democratic national headquarters at 2:30 a.m., that almost two years later the case would still be a hot issue in Congress and the courts.

The break-in ceased being a local police matter June 19, 1972, when the Justice Department announced a "full investigation" after it was discovered that one of the arrested men, James W. McCord Jr., was on the payroll of the Nixon re-election committee.

First Trial. On Sept. 15, 1972, the five burglars and two others involved were indicted, and the Justice Department said its investigation was over. At the trial in January 1973—presided over by U.S. District Judge John J. Sirica—five of the defendants bowed out early by pleading guilty, and the two others were convicted. It looked as if the matter would end there.

McCord Letter. But on March 19, McCord wrote Sirica an explosive letter, charging that he and his codefendants had been pressured to hide the truth, that perjury had been committed at the trial and that higher-ups were involved in a coverup. More revelations followed, and on April 30 Nixon announced the departure of his two top aides—H. R. Haldeman and John D. Ehrlichman—along with Attorney General Richard G. Kleindienst. He said the new attorney general, who turned out to be Elliot L. Richardson, could appoint a special prosecutor to get to the bottom of the case.

Senate Committee. Throughout the spring and summer, most of the visible Watergate drama centered in the televised hearings of the Senate Watergate investigating committee. But Special Prosecutor Archibald Cox got his share of headlines when the White House balked at his demands for tapes and documents. Their differences culminated Oct. 20 in the "Saturday night massacre"—Nixon ordered Cox fired, and Richardson and Deputy Attorney General William D. Ruckelshaus quit with him.

By that time, the public perception of the Watergate affair embraced a series of allegations against the administration, including political sabotage, campaign financing violations, extortion and political use of the FBI and Central Intelligence Agency.

New Prosecutor. In the wake of the widespread, emotional public protests over the Cox firing, the White House Nov. 1 named a new special prosecutor, Leon Jaworski, who vowed to operate with complete independence. And the House Judiciary Committee began an inquiry into the grounds for impeaching Nixon.

The Senate investigating committee resumed its public hearings in September after a two-month hiatus, but their original mass appeal was never rekindled. On Feb. 19, Committee Chairman Sam J. Ervin (D N.C.) said the panel would withdraw to write its report, leaving the courts and the House Judiciary Committee in the Watergate spotlight.

ence involving Nixon in the Watergate matter should be sent to the House instead of to the grand jury.

Jaworski told Sirica that he expected the trial of the seven men indicted to consume three to four months.

Sirica ordered all those involved in the case—the grand jurors, the attorneys, the defendants, witnesses and the special prosecutor's office—to avoid any comment outside the courtroom concerning the case, in order to guard the rights of the defendants to a fair trial. He told the grand jurors, 21 of whom were present, out of a total of 23, that they were not dismissed, but that they might be called back again in two weeks.

The Indictments

"Does the grand jury have anything to report?" asked Judge John J. Sirica. "Yes, your honor," replied the tall, bearded grand jury foreman, Vladimir N. Pregelj, handing to Sirica the indictments of seven men, all formerly connected to the Nixon administration, and a fat, brown, sealed envelope. Indicted after a 20-month grand jury investigation were:

• John N. Mitchell, 60, former attorney general and former campaign director of the Committee for the Re-election of the President—conspiracy to impede the Watergate investigation, obstruction of justice, making false declarations, perjury, lying to the FBI.

• H. R. Haldeman, 47, former White House chief of staff—conspiracy to impede the Watergate investigation, obstruction of justice, perjury.

• John D. Ehrlichman, 48, former assistant to the President for domestic affairs—conspiracy to impede the Watergate investigation, obstruction of justice, lying to FBI agents, making false declarations.

• Charles W. Colson, 42, former special counsel to the President—conspiracy to impede the Watergate investigation, obstruction of justice.

• Robert C. Mardian, 50, former assistant attorney general and former political consultant to Nixon's re-election committee—conspiracy to impede the Watergate investigation.

• Kenneth W. Parkinson, 46, the attorney representing the re-election committee—conspiracy to impede the Watergate investigation, obstruction of justice.

• Gordon Strachan, 30, former assistant to Haldeman and later general counsel to the United States Information Agency—conspiracy to impede the Watergate investigation, obstruction of justice, making false declarations.

All seven men were charged with conspiring to impede the investigation into the Watergate burglary. "It was part of the conspiracy," the indictment stated, "that the conspirators would corruptly influence, obstruct, and impede...the due administration of justice...for the purpose of concealing the identities of the persons who were responsible for, participated in, and had knowledge of (a) the activities which were the subject of the investigation and trial and (b) other illegal and improper activities."

The conspirators also worked, the indictment stated, to obstruct justice, to lie to government agencies and to defraud the government of its right to have the officials of the Central Intelligence Agency (CIA), the FBI and the Justice Department "transact their official business honestly and impartially, free from corruption, fraud,

Legal Status of Other Watergate-Related Defendants

As Special Prosecutor Leon Jaworski prepared to announce a new batch of Watergate indictments the week ending March 2, the box score of indictments and convictions related to the scandals up to that point looked like this:

Watergate Break-in. Three of the seven convicted conspirators had been released from prison while they appealed their sentences. They were Frank A. Sturgis, Bernard L. Barker and E. Howard Hunt Jr. Two others, Virgilio R. Gonzalez and Eugenio R. Martinez, expected to be paroled March 7. Of the two who pleaded not guilty, G. Gordon Liddy was serving a six- to 20-year prison term, and James W. McCord Jr. had not yet starting serving his sentence and reportedly was cooperating with prosecutors.

Coverup. Three former Nixon administration or re-election campaign officials—John W. Dean III, Frederick C. LaRue and Jeb Stuart Magruder—had pleaded guilty to obstruction of justice charges for covering up the true dimensions of the break-in. A fourth, Herbert L. Porter, had pleaded guilty to lying to the FBI during its early investigation of the incident. All four had agreed to cooperate with prosecutors in exchange for the reduced charges, and were yet to be sentenced.

Plumbers. Egil Krogh Jr., a former White House aide who headed the secret investigations unit called the "plumbers," was serving a six-month sentence for conspiring to violate the civil rights of Pentagon Papers defendant Daniel Ellsberg's psychiatrist. When Krogh pleaded guilty to the federal charge, an earlier California indictment against him for the 1971 break-in was dropped. The three others named in the California plumbers indictments had pleaded not guilty and were awaiting trial. They were Liddy; David R. Young Jr., a former White House aide, and John D. Ehrlichman, Nixon's former domestic affairs adviser.

Political Sabotage. Donald H. Segretti, who had confessed to running a political sabotage opera-

tion for the Republicans during the 1972 election, was serving a six-month prison term for conspiracy and distributing phony campaign literature. Nixon's former appointments secretary, Dwight L. Chapin, had pleaded not guilty to charges that he lied about his relationship with Segretti; his trial was scheduled for April 1. One of Segretti's agents in Florida, George Hearing, was serving a one-year sentence for violating state campaign laws.

Vesco Case. Former Attorney General John N. Mitchell and former Commerce Secretary Maurice L. Stans—the first cabinet heads to be indicted since the Teapot Dome scandals of the Harding administration—were on trial in New York City on charges that they attempted to block a government investigation of financier Robert L. Vesco in exchange for a $200,000 contribution to the Nixon campaign, and that they later lied about it.

Campaign Contributions. Nixon's long-time personal attorney and fund-raiser, Herbert W. Kalmbach, had pleaded guilty to violating federal campaign laws by participating in an illegal fund-raising committee in 1970 and by offering an ambassadorship in exchange for a contribution. While awaiting sentencing, Kalmbach reportedly was talking to prosecutors about the involvement of other top Nixon associates.

Jake Jacobsen, a former attorney for the American Milk Producers Inc., was under indictment for perjury in connection with donations by the producers to the Nixon campaign.

Federal judges had fined eight corporations and seven executives for making illegal contributions to the 1972 Nixon campaign, and a ninth company and an eighth executive were contesting a similar charge relating to a 1968 contribution to the Democrats. *(Kalmbach charge, p. 258; Jacobsen charge, p. 249; Porter charge, p. 211; corporate charges, p. 185, 164; earlier indictments and convictions box score, p. 171)*

improper and undue influence, dishonesty, unlawful impairment and obstruction.

"Among the means by which the conspirators would carry out the aforesaid conspiracy," the indictment continued, were the following:

"The conspirators would direct G. Gordon Liddy to seek the assistance of Richard G. Kleindienst, then attorney general...in obtaining the release from the District of Columbia jail of one or more of the persons who had been arrested on June 17, 1972, in the offices of the Democratic National Committee....

"...would at various times remove, conceal, alter and destroy...documents, papers, records and objects.

"...would plan, solicit, assist and facilitate the giving of false, deceptive, evasive and misleading statements and testimony.

"...would give false, misleading, evasive and deceptive statements and testimony.

"...would covertly raise, acquire, transmit, distribute and pay cash funds to and for the benefits of the defendants (in the original case)....

"...would make and cause to be made offers of leniency, executive clemency and other benefits to E. Howard Hunt Jr., G. Gordon Liddy, James W. McCord Jr. and Jeb. S. Magruder....

"...would attempt to obtain CIA financial assistance for persons who were subjects of the investigation....

"...would obtain information from the FBI and the Department of Justice concerning the progress of the investigation."

Forty-five overt acts were listed in support of the conspiracy charge, for which the maximum penalty is five years in prison and a $5,000 fine.

Obstruction of Justice. Mitchell, Haldeman, Ehrlichman, Strachan, Parkinson and Colson were also charged with one count of obstruction of justice for their

(Continued on p. 255)

Impeachable Offense: Opinion by Nixon Attorneys

Following are excerpts from a Feb. 28 analysis prepared by James D. St. Clair, John J. Chester, Michael A. Sterlacci, Jerome J. Murphy and Loren A. Smith, attorneys for President Nixon:

English Background of Constitutional Impeachment Provisions

"The Framers felt that the English system permitted men...to make arbitrary decisions, and one of their primary purposes in creating a Constitution was to replace this arbitrariness with a system based on the rule of law.... They felt impeachment was a necessary check on a President who might commit a crime, but they did not want to see the vague standards of the English system that made impeachment a weapon to achieve parliamentary supremacy....

"To argue that the President may be impeached for something less than a criminal offense, with all the safeguards that definition implies, would be a monumental step backwards into all those old English practices that our Constitution sought to eliminate. American impeachment was not designed to force a President into surrendering executive authority...but to check overtly criminal actions as they are defined by law....

"The terminology 'high crimes and misdemeanors' should create no confusion or ambiguity.... It was a unitary phrase meaning crimes against the state, as opposed to those against individuals.... It is as ridiculous to say that 'misdemeanor' must mean something beyond 'crime' as it is to suggest that in the phrase 'bread and butter issues' butter issues must be different from bread issues...."

The Constitutional Convention

"It is evident from the actual debate and from the events leading up to it that Morris' remark that 'An election of every four years will prevent maladministration,' expressed the will of the Convention. Thus, the impeachment provision adopted was designed to deal exclusively with indictable criminal conduct.... The Convention rejected all non-criminal definitions of impeachable offenses.... To distort the clear meaning of the phrase 'treason, bribery or other high crimes and misdemeanors' by including non-indictable conduct would thus most certainly violate the Framers' intent."

Legal Meaning of Impeachment Provision

"Just as statutes are to be construed to uphold the intent of the drafters...so should we uphold the intent of the drafters of the Constitution that impeachable offenses be limited to criminal violations. Also as penal statutes have been strictly construed in favor of the accused, so should we construe the impeachment provisions of the Constitution...."

American Impeachment Precedents

"Some of the proponents of presidential impeachment place great emphasis on the cases involving federal judges to support the proposition that impeachment will lie for conduct which does not of itself constitute an indictable offense. This view is apparently most appealing to those broad constructionists who favoring a severely weakened Chief Executive argue that certain non-criminal 'political' offenses may justify impeachment....

"The Framers...distinguished between the President and judges concerning the standard to be employed for an impeachment. Otherwise the 'good behavior' clause is a nullity....

"The precedent...asserted by the House in 1804 that a judge may be impeached for a breach of good behavior was reasserted again with full force over one hundred years later in 1912....

"The fact that the House...felt it necessary to make a distinction in the impeachment standards between the Judiciary and the Executive reinforces the obvious —that the words 'treason, bribery, and other high crimes and misdemeanors' are limited solely to indictable crimes and cannot extend to misbehavior....

"The acquittal of President Johnson over a century ago strongly indicates that the Senate has refused to adopt a broad view of 'other high crimes and misdemeanors'.... Impeachment of a President should be resorted to only for cases of the gravest kind—the commission of a crime named in the Constitution or a criminal offense against the laws of the United States. If there is any doubt as to the gravity of an offense or as to a President's conduct or motives, the doubt should be resolved in his favor. This is the necessary price for having an independent executive...."

Conclusion: Proper Standard for Presidential Impeachment

"Any analysis that broadly construes the power to impeach and convict can be reached only...by placing a subjective gloss on the history of impeachment that results in permitting the Congress to do whatever it deems most politic. The intent of the Framers, who witnessed episode after episode of outrageous abuse of the impeachment power by the self-righteous English Parliament, was to restrict the *political* reach of the impeachment power.

"Those who seek to broaden the impeachment power invite the use of power 'as a means of crushing political adversaries or ejecting them from office.'.... The acceptance of such an invitation would be destructive to our system of government and to the fundamental principle of separation of powers.... The Framers never intended that the impeachment clause serve to dominate or destroy the executive branch of the government....'"

(Continued from p. 253)

success in impeding the investigation and the due administration of justice. This obstruction was accomplished, the indictment stated, by providing cash and other benefits to the seven original Watergate defendants—Bernard L. Barker, Virgilio R. Gonzalez, Eugenio R. Martinez, McCord, Frank L. Sturgis and Hunt—"for the purpose of concealing...the identitites of the persons who were responsible for, participated in and had knowledge of the activities which were the subject of the investigation and trial." The maximum penalty for this charge is five years in prison and a $5,000 fine.

Mitchell. Because Mitchell was on trial in New York City on charges of impeding a federal investigation into the affairs of financier Robert L. Vesco, Sirica set arraignment of the seven defendants for March 9, a Saturday. *(Mitchell trial, p. 248)*

In addition to his indictment for conspiracy and obstruction of justice in the Watergate investigation, Mitchell was indicted on four different counts of lying—twice before the grand jury, once before the Senate Watergate committee and once to FBI agents.

• Mitchell told the grand jury in September 1972 that he had no idea of Liddy's intelligence-gathering activities. In April 1973 he denied being told of Liddy's involvement in the Watergate break-in before June 28, 1972. When he made these statements, "he then and there well knew (that they) were false," said the indictment.

• On July 10-11, 1973, Mitchell told the Senate committee that he had no idea on June 19, 1972, that Frederick C. LaRue, a former re-election committee official; Mardian; John W. Dean III, former counsel to the president, or Magruder knew of the "Gemstone" file. Mitchell said there was no discussion at a meeting with those persons that evening of destroying the file. Gemstone was a code name for a file on campaign espionage and sabotage. Mitchell knew this testimony was false, said the indictment.

• When Mitchell on July 5, 1972, told FBI agents that he knew nothing of the Watergate burglary other than what he had read in the newspapers, he was knowingly making "false, fictitious and fraudulent statements," said the indictment.

The maximum penalty for lying to the grand jury or to FBI agents is five years in prison and a $10,000 fine. For perjury before the Senate committee, the maximum penalty is five years in prison and a $2,000 fine.

Ehrlichman. In addition to charges of conspiracy and obstruction of justice, Ehrlichman was charged with two counts of lying to the grand jury and one count of lying to FBI agents.

• When Ehrlichman told FBI agents late in July 1973 that he had no information relating to the Watergate burglary other than what he had read in the newspapers, he was knowingly making "false, fictitious, and fraudulent statements," said the indictment.

• When Ehrlichman in May 1973 told the grand jury that he could not remember how he first learned that Liddy was involved in the Watergate break-in, he knew the statements were false, said the indictment.

• When Ehrlichman in May 1973 told the grand jury that he had not approved the raising of money for the defense of the original Watergate defendants and their families, and that he had not said this money-raising and its purpose should be kept secret, he knew those statements, too, were false, said the indictment.

Nixon on Impeachment

President Nixon declared at his Feb. 25 White House news conference that he did not believe he would be impeached and that he would not resign to save Republicans from losses at the polls in November.

"I want my party to succeed," Nixon said, "but more important, I want the presidency to survive. And it is vitally important in this nation that the presidency of the United States not be hostage to what happens to the popularity of a president at one time or another."

Nixon said he thought 1974 would be a good year for Republican candidates who stood behind the administration's record of peace and prosperity.

The President was less combative than at previous meetings with the press when questioned about Watergate-related matters. *(Excerpts, p. 264)*

Nixon revealed that he had refused a request to testify before a Watergate grand jury and that his counter-offer, to respond to questions in writing or to meet with the Watergate special prosecutor, had been turned down.

Impeachment. The President said he accepted the opinion of his White House counsel and some other constitutional lawyers that "a criminal offense on the part of the President is the requirement for impeachment," rather than some other criteria such as dereliction of duty.

Asked if it would not be in his best interest and that of the country to have the question of his involvement in Watergate resolved by impeachment, Nixon said: "Well, a full impeachment trial in the Senate under our Constitution comes only when the House determines that there is an impeachable offense. It is my belief that the House, after it conducts its inquiry, will not reach that determination. I do not expect to be impeached."

Nixon reiterated his position that he would cooperate with the House Judiciary Committee's staff investigation of impeachment trials so long as this did not interfere with his concept of executive privilege.

Taxes. Nixon said he would pay California income taxes if required to do so. He added that he would withdraw the federal income tax deduction he claimed for donating his vice presidential papers if it were determined that the deduction was improper. The President asserted at another point that similar deductions had been claimed in the past by a number of other public figures.

Kalmbach. Nixon denied that he had been consulted about an offer by his personal lawyer, Herbert W. Kalmbach, to a 1970 Republican campaign contributor, of a European ambassadorship in return for a $100,000 contribution. However, Nixon said, he had begun a query at the White House to determine who was responsible for approving the offer. "I would go further and say that ambassadorships cannot be purchased, and I would not approve an ambassadorship unless the man or woman was qualified, clearly apart from any contributions," Nixon said.

Haldeman. In addition to charges of conspiracy and obstruction of justice, Haldeman was also charged with three counts of perjury, all relating to his testimony before the Senate Watergate committee.

• When on July 30, 1973, he told the Senate committee that no one in the summer of 1972 was aware that the funds raised and provided to the Watergate defendants were a response to blackmail or were "hush money," Haldeman knew that these statements were false, stated the indictment.

• When on July 30-31, 1973, Haldeman told the committee that Nixon had told Dean on March 21, 1973, it would be wrong to pay the blackmail money Hunt was demanding, he knew that those statements also were false, the indictment said. This particular perjury charge appeared to lead back to Nixon himself, who had supported Haldeman's account of this conversation as accurate. *(Box p. 251)*

• When on Aug. 1, 1973, Haldeman said that there was no reference in the March 21 meeting to Magruder's committing perjury before the grand jury, he knew he was making a false statement, said the indictment.

Strachan. In addition to the charges of conspiracy and obstruction of justice, Strachan was also charged on one count of lying to the grand jury. Strachan told the grand jury on April 11, 1973, that on his own initiative he had taken $350,000 in cash in November 1972 from the safe where it had been kept and on his own initiative had returned it to Frederick LaRue rather than to the campaign committee treasurer. The indictment said he knew he was lying when he gave this testimony.

'High Crimes and Misdemeanors'

In the continuing debate over the definition of proper grounds for presidential impeachment, Nixon, the Justice Department and the President's lawyer, James D. St. Clair, all set out their definitions during the last week of February.

"You don't have to be a constitutional lawyer to know that the Constitution is very precise in defining what is an impeachable offense," said Nixon at his news conference Feb. 25. "It is the opinion of White House counsel and a number of other constitutional lawyers... that a criminal offense on the part of the President is the requirement for impeachment." *(Excerpts, p. 264)*

But this statement—and this narrow definition—were both at odds with the findings of the impeachment inquiry staff of the House Judiciary Committee, with the stance of the Republican leader of the House and with the views of a number of Judiciary Committee members.

On Feb. 22, House Minority Leader John J. Rhodes (R Ariz.) had defined an impeachable offense as not necessarily an indictable offense, but "probably...(also) an act or set of circumstances which would constitute a violation of the oath of officer or...the Constitution."

After the President's news conference, several members of the House Judiciary Committee disagreed with Nixon's narrow definition of an impeachable offense. The House has the power to impeach officials for a variety of actions—all serious but not necessarily all criminal, said Rep. Charles E. Wiggins (R Calif.). The Presi-

dent could be impeached for offenses "of a highly serious nature affecting the conduct of the nation's business," whether or not those offenses were crimes, said Charles W. Sandman (R N.J.). And Democratic committee member Jerome R. Waldie (D Calif.) said that "most people who have read the Constitution" would disagree with Nixon's interpretation of the impeachment language.

The Law of Impeachment. Releasing two portions of a five-part study by its Office of Legal Counsel on "The Law of Impeachment," the Justice Department Feb. 22 added still more to the debate over an impeachable offense. Prefaced by the statement that the views expressed in the study should not be taken as an official position of the Justice Department, Appendix I of the study dealt with "the concept of impeachable offense."

"All relevant clauses (in the Constitution itself) suggest the need for a criminal offense, although, of course, they do not expressly forbid an additional non-criminal penumbra," the study conceded.

"If there is one lesson to be learned from this material," it concluded, "it is that nothing can be considered resolved concerning the concept of impeachable offenses. The same basic arguments are repeated in each succeeding (impeachment) proceeding."

The Constitutional Standard. "The evidence is conclusive on all points; a President may only be impeached for indictable crimes. That is the lesson of history, logic, and experience," concluded "An Analysis of The Constitutional Standard for Presidential Impeachment," by the President's lawyers, headed by St. Clair. Released the afternoon of Feb. 28, the analysis took issue with another analysis made public by the impeachment inquiry staff a week earlier. *(p. 245)*

The men who wrote the Constitution reacted against the English practice of political impeachments—which demonstrated parliamentary supremacy—St. Clair's analysis stated. They rejected that use of impeachment in order to preserve an independent executive, it said. The language they adopted to define causes for impeachment, "treason, bribery, or other high crimes and misdemeanors" meant "such criminal conduct as justified the removal of an office holder from office. In light of English and American history and usage from the time of Blackstone onwards, there is no evidence to attribute anything but a criminal meaning to the unitary phrase 'other high crimes and misdemeanors.' "

Continuing to narrow the definition of "high crimes and misdemeanors," St. Clair interpreted the phrase as requiring not only "a criminal offense, but one of a very serious nature committed in one's governmental capacity."

Congress has clearly supported different standards for the impeachment of judges and for the impeachment of a president, wrote St. Clair; a judge who holds office for life "during good behavior" may be impeached for misbehavior which is not an indictable offense. On the other hand, "the use of a pre-determined criminal standard for the impeachment of a President is also supported by history, logic, legal precedent and a sound and sensible public policy."

The most notable lesson to be learned from the impeachment of Andrew Johnson, St. Clair wrote, "is that impeachment of a President should be resorted to only for cases of the gravest kind—the commission of a crime in the Constitution or a criminal offense against the laws of the United States." *(Excerpts from text, box, p. 254)*

Constitutional Confrontation

"I am prepared to cooperate with the committee in any way consistent with my constitutional responsibility to defend the office of the presidency against any action which would weaken that office and the ability to carry out the great responsibilities that any president will have," Nixon stated at his Feb. 25 news conference.

That same day, a letter had been sent from John M. Doar, special counsel to the House Judiciary Committee, to presidential counsel St. Clair, requesting many of the same documents and tapes that the White House had turned over voluntarily to the special prosecutor. The letter was expected to be only the first of a series of requests from the committee for information relevant to its inquiry into the evidence supporting the charges of impeachment against the President.

At an open meeting Feb. 22, Doar had told the House Judiciary Committee that it should not take the White House more than "a day or two" to comply with the initial committee request. No deadline was set for the White House response, but committee Democrats made clear that they would tolerate no delays. Doar said that if the request were rejected by the White House, he would return to the committee for a subpoena seeking that material. Albert E. Jenner Jr., minority counsel for the inquiry, said he felt it would be "asinine" for the White House to refuse to provide the committee with materials it already had provided to the grand jury.

One of the committee's Republican members warned: "If they're going to thwart our investigation down there, we're not going to be able to defend him...he's going to be in real trouble." Another, Robert McClory (R Ill.), expressed his confidence that the White House would cooperate fully with the committee, a feeling seconded by Edward Hutchinson (R Mich.), the committee's ranking Republican. Charles E. Wiggins (R Calif.) noted that President Andrew Johnson was successfully impeached only after he ignored congressional prerogatives.

Queried further at the Feb. 25 news conference concerning the extent of his cooperation with the committee, Nixon said that he would decide whether to turn over certain materials to the committee, depending on arrangements for the confidentiality of the materials and the risk that turning over the materials would jeopardize the rights of defendants in Watergate-related cases or impair the ability of the prosecution in those cases. *(Box, p. 255; excerpts, p. 264)*

Executive Privilege. A warning concerning the risk of asserting executive privilege in the face of an impeachment inquiry came to the White House Feb. 27 from an unexpected source—the Justice Department.

Appendix III of its study of the legal aspects of impeachment dealt with executive privilege. "Precedents relating to the subject of executive privilege in presidential impeachment are meager, confused, and inconclusive," it began. "In the only impeachment of a President in the nation's history, Andrew Johnson did not appear to give testimony and he did not assert the claim of executive privilege."

Presidential statements on the subject were not clear, stated the study, but the alternatives operated within a narrow range: the presidential power to invoke executive privilege in an impeachment proceeding was either nonexistent or subject to extraordinary restraint.

"Conceivably, in impeachment by the House or in the trial by the Senate, the President may feel that it is his constitutional duty not to disclose certain information which may endanger national security or the conduct of foreign affairs. It is unclear how the propriety of the President's refusal to make such information available may be tested.... A Chief Justice's ruling that the President may decline to disclose might then be overridden by the Senate, following established custom that (in an impeachment trial) the Senate has the last word on admissibility of evidence," said the study.

"If the President persisted in his refusal to comply, a constitutional confrontation of the highest magnitude would ensue," it concluded.

Post-Indictment Cooperation? Not only would he seek information from the White House directly, Doar had told the Judiciary Committee Feb. 22, but he also would continue to work with Jaworski to devise some method of cooperation and transfer of material between the impeachment inquiry staff and the staff of the special prosecutor. In the week ending with the long-awaited indictments from the grand jury, Jaworski himself indicated that such cooperation might be forthcoming after the indictments.

Nixon revealed at the press conference Feb. 25 that he had received, and rejected, a request from the grand jury that he appear and testify.

In an interview the following day with *The New York Times,* Jaworski made plain that the request for Nixon's testimony had come from the grand jury itself and not from the special prosecutor's office. Subsequent news accounts explained Jaworski's interest in making this distinction, reporting that after months of study, the special prosecutor's staff had decided that any evidence of presidential involvement in wrongdoing should go to the House Judiciary Committee, not to the grand jury.

Subpoena Rejected. Citing the example of Thomas Jefferson, who declined to appear to testify at the trial of Aaron Burr, Nixon Feb. 26 refused to comply with a California subpoena requiring his appearance at the trial of his former aide, John D. Ehrlichman, on charges arising out of the burglary of the office of Daniel Ellsberg's psychiatrist. A letter from St. Clair to the District of Columbia judge handling the matter explained that complying with such subpoenas would place a burden on the presidency making it impossible for the President to carry out his duties—and that a state court could not thereby infringe on the effective operation of the presidency. *(p. 227)*

Week's Watergate Chronology

Following is a day-to-day chronology of the week's events in the Watergate case: *(Previous Feb. 21 event, p. 250)*

FEB. 21

CIA Tape Destruction. Rep. Lucien N. Nedzi (D Mich.), chairman of the House Armed Services Intelligence Subcommittee, which in 1973 investigated Central Intelligence Agency (CIA) involvement in the Watergate affair, announced that the agency had destroyed no tapes of Watergate-related or presidential conversations when it routinely burned a batch of tapes in January 1973.

Kalmbach Guilty Plea

President Nixon's long-time personal lawyer and fund-raiser, Herbert W. Kalmbach, stood before U.S. District Judge John J. Sirica in Washington, D.C., Feb. 25 and pleaded guilty to two criminal charges stemming from his 1970 fund-raising activities. In exchange for the plea and an offer of cooperation, Watergate Special Prosecutor Leon Jaworski promised not to bring any other charges, provided the California attorney did not commit perjury.

The first charge, a felony, involved Kalmbach's raising of $2.8-million for 1970 Republican congressional candidates. The money was funneled through a secret political committee set up in the White House in violation of the Corrupt Practices Act of 1925, the campaign finance law then in effect.

The second charge was the result of an agreement reached by Kalmbach and Maryland Republican J. Fife Symington Jr. in 1970 that Symington would be given an ambassadorship in Europe in exchange for a $100,000 campaign contribution. Such an agreement was a misdemeanor violation of federal statutes barring the awarding of government jobs as political favors. The appointment never came through, but Symington refused to take back his contribution.

Together, the two charges could bring Kalmbach a maximum of three years in prison and $11,000 in fines. Judge Sirica postponed sentencing to await a pre-sentence report and released the attorney on his personal recognizance.

As he left the court, Kalmbach said he was still working as Nixon's personal attorney. But he announced the next day that he had resigned from the Newport Beach, Calif., law firm he founded in 1967. Officials of the California Bar Association said they would look into the question of whether Kalmbach should be disbarred.

Haldeman Involvement. After Kalmbach's guilty plea, reports circulated that he would testify that it was H. R. Haldeman, Nixon's former chief of staff, who organized and directed the secret 1970 fund-raising operation, which netted almost $4-million. *The Washington Post* reported Feb. 26 that Kalmbach had given prosecutors details of secret contributions and expenditures totaling about $6-million during the 1970 and 1972 campaigns.

In testimony before the Senate Watergate investigating committee July 16-17, 1973, Kalmbach admitted raising funds for the original Watergate break-in defendants. But he insisted that John D. Ehrlichman, a former top Nixon aide, had assured him the money was going for a legitimate legal defense fund. *(Testimony, Vol. I, p. 193)*

Nedzi said he based his conclusion on a report furnished by the agency, along with evidence already gathered by his subcommittee. *(Earlier report, p. 232)*

Milk Indictment. A federal grand jury indicted Jake Jacobsen, a former attorney for the Associated Milk Producers Inc., for perjury in connection with an alleged $10,000 payoff from the dairy group to the Nixon adminis-

tration for its 1971 decision to raise milk price supports. *(p. 249)*

FEB. 22

Suit Settlement. *The Washington Post* quoted Democratic National Chairman Robert S. Strauss as saying the national committee had reached "general agreement" on a settlement of its $6.4-million Watergate civil suit against the Committee for the Re-election of the President and its finance unit. The figure agreed upon reportedly was $775,000. *(Earlier development, p. 234)*

Impeachment Inquiry. John M. Doar, chief counsel to the House Judiciary Committee's impeachment investigation, reported to the committee that he had received from Special Prosecutor Leon Jaworski an index of all White House materials the prosecution had received during its investigation. Doar said he would use the list, which included about 700 pages of documents and 17 tapes, to draft his first specific request for White House materials.

Justice Department Study. The Justice Department issued two papers on the historical background of the impeachment process.

FEB. 25

Kalmbach Plea. Herbert W. Kalmbach, Nixon's personal lawyer and fund-raiser, pleaded guilty to charges brought by the special prosecutor that he had helped run an illegal congressional campaign committee in 1970 and had offered an ambassadorial assignment in exchange for a $100,000 campaign contribution. *(Box, this page)*

Nixon on Impeachment. In his first news conference in four months, Nixon asserted that the Constitution was "very precise" in specifying that impeachment should depend on proof of criminal misconduct and added: "I do not expect to be impeached." In response to a question, Nixon also revealed that he had declined, on constitutional grounds, the request of a federal grand jury for his testimony on Watergate matters. *(Box, p. 255)*

Impeachment Documents Request. The House Judiciary Committee sent White House special counsel James D. St. Clair a letter requesting documents and tapes already supplied to the special prosecutor for his Watergate investigations.

Senate Committee Appeal. The Senate Watergate investigating committee filed a 40-page brief in the U.S. Court of Appeals in Washington, D.C., in support of its appeal of a Jan. 25 district court ruling denying the committee access to five Watergate-related presidential tapes. *(Ruling, p. 228)*

FEB. 26

Nixon Refusal. Nixon refused on constitutional grounds to appear as a defense witness at the California trial of his former aide, John D. Ehrlichman, who faced charges for his role in the 1971 break-in at the office of Daniel Ellsberg's psychiatrist. In a letter from presidential counsel St. Clair to Washington, D.C., Superior Court Judge Harold H. Greene, the President also declined to attend a hearing the judge had scheduled for March 15 on whether or not Nixon would be required to appear at Ehrlichman's trial. *(Subpoena, p. 227)*

Rebozo Deposition. Nixon's friend, Charles G. Rebozo, said in a deposition that he never knew the exact purpose of $100,000 in cash given to him by a Howard Hughes employee in 1969 and 1970, but that he assumed it was a contribution to Nixon's 1972 campaign. Rebozo said he transferred the money to different envelopes when a dispute erupted in the Hughes organization—and eventually returned the cash untouched. The deposition was given to attorneys for Common Cause, an organization that was suing Nixon's re-election finance committee over alleged illegal campaign contributions. *(Previous development, p. 231)*

Military Spying. *The New York Times* reported that the special prosecution force had opened an investigation into Nixon's handling of alleged military spying on the executive branch in 1970-71. The Times said Feb. 24 that Nixon personally had blocked possible prosecution of two Pentagon officers accused of stealing White House foreign policy documents.

Gray on Wiretapping. The Times also reported that the prosecution team and a Senate Judiciary subcommittee were investigating the possibility that L. Patrick Gray III, Nixon's former nominee for FBI director, committed perjury during his 1973 confirmation hearings by denying any knowledge of FBI wiretaps on newsmen and government officials.

FEB. 27

Jaworski on Indictments. *The New York Times* quoted Special Prosecutor Jaworski as saying that the Watergate case had not yet "peaked" and that he expected new disclosures. Jaworski said his cooperation with the House Judiciary Committee's impeachment investigation probably would improve after the announcement of Watergate coverup indictments.

Ehrlichman Offer. John D. Ehrlichman, Nixon's former domestic affairs adviser, had rejected an offer by Jaworski to plead guilty to one federal charge in exchange for his cooperation with the prosecution, *The Los Angeles Times* reported. The report, confirmed by one of Ehrlichman's attorneys, said Jaworski had offered Ehrlichman immunity from further prosecution if he would plead guilty to violating the civil rights of Daniel Ellsberg's psychiatrist in the 1971 "plumbers" break-in. Egil Krogh Jr., another former White House aide, accepted such an offer. *(Krogh sentencing, p. 209)*

Justice Department Study. The Justice Department released an edited version of the final three sections of a five-part study on the historical background of impeachment. It said there was no precedent for a president to withhold information from an impeachment inquiry on grounds of executive privilege and warned of "a constitutional confrontation of the highest magnitude" if Nixon did so.

Saxbe on Impeachment. Attorney General William B. Saxbe told reporters Nixon would not be impeached unless the House Judiciary Committee and the special prosecutor "come up with things I'm not aware of."

Milk Contribution. During the trial of an antitrust suit against the American Milk Producers Inc. in San Antonio, Texas, it was revealed that the group's chief attorney had admitted the producers had made a

---

Poll Report

President Nixon's popularity rating improved two percentage points in the latest Gallup Poll. And, in another poll, the percentage favoring his resignation was three points lower than it had been a month earlier. *(Earlier poll, p. 237)*

Popularity. For the poll published Feb. 17, this question was asked 1,591 adults Feb. 1-4: "Do you approve or disapprove of the way Nixon is handling his job as president?"

	Latest	Jan. 18-21
Approve	28%	26%
Disapprove	59	64
No opinion	13	10

Resignation. Gallup pollsters asked the same sample, "Do you think President Nixon should resign from the presidency, or not?"

	Latest	Jan. 4-7
Should	42%	46%
Should not	49	46
No opinion	9	8

This question was asked: "Do you think President Nixon should be impeached and compelled to leave the presidency, or not?"

	Latest	Jan. 4-7
Yes	38%	37%
No	51	53
No opinion	11	10

Persons interviewed were shown four statements and asked which came closest to their point of view. The statements: "(A) Nixon planned the Watergate bugging from the beginning. (B) Nixon did not plan the bugging but knew about it before it took place. (C) Nixon found out about the bugging after it occured, but tried to cover it up. (D) Nixon had no knowledge of the bugging and spoke up as soon as he learned about it."

	Latest	Nov. 2-5, 1973
Planned	9%	10%
Knew about	28	32
Covered up	34	34
No knowledge	17	15
No opinion	12	9

$100,000 illegal contribution to the 1972 Nixon re-election committee and that the organization wanted the money returned.

White House Tapes Check. The Stanford Research Institute, an independent, nonprofit research center in Menlo Park, Calif., announced that it had been retained Jan. 20 by the White House "to provide experimental work and provide consultations on the White House tape recordings." On Jan. 15, a panel of court-appointed electronics experts reported that the 18-minute gap on one of the White House tapes was caused by several manual erasures. *(p. 201)*   √

IMPEACHMENT INQUIRY STAFF: LARGE, YOUNG AND BUSY

It is the youngest, largest and busiest of Washington's special legal teams. Its mission is to ascertain whether proper grounds exist for the House of Representatives to impeach, and the Senate to remove from office, President Richard M. Nixon.

The outcome and historic impact of the inquiry depends heavily on the integrity of the investigation conducted by the 43 attorneys of the House Judiciary Committee's special staff.

If the evidence they produce is judged sufficient to justify impeachment by the committee members, the House and the nation, then their findings will form the case for the prosecution, the case which House members will have to take to the Senate for trial. Should the staff have failed in that task, and the House members find themselves standing before the Senate inadequately equipped, they would be "up the creek without a paddle," as one Judiciary Committee Republican has warned.

So who are these lawyers hard at work on the second floor of the converted hotel behind the House office buildings? Where do they come from and what are their qualifications for this almost unprecedented task?

The answers are not easy to find. Extensive security arrangements insulate the attorneys from the public, the press and even from members of Congress. Their names and basic biographical data were made public by special counsel John M. Doar Feb. 5. But further inquiries concerning which were selected by Republicans, which headed the six task forces investigating various types of charges against the President, and which attorneys were working in which subject areas, were all met ·with the response that that information was to remain confidential—to protect staff members from possible harassment or pressure.

Even as Doar was selecting his staff, he barred all contact with the press, fearful of the news leaks which had resulted in so many front page stories during the investigations by the Senate Watergate Committee. He appointed Donald Coppock, a veteran of 32 years with the Border Patrol of the Justice Department's Immigration and Naturalization Service, to handle press relations for the inquiry staff.

And rules adopted Feb. 22 for the staff stated plainly: "The staff of the impeachment inquiry shall not discuss with anyone outside the staff either the substance or procedure of their work or that of the committee." *(Box p. 263)*

A Youthful Profile

Despite the tight lid on information, the basic data provided allows a profile of the staff to be traced. It resembles a newly organized, medium-size Washington law firm headed by two distinguished senior partners of wide reputation, with a few younger partners and a large number of associates only recently graduated from law school. The age range is from 66 to 25; the average age is 33. The salary range is from $36,000 to $14,000.

Compared to the other special legal teams in town, the impeachment inquiry staff is large. When supporting personnel—investigators, secretaries, clerks—are added to the 43 lawyers, the total is close to 100. With that weight, it outnumbers the 38 members of the House Judiciary Committee, all of whom are lawyers, the 17 attorneys and 64 total staff of the Senate Watergate Committee, and the 38 lawyers and 80 total staff of the special Watergate prosecutor's office.

The 43 attorneys selected—actually 41 when Doar and minority counsel Albert E. Jenner Jr. are excepted— were chosen from more than 400 applications. A dozen were selected by Jenner and the minority members of the committee, the remainder by Doar and the Democrats on the committee. The average age of those selected by the Republicans—36—is slightly above that of the Democratic choices—32.

The Leaders. Jenner, a Chicago attorney of considerable renown in legal circles, is the most senior and experienced member of the staff. Senior partner of the firm with which he has practiced for more than 40 years, Jenner looks younger than his 66 years, with his stylishly long silver sideburns, his well-tailored dark-striped suits and print bow ties.

Jenner had declined when asked by Judiciary Committee Chairman Peter W. Rodino Jr. (D N.J.) late in 1973 to consider the post of special counsel. Doar later accepted the position. Later, Jenner said, he accepted the post of minority counsel only after "the Illinois boys worked hard on me," presumably referring to Robert McClory (R Ill.) and Tom Railsback (R Ill.), the two Illinois Republicans on the Judiciary Committee.

The unity and bipartisan nature of the staff has been emphasized from the beginning of the inquiry, and blurring of party lines within the staff has been facilitated by the fact that neither Doar nor Jenner fits neatly into a party label. Jenner, a Republican, is also a lifelong

John M. Doar   **Albert E. Jenner Jr.**

Two Distinguished Senior Partners

Committee Staff: The Chiefs

John M. Doar, 52, special counsel in charge of impeachment inquiry staff: Minnesota native; graduate of University of California at Berkeley Law School, 1949; veteran of seven years in the Justice Department's civil rights division, the last two as assistant attorney general heading the division; selected as special counsel by Committee Chairman Peter W. Rodino Jr.; selection announced Dec. 20, 1973.

Albert E. Jenner Jr., 66, minority counsel selected early in January 1974: Chicago native; graduate of the University of Illinois Law School, 1930; senior partner of Chicago firm of Jenner and Block; veteran of 42 years practice of law.

Joseph A. Woods Jr., 48, senior associate special counsel in charge of constitutional and legal research: Alabama-born; classmate of Doar's at law school; California resident on leave from Oakland law firm of Donahue, Gallagher, Thomas and Woods, with which he has practiced since 1950.

Samuel Garrison III, 32, deputy minority counsel: native of Roanoke, Virginia; graduate of the University of Virginia Law School, 1966; former commonwealth's attorney for the city of Roanoke; associate minority counsel for the House Judiciary Committee, and special assistant to former Vice President Agnew; selected by the Republicans to work on the impeachment inquiry; began work Dec. 1, 1973.

Richard L. Cates, 48, senior associate special counsel overseeing factual research: graduate of the University of Wisconsin Law School, 1951; senior partner of Madison law firm of Lawton & Cates; on leave to work with the committee since Nov. 11, 1973.

Bernard W. Nussbaum, 36, senior associate special counsel overseeing factual research: New York native; graduate of Harvard Law School, 1961; former assistant U.S. attorney for the southern district of New York; partner in New York law firm of Wachtell, Lipton, Rosen & Katz.

Robert D. Sack, 34, senior counsel: Philadelphia native; graduate of Columbia University Law School, 1963; partner in Wall Street firm of Patterson, Belknap & Webb.

Robert A. Shelton, 32, senior counsel in charge of office security and management: Atlanta native; graduate of Harvard Law School, 1966; recently named partner of Baltimore firm of Venable, Baetjer, and Howard.

Richard H. Gill, 33, senior counsel: Alabama native; graduate of University of Virginia Law School, 1965; on leave of absence from the Montgomery law firm of Hobbs, Copeland, Franco & Screws.

Evan A. Davis, 30, senior counsel: New York native; graduate of Columbia Law School, 1969; former law clerk to Justice Potter Stewart; general counsel for New York City budget bureau and chief of the consumer protection division of the New York City Law Department.

friend of the family of the present Democratic senator from Illinois, Adlai E. Stevenson III, for whom he has attended at least one fund-raising dinner.

Doar, 52, practiced law with his family firm in New Richmond, Wis., during the 1950s, coming to Washington in the last days of the Eisenhower administration to join the newly created civil rights division of the Justice Department. Although a Republican by background, Doar stayed on into the crisis-filled civil rights days during the Kennedy and Johnson administrations, rising to head the division from 1965 until he left it in 1967. After six years of service in New York City, first as a member and president of the city school board and later as head of the Bedford-Stuyvesant Corporation, Doar was recalled to Washington to head the impeachment inquiry.

A tall, thin man with short graying curly hair and wire rim glasses, Doar speaks carefully and quietly with the air of a weary college professor. His clothes match his demeanor—conservative dark suits, white shirts and dark ties. But Doar is renowned for working days and nights with little rest.

The Deputies. Only one other member of the staff besides Doar is in his fifties, and only four are in their forties. Two of those are Joseph A. Woods, Jr., a classmate of Doar's at University of California Law School who left his Oakland law practice to head the constitutional and legal research unit of the impeachment inquiry staff, and Richard L. Cates, an attorney who took leave from his Madison, Wis., law firm to join the impeachment staff early in November 1973. Cates, with Bernard W. Nussbaum, 36, a New York lawyer, oversees the six task forces engaged in factual research.

Serving as Jenner's administrative deputy is Samuel Garrison III, 32, who joined the staff early in December, handling much of the minority's selection of staff attorneys. A native of the Virginia congressional district which sent Richard H. Poff (R Va. 1953-72) and then M. Caldwell Butler (R Va.) to Congress and the Judiciary Committee, Garrison joined the staff after working as congressional liaison on the Senate staff of Vice President Spiro T. Agnew.

The Staff. Of the other members of the staff, one—Edward S. Szukelewicz, a veteran of 22 years service in the Justice Department, chiefly in criminal investigation and prosecution—is in his fifties. Two attorneys other than Woods and Cates—Dagmar S. Hamilton, who served in the civil rights division with Doar, and John Edward Kennahan, former commonwealth's attorney for the city of Alexandria, Va.—are in their forties.

Of the remaining 34 members, half are in their thirties and half are in their twenties. Eight of the latter are members of the law school class of 1973.

Described as senior counsel are four of the other attorneys: Robert D. Sack, who came to the staff from a Wall Street law firm; Robert A. Shelton, who came from a Baltimore firm; Richard H. Gill, a Montgomery, Ala., attorney who attended the University of Virginia Law School with Garrison, and Evan A. Davis, former chief of the consumer protection division of the New York City Law Department.

Shelton, a recently appointed partner in the law firm with which committee member Paul S. Sarbanes (D Md.) formerly was associated, is in charge of the physical functioning of the office, but the duties of the other three senior counsel are unspecified.

(Continued on p. 263)

House Judiciary Committee Staff: The Indians

Fred H. Altshuler, 30, Detroit native; 1968 graduate of University of Chicago Law School; four years' work with California Rural Legal Assistance.

Thomas D. Bell, 28, Missouri native; 1971 graduate of the University of Wisconsin Law School; on leave from position held since 1972 as associate with the Doar family firm—Doar, Drill, Norman & Bakke.

William Paul Bishop, 26, Atlanta native; 1973 graduate of the University of Georgia Law School.

Robert L. Brown, 26, Alabama native; 1973 graduate of Rutgers Law School.

Michael M. Conway, 27, Missouri native; 1973 graduate of Yale Law School; on leave of absence from Chicago firm of Hopkins, Sutter, Owen, Mulroy & Davis.

Rufus Cormier Jr., 25, Texan and 1973 graduate of Yale Law School; on leave of absence from New York law firm of Paul, Weiss, Rifkind, Wharton & Garrison.

E. Lee Dale, 30, native of Pittsburgh; 1968 graduate of Vanderbilt Law School; practiced law with Denver firm of Dawson, Nagel, Sherman & Howard.

John B. Davidson, 30, native of Chicago; graduate of Harvard Business School and Harvard Law School, 1972; on leave of absence from employment with Chicago firm of Louis G. Davidson and Associates.

Chris Gekas, 27, Chicago native; 1970 graduate of the University of Illinois Law School; former member of legislation and special projects section of the criminal division, Department of Justice.

Dagmar S. Hamilton, 42, Philadelphia native; 1961 graduate of American University Law School; lawyer in civil rights division of Justice Department (1965-66); lecturer in Department of Government, University of Texas (1966-73).

David Gordon Hanes, 32, New York native; 1969 graduate of Columbia Law School; former senior law clerk to Chief Justice Warren E. Burger; associate with Washington firm of Wilmer, Cutler & Pickering.

John Edward Kennahan, 49, New York native; graduate of Georgetown University Law Center; former commonwealth's attorney for Alexandria, Va. (1969-73).

Terry Rhodes Kirkpatrick, 26, Virginia native; 1972 graduate of University of Arkansas Law School; special assistant for criminal matters, Arkansas Supreme Court.

John R. Labovitz, 30, native of Washington, D.C.; 1969 graduate of University of Chicago Law School; staff of President's Commission on Campus Unrest; research associate, Brookings Institution.

Lawrence Lucchino, 28, Pittsburgh native; 1972 graduate of Yale Law School.

R. L. Smith McKeithen, 30, North Carolina native; 1971 graduate of Columbia Law School; associate with Wall Street firm of Shearman and Sterling.

Robert Paul Murphy, 27, Maine native; 1973 graduate of Columbia Law School; formerly attorney-adviser with General Accounting Office.

James B. F. Oliphant, 35, New York native; 1966 graduate of University of Colorado Law School; veteran of four years' service in the organized crime and racketeering section of the criminal division, Justice Department (1968-72).

Richard H. Porter, 25, 1972 graduate of Yale Law School; associate with Milwaukee law firm of Foley and Lardner.

George G. Rayborn Jr., 36, Mississippi native; 1963 graduate of Rutgers Law School; three years' service with the Justice Department (1964-67); federal public defender in Los Angeles (1972-74).

James M. Reum, 27, Illinois native; 1972 graduate of Harvard Law School; associate with New York firm of Davis, Polk & Wardwell.

Hillary Rodham, 26, Chicago native; graduate of Yale Law School; formerly with Children's Defense Fund of the Washington Research Project.

Stephen A. Sharp, 26, Ohioan; 1973 graduate of University of Virginia Law School; law clerk and then attorney in office of general counsel, Federal Communications Commission.

Jared Stamell, 27, Detroit native; 1971 graduate of Harvard Law School; member of judiciary committee staff since early 1973 after year of service in Justice Department.

Roscoe B. Starek, III, 26, Minnesota native; 1973 graduate of American University Law School; member of staff of Sen. Charles H. Percy (R Ill.), then of staff of Senate Permanent Subcommittee on Investigations, and then of Federal Energy Office.

Garry William Sutton, 30, born in Canada; 1969 graduate of Harvard Law School; associate with Wall Street firm of Shearman and Sterling.

Edward S. Szukelewicz, 57, Brooklyn-born; 1940 graduate of St. John's University School of Law; veteran of 22 years' service in the Justice Department, criminal division.

Theodore Robert Tetzlaff, 30, Milwaukee native; 1969 graduate of Yale Law School; former associate acting director of legal services, Office of Economic Opportunity (1972-73); on leave from post as associate with Chicago firm of Jenner and Block.

Robert James Trainor, 27, New York native; 1971 graduate of Villanova Law School; member of committee staff since July 30, 1973, after serving as staff member for House Select Crime Committee.

Jean LaRue Traylor Jr., 36, Buffalo native; graduate of State University of New York at Buffalo Law School; formerly with criminal section of civil rights division of Justice Department.

Ben A. Wallis Jr., 37, Texan; 1966 graduate of University of Texas Law School; formerly vice president for development, Club Corporation of America.

William Floyd Weld, 28, New York native; 1970 graduate of Harvard Law School; associate with Boston firm of Hill and Barlow.

William Anthony White, 33, native of Washington, D.C.; 1969 graduate of Northwestern Law School; former U.S. attorney, District of Columbia (1970-73).

(Continued from p. 261)

Education, Experience

Harvard, Yale and Columbia Law Schools can claim the largest number of alumni on the impeachment inquiry staff, with seven, six and five attorneys, respectively. Seventeen other law schools are represented, from California (Doar and Woods) to the University of Illinois, Jenner's law school, to Rutgers and Villanova.

Four of the staff attorneys are black: Robert L. Brown, a 1973 graduate of Rutgers Law School, which is located in Newark—hometown of House Judiciary Committee Chairman Peter W. Rodino Jr. (D N.J.); Rufus Cormier Jr., a native of Beaumont, Texas, hometown of senior committee Democrat Jack Brooks (D Texas), and a 1973 graduate of Yale Law School; Richard H. Porter, a 1972 graduate of Yale Law School; and Jean LaRue Traylor Jr., who came to the staff from the Justice Department's civil rights division.

And two of the staff attorneys are women: Hamilton, who served in the civil rights division with Doar before moving to Austin, Texas, where she taught at the University of Texas, and Hillary Rodham, a recent graduate of Yale Law School.

Experience. Despite their description by Rodino and Edward Hutchinson (R Mich.), the committee's rank-ing Republican member, as "professional" and "highly qualified," only slightly more than half of the legal staff have actually engaged in the private practice of law during the last 10 years. Of these, 15 have practiced law for only three years or less. They come from several New York and Chicago law firms, and also from Milwaukee, Boston, Denver, Montgomery, Oakland and Baltimore. From the Doar family firm in New Richmond, Wis., came a young associate, Thomas D. Bell; from Jenner's Chicago law firm came another, Theodore Robert Tetzlaff.

Doar, Garrison and 14 of the other lawyers came to the staff from some sort of government or public service; three others came from legal aid work; one from teaching and one from business. Eight have had Justice Department experience: Doar, Hamilton, Szukelewicz, Traylor, Chris Gekas, James B. F. Oliphant, George G. Rayborn Jr., and Jared Stamell.

Republican Selections. Approximately one-third of the attorneys selected for the staff were chosen by Jenner, Garrison and the minority members of the committee. Besides Jenner and Garrison, they were Gekas, Szukelewicz, Tetzlaff, John Edward Kennahan, Oliphant, James M. Reum, Stephen A. Sharp, Roscoe B. Starek III, Ben A. Wallis Jr., William Floyd Weld and William Anthony White.

Relevant experience was clearly a criteria in the selection of these attorneys. From a background of prosecutorial experience come Garrison, who served as commonwealth's attorney for Roanoke, Va.; Kennahan, defeated in 1973 in his bid for a second term as commonwealth's attorney for Alexandria, Va.; White, who came from the office of the U.S. attorney for the District of Columbia, the office which initially prosecuted the Watergate burglars; Oliphant, Szukelewicz, and Wallis.

Adding political know-how are Garrison, fresh from the office of the vice president, and Starek, who joined the staff after working with Sen. Charles H. Percy (R Ill.), the Senate Permanent Subcommittee on Investigations, and the Federal Energy Office.

Tetzlaff is not an unknown in Washington, having served briefly as chief of legal services for the Office of Economic Opportunity, until he was fired early in 1973 by Howard J. Phillips, appointed acting OEO director by President Nixon to dismantle that office.

Cost. The largest chunk of the $1-million which the House provided to the committee in November to fund the initial months of the impeachment inquiry was for salaries.

The top six men on the inquiry staff—Doar, Jenner, Garrison, Woods, Cates and Nussbaum—are each paid at an annual rate of $36,000. No other salary levels were revealed.

But semi-annual reports, printed in the *Congressional Record* early in 1974, gave some indication of the salary level of those who already had joined the staff in 1973. Top among them was Kennahan, an experienced attorney, who was paid at an annual rate of about $26,-000 for the month that he worked for the inquiry staff in 1973. Robert James Trainor and Jared Stamell, both hired earlier in the year, were paid about $21,000 a year, while Traylor and Brown, who came to work the Monday after the "Saturday Night Massacre"—Oct. 23, 1973—were paid at an annual rate of about $18,000.   √

Staff Rules

Following are the staff rules adopted by the House Judiciary Committee Feb. 22:

The chairman and the ranking minority member have made the following rules for the staff:

1. The staff of the impeachment inquiry shall not discuss with anyone outside the staff either the substance or procedure of their work or that of the committee.
2. Staff offices on the second floor of the congressional annex shall operate under strict security precautions. One guard shall be on duty at all times by the elevator to control entry. All persons entering the floor shall identify themselves. An additional guard shall be posted at night for surveillance of the secure area where sensitive documents are kept.
3. Sensitive documents and other things shall be segregated in a secure storage area. They may be examined only at supervised reading facilities within the secure area. Copying or duplicating of such documents and other things is prohibited.
4. Access to classified information supplied to the committee shall be limited by the special counsel and the counsel to the minority to those staff members with appropriate security clearances and a need to know.
5. Testimony taken or papers and things received by the staff shall not be disclosed or made public by the staff unless authorized by a majority of the committee.
6. Executive session transcripts and records shall be available to designated committee staff for inspection in person but may not be released or disclosed to any other person without the consent of a majority of the committee.

NIXON FEB. 25 NEWS CONFERENCE: NO IMPEACHMENT SEEN

At his first press conference in four months, President Nixon Feb. 25 declared that he did not believe he would be impeached.

Nixon also said he would not resign in order to save Republicans from losses at the polls in November.

The President answered 20 questions during the nationally televised White House conference. Ten dealt with Watergate. Following are excerpts from the news conference:

Executive Privilege

THE PRESIDENT: Miss Thomas, I think you are No. 1 tonight.

Q: Mr. President, to heal the divisions in this country, would you be willing to waive Executive privilege to give the Judiciary Committee what it says it needs to end any question of your involvement in Watergate?

A: Mis Thomas, as you know, the matter of the Judiciary Committee's investigation is now being discussed by White House Counsel, Mr. St. Clair, and Mr. Doar. As I indicated in my State of the Union Address, I am prepared to cooperate with the committee in any way consistent with my constitutional responsibility to defend the office of the Presidency against any action which would weaken that office and the ability of future Presidents to carry out the great responsibilities that any President will have.

Mr. Doar is conducting those negotiations with Mr. St. Clair, and whatever is eventually arranged, which will bring a prompt resolution of this matter, I will cooperate in.

Cooperation with Committee

Q: Mr. President, to follow up Miss Thomas' question, you say you will cooperate with the Judiciary Committee, but you can't say yet precisely to what extent. Can you tell us if you anticipate you will be able to cooperate at least to the extent you cooperated with Mr. Jaworski in terms of turning over to the Judiciary Committee roughly the same tapes and documents that Mr. Jaworski has?

A: Well, this is a matter, Mr. Jarriel, that has been discussed by Mr. St. Clair with Mr. Doar and the decision will be made based on what arrangements are developed between the two for the confidentiality of those particular items where they must remain confidential, and also based on whether or not turning over to the committee will, in any way, jeopardize the rights of defendants or impair the ability of the prosecution to carry on its proper functions in the cases that may develop. It is a matter that we are talking about and it is a matter where we will be cooperative within those guidelines.

Impeachable Offense

Q: Mr. President, may I follow on to my colleague's question and also to Miss Thomas' question. Within the past week or ten days, the House Judiciary Committee and the Justice Department have issued differing interpretations of what by Constitution definition is an impeachable offense for a President.

Now, as we all know, you are an experienced student of the Constitution, and I think people would be interested to know what you consider to be an impeachable offense for a President, particularly on the dividing line, whether it requires the House to determine that they believe that the President may have committed a crime or whether dereliction of duty, not upholding the Constitution, is enough in itself to constitute an impeachable offense?

A: Well, Mr. Rather, you don't have to be a constitutional lawyer to know that the Constitution is very precise in defining what is an impeachable offense. And in this respect it is the opinion of White House counsel and a number of other constitutional lawyers, who are perhaps more up to date on this than I am at this time, that a criminal offense on the part of the President is the requirement for impeachment.

This is a matter which will be presented, however, to the committee by Mr. St. Clair in a brief which he presently is preparing.

Request for Testimony

Q: Mr. President, has the Special Prosecutor requested your testimony in any form; and if asked, will you testify?

A: Well, I believe it is a matter of record that the Special Prosecutor transmitted a request that I testify before the Grand Jury and on constitutional grounds, I respectfully declined to do so.

I did offer, of course, to respond to any interrogatories that the Special Prosecutor might want to submit or to meet with him personally and answer questions. And he indicated that he did not want to proceed in that way.

Impeachment Trial

Q: Mr. President, under the—however the impeachable offense is defined under the system, the impeachment proceeding is the courtroom of the President—you have said many times that these matters belong in the courts. So, won't it be in your best interest and in the best interest of the country to have this matter finally resolved in a proper judicial form, a full impeachment trial in the Senate?

A: Well, a full impeachment trial in the Senate under our Constitution comes only when the House determines that there is an impeachable offense. It is my belief that the House, after it conducts its inquiry, will not reach that determination. I do not expect to be impeached.

Advice to Candidates

Q: Mr. President, this is a political question.

A: The others weren't political?(Laughter)

Q: Jerry Ford's old House seat was won by a Democrat who campaigned mainly on the theme that you should be removed or impeached or that you should resign. What advice could you give Republican candidates this year to counter that argument?

A: First, I want Republican candidates to win where they are deserving candidates, and second, I recall the year 1948 when we confidently expected to gain in the House and when Mr. Fulbright, as you may recall, called for President Truman's resignation in the spring because the economy was in a slump, and President Truman had other problems, and we proceeded to campaign against Mr. Truman. He was the issue. We took a bad licking in the Congress in 1948.

What my advice to the candidates very simply would be is this: It is that nine months before an election, no one can predict what can happen in this country. What will affect the election in this year, 1974, is what always affects elections—peace and prosperity.

On the peace front, we are dong well, and I think we will continue to do well. With regard to the prosperity issue, the bread and butter issue, as I have already indicated, I think that this economy is going to be moving up.

I think, therefore, it will be a good year for those candidates who stand for the Administration.

Income Taxes

Q: Mr. President, as you prepare to sign your income tax returns for this year, do you intend to pay State or local income taxes, and have you had any second thoughts about your claimed deduction for the gift of the Vice Presidential papers?

A: With regard to any State taxes or concern, I will pay any that the law requires. As I understand, in California a ruling has been made, apparently, that even though I have a residence in California that there is not a requirement that I pay California taxes.

I would be glad to pay those taxes and, of course, deduct that from my Federal income tax liability as others can do if they desire to do so.

With regard to the gift of papers that I made to the Government, there is no question about my intent. All of my Vice Presidential papers were delivered to the Archives in March, four months before the deadline. The paper work on it apparently was not concluded until after that time.

This raises a legal question as to whether or not the deduction, therefore, is proper. That is why I voluntarily asked the Senate control committee of the House and Senate to look into the matter and to advise me as to whether or not the deduction was a proper one. If it was not a proper one, I, of course, will be glad to pay the tax.

No Resignation

Q: Mr. President, you have said on many occasions that you would not resign from the office to which you were elected, but what if within the next few months it became evident that your party was going to suffer a disastrous defeat in this year's election, would you then reconsider your resolve on this?

A: No. I want my party to succeed but more important, I want the Presidency to survive, and it is vitally important in this Nation that the Presidency of the United States not be hostage to what happens to the popularity of a President at one time or another. The stability of this office, the ability of the President to continue to govern, the ability, for example of this President to continue the great initiatives which have led to a more peaceful world than we have had for a generation, and to move on the domestic front in the many areas that I have described, all of these things, these goals, are yet before us.

We have a lot of work left to do, more than three years left to do, and I am going to stay here until I get it done.

Q: Mr. President, you have made a very strong defense on the confidentiality of Presidential documents and other matters, and you have launched a program to protect the privacy of citizens of the United States.

In light of this, would you explain how you happened to issue an Executive Order last year, once modified, to allow the Agriculture Department to examine key points of individual income tax returns of America's three million farmers and a Justice Department advisory opinion saying that this Executive Order should serve as a model for all the Federal Government departments?

A: Well, as a matter of fact, in the privacy message, which, as you know, I issued on Saturday, I did not raise this question specifically, but certainly I want that question, along with others, considered, because in this whole area of privacy, it isn't just a question of those who run credit bureaus and banks and others with their huge computers, but the Federal Government itself, in its activities, can very much impinge on the privacy of individuals.

This is a matter that I think should be considered by the commission that I have appointed which is chaired, as you know, by the Vice President.

Kalmbach Plea

Q: Thank you, Mr. President.

Your personal lawyer, Herb Kalmbach, entered a plea of guilty today to a criminal charge of accepting $100,000 in exchange for an Ambassadorial post. In your capacity as President you approve of Ambassadors and send the nominations to the Senate, were you consulted in any manner on this engagement, and this contribution, by Mr. Kalmbach, or anyone else in the White House, and have you done any research on this in the White House to determine who is responsible for it?

A: The answer to the first question is no; the answer to the second question is yes, and I would go further and say that Ambassadorships have not been for sale, to my knowledge; Ambassadorships cannot be purchased, and I would not approve an Ambassadorship unless the man or woman was qualified clearly apart from any contributions.

Fair Share of Taxes

Q: Mr. President, thank you very much. To follow on an earlier question about taxes, April 21, 1969 was a significant day for you in taxes and for the country, too. That is the notary date on the deed that allowed you to give your papers to the Government and pay just token taxes for two years. On that same date, you had a tax reform message in which you said, and I quote, "special preference in the law permit far too many Americans to pay less than their fair share of taxes. Too many others bear too much of the tax burden."

Now, Mr. President, do you think you paid your fair share of taxes?

A: Well, I would point out that those who made deductions such as I made in this particular instance, included John Kenneth Galbraith, Jerome Weisner, Vice President Humphrey, President Johnson, a number of others. I did not write that law. When it was brought to my attention, rather vigorously by President Johnson when I saw him shortly after my election, he thought that it would be wise for me to give my papers to the Government and take the proper deduction.

I did that. Under the circumstances, as you know now, that deduction is no longer allowed. As far as I am concerned, I think that was probably a proper decision.   √

JUDICIARY COMMITTEE EFFORTS TO GET SEALED REPORT

A bulging briefcase, a sealed envelope and more White House tapes were the stakes in the waiting game being played during the week ending March 9 by President Nixon, U.S. District Judge John J. Sirica and the House Judiciary Committee, which was investigating impeachment charges against Nixon.

The committee March 7 unanimously took the first step toward subpoenaing the briefcase and envelope by formally requesting them in a letter to Sirica, who received them March 1 from the Watergate grand jury. Despite an apparent grand jury request that the material be turned over to the committee, Sirica delayed a decision, concerned that his action might prejudice the trial of the seven men indicted in the Watergate coverup.

Despite published reports that the envelope contained findings of Nixon's involvement in the coverup—and assumptions that the briefcase contained supporting evidence—the White House officially adopted a position of neutrality on the disposition of the material. Objections to any release of it came, however, from lawyers for the seven indicted men. After a March 6 hearing to air the positions of the committee, the defendants, the White House and the special prosecutor's office, Sirica took the matter under advisement.

Acknowledging that "the whole focus is changing from a secret investigation by the grand jury to a House investigation," White House special counsel James D. St. Clair said March 6 that the President would turn over to the House committee all the material he had given the special prosecutor.

But the limits of this "forthcoming offer" were soon clear. At his press conference that evening, Nixon said he would not give the committee everything it might request and that he did not intend to allow it "to paw through" White House files.

And at a committee meeting March 7, committee counsel John M. Doar told the Judiciary members that St. Clair had failed to respond at all to the committee's request for certain tapes and documents not provided to the special prosecutor. "This seems to say to me," said Doar, " 'Your case against the President is simply the Watergate coverup.' This was an improper attempt by the White House to limit the scope of the committee inquiry," he said. "No one outside this committee," he added, "should set the limits of this inquiry."

Although a move was then made for the committee to subpoena the tapes that day, Doar and Albert E. Jenner Jr., the committee's special minority counsel, advised a delay—until the material provided by the White House could be examined and further discussion could be held with St. Clair.

Republican and Democratic members alike indicated their feeling that a subpoena for the material would be in order if their request were finally refused.

A second major indictment of former White House aides cast into relief the effort of the White House to limit the scope of the committee inquiry. On March 7, former presidential assistant John D. Ehrlichman, former White House special counsel Charles W. Colson and four other men were indicted for the burglary of the offices of Daniel Ellsberg's psychiatrist.

Committee Agreement

The committee's backbone was clearly stiffening as its requests for information met resistance—and an implied challenge to its pre-eminent role in the first phase of the impeachment process. By the end of the week, Republican and Democratic members appeared to be in agreement on the proper steps to obtain the information from the White House and Sirica.

After a two-hour closed briefing March 5, Committee Chairman Peter W. Rodino Jr. (D N.J.) announced that Doar and Jenner would appear before Sirica March 6 to request that the envelope and briefcase be given to the committee. Repeatedly, Rodino and Doar emphasized that the committee was in no way submitting itself to the jurisdiction of the court by making this appearance but that they were appearing at Sirica's invitation.

The Constitution explicitly grants the House the sole power of impeachment, a power the House formally delegated to the House Judiciary Committee for this inquiry. Thus the committee had an overriding constitutional responsibility that rendered it co-equal with any other branch of the government, committee members declared.

"The committee has a right to the material" in the envelope and briefcase, said Doar, and if Sirica did not give it over, the committee probably would subpoena it. "I am sure that the committee is of a mind to exercise its power and authority," added Rodino.

The chairman also disclosed that St. Clair, in reply to the committee's Feb. 25 request for information from the White House, had said that a full response would come March 6. No move to subpoena the material would come until after that, said Rodino, setting tentative committee meetings for March 7 and 8.

"It is the duty of the White House to cooperate, and I don't expect otherwise," said Edward Hutchinson (Mich.), ranking Republican on the committee, who added that he had approved the request "in its totality."

Status Report. "It is not yet possible to predict a date when this inquiry will be completed," reported the inquiry staff to the committee March 5. Most of the preliminary collection and analysis of materials was complete, the report said, and during the next two weeks the senior staff would "determine which factual categories require further investigation," so that the staff could begin to focus its energies more closely. *(Box, p. 267)*

In addition to the material requested by the committee Feb. 25, said the report, "there are additional specific items needed from the White House.... We are preparing the requests now."

Areas of Inquiry

These were the six major areas of charges against President Nixon that were under investigation by the special staff assembled by the House Judiciary Committee:

• **Domestic surveillance**—which included the activities of the investigative unit known as the White House "plumbers," the use of wiretaps to overhear the conversations of newsmen and White House personnel, and the offer of a possible post as FBI director, made by former presidential assistant John D. Ehrlichman to the federal judge who presided over the Pentagon Papers case. As of March 1, the inquiry staff reported that arrangements for interviewing witnesses on these charges had begun.

• **Intelligence operations related to the 1973 presidential election**—which included the "dirty tricks" campaign and coverup. A preliminary report on the information gathered on these matters was under review for a decision on "precisely what additional evidence and witness interviews are needed... to complete these investigations," the staff reported March 5.

• **Watergate break-in and coverup**—which included the possible use of "hush money" for the seven original Watergate defendants, the firing of the first Watergate special prosecutor, Archibald Cox, and the presidential tapes and their gaps. The preliminary reports in this area were under review; "testimony and exhibits sealed by court order in Watergate-related litigation have not yet been obtained," the staff reported March 5.

• **Personal finances**—which included the President's gift of his vice presidential papers to the government, the sale of his New York apartment and improvements to Key Biscayne, Fla., and San Clemente, Calif., homes and grounds. "For several months the federal income tax affairs of the President have been the subject of an extensive investigation by the Joint Committee on Internal Revenue Taxation.... The results...will become available shortly," the report stated. "The inquiry staff is prepared to begin immediately to assimilate the results.... Meanwhile, the inquiry staff is preparing tentative lists of witnesses...and documents to be sought."

• **Political use of executive agencies; campaign fund abuses**—which included 26 individual allegations, among them those concerning the contributions from milk producers and from financier Robert L. Vesco. Requests for information concerning these charges had gone from the committee to several executive departments and independent agencies, said the staff.

• **Other misconduct**—which included the bombing of Cambodia, the impoundment of funds and the dismantling of the Office of Economic Opportunity. The legal issues involved and past practices of other administrations in similar circumstances were under study, the staff reported. "Within the next two weeks senior members of the staff will determine which matters should be pursued further," the report said.

Court Arguments on Report

The answer to the committee's first request for documentation from the White House came the next morning in Sirica's courtroom, as a hearing began on what should be done with the grand jury's sealed report and the evidence that accompanied it.

"The President has authorized and directed me to tell Mr. Doar," said St. Clair, "that the President is prepared to turn over to the House committee all of the materials that he has furnished to the grand jury without limitation, and further that he is prepared to answer written interrogatories and participate in an oral interview in regard to his answers if that is deemed necessary."

Such an interview, St. Clair said during a recess in the proceeding, would probably take place in the White House, with Rodino and Hutchinson asking the questions without other legal counsel present. St. Clair first said it was possible that the President would be under oath during the interview, but after lunch he indicated that this would probably not be so. In his press conference that evening, Nixon indicated his feeling that it would be inappropriate for the President to be cross-examined in public but that he would not object to being questioned under oath. *(Box, p. 268)*

Confounding reports that the court hearing had been requested by the White House in order for it to object formally to Sirica's turning over the report to the committee, St. Clair told Sirica that the White House made no recommendation on the disposition of the report. "Whatever you decide to do with it is quite appropriate from our point of view," he said.

St. Clair expressed concern at the "serious breach of grand jury secrecy" that had produced front-page stories over the weekend of March 1. The stories said that the sealed envelope contained a report that the grand jury had found Nixon was implicated in the Watergate coverup. St. Clair labeled those stories a "gross distortion of the facts" concerning the contents of the envelope. Later in the day, Sirica stated that St. Clair had been allowed to read the summary report contained in that envelope before the March 6 hearing.

Pre-Trial Publicity. If the White House did not object to disclosure of the report by Sirica, John J. Wilson did. Wilson, the 73-year-old attorney representing former presidential assistants H. R. Haldeman and John D. Ehrlichman, challenged the grand jury's power to make the report and Sirica's power to release it.

Special grand juries, authorized by a 1970 administration-supported law, could issue such reports concerning the misbehavior of public officials, said Wilson—but a regular grand jury, such as this one, could not. "A regular grand jury," he asserted, "has no power to do other than indict or ignore."

Warning that he would appeal any decision to release the report, even to the House Judiciary Committee, Wilson argued the danger of prejudicial publicity, which he said would make it difficult or impossible to find an unbiased jury to try the Watergate coverup case. "Whether our clients are the targets of the report or are mentioned...this extra-judicial act prejudices their case, and should be expunged as illegal and improper," he said.

(Continued on p. 269)

Nixon News Conference: No Clemency, No Hush Money

More forcefully and in greater detail than ever before, President Nixon March 6 denied that he had authorized either clemency or the payment of hush money for the defendants in the 1972 Watergate break-in. But he acknowledged that he had discussed these matters in some detail before rejecting them.

Nixon used a nationally televised White House news conference as his forum for rebutting implications that had arisen the week before. One of the seven former White House aides or Nixon re-election committee officials indicted March 1 in the Watergate coverup was H. R. Haldeman, the President's former chief of staff. And one charge against Haldeman was that he had lied to the Senate Watergate investigating committee in saying that Nixon had told John W. Dean III, former presidential counsel, that "there is no problem in raising $1-million...but it would be wrong." *(p. 251)*

The conversation between Dean and Nixon occurred March 21, 1973, and was recorded on a White House tape. The tape was one of 19 turned over to Watergate Special Prosecutor Leon Jaworski. Its contents had not been made public. They were important to Nixon's credibility, because the President had corroborated Haldeman's version. Nixon acknowledged at the news conference that the transcript of the tape could be interpreted differently by different people, "but I know what I meant, and I also know what I did."

March 21 Meeting. In recounting the March 21 meeting with Dean, Nixon told reporters that he had learned for the first time at the meeting that money had been paid to the Watergate defendants for their silence, not just for their legal expenses. The President said he informed Dean, in these exact words: "It is wrong; that is for sure."

Nixon went on to say that he meant "the whole transaction was wrong, the transaction for the purpose of keeping this whole matter covered up.... I never at any time authorized clemency for any of the defendants. I never at any time authorized the payment of money to any of the defendants."

After four months without a news conference, Nixon held two within eight days. Watergate and related issues dominated the 35-minute session March 6. Fifteen of the 19 questions had something to do with the scandal or with the impeachment investigations that had sprung from it.

Judiciary Committee. Nixon expressed willingness to meet at some time with leaders of the House Judiciary Committee, which was conducting the impeachment investigation, and answer questions under oath. A prior step, responding in writing to the committee's questions, had been offered by Nixon's lawyer, James D. St. Clair. In court the day of the news conference, St. Clair had offered the committee all the records that had been given earlier to the special prosecutor.

In response to a later question, however, the President balked at a suggestion that giving the committee all the tapes and documents it sought would speed up settlement of the case. On the contrary, Nixon replied, it would delay a conclusion for as long as a year. Completion of the investigation could take months, he said, "if all that is really involved...is to cart everything that is in the White House down to a committee, and to have them paw through it on a fishing expedition."

But Nixon later repeated what he had said earlier —he wanted to remove the cloud over the White House. To do so, he said, he had cooperated with the special prosecutor and with the Judiciary Committee.

Cross-examination. Nixon said he would not go so far as to consent to cross-examination as a witness in the Watergate affair. "I will do nothing to weaken the office of the presidency," he said. "To submit to cross-examination under circumstances that would, in effect, put the President in the box when he was not indicted, in effect, by the House of Representatives—where he would be in the box if he went to the Senate—I think that would be improper."

Clemency for Aides. Granting clemency to his former associates who might be convicted of Watergate wrongdoing "would be improper," said Nixon, "and I will not engage in that activity." But he said he would not rule out clemency for an individual, "depending upon a personal tragedy or something of that sort."

Cincinnati Election. The upset election of a Democrat in Ohio's Republican 1st Congressional District March 5 might not be a clue to the results in November, Nixon advised, citing a handful of statistics from past off-year elections and Republican success in a California special election the same day as the one in Ohio.

"I believe that the dire predictions that are made as to what is going to happen in November because of what has been happening this spring will be proved to be wrong," the President predicted. It was an indirect reference to three Republican losses in the latest four House elections, losses attributed at least in part to voter disenchantment brought on by Watergate.

Impeachability. A questioner asked Nixon if he would consider perjury, obstruction of justice and conspiracy—the crimes in the previous week's indictments—impeachable offenses if they applied to him. Yes, he replied, adding, "I do not expect that the House committee will find that the President is guilty of any of these crimes to which you have referred."

The view of his attorneys toward impeachable offenses, described by some observers as a narrow view, was the "constitutional view," said Nixon.

Legal Expenses. The President said he would, if required to, pay for his own legal defense in an impeachment proceeding. "I should point out, however, that I am not a defendant until the House passes a bill of impeachment," he continued. "I would then be a defendant, and if the attorney general of the United States should rule that the President should pay for his defense, I will find somebody to loan me the money."

Mitchell-Stans Trial

The trial of two former members of President Nixon's cabinet on charges of conspiracy, obstruction of justice and perjury almost ended before it began. *(Trial opening, p. 248)*

Selection of a jury to hear the case against former Attorney General John N. Mitchell and former Commerce Secretary Maurice H. Stans was completed Feb. 28, clearing the way for the prosecution and defense to present their opening statements in U.S. District Court in New York City.

But immediately after the government finished laying out its case March 1, defense attorneys moved for a mistrial. Judge Lee P. Gagliardi said he would give their motion "serious consideration."

What upset Walter J. Bonner, chief counsel for Stans, and the judge was prosecutor James W. Rayhill's comparison of the trial jury with the grand jury that had indicted two of the President's former top lieutenants. In his statement, Rayhill said, "It is only by getting witnesses who tell the truth that our system of justice can work, and as you listen to the witnesses testifying before you, you put yourselves in the place of the grand jurors who investigated this case, citizens like yourselves...." At this point, Bonner interrupted to object.

The prosecution earlier had said it would show that Mitchell and Stans had tried to impede an investigation of international financier Robert L. Vesco by the Securities and Exchange Commission (SEC) in exchange for a secret cash contribution of $200,000 from Vesco to the Nixon re-election organization from Vesco, and then had tried to cover up the fact of the intervention and the payment. *(Indictment, Vol. I, p. 46)*

When the trial reconvened March 4, Judge Gagliardi denied the request for a mistrial. "It is clear," he said, "that an inference of guilt from the fact of the indictment was not planned by the prosecutor."

The defense then outlined its case, portraying the two former cabinet officers as men who had come up from the bottom, men who had worked their way through school at night to become wealthy and then devote their lives to their country.

After presenting its first five witnesses and getting into the record certain documents on telephone calls and meetings that it planned to use later, the government called up its first major witness, Harry L. Sears, a prominent New Jersey Republican politician who allegedly brought Vesco together with Mitchell and Stans. The government granted Sears full immunity from prosecution in return for his agreement to testify.

In his testimony March 5 and 6, Sears told of introducing Vesco to Mitchell and of inducing Mitchell to intervene in an SEC investigation into Vesco's affairs. Sears said he introduced Vesco to Mitchell at a political dinner in New Jersey in March 1971 and then began corresponding with and talking to the former attorney general about Vesco's problems with the SEC and, later in 1971, Vesco's jailing in Switzerland.

(Continued from p. 267)

Later in the hearing, Sirica asked Wilson what he thought about the position of neutrality the White House had taken on the question of disclosing the report to the House committee. "I don't care what the position of the White House is," responded Wilson testily. "I'm not working for the White House."

Discussing the problem of confidentiality and news leaks, Wilson said that the danger of prejudicial pretrial publicity stemming from Sirica's possible release of the report to the committee was aggravated by the fact that on Capitol Hill, "the leaks...are big enough to drive a truck through." *(Box, p. 270)*

Furthermore, he continued, under Rule 6(e) of the Federal Rules of Criminal Procedure, release of grand jury information was barred except in limited circumstances. The only one of those exceptions that might possibly be applicable, he said, was one that allowed release to a government official for use in future judicial proceedings. However, Wilson argued, the impeachment inquiry by the House committee was not a judicial proceeding.

Committee's Case. "Has there been any discussion by the committee of the advisability, the feasibility of delaying (its inquiry) until after the coverup trial?" asked Sirica of Doar. "I feel strongly, as Mr. Wilson does... concerning this problem of pre-trial publicity.... What harm would be done by waiting for this trial, which will begin Sept. 9?" he asked.

Both Doar and St. Clair opposed the suggestion of delay.

After Doar outlined for Sirica the rules the committee had adopted to ensure the confidentiality of material turned over to it for use in the investigation, Sirica pointed out. "You can't guarantee it (the confidentiality of the report) any more than I could the other day," he said, refering to the leak of a memo from the courthouse to the news media.

"This is the presidency" at issue, Jenner stated, rising to continue the committee's argument. "The people of this country are very anxious that...the House Judiciary Committee proceed with all deliberate speed" to resolve the matter of impeachment. "Your Honor has the briefcase.... You are a citizen. The House...respects you as an officer of a coordinate branch of the government, but however you came into possession of these documents, it is your responsibility to aid and assist the House...in discharging its predominant responsibility."

Wilson's points were sound but irrelevant, said Jenner. The situation, he said, was without precedent. The need to preserve the defendant's right to a fair trial could be met in a number of ways, he said, other than by keeping secret the contents of the report and the briefcase, even from the committee. Rule 6(e), which Wilson had cited as barring disclosure of the material, referred to matters occurring before a grand jury, not to related documents, said Jenner. That rule, said Jenner, was designed to protect persons under investigation before an indictment and to protect grand jurors from pressure. "It does not come into play in relation to the House...exercising its power to conduct an impeachment inquiry," he said.

"How you obtained the materials and whether the grand jury properly gave them to you is irrelevant," Jenner concluded. "It's what you do with them which is now of concern."

Government's Case. On behalf of the grand jury and the government, Philip A. Lacovara, counsel for the special prosecutor, argued that the grand jury had the authority to make the sealed report. He asked that Sirica grant the grand jury's request, presumably to pass on the materials to the House Judiciary Committee.

"This is an unprecedented situation.... We believe it would be unthinkable for any court to hold that this grand jury must remain mute" on matters relevant to the impeachment inquiry, he continued.

The contents of the envelope were not "an accusatory presentment," said Lacovara. Rule 6(e), he said, did not prevent their being passed on to the committee. "Neither Congress nor the (Supreme) Court (in approving this rule) would have cut off access of a grand jury involving matters of the highest national importance" by tieing the hands of a judge or jury and preventing the transfer of such information to the House, whose need for it must be considered of "supervening importance," he argued.

A Question of Limits

"It would be unthinkable for the committee to be unable to consider that material (in the envelope and briefcase) in its inquiry," reported Doar and Jenner to the committee March 7. Therefore, they recommended that the committee write Sirica requesting him to deliver the material to the committee "forthwith."

After some discussion, the committee by voice vote adopted a motion by Jack Brooks (D Texas) authorizing such a letter.

Queried by Jerome R. Waldie (D Calif.) about why St. Clair was allowed to read the two-page report in the sealed envelope, Doar said that he had no information on why that was permitted. "The President is being treated uniquely and extraordinarily by the court," protested Waldie.

Without specifically describing the materials requested, Doar then reported to the committee on his exchange of letters with St. Clair. Requested by the committee were:

• Some of the more than 700 documents and 19 tapes which the White House had already given special Watergate Prosecutor Leon Jaworski.

• A list of the materials for which Jaworski had asked but which had been refused to him.

• An outline of the indexing system for White House files.

• Six other tapes of presidential conversations relevant to the Watergate coverup.

In response, St. Clair said that "the specific materials you have requested that were furnished to the special prosecutor will be made available to you, together with any other materials which have been furnished the special prosecutor, without limitation....

"The President believes that the materials furnished voluntarily by him to the grand jury, which includes tapes of nineteen recorded presidential conversations and more than 700 documents are more than sufficient to afford the Judiciary Committee with the entire Watergate story. The special prosecutor himself has confirmed in the public press that the grand jury now knows the whole Watergate story.

"In addition to specific requests," St. Clair's letter continued, "you appear to have requested...access for

Leakage from Sirica's Court

"Leaks are a fact of life," remarked John J. Wilson, attorney for former presidential assistants John D. Ehrlichman and H.R. Haldeman, during his discussion in U.S. District Court March 6 concerning the dangers of pre-trial publicity.

"I found that out," responded Judge John J. Sirica grimly, referring to the leak of an inter-judge memorandum which he had written reporting that Watergate Special Prosecutor Leon Jaworski expected a total of 14 major indictments to come out of the work of his staff. One of the indictments was filed March 1; two more were filed March 7.

"Twelve More Watergate Indictments Expected," proclaimed *The Washington Star-News* on March 5, reporting the information contained in the Sirica memorandum and describing it as "the most explicit estimate on the scope of Jaworski's work to emerge publicly."

Obviously unhappy that the report had emerged into print, Sirica continued his response to Wilson in court March 6: "If I find out who leaked it," he said, "his job won't be worth a nickel—his or hers.... I thought it was a very terrible thing to do."

The six-page memo, which contained the Jaworski estimate given Sirica early in 1974, was written to support a suggestion by Sirica to the 14 other federal judges in his court that all the cases resulting from the Watergate indictments be tried by Gerhard A. Gesell, George L. Hart Sr. and Sirica himself. Sirica, scheduled to step down as chief judge of the federal court in Washington on March 19, already had assigned the coverup case to himself. Gesell was trying the Dwight Chapin case; and Hart, Sirica's successor as chief judge, had handled most of the illegal campaign contribution cases.

Sirica's memo suggested that setting up this three-judge Watergate group might be wise to ensure "fairness and uniformity (in sentencing, in particular) in an area where courts are often loudly criticized for inconsistency, and therefore, in the public mind, injustice." Such an unusual measure might also be justified, he wrote, by "recognition of the fact that the reputation of our court and the judiciary in general will be strongly influenced by the manner in which these unusual, and no doubt highly publicized, cases are handled."

Reaction to the suggestion from the other judges was apparently not unanimously enthusiastic, and the suggestion was tabled.

your staff to other Presidential papers, conversations and memoranda without apparent limitation except as the staff determines they are necessary for the investigation....

"The granting of a request for virtually unlimited access to presidential documents, conversations and other materials would, in the President's judgment, completely destroy the Presidency as an equal coordinate branch to our government and is beyond his constitutional ability to grant. Accordingly the President respectfully declines to grant such widespread access to these materials, assuming it is this that you have requested."

Poll Report

The public approval rating of President Richard M. Nixon remained close to its low point in the latest Gallup Poll published March 3. (*Earlier poll report, p. 259*)

Gallup asked 1,562 adults Feb. 8-11 and Feb. 15-18: "Do you approve or disapprove of the way Nixon is handling his job as President?"

	Latest	Feb. 1-4
Approve	27%	28%
Disapprove	63	59
No opinion	10	13

Stating that the committee should first define an impeachable offense before continuing with its inquiry, St. Clair also argued that "fundamental fairness would require that the allegations involving the President under investigation be identified so that the President could have at least some notice as to what allegations concerning him are the subject of this investigation.

"Surely a President is entitled to no less consideration than any other citizen...."

Setting forth the President's offer to respond to "relevant written interrogatories" and to meet with members of the committee, St. Clair then stated: "In the President's opinion, the Watergate matter and widespread allegations of obstruction of justice in connection therewith are at the heart of this matter. By making available to the committee without limitation all of the materials furnished to the grand jury...he feels that he will have provided the committee with the necessary materials to resolve any questions concerning him.

"He is confident that when these are reviewed, the committee will be satisfied that no grounds for impeachment exist."

Giving his view of the White House response, Doar told the committee: "This seems to say to me, 'Mr. Doar, your case against the President is simply the Watergate coverup. The evidence you need is just what we gave Jaworski. After you examine it, you will find that the President is not involved in the coverup.'"

Such a limiting response was inappropriate, he continued. "No one outside this committee should set the limits of this inquiry," he said.

However, said Doar, he and Jenner agreed that it would not be wise for the committee immediately to subpoena the White House material. "My judgment is that it would be well to examine and process the material from the White House, from Sirica, and to ask again of St. Clair for the six additional tapes," he said.

Despite Doar's recommendation that the material provided by the White House should be examined before a subpoena was issued for the additional information, Robert F. Drinan (D Mass.) proposed a subpoena. It would not be a "sign of weakness," said Doar, for the committee to delay issuing a subpoena until after the staff could examine the documents and tapes handed over and until Doar and Jenner could discuss the matter further with St. Clair.

But Drinan's move was considered premature by a majority of the committee's members, including Rodino, who asked Drinan to defer his motion in light of Doar's recommendation. Doar said he would talk to St. Clair that same day to be certain that there was no misunderstanding about the committee's request.

Key members of the committee on both sides of the aisle supported Doar—Charles E. Wiggins (R Calif.), John F. Seiberling (D Ohio), Tom Railsback (R Ill.), Don Edwards (D Calif.) and David W. Dennis (R Ind.). Dennis and Railsback made clear that they would support a subpoena "if it comes to that."

"We believe we can support fully...and justify the request for the additional six items," said Doar. The request to the White House for the list of materials refused to Jaworski also had been rejected, he said. St. Clair had suggested that the committee obtain the list from Jaworski himself.

"To delay issuance of the subpoena is to go the last mile with the President and his representatives," said John Conyers Jr. (D Mich.). And Drinan, admitting that bipartisan support of Doar's suggestion meant that "the votes aren't here" to approve his motion, withdrew it.

The Indictments

For the second time in a week, former White House officials were indicted by a federal grand jury in Washington, D.C. On March 7, the grand jury empaneled Aug. 13, 1973, to investigate Watergate-related matters handed up two indictments.

• For conspiracy to violate the rights of Dr. Lewis J. Fielding, Daniel Ellsberg's psychiatrist, by burglarizing his office, the grand jury indicted John D. Ehrlichman, 48, former assistant to the President for domestic affairs; Charles W. Colson, 42, former special counsel to the President; G. Gordon Liddy, 43, former staff assistant to the President; Bernard L. Barker, 56, and Eugenio Martinez, 51, convicted for the Watergate break-in; and Felipe De Diego, 51. Ehrlichman also was charged with lying to FBI agents and to the grand jury about his knowledge of the Fielding burglary.

Named as co-conspirators, but not indicted, were Egil Krogh Jr., who was serving a six-month prison term for his role in the Fielding burglary; E. Howard Hunt Jr., who was granted immunity by Sirica March 28, 1973, for his part in it, and David R. Young, another member of the White House "plumbers" investigative unit, who was granted immunity May 16, 1973. (*p. 209, p. 174*)

• For contempt of Congress as a result of his refusal to testify before the House Armed Services Special Subcommittee on Intelligence, the grand jury indicted Liddy. (*Vol. I, p. 218, 242-243*)

Part of the conspiracy which began about July 1, 1971, and continued until the time of the indictment, said the grand jury, was a plan "that the conspirators would, without legal process, probable cause, search warrant or other lawful authority, covertly and unlawfully enter the offices of Dr....Fielding...with intent to search for confidential information concerning Daniel Ellsberg, thereby injuring, oppressing, threatening, and intimidating Dr.... Fielding in the free exercise and enjoyment of the right and privilege secured him by the Fourth Amendment to the Constitution of the United States to be secure in his

Reaction to First Indictments

While most politicians avoided any comment on the March 1 Watergate indictments of former Nixon administration and campaign officials, several key officials in both parties predicted that pressure would be increased to impeach President Nixon. *(Indictment story, p. 251)*

The most outspoken reaction came from Oregon's Republican governor, Tom McCall. He urged Nixon to resign and spare the country the anguish of an impeachment trial. Speaking at a Republican conference in Seaside, Ore., McCall said, "The President is almost certain to be impeached and tried, and regardless of the outcome of the trial, both he and the country will lose."

Most politicians, however, shied away from calling on the President to step down. Rep. Albert H. Quie (R Minn.) acknowledged that "we're just plain stuck with him." But Quie warned that the indictments "increase the pressure.... We're one step closer to impeachment."

Rep. Richard Bolling (D Mo.) agreed. "There's more likelihood now of a bipartisan impeachment proceeding," he said.

Nixon himself reminded Americans that those indicted were presumed innocent unless proven guilty. "The indictments indicate the judicial process is finally moving toward resolution of the matter," said a statement approved by Nixon and released by White House deputy press secretary Gerald L. Warren.

Republicans tended to be more neutral in their public reaction to the indictments of former Attorney General John N. Mitchell, former presidential assistants John D. Ehrlichman, H.R. Haldeman, Charles W. Colson and Gordon Strachan, and re-election officials Kenneth W. Parkinson and Robert C. Mardian.

Appearing at the same conference as McCall, Sen. Robert W. Packwood (R Ore.) and former New York Gov. Nelson A. Rockefeller said that impeachment, not resignation, was the proper course to determine the President's responsibility for the alleged Watergate coverup.

Senate Democratic Whip Robert Byrd (W. Va.) warned that the indictments had a grim meaning for Nixon. "They pose serious implications for the President," he said, predicting that "public opinion is probably growing" for impeachment by the House.

Democratic liberals were especially harsh. Nixon's "soiled administration is now the chief threat to the presidency," said Sen. George S. McGovern (D S.D.), his party's presidential nominee in 1972.

Public reaction from most House Judiciary Committee members was relatively muted, but almost every member who commented agreed that the indictments would hasten the impeachment process under consideration by the committee. Rep. Charles E. Wiggins (R Calif.) said that in the aftermath of the indictments, "there is the greatest public interest to be served in a resolution of the serious allegations involving the President."

person, house, papers and effects against unreasonable searches and seizures, and that they would thereafter conceal such activities, so as to prevent Dr....Fielding from securing redress for the violation of such right and privilege." The break-in occurred Sept. 3, 1971.

Listing 19 overt acts in support of the conspiracy charge, the grand jury cast Ehrlichman, Colson, Krogh and Young in the roles of those who had conceived and authorized the burglary, which actually was carried out by Baker, De Diego and Martinez under the supervision of Liddy and Hunt. Liddy, Hunt, Barker and Martinez were convicted in the trial for the Watergate break-in in June 1972.

The maximum penalty for a conviction on the charge of conspiracy is $10,000 and a prison sentence of 10 years.

Ehrlichman. In addition to the charge of conspiracy, Ehrlichman was charged with four counts of lying, once to FBI agents and three times to the grand jury.

• Ehrlichman May 1, 1973, "did knowingly and willfully make false, fictitious and fraudulent statements" when he told FBI agents that "it had been over a year since he had seen anything on the 'Pentagon Papers' investigation, and that he had not seen any material covering the White House investigation of the...case for more than a year," the indictment stated.

• Ehrlichman May 14, 1973, told the grand jury that he did not know until after the Fielding burglary that the burglars were looking for a psychological profile of Ellsberg. When he made those statements, "he then and there well knew (that they) were false," the indictment claimed.

• Ehrlichman May 14, 1973, told the grand jury that he was not aware of the fact, before the Labor Day break-in, that an effort was directed toward obtaining information from Ellsberg or his psychiatrist. When he denied that knowledge, he knew his statements were false, according to the indictment.

• Ehrlichman May 14, 1973, told the grand jury that he knew of no files related to the Pentagon Papers investigation or other plumbers' operations in the possession of anyone except Krogh. When he made those statements, said the indictment, he knew they were false.

The maximum penalty for lying to FBI agents is a $10,000 fine and five years in prison. The maximum penalty for lying to a grand jury is the same.

Liddy. Liddy's indictment for contempt of Congress arose directly from his refusal to testify to the Armed Services Committee during its hearings into the alleged involvement of the Central Intelligence Agency in the Watergate break-in and electronic surveillance, the Watergate coverup and the Fielding burglary. Liddy appeared at an executive session of the subcommittee in 1973 but refused to testify.

The maximum penalty for contempt of Congress is a fine of $1,000 and a year in prison.

Week's Watergate Chronology

Following is a day-to-day chronology of the week's events in the Watergate case:

FEB. 28

Mitchell-Stans Trial. A jury of eight men and four women in U.S. District Court in New York City was selected and sequestered, opening the way for the start of the trial of former Attorney General John N. Mitchell and former Commerce Secretary Maurice H. Stans. *(Box, p. 269; p. 248)*

MARCH 1

Watergate Indictments. The Watergate grand jury indicted seven former White House aides or officials of President Nixon's re-election committee for conspiring to impede the investigation of the June 1972 break-in at the Democratic national headquarters. Three of Nixon's closest aides during his first term—former Attorney General Mitchell and former presidential assistants H.R. Haldeman and John D. Ehrlichman—were charged with conspiracy and obstruction of justice. Mitchell and Haldeman also were charged with giving false testimony to the Senate Watergate investigating committee, and Mitchell and Erlichman were charged with lying to FBI agents and the grand jury. Other former White House or campaign aides indicted were Charles W. Colson, Robert C. Mardian, Kenneth W. Parkinson and Gordon Strachan. *(Details, p. 251)*

Watergate Committee. The Senate voted to give the Select Committee on Presidential Campaign Activities an additional $300,000, bringing the committee's budget up to $1.8 million. *(p. 236)*

Mitchell-Stans Trial. U.S. District Judge Lee P. Gagliardi adjourned the Mitchell-Stans criminal trial to consider a defense motion for a mistrial after the prosecution, in its opening statement, told the jury that a grand jury of citizens such as they had found the case strong enough to merit indictment. *(Box, p. 269)*

MARCH 2

Watergate Indictments. A secret report given U.S. District Judge John J. Sirica March 1 by the Watergate grand jury described the jury's belief that Nixon was involved in a conspiracy to obstruct justice in the case, *The Washington Post* reported. The contents of the sealed report were of particular interest, because the indictment itself did not discuss Nixon's guilt or innocence. The Post said that the report contained about 50 paragraphs outlining the evidence against the President. The document reportedly cited specific acts by Nixon as well as a theory of the case that he participated in the conspiracy to obstruct justice.

MARCH 5

Impeachment Investigation. The House Judiciary Committee instructed its lawyers to tell Judge Sirica that the committee was entitled under the Constitution to any material relating to Nixon's conduct and that the committee was not subject to the jurisdiction of the courts. This represented the committee's first formal move to obtain the grand jury's secret report on Nixon's possible involvement in the Watergate coverup. *(Details, p. 266)*

Mayors on Watergate. Roy B. Martin Jr., mayor of Norfolk, Va., and head of the U.S. Conference of Mayors, said that Watergate had made it impossible "for government to govern." But Martin, the leader of Mayors for Nixon in 1972, called impeachment and trial of the President "disastrous for the country."

Mitchell-Stans Trial. Judge Gagliardi denied the defense motion for a mistrial, clearing the way for a continuation of the criminal trial for the two former administration officials.

Nixon Taxes. *The Washington Star-News* reported that the Joint Committee on Internal Revenue Taxation, which was examining Nixon's tax returns for the previous four years, at his request, would rule that he owed more than $300,000 in back taxes.

Nixon Claim. Nixon reasserted his claim that he told former presidential counsel John W. Dean III that it would be wrong to pay hush money to Watergate defendants. The White House statement said Nixon stood firmly by his statement at a press conference Aug. 22, 1973, when he called Haldeman's account of a March 1973 meeting with Nixon and Dean "accurate."

MARCH 6

Mitchell-Stans Trial. Federal prosecutors brought forward their first major witness, Harry L. Sears, who testified that he tried to use his friendship with Mitchell to help his own chief political contributor, Robert L. Vesco, end a Federal investigation of Mr. Vesco's financial dealings.

Nixon News Conference. In his second news conference in eight days, Nixon insisted that he never approved a promise of clemency for any of the Watergate defendants or authorized the payment of money to them in return for their silence. However, he acknowledged that the tape recording of his March 21, 1973, meeting with former aides Dean and Haldeman might lead to different conclusions. *(Details, box, p. 268)*

Watergate Data. James D. St. Clair, the President's special counsel, disclosed before Judge Sirica that Nixon had decided to give the House Judiciary Committee all the tapes and documents submitted to the Watergate grand jury.

MARCH 7

Watergate Indictments. The Watergate grand jury issued its indictments in the "plumbers" case involving the 1971 break-in at the office of Daniel Ellsberg's psychiatrist. Indicted on a charge of violating the civil rights of Dr. Lewis Fielding were former White House aides Erlichman and Colson, and Liddy, Bernard L. Barker, Eugenio R. Martinez and Felipe De Diego.

Liddy also was indicted for refusing to testify before a House committee, and Erlichman also was indicted on charges of lying to FBI agents and to the Watergate grand jury on activities of the "plumbers." *(Details, p. 271)*

The special prosecutor also filed an information charging Diamond International Corporation, maker of matches, paper and plastic products, and its vice president for public relations, Ray Dubrowin, with making non-willful illegal corporate campaign contributions of $5,000 to the Finance Committee to Re-elect the President and $1,000 to a representative of the 1972 Muskie presidential campaign. The company and Dubrowin pleaded guilty. The company was fined $5,000 and Dubrowin was fined $1,000.

Committee Request. The House Judiciary Committee voted unanimously to ask Judge Sirica to turn over to it the sealed Watergate grand jury report believed to deal with Nixon and the Watergate coverup. ✓

WHITE HOUSE CRITICISM OF HOUSE COMMITTEE INQUIRY

"I will not be a party to the destruction of the presidency of the United States," declared Richard M. Nixon March 15 to a friendly audience of some 3,000 businessmen and women at Chicago's Executives Club.

His answer, in response to a question on whether the damage of Watergate had made his resignation desirable, capped a week of White House counterattack against the House Judiciary Committee's impeachment inquiry, which the White House was clearly beginning to view as a threat to the independence of the executive branch. *(Text of answer, box, next page)*

The counterattack focused on the committee's request—sent to the White House Feb. 25—for certain materials not provided to Watergate Special Prosecutor Leon Jaworski. This, and other aspects of the request, were repeatedly criticized by White House spokesmen as overly broad, a mere "fishing expedition." Nixon continued this theme during his Chicago appearance, describing the cooperation with the House committee as "an unprecedented turnover of confidential materials...(including) several caseloads of documents covering items of everything from Cost of Living Council decisions with regard to the price of hamburger to oil and import quotas. The question now of course arises: 'Why not more?' Because the committee—or at least the staff members of the committee—and the chairman of the committee have indicated that they would like 42 more tapes...more documents, and in addition...an index of every document in the White House over the past five years so that their staff can determine what other documents or other information they need in order to find out whether there is an impeachable offense.

"With regard to additional requests," Nixon continued, "there are those who...would raise the question: 'Why not just give the members of the Judiciary Committee the right to come in and have all the tapes of every presidential conversation, a fishing license or a complete right...to go through all the presidential files in order to find out whether or not...some action had been taken which might be or might result in an impeachable offense?'

"The reason why we cannot go that far," explained Nixon, saying that in cooperating as he had he probably had already weakened the office of the presidency, "isn't a question that the President has something to hide. It is the fact that every president, Democrat and Republican, from the founding of this republic, has recognized the necessity of protecting the confidentiality of presidential conversations.... And if that confidentiality principle is completely destroyed, future presidents will not have the benefit of the kind of advice an executive needs to make the right decisions. He will be surrounded by a group of eunuchs, so far as their advice is concerned."

This defense, based on the need to preserve the presidency, fit with the statements of the President's chief defense counsel, James D. St. Clair, to *The New York Times* earlier in the week: "I don't represent Mr. Nixon personally; I represent him in his capacity as President."

But the White House counterattack—and the emphasis on the defense of the institution of the presidency—had less than beneficial results for Nixon's case on Capitol Hill. Stung by the White House refusal of the previous week to comply with its initial demand for information, and irritated further by White House tactics in criticizing that request, Republican and Democratic members of the House Judiciary Committee closed ranks.

Resentful of the White House effort to limit the scope of its inquiry and aware of the implicit challenge posed to the committee's prerogatives, several of the Republican members spoke out during the week in defense of the committee's request and its authority. Although the committee leadership and its special counsel restrained efforts on the part of some Democratic members to issue a subpoena to the White House for the information, the support for such a subpoena was clear on both sides of the committee's roster.

And the questions remained concerning the discrepancy in two of Nixon's public statements concerning the date he learned of "hush money" payments to the original Watergate defendants. St. Clair said that Nixon, as the nation's chief law enforcement officer, only had to see that an investigation of the matter was underway. But Attorney General William B. Saxbe made clear that the President "was no different than any other citizen" in his duty to report any crime.

Republican Warnings

Under the stream of White House criticism of its request for information, the House Judiciary Committee closed ranks to defend its rights and its reasonableness. Republican members, pushed to a choice between the man in the White House and the House committee, chose the committee. William S. Cohen (R Maine) told newsmen March 14 that whatever factions had existed within the committee were disappearing under White House pressure.

Republican members—and one former member, Vice President Gerald R. Ford—used the news media during the week to send a message to the White House to comply with the request.

Appearing March 10 on the ABC-TV news program, "Issues and Answers," Robert McClory (R Ill.), the second-ranking Republican on the committee, and Robert W. Kastenmeier (D Wis.), a senior committee Democrat, expressed unusually harmonious views. Both warned that the White House would be wise to provide the requested documents. Continued refusal would without doubt provoke a committee subpoena, they said. And Kastenmeier,

Nixon on Resignation: No Plans for 'An Easy Cop-out'

In a question-and-answer session before the Executives Club of Chicago March 15, President Nixon was asked: "Do you not think that the entire incident (Watergate) has begun to affect the quality of life in this country, particularly the great deal of uncertainties that people have about it, and also has begun to affect the concept of ethics, particularly in our young people? And for these reasons alone, would it not be better if you resigned at this time and allowed yourself the public forum as a private citizen to answer all accusations on all parts?"

This was Nixon's answer, as transcribed by Congressional Quarterly from a tape recording:

"Let me respond...first, by saying that of course Watergate has had a disturbing effect not only on young people but on other people. It was a wrong and very stupid action, to begin with. I have said that, I believe it now.

"Second, as far as Watergate is concerned, it has been carried on, it has been, I believe, over-publicized, and a lot of charges have been made that frankly have proved to be false. I'm sure that many people in this audience have read at one time or other either in your news magazines, possibly in a newspaper, certainly heard on television and radio, such charges as this:

• "That the President helped to plan the Watergate thing before and had knowledge of it.

• "That the President was informed of the coverup on September the 15th of 1973 (sic).

• "That the President was informed that payments were being made on March the 13th, and that a blackmail attempt was being made in the White House on March the 13th rather than on March 21st, when I said was the first time that those matters were brought to my attention.

• "That the President had authorized the issuance of clemency or a promise of clemency to some of the defendants, and that the President had ordered the burglarizing, again a very stupid act, part in the fact of its being wrong and illegal, of Dr. Ellsberg's psychiatrist's office in California.

"Now all of those charges have been made. Many of the Americans, perhaps the majority, believe them. They are all totally false, and the investigations will prove it. Whatever the Congress does, the tapes, etc., when they all come out, will establish that they are false.

"The President learned for the first time on March 21 of 1973 that the blackmail attempt was being made in the White House—not on March 13.

"The President learned for the first time at that time that payments had been made to the defendants, and let me point out that payments had been made. But correcting what may have been a misapprehension when I spoke to the press on March the 6th in Washington, it was alleged that the payments that had been made to defendants were made for the purpose of keeping them still. However, Mr. Ehrlichman, Mr. Haldeman, Mr. Mitchell have all denied that that was the case, and they certainly should be allowed the right in court to establish their innocence or guilt without our concluding that that was the case.

"Be that as it may, Watergate has hung over the country, and it continues to hang over the country. It will continue to as the Judiciary Committee continues its investigation, not only of the voluminous documents that we have already presented to the special prosecutor; not only of all the material they have from the Ervin committee that has conducted months of hearings —and they have access to that—but in addition, scores of tapes and thousands of documents more, which would mean that not just one year, but two years or three years we're going to have this hanging over the country.

"That's why I want a prompt and just conclusion and will cooperate...with the committee, consistent with my responsibilities to defend the office of the presidency, to get that prompt and just conclusion.

"Now under these circumstances, because the impression has been created, as you have very well indicated, doubts, mistrust of the President, I recognize that. Why doesn't the President resign? Because if the President resigned when he was not guilty of charges, then every president in the future could be forced out of office by simply leveling the charges and getting the media to carry them, and getting a few congressmen and senators who were on the other side to exploit them.

"Why doesn't the President resign because his popularity is low? I already have referred to that question, because if the time comes in this country when a president makes decisions based on where he stands in the polls rather than what is right or what is wrong, we'll have a very weak president. The nation and the world needs a strong president.

"Now, personally, I will say finally, from a personal standpoint, resignation is an easy cop-out. Resignation, of course, might satisfy some of my good, friendly partisans who would rather not have the problem of Watergate bother them. On the other hand, apart from the personal standpoint, resignation of this President on charges of which he is not guilty, resignation simply because he happened to be low in the polls, would forever change our form of government. It would lead to weak and unstable presidencies in the future, and I will not be a party to the destruction of the presidency of the United States."

going one step further, said that, should the President defy a subpoena and be found in contempt of Congress, that in itself would be grounds for impeachment. This view was endorsed by Judiciary Committee special counsel John M. Doar at a committee meeting March 7.

Appearing the next day on the NBC-TV "Today" show, McClory said that the committee undoubtedly would subpoena the materials if the White House refused to provide them. "It's by far in the best interest of the country and of the President to get this over expeditiously,"

A Question of Criminality Over 'Hush Money' Statements

"Who ever having knowledge of the actual commission of a felony...conceals and does not as soon as possible make known the same to some judge or other person in civil or military authority under the United States shall be fined not more than $500 or imprisoned not more than three years or both."—U.S. Code, Title 18, Section 4

Did President Nixon violate this criminal law by deliberately concealing the knowledge, which he said he acquired March 21, 1973, that "hush money" had been paid to the original defendants in the Watergate burglary case?

"Yes," answered one of those defendants, James W. McCord Jr. "No," responded Nixon's chief defense lawyer, James D. St. Clair.

McCord's claim was based on the revised version of the March 21 meeting that Nixon set forth in his March 6 news conference, when he said that John W. Dean III, a former presidential counsel, "for the first time...told me that payments had been made to defendants for the purpose of keeping them quiet, not simply for their defense."

Nixon said that he disapproved of the payment of such "hush money." *(p. 268)*

This version of a particular aspect of the meeting appeared inconsistent with Nixon's Aug. 15, 1973, news conference description: "I was then told that funds had been raised for payments to the defendants with the knowledge and approval of persons both on the White House staff and at the re-election committee. *But I was only told that the money had been used for attorneys' fees and family support, not that it had been paid to procure silence from the recipients."* (Italics added.)

The White House refused to comment on the seeming discrepancy and described it simply as a problem of "semantics."

McCord Letter. In a three-page letter written March 7 and sent to various news organizations, McCord wrote that the case against him and the other six original defendants would have been dismissed immediately—and their convictions overturned—if Nixon had made public his knowledge of the "hush money" payments. McCord noted that the day before the March 21 meeting, he had written a letter to Judge John J. Sirica asserting that "there was political pressure applied to the defendants to plead guilty and remain silent." The revelation of the use of "hush money" would have supported that assertion, McCord claimed.

The President's concealment of this knowledge of a crime was in itself the crime of misprision (concealment) of a felony, wrote McCord. Nixon did not make this known to Sirica, to the attorney general or to the head of the FBI. This combination of government and presidential wrongdoing "fatally infected" the trial of McCord and the other men arrested for the burglary of the Democratic national headquarters, he concluded.

St. Clair Rebuttal. In an interview with *The New York Times* March 11, St. Clair took issue with McCord. "The President is the chief law enforcement officer of the country," he said; his obligation when informed of a crime is simply to see that the judicial process is set in motion. The President did that, said St. Clair, citing the recent indictments for the Watergate coverup. *(p. 271, 229)*

St. Clair conceded that people could differ on whether or not Nixon should have immediately reported the payment of "hush money" to the defendants. But, given the President's position at the top of the law enforcement structure, said St. Clair, there was little substance to the question of whether or not Nixon was guilty of misprision of a felony.

he said. "The only way for that to happen is to get good cooperation from the White House."

Committee Democrat Don Edwards (D Calif.), also appearing on the program, denied that the committee demands were unreasonable. They were "specifically described" in the requesting letter, he said. "There isn't the slightest intention of anybody on the Judiciary Committee of going over to the White House on a fishing expedition or pawing through documents," he said, responding to a comment by Nixon at his March 6 news conference. *(p. 268)*

Ford told reporters March 12 that he felt Nixon had the right to judge the validity of the committee's requests, but that "a totally adamant attitude (on the part of the White House refusing to give up the documents)...could just be one of those catalysts" galvanizing impeachment. He said he did not think that such an attitude presently existed. Whether refusal to honor a committee subpoena would be an impeachable offense, Ford said he was not sure, "but it certainly adds fuel to the fire."

Sen. Charles H. Percy (R Ill.) said March 14 that he would vote to convict Nixon in a Senate trial if Nixon refused to comply with a committee subpoena that the Supreme Court upheld.

'A Fishing Expedition...'

At the March 7 committee meeting, Doar had described the contents of the letter he had sent Feb. 25 to White House special counsel James D. St. Clair, requesting material for the inquiry. Among committee members, only Chairman Peter W. Rodino Jr. (D N.J.) had seen the final draft of the letter. Ranking Republican Edward Hutchinson (R Mich.) had seen and approved a preliminary draft. To protect confidentiality, none of the other committee members had been allowed to see the letter. Elizabeth Holtzman (D N.Y.) said March 7 that she had asked Doar for a copy of the letter earlier and been refused.

Doar described the material requested in the letter as composed of four categories:

• Some of the more than 700 documents and 19 tapes that the White House already had given Watergate Special Prosecutor Leon Jaworski.

• A list of the materials for which Jaworski had asked but which had been refused him by the White House.

• An outline of the indexing system for White House files.

• Six other tapes of presidential conversations relevant to the questions raised by the Watergate coverup allegations.

The first request was granted by the White House, which said March 6 that the committee could have all the information and material that had been given by the White House to Jaworski. That should be sufficient, implied the letter of that date from St. Clair to Doar. The material was delivered to the committee the week of March 8-15.

The other requests apparently were rejected by the White House. On March 13, Jaworski provided the committee the list of material he had requested but not received from the White House. *(p. 270-271)*

St. Clair apparently interpreted the request for an outline of the indexing system as a request for unlimited access to the White House files; "such widespread access" could not properly be granted, he said March 6. In his news conference that evening, Nixon agreed, making 'his "fishing expedition" reference.

Following this lead, the White House repeatedly described the committee's request in such terms during the week ending March 16. Central to the White House response was the committee request for additional tapes that Jaworski had not been given.

Apparently attempting to discredit Doar and to imply that he had "hoodwinked" the committee by his March 7 description of the materials requested, an unnamed White House official (later disclosed to be Kenneth W. Clawson, director of communications) released part of Doar's Feb. 25 letter to the press March 11.

The leak—which infuriated members of the committee who had not seen the letter—was to correct the "misapprehension" that the committee had requested only six more tapes. In fact, said Clawson, the request involved a total of 42 tape recordings or segments of recordings. The letter revealed the committee's desire for "carte blanche to rummage through every nook and cranny in the White House on a fishing expedition," he said.

The recordings requested, of whatever number, related to six separate sets of conversations:

• Conversations on or about Feb. 20, 1973, between Nixon and H. R. Haldeman, then White House chief of staff, about the appointment of the deputy presidential re-election campaign chairman, Jeb Stuart Magruder, to a government post. Eventually Magruder was named head of the Office of Policy Development for the Commerce Department, a post that did not require Senate confirmation, a process that might have led to discovery of his role in the coverup.

• Conversations on or about Feb. 27, 1973, between Nixon, Haldeman and then presidential assistant John D. Ehrlichman concerning the assignment of John W. Dean III, then White House counsel, to work with the President on Watergate and Watergate-related matters. Dean testified to the Senate Watergate committee that after such a meeting, he met with Nixon for the first

Coverup, Break-in Arraignments

In a brief proceeding, dramatic only because of the positions once held by the defendants, seven former high-ranking White House and presidential campaign aides were arraigned in Washington, D.C., March 9 on charges that they conspired to obstruct justice by covering up White House involvement in the Watergate burglary.

"Not guilty to all counts," pleaded former Attorney General John N. Mitchell, former presidential assistants John D. Ehrlichman and H. R. Haldeman, former White House special counsel Charles W. Colson, former White House aide Gordon Strachan and former presidential re-election committee officials Robert C. Mardian and Kenneth W. Parkinson. All seven men were released without bail but were required to surrender their passports to preclude foreign travel. *(Indictments, p. 252)*

Judge John J. Sirica, who would conduct the trial of the seven men, gave the defendants until May 1 to file pretrial motions; the Watergate special prosecutor had until June 3 to respond to the motions. The trial date was set tentatively for Sept. 9.

Break-in. Erlichman and Colson also entered pleas of not guilty March 9 to all counts on which they were indicted March 7 for their alleged involvement in the 1971 burglary by White House "plumbers" of the office of Daniel Ellsberg's psychiatrist. The four others charged with conspiracy to participate in the burglary were arraigned March 14 in Washington. All four pleaded not guilty to all counts with which they where charged. *(Indictments, p. 271)*

Removing a major complication in the federal trial of Ehrlichman and G. Gordon Liddy on the latter charges, the Los Angeles County district attorney March 11 agreed to drop the charges of conspiracy and burglary brought against Ehrlichman, Liddy and David R. Young Jr. under state law for their part in the break-in. A charge of perjury under state law against Ehrlichman would not be dropped, however. Dismissal of these charges against Young, the former co-director of the "plumbers" who was named as an unindicted co-conspirator in the March 7 indictment, cleared him of all outstanding criminal charges.

The move to dismiss the state charges was explained as an effort to ensure fairness to the defendants, who otherwise would be tried in two different jurisdictions for basically the same actions. "Many of these issues involve matters of national interest, and, therefore, would best be decided in the federal court system," said the district attorney. The perjury charge against Ehrlichman would remain, because it dealt "solely...(with) a state interest," he said.

Dismissal of the case also would render moot the subpoena issued by a California state judge Jan. 29 ordering Nixon to appear as a material witness in the state trial of Ehrlichman, Liddy and Young. Nixon had formally refused Feb. 26 to comply, basing his refusal on constitutional grounds. *(p. 258, 227)*

time since Sept. 15, 1972 and told the President that "I had only managed to contain the matter during the campaign but that I was not sure it could be contained indefinitely." He was referring to the coverup of White House involvement in the Watergate break-in.

• Conversations on the afternoon of March 17, 1973, and in the evening of March 20, 1973, between Dean and Nixon. At the March 17 meeting, Dean apparently told Nixon of the break-in at the office of Daniel Ellsberg's psychiatrist by the White House "plumbers." During the March 20 conversation, Dean said, he told Nixon he needed to talk to him because "I did not think he fully realized all the facts (about the Watergate matter) and the implication of those facts for people at the White House as well as himself."

• Conversations on the morning of March 27 and the afternoon of March 30 between Nixon and Ehrlichman. Nixon had said that at this time he directed Ehrlichman to investigate the Watergate matter.

• All conversations between Haldeman, Nixon and Ehrlichman April 14-17, 1973. During this period, Nixon had said, Ehrlichman reported on his investigation.

• All conversations between Nixon and then Attorney General Richard G. Kleindienst and between Nixon and Henry Petersen, assistant attorney general in charge of the criminal division, April 15-18, 1973.

"This release of the letter," said committee Democrat Jack Brooks (D Texas) March 12, "is an affront to the comity between the White House and the Congress of the United States, and I think the hucksterism of the White House should not detract from the decency and forbearance of the committee."

But the White House criticism continued. Seconding a suggestion St. Clair had made in his letter responding to the committee request, presidential press secretary Ronald L. Ziegler said March 12 that the breadth of the committee's request demonstrated the need for an authoritative definition of an impeachable offense. It would be "constitutionally irresponsible" for the President to grant the committee all it had requested, he said: "The mere fact of an impeachment inquiry does not give Congress the right to back up a truck and haul off White House files."

The information already given the committee, said Ziegler, related to many other matters than the coverup. "Once they begin to assess what we are now...furnishing, they will conclude that they have sufficient materials to complete their inquiry...quickly," he said.

Later in the afternoon of March 12, Bryce N. Harlow, counselor to the President, said that Nixon had not foreclosed releasing the additional tapes to the committee, but that the President felt that the committee itself, not the inquiry staff, should decide what it really needed.

Committee Unity

Delaying the move to subpoena the White House documents, Rodino decided that the committee's regular meeting March 12 would consider matters other than impeachment. But the irritation of committee Democrats over White House criticism brought about a caucus of committee Democrats March 13.

Still advising caution, and reminding committee members that they were dealing only with St. Clair, not with Ziegler or Clawson, Doar and Rodino managed

Mitchell-Stans Trial

As the government completed taking testimony March 11 from Harry L. Sears, the New Jersey Republican politician who was the key prosecution witness in the trial of John N. Mitchell and Maurice H. Stans, it faced a two-pronged dilemma. First, it had to discredit those parts of Sears' testimony that could help the two former Nixon aides. Second, it had to corroborate other aspects of his testimony that it was using to build the conspiracy, obstruction of justice, and perjury case against the defendants. *(Earlier story, p. 269)*

While he testified for the prosecution, Sears had described conversations with Mitchell, Stans and Robert L. Vesco, the fugitive financier, and with William J. Casey, former chairman of the Securities and Exchange Commission (SEC), and SEC staff members. The Sears testimony laid the groundwork for the government's case that Vesco made an illegal $200,000 cash gift to the Nixon re-election campaign in return for Stans' and Mitchell's help in obstructing an SEC investigation into his tangled financial activities. The two former cabinet officers also were charged with perjury before the grand jury that indicted them.

Although he was a chief prosecution witness, Sears was also a problem witness for the prosecution. He testified for the government only reluctantly and admitted that he still considered himself a friend of Mitchell.

His trial testimony differed at times from his testimony before the grand jury, and government attorneys at times had no idea how Sears would answer questions they asked.

Cross-Examination. In his cross-examination of Sears, Peter E. Fleming Jr., Mitchell's attorney, attempted to dilute the impact of Sears' prosecution testimony. Instead of emphasizing the discrepancies between Sears' statements at the trial and his prior statements during 10 private appearances before the grand jury, Fleming appeared to suggest that either all memories are fallible or that the prosecutors had coached Sears in the responses they wanted.

Sears was an obliging witness for the defense. For example, Sears said on March 7 that he told Mitchell about the $200,000 contribution a few hours after he delivered it to Stans. But on March 12, Sears said under cross-examination that he had told the grand jury in 1973 that he never discussed the contribution with Mitchell.

The apparent defense strategy in the trial's early stages was to picture the alleged conspirators as a group of men helping each other out, as friends sometimes do.

The government already had recognized its problem with Sears and on March 6 had asked U.S. District Judge Lee P. Gagliardi to rule him a hostile witness. Gagliardi refused but permitted government lawyers to ask him leading questions.

to "cool the waters," said Rep. William L. Hungate (D Mo.).

"We're moving strongly and firmly ahead," said Rep. Jerome R. Waldie (D Calif.). "We're just not rushing." And even Robert F. Drinan (D Mass.), who had moved March 7 to subpoena the White House documents, said that Doar had convinced him that the committee should build a careful case "before moving further (in order to) avoid forcing a showdown on the wrong issue at the wrong time."

But a feeling of the inevitability of an eventual subpoena was evident among a number of the committee members. Several Republicans stated their readiness to back a committee subpoena. As Brooks put it: "I think they've turned the hourglass up, and the sand has started to fall through.... It's just a matter of time" before the committee would have to subpoena the information.

Hutchinson and Rodino, appearing with Doar and special minority counsel Albert E. Jenner Jr. at a news conference March 13, stood firmly together in defense of the committee's request.

"We believe these conversations are necessary to a full and complete explanation of the events...in connection with the so-called Watergate coverup and the President's relation with it," said Rodino. "We expect full cooperation from all persons. The Constitution permits nothing less."

"What we have asked for is very reasonable and very relevant," said Hutchinson. "It is necessary to the inquiry. There would be no inquiry if there were no suspicions about the President's actions in connection with the so-called Watergate coverup."

St. Clair was well aware that the request was no "fishing expedition," said committee special counsel Doar and Jenner. "We spent two and one-half hours with him on Monday (March 11) going over in detail what we wanted and why. There is no misunderstanding on his part of what the committee request is," said Jenner.

The suggestion that the committee adopt an authoritative definition of an impeachable offense was rejected by both committee leaders, who held that each member must make that determination for himself. A committee-approved definition could not effectively bind any member; the attempt to reach such a definition would be "time-consuming and futile," said Hutchinson.

Another suggestion, from Sen. Norris Cotton (R N.H.), who had said that Nixon had indicated to him that he was thinking of finding some trustworty third party to decide which White House materials were relevant and should be handed over to the committee, also was rejected. "That would be totally inappropriate," said Hutchinson.

The Sealed Report

Early in the week, it was disclosed that St. Clair had requested Judge John J. Sirica, if he should decide to give to the House committee the sealed report, briefcase and summary he had received from the Watergate grand jury March 1, to allow St. Clair to review the report. The House committee wrote Sirica a letter March 12, asking that he reject this request. Sirica's ruling on the matter had been expected during the week ending March 16, but on March 15 it was announced that it would not be released until March 18.

The report that Jaworski had determined that a president should not be indicted before he was impeached was confirmed March 11, when a spokesman for Jaworski's office said that Jaworski had advised the Watergate grand jury that it would not be responsible for them to indict Nixon if the jury found him involved in improper activity related to the Watergate break-in and coverup.

Instead, Jaworski suggested that the House Judiciary Committee was the proper forum for evidence relating to such involvement of a President. The spokesman said that Jaworski felt that "the trauma the nation would suffer in the interim—let alone the scar such action would leave on the institution of the presidency—renders (indictment of a President) inadvisable regardless of whether the evidence otherwise would warrant it."

Presidential Tax Troubles

Nixon's tax problems, not his involvement in the Watergate coverup, might be the crucial development that could force him to resign. That was how, in an interview March 8, Rep. Wilbur D. Mills (D Ark.) viewed the potentially explosive issue of the President's income tax payments.

Mills, vice chairman of the Joint Committee on Internal Revenue Taxation, which was investigating Nixon's tax returns for 1969 through 1972, said the committee's findings would increase pressure on the President to step down. The committee was expected to report on its investigation in April.

Mills, also chairman of the House Ways and Means Committee, did not predict Nixon's resignation outright. But he did say the President should resign. Asked why, he replied, "That will come out later. You will know about it in 30 or 40 days." Mills refused to discuss what the committee report would say, but he dropped several hints that it would be devastating and would seriously damage Nixon's already weakened political position.

Reports that the joint committee would find that the President had erred in taking substantial deductions for the donation of his vice presidential papers to the National Archives began to appear March 5. But Mills' comments were the first public indication that Nixon could expect serious trouble from the report. "Those I have talked to are dissatisfied with the President's handling of his tax returns," Mills said.

White House Reaction. An already sensitive White House responded sharply to Mills' comments. An official who asked not to be named said March 8, "Congressman Mills is taking a dirty, cheap shot that is unbecoming his place as a respected member of Congress. Utilizing a scare tactic by referring to a report which I believe is non-existent is the lowest form of political demagoguery."

On March 12, Bryce N. Harlow, counselor to the President, stepped up the White House counterattack against Mills, calling on the Arkansan to "put up or shut up."

But Mills held firm. He reportedly told other members of Congress who called him about his earlier statement that the American people would be outraged when they saw the forthcoming report, because, he said, there would be so many different items on which the legality, or at least the morality, of Nixon's claims would be questioned.

Poll Report

A majority of the people questioned in the latest Harris Survey said they thought impeachment charges should be brought against President Nixon if he did not give the House Judiciary Committee the information it sought. A larger majority thought he would withhold information. (*Earlier poll report, p. 271*)

Interviewing was conducted Feb. 18-22 for the poll, published March 11. These were the questions asked of 1,665 households:

"Do you feel President Nixon has been frank and honest in the Watergate affair, or do you feel that he has withheld important information on it?"

	Latest	January
Frank, honest	18%	18%
Withheld facts	71	73
Not sure	11	9

"Do you think President Nixon will turn over all the evidence to the House Judiciary Committee, or do you think he will withhold important information from them?"

Turn over	17%
Withhold	64
Not sure	19

"If President Nixon fails to turn over the information the House Judiciary Committee wants, do you think that committee should vote to bring up impeachment charges against the President, or not?"

Should	54%
Should not	32
Not sure	14

Other Developments. The President had suggested in June 1969 that members of his staff be given access to the tax returns of former presidents so that he could learn what deductions they had taken, according to an internal White House memorandum leaked to the press March 11.

California State Controller Houston I. Flournoy, chairman of the state franchise tax board, said March 5 that Nixon might have to pay state capital gains taxes on San Clemente property he had sold. (*Nixon's tax problems, p. 181*)

Week's Watergate Chronology

Following is a day-to-day chronology of the week's events in the Watergate case: (*Earlier March 7 events, p. 273*)

MARCH 7

Mitchell-Stans Trial. Government witness Harry L. Sears alleged that John N. Mitchell, the former attorney general, called William J. Casey, chairman of the Securities and Exchange Commission (SEC), to arrange a meeting between Sears and Casey within hours after Robert L. Vesco, the international financier, contributed $200,000 in cash to Nixon's re-election campaign. Sears said he, Casey and other SEC officials discussed the commission's investigation of Vesco's financial operation. (*Box, p. 278*)

MARCH 8

Nixon on Reform. Nixon unveiled a campaign reform plan that would set limits on campaign contributions, bar cash contributions over $50 and restrict the campaign activities of large, special-interest organizations. The President reiterated his strong opposition to public financing of elections.

Mitchell-Stans Trial. In his fourth day on the witness stand, Sears testified that Vesco tried to use Nixon's two brothers, F. Donald and Edward, to stop the SEC investigation of his financial dealings. Sears also said that Vesco had made efforts to frighten former Attorney General Mitchell into quashing the investigation by threatening to expose his Nixon campaign contribution.

McCord on Hush Money. James W. McCord, one of the original Watergate conspirators, accused Nixon of having "deliberately concealed and suppressed" knowledge of hush-money payments to Watergate defendants. Had the President spoken out when he first learned of the payments, the convictions of the Watergate conspirators "would have been overturned," McCord said. (*Box, p. 276*)

Nixon Tax Returns. Rep. Wilbur D. Mills (D Ark.), vice chairman of the Joint Committee on Internal Revenue Taxation, predicted that the committee's study of the President's disputed tax returns would be so damaging that pressure would increase for Nixon's resignation. (*Details, p. 279*)

MARCH 9

Watergate Arraignment. Seven former presidential and Nixon re-election aides indicted for covering up the Watergate burglary pleaded not guilty before U.S. District Judge John J. Sirica in Washington. Two of the seven, John D. Ehrlichman and Charles W. Colson, also pleaded not guilty to charges related to their alleged involvement with the burglary of the office of Daniel Ellsberg's psychiatrist. (*Box, p. 267*)

MARCH 11

Ellsberg Burglary Charges. Los Angeles County District Attorney Joseph Busch agreed to seek dismissal of California charges against former White House aides Ehrlichman, G. Gordon Liddy and David R. Young for alleged involvement in the 1971 burglary of the psychiatrist's office. State perjury charges against Ehrlichman were still pending.

Fraud Investigation. Nixon's 1969 income tax return, which included the deduction of the donation of his vice presidential papers, was the subject of a criminal fraud investigation by the Internal Revenue Service, *Newsweek* magazine reported.

Nixon Tax Request. Quoting an internal White House memorandum, *The New York Times* reported that the President had suggested in June 1969 that members of his staff be given access to the tax returns of former presidents so he could learn what tax deductions they had taken. The memorandum was written by John D. Ehrlichman, then an adviser to the President.

Mitchell-Stans Trial. The prosecution read a seven-page, unsigned typewritten memorandum allegedly written by Robert L. Vesco, that depicted Vesco as being so frantic about an SEC investigation into his financial operations that he warned F. Donald Nixon, the President's brother, that there would be national and international repercussions if the investigation were not halted.

Meanwhile, it was reported that F. Donald Nixon, whose name had been mentioned several times in trial testimony, was trying to quash, on grounds of ill health, a subpoena requiring him to testify at the trial.

Judiciary Committee Request. By leaking to the press the House Judiciary Committee's Feb. 25 letter requesting information from the White House, the White House revealed that the committee had asked for tapes of 42 presidential conversations, tapes not provided to the special Watergate prosecutor.

St. Clair Interview. In an interview with *The New York Times,* James D. St. Clair, the President's chief defense lawyer, defended Nixon against suggestions that he violated the law when he did not report to federal prosecutors as soon as he found out that hush money had been paid to the Watergate burglars. *(Box, p. 276)*

Ford Hedge. In a political appearance in Boston, Vice President Gerald R. Ford appeared to hedge his support of Nixon, saying that he was still convinced that Nixon was not involved in Watergate or its coverup but then adding, "But time will tell."

Jaworski Advice. Leon Jaworski, the Watergate special prosecutor, had advised the Watergate grand jury that it would not be "responsible conduct" to indict Nixon, according to a spokesman for his office. His advice included the suggestion that the House Judiciary Committee was the proper body to consider evidence relating to a president.

Nixon Defense. Responding to Rep. Mills' prediction that a congressional committee report on the President's tax returns would increase pressure for his resignation, Bryce N. Harlow, counselor to the President, accused Mills of engaging in McCarthy-like tactics. Harlow told Mills to "put up or shut up."

MARCH 12

White House Unwillingness. Ronald L. Ziegler, Nixon's press secretary, suggested that the President would be unwilling to supply the additional tapes requested by the House Judiciary Committee for its impeachment inquiry until the committee defined an impeachable offense.

Ford Reaction. Vice President Ford told newsmen that White House refusal to comply with a House subpoena, should one be issued for the materials, might be the catalyst that would bring about Nixon's impeachment.

Hush Money. The Watergate grand jury concluded that a disputed hush money payment to the attorney for conspirator E. Howard Hunt Jr. was made on the evening of March 21, 1973, less than 12 hours after a White House meeting of Nixon, Haldeman, Ehrlichman and John W. Dean III, *The New York Times* reported.

Mitchell-Stans Trial. Under defense cross-examination, Harry L. Sears asserted that "never at any time" did he ask John N. Mitchell to "fix" a case against Robert L. Vesco, the fugitive financier.

St. Clair Interview. In an interview in *The New York Times,* James D. St. Clair, Nixon's lawyer, said he represented "the office of the presidency," not the individual occupant of that office. In describing his work, St. Clair said he had spent much of this time trying to ensure that there were no unwarranted incursions on the executive branch by the judicial and legislative branches.

Presidential Tax Returns. Nixon denied that he ever saw the tax returns of former presidents and did not recall asking for them, according to Ziegler, his press secretary.

Milk Money. The Associated Milk Producers had once agreed to give Herbert W. Kalmbach, Nixon's one-time fund-raiser and personal lawyer, a $300,000 campaign contribution in return for having a civil antitrust suit against the Texas-based co-op killed, Dwight L. Morris, a former secretary to the milk producers, said in a statement filed in U.S. District Court in Kansas City, Mo. Morris said Kalmbach had canceled the plan late in 1972.

Trust Fund. The Finance Committee to Re-elect the President had been closed down and had transferred the $3.57-million it held to a trust fund, it was reported. Trustees of the fund told the General Accounting Office in their first financial report that they would continue to pay legal fees and other expenses, including an estimated $775,000 to settle major lawsuits arising from the Watergate break-in.

MARCH 13

Judiciary Committee Stand. Chairman Peter W. Rodino (D N.J.) and Rep. Edward Hutchinson (R Mich.), ranking minority member of the House Judiciary Committee, insisted that requests for additional material from the White House for the impeachment inquiry were reasonable and relevant and had to be complied with.

Saxbe Comments. Attorney General William B. Saxbe said that the President was "no different than any other citizen" when it came to the duty to report immediately any information he received about the commission of crimes. But Saxbe refused to say whether Nixon ignored this duty when he failed to tell federal prosecutors, as soon as he learned, about hush-money payments to the original Watergate defendants.

Mitchell-Stans Trial. Laurence B. Richardson Jr., the government's second major witness in the conspiracy trial of the two former Nixon lieutenants, testified that within minutes after Robert L. Vesco promised to contribute $500,000 to Nixon's re-election campaign, Maurice H. Stans tried to get him an appointment for that same day with John N. Mitchell to discuss an SEC investigation of his financial dealings.

Charges Dropped. Los Angeles Superior Court Judge Gordon Ringer officially dropped burglary and conspiracy charges against John D. Ehrlichman, David Young and G. Gordon Liddy, three former White House aides, for the break-in at the office of Dr. Lewis J. Fielding, Daniel Ellsberg's psychiatrist. ✓

PRESIDENT NIXON'S CONSERVATIVE SUPPORT WANES

Apparently unconvinced by the recent flurry of public presidential appearances, key conservatives warned President Nixon during the week ending March 22 that the course he was following with regard to the impeachment inquiry underway in the House and the Watergate scandals in general was a perilous one. And public opinion polls released March 20 showed Nixon at his lowest point in public standing with the approval of only 25 or 26 per cent of the American people.

In an unexpected blow to the White House which fellow Republicans described as "profound" and "devastating," Sen. James L. Buckley (Cons-R N.Y.) March 19 called for Nixon's resignation.

But some critics opposed this suggestion. One was Walter Flowers (D Ala.), considered one of the few Democratic members of the House committee who might oppose impeachment. In a significant speech before the committee March 20, Flowers urged Nixon instead to cooperate with the committee, and to stop "playing games with our Constitution, the Congress...and the American people" by claiming to be cooperating while he was actually confusing the issue.

Also angered by the White House attack on the House Judiciary Committee's request for information for the impeachment inquiry, Rep. Lawrence J. Hogan (R Md.) warned March 15 that if the President continued such an attitude, "he will lose even those on the committee who are trying to keep an open mind on the impeachment issue." Hogan, a member of the committee, had been considered one of Nixon's staunchest supporters. (White House criticism, p. 244)

Pressure on the White House for information pertinent to the investigations underway in the House and before federal grand juries continued. While counsel for the impeachment inquiry continued negotiating with the White House for needed information, the court of appeals, District of Columbia circuit, March 21 upheld Judge John J. Sirica's March 18 order granting to the House committee the sealed report which he had received March 1 from the original Watergate grand jury. Attorneys for defendants in the Watergate coverup case, who opposed giving the report to the committee, were given until late March 25 to appeal this decision to the Supreme Court. (Story p. 283)

And it was disclosed March 21 that special Watergate prosecutor Leon Jaworski had on March 15 subpoenaed the White House for additional information. The deadline for White House response to the subpoena was March 25.

The Nature of The Inquiry

"In order for me to represent the President adequately, it is imperative that I be allowed to participate in any prehearing discovery, as well as in any hearing conducted by the committee," presidential counsel James D. St. Clair wrote John M. Doar, special counsel for the House Judiciary Committee.

Based on historical precedent, this request sparked considerable disagreement within the committee as to the proper response—and thrust the committee into an attempt to analyze the precise nature of the inquiry going on under its jurisdiction. Most of the briefing sessions held by the committee March 20 and 21 were spent in discussion of this subject; the matter was not resolved by the week's end. Republican members generally favored granting St. Clair's request in the interest of fairness. Democrats opposed, saying that they were not conducting an adversary proceeding.

St. Clair requested the right to be present at non-public sessions when the committee staff, for example, took depositions—compelled sworn statements—from witnesses. He also asked for the right to cross-examine witnesses. In addition, he asked the right to participate in committee hearings, to call and subpoena witnesses, and to cross-examine the committee's witnesses.

Erupting in opposition to this request which he said would be "foolishness" for the committee to consider, senior Democrat Jack Brooks (D Texas) exclaimed: "Our basic problem is who is going to run this inquiry.... Mr. St. Clair or the House through this committee?... We're not having a trial." There was no reason for the committee to allow St. Clair to "put the evil eye" on witnesses, he said.

But Tom Railsback (R Ill.) March 21, pointed out that "since 1876...every respondent in every such inquiry which resulted in impeachment has been permitted on his request the privilege of having counsel present. In addition...the respondent or his counsel has been granted the privilege of cross-examining witnesses, raising objections and testifying in his own behalf.... If we don't give the right to be present (to the President and St. Clair), we are risking a real partisan confrontation (among committee members)."

"This issue goes to the heart of these proceedings," Judiciary Committee Chairman Peter W. Rodino Jr. (D N.J.) said.

If the committee was acting as a grand jury, the analogy often used to explain the House function in impeachment, then it would be unlikely to grant St. Clair's request. Persons under investigation by a grand jury are not allowed the company of counsel before the grand jury, or the right of cross-examination.

But if the committee found that it was actually conducting an adversary accusatory proceeding, then it would be logical to allow St. Clair the rights he requested.

Rejecting this latter finding, Edward Mezvinsky (D Iowa) told the committee March 21: "Our inquiry is not the arena for an adversary prceeding.... What we're doing is searching for the evidence and there is no opposition role in the script."

The grand jury analogy did not hold in the case of public sessions, William S. Cohen (R Maine) said. A grand jury investigated in secret; similar actions taken in public became accusatory. And Wiley Mayne (R Iowa) charged that the committee would be engaged in its own "coverup" if it denied St. Clair's request.

Expressing his concern that the committee not become polarized over this matter, Don Edwards (D Calif.) urged "an exhaustive and explicit study of the precedents" before the committee decided. "This is an entirely unique situation...entirely distinguishable from all that has gone before," said Robert F. Drinan (D Mass.), claiming a lack of cooperation with the committee by the White House. He implied that if the requested materials were supplied, then the committee might allow St. Clair to be present at its proceedings.

Cross-examination of committee witnesses by St. Clair would not necessarily make the proceedings adversary, said ranking Republican Edward Hutchinson (R Mich.): "I don't see how we can deny the President's counsel the privilege of appearing if he requests it."

"We are at the investigatory stage...developing the facts of the case," said Doar, "and I know of no circumstances in which counsel (for the person investigated) is allowed to participate at this point." Seconding this point, Ray Thornton (D Ark.) described it as "premature and improper to allow outside counsel to participate" in this phase of the inquiry.

Progress Report. Doar told the committee members March 20 that the inquiry staff had received almost all the material requested from the Senate Watergate committee, and all but one of the items which the White House had given the special prosecutor's office. In addition, he said, interviews with witnesses had begun, and there had been no difficulty in obtaining information from executive departments.

On March 18, Doar and Albert E. Jenner Jr., special minority counsel, had met again with St. Clair to discuss the request of the committee Feb. 25 for the 40-odd recorded conversations relating to the Watergate coverup. The attorneys reviewed again each of the items and the reason it was needed by the inquiry staff. Total time involved in the conversations sought was "substantially less than 20 hours," said Doar, who said he and Jenner made clear their feeling that "the committee would be unswerving in its determination to get (this and other relevant) information."

"We were very, very specific with Mr. St. Clair as to the purpose, need and relevance" of these tapes, Jenner added.

On his part, Doar said, St. Clair explained that the decision to release the tapes would be Nixon's, not his. He also expressed the hope that the committee would first analyze the materials it had already received before making additional requests and that those requests would be as precise and narrow as possible.

Doar explained that there had been no further discussion of the committee's controversial request for an outline of the index of White House files—as a preliminary step toward specific requests for certain files—since St. Clair had informed him March 6 that there was no such index.

Negotiations were continuing on the request for the additional recorded conversations, Doar said. Noting that President Nixon's recent public statements had evidenced adamant opposition to granting any further material to the committee, Jerome R. Waldie (D Calif.) asked Doar and Jenner: "Whom are we to believe, the President or his attorney?... If the President is speaking for himself, are we not wasting our time talking to Mr. St. Clair?... I have a feeling," he continued, "that if the evidence we've requested were not incriminating, the President himself would rent a U-Haul truck to send it up here."

Flowers, considered one of the least likely Democratic committee members to support impeachment, released a blast of criticism at Nixon March 20: "It is high time that this President stopped playing games.... On the one hand we hear on television about full cooperation...but we see developing the intricate maneuvers of a strategy to limit this committee and confuse the issue."

Sirica's Decision

"We deal in a matter of the most critical moment to the nation, an impeachment investigation involving the President of the United States. It would be difficult to conceive of a more compelling need than that of this country for an unswervingly fair inquiry based on all the pertinent information," Judge Sirica ruled March 18. He ordered that the House Judiciary Committee should be given the sealed report and locked briefcase that he received March 1 from the original Watergate grand jury. *(p. 251, 266)*

There was no doubt why the grand jury had requested that the report and briefcase be forwarded to the committee. During its investigation into the Watergate break-in and coverup, the jury had heard evidence material to the impeachment inquiry under way in the House committee. The report was "a simple and straightforward compilation of information gathered by the grand jury," said Sirica; "it draws no accusatory conclusions.... It renders no moral or social judgments." *(Box, next page)*

Turnover of the report and briefcase to the House Judiciary Committee had not officially been opposed by the White House.

Opposition had come from the defense attorneys representing the seven former presidential staff and Nixon campaign officials indicted March 1 for their involvement in the coverup.

Led by John J. Wilson, attorney for H. R. Haldeman and John D. Ehrlichman, the defense attorneys had contended that the grand jury had no power to issue such a report, that Sirica had no power to release it, even to the House Judiciary Committee, and that release of it, even to the committee, would result in publicity prejudicing the defendants' right to a fair trial. *(p. 266)*

After an examination of the history and precedents, Sirica concluded that the first argument did not hold up: "The court...would be unjustified in holding that the grand jury was without authority to hand up this report."

Under the circumstances of this case, Sirica held that he did have the authority to pass the report on to the impeachment inquiry. "The grand jury has recommended disclosure; not public dissemination, but delivery to the... committee with a request that the report be used with due regard for the constitutional rights of persons under indictment," he wrote.

(Continued on p. 285)

Excerpts of Sirica's Opinion on Grand Jury Report

Following are excerpts of the March 18 opinion of U.S. District Judge John J. Sirica that a grand jury report should be turned over to the House Judiciary Committee:

"On March 1, 1974, in open court, the June 5, 1972 Grand Jury lodged with the Court a sealed Report... accompanied by a two-page document entitled *Report and Recommendation* which is in effect a letter of transmittal...(which) further strongly recommends that accompanying materials be submitted to the Committee on the Judiciary of the House.... The Grand Jury states it has heard evidence that it regards as having a material bearing on matters within the primary jurisdiction of the Committee in its current inquiry, and notes further its belief that it ought now to defer to the House of Representatives for a decision on what action, if any, might be warranted in the circumstances....

"Having carefully examined the contents of the Grand Jury Report, the Court is satisfied that there can be no question regarding their materiality to the House Judiciary Committee's investigation.... It is the Committee's responsibility to determine the significance of the evidence, and the Court offers no opinion as to relevance. The questions that must be decided, however, are twofold: (1) whether the Grand Jury has the power to make reports and recommendations, (2) whether the Court has power to disclose such reports, and if so, to what extent."

Grand Jury Power. "I....(T)he instant Report is not the first delivered up by a grand jury, and... indeed grand juries have historically published reports on a wide variety of subjects....

"On this historical basis, with reliance as well upon principles of sound public policy, a number of federal courts have upheld and defined the general scope of grand jury reportorial prerogatives....

"The Report here at issue...draws no accusatory conclusions. It deprives no one of an official forum in which to respond. It is not a substitute for indictments where indictments might properly issue. It contains no recommendations, advice or statements that infringe on the prerogatives of other branches of government. Indeed, its only recommendation is to the Court, and rather than injuring separation of powers principles, the Jury sustains them by lending its aid to the House in the exercise of that body's constitutional jurisdiction. It renders no moral or social judgments. The Report is a simple and straightforward compilation of information gathered by the Grand Jury, and no more.

"Having considered the cases and historical precedents...it seems to the Court that it would be unjustified in holding that the Grand Jury was without authority to hand up this report...."

Court Disclosure. "II. Beyond the question of issuing a report is the question of disclosure. It is here that grand jury authority ends and judicial authority becomes exclusive....

"We begin here with the fact that the Grand Jury has recommended disclosure; not public dissemination, but delivery to the House Judiciary Committee with a request that the Report be used with due regard for the constitutional rights of persons under indictment. Where, as here, a report is clearly within the bounds of propriety, the Court believes that it should presumptively favor disclosure to those for whom the matter is a proper concern and whose need is not disputed....(D)elivery to the Committee is eminently proper, and indeed, obligatory. The Report's subject is referred to in his public capacity, and on balance with the public interest, any prejudice to his legal rights caused by disclosure to the Committee would be minimal...The Report is not an indictment, and the President would not be left without a forum in which to adjudicate any charges aginst him that might employ Report materials....

"Here, for all purposes relevant to this decision, the Grand Jury has ended its work. There is no need... to protect grand jury deliberations, to safeguard unaccused or innocent persons with secrecy. The person on whom the Report focuses, the President of the United States, has not objected to its release to the Committee. Other persons are involved only indirectly.... We deal in a matter of the most critical moment to the Nation, an impeachment investigation involving the President of the United States. It would be difficult to conceive of a more compelling need than that of this country for an unswervingly fair inquiry based on all the pertinent information.

"These considerations might well justify even a public disclosure of the Report, but are certainly ample basis for disclosure to a body that in this setting acts simply as another grand jury. The Committee has taken elaborate precautions to insure against unnecessary and inappropriate disclosure of these materials....

"Finally, it seems incredible that grand jury matters should lawfully be available to disbarment committees and police disciplinary investigations and yet be unavailable to the House of Representatives in a proceeding of so great import as an impeachment investigation....

"Principles of grand jury secrecy do not bar this disclosure."

Defendants' Dubious Standing. "III. .... The only individuals who object to such order are defendants in the *United States v. Mitchell, et al.* case currently pending in this court. Their standing is dubious at best given...that 1) their mention in the Report is incidental, (2) their trials will provide ample opportunity for response to such references, none of which go beyond allegations in the indictment, and (3) considerations of possible adverse publicity are both premature and speculative. Their ability to seek whatever appellate review of the Court's decision might be had, is therefore questionable. Nevertheless, because of the irreversible nature of disclosure, the Court will stay its order for two days...to allow defendants an opportunity to pursue their remedies, if any, should they desire...."

Buckley on Nixon Resignation

Sixteen months after he strongly backed President Nixon's re-election, Sen. James L. Buckley (Cons-R N.Y.) broke with the President and urged him to resign to pull the country out of the "Watergate swamp."

Buckley, the first conservative Republican in Congress to call for Nixon's resignation, told a March 19 news conference that the Watergate crisis had become so serious that it threatened the stability of the government and the nation. The senator, however, offered no judgment on the President's guilt or innocence. What concerned him most, he said, was the possible damage that might be done by a prolonged impeachment trial.

"Can anyone imagine that such a trial could bring the nation back on an even keel and steady course; that it could fail to hurt the presidency itself?" he asked. Buckley called on Nixon to make a "free, positive and magnanimous act on his part." His resignation "would be an act of sacrifice for the achievement of the goals that he has proclaimed," said the New Yorker.

But he called for resignation instead of impeachment because, he said, "the impeachment process cannot possibly resolve the crisis. It can only exacerbate it still more."

Referring to Nixon's argument that his resignation from the presidency would weaken the office, Buckley said the office would be strengthened if he stepped down. "Precisely the opposite is the case in order to preserve the Presidency," said Buckley. "Richard Nixon must resign as President. If future presidents are to carry out their grave responsibilities in the free and unfettered manner President Nixon desires, they must be able to inherit an office that has not been irrevocably weakened by a long, slow, agonizing, inch-by-inch process of attrition."

Buckley offered a bleak appraisal of Nixon's ability to survive Watergate if he decided to hang on. "The President's current rating in the polls does not reflect a dissatisfaction with one or two or a dozen specific issues," he said. "Rather it reflects a cumulative loss of faith that has eroded his credibility and moral authority; a loss that, in my judgment, is beyond repair. This goes to the heart of the crisis of regime that is unique to Watergate."

Buckley said he decided to speak out because the Watergate affair was no longer a "troublesome episode" but had "plunged our country into what historians call a 'crisis of the regime.' A crisis of the regime is a disorder, a trauma, involving every tissue of the nation, conspicuously including its moral and spirital dimensions."

The crisis in the United States, he said, could be seen in the "spreading cynicism about those in public life and about the political process itself," the "perception of corruption that has effectively destroyed the President's ability to speak from a position of moral leadership."

(Continued from p. 283)

"Delivery to the committee is eminently proper, and indeed, obligatory," Sirica concluded. "The report's subject is referred to in his public capacity, and on balance with the public interest, any prejudice to his legal rights caused by disclosure to the committee would be minimal.... The President would not be left without a forum in which to adjudicate any charges against him that might employ report materials...."

Inapplicable Rule. The much-discussed rule 6(e) of federal criminal procedure barring disclosure of matters occurring before a grand jury did not bar this type of disclosure, Sirica held. The grand jury had "for all purposes relevant to this decision" completed its work, he wrote. "There is no need to protect against flight on anyone's part, to prevent tampering with or restraints on witnesses or jurors, to protect grand jury deliberations, to safeguard unaccused or innocent persons with secrecy. The person on whom the report focuses, the President of the United States, has not objected to its release.... Other persons are involved only indirectly."

The considerations of national interest might even justify public disclosure of the report, Sirica suggested, but were certainly "ample basis for disclosure to a body that in this setting acts simply as another grand jury."

With regard to Wilson's concern about pretrial publicity, Sirica pointed to the "elaborate precautions" the committee had taken to avoid unnecessary disclosure of confidential information it received in the course of the inquiry. He could not, he wrote, withhold the report "on the basis of speculation that leaks will occur, added to the further speculation that resultant publicity would prejudice the rights of defendants" in the cover-up case. *(p. 247)*

Appeal Doubts. Although he delayed the effect of his order for two days to allow an appeal, which Wilson had promised in the event of such a ruling, Sirica expressed doubt that the coverup defendants were in a proper legal position to appeal the ruling. Mention of them in the report was incidental, he said; they could respond to any such references at their trial; none of the references went beyond the charges against them in the indictment; it was premature and speculative to worry about adverse publicity.

Nixon had requested that St. Clair be allowed to review the contents of the report if it were to be turned over to the committee. Sirica left a decision on this request to Rodino. In closing, Sirica added his request to that of the grand jury, that the committee consider and use the report "with due regard for avoiding any unnecessary interference with the court's ability to conduct fair trials of persons under indictment."

Appeals. Wilson, in behalf of Haldeman, and John M. Bray, representing former Haldeman aide Gordon Strachan, asked Sirica March 20 to delay the effect of his order until the appeals court ruled on their appeal. The special prosecutor's office opposed his request. Sirica rejected the request but gave the attorneys an additional 24 hours, until 4 p.m. March 21, to make their appeal.

In a special hearing before the appeals court, District of Columbia circuit, on the morning of March 21, Wilson and Bray asked the court to order Sirica not to give the grand jury report to the House Judiciary Committee. Again the special prosecutor's office opposed this request.

Mitchell-Stans Trial

Rose Mary Woods, Nixon's personal secretary, added an element of drama March 19 at the New York City trial of John N. Mitchell and Maurice H. Stans when she brought, in her attache case, a secret White House campaign donor list known irreverently as "Rose Mary's baby."

The existence of the list became known in 1973 because of a Common Cause suit against the Finance Committee to Re-elect the President. But the list, which included pre-April 7, 1972, contributions by corporation totals rather than by the names of individual donors, never had been publicly available until Miss Woods appeared at the trial of the two former top Nixon lieutenants. *(Earlier trial story, p. 278)*

The significance of the list was that the secret campaign contributions by companies showed that defense contractors and oil firms were the major money-givers. *(Box, p. 287)*

The list also confirmed that large numbers of executives made hundreds of thousands of dollars in undisclosed contributions to Nixon in 1972.

The largest contribution came from the Amerada Hess Corporation, the oil company that faced a Department of Interior investigation of its oil refinery operations in the Virgin Islands at the time it made a donation of $250,000. More than half the contribution already had been identified on previous campaign filings as having come from individuals associated with Hess, but the White House list confirmed that money was actually part of the company's package.

A few weeks after the contribution was made in April 1972, the Interior Department closed out its investigation of Hess without taking any action.

William E. Simon, the Federal Energy Office director, also appeared on the list as the executive from Salomon Brothers, a New York investment house, who arranged the firm's $100,000 Nixon contribution.

Trial Testimony. In the trial itself, the government was still having difficulty March 20 proving its conspiracy, obstruction of justice and perjury case against Mitchell and Stans, two former Nixon cabinet officers, for their alleged dealings with Robert L. Vesco, the fugitive financier. By March 20, the jurors had heard testimony from Harry L. Sears, who allegedly tried to help Vesco quash a Securities and Exchange Commission (SEC) investigation of his financial operations; Laurence B. Richardson Jr., a former Vesco business associate; Daniel Hofgren, a former Nixon fundraiser, and William J. Casey, the SEC chairman when Vesco allegedly tried to stop the commission's probe.

The prosecution had tried to show how Mitchell, Nixon's former attorney general, and Maurice H. Stans, a former commerce secretary, solicited a $200,000 cash contribution from Vesco in return for attempts to stop the SEC's investigation of him. But the witnesses had fuzzy memories, and, through their answers under cross-examination, disclaimed that they were trying to fix the case.

In the government's attempt to build its perjury case against the two men, Hofgren testified March 15 that Mitchell had told him to stay away from any questions about Vesco. Mitchell already had told the grand jury that he never told Hofgren to stay away from anything.

Nixon's Houston Appearance

President Nixon said March 19 that Sen. James L. Buckley's (Cons-R N.Y.) statement that he should resign had not caused him to reassess his position on resignation. *(Buckley statement, box, opposite page; earlier Nixon statement, p. 275)*

During a question-and-answer session before the National Association of Broadcasters in Houston, Texas, Nixon said: "...While it might be an act of courage to run away from a job that you were elected to do, it also takes courage to stand and fight for what you believe is right, and that is what I intend to do."

For a President to resign in the face of charges against him that he knew to be false, said Nixon, "might be good politics, but it would be bad statesmanship. And it would mean that our system of government would be changed for all presidents and all generations in the future."

Impeachment is the constitutional method for removing a president from office for committing crimes, Nixon went on. Resigning as a result of false charges and low poll ratings, he said, "would mean then that every future president would be presiding over a very unstable government in the United States of America."

Confidentiality. Nixon repeated his determination to protect the principle of presidential confidentiality in the face of demands by the House Judiciary Committee's special impeachment study staff that he turn over more Watergate-related tapes and documents.

"It is difficult to find a proper way to meet the demands of the Congress," he said. "I am trying to do so and trying to be as forthcoming as possible. But I also have another responsibility. I must think not of myself, but I must think also of future presidents of this country, and I am not going to do anything and I am not going to give up to any demand that I believe would weaken the presidency of the United States. I will not participate in the destruction of the office of the president of the United States while I am in this office."

Nixon argued that to give the committee staff free access to presidential documents and tapes would reduce the candor of future presidential advisers, since they would be afraid that their private conversations might eventually become public knowledge. If this became the case, Nixon said, a president "isn't going to get the variety of views he needs to make the right kind of decision."

The President told the broadcasters and a national television audience that the White House was still discussing with committee counsel John M. Doar the extent of Nixon's cooperation with the staff. He declared that the committee "has enough information to conduct its investigation and to see whether any charges it may have against the President are true or false."

At the same time, Nixon urged the committee to resolve the impeachment issue speedily. "...Dragging out Watergate drags down America...," he said.

Nixon's Corporate Contributors

Following are the corporate contributions made before April 7, 1972, to the Nixon re-election campaign as reported on a secret list kept by Rose Mary Woods, President Nixon's private secretary. The list also included the names of the executives whose individual contributions were grouped together for total corporate donations.

Amerada Hess Corporation, New York, oil—$250,000.
Anheuser-Busch Inc., St. Louis, brewers—$56,353.
Bethlehem Steel Corporation, Bethlehem, Pa.—$49,002.
Bristol-Meyers Company, New York, drugs—$50,000.
Chrysler Corporation, Detroit, automobiles—$133,844.
Dart Industries, Los Angeles, retail drug sales—$50,826.
Disney Productions Inc., Burbank, Calif., motion pictures—$34,475.
E. I. du Pont de Nemours and Company, Wilmington, Del., chemicals—$60,000.
Ernst and Ernst, Cleveland, accountants—$88,000.
General Dynamics Corporation, St. Louis, defense contractors—$83,717.
General Motors Corporation, Detroit, automobiles—$51,012.
Lehman Brothers Corporation, New York, stock brokers—$86,289.
Ling-Temco-Vought Corporation, Dallas, defense and aerospace contractor—$95,250.
Litton Industries, Los Angeles, defense contractor—$86,095.
Marathon Oil Company, Findlay, Ohio—$40,000.
McDonnell-Douglas Corporation, St. Louis, defense and aerospace contractor—$34,528.
Minnesota Mining and Manufacturing Corporation, St. Paul, Minn.—$142,741.
Mutual of Omaha, Omaha, Neb., insurance—$34,325.
National Homes Corporation, Lafayette, Ind., prefabricated structures—$50,000.
North American Rockwell Corporation, El Segundo, Calif., aerospace and defense contractor—$98,270.
Northrop Corporation, Los Angeles, aerospace and defense contractor—$100,000.
Price-Waterhouse Company, New York, accountants—$102,000.
St. Regis Paper Company, New York—$19,000.
Salomon Brothers, New York, brokers—$100,000.
Charles E. Smith and Company, Washington, real estate—$55,000.
Texas Eastern Transmission Company, Houston, gas pipeline—$30,000.
Texas Instruments Company, Dallas, electronics—$111,949.
Westinghouse Electric Company, Pittsburgh—$35,460.

Week's Watergate Chronology

Following is a day-to-day chronology of the week's events in the Watergate case:

MARCH 14

Ellsberg Burglary. Four men, three of them members of the original Watergate burglary team, pleaded not guilty in U.S. District Court in Washington to charges in connection with the break-in at the office of Dr. Lewis J. Fielding, Daniel Ellsberg's psychiatrist. The four were G. Gordon Liddy, Bernard L. Barker and Eugenio R. Martinez, the original Watergate burglars, and Felipe de Diego. *(p. 277)*

Milk Money. A report made public in U.S. District Court in Kansas City, Mo., during a pretrial hearing on an antitrust suit disclosed that Associated Milk Producers Inc., the nation's largest dairy cooperative, had apparently paid more than $100,000 in corporation funds to print and distribute during the 1968 presidential campaign copies of a book of President Johnson's speeches.

Prepared by an Arkansas law firm at the request of the co-op's board of directors, the investigative report also told about a telephone conversation between the corporation's general manager, George Mehren, and Herbert W. Kalmbach, then a Nixon fund-raiser, about the time of an alleged deal to kill an antitrust suit against the dairy group.

McCord Request. James W. McCord, one of the original Watergate conspirators, formally asked U.S. District Judge John J. Sirica to vacate his conviction on the ground that Nixon tainted the case by failing a year earlier to report that he had been told hush money was paid to Watergate defendants. *(p. 276)*

Cost Council Investigation. The Watergate special prosecutor, it was disclosed, was investigating charges of illegal political influence in three decisions by the Cost of Living Council before the 1972 election. The decisions permitted a price increase by McDonald's Corporation and removed controls on silver futures contracts and on the motion picture industry.

Reinecke Test. Lt. Gov. Edwin Reinecke (R Calif.) said the Watergate special prosecutor was to arrange a lie detector test he had sought. Reinecke had asked for the test to prove that he was not perjuring himself when he testified before the Senate Judiciary Committee in 1972 about the offer of International Telephone and Telegraph Corporation's offer to underwrite the 1972 Republican national convention.

Mitchell-Stans Trial. Laurence B. Richardson Jr., the former president of Robert L. Vesco's International Controls Corporation and the second major prosecution witness in the perjury trial of the two former cabinet officials, testified that he was just a "messenger" and not a "bag man" or "fixer" when he delivered $200,000 in cash and a message from Vesco to Maurice H. Stans, former head of the Nixon campaign finance unit. Richardson told of his falling out with Vesco because of what he considered to be Vesco's wrongdoings.

MARCH 15

Silbert Defense. Earl J. Silbert, the assistant U.S. attorney who tried the first Watergate case, defended his handling of the case in a 31-page letter to the Senate Judiciary Committee. Silbert wrote that he never figured out the motivation for the Watergate burglary and bugging.

Nixon Tax Returns. Rep. James A. Burke (D Mass.), a member of the Joint Committee on Internal Revenue Taxation, which was investigating Nixon's income tax returns, said the committee report "will in many ways be worse (for the White House) than the Watergate case."

Milk Case. Jake Jacobsen, a former lawyer for Associated Milk Producers Inc., pleaded not guilty to a charge of lying to the Watergate grand jury about an alleged $10,000 payoff for the Nixon administration's 1971 increase in milk support prices. *(Indictment, p. 249)*

Nixon Deed. An original deed donating Nixon's vice presidential papers to the National Archives was thrown away, according to Frank De Marco, Nixon's tax lawyer. The deed was considered a key document in the controversy in Nixon's deduction of his vice presidential papers. *(Earlier story, p. 279)*

Woods Subpoena. Rose Mary Woods, Nixon's personal secretary, accepted a subpoena requiring her to testify before the Senate Watergate Committee about a $100,000 campaign contribution from billionaire Howard Hughes. *(Earlier Woods testimony, p. 170)*

Nixon Speech. In an appearance before the Executives Club of Chicago, Nixon declared that he would not resign and would not "be a party to the destruction of the presidency of the United States." Nixon also told the Chicago businessmen that congressional investigators had found no evidence that he committed tax fraud, although he might wind up owing "more taxes." *(p. 275)*

Election Reform. In the Democratic Party reply to Nixon's campaign reform proposals, Sen. John O. Pastore (D R.I.) rejected the President's recommendations as inadequate and called on Nixon to endorse public financing of elections "to end political payola."

Mitchell-Stans Trial. Daniel Hofgren, a Washington investment banker who was a Nixon fund-raiser in 1972, testified that he had asked John N. Mitchell if he had had a meeting with Robert L. Vesco on the financier's problems and was told, "You stay away from that." Hofgren's testimony contradicted previous grand jury testimony by Mitchell that he "never told Mr. Hofgren to stay away from anything."

MARCH 16

Nixon's Taxes. Congressional investigators and the Internal Revenue Service had challenged as seriously inflated, and for some years possibly fictitious, the deductions for California gasoline taxes that Nixon had taken on his federal tax returns, *The New York Times* reported.

Sale of Ambassadorships. The Times also disclosed that the White House had refused a request by the Watergate special prosecutor for documents believed to bear on the alleged awarding of diplomatic posts in return for large contributions to the 1972 Republican campaign.

MARCH 17

Mills Prediction. Rep. Wilbur D. Mills (D Ark.) predicted that Nixon would be out of office by November because of Republican pressure and public disapproval of his income tax payments.

MARCH 18

Sirica Decision. U.S. District Judge John J. Sirica ruled that the secret Watergate grand jury report and accompanying material believed to deal with Nixon's possible involvement in the Watergate scandal and cover-up be turned over to the House Judiciary Committee. *(Details, p. 283)*

Mitchell-Stans Trial. Rose Mary Woods, Nixon's secretary, testified in the Mitchell-Stans trial that the name of Robert L. Vesco was absent from a list of pre-April 7, 1972, contributors that had been sent to her. However, she said under cross-examination that Vesco's name had been included on a second list of the largest contributors to the Nixon campaign. *(Details, p. 286)*

MARCH 19

Buckley Call. Sen. James L. Buckley (Cons-R N.Y.) became the first conservative Republican in Congress to call on Nixon to resign because of the Watergate scandal. *(Box, p. 285)*

Nixon Rebuttal. In an appearance before the National Association of Broadcasters in Houston, the President said Buckley's resignation call had not caused him to reassess his position, and he again promised not to resign. "It...takes courage to stand and fight for what you believe is right," he said. "It may be good politics (to resign), but not statesmanship." *(Box, p. 286)*

Secret List. A secret donors list prepared by Rose Mary Woods from the 1972 Nixon campaign drive and made public for the first time at the Mitchell-Stans trial disclosed that defense contractors and oil firms were high on the list. *(Box, p. 287)*

MARCH 20

Reagan Defense. Gov. Ronald Reagan (R Calif.) defended Nixon against calls for his resignation, saying that it would be worse for the country if Nixon quit under pressure than if he had to endure an impeachment trial.

Sirica Decision Appeal. John J. Wilson, the lawyer for H. R. Haldeman and John D. Ehrlichman, asked the District of Columbia Court of Appeals to bar Judge Sirica from turning over the Watergate grand jury's secret report to the House Judiciary Committee.

Saxbe Offer. Attorney General William B. Saxbe said he had told Justice Department employees they could volunteer for Nixon's Watergate defense team and be assured of getting their former jobs back later.

St. Clair Request. James D. St. Clair, Nixon's defense lawyer, asked the House Judiciary Committee for the right to cross-examine witnesses, not only during public hearings but also as the staff assembled evidence.

At separate closed caucuses, the House Judiciary Committee's Democratic majority agreed to oppose the request, while the Republican minority decided to support it.

Rhodes Proposal. House Minority Leader John J. Rhodes (R Ariz.) called on the House Judiciary Committee to limit its impeachment investigation to a few specific areas. As a way out of the committee-White House impasse over 42 tapes, Rhodes proposed turning them over to a third party who would review them and decide if they were relevant.

Watergate Report. The Justice Department should be prohibited from advising a president politically or personally, a report prepared for the Senate Watergate Committee recommended. The report also said that the "abuses associated with Watergate" were caused in part by a serious and possibly illegal concentration of power in the presidency.

Mitchell-Stans Trial. William J. Casey, former chairman of the Securities and Exchange Commission (SEC), said that John W. Dean III, when he was White House counsel, tried to get the SEC to delay questioning secretaries of Robert L. Vesco until after the 1972 election. The government claimed that Dean telephoned Casey at John N. Mitchell's request, but Casey said Dean did not mention Mitchell. √

A SMALL NIXON DEFENSE TEAM HAS RECRUITING PROBLEMS

By the end of March 1973, less than six weeks before the special House Judiciary Committee staff was due to report on whether proper grounds existed for the impeachment of President Nixon, the White House legal defense team had one particularly salient feature.

It was small.

James D. St. Clair, the experienced Boston trial lawyer who would most likely defend Nixon in a Senate impeachment trial, had only four staff lawyers working for him as of March 21, compared to the 43 lawyers on the Judiciary Committee's impeachment study staff.

Counting staffs of the Senate Watergate Committee and special prosecutor Leon Jaworski, the White House faced an array of almost 150 adversaries.

St. Clair had the services of one other full-time lawyer, special counsel to the President John J. Chester, and a $100-a-day consultant, Jerome J. Murphy. Counting St. Clair and the four staff lawyers, this brought the active impeachment defense team to a grand total of seven.

Also listed by the White House as members of the legal team were J. Fred Buzhardt Jr., counsel to the President; presidential Assistant Leonard Garment, and consultants Charles A. Wright, Thomas P. Marinis and Samuel J. Powers. *(Box, this page)*

However, White House spokesmen acknowledged that none of these was actively involved in the impeachment duel with the Judiciary Committee staff.

Casualty Rate

The casualty rate among White House lawyers had been high.

With the March 15 departure of Robert T. Andrews, a 54-year-old lawyer who had been the senior member of St. Clair's staff, the dismantling of the original Watergate legal defense team that had come in with Buzhardt on May 10, 1973, was complete. "I only stayed over to help with the transition," said Andrews, who returned to his former job as deputy assistant general counsel for the Defense Department.

The first victim was presidential counsel John W. Dean III, whom Nixon fired April 30, 1973, charging that he had withheld information from the President about the Watergate coverup.

The next was Wright, who had come to the White House to construct a constitutional argument supporting Nixon's refusal to turn over Watergate tapes and documents to Judge John J. Sirica and the Watergate grand jury. Wright returned to his post as a law professor at the University of Texas shortly after Nixon reversed his stand on the tapes in the wake of the Oct. 20 firing of special Watergate prosecutor Archibald Cox. Amid what the White House called a "firestorm" of public reaction to the firing, and demands in Congress for impeachment, Nixon announced that he would release the tapes.

The next ones to go were Buzhardt and Garment, who headed the legal team until St. Clair took over on Jan. 5. They were both promoted out of the job after Buzhardt became a target of criticism within the administration following his handling of the mysterious gaps that

Consultants

Jerome J. Murphy, 31, consultant to the President since Dec. 15, 1973, $100 a day; a native of St. Louis, Mo. Murphy was a 1964 graduate of Notre Dame University and received a law degree from St. Louis University in 1968. He was an assistant U.S. attorney and district counsel for the Drug Enforcement Administration Task Force in St. Louis before joining the White House team.

Also listed as consultants but not active in the impeachment fight as of early March 1974 were:

Charles A. Wright, 46, consultant to the President since June 6, 1973, $150 a day; law professor at the University of Texas.

Thomas P. Marinis Jr., 30, consultant to the President since June 6, 1973, $150 a day; member of the Houston law firm of Vinson, Elkins, Searls, Connally & Smith and a former student of Wright.

Samuel J. Powers, 56, consultant to the President since Nov. 5, 1973, $150 a day; a member of the Miami, Fla., law firm of Blackwell, Walker & Green.

appeared in the tapes that Nixon finally turned over to Sirica. Buzhardt testified before Sirica on Nov. 29 that when he first discovered the 18½-minute gap in a conversation between Nixon and aide H. R. Haldeman, recorded three days after the Watergate break-in, Buzhardt did not think there was any "innocent explanation" for it.

Recruiting Problems. As Andrews left, St. Clair was preparing to hire "five or six" more staff lawyers, some or all of them from the civil division of the Justice Department, Congressional Quarterly learned.

St. Clair could not be reached to answer why the staff additions were coming so late. However, a spokesman for St. Clair told Congressional Quarterly, "I don't think anyone really has had much time to actively go out and recruit staff lawyers. It's sort of catch as catch can around here because everybody's so darned busy."

The White House had not been very successful in attracting new staffers. Congressional Quarterly learned that St. Clair's predecessor, Buzhardt, had invited applications from at least two repositories of government lawyers—the U.S. attorney's office for the District of Columbia and the Justice Department's office of legal counsel. The office of legal counsel had been responsible for preparing a lengthy study of impeachment under the direction of then Acting Attorney General Robert H. Bork, which was partly the reason for the White House interest.

No one from the office of legal counsel volunteered, and only one person signed on from the U.S. attorney's office: John A. McCahill, a 34-year-old assistant U.S. attorney who had been planning to leave government service and go into private law practice. McCahill joined the staff Nov. 27, 1973.

"It looked like just the most exciting case of the century regardless of what your political viewpoints are,"

Chiefs

James D. St. Clair, 53, special counsel to the President since Jan. 5, $42,500: a top-ranking Boston trial lawyer with a reputation as a painstakingly thorough preparer of cases and a brilliant courtroom tactician with an almost uncanny recall of details; a member of the Boston firm of Hale & Dorr before he came to the White House; served on the staff of Joseph N. Welch, another member of Hale & Dorr, whose televised clashes with the late Sen. Joseph R. McCarthy (R Wis. 1947-57) as special Army counsel helped end the so-called McCarthy era; a native of Akron, Ohio; a 1941 graduate of the University of Illinois with a law degree from Harvard University, awarded in 1947.

John J. Chester, 53, special counsel to the President since Jan. 30, $40,000: a native of Columbus, Ohio, and a 1942 graduate of Amherst College; law degree from Yale University in 1948. Chester practiced law in Columbus as a partner in the firms of Chester and Chester (1948-57), Chester and Rose (1957-70) and Chester, Hoffman, Park, Willcox and Rose (1970-74). He was elected as a representative to the Ohio General Assembly from Franklin County in 1952, 1954 and 1956.

Also on the White House legal team but not actively involved in the impeachment fight were **J. Fred Buzhardt Jr.,** 50, counsel to the President since Jan. 5, $42,500; and **Leonard Garment,** assistant to the President since Jan. 5, $42,500.

Staff

Cecil Emerson, 39, defense team since Nov. 25, 1973, $32,031: received law degree from Baylor University in 1965; was an assistant district attorney and assistant U.S. attorney in Dallas, Texas, and regional director of the Dallas Drug Enforcement Administration Task Force before coming to the White House.

John A. McCahill, 34; defense team since Nov. 27, 1973, $24,247, paid out of Agriculture Department funds: a 1962 graduate of Columbia, McCahill received a law degree from Catholic University in 1969; was an assistant U.S. attorney in the District of Columbia before joining the White House.

Michael Sterlacci, 31; defense team since Dec. 10, 1973, $24,247, paid out of Transportation Department funds: a 1965 graduate of Seton Hall; received a law degree from George Washington University in 1968; was the assistant general counsel of the United States Information Agency before coming to the White House.

Loren A. Smith, 29, defense team since Nov. 27, 1973, $17,497, paid out of Federal Communications Commission (FCC) funds: a 1966 graduate of Northwestern University; received a law degree from Northwestern in 1969; worked in the general counsel's office of the FCC before joining the White House.

McCahill told Congressional Quarterly. "They explained to me that it would be a strictly professional job and I would not be part of the political staff. I would be a lawyer doing work as if I were in a private law firm. I took it on that basis and that's the way it's been. I think it's a privilege to be involved in a case of this magnitude."

Of those contacted, the lawyers who decided to pass up the job cited two main reasons: fear of not being able to return to their jobs once their stint with St. Clair had ended, and a general conviction among many that Nixon was not telling his attorneys the full extent of his involvement in Watergate.

At a meeting with reporters March 20, Attorney General William B. Saxbe deplored this attitude and assured Justice Department lawyers that they could volunteer for assignment to the White House on the understanding that their jobs would be waiting for them when they returned.

"I'm astounded sometimes by the attitude that people have that the President is not entitled to defend himself," Saxbe said.

Evidently many of the lawyers were unconvinced.

'Have to Be Nuts.' "I think you'd have to be nuts to work there (in the White House)," one lawyer said. "I think some of Nixon's past lawyers, like Wright and Buzhardt, have really been hurt. A smart client in a murder case will come to you and tell you what he did, how he did it, why he did it, and you can deal with the evidence. But when every day you think of a strategy and the prosecution comes out with some document that your client never told you they had, and knocks you off at the pass, you don't look too good as a lawyer. At least you expect them to level with you, and the White House is liable to leave you dangling in the wind, as they put it."

A lawyer who said he was tempted by the offer declared, "I wanted at least to consider it overnight. I don't know how many times I would have the opportunity to work in the White House. But I think the proper role for a lawyer is to believe in his client..."

"Most of the people in this office are young and only two or three years out of law school," said another lawyer. "If they got into a situation that was over their heads, it could really damage their careers. I'm speaking for myself, too."

Though St. Clair could not be reached for comment, former senior staff member Andrews acknowledged that the White House had encountered trouble assembling a suitable staff.

"We had some overzealous applicants, and they aren't so good," Andrews said. "And there was a feeling on the part of some that somehow they would be tied to their client. I think it's unfortunate that some people feel this way. Even a bad guy or somebody who's been up the river before is entitled to representation, and the man who represents him is not considered a bad guy too."

Other Staffers. In addition to McCahill, St. Clair's staff as of March 19 consisted of:

• Cecil Emerson, 39, a former assistant district attorney and assistant U.S. attorney in Dallas, Texas, and regional director of the Dallas Drug Enforcement Administration Task Force before joining the White House team Nov. 25, 1973;

(Continued on p. 292)

Impeachable Offense: Opinion of Nixon Attorneys

Following are excerpts from a Feb. 28 analysis prepared by James D. St. Clair, John J. Chester, Michael A. Sterlacci, Jerome J. Murphy and Loren A. Smith, attorneys for President Nixon:

English Background of Constitutional Impeachment Provisions

"The Framers felt that the English system permitted men...to make arbitrary decisions, and one of their primary purposes in creating a Constitution was to replace this arbitrariness with a system based on the rule of law.... They felt impeachment was a necessary check on a President who might commit a crime, but they did not want to see the vague standards of the English system that made impeachment a weapon to achieve parliamentary supremacy....

"To argue that the President may be impeached for something less than a criminal offense, with all the safeguards that definition implies, would be a monumental step backwards into all those old English practices that our Constitution sought to eliminate. American impeachment was not designed to force a President into surrendering executive authority...but to check overtly criminal actions as they are defined by law....

"The terminology 'high crimes and misdemeanors' should create no confusion or ambiguity.... It was a unitary phrase meaning crimes against the state, as opposed to those against individuals.... It is as ridiculous to say that 'misdemeanor' must mean something beyond 'crime' as it is to suggest that in the phrase 'bread and butter issues' butter issues must be different from bread issues...."

The Constitutional Convention

"It is evident from the actual debate and from the events leading up to it that Morris' remark that 'An election of every four years will prevent maladministration,' expressed the will of the Convention. Thus, the impeachment provision adopted was designed to deal exclusively with indictable criminal conduct.... The Convention rejected all non-criminal definitions of impeachable offenses.... To distort the clear meaning of the phrase 'treason, bribery or other high crimes and misdemeanors' by including non-indictable conduct would thus most certainly violate the Framers' intent."

Legal Meaning of Impeachment Provision

"Just as statutes are to be construed to uphold the intent of the drafters...so should we uphold the intent of the drafters of the Constitution that impeachable offenses be limited to criminal violations. Also as penal statutes have been strictly construed in favor of the accused, so should we construe the impeachment provisions of the Constitution...."

American Impeachment Precedents

"Some of the proponents of presidential impeachment place great emphasis on the cases involving federal judges to support the proposition that impeachment will lie for conduct which does not of itself constitute an indictable offense. This view is apparently most appealing to those broad constructionists who favoring a severely weakened Chief Executive argue that certain non-criminal 'political' offenses may justify impeachment....

"The Framers...distinguished between the President and judges concerning the standard to be employed for an impeachment. Otherwise the 'good behavior' clause is a nullity....

"The precedent...asserted by the House in 1804 that a judge may be impeached for a breach of good behavior was reasserted again with full force over one hundred years later in 1912....

"The fact that the House...felt it necessary to make a distinction in the impeachment standards between the Judiciary and the Executive reinforces the obvious —that the words 'treason, bribery, and other high crimes and misdemeanors' are limited solely to indictable crimes and cannot extend to misbehavior....

"The acquittal of President Johnson over a century ago strongly indicates that the Senate has refused to adopt a broad view of 'other high crimes and misdemeanors'.... Impeachment of a President should be resorted to only for cases of the gravest kind—the commission of a crime named in the Constitution or a criminal offense against the laws of the United States. If there is any doubt as to the gravity of an offense or as to a President's conduct or motives, the doubt should be resolved in his favor. This is the necessary price for having an independent executive...."

Conclusion: Proper Standard for Presidential Impeachment

"Any analysis that broadly construes the power to impeach and convict can be reached only...by placing a subjective gloss on the history of impeachment that results in permitting the Congress to do whatever it deems most politic. The intent of the Framers, who witnessed episode after episode of outrageous abuse of the impeachment power by the self-righteous English Parliament, was to restrict the *political* reach of the impeachment power.

"Those who seek to broaden the impeachment power invite the use of power 'as a means of crushing political adversaries or ejecting them from office.'.... The acceptance of such an invitation would be destructive to our system of government and to the fundamental principle of separation of powers.... The Framers never intended that the impeachment clause serve to dominate or destroy the executive branch of the government...."

Tax Lawyers

H. Chapman Rose, 67, donating his services as a tax consultant to President Nixon, according to a White House spokesman. Rose served in the Eisenhower administration as assistant secretary of the treasury (1953-55) and as under secretary of the treasury (1955-56). He was a partner in the 137-member Cleveland, Ohio, law firm of Jones, Day, Cockley & Reavis, which specialized in corporation, tax, trust and estate planning law. Clients included Chrysler, General Motors and Republic Steel. A native of Columbus, Ohio, Rose was a 1928 graduate of Princeton University. He received a law degree from Harvard University in 1931 and served as secretary to Supreme Court Justice Oliver Wendell Holmes in 1931 and 1932.

Kenneth W. Gemmill, 64, also donating his services as a tax consultant, according to the White House. Gemmil was an assistant to the treasury secretary under the Eisenhower administration in 1953 and 1954 and was acting chief counsel of the Internal Revenue Service in 1953. He was a partner in the 118-member law firm of Dechert, Price & Rhoads with main offices in Philadelphia and branches in Harrisburg, Pa., Washington, D.C., and Brussels, Belgium. Born in Ivyland, Pa., Gemmill was a 1932 graduate of Princeton University and received a law degree from the University of Pennsylvania in 1935.

Preparers. The consultants who prepared Nixon's tax returns were Frank DeMarco, a member of the firm of Kalmbach, DeMarco, Knapp & Chillingworth of Los Angeles and Newport Beach, Calif., and Arthur Blech, a certified public accountant with his own firm in Los Angeles.

(Continued from p. 290)

• Michael Sterlacci, 31, who was assistant general counsel of the United States Information Agency (USIA) before coming to the White House Dec. 10, 1973; and

• Loren A. Smith, 29, who worked in the general counsel's office of the Federal Communications Commission (FCC) before signing with St. Clair Nov. 27, 1973.

Salaries. The mechanism by which McCahill's and Sterlacci's salaries were being paid was somewhat unusual.

With the exception of Emerson, who was being paid from White House funds, the staff lawyers were classified as agency employees "detailed" to the White House—a practice whereby the White House obtained staffers without having to pay them out of the White House budget.

Normally, "detailees" would return to their agencies after they had completed their assignments. However, only Smith's salary, $17,497 a year, was being paid by the agency from which he had come.

McCahill and Sterlacci were being paid $24,247 a year each from agencies for which they had never worked: the Departments of Agriculture and Transportation, respectively.

A White House spokesman said the salary arrangements for McCahill and Sterlacci were a matter of "finding a convenient payroll to put them on." The USIA, for which Sterlacci had worked, was not a large enough agency to continue carrying him on its payroll, and McCahill had quit the U.S. attorney's office, according to the White House.

The two other members of St. Clair's team were being paid from White House funds.

St. Clair's associate, John Chester, a 53-year-old Columbus, Ohio, lawyer, was named special counsel to the President on Jan. 30 at a salary of $40,000.

Jerome Murphy, 31, was named a consultant to the President on Dec. 15, 1973, at a fee of $100 a day.

Income Taxes

Absent from the official White House roll of lawyers, but occasionally seen in the Executive Office Building next to the White House, were two prominent tax lawyers: H. Chapman Rose and Kenneth W. Gemmill.

Rose and Gemmill, both former Treasury Department officials during the Eisenhower administration and described by the White House as "old friends of the President," were donating their services to Nixon as consultants in the dispute over Nixon's income tax returns, a White House spokesman told Congressional Quarterly. *(Box, this page)*

Defense Strategy. The absence of Rose and Gemmill from government payrolls might have lent weight to what appeared to be shaping up as a key position in Nixon's defense strategy against impeachment. Rep. Wilbur D. Mills (D Ark.), chairman of the Joint Committee on Revenue Taxation, was predicting that his committee's staff study of Nixon's tax returns would increase pressure on Nixon to resign.

The position, some observers predicted, would be that charges of tax evasion were not proper grounds for impeachment since Nixon's tax affairs were not connected with his performance of official duties.

This argument was intimated in a Feb. 28 analysis of the constitutional standard for presidential impeachment, prepared by St. Clair, Chester, Sterlacci, Murphy and Smith.

The analysis contained the following declaration: "The words (in the Constitution) 'Treason, Bribery or other high Crimes and Misdemeanors,' construed either in the light of present day usage or as understood by the framers of the late 18th century, mean what they clearly connote—criminal offenses. Not only do the words inherently require a criminal offense, but one of a very serious nature committed in one's governmental capacity."

WITH NO FANFARE: A TURNOVER OF GRAND JURY EVIDENCE

For the beleaguered Nixon administration, March—which had come roaring in with the March 1 indictments of former White House and administration officials for obstruction of justice—ended with deceptive calm.

Beneath the quiet of the week ending March 30 lay the same undecided questions of confrontation and co-operation that had occupied all three branches of the government in the preceding weeks. With no fanfare, Federal Judge John J. Sirica March 26 handed over to the House impeachment inquiry the sealed grand jury report and locked briefcase of evidence which the grand jury had entrusted to him March 1.

While the inquiry staff of the House Judiciary Committee worked to analyze the voluminous material received already from the White House and other sources, the committee's month-old request for additional presidential tapes hung unresolved at the White House. There too lay a subpoena from Watergate Special Prosecutor Leon Jaworski, issued for additional material March 15, with the deadline for compliance extended at White House request from March 25 to March 29.

On the morning of March 29, it was announced that last-minute negotiations would be held that afternoon between White House and prosecution force attorneys. Just before noon, however, presidential press secretary Ronald L. Ziegler hurriedly announced that the White House would supply Jaworski with the materials sought in the subpoena. Neither side elaborated on what was in the subpoena. The negotiation session was canceled.

To avoid further partisan wrangling over the rights accorded White House defense counsel James D. St. Clair in the impeachment inquiry, the Judiciary Committee did not meet on the matter of impeachment during the week. St. Clair and the inquiry staff were preparing memoranda setting out the arguments for granting and denying certain rights to the legal counsel representing an official subject of an impeachment inquiry. The committee was not expected to resolve the issue at least until the memoranda had been presented.

From Court to Committee. The potentially crucial, but undramatic, transfer of the grand jury report and evidence from the court to the committee followed a decision by attorneys for former White House chief of staff H.R. Haldeman and his former aide, Gordon Strachan, to concede defeat in their legal battle to bar disclosure of the report to anyone. Attorneys for Haldeman and Strachan, two of the seven defendants in the Watergate coverup case, had argued that handing over the report to the House inquiry inevitably would lead to leaks and pretrial publicity jeopardizing their clients' right to a fair trial. After Sirica and the court of appeals, District of Columbia circuit, had rejected their arguments, the attorneys declined to appeal to the Supreme Court, feeling that they had "exhausted all reasonable avenues for relief."

The deadline for their appeal expired at 5 p.m. March 25. At 9:30 a.m. March 26, special impeachment inquiry counsel John M. Doar and Albert E. Jenner Jr. appeared at the federal courthouse at the foot of Capitol Hill. After a two-hour closed session with Sirica and a representative of the special prosecutor's office, during which the items in the briefcase were examined to ensure that they were all there, Doar and Jenner emerged with the controversial materials.

They took the materials directly to the tightly guarded impeachment inquiry offices, where access to them was governed by the committee's special procedures. Access was allowed initially only to Doar, Jenner and the committee chairman, Peter W. Rodino Jr. (D N.J.), and to the committee's ranking Republican, Edward Hutchinson (R Mich.).

Rodino and Hutchinson began examining the grand jury report and evidence March 27. After three hours of reading and listening, then each reported briefly to other members of the committee—without revealing details of the contents.

Continued Criticism. Late in the previous week, Senate Minority Leader Hugh Scott (R Pa.) revealed that in a March 19 meeting with St. Clair, he had warned the White House that a confrontation with Congress over the additional information and tapes requested by the impeachment inquiry would endanger President Nixon's fate in both the House and the Senate. *The Los Angeles Times* March 23 carried a story reporting that the White House had, apparently as a result of Scott's warning, decided to give the additional tapes to the committee. In another story, the Times stated that the tape recording of the crucial March 21, 1973, meeting between John W. Dean III, former White House counsel, and the President unambiguously pointed toward the President's involvement in the coverup.

Angrily denying both reports, presidential press secretary Ronald L. Ziegler attacked the committee for "this lack of regard for the responsible handling of materials provided to the committee." This, he continued, "cannot help but influence the White House with respect to providing additional materials in the future."

But the next day, Howard H. Baker Jr. (R Tenn.), ranking Republican on the Senate Watergate committee, urged Nixon to give the House investigators all relevant tapes and documents. Appearing on the CBS-TV program "Face the Nation," Baker said that Nixon should not rely on "narrow legalism" to withhold information, but should give the committee anything that was arguably relevant. He suggested that the President make public the controversial March 21, 1973, tape of his conversation with Dean.

On the other hand, Baker advised the House committee to honor "whatever reasonable request the President makes, such as the presence of counsel in the principal deliberations and investigation of the committee."

Continuing his criticism of the inquiry staff, Ziegler suggested March 25 that the staff accelerate its pace

(Continued on p. 295)

Milk Money: Steady Flow to Republicans, Democrats

As the Senate debated a proposal for public financing of political campaigns during the week that ended March 30, fresh revelations of illegal or questionable contributions to past races made front-page news. The names of prominent Democrats as well as Republicans showed up in the stories, which were based on a study of political activities by the nation's largest dairy cooperative, Associated Milk Producers Inc. (AMPI).

AMPI's board of directors commissioned a law firm to prepare the report after the co-op came under fire for its financial dealings with the Nixon administration. The document was submitted to the U.S. District Court in Kansas City, Mo., where the Justice Department was conducting an antitrust suit against AMPI and two other milk cooperatives, and was made public March 14. The Watergate special prosecution force and the Senate investigating committee received copies.

Money for Democrats. The milk group's large campaign contributions and pledges to President Nixon had been under investigation for almost a year—and AMPI was being sued by associates of consumer advocate Ralph Nader for allegedly convincing the administration to raise milk price supports in 1971 in exchange for campaign money. But the new report showed that AMPI had an earlier political connection to Democrats. *(Nixon position, p. 191)*

The 1968 presidential campaign of Sen. Hubert H. Humphrey (D Minn.) and the 1972 campaign of Rep. Wilbur D. Mills (D Ark.) received AMPI money, as did Humphrey's 1970 Senate race, the report said. Both men denied any knowledge that the funds had come from a corporate source and were thus illegal.

An audit accompanying the report on AMPI's political activities listed contributions of $91,691 to Humphrey's presidential campaign and $34,500 to his Senate race, according to the Associated Press. But the auditors cautioned that the figures might be incomplete, and various news reports gave different figures.

The 1968 contribution was used to pay the salary and travel expenses of a campaign worker, reimburse individuals who made political donations to Humphrey, and defray miscellaneous political expenses, the report said.

To help Mills backers drum up a presidential campaign, the report said, AMPI paid the salary and apartment rent of a full-time campaign worker in late 1971 and early 1972. Another worker's rent and rented furniture for both were also covered.

It was the second admission of illegal corporate donations to Mills' unsuccessful 1968 presidential bid. Gulf Oil Corporation and one of its executives had pleaded guilty Nov. 13, 1973, to contributing $15,000 in company funds to Mills, who later repaid Gulf out of his own pocket. *(Gulf plea, p. 133)*

Johnson Ties. The AMPI report also revealed the group's political ties with the late President Johnson, although contributions were not mentioned. Before Johnson announced in 1968 that he would not run for re-election, for example, the report said AMPI paid a total of $104,521 to print and distribute a booklet of Johnson speeches and color photographs entitled *No Retreat from Tomorrow*. It appeared "to have been designed as a memento for campaign contributors," a March 27 *Washington Post* article said.

Several former Johnson officials figured in the report. Jake Jacobsen, a former Johnson White House aide who became an AMPI lawyer, was said to have requested and been granted a $10,000 cash fund "for the use of Mr. John B. Connally," then treasury secretary, in 1971. Jacobsen, who was quoted as saying Connally refused the money twice, was indicted Feb. 21 for lying to a Watergate grand jury about the fund. He pleaded not guilty. *(p. 249)*

Payback Scheme. Although the Democrats continued to receive AMPI funds, the co-op's executives decided to "make peace" with the Republicans after Nixon's election in 1968, the report said. In August 1969, they arranged for delivery of a suitcase packed with $100,000 in $100 bills to the President's personal attorney, Herbert W. Kalmbach.

The report detailed an elaborate scheme the dairy executives devised to disguise the contribution when they realized several days later that it was illegal, according to the study. An attorney for AMPI admitted in 1974 that the contribution violated federal election law. *(p. 259)*

The executives took out a $10,000 bank loan to replace the cash withdrawn from their political fund, and then set out to repay it by collecting funds on false pretexts from lawyers and public relations experts on retainer to the co-op, the report stated. A number of those men, all of whom later denied knowing the real purpose of their donations, turned out to be well-known Democrats. They included attorney Richard Maguire, a former treasurer of the Democratic National Committee; Ted Van Dyk and Kirby Jones, public relations men who took important jobs in the 1972 presidential campaign of Sen. George McGovern (D S.D.), and Rep. James R. Jones (D Okla.), then a Tulsa attorney.

Van Dyk told *The Washington Post* that he gave the AMPI executives $20,000 as a contribution toward a bonus for the group's Washington representative in December 1969, and was later reimbursed by billing AMPI for his regular services. "I assumed they wanted to do it that way so that other guys at AMPI wouldn't find out about it and get upset," he explained. "I had no reason to think there was anything under the table about this at all."

Rep. Jones said he made two payments of $5,000 each in 1969 and 1970 to help launch AMPI's political committee. And although the report showed he received more than his regular annual retainer in 1969-70, he denied having been repaid for the donation. Jones added that he would be "damned mad" if the money went to Nixon instead of to Democrats, as he was promised.

(Continued from p. 293)

and "perhaps work late into the evenings" to complete analyzing the information it already had received. The White House felt that this phase of the inquiry should be complete "within a matter of weeks," said Ziegler. "They have enough lawyers," he added, referring to the size of the inquiry staff compared with the small White House defense team. (p. 289)

"We stand ready to cooperate," said Ziegler, after the committee staff completed the initial phase of its work.

A spokesman for the committee staff said that members of the inquiry task forces already had been working nights and weekends, before Ziegler's suggestion.

Characterizing Nixon's attacks on the committee as "a wild defensive maneuver...almost beneath the dignity of the office of the President," House Speaker Carl Albert (D Okla.) March 25 criticized such reaction as "damaging the atmosphere...in the House" toward Nixon.

"I think the President would be well advised to cooperate," said Albert in an interview with Public Broadcasting Service. "There's nothing that can be done when one of the big issues is coverup."

In a speech March 27, Assistant Senate Majority Leader Robert C. Byrd (D W.Va.) also criticized the White House handling of the matter. Nixon was attempting to sabotage the impeachment inquiry, he said, using television to "launch subtle, but sustained and unjustified, attacks upon the legislative branch." This strategy, said Byrd, "can only mislead the people...it is calculated to sabotage the legitimate and constitutional impeachment inquiry by the House...and avoid the disaster of a possible trial and conviction by the Senate."

Mitchell-Stans Trial

A star witness for the second time since he lost his job as counsel to President Nixon, John W. Dean III attracted a crowd of eager spectators to the New York City courtroom where the trial of two former Nixon cabinet officers began its sixth week March 25.

Dean had been expected to testify March 21, but the illness of a juror prompted U.S. District Judge Lee P. Gagliardi to recess the trial and postpone his appearance. That heightened the anticipation for Dean's March 25 appearance, just as the drama of his debut at the Senate Watergate committee in June 1973 had been enhanced by a last-minute week-long delay. (Testimony, Vol. I, p. 151)

Government prosecutors were counting on Dean as a key supporter of their conspiracy, obstruction of justice and perjury charges against former Attorney General John N. Mitchell and former Commerce Secretary Maurice H. Stans. Previous prosecution witnesses had been equivocal or hostile to the prosecutor's case and had proclaimed their friendship for the defendants. (Previous trial story, p. 286)

Mitchell and Stans were accused of interfering with a Securities and Exchange Commission (SEC) investigation of the business activities of financier Robert L. Vesco in exchange for a secret $200,000 campaign contribution —and of lying about their attempts to cover up the gift. Dean was named as a co-conspirator in the case but was not indicted.

Mitchell, Stans Attacked. He had been known as "Mr. Mitchell's man at the White House," Dean said,

but his courtroom testimony supported charges of perjury and conspiracy against his former mentor. Mitchell had told the grand jury he never discussed the Vesco case; but, according to Dean, he and Mitchell had conferred on the subject at least 19 times. During one of those conversations, Dean alleged, Mitchell asked him to try to delay part of the SEC investigation until after the 1972 presidential election.

Buttressing the government's conspiracy charges, Dean testified that he met with Stans and Mitchell twice in November 1972 to discuss Vesco's cash gift, and that the two men had expressed concern that the contribution would come to light before election day. At the second meeting, at which Mitchell and Stans agreed to refund the cash, Dean said, Stans mentioned that he had contacted the SEC's general counsel, G. Bradford Cook, and thought Cook "might be helpful" in covering up the contribution.

Testifying at the trial March 27, Cook said he had deleted a paragraph mentioning the $200,000 gift from the SEC's complaint against Vesco—at Stans' request. Cook became SEC chairman in March 1973, but resigned in May after the Vesco indictment disclosed that he had talked to Stans about the case. (Vol. I, p. 67-68)

Cook's predecessor as SEC chairman, William J. Casey, had testified a week earlier that he did not learn of the Vesco contribution until it was made public in early 1973. But Dean contradicted that assertion, saying that he told Casey about the gift in the fall of 1972, while the investigation was still in progress.

Another surprise during Dean's first day in the witness chair was his assertion that Mitchell had called him on March 20, 1973, with a request that Dean complain to then Attorney General Richard G. Kleindienst about the "runaway" New York grand jury that was questioning Mitchell about the Vesco case.

Defense Counterattack. Defense attorneys armed with partial transcripts of three White House tapes attacked Dean's credibility March 26, injecting the specter of Watergate in the process. The judge had instructed the government to provide the defense with certain White House tapes as a condition of Dean's appearance.

Mitchell's chief lawyer, Peter Fleming Jr., referred to a March 20, 1973, conversation between Nixon and Dean during which Dean mentioned the "runaway grand jury" but said nothing about Mitchell's request for Dean to call Kleindienst. "Mr. Dean, wasn't this a period of your life when you were telling the President all the truth?" he asked. "Yes, indeed," Dean responded.

Fleming said the transcript showed Mitchell's real concern was the grand jury's interest in the activities of Nixon's relatives, Watergate conspirator E. Howard Hunt Jr. and Republican campaign saboteur Donald H. Segretti.

At that, Stans' lawyer moved for a mistrial on grounds that prejudicial Watergate material had been injected into the trial. Judge Gagliardi refused.

In another attempt to discredit Dean's testimony, the defense attorneys led him through a recitation of his involvement in the Watergate coverup and disbarment from practicing law in Virginia. Observers remarked that throughout the tough cross-examination, Dean maintained the same dispassionate precision he displayed during the Watergate hearings.

Poll Report

President Nixon's popularity dropped to its all-time low in both the Gallup Poll and the Harris Survey published March 21. *(Earlier poll report, p. 280)*

Both polls reflected the indictment March 1 of seven former White House or Nixon re-election campaign aides for their alleged involvement in the Watergate coverup. Neither poll reflected the President's news conferences and speeches in which he explained his positions on the scandal and on the House impeachment investigation. Gallup's interviews were conducted Feb. 22-25 and March 1-4. Harris' were conducted March 3-7.

Gallup. This question was asked in the Gallup survey: "Do you approve or disapprove of the way Nixon is handling his job as President?"

	Latest	February
Approve	25%	27%
Disapprove	64	63
No opinion	11	10

Harris. Nixon's rating in the Harris Survey was one point higher than in the Gallup Poll. But it was three points lower than the Harris rating in February.

Positive	26%
Negative	71
Not sure	3

Week's Watergate Chronology

Following is a day-to-day chronology of the week's events in the Watergate case:

MARCH 21

Nixon Homes. A House Government Operations subcommittee investigating federal expenditures for Nixon's San Clemente, Calif., and Key Biscayne, Fla., homes reported that the government had spent $17-million over the past five years. In addition to the $10-million in fixed expenditures already disclosed, the report said that $7.1-million was spent for "personnel permanently assigned" to the California and Florida houses. *(Earlier story, Vol. I, p. 271)*

Rodino Reply. Responding to Nixon counsel James D. St. Clair's request to cross-examine witnesses and introduce evidence at the House Judiciary Committee's impeachment inquiry, Chairman Peter W. Rodino (D N.J.) warned that the White House bid for an adversary role could turn the House proceedings into a full-scale trial and thus usurp the Senate's constitutional role as the sole judge of Nixon's conduct in office. *(p. 282)*

Sirica Upheld. The District of Columbia Court of Appeals, in a 5-to-1 decision, upheld U.S. District Judge John J. Sirica's earlier decision to turn the Watergate grand jury's sealed report on possible Nixon involvement in the Watergate scandal over to the House Judiciary Committee. *(p. 283)*

Jaworski Subpoena. Leon Jaworski, special Watergate prosecutor, disclosed that he had subpoenaed additional documents from the White House files. Neither Gerald L. Warren, deputy White House press secretary, nor Jaworski would disclose any details about the subpoena, but Jaworski told reporters that there could be further subpoenas "relating to areas under investigation."

Mitchell-Stans Trial. The trial of two of Nixon's former top aides was adjourned for four days when one of the jurors became ill. Before adjournment, U.S. District Judge Lee P. Gagliardi ordered the government to turn over to the defendants portions of a transcript of a tape of John W. Dean III talking to the President.

White House Offer. Presidential counselor Bryce W. Harlow suggested that Nixon would be willing to have St. Clair, his lawyer, screen transcripts of the disputed 42 tapes and then turn the edited transcripts over to the House Judiciary Committee for its impeachment inquiry.

Milk Fund. Bob Lilly, legislative director of Associated Milk Producers Inc., a Texas-based milk cooperative, said he used the Texas deputy agriculture commissioner as "a conduit for political funds" to state legislators in the off-election year of 1969, according to a report prepared for the milk co-op by a Little Rock, Ark., law firm that was made public in U.S. District Court in Kansas City, Mo. *(p. 294)*

MARCH 22

White House Tapes. At least one of 17 wiretaps authorized by Nixon for "national security" reasons provided the White House with political intelligence about the presidential campaign of Sen. Edmund S. Muskie (D Maine). The tap was on the home telephone of Morton H. Halperin, a former National Security Council official who joined the Muskie staff. The disclosure came as Mr. Halperin won a U.S. District Court order in Washington ordering the Nixon administration to turn over to Halperin the records of the wiretap. *(Earlier story, Vol. I, p. 259)*

March 21 Tape. The tape recording of Nixon's March 21, 1973, conversation with John W. Dean III about hush money to silence the Watergate defendants was "explosive" and "unambiguous," *The Los Angeles Times* reported two government sources familiar with the tape as saying. A spokesman for the Watergate special prosecutor refused comment. White House deputy press secretary Gerald L. Warren said, "We expected this type of story...to be planted."

Nixon Retirement. Nixon's older brother, F. Donald, would retire in April as an executive of the Marriott Corporation, a company spokesman announced.

MARCH 23

Milk Co-op Aid. American Milk Producers Inc. spent $137,000 in corporate funds on computer mailing lists for campaign use by midwestern Democrats, including Senators Hubert H. Humphrey (D Minn.) and James Abourezk (D S.D.) in 1971, according to court documents and a report disclosed in U.S. District Court in Kansas City, Mo.

Nixon Tax Lawyers. The White House said that Herbert W. Kalmbach and Frank De Marco Jr., the two lawyers who advised Nixon on his personal income taxes, would be released from attorney-client confidentiality to testify before the Joint Committee on Internal Revenue Taxation that was probing the President's tax returns.

MARCH 24

Rebozo Testimony. Charles G. Rebozo, the President's close friend, was unable to recall with certainty for the Senate Watergate committee several details of his receipt of a $100,000 cash payment he received from the Howard Hughes organization nearly four years earlier, according to sources close to the committee's investigation. The most crucial problem was Rebozo's inability to remember attending a meeting, to which he had previously alluded, that he had with Nixon and a Hughes representative at Nixon's San Clemente estate in July 1970.

More Milk Aid. The brief presidential campaign of Rep. Wilbur D. Mills (D Ark.) received early financial support in corporate contributions from American Milk Producers Inc. According to a report on the group's political dealings, two top workers in the Mills campaign were paid in corporate funds from the Texas-based co-op.

Media Suits. The Watergate special prosecution force said it had found no evidence that antitrust suits the Justice Department filed against three television networks were improperly motivated.

Nixon Audit. The White House denied a report in *The Baltimore Sun* that the President's 1968 income tax return was being examined by Internal Revenue Service agents. The Sun said that one of the main items being challenged was a deduction, as a business expense, of 25 per cent of the depreciation of the New York cooperative apartment formerly owned by the Nixons.

Finch Comments. Former presidential aide Robert Finch blamed former Nixon advisers H. R. Haldeman and John D. Ehrlichman, among others, for the problems of Watergate, but added that Nixon, his friend of 25 years, must bear part of the responsibility. "The President's not without blame" for Watergate, Finch said in an interview. "After all, in the final analysis, the President came down in support of their—Haldeman, Erlichman and others—control of the staff, as against listening to me or somebody else."

MARCH 25

Mitchell-Stans Trial. Former White House counsel John Dean testified that former Nixon lieutenants John N. Mitchell and Maurice H. Stans had made determined efforts to keep Robert L. Vesco's financial scandal secret until after election day in 1972. "The whole thing is something we just don't need before the election," Dean quoted Mitchell as saying. *(Details, p. 295)*

Milk Money Cover. Several prominent Democrats were used by American Milk Producers Inc. in an elaborate scheme to cover up a $100,000 cash contribution for President Nixon, it was reported.

Evidence to House. Attorneys for the House Judiciary Committee's impeachment inquiry received from U.S. District Judge John J. Sirica the briefcase of evidence and the two-page report that the Watergate grand jury wanted turned over to the impeachment inquiry. *(Earlier story, p. 273)*

Albert Warning. House Speaker Carl Albert (D Okla.) warned Nixon that he was making a mistake

if he thought he could base a successful defense against impeachment solely on tough political statements and attacks on the House Judiciary Committee. "If the President is trying to win this...by going out and making speeches and charges in political audiences or semi-political audiences, I think he's making a mistake," Albert said.

MARCH 26

McCord Papers. *The Chicago Tribune* reported that a Central Intelligence Agency (CIA) agent burned papers in James W. McCord's home after the Watergate break-in to destroy anything linking McCord to the CIA. However, Rep. Lucien N. Nedzi (D Mich.), chairman of the House Intelligence Subcommittee, said his investigation of the incident produced no evidence either that the CIA was involved or that McCord's wife or the CIA agent were destroying evidence.

More Milk Disclosures. American Milk Producers Inc. (AMPI) paid Lady Bird Johnson's family corporation $94,000 a year for use of an airplane hangared at the LBJ ranch, the Associated Press disclosed. An internal audit of AMPI showed that the co-op paid at least $91,691 in corporate money to support Hubert H. Humphrey's 1968 presidential campaign and $34,500 to his 1970 senatorial campaign.

Mitchell-Stans Trial. In his cross-examination of John W. Dean III, the lawyer for John N. Mitchell had Dean admit that he did not tell Nixon the whole story about Mitchell's involvement in the Vesco investigation.

White House Document. The White House prepared a document arguing that the House Judiciary Committee would be "severely prejudicing" Nixon's rights if it refused to allow his counsel to represent him and cross-examine witnesses in its impeachment inquiry.

Target Date. House Judiciary Committee Chairman Peter W. Rodino Jr. said that it "doesn't really seem likely" that the committee could complete its impeachment inquiry by April 30. It might take another month, he said.

MARCH 27

Mitchell-Stans Trial. Maurice H. Stans was depicted in testimony as seeking to limit a Securities and Exchange Commission (SEC) inquiry of financier Robert L. Vesco. G. Bradford Cook, former SEC general counsel and chairman, said at the trial that in late 1972 Stans asked him to reword part of an SEC charge against Vesco to avoid disclosing Vesco's secret cash contribution to Nixon. Cook said he had the paragraph changed.

Byrd Statement. Robert C. Byrd (D W.Va.), the Senate Democratic whip, criticized Nixon's stance on impeachment as an effort to sabotage the House investigation by portraying Congress as out to get him and by creating "underdog sympathy" for himself.

More Tapes Missing. Some of the 42 Nixon tapes the House Judiciary Committee sought might not exist, Ronald L. Ziegler, Nixon's press secretary, hinted. It would depend on whether the conversations took place in rooms with recording equipment, he said. However, Ziegler said he was sure none of the tapes had been tampered with. √

NIXON AGREES TO PAY $467,000 IN BACK TAXES

Six months after it was disclosed that he had paid only nominal sums in federal income taxes during his first term as President, Richard M. Nixon April 3 received a bill for nearly half a million dollars in taxes he allegedly should have paid for those years.

The financial impact of the finding was staggering, even for a man whose annual salary was $200,000. But in December, Nixon had asked the Joint Committee on Internal Revenue Taxation to review his tax returns for 1969 through 1972. Those returns had been the subject of much speculation and questioning after disclosure of his small tax payments and of the circumstances surrounding his major tax deduction over those years, his gift of vice presidential papers to the National Archives.

The President had said that he would abide by the finding of the joint committee. The committee's staff report was released April 3, finding that the President owed $476,531 in taxes and interest. An Internal Revenue Service (IRS) report that the President had received April 2, which was not made public, contained similar findings.

Nixon announced April 3 that he would not contest the findings but would pay the IRS bill of more than $467,000. The White House later said that this payment would "almost wipe out" the President's personal savings and probably would force him to obtain a loan in order to pay the entire amount.

The political impact of the tax matter—a crucial question for a President already the subject of a House impeachment inquiry—was unclear as the week ended. As Robert W. Kastenmeier (D Wis.), a senior Democrat on the House committee in charge of that inquiry, explained: "The tax report will not enhance in any way the President's standing with the public or the committee.... Prompt payment...may mitigate somewhat the damage which has been done."

Few mustered an argument to back up the claim that Nixon would benefit from a finding that he had not paid the taxes he should have paid during his first term.

Even before the disclosure of the tax findings, key Republicans had continued to make clear their distance from the problems surrounding the President. At a meeting of Republican leaders from the Midwest on March 30, Vice President Ford directed stinging criticism at the Committee for the Re-election of the President: "The political lesson of Watergate is this. Never again must America allow an arrogant, elite guard of political adolescents like CREEP to bypass the regular party organization and dictate the terms of a national election."

Nixon's continued refusal to give the House Judiciary Committee the material it had requested seemed to be moving the committee toward subpoenaing that material. The committee set an April 9 deadline for a White House response, and even conservative Republican members were indicating their support for a subpoena if necessary.

Nixon's Tax Problems

Members of Congress had mixed views of what effect Nixon's income tax affairs would have on impeachment proceedings or a possible resignation.

Nixon announced April 3 that he would pay about $467,000 in taxes and interest that the Internal Revenue Service had informed him he owed. The announcement came less than five hours after the Joint Committee on Internal Revenue Taxation released a staff study claiming that Nixon owed $476,431 in taxes and interest.

"I don't think this will have any direct effect on impeachment, since his taxes are not an issue in the impeachment question," said Sen. Wallace F. Bennett (R Utah), the ranking Senate minority member of the committee. Bennett expressed relief that Nixon had agreed to pay the back taxes without challenging them in court. "I am glad he did this, because, coming just 10 days before April 15, this sets a wonderful example for the American taxpayer," he said.

But the committee vice chairman, Rep. Wilbur D. Mills (D Ark.), repeated his earlier assertion that the staff report would put pressure on Nixon to resign. *(Earlier statement, p. 288)*

The chairman of the House Republican Conference, Rep. John B. Anderson (R Ill.), said Nixon's decision to pay was "more seemly than going into tax court and litigating." But, he said, "It would be almost fatuous to deny that this is a minus in the whole equation as far as the President is concerned."

White House Response. In announcing that Nixon would pay the amount set by the IRS, the White House noted that the still-secret IRS report "rebuts any suggestion of fraud on the part of the President," and the Joint Committee staff's report "offers no facts which would support any such charge."

The White House said Nixon had decided to pay the taxes even though he was convinced his lawyers "can make a very strong case" against the major adverse findings. The White House said he would pay up without quarrel because of his Dec. 8, 1973, pledge to abide by the findings of the Joint Committee.

"In view of the fact that the staff report indicates that the proper amount to be paid must be determined by the Internal Revenue Service, he (Nixon) has today instructed payment of the $432,787.13 set forth by the Internal Revenue Service, plus interest," the White House said. *(Text of statement, p. 299; excerpts of committee report, p. 307; Nixon's financial disclosure and joint committee profile, p. 181, 182)*

Financial Blow. The decision by Nixon to pay the taxes dealt a heavy blow to his financial status. In Nixon's December financial disclosure, the White House cited an audit performed by the accounting firm of Coopers &

Lybrand, which showed that as of May 31, 1973, Nixon and his wife had cash holdings of about $433,000.

A White House official said Nixon probably would use part of his savings to pay the $467,000 the IRS said he owed. He probably would "get a loan to pay the rest of it," the official said. No family "likes to wipe out its entire savings," he added.

The Wall Street Journal noted April 4 that Nixon legally would have three years after paying the taxes in which he could contest the IRS rulings in the courts and seek a refund. A White House spokesman declined to say precisely when Nixon would pay the additional taxes, declaring that it was "a matter between the President and the IRS."

Committee Actions. The joint committee voted April 3 to release the staff report in order to prevent leaks while the committee considered what action it should take on the politically explosive matter. Nixon relieved the committee of that problem when he announced that he would pay.

The committee "has viewed its staff report on the President's taxes for the years 1969 through 1972,"

White House Statement on Taxes

Following is the text of a statement issued by the White House April 3 on the President's decision to settle his back taxes:

We have learned of the decision by the Joint Committee on Internal Revenue Taxation to release a staff analysis of the President's taxes before the Committee itself has had opportunity to evaluate the staff views, and before the President's tax counsel could advise the Committee of their views on the many legal matters in dispute in that report.

Yesterday the President received a statement from the Internal Revenue Service indicating its view, also, that he should pay an additional tax.

The President's tax counsel have advised him that the positions they have sought to present to the Committee, as outlined in their brief, are valid and compelling. His intent to give the papers was clear. Their delivery was accomplished in March, 1969, four months before the July deadline. His intent as to the amount of the gift was stated to his counsel. Because of these facts the President's tax counsel strongly affirm that those various issues could be sharply and properly contested in court proceedings such as are open to an ordinary taxpayer to review the decisions of the Internal Revenue Service.

The President believes that his tax counsel can make a very strong case against the major conclusions set forth in the Committee's staff report. However, at the time the President voluntarily requested the Committee to conduct its examination of his tax returns, he stated that he would abide by the Committee's judgment. In view of the fact that the staff report indicates that the proper amount to be paid must be determined by the Internal Revenue Service, he has today instructed payment of the $432,787.13 set forth by the Internal Revenue Service, plus interest.

It should be noted that the report by the Internal Revenue Service rebuts any suggestion of fraud on the part of the President. The Committee's staff report offers no facts which would support any such charge.

Any errors which may have been made in the preparation of the President's returns were made by those to whom he delegated the responsibility for preparing his returns and were made without his knowledge and without his approval.

a spokesman said April 4 in a prepared statement. "While we have not completely analyzed all of the technical aspects of the report, the members agree with the substance of most of the recommendations made by the staff."

Because of Nixon's decision to pay, the spokesman declared, the committee "has decided to conclude its examination of the President's returns. The committee commends the President for his prompt decision to make these tax payments."

Sen. Carl T. Curtis (R Neb.), a member of the committee, said in a statement, "I concur in the motion to conclude the examination but dissent from the concurrence with the staff report." Curtis April 3 had pointed to conflicting information in the staff report and had called for a court proceeding to clarify any disputes.

The committee chairman, Sen. Russell B. Long (D La.), said April 4, "There are some items where the staff may have been too tough on the President. Auditors are like that. When the IRS gets after you, they range from hard to fair."

According to the report, the staff shared information with the IRS and in some cases conducted joint interviews.

The report covered 10 areas in which it cited "deficiencies" in Nixon's tax returns for the years 1969 through 1972. Because the statute of limitations for the payment of back taxes had run out for 1969, the staff noted that payment by Nixon of additional taxes for that year "would be voluntary." The staff did not include interest for that year in its recommended levy.

The staff found that Nixon owed $171,055 in additional taxes for 1969 and the following amounts, including interest, for the other years: $110,048 for 1970, $100,214 for 1971 and $95,114 for 1972.

Papers. A major part of the 210-page staff report and its 783-page documentary appendix dealt with charitable deductions taken by Nixon for the gift of his vice presidential papers from 1969 through 1972.

The $482,018 total taken in deductions for the papers "should not, in the staff's view, be allowed because the gift was made after July 25, 1969, the date when the provisions of the Tax Reform Act of 1969 disallowing such deductions became effective," the report stated.

In the introduction to the report, the staff declared its belief that it should not consider "whether there was, or was not, fraud or negligence" in the preparation of Nixon's returns, because to do so might prejudge impeachment proceedings. However, the section of the report dealing with the papers cited inconsistencies in some of the accounts of Nixon's intent to donate the papers and when they were legally turned over.

"(T)he staff believes that for purposes of the tax deduction there needs to be some expression that the delivery of these papers represented a gift of a specific portion of the papers," according to the report. "The staff has no evidence that any such expression, either oral or written, was made on or before July 25, 1969; and no one at the National Archives or the General Services Administration has indicated any awareness that any portion of the papers delivered on March 26-27, 1969, was to be given to the United States as of that date. They believed, rather, that the papers were delivered for storage purposes and that there would be future gifts from among the papers that had been delivered, but not that a gift had been made as of that date."

Nixon's tax lawyers conceded that the deed transferring the papers was not signed until April 1970, about nine months after the law allowing such deductions was changed. They contended, however, that the deed replaced an earlier deed which they said had been destroyed and that, for this reason, the 1970 deed was back-dated.

The committee staff rejected this explanation and noted that the deed was not signed by Nixon, but by Edward Morgan, then a presidential counselor. The staff said there was "no evidence that he was authorized to sign for the President."

San Clemente. The staff claimed that, because of erroneous estimates involved in Nixon's sale of a large parcel of his San Clemente, Calif., estate to his friends, Charles G. Rebozo and Robert Abplanalp, in 1970, a capital gain of $117,836 should have been declared.

Nixon's tax accountant had held that the President did not receive any gain on the sale, even though independent auditors who reviewed Nixon's finances at his request found that he should have declared a capital gain of $117,370.

The committee staff's finding was based on its commission of a Santa Ana, Calif., engineering firm and a local real estate appraisal to determine independently the fair market value of the property sold and the property retained.

New York City. Concluding that Nixon's principal residence was not San Clemente, as his tax accountants had held, the committee staff found that Nixon was not allowed to defer recognition of his capital gain on the 1969 sale of his New York City cooperative apartment.

Nixon had argued that he did not move to declare a capital gain because he had reinvested the proceeds of the New York sale in the San Clemente property, which he declared was his principal residence. The staff held that Nixon should have declared a $151,848 capital gain.

Business Expenses. The staff recommended disallowance of four categories of business expenses that the President had claimed as deductions: business use of his San Clemente residence, business use of his Key Biscayne, Fla., residence, depreciation expenses of a cabinet table he bought for use in the White House and business expenses that the staff found could not be adequately substantiated. The President had claimed a total of $85,399 in deductions.

The staff suggested the government should reimburse Nixon for his furniture expenditures and pay Nixon $4,816.84 for the cabinet table.

Florida. The committee staff declared that the President should have reported $11,617 in capital gains from the 1972 sale of a Florida lot. Nixon reported a gain on 60 per cent of the sale, but his daughter, Tricia Nixon Cox, reported the rest. The staff held that the entire amount should have been reported by the President.

Aircraft. While accepting the argument that all of Nixon's use of government aircraft was connected with his duties as President, the staff held

Personal vs. Official Expenses

Much of the taxation committee staff's time was spent determining just how many government services provided to Nixon were related to his office as President and thus were not declarable as personal income.

Handrails. One item that the staff believed served no presidential imperative was the installation of handrails at Nixon's San Clemente estate. "The installation of the new wrought iron handrail and the remodeling of the existing redwood handrail leading to the beach were not for security purposes," the staff concluded. "While there is a safety element present, the hazard involved is the same as anyone having a private beach would face, i.e., the danger of slipping, and is not related to the President's position.... Thus, the staff believes that the full cost of these improvements should be taxable income to the President."

Airplanes. Another problem was whether or not any of the President's use of government aircraft to fly from Washington, D.C., to his private residences and back was of a personal nature and should be declared as income.

"A President cannot take 'personal trips' or 'trips...for vacation purposes' on Air Force One," argued Nixon's tax lawyers, Kenneth W. Gemmill and H. Chapman Rose, in an April 1 response to the committee chairman, Sen. Russell B. Long (D La.). "Every President carries with him as he travels his Constitutional burdens of, among other things, Commander-in-Chief of the Armed Forces, chief administrative officer of the Executive Branch, and Chief of State charged with our Nation's dealings with foreign powers.... No President, therefore, has 'vacations' or 'personal trips' as people normally envisage those terms. He is on official business day and night as long as he holds office."

While pointing out that some of the President's use of government aircraft "could be classified as primarily personal since the flights take him to locations where he spends a significant part of his time on vacation," the staff agreed not to recommend that such flights be charged as personal income.

However, the staff differed with Nixon's lawyers on the use of such flights by the President's family and friends. "The staff believes...that the President does receive economic benefit and that an amount should be included in his income subject to tax with respect to the personal use of Government planes by his family and personal friends," the staff report stated.

that the personal use of such aircraft by Nixon's family and friends should be classified as taxable income totaling $27,015.19. *(Box, this page)*

Improvements. The staff combed through government-financed improvements to Nixon's Key Biscayne and San Clemente residences and found "those undertaken primarily for the President's personal benefit" to be worth $92,298, which the staff concluded should be declared as taxable income. At San Clemente, these improvements included an exhaust fan, den windows, heating system, gazebo, boundary surveys, sewer, handrails, paving cabana, stair rail to a beach, railroad crossing and warning signals, landscape construction and maintenance. Key Biscayne improvements included a shuffleboard court, fence and hedge system, landscape construction and maintenance.

Sales Tax. The staff declared that Nixon should be allowed an additional $1,007 in sales tax deductions.

Gasoline Tax. Nixon's deductions of $148 for gasoline tax should not be allowed, the staff held; but $10 more than the President claimed in 1972 could be allowed.

Other Items. The staff commented briefly on a number of other parts of Nixon's returns, which included items that it said should have been reported as income but which "are entirely offset by deductions and hence do not increase taxable income."

A Committee Deadline

"The patience of this committee is now wearing thin," said House Judiciary Committee Chairman Peter W. Rodino (D N.J.) April 4. His warning opened a committee briefing on the impeachment inquiry and led up to an announcement that the committee was setting an April 9 deadline for the White House response to its six-week-old request for information. *(p. 257, 270)*

"When we made our request, we made it not out of curiosity, not because we were prosecutors, but because it is our responsibility," Rodino continued, referring to the committee's Feb. 25 request for some 40 recorded conversations between the President and his aides. "We have tried to pursue it in a spirit of accommodation.... Yet there comes a time when patience and accommodation can begin to undermine the process...."

Chapin Trial: Nixon Aide Convicted of Perjury Charges

Dwight L. Chapin, President Nixon's former appointments secretary, was convicted April 5 of two counts of perjury. He was acquitted of a third count. Sentencing was set for May 15; the maximum possible penalty was 10 years in prison and $20,000 in fines.

Chapin, the handsome young man who scheduled the President's appointments and trips during Nixon's first term, went on trial April 1, charged with four counts of lying to the Watergate grand jury in April 1973. According to the indictment, he lied when asked about his relationship to, knowledge of and role in the "dirty tricks" campaign conducted in 1972 by a college friend, Donald H. Segretti.

Chapin, 33, appeared before the grand jury a month after he had left his White House job as deputy assistant to the President to assume an executive position with United Air Lines. The statements he made, which assistant special prosecutor Richard J. Davis described as "deliberate lies," included:

• His denial that he had discussed with Segretti —or knew of—the distribution of fake campaign literature.

• His statement that he had advised Segretti, who had called Chapin to say he was concerned about being contacted by the FBI, to talk with the FBI agents.

• His statement that he did not recall telling Segretti to focus his efforts on one Democratic presidential candidate, Sen. Edmund S. Muskie of Maine.

• His denial of knowledge of the salary and expense arrangements between Segretti and Herbert W. Kalmbach, Nixon's former personal lawyer.

This last charge was dismissed by Federal Judge Gerhard A. Gesell April 3 at the conclusion of the prosecution's case. The evidence on that count was "fuzzy," Gesell said, and Segretti's salary was merely a "housekeeping detail."

The jury found Chapin guilty of lying about his conversations with Segretti concerning campaign literature and concentration of the "dirty tricks" on Muskie. It found him not guilty of lying concerning his advice to Segretti about the FBI.

The trial lasted only three days after the jurors were selected on April 1. Davis sought to prove that Chapin had willfully lied under oath before the grand jury. He called four witnesses—Segretti, Kalmbach, former presidential counsel John W. Dean III and Angelo Lano, the FBI agent in charge of investigating the "dirty tricks" campaign. All of the first three prosecution witnesses already had pleaded guilty to some Watergate-related offenses; Segretti had completed serving a 4½-month prison sentence only days before his testimony April 2.

Defense Attorney Jacob Stein described Chapin's testimony as misstatements, due chiefly to his busy White House schedule and lack of attention to details concerning the Segretti operation, and to his poor memory. "There are differences (in the testimony of Chapin and that of Segretti, for example), but nobody's lying," Stein argued. The witnesses for the defense were Chapin, his former personal secretary in the White House, Nell Yates, and John C. Whitaker, under secretary of interior and a former White House aide. The case went to the jury April 4.

In his testimony, Chapin acknowledged hiring Segretti to "cause confusion" among the campaign efforts of Democratic presidential hopefuls, and his efforts to keep secret the White House involvement in the operations. He said he did not keep a close watch over those operations, noting that during some of the time involved he was traveling to China and the Soviet Union to plan the President's trips to those countries.

Chapin, who worked for H. R. Haldeman both in the White House and in the early 1960s in an advertising agency, said that he had hoped to avoid implicating Haldeman, Nixon's former chief of staff, in the "dirty tricks" operation. But he admitted that he told the grand jury, when questioned directly, that Haldeman had approved the hiring of Segretti. Chapin also admitted that he had made "misstatements" to FBI agents investigating his relationship with Segretti. He gave them false information, he said, because he was concerned about leaks.

"We shall not be thwarted by inappropriate legalisms or by narrow obstacles to our inquiry," Rodino said. "We will subpoena them (the sought-after tapes) if we must."

In response to a request from presidential special counsel James D. St. Clair, special committee counsel John M. Doar would send yet another letter to the White House "setting forth specifically why the committee has the responsibility to examine the particular conversations" it sought. That letter would set April 9 as the deadline for a White House response.

"The committee has displayed a large amount of patience," ranking Republican Edward Hutchinson (R Mich.) agreed. Obviously, he continued, the matter could be settled "more expeditiously" if the White House would provide the committee with the requested material. "We're not after irrelevant material or state secrets," he said, "but simply the information which is going to bring this matter to a conclusion."

Doar's letter to St. Clair followed a series of meetings between Doar, special committee minority counsel Albert E. Jenner Jr. and St. Clair. It made clear that the committee sought the tapes to see if they had any bearing on the President's knowledge of or involvement in the obstruction of the investigations into the Watergate affair or into the work of the White House investigative unit known as the plumbers.

The April 9 deadline was simply stated at the end of the letter. Committee members refused to label the deadline an ultimatum, but sentiment to settle the matter and move on was clear. Wiley Mayne (R Iowa), one of the most conservative members of the committee, declared April 4: "We've certainly waited long enough. We should issue a subpoena if that's what is necessary."

The Counsel's Role. The role which the President's counsel should play in the committee inquiry was the subject of three documents presented to committee members April 4. One from St. Clair, backed by another prepared by the inquiry staff at the request of Republican members, supported the White House request "to participate fully in all proceedings." A third, prepared at the direction of Chairman Rodino by the inquiry staff, set out historical precedents and indicated that the committee had wide discretion in deciding what St. Clair's role should be. It noted, too, that that decision could be deferred until a later stage in the proceedings.

The latter memo also proposed a way in which the committee might assess the evidence assembled on the charges against the President. Initially, the memo proposed, the staff would give each committee member a notebook, setting out the relevant facts which the staff believed were established by the evidence. Each statement would be annotated to indicate what related evidence supported it.

At the same time, an index would be given to the committee reflecting all the material accumulated by the staff. Counsel would go over the evidence paragraph by paragraph with the committee. Then the committee would discuss the evidence, including the need for additional material or testimony. The committee might also then decide to inquire into additional matters which the staff had not previously investigated.

Three points would have to be decided by the committee in regard to this procedure, if it were followed,

Reinecke Indictment

California Lt. Gov. Ed Reinecke was indicted by a Watergate grand jury April 3 on three counts of lying to the Senate Judiciary Committee about Republican Party dealings with the International Telephone and Telegraph Corporation (ITT).

At a press conference in Sacramento, Calif., after the indictment was announced in Washington, D.C., Reinecke proclaimed his innocence and vowed to continue his race for the Republican gubernatorial nomination. "I will not plead guilty. There will be no plea bargaining whatsoever," he said.

ITT Testimony. The charges against Reinecke were based on his April 19, 1972, testimony before the Judiciary Committee, which was considering the nomination of Richard G. Kleindienst as attorney general. At Kleindienst's request, the committee was investigating allegations that the Nixon administration had granted ITT a favorable settlement of an anti-trust suit in exchange for a pledge of financial support for the 1972 Republican convention, then planned for San Diego, Calif.

The San Diego convention plans were canceled after an alleged internal ITT memo linking the pledge and the settlement was leaked to the press March 1, 1972. The memo was dated June 25, 1971; the anti-trust settlement was announced one month later, on July 31. Reinecke and former Attorney General John N. Mitchell were named in the memo as members of a small group that was aware of ITT's campaign pledge.

Reinecke told reporters in March 1972 that he and Mitchell had discussed the ITT pledge in May 1971. But before the Judiciary Committee in April 1972, he revised that to say he and Mitchell had not discussed the promised contribution until September 1971, after the anti-trust settlement had been announced.

He also told the committee that he "had no way of knowing" whether Mitchell knew of ITT's financial commitment before their September discussion. On those points, the indictment charged, Reinecke had been lying.

The third perjury charge related to the California Republican's assertion to the committee that he first had considered trying to have the 1972 convention held in San Diego during a reception for the city's businessmen in Washington, D.C., on April 27, 1971.

The Reinecke indictment raised questions about Mitchell's testimony before the Senate Judiciary Committee March 14-15, 1972. Asked if he had discussed the ITT campaign pledge with Reinecke in April or May 1971, Mitchell said no, and suggested that Reinecke had him mixed up with someone else.

Reinecke reportedly had told federal prosecutors in early 1974 that he was willing to testify against Mitchell on that point, but insisted that he had been genuinely confused during his Senate appearance and had not knowingly lied. *(Kleindienst involvement, p. 102)*

said Doar: Would St. Clair be given the notebook of proposed statement of facts? Would he have access to the evidence backing up the facts and if so, to what extent? Would he be allowed to question and call his own witnesses? Doar indicated that he felt that St. Clair should be given the notebook when committee members received it, but he did not express his opinion on the other questions.

Endorsing the suggested procedure, Jenner said that in his long career as a trial lawyer, it had been his practice to use this method to prepare for the presentation of a case in court.

Continuing to discuss the matter of St. Clair's proper role, Jack Brooks (D Texas) pointed out that during the impeachment inquiry into the conduct of Supreme Court Justice William O. Douglas in 1970, then-Rep. Gerald R. Ford (R Mich.) had argued against allowing Douglas or his lawyer to participate in the committee proceedings, saying that such a role would result in a "whitewash." In response, Tom Railsback (R Ill.) cited Douglas' lawyer as saying that he and Douglas had the right to be present at every committee session involving evidence.

Expressing support for St. Clair's request to participate, at least at some stage in the committee's work, Walter Flowers (D Ala.) commented that the committee seemed to have "the cart before the horse.... St. Clair ought to have that privilege at some point, but the members of this committee haven't had that privilege yet." Flowers was referring to the committee's procedures which precluded members other than Rodino and Hutchinson from seeing the evidence until it was presented to them by the staff. *(p. 247)*

The Committee's Schedule. In response to further questions, Doar said that he hoped to have staff work completed "to the maximum extent possible" before beginning the presentation of evidence to the committee early in May.

Some of the 50-odd charges against President Nixon would not be contained in the initial statement of facts, he said. "With respect to some of the charges, Mr. Jenner and I are prepared to recommend that...we drop some," especially in the area of alleged political use of executive agencies, he said. *(Box, p. 267)*

Remarking critically upon the fact that the committee had had only a few business meetings on the matter of impeachment since the issue was referred to it in October, Republican members urged Rodino to convene such a meeting during the week of April 8, before the House recessed April 11 for Easter.

Hutchinson "implored" Rodino to call such a meeting; McClory seconded that request, stating that the committee needed to adopt rules of procedure, including those defining St. Clair's role, before beginning to assess the evidence. St. Clair should be present at the initial presentation, McClory said, "to object or comment on the presentation...of statements of fact."

Railsback joined in support of the request for a business meeting with David W. Dennis (R Ind.), who said that "if we had a meeting we could thrash some of this out" in regard to St. Clair's role, and possible streamlining of some of the charges.

"The time is long past due for some action by the committee itself," declared Mayne, critical of the "very leisurely pace" at which the committee had proceeded on

impeachment. In the six months since impeachment resolutions were referred to the committee, "we've had only three business meetings" on the subject, he complained, and at those "you, Mr. Chairman, have very severely circumscribed the agenda." On the top of the agenda for the desired business meeting, Mayne said, were action to get the tapes from the White House, a decision to eliminate some of the charges against the President—"we all know a lot of those have no chance of being the basis of impeachment"—and a decision on St. Clair's role.

Mitchell-Stans Trial

The government rested its case against former Nixon administration officials John N. Mitchell and Maurice H. Stans April 3. Prosecutors had called 40 witnesses during the first seven weeks of the trial, which opened Feb. 19 in New York City. Many of them proved reluctant, or unwilling, to support the government's case.

As expected, defense attorneys promptly moved to dismiss the four counts of conspiracy and obstruction of justice against their clients on grounds that the government had failed to produce hard evidence. Mitchell and Stans were accused of attempting to block a Securities and Exchange Commission (SEC) investigation of financier Robert L. Vesco in exchange for a secret $200,000 contribution to President Nixon's re-election campaign, which the two former cabinet officials headed.

"At best, the evidence tends to support an intention on Vesco's part to influence the investigation, but no evidence supports anyone's agreement therewith," a joint defense motion argued, "and most significantly in terms of this trial, there is no evidence that either Mitchell or Stans discharged Vesco's purpose."

No attempt was made to dismiss the six counts of perjury each defendant faced for his testimony before the grand jury that indicted them May 10, 1973—charges that were thought to be the government's strongest suit. Prosecutors spent most of their last morning April 3 reading from transcripts of that testimony for the jury's benefit.

U.S. District Judge Lee P. Gagliardi had said earlier that he probably would dismiss at least one of the three obstruction of justice charges because of overlapping. If all but the perjury charges were dismissed, defense attorneys were expected to move for a new trial on grounds that the jury had been prejudiced by testimony irrelevant to the charges.

Cook, Sporkin Testimony. The government concluded its case with testimony from two former SEC officials and one of the President's brothers. G. Bradford Cook, who appeared March 27-29, offered the most damaging evidence against Stans, but was forced to admit his own perjury in the process. Cook had become the youngest SEC chairman in history in March 1973, but resigned in disgrace after the Vesco indictments implicated him in the alleged obstruction of the case. *(Previous trial coverage, p. 295)*

Cook testified March 27 and 28 that while he was an SEC staff member in charge of the Vesco investigation and an aspirant to the chairmanship, he had discussed the case with Stans and agreed to remove a passage of the agency's complaint against the financier that would have revealed Vesco's secret $200,000 gift.

When a New York grand jury began investigating the case later, Cook said, he and Stans agreed not to mention their discussions of the complaint. Cook described a meeting in the White House dining room March 7, 1973, at which he claimed Stans said to him: "Brad, let's have one of those conversations that doesn't take place." Stans then explained that he had testified before the grand jury two days before without mentioning the discussions, and received Cook's assurance that he would do the same, Cook testified.

Under harsh questioning by defense attorneys trying to discredit him, Cook admitted March 29 that he lied or gave incomplete answers during three grand jury appearances and three congressional hearings on the SEC case during the spring of 1973. He had been less then truthful, Cook said, out of loyalty to Stans and because "I did not want to bring any discredit or dishonor to the commission." But, he insisted, "I am not lying now."

Stanley Sporkin, director of the SEC's enforcement division, testified April 1 that he had been pressured by superiors to delay the commission's investigation of Vesco until after the 1972 election in order to avoid any political embarrassment for the President. But he offered no direct evidence linking Mitchell or Stans to the pressure.

Nixon Testimony. The government's last major witness was the President's younger brother, F. Donald Nixon, who unsuccessfully had tried to avoid testifying because of ill health. In an April 2 appearance that lasted less than half an hour, Nixon told the jury that one of Vesco's lawyers had asked him shortly before the 1972 election to warn the President that Vesco's secret contribution would be made public if the SEC's investigation were not dropped.

He refused to relay the warning, Nixon said, and instead referred the lawyer, Howard Cerny, to Mitchell. "I have never taken anything directly to (the President), nor have I used that office for any purpose for myself or for any client or people I work for," he said.

Vesco contacted him again the weekend after the election, Nixon said, asking for help in delivering a message to Mitchell. Nixon said he agreed to ask the manager of the New York City hotel where Mitchell was staying to deliver an envelope from Vesco. If the envelope contained another threat about the contribution, as the government claimed, the attempt was futile. The SEC filed its charges against Vesco on Nov. 27, 1972.

The President's brother, who was about to retire from the Marriott Corporation (owner of the hotel where Mitchell was staying in November 1972), testified that Cerny, Mitchell and Stans were his friends and that he had met Vesco several times. He said he did not know where his son, Donald A. Nixon, was working, but it was widely known that the President's nephew had been Vesco's personal aide.

Defense attorneys were expected to call President Nixon's other brother, Edward, sometime after they began presenting their case April 5.

Week's Watergate Chronology

Following is a day-to-day chronology of the week's events in the Watergate case: (*Earlier March 27 events, p. 297*)

Opinions on Impeachment

Congressional leaders disagreed over the likelihood of the House of Representatives impeaching President Nixon.

Senate Majority Leader Mike Mansfield (D Mont.) said at a breakfast meeting March 28 several Democratic members of the House had told him "the votes are there" in the House for impeachment.

However, Senate Minority Leader Hugh Scott (R Pa.) told Congressional Quarterly that any such judgment was premature until the House Judiciary Committee had received articles of impeachment from its special impeachment inquiry staff. "Until the articles are presented, anyone doing any counting is doing a lot of guesswork," Scott said through a spokesman. "It depends on whom you talk to at this stage." Scott added that he had not taken any head count, and while he was "not quarreling" with Mansfield, he believed that Mansfield was "just thinking out loud."

House Minority Leader John J. Rhodes (R Ariz.) took a somewhat harder stance during an interview with a *Washington Post* reporter, published March 29. "I don't feel the votes are there now to impeach him," Rhodes said.

But Senate Minority Whip Robert P. Griffin (R Mich.) declared that the likelihood of Nixon's impeachment by the House "seems much greater today than it did a month or two ago."

At his breakfast meeting with reporters, Mansfield said a Senate trial of Nixon could start "within a week or two" of a House impeachment vote. The trial should be televised, Mansfield said, and its timing should not be affected by the November elections. "The election will be secondary," he said.

MARCH 27

Connally Tape. The Watergate special prosecutor had obtained a tape recording of a phone conversation between Nixon and former Treasury Secretary John B. Connally about the controversial 1971 White House decision to increase milk price support, according to news reports. In the phone conversation, Connally evidently recommended higher price supports, the reports stated. (*Previous stories, p. 296, 294*)

MARCH 28

Saxbe Criticized. Sen. Sam J. Ervin Jr. (D N.C.), chairman of the Watergate investigating committee, accused Attorney General William B. Saxbe of violating a pledge to keep out of the Watergate case. Ervin made his charge after the Department of Justice filed a friend-of-the-court brief in the Senate tapes suit against President Nixon.

Break-In Memo. Sen. Lowell P. Weicker Jr. (R Conn.) revealed a memorandum written on White House stationery to former White House counsel John W. Dean III discussing the possibility of a break-in at the offices of Potomac Associates, a Washington research organization. The memo was written by former White House aide John J. Caulfield and was dated July 6, 1971.

Mitchell-Stans Trial. G. Bradford Cook, former general counsel and chairman of the Securities and Exchange Commission (SEC), testified that he agreed, at the request of Maurice H. Stans, to lie to a federal grand jury investigating Robert L. Vesco's secret cash contribution to the Nixon re-election campaign in order to corroborate Stans' own testimony to the grand jury. He said he lied only twice to the grand jury before changing his mind and deciding to tell the truth. *(Details, p. 303)*

Kleindienst Information. Former Attorney General Richard G. Kleindienst reportedly told the FBI that he had no explanation for having withheld from federal prosecutors for nearly a year information that would have linked John N. Mitchell's name with the five men arrested in the Watergate burglary. G. Gordon Liddy, one of the convicted Watergate burglars, invoked Mitchell's name in a conversation with Kleindienst on June 17, 1972, in urging that the five burglars be released, *The New York Times* reported.

Kleindienst Plea Bargaining. *The Washington Post* reported that Kleindienst was plea bargaining with the Watergate special prosecutor and tentatively had agreed to plead guilty to a misdemeanor charge in connection with his 1972 congressional testimony about the International Telephone and Telegraph Corporation anti-trust case.

Mansfield on Impeachment. Senate Majority Leader Mike Mansfield (D Mont.) said he believed "the votes are there" in the House to impeach Nixon. *(Box, p. 304)*

Griffin on Impeachment. Senate Minority Whip Robert P. Griffin (R Mich.) said the likelihood of the President's impeachment by the House "seems much greater today than it did a month or two ago."

Missing Tapes. Gerald L. Warren, deputy White House press secretary, said it was a matter of court record that at least 10 of the 42 presidential conversations sought by the House Judiciary Committee had never been recorded. He would not say whether others also were not on tape.

MARCH 29

Percy Warning. Sen. Charles H. Percy (R Ill.) warned a group of midwestern Republicans that their most immediate problem was the possibility that Nixon might be forced out of office.

Humphrey, Tower Comments. Sen. Hubert H. Humphrey (D Minn.) said "it appears to me that...the majority of the members of the House now (are) for the impeachment charges."

Sen. John G. Tower (R Texas) said he thought the House was still short of an impeachment majority but added that "the atmosphere of confrontation" that had developed in the previous two weeks between Nixon and the House Judiciary Committee had damaged the President's standing.

Subpoenaed Data. The White House agreed to surrender all the material subpoenaed March 15 by the Watergate special prosecutor. *(p. 296, 288)*

Mitchell-Stans Trial. G. Bradford Cook, former SEC chairman, admitted that he had lied under oath on three occasions to the grand jury that investigated the Vesco case and twice to congressional committees. He did it, he said, to protect Maurice H. Stans as well as the reputation of the SEC.

Campaign Trustees. Charles E. Potter and Guilford Dudley Jr., two trustees of the leftover 1972 campaign funds of the Nixon re-election committee, ended a policy that allowed use of the money to pay legal fees of former campaign officials found guilty of misdemeanors. *(p. 281)*

MARCH 30

Ford Attack. In a speech to midwestern Republicans in Chicago, Vice President Ford said of Nixon's 1972 re-election committee: "Never again must Americans allow an arrogant elite guard of political adolescents like CREEP to bypass the regular Republican Party organization. It is we, not they, who should dictate the terms of a national election."

MARCH 31

Ehrlichman Lawyer. Former White House adviser John D. Ehrlichman replaced John J. Wilson with William S. Frates as his defense attorney. Ehrlichman reportedly decided to replace Wilson because of a potential conflict of interest with former White House chief of staff H. R. Haldeman, who also was represented by Wilson.

Papers Culled. The pre-presidential papers for which Nixon claimed a $576,000 tax deduction were culled to eliminate "sensitive" documents, even though Nixon turned the papers over to the National Archives with the specification that no unauthorized person could see them until he left the White House, *The New York Times* reported.

APRIL 1

White House Request. Nixon's tax lawyers asked to appear before the Joint Congressional Committee on Internal Revenue Taxation to dispute a committee staff report that Nixon improperly took large tax deductions on the donation of his vice presidential papers and the sale of property at San Clemente.

Mills Prediction. Rep. Wilbur D. Mills (D Ark.), chairman of the House Ways and Means Committee, predicted that a majority of the House was ready to vote to impeach Nixon. Mills said he detected a changed in the House mood in recent weeks to a pro-impeachment position largely because of "what the membership feels is lack of cooperation on the part of the White House" with the House Judiciary Committee.

Mitchell-Stans Trial. Stanley Sporkin, the head of the SEC's investigation of financier Robert L. Vesco, described six attempts to interfere in the case by former SEC Chairmen G. Bradford Cook and William J. Casey to avoid political embarrassment.

Televising an Impeachment: A Disputed Proposition

Senate Majority Leader Mike Mansfield's (D Mont.) March 28 assertion that a Senate impeachment trial should be televised touched off a controversy over the role of television in impeachment proceedings.

The immediate response from several Republicans was that Mansfield's statement was premature. "We are not addressing that issue until someone sends a resolution dealing with it to the Senate Rules Committee," a spokesman for Senate Minority Leader Hugh Scott (R Pa.) told Congressional Quarterly.

"I think we ought to wait until we know if there's going to be a Senate trial before we talk about that," said Rep. David W. Dennis (R Ind.), a member of the House Judiciary Committee. "I'm not crazy about televising any proceedings, because I think they tend to lend a circus atmosphere."

Mansfield made the statement during a breakfast meeting with reporters at which he also said some members of the House had told him they believed there were enough votes to impeach Nixon. *(Box, p. 304)*

A spokesman for Assistant Majority Leader Robert C. Byrd (D W.Va.) said he endorsed Mansfield's suggestion that the Senate proceedings be televised. Byrd, a long-time advocate of opening the Senate to television cameras, had suggested that any impeachment trial should be televised during a March 3 interview on NBC-TV's "Meet the Press."

Rep. Charles E. Wiggins (R Calif.), another member of the Judiciary Committee, told Congressional Quarterly he was doubtful that television coverage in the Senate would be proper. "The most important consideration is that this trial be fair and it ascertain the truth under a mechanism that insulates it from outside pressures and passions," Wiggins said. "That's much more important in my opinion than the value of some public access to the proceedings through television."

Senate sources noted that a resolution calling for televising an impeachment trial probably would not be introduced until after the House Judiciary Committee had acted on its staff's impeachment inquiry. "It would be anticipatory to act before that," said one source.

House Attitudes

In the meantime, support for televising a House floor debate on impeachment gathered strength in the wake of Mansfield's statement.

Rep. Sidney R. Yates (D Ill.) introduced a resolution (H Res 1028) April 4 calling for televising of House proceedings. Yates originally introduced a resolution (H Res 802) Jan. 31, 1973, seeking to open the chamber to

radio and television. Since then he had been joined by 43 cosponsors, 36 Democrats and seven Republicans.

"Putting the House on the air would prove to be an invaluable way of enlightening our constituents on the meaning and importance of the constitutional process of impeachment," Yates said in an April 2 "Dear Colleague" letter seeking more cosponsors for his resolution. "Broadcasting the proceedings will provide a sense of immediacy and an all-pervasive eye and ear on the events which will transpire; thereby, giving our citizens a sense of participating in the operation of their government."

While he was firmly opposed to televising the Judiciary Committee's impeachment proceedings, Wiggins said he was less concerned about opening the floor of the House to television. "Television coverage of the House might prejudice a Senate trial," Wiggins said. "But the reality is, whether it's covered by television or not, it's going to be given such broad coverage that a senator would have to be literally isolated in an igloo somewhere to not be affected and be aware of what's going on. We're ultimately going to have to be confident that senators mean their oath when they take the oath to be guided solely by the evidence."

No Precedents

Live radio and television coverage of House or Senate proceedings, except for some joint sessions, apparently was unprecedented.

The Senate long had consented to live broadcasts of committee proceedings. The House banned such coverage from 1952 until late 1970, when the Legislative Reorganization Act carried a provision authorizing it at the discretion of a majority of each House committee.

Rule 4 of the Senate Manual's guidelines for the regulation of the Senate wing states, "The taking of pictures of any kind is prohibited in the Senate chamber, the Senate reading rooms, the Senate cloak rooms and the private dining room of the Senate." A Senate Rules Committee spokesman said that rule had been waived only twice in recent years, both times for the taking of still pictures of sessions for historical purposes.

Under existing rules, televising of Senate committee proceedings had to be cleared with the chairman of the committee involved and with the Senate Rules Committee. The Senate sergeant at arms had to give permission for filming anywhere in the Senate wing of the Capitol building itself.

There were two areas on the grounds of the Capitol where television crews could operate without specific permission: a grassy triangle across from the Senate steps and an area at the bottom of the hill on which the Capitol building is located.

Chapin Trial. A jury was selected and sequestered in Washington for the trial of Dwight L. Chapin, Nixon's former appointments secretary, who was charged with lying to a grand jury. *(Box, p. 301)*

APRIL 2

Jaworski Complaint. Leon Jaworski, the Watergate special prosecutor, said that Nixon had not given him all the information he subpoenaed. White House spokesman Gerald L. Warren said the President, complying March 29 with the subpoena, had given the special prosecutor "all relevant material" sought. Warren indicated that some requested data had been withheld. Later a spokesman for Jaworski's office told reporters that investigators still had a number of outstanding requests, apparently for documents the subpoena did not include.

Nixon's Taxes. Nixon's tax lawyers, Kenneth Gemmill and H. Chapman Rose, met with staff members of the Joint Congressional Committee on Internal Revenue Taxation, the committee investigating the President's taxes, and contended that Nixon had acted legally in taking a $576,000 deduction for his vice presidential papers. The two attorneys also asked to present the White House side of the case when the committee took up the staff report on Nixon's taxes.

Nixon Position. A spokesman for Nixon refused to repeat the President's earlier pledge to pay any back taxes that might be recommended by the joint committee investigating his returns for 1969 through 1972. *(Nixon promise, p. 181)*

Mitchell-Stans Trial. F. Donald Nixon, the President's brother, testified that he rebuffed an effort by a friend of Robert L. Vesco to get a message to the President that Vesco's secret contribution might be exposed before election day. But Nixon's brother did suggest to Vesco's lawyer that John N. Mitchell might be the man to talk to, he testified.

Chapin Trial. Campaign saboteur Donald H. Segretti said he kept Dwight L. Chapin, Nixon's former appointments secretary, informed of attempts to sabotage 1972 Democratic presidential candidacies. Herbert W. Kalmbach, Nixon's former personal lawyer and political fund-raiser, testified that he paid Segretti with surplus funds from the 1968 Nixon campaign. Both Segretti and Kalmbach said Chapin was familiar with Segretti's activities.

Nixon Tapes. John J. Chester, an attorney for President Nixon, told the U.S. Court of Appeals in Washington that public disclosure of five tape recordings of conversations between the President and John W. Dean III would have a "profound impact on public opinion." Chester made his remarks at a hearing on a subpoena by the Senate Watergate committee for the five tapes.

APRIL 3

Tax Report. The staff of the Joint Committee on Internal Revenue Taxation found that Nixon owed $476,431, including interest, on back taxes for 1969 through 1972. The staff found that Nixon was not entitled to a deduction for the gift of his vice presidential papers and that he should have paid capital gains tax for the sale of some San Clemente, Calif., property and a New York City apartment. *(Details, p. 298)*

Nixon Payment. Five hours after receiving the staff report, the White House said that the President would pay $432,787.13, plus interest, that the Internal Revenue Service ruled was due. The President rejected advice from his lawyers that he could make "a very strong case" against the findings. *(Box, p. 299)*

Reinecke Indictment. Lt. Gov. Ed Reinecke (R Calif.) was indicted by a Watergate grand jury for having lied three times to a Senate committee about when he informed John N. Mitchell of an International Telephone and Telegraph Corporation pledge of money for the 1972 Republican national convention. Reinecke said he would fight the charges and not halt his drive for the Republican gubernatorial nomination. *(Box, p. 302)*

Mitchell-Stans Trial. The prosecution rested its case after calling its 40th witness, the Nixon campaign official who gave back to Robert L. Vesco his $200,000 secret contribution.

Chapin Trial. Dwight L. Chapin testified that H. R. Haldeman had approved the hiring of political saboteur Donald Segretti. Chapin denied lying to a grand jury about his own knowledge of Segretti's work, and one of the four counts against him was dropped.

Javits Statement. Sen. Jacob K. Javits (R N.Y.) warned Nixon against playing "impeachment politics" by trimming his legislative programs "to please a given number of senators: 33 plus one."

TEXT OF STAFF REPORT

Following is the text of the introduction and summary of recommendations from the report by the staff of the Joint Committee on Internal Revenue Taxation on President Nixon's income taxes.

INTRODUCTION

On December 8, 1973, President Nixon made public his tax returns and asked the Joint Committee on Internal Revenue Taxation to examine whether two transactions, a gift of his papers claimed as a deduction in 1969 and the sale of 23 acres of land at San Clemente, were correctly reported on his tax returns. The full text of the letter dated December 8, 1973, which President Nixon wrote to Chairman Wilbur D. Mills is as follows:

"Dear Mr. Chairman: Recently there have been many questions in the press about my personal finances during my tenure as President.

"In order to answer these questions and to dispel public doubts, I am today making public a full accounting of my financial transactions since I assumed this office. This accounting includes copies of the income tax returns that Mrs. Nixon and I have filed for the years 1969—72; a full, certified audit of our finances; a full, certified report on the real and personal property we own; an analysis of our financial transactions, including taxes, from January 1, 1969 through May 31, 1973, and other pertinent documents.

"While these disclosures are the most exhaustive ever made by an American President, to the best of my knowledge, I recognize that two tax-related items may continue to be a subject of continuing public questioning. Both items are highly complex and, in the present environment, cannot easily be resolved to the public's satisfaction even with full disclosure of information.

"The first transaction is the gift of certain pre-Presidential papers and other memorabilia which my wife and I claimed as a tax deduction of $576,000 on our 1969 return and have carried forward, in part, in each subsequent year. The second item in question is the transfer by us, through the Title Insurance and Trust Co., to the B&C Investment Co. of the beneficial interest in 23 acres of land in San Clemente, California in 1970. I have been consistently advised by counsel that this transaction was correctly reported to the Internal Revenue Service. The IRS has also reviewed these items and has advised me that they were correctly reported.

"In order to resolve these issues to the full satisfaction of the American people, I hereby request the Joint Committee on

Internal Revenue Taxation to examine both of these transactions and to inform me whether, in its judgment, the items have been correctly reported to the Internal Revenue Service. In the event that the committee determines that the items were incorrectly reported, I will pay whatever tax may be due. I also want to assure you that the committee will have full access to all relevant documents pertaining to these matters and will have the full cooperation of my office.

"I recognize that this request may pose an unusual challenge for the committee, but I believe your assistance on this matter would be a significant public service.

"With warmest regards,

"Sincerely,   s/RICHARD NIXON."

On December 12, 1973, the Joint Committee on Internal Revenue Taxation met in executive session and decided to conduct a thorough examination of the President's income tax returns for the years 1969 through 1972 and to submit a report to the President and to the Congress on its findings.

The committee decided not to confine its examination to the two items mentioned by President Nixon in his letter quoted above, but rather to examine all tax items for the years 1969 through 1972. (President Nixon's tax returns for these years are reproduced in Exhibits XI—1 to XI—4 in the Appendix.) The committee believed that the broader examination was necessary in part because various items on a tax return are often so interrelated that distortions result if a comprehensive review is not made. Probably more important, however, is that so many questions have been raised about the tax returns of the President for these years that the committee believed the general public can only be satisfied by a thorough examination of the President's taxes. From the standpoint of the tax system alone, this confidence of the general public is essential since ours is basically a voluntary assessment system which has maintained its high level of effectiveness only because the general public has confidence in the basic fairness of the collection system.

At its meeting, the committee instructed its staff to conduct a thorough examination of the President's tax matters for the years 1969-1972 and to prepare a report to the committee on its findings. This is that report.

The staff first would like to thank the Internal Revenue Service for its fine cooperation in the examination of these returns. In every respect, the staff found the Internal Revenue Service cooperative and helpful. About the same time President Nixon asked the Joint Committee to examine his returns, the Internal Revenue Service began an examination of the President's return for 1970 and reopened the years 1971 and 1972 (the general statute of limitations having expired on the 1969 return). The staff has exchanged information with the Internal Revenue Service in numerous cases, and the two also have conducted many joint interviews. However, the conclusions reached in this report are those of the staff alone and in no way are intended as indicative of any reexaminations made by the Internal Revenue Service.

Generally, it is the responsibility of the taxpayer to substantiate his deductions or to show why other items should not be included in his return. However, in this case, because of the office held by the taxpayer, it has not been possible to call upon him for the usual substantiation. The unique position of the Presidency has also raised other questions in these returns which the staff comments on at the appropriate points in this report. Although the staff has not been able to contact the taxpayer in this case, he has been represented by counsel, Kennth W. Gemmill and H. Chapman Rose. The counsel have been helpful in the staff examination of the President's returns, and they have supplied most of the information requested. [1]

In its examination of the President's tax returns, the staff conducted approximately 30 interviews with persons involved in different aspects of the President's tax matters. In a number of cases, this represents more than one interview with the same person. In addition, the staff has made contact with numerous other possible sources of information, has on two occasions sent staff members to California to consider various tax issues, and on another occasion has sent staff personnel to New York to carry out the examination. This is in addition to information the staff received through numerous investigations made by the Internal Revenue Service personnel. Finally, the staff has employed experts to help it appraise the value of the San Clemente property—an engineering firm and an appraisal firm, both in California. The staff believes that it has conducted an extensive examination.

As is true in any examination of a tax return, however, it is not possible to give assurance that all items of income have been included. The staff report contains recommendations on two categories of income which it believes should have been included but were not; namely, improvements made by the Government to the San Clemente and Key Biscayne properties which the staff believes primarily represent personal economic benefits to the President, and economic benefits obtained by family and friends from the use of Government aircraft for personal purposes.

The staff did not examine the President's income tax returns for years prior to 1969. In the course of its examination of the returns for 1969-1972, however, the staff found that because of interrelationships of prior years' returns it was necessary to consider a limited number of items relating to prior years' returns, since they affect returns for the years in question. In addition, the staff has limited its recommendations to income tax matters, although in this examination it found instances where the employment taxes were not paid and gift tax returns not filed.

The staff has made no attempt in this report to draw any conclusions whether there was, or was not, fraud or negligence [2] involved in any aspect of the returns, either on the part of the President or his personal representatives. The staff believes that it would be inappropriate to consider such matters in view of the fact that the House Judiciary Committee presently has before it an impeachment investigation relating to the President and that members of the Joint Committee on Internal Revenue Taxation, along with members of the House and Senate, may subsequently be called upon to pass judgment on any charges which may be brought as a result of that investigation. The staff believes that neither the House nor the Senate members of the Joint Committee would want to have pre-judged any issue which might be brought in any such proceedings.

The staff in preparing this report recognizes that an examination by a committee staff, possibly with the publication of the recommendations does not retain for the taxpayer his usual rights of review which are available to him under the appellate procedure in the Internal Revenue Service and through the courts. For this reason, the staff has attempted to examine mat-

---

1 The exceptions are listed here. (1) The Chairman of the Joint Committee requested information on flights taken by the President and his family on Government airplanes. This information was supplied only with respect to flights where the family were passengers but the President was not. The President's counsel responded to Chairman Long's letter on April 1, 1974, that this information would not be furnished and indicated the reasons. The response is shown in the Appendix in Exhibit XII-3.

(2) Because of the absence of the normal contact with the taxpayer, toward the end of its investigation the staff also submitted a series of questions for consideration by the President. The questions submitted relate to issues still not fully answered after many interviews were conducted with other persons involved in one way or another with the President's tax matters. These questions are shown in the Appendix Exhibit XII-1. The staff recognizes that these questions were submitted late in the examination period and that this may well account for the fact that the staff has not yet received an answer. It is still hoped, however, that answers will be forthcoming and that these can be made public.

(3) The staff also requested information from the President's representatives with respect to a so-called "Special Projects Fund." The staff was made aware that certain expenditures out of this fund possibly had been made for personal items of the President relating to his San Clemente residence. For this reason, the staff requested a statement from the President's representatives on which of the expenditures made out of that fund were for the President's personal benefit. The staff's letter to the President's representatives on this matter is shown in Exhibit XII-2. On April 1, 1974, the President's counsel responded to this request and indicated that on the basis of an investigation there was found only one possible occasion on which a personal expense of President Nixon was paid out of the Special Projects Fund. This was for $6.30, which was a reimbursement for an expenditure for light bulbs at San Clemente. The staff has no way to verify whether these were all the expenditures made other than the letter. The letter is shown in Exhibit XII-4.

2 The addition to tax for negligence itself, of course, is not a fraud issue and applies when there is no intent to defraud (see I.R.C. section 6653(a)).

ters with great care before making a recommendation which will result in greater tax payments. At the same, however, the staff has attempted to follow the standards which it believes, under the law, are required to be applicable to taxpayers generally, and the staff has not withheld recommendations because of the office of the taxpayer involved. The staff, in any case, believes it should be emphasized that this is a report only. It is not a demand for payment of taxes. Any tax payment is a matter for consideration by the taxpayer and the Internal Revenue Service.

SUMMARY OF RECOMMENDATIONS

The report which follows is divided into ten separate parts. Each of these deals with one or more major questions with respect to the tax returns of the President. In most cases the report indicates first the scope of the examination and then presents an analysis of points of law which may be involved. This is followed by a summary of staff recommendations, and finally the staff presents an analysis of these recommendations.

The staff recommendations would make the following increases in the President's taxes for the years involved:

Year	Proposed Deficiency	Interest *1*	Deficiency plus interest
1969	$171,055	(2)	$171,055 2
1970	93,410	$16,638	110,048
1971	89,667	10,547	100,214
1972	89,890	5,224	95,114
Total	$444,022	$32,409	$476,431

1 Interest to April 3, 1974.
2 Since 1969 is a closed year and any payment by the President would be voluntary, the staff did not include an interest payment for the deficiency in this year. However, if interest were to be included, the amount would be $40,732.

Should the President decide to reimburse the Government for the General Services Administration improvements which the staff believes were primarily personal in nature, he would pay $106,262. In addition, if he should decide to reimburse the Government for the amount determined by the staff to represent the cost for the personal trips of his family and friends, this would amount to $27,015. On the other hand, if the President were to receive reimbursement for the expense which he paid for the table located in the cabinet room in the White House for which the staff believes the Government should have paid, the amount he should receive would be $4,816.84. If the President were to make the reimbursements referred to above, he would be allowed to take deductions in the year of the payments, since the amounts were treated as taxable income in the years under examination in which they occurred.

The major causes of the deficiencies resulting from the staff examination are set forth below.

(1) The charitable deductions ($482,018) taken for a gift of papers from 1969-1972 should not, in the staff's view, be allowed because the gift was made after July 25, 1969, the date when the provisions of the Tax Reform Act of 1969 disallowing such deductions became effective. The staff believes that in view of the restrictions and retained rights contained in the deed of the gift of papers, that the deed is necessary for the gift. The deed (dated March 27, 1969) which purportedly was signed on April 21, 1969, was not signed (at least by all parties) until April 10, 1970 and was not delivered until after that date. It should also be noted that this deed was signed by Edward Morgan (rather than the President), and the staff found no evidence that he was authorized to sign for the President. In addition, the deed stated that its delivery conveyed title to the papers to the United States and since the deed was not delivered until after April 10, 1970, it is clear that title could not have been conveyed by way of the deed until after July 25, 1969. Furthermore, because the gift is so restricted, in the opinion of the staff, it is a gift of a future interest in tangible personal property, which is not deductible currently under law, even if the gift was valid in all other respects; that is, it had been made and the deed

delivered prior to July 25, 1969. President Nixon's 1968 gift of papers contains the same restrictions as the second gift so that in the staff's opinion it, too, is a nondeductible gift of a future interest. As a result, the staff believes that the amount of the 1968 gift in excess of what was deducted in 1968 is not available to be carried over into 1969.

(2) In 1970, no capital gain was reported on the sale of the President's excess San Clemente acreage. The staff believes that there was an erroneous allocation of basis between the property retained and the property sold and that a capital gain of $117,836 should have been reported.

(3) The staff believes that the President is not allowed to defer recognition of his capital gain on the sale of his New York City cooperative apartment because it does not view the San Clemente residence in which he reinvested the proceeds of the sale (with one year) as his principal residence. Also, the staff believes this gain is larger than the $142,912 reported on the 1969 tax return, because the President's cost basis should be reduced by the depreciation and amortization allowable on the New York apartment resulting from its use in a trade or business by Mr. Nixon. The staff determined that the amount of depreciation and amortization allowable is $8,936. The staff measures the total capital gain at $151,848, which in its view should be reported as income in 1969.

(4) The staff believes that depreciation on the San Clemente house and on certain furniture purchased by the President, business expense deductions taken on the San Clemente property, as well as certain expenditures from the White House "guest fund" are not proper business expenses and are not allowable deductions. These deductions totalled $85,399 during the years under examination. In the case of the purchase of part of the furniture, however, the staff believes the Government should reimburse President Nixon for his expenditure.

(5) In the case of capital gain on the sale of the Cape Florida Development lots in 1972, 60 percent was reported by President Nixon and 40 percent was reported by his daughter Patricia. The staff believes the entire amount should be reported as income to the President. Thus, in the view of the staff, he should report $11,617 (this is the amount allocated to his daughter from the installment payment in 1972) as a capital gain in 1972 and the remainder of the gain 1973. On this basis, Mrs. Cox should also file an amended return and not include any of this gain for 1972 (or in 1973). Also, on this basis President Nixon could deduct as interest part of the payment he made in 1973 to Patricia on the money she loaned him. She, of course, should report the interest as income in 1973.

(6) The staff believes President Nixon should declare as income the value of flights in Government planes taken by his family and friends when there was no business purpose for the furnishing of the transportation. The staff was given no information about family and friends on flights where the President was a passenger. However, for other flights the first-class fare costs of his family and friends are estimated to be $27,015 for the years 1969 through 1972. From April 1971 through March 1972 and again after November 7, 1972, President Nixon paid for most of such travel expense himself.

(7) The staff believes that President Nixon should declare as income $92,298 in improvements made to his Key Biscayne and San Clemente estates. The only improvements taken into account for this purpose, the staff believes, were those undertaken primarily for the President's personal benefit.

(8) The staff believes the President should be allowed an additional $1,007 in sales tax deductions.

(9) The staff believes that $148 of gasoline tax deductions should not be allowed for 1969 through 1971. However, the staff has determined that an additional $10 in gasoline tax deductions is allowable for 1972.

(10) Several other income items should be reported on President Nixon's tax returns, although these are entirely offset by deductions and hence do not increase taxable income.

Each adjustment in tax by year is shown in Table 1. *(next page)*

Recommended Deficiency and Interest, 1969-72

SCHEDULE A	1969	1970	1971	1972
1. Income as reported on return (AGI)	$328,162	$262,943	$262,385	$268,778
2. Additions to income	142,367	85,994	13,592	18,011
a. Gain on sale of New York apartment (50% of NLTCG)[1]	$ 75,924			
b. Improvements to San Clemente and Key Biscayne properties	62,442	$ 17,800	$ 8,956	$ 3,101
c. Personal use of government airplanes by family and friends	4,001	9,276	4,636	9,102
d. Gain on sale of San Clemente property (50% of NLTCG)		58,918		
e. Gain on sale of Florida lots (50% of NLTCG)			5,808	
3. Deductions from income improperly taken as itemized deductions (item 6)[2]	—6,294	—5,510	—5,517	—5,332
4. Corrected income (AGI) (1 + 2 — 3)	464,235	343,427	270,460	281,457
5. Deductions reported on return	178,535	307,182	255,677	247,570
6. Deductions improperly taken as itemized deductions but allowable in arriving at AGI (item 3)[2]	—6,294	—5,510	—5,517	—5,332
7. Deductions not allowable	$177,184	$140,976	$152,102	$157,303
a. Charitable contribution deduction for gift of papers	95,298	123,959	128,668	134,093
b. Amounts treated on return as business deductions	21,833	16,954	23,402	23,210
i. San Clemente residence	4,700	7,808	10,237	9,422
ii. Key Biscayne residence	292	646	614	583
iii. Depreciation of White House furniture		1,347	1,095	889
iv. Guest fund deductions	16,841	7,153	11,456	12,316
c. Gasoline tax	53	63	32	
8. Additional deductions allowed:				
a. Sales tax	1,274			
b. Gasoline tax				10
9. Allowable itemized deductions (5—6—7 +8)	56,331	160,696	98,058	84,949
10. Corrected taxable income (4—9—personal exemptions)[3]	406,104	180,856	171,052	195,012
11. Ordinary tax determined on corrected taxable income	137,394	58,820	90,545	86,927
12. Alternative capital gain tax (if applicable)	84,185	32,512		7,261
13. Total corrected ordinary income tax liability (11 + 12)	243,737	94,203	90,545	94,188
14. Total tax (13 plus minimum tax)	[4]243,737	[5]94,203	90,545	94,188
15. Tax as shown on return	72,682	793	878	4,298
16. Deficiency (14—15)	171,055	93,410	89,667	89,890
17. Interest	[6]	16,638	10,547	5,224
18. Total deficiency and interest	171,055	110,048	100,214	95,114

[1] Net long term capital gain.

[2] This amount represents those deductions claimed because of the business use of the Key Biscayne residence. The President had claimed these expenses as itemized deductions, but the committee staff believes that they should be allowed as expenses incurred in connection with maintaining investment property (sec. 212). This means that it now is a deduction to arrive at AGI, rather than an itemized deduction and is treated accordingly.

[3] Personal exemptions for 1969 totaled $1,800 ($600 x 3); $1,875 for 1970 ($625 x 3); $1,350 for 1970 ($675 x 2); and $1,500 for 1972 ($750 x 2).

[4] Includes $22,158 of income tax surcharge at 10 per cent.

[5] Includes $22,283 of income tax surcharge at 2.5 per cent and minimum tax of $588.

[6] Since 1969 is a closed year and any payment by the President would be voluntary, the staff did not include an interest payment for the deficiency in this year. However, if interest were to be included, the amount would be $40,732.

SOURCE: Staff report, Joint Committee on Internal Revenue Taxation

WATERGATE: A HISTORIC SUBPOENA TO THE PRESIDENT

Marking out clear limits to Republican support for President Nixon on Capitol Hill, key Republicans in both chambers sent strong warnings to the White House during the week ending April 13, climaxed by a bipartisan subpoena to the President from the House Judiciary Committee.

The dilatory tactics of the White House in dealing with the request of the committee's impeachment inquiry for information "make it very difficult for minority members," said Rep. Hamilton Fish Jr. (R N.Y.) before voting for the subpoena April 11. Fish described the White House response as "outrageous." Nixon supporter Edward Hutchinson (R Mich.) agreed regretfully that it was "offensive to the House."

Earlier in the week, six Senate Republicans, all holding leadership posts, warned Nixon that "the first article in the bill of impeachment very well could be contempt of Congress," if Nixon did not quickly furnish the impeachment inquiry with all the materials it needed. Minority Leader Hugh Scott (Pa.), Assistant Minority Leader Robert P. Griffin (Mich.), John G. Tower (Texas), Wallace F. Bennett (Utah), Norris Cotton (N.H.) and Bill Brock (Tenn.) sent their message April 9 through Dean Burch, counselor to the President.

The President was running his own case, said a former member of the White House defense team, implying that the delaying moves in supplying the House with information originated with Nixon, not his counsel, James D. St. Clair. (Box, p. 313)

After the White House received the subpoena, Press Secretary Ronald L. Ziegler said that by April 25 the White House would give the inquiry materials which would be "comprehensive and conclusive in regard to the President's actions," and that compliance would be as full as "consistent with his constitutional responsibilities."

"Realistically," noted an inquiry staff memo, "the President cannot be compelled to comply with a subpoena." If the President did not comply, it was unlikely that the House would move to attempt to enforce the subpoena, but would simply take into account, along with the other charges against Nixon, his non-compliance.

A Committee Subpoena

Undeterred by a last-minute telephone call from St. Clair, the Judiciary Committee on the afternoon of April 11 voted 33-3 to subpoena the President in order to obtain the records of certain conversations which the staff judged would be potentially helpful in determining Nixon's knowledge of or participation in the Watergate coverup.

After several hours of heated discussion, including two party-line votes on related matters, the committee united to adopt a Republican amendment making the subpoena more specific in describing the items at which

it was directed. Then the committee voted to authorize issuance of the subpoena. Voting against issuance were the ranking committee Republican, Hutchinson, who cast the proxy vote of Charles E. Wiggins (R Calif.) against the subpoena as well, and Trent Lott (R Miss.). Absent and not voting were Charles W. Sandman Jr. (R N.J.) and Harold V. Froehlich (R Wis.).

It was the first time in history that a President had been subpoenaed to furnish information to an inquiry investigating impeachment charges against him. In 1973, when the special prosecutor and the Senate Watergate committee issued subpoenas to Nixon, he became the first president since Thomas Jefferson to be served with a subpoena. (p. 230)

Demanded by the subpoena—which contained a deadline of 10 a.m. April 25, exactly two months after the original request for the information—were tapes and other records of more than 40 presidential conversations. They were described by the committee as:

• Between the President and H. R. Haldeman, then White House chief of staff, on Feb. 20, 1973, concerning the possible appointment of campaign aide Jeb Stuart Magruder to a government post.

• Among Nixon, Haldeman and John D. Ehrlichman, then Nixon's domestic affairs adviser, on Feb. 27, 1973, concerning the assignment of White House counsel John W. Dean III to work with the President on Watergate.

• Between the President and Dean on March 17, 1973.

• Between Nixon and Ehrlichman on March 27 and March 30, 1973.

• All conversations between Nixon and Haldeman and Nixon and Ehrlichman April 14-17, 1973.

• All conversations between Nixon and then Attorney General Richard G. Kleindienst and between Nixon and Assistant Attorney General Henry Petersen April 15-18, 1973. (p. 277-278)

St. Clair Response. In a belated response to the committee deadline of April 9 for a White House response to the Feb. 25 request for this information, St. Clair wrote that "a review of the materials was underway" and probably would be completed by April 22, when Congress returned from its Easter recess. "We expect...that the additional materials furnished at that time will permit the committee to complete its inquiry promptly," he wrote. (p. 301)

Republican committee members joined their Democratic colleagues in making plain their disappointment at this reply. "This is an additional dilatory tactic by the President's lawyers....an unconscionable delay," said Lawrence J. Hogan (R Md.). "We don't want to be unreasonable, but this response is unacceptable," agreed Tom Railsback (R Ill.). "It certainly creates a presumption that the President is withholding damaging evidence," said M. Caldwell Butler (R Va.).

Forty-five minutes before the April 11 committee meeting began—to consider a subpoena—St. Clair called special committee counsel John M. Doar and asked whether a subpoena would be avoided if the White House, within a day or two, gave the committee the first four items requested. Doar said he could not reply for the committee but would deliver the message.

The last-minute compromise offer swayed a number of committee Republicans who had come ready to back a subpoena. Democrats were not so influenced. "It's a little late to make a deal," said Robert W. Kastenmeier (D Wis.).

Amendments. In a party-line vote of 21-17, the Democrats overruled Republican opposition to a rule limiting debate on the subpoena to one minute per member. David W. Dennis (R Ind.) then proposed to amend the subpoena to limit it to the four items the White House appeared ready to provide, to avoid a "blanket subpoena" and the risk of "getting slapped down." But the committee rejected this amendment, 22-16, with Butler joining the Democrats in opposition.

Delbert Latta (R Ohio), a senior member of the House who had recently joined the Judiciary Committee to fill a vacancy, then proposed an amendment to make more specific the dates and times of the known conversations sought by the committee within the last two categories. Latta also moved to recess until after lunch; the committee agreed by voice vote.

Republican committee members, led by Robert McClory (Ill.), tried during the luncheon recess to obtain more specific assurances from St. Clair concerning the furnishing of needed materials. Their failure assured bipartisan support for the subpoena. When the committee reconvened, the Latta amendment was quickly adopted by voice vote after Rodino expressed his support for it. The subpoena was then approved, with only three dissenting votes.

Re-emphasizing committee determination to move ahead, Rodino announced that during the first week after the recess, the committee would discuss narrowing the scope of the inquiry by dropping some of the matters under investigation. The week of April 29, he said, the committee would consider the rules needed to guide its evidentiary hearings, expected to begin May 7.

Counsel's Role. Even as the committee readied a subpoena for the White House, some agreement was reached on the role for the President's counsel in the evidentiary proceedings. *(p. 302, 282)*

Although the committee Democrats had at first reacted negatively to St. Clair's request for full participation in the proceedings, they agreed, at a committee caucus April 9, to allow St. Clair a certain role. Rodino said April 11 he would support granting the President's counsel:

• The privilege of attending the initial presentation of the evidence to the committee and of receiving copies of whatever documents and materials committee members were given.

• The opportunity, at the end of the presentation, to make his views known to the committee concerning the evidence and to recommend that certain witnesses be called.

• The opportunity to question witnesses "as the committee deems appropriate," if and when the committee called any witnesses.

Nixon's Taxes. Any hope that Nixon's pledge to pay his back taxes would end the matter was proved

Porter Sentencing

Herbert L. Porter, the Nixon re-election committee official who scheduled the "surrogate speakers" program during the 1972 presidential campaign, was sentenced April 11 to serve 30 days in prison. The sentence, handed down by U.S. District Judge William B. Bryant in Washington, D.C., followed Porter's Jan. 28 plea of guilty to a charge that he had lied to FBI agents investigating the Watergate break-in. *(p. 211)*

The charge carried a maximum penalty of five years in prison and a $10,000 fine, but Richard Ben-Veniste, the assistant special prosecutor, said that Porter's involvement in the coverup was "less in degree than others who pleaded guilty to felony charges." Bryant sentenced Porter to five to 15 months in prison, then suspended all but 30 days of the sentence.

vain during the week after the Internal Revenue Service (IRS) and a joint congressional committee had presented him with reports assessing his back-tax bill at almost $500,000. *(p. 298)*

The question of whether fraud was involved in the preparation of the tax returns was clearly within the scope of the impeachment inquiry, said special committee counsel John M. Doar April 8. And so the IRS had been asked to turn over the records of its investigation to the inquiry staff.

The President's involvement in possible tax fraud was "an area that the Judiciary Committee must dispose of," said Attorney General William B. Saxbe April 9. But he acknowledged that weeks or months before the IRS and congressional reports on presidential taxes, information on the matter had gone to the special Watergate prosecutor.

The New York Times reported April 11 that Donald C. Alexander, commissioner of internal revenue, had asked the special prosecutor to begin a federal grand jury investigation into a possible criminal conspiracy concerning Nixon's disallowed claim of a $576,000 tax deduction for his vice presidential papers.

In California, the executive officer of the state franchise board announced April 12 that Nixon owed $4,263.72 in back taxes to the state for 1969 and 1970, plus a penalty of $39.17 for 1970.

Mitchell-Stans Trial

Precisely two years after $200,000 in $100 bills was delivered to Nixon's re-election campaign finance chairman, Maurice H. Stans, former Attorney General John N. Mitchell took the witness stand in a federal courtroom. Mitchell denied charges that he and Stans, in return for the secret contribution from financier Robert L. Vesco, had tried to block an investigation of Vesco by the Securities and Exchange Commission (SEC).

Mitchell, taking the stand April 10 in U.S. District Court in New York City, said that he did not recall meeting Vesco until late spring 1972, after the contribution had been made.

Former New Jersey Republican leader Harry L. Sears had testified earlier that he had introduced Vesco and Mitchell a year before that. *(Earlier trial story, p. 303)*

(Continued on p. 314)

Former White House Lawyer: Nixon 'Runs His Own Case'

President Nixon, who had claimed the Watergate scandals arose because he was not personally running his 1972 presidential campaign, was running his own defense against impeachment, according to a former White House lawyer.

"Nixon is probably the most unique client in the world, and he runs his own case," said Cecil Emerson, who until resigning at the end of March was the senior lawyer on the staff of White House special counsel James D. St. Clair. Emerson said Nixon himself was directing St. Clair's resistance to the House Judiciary Committee's attempt to force the White House to hand over 42 recorded conversations between Nixon and his aides. *(Details, p. 311)*

The ex-White House lawyer referred to public statements by Nixon to the effect that he objected to committee staff lawyers searching through White House documents and tapes on a wholesale basis. Allowing a client to dictate legal strategy such as this to his counsel "is totally foreign to a lawyer like St. Clair," Emerson said in an April 9 telephone interview from Dallas, Texas, with Congressional Quarterly. "You could tell him to get another lawyer, but you just can't do that with the President. So when (White House chief of staff Alexander M.) Haig and Nixon say, 'We want to do it this way,' Jim has got to figure out an honorable, ethical, moral, legal way to do it."

However, St. Clair was convinced of Nixon's innocence in Watergate and related scandals and was prepared to move beyond procedural disputes with the House Judiciary Committee and launch an "affirmative defense" of Nixon, Emerson said. "Mr. St. Clair, in my opinion, has the utmost confidence in the President's innocence," Emerson declared. "As soon as they (the committee) define what's an impeachable offense—and I think they're going to have to do that very soon—then you'll see an affirmative defense taking place."

James D. St. Clair

Emerson said he based his judgment of St. Clair's belief in Nixon's innocence on conversations he had with St. Clair before leaving his staff. St. Clair was the only member of the White House legal team who had direct access to the President.

Emerson, 39, returned to Dallas to accept an offer from a private law firm after a four-month stay at the White House. He had been an assistant district attorney and assistant U.S. attorney in Dallas and regional director of the city's Drug Enforcement Administration task force before joining Nixon's defense team. After leaving the White House, Emerson became the counsel for a group of Dallas businessmen who were seeking to buy Nixon's presidential papers and donate them to a school or a public library.

St. Clair's delay in responding to the Judiciary Committee's Feb. 25 request for materials led some members of the committee to accuse the White House of foot-dragging. Some observers speculated that the delay was an attempt to provoke the committee into issuing a subpoena—which it voted April 11 to do, with only three dissenting votes—and thus to focus the impeachment issue on a procedural point rather than on any substantive Watergate-related charges against Nixon.

St. Clair was not available to respond to the direct question of whether he believed in his client's innocence, as Emerson claimed. Since coming to the White House Jan. 5, St. Clair had been careful in his public statements to draw a line between his legal representation of the office of the presidency rather than of its individual occupant, Nixon.

"I don't represent Mr. Nixon personally. I represent him in his capacity as President," St. Clair told a reporter March 12. This position mirrored Nixon's own public statements that his refusals in the past to turn over tapes and documents to the Senate Watergate committee and the Watergate special prosecutor were based on his belief that the confidentiality of presidential conversations had to be protected. Nixon's Oct. 20, 1973, firing of Special Prosecutor Archibald Cox stemmed from the President's refusal to release Watergate tapes.

Emerson rejected the suggestion that Nixon was not informing St. Clair of the full extent of his involvement in the Washington scandals. However, he said the Nixon-St. Clair relationship had only recently become a close one. "The relationship started out just like any attorney-client relationship, with a bit of sizing up of one another, particularly Nixon sizing up St. Clair to see whether he was heavy enough to handle his business," Emerson said.

There was some dissatisfaction among staff lawyers over Nixon's refusal to deal directly with anyone on the legal team except St. Clair, Emerson said. But, he added, "I could say I'm upset because President Nixon didn't call me in there and have me do something instead of Jim, but that's just not the facts of life...."

Emerson compared the Nixon-St. Clair relationship to that of a senior partner of a law firm that has taken on a major case involving a large corporation "where the president of the corporation is very much interested in the thing." The corporate head "doesn't want to talk to any junior partner; he wants to talk to the senior man, the number one man who is handling the case," said Emerson.

Emerson had high praise for St. Clair. "He gets into his office at a normal hour and he leaves at a normal hour, but he works all the time," he said. "He's just a constant, steady worker.... I was right there in the same office with him and very close to him, personally and professionally, and I have never seen him frustrated. He's the type of person who if he can't get in the front door on something he'll go around to the window or the back door or come through the chimney."

Impeachment and Foreign Policy

The effect of the Watergate scandal on U.S. foreign policy aroused some concern on Capitol Hill. One member of Congress introduced legislation to curtail President Nixon's foreign policy activities during impeachment proceedings, and several others called for postponement of the President's trip to Moscow, expected sometime in June.

Aspin Resolutions. Rep. Les Aspin (D Wis.)— declaring that impeachment "with each passing day...becomes more and more likely"—introduced three concurrent resolutions April 4 aimed at defining "the role of the President and Congress during the twilight zone between the time the House of Representatives votes a bill of impeachment and the final disposition of those charges by the Senate."

• The first resolution (H Con Res 461) would require the secretary of defense, the secretary of state and the director of the Central Intelligence Agency to give regular foreign policy briefings to the Vice President and the congressional leadership during impeachment proceedings. Asserting that it was still unknown whether the military alert during the October 1973 Middle East conflict was "a real one or a limited one or just plain phony," Aspin said his resolution would provide the country with "some assurance that an emergency is genuine."

• The second resolution (H Con Res 462) would bar the President from making or signing any international agreements during the impeachment period because of what Aspin described as both the temptation to give too much away in order to conclude a historical treaty and the likelihood of sell-out charges.

• The third resolution (H Con Res 463) would both bar the President from traveling abroad on government business and any foreign head of state from making an official trip to the United States during impeachment proceedings. Aspin specifically asked Nixon to postpone his trip to Moscow if it fell in the period of a Senate trial.

Other Opposition. Other legislators made similar requests. Sen. James L. Buckley (Cons-R N.Y.) strongly recommended April 9 against a presidential trip to Moscow during impeachment proceedings. He said Secretary of State Henry A. Kissinger's trip to Moscow in March had "made it clear that the President's political difficulties at home have served to harden Soviet attitudes and positions. This is hardly an atmosphere that is conducive to fruitful negotiations." Buckley also asserted that any negotiations between the two superpowers would be viewed by the Europeans with the "deepest concern" because of the political climate in the United States and the problems in U.S.-European relations.

Opposition to a Moscow trip also was voiced by Senators Henry M. Jackson (D Wash.), Marlow W. Cook (R Ky.) and Dick Clark (D Iowa), according to an April 4 *Washington Star-News* article which said that the discussion had been touched off April 3 when Sen. Jacob K. Javits (R N.Y.) warned the President not to play "impeachment politics on domestic legislation or foreign policy."

(Continued from p. 312)

Mitchell admitted that, on Sears' request, he had arranged a meeting in February 1972 among Sears, an attorney representing Vesco and William Casey, then chairman of the SEC. But he did not know then of Vesco's intention to make the contribution, Mitchell said, and did not consider or intend that what he was doing would impede the SEC investigation.

Before the defense began presenting its case, Judge Lee P. Gagliardi April 5 dismissed one of the obstruction of justice charges against Mitchell and Stans. He left undisturbed the conspiracy charge and the two other obstruction of justice charges against both, and the six perjury charges against each one of them.

Other Defense Witnesses. President Nixon's youngest brother, Edward C. Nixon, was the first defense witness. He appeared April 5, three days after his brother, F. Donald Nixon, had testified briefly as a reluctant witness for the government. Edward Nixon told the jury that Stans had said in 1972 that Vesco's $200,000 campaign contribution could be made in cash or by check.

This contradicted the testimony of two prosecution witnesses, Sears and Laurence B. Richardson Jr., and went to the heart of one of the perjury charges against Stans. Stans had told the investigating grand jury that the decision to make the contribution in cash was not his but Vesco's.

Three attorneys who had represented Vesco or an associate during the SEC investigation testified April 8. Sherwin J. Markman conceded that Vesco had bypassed him and set up meetings on his own with SEC personnel. Martin Mensch and Arthur Liman explained how they had been retained only the day before Vesco and an associate, Richard Clay, were to appear before the SEC. As a result, the attorneys said, the only advice they could then give their new clients was to take the protection of the Fourth, Fifth and Sixth Amendments to the Constitution to avoid answering questions.

Former Secretary of Health, Education and Welfare Robert H. Finch, former re-election committee spokesman DeVan L. Shumway and W. Clement Stone, a Chicago millionaire who gave more than $2-million to the Nixon campaign, testified for the defense April 9. Finch and Shumway testified about the White House decision to promise anonymity to campaign contributors who made their gifts before the April 7, 1972, starting date of the new campaign financing law.

Stone testified briefly about his contribution. He was the first in a series of large campaign donors whom the defense had planned to call to show that they expected nothing in return for their contributions.

But, in a blow to the defense, Judge Gagliardi ruled that such testimony was irrelevant. He also found it irrelevant for the defense to call former political campaign managers to testify that Stans had followed accepted campaign tactics in his 1972 fund-raising.

Week's Watergate Chronology

Following is a day-to-day chronology of the week's events in the Watergate case:

APRIL 4

Tapes Deadline. The House Judiciary Committee gave Nixon until April 9 to decide whether or not to turn over 42 presidential tape recordings for its impeachment inquiry. The deadline was set in a letter to the White House from Chairman Peter W. Rodino Jr. (D N.J.) and Rep. Edward Hutchinson (R Mich.), the committee's ranking minority member. *(p. 301)*

Doar Timetable. John M. Doar, counsel for the Judiciary Committee's impeachment inquiry, said he would be ready after May 1 to give committee members a written summary of tape recordings, grand jury testimony and other evidence that might touch on any presidential involvement in the Watergate scandal. *(p. 303)*

Nixon's Taxes. The Joint Committee on Internal Revenue Taxation received a report prepared by its staff on Nixon's taxes and sent the report to the House Judiciary Committee. *(p. 298)*

Paying the back taxes and interest, estimated at $465,000, would almost wipe out Nixon's assets, said Gerald L. Warren, the President's deputy press secretary. He said that Nixon probably would borrow money to pay the debt.

California Controller Houston I. Flournoy said it was likely that Nixon would be required to pay state taxes on the 1970 sale of part of his San Clemente estate.

Mitchell-Stans Trial. Prosecutors revealed that they had evidence that Robert L. Vesco's secret cash contribution to the 1972 Nixon campaign was used to finance the Watergate break-in. *(Earlier story, p. 303)*

IRS on Nixon. The Internal Revenue Service (IRS) said it would not seek to impose any penalty on Nixon for civil fraud in connection with his tax returns for 1969 through 1972. The IRS also said it was closing its audit of the case.

APRIL 5

Mitchell-Stans Trial. Edward C. Nixon, the President's younger brother, testified as the first witness for the defense. He said that he had told Robert L. Vesco to contribute cash to the President's re-election campaign if he wanted to keep the payment secret. Nixon said that Maurice H. Stans, the President's chief fund-raiser in 1972, told him that the re-election committee had no preference as to whether the contribution was made in cash or by check.

Chapin Verdict. Dwight L. Chapin was convicted by a U.S. District Court jury in Washington of deliberately lying twice to the Watergate grand jury about his connection with political saboteur Donald Segretti. *(p. 301)*

Kalmbach Testimony. President Nixon's former attorney, Herbert W. Kalmbach, testified under oath that portions of a secret $100,000 campaign contribution from billionaire Howard Hughes were either loaned or given to Rose Mary Woods, the President's private secretary, and to F. Donald Nixon, the President's brother, *The Washington Post* reported. The Post quoted informed sources as saying that Kalmbach testified in secret that he learned of the alleged gifts or loans in a conversation with Charles G. (Bebe) Rebozo, Nixon's close friend. Kalmbach's testimony contradicted sworn testimony by Rebozo, who had insisted he kept the $100,000 in a safe deposit box for three years and then returned it to Hughes, and by Miss Woods, who said she never received any money from Rebozo.

Steinbrenner Indictment. George M. Steinbrenner III, chairman of the American Shipbuilding Company and

Poll Report

President Nixon's standing in the latest Harris Survey rose five percentage points above his all-time low of a few weeks earlier. Interviewing for the poll was done March 24-29, before public disclosure April 3 that Nixon owed more than $467,000 in unpaid back taxes and interest. *(Earlier poll report, p. 296)*

Harris interviewers asked 1,495 households nationwide for the poll published April 8: "How would you rate the job President Nixon is doing as President—excellent, pretty good, only fair, or poor?"

	Latest	Early March
Good-excellent	31%	26%
Fair-poor	66	71
Not sure	3	3

principal partner in the New York Yankees, was indicted in U.S. District Court in Cleveland for making illegal contributions to the campaigns of Nixon and to Democratic congressional candidates through an elaborate kickback scheme. The 15-count indictment accused Steinbrenner of attempting to obstruct two grand jury probes by destroying and falsifying records and ordering company officers to lie to FBI agents and grand juries in Cleveland and Washington.

Ford on Tapes. Vice President Ford said he hoped a compromise might be reached on the tapes issue "so that the facts could be the determining factor and not an institutional conflict." Speaking in Denver, Ford expressed concern that a "head-to-head confrontation" between the White House and the House Judiciary Committee over the committee's request for 42 tapes might increase the chances of Nixon's impeachment.

DeMarco Statement. Frank DeMarco Jr., the President's tax lawyer, said it was "ridiculous" to believe that Nixon did not know about his tax returns. "What we did was go over the return page by page," De Marco said.

Kalmbach Testimony. Herbert Kalmbach testified that Charles G. Rebozo told him that Nixon personally requested that Rebozo and Kalmbach meet in the spring of 1973 to discuss what to do about a $100,000 cash contribution from billionaire Howard Hughes, *The Washington Post* reported.

APRIL 6

Weicker Charge. Sen. Lowell P. Weicker Jr. (R Conn.) charged that the Internal Revenue Service (IRS) had acted as "a lending library for the White House" in supplying sensitive tax data on political friends and foes of Nixon.

APRIL 7

IRS Admission. Donald C. Alexander, IRS commissioner, acknowledged in a television interview that the IRS "did not do as thorough an audit as it should have done some 10 months ago" in examining Nixon's tax returns.

Nixon's Taxes. Arthur Blech, Nixon's accountant who prepared his contested tax returns, said he was ordered by White House aides to take some of the deductions from Nixon's taxable income that were declared improper by a congressional investigation April 3.

APRIL 8

Nixon's Taxes. Nixon's handling of his income taxes was being investigated by the House Judiciary Committee's impeachment staff for possible fraud, it was disclosed. John M. Doar, the impeachment inquiry's chief counsel, said IRS records dealing with Nixon's tax matters had been requested along with other tax information. Several committee members said they would regard evidence of criminal fraud in Nixon's tax returns as potential grounds for impeachment.

Weicker Allegations. Sen. Lowell P. Weicker Jr. (R Conn.) made public documents he had given to three Senate committees holding joint hearings on government surveillance activities. The documents indicated that the White House had frequent access to IRS files, which it used to harass political and ideological opponents. Weicker charged that an administration study group set up in mid-1969 to gather tax information on "activist organizations" collected files on about 10,000 taxpayers until the unit was disbanded in August 1973. He also produced what he said was evidence of 54 investigations of White House "enemies" conducted by Anthony Ulasewicz, a retired detective from New York.

Mansfield Criticism. Senate Majority Leader Mike Mansfield (D Mont.) criticized polls and speculation about the outcome of an impeachment vote. If the Senate had to hold an impeachment trial, he said, he would try to make the proceedings as nonpartisan as possible. He also said the trial should be televised. *(Earlier story, p. 306)*

Republican Charges. Seven Republican members of the House Judiciary Committee assailed the committee's leadership and staff for moving too slowly in the impeachment investigation. Rep. Robert McClory (R Ill.) said the proceedings should be speeded up, with daily committee meetings if necessary.

Mitchell-Stans Trial. Three lawyers testified for the defense in an effort to establish that Robert L. Vesco was being harassed by the Securities and Exchange Commission (SEC) and that he sought relief from that harassment.

Rebozo-Kalmbach Meeting. William S. Frates, the lawyer for Charles G. Rebozo, acknowledged that Rebozo had discussed, at Nixon's suggestion, a $100,000 campaign contribution from Howard Hughes during a White House meeting in April 1973 with Herbert W. Kalmbach. Frates denied to *The New York Times* that Rebozo had told Kalmbach, as Kalmbach reportedly had testified to the Senate Watergate committee, that he disbursed the cash to the President's two brothers, Edward C. and F. Donald, the President's personal secretary, Rose Mary Woods, and others.

APRIL 9

Tapes Delay. The White House told the House Judiciary Committee that it needed more time to decide how to respond to the committee's request for tape recordings of 42 presidential conversations relating to Watergate. In a letter to the committee, James D. St. Clair, Nixon's chief defense lawyer, wrote that Nixon would be ready by April 22 to furnish materials that "will enable the committee to complete its inquiry promptly." But St. Clair gave the committee no pledge to turn over all the materials the committee had sought. *(Details, p. 311; tapes request, p. 258)*

St. Clair Role. The Democratic majority on the House Judiciary Committee informally agreed to allow St. Clair to play a limited role in the impeachment inquiry. Nixon's lawyer would be allowed to sit in as an observer in sessions at which the evidence on the President's conduct in office was presented to the committee.

Nixon's Taxes. The Internal Revenue Service referred to the Watergate special prosecutor the question of whether there was fraud in the preparation of Nixon's tax returns, Attorney General William B. Saxbe disclosed.

Mitchell-Stans Trial. U.S. District Judge Lee P. Gagliardi made two rulings that seriously restricted the defense of John N. Mitchell and Maurice H. Stans in their criminal conspiracy trial. *(Details, p. 312)*

APRIL 10

Mitchell-Stans Trial. John N. Mitchell took the witness stand in his criminal conspiracy trial and denied that he ever tried to fix or impede a Securities and Exchange Commission investigation of Robert L. Vesco in return for a contribution to Nixon's re-election campaign.

Request for Judge Change. John D. Ehrlichman, John N. Mitchell, Charles W. Colson and Gordon C. Strachan, defendants in the Watergate coverup trial, filed motions in U.S. District Court in Washington asking that Judge John J. Sirica be disqualified from conducting the trial because he had "an unshakeable personal bias in favor of the prosecution."

Reinecke Plea. Lt. Gov. Ed Reinecke (R Calif.) pleaded not guilty in U.S. District Court in Washington to charges of lying to the Senate Judiciary Committee about the International Telephone and Telegraph Corporation's offer to help pay for the 1972 Republican convention. Reinecke asked for a trial before the June 4 primary in California. *(Reinecke indictment, p. 302)*

Nixon Taxes. IRS Commissioner Donald C. Alexander asked that the Watergate special prosecutor initiate a grand jury investigation into a possible criminal conspiracy stemming from Nixon's claim of a $576,000 tax deduction for his vice presidential papers, *The New York Times* reported.

Connally Report. John B. Connally, former secretary of the treasury, was under investigation by the Watergate prosecutor for bribery, columnist Jack Anderson reported. Connally denied the report. Anderson wrote that FBI investigators assigned to the special prosecutor's office had evidence that Connally pocketed $10,000 from the Associated Milk Producers Inc., and that Connally returned the cash after the dairy group came under investigation. *(Earlier milk money story, p. 294)*

√

JAWORSKI SUBPOENAS 60 ADDITIONAL CONVERSATIONS

"With regard to cooperation, as you probably are aware, we have cooperated with the Rodino committee, the Judiciary Committee of the House of Representatives, by my directing that all of the materials that were furnished to the special prosecutor have been turned over to the Judiciary Committee.... Being reasonable, it seems to me, would be that the committee should first examine what it has, because Mr. Jaworski, the special prosecutor, said that he had what he considered to be the full story of Watergate, and we want the full story out."

—President Nixon during question-and-answer session before the Executives' Club of Chicago, March 15, 1974

"On March 12, 1974, I wrote to you requesting access to certain taped conversations.... If the President declines to produce these materials.... I am compelled by my responsibilities to seek appropriate judicial process."

—Watergate Special Prosecutor Leon Jaworski in an April 11, 1974, letter to special presidential counsel James D. St. Clair

The efforts of investigators to obtain information from the White House became a triangular tug-of-war April 18 when, at the request of Watergate Special Prosecutor Leon Jaworski, Judge John J. Sirica issued a subpoena ordering President Nixon to furnish Jaworski with the tapes and records of more than 60 conversations that took place between June 1972 and June 1973.

Jaworski made the request April 16, stating that the information contained in the records was needed in order for the government and the defendants in the Watergate coverup case to build their cases. The White House said it would have no comment until its lawyers had studied the request. Two of the defendants in the coverup case, Charles W. Colson and Robert C. Mardian, joined Jaworski's request for the subpoena. The case was scheduled for trial Sept. 9.

Weary of three months of fruitless negotiations to obtain the information without a subpoena, Jaworski had asked that Sirica set April 23—one week from the date of the request—as the deadline for a White House reply to the subpoena. Sirica, issuing the order two days later, set a deadline of May 2, two weeks from the date of the subpoena. The subpoena to Nixon issued April 11 by the House Judiciary Committee for records of more than 40 conversations contained a deadline of April 25. *(p. 311)*

Turning inside out his pledge in March that he would give the House committee everything he had given the special prosecutor, Nixon apparently had told Jaworski in early April, through St. Clair, that he would receive any materials that Nixon had given the House committee. And he apparently added that he would not consider other materials Jaworski had requested until he had decided what to give the Judiciary Committee.

Maintaining the committee's right to decide what was and was not relevant to its inquiry, Judiciary Committee Chairman Peter W. Rodino Jr. (D N.J.) reacted adversely April 18 to reports that the White House was screening the tapes requested in order to eliminate irrelevant portions from those that would be given to the committee. Such White House editing, said Rodino on the NBC-TV "Today" show, "would mean that the White House would be making the final determination.... This could not be a proper...comprehensive inquiry unless we were to make the determination as to what is necessary."

If the President did not fully comply with the committee subpoena, said Rodino, that noncompliance "could be considered as a possible ground of impeachment." A study prepared by the impeachment inquiry staff supported that statement after an analysis of the various ways in which the committee and the House could deal with presidential noncompliance. *(Box, p. 979)*

Separate Requests. In a letter April 11 to presidential counsel James D. St. Clair, explaining why he would request the additional subpoena, the third from the special prosecutor's office to the White House, Jaworski tried to separate his request from that of the committee. "I have emphasized repeatedly that our request is in no way tied to the requests of the House Judiciary Committee," he wrote. "The requests are distinguishable both factually and legally. Nevertheless, you have refused to consider them separately, and you have been unable to tell us the criteria that will govern the President's response."

But some of the conversations in which the impeachment inquiry was interested, and for which Jaworski also sought records and recordings, were the same. Jaworski sought material related to:

• Conversations during the week after the June 17, 1972, break-in at Democratic national headquarters in Washington's Watergate office building, including three between Nixon and Colson and three between Nixon and his then chief of staff, H.R. Haldeman.

• A number of conversations between Nixon and Colson, former White House counsel John W. Dean III, Haldeman and former domestic affairs adviser John D. Ehrlichman during March and April 1973, including six conversations on April 14, seven on April 16, four on April 17 and six on April 25. Many of these also were sought by the subpoena from the House committee.

• Two conversations between Nixon and Haldeman on June 4, 1973, after Haldeman had left his White House post. It was the day that Nixon went to Camp David, Maryland, and listened to some of the tapes. Both conversations were telephone conversations.

Jaworski explained that he was asking for the subpoena, and the early reply date, "solely for the purpose of preventing any postponement of the trial or delay during the conduct of the trial." He said that if the requested material were supplied, it would have to be analyzed—"an arduous and time-consuming task." If the White House should contest the subpoena, Jaworski said, "it would be best for all concerned that such limitation be initiated promptly in order to avoid the possibility of postponing the trial."

Warning from Scott. Applying another spur to White House cooperation, Senate Minority Leader Hugh Scott (R Pa.) warned that Nixon's refusal to cooperate with the House committee could lead to his impeachment. In a letter to his constituents made public April 18, Scott stated: "It would be a grave danger and with serious consequences possibly leading to impeachment if the President would not cooperate with the committee and decided against furnishing the necessary facts requested by the committee." He said that he was urging both sides to cooperate in reaching an acceptable compromise on the necessary material.

Lowenstein Suit. In another Watergate-related development, former Rep. Allard K. Lowenstein (D N.Y. 1969-71) filed suit April 18 against five former White House officials for conspiring through an "enemies list" to defeat him in 1972. He also accused the FBI of investigating him unlawfully and the Internal Revenue Service of auditing his tax returns to harass him.

The former White House officials named in the suit were H.R. Haldeman, John D. Ehrlichman, Charles W. Colson, John W. Dean III and Lawrence M. Higby. Among others named as defendants in the civil suit, filed in U.S. District Court in Brooklyn, were several FBI and IRS officials.

Mitchell-Stans Trial

The defendants themselves, John N. Mitchell and Maurice H. Stans, took the witness stand during the week ending April 20 in their trial on perjury, conspiracy and obstruction of justice changes. Their accounts of how they treated the secret $200,000 cash contribution to the Nixon re-election campaign from financier Robert L. Vesco, and the financier's problems with the Securities and Exchange Commission (SEC), differed greatly from the version the government had presented.

Mitchell, former attorney general and director of Nixon's re-election campaign, maintained his innocence in testimony April 15 after his lawyer had finished direct examination. The trial was being held in U.S. District Court in New York City.

"Are you guilty or not guilty?" attorney Peter Fleming Jr. asked Mitchell, his client.

"Absolutely not guilty to any of the charges," was Mitchell's firm response.

Earlier, Mitchell had denied that he and Stans had tried to block an SEC investigation of Vesco's financial dealings in return for a secret contribution to the Nixon re-election campaign. *(p. 312)*

Mitchell held to that line under persistent cross-examination. The prosecution quizzed him April 15 and 16. John R. Wing, the chief prosecutor, again and again received from Mitchell direct contradictions of the government's evidence. In response to Wing's questions, Mitchell was led either to deny that a conversation or event occurred or that he had no recollection of them.

Contradictions. In the process, Mitchell directly contradicted the testimony of four of the government's

Poll Report

For the first time, a plurality of persons interviewed by the Harris Survey agreed that President Nixon should be impeached and removed from office. The poll was published April 13. *(Earlier poll report, p. 315)*

These were the percentages in the survey, conducted March 24-29 in 1,495 households nationwide:

Should be impeached	43%
Should not	41
Not sure	14

A majority agreed with a statement that if Nixon "fails to turn over the information the House Judiciary Committee wants, then that committee should vote to bring impeachment charges against the President."

Agreed	55%
Disagreed	33
Not sure	12

A majority said they did not expect Nixon to give the Judiciary Committee all the material it sought.

Expected	19%
Did not expect	67
Not sure	14

A larger majority gave the President, Harris wrote, "overwhelmingly negative marks...on the way he is cooperating with the impeachment proceedings."

Positive	21%
Negative	72
Not sure	7

The same survey found that more persons believed John W. Dean III, Nixon's chief accuser and a former presidential counsel, than believed the President. This was the question: "Who do you think has been more truthful about the Watergate cover-up—President Nixon or John Dean?"

	Latest	July 1973
Nixon	29%	38%
Dean	46	37
Not sure	25	25

key witnesses against him—Daniel W. Hofgren, former vice chairman of the Finance Committee to Re-elect the President; Harry L. Sears, a former Vesco attorney; John W. Dean III, former White House counsel, and William J. Casey, former SEC chairman.

Hofgren had said he was present March 8, 1972, when Vesco offered a large contribution to Stans and described Vesco's SEC problems. That evening, Hofgren testified, he met Mitchell at a political dinner, mentioned Vesco and was told, "Dan, you stay away from that."

One of the perjury counts against Mitchell charged that he had lied when he told the grand jury he never had such a conversation with Hofgren. Mitchell April 15 said again that the conversation had not occurred.

On direct examination, Mitchell conceded that he had telephoned the Justice Department in June, July or August 1972 at the request of Sears to check on whether the SEC had referred its Vesco inquiry to the Justice Department for a criminal investigation. Mitchell said he called someone—possibly then Attorney General Richard G. Kleindeinst—and was told that the SEC had not done so.

Under cross-examination, Mitchell:

• Said he had no idea why his initials were put next to a listing of the Vesco contribution.

• Repeated that he did not recall discussing Vesco with Sears before Nov. 30, 1971.

• Asserted that "if Vesco thought he was going to get a favor (in return for his contribution), he would be looking for something more than just a meeting with the chairman of the SEC."

• Said he recalled making only one telephone call, in February 1972, asking Casey, then SEC chairman, to see Sears and listen to his complaint that the SEC staff was harassing Vesco. Mitchell claimed there was nothing improper about that call.

Cross-examination of Mitchell was completed April 16. He continued to deny the testimony by Dean, a key witness against him, especially on perjury counts, concerning Mitchell's appearance before the grand jury in 1973.

Dean said Mitchell told him he had "a hell of a grilling" by "those little bastards" in the U.S. attorney's office and that it was a "runaway grand jury." According to Dean, Mitchell asked him to call Kleindeinst "and tell him what's going on...." Dean said he had called Kleindeinst.

Mitchell, however, denied that story under cross-examination. He had called Dean about another matter, and told him about appearing before the grand jury, Mitchell said. But he said he had been questioned politely by the government attorneys.

Introduced in the trial was a transcript of a White House tape recording of a conversation between Dean and Nixon on March 20, 1973. According to the transcript, Dean had said that Mitchell had had a "grilling" by a "runaway grand jury." Mitchell April 16 attributed Dean's description to a "lively imagination."

Kleindeinst appeared as the defense's last witness April 16 in an attempt to corroborate Mitchell's testimony on the Dean-Mitchell phone conversation. Kleindeinst said he could not recall the conversations that Dean testified he had had with him about the case. But he would not deny that they had occurred.

Stans Testimony. Stans, the former accountant who rose to high posts in the Eisenhower and Nixon administrations and who was Nixon's re-election finance chairman, took the stand April 17 to present his story of what occurred with the Vesco contribution and SEC investigation. Like his codefendant, Mitchell, he denied the testimony of government witnesses against him and said none of his activities had been illegal or improper.

There was no payoff, no *quid pro quo* in return for Vesco's contribution, Stans said. "Vesco made the contribution in private, and privacy was his constitutional right under the law," he testified.

The foundation of Stans' defense was that he was obligated to protect the privacy of Vesco and other large contributors who sought legal anonymity by giving donations before the 1971 Federal Election Campaign Act took effect April 7, 1972. That law required the reporting of campaign contributions.

Stans denied the trial accounts of Dean, Sears, G. Bradford Cook, former SEC counsel and chairman, and Laurence B. Richardson Jr., a former Vesco associate. Specifically, he denied that he called Mitchell's office for an appointment for Vesco or said anything about arranging a meeting with SEC Chairman Casey after Vesco told him he wanted to make a large contribution. He also denied that he had asked Vesco to make his contribution before April 7 or to make it in cash. Stans denied that Richardson had referred to the "SEC problem" or that Stans' response was, "Mitchell and Sears are handling that," when Richardson delivered the money to him.

The former fund-raiser said he did not tell anyone from whom the $200,000 contribution came, but instructed an aide on the spur of the moment to list it under Mitchell's name, since "it came through Sears," a friend of Mitchell. Stans swore that it was Cook, then SEC counsel, who volunteered without Stans' asking to drop all mention of the $200,000 from the commission's formal complaint against Vesco on Nov. 27, 1972. Cook had testified that it was Stans who had indicated he wanted the paragraph about the $200,000 dropped from the SEC complaint.

As the trial ended April 17, Judge Lee P. Gagliardi had under advisement a defense request that Stans' lawyers be permitted to tell the jury about the serious blood illness Mrs. Stans was suffering from at the time her husband appeared before the grand jury concerning the Vesco contribution. The defense claimed that the pressure Stans was under because of his wife's health might have caused various contradictions in his grand jury testimony.

Week's Watergate Chronology

Following is a day-to-day chronology of the week's events in the Watergate case:

APRIL 11

Nixon Subpoena. The House Judiciary Committee voted 33-3 to subpoena presidential tape recordings of more than 40 conversations that the committee believed necessary for its impeachment investigation. The committee set April 25 as the deadline for compliance. *(p. 311)*

Ronald L. Ziegler, Nixon's press secretary, indicated that Nixon probably would turn over some but not all of the materials subpoenaed by the committee. Ziegler said the President would respond to the subpoena after Congress returned April 22 from its Easter recess.

St. Clair Role. Chairman Peter W. Rodino Jr. (D N.J.) of the Judiciary Committee said he was willing, in principle, to let James D. St. Clair, Nixon's defense counsel, be present when the committee heard impeachment evidence in May.

Presidential Noncompliance: A Committee Staff Analysis

Aware of the possibility that President Nixon might not comply with the subpoena issued to him April 11 by the House Judiciary Committee, the staff of the impeachment inquiry that morning presented the committee members with a memorandum. It supported the committee's right to issue such a subpoena and discussed the various ways in which the committee might deal with presidential noncompliance. Three ways were mentioned: the contempt processes of the House itself, the courts, or simply taking noncompliance into account in evaluating the charges against the President during the impeachment inquiry. *(p. 311)*

Excerpts from the memorandum follow:

INTRODUCTION

The Constitution vests in the House of Representatives the sole power of impeachment. Implicit in the power to impeach are the power to inquire and the power to compel the giving of evidence. The full investigative power of the House has been delegated to the Committee on the Judiciary by H Res 803, adopted Feb. 6, 1974.

....The power to inquire necessarily implies the further power to compel the production of testimonial and other evidence, to enforce compliance with a subpoena, and to punish noncompliance. This memorandum discusses the alternative methods that are available to the House for this purpose.

Each...presents problems, especially in the case of a subpoena...directed to the President. If the President refuses to comply, the practical difficulties of enforcing the subpoena may well be insurmountable, and for this reason this memorandum also raises the possibility that factual inferences may be drawn from presidential noncompliance with a subpoena or that noncompliance may itself be a ground for impeachment.

...There is every reason to assume that the President would comply with a subpoena, lawfully issued by the committee for the purpose of its inquiry.

...If the President complies...the committee and the House will be in a better position to evaluate fully and on the merits whether or not grounds for impeachment exist. Such an evaluation is preferable to one based on incomplete evidence or partly on the President's refusal to produce further evidence the committee considers necessary for its inquiry.

DIRECT ENFORCEMENT THROUGH THE PROCESSES OF THE HOUSE

The House has the power to hold in contempt a person who has disobeyed its subpoena.... (B)y order or resolution of the House he may be incarcerated for a period not lasting beyond the term of the House of Representatives that imprisoned him. Alternatively, it would appear that the House may merely reprimand or censure him without directing his further imprisonment.

...The courts have been reluctant to intervene to quash a congressional investigative subpoena at the insistence of the subpoenaed party.... (A) court...is limited to determining whether the action of the House...was within its jurisdiction....

ENFORCEMENT THROUGH THE JUDICIAL PROCESS

Because the powers of impeaching and removing federal officials are vested by the Constitution exclusively in the Congress, it may be thought inappropriate to seek the aid of the judicial branch in exercising these powers. Moreover, as a practical matter, the courts have no more means to enforce compliance with process in a presidential impeachment inquiry that are not also available to the House itself through its own procedures.

The usual mode of enforcement of congressional subpoenas is for Congress to refer contempts to the appropriate U.S. attorney for criminal prosecution....

...Criminal proceedings, however, would pose a number of problems for this inquiry, including delay, the uncertainty of relying upon the executive branch to prosecute the chief executive, and doubt whether an incumbent President may be prosecuted for a criminal offense before his impeachment and removal from office.

A civil proceeding to compel compliance by the President might lie under (the portion of federal law) conferring jurisdiction on the federal district courts to hear "any action in the nature of a *mandamus* to compel an officer or employee of the United States or any agency thereof to perform a duty owed to the plaintiff...." It might be argued that the obligation to obey a subpoena does not fall within the statutory definition, leading to delay while that threshold jurisdictional issue was litigated.

While civil proceedings might be brought under other existing statutes, they may also raise jurisdictional issues.... New legislation probably could resolve other litigation difficulties. Consideration should be given, however, to the time required for the passage of legislation, the possibility of a presidential veto....

NONCOMPLIANCE AND THE IMPEACHMENT INQUIRY

Realistically, the President probably cannot be compelled to comply with a *subpoena duces tecum* by use of the processes of either the House or the courts. Rather than being considered solely in terms of the availability of coercive means of enforcement, however, noncompliance may also be addressed in terms of its effect in the impeachment proceeding itself.... There is no direct precedent....

...Noncompliance by the President with a subpoena issued by the committee could be taken into account in the impeachment inquiry in two ways:

First, under some circumstances, an inference negative to the President might be drawn from his refusal to produce materials sought by the committees.

Second, unjustified noncompliance might be considered independently in determining whether sufficient grounds exist for impeachment of the President. For example, contempt of the House...is prosecutable as a federal crime. And unjustified disobedience of a subpoena issued by a committee exercising the sole power of impeachment would be an action in derogation of the authority explicitly vested by the Constitution in the House of Representatives.

Porter Sentencing. Herbert L. Porter, a former aide in the Nixon re-election campaign, received a 15-month jail sentence from U.S. District Judge William B. Bryant in Washington for lying to the FBI during its Watergate inquiry. The judge suspended all except 30 days of the sentence. *(p. 312)*

Rebozo, Abplanalp Tax Returns. Leon Jaworski, the Watergate special prosecutor, subpoenaed the federal income tax returns of Charles G. Rebozo and Robert H. Abplanalp, two of Nixon's closest friends, in the investigation of a $100,000 campaign contribution from Howard R. Hughes, *The New York Times* reported.

Senate Warning. Six Republican leaders in the Senate issued a unanimous warning to Nixon that unless he promptly produced all materials being sought by the House Judiciary Committee, he was "aching for impeachment." *(p. 311)*

APRIL 12

California Tax. The franchise tax board of the state of California ruled that President and Mrs. Nixon owed $4,302 for 1969 and 1970 on the part of their income earned in that state. Martin Huff, executive officer of the board, said the assessment resulted from an inquiry requested by the Joint Committee on Internal Revenue of the California Legislature.

IRS Contact. The Senate Watergate committee obtained the name of the former federal tax official alleged to have furnished the White House with tax data on its friends and enemies. John J. Caulfield, Nixon's former law enforcement adviser, named as his primary Internal Revenue Service (IRS) contact Vernon D. (Mike) Acree, U.S. commissioner of customs and former assistant IRS commissioner for inspections.

APRIL 13

Abplanalp Charge. Robert H. Abplanalp accused investigators of the Senate Watergate committee of "reckless conjecturing" as he again denied that he ever discussed a $100,000 donation by Howard Hughes to the Nixon re-election campaign. Abplanalp said that he met with Charles G. Rebozo on a fishing trip before the cash was returned to a Hughes employee.

APRIL 14

Ford on Tapes. Vice President Ford said he sought to work out a compromise between the House Judiciary Committee and the White House to avoid a confrontation over the tapes that the committee sought. This reportedly was the first indication that Ford had been involved in trying to head off the committee's subsequent decision to subpoena the tapes.

APRIL 15

Illegal Contributions. The Securities and Exchange Commission (SEC) charged the American Ship Building Company and its chairman, George M. Steinbrenner III, with filing false reports to hide its illegal corporate campaign gifts to Nixon, Sen. Vance Hartke (D Ind.) and Sen. Daniel K. Inouye (D Hawaii). The SEC sued to force Steinbrenner to repay the company. *(Steinbrenner indictment, p. 315)*

Mitchell-Stans Trial. John N. Mitchell testified that while he was attorney general, he "willingly contacted" the chairman of the SEC in behalf of Robert L. Vesco, who was being investigated by the agency. He said, however, that his action had not been improper. *(Earlier story, p. 312)*

Gifts to Nixon Nixon received more than $47,000 in unsolicited cash and pledges to help pay his back income taxes, but he decided to pay "every penny" himself, the White House said.

Connally Probe. The Watergate special prosecutor asked the White House for tapes of conversations between Nixon and John B. Connally, former treasury secretary, on milk matters, columnist Jack Anderson reported. The prosecutors wanted to learn what the President and Connally said about the dairy industry's push for higher milk price supports in 1971 and 1972. *(Earlier milk story, p. 316)*

APRIL 16

Another Subpoena. Leon Jaworski, the Watergate special prosecutor, asked U.S. District Judge John J. Sirica for a subpoena of tapes and documents covering 64 conversations between Nixon and four of his top former aides—John W. Dean III, Charles W. Colson, H. R. Haldeman and John D. Ehrlichman. *(Details, p. 317)*

Mitchell-Stans Trial. Lawyers for John N. Mitchell ended their defense by calling former Attorney General Richard G. Kleindeinst to testify at the perjury and conspiracy trial of Mitchell and Maurice H. Stans. *(Details, p. 318)*

Ehrlichman Attitude. Close friends of former Nixon aide John D. Ehrlichman said that Ehrlichman had privately expressed disenchantment with the President and had told them he was considering reaching a settlement on the Watergate-related charges pending against him, *The Los Angeles Times* reported.

APRIL 17

Mitchell-Stans Trial. Maurice H. Stans, former commerce secretary and chief Nixon re-election fundraiser, took the stand at his perjury and conspiracy trial and testified that he and John N. Mitchell once had discussed whether it was proper to accept a campaign contribution from Robert L. Vesco. They decided it was, Stans said, because Harry L. Sears, a former Vesco associate, had told them that a Securities and Exchange Commission investigation of Vesco was winding down. Stans also said he kept Vesco's gift secret because "privacy was his (Vesco's) constitutional right under the law."

Colson Request. Charles W. Colson, a former Nixon aide, joined Watergate Special Prosecutor Jaworski in asking the U.S. District Court in Washington to subpoena records of 64 Nixon conversations. Colson wanted to use the material to help prepare his defense against charges of conspiring to cover up Watergate.

Ehrlichman Denial. John D. Ehrlichman denied news reports that he was bargaining with the Watergate special prosecutor about a possible guilty plea to a reduced charge. The former Nixon assistant said he would prove his innocence of charges of conspiring to cover up Watergate.

Reinecke Trial Date. U.S. District Judge Barrington D. Parker set May 13 as the date for a hearing on pretrial motions in the perjury trial of Lt. Gov. Ed Reinecke (R Calif.). Reinecke's trial in Washington, D.C., was expected to begin May 14 or 15. He had asked that the date be moved up to before the June 4 California primary. *(Reinecke plea, p. 316)* √

A FIVE-DAY EXTENSION OF TAPES DEADLINE

An acquiescent House Judiciary Committee, during the week ending April 27, granted a White House request for a five-day extension of the deadline for responding to a subpoena of more tapes and records of presidential conversations. The deadline was changed from April 25 to April 30.

In New York City, the government's case against former Attorney General John N. Mitchell and former Commerce Secretary Maurice H. Stans went to a jury in U.S. District Court. The two former cabinet officers and Nixon re-election campaign officials were charged with perjury and obstruction of justice relating to their efforts in behalf of indicted financier Robert L. Vesco.

On April 25, the Judiciary Committee received a staff report on the status of its investigation into charges against President Nixon. The staff recommended narrowing the charges so that the committee could concentrate on:

• The Watergate break-in and coverup.
• Other domestic surveillance and intelligence operations directed by the White House.
• The Vesco matter and three other sets of charges that the administration had used government power to help its friends or harm its critics.
• The possibility that Nixon was guilty of tax fraud in the way he deducted his gift of vice presidential papers to the National Archives.

It was revealed that the Judiciary Committee was seeking still more information from the White House. A letter requesting further material was sent on April 19. No immediate response was reported.

Judiciary Committee Actions

With few objections, the House Judiciary Committee voted 34-4 April 25 to grant the White House request that President Nixon have five additional days—until April 30—to respond to the committee's April 11 subpoena. Voting against the extension were Jerome R. Waldie (D Calif.), Robert F. Drinan (D Mass.), Charles B. Rangel (D N.Y.) and Elizabeth Holtzman (D N.Y.).

'When the Going Was Difficult...'

Addressing the annual convention of the Mississippi Economic Council-State Chamber of Commerce April 25 in Jackson, President Nixon dwelt on the future, alluding only indirectly to the difficulties of the present.

Nixon predicted that 1976 "will be the best in America's history, the most prosperous, the most free." He forecast a future president's words concerning the present generation: "They did not fail when the going was very difficult and when American leadership was so important in the world."

"We're backing down," said Waldie, from the determination expressed in the earlier vote to subpoena the President.

"We've leaned over so far backwards (to be fair) that I fear some of us have fallen over," said Holtzman.

"We will not be diverted," said Chairman Peter W. Rodino Jr. (D N.J.), from the committee's duty to reach a reasonable judgment on the charges of impeachable acts.

Granting the additional time, said Walter Flowers (D Ala.), would "place a stronger burden on the White House to agree with our request."

Barbara Jordan (D Texas) expressed willingness to grant the President "due process quadrupled." The five-day extension, she said, would show the committee's willingness "to demonstrate clearly that we are not out to kill the king."

The April 22 request for more time, made by special White House counsel James D. St. Clair, was accompanied by no assurance of eventual compliance, said special committee counsel John M. Doar. Earlier in the week, Rodino and other committee members had reacted disapprovingly to reports that the White House would give the committee edited transcrips of the taped conversations sought.

To provide the committee with a mechanism to deal with White House claims that sought-after materials were irrelevant, protected by executive privilege or too sensitive because of national security to be disclosed, Charles E. Wiggins (R Calif.) made a motion April 25 to set up procedures for committee responses to such claims. The motion was to be considered the next week when the committee took up questions of procedure.

A Narrowing Inquiry. To better focus the energies of the 101-member impeachment inquiry staff, the staff April 25 recommended discontinuing the investigation of:

• Most of the questions concerning Nixon's personal finances.
• Half of the charges of administration misuse of government agencies in response to large campaign contributions.
• Charges related to the impoundment of funds and the dismantling of the Office of Economic Opportunity.

The committee did not approve the staff report on April 25. Members made it obvious that ceasing an investigation of a particular charge should not foreclose later reopening of the investigation. Nor should it be seen, they said, either as a dismissal of the charge or a vindication of the President.

Nixon Taxes. Summarizing the report on Nixon's taxes by the Joint Committee on Internal Revenue Taxation, the staff report stated that if the Judiciary Committee chose to pursue the issue of possible tax fraud, it would have to conduct its own investigation. Although Watergate Special Prosecutor Leon Jaworski had been delegated responsibility to investigate possible tax fraud, that investigation, said the report, was unlikely to be complete in time to help the committee in its decision on impeachment.

Doar said that he had not yet formally requested the Internal Revenue Service report on Nixon's taxes, which had not been made public. He said he intended to do so after completing discussions and exchanging information with the staff and members of the joint committee. "There was no feasible way to develop this factual material without the joint committee's work," Doar reminded the Judiciary Committee.

The disallowed gift of Nixon's pre-presidential papers to the National Archives was the chief matter of relevance to the impeachment inquiry, said Doar, who also said that he had a tax fraud expert on his staff.

Campaign Favors. About half of the charges of misuse of government power to favor friends and to harm critics of the administration did not appear to deserve further investigation by the impeachment staff, the report stated. But "the staff is continuing its inquiry into some of these allegations," said the report, "focusing primarily on the Howard Hughes $100,000 contribution, the contribution by Robert L. Vesco, the contributions by representatives of the dairy industry and the financial pledge by a subsidiary of ITT related to the 1972 Republican National Convention.

"The purpose of the inquiry is to determine the extent, if any, of Presidential responsibility for unlawful campaign contributions and illegal or improper executive branch action in response to them," the report stated. Among related charges still under investigation were the "sale" of ambassadorships, the commutation of prison sentences, misuse of the Federal Communications Commission and the antitrust division of the Justice Department to retaliate against media criticism, and misuse of the Internal Revenue Service.

Because "there is no substantial evidence known to the staff...or the evidence is insufficient to justify devoting the resources required to complete a thorough investigation," the staff was inclined not to pursue further charges that campaign contributions were obtained through promises of government favors or retaliation. In addition, the staff recommended that no further investigation be undertaken into charges that specific favors— the granting or denial of bank charters, the dropping of lawsuits, permission to increase prices, withholding of certain safety standards—were granted to campaign contributors or presidential friends.

Other Misconduct. The staff review of evidence supporting the charge that Nixon had acted illegally and unconstitutionally in authorizing the secret bombing of Cambodia between March 1969 and August 1973 was incomplete, said the report. And, it continued, the staff was awaiting the report of the Senate Armed Services Committee on the matter. Special minority counsel Albert E. Jenner Jr. said that as soon as Rodino and ranking Republican member Edward Hutchinson (R Mich.) could pay a courtesy visit to Senate Armed Services Committee Chairman John C. Stennis (D Miss.), the inquiry staff would begin receiving the printer's proofs of the Senate committee report. Within seven to 10 days after that, said the report, the staff could report further to the committee.

Charges related to the impoundment of funds and the dismantling of the Office of Economic Oppor-

tunity involved "substantially similar issues," reported the inquiry staff. More than 50 court decisions had been issued on the question of impoundment, most finding it illegal—although the administration was able to present respectable arguments in support of its position, said the report. Because impoundment was a public affair, had diminished as a result of adverse court rulings and could be resolved in court, "the staff is not presently conducting further investigation with respect" to these two categories, the report stated.

Mitchell-Stans Trial

The jurors who must weigh the strength of the government's perjury, conspiracy and obstruction of justice charges against John N. Mitchell and Maurice H. Stans finally began deliberating the case on April 25, 10 weeks after the trial of the two former Nixon cabinet officers began.

During the 45 days they spent in U.S. District Court in New York City, the jurors had heard 59 witnesses—45 of them testifying for the government, 15 for the defense and three for both sides. Some 300 documents were submitted as evidence. *(Earlier story, p. 318)*

Stans Summation. Before Judge Lee J. Gagliardi made his charge to the jury, the defense and prosecution spent almost 2½ days summing up their cases. Walter J. Bonner, Stans' lawyer, made an emotional defense April 23. His aim was not so much to rebut the government's testimony in the trial as to create for the jury the notion that it was unbelievable to suppose that Stans would commit a crime.

Bonner pictured the white-haired, 66-year-old Stans as a man so accustomed to handling vast sums of money that it was incredible to think he was impressed by financier Robert L. Vesco's $200,000 contribution. Bonner accused the government of being afflicted with a disease he called "Vescoitis." "It was conceived in the test tubes of the prosecution and it has permeated the life of my client...for a full year. It has permeated this courtroom," he said.

Through the weeks of the trial, Bonner said, he had tried to "help cure that disease, to kill it and to stamp it out so that we will have no more of it." His client, Bonner continued, "has been treated in this courtroom as though his heart and mind and soul were wrapped up with and dedicated to a man named Robert L. Vesco. It is not true," he said. "You have learned that we met him once."

Bonner tried to disparage the prosecution testimony given by John W. Dean III, the former White House counsel who was an unindicted co-conspirator in the case. "Can you believe Dean?" Bonner asked. "Hell, he wouldn't even tell you" the truth about his conversations with Stans.

Bonner dismissed the notion that Stans would attempt to fix Vesco's problems with the Securities and Exchange Commission in return for a contribution. "This man is anything but a damned fool," he said of his client. "For God's sake, if he were involved in a fix, he sure as hell would have sent someone to get the money down in D.C."

Mitchell Summation. In his summation, which followed Bonner's, Peter Fleming Jr., Mitchell's lawyer, spoke caustically April 24 of the government's case as "a prosecutorial vision." Fleming ridiculed the charges against his client and Stans, saying, "This must be the

(Continued on p. 325)

J. Fred Buzhardt: From Shadows Back to Spotlight

More than three months after he was replaced by Boston lawyer James D. St. Clair as President Nixon's chief Watergate lawyer, presidential counsel J. Fred Buzhardt emerged as one of Nixon's principal advisers.

Buzhardt, once widely thought to have lost Nixon's confidence because of his handling of Watergate, was in charge of the tapes sought by the House Judiciary Committee and Special Prosecutor Leon Jaworski, according to former White House lawyer Cecil Emerson.

Emerson, 39, who left at the end of March after a four-month period working for St. Clair, claimed that Buzhardt was the "political man" on the legal team and was a "Nixon loyalist." He was closer to Nixon personally and had more influence than St. Clair, whom Emerson described as the "professional" who was charged with representing White House positions to the committee and the special prosecutor. Buzhardt was "in the driver's seat" in running White House strategy, and Nixon was dictating the strategy, according to Emerson.

White House Reaction. The White House reacted strongly to Emerson's claims, originally published in an interview with Congressional Quarterly, that St. Clair was not in full control of the case. *(p. 313)*

Reacting to Emerson's assertion that St. Clair believed Nixon to be innocent of the Watergate cover-up, St. Clair said, "For a lawyer to pass judgment on any case is inappropriate. On the other hand, I'm satisfied that the President is not guilty of the matter about which I believe he is being charged (the coverup)."

J. Fred Buzhardt

Asked about St. Clair's status, White House Press Secretary Ronald L. Ziegler said he was "very much in control of the entire legal operation. The President looks to him for advice." Ziegler disparaged Emerson's views. "You just have to consider the source of the statements," Ziegler said.

Although St. Clair and Buzhardt had "differences of view that shift from time to time," it was "misleading and even fatuous to say there's a conflict of opinion" between them on basic legal strategy, a senior White House official told Congressional Quarterly.

Buzhardt's Function. For all that, the White House evidently was not willing to allow St. Clair to make his own judgment on how many of the tapes subpoenaed by the Judiciary Committee and by Jaworski should be turned over. Congressional Quarterly learned that it was Buzhardt, not St. Clair, who was reviewing the tapes. "He's been listening to them so long that his ears are below the surface of his skull," said one source. Another source said Buzhardt was working virtually around the clock to review the materials.

Buzhardt's stay at the White House had not been smooth. He joined the White House staff to head the Watergate defense on May 11, 1973, less than two weeks after the resignations of top Nixon aides H. R. Haldeman and John D. Ehrlichman and Attorney General Richard G. Kleindienst, and the firing of John W. Dean III.

On June 27, 1973, Buzhardt issued a 12-page memo attacking Dean's credibility as the former White House counsel was in the midst of testifying before the Senate Watergate committee. Dean characterized the memo as having been pieced together from newspaper accounts, and the next day the White House said it had been released without Nixon's approval and did not "represent the White House position."

Buzhardt then was involved in a series of White House embarrassments in Judge John J. Sirica's courtroom over missing and erased tapes. Pressed by tenacious prosecutors on Jaworski's staff, Buzhardt himself was finally forced onto the witness stand Nov. 29. He testified that he saw "no innocent explanation" for an 18½-minute gap he had discovered in one of the tapes.

Ziegler the next day told reporters that the White House's poor showing in the missing and erased tapes matter may have resulted from "overwork" of Buzhardt's staff. Ziegler issued such a lukewarm endorsement of Buzhardt that some observers concluded Buzhardt had lost Nixon's confidence.

Disappearance and Re-emergence. A month later St. Clair replaced Buzhardt, who was promoted to the job of presidential counsel. Buzhardt dropped from public view for about 2½ months. White House spokesmen minimized his role until Emerson began speaking up.

A senior White House aide close to Buzhardt denied that Buzhardt had been forced out of his job as head of the legal team. Instead, said the official, Buzhardt and Nixon's other chief Watergate lawyer, Leonard Garment, were removed at their own recommendation. Garment returned to his old job as assistant to Nixon.

"There was a strong feeling in November (during the controversy over the missing and erased tapes) that the lawyers in the case were growing weary and somewhat scarred by the media," the official told Congressional Quarterly. "Most of the leading counsel (Buzhardt and Garment) were quite close to the principals involved in the matter, and it didn't take a great deal of thinking to figure out that it might be well to get some independent, detached professional involved in the case."

This source laid Ziegler's statements that Buzhardt's staff was at fault during the White House courtroom embarrassments to the then "extremely confused and confusing time."

"Fred has been a little bit badly treated by contemporary accounts," a White House official told Congressional Quarterly. "But he's professional enough to accept them gracefully and silently. The whole story will have to wait a year or two, when we have a revisionist view of Watergate—out of a law review."

only fix in modern times, or ancient times, or biblical times, when the payoff was made in April and afterwards everything gets worse."

Like Bonner, Fleming asked the jury to chose between his client and John Dean. Whom did they believe, Dean or Mitchell? he asked. What was the government's motive for bringing the case?

Government Summation. Emphasizing the perjury charges against the two defendants, John R. Wing, the government's chief prosecutor, told the jury April 24 that "what this case involves is telling the truth." Mitchell and Stans "sat at the very pinnacle of government" and thought "they were above the law," he said. "There exists in this country a principle that no man is above the law. It applies to you and to me, to Mr. Mitchell and Mr. Stans. They felt they were above the law—that it didn't apply equally to them.

"Start out knowing for sure one thing that can't be in dispute. Some people who came before you and raised their hand and took their oath have lied to you—make no mistake about it."

Stans' Earlier Testimony. Stans had acknowledged April 18 that there were discrepancies between his testimony at his trial and his testimony before the grand jury investigating Vesco's secret $200,000 cash contribution to the Nixon re-election campaign. Stans was permitted by Judge Gagliardi to say that his memory of events from August to December 1972 was shaky when he testified to a grand jury in 1973, because his wife was critically ill and hospitalized during that period.

Although he denied, "On my oath, I never did anything to help Robert Vesco in any way, and I never asked anyone to do anything to help him," Stans conceded, under cross-examination by Wing, discrepancies with his other testimony. Stans said Vesco did not receive a thank-you letter for his contribution, as did many other donors of money before new laws took effect on April 7, 1972. And he admitted that others who promised gifts before April 7 were not told that they could deliver later, as was the case with Vesco.

Rebuttal Testimony. The prosecution April 22 put nine witnesses on the stand to rebut the defense as testimony in the trial ended.

The two key witnesses were Dean and Sally Quinn, a reporter with *The Washington Post.* Dean testified mainly against Stans. The former commerce secretary had testified that he twice had withheld information about Vesco's cash contribution from the Securities and Exchange Commission (SEC) on the advice of Dean. On both occasions, Stans said, he asked whether he should volunteer information to his friend G. Bradford Cook, who was then in charge of the SEC's investigation of Vesco, but was advised by Dean that this would not be necessary unless the SEC made a formal inquiry.

Dean said the matter was not discussed either time.

Quinn testified that she spoke to Mitchell on March 8, 1972, at a reception before a Republican fund-raising dinner in a Washington hotel. Mitchell had testified that he arrived after the reception had ended and most of the guests were seated in the dining room.

The issue concerned one of the perjury counts against Mitchell. Daniel W. Hofgren, a former Stans aide, had testified that he was at the March 8 reception, had mentioned Vesco to Mitchell and was told, "Dan, you stay away from that." Mitchell denied in grand jury and trial testimony that the conversation took place or that he even saw Hofgren.

Week's Watergate Chronology

Following is a day-to-day chronology of the week's events in the Watergate case:

APRIL 18

Another Subpoena. U.S. District Judge John J. Sirica issued a subpoena commanding President Nixon to turn over tape recordings and other records of 64 White House conversations relating to the Watergate coverup to Watergate Special Prosecutor Leon Jaworski. *(p. 317)*

Compromise Barred. Chairman Peter W. Rodino Jr. (D N.J.) of the House Judiciary Committee ruled out any compromise with the White House over the committee's request for tape recordings of 41 or 42 Watergate-related conversations. Rodino said it would be unacceptable for Nixon's lawyers to decide unilaterally which portions of the recordings were relevant to the committee's impeachment inquiry.

Guilty Plea. John H. Melcher Jr., executive vice president of the American Ship Building Company, pleaded guilty to concealing an illegal $25,000 contribution to Nixon's re-election campaign. The surprise plea was reported to indicate that Melcher would testify against George M. Steinbrenner III, the firm's president. *(Steinbrenner indictment, p. 315)*

Bar Inquiry. The New York City Bar Association said it was conducting an investigation that possibly could lead to the disbarment in that state of Nixon, former Attorney General John N. Mitchell and several former White House aides.

Mitchell-Stans Trial. The government began its cross-examination of Maurice H. Stans, hinting to the jury that Stans had concealed campaign funds allegedly used to help finance the Watergate break-in. The prosecution also tried to show that Stans had lied to the grand jury investigating his case and that he kept virtually no records of millions of dollars he collected for the campaign. *(Details, p. 323)*

Sidona Offer. In a development related to the Mitchell-Stans trial and the Watergate case, Stans testified at his criminal trial that Michele Sidona, an Italian financier, offered a secret $1-million contribution to the Nixon re-election campaign. Stans said he rejected the contribution, offered shortly before the 1972 election, because Sidona "wanted the assurance that he would have anonymity, that there would be no publicity about his contribution."

APRIL 19

Mitchell-Stans Trial. The defense for Mitchell and Stans rested, with Stans conceding there were discrepancies between his grand jury and trial testimony but denying they were lies.

Information Order. U.S. District Judge Gerhard A. Gesell ordered Special Prosecutor Jaworski to give him and the defendants in the Ellsberg break-in case any evidence Jaworski might have about Nixon's possible personal involvement. The judge ordered Jaworski to respond by April 20 to the question of whether Nixon might have authorized or known in advance of the burglary attempt.

Steinbrenner Plea. George M. Steinbrenner III, chief executive of the American Ship Building Company, pleaded not guilty to charges of contributing illegally to 1972 election campaigns. *(Securities and Exchange Commission action, p. 321)*

Rodino Warning. Chairman Rodino of the House Judiciary Committee warned Nixon that the committee's impeachment inquiry probably would require even more tapes and documents than those already subpoenaed. Rodino told the White House in a letter that there probably would be further requests beyond those covered by the subpoena April 11. *(Committee subpoena, p. 311)*

Milk Money. Jake Jacobsen, a former lawyer for the Associated Milk Producers Inc., sent word to the Watergate special prosecutor that he was prepared to testify that former Treasury Secretary John B. Connally took $10,000 for helping the giant dairy cooperative, according to an informed source quoted by the Associated Press. Sources reported that Jacobsen was prepared to testify against his former close associate if the government would reduce charges against him. *(Milk money, p. 294)*

APRIL 20

Connally Denial. Former Treasury Secretary Connally denied he pocketed a $10,000 payoff by the dairy industry for his efforts to increase the federal subsidy on milk.

IRS Obstruction Charge. Investigators for the Senate Watergate committee accused the Internal Revenue Service (IRS) of obstructing the committee's inquiry into a $100,000 Nixon campaign donation from billionaire Howard Hughes, *The New York Times* reported. In a nine-page report sent to committee members April 15, Terry F. Lenzner, the committee's assistant chief counsel, charged that the IRS had, in effect, defied a Senate resolution by refusing to provide tax returns and other data to the committee.

APRIL 22

More Tapes Sought. The House Judiciary Committee reportedly asked President Nixon for additional tape recordings and documents dealing with Watergate and alleged political influence in government anti-trust and milk price support decisions. The new information requested involved the 1971 settlement of the government's anti-trust suit against the International Telephone and Telegraph Corporation and the White House decision in 1971 to raise the level of federal milk price supports. *(Earlier subpoena, p. 311)*

White House-IRS Link. Investigators for the Senate Watergate committee were reported by *The New York Times* to believe that the White House played a major role in coordinating the IRS investigation of Howard Hughes' $100,000 campaign contribution.

Strauss Warning. Robert S. Strauss, chairman of the Democratic National Committee, urged Democratic governors meeting in Chicago to stop calling for Nixon's resignation. "I ask you what horrors await this nation if he (Nixon) is able to portray himself as a resigned martyr," Strauss said.

Mitchell-Stans Trial. The prosecution called nine rebuttal witnesses, including former White House counsel John W. Dean III and *Washington Post* reporter Sally Quinn, in the last day of testimony in the trial of Mitchell and Stans. Dean contradicted Stans' testimony about two conversations they had in November 1972.

Hunt Finances. Watergate conspirator E. Howard Hunt Jr. purchased more than $100,000 worth of stock in 1973 at the same time he was allegedly demanding $120,000 in hush money from the White House, *The Los Angeles Times* reported. The stock was probably bought with part of the $260,000 Hunt collected in flight insurance after his wife died in a plane crash Dec. 8, 1972, according to his brokerage records, the Times report stated.

APRIL 23

Mitchell-Stans Trial. Walter J. Bonner, lawyer for Maurice H. Stans, spent five hours presenting his summary statement. Bonner depicted Stans as a man of integrity, honor and character who could not be bought off with a $200,000 contribution.

Deadline Eased. The White House asked the Judiciary Committee for another five days to respond to the committee's subpoena for tape recordings of more than 40 Watergate-related conversations. Chairman Rodino said he expected the committee to approve the request at its April 25 meeting. *(Subpoena issued, p. 311)*

Nixon, Rebozo Data. In an abrupt reversal, the IRS agreed to provide the Senate Watergate committee with politically sensitive tax returns and other materials from its files on F. Donald Nixon and Charles G. Rebozo, according to sources quoted by *The New York Times.*

Rodino Statement. Rodino issued a statement confirming that the Judiciary Committee had asked the White House April 22 for additional tape recordings and documents covering three areas of the impeachment inquiry—the alleged Watergate coverup, contributions by the dairy industry to Nixon's re-election campaign, and the ITT case.

APRIL 24

Mitchell-Stans Trial. John N. Mitchell's lawyer summed up his client's case, accusing the government of abusing its power by prosecuting the former attorney general with insufficient evidence. The government began its summation.

Jaworski Investigation. The Watergate special prosecutor's investigation into illegal campaign donations broadened into an investigation of federal officials who might have done favors for the big donors, according to sources close to the inquiry who were quoted by *The New York Times.*

Spater Reprimand. American Airline's former chairman, George Spater, was reprimanded by a New York City Bar Association committee for arranging an illegal $55,000 corporate gift to Nixon's re-election campaign. But the committee decided against disbarment of Spater. *(Spater fine, p. 61)* √

TRANSCRIPTS: A DRAMATIC PUBLIC DISCLOSURE BY NIXON

Breaking his own rule that private presidential conversations were protected by the doctrine of executive privilege, President Nixon April 30 turned over to the House Judiciary Committee heavily edited transcripts of 46 tapes of discussions between Nixon and his advisers concerning Watergate. The White House the same day also released to the public a 1,308-page volume containing the transcripts.

"I realize these transcripts will provide grist for many sensational stories in the press," Nixon said in announcing his decision during a nationwide television address April 29. "Parts will seem to be contradictory with one another, and parts will be in conflict with some of the testimony given in the Senate Watergate committee hearings."

The President said he had been reluctant to release the tapes, "not just because they will embarrass me and those with whom I have talked, which they will—not just because they will become the subject of speculation and even ridicule—which they will—and not just because certain parts of them will be seized upon by political and journalistic opponents—which they will."

Nixon said he also was concerned with violating the confidentiality of presidential conversations and with "the human impact" that disclosure would have on those involved. However, he added, "the basic question at issue today is whether the President personally acted improperly in the Watergate matter," as charged by former White House counsel John W. Dean III during the 1973 Senate Watergate committee hearings. "Month after month of rumor, insinuation and charges by just one Watergate witness—John Dean—suggested that the President did act improperly," said Nixon.

"From the beginning," he declared, "I have said that in many places on the tapes there were ambiguities—statements and comments that different people with different perspectives might interpret in drastically different ways. But although the words may be ambiguous—though the discussions may have explored many alternatives—the record of my actions is totally clear now, and I still believe it was totally correct then."

Judiciary Committee Role. The turnover of the transcripts was a response to an April 11 House Judiciary Committee subpoena for 42 tapes of conversations. The committee originally had requested the tapes on Feb. 25.

Although refusing to turn over the tapes themselves, Nixon offered to allow Committee Chairman Peter W. Rodino (D N.J.) and ranking Republican member Edward Hutchinson (R Mich.) to listen to the tapes and verify the accuracy of the transcripts.

The committee voted May 1, 20-18, to inform Nixon that he had not complied with the committee's subpoena. The vote split generally along party lines.

"The procedure suggested by the President for Mr. Hutchinson and me to come to the White House to review the subpoenaed tape recordings to determine the rele-

Advance Tip-off on Transcripts

On April 26, three days before President Nixon's televised announcement that he would release voluminous transcripts of his taped conversations, White House counselor Dean Burch told the Republican National Committee in a Washington, D.C., speech:

"Early next week, when the President responds to the committee subpoena, a massive body of evidence will supplant charges and allegations and innuendo, and out of this factual record the whole story will emerge and the whole truth become known. The body of evidence will be substantial. It will be relevant. It will be compelling and persuasive. I genuinely believe, beginning early next week, that the end of Watergate will be in sight."

Burch pleaded for loyalty to the President in the same speech. He called Nixon's functions as President and Republican leader "indistinguishable" and said, "Our hopes and our goals and our fortunes are as one." No one applauded.

Ford Speech. In a speech prepared for delivery April 27 in Tulsa, Okla., Vice President Ford made a similar appeal for Republican unity. "Let us return to the ABCs of politics and reject the endless exploitation of the controversy that has been generated about our President," he said.

vance and accuracy of the partial transcripts is not compliance with our subpoena," Rodino said May 1.

Republican Support. The President found some outspoken support for his position among Republicans. "I have no patience with people who whine and say, 'But the President didn't do it the way we wanted,' " said Sen. Barry Goldwater (R Ariz.). "...I believe the President has gone as far as he possibly could on the question of materials sought by the House Judiciary Committee."

Rep. Charles Wiggins (R Calif.), an influential member of the Judiciary committee, declared April 30, "I view the submission of the President to be a good-faith effort on his part to comply with the legitimate demands of our committee for evidence."

Numerous Deletions. The transcripts were laced with parenthetical notes such as "materials unrelated to presidential actions deleted," "unintelligible," "inaudible" and "expletive omitted." Many of these deletions interrupted sections of the transcript so as to obscure meanings. In an interview with CBS news announcer Walter Cronkite, White House lawyer James D. St. Clair acknowledged that no attempts had been made to improve the quality of the tapes by electronic means.

Critics pointed out that without possession of the tapes themselves, the committee had no way of determining whether the tapes had been tampered with before the transcripts were made. This possibility was raised when CBS reported May 2 that friends of Dean quoted him as saying the transcripts did not contain a lengthy discussion on Sept. 15, 1972, between Dean and Nixon about using the Internal Revenue Service (IRS) to harass enemies of the administration and a report on an IRS investigation of Lawrence F. O'Brien, then chairman of the Democratic National Committee.

Other Actions. In other developments during the week ending May 4:

• White House lawyers May 1 moved to quash a special Watergate prosecution subpoena for tapes and records of 64 White House conversations relating to the coverup.

• White House chief of staff Alexander M. Haig Jr., appearing under subpoena at a May 2 closed meeting of the Senate Watergate committee, presented a letter from Nixon instructing him not to answer any questions. Nixon had promised on May 22, 1973, that "executive privilege will not be invoked as to any testimony concerning possible criminal conduct or discussions of possible criminal conduct, in matters presently under investigation, including the Watergate affair and the alleged coverup."

Contents of Summary, Transcripts

To ensure that Nixon at least had a good first hearing in the press, the White House handed out a 50-page summary of the transcripts, giving the tapes an interpretation favorable to the President, shortly after the complete transcripts had gone to the House Judiciary Committee by station wagon at 10:30 a.m. April 30. Blue paperback copies of the transcripts, as thick as the Manhattan telephone directory, were not released at the White House press room until shortly after 3 p.m., less than two hours before deadlines for evening television newscasts.

Thus the nation's afternoon newspapers had only the interpretive summary, written in the style of a legal brief, to write about. And because of the volume of the complete transcripts and the timing of their release, the evening news programs and the next day's morning papers had time to prepare only cursory stories.

Nixon on Watergate

In the year after President Nixon first went on live television and radio to address the nation about Watergate, he made three prepared speeches and issued six white papers dealing with Watergate-related matters.

On April 30, 1973, Nixon appeared on television to announce the resignation of presidential aides H. R. Haldeman and John D. Ehrlichman. In a prepared statement Aug. 15, 1973, Nixon made references to the Senate Watergate hearings. On April 29, 1974, he announced that he would release edited transcripts of tapes subpoenaed by the House Judiciary Committee.

Nixon's white papers commenting on events connected with Watergate were issued April 30, 1973; May 22, 1973; Aug. 15, 1973; Nov. 12, 1973; Jan. 8 and April 29, 1974.

"Frankly, the President wanted to get his case out to the American people before the critics started in on the President," a White House official acknowledged to a *Washington Post* reporter. "We thought this was the best way to do it."

Claims of Innocence. The thrust of the summary was to substantiate Nixon's claims that he was innocent of criminal behavior and to discredit his former counsel, Dean.

"Throughout the period of the Watergate affair the raw material of these recorded confidential conversations establishes that the President had no prior knowledge of the break-in and that he had no knowledge of any coverup prior to March 21, 1973," according to the summary. "In all of the thousands of words spoken, even though they often are unclear and ambiguous, not once does it appear that the President of the United States was engaged in a criminal plot to obstruct justice."

One of the ambiguities the summary sought to resolve in Nixon's favor was part of a Sept. 15, 1972, conversation in which Nixon congratulated Dean for doing a good job. The transcript quoted Nixon as telling Dean, "Oh, well, this is a can of worms as you know a lot of this stuff that went on. And the people who worked this way are awfully embarrassed. But the way you have handled all this seems to me has been very skillful putting your fingers in the leaks that have sprung here and sprung there."

According to the summary, "This was said in the context not of a criminal plot to obstruct justice, as Dean alleges, but rather in the context of the politics of the matter, such as civil suits, counter-suits, Democratic efforts to exploit Watergate as a political issue and the like. The reference to 'putting your finger in the leaks' was clearly related to the handling of the political and public relations aspect of the matter...."

However, critics were quick to point out that the passage could also be interpreted to show Nixon congratulating Dean on his handling of a coverup. The transcript showed that Nixon's comment was made after Dean had assured him that "Nothing is going to come crashing down to our surprise," and the summary deleted Nixon's question immediately after his remarks about "leaks": "The Grand Jury is dismissed now?"

Later in the conversation, Nixon commented, according to the transcript: "The worst may happen but it may not. So you just try to button it up as well as you can and hope for the best, and remember basically the damn business is unfortunately trying to cut our losses."

Discrediting Dean. In attempting to discredit Dean, the summary cited inconsistencies between his testimony before the Senate Watergate committee and the transcribed conversations.

In one instance, Dean had testified that he told Nixon about money demands and threats of blackmail from Watergate defendants on March 13, 1973. "He said he was 'very clear' about this date," according to the summary. "It now develops that the conversations with the President, on the date of which Dean was so clear, did not in fact take place until the morning of March 21, 1973, as the President had always contended.... This discrepancy in Dean's testimony from the tapes of these two meetings is surprising in the light of Dean's self-professed excellent memory...."

The summary claimed the transcripts disproved Dean's assertion that Nixon "never at any time" asked him during a March 22, 1973, meeting, also attended by H.R. Haldeman, to deliver to Nixon a written report on his knowledge of Watergate.

In a more veiled attack on Dean, the summary referred to the trials of former Secretary of Commerce Maurice H. Stans and former Attorney General John N. Mitchell, whose acquittals were seen as damaging Dean's credibility. Dean had been one of the prosecution's main witnesses. *(Box, p. 333)*

The acquittals "demonstrate the wisdom of the President's actions in insisting that the orderly process of the judicial system be utilized to determine the guilt or innocence of individuals charged with crime, rather than participating in trials in the public media," according to the summary.

Hush Money to Hunt. While acknowledging that many of the transcribed exchanges between Nixon and his aides were ambiguous and that "someone with a motive to discredit the President could take (them) out of context and distort to suit his own purposes," the summary argued that a complete reading of the transcripts would show Nixon's innocence. However, the full transcripts showed that Nixon at least considered the option of paying hush money to Watergate defendant E. Howard Hunt Jr.

In a critical March 21 meeting, Dean told Nixon there would be "a continual blackmail operation" by the Watergate defendants, who were threatening to make public their involvement in the break-in of Daniel Ellsberg's psychiatrist's office. The "problem" of blackmail "will not only go on now, but it will go on while these people are in prison, and it will compound the obstruction of justice situation," Dean told Nixon. This appeared in the edited transcript:

Dean: It will cost money. It is dangerous. People around here are not pros at this sort of thing. This is the sort of thing Mafia people can do: washing money, getting clean money, and things like that. We just don't know about those things, because we are not criminals and not used to dealing in that business.

Nixon: That's right.

Dean: It is a tough thing to know how to do.

Nixon: Maybe it takes a gang to do that.

Dean: That's right. There is a real problem as to whether we could even do it. Plus there is a real problem in raising some money. Mitchell has been working on raising some money. He is one of the ones with the most to lose. But there is no denying the fact that the White House, in (John D.) Ehrlichman, Haldeman and Dean are involved in some of the early money decisions.

Nixon: How much money do you need?

Dean: I would say these people are going to cost a million dollars over the next two years.

Nixon: We could get that. On the money, if you need the money you could get that. You could get a million dollars. You could get it in cash. I know where it could be gotten. It is not easy, but it could be done. But the question is who the hell would handle it? Any ideas on that?

Dean: That's right. Well, I think that is something that Mitchell ought to be charged with.

Nixon: I would think so too.

There followed a discussion of how the money might be raised and delivered. Later the conversation turned to what Dean called the likelihood that Hunt and the

Agnew's Maryland Disbarment

The Maryland Court of Appeals unanimously decided May 2 to disbar former Vice President Spiro T. Agnew, saying in its decision that Agnew was guilty of a crime "infested with fraud, deceit and dishonesty."

The court's decision, made seven months after Agnew resigned as vice president after being accused of taking kickbacks from contractors while governor of Maryland and vice president, effectively barred him from practicing law in Maryland. Its practical effect, however, was almost certain to make it impossible for him to practice law elsewhere in the country, because most states generally refuse to admit to the bar lawyers who have been disbarred in other states.

Written by Associate Judge J. Dudley Diggs, the decision was especially critical of Agnew's conduct in taking kickbacks and evading income taxes. "It is difficult to feel compassion for an attorney who is so morally obtuse that he consciously cheats for his own pecuniary gain that government he has sworn to serve, completely disregards the words of the oath he uttered when first admitted to the bar, and absolutely fails to perceive his professional duty to act honestly in all matters," the decision stated.

Joining in the 13-page decision were Chief Judge Robert C. Murphy, Associate Judges Irving A. Levine and John C. Eldridge and three Court of Special Appeals judges—Charles E. Orth Jr., James C. Morton and C. Audry Thompson.

Because of Agnew's no-contest plea in U.S. District Court in Baltimore Oct. 10, 1973, to a single charge of tax evasion, the court said that "to do otherwise than disbar" Agnew "would constitute a travesty of our responsibility."

The court said that such a crime "clearly comes within that category we have previously discussed that will result in automatic disbarment when the respondent fails to demonstrate by clear and convincing evidence a compelling reason to the contrary. "On the record before us, we perceive no mitigating circumstances—in fact, all that appears tends to aggravate the gravity of the offense."

Agnew and his lawyers had tried to head off his disbarment since his first appearance Dec. 18, 1973, before a special three-judge panel in Annapolis. He pleaded then with the court "not to strip me of my means of livelihood."

On Jan. 14, the panel unanimously recommended to the Court of Appeals that Agnew be disbarred, because the former vice president's "deceitful and dishonest" conduct made him "unfit to continue as a member of the bar."

Agnew and his lawyers had argued that the no-contest plea to evading nearly $30,000 in federal income taxes while governor of Maryland in 1967 was a private matter and that his former public positions should not be considered by the court. They also contended that the court should accept as a mitigating factor the fact that Agnew was not convicted of cheating a client.

other defendants would demand clemency, which Nixon seemed to rule out for political reasons.

Dean: They all are going to expect to be out and that may put you in a position that is just untenable at some point. You know, the Watergate hearings just over, Hunt now demanding clemency or he is going to blow. And politically, it's impossible for you to do it. You know, after everybody—

Nixon: That's right!

Dean: I am not sure that you will ever be able to deliver on the clemency. It may be just too hot.

Nixon: You can't do it politically until after the '74 elections, that's for sure. Your point is that even then you couldn't do it.

Dean: That's right. It may further involve you in a way you should not be involved in this.

Nixon: No—it is wrong that's for sure.

Later in the same meeting Nixon seemed to rule out the payment of hush money as well.

Nixon: If, for example, you say look we are not going to continue to—let's say, frankly, on the assumption that if we continue to cut our losses, we are not going to win. But in the end, we are going to be bled to death. And in the end, it is all going to come out anyway. Then you get the worst of both worlds. We are going to lose, and people are going to—

Haldeman: And look like dopes!

Nixon: And in effect, look like a cover-up. So that we can't do.

A few moments later Nixon added, "First it is going to require approximately a million dollars to take care of the jackasses who are in jail. That can be arranged. That could be arranged. But you realize that after we are gone, and assuming we can expend this money, then they are going to crack and it would be an unseemly story...."

Battle with Democrats. The transcripts shed light on Nixon's view of his Watergate troubles as a political vendetta on the part of the Democrats. In a Feb. 28, 1973, discussion with Dean on how to prepare for upcoming congressional hearings on Watergate, Nixon remarked, "It seems like a terrible waste of your time. But it is important in the sense that all this business is a battle and they are going to wage the battle. A lot of them have enormous frustrations about those elections, state of their party, etc. And their party has its problems...."

In the same discussion, Nixon acknowledged the importance of the affair but seemed to indicate belief that his lack of involvement in the actual break-in would keep him from harm.

Dean: We have come a long road on this thing now. I had thought it was an impossible task to hold together until after the election until things started falling out, but we have made it this far and I am convinced we are going to make it the whole road and put this thing in the funny pages of the history books rather than anything serious because actually—

Nixon: It will be somewhat serious but the main thing, of course, is also the isolation of the President.

Dean: Absolutely! Totally true!

Nixon: Because that, fortunately, is totally true.

Dean: I know that sir!

The Private Man. Besides illuminating matters of substance involving Watergate, the transcripts showed a picture of Nixon, the private man, in confidential discussions with aides, that differed dramatically from the decorous public image he had sought to project. In private, Nixon's language was often coarse and blunt, particularly in his characterizations of other public figures.

"I tried to get it through his thick skull," Nixon said of Sen. Howard Baker (R Tenn.) during a Feb. 28, 1973, discussion of Nixon's belief that hearsay evidence should not be permitted in the Senate Watergate committee hearings. Baker was vice chairman of the committee.

During the Sept. 15, 1973, meeting with Haldeman and Dean, Nixon ordered that "the most comprehensive notes" be kept on "all those who tried to do us in," evidently referring to Democrats who were pressing the Watergate investigation.

"They didn't have to do it," Nixon said. "If we had had a very close election and they were playing the other side I would understand this. No—they were doing this quite deliberately and they are asking for it and now they are going to get it. We have not used the power in this first four years as you know, We have never used it. We have not used the Bureau (FBI) and we have not used the Justice Department but things are going to change now. And they are either going to do it right or go."

Dean asserted that the Nixon campaign team was then being audited by the General Accounting Office at the request of House Speaker Carl Albert (D Okla.)—the third man in line for the presidency.

"That surprises me," said Nixon.

"Well, (expletive deleted) the Speaker of the House," said Haldeman. "Maybe we better put a little heat on him."

"I think so too," said Nixon.

As embarrassing as some of these disclosures were, Nixon evidently was staking his presidency on the hope that the House of Representatives would not find impeachable offenses in any of them, or if they did, that the Senate would not find in them grounds for conviction.

A Finding of Non-Compliance

"There is no question that, whatever else the President may have done or been thought to have done on Monday evening, and whatever individual members of this committee may think of the merits of that action, the President has not complied with our subpoena," Judiciary Committee Chairman Rodino said May 1.

But there was a question within the Judiciary Committee as to the proper response from the committee to the President's move. At an unusual evening meeting May 1, which adjourned near midnight, this question was discussed at length.

Some Republicans felt that confrontation with the White House should be avoided at all costs. Ranking Republican Edward Hutchinson (R Mich.) warned that the men who constructed a government of separated powers never contemplated a confrontation between the branches of the government. "Confrontation never works," he said; "it produces only stalemates."

But there was a conflicting view, propounded by Jerome R. Waldie (D Calif.), that impeachment itself was the "ultimate confrontation of the legislative branch with the executive branch."

Middle Road. Following a middle road, the committee rejected a motion recommending that the President be found in contempt of Congress. Instead, it authorized a terse letter to Nixon informing him that the committee found that he had not complied with its subpoena. The letter, from Rodino to Nixon, simply advised the President that the committee "finds that as of 10:00 a.m. April 30, you have failed to comply with the committee's subpoena of April 11, 1974."

Basic to the committee's decision was the members' feeling that they should have the best evidence possible on which to make a judgment on the charges against the President—and that the White House transcripts were not that best evidence. As James R. Mann (D S.C.), one of the more conservative Democratic members of the committee, explained it: "The tapes which were subpoenaed and an expert analysis of the tapes are essential to obtain the whole truth.... How can anyone object to the whole truth? ...Unless I get it I am handicapped in my service to the American people in determining this issue."

The committee's position was further outlined by Rodino: "We did not subpoena an edited White House version of partial transcripts of portions of presidential conversations. We did not subpoena a presidential interpretation of what is necessary or relevant for our inquiry. And we did not subpoena a lawyer's argument presented before we have heard any of the evidence.

"Under the Constitution," Rodino reminded the committee, "it is not within the power of the President to conduct an inquiry into his own impeachment, to determine which evidence, and what version or portion of that evidence, is relevant and necessary to such an inquiry. These are matters which, under the Constitution, only the House has the sole power to determine. The President's suggestion that the committee have only the transcripts is not something that I or any member of the committee can explain to the American people. It would only raise questions about the committee's inquiry. The committee must follow the appropriate, the proper, the lawful way as it moves ahead."

Debate Over Letters. The letter to the President—authorized by a motion proposed by Harold D. Donohue (D Mass.) as amended to include a text of the letter by Jack Brooks (D Texas)—was approved by the committee by a narrow margin, divided along party lines, 20-18. John Conyers Jr. (D Mich.) and Waldie, both in favor of citing the President for contempt, voted against the motion. Had they been joined by every Republican member, the motion would have failed on a tie vote, 19-19. But William S. Cohen (R Maine) crossed party lines to vote in favor of the Brooks-Donohue motion, providing the margin of approval.

Earlier, the committee had rejected, 11-27, a compromise letter proposed by Cohen which would have advised Nixon that the transcripts were not "full compliance" and that the committee should have the option of reviewing the original tapes, with the assistance of counsel and technical experts. But this proposal was objected to by members on both sides. Most Democrats found it too soft, while some Republicans opposed any such letter.

Voting with Cohen for his proposal were Walter Flowers (D Ala.), Mann, Wayne Owens (D Utah), Del-

---

Spoken vs. Written Words

Critics of President Nixon's April 29 announcement that he would release transcripts of taped conversations, instead of the tapes themselves, complained that transcripts alone would be inadequate. Missing, they said, would be the intonations, inflections and pauses that often reveal the true meaning of the spoken word.

At a news conference Sept. 5, 1973, Nixon had some bitter observations about the delivery of television commentators. It was difficult, he said, "for four months to have the President of the United States by innuendo, by leak, by, frankly, leers and sneers of commentators, which is their perfect right, attacked in every way without having some of that confidence being worn away." *(News conference text, p. 22)*

---

bert L. Latta (R Ohio), Tom Railsback (R Ill.), Charles E. Wiggins (R Calif.), David W. Dennis (R Ind.), Hamilton Fish Jr. (R N.Y.), Wiley Mayne (R Iowa) and M. Caldwell Butler (R Va.). The committee then rejected, 18-20, a motion by Latta to table the Brooks-Donohue motion; Conyers joined the Republicans in voting to table it.

Pointing out that May 1 was "Law Day," Conyers then moved that the committee recommend to the House that Nixon be cited for contempt of Congress for failing to comply with the committee's lawful subpoena. "Law Day," suggested Conyers, was an appropriate occasion for the committee "to enforce the law on the President of the United States."

The committee rejected the motion, with only five members supporting it: Conyers, Waldie, Robert W. Kastenmeier (D Wis.), Charles B. Rangel (D N.Y.) and Elizabeth Holtzman (D N.Y.). Robert F. Drinan (D Mass.) abstained on the vote; the other 32 members opposed it. The committee then adjourned; it was almost midnight.

What Degree of Compliance? During hours of discussion on the evening of May 1 concerning the degree of compliance which the massive White House transcripts represented, no member of the committee suggested that they fully complied with the committee subpoena seeking tapes, dictabelts, notes, memoranda or other records of 42 presidential conversations. But there was a diversity of views on the degree of compliance.

No tapes of any of the conversations had been provided. The transcripts of most of the requested conversations had been provided, however, said special committee counsel John M. Doar. The sought-after conversations for which transcripts were not produced included a Feb. 20, 1973, conversation between the President and H. R. Haldeman, a Feb. 27, 1973, conversation between Nixon and John D. Ehrlichman and several of the conversations with Haldeman, Ehrlichman and other aides or officials during the period from April 15-18, 1973.

Furthermore, reported Doar, no notes, memoranda, dictabelts or other records of any of the conversations had been provided to the committee, and no explanation for the lack of these records had been given. Under questioning from several Republican members, Doar admitted that he had no personal knowledge of the existence of notes or dictabelts related to the specific conversations requested. He cited presidential statements and the testimony of various presidential aides concerning the existence of their notes, presidential notes and dictabelts produced by Nixon as part of his personal diary—in general, but not specifically related to the conversations sought.

If these records did not exist, Doar said, the President could have said so in his response to the subpoena. He did not.

Monitoring the Tapes. Referring to the President's suggestion that Rodino and Hutchinson listen to the tapes to verify the authenticity of the transcripts, Rodino asked Doar: "In your professional opinion, is it prudent for me and Mr. Hutchinson to make a judgment on the relevance of tapes not transcribed?"

"No," responded Doar, pointing to the need for those who listen to the tapes for that purpose to be thoroughly grounded in all the facts involved in the charges. Rodino agreed, calling it "absolutely impossible" for him to discharge adequately such a responsibility to the committee, to authenticate the tapes without the assistance of counsel and technical experts.

"These transcripts are not accurate," said Doar, referring to those provided by the White House. "I'm not suggesting intentional distortion," he said, "but with time, patience, energy and good equipment, they can be improved." With better equipment than the White House had, he said—and "superior diligence"—the impeachment inquiry staff had produced a better and more complete transcript of at least one tape already in the staff's possession, that of the March 21, 1973, meeting between Dean and Nixon.

"Do you mean that some of the 'deletions' and 'inaudibles' on the March 21 transcript have been deciphered with our equipment?" asked Waldie. "Yes," responded Doar, who emphasized to the committee that he felt there was "a very significant difference" between reading a transcript and listening to a tape.

Referring to the contents of the transcripts, Lawrence J. Hogan (R Md.) said that he had "come to the inescapable conclusion that he (Nixon) must have forgotten that the tapes were being made." Later he added that he felt that in many places the expletives deleted "seem to be essential to the meaning of the statement" from which they were removed.

Prevalent Dissatisfaction. Some dissatisfaction with the President's response was expressed by almost every committee member. But Wiggins urged that, although the form of the response was insufficient, the committee defer action on any response until its members had the opportunity to consider the substance of the transcripts. Since receiving the 1,300-page transcripts, he said, he had "diligently pursued the information" they contained, but was only through 200 pages. "We should not pursue the form (the tapes)," he said, "if the substance meets our needs."

Members of the committee were also disturbed by the medium that Nixon had chosen for his response. Mann chided Nixon for "mounting his electronic throne" instead of simply informing the committee of which materials it sought did or did not exist.

Flowers expressed similar concern about the forum chosen by the President to respond. He pointed out that the contents of the tapes still would be confidential if Nixon had just turned them over to the committee, instead of going public.

Procedural Plans. "We are going to go ahead," Rodino affirmed on the evening of May 1, informing committee members that the initial presentation of evidence would begin the next week, probably in closed session. Later he said that the committee members should expect to work mornings and afternoons, three days a week, hearing the evidence. Estimates of the time needed for this presentation ranged from five days to six weeks.

In preparation for receiving the evidence, the committee turned its attention to the rules of procedure that would guide the presentation. On May 1, the Judiciary Subcommittee on Courts, Civil Liberties and the Administration of Justice met to consider the rules drafted by the impeachment inquiry staff—and unanimously reported them to the full committee with several amendments.

The next day the full committee considered the rules and amendments at morning and afternoon sessions. The version adopted late on the afternoon of May 2 included several key points:

• The sessions at which the committee would receive from the staff a presentation of pertinent information would be hearings, open to the public unless closed by committee vote.

• Nixon as well as St. Clair would be invited to attend the presentation, and all hearings at which witnesses were heard by the committee, including any such hearings held in executive session.

• St. Clair could be invited to submit requests that the committee hear additional witnesses or receive additional evidence.

• St. Clair could raise objections relating to the examination of witnesses or the admissibility of evidence; such objections would be ruled on by the chairman, and his rulings would be final unless overruled by a majority of the committee members present.

• St. Clair could question any witness, subject to instructions from the chairman.

"The members...have leaned over backward to ensure fairness to St. Clair," said Rodino, noting the privileges the President's counsel could be granted under the rules. All attempts to expand or limit those privileges—through amendments suggested by committee members—were rejected.

By voice vote, the committee rejected an amendment proposed by George E. Danielson (D Calif.) removing from the rules the presidential counsel's right to object to the examination of a witness or the admissibility of evidence. Danielson proposed the amendment, he said, because of concern that giving St. Clair this right would allow him to obstruct the proceedings. Rodino made clear that he would not tolerate any such obstruction.

On the other hand, the committee also rejected, by a vote of 15-23, an amendment proposed by Dennis that would have given St. Clair the right to examine and cross-examine, not just question, any witness.

The committee by voice vote adopted an amendment allowing radio and television coverage of any open hearings, a proposal made by Robert McClory (R Ill.). By a vote of 19-17, an amendment was adopted setting 10 rather than 20 members as the number that would constitute a quorum for the hearings.

Mitchell-Stans Trial: Acquittal on All 15 Counts

After deliberating four days, a U.S. District Court jury in New York City April 28 acquitted John N. Mitchell and Maurice H. Stans of all charges in their criminal conspiracy case. The verdict came on the 48th day of the trial of the two former Nixon cabinet officers and was reached after the nine men and three women deliberated for 26 hours. *(Earlier story, p. 323)*

Mitchell and Stans, former key figures in President Nixon's 1972 re-election campaign, had been charged with 15 counts of conspiracy, perjury and obstruction of justice.

Their trial, which began Feb. 21, marked the first time in the nation's history that two former cabinet officers had been tried together and the first trial of former cabinet officers since the Teapot Dome scandal of the 1920s.

The government had alleged that the two former Nixon aides attempted to impede a Securities and Exchange Commission (SEC) investigation of Robert L. Vesco, the fugitive financier, in return for a secret $200,000 cash contribution from Vesco to Nixon's 1972 re-election drive. The defense lawyers claimed that Mitchell and Stans never had attempted to "fix" the SEC investigation into Vesco's tangled financial dealings and that the prosecution's chief witnesses were not telling the truth.

John N. Mitchell

In interviews after the verdicts were announced, the jurors said that they had voted to acquit Mitchell and Stans because they could not believe the testimony of key government witnesses. They used the words "incredible" or "unbelievable" when they talked about John W. Dean III, G. Bradford Cook, William J. Casey, Harry L. Sears and Laurence Richardson Jr., major prosecution witnesses.

"I don't want to say Mr. Dean was lying, but he was often unbelievable," said Sybil Kucharski, the 21-year-old forewoman of the jury. Referring to Mitchell and Stans, she said, "We didn't feel they had any reason to lie. We didn't feel they had the need. They were credible men."

Kucharski and five other jurors said in interviews that they saw nothing improper in what the two former administration officials had done for Vesco. "We didn't put them above the law," she said. "But we felt they were doing things in the course of the normal working day. They weren't sneaking around or anything."

Maurice H. Stans

The acquittal verdict emphasized the importance of the Watergate tape recordings in other criminal and impeachment proceedings. Dean, the former presidential counsel who was a key witness for the prosecution, was expected to be a major government witness in the forthcoming Watergate conspiracy trial of Mitchell, H.R. Haldeman, John D. Ehrlichman and four others. He also was the principal accuser of Nixon in the alleged White House effort to obstruct the Watergate investigation.

The White House said that "the President was very pleased for the two men and their families."

Vesco, too, expressed satisfaction.

District Court Action

On the second front of his battle of the tapes, Nixon sent his attorneys to court May 2 to seek the quashing of the Watergate special prosecutor's subpoena for tapes and documents relating to 64 post-Watergate conversations, most of them involving the President himself.

U.S. District Judge John J. Sirica set a hearing for May 8 on the motion to quash. He gave the special prosecutor and any of the seven defendants in the Watergate coverup case until 2 p.m. May 6 to reply to the President's motion, and the White House until May 8 to respond.

Sirica issued the subpoena April 18 at the request of Special Prosecutor Leon Jaworski. Jaworski said the information contained in the records was needed by both the government and the defendants to build their cases for the coverup trial, scheduled to begin Sept. 9. Two of the defendants, Charles W. Colson and Robert C. Mardian, joined in Jaworski's request for the subpoena. *(p. 317)*

Executive Privilege Question. The subpoenaed tapes and documents related to conversations between June 1972—the month of the Watergate break-in—and June 1973. In arguments before Sirica May 2, Philip A. Lacovara, counsel to the special prosecutor, pointed out that 20 of the tapes called for were among those for which the President released transcripts April 30. Therefore, Lacovara suggested, executive privilege had been waived regarding those conversations, and Sirica could rule immediately that those tapes should be turned over.

White House attorney John A. McCahill, however, said executive privilege had been waived only for the transcripts, not for the tapes themselves.

One possible exception was suggested in the President's motion. If any of the defendants in the coverup case could demonstrate that the presidential files contained information that would support their claims of innocence, the motion said, "the President would be willing to consider whether a defendant's need for access outweighs the public interest in maintaining confidentiality."

Impeachment Inquiry Money

A new deadline for the work of the House Judiciary Committee's impeachment inquiry staff—June 30—and an explanation of the cost of that staff's work were made public April 29 as the House approved additional funds for the work of the committee.

By voice vote, the House approved H Res 1027, which provided an additional $979,000 for the committee during the remainder of the 93rd Congress. Most of this total, $733,759, was to be used to pay the expenses of the staff investigating charges of impeachable offenses against President Nixon.

Committee Chairman Peter W. Rodino Jr. (D N.J.) said April 29 that the cost of the inquiry from November 1973 until the end of March 1974 had been $438,365. The total estimated cost for the inquiry through June 30 would be about $1.2-million, he said.

Transcripts' Impact. The presidential brief suggested that in view of the release of the 20 edited transcripts, Jaworski might want to "reassess his need" for the material. The prosecutors had argued in the past, however, that transcripts were not satisfactory as evidence as long as tapes themselves existed.

The brief also questioned whether many of the subpoenaed conversations would be admissible in a criminal trial. "For example, the recorded conversations between President Richard M. Nixon and John Dean, neither of whom are named parties in the current proceeding, can only be categorized as inadmissible hearsay," the brief stated.

The possibility that the President might appeal an unfavorable ruling on the subpoena request to the Supreme Court also was raised in the brief. He had not done so in past battles over subpoenas, always complying with them after seeking delays and compromises. He appealed to the U.S. Circuit Court of Appeals in the first subpoena case in the summer of 1973, but lost 5-2 and subsequently turned over the material.

The President's lawyers had argued that "a president is not subject to compulsory process from a court."

Nixon personally invoked executive privilege in the case of the latest subpoena. He said he had decided that disclosure of any more of his conversations "would be contrary to the public interest."

His special counsel, James D. St. Clair, said the Watergate prosecutors were plainly embarked on a "fishing expedition" and that "absolutely no attempt has been made by the special prosecutor to establish either the admissibility or relevancy of any of the requested items."

Other Motions. Among a flurry of motions filed by the seven coverup defendants May 1 in U.S. District Court in Washington, D.C., was one by H. R. Haldeman, the former White House chief of staff, asking the court to permit him to "inspect and test" the original tapes of all his conversations with President Nixon to help him prepare his defense. He also asked to be allowed to inspect the machines used to record the conversations and later to transcribe the tapes, "to determine whether (they) were operating properly."

Haldeman and the other defendants also asked that the charges against them be dismissed on grounds of extensive pretrial publicity about the case. Several defendants asked to be tried separately and to have their trials moved out of Washington.

Jaworski was given until June 5 to respond to the defense motions. Similar motions were filed by the six defendants charged with conspiracy in the break-in at the office of Daniel Ellsberg's psychiatrist. That case was scheduled for trial June 17.

Week's Watergate Chronology

Following is a day-to-day chronology of the week's events in the Watergate case:

APRIL 25

Mitchell-Stans Trial. The case against John N. Mitchell and Maurice H. Stans went to the jury after a 3½-hour instruction from Judge Lee P. Gagliardi.

Tapes Deadline. The House Judiciary Committee voted 34-4 to extend for five days Nixon's deadline to answer its subpoena for tapes. (Nixon request, p. 322)

Reduced Charges. The Judiciary Committee's impeachment staff reported that it could find no substance to 15 relatively peripheral allegations of wrongdoing against Nixon and that it was focusing its inquiry on 41 other charges. (p. 322)

Tax Probe. The question of tax fraud in Nixon's disallowed deduction for the gift of his vice presidential papers was being studied by the House Judiciary Committee impeachment staff, majority counsel John M. Doar said. (p. 322)

APRIL 26

Reinecke Trial. California Lt. Gov. Ed Reinecke's (R) lawyers withdrew their request for a hurry-up trial for perjury. U.S. District Judge Barrington D. Parker said Reinecke's lawyers had asked for a delay because "they said they think the case is of such magnitude that it requires more time to prepare for trial." (Earlier story, p. 321)

Sirica Defense. Watergate prosecutors maintained that attempts to disqualify U.S. District Judge John J. Sirica from the Watergate coverup trial were groundless and even scurrilous in some respects. (Earlier story, p. 316)

White House Warning. White House counselor Dean Burch told officials at a Republican National Committee meeting in Washington that they could not afford to desert Nixon in the wake of the Watergate-induced election losses, because "our fortunes are as one."

Watergate Report. Senate Watergate investigators concluded that excessive secrecy and concentration of power in the presidency gave rise to the Watergate scandal, and they drafted recommendations to diffuse that power drastically as a safeguard against any recurrence, according to United Press International. UPI obtained a copy of the draft report that recommended that White

(Continued on p. 336)

'Hush Money': A Continuing Problem of Interpretation

Did President Nixon approve payment of "hush money" to the original Watergate defendants? The answer to that question was crucial to proving or disproving charges that Nixon himself participated in the Watergate coverup, obstructing the investigation into the break-in at the national Democratic headquarters on June 17, 1972.

Four times in public between August 1973 and April 1974, Nixon gave his account of a March 21, 1973, conversation with John W. Dean III, then his counsel, at which the subject of "hush money" was broached. The four versions did not agree on all points, leaving some questions unanswered. The transcript of that conversation was released April 30.

Aug. 22, 1973. At a news conference in San Clemente, Calif., Nixon related his recollections of the conversation, saying that he had told Dean that to pay 'hush money' would be wrong and would not work:

"Basically, what Mr. Dean was concerned about on March 21 was not so much the raising of money for the defendants but the raising of money for the defendants for the purpose of keeping them still. In other words so-called hush money.

"The one would be legal, in other words raising the defense funds for any group, any individual, as you know is perfectly legal and is done all the time. But you raise funds for the purpose of keeping an individual from talking, that's obstruction of justice.

"Mr. Dean said also, on March 21, that there was an attempt to, as he put it, to blackmail the White House, to blackmail the White House by one of the defendants...."

"My reaction very briefly was this: I said as you look at this, I said isn't it quite obvious, first, that if it going to have any chance to succeed, that these individuals aren't going to sit there in jail for four years, they're going to have clemency. Isn't that correct?

"He said yes.

"I said we can't give clemency....

"Then I went to another point. The second point is that isn't it also quite obvious, as far as this is concerned, that while we could raise the money, and he indicated in answer to my question that it would probably take a million dollars over four years to take care of this defendant and others on this kind of basis, the problem was, how do you get the money to them. And also, how do you get around the problem of clemency because they're not going to stay in jail simply because their families are being taken care of.

"And so that was why I concluded, as Mr. Haldeman recalls, perhaps and did testify very effectively, when I said, John, it's wrong, it won't work, we can't give clemency, and we've got to get this story out.'"

March 6, 1974. Nixon was asked at a White House news conference to explain again his reaction to the report of the hush money effort, in light of the indictment of his former chief of staff, H. R. Haldeman, for perjury for telling the Senate Watergate committee that Nixon had said such payments would be wrong. Nixon reiterated his account of the March 21 meeting:

"On that occasion, Mr. Dean asked to see me, and when he came into the office, soon after his arrival he said that he wanted to tell me some things that he had not told me about the Watergate matter. And for the first time on March 21, he told me that payments had been made to defendants for the purpose of keeping them quiet, not simply for their defense.

"If it had been simply for their defense, that would have been proper, I understand. But if it was for the purpose of keeping them quiet—you describe it as hush money—that, of course, would have been an obstruction of justice.

"I examined him at great length. We examined all of the options at great length during our discussion, and we considered them on a tentative basis....

"Then we came to what I considered to be the bottom line. I pointed out that raising the money, paying the money, was something that could be done, but I pointed out that was linked to clemency, that no individuals is simply going to stay in jail because people are taking care of his family or his counsel, as the case might be, and that unless a promise of clemency was made that the objective of so-called hush money would not be achieved....

"I then said that to pay clemency was wrong. In fact, I think I quote it directly. I said, 'It...is wrong; that is for sure....' "

March 15, 1974. Nixon again related, more briefly, his recollection of the March 21, 1973, meeting in a question-and-answer session at the Executives' Club of Chicago:

"The President learned for the first time on March 21st of 1973 that a blackmail attempt was being made on the White House, not on March 13. The President learned for the first time at that time that payments had been made to the defendants, and let me point out that payments had been made—but correcting what may have been a misapprehension when I spoke to the press on March 6 in Washington—it was alleged that the payments that had been made to defendants were for the purpose of keeping them silent."

April 29, 1974. In his televised speech to the nation, Nixon again expounded his version of the conversation at that meeting, one of those for which the tape was sought by both the special prosecutor and the House Judiciary Committee. He prefaced his account with the statement that "in many places on the tapes there were ambiguities—statements and comments that different people with different perspectives might interpret in drastically different ways":

"I returned several times to the immediate problem posed by Mr. Hunt's blackmail threat, which to me was not a Watergate problem, but one which I regarded, rightly or wrongly, as a potential national security problem of very serious proportions. I considered long and hard whether it might in fact be better to let the payment go forward, at least temporarily, in the hope that this national security matter would not be exposed in the course of uncovering the Watergate cover-up.

"I believed then, and I believe today, that I had a responsibility as President to consider every option—including this one—where production of sensitive national security matters was at issue, protection of such matters. In the course of considering it and of 'just thinking out loud,' as I put it at one point, I several times suggested that meeting Hunt's demands might be necessary.

"But then I also traced through where that would lead. The money could be raised. But money demands would lead inescapably to clemency demands and clemency could not be granted. I said, and I quote directly from the tape: 'It is wrong, that's for sure.' "

House powers be diluted by giving more independence to government agencies, particularly the Justice Department, FBI, Internal Revenue Service and Central Intelligence Agency.

Funds Cache. Former presidential assistant H. R. Haldeman kept in his White House safe a private cash "gift" fund from which selected White House aides were paid $1,000 or more each in moving expenses when they joined or left the Nixon administration, according to sworn testimony by Lawrence Higby, a former aide to Haldeman. Higby testified, in a newly unsealed deposition, in a civil suit growing out of the Watergate affair.

APRIL 28

Mitchell-Stans Trial. Mitchell and Stans were acquitted of all counts of criminal conspiracy, obstruction of justice, and perjury in connection with a secret $200,000 cash contribution to Nixon's 1972 re-election campaign. *(Box, p. 333)*

Richardson on Tapes. Former Attorney General Elliot L. Richardson said that "the case is closed" on whether Nixon was guilty or innocent of criminal offenses in the Watergate scandals. The disputed Watergate tapes "could very well tip it one way or another," he said on NBC-TV's "Meet the Press."

Javits Suggestion. Sen. Jacob K. Javits (R N.Y.) said that if the House voted impeachment, Nixon should turn over his office to Vice President Ford for the duration of the trial in the Senate. Javits also said the Republican Party was "doomed to disaster" in the fall elections if it tied its fate to Nixon.

APRIL 29

Nixon Response. Nixon announced in a 35-minute speech on national television that he would turn over to the House Judiciary Committee and would make public April 30 the edited transcripts of some Watergate conversations. The speech included a sharp attack on John W. Dean III, the principal accuser of Nixon at the 1973 Senate Watergate hearings. *(Details, p. 327)*

Gurney Indictment. Sen. Edward J. Gurney (R Fla.), a member of the Senate Watergate committee, was indicted by a county grand jury in Tallahassee, Fla., on charges of violating state election laws, a Gurney aide announced in Washington. Gurney declared his innocence.

Impeachment Investigation Funds. The House voted to give the House Judiciary Committee $733,000 more for its impeachment inquiry. *(Box, p. 334)*

Dismissal Asked. California Lt. Gov. Reinecke asked the U.S. District Court in Washington to dismiss an indictment against him, saying that Watergate Special Prosecutor Jaworski had promised not to prosecute him. Reinecke said that, relying on that promise, he had cooperated with Jaworski and provided information and evidence about an alleged offer of the International Telephone and Telegraph Corporation to help finance the 1972 Republican national convention, at first scheduled for San Diego.

Order to Colson. Nixon ordered former White House aides Charles W. Colson and H. R. Haldeman to do "whatever has to be done...whatever the cost" to stop leaks of classified government information, Colson

said in a sworn affidavit filed in U.S. District Court in Washington.

APRIL 30

Nixon Transcripts. The transcripts of recordings of Nixon's Watergate conversations related to the coverup were released. *(Details, p. 333)*

Nixon's Refusal. James D. St. Clair, Nixon's Watergate lawyer, said he would move to quash the Watergate special prosecutor's subpoena calling on the President to supply by May 2 tape recordings and documents relating to 64 conversations between Nixon and four of his former aides. *(Earlier story, p. 325)*

Sirica Refusal. Judge John J. Sirica refused to disqualify himself from presiding at the Watergate coverup conspiracy trial of seven former Nixon aides.

Nixon Taxes. Nixon paid his tax deficiency of $432,000 plus interest and probably did not have to borrow money to do it, a source familiar with Nixon's financial affairs was quoted by *The Washington Post* as saying.

Ehrlichman Defense. Nixon in April 1973 specifically described the break-in at the office of Dr. Lewis Fielding, Daniel Ellsberg's psychiatrist, as "in furtherance of national security and fully justified by the circumstances," former presidential aide John D. Ehrlichman said in an affidavit filed in U.S. District Court in Washington.

Silbert Probe. Sen. Sam J. Ervin Jr. (D N.C.) asked the Senate Judiciary Committee to conduct an investigation of the Justice Department's handling of Watergate before acting on the nomination of Earl J. Silbert to become U.S. attorney for the District of Columbia.

MAY 1

Nixon Refusal. Nixon personally refused to hand over the tapes and documents subpoenaed by Special Prosecutor Jaworski for the Watergate coverup trials. Formally invoking executive privilege in a one-page statement submitted to U.S. District Judge John J. Sirica, Nixon said he had decided that disclosure of more of his conversations "would be contrary to the public interest."

Transcript Inaccuracies. John M. Doar, impeachment counsel to the House Judiciary Committee, told the committee that discrepancies were found between the transcripts of tape recordings Nixon released and transcripts of the recording made by the committee's technical staff. Doar said he was not "suggesting any intentional distortions."

No More Material. Presidential lawyer James D. St. Clair indicated that the White House would resist turning over to the House Judiciary Committee the additional material it had requested in its impeachment inquiry. *(p. 326)*

St. Clair Role. A House Judiciary subcommittee approved on a 7-0 vote rules permitting Nixon's lawyer to participate in committee consideration of the impeachment case, but under conditions preventing obstruction. *(St. Clair request, p. 316)*

Haldeman Request. Former presidential assistant H. R. Haldeman asked the U.S. District Court in Washington to permit him to "inspect and test" the original tapes of all his conversations with Nixon to help him pre-

The Tapes: A Nine-Month Battle for Disclosure

The public revelation that many presidential conversations had been tape-recorded since early 1971 was made on July 16, 1973, at hearings of the Senate Watergate investigating committee. The man who opened up the stunning new chapter in the scandal was Alexander P. Butterfield, head of the Federal Aviation Administration and a former White House aide.

Butterfield's testimony triggered a continuing struggle over disclosure of the contents of the tapes. Following is a chronology of important dates in that struggle:

July 17-23, 1973: The Senate Watergate committee and then Watergate Special Prosecutor Archibald Cox asked for certain Watergate-related tapes. After Nixon refused to release the tapes, the committee and Cox issued subpoenas demanding them.

July 26: Cox requested U.S. District Judge John J. Sirica to sign a show-cause order directing Nixon to indicate why the tapes should not be turned over by Aug. 7.

Aug. 9: The Senate committee filed suit in U.S. District Court in Washington, D.C., in an attempt to gain access to the tapes.

Aug. 22: Cox and Charles Alan Wright, then consultant to White House counsel J. Fred Buzhardt, argued their cases before Sirica.

Aug. 29: Sirica ordered Nixon to make the tapes available to him for a decision on their use by the Watergate grand jury. The President refused.

Sept. 7: Cox asked the U.S. Court of Appeals to grant the grand jury direct access to the tapes.

Sept. 11: Wright, Cox and Sirica's two attorneys argued Sirica's Aug. 29 ruling before the Court of Appeals.

Sept. 13: The seven Court of Appeals judges issued a unanimous memorandum urging Nixon and Cox to settle the tapes dispute out of court.

Oct. 12: In a 5-2 decision, the appeals court upheld Sirica.

Oct. 19: Nixon said he would not comply with the order to give Sirica the tapes but would not appeal the tapes decision to the Supreme Court.

Oct. 23: Wright reversed the previous position and announced that Nixon would turn over the tapes and other documents to the court.

Oct. 31: Buzhardt said two of the nine tapes requested never existed.

Nov. 21: White House attorneys told Sirica that an 18½-minute segment was erased from the June 20,

1972, tape of a conversation between Nixon and H. R. Haldeman, his former chief of staff.

Nov. 26: White House attorneys turned over the existing subpoenaed tapes and related materials to the court.

Dec. 3: Sirica began his private review of the subpoenaed tapes.

Dec. 19: Sirica ruled that nearly all of two subpoenaed tapes and part of a third be turned over to Leon Jaworski, Watergate special prosecutor.

Jan. 15, 1974: Technical experts reported to the court that the 18½-minute gap was the result of five separate manual erasures.

Feb. 6: The House by a 410-4 vote approved H Res 803, authorizing the House Judiciary Committee to conduct an impeachment inquiry and granting it special subpoena power during the inquiry.

Feb. 25: The House Judiciary Committee sent James D. St. Clair, special White House counsel, a letter requesting tapes and documents related to presidential conversations, including some of those already provided to the special prosecutor.

March 6: St. Clair told Sirica that Nixon had decided to give the House committee all the tapes and documents submitted to the Watergate grand jury.

March 11: The White House leaked the committee's Feb. 25 letter, disclosing its request for 42 additional tapes.

March 12: Ronald L. Ziegler, Nixon's press secretary, said that the President would be unwilling to supply additional tapes until the House Judiciary Committee defined impeachable offenses.

March 25: The Watergate grand jury's report on Nixon was turned over to the House committee.

April 4: The House Judiciary Committee gave Nixon until April 9 to decide whether to turn over the 42 presidential tape recordings.

April 9: White House attorneys told the committee that they needed more time to decide how to respond.

April 11: The House Judiciary Committee voted 33-3 to subpoena the tapes requested March 11.

April 18: Jaworski issued another subpoena for tapes, memos and other materials relating to 64 conversations of Nixon.

April 29: Nixon announced on national television that he would release the next day edited transcripts of certain tapes in response to the April 11 committee subpoena.

pare a defense in the Watergate coverup case. Haldeman also asked the court to allow him to inspect the machines used to record the conversations and later to transcribe Nixon's secret tapes "to determine whether those machines were operating properly." *(Haldeman indictment, p. 256)*

Northrop Fine. The Northrop Corporation and its chairman, Thomas V. Jones, were each fined $5,000 by U.S. District Judge George L. Hart in Washington

after pleading guilty to charges of illegally contributing $150,000 in company funds to Nixon's 1972 re-election campaign. *(Northrop contribution, p. 287)*

Colson Refusal. Charles W. Colson, a former Nixon aide, refused an offer from Watergate Special Prosecutor Jaworski to plead guilty to a misdemeanor, according to United Press International. *(Colson indictments, p. 251, 271)*

Appendix

THE TRANSCRIPTS: EXTRAORDINARY WHITE HOUSE DOCUMENT

It was, beyond question, one of the most remarkable documents ever to come out of the White House.

The volume of Watergate-related tape transcripts made public by President Nixon April 30 contained the "brutal candor" that he had promised, even though the White House had excised the coarsest language and the rawest characterizations of persons.

But the 1,308-page book did little to resolve the major question remaining from the inquiries into the June 17, 1972, break-in at the Democratic National Committee offices and the subsequent coverup: What did the President know and when did he learn it?

If anything, Nixon's disclosure of the transcripts increased pressure on him to resign or be impeached. Reading the transcripts was like peering into the soul of the Nixon presidency, and many of those who took the trouble —including some Nixon supporters—did not like what they saw.

One who peered in, Senate Minority Leader Hugh Scott (R Pa.), said after reading 800 pages that the transcripts revealed "a shabby, disgusting, immoral performance" by all of those involved in the recorded conversations. "I am enormously disturbed that there was not enough showing of moral indignation," Scott said.

Scott had said in January that the White House had shown him transcripts proving John W. Dean III, Nixon's former counsel, had lied in accusing the President of complicity in the coverup.

The transcripts cost Nixon the support of *The Chicago Tribune*, conservative voice of the American heartland where Nixon counted much of his constituency. No one reading the transcripts, the Tribune wrote in a May 9 editorial, could "continue to think Mr. Nixon has upheld the standards and high dignity of the presidency.

"He is humorless to the point of being inhumane," the editorial said. "He is devious. He is vacillating. He is profane. He is willing to be led. He displays dismaying gaps in his knowledge...his loyalty is minimal."

As the House Judiciary Committee began hearings May 9 on whether or not Nixon should be impeached, Rep. John B. Anderson of Illinois, chairman of the House Republican Conference, said that the President should resign. Another Republican official, House Minority Leader John J. Rhodes of Arizona, said that Nixon should consider stepping down.

To counter Scott and others who found in the transcripts indications that the Nixon presidency was amoral or immoral, the Rev. John McLaughlin, a Jesuit priest and deputy assistant to the President, said that such a suggestion was "erroneous, unjust and contains an element of hypocrisy."

Contents. It was in response to the House Judiciary Committee's subpoena of the tapes of 42 recorded conversations that the President submitted the transcripts and made them public at the same time. The committee May 1 voted to send Nixon a letter saying that the transcripts "failed to comply with the committee's subpoena of April 11, 1974." *(p. 331)*

The transcripts actually covered 46 conversations, four more than the committee subpoenaed. The White House presumably offered the four extra transcripts so that excerpts from them could be used in a 50-page White House summary that prefaced the transcript volume.

All four extra transcripts were mentioned in the summary, which argues that the tapes, taken in their entirety, prove Nixon's innocence in the coverup. "In all of the thousands of words spoken, even though they often are unclear and ambiguous, not once does it appear that the President of the United States was engaged in a criminal plot to obstruct justice," the brief states. *(Text, p. 412)*

The transcripts covered only a portion of the tapes sought by the Senate Watergate committee and the special prosecutor, Leon Jaworski, who also was seeking White House tapes of recorded conversations dealing with dairy industry campaign contributions, settlement of antitrust charges against International Telephone and Telegraph Corporation, and other matters. *(Boxes on tapes and subpoenas, p. 343, 344)*

But Nixon made it clear that no further tapes or other materials related to Watergate would be released. His lawyer, James D. St. Clair, said May 7 that the President believed that all relevant material on Watergate had been turned over to the authorities and that "the full story is out."

In all, the transcripts covered 1,254 pages, not counting the summary or contents pages.

Highlights. "I realize that these transcripts will provide grist for many sensational stories in the press," the President said in an April 29 televised speech announcing his decision to release the transcripts. *(Text, p. 408)*

The prediction was accurate. For all the deletions of profanity, "inaudible" or "unintelligible" comments and irrelevancies, the transcripts provided material for countless stories. Among them:

• The transcripts show Nixon as being motivated throughout the covered period (Sept. 15, 1972, to April 30, 1973) by a strong desire to protect his former two closest aides, H. R. Haldeman and John D. Ehrlichman. The pages are studded with emotional Nixon references to them. The book ends with the April 30, 1973, speech in which Nixon announced the resignations of Dean, Haldeman and Ehrlichman. In it, he praised Haldeman and Ehrlichman as "two of the finest public servants it has been my privilege to know." But he had no such words for Dean.

• Haldeman and Ehrlichman, who later were indicted in connection with the coverup, appear in the transcripts as acting as Nixon's peers, rather than subordinates, often telling him what to do rather than suggesting. In contrast, Dean in the early pages shows such deference to Nixon that the transcript typist felt obliged to use exclamation points to show the exuberance of his "Yes, sirs!" and other responses.

• The transcripts show Nixon viewing the Watergate investigation as a vendetta by his Democratic opponents in general and Sen. Edward M. Kennedy (D Mass.) in particular. In a March 13, 1973, discussion with the President, Dean suggests that some sleuthing might turn up Democratic scandals. "If he would get Kennedy into it, too, I would be a little bit more pleased," Nixon replies. On Feb. 28, 1973, Nixon told Dean during a discussion of the then upcoming Senate Watergate hearings that "the fine hand of the Kennedys is behind this whole hearing. There is no doubt about it...."

• The transcripts trace John Dean's transformation—in the eyes of Nixon, Haldeman and Ehrlichman—from trusted aide to White House enemy.

• Assistant Attorney General Henry E. Petersen is depicted as keeping the White House informed on the progress of the Watergate investigation. Nixon apparently relayed some of this information to Haldeman and Ehrlichman, even though Petersen had informed them that they were potential defendants in the case.

• The transcripts give hints, but not answers, to what the President knew and when he knew it. They give no indication that he knew in advance of the break-ins at the Watergate or at the office of the psychiatrist for Daniel Ellsberg, who disclosed the Pentagon Papers. Nixon in fact expresses incredulity that these break-ins happened and that his aides would have approved of them. But the transcripts establish that Nixon knew by March 21, 1973, that an illegal coverup existed and that he did not rush to remedy it. They indicate that he knew that Jeb Stuart Magruder, his former campaign deputy, had perjured himself before Magruder pleaded guilty to that crime; but there is no indication that Nixon reported this to the Justice Department.

• On the issue of "hush money" and clemency for the Watergate burglars, it is clear that Nixon opposed giving them executive clemency, but it is not clear whether his reasons were moral or political. The transcripts show Nixon considering the payment of hush money as an option, but it is not clear that he ordered the payments. He viewed the payments as a way of "buying time." At one point, he tells Dean that it appears he has "no choice" but to raise $120,000 demanded by one of the Watergate conspirators, E. Howard Hunt Jr. He asks Dean if it isn't true that "you damn well better get that done."

• Although the White House said that "characterization of third persons, in fairness to them," was deleted, the transcripts contain many instances where the President and his aides characterize members of Congress and other persons in uncomplimentary terms. Nixon describes his original nominee for FBI director, L. Patrick Gray III, as "a little bit stupid." Dean says that Sen. Sam J. Ervin Jr. (D N.C.), chairman of the Watergate committee, is "merely a puppet for Kennedy in this whole thing." Haldeman calls Lowell P. Weicker Jr. (R Conn.), a member of the Ervin committee, "too buzzy, stupid." Nixon refers to Dean, after he had begun talking to the federal prosecutors, as "a loose cannon." Nixon refers to the original seven Watergate defendants as "the jackasses who are in jail." *(Partial list of persons mentioned in the transcripts, p. 421)*

Gaps and Silences. Nixon said in his April 29 speech that the transcripts would contain ambiguities and contradictions that could be subject to different interpretations.

But reporters found other problems with the transcripts for which the White House had no ready answer. For example, *The New York Times* reported May 7 that there were indications of unaccountable silences or gaps

in transcripts of an April 14, 1973, conversation of Nixon, Haldeman and Ehrlichman and a March 22, 1973, meeting of Nixon, Dean, Haldeman, Ehrlichman and John N. Mitchell, former manager of the Nixon re-election campaign.

At one point in the April 14 transcript, Nixon mentions the time as "quarter after" without giving the hour. Eight pages later, Haldeman says it is "11 o'clock." The Times reported that "although 45 minutes appear to have elapsed between the two remarks, it requires less than 10 minutes to read the eight pages of intervening dialogue aloud in a conversational manner, with ample time for reflective pauses."

The Times article noted that the March 22 meeting was reported as lasting from 1:57 to 3:34 p.m. But the transcript ends immediately after Ehrlichman mentions that "it is 3:16."

In a similar development, *The Washington Post* reported May 8 that "informed sources" said there were numerous periods of unexplained silences lasting as long as several minutes each in the tapes from which the transcripts were made.

Since the White House taping system was sound-activated, the tape should not have been running while the room was silent. The Post reported that information from "persons in the White House involved in preparing the edited transcripts suggests that the cause of the newly discovered silences...is not known."

Regarding the numerous "inaudibles" and "unintelligibles" noted in the transcripts, presidential counsel J. Fred Buzhardt said May 6 that many of these could have been caused by "swurping" noises on the tapes as the machines picked up speed after turning on automatically.

The *Post* reported May 14 that "as the result of an apparent accident, the edited White House transcripts contain two different versions of a portion of the same conversation" on April 16, 1973, between Nixon and Assistant Attorney General Petersen. The article said that the apparent mistake, acknowledged by the White House, "demonstrates the problems in making an accurate transcript."

The conversation, duplicated on three consecutive pages with variations in some words and phrases, deals with the preparation of a public statement Nixon made the following day about the Watergate scandal.

Special prosecutor Leon Jaworski and the House Judiciary Committee had contended throughout the tapes controversy that only the actual tapes would constitute acceptable evidence in their investigations.

Best Seller. The massive, blue-bound volume, officially entitled *Submission of Recorded Presidential Conversations to the Committee on the Judiciary of the House of Representatives by President Richard Nixon,* achieved the status of a best seller as soon as it was released.

The Government Printing Office (GPO) as of May 9 had distributed or sold, at $12.25 each, 15,000 copies of the transcript volume, and the GPO anticipated a total demand of 50,000 copies.

Two private publishing houses, Dell in conjunction with *The Washington Post* and Bantam in conjunction with *The New York Times,* published the full text in paperbacks. The two publishers planned to print a combined total of 1,500,000 copies.

(Continued on p. 345)

The Tapes, Subpoenas and Transcripts

From disclosure of their existence in July 1973 to publication of voluminous edited transcripts in April 1974, the trail of the White House tapes had been a tangled one. *(Chronology, p. 337)*

The first two subpoenas for White House tapes were issued July 23, 1973. Later subpoenas, containing more sweeping demands than the first, led to the President's April 30 release of the edited transcripts.

Following is a rundown of what tapes were subpoenaed by the Senate Watergate committee, the House Judiciary Committee and the special prosecutor—and what they had obtained by early May 1974.

Senate Subpoenas. The Senate Watergate committee July 23, 1973, issued two subpoenas, one of them for White House tapes containing five conversations between Nixon and John W. Dean III, then his White House counsel, on Sept. 15, 1972, Feb. 28, March 13, and March 21, 1973 (two conversations).

The White House refused to comply with this subpoena; the courts refused to enforce it. The edited transcripts of these five conversations were released by the White House April 30, 1974.

On Dec. 18, 1973, the committee issued three more subpoenas, two of which sought approximately 40 tapes containing 500 conversations which took place between Jan. 1, 1971, and Dec. 18, 1973. These subpoenas too were rejected by the White House.

Special Prosecutor. The special Watergate prosecutor, on behalf of the grand jury investigating the Watergate break-in and coverup, July 23, 1973, obtained a subpoena for White House tapes of nine conversations, including four of the five sought by the Senate committee. The others were two conversations on June 20, 1972—one among Nixon, H. R. Haldeman and John D. Ehrlichman, and a telephone conversation among Nixon, Mitchell and Haldeman; a March 22, 1973, conversation among Nixon, Dean, Haldeman, Ehrlichman and Mitchell; and an April 15, 1973, conversation between Nixon and Dean.

After much litigation and arguing, the White House in October agreed to turn over the tapes to Judge John J. Sirica, for a ruling on the claims of executive privilege raised to protect them from disclosure to the grand jury. It later was revealed that two of the sought-after tapes did not exist—the June 20 Nixon-Mitchell telephone conversation and the April 15 Nixon-Dean conversation—and that the June 20 Nixon-Haldeman-Ehrlichman tape contained an 18½-minute "hum" or gap. After examining the tapes, Sirica upheld claims of privilege concerning parts of the June 20, June 30 and Sept. 15 tapes—turning over the non-privileged parts and the other four tapes to the special prosecutor and the grand jury in December.

At least some, if not all, of these tapes were contained in a bulging briefcase the grand jury gave to Sirica March 1, and which Sirica later transferred to the House Judiciary Committee.

Also in December, Special Prosecutor Leon Jaworski received the tape of a March 23, 1971,

White House meeting concerning the increase in milk price supports—from the White House—and a "significant number" of other tapes concerning Watergate, dairy industry campaign contributions and the settlement of antitrust charges against the International Telephone and Telegraph Corp. All of these tapes presumably were given by the White House to the House committee in March 1974.

Jaworski on April 16, 1974, obtained another subpoena for White House tapes. This subpoena sought tapes of 64 White House conversations among Nixon, former White House counsel Charles W. Colson, Haldeman, Ehrlichman and Dean between June 20, 1972, and June 4, 1973. White House lawyers moved May 2 to quash this subpoena; a hearing was set for May 13.

Transcripts of 20 of these subpoenaed conversations were contained in the volume released April 30.

Judiciary Committee. The House Judiciary Committee investigating charges of impeachable offenses against Nixon asked the White House Feb. 25 for several categories of information—including some of the 19 tapes already provided to the special prosecutor, and 42 additional tapes. On March 6 the White House replied that it would give the committee everything it had given the special prosecutor, but no more.

After negotiating in vain, the committee April 11 subpoenaed the 42 tapes. Transcripts for 31 of them were provided in the April 30 volume. The conversations for which no transcript was provided included:

• One on Feb. 20, 1973, between Nixon and Haldeman.

• One on Feb. 27, 1973, between Nixon and Ehrlichman.

• Four on April 15, 1973, in the Executive Office Building after the tape machine there ran out and ceased to record—three conversations among Nixon, Haldeman and Ehrlichman and one among Nixon, Attorney General Richard G. Kleindienst and Assistant Attorney General Henry Petersen.

• Five telephone conversations on April 15 and early April 16—one between Nixon and Kleindienst, one between Nixon and Petersen, one between Nixon and Haldeman and two between Nixon and Ehrlichman.

The committee April 19 requested the tapes of an additional 141 White House conversations. No official description of the request was released, but it was reported to seek 75 conversations related to the Watergate coverup, 46 conversations related to the increase in milk price supports approved by the administration in March 1971, and 20 conversations related to the 1971 settlement of the antitrust charges against ITT. Most of the milk-related discussions took place between March 12 and 25, 1971, according to committee documents, involving Nixon, Ehrlichman, Colson, former Treasury Secretary John B. Connally, and former Nixon aide Murray M. Chotiner. The ITT-related conversations occurred chiefly between Feb. 29 and April 5, 1972, involving Nixon, Haldeman, Ehrlichman, Colson and Mitchell.

Transcripts: Who Wanted the Tapes and What They Cover

The edited transcripts of 46 conversations were made public April 30. Following is a list of each conversation, and who, if anyone, subpoenaed the related tape:

Sept. 15, 1972, evening meeting of President Nixon, H.R. Haldeman and John W. Dean III. Part of this tape was in the hands of the House Judiciary Committee. It was sought by the special prosecutor and the Senate Watergate committee. Judge John J. Sirica gave it to the special prosecutor in December 1973.

Feb. 28, 1973, morning meeting of Nixon, Dean. The Senate committee sought this tape.

March 13, 1973, mid-day meeting Nixon, Dean. The House committee already had this tape, which Sirica gave to the special prosecutor after he and the Senate committee subpoenaed it.

March 17, 1973, afternoon meeting Nixon, Dean. **March 20, 1973,** evening telephone conversation Nixon, Dean. Both tapes were subpoenaed by both committees and the special prosecutor.

March 21, 1973, morning meeting of Nixon, Dean and Haldeman; afternoon meeting of Nixon, Dean, Haldeman and John D. Ehrlichman; **March 22, 1973,** afternoon meeting of same plus John N. Mitchell. All three were in the hands of the House committee. They had been subpoenaed by the Senate committee and the special prosecutor; the latter had received them from Sirica in December 1973.

March 27, 1973, mid-day meeting of Nixon, Haldeman, Ehrlichman, and Ronald L. Ziegler. The House committee and the special prosecutor both sought this tape.

March 28, 1973, telephone conversation between Ehrlichman and Attorney General Richard G. Kleindienst. Not sought by subpoena.

March 30, 1973, noon meeting of Nixon, Ehrlichman, Ziegler. This was subpoenaed by the House committee and the special prosecutor.

April 8, 1973, early-morning telephone conversation between Nixon and Ehrlichman. Not subpoenaed.

April 14, 1973, morning meeting of Nixon, Haldeman, Ehrlichman; afternoon meeting of Nixon and Haldeman; afternoon meeting of Nixon, Haldeman, Ehrlichman; late-afternoon meeting of Nixon, Haldeman, Ehrlichman. These four tapes were subpoenaed by both committees and the special prosecutor.

April 14, 1973, telephone conversation between Ehrlichman and Kleindienst. Not subpoenaed.

April 14, 1973, late-night telephone conversation between Nixon, Haldeman; late-night telephone conversation between Nixon, Ehrlichman; **April 15, 1973,** morning meeting between Nixon, Ehrlichman. These three were subpoenaed by both committees and the special prosecutor.

April 15, 1973, afternoon meeting of Nixon, Kleindienst. This tape was subpoenaed by the two committees. The White House gave it to Sirica.

April 15, 1973, afternoon telephone conversation between Nixon, Haldeman. Both committees subpoenaed this tape as did the special prosecutor.

April 15, 1973, afternoon telephone conversation between Nixon, Kleindienst. Both committees subpoenaed this tape.

April 15, 1973, telephone conversation between Haldeman and aide Lawrence M. Higby. Not subpoenaed.

April 15, 1973, four evening telephone conversations between Nixon and Assistant Attorney General Henry E. Petersen. All subpoenaed by both committees.

April 16, 1973, morning meeting of Nixon, Haldeman and Ehrlichman. This was subpoenaed by both committees and the special prosecutor.

April 16, 1973, morning meeting of Nixon and Dean. This tape was subpoenaed by the Senate committee and was given to Sirica, by the White House in 1973.

April 16, 1973, morning meeting of Nixon, Haldeman, and Ehrlichman; noon meeting of Nixon and Haldeman. Both were subpoenaed by both committees and the special prosecutor.

April 16, 1973, afternoon meeting of Nixon and Petersen. This tape was sought by both committees.

April 16, 1973, afternoon meeting of Nixon, Ehrlichman and Ziegler. Both committees and the special prosecutor subpoenaed this tape.

April 16, 1973, afternoon meeting of Nixon and Dean. The Senate Watergate committee subpoenaed this tape which the White House had earlier given to Sirica.

April 16, 1973, evening telephone conversation of Nixon and Petersen. This tape was subpoenaed by both committees.

April 17, 1973, morning meeting of Nixon and Haldeman; afternoon meeting of Nixon, Haldeman, Ehrlichman and Ziegler, these two tapes were subpoenaed by the special prosecutor and by both committees.

April 17, 1973, afternoon telephone conversation between Nixon and Ehrlichman; afternoon meeting between Nixon and Petersen. Both conversations were subpoenaed by both committees.

April 17, 1973, afternoon meeting of Nixon, Haldeman, Ziegler and Ehrlichman. Both committees and the special prosecutor subpoenaed this tape.

April 17, 1973, afternoon meeting of Nixon, Secretary of State William P. Rogers, Haldeman and Ehrlichman. This tape was subpoenaed by both committees and the special prosecutor.

April 18, 1973, afternoon telephone conversation of Nixon and Petersen. Both committees subpoenaed it.

April 19, 1973, evening meeting of Nixon with lawyers Frank Strickler and John J. Wilson. The Senate committee subpoenaed this tape.

April 27, 1973, afternoon meeting of Nixon and Petersen; evening meeting of Nixon, Petersen and Ziegler. Neither tape was subpoenaed.

(Continued from p. 342)

The Chicago Tribune published the full text May 1 and sold 800,000 copies. Other major newspapers serialized the text or published sizable excerpts.

Nixon and the Press. Reporters looking into the transcripts found that Nixon and the men around him often were looking the other way—at the press. The transcripts are replete with disdainful remarks about the news media.

For example, several of the conversations took place on April 14, 1973, before Nixon, Haldeman and Ehrlichman attended the annual White House Correspondents' Association dinner at which *Washington Post* reporters Bob Woodward and Carl Bernstein were honored for their Watergate coverage.

"I am going to go see Bernstein and what's-his-name get their awards," Ehrlichman says at one point.

"Well, you fellows need a rest," Nixon says later. Haldeman replies, "Rest? There's that damn dinner."

"We'll grin at the White House correspondents," Ehrlichman says. "That's no rest, that's work," Haldeman replies.

Media on Transcripts. Reportage of the Watergate transcripts often mentioned that the conversations are not necessarily typical.

NBC's John Chancellor, for example, said at the end of a May 5 special on the transcripts that "we must keep in mind that they necessarily deal with a President in trouble trying to fight his way out. Not all White House conversations read the way these do."

"Having said that," Chancellor continued, "it must also be said that in reading it all as some of us here have had to do, it is the most melancholy book around today. It is a document long on suspicion, distrust and deviousness; short on faith, hope and charity. It is fascinating and depressing, but more depressing than fascinating. And in that it's a good symbol of the Watergate mess."

Excerpts Follow. Nixon said that the transcripts should be read in their entirety. "To anyone who reads his way through this mass of materials as I have provided it," he said April 29, "it will be totally, abundantly clear that as far as the President's role with regard to Watergate is concerned, the entire story is here."

But "reading it all" is a monumental job, and for that reason Congressional Quarterly analyzed the transcripts and grouped the excerpts to show the major things the President and his top aides said in the following subject areas:

- Congress and how to deal with it; *(this page)*
- Nixon's knowledge of the Watergate break-in and the coverup; *(p. 348)*
- The issues of 'hush money' and clemency for the Watergate burglars; *(p. 354)*
- The role of Henry Petersen and the Justice Department; *(p. 361)*
- The fall of John Dean; *(p. 367)*
- Administration attitudes toward the press. *(p. 375)*

In the verbatim excerpts, Nixon is identified as **P** for President, Dean as **D**, Haldeman as **H**, Ehrlichman as **E**, Petersen as **HP**, Lawrence M. Higby as **LH** and Ronald L. Ziegler as **Z**. √

The Administration and Congress

The derisive remarks about Congress that lace the edited transcripts of White House conversations between President Nixon and his top aides drew reactions on Capitol Hill ranging from knowing nods to outrage.

"I wasn't really surprised" that the Nixon team held Congress in such low regard, said Sen. Howard H. Baker Jr. (R Tenn.). "We suspected in varying degrees for a long time that this was the attitude."

At one point Nixon called Congress "irrelevant because they are so damned irresponsible, as much as we would like to say otherwise." At another point H.R. Haldeman, then Nixon's chief of staff, said of House Speaker Carl Albert (D Okla.)—the third man in the line of succession for the presidency, "Well, (expletive deleted) the speaker of the House."

"I wasn't startled at the language," said Baker, vice chairman of the Senate Watergate commitee, who Nixon at one point referred to as having a "thick skull" and at another stage characterized as a "smoothy."

Most of us have been up there (at the White House) at one time or another and we know that most presidents are human and sometimes speak in hyperbole and tend to "exaggerate," Baker told Congressional Quarterly. "Lyndon Johnson could have deleted a few expletives himself."

However, Rep. Jerome Waldie (D Calif.), one of Nixon's chief critics on the House Judiciary Committee, said he was "surprised" at the bluntness of some of the remarks.

"I was surprised and depressed to think that those people have controlled this country for the years they have and are still in control of it," Waldie said. "But if there's any group of people whose opinion about Congress would not be valued by me, it's that shabby, sleazy group."

Sen. Edward M. Kennedy (D Mass.), who the transcripts show the White House believed to have been the moving force behind the Watergate committee hearings, called remarks about him "paranoid."

"There's always a sort of adversary relationship between the White House and Congress no matter who's in the White House," said Kennedy spokesman Richard C. Drayne. "They're trying to get things passed through Congress and trying to get their own way. I'm sure Lyndon Johnson sat around and said nasty things about Congress, but I'm sure he had a great deal of respect for it. There's always been a mutual respect which I think has never been true with Nixon. I think they had a particular scorn for the Congress."

Nixon and his aides were harsh on Congress as an institution and on individual members as well. Following are pertinent excerpts:

Meeting of Nixon and Dean Feb. 28, 1973, in Oval Office (12:42-2p.m.):

P. Congress, is, of course, on its (inaudible). And yet they are so enormously frustrated that they are exhausted. Isn't that the point?

D. I think there is a lot of that.

P. It is too bad. We can take very little comfort from it because we have to work with them. But they become irrelevant because they are so damned irresponsible, as much as we would like to say otherwise.

D. Yes, sir. I spent some years on the Hill myself and one of the things I always noticed was the inability of the Congress to deal effectively with the executive branch because they have never provided themselves with adequate staffs, had adequate information available—

"We are in it together. This is a war. We take a few shots and it will be over. We will give them a few shots and it will be over. Don't worry. I wouldn't want to be on the other side right now. Would you?"

—President Nixon to John Dean III
Sept. 15, 1972

P. Well now they have huge staffs compared to what we had.
D. Well they have huge staffs, true, as opposed to what they had years ago, But they are still inadequate to deal effectively—"
P. (Expletive deleted) Don't try to help them out!

Sen. Sam Ervin (D N.C.), chairman of the Senate Watergate committee, "away from his staff is not very much," Dean said during a March 22 discussion of strategy in trying to get Ervin to agree to a compromise on procedures for the then-pending hearings. If the Nixon team could get Ervin into the White House to discuss the matter, "...I think he might just give up the store himself right there and lock himself in," Dean suggested.

Many other references to Congress and individual members were unclear from the transcripts because they were "inaudible" or "untelligible" according to the White House version.

The transcripts show, however, that the general feeling on the part of Nixon and his aides was that their Watergate troubles were the result of a political vendetta being waged by the Democrats. The mood seemed to change from one of vindictiveness toward the Democats during the early stages to helpless rage during the climactic days leading up to Nixon's April 30, 1973, statement announcing the firing of Dean and the resignations of top aides Haldeman and John D. Ehrlichman and Attorney General Richard Kleindienst.

Excerpts follow on how Nixon vowed to seek revenge on his adversaries.

Meeting of Nixon, Haldeman and Dean Sept. 15, 1972 in the Oval Office (5:27—6:17 p.m.):

P. We are all in it together. This is a war. We take a few shots and it will be over. We will give them a few shots and it will be over. Don't worry. I wouldn't want to be on the other side right now. Would you?
D. Along that line one of the things I've tried to do, I have begun to keep notes on a lot of people who are emerging as less than our friends because this will be over some day and we

shouldn't forget the way some of them have treated us.
P. I want the most comprehensive notes on all those who tried to do us in. They didn't have to do it. If we had had a very close election and they were playing the other side I would understand this. No—they were doing this quite deliberately and they are asking for it and they are going to get it. We have not used the power in this first four years you know. We have never used it. We have not used the Bureau and we have not used the Justice Department but things are going to change now. And they are either going to do it right or go.

"Another thing. I would like the libel suits. I think both of you, and Bob particularly, you ought to get yourself a libel lawyer, Bob, and check the or have Wilson check and use the most vicious libel lawyer there is. I'd sue every (expletive deleted) (unintelligible).

—President Nixon to H. R. Haldeman
and John Dean, April 17, 1973

D. What an exciting prospect.
P. Thanks. It has to be done. We have been (adjective deleted) fools for us to come into this election campaign and not do anything with regard to the Democratic Senators who are running, et cetera. And who the hell are they after? They are after us. It is absolutely ridiculous. It is not going to be that way any more.

During the same meeting, Dean reported that a General Accounting Office auditor was investigating the White House at the request of Speaker Albert:

P. That surprises me.
H. Well, (expletive deleted) the speaker of the House. Maybe we better put a little heat on him.
P. I think so too.
H. Because he has a lot worse problems than he is going to find down here.
D. That's right.
H. That is the kind of thing that, you know, we really ought to do is call the speaker and say, "I regret to say your calling the GAO down here because of what it is going to cause us to do to you."
P. Why don't you see if Harlow will tell him that.
H. Because he wouldn't do it—he would just be pleasant and call him Mr. Speaker.

After the transcripts were released Albert termed the report that he had ordered a White House investigation by the GAO a "fabrication."

The conversation turned to Rep. Wright Patman's (D Texas) House Banking and Currency committee, which was then planning hearings that would have dealt with Watergate, and whether the White House could "be successful in turning them off," in Dean's words.

"(W)e are looking at all the campaign reports of every member of that committee because we are convinced that none of them complied exactly with the law either," said Dean. "If they want to play rough—some day we better say, 'Gentlemen, we want to call your attention that you have not complied with A, B, C, and F and we are not going to hold that a secret if you start talking campaign violations here.'"

Blaming the administration's Watergate problems on the Democrats, and Kennedy in particular, became a recurring theme in the conversations.

In the Feb. 28, 1973, (9:12—10:23 a.m.) discussion:

D. I am convinced that he (Ervin) has shown that he is merely a puppet for Kennedy in this whole thing. The fine hand of the Kennedy's is behind this whole hearing. There is no doubt about it. When they considered the resolution on the Floor of the Senate I got the record out to read it. Who asked special permission to have their staff man on the floor? Kennedy brings this man Flug out on the floor when they are debating a resolution. He is the only one who did this. It has been Kennedy's push quietly, his constant investigation. His committee did the (untelligible) subpoenas to get at Kalmbach and all these people.

P. Uh, huh.

D. He has kept this quiet and constant pressure on this thing. I think this fellow Sam Dash, who has been selected counsel, is a Kennedy choice. I think this is also something we will be able to quietly and slowly document. Leak this to the press, and the parts and cast become much more apparent.

P. Yes, I guess the Kennedy crowd is just laying in the bushes waiting to make their move.

The White House kept careful track of which members of Congress could be counted upon for support, as well. Baker and Sen. Edward J. Gurney (R Fla.) were considered loyalists on the Watergate committee, and Sen. Barry Goldwater was seen as a conduit for making public the White House position that Nixon's own campaign had been the target of "dirty tricks." Dean outlined some of his efforts to mount a "counteroffensive" to take some attention away from the Watergate charges against the administration. Part of the plan was to have White House aide William Baroody write a speech for Goldwater.

Meeting of Nixon and Dean March 13, 1973 (12:42—2 p.m.):

D. I have all of the information that we have collected. There is some there, and I have turned it over to Baroody. Baroody is having a speech drafted for Barry Goldwater. And there is enough material there to make a rather sensational speech just by: Why in the hell isn't somebody looking into what happened to President Nixon during his campaign? Look at these

events! How do you explain these? Where are the answers to these questions? But, there is nothing but threads. I pulled all the information....

P. Also, the senator should then present it to the Ervin Committee and demand that that be included. He is a senator, a senator....

D. What I am working on there for Barry is a letter to Senator Ervin that this has come to my attention, and why shouldn't this be a part of the inquiry? And he can spring out 1964 and quickly to '72. We've got a pretty good speech there, if we can get our materials.

P. Good!

At the outset, Watergate committee member Lowell P. Weicker Jr. (R Conn.) was regarded with uncertainty as to whether he was a friend or a foe.

"I would suspect if we are going to get any insight to what that committee is going to do, it is going to be through Gurney," Dean told Nixon Feb. 28. "I don't know about Weicker, where he is going to fall out on this thing."

By March 27, Nixon was asking Ehrlichman, "What the hell makes Weicker tick?" "Nobody's been able to figure that out," Ehrlichman replied.

Shortly after Nixon had announced he was "investigating serious charges which have come to my attention" regarding Watergate, he and his chief aides met in an angry mood. The talk turned to Weicker and whether the senator's congressional immunity against libel would shield him from the wrath of the White House:

P. Another thing. I would like the libel suits. I think both of you, and Bob particularly, you ought to get yourself a libel lawyer, Bob, and check the or have Wilson check and use the most vicious libel lawyer there is. I'd sue every (expletive deleted) (unintelligible.) There have been stories over this period of time. That will make—that also helps with public opinion. Sue right down the line. It doesn't make any difference now about the taking depositions and the rest, does it? The important thing is the story's big and I think you ought to go out and sue people for libel.

H. Do you mean Senator Weicker?

P. He's covered.

E. Oh, he's not, not when he was on Issues and Answers.

H. (unintelligible) or using newspaper interviews.

E. That's right.

H. It was not on the floor, he's too buzzy, stupid.

P. The point is the thing with Weicker (unintelligible) is whether he said—how did he say that? Was it libelous?

H. I think so. I better ask a lawyer.

P. Was he that specific?

H. He was damned specific.

P. That Haldeman knew?

H. Yes. "That Haldeman directed and Haldeman was in personal command of all personnel." I repeat, "all personnel at the Re-election Committee."

P. Good, sue him.

The President's men decided against libel suits. But clearly, by April 17, the White House had discovered that Weicker was not a friend. √

Nixon's Knowledge of Watergate

What did President Nixon know about Watergate? What did he know about the coverup of Watergate? What did he know about the Ellsberg break-in and other Watergate-related events? What did he know, as Sen. Howard H. Baker Jr. (R Tenn.) asked repeatedly, and when did he learn it? What did he do when he learned of wrongdoing? In short, did the President of the United States act to "prick the boil," as he put it, or did he join in the coverup and by so doing make himself criminally culpable? The edited transcrips offer no definitive answers; but they provide hints.

The Watergate Break-in. Nothing in the edited transcript even suggests that the President had any prior knowledge of the entry into the Democratic National Committee. Indeed, there are instances in which Nixon declares how shocked he was to learn that his campaign organization had been linked to the crime.

Following are pertinent excerpts:

Meeting of the President and Dean in the Oval Office, Feb. 28 (9:12-10:23 a.m.):

P. ...I will never forget when I heard about this (adjective deleted) forced entry and bugging. I thought what the hell is this? What is the matter with these people? Are they crazy? I thought they were nuts! A prank! But it wasn't. It wasn't very funny. I think that our Democratic friends know that, too. They know what the hell it was. They don't think we'd be involved in such.

Meeting of the President, Haldeman, Ehrlichman, Dean and Ziegler, EOB Office, March 27 (11:10 a.m.-1:30 p.m.):

P. Well, the thing is too, that I know they talk about this business of (former campaign official Jeb Stuart) Magruder's, saying that Haldeman had ordered, the President had ordered, etc., of all people who was surprised on the 17th of June—I was in Florida—was me. Were you there?

E. No, I was here.

P. Who was there?

E. I called (former White House aide Charles) Colson, Haldeman and Ziegler and alerted them to this.

P. And I read the paper. What in the name of (expletive removed) is this? I just couldn't believe it. So you know what I mean—I believe in playing politics hard, but I am also smart. What I can't understand is how Mitchell would ever approve.

H. That's the thing I can't understand here.

Later, in the same conversation, Nixon took a different view of Mitchell's possible involvement in the break-in.

P. You know Mitchell could be telling the truth and (convicted Watergate defendant G. Gordon) Liddy could be too. Liddy just assumed he had abstract approval. Mitchell could say, "I know I never approved this damn plan." You've got

to figure the lines of defenses that everybody's going to take here. That's Mitchells. Right?...

The Coverup. On the morning of March 21, 1973, John Dean told Nixon the coverup of Watergate—he called it a "cancer" —was enveloping the presidency. Nixon would later say publicly that this was his first indication of a coverup involving his close associates. Dean, however, would testify that Nixon already knew of

---

"...I will never forget when I heard about this (adjective deleted) forced entry and bugging. I thought what the hell is this? What is the matter with these people? Are they crazy? I thought they were nuts! A prank! But it wasn't. It wasn't very funny...."

—President Nixon to John W. Dean III,
Feb. 28, 1973

---

the coverup. What he did not know according to Dean, was that it was collapsing. The transcripts do not settle that Nixon-Dean conflict but they do establish that by 11:55 a.m. March 21, 1973, the President knew an illegal coverup existed.

Following are pertinent excerpts:
Meeting of the President, Dean and Haldeman in the Oval Office, March 21, 1973 (10:12-11:55 a.m.):

D. The reason that I thought we ought to talk this morning is because in our conversations, I have the impression that you don't know everything I know and it makes it very difficult for you to make judgments that only you can make on some of these things and I thought that—

P. In other words, I have to know why you feel that we shouldn't unravel something?

D. Let me give you my overall first.

P. In other words, your judgment as to where it stands, and where we will go.

D. I think that there is no doubt about the seriousness of the problem we've got. We have a cancer within, close to the Presidency, that is growing. It is growing daily. It's compounded, growing geometrically now, because it compounds itself. That will be clear if I, you know, explain some of the details of why it is. Basically, it is because (1) we are being blackmailed; (2) People are going to start perjuring themselves very quickly that have not had to perjure themselves to protect other people in the line. And there is no assurance—

P. That that won't bust?

D. That that won't bust...

Dean proceeded to tell Nixon the story of Watergate, from the very beginning. Piecing together fact and supposition, Dean, according to the transcript, viewed the break-in at Democratic headquarters as the work of zealots like Gordon Liddy. Their go-ahead, asserted Dean, was probably accidentally given, the result of misunderstandings and poor communications between the White House and the Commitee to Re-elect the President. Dean took the president through the conviction of the original seven Watergate defendants.

D. Alright now, we have gone through the trial. I don't know if (John) Mitchell has perjured himself in the Grand Jury or not.

P. Who?

D. Mitchell. I don't know how much knowledge he actually had. I know that Magruder has perjured himself in the Grand Jury. I know that (former campaign official) Porter has perjured himself in the Grand Jury.

P. Who is Porter? (unintelligible)

D. He is one of Magruder's deputies. They set up this scenario which they ran by me. They said, "How about this?" I said, "I don't know. If this is what you are going to hang on, fine."

P. What did they say in the Grand Jury?

D. They said, as they said before the trial in the Grand Jury, that Liddy had come over as Counsel and we knew he had these capacities to do legitimate intelligence. We had no idea what he was doing. He was given an authorization of $250,000 to collect information, because our surrogates were out on the road. They had no protection, and we had information that there were going to be demonstrations against them, and that we had to have a plan as to what liabilities they were going to be confronted with and Liddy was charged with doing it. We had no knowledge that he was going to bug the DNC.

P. The point is, that is not true?

D. That's right.

P. Magruder did know it was going to take place?

D. Magruder gave the instructions to be back in the DNC.

P. He did?

D. Yes.

P. You know that?

D. Yes.

P. I see. O.K.

D. I honestly believe that no one over here knew that. I know that as God is my maker, I had no knowledge that they were going to do this.

P. Bob didn't either, or wouldn't have known that either. You are not the issue involved. Had Bob known, he would be.

D. Bob—I don't believe specifically knew that they were going in there.

P. I don't think so.

D. I don't think he did. I think he knew that there was a capacity to do this but he was not given the specific direction.

P. Did (Haldeman deputy Gordon) Strachan know?

D. I think Strachan did know.

P. (unintelligible) Going back into the DNC—Hunt, etc.—this is not understandable!

D. So—those people are in trouble as a result of the Grand Jury and the trial. Mitchell, of course, was never called during the trial. Now—

P. Mitchell has given a sworn statement, hasn't he?

D. Yes, Sir.

P. To the Jury?

D. To the Grand Jury.—

* * * *

D. I don't know what he (Mitchell) said. I have never seen a transcript of the Grand Jury. Now what has happened post June 17? I was under pretty clear instructions not to investigate this, but this could have been disastrous on the electorate if all hell had broken loose. I worked on a theory of containment—

P. Sure.

D. To try to hold it right where it was.

P. Right.

D. There is no doubt that I was totally aware of what the Bureau was doing at all times. I was totally aware of what the Grand Jury was doing. I knew what witnesses were going to be called. I knew what they were asked, and I had to.

P. Why did (Asst. Attorney General Henry) Peterson play the game so straight with us?

D. Because Peterson is a soldier. He kept me informed. He told me when we had problems, where we had problems and the like. He believes in this Administration. This Administration has made him. I don't think he has done anything improper, but he did make sure that the investigation was narrowed down to the very, very fine criminal thing which was a break for us. There is no doubt about it.

P. Do you honestly feel that he did an adequate job?

D. They ran that investigation out to the fullest extend they could follow a lead and that was it.

P. But the way point is, where I suppose he could be criticized for not doing an adequate job. Why didn't he call Haldeman? Why didn't he get a statement from Colson? Oh, they did get Colson!

D. That's right. But as based on their FBI interviews, there was no reason to follow up. There were no leads there. Colson said, "I have no knowledge of this" to the FBI. Strachan said, "I have no knowledge." They didn't ask Strachan any questions about Watergate. They asked him about (former campaign operative) Segretti. They said, "what is your connection with Liddy?" Strachan just said, "Well, I met him over there." They never really pressed him. Strachan appeared, as a result of some coaching, to be the dumbest paper pusher in the bowels of the White House.

P. I understand.

D. Alright. Now post June 17th: These guys immediately—It is very interesting. (Dean sort of chuckled) Liddy, for example, on the Friday before—I guess it was on the 15th, no, the 16th of June—had been in Henry Peterson's office with another member of my staff on campaign compliance problems. After the incident, he ran (Attorney General) Kleindienst down at Burning Tree Country Club and told him "you've got to get my men out of jail." Kleindienst said, "You get the hell out of here, kid. Whatever you have to say, just say to somebody else. Don't bother me." But this has never come up. Liddy said if they all got counsel instantly and said we will ride this thing out. Alright, then they started making demands. "We have to have attorneys fees. We don't have any money ourselves, and you are asking us to take this through the election." Alright, so arrangements were made through Mitchell, initiating it. And I was present in discussions where these guys had to be taken care of. Their attorneys fees had to be done. Kalmbach was brought in. Kalmbach raised some cash.

P. They put that under the cover of a Cuban Committee, I suppose?

D. Well, they had a Cuban Committee and they had—some of it was given to (convicted Watergate conspirator Howard) Hunt's lawyer, who is turn passed it out. You know, when Hunt's wife was flying to Chicago with $10,000 she was actually, I understand after the fact now, was going to pass that money to one of the Cubans—to meet him in Chicago and pass it to somebody there.

P. (unintelligible) but I would certainly keep that cover for whatever it is worth.

D. That's the most troublesome post-thing because (1) Bob (Haldeman) is involved in that; (2) John (Ehrlichman) is involved in that; (3) I am involved in that; (4) (John) Mitchell is involved in that. And that is an obstruction of justice.

P. In other words the bad it does. You were taking care of witnesses. How did Bob get in it?

D. Well, they ran out of money over there. Bob had $350,000 in a safe over here that was really set aside for polling purposes. And there was no other source of money, so they came over and said you all have got to give us some money. I had to go to Bob and say, "Bob, they need some money over there." He said "What for." So I had to tell him what it was for because he wasn't just about to send money over there willy-nilly. And John was involved in those discussions. And then we decided there was no price too high to pay to let this thing blow up in front of the election.

P. I think we should be able to handle that issue pretty well. May be some lawsuits.

Dean told Nixon of the "blackmail" which he said Hunt was attempting to extract. The two men discussed whether and how to continue it. Dean shifted the discussion back to his original theme.

D. ....When I say this is a growing cancer, I say it for reasons like this. (Former White House aide Egil) Bud Krogh, in his testimony before the Grand Jury, was forced to perjure himself. He is haunted by it. Bud said, "I have not had a pleasant day on my job." He said, "I told my wife all about this. The curtain may ring down one of these days, and I may have to face the music, which I am perfectly willing to do."

P. What did he perjure himself on, John?

D. Did he know the Cubans. He did.

P. He said he didn't?

D. That is right. They didn't press him hard.

P. He might be able to—I am just trying to think. Perjury is an awful hard rap to prove. If he could just say that I—Well, go ahead.

D. Well, so that is one perjury. Mitchell and Magruder are potential perjurers. There is always the possibility of any one of these individuals blowing. Hunt. Liddy. Liddy is in jail right now, serving his time and having a good time right now. I think Liddy in his own bizarre way the strongest of them. So there is that possibility.

P. Your major guy to keep under control is Hunt?

D. That is right.

P. I think. Does he know a lot?

D. He knows so much. He could sink Chuck Colson. Apparently he is quite distressed with Colson. He thinks Colson has abandoned him. Colson was to meet with him when he was out there after, you know, he had left the White House. He met with him through his lawyer. Hunt raised the question he wanted money. Colson's lawyer told him Colson wasn't doing anything with money. Hunt took offense with that immediately, and felt Colson had abandoned him.

P. Just looking at the immediate problem, don't you think you have to handle Hunt's financial situation damn soon?

D. I think that is—I talked with Mitchell about that last night and—

P. It seems to me we have to keep the cap on the bottle that much, or we don't have any options.

D. That's right.

P. Either that or it all blows right now?

D. That's the question.

P. We have Hunt, Krogh. Well go ahead with the other ones.

D. Now we've got (Nixon attorney Herbert) Kalmbach. Kalmbach received, at the close of the '68 campaign in January of 1969, he got a million $700,000 to be custodian for. That came down from New York, and was placed in safe deposit boxes here. Some other people were on the boxes, and ultimately, the money was taken out to California. Alright, there is knowledge of the fact that he did start with a million seven. Several people know this. Now since 1969, he has spent a good deal of this money and accounting for it is going to be very difficult for Herb. For example, he has spent close to $500,000 on private polling. That opens up a whole new thing. It is not illegal, but more of the same thing.

Scattered throughout the transcripts are conversations assessing the culpability of different members of the Nixon team. Hardheaded judgments are offered as to who faces criminal charges of perjury and obstruction of justice.

Following are pertinent excerpts:

Meeting of the President and Dean in the Oval Office, March 13:

P. Let's face it, I think they are really after Haldeman.

D. Haldeman and Mitchell.

P. Colson is not big enough name for them. He really isn't. He is you know, he is on the government side, but Colson's name doesn't bother them so much. They are after Haldeman and after Mitchell. Don't you think so?

D. Sure. They are going to take a look and try to drag them, but they're going to be able to drag them into the election—

P. In any event, Haldeman's problem is Chapin isn't it?

D. Bob's problem is circumstantial.

P. Why is that? Let's look at the circumstantial. I don't know, Bob didn't know any of those people like the Hunts and all that bunch. Colson did, but Bob didn't. OK?

D. That's right.

P. Now where the hell, or how much Chapin knew I will be (expletive deleted) if I know.

D. Chapin didn't know anything about the Watergate.

P. Don't you think so?

D. Absolutely not.

P. Strachan?

D. Yes.

P. He knew?

D. Yes.

P. About the Watergate?

D. Yes.

P. Well, then, he probably told Bob. He may not have.

D. He was judicious in what he relayed, but Strachan is as tough as nails. He can go in and stonewall, and say, "I don't know anything about what you are talking about." He has already done it twice you know, in interviews.

P. I guess he should, shouldn't he? I suppose we can't call that justice, can we?

D. Well, it is a personal loyalty to him. He doesn't want it any other way. He didn't have to be told. He didn't have to be asked. It just is something that he found was the way he wanted to handle the situation.

P. But he knew? He knew about Watergate? Strachan did?

D. Yes.

P. I will be damned! Well that is the problem in Bob's case. Not (Presidential Appointments Secretary) Chapin then, but Strachan. Strachan worked for him, didn't he?

D. Yes. They would have one hell of a time proving that Strachan had knowledge of it, though.

P. Who knew better? Magruder?

D. Magruder and Liddy.

P. Oh, I see. The other weak link for Bob is Magruder. He hired him et cetera.

D. That applies to Mitchell, too.

P. Mitchell—Magruder. Where do you see Colson coming into it? Do you think he knew quite a bit and yet, he could know quite a great deal about a lot of other things and not know a lot about this. I don't know.

D. Well I have never—

P. He sure as hell knows Hunt. That we know. Was very close to him.

D. Chuck has told me that he had no knowledge, specific knowledge, of the Watergate before it occurred. There have been tidbits that I have raised with Chuck. I have not played any games with him. I said, "Chuck, I have indications—"

P. What indications? The lawyer has to know everything.

D. That's right. I said, "Chuck, people have said that you were involved in this, involved in that, involved in all of this. He said, "that is not true, etc." I think that Chuck had knowledge that something was going on over there, but he didn't have any knowledge of the details of the specifics of the whole thing.

P. There must have been an indication of the fact that we had poor pickings. Because naturally anybody, either Chuck or Bob, were always reporting to me about what was going on. If they ever got any information they would certainly have told me that we got some information, but they never had a thing to report. What was the matter? Did they never get anything out of the damn thing?

D. I don't think they ever got anything, sir.

P. A dry hole?

D. That's right.

P. (Expletive deleted)

D. Well, they were just really getting started.

P. Yeah. Bob one time said something to me about something, this or that or something, but I think it was something about the Convention, I think it was about the convention problems they were planning something. I assume that must have been MacGregor— not MacGregor, but Segretti.

D. No, Segretti wasn't involved in the intelligence gathering piece of it at all.

P. Oh, he wasn't? Who the hell was gathering intelligence?

D. That was Liddy and his outfit.

Meeting of the President and Ehrlichman in the Oval Office, April 15 (10:35-11:15 a.m.):

E. Not yet. Not yet.

P. He's a good man—good man.

E. I think he, I think he'll do fine. You see...

P. (Unintelligble) you expect anyone (unintelligible) I was cogitating last night, and we've got the people that can—I mean on the obstruction of justice thing, which I think is our main problem at this time—well of course it is the main problem because it involved the other people.

E. Yeah.

P. Otherwise it's just Chapin.

E. Yes, Chapin.

P. and Mitchell.

E. Yeap.

P. Magruder.

E. Yeah.

P. Possibly Dean, but a....

E. (Former Assistant Attorney General and campaign official Robert) Mardian and (former campaign official Fred) LaRue.

P. (Unintelligible) on the (unintelligible) of the case?

E. LaRue.

P. They got him on that too?

E. Yeah. Yeah.

P. You mean Magruder has?

E. Yeah.

P. That's going to be hard. This fellow's lied twice to (unintelligible)?

E. That's right. That's true.

P. The people you've got with obstruction are Hunt and Goldblatt and Bittman, right?

E. Oh, (Henry) Rothblatt the lawyer (Lawyer for four of the original Watergate defendants)

P. Rothblatt?

E. Yeah, right. Well, I don't think (Hunt lawyer William) Bittman is going to testify. I would be very surprised if he did.

P. Why?

E. Well.

P. Get him involved in obstruction of justice?

E. Well I just don't think—I think, I'm just guessing here, my guess is that he's worked himself out a haven in all of this.

P. Wouldn't serve his interests to get involved in the obstruction of justice. He's basically almost a bag man, not a bag man, but a message carrier, isn't he?

E. No. No.—was an instigator—. He was concerned about his fee. And a...

P. Oh really John?

E. Yeah. Yeah. So he was one of the active promoters.

* * * *

P. I think (unintelligible) it was—nobody was trying to keep him from telling the truth to the Grand Jury—to shut him up to the Grand Jury?

E. I can say in truth and candor that Dean never explained to me that there was any kind of a deal to get these guys to lie or to change their stories or to refuse to testify to the trial of the action or anything of that kind. That was just never discussed. So I don't feel too uncomfortable with this.

At that same meeting, according to the transcript, Ehrlichman told Nixon that Dean had passed along secret information on the Watergate grand jury's investigation to Mardian, who in turn used that information to perpetuate the coverup by inducing witnesses to lie to the grand jury.

E. Yeah. He—well, this is kind of interesting. I may have told you about this, but the U.S. Attorney now feels that Dean overreached them by providing information out of the Grand Jury to the Committee for the Re-election. I think that may be legitimate criticism if he in fact did that. On the other hand, for him to provide us with information inside, for the orderly operation of the government, is another matter. That's two quite different things. If you peddle information from a Grand Jury to the outside, or if you peddle it inside to people who are responsible.

P. (Unintelligible)

E. Oh that was, let me think.

P. (Unintelligible) Grand Jury at that point.

E. He had information on who was going to be called as witnesses so that apparently Mardian was able to get around and coach witnesses.

P. Did Mardian coach them?

E. In some cases Mardian, I guess, was very heavy-handed about it, and—

P. Well, is there anything wrong with that?

E. Yeah, well there's something wrong with—

P. He was not their attorneys is the problem?

E. Well, no, the problem—the problem is he asked them to say things that weren't true.

P. Oh.

E. When I say coach I use the word loosely, and —

P. (Unintelligible)

E. Well no, a fellow over there named Porter—Bart Porter for one.

P. Where is he now, in jail?

E. No, he's in business somewhere, and he will probably be indicted.

P. They coached him to what, did he say?

E. Say.

P. Was he—he was one of the buggers over there?

E. No-no. Oh no, he worked for the Committee, worked for the Committee, but they asked him about higher-ups and about whether there was any (unintelligible) and so on and so forth.

P. How was he in the deal? How would he know about it?

E. He worked over there in Magruder's office, and he apparently passed money to Liddy from Sloan and was privy to quite a lot of the information.

P. I thought John (unintelligible) Liddy to take money for that (unintelligible).

E. Apparently he did. Well I don't mean after—I mean to pay for equipment and to.

P. Oh (unintelligible)

E. That's right.

P. Why the hell didn't the Grand Jury indict him?

E. Well because they didn't have the, they didn't have the evidence. There was a cover story which Mardian and others cooked up, and Porter, who corroborated the cover story, is now indictible for perjury. He is a little fish who got caught in the net.

P. Poor son of a bitch. It's wrong. It's wrong.

E. The whole things is just monumentally tragic.

P. It is. Now don't let it get you down.

E. Well that's right, that's right, and it'll pass.

P. Dean is concerned, and concerns me.

E. Yeah.

P. I don't think he could have been that active in the pre—the post yes—the pre things. Magruder, Magruder may be (unintelligible) a little (unintelligible) in some of that stuff.

The Other Break-ins. The transcripts link the White House to two other break-ins. One took place in 1971 at the Los Angeles office of Dr. Lewis Fielding, psychiatrist of Daniel Ellsberg. The other, in 1972, involved cracking the safe of Las Vegas publisher Hank Greenspun. The transcripts disclose no indication that the President reported either crime to law enforcement officials when he learned of them.

Following are pertinent excerpts:

Meeting of the President and Dean in the Oval Office on March 17:

D. ...The other potential problem is Ehrlichman's and this is—

P. In connection with Hunt?

D. In connection with Hunt and Liddy both.

P. They worked for him?

D. They—these fellows had to be some idiots as we've learned after the fact. They went out and went into Dr. Ellsberg's doctor's office and they had, they were geared up with all this CIA equipment—cameras and the like. Well they turned the stuff back in to the CIA some point in time and left film in the camera. CIA has not put this together, and they don't know what it all means right now. But it wouldn't take a very sharp investigator very long because you've got pictures in the CIA files that they had to turn over to (unintelligible).

P. What in the world—what in the name of God was Ehrlichman having something (unintelligible) in the Ellsberg (unintelligible)?

D. They were trying to—this was a part of an operation that—in connection with the Pentagon papers. They were—the whole thing—they wanted to get Ellsberg's psychiatric records for some reason. I don't know.

P. This is the first I ever heard of this. I, I (unintelligible) care about Ellsberg was not our problem.

D. That's right.

P. (Expletive deleted)

D. Well, anyway, (unintelligible) it was under an Ehrlichman structure, maybe John didn't ever know. I've never asked him if he knew. I didn't want to know.

Meeting of the President, Dean and Haldeman in the Oval Office on March 21 (10:12-11:55 a.m.):

P. What is the answer on this? How you keep it out, I don't know. You can't keep it out if Hunt talks. You see the point is irrelevant. It has gotten to this point—

D. You might put it on a national security grounds basis.

H. It absolutely was.

D. And say that this was—

H. (unintelligible)—CIA—

D. Ah—

H. Seriously,

P. National Security. We had to get information for national security grounds.

D. Then the question is, why didn't the CIA do it or why didn't the FBI do it?

P. Because we had to do it on a confidential basis.

H. Because we were checking them.

P. Neither could be trusted.

H. It has basically never been proven. There was reason to question their position.

P. With the bombing thing coming out and everything coming out, the whole thing was national security.

D. I think we could get by on that.

P. On that one I think we should simply say this was a national security investigation that was conducted. And on that basis, I think the same in the drug field with Krogh. Krogh could say feels he did not perjure himself. He could say it was a national security matter. That is why—

D. That is the way Bud rests easy, because he is convinced that he was doing. He said there was treason about the country, and it could have threatned the way the war was handled and (expletive deleted)—

P. Bud should just say it was a question of national security, and I was not in a position to divulge it. Anyway, let's don't go beyond that....

Meeting of the President, Haldeman and Ehrlichman, Oval Office, April 14, 1973 (8:55-11:31 a.m.):

P. Question, for example, is Hunt prepared to talk on other activities that he is engaged in?

E. Well, I think, I couldn't derive that.

P. You mean is he going to blow the White House on the—

E. I couldn't get that at all.

P. The U.S. Attorney, I would assume, would not be pressing on that.

E. Ordinarily not. McCord volunteered this Hank Greenspun thing, gratuitously apparently, not—

P. Can you tell me is that a serious thing? Did they really try to get into Hank Greenspun?

E. I guess they actually got in.

P. What in the name of (expletive deleted) though, has Hank Greenspun got with anything to do with Mitchell or anybody else?

E. Nothing. Well, now, Mitchell. Here's—Hughes. And these two fellows, Colson and (David) Shapiro (Colson's attorney and law partner), Colson threw that out.

P. Hughes on whom?

E. Well, you know the Hughes thing is cut into two factions—

E. I don't even know—but they're fighting.

P. Yeah.

E. Bennett, Senator Bennett's son, for whom Hunt worked,

P. Oh?

E. Represents one of those factions.

P. So he ordered the bugging?

E. I don't know. I know the (unintelligible) say it's a bag job.

H. They busted his safe to get something out of it. Wasn't that it?

E. No. They flew out, broke his safe, got something out (unintelligible). Now as they sat there in my office—

P. Other delicate things, too. You've got apart from my from my poor brother, which unfortunately or fortunately was a long time ago but, more recently, you've got Hubert Humphrey's son works for him and, of course, they're tied in with (Democratic National Chairman Lawrence) O'Brien I suppose. But maybe they were trying to get it for that reason.

'Hush Money' and Clemency

Did President Nixon authorize the payment of "hush money" to the Watergate defendants? Did he agree to grant clemency to persons convicted in connection with the break-in at Democratic national headquarters on June 17, 1972? The answer to these questions was crucial to the House Judiciary Committee in trying to decide whether Nixon himself participated in the Watergate cover-up.

The edited transcripts of recorded talks the White House gave to the committee and made public April 30 were, as Nixon said, subject to different interpretations. But the conversations between the President and key aides did provide some indications of Nixon's role.

Although he expressed sympathy for the clemency bid of convicted Watergate conspirator E. Howard Hunt Jr., whose wife had been killed in a plane crash, Nixon ultimately concluded that clemency could not be granted to any of those imprisoned until after the 1974 elections, if then. "No—it is wrong that's for sure," Nixon said.

What the transcripts did not make clear was whether Nixon viewed such action as morally wrong, or simply politically unwise.

On the issue of hush money, the transcripts were more ambiguous. They clearly showed that Nixon at least considered the option of paying off Hunt to keep him from revealing his involvement in the break-in of Daniel Ellsberg's psychiatrist's office. But they provided no firm evidence that such a payment was made on Nixon's instructions. Nixon appeared to view the payment of hush money only as a method of "buying time." In the end, he said, "we are going to be bled to death," and "it is all going to come out anyway."

Money for blackmail payments loomed as a major problem. Although Nixon said it would be possible to get the $1-million that White House counsel John W. Dean III said would be needed over the next two years, handling of the money promised to be difficult. "This is the sort of thing Mafia people can do," Dean said. Nixon agreed with Dean that White House people were "a bunch of amateurs," who did not know how to "wash" money.

The transcripts also showed a pervasive concern over obstruction of justice charges should hush money payments be revealed. The "motive" of the payments was discussed repeatedly. The hush money motive apparently was seldom mentioned explicitly, although presidential assistant John D. Ehrlichman, for one, said that "it was certainly understood."

Dean Disclosures. In a March 21, 1973, meeting with President Nixon, Dean reviewed past payments to the Watergate defendants and said that he, White House chief of staff H. R. Haldeman, Ehrlichman and John N. Mitchell, former attorney general and Nixon campaign chief, were involved in possible obstruction of justice. *(Complete text of March 21 transcript, p. 394)*

Dean's disclosure of Hunt's "blackmail" threats led to a discussion of hush money and clemency that formed the basis for subsequent conversations. Nixon appeared to agree that it would be "worthwhile" to pay Hunt as a means of "buying time." Ehrlichman later quoted Mitchell as saying that problem had been "taken care of." As for clemency, Nixon and Dean concluded it would be impossible at least until after the 1974 elections.

Meeting of the President, Dean and Haldeman in the Oval Office March 21, 1973 (10:12-11:55 a.m.):

Dean tells Nixon that Hunt is demanding an additional $72,000 for his own personal expenses and $50,000 for legal fees. Unless the money is paid, Hunt threatens to expose the "seamy things" he has done for Ehrlichman.

P. Was he talking about Ellsberg (Daniel Ellsberg, who faced charges in the Pentagon Papers case):

D. Ellsberg, and apparently some other things. I don't know the full extent of it.

P. I don't know about anything else.

D. I don't know either, and I hate to learn some of these things. So that is that situation. Now, where are at the soft points? How many people know about this? Well, let me go one step further in this whole thing. The Cubans that were used in the Watergate were also the same Cubans that Hunt and Liddy used for this California Ellsberg thing, for the break in out there. So they are aware of that. How high their knowledge is, is something else. Hunt and Liddy, of course, are totally aware of it, of the fact that it is right out of the White House.

P. I don't know what the hell we did that for!

D. I don't know either.

Dean goes on to list others with knowledge of the affair, including the Watergate defendants' lawyers, lawyers for the Nixon re-election committee, "an awful lot of the principals involved" and "some people's wives." Dean says Mrs. Hunt—"the savviest woman in the world"—"had the whole picture together."

P. Did she?

D. Yes. Apparently, she was a pillar of strength in that family before the death.

P. Great sadness. As a matter of fact, there was a discussion with somebody about Hunt's problem on account of his wife and I said, of course commutation could be considered on the basis of his wife's death, and that is the only conversation I ever had in that light.

D. Right.

D. So that is it. That is the extent of the knowledge. So where are the soft spots on this? Well, first of all, there is the problem of the continued blackmail which will not only go on now, but it will go on while these people are in prison, and it will compound the obstruction of justice situation. It will cost money. It is dangerous. People around here are not pros at this sort of thing. This is the sort of thing Mafia people can do: washing money, getting clean money, and things like that. We just don't know about those things, because we are not criminals and not used to dealing in that business.

P. That's right.

D. It is a tough thing to know how to do.

P. Maybe it takes a gang to do that.

D. That's right. There is a real problem as to whether we could even do it. Plus there is a real problem in raising money. Mitchell has been working on raising some money. He is one of the ones with the most to lose. But there is no denying the fact that the White House, in Ehrlichman, Haldeman and Dean are involved in some of the early money decisions.

P. How much money do you need?

D. I would say these people are going to cost a million dollars over the next two years.

P. We could get that. On the money, if you need the money you could get that. You could get a million dollars. You could get it in cash. I know

---

"...(I)t is going to require approximately a million dollars to take care of the jackasses who are in jail....
—President Nixon to John W. Dean III
March 21, 1973

---

where it could be gotten. It is not easy, but it could be done. But the question is who the hell would handle it? Any ideas on that?

D. That's right. Well, I think that is something that Mitchell ought to be charged with.

P. I would think so too.

D. And get some pros to help him.

A short time later, Nixon asks:

P. What do you think? You don't need a million right away, but you need a million? Is that right?

D. That is right.

P. You need it in cash don't you? I am just thinking out loud here for a moment. Would you put that through the Cuban Committee:

D. No.

P. It is going to be checks, cash money, etc. How if that ever comes out, are you going to handle it? Is the Cuban Committee an obstruction of justice, if they want to help?

D. Well they have priests in it.

P. Would that give a little bit of a cover?

D. That would give some for the Cubans and possibly Hunt. Then you've got Liddy. McCord (Watergate conspirators Hunt, G. Gordon Liddy and James W. McCord Jr.) is not accepting any money. So he is not a bought man right now.

After a brief discussion of other matters, the conversation returns to Hunt's demands.

P. Your major guy to keep under control is Hunt?

D. That is right.

P. I think. Does he know a lot?

D. He knows so much. He could sink (former presidential special counsel Charles W.) Chuck Colson. He thinks Colson has abandoned him. Colson was to meet with him when he was out there after, you know, he had left the White House. He met with him through his lawyer. Hunt raised the question he wanted money. Colson's lawyer told him Colson wasn't doing anything with money. Hunt took offense with that immediately, and felt Colson had abandoned him.

P. Just looking at the immediate problem, don't you think you have to handle Hunt's financial situation damn soon?

D. I think that is—I talked with Mitchell about that last night and—

P. It seems to me we have to keep the cap on the bottle that much, or we don't have any options.

D. That's right.

P. Either that or it all blows right now?

D. That's the question.

Later in the conversation, when Nixon questions Dean's assertion that he, Dean, had obstructed justice, Dean replies:

D. Well, I have been a conduit for information on taking care of people out there who are guilty of crimes.

P. Oh, you mean like the blackmailers?

D. The blackmailers. Right.

P. Well, I wonder if that part of it can't be—I wonder if that doesn't—let me put it frankly: I wonder if that doesn't have to be continued? Let me put it this way: let us suppose that you get the million bucks, and you get the proper way to handle it. You could hold that side?

D. Uh, huh.

P. It would seem to me that would be worthwhile.

D. Well, that's one problem.

P. I know you have a problem here. You have the problem with Hunt and his clemency.

D. That's right. And you are going to have a clemency problem with the others. They all are going to expect to be out and that may put you in a position that is just untenable at some point. You know, the Watergate Hearings just over, Hunt now demanding clemency or he is going to blow. And politically, it's impossible for you to do it. You know, after everybody—

P. That's right!

D. I am not sure that you will ever be able to deliver on the clemency. It may be just too hot.

P. You can't do it politically until after the '74 elections, that's for sure. Your point is that even then you couldn't do it.

D. That's right. It may further involve you in a way you should not be involved in this.

P. No—it is wrong that's for sure.

The question of continued payments is less easily resolved:

D. What I am coming in today with is: I don't have a plan on how to solve it right now, but I think it is at the juncture that we should begin to think in terms of how to cut the losses; how to minimize the further growth of this thing, rather than further compound it by, you know, ultimately paying these guys forever. I think we've got to look—

P. But at the moment, don't you agree it is better to get the Hunt thing that's where that—

D. That is worth buying time on

P. That is buying time, I agree.

Later, Nixon pursues this line:

P. If, for example, you say look we are not going to continue to—let's say, frankly, on the assumption that if we continue to cut our losses, we are not going to win. But in the end, we are going to be bled to death. And in the end, it is all going to come out anyway. Then you get the worst of both worlds. We are going to lose, and people are going to—

H. And look like dopes!

P. And in effect, look like a cover-up. So that we can't do.

Still later:

P. Another way to do it then Bob, and John realizes this, is to continue to try to cut our losses. Now we have to take a look at that course of action. First it going to require approximately a million dollars to take care of the jackasses who are in jail. That can be arranged. That could be arranged. But you realize that after we are gone, and assuming we can expend this money, then they are going to crack and it would be an unseemly story.

Finally, reverting to Hunt's threats to testify, Nixon apparently reaches a decision:

P. That's why for your immediate things you have no choice but to come up with the $120,000, or whatever it is. Right?

D. That's right.

P. Would you agree that that's the prime thing that you damn well better get that done?

Meeting of the President, Haldeman and Ehrlichman in the Executive Office Building April 14, 1973 (8:55-11:31 a.m.):

Nixon returns to the issue of Hunt's payoff demand:

P. This business, somebody in—Dean, Dean. Dean asked, told me about the problem of Hunt's lawyer. This was a few weeks ago. Needed sixty thousand or forty thousand dollars or something like that. You remember? I said I don't know where you can get it. I said, I mean, I frankly felt he might try to get it but I didn't know where. And then, he left it up with Mitchell and Mitchell said it was taken care of and after (unintelligible). Did he talk to you about that?

E. He talked to me about it. I said, John, I wouldn't have the vaguest notion where to get it.

P. Yeah.

E. I saw him later in the day. I saw Mitchell later in the day—

P. What happened?

E. And he just said, "It's taken care of."

Meeting of the President and Dean in the Oval Office, April 16, 1973 (10:00-10:40 a.m.):

Nixon asks Dean to sign a letter of resignation so that he would have it in hand in case someone says, " 'What the hell. After Dean told you all of this, what did you do?' "

Later Nixon tells Dean that Assistant Attorney General Henry E. Petersen "seems to think that the obstruction of justice thing is a (expletive deleted) hard thing to prove in court." Nixon goes on to ask Dean a series of questions about Hunt's demands for money.

P. What was the situation, John? The only time I ever heard any discussion of support for the defense fund was (inaudible). I guess I should have assumed somebody was helping them. I must have assumed it. But I must say people were good in a way because I was busy. Was when you mentioned to me something about hard-hitting problem. But that was handled by Mitchell. Was that true or what?

D. The last time we had a request was the week before sentencing.

P. He hit you at a dinner or something?

D. No, no. (Paul L.) O'Brien, who was one of the lawyers who was representing the Re-Election Committee, was asked by Hunt to meet with him. He came to me after the meeting and said that Hunt asked that the following message be passed to you. I said, "why me?" He said, "I asked Hunt the same question."

P. You, Dean—or me, the President?

D. Passed to me, Dean.

P. He had never asked you before?

D. No.

P. Let me tell you. What did you report to me on though. It was rather fragmentary, as I recall it. You said Hunt had a problem—

D. Very fragmentary. I was—

P. I said, "Why, John, how much is it going to cost to do this?" That is when I sent you to Camp David and said (expletive removed) "Let's see where this thing comes out."

D. That's right.

P. And you said it could cost a million dollars.

D. I said it conceivably could. I said, "If we don't cut this thing—"

P. How was that handled? Who handled the money?

D. Well, let me tell you the rest of what Hunt said. He said, "You tell Dean that I need $72,000 for my personal expenses, $50,000 for my legal fees and if I don't get it I am going to have some things to say about the seamy things I did at the White House for John Ehrlichman." Alright I took that to John Ehrlichman. Ehrlichman said, "Have you talked to Mitchell about it?" I said, "No, I have not." He said, "Well, will you talk to Mitchell?" I said, "Yes I will." I talked to Mitchell. I just passed it along to him. And then we were meeting down here a few days later in Bob's office with Bob and Ehrlichman, and Mitchell and myself, and Ehrlichman said at that time, "Well is that problem with Hunt straightened out?" He said it to me and I said "Well, ask the man who may know: Mitchell." Mitchell said, "I think that problem is solved."

P. That's all?

D. That's all he said.

P. In other words, that was done at the Mitchell level?

D. That's right.

P. But you had knowledge; Haldeman had knowledge; Ehrlichman had knowledge and I suppose I did that night. That assumes culpability on that, doesn't it?

D. I don't think so.

P. Why not? I plan to be tough on myself so I can handle the other thing. I must say I did not even give it a thought at the time.

D. No one gave it a thought at the time.

P. You didn't tell me this about Ehrlichman, for example, when you came in that day.

D. I know.

P. You simply said, "Hunt needs this money." You were using it as an example of the problems ahead.

D. I have tried all along to make sure that anything I passed to you myself didn't cause you any personal problems.

Clemency Promises. Although Nixon and Dean concluded in their March 21 meeting that clemency could not be considered at least until after the 1974 elections, the clemency issue continued to come up in later meetings. Of particular concern to Nixon and his aides were assurances of clemency that Charles Colson, who had left the White House, was thought to have made to Hunt.

Meeting of the President, Haldeman and Ehrlichman in the Executive Office Building April 14, 1973 (8:55-11:31 a.m.):

Nixon asks if Hunt will testify that Colson promised him clemency.

E. No. Apparently not.

P. You see the only possible involvement of the President in this is that, now apparently John, either you or Bob or Dean, somebody told me they said, told Colson not to discuss it with me.

E. I did.

P. You did? How did it get to you then John? How did you know that the matter had to be discussed with (William O.) Bittman (Hunt's lawyer) or something like that?

E. Well, I—

P. When did this happen? As I remember a conversation this day was about five thirty or six o'clock that Colson only dropped it in sort of parenthetically, said I had a little problem today, talking about Hunt, and said I sought to reassure him, you know, and so forth. And I said, well. Told me about Hunt's wife. I said it was a terrible thing and I said obviously we will do just, we will take that into consideration. That was the total of the conversation.

Ehrlichman describes his own conversations with Colson about Hunt:

E. And he said, "What can I tell him about clemency or pardon." And I said, "You can't tell him anything about clemency or pardon." And I said, "Under no circumstances should this ever be raised with the President."

Subsequently, Ehrlichman says Colson told him that "he was very skillful in avoiding any commitment" in talking with Hunt's lawyer. Haldeman then interjects that Colson "said you (Ehrlichman) and Dean told him to promise clemency, but that he was smarter than you and didn't."

Later, Nixon asks how the problem of clemency is to be handled.

H. Well, you don't handle it at all. That's Colson's, cause that's where it comes from.

E. That was the line of communication—

P. Colson to Bittman. I guess that's the only thing we have on that—except Mitchell, apparently had said something about clemency to people.

H. To Liddy.

P. And Mitchell has never, never—Has he ever discussed clemency with you?

E. No.

P. Has he ever discussed it with you?

H. No.

P. (unintelligible) We were all here the room.

H. Well, may have said, "Look we've got to take care of this."

P. But's he's never said, "Look you're going to get a pardon from these people when this is over." Never used any such language around here, has he, John?

E. Not to me.

H. I don't think so.

P. With Dean has he?

E. Well I don't know. That's a question I can't answer.

P. Well, but Dean's never raised it.

Meeting of the President and Dean in the Oval Office April 16, 1973 (10:00-10:40 a.m.):

P. Well, you take, for example, the clemency bit. That is solely Mitchell apparently and Colson's talk with Bittmann where he says he will do everything I can because as a friend.

D. No, that was with Ehrlichman.

P. Hunt?

D. That was with Ehrlichman.

P. Ehrlichman with whom?

D. Ehrlichman, and Colson and I sat up there. Colson presented his story to Ehrlichman regarding it and then John gave Chuck very clear instructions on going back and telling him, "Give him the inference he's got clemency but don't give him any commitment."

P. No commitment.

D. Right.

P. That's alright. No commitment. I have a right to say here—take a fellow like Hunt or a Cuban whose wife is sick or something and give them clemency for that purpose—isn't that right?

D. That's right.

P. But John specifically said, "No commitment," did he?

D. Yes.

P. And then Colson went on apparently to—

D. I don't know how Colson delivered it—

P. To Hunt's lawyer—isn't that your understanding?

D. Yes, but I don't know what he did or how—

P. Where did this business of the Christmas thing get out, John? What in the hell is that all about it? That must have been Mitchell, huh?

D. No, that was Chuck again.

P. That they would all be out by Christmas?

D. No, I think he said something to the effect that Christmas is the time the clemency generally occurs.

P. Oh yeah. Well, I don't think that is going to hurt him. Do you?

D. No.

P. Clemency is one thing. He is a friend of Hunt's. I am just trying to put the best face on it, but if it is the wrong thing to do I have to know.

Money for Payments. The problem of obtaining money for payments to the Watergate defendants was a source of continuing concern to participants in the conversations. President Nixon reacted with shock when told by Dean March 21 that campaign aide Frederick C.

LaRue had "started out going out trying to solicit money from all kinds of people," including Nixon re-election fund raiser Thomas A. Pappas. Other sources of money were discussed, including funds held by Nixon lawyer Herbert W. Kalmbach and $350,000 in cash held by Haldeman, most of which ultimately was returned to the re-election committee.

Meeting of the President, Dean and Haldeman in the Oval Office March 21, 1973 (10:12-11:55 a.m.):

Nixon says that "we could get the money" and that "Mitchell could provide the way to deliver it." Haldeman cautions: "I don't see how there is any way that you can have the White House or anybody presently in the White House involved in trying to gin out this money."

D. We are already deeply enough in that. That is the problem, Bob.

P. I thought you said—

H. We need more money.

D. Well, in fact when—

P. Kalmbach?

D. Well, Kalmbach.

H. He's not the one.

D. No, but when they ran out of that money, as you know it came out of the 350,000 that was over here.

P. And they knew that?

D. And I had to explain what it was for before I could get the money.

H. In the first place, that was put back to LaRue.

D. That's right.

H. It was put back where it belonged. It wasn't all returned in a lump sum. It was put back in pieces.

D. That's right.

P. Then LaRue used it for this other purpose?

D. That's right.

Later, pre-election payments to the defendants are discussed.

D. These fellows could have sold out to the Democrats for one-half a million.

P. These fellows though, as far as what has happened up to this time, are covered on their situation, because the Cuban Committee did this for them during the election?

D. Well, yeah. We can put that together. That isn't of course quite the way it happened, but—

P. I know, but that's the way it is going to have to happen.

D. It's going to have to happen.

As the meeting continues, Dean says that "one of the real problems" is that "they haven't been able to raise a million dollars in cash." The need for secrecy appears to be a major stumbling block.

D. It sounds easy to do and everyone is out there doing it and that is where our breakdown has come every time.

P. Well, if you had it, how would you get it to somebody?

D. Well, I got it to LaRue by just leaving it in mail boxes and things like that. And someone phones Hunt to come and pick it up. As I say, we are a bunch of amateurs in that business.

H. That is the thing that we thought Mitchell ought to be able to know how to find somebody who would know how to do all that sort of thing, because none of us know how to.

D. That's right. You have to wash the money. You can get a $100,000 out of a bank, and it all comes in serialized bills.

P. I understand.

D. And that means you have to go to Vegas with it or a bookmaker in New York City. I have learned all these things after the fact. I will be in great shape for the next time around.

H. (Expletive deleted)

P. Well, of course you have a surplus from the campaign. Is there any other money hanging around?

H. Well, what about the money we moved back out of here?

D. Apparently, there is some there. That might be what they can use. I don't know how much is left.

P. Kalmbach must have some.

D. Kalmbach doesn't have a cent.

P. He doesn't?

H. That $350,000 that we moved out was all that we saved. Because they were afraid to because of this. That is the trouble. We are so (adjective deleted) square that we get caught at everything.

Obstruction of Justice. The question of motives was a recurrent theme throughout the transcripts. Those who had knowledge of, or played an active role in, the payments to the Watergate defendants exhibited a nagging concern over whether they were liable to charges of obstruction of justice. At issue was the question of whether the payments were made for the purpose of handling legal fees and family support or whether they were hush money intended to ensure the defendants' silence.

Meeting of the President, Haldeman and Ehrlichman in the Executive Office Building April 14, 1973 (8:55-11:31 a.m.):

Ehrlichman reports that Hunt apparently is prepared to testify that the payments were hush money:

P. Hunt then is going to go. Now that raises the problem on Hunt with regard to Kalmbach. He has possible vulnerability as to whether he was aware, in other words, the motive, the motive,—

E. This doesn't add anything to do with Kalmbach's problem at all.

P. What happened on that? Dean called Kalmbach? And what did Dean call Kalmbach about?

E. He said we have to raise some money in connection with the aftermath, and I don't know how he described it. Herb said how much do you need, and

P. It was never discussed then?

E. Presumably Dean told him, and Herb went to a couple of donors and got some money and sent it back.

H. Dean says very flatly that Kalmbach did not know the purpose of the money and has no problem.

P. Dean did know the purpose? Hunt testifies—so basically then Hunt will testify that it was so-called hush money. Right?

E. I think so....

Subsequently, Haldeman remarks that "the line they used around here" was "that we've got to have money for their legal fees and family."

P. Support. Well, I heard something about that a much later time.
H. Yeah.
P. And, frankly, not knowing much about obstruction of justice, I thought it was perfectly proper.
E. Well, it's like—
P. Would it be perfectly proper?
E. The defense of the—
P. Berrigans?
E. The Chicago Seven.
P. The Chicago Seven?
H. They have a defense fund for everybody.
P. Not only a defense fund—they take care of the living expenses, too...Despite all this about legal fees, they take care of themselves. They raise—you remember the Scottsboro case? The Communist front raised a million dollars for the Scottsboro people. Nine hundred thousand went into the pockets of the Communists. So it's common practice.
E. Yeah.
P. Nevertheless, that Hunt then saying there was a pay-off.

Meeting of the President, Haldeman and Ehrlichman in the Executive Office Building April 14, 1973 (8:55-11:31 a.m.):

The conversation focuses on the number of persons who knew about the payments to the Watergate defendants and the implications of that knowledge:

P. Well, I knew it. I knew it.
E. And it was not a question of whether—
P. I must say though, I didn't know it but I must have assumed it though but you know, fortunately—I thank you both for arranging it that way and it does show the isolation of the President, and here it's not so bad—But the first time that I knew that they had to have the money was the time when Dean told me that they needed forty thousand dollars. I had been, frankly, (unintelligible) papers on those little envelopes. I didn't know about the envelopes (unintelligible) and all that stuff.
E. The point is that if Dean's, if the wrongdoing which justifies Dean's dismissal is his knowledge that that operation was going on, then you can't stop with him. You've got to go through a whole place wholesale.
P. Fire the whole staff.

"That's right," Ehrlichman agrees. The conversation then turns to Dean's motive and role, with Ehrlichman stating: "...I don't think Dean's role in the aftermath, at least from the facts that I know now, achieves a level of wrongdoing that requires you to terminate him."

H. What Dean did, he did with all conscience in terms that the higher good.
P. Dean, you've got to have a talk with Dean. I feel that I should not talk to him.

E. I have talked to him.
P. I mean about motive.
E. I have talked to him.
P. What's he say about motive. He says' it was hush-up?
E. No. He says he knew, he had to know that people were trying to bring that result about.
P. Right.
E. And he says, you know, the way I got into this was I was I would go to meetings in campaign headquarters and we'd get through the meeting and Mitchell and LaRue would say to—Mardian and LaRue would say to Mitchell, "You've got to do something about this." And Mitchell's stock answer was, to turn to John Dean and say, "What are you going to do?" And so John said, "I got to be kind of a water carrier. I'd come back from those meetings and I'd come in to see Bob," or me or somebody else, and say, "Well Mitchell's got this big problem." And then he'd say, "They'd say to me, 'well I don't know what I'll do about it.' "
P. When he came in to see Bob and you what would he say was the problem?
E. He'd say, "These guys, Hunt's getting jittery, and says that he's got to have umpty-ump thousand dollars, and Mitchell's terribly worried about it," and it was never expressed, but it was certainly understood—
P. On the question of motive then, though, I guess in those conversations with you with respect to motive was never discussed.
E. Never discussed with me in those terms.
P. Right. The motive was to help defendants who were, by golly, who had worked for the campaign committee.

Meeting of the President and Ehrlichman in the Oval Office April 15, 1973 (10:35-11:15 a.m.):

During a discussion of obstruction of justice, Nixon asks: "What was involved? I mean, from our side, our guys."

E. Well you had defendents who were concerned about their families. That's understandable. You had lawyers who were concerned about their fees and that's less understandable.
P. Oh yes. It's understandable.
E. Well I mean in terms of the end result. You had a campaign organization that was concerned about the success of its campaign....
P. Yes.
E. and didn't want these fellows to say anything in public that would disrupt the campaign.
P. Is that legitimate to want people not to say it out in public which (unintelligible)?
E. I think so. I think so. And then you had a....
P. No, but I mean, say something in public that would disrupt the campaign or because it would embarrass people?
E. Sure.
P. Cover up, you mean?
E. It would impeach the campaign in effect. But at the same time a lot of those same people who

had that legitimate motive—Hello (unintelligible) (Voice: Hello, sir. (door opens and closes)) they had the same people who had that legitimate motive had an illegitimate motive because they were involved in protecting their own culpability and here we're talking about LaRue, (Nixon campaign official Jeb Stuart) Magruder, Mitchell possibly. (Unintelligible) they wanted the defendents to shut up in court?

E. Certainly, certainly.

P. So you would say, you could say....

E. You have.

In a discussion of Dean's situation, Ehrlichman says that if he were Dean, "I would develop a defense that I was being manipulated by people who had a corrupt motive for ostensibly a benign motive."

Turning to his own motives, Ehrlichman recalled that Howard Hunt had written 40 books.

E. Howard Hunt was worried about the support of his family. And I could see Howard Hunt writing an inside expose of how he broke into the Democratic National Headquarters at the request of the Committee to Re-elect the President.

P. Yeah.

E. Now, if I had a choice between getting contributions for the support of Howard Hunt's family.

P. Yeah. And that's...

E. And that was pretty easy.

Further, Ehrlichman added:

E. I can say in truth and candor that Dean never explained to me that there was any kind of a deal to get these guys to lie or to change their stories or to refuse to testify to the trial of the action or anything of that kind. That was just never discussed. So I don't feel too uncomfortable with this.

Meeting of the President and Kleindienst in the Executive Office Building April 15, 1973 (1:12-2:22 p.m.):

At Nixon's request Attorney General Richard G. Kleindienst explains the legal distinction between legitimate defense support payments and obstruction of justice:

P. Of course I was thinking of the Berrigans and all the funds that have been raised through the years, Scottsboro, etc. Nobody ever raised any question about it. If you raise money for the defense and it's for support—and Ellsberg (expletive removed) in Ellsberg, the defense—

K. And likewise in this case. If I had committed a crime and you know about it and you say, "Kleindienst, you go in the Court and plead guilty to the commission of that crime and here is ten thousand dollars, you know, to tide you over and so forth."

P. That isn't a crime?

K. No. On the other, if you know that I committed a crime.

P. Right.

K. And you say, "you go in there and plead guilty, and here is twenty-five thousand dollars on the condition that thereafter you'll say nothing. You just make the plea, take the Fifth Amend-

ment, the judge cites you for contempt, you've got to continue to testify you don't. You do not take it." Then you are now in a position of obstructing justice.

Meeting of the President, Haldeman, Ehrlichman and Zeigler in the Oval Office April 17, 1973 (12:35-2:20 p.m.):

Nixon refers to what Dean previously told him about payments to the Watergate defendants, and there is a discussion of what to do with Dean. Nixon then turns to a rationale for the payments:

P. Have you thought when you say before it gets to (unintelligible) thing out of the way. Have you given any thought to what the line ought to be—I don't mean a lie—but a line, on raising the money for these defendants? Because both of you were aware of what was going on you see—the raising of the money—you were aware of it, right?

E. Yes, sir.

P. And you were aware—You see, you can't go in and say I didn't know what in hell he wanted the $250 for.

H. No—I've given a great deal of thought (unintelligible)

P. Well I wonder. I'm not—look—I'm concerned about the legal thing Bob, and so forth. You say that our purpose was to keep them from talking to the press.

E. Well, that was my purpose—and before I get too far out on that, ah, I want to talk to an attorney and find out what the law is—which I have not yet done.

P. Right!

H. That's just what I want to do too. This is only a draft.

P. Right. Good. The only point is I, I think it is not only that but you see that involves all our people. That's what I feel—it involves Kalmbach—

E. Well.

P. And what to hell Kalmbach was told.

E. Well, Mr. President, when the truth and fact of this known, that building next door is full of people who knew that money was being raised for these people.

P. EOB?

E. Yes, sir, just full of them.

P. Many who know, but there were not so many actors. In other words, there's a difference between actors and noticees.

E. O.K. Well, apparently not, because I'm not an actor, ah—

Nixon and Haldeman review Dean's initial account of Hunt's blackmail demands. Both agree that although they explored the possibility of raising money for such a purpose, neither of them had told Dean to go get the money.

"I said you got to talk to Mitchell," Haldeman said. "This is something you've got to work out with Mitchell—not here—there's nothing we can do about it here."

Shortly thereafter, Nixon said: "Well (inaudible). I suppose we should have cut—shut it off, 'cause later on you met in your office and Mitchell said, 'That was taken care of.'"

Petersen and the White House

The transcripts disclosed how Henry E. Petersen, assistant attorney general in charge of the criminal division of the Justice Department, kept the White House closely informed about the progress of the government's investigation of Watergate.

First dealing with Dean and then at times in daily contact with Nixon, Petersen provided information about grand jury testimony and potential witnesses, what potential witnesses were telling the Watergate prosecutors, then led by assistant U.S. attorney Earl J. Silbert, and kept Nixon abreast of the status of the inquiry.

Nixon at times apparently relayed this information to his two top advisers, Ehrlichman and Haldeman, even though Petersen had told Nixon that both were potential defendants in the criminal trials that were likely to result from the inquiry. The transcripts show Nixon at one point advising Ehrlichman and Haldeman to prepare defenses against possible charges against them.

Petersen repeatedly assured Nixon of his belief that Nixon was not involved in the case, and in any event that Petersen did not believe it was the duty of the Justice Department to investigate the President himself.

The New York Times reported May 3 that the prosecution team headed by Silbert warned Petersen that Petersen himself was scheduled to be a key witness against Dean and therefore he should not continue advising Nixon. As a result of Petersen's refusal to stop sharing information with the President, the Silbert team broke contact with Petersen on April 25.

After release of the transcripts Petersen May 2, 1974, defended his actions.

"I'm not a whore," Petersen said during a brief meeting with newsmen outside his office. "I walked through a minefield and came out clean. You newspaper people are disappointed that I'm not a whore."

"First of all, Henry was dealing with the President," said one Justice official, who asked not to be named, in offering an explanation for Petersen's actions. "Here he is: a guy who started his government career as an FBI messenger, and now he's dealing with Nixon. It was very overwhelming. And then, I think he worried that if he got out—recused himself—it would be a terrible blow to his reputation."

Petersen and Dean. The tapes show that Petersen began passing information about the government's Watergate inquiry during the early stages of the case. This apparently led to White House staffers coaching some of those who were subsequently called to testify before the Watergate grand jury.

During the March 21, 1973, meeting Dean told Nixon that after the June 17, 1972 break-in and arrests, "I was under pretty clear instructions not to investigate this, but this could have been disastrous on the electorate if all hell had broken loose. I worked on a theory of containment."

Meeting of Nixon, Dean and Haldeman, Oval Office, March 21, 1973 (10:12—11:55):

P. Sure.

D. To try to hold it right where it was.

P. Right.

D. There is no doubt that I was totally aware of what the Bureau was doing at all times. I was totally aware of what the Grand Jury was doing. I knew what witnesses were going to be called. I knew what they were asked, and I had to.

P. Why did Peterson play the game so straight with us?

D. Because Peterson is a soldier. He kept me informed. He told me when we had problems, where we had problems and the like. He believes in you and he believes in this Administration. This Administration has made him. I

"I was totally aware of what the grand jury was doing. I knew what witnesses were going to be called. I knew what they were asked, and I had to."

—John Dean III to President Nixon
March 21, 1973

---

don't think he has done anything improper, but did make sure that the investigation was narrowed down to the very, very fine criminal thing which was a break for us. There is no doubt about it.

P. Do you honestly feel that he did an adequate job?

D. They ran that investigation out to the fullest extend they could follow a lead and that was it.

P. But the way point is, where I suppose he could be criticized for not doing an adequate job. Why didn't he call Haldeman? Why didn't he get a statement from Colson? Oh, they did get Colson!

D. That's right. But as based on their FBI interviews, there was no reason to follow up. There were no leads there. Colson said, "I have no knowledge." They didn't ask Strachan any questions about Watergate. They asked him about Segretti. They said, "what is your connection with Liddy?" Strachan just said, "Well, I met him over there." They never really pressed him. Strachan appeared, as a result of some coaching, to be the dumbest paper pusher in the bowels of the White House.

P. I understand.

Nixon and Ehrlichman at one point discussed the coaching of witnesses based on Dean's information from the Grand Jury.

Meeting of Nixon and Ehrlichman in the Oval Office, April 15, 1973 (10:35—11:15 a.m.):

E. ...I may have told you about this, but the U.S. Attorney now feels that Dean overreached them by providing information out of the Grand Jury to the Committee for the Re-election. I think that may be legitimate criticism if he in fact did that. On the other hand, for him to provide us with information inside, for the orderly operation of the government, is another matter. That's two quite different things. If you peddle information from a Grand Jury to the outside, or if you peddle it inside to people Who are responsible.

P. (Unintelligible)

E. Oh that was, let me think.

P. (Unintelligible) Grand Jury at that point.

E. He had information on who was going to be called as witnesses so that apparently Mardian was able to get around and coach witnesses.

P. Did Mardian coach them?

E. In some cases Mardian, I guess, was very heavy-handed about it, and—

P. Well, is there anything wrong with that?

E. Yeah, well there's something wrong with—

P. He was not their attorneys is the problem?

E. Well, no, the problem—the problem is he asked them to say things that weren't true.

P. Oh.

E. When I say coach I use the word loosely, and—

P. (Unintelligible)

In one of Nixon's subsequent meetings with Petersen, Petersen acknowledged that Dean had made use of grand

---

"That comes out to a misprision of a felony. Misprision is a statute that is hardly ever enforced. You could put everybody in jail I suppose if you tried to."

—Henry Petersen to President Nixon
April 16, 1973

---

jury information—which Petersen said Dean "was allegedly developing for you as President's counsel to keep you informed of what was going on."

Meeting of Nixon and Petersen in the Executive Office Building, April 16, 1973 (1:39—3:25 p.m.):

HP I told Dean that he (Magruder) made a good witness in his own behalf.

P. But the Jury didn't believe him?

HP. But the Jury had some difficulty in accepting the story with respect to the money—that is—that anyone could...

P. Oh you mean the money for the bugging.

HP. (inaudible) hundred thousand dollars and not ask what the hell Liddy was doing with it, which is what Magruder was testifying to.

P. OK—go ahead.

HP. Dean then calls Magruder, according to Magruder, and says Petersen says you've passed. Now that has great relevance in terms of the subornation of perjury charge. And the possibilities are...

P. Well, when (inaudible) after—Dean said, you passed?

HP. Yeah—the possibility is that I could be witness.

P. Dean told Magruder—you passed. That's what Magruder says.

HP. That's right.

P. So you—and that—how's that involve subornation and perjury? Oh, I see.

HP. See they previously could engage in the cultured story—then go in. Dean was party to that. After he testifies, Dean calls me and says how did he do? I tell him. Dean then passes it on to Magruder, in effect—and "I told you it would be all right if you just testify the way we said, Petersen says you passed." I—conceivably, I could be a witness on that issue.

P. But

HP. Silbert

P. Is?

HP. No, no sir—he is not (inaudible). (Inaudible) it.

P. (Inaudible) not supposed to talk to you—and you were not supposed to tell Dean (inaudible).

HP. I didn't tell him (inaudible).

P. He's conducting an investigation for the President.

HP. That's right.

P. Damnit, I'm entitled to know this.

HP. And I can tell under the rule

P. Yeah.

HP. Those that (inaudible) to the extent that it's necessary to discharge my obligation

P. Yeah.

HP. And I didn't tell him any testimony in any event.

P. I see.

HP. I told him what occurred, that is to say the Grand Jury didn't believe his story—yes he was a good witness on his own behalf.

P. That's right.

HP. But I don't think. That's

P. You characterized it rather than give him the substance of it.

HP. That's right. That's right.

Petersen and Nixon. Nixon put Petersen in charge of the Watergate inquiry on April 15, 1973—a Sunday. According to the White House, the tape ran out before they had their first meeting that day. But a telephone conversation that evening showed Peterson providing information of the status of the inquiry and indicated he had given Nixon a fuller briefing earlier in the day. Nixon seemed particularly interested in learning whether Dean had struck a bargain with the prosecutors. Dean had begun secretly talking to the prosecutors as early as May 8 under an agreement that they would not use his information unless the prosecutors granted Dean immunity from prosecution. Earlier tapes indicated that Nixon knew that Dean's testimony would implicate Ehrlichman and Haldeman in the coverup.

Telephone conversation between Nixon and Petersen, April 15, 1973 (8:14—8:18 p.m.):

P. ...Anything further you want to report tonight before our meeting tomorrow at 12:30?

HP. Not anything that specially, that I didn't give you today.

P. Nothing that adds to what we had earlier, huh?

HP. That's right—they concluded the meeting with Dean. His counsel says he will not permit him to plead; that a—

P. Permit him to plead? What do you mean by that?

HP. To plead guilty. In other words, he will go to trial.

P. He is going to plead not guilty, huh?

HP. That's right, unless we come to some agreement with him. His counsel's position is that it would be a travesty to try Dean and not try Ehrlichman and Haldeman.

P. Uh, huh.

HP. That is the basic information to the extent that it developed in these preliminary negotiations isn't much more than I gave you.

P. Well, let me ask you this. Based on this, though, you mean that inhibits you from using the information the, or do you use it, or how do you do it, or do you use it for leads, but you can't use it unless he pleads? right?

HP. We cannot use it for any purpose unless he pleads.

P. For no purpose?

HP. That's right. That's incorrect, unless we strike some agreement with him.

P. Hmp.

Nixon loyalty to aides. Nixon's fierce loyalty to Ehrlichman and Haldeman was underscored at a meeting with his two aides during which they discussed the threat of Dean's possible testimony if Nixon were to fire him.

Meeting of Nixon, Haldeman, Ehrlichman and Ziegler, Oval Office, April 17, 1973 (12:35—2:20 p.m.):

P. Well, the point is can we survive it (the testimony)?

E. Well—

P. Can Haldeman and Ehrlichman survive it. The point that I—Let me say this. I know your (unintelligible) It's a hell of a lot different that John Dean. I know that as far as you're concerned, you'll go out and throw yourselves on a damned sword. I'm aware of that. I'm trying to think the thing through with that in mind because, damn it, you're the two most valuable members on the staff. I know that. The problem is, you're the two most loyal and the two most honest. We don't have to go into that. You know how I feel about that. It's not bull—it's the truth. The problem we got here is this. I do not want to be in a position where the damned public clamour makes, as it did with Eisenhower, with Adams, makes it necessary or calls—to have Bob come in one day and say, "Well Mr. President, the public—blah blah blah—I'm going to leave." Now that's the real problem on this damned thing and I don't think that kicking Dean out of here is going to do it. Understand, I'm not ruling out kicking him out. But I think you got to figure what to hell does Dean know. What kind of blackmail does he have? I don't know what all he does—

The tapes show that Petersen apparently did not detect the intensity of this attitude of protectiveness on the part of Nixon, which led to some conversations that seemed at cross purposes.

During a key meeting, Petersen suggested that Haldeman and Ehrlichman would have to resign—not necessarily because they were guilty of crimes, but for the sake of preserving the public image of the White House. Petersen gave Nixon information about what Dean and Magruder had been telling the prosecutors. The information implicated Haldeman in the Watergate break-in and Ehrlichman in the coverup. Nixon defended Haldeman on the grounds that while Haldeman might not have actively halted the bugging operation, he had not approved it. Petersen then told Nixon if Haldeman had known about it and not stopped it, he was guilty of a crime.

Meeting of Nixon and Petersen in the Executive Office Building, April 16, 1973 (1:39—3:25 p.m.):

P. That would not make Haldeman liable in this case— the very fact he didn't stop it. He didn't have the responsibility. I am looking at it just from a legal standpoint. Now understand, from a public standpoint it's devastating. You think he would be liable for not issuing an order to (inaudible). I suppose if Dean was his subordinate. (Inaudible)

HP. (Inaudible) a subordinate. It depends on who has authority to act with respect to the budget proposals?

P. Haldeman (inaudible).

HP. He did not have any authority?

P. No sir—none, none—all Mitchell—campaign funds. He had no authority whatever. I wouldn't let him (inaudible).

HP. Then you're left with the fact that he has knowledge of

P. That's right.

HP. but he doesn't act upon.

P. Knowledge of a proposal?

HP. that comes out as a misprision of a felony.

P. Huh?

HP. That comes out to a misprision of a felony. Misprision is a statute that is hardly ever enforced. You could put everybody in jail I suppose if you tried to.

P. Knowledge and so on?

HP. That's right.

P. Knowledge it's being considered.

HP. That's right. (Inaudible) type of thing—

P. (Inaudible) say specifically that he discussed the budget proposal with Haldeman! Well I'll be damned!

In a meeting with Ehrlichman and Ziegler immediately following this conversation Nixon told Ehrlichman, "I've got Petersen on a short leash."

Nixon Pledge. In their next conversation Nixon assured Petersen he would not pass along to anyone Petersen's information about the grand jury. Petersen then told Nixon that LaRue had testified freely.

Telephone conversation between Nixon and Petersen, April 16, 1973 (8:58—9:14 p.m.):

P. ...Let me say first, I just want to know if there are any developments I should know about and, second, that of course, as you know, anything you tell me, as I think I told you earlier, will not be passed on.

HP. I understand, Mr. President.

P. Because I know the rules of the Grand Jury.

HP. Now—LaRue was in and he was rather pitiful. He came down with O'Brien and said he didn't want private counsel at all. He just wanted to do what he did. He told John Mitchell that it was "all over."

P. He said he had told John Mitchell that?

HP. Yes, He, LaRue, admits to participating in the (unintelligible) and obstruction of justice.

Petersen then gave Nixon a report of what Dean had been telling the prosecutors. He told Nixon that Colson and Kalmbach would be called as grand jury witnesses as a result of Dean's information. At one point Nixon said he needed this information "to get the timing, you see, with regard to whatever I say," presumably meaning in public statements.

HP. Ah, then you also asked about Colson. Colson and Dean were together with Ehrlichman when Ehrlichman advised about Hunt to get out of town and thereafter—

P. Colson was there?

HP. Colson was there so he is going to be in the Grand Jury. With respect to Haldeman, another matter. In connection with payments of money after—

P. the fact.

HP. June 17th, Mitchell requested Dean to activate Kalmbach. Dean said he didn't have that authority and he went to Haldeman.

P. Uh, huh.

HP. Haldeman gave him the authority.

P. Haldeman gave him the authority.

P. Uh, huh.

HP. He then got in touch with Kalmbach to arrange for money, the details of which we really don't know as yet.

P. Right.

HP. So Kalmbach is also a Grand Jury witness to be called. And I think those are the only additional developments.

P. Right. What is your situation with regard to negotiation with Dean and your negotiation with regard to testimony by Magruder?

P. Trying to get the timing, you see, with regard to whatever I say.

HP. Magruder's lawyers are still waiting to get back to him.

P. I see.

Petersen then advised Nixon that Haldeman and Ehrlichman were likely to be indicted.

HP. ...In terms of the things we are concerned with, we don't feel like we ought to put Haldeman and Ehrlichman in there as unindicted coconspirators at this point, but we are afraid not to. If we don't and it gets out, you know, it is going to look like a big cover-up again.

P. Hmph.

HP. So we are trying to wrestle our way through that.

P. Whether you indict Haldeman and Ehrlichman along with the others, huh?

HP. Well we would name them at this point only as unindicted coconspirators, but anybody who is named as an unindicted coconspirator in that indictment is in all probability going to be indicted later on.

The same conversation shows Nixon keeping track of Dean's negotiations with the prosecutors—upon which hinged the use of Dean's information against Haldeman and Ehrlichman.

P. ...What about Dean—in his case you are still negotiating, huh?

HP. Well, we are still tying down facts with him and we want to get as much as we can.

P. And basically with him, the point is you've got to get enough facts to justify giving him immunity? Right?

HP. Enough to make the decision, yes sir.

P. Depends on how much he tells you, is that it?

HP. Right. And more than that, how much of it we can corroborate.

P. If you can't corroborate enough then he doesn't get off, is that it?

HP. Well, if we can't corroborate it, that's right. We can't very well immunize him and put him head to head against a witness who is going to beat him.

P. I see. Well his people are playing it pretty tough with you then?

HP. Yes sir.

P. I guess we'd do that too, I suppose.

HP. Indeed so.

At the end of the conversation Nixon said, "Well if anything comes up, call me even if it is the middle of the night. OK?"

"I will indeed," Petersen replied.

The following morning Nixon passed to Haldeman Petersen's information about LaRue's testimony, what Dean had told the prosecutors regarding White House payment of hush money, and the fact that Kalmbach was to be called.

Meeting of Nixon and Haldeman, Oval Office, April 17, 1973 (9:47-9:59 a.m.):

P. ...Another thing, if you could get John and yourself to sit down and do some hard thinking about what kind of strategy you are going to have with the money. You know what I mean.

H. Yeh.

(Material unrelated to President's actions deleted.)

P. Look, you've got to call Kalmbach so I want to be sure. I want to try to find out what the hell he is going to say he told Kalmbach? What did Kalmbach say he told him? Did he say they wanted this money for support or—

H. I don't know. John has been talking to Kalmbach.

P. Well, be sure that Kalmbach is at least aware of this, that LaRue has talked very freely. He is a broken man.

Dean Immunity. In a subsequent conversation about whether to give Dean immunity or not, Nixon orders Petersen directly to "let me handle Haldeman and Ehrlichman."

Meeting of Nixon and Petersen, Oval Office, April 17, 1973 (2:46—3:49 p.m.):

HP. The thing that scares the hell out of me is this—suppose Dean is the only key to Haldeman and Ehrlichman and the refusal to immunize Dean means that Haldeman and Ehrlichman go free. That is the decision that we are going to ultimately come down to.

P. Well you will have to come into me with what you've got (inaudible) then there...

HP. I will

P. and let me handle Haldeman and Ehrlichman.

HP. I will sir.

P. Do you get my point?

HP. Yes, sir.

P. If it comes down to that—I may have to move on Haldeman and Ehrlichman—then for example you come to me and say look here's what —Look I am not going to do anything to Haldeman and Ehrlichman just because of what Dean says—I can't do that. Its got to be corroborated.

HP. I agree with that.

P. Do you agree with that?

HP. Yes sir—I am not going to do anything with those two unless it is corroborated either.

P. Dean is—I find, has told two or three different stories. I didn't realize it until lately. I guess when a guy is scared he doesn't—

HP. He is a man under great pressure.

P. Sure, I feel for the poor—

HP. So do I. He took a lot—he knows

P. He is a fine lawyer

Later in the same conversation Petersen said that uncorroborated testimony from Dean against Ehrlichman might not be enough grounds to prosecute Ehrlichman but would be grounds for firing him.

P. ...Let's suppose you cannot get anybody to corroborate that—All right, then the question is, however, then that is one thing. If on the other hand—you wouldn't sack Ehrlichman for that?

HP. Mr. President, I wouldn't prosecute Ehrlichman for that.

P. But you might sack him?

HP. Yes sir.

P. Now the second point is, let us suppose...

HP. I mean if he were a junior partner in the Petersen-Nixon law firm out in Oskosh, I would not. But as senior advisor to the President of the United States I would. That is the difference.

P. Yeah....

Petersen continued to press the case for immunizing Dean. But Nixon argued against immunizing Dean for giving testimony that could not be corroborated because, Nixon said, it might appear that Petersen had made a deal with Dean because of their close relationship during the early days of the inquiry.

P. And it's a bad rap, but ah, I'm (inaudible).

HP. But we are not going to do that Mr. President —we are going to have...will have corroborative witnesses all along the line,

P. Yes, sure

HP. But I see the problem and I feel—I think we are looking at it a little bit differently—.

P. Sure.

HP. And I see the problem in two dimensions and, of course, I see it in this respect as a neophite. Obviously you and Bill Rogers are much more experienced in these affairs than I, but maybe because I am a neophite and one of the public I

HP. I see it perhaps more clearly—at least from a different point of view. It seems to me

P. It's the taint

HP. that it's just the things that they have done impairs you.

P. I understand. Understand and I agree with you on that. My point though now is a different one—it is the question of the immunity. That worries hell out of me.

HP. Well that—

P. The immunity worries me for the reason that it just is...I don't think it's good to give it. I don't think in view of the fact that we had this hell of a flap—you know that is the reason Gray wasn't confirmed—because of Dean.

HP. Well Mr. President—

P. We go in and give it.

HP. if I could only put your mind at ease—I have arguing with those prosecutors for three days on this issue—

P. I think you've got to understand, I am not saying this because of Haldeman—I am not suggesting this about Strachan or a secretary or anybody else—no immunity all the way down the line, but it occurred to me that particularly in talking to Rogers said how in the hell can they give John Dean immunity after he's the guy that sunk Pat Gray.

HP. Well if I sound like a devil's advocate—I am. I have been saying the same to the prosecutors— how in the hell can I immunize John Dean?

P. That's the point. Well, I feel it strongly—I mean—just understand I am not trying to protect anybody—I want the damn facts if you can get the facts from Dean and I don't care whether—

HP. Mr. President, if I thought you were trying to protect somebody, I would have walked out.

Breakoff. In their ninth recorded conversation— three days before Nixon announced the firing of Dean and the resignations of Haldeman, Ehrlichman and Kleindienst—Petersen told Nixon that the Watergate prosecutors, in a "crisis of confidence," had protested Petersen's policy of sharing information with Nixon. Nevertheless, Nixon continued to insist on further information about what Dean was telling the prosecutors.

Toward the end of the conversation Petersen reiterated his belief that it was not the responsibility of the Justice Department to investigate Nixon personally.

The following conversation is reproduced in its entirety.

Meeting of Nixon and Petersen in the Oval Office, April 27, 1973 (5:37—5:43 p.m.):

P. Come in.

HP. How are you today?

P. How was your hard day?

HP. I'm sure no harder than yours, sir.

P. Sit down, sit down. I was down in Mississippi today. We have gotten a report that, ah, that really we've got to head them off at the pass. Because it's so damned—so damn dangerous to the Presidency, in a sense. There's a reporter by the name of Hersh of the *New York Times* you probably know.

HP. He's the fellow that did the Vietnam stories.

P. Right. Who told Bittman, who told O'Brien, apparently that they have information—Hersh has information I don't know. You can't ever tell who is saying "this is from Hersh" or "this is from Bittman." Information indicating that Dean has made statements to the prosecuting team implicating the President. And whether—and whether—the *Post* has heard similar rumors. Now, Henry, this I've got to know. Now, understand—I have told you everything I know about this thing.

HP. I don't have any problem with that, Mr. President, and I'll get in touch with them immediately, but—

P. Who?

HP. With Titus, Silbert and Glanzer and Campbell? Who are—

P. Do you mind calling them right now?

HP. No, sir.

P. OK. Say, "Now look. All of your conversations with Dean and Bittman, do they implicate the President?" Because we can't—I've got—if the U.S. Attorney's office and, ah

HP. Mr. President, (unintelligible) I had them over there—we had a kind of crisis of confidence night before last. I left to come over here and I left my two principal assistants to discourse with Silbert and the other three. And in effect it concerned me—whether or not they were at ease with my reporting to you, and I pointed out to them that I had very specific instructions, discussed that with them before on that subject, and—well

P. Yes.

HP. As a consequence—I kind of laid into Titus yesterday and it cleared the air a little bit, but there is a very suspicious atmosphere. They are concerned and scared. Ah—and I will check on this but I have absolutely no information at this point that—

P. Never heard anything like that—

HP. No, sir. Absolutely not.

P. My gosh—As I said—

HP. Mr. President, I tell you, I do not consider it, you know, I've said to Titus, "We have to draw the line. We have no mandate to investigate the President. We investigate Waterate." and I don't know where that line draws, but we have to draw that all the time.

P. Good. Because if Dean if implicating the Presidency—we are going to damned well find out about it. That's—that's—because let me tell you the only conversations we ever had with him, was that famous March 21st conversation I told you about, where he told me about Bittman coming to him. No, the Bittman request for

$120,000 for Hunt. And I then finally began to get at them. I explored with him thoroughly, "Now what the hell is this for?" He said "It's because he's blackmailing Ehrlichman." Remember I said that's what it's about. And Hunt is going to recall the seamy side of it. And I asked him, "Well how would you get it? How would you get it to them?" so forth. But my purpose was to find out what the hell had been going on before. And believe me, nothing was approved. I mean as far as I'm concerned—as far as I'm concerned turned it off totally.

HP. Yeah. My understanding of law is—my understand of our responsibilities, is that if it came to that I would have to come to you and say, "We can't do that." The only people who have jurisdiction to do that is the House of Representatives, as far as I'm concerned.

P. That's right. But I want you to know, you tell me, because as far as I'm concerned—

HP. I'll call them. Do you want me to call from here or outside?

P. Use the Cabinet Room and you will be able to talk freely. And who will you call, who will you talk to there?

HP. I'll call Silbert. If he's not there, I'll get Titus.

P. You'll say that "This is the story some *New York Times* reporter has and Woodward of the *Post*, but Hersh is reporting that Dean had made a statement to the prosecutors." Now understand that this is not a Grand Jury thing. Now damnit, I want to know what it is.

HP. I'll call right away.

P. And I need to know.

HP. Yes, sir.

Petersen's conversation with the prosecutors is not shown in the transcripts. A short time later he reported back to the President.

Meeting of Nixon, Petersen and Ziegler in the Oval Office, April 27, 1973 (6:04—6:48 p.m.):

HP. There's no more on that other than I've just told you.

P. Why in the hell can't we stop though—the paper that Hersh—to think that to bring the President with a thing like that. (expletive removed), you know. Understand. Let me say this. If it were in with the Grand Jury I want to know that too.

HP. All right. Well—

P. (expletive removed). You've got to believe me. I am after the truth, even if it hurts me. But believe me, it won't.

HP. I understand that, you see. But, you know—

P. Just like it won't hurt you. We are doing our job. And somebody was in here the other day and they were saying, well, Dean is going to blackmail you because of something you're supposed to have told me. And I said, (expletive removed) I said, you have a right to tell me what was going on.

But with the April 25 break with his Justice Department subordinates, Petersen's usefulness to Nixon in providing information evidently had ended.

The Fall of John Dean

For five days—from June 25 to 29, 1973—John W. Dean III sat unflustered before the Senate Watergate committee and laid out, in flat, phlegmatic tones, a dramatic televised indictment of President Nixon and some of his closest aides for attempting to cover up the Watergate scandal.

Dean, who served as the President's counsel for three years until he was fired April 30, 1973, presented the first insider's account of what allegedly went on within the White House to try to suppress the burgeoning scandal.

One of the top White House strategists in the alleged coverup, Dean went before the Senate committee after falling out with Nixon and his two principal advisers, H. R. Haldeman and John D. Ehrlichman.

The White House transcripts of some of the President's Watergate-related conversations—made public a year to the day after his dismissal—help trace the change in Dean's position from the trusted lieutenant who drew up the White House enemies list to a White House enemy himself.

Dean as Trusted Aide. The transcripts open Sept. 15, 1972, with a meeting between the President, Haldeman and Dean in Nixon's White House office. The meeting was a wide-ranging affair with Dean loyally and eagerly following the President's orders and making suggestions.

Dean assured Nixon that the Watergate break-in case would not turn out to be an embarrassment to him. "Three months ago," he said, "I would have had trouble predicting there would be a day when this would be forgotten, but I think I can say that 54 days from now nothing is going to come down crashing to our surprise."

Nixon then complimented Dean for the way he had handled the case so far. "...(T)he way you have handled all this seems to me has been very skillful putting your fingers in the leaks that have sprung here and sprung there," Nixon said.

Later in that meeting, the President and Dean turned to the attacks on the White House by supporters of Sen. George McGovern (D S.D.) the 1972 Democratic presidential candidate, and what the President wanted done to those persons making the charges.

Meeting of Nixon, Haldeman and Dean in the Oval Office, Sept. 15, 1972 (5:27—6:17 p.m.):

P. We are all in it together. This is a war. We take a few shots and it will be over. We will give them a few shots and it will be over. Don't worry. I wouldn't want to be on the other side right now. Would you?

D. Along that line, one of the things I've tried to do, I have begun to keep notes on a lot of people who are emerging as less than our friends because this will be over some day and we shouldn't forget the way some of them treated us.

P. I want the most comprehensive notes on all those who tried to do us in. They didn't have to do it. If we had had a very close election and they were playing the other side I would understand this. No—they were doing this quite deliberately and they are asking for it and they are going to get it. We have not used the power in this first four years as you know. We have never used it. We have not used the Bureau (the Federal Bureau of Investigation) and we have not used the Justice Department but things are going to change now. And they are either going to do it right or go.

D. What an exciting prospect.

P. Thanks. It has to be done....

Watergate Unraveling. By the time of the next transcript five months later, the Watergate case had begun to unravel. James W. McCord Jr., one of the original Watergate conspirators, had written a letter to U.S. District Court Judge John J. Sirica saying that higher officials in the Nixon administration were involved.

"They do not ultimately solve what I see as a grave problem of a cancer growing around the presidency. This creates another problem."

—John Dean to President Nixon
March 21, 1973

The Senate had established a special committee to investigate the case. And Judge Sirica was not satisfied that federal prosecutors had probed deep enough in developing their case.

Dean continued to play a leading role in the White House in handling the case, and he and the President talked about the latest developments in the Oval Office Feb. 28, 1973 for over an hour between 9:12 and 10:23 a.m.

Toward the end of their conversation, an optimistic Dean told Nixon, "...We have come a long way on this thing now. I had thought it was an impossible task to hold together until after the election until things started falling out, but we have made it this far and I am convinced we are going to make it the whole road and put this thing on the funny pages of the history books rather than anything serious because actually—"

"It will be somewhat serious," the President replied, "but the main thing, of course, is also the isolation of the President."

"Absolutely! Totally true!" said Dean.

Dean emphasized in discussing tactics for dealing with the Senate Watergate committee, that "the President should not become involved in any part of this case."

Two weeks later, Dean and Nixon talked again about matters related to the Watergate, such as Judge Sirica, the Senate confirmation hearings of L. Patrick Gray III as FBI director and the money demands of the Watergate burglars.

Throughout the one-and-a-half hour March 13, 1973, conversation, the President kept asking Dean his advice on handling certain aspects of the case. Toward the end, he asked Dean, "Is it too late to go the hangout road?"

"Yes, I think it is...," Dean replied. His reason was that "there is a certain domino situation here. If some things start going, a lot of other things are going to start going, and there can be a lot of problems if everything starts falling. So there are dangers, Mr. President. I would be less than candid if I didn't tell you there are. There is a reason for not everyone going up and testifying."

Report Proposed. In an early evening telephone conversation with Nixon March 20, 1973, Dean suggested giving Nixon a report. Nixon, in turn suggested, a "general statement" that he could "put out" to "reassure" his supporters.

"You could do it orally, even if you don't want to make the written statement," Nixon said. "...(W)e need something to answer somebody, answer things, you know they say, 'What are you basing this on,' I can say, 'Well, my counsel has advised me that'—...I don't want a, too much in chapter and verse...."

"An all around statement," Dean interjected.

"That's right. Try just something general," Nixon said.

To this point, the President's request for the report from Dean appeared innocuous. But Nixon's suggestion that Dean draft a report for him became a major turning point in the relationship between the two men. It did not affect their relationship at first but the transcripts of

---

"In other words, rather than fighting it, we are not fighting the committee, of course—we are fighting the situation thing."

—President Nixon to John Ehrlichman
March 22, 1973

---

subsequent conversations show how the issue of the report and Dean's failure to write it were used by the President and his two closest assistants, Haldeman and Ehrlichman, to blame Dean for the White House's failure to uncover the case.

The day after the idea of a report was suggested, the crucial March 21, 1973 morning meeting took place in the Oval Office. Nixon and Dean were alone for about half of the conversation, until Haldeman joined them.

It was in that meeting that Dean warned Nixon that a "cancer" was growing near the presidency—the Watergate coverup—and that it could seriously threaten the President.

"I think that there is no doubt about the seriousness of the problem we've got," Dean said. "We have a cancer within, close to the Presidency, that is growing. It is growing daily. It's compounded, growing geometrically now, because it compounds itself. That will be clear if I, you know, explain some of the details of why it is. Basically, it is because (1) we are being blackmailed; (2) People are going to start perjuring themselves very quickly that have not had to perjure themselves

to protect other people in the line. And there is no assurance—"

"That that won't bust?" said the President.

"That that won't bust," replied Dean. "So let me give you the sort of basic facts, talking first about the Watergate; and then about (political saboteur Donald H.) Segretti; and then about some of the peripheral items that have come up...."

Dean then explained the genesis of the Nixon re-election committee's intelligence-gathering operations that led to the Watergate break-in.

The conversation also dealt with blackmail money payments and executive clemency—the $120,000 payment to E. Howard Hunt Jr., one of the Watergate conspirators, and the political problems surrounding the granting of executive clemency.

A second March 21 meeting covered in the transcripts (5:20-6:01 p.m.) had a bearing on Dean's relationship with the President.

The conversation, which included Nixon, Dean, Haldeman and Ehrlichman, took place in the President's office in the Executive Office Building. During it, Ehrlichman suggested that Dean write a memorandum to Nixon on Watergate that the President would use, if he needed, to extricate himself from the scandal by saying, "I relied on this."

The four men also discussed how to handle the problem caused by the disclosure that 'hush money' payments had been made in the past and the fact that some people might have to be sacrificed to protect the White House. To continue the payments would look like a cover-up, the President said. The alternative, he added, was to take a look at those losses and decide who must be sacrificed.

John N. Mitchell, the former Attorney General, and Jeb Stuart Magruder, deputy director of the Committee for the Re-election of the President, were mentioned as likely possibilities. Perhaps, suggested Dean, they should "draw numbers with names out of a hat to see who gets hurt and who doesn't...."

Meeting of President, Haldeman, Ehrlichman and Dean in the President's office in the Executive Office Building March 21, 1973 (5:20-6:01 p.m.)

P. Also, that there has been such a lot of—put out about what you have done without referring to the fact, without being defensive about it, you intended to—This should not be a letter to Eastland. I think this should be a letter to me. You could say that, "Now, now that hearings are going on, I can now give a report that we can put out."

H. That is what you can say. In other words, he gives you a report because you asked him for it, regardless of the timeliness.

D. I am not thinking of that. Don't worry about that. I have no problem with the timing. It is just that Liddy and McCord are still out on appeal. That is why I haven't tried to do this before.

H. We are going to have a big period of that. I think you could say—

E. You could say, "I have a report. I don't want to show it. I would not want it published because some fellow's trial of the case is still on."

P. Let me say this. The problem with, is: I don't believe that helps on our cause. The fact that cover up—I am not sure. Maybe I am wrong. The fact that the President says, "I have shown (Senate Watergate committee chairman Sam J. Ervin Jr.) Ervin." Remember we had nobody there. I think that something has to go first. We need to put out something.

H. If we worry about the timeliness, and try to hang it on a sense thing, then we have to ignore the trial, and say Dean has given you a report. We basically said it was an oral report. The thing is that Dean has kept you posted from time to time with periodic oral reports as this thing, as it becomes convenient. You have asked him now to summarize those into an overall summary.

P. Overall summary. And I will make the report available to the Ervin Committee. And then I offer the Ervin Committee report this way, I say, "Dear Senator Ervin. Here is the report before your hearings. You have this report, and as I have said previously, any questions that are not answered here, you can call the White House staff member, and they will be directed to answer any questions on an informal basis." (inaudible)

H. Yeah.

E. Let's suppose you did do that. You did as to the burglary, you did it as to Segretti and you made some passing comments to money, right? You send her up there. Let's suppose I am called at some time. Our position on that is that I wasn't a prosecutor, that he was sent out to do an investigation on (Pentagon Papers disseminator Daniel) Ellsberg. And when we discovered what he was up to, we stopped him. Now, I suppose that lets Ellsberg out, because there are search and seizure things here that may be sufficient at least for a mistrial, if not for—

P. Isn't that case about finished yet?

E. Oh, it will go a little while yet. Let's suppose that occurred. That was a national security situation. The man exercised bad judgment, and I think it is inarguable that he should never have been permitted to go to the Committee after that episode, having reflected on his judgemnt that way. But beyond that, the question is did he completely authorize (inaudible)

P. Yeah. Getting back to this, John. You still tilt to the panel idea yourself?

D. Well, I see in this conversation what I have talked about before. They do not ultimately solve what I see as a grave problem of a cancer growing around the Presidency. This creates another problem. It does not clean the problem out.

P. Well,

E. But doesn't it permit the President to clean it out at such time as it does come up? By saying, "Indeed, I relied on it. And now this later thing turns up, and I don't condone that. And if I had known that before, obviously I would have run it down."

P. Here's what John is to. You really think you've got to clean the cancer out now, right?

D. Yes sir.

P. How would you do that? Do you see another way? Without breaking down our executive privilege.

D. I see a couple of ways to do it.

P. You certainly don't want to do it at the Senate, do you?

D. No sir, I think that would be an added trap.

P. That's the worst thing. Right. We've got to do it. We aren't asked to do it.

D. You've got to do it, to get the credit for it. That gets you above it. As I see it, naturally you'll get hurt and I hope we can find the answer to that problem.

E. Alright, suppose we did this? Supposing you write a report to the President on everything you know about this. And the President then, prior to seeing it, says "Did you send the report

---

"(M)itchell's case is a killer. Dean's case is the question. And I do not consider him guilty. Now that's all there is to that."

—President Nixon to aides
April 14, 1973

---

over to the Justice Department?" When it goes he says, (unintelligible) has been at work on this. My Counsel has been at work on this. Here are his findings."

P. Where would you start? I don't know where it stops. (White House press secretary Ronald L.) Ziegler? The Vice President (Spiro T. Agnew)?

H. Well, re Magruder over at Commerce. Obviously you would send a report over that said Magruder did this and that. Well, that is what he is talking about apparently.

P. And then Magruder. The fellow is a free agent.

H. The free agent.

P. Who according to the Hunt theory, could pull others down with him.

H. Sure. What would happen? Sure as hell we have to assume Dwight would be drawn in.

D. Draw numbers with names out of a hat to see who gets hurt and who doesn't. That sounds about as fair as you can be, because anyone can get hurt.

Camp David Report. The following day—March 22—Haldeman, Ehrlichman, Dean, and Mitchell met with the President. The two-hour conversation, during which they considered the forthcoming Senate Watergate investigation, was rambling and largely inconclusive.

The main development coming out of the session was that Dean was ordered by the President to "hold up for the weekend" at Camp David to work on a Watergate report. Nixon considered publication of Dean's findings but nothing was decided on.

Meeting of the President, Haldeman, Ehrlichman, Mitchell and Dean in the President's office in the old

Executive Office Building March 22, 1973 (1:57-3:43 p.m.)

D. I think the proof is in the pudding, so to speak—it is how this document is written and until I sit down and write that document. I have done part of it so to speak. I have done the Segretti thing and I am relatively satisfied that we don't have any major problems there. As I go to part A—to the Watergate—I haven't written—I haven't gone through the exercise yet in a real effort to write such a report, and I really can't say until I do it where we are and I certainly think it is something that should be done though.

P. What do you say on the Watergate (inaudible)

D. We can't be complete if we don't know, all we know is what, is what—

P. It is a negative in setting forth general information involving questions. Your consideration—your analysis, et cetera. You have found this, that. Rather than going into every news story and every charge, et cetera, et cetera. This, this this, —put it down—I don't know but

D. I don't think I can do it until I sit down this evening and start drafting.

H. I think you ought to hold up for the weekend and do that and get it done.

P. Sure.

H. Give it your full attention and get it done.

P. I think you need—why don't you do this? Why don't you go up to Camp David?

D. I might do it, I might do it.

P. Completely away from the phone. Just go up there and (inaudible) I want a written report.

E. That would be my scenario. He presents it to you at your request. You then publish—(inaudible)

E. I know that but I don't care.

H. You are not dealing with the defendants on trial. You are only dealing with White House involvement. You are not dealing with the campaign.

D. That's where I personally....

P. You could write it in a way that you say this report was not comment on et cetera, et cetera, but, "I have reviewed the record, Mr. President and without at all compromising the right of defendents and so forth, some of whom are on appeal, here are the facts with regard to members of the White House staff et cetera, et cetera, that you have asked me about. I have checked the FBI records; I have read the Grand Jury transcripts —et cetera, et cetera.

E. As a matter of fact you could say, "I will not summarize some of the FBI reports on this stuff because it is my understanding that you may wish to publish this." Or you may allude to it in that way without saying that fact. Just say that I do not summarize all the FBI documents and so forth.

D. It is my understanding that all the FBI reports have been turned over to the Ervin Committee.

H. Not everything. He has only seen half of them.

D. Another vehicle might be, take the report I write and give it to Ervin and (Sen. Howard H.) Baker (R Tenn.) under the same terms that they got the FBI reports. You could say, "Now, this has

innuendo in it—and from this the press might assume things that shouldn't be assumed, but I want you to know everything we know." And publicly state that, "I have turned over a Dean Report to your Committee." Then begin to say that, "You see that various people have various ingredients which may be of assistance in testifying. But it is not worth their coming up here to be able to repeat to the Committee what is here in this report in some forum where they are going to be treated like they are in a circus. But I am also willing, based on this document, to set some ground rules for how we can have these people appear before the Committee."

H. In case of that the Committee would issue a warrant on our phone calls. Bully!

P. That's right.

H. That is all I know about the damn thing is that the Secret Service at some point has been bugged.

D. And that could go on forever with you on that tack. I could draw these things like this Staff into this report and have (Attorney General Richard G.) Kleindienst come get it and give it to Ervin in confidence—I am not talking about documents you see. I am talking about something we can spread as facts. You see you could even write a novel with the facts.

P. Inaudible

D. Inaudible

P. Inaudible

E. My thought is—

P. In other words, rather than fighting it, we are not fighting the Committee, of course—we are fighting the situation thing.

E. And I am looking to the future, assuming that some corner of this thing comes unstuck, you are then in a position to say, "Look, that document I published is the document I relied on, that is, the report I relied on."

P. This is all we knew.

H. That is all the stuff we could find out—

E. And now this new development is a surprise to me —I am going to fire A,B,C and D, now.

Only at the end of the meeting was there a hint of nervousness as the following exchange indicated.

P. Do you think we want to go this route now? Let it hang out so to speak?

D. Well, it isn't really that—

H. It's a limited hang out.

D. It is a limited hang out. It's not an absolute hang out.

P. But some of the questions look big hanging out publicly or privately.

D. What it is doing, Mr. President, is getting you up above and away from it. That is the most important thing.

On March 27, 1973, the question of Dean's appearance before the federal grand jury investigating Watergate came up in a talk between the President, Haldeman, Ehrlichman and Ziegler. Nothing was decided then. But on April 8, Ehrlichman informed Nixon during a telephone coversation that Dean felt the "smartest thing that he, Dean, could do" would be to testify before the grand jury and "appear cooperative."

The President replied, "Right."

That same day, Dean had in fact met secretly with federal prosecutors for the first time.

Situation Deteriorates. For the White House, the situation continued to deteriorate rapidly and by the weekend of April 14-15, it had become ominous. On those two days, 16 conversations took place that involved the President, Haldeman, Ehrlichman, Haldeman's assistant Lawrence M. Higby, Attorney General Kleindeinst, and Assistant Attorney General Henry E. Petersen.

Dean was a central figure in most of the conversations, and the transcripts indicate it was dawning on the President, after he learned that Dean was talking to the prosecutors that he, Dean, had become a threat.

Meeting of the President, Haldeman and Ehrlichman in the President's office in the Old Executive Office Building April 14, 1973 (8:55-11:31 a.m.)

P. My point is that if three of us talk here, I realize that, frankly—Mitchell's case is a killer. Dean's case is the question. And I do not consider him guilty. Now that's all there is to that. Because if he—if that's the case, then half the staff is guilty.

E. That's it. He's guilty of really no more except in degree.

* * *

H. You won't have to appeal to him on that because he's made the point you know that if Dean testifies it's going to unscramble the whole omelet.

P. That's why I don't want to leave it at the point that Dean's or Magruder's or anyones testimony is essential to Mitchell's—

E. That's right.

P. You see that's the point of that. On the Dean thing, I I wouldn't say that the President has stood, frankly, John, on executive privilege thing, because it's up to (unintelligible) and so forth.

Late in the evening (11:22-11:53 p.m.) of April 14, the President called Ehrlichman. As the conversation was ending, Nixon suggested that Dean would talk with Kleindeinst "in confidence" about a Watergate-related matter.

However, Ehrlichman warned him against that. "I am not sure," Ehrlichman said. "I just don't know how much to lean on that reed at the moment."

The next day, April 15, Kleindeinst met with the President and told him about his all-night session with Petersen, Assistant U.S. Attorney Earl J. Silbert and U.S. Attorney Harold H. Titus Jr. about the Watergate case.

"The purpose of it (the meeting) was to give me the benefit of what had transpired on Thursday, Friday and Saturday with Magruder, and then what had been transpiring for a week with John Dean and his attorneys," Kleindeinst said.

The Attorney General said that Dean might implicate Haldeman and Ehrlichman, and reported that the prosecutors had told him that Dean will be indicted on Magruder's testimony.

Kleindeinst told Nixon that Dean's principal charges against Ehrlichman were that Ehrlichman had once proposed throwing documents into the Potomac River and

that on another occasion he had ordered Hunt to flee the country.

During the day, Haldeman's aide Lawrence Higby called Haldeman to relay a message from Dean.

Telephone conversation between Higby and Haldeman April 15, 1973.

LH. John Dean just called me. He had a message he wanted to relay to the President through you. He would not speak directly to you.

H. Alright.

LH. (1) I hope you understand my actions are motivated totally out of loyalty to you, the President.

H. Wait a minute.

LH. totally out of loyalty to you and the President.

H. Yep.

LH. And if it's not clear now—

H. Uh, huh.

LH. it will become clear.

H. Wait a minute.

LH. (2) Ehrlichman requested to meet tonight—

H. Yeah.

LH. but I feel inappropriate at this time.

H. Just a minute. Ok.

LH. I am ready and willing to meet with you, meaning the President, at any time to discuss these matters.

H. Just a minute.

LH. (3) I think you, meaning the President, should take your counsel from Henry Petersen who I assure you does not want the Presidency hurt.

H. Hmph.

LH. That was the end of his message. He was calling you from his home, the operator said.

Later that day (8:14-8:18 p.m.) Nixon called Petersen at home to continue a discussion of developments in the Watergate case. Petersen told the President that Dean's lawyer "says he will not permit him to plead...."

"Permit him to plead? What do you mean by that," asked the President.

"To plead guilty," said Petersen. "In other words he will go to trial."

Petersen said that Dean's lawyer was trying to reach an agreement with the prosecutors. "His counsel's position is that it would be a travesty to try Dean and not try Ehrlichman and Haldeman," he said. "That is the basic information to the extent that it developed in these preliminary negotiations isn't much more than I gave you."

The President then asked, "Well, let me ask you this. Based on this, though, you mean that inhibits you from using the information then, or do you use it, or how do you do it, or do you use it for leads, but you can't use it unless he pleads? Right?"

"We cannot use it for any purpose unless he pleads," replied Petersen.

"For no purpose?" said the President.

Petersen answered, "That's right. That's incorrect, unless we strike some agreement with him."

Nixon called back Petersen later that night and told him he had heard Dean's story and had asked Dean to resign. Petersen advised against asking for the White House counsel's resignation.

Telephone conversation between the President and Petersen April 15, 1973 (11:45-11:53 p.m.)

P. Fine. Second, I have met with Dean. I got him in finally and heard his story and I said directly to him, "Now when do you want to resign?" And, he said, "Well I will resign but I would prefer to wait until I have testified." Now I want to ask your judgment on that. I can bring him in in the morning and tell him, "Look, I want your resignation."

P. But, what do you want me to do? I don't want to interfere with your process?

HP. Mr. President, I don't think that we ought to—

P. Tip our hand?

HP. Not yet. He is the first one who has really come in.

P. Oh, I see.

HP. He came in a week ago Sunday.

P. Right. Let me say this. The main thing Henry we must not have any question, now, on this, you know I am in charge of this thing. You are and I am. Above everything else and I am following it every inch of the way and I don't want any question, that's of the fact that I am a way ahead of the game. You know, I want to stay one step ahead of the curve. You know what I mean?

HP. I understand.

P. So - if you think on Dean -

HP. I think we ought to hold the line.

P. Alright and you will let me know.

HP. Yes, sir. I will indeed.

P. as soon as -then I will call him in and naturally he will have to resign.

HP. Yes, sir.

P. Now Haldeman and Ehrlichman - I have informed both of them of the charges that have been generally made and I have said that if they stand up, and I didn't have to say it. They said well, of course, we will, we don't want to be an embarrassment. They are good guys. But my feeling with both of them, and it is only a question, and we talked today of when—no, it is whether, also, but I think you've got to hear (Haldeman assistant Gordon C.) Strachan and I think you've got to hear Dean and then I suppose you would want to hear them or do you think we should move on them before? Or do you want to think of that overnight?

HP. We would like to wait. We would like to wait, Mr. President.

P. Because like today, you were suggesting that we call them all in and have them resign and I just wanted to be sure you didn't think I should do that because I am perfectly prepared to.

HP. That is really your judgment. I think ultimately that is going to have to be done.

P. Yeah. But your point is that as far as the case is concerned, you are telling me now that it is best to wait. Is that the point?

HP. On Dean, yes. And on Ehrlichman/Haldeman - I suppose until we hear their testimony, which is, well we want to put them off until we can fashion all the—

P. All the others.

HP. things into a pattern.

Dean as Enemy. After the hectic weekend, the President, Haldeman and Ehrlichman held what appeared to be a strategy planning session April 16 to discuss how to handle the problem posed by Dean and contain his revelations. Dean by this time was perceived by Nixon as a serious threat.

During the conversation, that lasted from 9:50 to 9:59 a.m., Ehrlichman advised Nixon that "if I am going to be splashed on this thing you are better off now having another scrap with Dean."

Ehrlichman proposed that Nixon get letters from Dean that Nixon could release at his discretion.

"I think that the point is that in picking up these letters from him (Dean), it would be the agreement that neither he nor you would announce it immediately. So the announcement would be your discretion," Ehrlichman said.

"Right," Nixon said.

Immediately after that meeting, Nixon met with Dean in his Oval Office for 40 minutes for what was probably one of the tensest episodes portrayed in the transcripts. The President appeared to be seeking some way to remove Dean from the White House.

Nixon immediately brought up "the resignations... that I should have in hand. Not to be released."

Meeting between the President and Dean in the Oval Office April 16, 1973 (10-10:40 a.m.)

P. But that I should have in hand something or otherwise they will say, "What the hell. After Dean told you all of this, what did you do?" You see?

D. Uh, huh.

P. I talked to Petersen about this other thing and I said, "Now what do you want to do about this situation on Dean, et cetera?" And he said, well, he said I don't want to announce anything now. You know what I mean.

D. Uh, huh.

P. But what is your feeling on that? See what I mean?

D. Well I think it ought to be Dean, Ehrlichman and Haldeman.

P. Well, I thought Dean at this moment.

D. Alright.

P. Dean at this moment because you are going to be going and I will have to handle them also. But the point is, what is your advice? You see the point is, we just typed up a couple just to have here which I would be willing to put out. You know.

D. Uh, huh.

P. In the event that certain things occur.

D. I understand.

P. To put—just putting. What is your advice?

D. I think it would be good to have it on hand, and I would think to be very honest with you—

P. Have the others too?

D. Yeah, have the others too.

P. Well as a matter of fact, they both suggested it themselves so I've got that—I am sorry, Steve, I hit the wrong bell.

D. (Half laugh)

P. So I have already done that with them.

D. Alright.

P. They said look whatever—and I want to get your advice on them, too. And what I would think we would want to do is to have it in two different forms here and I would like to discuss with you the forms. I seems to me that your form should be to request an immediate leave of absence. That would be one thing. The other, of course, would be just a straight resignation.

D. Uh, huh.

P. First, what I would suggest is that you sign both. That is what I had in mind. And then we'll talk about after—you don't know yet what you're. For example, if you go in and plead guilty you would have to resign.

D. That is right.

P. If on the other hand, you're going in on some other basis, then I think the leave of absence is the proper thing to do.

D. Uh, huh, I would think so.

P. And that is the way I would discuss it with others, too. If you have any other thoughts, let me know. I am not trying to press you on the thing. I just want to be sure John's got the record of anything that I should have here.

D. I think it is a good idea. I frankly do. But I think if you do it, for one, I think you have problems with others too Mr. President.

P. I already have the others.

D. That is what I am trying to advise you on—

P. But on theirs, both, it is all pending their appearance, et cetera. That isn't yours. Nothing is going to be said but I have to have it in hand by reason, as I told them as a matter of fact after our talk last night. I told them that I have to have these in hand so that I can move on this if Petersen is going to report to me every day. I said now Petersen, "If you get this stuff confirmed, I need to know." He said, well, I asked him specifically, "what do you do? Who is going to be today?" And he said, "well, Strachan." There are three today I think. Who is the third one?

D. I don't know.

P. That's right! You're not supposed....

D. (Laughter)

P. Then, OK.

D. What I would like to do is draft up for you an alternative letter putting in both options and you can just put them in the file. Short and sweet.

P. Alright. Fine. I had dictated something myself. All my own which, if you can give me a better form, fine. I just want you to do it either way. Do you? Or do you want to prepare something?

D. I would like to prepare something.

P. Good. Alright. Fine. Why don't you take this? You can take those as an idea and have something. I've got to see Petersen at 1:30.

D. Alright.

P. Understand I don't want to put anything out because I don't want to jeopardize your position at all. You have a right to, just as everybody else has. You have taken a hell of a load here but I just feel that since what you said last night that we've got to do it and with Haldeman and Ehr-

lichman I have leave of absences from them. Which, however, I will not use until I get the word from Petersen on corroboration which he advised himself. I talked to him after you left—about 11:45 and let (him—characterization omitted) know how hard we work around here.

Later in the meeting, Nixon inquired about questions that might be presented to Dean by the prosecutors and he seemed to try to coach Dean on the answers, particularly on the issues of the payments to Hunt and on bugging operations. He urged Dean to invoke executive privilege on "the electronic stuff."

Nixon at one point turned to the Alger Hiss case and used it to admonish Dean not to lie.

P. Oh yes, I remember. You told me that. I guess everybody told me that. Dean said, "I am not going down there and lie," because your hand will shake and your emotions. Remember you told me that.

D. Yes, I said that. I am incapable of it.

P. Thank God. Dont' ever do it, John. Tell the truth. That is the thing I have told everybody around here. (expletive omitted) tell the truth! All they do John is compound it.

P. That (characterization omitted) Hiss would be free today if he hadn't lied. If he had said, "Yes I knew Chambers and as a young man I was involved with some Communist activities but I broke it off a number of years ago." And Chambers would have dropped it. If you are going to lie, you go to jail for the lie rather than the crime. So believe me, don't ever lie.

D. The truth always emerges. It always does.

P. Also there is a question of right and wrong too.

D. That's right.

P. Whether it is right and whether it is wrong. Perhaps there are some gray areas, but you are right to get it out now.

D. I am sure.

Ten minutes after Dean left the Oval Office, Ehrlichman and Haldeman entered for another talk with the President.

Nixon reported success in dealing with Dean.

Meeting between President, Haldeman and Ehrlichman in Oval Office April 16, 1973 (10:50-11:04 a.m.)

H. The scenario worked out pretty well. Yeah—

P. Well, John, let me say this is quite the operator. We first talked about the work he did before this began. I said that I wanted him to know that it is national security work. He said I consider it so. I said, "Have you told anybody about it?" He said, "No. I don't intend to. I don't intend to say a thing more than I need to say in answering questions with regard to this matter, and I will not comment on anything else of course. I will not comment on any conversation I have had with the President." So far as he is concerned, that operation will not be discussed. Of course, the problem I suppose is as far as others are concerned or were involved. But if they do John, I would play it straight out. Damn it, of course we do this.

And the President and his two aides decided to use Dean's alleged failure to draft his Watergate report as Nixon's reason for entering the case and conducting his own investigation.

P. Incidentally, I don't think it will gain us anything by dumping on the Dean Report as such.
E. No.
P. What I mean is I would say I was not satisfied that the Dean Report was complete and also I thought it was my obligation to go beyond that to people other than the White House.
E. Ron has an interesting point. Remember you had John Dean go to Camp David to write it up. He came down and said, "I can't."
P. Right.
E. That is the tip off and right then you started to move.
P. That's right. He said he could not write it.
H. Then you realized that there was more to this than you had been led to believe. (unintelligible)
P. How do I get credit for getting Magruder to the stand?
E. Well it is very simple. You took Dean off of the case right then.
H. Two weeks ago, the end of March.
P. That's right.
E. The end of March. Remember that letter you signed to me?
P. Uh, huh.
E. 30th of March.
P. I signed it. Yes.
E. Yes sir, and it says Dean is off of it. I want you to get into it. Find out what the facts are. Be prepared to—
P. Why did I take Dean off? Because he was involved? I did it, really, because he was involved with Gray.
E. Well there was a lot of stuff breaking in the papers, but at the same time—
H. The scenario is that he told you he couldn't write a report so obviously you had to take him off.
P. Right, right.
E. And so then we started digging into it and we went to San Clemente....

In a conversation later that day with Ehrlichman and Ziegler, Nixon discussed what he had learned from Assistant Attorney General Petersen about the threat Dean posed to the White House inner circle.

Meeting between the President, Ehrlichman and Ziegler in the President's office in the Executive Office Building April 10, 1973 (3:27—4:04 p.m.)

P. I asked about the timing on Dean. They haven't got a deal on him because—in fact his lawyers made an interesting comment. He said Dean shouldn't do anything to upset the unmaking of Haldeman and Ehrlichman and Mitchell, and if they don't get immunity they're going to try this Administration and the President. His lawyer, Schaffer (Charles N. Shaffer). Petersen says that's quite common. Everybody shouts to everybody. I'm getting (unintelligible) difficult (unintelligible). After all, the business of the—about the Dean report, why end it that way?

Dean will stick to the position. John, you can see how he's going to (unintelligible) Ehrlichman. You know, he did make some movement on his own in this thing. I've asked Dean a specific question. "Haldeman/Ehrlichman, did they know in advance?" He said, "No." I said, "I've asked you again, I've asked you." He told me that (unintelligible) Well Dean said after a second meeting over there he went over and saw Haldeman and said, "We oughtn't to be in this. Haldeman said, I agree. I said, "Well, what's wrong with that." He said, "Well, Haldeman, by failing to act—"

Dean had a second meeting between 4:07-4:35 p.m. with Nixon April 16 at which they discussed his, Dean's, draft resignation statement. Although nothing was decided upon at the session, Dean made clear to Nixon his concern that he would become the "scapegoat" for Haldeman and Ehrlichman.

The President's anger against Dean surfaced the following day, April 17, during a talk with Haldeman. Nixon passed along information to Haldeman he had received from Petersen. But as the meeting ended, he lashed out at Dean.

Meeting between President and Haldeman in the Oval Office April 17, 1973 (9:47-9:59 a.m.)

P. That's right. The other point is the other element. The question now that is coming as far as Dean is concerned. He basically is the one who surprises me and disappoints you to an extent because he is trying to save his neck and doing so easily. He is not, to hear him tell it, when I have talked to him, he is not telling things that will, you know—
H. That is not really true though. He is.
P. I know, I know, I know. He tells me one thing and the other guy something else. That is when I get mad. Dean is trying to tell enough to get immunity and that is frankly what it is Bob.
H. That is the real problem we've got. It had to break and it should break but what you've got is people within it, as you said right at the beginning, who said things and said them, too, exactly as Dean told them. The more you give them the better it will work out.

A decision to cut off all contact with Dean was made two and a half hours later during a meeting of Nixon, Haldeman, Ehrlichman and Zeigler that lasted from 12:35 to 2:20 p.m. Nixon discussed with his aides how best to stop talking to Dean without hurting Haldeman's and Ehrlichman's positions in the unfolding Watergate cover-up investigation.

Thirteen days later, Nixon fired Dean. In an April 30 television speech, the President took responsibility for Watergate and announced that, "in one of the most difficult decisions of my presidency, I accepted the resignations of my closest associates in the White House—Bob Haldeman, John Ehrlichman—two of the finest public servants it has been my privilege to know."

After announcing Kleindienst's resignation, the President, almost as an afterthought, mentioned Dean. "The counsel to the President, John Dean, has also resigned," he said.

Nixon and the Press

As the Watergate coverup unraveled, Richard Nixon went on national television to pledge to get the full story out to the American people. "I was determined," he said in his April 30, 1973, speech, "that we should get to the bottom of the matter, and that the truth should be fully brought out—no matter who was involved."

Yet the actions of the President and his closest White House aides—John D. Ehrlichman, H.R. Haldeman and John W. Dean III—as disclosed in the edited White House transcripts of the Watergate-related conversations, show that they often followed the opposite course.

From almost the moment that the scandal began to threaten them, they treated it largely as a public relations and press problem. Judging from their remarks, it was to them basically a problem to be handled by seizing the initiative, by minimizing the public impact, by cutting losses and by attempting not to appear defensive.

The conversations between Nixon and his key advisers usually were not over how to fully disclose details of the scandal but how to reveal as little as possible and how to put the best face on the disclosures.

Their ultimate aim was best captured in the middle of a two-hour conversation by the President, Haldeman and Ehrlichman on April 17, 1973 (12:35-2:20 p.m.):

"You know where the Watergate story is in *The Washington Post* today? Page 19," Haldeman said.

Ehrlichman then made an "unintelligible" remark.

"I know, I know," Nixon said. "And it'll be page 19 five months from now if we handle it right."

To "handle it right," Nixon and his aides spent much of their time working out "scenarios" to get the President "out in front" as the scandal unfolded and to "isolate" him from its consequences and involvement.

They were deeply concerned about the press—how it reported Watergate and what it reported. They considered ways of manipulating and intimidating it to restrict its Watergate coverage. Always in the background was Nixon's long-running hostility toward the press.

'Isolation of the President.' "It will be somewhat serious," the President remarked to Dean about Watergate Feb. 28, 1973, "but the main thing, of course, is also the isolation of the President."

Nixon and Dean had met for an hour and 10 minutes that day and they talked about the formation of the Senate Watergate committee earlier that month, on Feb. 7, and the best way for the White House to handle its investigation. The "isolation" of the President was the paramount problem for Nixon and his inner circle and the strategies they devised were aimed at doing just that.

They took several approaches.

Information from the White House would be held to an absolute minimum. At his infrequent news conferences, the President would take the "no comment" route. The President and Dean decided on that tack during a March 13, 1973, conversation, two days before a presidential news conference. The two men talked about questions they expected to be asked and Dean coached him on a variety of "no comments."

Meeting of the President, Haldeman and Dean in the Oval Office, March 13, 1973 (12:42-2:00 p.m.):

P. Well, now, with regard to the question, etc., it would be my opinion not to dodge it just because there are going to be questions.

D. Well you are probably going to get more questions this week. And the tough questions. And some of them don't have easy answers. For example, did Haldeman know that there was a Don Segretti (political saboteur Donald H. Segretti) out there? That question is likely.

P. Did he? I don't know.

D. Yes, he had knowledge that there was somebody in the field doing prankster-type activities.

P. Well, I don't know anything about that. What about that. What about my taking, basically, just trying to fight this thing one at a time. I am only going to have to fight it later, and it is not going to get any better. I think the thing to say is, "this is a matter being considered by the Committee and I am not going to comment on it." I don't want to get into the business of taking each charge that comes up in the Committee and commenting on it: "It is being considered by the Committee. It is being investigated and I am not going to comment on it."

D. That is exactly the way I have drafted these. I have checked them generally.

P. I will just cut them off. I think, John, if I start breaking down, you see like I have done the Court thing on the Watergate stuff, I am not going to comment on it. I know all of these questions. I am not going to comment on it. That is a matter for the Committee to determine. Then, I will repeat the fact that as far as the Watergate matter is concerned, I am not going to comment on it, on anything else. Let the Committee find out. What would you say? You don't agree with that?

D. Well, the bottom line, on a draft that (unintelligible). But if you have nothing to hide, Mr. President, here at the White House, why aren't you willing to spread on the record everything you know about it? Why doesn't the Dean Report be made public? Why doesn't everything come out? Why does Ziegler stand up there and bob and weave, and no comment? That's the bottom line.

P. Alright. What do you say to that?

D. Well,...

P. We are furnishing information. We will...

D. We have cooperated with the FBI in the investigation of the Watergate. We will cooperate with the investigation of, the proper investigation by the Senate.

P. We will make statements.

D. And indeed we have nothing to hide.

P. All this information, we have nothing to hide. We have to handle it. You see, I can't be in the position of basically hunkering down because you have a lot of tough questions on Watergate, and not go out and talk on their issues because it is not going to get better. It is going to get worse.

D. I would agree. I think its cycled somewhat. I think after the Gray thing (hearings on L. Patrick Gray III's nomination as FBI director) takes one course or the other, there will be a dead period of news on Watergate until the Ervin Hearings start again. This has obviously sparked the news again.

P. Well, let me just run over the questions again. If it is asked, what about Mr. Haldeman, Mr. Segretti, etc., etc. that is a matter being considered by the Senate Committee and I am not going to comment on it.

D. That is correct. That is specifically in their resolution.

P. I am not going to comment on something being investigated by the Committee. As I have already indicated, I am just not going to comment. Do you approve such tactics? Another question—?

D. Did Mr. (former Nixon appointments secretary Dwight L.) Chapin's departure have something to do with his involvement with Mr. Segretti?

P. (inaudible) What about Mr. Dean? My position is the same. We have cooperated with the Justice Department, the FBI—completely tried to furnish information under our control in this matter. We will cooperate with the Committee under the rules I have laid down in my statement on Executive Privilege. Now what else?

D. Well, then you will get a barrage of questions probably, on will you supply—will Mr. Haldeman and Mr. Ehrlichman and Mr. Dean go up to the Committee and testify?

P. No absolutely not.

D. Mr. (former Nixon special counsel Charles W.) Colson?

P. No. Absolutely not. It isn't a question of not—Ziegler or somebody had said that we in our executive privilege statement it was interpreted as meaning that we would not furnish information and all that. We said we will furnish information, but we are not going to be called to testify. That is the position. Dean and all the rest will grant you information. Won't you?

D. Yes. Indeed I will!

P. My feeling, John, is that I better hit it now rather than just let it build up where we are afraid of these questions and everybody, etc., and let Ziegler go out there and bob and weave around. I know the easy thing is to bug out, but it is not...

D. You're right. I was afraid. For the sake of debate, but I was having reservations. It is a bullet biter and you just have to do it. These questions are just not going to go away. Now the other thing that we talked about in the past, and I still have the same problem, is to have a "here it all is" approach. If we do that...

P. And let it all hang out.

D. And let it all hang out. Let's with a Segretti—etc.

P. We have passed that point.

D. Plus the fact, they are not going to believe the truth! That is the incredible thing!

P. They won't believe the truth, and they have committed seven people!

D. That's right! They will continually try to say that there is (unintelligible),

P. They hope one will say one day, "Haldeman did it," and one day, one will say I did it. When we get to that question—they might question his political savvy, but not mine! Not on a matter like that!

The "scenario" called for presidential statements on Watergate to contain as little detailed information as possible and for their preparation by Dean and other White House aides whom Nixon could refer to for indications that the President was acting.

In an early evening telephone conversation with Nixon on March 20, 1973, Dean suggested giving the President a report on Watergate to relieve outside pressure for a White House statement. The President, in turn, suggested a "general statement" that would "reassure" his supporters.

"We need something to answer somebody, answer things," Nixon said. "You know they say, 'What are you basing this on,' I can say, 'Well, my counsel advised me that'—...I don't want a, too much in chapter and verse...."

"An all around statement," Dean said.

"That's right. Try just something general," the President said.

Wording of Statements. The transcripts indicate that White House statements were carefully worded so as not to help Watergate investigators by disclosing the existence of documents that then could be subpoenaed. Ehrlichman and Ziegler discussed a possible statement by Nixon on the coverup charges at a March 30, 1973, meeting with the President. During the conversation, they decided that Ziegler would not mention at a press briefing anything about sworn affidavits from White House staff members denying knowledge of the coverup.

Meeting between the President, Ehrlichman and Ziegler in the Oval Office, March 30, 1973 (12:02-12:18 p.m.):

P. Yeah—Yeah—the President called for—fine. Every member of the White House staff who has been mentioned (unintelligible) mentioned as a —has submitted a sworn affidavit to me denying any knowledge of.

E. Any prior knowledge.

P. Any knowledge of or participation in. Could we say this?

E. No—I wouldn't.

P. Why? Not true? Too defensive?

E. Well, number one—it's defensive—it's self-serving. Number two—then that establishes the existence of a piece of paper that becomes a focal point for a subpoena and all that kind of thing.

Settings for Disclosure. The President, Haldeman, Ehrlichman and Dean sought to limit the scope of the Watergate investigation. They discussed the best settings in which to make Watergate disclosures and to control how the information would be released. At one point (March 21, 1973, 10:12-11:55 a.m.), they talked about going the grand jury route.

"The Grand Jury appeals to me from the standpoint, the President makes the move," Nixon said. "All these charges being bandied about, etc., the best thing to do is that I have asked the Grand Jury to look into any further charges. All charges have been raised. That is the place to do it, and not before a Committee of the Congress. Right?"

But the President, Haldeman and Dean reached no decision then.

Six days later, on March 27, they discussed creating a "superpanel"—a commission of judges or other prominent citizens to determine the involvement of White House officials—to handle the widening problem. But the President rejected that idea.

Out in Front. The President and his men weighed strategies to get him "out front" as they began to lose control of the coverup investigation.

In a March 27, 1973, conversation, the President, Haldeman, Ehrlichman and Ziegler talked about the establishment of the Presidential superpanel to investigate Watergate. They also discussed other options, such as a White House-controlled investigation that would send witnesses before the federal grand jury presided over by Judge John J. Sirica of the U.S. District Court for the District of Columbia.

During that meeting, this dialogue ensued:

P. Yeah. Another alternative that I thought of, rather than set up another procedure, call the Judge in and say, "Judge, we will carry out this investigation by sending them all down here and you can question them. I want everybody here and I want you to get to the bottom of this thing. You will have my total backing." Now that is another way to do it.

E. That's ok, as long as you then get out front.

The nonexistent Dean report on Watergate also was viewed in that light, especially after Dean's falling out with the President, Haldeman and Ehrlichman. The President and his aides discussed how to use the "Dean report" to give the President credit for investigating the coverup.

Meeting of the President, Haldeman and Ehrlichman in the Oval Office, April 16, 1973 (10:50-11:04 a.m.):

E. Ron (Ziegler, Nixon's press secretary) has an interesting point. Remember you had John Dean go to Camp David to write it (the Watergate report) up. He came down and said, "I can't".

P. Right.

E. That is the tip off and right then you started to move.

P. That's right. He said he could not write it.

H. Then you realized that there was more to this than you had been led to believe. (unintelligible)

P. How do I get credit for getting (former Nixon campaign deputy Jeb Stuart) Magruder to the stand?

E. Well it is very simple. You took Dean off of the case right then.

* * *

P. Why did I take Dean off? Because he was involved? I did it, really, because he was involved with Gray.

E. Well there was a lot of stuff breaking in the papers, but at the same time—

H. The scenario is that he told you he couldn't write a report so obviously you had to take him off.

P. Right, Right.

Handling the Press. Despite his professed indifference to the press, the President, according to the transcripts, spent much time talking with his aides about press coverage of Watergate and how to handle the news media. They watched the newspapers each day, were aware of stories by individual reporters, and paid careful attention to press reaction.

They also considered trying to use the press for leaks. On March 27, 1973, as the White House position deteriorated, Nixon, Haldeman, Ehrlichman and Ziegler met to decide how to handle the situation. Finally, the President told Ziegler, "...Just get out there (at a press briefing) and act like your usual cocky, confident self."

Other excerpts from that meeting:

Z. Then if I am asked a question about whether or not Dean would appear before the grand jury, if I am asked that question—

P. Yeah.

Z. How should I handle that?

P. That's tough.

Z. I could—Two options: one would be to say that (unintelligible) the other would be to say (unintelligible).

* * *

P. Why don't you say, "We have indicated cooperation and when we see the form of the request, or whatever it is—"

Z. "These matters must proceed in an orderly manner and I am not going to get up here and comment on the possibility of—"

P. "of future action" (unintelligible)

E. The other thing you might do is—this would put our friend John Dean III in a tough spot—say, "while there have been some accusations against him, he's really in the poorest position to defend himself of anybody in the government."

At other times, Ziegler got terser orders. "Kill it, kill it," was Nixon's order to his press secretary about a rumored story in *The Washington Post* and *The New York Times.*

Use of Leaks. On several occasions, the President and his aides talked about leaking stories that would embarrass the Democrats. One such story involved information (which Dean said he had obtained from former FBI official William C. Sullivan) that the Johnson administration allegedly had bugged the 1968 campaign plane of Spiro T. Agnew and had conducted surveillance of Sen. Barry Goldwater (R Ariz.) during his 1964 presidential campaign.

Meeting of the President, Haldeman and Dean in the Oval Office, March 13, 1973 (12:42-2:00 p.m.):

D. I have a thing on (former FBI official William) Sullivan I would like to ask you. Sullivan, as I told you, had been talking with me and I said Bill I would like for my own use to have a list of some of the horribles that you are aware of. He hasn't responded back to me, but he sent me a note yesterday saying John I am willing at any time to testify to what I know if you want me to. What he has, as we already know, he has something that has a certain degree of a dynamite situation already—the '68 presidency, surveillance of Goldwater.

P. I thought he said he saw that the '68 bugging was ordered, but he doesn't know whether it was carried out.

D. That's right.

P. But at least he would say (inaudible).

D. Well, I have never talked with Bill about it. I have never gone into details, because he has always been very close about it, but he is now getting to the point if we wanted him to do this, someone—and I don't think the White House should do it—should sit down with him and really take down some notes of what he does know, how strong it is, what he can substantiate.

P. Who the hell could do it if you don't?

D. Well, probably there is no one.

P. That is the problem.

D. Now the other thing, if we are going to use a package like this: Let's say in the Gray hearings—where everything is cast that we are the political people and they are not—that (the late FBI director, J. Edgar) Hoover was above reproach, which is just not accurate, total (expletive deleted). The person who would destroy Hoover's image is going to be this man Bill Sullivan. Also it is going to tarnish quite severely....

P. Some of the FBI.

D. ...some of the FBI. And a former President. He is going to lay it out, and just all hell is going to break loose once he does it. It is going to change the atmosphere of the Gray hearings and it is going to change the atmosphere of the whole Watergate hearings. Now the risk....

P. How will it change?

D. Because it will put them in context where government institutes were used in the past for the most flagrant political purposes.

P. How can that help us?

D. How does it help us?

P. I am being the devil's advocate....

D. I appreciate what you are doing. It is a red herring. It is what the public already believes. I think the people would react: (expletive deleted), more of that stuff! They are all bad down there! Because it is a one way street right now....

P. Do you think the press would use it? They may not play it.

D. It would be difficult not to. Ah, it would be difficult not to.

Later in the meeting, they talked about where to leak the story. "Maybe we need to go to *U.S. News,* sir," Dean said, referring to *U.S. News & World Report,* the weekly news magazine.

"Have him (Sullivan) give an interview to *U.S. News,* 'Wires in the Sky' or something," the President said.

Nixon then suggested "a respected reporter—why not give it to Mollenhoff?"

Clark R. Mollenhoff, Washington bureau chief of the *Des Moines Register and Tribune,* served as a special counselor to the President from July 1969 to July 1970.

D. Well that is interesting, Mollenhoff is close, but our guy gets near Mollenhoff. Mollenhoff may not do anything.

P. No, and we are in a position with Mollenhoff that he has been fighting us some. Maybe Mollen-

hoff would be a pretty good prospect for this thing. It is the kind of story he loves, but he digs on something. You couldn't call him, however, (inaudible)—The (characterization deleted) loves to talk soo much, although he is a hell of a guy.

D. Ok. Can I call Clark and say "listen Clark, a guy brought me a piece of dynamite that I don't even want in the White House?"

P. He will write that, won't he?

D. Yeah. Because that doesn't look like a set up deal. Well Clark Mollenhoff is the first guy to uncover a shield of anything, and he will say no way—

P. But he would do it. That is very important piece....

Criticism of Press. Nixon and his aides paid close attention to the reporting on Watergate and were mostly critical of it.

At their March 13, 1973, meeting, Dean said to the President about a NBC Nightly News report:

"That NBC thing last night, which is just a travesty as far and we're talking about shabby journalism, they took the worst edited clips out of context, with Strachan saying he was leaving. And then had a little clip of Ron saying, 'I deny that.' And he was denying something other than what they were talking about in their charge. It was incredible. Someone is going through and putting that altogether right now and Ron ought to be able to (unintelligible) to that one on NBC. It was a very, very dishonest television reporting of sequence of events, but out of sequence."

In an April 15, 1973, conversation (10:35-11:15 a.m.), the President and Ehrlichman talked about a story by Haynes Johnson of *The Washington Post.*

"I read (unintelligible) front page the Haynes Johnson (unintelligible) story today about—story on (unintelligible).

"I haven't had a chance to read that," Ehrlichman said. "I saw the headlines."

"It's not corroborated of course," Nixon said, "but they said their survey of the country and all showed that the President's support regarding the war was not (unintelligible)—the economy is the problem (unintelligible) but the overriding issues that are (unintelligible) Watergate. (unintelligible), but John that is just not true."

A few seconds later, Ehrlichman said of Johnson, he "is notorious for finding what's he's looking for."

Earlier in their conversation, Nixon and Ehrlichman talked about press coverage of Watergate.

E. We are at kind of an ebb tide right now in this whole thing, in terms of the media, as I see it. They are a little afraid to get too far out on a limb on this 'cause they think something's going on with the committee negotiations, and there's no new news breaking, and so they are kind of.

P. Waiting.

E. Waiting.

P. Yeah,—they'll get a full tide when they get to the Grand Jury.

E. Well sure, but now is a good time for us to fill that vacuum.

P. Oh yes—a little news.

E. Yeah.

P. Sure—let 'em know other things are going on.

The President's hostility toward the press came out in a conversation he had with Dean on Feb. 28, 1973, in which they discussed a civil suit in which newsmen were subpoenaed.

Meeting between the President and Dean in the Oval Office, Feb. 28, 1973 (9:12-10:23 a.m.):

P. Well, one hell of a lot of people don't give one damn about this issue of the suppression of the press, etc. We know that we aren't trying to do it. They all squeal about it. It is amusing to me when they say—I watched the networks and I thought they were restrained. What (expletive omitted) do they want them to do—go through the 1968 syndrome when they were 8 to 1 against us. They are only three to one this time. It is really sickening though to see these guys. These guys have

always figured we have the press on our side. You know we receive a modest amount of support—no more. Colson sure making them move it around, saying we don't like this or that and (inaudible)

D. Well, you know Colson's threat of a law suit which was printed in Evans and Novak (columnists Rowland Evans Jr. and Robert D. Novak) had a very sobering effect on several of the national magazines. They are now checking before printing a lot of this Watergate junk they print. They check the press office trying to get confirmation or denial, or call the individuals involved. And they have said they are doing it because they are afraid of a libel suit on them. So it did have a sobering effect. We will keep them honest if we can remind them that they can't print anything and get away with it. √

White House Edited Transcripts of Presidential Conversations

Meeting: The President, Haldeman and Dean, Oval Office, Sept. 15, 1972, (5:27—6:17 p.m.):

Following is the text of a recorded conversation among President Nixon, presidential counsel John W. Dean III, and White House chief of staff H.R. Haldeman on Sept. 15, 1972.

On the same day, a federal grand jury indicted G. Gordon Liddy, E. Howard Hunt Jr. and five other men in connection with the break-in at the Watergate offices of the Democratic National Committee.

Dean testified before the Senate Watergate committee in June 1973 that this was the first conversation he had with Nixon about Watergate, that the President congratulated him about doing "a good job," and that he left the meeting "with the impression that the President was well aware of what had been going on regarding the success of keeping the White House out of the Watergate scandal...."

The transcript, among those supplied to the House Judiciary Committee April 30, 1974, was edited by the White House to delete expletives, personal characterizations and irrelevancies. The participants are identified by initials—P for President, D for Dean and H for Haldeman.

This opens just as Dean comes in the door.

P. Hi, how are you? You had quite a day today didn't you. You got Watergate on the way didn't you?

D. We tried.

H. How did it all end up?

D. Ah, I think we can say well at this point. The press is playing it just as we expect.

H. Whitewash?

D. No, not yet—the story right now—

P. It is a big story.

H. Five indicted plus the WH former guy and all that.

D. Plus two White House fellows

H. That is good that takes the edge off whitewash really that was the thing (Nixon campaign manager John N.) Mitchell kept saying that to people in the country Liddy and Hunt (G. Gordon Liddy and E. Howard Hunt Jr., Watergate conspirators) were big men. Maybe that is good.

P. How did MacGregor (Clark MacGregor, who succeeded Mitchell as campaign manager) handle himself?

D. I think very well he had a good statement which said that the Grand Jury had met and that it was now time to realize that some apologies may be due.

H. Fat chance.

D. Get the damn (inaudible)

H. We can't do that.

P. Just remember, all the trouble we're taking, we'll have a chance to get back one day. How are you doing on your other investigations?

H. What has happened on the bug?

P. What bug?

D. The second bug there was a bug found in the telephone of one of the men at the DNC (Democratic National Committee).

P. You don't think it was left over from the other time?

D. Absolutely not, the Bureau has checked and re-checked the whole place after that night. The man had specifically checked and re-checked the telephone and it was not there.

P. What the hell do you think was involved?

D. I think DNC was planted.

P. You think they did it?

D. Uh huh

P. (Expletive deleted)—do they really want to believe that we planted that?

H. Did they get anything on the finger prints?

D. No, nothing at all—either on the telephone or on the bug. The FBI has unleashed a full investigation over at the DNC starting with (Democratic chairman Lawrence F.) O'Brien right now.

H. Laughter. Using the same crew—

D. The same crew—the Washington Field Office.

P. What kind of questions are they asking him?

D. Anything they can think of because O'Brien is charging them with failing to find all the bugs.

H. Good, that will make them mad.

D. So (acting FBI director L. Patrick) Gray is pissed and his people are pissed off. So maybe they will move in because their reputation is on the line. I think that is a good development.

'A Good Development'

P. I think that is a good development because it makes it look so (adjective deleted) funny. Am I wrong?

D. No, no sir. It looks silly. If we can find that the DNC planted that, the whole story will reverse.

P. But how could they possible find it, though?

D. Well, they are trying to ascertain who made the bug. It is a custom made product. If they can get back to the

---

"I want the most comprehensive notes on all those who tried to do us in.... We have not used the Bureau and we have not used the Justice Department but things are going to change now. And they are either going to do it right or go."

—President Nixon to John W. Dean III and H.R. Haldeman Sept. 15, 1972

---

man who manufactured it and who he sold it to and how it came down through the chain.

P. Boy, You never know when those guys get after it—they can really find it.

D. The resources that have been put against this whole investigation to date are really incredible. It is truly a larger investigation than was conducted against the after inquiry of the JFK assassination.

P. Oh.

D. Good statistics supporting the finding.

H. Isn't that ridiculous—this silly thing.

P. Yes (Expletive deleted). (Sen. Barry) Goldwater (R Ariz.) put it in context when he said "(expletive deleted) everybody bugs everybody else. You know that."

D. That was priceless.

P. It happens to be totally true. We were bugged in '68 on the plane and in '62 even running for Governor—(expletive deleted) thing you ever saw.

D. It is a shame that evidence to the fact that that happened in '68 was never around. I understand that only the former Director had that information.

H. No, that is not true.

D. There was evidence of it?

H. There are others who have information.

P. How do you know? Does DeLoache (Cartha D. De Loach, a former assistant FBI director) know?

D. DeLoache?

H. I have some stuff too—on the bombing incident and too in the bombing halt stay.

P. The difficulty with using it, of course, is it reflects on (former President Lyndon B.) Johnson. If it weren't for that, I would use it. Is there any way we could use it without using his name—saying that the DNC did it? No—the FBI did the bugging.

D. That is the problem—would it reflect on Johnson or (former Vice President Hubert H.) Humphrey?

H. Johnson. Humphrey didn't do it.

P. Oh, hell no.

H. He was bugging Humphrey, too.

P. (Expletive deleted)

P. Well, on the other hand. I want you to ask (former Treasury Secretary John B.) Connally. What crazy things we do. That this might help with the bombing. I don't think he will talk to Johnson—and also it would reflect on the Bureau. They hate to admit that.

H. It is a rough one on them with all this stuff that they don't do Congressmen, etc.

P. It isn't worth it—the hell with it. What is the situation on the little red box? Have they found the box yet?

D. Gray has never had access to the box. He is now going to pursue the box. I spoke to him just about thirty minutes ago. Pat said "I don't know about the box. Don't know

---

"(T)his thing is just one of those side issues and a month later everybody looks back and wonders what all the shooting was about...."

—President Nixon to John N. Mitchell
Sept. 15, 1972

---

where it is now. We never had an opportunity before when it was first released in the press that there was a box to go in but we have decided now we have grounds to go in and find it."

H. The latest public story was that she handed it over to Edward Bennett Williams (a Washington lawyer).

D. That is right.

H. The Bureau ought to go into Edward Bennett Williams and start questioning him and have him tied up for a couple of days.

P. Yeah, I hope they do. The Bureau better get over pretty quick and get that little red box. We want it cleared up. We want to get to the bottom of it. If any body is guilty over here we want to know.

H. It will probably be in the news!

D. You might be interested in some of the allocations we got. The Stans (Maurice H. Stans, finance director of the Nixon campaign) libel action was assigned to Judge Ritchie (Judge Charles R. Richey of the U.S. District Court for the District of Columbia).

P. (Expletive deleted)

D. Well now that is good and bad. Judge Richey is not known to be one of the (inaudible) on the bench, that is considered by me. He is fairly candid in dealing with

people about the question. He has made several entrees off the bench—one to (Attorney General Richard G.) Kleindienst and one to Roemer McPhee (H. Roemer McPhee, a Republican Party lawyer) to keep Roemer abreast of what his thinking is. He told Roemer he thought Maury ought to file a libel action.

P. Did he?

H. Can he deal with this concurrently with the court case?

D. Yeah. The fact that the civil case drew to a halt—that the depositions were halted he is freed.

H. It was just put off for a few days, wasn't it?

D. It did more than that—he had been talking to (Earl J.) Silbert, one of the Assistant U.S. Attorneys down here. Silbert said, "We are going to have a hell of a time drawing these indictments because these civil depositions will be coming out and the Grand Jury has one out on this civil case but it is nothing typical."
Someone asked the President if he wanted Mitchell's call—he said, "Yeah."

D. Based on that when Silbert had told Richey this and with a casual encounter—in fact it was just in the hall, so Richey stopped the civil case so Silbert can get the indictment down.
Telephone call from John Mitchell:
Hello.

P. —comments only from here on until end of call:
Well are you still alive.
I was just sitting here with John Dean and he tells me you were going to be sued or something. Good, Good. Yeah. Good. Sure. Well I tell you just don't let this keep you or your colleagues from concentrating on the big game. This thing is just one of those side issues and a month later everybody looks back and wonders what all the shooting was about. OK, John. Good night. Get a good night's sleep. And don't bug anybody without asking me? OK? Yeah. Thank you.

D. Three months ago I would have had trouble predicting there would be a day when this would be forgotten, but I think I can say that 54 days from now nothing is going to come crashing down to our surprise.

P. That what?

D. Nothing is going to come crashing down to our surprise.

'Way You Have Handled All This...Skillful'

P. Oh well, this is a can of worms as you know a lot of this stuff that went on. And the people who worked this way are awfully embarrassed. But the way you have handled all this seems to me has been very skillful putting your fingers in the leaks that have sprung here and sprung there. The Grand Jury is dismissed now?

D. That is correct. They have completed and they have let them go so there will be no continued investigation prompted by the Grand Jury's inquiry. the GAO (General Accounting Office) report referred over to Justice is on a shelf right now because they have hundreds of violations—they have violations of (Sen. George) McGovern (D S.D.), of (Sen.) Humphrey (D Minn.), violations of (Sen. Henry M.) Jackson (D Wash.), and several hundred Congressional violations. They don't want to start prosecuting one any more than they prosecute the other.

P. They definitely will not prosecute us unless they prosecute the others.

D. Well, we are talking about technical violations referred over also.

P. What about watching the McGovern contributors and all that sort of thing?

D. We have (inaudible) eye out on that. His I understand is not in full compliance.

P. He asked?

D. No.

P. Well, not yet. His 300 committees—have they all reported yet?

D. We have a couple delinquent state committees.

P. It said in the paper that McGovern had 300 committees reported.

D. No, they have not. There are a lot of things he has never done—as he has never disclosed the fact that he has some 300 committees. *The Wall Street Journal* piece that picked it up and carried that story brought out his committees.

P. Can we say anything publicly about it?

D. Purpose there hasn't been a tax sham—it is hard to comprehend why he set up that many committees. He doesn't have that many large contributors, but they may have to disburse through a great number of smaller committees.

H. Unless someone is stealing $900,000.

D. That's right.

P. It could be. That could be possible.

H. He may be getting $900,000 from somebody. He may have two or three angels.

P. I don't think he is getting a hell of a lot of small money. I don't believe (expletive deleted) Have you had the P.O. checked yet?

H. That is John's area. I don't know.

P. Well, let's have it checked.

D. Well as I see it, the only problems we may have are the human problems and I will keep a close watch on that.

P. Union?

D. Human.

H. Human frailities.

D. People get annoyed—some finger pointing—false accusations—any internal dissension of any nature.

P. You mean on this case?

D. On this case. There is some bitterness between the Finance Committee and the Political Committee—they feel they are taking all the heat and all the people upstairs are bad people—not being recognized.

'This Is a War'

P. We are all in it together. This is a war. We take a few shots and it will be over. We will give them a few shots and it will be over. Don't worry. I wouldn't want to be on the other side right now. Would you?

D. Along that line, one of the things I've tried to do, I have begun to keep notes on a lot of people who are emerging as less than our friends because this will be over some day and we shouldn't forget the way some of them have treated us.

P. I want the most comprehensive notes on all those who tried to do us in. They didn't have to do it. If we had had a very close election and they were playing the other side I would understand this. No—they were doing this quite deliberately and they are asking for it and they are going to get it. We have not used the power in this first four years as you know. We have never used it. We have not used the Bureau and we have not used the Justice Department but things are going to change now. And they are either going to do it right or go.

D. What an exciting prospect.

P. Thanks. It has to be done. We have been (adjective deleted) fools for us to come into this election campaign and not do anything with regard to the Democratic Senators who are running, et cetera. And who the hell are they after? They are after us. It is absolutely ridiculous. It is not going to be that way any more.

H. Really, it is ironic that we have gone to extremes. You and your damn regulations. Everybody worries about not picking up a hotel bill.

D. I think you can be proud of the White House staff. It really has had no problems of that sort. And I love this

GAO audit that is going on now. I think they have some suspicion that even a cursory investigation is going to discover something here. I don't think they can find a thing. I learned today, incidentally, and have not confirmed it, that the GAO auditor who is down here is here at the Speaker of the House's request.

P. That surprises me.

'Put a Little Heat on Him'

H. Well, (expletive deleted) the Speaker of the House. Maybe we better put a little heat on him.

P. I think so too.

H. Because he has a lot worse problems than he is going to find down here.

D. That's right.

H. That is the kind of thing that, you know, we really ought to do is call the Speaker and say, "I regret to say your calling the GAO down here because of what it is going to cause us to do to you."

P. Why don't you see if (former presidential counselor Bryce N.) Harlow will tell him that.

H. Because he wouldn't do it—he would just be pleasant and call him Mr. Speaker.

D. I suppose the other area we are going to see some publicity on in the coming weeks because I think now that the indictments are down there will be a cresting on that— the white wash—the civil rights cases in advance. But (Rep.) Wright Patman's (D Texas) hearings—his banking

---

"This is a war.... I wouldn't want to be on the other side right now. Would you?"

—President Nixon to John W. Dean III
and H.R. Haldeman
Sept. 15, 1972

---

and currency committee—whether we will be successful in turning that off or not I don't know. We have a plan where (Henry B.) Rothblatt and (William O.) Bittman who were counsel for the seven who were indicted today are going to go up and visit the five top members and say that if you commence hearings you are going to jeopardize the civil rights of these individuals in the worst way and they will never get a fair trial.

P. Why not ask that they request to be heard by the committee?

D. They could say, "If you do commence with these hearings we intend to come up and say what you are doing to the rights of individuals." Something to that effect.

P. They could even get a motion in court to get the thing dismissed.

H. Going the other way—

P. Getting the criminal charges dismissed on the grounds of civil rights.

D. We have someone approaching the ACLU (American Civil Liberties Union) for these guys—having them exert some pressure because we don't just want Stans up there in front of the cameras with Patman asking all these questions. It is going to be the whole thing over and over again. I understand too, or I have been told, that John Connally is close to Patman and if anyone could talk turkey to Patman, Connally could. (House Minority Leader Gerald R.) Jerry Ford (R Mich.) is not really taking an active interest in this matter that is developing so Stans is going to see Jerry Ford and try to brief him and explain to him the problems he has.

The other thing we are going to do—we are looking at all the campaign reports of every member of that committee because we are convinced that none of them complied exactly with the law either. If they want to play rough —some day we better say, "Gentlemen, we want to call your attention that you have not complied with A,B,C, and F and we are not going to hold that a secret if you start talking campaign violations here."

P. What about Ford? Do you think so? Connally can't because of the way he is set up. If anybody can do it, Connally could, but if Ford can get the minority members. They have some weak men and women on that committee, unfortunately. (Rep. Margaret M.) Heckler (R Mass.) is alright.

D. Heckler was great.

P. (Rep. William B.) Widnall (R N.J.), et cetera. Jerry should talk to Widnall. After all, if we ever win the House, Jerry will be the Speaker and he could tell him if he did not get off—he will not be Chairman ever.

D. That would be very helpful to get all of these people at least pulling together. If Jerry could get a little action on this.

H. Damn it Jerry should. That is exactly the thing he was talking about, that the reason they are staying is so that they can run investigations.

P. The point is that they ought to raise hell about these hearings. I don't know that the counsel calls the members of the committee often. I think if they have to have this blunderbuss in the public arena then this is all it is.

D. That is the last forum where we have the least problem right now. (Sen. Edward M.) Kennedy (D Mass.) has already said he may call hearings of the Administrative

---

"Well, (expletive deleted) the speaker of the House. Maybe we better put a little heat on him."

—H.R. Haldeman to President Nixon
and John W. Dean III
Sept. 15, 1972

Practices sub-committee. As these committees spin out oracles we used to get busy on each one. I stopped doing that about two months ago. We just take one thing at a time.

'Trying to Cut Our Losses'

P. You really can't sit and worry about it all the time. The worst may happen but it may not. So you just try to button it up as well as you can and hope for the best, and remember basically the damn business is unfortunately trying to cut our losses.

D. Certainly that is right and certainly it has had no effect on you. That's the good thing.

H. No, it has been kept away from the White House and of course completely from the President. The only tie to the White House is the (former presidential special counsel Charles W.) Colson effort they keep trying to pull in.

D. And, of course, the two White House people of lower level —indicted—one consultant and one member of the Domestic Staff. That is not very much of a tie.

H. That's right. Or (convicted mass murderer Charles M.) Manson. (expletive deleted). If they had been killers. Isn't that true?

H. It is certainly true.

P. These (characterization deleted) they have had no way. They ought to move the trial away from—

D. There has been extensive clipping on the part of the counsel in this case. They may never get a fair trial. They may never get a jury that will convict them. The *Post*, you know, that they have a real large team as-

---

"(T)he worst may happen but it may not. So you just try to button it up as well as you can and hope for the best, and remember basically the damn business is unfortunately trying to cut our losses."

—President Nixon to John W. Dean III
Sept. 15, 1972

---

signed to cover this case. Believe me, the Maury Stans story about his libel suit that had so much coverage in the *Evening News* they put way back on page 8 of the *Post* and did not even cover it in total.

H. Yes, I will talk to Bill.

D. I think Dick Cook (White House lobbyist Richard K. Cook) has been working on it.

P. Maybe Mitchell should do.

H. Could Mitchell do it?

P. No.

D. I don't think it would be good to draw him into it. I think Maury could talk to Ford if that would do any good. I think Maury ought to brief Ford on exactly what his whole side of the story is. Maury understands the law.

H. I will talk to Cook.

P. Maybe (presidential assistant John D.) Ehrlichman should talk to him. Ehrlichman understands the law.

H. Is that a good idea? Maybe it is.

'...It Comes from the Top'

P. I think maybe that is the thing. This is a big play. He has to know that it comes from the top. While I can't talk for myself he has to get at this and—the thing up.

D. Well, if we got that slide up there—it is a tragedy to let them have a field day up there.

P. What is the first move? When does he call his witnesses?

D. Well, he has not even gotten the vote of his committee— he hasn't even convened his committee as to whether he can call hearings. That is why he won't come Monday morning. His attorney is going to arrive on the doorstep

---

"Certainly that is right and certainly it has had no effect on you. That's the good thing."

—Dean's reply to President Nixon

---

of the chairman and to tell him what to do and he proceeds. One of the members of the committee, (Rep. Garry) Jerry Brown (R Mich.), wrote Kliendienst a letter saying, "If the chairman holds committee hearings on this, isn't this going to jeopardize your criminal case?"

P. That is smart politics for Michigan and some tie into Ford. He is a very smart fellow.

D. Good lawyer and being helpful. He is anxious to help.

P. Tell Ehrlichman to get Brown and Ford in together and they can work out something. They ought to get off their —and push it. No use to let Patman have a free ride here.

D. Well we can keep them well briefed on moves if they will move when we provide them with the strategy. And we will have a raft of depositions going the other way soon.

"P. But he knew? He knew about Watergate? Strachan did?

"D. Yes.

"P. I will be damned!"

—President Nixon and John W. Dean III
March 13, 1974

We will be hauling the O'Briens in and the like on our due process soon.

P. What did they ask—any questions?

D. No. I saw Rothblatt laughing at the start of the symposium. He is quite a character. He has been getting into the sex life of some of the members of the DNC.

P. Why? What is the justification?

D. Well, he is working on the entrapment theory that they were hiding something and they had secret information of theirs to hide and if they could someway conspire to bring this thing about themselves. It is a way-out theory that no one had caught.

H. (Laughter)

D. He had scheduled Patricia (Roberts) Harris (Democratic Party official in 1972) and she did not show up. She went to the beauty parlor instead so he went down to the Court House and she had been directed to show up and then the next day the Judge cut all the depositions

---

"P.. Is it too late to go the hang-out road?

"D. Yes, I think it is...."

—President Nixon and John W. Dean III
March 13, 1973

---

off. But he had a host of wild questions about where O'Brien got his compensation when he was Chairman. Not that he would know anything about that, but it was just an interesting question he might want to ask the Chairman under oath.

H. That's what Gibbons said—the same hunting license that gave them.

D. No—that is right.

H. So we can play the same game they are playing. We ought to be able to do better at it.

P. Well.

H. Are those depositions sealed?

D. That's right.

H. They are?

D. But that argues that they will want them unsealed less than we will, and we may be arguing at some point to get them unsealed.

P. Yeah.

D. I think what is going to happen on the civil case is that the Judge is going to dismiss the complaint that is down there right now. They will then file a new complaint

which will come back to (Judge) Richey again. That will probably happen the 20th, 21st, 22nd. Then 20 days will run before any answers have to be filed and the depositions will be commenced so we are eating up an awful lot of time.

P. Why will the Judge dismiss the complaint?

D. Probably on the middle ground—both on the substantive ground that they haven't stated a good cause of action —that there is improper class actions filed. O'Brien doesn't indeed represent any class. And he will just dismiss it on the merits. It is not a good complaint. He has already shaved it down to almost nothing on his original order. They will then have to re-design it in a much narrower action but the Judge himself can't

---

"P. ...Apparently you haven't been able to do anything on my project of getting on the offensive?

"D. But I have sir, to the contrary!"

—President Nixon and John W. Dean III
March 13, 1973

---

suggest something to counsel. He has to do a cute argument here. If he dismisses on the merits, that they can't file another suit. They are out of the court totally.

H. But our two suits go hang?

D. We have two suits—we have the abuse of process and the libel suit.

H. We can take depositions on both of those?

D. Absolutely.

P. Hell yes.
(Inaudible)

H. (Laughter)

D. We can blunder down the road anyway.

NOTE

(Further conversation following unrelated to Watergate.)

Meeting: The President, Haldeman and Dean, Oval Office, March 13, 1973 (12:42-2 p.m.):

Following is the text of a recorded conversation between President Nixon and his counsel, John W. Dean III, on March 13, 1973. White House chief of staff H. R. Haldeman participates briefly in the beginning of the conversation. In his testimony to the Senate Watergate committee, Dean said that in this conversation he and Nixon discussed the money demands of the Watergate burglars and that the President said it would be 'no problem' to raise $1-million. There is no reference to these subjects in the White House transcript of the March 13 conversation. This discussion is contained in the March 21, 1973, transcript. (March 21 text, p. 394)

Highlights of the following conversation include:
• Nixon and Dean discuss the idea of former White House aide Charles W. Colson as a consultant so that he would not have to testify.
• Nixon asks if Dean needs Internal Revenue Service information for the counter-offensive.
• Nixon hears of the involvement of Gordon C. Strachan, former aide to Haldeman.

• *Nixon states that his nominee for FBI director, L. Patrick Gray III, "should not be head of the FBI."*

The transcript was edited by the White House to delete expletives, personal characterizations and irrelevancies. Nixon is identified as P (for President), Dean as D and Haldeman as H.

H. Say, did you raise the question with the President on (former presidential special counsel Charles W.) Colson as a consultant?

D. No, I didn't.

H. Was that somebody else?

D. The thought was as a consultant, without doing any consulting, he wants it for continued protection on—

H. Solely for the purpose of executive privilege protection, I take it.

D. It is one of those things that is kept down in the personnel office, and nothing is done on it.

P. What happens to (White House appointments secretary Dwight L.) Chapin?

D. Well, Chapin doesn't have quite the same problem in appearing as Colson will.

H. Yeah—you have the same problems of Chapin appearing as Colson.

P. Well, can't—that would such an obvious fraud to have both of them as consultants, that that won't work. I think he is right. You would have to leave Chapin.

H. Well, you can't make Chapin a consultant, because we have already said he is not.

D. Yeah.

H. Because we wanted the separation. The question is, are you then, as of now, the way they have interpreted executive privilege, is that you are not going to let Chapin testify.

P. Anybody.

H. Because it applies to executive privilege by the former people in relation to matters while they were here.

D. And the problem area is....

H. And that same thing would apply to Colson.

D. Well, yes, if Chuck were truly going to be doing nothing from this day on.

H. That's alright. He is concerned with what he is doing. Colson is concerned with what he is doing from now on, and he would apply the consulting tactic if he were called with regard to actions taken now...

D. That's right.

H. that relate to the Watergate action.

D. The problem is, I think, he will be out stirring up counter-news attacks and things of this nature.

P. (expletive deleted) Is he supposed to do that and be consulting with the President on it?

D. No, no. But he is consulting. It is a wide open consultantship. It doesn't mean he would be consulting with you.

H. Yeah. Your idea was just to put this in the drawer, in case.

D. Put it in the drawer, and then decide it.

H. It would be a consultant without pay.

D. I wouldn't even tell Chuck this. Just tell Chuck there is something in the drawer.

H. There is no reason to tell Chuck is there? Why....

P. I would tell Chuck. Tell him he is not to say anything, frankly.

H. The point would be to date it back on Saturday, so it is that day.

D. Continuous.

P. His consultant fee stopped for the present time, but he is still available for purposes of consulting on various problems and the like.

D. Right.

P. Unpaid consultants?

D. Yes.

H. We have some of those.

D. Good ones.

P. Well, what are the latest developments Bob should get something on?

D. Yeah.

P. Before we get into that I was wondering about that jackassery about some kid who (unintelligible)—which of course is perfectly proper course of action if it works. I would expect we were heavily infiltrated that way too.

D. The only problem there Mr. President is that....

P. Did he get paid?

D. He was paid.

P. By check?

D. He was paid by personal check of another person over there who, in turn, was taking it out of expense money. The ultimate source of the money—and this is ticklish —is that it is pre-April 7th money, and there could be some potential embarrassment for Ken Reitz (Kenneth C. Rietz, Nixon's 1972 youth director) along the way.

P. Oh!

D. So he is. But I think it is a confined situation. Obviously it is something that will come up in the Ervin Committee, but it is not another new Liddy-Hunt (Watergate conspirators G. Gordon Liddy and E. Howard Hunt Jr.) operation.

P. It is just a (adjective deleted) thing.

D. Oh, it is.

P. What happened to the kid? Did he just decide to be a hero?

D. That's right. He probably chatted about it around school, and the word got out, and he got confronted with it and he knew he had chatted about it, so there he was. Its absurd, it really is. He didn't do anything illegal.

P. Illegal? Of course not! Apparently you haven't been able to do anything on my project of getting on the offensive?

D. But I have sir, to the contrary!

P. Based on Sullivan, have you kicked a few butts around?

D. I have all of the information that we have collected. There is some there, and I have turned it over to Baroody (presidential special assistant William J. Baroody Jr.). Baroody is having a speech drafted for (Sen.) Barry Goldwater (R Ariz.). And there is enough material there to make a rather sensational speech just by: Why in the hell isn't somebody looking into what happened to President Nixon during his campaign? Look at these events! How do you explain these? Where are the answers to these questions? But, there is nothing but threads. I pulled all the information.

P. Also, the Senator should then present it to the Ervin Committee and demand that that be included. He is a Senator, a Senator....

D. What I am working on there for Barry is a letter to Senator Ervin that this has come to my attention, and why shouldn't this be a part of the inquiry? And he can spring out 1964 and quickly to '72. We've got a pretty good speech there, if we can get out our materials.

P. Good!

D. So it's in the mill.

H. We have finally started something.

P. (expletive deleted) Why haven't we had anyone involved in it before? Just didn't have enough stuff? For example, investigations were supposed to have been taken for the 34 (unintelligible) contributed to (1972 Democratic presidential nominee George) McGovern. And they say (expletive deleted) it is all hanky-panky, and their records are just too bad to find out. Is that the problem?

H. Won't that be an issue?

D. That will be an issue. There is a crew working that, also.

'Need Any IRS Stuff?'

P. Do you need any IRS (Internal Revenue Service) stuff?

D. There is no need at this hour for anything from IRS, and we have a couple of sources over there that I can go to. I don't have to go around with (IRS commissioner) Johnnie (M.) Walters or anybody, but we can get right in and get what we need. I have been preparing the answers for the briefing book and I just raised this with Ron; in my estimation, for what it is worth, that probably this week will draw more Watergate questions than any other week we are likely to see, given the Gray (Acting FBI Director L. Patrick Gray III) hearings, the new revelations—they are not new, but they are now substantiated—about (Nixon personal attorney Herbert W.) Kalmbach and Chapin that have been in the press.

P. To the effect of what phase?

D. That Chapin directed Kalmbach to pay (Donald H.) Segretti, the alleged saboteur, somewhere between $35 and $40,000. There is an awful lot of that hot in the press now. There is also the question of Dean appearing, not appearing—Dean's role. There are more stories in the *Post* this morning that are absolutely inaccurate about my turning information over to the Re-Election Committee for some woman over there. Mrs. (Judy) Hoback signed an affidavit and gave it to (Sen.) Birch Bayh (D Ind.), and said that "I was brought into (former Nixon campaign deputy manager Robert C.) Bob Mardian's office within 48 hours after a private interview I had with the jury and confronted with it." How did they know that? It came from internal sources over there. That's how they knew it!

P. From what?

D. Internal sources—this girl had told others that she was doing this, and they just told. They just quickly sent it to the top that she was out on her own.

P. Did she quit?

D. She did. There have been two or three of those.

H. Why did she do that? Was she mad?

D. She is a registered Democrat.

H. Why did we take her in?

D. To this day, I do not know what she was doing.

P. Who was she working for?

D. She worked in (Nixon campaign finance director Maurice H.) Stans' operation.

P. Why did he have her working for him?

D. It wasn't a good move. In fact that was one of our problems—the little pocket of women who worked for Maury Stans. There is no doubt that things would have sailed a lot smoother without that pack. Not that they have or had anything that was devastating.

P. Well, now, with regard to the question, etc., it would be my opinion not to dodge it just because there are going to be questions.

D. Well you are probably going to get more questions this week. And the tough questions. And some of them don't have easy answers. For example, did Haldeman know that there was a Don Segretti out there? That question is likely.

P. Did he? I don't know.

D. Yes, he had knowledge that there was somebody in the field doing prankster-type activities.

P. Well, I don't know anything about that. What about my taking, basically, just trying to fight this thing one at a time. I am only going to have to fight it later, and it is not going to get any better. I think the thing to say is, "this is a matter being considered by the Committee and I am not going to comment on it." I don't want to get into the business of taking each charge that comes

up in the Committee and commenting on it: "It is being considered by the Committee. It is being investigated and I am not going to comment on it."

D. That is exactly the way I have drafted these. I have checked them generally.

P. I will just cut them off. I think, John, if I start breaking down, you see like I have done the Court thing on the Watergate stuff, I am not going to comment on it. I know all of these questions. I am not going to comment on it. That is a matter for the Committee to determine. Then, I will repeat the fact that as far as the Watergate matter is concerned, I am not going to comment on it, on anything else. Let the Committee find out. What would you say? You don't agree with that?

D. Well, the bottom line, on a draft that (unintelligible). But if you have nothing to hide, Mr. President, here at the White House, why aren't you willing to spread on the record everything you know about it? Why doesn't the Dean Report be made public? Why doesn't everything come out? Why does (White House press secretary Ronald L.) Ziegler stand up there and bob and weave, and no comment? That's the bottom line.

P. Alright. What do you say to that?

D. Well,....

P. We are furnishing information. We will....

D. We have cooperated with the FBI in the investigation of the Watergate. We will cooperate with the investigation of, the proper investigation by the Senate.

P. We will make statements.

D. And indeed we have nothing to hide.

P. All this information, we have nothing to hide. We have to handle it. You see, I can't be in the position of basically hunkering down because you have a lot of tough questions on Watergate, and not go out and talk on their issues because it is not going to get better. It is going to get worse.

D. I would agree. I think its cycled somewhat. I think after the Gray thing takes one course or the other, there will be a dead period of news on Watergate until the Ervin Hearings start again. This has obviously sparked the news again.

P. Well, let me just run over the questions again. If it is asked, what about Mr. Haldeman, Mr. Segretti, etc., etc. that is a matter being considered by the Senate Committee and I am not going to comment on it.

D. That is correct. That is specifically in their resolution.

P. I am not going to comment on something being investigated by the Committee. As I have already indicated, I am just not going to comment. Do you approve such tactics? Another question—?

D. Did Mr. Chapin's departure have something to do with his involvement with Mr. Segretti?

P. (inaudible) What about Mr. Dean? My position is the same. We have cooperated with the Justice Department, the FBI—completely tried to furnish information under our control in this matter. We will cooperate with the Committee under the rules I have laid down in my statement on Executive Privilege. Now what else?

D. Well, then you will get a barrage of questions probably, on will you supply—will Mr. Haldeman and Mr. (presidential assistant John D.) Ehrlichman and Mr. Dean go up to the Committee and testify?

P. No, absolutely not.

D. Mr. Colson?

P. No. Absolutely not. It isn't a question of not—Ziegler or somebody had said that we in our executive privilege statement it was interpreted as meaning that we would not furnish information and all that. We said we will furnish information, but we are not going to be called to testify. That is the position. Dean and all the rest will grant you information. Won't you?

D. Yes. Indeed I will!

P. My feeling, John, is that I better hit it now rather than just let it build up where we are afraid of these questions and everybody, etc., and let Ziegler go out there and bob and weave around. I know the easy thing is to bug out, but it is not....

D. You're right. I was afraid. For the sake of debate, but I was having reservations. It is a bullet biter and you just have to do it. These questions are just not going to go away. Now the other thing that we talked about in the past, and I still have the same problem, is to have a "here it all is" approach. If we do that....

'Let it All Hang Out'

P. And let it all hang out.

D. And let it all hang out. Let's with a Segretti—etc.

P. We have passed that point.

D. Plus the fact, they are not going to believe the truth! That is the incredible thing!

P. They won't believe the truth, and they have committed seven people!

D. That's right! They will continually try to say that there is (unintelligible),

P. They hope one will say one day, "Haldeman did it," and one day, one will say I did it. When we get to that question—they might question his political savvy, but not mine! Not on a matter like that!

D. I have a thing on Sullivan (William C. Sullivan, assistant to former FBI director J. Edgar Hoover) I would like to ask you. Sullivan, as I told you, had been talking with me and I said Bill I would like for my own use to have a list of some of the horribles that you are aware of. He hasn't responded back to me, but he sent me a note yesterday saying John I am willing at any time to testify to what I know if you want me to. What he has, as we already know, he has something that has a certain degree of a dynamite situation already— the '68 Presidency, surveillance of Goldwater.

P. I thought he said he saw that the '68 bugging was ordered, but he doesn't know whether it was carried out.

D. That's right.

P. But at least he would say (inaudible).

D. Well, I have never talked with Bill about it. I have never gone into details, because he has always been very close about it, but he is now getting to the point if we wanted him to do this, someone—and I don't think the White House should do it—should sit down with him and really take down some notes of what he does know, how strong it is, what he can substantiate.

P. Who the hell could do it if you don't?

D. Well, probably there is no one.

P. That is the problem.

D. Now the other thing, if we were going to use a package like this: Let's say in the Gray hearings—where everything is cast that we are the political people and they are not—that Hoover was above reproach, which is just not accurate, total (expletive omitted). The person who would destroy Hoover's image is going to be this man Bill Sullivan. Also it is going to tarnish quite severely....

P. Some of the FBI.

D. ...some of the FBI. And a former President. He is going to lay it out, and just all hell is going to break loose once he does it. It is going to change the atmosphere of the Gray hearings and it is going to change the atmosphere of the whole Watergate hearings. Now the risk....

P. How will it change?

D. Because it will put them in context of where government institutes were used in the past for the most flagrant political purposes.

P. How can that help us?

D. How does it help us?

P. I am being the devil's advocate....

D. I appreciate what you are doing. It is a red herring. It is what the public already believes. I think the people would react: (expletive deleted), more of that stuff! They are all bad down there! Because it is a one way street right now....

P. Do you think the press would use it? They may not play it.

D. It would be difficult not to. Ah, it would be difficult not to.

P. Why is Sullivan willing to do this?

D. I think the quid pro quo with Sullivan is that he wants someday back in the Bureau very badly.

P. That's easy.

D. That's right.

P. Do you think after he did this, the Bureau would want him back? Would they want him back?

'Domestic...Intelligence System'

D. I think probably not. What Bill Sullivan's desire in life is, is to set up a domestic national security intelligence system, a White House program. He says we are deficient. He says we have never been efficient, because Hoover lost his guts several years ago. If you recall he and Tom Huston (White House aide Tom Charles Huston) worked on it. Tom Huston had your instructions to go out and do it and the whole thing just crumbled.

P. (inaudible)

D. That's all Sullivan really wants. Even if we could put him out studying it for a couple of years, if you could put him out in the CIA or someplace where he felt—put him there....

P. We will do it.

D. I think that is a simple answer. Let me just simply raise it with him.

P. There is no problem with Sullivan. He is a valuable man. Now would the FBI turn on him (characterization deleted)?

D. There would be some effort at that. That's right they would say he was disgruntled. He was canned by Hoover. He is angry, he is coming back. But I would think a lot of that would be lost in the shuffle of what he is laying out. I don't know if he has given me his best yet. I don't know whether he's got more ammunition than he has already told me. I will never forget a couple off-the-cuff remarks.

P. Why do you think he is now telling you this? Why is he doing this now?

D. Well, the way it came out when *Time* Magazine broke on the fact that it charged that the White House had directed that newsmen and White House staff people be subjected to some sort of surveillance for national security reasons. I called, in tracking down what happened, I called Sullivan and I said, "don't you think you ought to come over and talk to me about it and tell me what you know." I was calling to really determine whether he was a leak. I was curious to know where this might have come from because he was the operative man at the Bureau at the time. He is the one who did it. He came over and he was shocked and distraught and (unintelligible). Then, after going through with his own explanation of all what had happened, he started volunteering this other thing. He said John this is the only thing I can think of during this Administration that has any taint of political use but it doesn't really bother me because it was for national security purposes. These people worked with sensitive material on Vietnam that was getting out to reporters.

P. Of course, the stuff was involved with the (expletive deleted) Vietnam war.

D. That's right. Then he told me about going to (location and name deleted) and all that, and he said, "John that doesn't bother me, but what does bother me is that you all have been portrayed as politically using"—

P. And we never did.

D. And we never have! And he said the Eisenhower Administration didn't either.

P. Never.

D. He said the only times that he can recall that there has been a real political use has been during Democratic tenure. I said for example, Bill, what are you talking about? Then he told me of the Walter (W.) Jenkins (former aide to President Lyndon B. Johnson) affair, when (former FBI assistant director Cartha D.) DeLoach and (former Supreme Court Justice Abe) Fortas, etc.—

P. The Kennedy's, let me say, used it politically in that steel thing. That was not national security was it?

D. I asked somebody about that and they told me what happened. They were being defensive of Kennedy, and so he was saying that Kennedy had given Hoover orders and Hoover, being typical in his response, tried to get it yesterday as far as the answer for the President. And that is why sending people out in a plane in the middle of the night really fell on Hoover. This might be rumor over there, who knows?

P. It is still wrong!

D. Sure.

P. (expletive deleted) Can you imagine if a steel company or an automobile company had raised hell about something (Environmental Protection Agency director William D.) Ruckelshaus does, and we send FBI agents out to arrest? (expletive deleted) Does he know about the bugging in '68?

D. Yep! I think he would tell everything. He knows!

P. You do?

D. Uh huh. That's what I am saying he is a bomb!

P. You think we could get him to do this?

D. That is the real problem. How it could be done, how it could be structured. He sent me this note and I called up and said, "Bill, I appreciate getting that note very much. It takes a lot of guts to send a note like that to me." He said, "it has been a pleasure to see a man standing up blowing up a little smoke up him and the like." He said, "well, I mean it! I am perfectly willing to do anything you want. If you want me to go up and testify, I will." I said, "well how much, you have just given me some tidbits in our conversation and I would really like to again repeat: can you put together what you do know; just for your own use, put it together on a pad—just your own recollections; and also tell me how you can substantiate them;—what kind of cross-examination you might be subject to on it if you did testify." So he is doing that. The question I have had is, how in the world can we program something like this? I just have a feeling that it would be bad for one Bill Sullivan to quietly appear on some Senator's doorstep, and say, "I have the information you ought to have." Well, "where did you get it?" "Why are you up here?" "Well the White House sent me." That would be bad! The other thing is, maybe this information could be brought to the attention of the White House, and the White House could say to (Sen. James O.) Eastland (D Miss.), "I think you ought to call an executive session and hear his testimony. This is quite troublesome, the information that has been presented to us. It is so troublesome, we can't hold it here and hope to be less comfortable."

P. Why couldn't we have him just present it to Eastland? Why an executive session? That doesn't serve—

D. Well, the first approach would be enough of the story, not to tarnish the names, but it would leak out of there quite obviously. If it doesn't we could make sure it did.

D. If Sullivan went up to Eastland cold, say, or (Sen. Roman L.) Hruska (R Neb.), I think they would say, "go on down back to the Department of Justice where you work, and let's not start all this."

P. Suppose, another thing, Pat Gray knows anyone, or Hruska on the Committee, who is a tiger on our side on the committee—

'Gurney Has Been Good'

D. (Sen. Edward J.) Gurney (R Fla.) has been good. He was good on the ITT Committee. He will study, he will get prepared.

P. Could we go after the Bureau? I don't know whether we could or not.

D. Not quite after the Bureau. What they are doing is taking the testimony of somebody who is going after the Bureau.

P. I know that. I am just thinking. They will look down the road and see what the result of what they are doing is, won't they? I would think so. Would they go after Johnson? Let's look at the future. How bad would it hurt the country, John, to have the FBI so terribly damaged?

D. Do you mind if I take this back and kick it around with (presidential special counsel Richard A.) Dick Moore? These other questions. I think it would be damaging to the FBI, but maybe it is time to shake the FBI and rebuild it. I am not so sure the FBI is everything it is cracked up to be. I am convinced the FBI isn't everything the public think it is.

P. No.

D. I know quite well it isn't.

P. If we can get (District of Columbia police chief) Jerry (V.) Wilson in there—What is your feeling at the moment about Gray? Can he hang in there? Should he?

D. They have an executive session this afternoon to invite me to testify.

P. Sure.

D. There is no question, they are going to invite me to testify. I would say, based on how I handle: (1) the formal letter that comes out of the Committee asking for information, and I programmed that if they do get specific as to what in the hell they do want to know, that I've got to lay it out in a letter sent down here so I can be responsive, fully responsive.

P. Respond to the letter in full!

D. I feel I can respond to the letter in full. I feel I have nothing to hide, as far this issue Gray raised.

P. Would you respond under oath?

D. I think I would be willing to, yes, give it under oath.

P. That is what I would say: that is, what I would prepare in the press thing. He will respond under oath in a letter. He will not appear in a formal session. They might then say, "would he be willing to be questioned under oath?"

D. That is not what the question is. Yes, I would be willing to be questioned under oath, but we are not going up.

P. No, no! Here?

D. No. I think that would be a hell of a bad precedent.

P. Just so we don't cross that bridge. I agree, but you would respond in writing. That's it. OK.

D. After that, if we have been responsive, their argument for holding up Gray's confirmation based on me should be gone. Sure, it can raise more questions than answers, but it should work. The effect of the letter we have taken the central points that they want answers to, given them the responses, given them something in Eastland's hand. And he can say, "alright, it is time to vote. And Eastland says he has the votes to get Gray through. Now, what happens on the Senate Floor is something else, because (Sen. Robert C.) Byrd (D W.Va.) is posing very perceptive, and controlling that Southern bloc.

P. Uh, uh! October! Byrd is running for leader of the whole Senate.

D. But (Senate majority leader Mike) Mansfield (D Mont), on the other hand, has come out and said he would support Gray's confirmation.

P. My feeling is that they would like to have an excuse not to. And maybe they will use not you. But about these hearings—

D. Well if they say they have to hold up Gray's confirmation until the Watergate Hearings are completed—

P. That's great!

D. That's the vehicle.

'Gray...Should Not Head FBI'

P. That's a vote really for us, because Gray, in my opinion, should not be the head of the FBI. After going through the hell of the hearings, he will not be a good Director, as far as we are concerned.

D. I think that is true. I think he will be a very suspect Director. Not that I don't think Pat won't do what we want—I do look at him a little differently than Dick in that regard. Like he is still keeping in close touch with me. He is calling me. He has given me his hot line. We talk at night, how do you want me to handle this, et cetera? So he still stays in touch, and is still being involved, but he can't do it because he is going to be under such surveillance by his own people—every move he is making—that it would be a difficult thing for Pat. Not that Pat wouldn't want to play ball, but he may not be able to.

P. I agree. That's what I meant.

D. Pat has already gotten himself in a situation where he has this (W.) Mark Felt as his number two man. These other people have surrounded him. He could have gotten a Wilson in there you know. Like this: saying, "Gentlemen, I am putting my own team in, and I am going to put in a team I have met around the country who are good office directors; Sacks out of Chicago," or whatever, and just put his own team together for the Headquarter's Office.

P. That's the way it should be done.

D. Gray should have walked in and made these major personnel decisions. I wouldn't be surprised if death of his nomination occurs if they say they cannot go forward with Gray's hearings because of the Watergate.

P. Where would that be done, John, at what point?

D. It would simply be voted first in the Judiciary Committee. The question is, then, whether it will be put on the calendar by the leadership.

P. The leadership might determine that we will not put it on the calendar until after the Watergate Hearings. Then Gray would, in turn, say that he will not wait that long.

D. "Gentlemen, this is damaging to the leadership of the FBI, and I will have to withdraw based on this." What would be nice for all is to get Gray voted out of the Committee, with a positive vote, enough to get him out of the Committee, and then lock him in limbo there.

P. What is Moore's judgment about Sullivan? What does he think?

D. He said it speaks dynamite. And we both feel that it is the way it would be done, that would be the secret. How it is done? Whether it is the sort of thing that you leak out and do? It would have to be very carefully thought through. We would have to decide, should the White House not be involved or should we be involved? If we are going to play with it, we are probably going to say that we are involved and structure it in a way that there is nothing improper with our involvement.

P. The difficulty with the White House being involved is that if we are involved in this (expletive deleted) that is why it ought to be that he just....

D. I suppose the answer is to say to him, "you have intimated a few things to me, the proper place to take that information is to the Senate Judiciary Committee or to the Attorney General, possibly." And then have him take it to the Committee. Or is that too close to the President still?

P. Well, he works for the Attorney General, doesn't he?

D. If he takes it to (Attorney General Richard G.) Kleindienst, Kleindienst is going to say, "Bill just don't do it because you are going to take DeLoach's name down with it, and DeLoach is a friend of ours."

P. (Expletive deleted)

D. Something I have always thought.

P. Nobody is a friend of ours. Let's face it! Don't worry about that sort of thing.

D. Something I can kick around with Dick Moore. But first of all, it will have to be thought through every inch of the way. Either late yesterday afternoon—it wasn't when I talked with Bob—he was quite excited about it. Ehrlichman said, gave a very good, "uh huh." I said I am not going to rush anything on this. We have a little bomb here that we might want to drop at one time down the road. Maybe the forum to do it is is something totally out of context between the Gray hearings and the Watergate hearings. Maybe we need to go to the *U.S. News,* sir. Who knows what it would be, but we ought to consider every option, now that we've got it.

P. Rather than going to a hearing, do "Meet the Press," and that will force the hearing to call him. That is quite the way to do it. Have him give an interview to *U.S. News* "Wires in the Sky" or something. A respected reporter—why not give it to Molenhoff (Clark R. Mollenhoff of the *Des Moines Register and Tribune*)?

D. Well that is interesting. Mollenhoff is close, but our guy gets near Mollenhoff. Mollenhoff may not do anything.

P. No, and we are in a position with Mollenhoff that he has been fighting us some. Maybe Mollenhoff would be a pretty good prospect for this thing. It is the kind of a story he loves, but he digs on something. You couldn't call him, however, (inaudible)—The (characterization deleted) loves to talk too much, although he is a hell of a guy.

D. Ok. Can I call Clark and say "listen Clark, a guy has brought me a piece of dynamite that I don't even want in the White House?"

P. He will write that, won't he?

D. Yeah. Because that doesn't look like a set up deal. Well Clark Mollenhoff is the first guy to uncover a shield of anything, and he will say no way—

P. But he would do it. That is very important piece. (unintelligible) Getting back, don't you feel that is the need here to broaden the scope?

D. The focus is right on us. That's the problem.

P. Nothing on the Democrats. —Nothing on what the previous three Administrations did?

'Shabby Journalism'

D. Nothing. If Hunt is still a walking story we'll pull out of this thing. You can't find anybody who even knows what is happening. Although it has increased in the network coverage. That NBC thing last night, which is just a travesty as far and we're talking about shabby journalism, they took the worst edited clips out of context, with (Haldeman assistant Gordon C.) Strachan saying he was leaving. And then had a little of clip of Ron saying, "I deny that." And he was denying something other than what they were talking about in their charge. It was incredible. Someone is going through and putting that altogether right now and Ron ought to be able to (unintelligible) to that one on NBC. It was a very, very dishonest television reporting of sequence of events, but out of sequence.

P. You see, John, when that Ervin gets up there—and a lot of Republicans even think he is a great Constitutional lawyer—it just makes us wonder about our even sending Gray up. Who knows?

D. Who knows? That is right. If you didn't send him up, why didn't you send him up. Because he was—

P. I know, but that is one thing: You send somebody else up to take them on, not a big clown. You know what I mean?

P. I won't even announce any appointments. I think the problem of the Senate was with all this stuff hanging out there in the Ervin Committee.

D. Well one thing, the saturation level of the American people on this story is cracking. The saturation level in this city is getting pretty high now, and they can't take too much more of this stuff.

P. Think not?

D. There is nothing really new coming out.

P. I talked with some kid and he said I don't think that anybody incidentally would care about anybody infiltrating the peace movement that was demonstrating against the President, particularly on the War in Vietnam. Do you think so?

D. No!
Anyway, I don't care about that. What happened to this Texas guy that gets his money back? Was he—

D. All hell broke loose for him that week. This was Allan

P. No, no. Allan—

D. Allan, not Duncan nor (unintelligible). All hell broke loose for Allan for this reason: He—the money apparently originally came out of a subsidiary of one of Allan's corporations down in Mexico. It went to a lawyer in Mexico who put it down as a fee billed to the subsidiary, and then the lawyer sent it back into the States, and it came back up here. But the weakness of it is that the Mexican lawyer: (1) didn't have a legitimate fee; (2) It could be corporate contribution. So Allan had personally put a note up with the corporation to cover it. Allan, meanwhile, is having problems with his wife, and a divorce is pending. And tax problems—

P. (inaudible) Watergate—

D. I don't know why that went in the letter. It wasn't used for the Watergate. That is the interesting thing.

P. It wasn't?

D. No it was not. What happened is that these Mexican checks came in. They were given to Gordon Liddy, and said, "why don't you get these cashed?" Gordy Liddy, in turn, put them down to this fellow (Watergate conspirator Bernard) Barker in Florida, who said he could cash these Mexican checks, and put them with your Barker's bank account back in here. They could have been just as easily cashed at the Riggs Bank. There was nothing wrong with the checks. Why all that rigamorole? It is just like a lot of other things that happened over there. God knows what it was all done. It was totally unnecessary, and it was money that was not directly involved in the Watergate. It wasn't a wash operation to get money back to Liddy and the like.

P. Who is going to be the first witness up there?

D. Sloan (Hugh W. Sloan Jr., treasurer of the Nixon re-election finance committee).

P. Unfortunate.

D. No doubt about it—

P. He's scared?

'He's Scared, He's Weak'

D. He's scared, he's weak. He has a compulsion to cleanse his soul by confession. We are giving him a lot of stroking. Funny thing is this fellow goes down to the Court House here before Sirica (Judge John J. Sirica of the U.S. District Court for the District of Columbia),

testifies as honestly as he can testify, and Sirica looks around and called him a liar. He just said—Sloan just can't win! So Kalmbach has been dealing with Sloan. Sloan is like a child. Kalmbach has done a lot of that. The person who will have a greater problem as a result of Sloan's testimony is Kalmbach and Stans. So they are working closely with him to make sure that he settles down.

P. Kalmbach will be a good witness, knowing what Kalmbach has been through.

D. Kalmbach has borne up very well. In fact, I decided he may be—

P. Kalmbach is somewhat embarrassed, as he is, they say lawyer for the President. Well, hell I don't need a lawyer. He and (Frank) DeMarco (Jr.), his other partner, handle our pay out there.

D. He is sensitive on that point. He saw a transcript of a briefing where Ron was saying, "well he is really not, right nomenclature, 'personal attorney.'" Herb said, "well, gee whiz. I don't know whether Ron knows what all I do." And I said, "well, don't worry about it."

P. What I meant is—I don't care about it, but I mean—it is just the fact that it is played that way, that he is in talking to me all the time. I don't ask him anything. I don't talk to him about anything. I don't know, I see Herb once a year when we see and sign the income tax returns.

D. That's right!

P. Now, true, he handles our San Clemente property and all the rest, but he isn't a lawyer in the sense that most people have a lawyer.

D. No, no. Although when you had an estate claim, he has some dove-tailing on it.

P. Anyway we don't want to back off of him.

D. No, he is solid.

P. He will—how does he tell his story? He has a pretty hard row to hoe—he and Stans have.

D. He will be good. Herb is the kind of guy who will check, not once nor twice, on his story—not three times—but probably fifty to a hundred times. He will go over it. He will know it. There won't be a hole in it. Probably he will do his own Q & A. He will have people cross-examine him from ten ways. He will be ready as (former Nixon campaign director) John Mitchell will be ready as Maury Stans will be ready.

P. Mitchell is now studying, is he?

D. He is studying. Sloan will be the worst witness. I think (former Nixon re-election campaign official Jeb Stuart) Magruder will be a good witness. This fellow, Bart Porter (Herbert L. Porter, former official of the Nixon re-election committee), will be a good witness. They have already been through Grand Jury. They have been through trial. They did well. And then, of course, people around here.

P. None will be witnesses.

D. They won't be witnesses?

P. Hell, no. They will make statements. That will be the line which I think we have to get across to Ziegler in all his briefings where he is constantly saying we will provide information. That is not the question. It is how it is to be furnished. We will not furnish it in a formal session. That would be a break down of the privilege. Period. Do you agree with that?

D. I agree. I agree. I have always thought that's the bottom line, and I think that is the good thing that is happening in the Gray hearings right now. If they send a letter down with specific questions, I send back written interrogatories sworn. He knows, the lawyer, that you can handle written interrogatories, where cross examination is another ball game.

P. That's right!

D. You can make a person look like they're inaccurate even if they are trying to tell the truth.

P. Well now, really, you can't mean that! All the face-making and all that. Written interrogatories you can handle?

D. Can be artfully, accurately answered and give the full information.

P. (unintelligible) Well, what about the sentencing: When the hell is he going to sentence?

D. We thought he was going to sentence last Friday.

P. I know he should have.

D. No one knows what in the world Sirica is doing. It is getting to be a long time now. It frankly is, and no one really has a good estimation of how he will sentence. There is some feeling that he will sentence Liddy the heaviest. Liddy is already in jail, he is in Danbury. He wants to start serving so he can get good time going. Hunt, he will probably be very fair with.

P. Why?

D. He likes Hunt—he thought Hunt was being open with him and being candid, and Hunt gave a statement in open court that he didn't know of any higher ups involved and Hunt didn't put him through the rigors of trial. Hunt was a beaten man who had lost his wife, was ill, and still they tried to move to have him severed from the trial. And Hunt did not try to cause a lot of problems. (Hunt attorney William O.) Bittman was co-operative, whereas Liddy played the heavy in the trial. His lawyer raised all the objections and the like, and embarrassed the Judge for some in-chambers things he had said.

P. But Liddy is going to appeal the sentence?

D. Liddy is going to appeal the decision, the trial. He will appeal that.

P. He will appeal the trial? He was convicted!

D. There is an outside chance that this man, this Judge, has gone so far in his zeal to be a special prosecutor—

P. Well some of those statements from the Bench—

D. Incredible statements!

P. To me, incredible!

D. Commenting on witnesses testimony before the Jury, was just incredible. Incredible! So there may be a mistrial. Or maybe a reversible error.

P. What about the Cubans?

D. The Cubans will probably be thought of as hired hands, and receive nowhere near the sentence of Liddy, I would think. Not all of them. Barker, the lead Cuban, may get more than the others. It is hard to say. I just don't have any idea. Sirica is a strange man. He is known as a hanging judge.

P. (unintelligible)

D. That's right. He's tough. He is tough. The other thing, Sirica, there was some indication that Sirica might be putting together a panel. There is a system down there now, based on informal agreement, where a sentencing judge convenes a panel of his own to take advice from. if Sirica were being shrewd, he just might get himself a panel and take their recommendations.

P. When will the Ervin thing be hitting the fan most any day, thinking from the standpoint of time?

D. Well, I would say the best indications we have now is that public hearings will probably start about the first of May. Now, there will probably be a big bang of interest, initially. We have no idea how they will proceed yet. We do have sources to find that out, other than (Sen. Howard H.) Baker (R Tenn.). Incidentally, Kleindienst had called Ervin again, returned the call. Ervin is going to see him this week with Baker.

'Hearings...Three Weeks'

P. Public hearings the first of May. Well it must be a big show. Public hearings. I wouldn't think though, I know from experience, my guess is that I think they could get

through about three weeks of those and then I think it would begin to peter out somewhat. Don't you agree?

D. No, I—

P. ITT went longer, but that was a different thing, and it seemed more important.

D. When I told Bob, oh, several months ago, I hope they don't think (unintelligible). He said the way they could have those hearings and do a masterful job on it would be to hold one hearing a week on Thursdays, Thursday mornings, they cover it live. That way, you get the networks that night; the national magazines that week; get the weekend wrap-ups. You can stretch this thing out by, really.

P. Our members of the Committee at least should say, let's get it over with, and go through five day sessions, etc.

D. Well you see, I don't think they are that perceptive. They just think they are.

P. Well, so be it. I noticed in the news summary (White House aide Patrick J.) Buchanan was viewing with alarm the grave crisis in the confidency of the Presidency, etc.

D. Well the best way—

P. How much?

D. Pardon?

P. How much of a crisis? It will be—I am thinking in terms of—the point is, everything is a crisis. (expletive deleted) it is a terrible lousy thing—it will remain a crisis among the upper intellectual types, the soft heads, our own, too—Republicans—and the Democrats and the rest. Average people won't think it is much of a crisis unless it affects them. (unintelligible)

D. I think it will pass. I think after the Ervin hearings, they are going to find so much—there will be some new revelations. I don't think that the thing will get out of hand. I have no reason to believe it will.

P. Oh, yes—there would be new revelations.

D. They would be quick (inaudible) They would want to find out who knew—

P. Is there a higher up?

D. Is there a higher up?

P. Let's face it, I think they are really after Haldeman.

D. Haldeman and Mitchell.

P. Colson is not big enough name for them. He really isn't. He is, you know, he is on the government side, but Colson's name doesn't bother them so much. They are after Haldeman and after Mitchell. Don't you think so?

D. Sure. They are going to take a look and try to drag them, but they're going to be able to drag them into the election—

P. In any event, Haldeman's problem is Chapin isn't it?

D. Bob's problem is circumstantial.

P. Why is that? Let's look at the circumstantial. I don't know, Bob didn't know any of those people like the Hunts and all that bunch. Colson did, but Bob didn't. OK?

D. That's right.

P. Now where the hell, or how much Chapin knew I will be (expletive deleted) if I know.

D. Chapin didn't know anything about the Watergate.

P. Don't you think so?

'Strachan...He Knew'

D. Absolutely not.

P. Strachan?

D. Yes.

P. He knew?

D. Yes.

P. About the Watergate?

D. Yes.

P. Well, then, he probably told Bob. He may not have.

D. He was judicious in what he relayed, but Strachan is as tough as nails. He can go in and stonewall, and say, "I don't know anything about what you are talking about." He has already done it twice you know, in interviews.

P. I guess he should, shouldn't he? I suppose we can't call that justice, can we?

D. Well, it is a personal loyalty to him. He doesn't want it any other way. He didn't have to be told. He didn't have to be asked. It just is something that he found was the way he wanted to handle the situation.

P. But he knew? He knew about Watergate? Strachan did?

D. Yes.

P. I will be damned! Well that is the problem in Bob's case. Not Chapin then, but Strachan. Strachan worked for him, didn't he?

D. Yes. They would have one hell of a time proving that Strachan had knowledge of it, though.

P. Who knew better? Magruder?

D. Magruder and Liddy.

P. Oh, I see. The other weak link for Bob is Magruder. He hired him et cetera.

D. That applies to Mitchell, too.

P. Mitchell—Magruder. Where do you see Colson coming into it? Do you think he knew quite a bit and yet, he could know quite a great deal about a lot of other things and not know a lot about this. I don't know.

D. Well I have never—

P. He sure as hell knows Hunt. That we know. Was very close to him.

D. Chuck has told me that he had no knowledge, specific knowledge, of the Watergate before it occurred. There have been tidbits that I have raised with Chuck. I have not played any games with him. I said, "Chuck, I have indications—"

P. What indications? The lawyer has to know everything.

D. That's right. I said, "Chuck, people have said that you were involved in this, involved in that, involved in all of this. He said, "that is not true, etc." I think that Chuck had knowledge that something was going on over there, but he didn't have any knowledge of the details of the specifics of the whole thing.

P. There must have been an indication of the fact that we had poor pickings. Because naturally anybody, either Chuck or Bob, were always reporting to me about what was going on. If they ever got any information they would certainly have told me that we got some information, but they never had a thing to report. What was the matter? Did they never get anything out of the damn thing?

D. I don't think they ever got anything, sir.

'A Dry Hole'

P. A dry hole?

D. That's right.

P. (Expletive deleted)

D. Well, they were just really getting started.

P. Yeah. Bob one time said something to me about something, this or that or something, but I think it was something about the Convention, I think it was about the convention problems they were planning something. I assume that must have been MacGregor—not MacGregor, but Segretti.

D. No, Segretti wasn't involved in the intelligence gathering piece of it at all.

P. Oh, he wasn't? Who the hell was gathering intelligence?

D. That was Liddy and his outfit.

P. Apart from Watergate?

D. That's right. Well you see Watergate was part of intelligence gathering, and this was their first thing. What happened is—

P. That was such a stupid thing!

D. It was incredible—that's right. That was Hunt.

P. To think of Mitchell and Bob would have allowed—would have allowed—this kind of operation to be in the campaign committee!

D. I don't think he knew it was there.

P. I don't think that Mitchell knew about this sort of thing.

D. Oh, no, no! Don't misunderstand me. I don't think that he knew the people. I think he knew that Liddy was out intelligence gathering. I don't think he knew that Liddy would use a fellow like (Watergate conspirator James W.) McCord, (expletive removed), who worked for the Committee. I can't believe that.

P. Hunt?

D. I don't think Mitchell knew about Hunt either.

P. Well Mitchell thought, well, gee, and I hired this fellow and I told him to gather intelligence. Maybe Magruder says the same thing.

D. Magruder says—as he did in the trial—well, of course, my name has been dragged in as the guy who sent Liddy over there, which is an interesting thing. Well what happened they said is that Magruder asked—he wanted to hire my deputy over there as Deputy Counsel and I said, "No way. I can't give him up."

P. Was Liddy your deputy?

D. No, Liddy never worked for me. He wanted this fellow Fred (F.) Fielding who works for me. Look, he said, Magruder said to me, "will you find me a lawyer?" I said, "I will be happy to look around." I checked around the White House, (Egil) Krogh (Jr.) said, "Liddy might be the man to do it—he would be a hell of a writer. He has written some wonderful legal opinions over here for me, and I think he is a good lawyer." So I relayed that to Magruder.

P. How the hell does Liddy stand up so well?

'A Strange Man'

D. He's a strange man, Mr. President.

P. Strange or strong?

D. Strange and strong. His loyalty is—I think it is just beyond the pale. Nothing—

P. He hates the other side too, doesn't he?

D. Oh, absolutely! He really is.

P. Is it too late to go the hang-out road?

D. Yes, I think it is. The hang-out road—

P. The hang-out road (inaudible).

D. It was kicked around Bob and I and—

P. Ehrlichman always felt it should be hang-out.

D. Well, I think I convinced him why he would not want to hang-out either. There is a certain domino situation here. If some things start going, a lot of other things are going to start going, and there can be a lot of problems if everything starts falling. So there are dangers, Mr. President. I would be less than candid if I didn't tell you there are. There is a reason for not everyone going up and testifying.

P. I see. Oh no, no, no! I didn't mean to have everyone go up and testify.

D. Well I mean they're just starting to hang-out and say here's our story—

P. I mean put the story out PR people, here is the story, the true story about Watergate.

D. They would never believe it. The two things they are working on are Watergate—

P. Who is "they?"

D. The press, (inaudible), the intellectuals,—

P. The Packwoods?

D. Right—They would never buy it as far as one White House involvement in Watergate which I think there is just none for that incident which occurred at the Democratic National Headquarters. People here we just did not know that was going to be done. I think there are some people who saw the fruits of it, but that is another story. I am talking about the criminal conspiracy to go in there. The other thing is that the Segretti thing. You hang that out, and they wouldn't believe that. They wouldn't believe that Chapin acted on his own to put his old friend Segretti to be a (political prankster) Dick Tuck on somebody else's campaign. They would have to paint it into something more sinister, more involved, part of a general plan.

P. Shows you what a master Dick Tuck is. Segretti's hasn't been a bit similar.

D. They are quite humorous as a matter of fact.

P. As a matter of fact, it is just a bunch of (characterization deleted). We don't object to such damn things anyway. On, and on and on. No, I tell you this is the last gasp of our hardest opponents. They've just got to have something to squeal about it.

D. It is the only thing they have to squeal—

P. (Unintelligible) They are going to lie around and squeal. They are having a hard time now. They got the hell kicked out of them in the election. There is not a Watergate around in this town, not so much our opponents, even the media, but the basic thing is the establishment. The establishment is dying, and so they've got to show that the despite the successes we have had in foreign policy and in the election, they've got to show that it is just wrong just because of this. They are trying to use this as the whole thing.

D. Well, that is why I keep coming back to this fellow Sullivan. It could change the picture.

P. How could it change though? Saying here is another—

D. Saying here is another and it happens to be Democrats. You know, I know I just—

'If...Get Kennedy Into It'...

P. If he would get (Sen. Edward M.) Kennedy (D Mass.) into it, too, I would be a little more pleased.

D. Let me tell you something that lurks at the bottom of this whole thing. If, in going after Segretti, they go after Kalmbach's bank records, you will recall sometime back—perhaps you did not know about this—I apologize. That right after Chappaquidick somebody was put up there to start observing and within six hours he was there for every second of Chappaquidick for a year, and for almost two years he worked for (Treasury aide John J.) Jack Caulfield.

P. Oh, I have heard of Caulfield.

D. He worked for Caulfield when Caulfield worked for John, and then when I came over here I inherited Caulfield and this guy was still on this same thing. If they get to those bank records between the start of July of 1969 through June of 1971, they say what are these about? Who is this fellow up in New York that you paid? There comes Chappaquidick with vengeance. This guy is a twenty year detective on the New York City Police Department.

P. In other words we—

D. He is ready to disprove and how that—

P. (unintelligble)

D. If they get to it—that is going to come out and this whole thing can turn around on that. If Kennedy knew the bear trap he was walking into—

P. How do we know—why don't we get it out anyway?

D. Well, we have sort of saved it.

P. Does he have any records? Are they any good?

D. He is probably the most knowledgeable man in the country. I think he ran up against walls and they closed the records down. There are things he can't get, but he can ask all of the questions and get many of the answers as a 20 year detective, but we don't want to surface him right now. But if he is ever surfaced, this is what they will get.

P. How will Kalmbach explain that he hired this guy to do the job on Chappaquidick? Out of what type of funds?

D. He had money left over from the pre-convention—

P. Are they going to investigate those funds too?

D. They are funds that are quite legal. There is nothing illegal about those funds. Regardless of what may happen, what may occur, they may stumble into this in going back to, say 1971, in Kalmbach's bank records. They have already asked for a lot of his bank records in connection with Segretti, as to how he paid Segretti.

P. Are they going to go back as far as Chappaquidick?

D. Well this fellow worked in 1971 on this. He was up there. He has talked to everybody in that town. He is the one who has caused a lot of embarrassment for Kennedy already by saying he went up there as a newspaperman, by saying; "Why aren't you checking this? Why aren't you looking there?" Calling the press people's attention to things. Gosh, the guy did a masterful job. I have never had the full report.

P. Coming back to the Sullivan thing, you will now talk to Moore and then what?

D. I will see if we have something that is viable. And if it's—

P. You plan to talk with him again.

D. Yes he asked me last night to give him a day or so to get all his recollections together, and that was yesterday. So I thought I would call him this evening and say, "Bill, I would just like to know—"

P. You see, right after you talk to him it will become known. So maybe the best thing to say is that he is to turn this over and be maligned. But anyway, the Committee is going to say the White House turned over information on the FBI. I don't know how the (expletive deleted) we get it down there?

D. I think I can kick it around with Dick Moore. He and I do very well just bouncing these things back and forth and coming up with something. We would never be embarrassed about it.

P. To give it to a newsman, it would be a hell of a break for a newspaper, a hell of a story! The *Star* just run a whole story on a real bomb on the FBI. Then the Committee member, the man you would use, for example, in this case would be to call Gurney, and to say, "Look! We are on to something very hot here. I can't tell you any more. Go after it, you'll get your other end this fall." Then he goes. It seems to me that's a very effective way to get it out.

D. Uh huh. It seems to me that I don't think Sullivan would give up the White House. Sullivan—if I have one liability in Sullivan here, it is his knowledge of the earlier (unintelligible) that occurred here.

P. That we did?

D. That we did.

P. Well, why don't you just tell him—he could say, "I did no political work at all. My work in the Nixon Administration was solely in the national security." And that is thoroughly true!

D. That is true.

P. Well, good luck.

D. Thank you, sir.

P. It is never dull is it?

D. Never.   ✓

White House Transcript of Celebrated March 21, 1973, Meeting

Following is the text of the most controversial of the transcripts President Nixon furnished to the House Judiciary Committee April 30, 1974. The transcript, as edited by the White House, is of a recorded conversation in the Oval Office March 21, 1973, among Nixon, presidential counsel John W. Dean III and White House chief of staff H. R. Haldeman.

The three men discussed the possibility that the Watergate burglars might demand up to $1-million for their silence. In his Senate Watergate committee testimony, Dean contended that this conversation took place March 13, before a payment had been made to an attorney for one of the burglars, E. Howard Hunt Jr.

Participants in the conversation are identified by initials—P for the President, D for Dean and H for Haldeman.

P. Well, sit down, sit down.

D. Good morning.

P. Well what is the Dean summary of the day about?

D. John caught me on the way out and asked me about why (Acting FBI Director L. Patrick) Gray was holding back on information, if that was under instructions from us. And it was and it wasn't. It was instructions proposed by the Attorney General, consistent with your press conference statement that no further raw data was to be turned over to the full committee. And that was the extent of it. And then Gray, himself, who reached the conclusion that no more information should be turned over, that he had turned over enough. So this again is Pat Gray making decisions on his own on how to handle his hearings. He has been totally (unintelligible) to take any guidance, any instruction. We don't know what he is going to do. He is not going to talk about it. He won't review it, and I don't think he does it to harm you in any way, sir.

P. No, he is just quite stubborn and also he isn't very smart. You know—

D. He is bullheaded.

P. He is smart in his own way but he's got that typical (expletive deleted) this is right and I am going to do it.

D. That's why he thinks he is going to be confirmed. He is being his own man. He is being forthright and honest. He feels he has turned over too much and so it is conscious decision that he is harming the Bureau by doing this and so he is not going to.

P. We have to get the boys off the line that this is because the White House told him to do this and everything. And also, as I told (presidential assistant John D.) Ehrlichman, I don't see why our little boys can't make something out of the fact that (expletive deleted) this is the only responsible position that could possibly be made. The FBI cannot turn over raw files. Has anybody made that point? I have tried to several times.

D. Sam Ervin (chairman of the Senate Watergate committee) has made that point himself. In fact, in reading the transcript of Gray's hearings, Ervin tried to hold Gray back from doing what he was doing at the time he did it. I thought it was very unwise. I don't think that anyone is criticizing your position on it.

P. Let's made a point that raw files, I mean that point should be made that we are standing for the rights of innocent individuals. The American Civil Liberties Union is against it. We are against it. (Former FBI Director J. Edgar) Hoover had the tradition, and it will continue to be the tradition. All files are confidential. See if we can't get someone inspired to put that out. Let them see what is in one.

D. (expletive deleted) You—

P. Any further word on (Hoover's former assistant, William C.) Sullivan? Is he still—

D. Yes, he is going to be over to see me today, this morning someplace, sometime.

P. As soon as you get that, I will be available to talk to you this afternoon. I will be busy until about one o'clock. Anytime you are through I would like to see what it is he has. We've got something but I would like to see what it is.

D. The reason that I thought we ought to talk this morning is because in our conversations, I have the impression that you don't know everything I know and it makes it very difficult for you to make judgments that only you can make on some of these things and I thought that—

P. In other words, I have to know why you feel that we shouldn't unravel something?

D. Let me give you my over-all first.

P. In other words, your judgment as to where it stands, and where we will go.

'A Cancer...That Is Growing'

D. I think that there is no doubt about the seriousness of the problem we've got. We have a cancer within, close to the Presidency, that is growing. It is growing daily. It's compounded, growing geometrically now, because it compounds itself. That will be clear if I, you know, explain some of the details of why it is. Basically, it is because (1) we are being blackmailed; (2) People are going to start perjuring themselves very quickly that have not had to perjure themselves to protect other people in the line. And there is no assurance—

P. That that won't bust?

D. That that won't bust. So let me give you the sort of basic facts, talking first about the Watergate; and then about (political saboteur Donald H.) Segretti; and then about some of the peripheral items that have come up. First of all on the Watergate: how did it all start, where did it start? O.K.! It started with an instruction to me from Bob Haldeman to see if we couldn't set up a perfectly legitimate campaign intelligence operation over at the Re-Election Committee. Not being in this business, I turned to somebody who had been in this business, (Treasury aide John J.) Jack Caulfield. I don't remember whether you remember Jack or not. He was your original bodyguard before they had the candidate protection, an old city policeman.

P. Yes, I know him.

D. Jack worked for John and then was transferred to my office. I said Jack came up with a plan that, you know—a normal infiltration, buying information from secretaries and all that sort of thing. He did, he put together a plan. It was kicked around. I went to Ehrlichman with it. I went to Mitchell with it, and the consensus was that Caulfield was not the man to do this. In retrospect, that might have been a bad call because he is an incredibly cautious person and wouldn't have put the situation where it is today. After rejecting that, they said we still need something so I was told to look around for someone who could go over to 1701 (1701 Pennsylvania Ave., NW, Nixon re-election committee headquarters) and do this. That is when I came up with Gordon Liddy. They needed a lawyer. Gordon had an intelligence background from his FBI service. I was aware of the fact that he had done some extremely sensitive things for the White House while he had been at the White House and he had apparently done them well. Going out into Ellsberg's (Daniel Ellsberg released the Pentagon Papers) doctor's office—

P. Oh, yeah.

D. And things like this. He worked with leaks. He tracked these things down. So the report that I got from (White House aide Egil) Krogh was that he was a hell of a good man and not only that a good lawyer and could set up a proper operation. So we talked to Liddy. He was interested in doing it. I took Liddy over to meet (campaign director John N.) Mitchell. Mitchell thought highly of him because Mitchell was partly involved in his coming to the White House to work for Krogh. Liddy had been at Treasury before that. Then Liddy was told to put together his plan, you know, how he would run an intelligence operation. This was after he was hired over there at the Committee. (Nixon campaign aide Jeb Stuart) Magruder called me in January and said I would like to have you come over and see Liddy's plan.

P. January of '72?

D. January of '72.

D. "You come over to Mitchell's office and sit in a meeting where Liddy is going to lay his plan out." I said I don't really know if I am the man, but if you want me there I will be happy to. So I came over and Liddy laid out a million dollar plan that was the most incredible thing I have ever laid my eyes on: all in codes, and involved black bag operations, kidnapping, providing prostitutes to weaken the opposition, bugging, mugging teams. It was just an incredible thing.

P. Tell me this: Did Mitchell go along—?

D. No, no, not at all, Mitchell just sat there puffing and laughing. I could tell from—after Liddy left the office I said that is the most incredible thing I have ever seen. He said I agree. And so Liddy was told to go back to the drawing board and come up with something realistic. So there was a second meeting. They asked me to come over to that. I came into the tail end of the meeting. I wasn't there for the first part. I don't know how long the meeting lasted. At this point, they were discussing again bugging, kidnapping and the like. At this point I said right in front of everybody, very clearly, I said, "These are not the sort of things (1) that are ever to be discussed in the office of the Attorney General of the United States—that was where he still was—and I am personally incensed." And I am trying to get Mitchell off the hook. He is a nice person and doesn't like to have to say no when he is talking with people he is going to have to work with.

P. That's right.

D. So I let it be known. I said "You all pack that stuff up and get it the hell out of here. You just can't talk this way in this office and you should re-examine your whole thinking."

P. Who all was present?

D. It was Magruder, Mitchell, Liddy and myself. I came back right after the meeting and told Bob, "Bob, we have a growing disaster on our hands if they are thinking this way," and I said, "The White House has got to stay out of this and I, frankly, am not going to be involved in it." He said, "I agree John." I thought at that point that the thing was turned off. That is the last I heard of it and I thought it was turned off because it was an absurd proposal.

P. Yeah.

D. Liddy—I did have dealings with him afterwards and we never talked about it. Now that would be hard to believe for some people, but we never did. That is the fact of the matter.

P. Well, you were talking with him about other things.

D. We had so many other things.

P. He had some legal problems too. But you were his adviser, and I understand you had conversations about the campaign laws, etc. Haldeman told me that you were handling all of that for us. Go ahead.

D. Now. So Liddy went back after that and was over at 1701, the Committee, and this is where I come into having put the pieces together after the fact as to what I can put together about what happened. Liddy sat over there and tried to come up with another plan that he could sell. (1) They were talking to him, telling him that he was putting too much money in it. I don't think they were discounting the illegal points. Jeb is not a lawyer. He did not know whether this is the way the game was played and what it was all about. They came up, apparently, with another plan, but they couldn't get it approved by anybody over there. So Liddy and Hunt apparently came to see (White House counsel Charles W.) Chuck Colson, and Chuck Colson picked up the telephone and called Magruder and said, "You all either fish or cut bait. This is absurd to have these guys over there and not using them. If you are not going to use them, I may use them." Things of this nature.

P. When was this?

D. This was apparently in February of '72.

P. Did Colson know what they were talking about?

D. I can only assume, because of his close relationship with Hunt, that he had a damn good idea what they were talking about, a damn good idea. He would probably deny it today and probably get away with denying it. But I still—unless Hunt (Watergate conspirator E. Howard Hunt Jr.) blows on him—

P. But then Hunt isn't enough. It takes two doesn't it?

D. Probably. Probably. But Liddy was there also and if Liddy were to blow—

'Criminal Liability in White House'

P. Then you have a problem—I was saying as to the criminal liability in the White House.

D. I will go back over that, and take out any of the soft spots.

P. Colson, you think was the person who pushed?

D. I think he helped to get the thing off the dime. Now something else occurred though—

P. Did Colson—had he talked to anybody here?

D. No. I think this was—

P. Did he talk with Haldeman?

D. No, I don't think so. But here is the next thing that comes in the chain. I think Bob was assuming, that they had something that was proper over there, some intelligence gathering operation that Liddy was operating. And through (Haldeman assistant Gordon C.) Strachan, who was his tickler, he started pushing them to get some information and they—Magruder—took that as a signal to probably go to Mitchell and to say, "They are pushing us like crazy for this from the White House. And so Mitchell probably puffed on his pipe and said, "Go ahead," and never really reflected on what it was all about. So they had some plan that obviously had, I gather, different targets they were going to go after. They were going to infiltrate, and bug, and do all this sort of thing to a lot of these targets. This is knowledge I have after the fact. Apparently after they had initially broken in and bugged the DNC (Democratic National Committee) they were getting information. The information was coming over here to Strachan and some of it was given to Haldeman, there is no doubt about it.

P. Did he know where it was coming from?

D. I don't really know if he would.

P. Not necessarily?

D. Not necessarily. Strachan knew it. There is no doubt about it, and whether Strachan—I have never come to press these people on these points becaue it hurts them to give up that next inch, so I had to piece things together. Strachan was aware of receiving information, reporting to Bob. At one point Bob even gave instructions to change their capabilities from (Sen. Edmund S.) Muskie to (Sen. George) McGovern, and passed this back through Strachan to Magruder and apparently to Liddy. And Liddy was starting to make arrangements to go in and bug the McGovern operation.

P. They had never bugged Muskie, though, did they?

D. No, they hadn't, but they had infiltrated it by a secretary.

P. By a secretary?

D. By a secretary and a chauffeur. There is nothing illegal about that. So the information was coming over here and then I, finally, after—. The next point in time that I became aware of anything was on June 17th when I got the word that there had been this break in at the DNC and somebody from our Committee had been caught in the DNC. And I said, "Oh, (expletive deleted)." You know, eventually putting the pieces together—

P. You knew what it was.

D. I knew who it was. So I called Liddy on Monday morning and said, "First, Gordon, I want to know whether anybody in the White House was involved in this." And he said, "No, they weren't." I said, "Well I want to know how in (adjective deleted) name this happened." He said, "Well, I was pushed without mercy by Magruder to get in there and to get more information. That the information was not satisfactory. That Magruder said, 'The White House is not happy with what we are getting.'"

P. The White House?

D. The White House. Yeah!

P. Who do you think was pushing him?

D. Well, I think it was probably Strachan thinking that Bob wanted things, because I have seen that happen on other occasions where things have said to have been of very prime importance when they really weren't.

P. Why at that point in time I wonder? I am just trying to think. We had just finished the Moscow trip. The Democrats had just nominated McGovern. I mean, (expletive deleted), what in the hell were these people doing? I can see their doing it earlier. I can see the pressures, but I don't see why all the pressure was on them.

D. I don't know, other than the fact that they might have been looking for information about the conventions.

P. That's right.

D. Because, I understand that after the fact that there was a plan to bug (Democratic chairman Lawrence) Larry O'Brien's suite down in Florida. So Liddy told me that this is what had happened and this is why it had happened.

P. Where did he learn that there were plans to bug Larry O'Brien's suite?

D. From Magruder, long after the fact.

P. Magruder is (unintelligible)

D. Yeah. Magruder is totally knowledgeable on the whole thing.

P. Yeah.

D. Alright now, we have gone through the trial. I don't know if Mitchell has perjured himself in the Grand Jury or not.

P. Who?

D. Mitchell. I don't know how much knowledge he actually had. I know that Magruder has perjured himself in the Grand Jury. I know that Porter has perjured himself in the Grand Jury.

P. Who is (Herbert L.) Porter? (unintelligible)

D. He is one of Magruder's deputies. They set up this scenario which they ran by me. They said, "How about this?" I said, "I don't know. If this is what you are going to hang on, fine."

P. What did they say in the Grand Jury?

D. They said, as they said before the trial in the Grand Jury, that Liddy had come over as Counsel and we knew

he had these capacities to do legitimate intelligence. We had no idea what he was doing. He was given an authorization of $250,000 to collect information, because our surrogates were out on the road. They had no protection, and we had information that there were going to be demonstrations against them, and that we had to have a plan as to what liabilities they were going to be confronted with and Liddy was charged with doing this. We had no knowledge that he was going to bug the DNC.

P. The point is, that is not true?

D. That's right.

P. Magruder did know it was going to take place?

D. Magruder gave the instructions to be back in the DNC.

P. He did?

D. Yes.

P. You know that?

D. Yes.

P. I see. O.K.

'No One Over Here Knew That'

D. I honestly believe that no one over here knew that. I know that as God is my maker, I had no knowledge that they were going to do this.

P. Bob didn't either, or wouldn't have known that either. You are not the issue involved. Had Bob known, he would be.

D. Bob—I don't believe specifically knew that they were going in there.

P. I don't think so.

D. I don't think he did. I think he knew that there was a capacity to do this but he was not given the specific direction.

P. Did Strachan know?

D. I think Strachan did know.

P. (unintelligible) Going back into the DNC—Hunt, etc.— this is not understandable!

D. So—those people are in trouble as a result of the Grand Jury and the trial. Mitchell, of course, was never called during the trial. Now—

P. Mitchell has given a sworn statement, hasn't he?

D. Yes, Sir.

P. To the Jury?

D. To the Grand Jury.—

P. You mean the Goldberg arrangement?

D. We had an arrangement whereby he went down with several of them, because of the heat of this thing and the implications on the election, we made an arrangement where they could quietly go into the Department of Justice and have one of the assistant U.S. Attorneys take their testimony and then read it before the Grand Jury.

P. I thought Mitchell went.

D. That's right, Mitchell was actually called before the Grand Jury. The Grand Jury would not settle for less, because the jurors wanted him.

P. And he went?

D. And he went.

P. Good!

D. I don't know what he said. I have never seen a transcript of the Grand Jury. Now what has happened post June 17? I was under pretty clear instructions not to investigate this, but this could have been disastrous on the electorate if all hell had broken loose. I worked on a theory of containment—

P. Sure.

D. To try to hold it right where it was.

P. Right.

D. There is no doubt that I was totally aware of what the Bureau was doing at all times. I was totally aware of what the Grand Jury was doing. I knew what witnesses were going to be called. I knew what they were asked, and I had to.

P. Why did (Assistant Attorney General Henry E.) Petersen play the game so straight with us?

D. Because Petersen is a soldier. He kept me informed. He told me when we had problems, where we had problems and the like. He believes in you and he believes in this Administration. This Administration has made him. I don't think he has done anything improper, but he did make sure that the investigation was narrowed down to the very, very fine criminal thing which was a break for us. There is no doubt about it.

P. Do you honestly feel that he did an adequate job?

D. They ran that investigation out to the fullest extent they could follow a lead and that was it.

P. But the way is, where I suppose he could be criticized for not doing an adequate job. Why didn't he call Haldeman? Why didn't he get a statement from Colson? Oh, they did get Colson!

D. That's right. But as based on their FBI interviews, there was no reason to follow up. There were no leads there. Colson said, "I have no knowledge of this" to the FBI. Strachan said, "I have no knowledge." They didn't ask Strachan any questions about Watergate. They asked him about Segretti. They said, "what is your connection with Liddy?" Strachan just said, "Well, I met him over there." They never really pressed him. Strachan appeared, as a result of some coaching, to be the dumbest paper pusher in the bowels of the White House.

P. I understand.

D. Alright. Now post June 17th: These guys immediately—It is very interesting. (Dean sort of chuckled) Liddy, for example, on the Friday before—I guess it was on the 15th, no, the 16th of June—had been in Henry Petersen's office with another member of my staff on campaign compliance problems. After the incident, he ran (Attorney General Richard G.) Kleindienst down at Burning Tree Country Club and told him "you've got to get my men out of jail." Kleindienst said, "You get the hell out of here, kid. Whatever you have to say, just say to somebody else. Don't bother me." But this has never come up. Liddy said if they all got counsel instantly and said we will ride this thing out. Alright, then they started making demands. "We have to have attorneys fees. We don't have any money ourselves, and you are asking us to take this through the election." Alright, so arrangements were made through Mitchell, initiating it. And I was present in discussions where these guys had to be taken care of. Their attorneys fees had to be done. (Nixon personal attorney Herbert W.) Kalmbach was brought in. Kalmbach raised some cash.

P. They put that under the cover of a Cuban Committee, I suppose?

D. Well, they had a Cuban Committee and they had—some of it was given to Hunt's lawyer, who in turn passed it out. You know, when Hunt's wife was flying to Chicago with $10,000 she was actually, I understand after the fact, now, was going to pass that money to one of the Cubans—to meet him in Chicago and pass it to somebody there.

'Keep That Cover'

P. (unintelligible) but I would certain keep that cover for whatever it is worth.

D. That's the most troublesome post-thing because (1) Bob is involved in that; (2) John is involved in that; (3) I am involved in that; (4) Mitchell is involved in that. And that is an obstruction of justice.

P. In other words, the bad it does. You were taking care of witnesses. How did Bob get in it?

D. Well, they ran out of money over there. Bob had $350,000 in a safe over here that was really set aside for polling purposes. And there was no other source of money, so they came over and said you all have got to give us some money. I had to go to Bob and say, "Bob, they need some money over there." He said "What for." So I had to tell him what it was for because he wasn't just about to send money over there willy-nilly. And John was involved in those discussions. And then we decided there was no price too high to pay to let this thing blow up in front of the election.

P. I think we should be able to handle that issue pretty well. May be some lawsuits.

D. I think we can too. Here is what is happening right now. What sort of brings matters to the (unintelligible). One, this is going to be a continual blackmail operation by Hunt and Liddy and the Cubans. No doubt about it. And McCord (Watergate conspirator James W. McCord Jr.), who is another one involved. McCord has asked for nothing. McCord did ask to meet with somebody, with Jack Caulfield who is his old friend who had gotten him hired over there. And when Caulfield had him hired, he was a perfectly legitimate security man. And he wanted to talk about commutation, and things like that. And as you know Colson has talked indirectly to Hunt about commutation. All of these things are bad, in that they are problems, they are promises, they are commitments. They are the very sort of things that the Senate is going to be looking most for. I don't think they can find them, frankly.

P. Pretty hard.

D. Pretty hard. Damn hard. It's all cash.

P. Pretty hard I mean as far as the witnesses are concerned.

D. Alright, now, the blackmail is continuing. Hunt called one of lawyers from the Re-Election Committee on last Friday to leave it with him over the weekend. The guy came in to see me to give a message directly to me. From Hunt to me.

P. Is Hunt out on bail?

D. Pardon?

P. Is Hunt on bail?

D. Hunt is on bail. Correct. Hunt now is demanding another $72,000 for his own personal expenses; another $50,000 to pay attorneys fees; $120,000. Some (1) he wanted it as of the close of business yesterday. He said, "I am going to be sentenced on Friday, and I've got to get my financial affairs in order." I told this fellow O'Brien (Paul L. O'Brien, an attorney for the Nixon re-election committee). "If you want money, you came to the wrong man, fellow. I am not involved in the money. I don't know a thing about it. I can't help you. You better scramble about elsewhere." O'Brien is a ball player. He carried tremendous water for us.

P. He isn't Hunt's lawyer?

D. No he is our lawyer at the Re-Election Committee.

P. I see.

D. So he is safe. There is no problem there. So it raises the whole question. Hunt has now made a direct threat against Ehrlichman. As a result of this, this is his blackmail. He says, "I will bring John Ehrlichman down to his knees and put him in jail. I have done enough seamy things for he and Krogh, they'll never survive it."

P. Was he talking about Ellsberg?

D. Ellsberg, and apparently some other things. I don't know the full extent of it.

P. I don't know about anything else.

D. I don't know either, and I hate to learn some of these things. So that is that situation. Now, where are at the soft points? How many people know about this? Well, let me go one step further in this whole thing. The

Cubans that were used in the Watergate were also the same Cubans that Hunt and Liddy used for this California Ellsberg thing, for the break in out there. So they are aware of that. How high their knowledge is, is something else. Hunt and Liddy, of course, are totally aware of it, of the fact that it is right out of the White House.

P. I don't know what the hell we did that for!

D. I don't know either.

P. What in the (expletive deleted) caused this? (unintelligible)

D. Mr. President, there have been a couple of things around here that I have gotten wind of. At one time there was a desire to do a second story job on the Brookings Institute where they had the Pentagon papers. Now I flew to California because I was told that John had instructed it and he said, "I really hadn't. It is a misimpression, but for (expletive deleted), turn it off." So I did. I came back and turned it off. The risk is minimal and the pain is fantastic. It is something with a (unintelligible) risk and no gain. It is just not worth it. But—who knows about all this now? You've got the Cubans' lawyer, a man by the name of (Henry R.) Rothblatt, who is a no good, publicity seeking (characterization deleted), to be very frank with you. He has had to be pruned down and tuned off. He was canned by his own people because they didn't trust him. He didn't want them to plead guilty. He wants to represent them before the Senate. So F. Lee Bailey, who was a partner of one of the men representing McCord, got in and cooled Rothblatt down. So that means that F. Lee Bailey has knowledge. Hunt's lawyer, a man by the name of (William O.) Bittmann, who is an excellent criminal lawyer from the Democratic era of Bobby Kennedy, he's got knowledge.

P. He's got some knowledge?

D. Well, all the direct knowledge that Hunt and Liddy have, as well as all the hearsay they have. You have these two lawyers over at the Re-election Committee who did an investigation to find out the facts. Slowly, they got the whole picture. They are solid.

P. But they know?

D. But they know. You've got, then an awful lot of the principals involved who know. Some people's wives know. Mrs. Hunt was the savviest woman in the world. She had the whole picture together.

P. Did she?

D. Yes. Apparently, she was the pillar of strength in that family before the death.

P. Great sadness. As a matter of fact, there was a discussion with somebody about Hunt's problem on account of his wife and I said, of course commutation could be considered on the basis of his wife's death, and that is the only conversation I ever had in that light.

D. Right.

D. So that is it. That is the extent of the knowledge. So where are the soft spots on this? Well, first of all, there is the problem of the continued blackmail which will not only go on now, but it will go on while these people are in prison, and it will compound the obstruction of justice situation. It will cost money. It is dangerous. People around here are not pros at this sort of thing. This is the sort of thing Mafia people can do: washing money, getting clean money, and things like that. We just don't know about those things, because we are not criminals and not used to dealing in that business.

P. That's right.

D. It is a tough thing to know how to do.

P. Maybe it takes a gang to do that.

D. That's right. There is a real problem as to whether we could even do it. Plus there is a real problem in raising money. Mitchell has been working on raising some money. He is one of the ones with the most to lose. But there is no denying the fact that the White House, in Ehrlichman, Haldeman and Dean are involved in some of the early money decisions.

P. How much money do you need?

D. I would say these people are going to cost a million dollars over the next two years.

P. We could get that. On the money, if you need the money you could get that. You could get a million dollars. You could get it in cash. I know where it could be gotten. It is not easy, but it could be done. But the question is who the hell would handle it? Any ideas on that?

D. That's right. Well, I think that is something that Mitchell ought to be charged with.

P. I would think so too.

D. And get some pros to help him.

P. Let me say there shouldn't be a lot of people running around getting money—

D. Well he's got one person doing it who I am sure is—

P. Who is that?

D. He has Fred LaRue (Frederick C. LaRue, a Nixon campaign aide) doing it. Now Fred started out going out trying to solicit money from all kinds of people.

P. No!

D. I had learned about it, and I said, "(expletive deleted) It is just awful! Don't do it!" People are going to ask what the money is for. He has apparently talked to Tom Pappas (Thomas A. Pappas, a Nixon fund raiser).

P. I know.

D. And Pappas has agreed to come up with a sizeable amount, I gather.

P. What do you think? You don't need a million right away, but you need a million? Is that right?

D. That is right.

P. You need it in cash don't you? I am just thinking out loud here for a moment. Would you put that through the Cuban Committee:

D. No.

P. It is going to be checks, cash money, etc. How if that ever comes out, are you going to handle it? Is the Cuban Committee an obstruction of justice, if they want to help?

D. Well they have priests in it.

P. Would that give a little bit of a cover?

D. That would give some for the Cubans and possibly Hunt. Then you've got Liddy. McCord is not accepting any money. So he is not a bought man right now.

P. OK. Go ahead.

D. Let me continue a little bit right here now. When I say this is a growing cancer, I say it for reasons like this. Bud Krogh, in his testimony before the Grand jury, was forced to perjure himself. He is haunted by it. Bud said, "I have not had a pleasant day on my job." He said, "I told my wife all about this. The curtain may ring down one of these days, and I may have to face the music, which I am perfectly willing to do."

P. What did he perjure himself on, John?

D. Did he know the Cubans. He did.

P. He said he didn't?

D. That is right. They didn't press him hard.

P. He might be able to—I am just trying to think. Perjury is an awful hard rap to prove. If he could just say that I—well, go ahead.

D. Well, so that is one perjury. Mitchell and Magruder are potential perjurers. There is always the possibility of any one of these individuals blowing. Hunt. Liddy. Liddy is in jail right now, serving his time and having a good time right now. I think Liddy in his own bizarre way the strongest of all of them. So there is that possibility.

P. Your major guy to keep under control is Hunt?

D. That is right.

P. I think. Does he know a lot?

D. He knows so much. He could sink Chuck Colson. Apparently he is quite distressed with Colson. He thinks Colson has abandoned him. Colson was to meet with him when he was out there after, you know, he had left the White House. He met with him through his lawyer. Hunt raised the question he wanted money. Colson's lawyer told him Colson wasn't doing anything with money. Hunt took offense with that immediately, and felt Colson had abandoned him.

P. Just looking at the immediate problem, don't you think you have to handle Hunt's financial situation damn soon?

D. I think that is—I talked with Mitchell about that last night and—

P. It seems to me we have to keep the cap on the bottle that much, or we don't have any options.

D. That's right.

P. Either that or it all blows right now?

D. That's the question.

P. We have Hunt, Krogh. Well go ahead with the other ones.

D. Now we've got Kalmbach. Kalmbach received, at the close of the '68 campaign in January of 1969, he got a million $700,000 to be custodian for. That came down from New York, and was placed in safe deposit boxes here. Some other people were on the boxes. And ultimately, the money was taken out to California. Alright, there is knowledge of the fact that he did start with a million seven. Several people know this. Now since 1969, he has spent a good deal of this money and accounting for it is going to be very difficult for Herb. For example, he has spent close to $500,000 on private polling. That opens up a whole new thing. It is not illegal, but more of the same thing.

P. Everybody does polling.

D. That's right. There is nothing criminal about it. It's private polling.

P. People have done private polling all through the years. There is nothing improper.

D. That's right. He sent $400,000, as he has described to me, somewhere in the South for another candidate. I assume this was 400,000 that went to (Alabama Gov. George C.) Wallace.

P. Wallace?

D. Right. He has maintained a man who I only know by the name of "Tony," who is the fellow who did the Chappaquiddick study.

P. I know about that.

D. And other odd jobs like that. Nothing illegal, but closer. I don't know of anything that Herb has done that is illegal, other than the fact that he doesn't want to blow the whistle on a lot of people, and may find himself in a perjury situation. Well, what will happen when they call him up there—and he has no immunity? They will say, "How did you pay Mr. Segretti?" He will say, "Well, I had cash on hand." "How much cash did you have on hand?" Where does it go from there? Where did you get the cash? A full series of questions. His bank records indicate he had cash on hand, because some of these were set up in trustee accounts.

P. How would you handle him, John, for example? Would you just have him put the whole thing out? I don't mind the $500,000 and the $400,000.

D. No—that doesn't bother me either. As I say, Herb's problems are politically embarrassing, but not criminal.

P. Well he just handled matters between campaigns. These were surveys etc., etc. There is no need to account for that.

There is no law that requires his accounting for that.

D. Ah, now—

P. Sources of money. There is no illegality in having a surplus in cash after a campaign.

D. No, the money—it has always been argued by Stans that it came in the pre-convention primary for the 1968 race, and it was just set aside. That all can be explained.

P. How about the other probabilities?

'Runaway Grand Jury'

D. We have a runaway Grand Jury up in the Southern District. They are after Mitchell and (campaign finance director Maurice H.) Stans on some sort of bribe or influence peddling with (financier Robert L.) Vesco. They are also going to try to drag Ehrlichman into that. Apparently Ehrlichman had some meetings with Vesco, also. Don Nixon Jr. (Donald A. Nixon, the President's nephew) came in to see John a couple of times about the problem.

P. Not about Vesco, but about Don Jr.? Ehrlichman never did anything for Vesco?

D. No one at the White House has done anything for Vesco.

P. Well Ehrlichman doesn't have to appear there?

D. Before that Grand Jury? Yes he could very well.

P. He couldn't use Executive Privilege?

D. Not really. Criminal charge, that is a little different. That would be dynamite to try to defend that.

P. Use the Flanigan analogy?

D. Right! That's pretty much the over-all picture. And probably the most troublesome thing is the Segretti thing. Let's get down to that. Bob has indicated to me that he has told you a lot of it, that he, indeed did authorize it. He did not authorize anything like ultimately evolved. He was aware of it. He was aware that (Nixon appointments secretary Dwight L.) Chapin and Strachan were looking for somebody. Again, this is one that has potential that Dwight Chapin should have a felony in this. He has to disprove a negative. The negative is that he didn't control and direct Segretti.

P. Wouldn't the felony be perjury again?

D. No, the felony in this instance would be a potential use of one of the civil rights statutes, where anybody who interferes with the campaign of a candidate for national office.

P. Why isn't it under civil rights statutes for these clowns demonstrating against us?

D. I have argued for that very purpose.

P. Really?

D. Yes, I have.

P. We were closer—nuts interfering with the campaign.

D. That is exactly right.

P. I have been sick about that because it is so bad the way it has been put out on the PR side. It has ended up on the PR side very confused.

D. What really bothers me is this growing situation. As I say, it is growing because of the continued need to provide support for the Watergate people who are going to hold us up for everything we've got, and the need for some people to perjure themselves as they go down the road here. If this thing ever blows, then we are in a coverup situation. I think it would be extremely damaging to you and the—

P. Sure. The whole concept of Administration justice. Which we cannot have!

D. That is what really troubles me. For example, what happens if it starts breaking, and they do find a criminal case against a Haldeman, a Dean, a Mitchell, an Ehrlichman? That is—

P. If it really comes down to that, we would have to (unintelligible) some of the men.

D. That's right. I am coming down to what I really think, is that Bob and John and John Mitchell and I can sit down and spend a day, or however long, to figure out one, how this can be carved away from you, so that it does not damage you or the Presidency. It just can't! You are not involved in it and it is something you shouldn't—

P. That is true!

D. I know, sir. I can just tell from our conversation that these are things that you have no knowledge of.

P. You certainly can! Buggings, etc.! Let me say I am keenly aware of the fact Colson, et al., were doing their best to get information as we went along. But they all knew very well they were supposed to comply with the law. There was no question about that! You feel that really the trigger man was really Colson on this then?

D. No. He was one of us. He was just in the chain. He helped push the thing.

P. All I know about is the time of ITT, he was trying to get something going there because ITT was giving us a bad time.

D. I know he used Hunt.

P. I knew about that. I didn't know about it, but I knew there was something going on. But I didn't know it was a Hunt.

D. What really troubles me is one, will this thing not break some day and the whole thing—domino situation—everything starts crumbling, fingers will be pointing. Bob will be accused of things he has never heard of and deny and try to disprove it. It will get real nasty and just be a real bad situation. And the person who will be hurt by it most will be you and the Presidency, and I just don't think—

P. First, because I am an executive I am supposed to check these things.

D. That's right.

P. Let's come back to this problem. What are your feelings yourself, John? You know what they are all saying. What are your feelings about the chances?

D. I am not confident that we can ride through this. I think there are soft spots.

P. You used to be—

D. I am not comfortable for this reason. I have noticed of recent—since the publicity has increased on this thing again, with the Gray hearings, that everybody is now starting to watch after their behind. Everyone is getting their own counsel. More counsel are getting involved. How do I protect my ass.

P. They are scared.

D. That is bad. We were able to hold it for a long time. Another thing is that my facility to deal with the multitude of people I have been dealing with has been hampered because of Gray's blowing me up into the front page.

P. Your cover is broken?

D. That's right and its—

P. So what you really come to is what we do. Let's suppose that you and Haldeman and Ehrlichman and Mitchell say we can't hold this? What then are you going to say? What are you going to put out after it. Complete disclosure, isn't that the best way to do it?

D. Well, one way to do it is—

P. That would be my view.

D. One way to do it is for you to tell the Attorney General that you finally know. Really, this is the first time you are getting all the pieces together.

P. Ask for another Grand Jury?

D. Ask for another Grand Jury. The way it should be done though, is a way—for example, I think that we could avoid criminal liability for countless people and the ones that did get it could be minimal.

P. How?

D. Well, I think by just thinking it all through first as to how. You know, some people could be granted immunity.

P. Like Magruder?

'Some People Are Going...to Jail'

D. Yeah. To come forward. But some people are going to have to go to jail. That is the long and short of it, also.

P. Who? Let's talk about—

D. Alright. I think I could. For one.

P. You go to jail?

D. That's right.

P. Oh, hell no! I can't see how you can.

D. Well, because—

P. I can't see how. Let me say I can't see how a legal case could be made against you, John.

D. It would be tough but, you know, I can see people pointing fingers. You know, to get it out of their own, put me in an impossible position. Just really give me a (unintelligible).

P. Oh, no! Let me say I got the impression here—But just looking at it from a cold legal standpoint: you are a lawyer, you were a counsel—doing what you did as counsel. You were not—What would you go to jail for?

D. The obstruction of justice.

P. The obstruction of justice?

D. That is the only one that bothers me.

P. Well, I don't know. I think that one. I feel it could be cut off at the pass, maybe, the obstruction of justice.

D. You know one of the—that's why—

P. Sometimes it is well to give them something, and then they don't want the bigger push?

D. That's right. I think that, I think that with proper coordination with the Department of Justice, Henry Petersen is the only man I know bright enough and knowledgeable enough in the criminal laws and process that could really tell us how this could be put together so that it did the maximum to carve it away with a minidamage to individuals involved.

P. Petersen doesn't know does he?

D. That's right. No, I know he doesn't know. I know he doesn't now. I am talking about somebody who I have over the years grown to have enough faith in—you constantly. It would have to put him in a very difficult situation as the Head of the Criminal Division of the United States Department of Justice, and the oath of office—

P. No. Talking about your obstruction of justice, though, I don't see it.

D. Well, I have been a conduit for information on taking care of people out there who are guilty of crimes.

P. Oh, you mean like the blackmailers?

D. The blackmailers. Right.

P. Well, I wonder if that part of it can't be—I wonder if that doesn't—let me put it frankly: I wonder if that doesn't have to be continued? Let me put it this way: let us suppose that you get the million bucks, and you get the proper way to handle it. You could hold that side?

D. Uh, huh.

P. It would seem to me that would be worthwhile.

D. Well, that's one problem.

P. I know you have a problem here. You have the problem with Hunt and his clemency.

D. That's right. And you are going to have a clemency problem with the others. They are all going to expect to be out and that may put you in a position that is just untenable at some point. You know, the Watergate Hearings just over, Hunt now demanding clemency or he is going to blow. And politically, it's impossible for you to do it. You know, after everybody—

P. That's right!

D. I am not sure that you will ever be able to deliver on the clemency. It may be just too hot.

P. You can't do it politically until after the '74 elections, that's for sure. Your point is that even then you couldn't do it.

D. That's right. It may further involve you in a way you should not be involved in this.

P. No—it is wrong that's for sure.

D. Well—there have been some bad judgments made. There have been some necessary judgments made.

P. Before the election?

D. Before the election and in the wake the necessary ones, you know, before the election. You know, with me there was no way, but the burden of this second Administration is something that is not going to go away.

P. No, it isn't.

D. It is not going to go away, Sir!

P. It is not going to go away.

D. Exactly.

P. The idea, well, that people are going to get tired of it and all that sort of thing.

D. Anything will spark it back into life. It's got to be,—It's got to be—

P. It is too much to the partisan interest to others to spark it back into life.

D. And it seems to me the only way—

P. Well, also so let's leave you out of it. I don't think on the obstruction of justice thing—I take that out. I don't know why, I think you may be over that cliff.

D. Well, it is possible.

P. Who else do you think has—

D. Potential criminal liability?

P. Yeah.

D. I think Ehrlichman does. I think that uh—

P. Why?

D. Because of this conspiracy to burglarize the Ellsberg doctors' office.

P. That is, provided Hunt's breaks?

D. Well, the funny—let me say something interesting about that. Within the files—

P. Oh, I thought of it. The picture!

D. Yes, sir. That is not all that buried. And while I think we've got it buried, there is no telling when it is going to pop up. Now the Cubans could start this whole thing. When the Ervin Committee starts running down why this mysterious telephone was here in the White House listed in the name of a secretary, some of these secretaries have a little idea about this, and they can be broken down just so fast. That is another thing I mentioned in the cycle—in the circle. Liddy's secretary, for example, is knowledgeable. Magruder's secretary is knowledgeable.

P. Sure. So Ehrlichman on the—

D. What I am coming in today with is: I don't have a plan on how to solve it right now, but I think it is at the juncture that we should begin to think in terms of how to cut the losses; how to minimize the further growth of this thing, rather than further compound it by, you know, ultimately paying these guys forever. I think we've got to look—

P. But at the moment, don't you agree it is better to get the Hunt thing that's where that—

D. That is worth buying time on.

P. That is buying time, I agree.

D. The Grand Jury is going to reconvene next week after Sirica sentences. But that is why I think that John and Bob have met with me. They have never met with Mitchell on this. We have never had a real down and out with everybody that has the most to lose and it is the most danger for you to have them have criminal liabilities. I think Bob has a potential criminal liability, frank-

ly. In other words, a lot of these people could be indicted.

P. Yeah.

D. They might never be convicted but just the thought of spending nights—

P. Suppose they are?

D. I think that would be devastating.

P. Suppose the worst—that Bob is indicted and Ehrlichman is indicted. And I must say, we just better then try to tough it through. You get the point.

D. That's right.

P. If they, for example, say let's cut our losses and you say we are going to go down the road to see if we can cut our losses and no more blackmail and all the rest. And then the thing blows cutting Bob and the rest to pieces. You would never recover from that, John.

D. That's right.

'Better to Fight It Out'

P. It is better to fight it out. Then you see that's the other thing. It's better to fight it out and not let people testify, and so forth. And now, on the other hand, we realize that we have these weaknesses.—that we have these weaknesses—in terms of blackmail.

D. There are two routes. One is to figure out how to cut the losses and minimize the human impact and get you up and out and away from it in any way. In a way it would never come back to haunt you. That is one general alternative. The other is to go down the road, just hunker down, fight it at every corner, every turn, don't let people testify—cover it up is what we really are talking about. Just keep it buried, and just hope that we can do it, hope that we make good decisions at the right time, keep our heads cool, we make the right moves.

P. And just take the heat?

D. And just take the heat.

P. Now with the second line of attack. You can discuss this (unintelligible) the way you want to. Still consider my scheme of having you brief the Cabinet, just in very general terms and the leaders in very general terms and maybe some very general statement with regard to my investigation. Answer questions, basically on the basis of what they told you, not what you know. Haldeman is not involved. Ehrlichman is not involved.

D. If we go that route Sir, I can give a show we can sell them just like we were selling Wheaties on our position. There's no—

P. The problem that you have are these mine fields down the road. I think the most difficult problem are the guys who are going to jail. I think you are right about that.

D. I agree.

P. Now. And also the fact that we are not going to be able to give them clemency.

D. That's right. How long will they take? How long will they sit there? I don't know. We don't know what they will be sentenced to. There's always a chance—

P. Thirty years, isn't it?

D. It could be. You know, they haven't announced yet, but it—

P. Top is 30 years, isn't it?

D. It is even higher than that. It is about 50 years. It all—

P. So ridiculous!

D. And what is so incredible is, he is (unintelligible).

P. People break and enter, etc., and get two years. No weapons! No results! What the hell are they talking about?

D. The individuals who are charged with shooting (Sen.) John Stennis are on the street. They were given, you know, one was put out on his personal recognizance rather than bond. They've got these fellows all stuck with $100,000 bonds. It's the same Judge, (John J.) Sirica, let one guy who is charged with shooting a United States Senator out on the street.

P. Sirica?

D. Yes—it is phenomenal.

P. What is the matter with him? I thought he was a hard liner.

D. He is. He is just a peculiar animal, and he set the bond for one of the others somewhere arount 50 or 60,000. But still, that guy is in. Didn't make bond, but still 60 thousand dollars as opposed to $100,000 for these guys is phenomenal.

P. When could you have this meeting with these fellows as I think time is of the essence. Could you do it this afternoon?

D. Well, Mitchell isn't here. It might be worth it to have him come down. I think that Bob and John did not want to talk to John Mitchell about this, and I don't believe they have had any conversation with him about it.

P. Well, I will get Haldeman in here now.

D. Bob and I have talked about it, just as we are talking about it this morning. I told him I thought that you should have the facts and he agrees. Of course, we have some tough problems down the road if we—(inaudible) Let me say (unintelligible) How do we handle all (unintelligible) who knew all about this in advance. Let me have some of your thoughts on that.

D. Well we can always, you know, on the other side charge them with blackmailing us. This is absurd stuff they are saying, and

P. See, the way you put it out here, letting it all hang out, it may never get there.

Haldeman Entrance

(Haldeman enters the room)

P. I was talking to John about this whole situation and he said if we can get away from the bits and pieces that have broken out. He is right in recommending that there be a meeting at the very first possible time. I realize Ehrlichman is still out in California but, what is today? Is tomorrow Thursday?

H. (unintelligible)

D. That's right.

P. He does get back. Could we do it Thursday? This meeting—you can't do it today, can you?

D. I don't think so. I was suggesting a meeting with Mitchell.

P. Mitchell, Ehrlichman, yourself and Bob, that is all. Now, Mitchell has to be there because he is seriously involved and we are trying to keep him with us. We have to see how we handle it from here on. We are in the process of having to determine which way to go, and John has thought it through as well as he can. I don't want Moore (Richard A. Moore, special presidential counsel) there on this occasion. You haven't told Moore all of this, have you?

D. Moore's got, by being with me, has more bits and pieces. I have had to give him,

P. Right.

D. Because he is making judgments—

P. The point is when you get down to the PR, once you decide it, what to do, we can let him know so forth and so on. But it is the kind of thing that I think what really has to happen is for you to sit down with those three and for you to tell them exactly what you told me.

D. Uh, huh.

P. It may take him about 35 or 40 minutes. In other words he knows, John knows, about everything and also what all the potential criminal liabilities are, whether it is—like that thing—what, about obstruction?

D. Obstruction of justice. Right.

P. So forth and so on. I think that's best. Then we have to see what the line is. Whether the line is one of continuing to run a kind of stone wall, and take the heat from that, having in mind the fact that there are vulnerable points there;—the vulnerable points being, the first vulnerable points would be obvious. That would be one of the defendents, either Hunt, because he is most vulnerable in my opinion, might blow the whistle and his price is pretty high, but at least we can buy the time on that as I pointed out to John. Apparently, who is dealing with Hunt at the moment now? Colson's—

D. Well, Mitchell's lawyer and Colson's lawyer both.

P. Who is familiar with him? At least he has to know before he is sentenced.

H. Who is Colson's lawyer? Is he in his law firm?

D. (David) Shapiro. Right. The other day he came up and—

H. Colson has told him everything, hasn't he?

D. Yep, I gather he has. The other thing that bothered me about that is that he is a chatterer. He came up to Fred (F.) Fielding, of my office, at Colson's going away party. I didn't go over there. It was the Blair House the other night. He said to Fred, he said, "well, Chuck has had some mighty serious words with his friend Howard and has had some mighty serious messages back." Now, how does he know what Fielding knows? Because Fielding knows virtually nothing.

P. Well,—

H. That is where your dangers lie, in all these stupid human errors developing.

P. Sure. The point is Bob, let's face it, the secretaries, the assistants know all of this. The principals may be as hard as a rock, but you never know when they, or some of their people may crack. But, we'll see, we'll see. Here we have the Hunt problem that ought to be handled now. Incidentally, I do not feel that Colson should sit in this meeting. Do you agree?

D. No. I would agree.

P. Ok. How then—who does sit on Colson? Because somebody has to, don't they?

D. Chuck—

P. Talks too much.

D. I like Chuck, but I don't want Chuck to know anything that I am doing, frankly.

P. Alright.

H. I think that is right. I think you want to be careful not to give Chuck any more knowledge than he's already got.

D. I wouldn't want Chuck to even know of the meeting, frankly.

P. Ok. Fortunately, with Chuck it is very—I talk to him about many, many political things, but I have never talked with him about this sort of thing. Very probably, I think he must be damn sure that I didn't know anything. And I don't. In fact, I am surprised by what you told me today. From what you said, I gathered the impression, and of course your analysis does not for sure indicate that Chuck knew that it was a bugging operation.

D. That's correct. I don't have—Chuck denies having knowledge.

P. Yet on the other side of that is that Hunt had conversations with Chuck. It may be that Hunt told Chuck that it was bugging, and so forth and so on.

D. Uh, uh, uh, uh. They were very close. They talk too much about too many things. They were intimate on this sort of—

H. That's the problem. Chuck loves (unintelligible). Chuck loves what he does and he loves to talk about it.

P. He also is a name dropper. Chuck may have gone around and talked to Hunt and said, well I was talking to the President, and the President feels we ought to get information about this, or that or the other thing, etc.

D. Well, Liddy is the same way.

P. Well, I have talked about this and that and the other thing. I have never talked to anybody, but I have talked to Chuck and John and the rest and I am sure that Chuck might have even talked to him along these lines.

H. Other than—Well, anything could have happened. I was going—

D. I would doubt that seriously.

H. I don't think he would. Chuck is a name dropper in one sense, but not in that sense. I think he very carefully keeps away from that, except when he is very intentionally bringing the President in for the President's purposes.

P. He had the impression though apparently he, as it turns out, he was the trigger man. Or he may well have been the trigger man where he just called up and said now look here Jeb go out and get that information. And Liddy and Hunt went out and got it at that time. This was February. It must have been after—

D. This was the call to Magruder from Colson saying, "fish or cut bait." Hunt and Liddy were in his office.

H. In Colson's office?

D. In Colson's office. And he called Magruder and said, "Let's fish or cut bait on this operation. Let's get it going."

H. Oh, really?

D. Yeah. This is Magruder telling me that.

H. Of course. That—now wait, Magruder testified—

D. Chuck also told me that Hunt and Liddy were in his office when he made the call.

H. Oh, ok.

D. So it was corroborated by the principal.

H. Hunt and Liddy haven't told you that, though?

D. No.

H. You haven't talked to Hunt and Liddy?

D. I talked to Liddy once right after the incident.

P. The point is this, that it is now time, though, that Mitchell has got to sit down, and know where the hell all this thing stands, too. You see, John is concerned, as you know, about the Ehrlichman situation. It worries him a great deal because, and this is why the Hunt problem is so serious, because it had nothing to do with the campaign. It has to do with the Ellsberg case. I don't know what the hell the—(unintelligible)

H. But what I was going to say—

P. What is the answer on this? How you keep it out, I don't know. You can't keep it out if Hunt talks. You see the point is irrevelant. It has gotten to this point—

'National Security Grounds'

D. You might put it on a national security grounds basis.

H. It absolutely was.

D. And say that this was—

H. (unintelligible)—CIA—

D. Ah—

H. Seriously,

P. National Security. We had to get information for national security grounds.

D. Then the question is, why didn't the CIA do it or why didn't the FBI do it?

P. Because we had to do it on a confidential basis.

H. Because we were checking them.

P. Neither could be trusted.

H. It has basically never been proven. There was reason to question their position.

P. With the bombing thing coming out and everything coming out, the whole thing was national security.

D. I think we could get by on that

P. On that one I think we should simply say this was a national security investigation that was conducted. And on that basis, I think the same in the drug field with

Krogh. Krogh could say he feels he did not perjure himself. He could say it was a national security matter. That is why—

D. That is the way Bud rests easy, because he is convinced that he was doing. He said there was treason about the country, and it could have threatened the way the war was handled and (expletive deleted)—

P. Bud should just say it was a question of national security, and I was not in a position to divulge it. Anyway, let's don't go beyond that. But I do think now there is a time when you just don't want to talk to Mitchell. But John is right. There must be a four way talk of the particular ones you can trust here. We've got to get a decision on it. It is not something—you have two ways basically. You really only have two ways to go. You either decide that the whole (expletive deleted) thing is so full of problems with potential criminal liabilities, which most concern me. I don't give a damn about the publicity. We could rock that through that if we had to let the whole damn thing hang out, and it would be a lousy story for a month. But I can take it. The point is, that I don't want any criminal liabilities. That is the thing that I am concerned about for members of the White House staff, and I would trust for members of the Committee. And that means Magruder.

D. That's right. Let's face it. I think Magruder is the major guy over there.
   I think he's got the most serious problem.

P. Yeah.

H. Well, the thing we talked about yesterday. You have a question where you cut off on this. There is a possibility of cutting it at Liddy, where you are now.

P. Yeah.

D. But to accomplish that requires a continued perjury by Magruder and requires—

P. And requires total commitment and control over all of the defendants which—in other words when they are let down—

H. But we can, because they don't know anything beyond Liddy.

D. No. On the fact that Liddy, they have hearsay.

H. But we don't know about Hunt. Maybe Hunt has that tied into Colson. We don't know that though, really.

P. I think Hunt knows a hell of a lot more.

D. I do too. Now what McCord does—

H. You think he does. I am afraid you are right, but we don't know that.

P. I think we better assume it. I think Colson—

D. He is playing hard ball. He wouldn't play hard ball unless he were pretty confident that he could cause an awful lot of grief.

H. Right.

P. He is playing hard ball with regard to Ehrlichman for example, and that sort of thing. He knows what he's got.

H. What's he planning on, money?

D. Money and—

H. Really?

P. It's about $120,000. That's what, Bob. That would be easy. It is not easy to deliver, but it easy to get. Now,

H. If the case is just that way, then the thing to do if the thing cranks out.

P. If, for example, you say look we are not going to continue to—let's say, frankly, on the assumption that if we continue to cut our losses, we are not going to win. But in the end, we are going to be bled to death. And in the end, it is all going to come out anyway. Then you get the worst of both worlds. We are going to lose, and people are going to—

H. And look like dopes!

P. And in effect, look like a cover-up. So that we can't do. Now the other line, however, if you take that line, that we are not going to continue to cut our losses, that means then we have to look square in the eye as to what the hell those losses are, and see which people can—so we can avoid criminal liability. Right?

D. Right.

P. And that means keeping it off you. Herb has started this Justice thing. We've got to keep it off Herb. You have to keep it, naturally, off of Bob, off Chapin, if possible, Strachan, right?

D. Uh, huh

P. And Mitchell. Right?

D. Uh, huh

H. And Magruder, if you can.

P. John Dean's point is that if Magruder goes down, he will pull everybody with him.

H. That's my view. Yep, I think Jeb, I don't think he wants to. And I think he even would try not to, but I don't think he is able not to.

D. I don't think he is strong enough.

'Jackasses Who Are in Jail'

P. Another way to do it then Bob, and John realizes this, is continue to try to cut our losses. Now we have to take a look at that course of action. First it is going to require approximately a million dollars to take care of the jackasses who are in jail. That can be arranged. That could be arranged. But you realize that after we are gone, and assuming we can expend this money, then they are going to crack and it would be an unseemly story. Frankly, all the people aren't going to care that much.

D. That's right.

P. People won't care, but people are going to be talking about it, there is no question. And the second thing is, we are not going to be able to deliver on any of a clemency thing. You know Colson has gone around on this clemency thing with Hunt and the rest?

D. Hunt is now talking about being out by Christmas.

H. This year?

D. This year. He was told by O'Brien, who is my conveyor of doom back and forth, that hell, he would be lucky if he were out a year from now, or after Ervin's hearings were over. He said how in the Lord's name could you be commuted that quickly? He said, "Well, that is my commitment from Colson."

H. By Christmas of this year?

D. Yeah.

H. See that, really, that is verbal evil. Colson is— That is your fatal flaw in Chuck. He is an operator in expediency, and he will pay at the time and where he is to accomplish whatever he is there to do. And that, and that's—I would believe that he has made that commitment if Hunt says he has. I would believe he is capable of saying that.

P. The only thing we could do with him would be to parole him like the (unintelligible) situation. But you couldn't buy clemency.

D. Kleindienst has now got control of the Parole Board, and he said to tell me we could pull paroles off now where we couldn't before. So—

H. Kleindienst always tells you that, but I never believe it.

P. Paroles—let the (unintelligible) worry about that. Parole, in appearance, etc., is something I think in Hunt's case, you could do Hunt, but you couldn't do the others. You understand.

D. Well, so much depends on how Sirica sentences. He can sentence in a way that makes parole even impossible.

P. He can?

D. Sure. He can do all kind of permanent sentences.

P. (unintelligible)

D. Yeah. He can be a (characterization deleted) as far as the whole thing.

H. Can't you appeal an unjust sentence as well as an unjust?

D. You have 60 days to ask the Judge to review it. There is no Appellate review of sentences.

H. There isn't?

P. The judge can review it.

H. Only the sentencing judge can review his own sentence?

P. Coming back, though, to this. So you got that hanging over. Now! If—you see, if you let it hang there, you fight with them at all or they part—The point is, your feeling is that we just can't continue to pay the blackmail of these guys?

D. I think that is our great jeopardy.

P. Now, let me tell you. We could get the money. There is no problem in that. We can't provide the clemency. Money could be provided. Mitchell could provide the way to deliver it. That could be done. See what I mean?

H. Mitchell says he can't, doesn't he?

D. Mitchell says—there has been an interesting phenomena all the way along. There have been a lot of people having to pull oars and not everybody pulls them all the same time, the same way, because they develop self-interests.

H. What John is saying, everybody smiles at Dean and says well you better get something done about it.

D. That's right.

H. Mitchell is leaving Dean hanging out on him. None of us, well, maybe we are doing the same thing to you.

D. That's right.

H. But let me say this. I don't see how there is any way that you can have the White House or anybody presently in the White House involved in trying to gin out this money.

D. We are already deeply enough in that. That is the problem, Bob.

P. I thought you said—

H. We need more money.

D. Well, in fact when—

P. Kalmbach?

D. Well, Kalmbach

H. He's not the one.

D. No, but when they ran out of that money, as you know it came out of the 350,000 that was over here.

P. And they knew that?

D. And I had to explain what it was for before I could get the money.

H. In the first place, that was put back to LaRue.

D. That's right.

H. It was put back where it belonged. It wasn't all returned in a lump sum. It was put back in pieces.

D. That's right.

P. Then LaRue used it for this other purpose?

D. That's right.

H. And the balance was all returned to LaRue, but we don't have any receipt for that. We have no way of proving it.

D. And I think that was because of self-interest over there. Mitchell—

H. Mitchell told LaRue not to take it at all.

D. That's right.

H. That is what you told me.

D. That's right. And then don't give them a receipt.

P. Then what happened? LaRue took it, and then what?

D. It was sent back to him because we just couldn't continue piecemeal giving. Every time I asked for it I had to tell Bob I needed some, or something like that, and he had to get Gordon Strachan to go up to his safe and take it out and take it over to LaRue. And it was just a forever operation.

P. Why did they take it all?

D. I just sent it along to them.

H. We had been trying to get a way to get that money back out of here anyway. And what this was supposed to be was loans. This was immediate cash needs that was going to be replenished. Mitchell was arguing that you can't take the $350,000 back until it is all replenished. Isn't that right?

D. That is right.

H. They hadn't replenished, so we just gave it all back anyway.

P. I had a feeling we could handle this one.

D. Well, first of all, I would have a hell of a time proving it. That is one thing.

P. I just have a feeling on it. Well, it sounds like a lot of money, a million dollars. Let me say that I think we could get that. I know money is hard to raise. But the point is, what we do on that—Let's look at the hard problem—

D. That has been, thus far, the most difficult problem. That is why these fellows have been on and off the reservation all the way along.

P. So the hard place is this. Your feeling at the present time is the hell with the million dollars. I would just say to these fellows I am sorry it is all off and let them talk. Alright?

D. Well,—

P. That's the way to do it isn't it, if you want to do it clean?

'What Do You Need Tomorrow?'

H. That's the way. We can live with it, because the problem with the blackmailing, that is the thing we kept raising with you when you said there was a money problem. When you said we need $20,000, or $100,000, or something. We said yeah, that is what you need today. But what do you need tomorrow or next year or five years from now?

P. How long?

D. That was just to get us through November 7th, though.

H. That's what we had to have to get through November 7th. There is no question.

D. These fellows could have sold out to the Democrats for one-half a million.

P. These fellows though, as far as what has happened up to this time, are covered on their situation, because the Cuban Committee did this for them during the election?

D. Well, yeah. We can put that together. That isn't of course quite the way it happened, but—

P. I know, but that's the way it is going to have to happen.

D. It's going to have to happen.

P. Finally, though, so you let it happen. So then they go, and so what happens? Do they go out and start blowing the whistle on everybody else? Isn't that what it really gets down to?

D. Uh, huh.

P. So that would be the clean way—Right!

D. Ah—

P. Is that—you would go so far as to recommend that?

D. No, I wouldn't. I don't think necessarily that is the cleanest way. One of the things that I think we all need to discuss is, is there some way that we can get our story before a Grand Jury, so that they can really have investigated the White House on this. I must say that I have not really thought through that alternative. We have been so busy on the other containment situation.

P. John Ehrlichman, of course, has raised the point of another Grand Jury. I just don't know how you could do it. On what basis. I could call for it, but I—

D. That would be out of the question.

P. I hate to leave with differences in view of all this stripped land. I could understand this, but I think I want another Grand Jury proceeding and we will have the White House appear before them. Is that right John?

D. Uh huh.

P. That is the point, see. Of course! That would make the difference. I want everybody in the White House called. And that gives you a reason not to have to go before the Ervin and Baker Committee. It puts it in an executive session, in a sense.

H. Right.

D. That's right.

H. And there would be some rules of evidence, aren't there?

D. There are rules of evidence.

P. Rules of evidence and you have lawyers.

H. You are in a hell of a lot better position than you are up there.

D. No, you can't have a lawyer before the Grand Jury.

P. Oh, no. That's right.

H. But you do have rules of evidence. You can refuse to talk.

D. You can take the 5th Amendment.

P. That's right.

H. You can say you have forgotten too can't you?

D. Sure but you are chancing a very high risk for perjury situation.

P. But you can say I don't remember. You can say I can't recall. I can't give you answer to that that I can recall.

H. You have the same perjury thing on the Hill don't you?

D. That's right.

P. Oh hell, yes.

H. And the Ervin Committee is a hell of a lot worse to deal with.

D. That's right.

P. The Grand Jury thing has its in view of this thing. Suppose we have a Grand Jury thing. What would that do to the Ervin Committee? Would it go right ahead?

D. Probably. Probably.

P. If we do that on a Grand Jury, we would then have a much better cause in terms of saying, "Look, this is a Grand Jury, in which the prosecutor—How about a special prosecutor? We could use Peterson, or use another one. You see he is probably suspect. Would you call in another prosecutor?

D. I would like to have Petersen on our side, if I did this thing.

P. Well, Petersen is honest. There isn't anybody about to question him is there?

D. No, but he will get a barrage when these Watergate hearings start.

P. But he can go up and say that he has been told to go further with the Grand Jury and go in to this and that and the other thing. Call everybody in the White House, and I want them to come and I want them to go to the Grand Jury.

D. This may happen without even our calling for it when these—

P. Vesco?

D. No. Well, that is one possibility. But also when these people go back before the Grand Jury here, they are going to pull all these criminal defendants back before the Grand Jury and immunize them.

P. Who will do this?

D. The U.S. Attorney's Office will.

I. To do what?

D. To let them talk about anything further they want to talk about.

I. But what do they gain out of it?

D. Nothing.

P. To hell with it!

D. They're going to stonewall it, as it now stands. Excepting Hunt. That's why his threat.

H. It's Hunt opportunity.

'Come Up With $120,000'

P. That's why for your immediate things you have no choice but to come up with the $120,000, or whatever it is. Right?

D. That's right.

P. Would you agree that that's the prime thing that you damn well better get that done?

D. Obviously he ought to be given some signal anyway.

P. (Expletive deleted), get it. In a way that—who is going to talk to him? Colson? He is the one who is supposed to know him?

D. Well, Colson doesn't have any money though. That is the thing. That's been one of the real problems. They haven't been able to raise a million dollars in cash. (unintelligible) has been just a very difficult problem as we discussed before. Mitchell has talked to Pappas, and John asked me to call him last night after our discussion and after you had met with John to see where that was. And I said, "Have you talked to Pappas?" He was at home, and Martha picked up the phone so it was all in code. I said, "Have you talked to the Greek?" And he said, "Yes, I have." I said, "Is the Greek bearing gifts?" He said, "Well, I'll call you tomorrow on that."

P. Well look, what it is you need on that? When—I am not familiar with the money situation.

D. It sounds easy to do and everyone is out there doing it and that is where our breakdown has come every time.

P. Well, if you had it, how would you get it to somebody?

D. Well, I got it to LaRue by just leaving it in mail boxes and things like that. And someone phones Hunt to come and pick it up. As I say, we are a bunch of amateurs in that business.

H. That is the thing that we thought Mitchell ought to be able to know how to find somebody who would know how to do all that sort of thing, because none of us know how to.

D. That's right. You have to wash the money. You can get a $100,000 out of a bank, and it all comes in serialized bills.

P. I understand.

D. And that means you have to go to Vegas with it or a bookmaker in New York City. I have learned all these things after the fact. I will be in great shape for the next time around.

H. (Expletive deleted)

P. Well, of course you have a surplus from the campaign. Is there any other money hanging around?

H. Well, what about the money we moved back out of here?

D. Apparently, there is some there. That might be what they can use. I don't know how much is left.

P. Kalmbach must have some.

D. Kalmbach doesn't have a cent.

P. He doesn't?

H. That $350,000 that we moved out was all that we saved. Because they were afraid to because of this. That is the trouble. We are so (adjective deleted) square that we get caught at everything.

P. Could I suggest this though: let me go back around—

H. Be careful—

P. The Grand Jury thing has a feel. Right? It says we are cooperating well with the Grand Jury.

D. Once we start down any route that involves the criminal justice system, we've got to have full appreciation that there is really no control over that. While we did an amazing job of keeping us in on the track before while the FBI was out there, and that was the only way they found out where they were going—

P. But you've got to (unintelligible) Let's take it to a Grand Jury. A new Grand Jury would call Magruder again, wouldn't it?

D. Based on what information? For example, what happens if Dean goes in and gives a story. You know, that here is the way it all came about. It was supposed to be a legitimate operation and it obviously got off the track. I heard—before, but told Haldeman that we shouldn't be involved in it. Then Magruder can be called in and questioned again about all those meetings and the like. And it again he'll begin to change his story as to what he told the Grand Jury the last time. that way, he is in a perjury situation.

H. Except that is the best leverage you've got with Jeb. He has to keep his story straight or he is in real trouble, unless they get smart and give him immunity. If they immunize Jeb, then you have an interesting problem.

D. We have control over who gets immunized. I think they wouldn't do that without our—

P. But you see the Grand Jury proceeding achieves this thing. If we go down that road—(unintelligible) We would be cooperating. We would be cooperating through a Grand Jury. Everybody would be behind us. That is the proper way to do this. It should be done in the Grand Jury, not up there under the kleig lights of the Committee. Nobody questions a Grand Jury. And then we would insist on Executive Privilege before the Committee, flat out say, "No we won't do that. It is a matter before the Grand Jury, and so on, and that's that."

H. Then you go the next step. Would we then—The Grand Jury is in executive session?

D. Yes, they are secret sessions.

H. Alright, then would we agree to release our Grand Jury transcripts?

D. We don't have the authority to do that. That is up to the Court and the Court, thus far, has not released the ones from the last Grand Jury.

P. They usually are not.

D. It would be highly unusual for a Grand Jury to come out. What usually happens is—

H. But a lot of the stuff from the Grand Jury came out.

P. Leaks.

D. It came out of the U.S. Attorney's office, more than the Grand Jury. We don't know. Some of the Grand Jurors may have blabbered, but they were—

P. Bob, it's not so bad. It's bad, but it's not the worst place.

H. I was going the other way there. I was going to say that it might be to our interest to get it out.

P. Well, we could easily do that. Leak out certain stuff. We could pretty much control that. We've got so much more control. Now, the other possibility is not to go to the Grand Jury. We have three things. (1) You just say the hell with it, we can't raise the money, sorry Hunt you can say what you want, and so on. He blows the whistle. Right?

D. Right.

P. If that happens, that raises some possibilities about some criminal liabilities, because he is likely to say a hell of a lot of things and will certainly get Magruder in on it.

D. It will get Magruder. It will start the whole FBI investigation going again.

P. Yeah. It would get Magruder, and it could possibly get Colson.

D. That's right. Could get—

P. Get Mitchell. Maybe. No.

H. Hunt can't get Mitchell.

D. I don't think Hunt can get Mitchell. Hunt's got a lot of hearsay.

P. Ehrlichman?

D. Krogh could go down in smoke. .

P. On the other hand—Krogh says it is a national security matter. Is that what he says?

D. Yeah, but that won't sell ultimately in a criminal situation. It may be mitigating on sentences but it won't, in the main matter.

P. Seems we're going around the track. You have no choice on Hunt but to try to keep—

D. Right now, we have no choice.

P. But my point is, do you ever have any choice on Hunt? That is the point. No matter what we do here now, John, whatever he wants if he doesn't get it—immunity, etc., he is going to blow the whistle.

D. What I have been trying to conceive of is how we could lay out everything we know in a way that we have told the Grand Jury or somebody else, so that if a Hunt blows, so what's new? It's already been told to a Grand Jury and they found no criminal liability and they investigated it in full. We're sorry fellow—And we don't, it doesn't—

P. (Unintelligible) for another year.

D. That's right.

P. And Hunt would get off by telling them the Ellsberg thing.

D. No Hunt would go to jail for that too—he should understand that.

P. That's a point too. I don't think I would throw that out. I don't think we need to go into everything. (adjective deleted) thing Hunt has done.

D. No.

P. Some of the things in the national security area. Yes.

H. Whoever said that anyway. We laid the groundwork for that.

P. But here is the point, John. Let's go the other angle, is to decide if you open up the Grand Jury: first, it won't be any good, it won't be believed. And then you will have two things going: the Grand Jury and the other things, committee, etc. The Grand Jury appeals to me from the standpoint, the President makes the move. All these charges being bandied about, etc., the best thing to do is that I have asked the Grand Jury to look into any further charges. All charges have been raised. That is the place to do it, and not before a Committee of the Congress. Right?

D. Yeah.

P. Then, however, we may say, (expletive deleted), we can't risk that, or she'll break loose there. That leaves you to your third thing.

D. Hunker down and fight it.

P. Hunker down and fight it and what happens? Your view is that it is not really a viable option.

D. It is a high risk. It is a very high risk.

P. Your view is that what will happen on it, that it's going to come out. That something is going to break loose, and—

D. Something is going to break and—

P. It will look like the President

D. is covering up—

P. Has covered up a huge (unintelligible)

D. That's correct.

H. But you can't (unaudible)

P. You have now moved away from the hunker down—

D. Well, I have moved to the point that we certainly have to take a harder look at the other alternative, which we haven't before.

P. The other alternative is—

D. Yes, the other choices.

'Middle Ground of Grand Jury'

P. As a matter of fact, your middle ground of Grand Jury. I suppose there is a middle ground of a public statement without a transcript.

D. What we need also, Sir

H. But John's view is if we make the public statement that we talked about this morning, the thing we talked about last night—each of us in our hotel, he says that will immediately lead to a Grand Jury.

P. Fine—alright, fine.

H. As soon as we make that statement, they will have to call a Grand Jury.

P. They may even make a public statement before the Grand Jury, in order to—

H. So it looks like we are trying to do it over.

D. Here are public statements, and we want full Grand Jury investigations by the U.S. Attorney's office.

P. If we said that the reason we had delayed this is until after the sentencing— You see that the point is that the reason time is of the essence, we can't play around on this. If they are going to sentence on Friday, we are going to have to move on the (expletive deleted) thing pretty fast. See what I mean?

D. That's right.

P. So we really have a time problem.

D. The other thing is that the Attorney General could call Sirica, and say that, "The government has some major developments that it is considering. Would you hold sentencing for two weeks?" If we set ourselves on a course of action.

P. Yep, yep.

D. See, the sentencing may be in the wrong perspective right now. I don't know for certain, but I just think there are some things that I am not at liberty to discuss with you, but I want to ask that the Court withhold two weeks sentencing.

H. So then the story is out: "Sirica delays sentencing Watergate"—

D. I think that could be handled in a way between Sirica and Kleindienst that it would not get out. Kleindienst apparently does have good rapport with Sirica. He has never talked since this case developed, but—

P. That's helpful. So Kleindienst should say that he is working on something and would like to have a week. I wouldn't take two weeks. I would take a week.

D. I will tell you the person that I feel we could use his counsel on this, because he understands the criminal process better than anybody over here does.

P. Petersen?

D. Yes, Petersen. It is awkward for Petersen. He is the head of the criminal division. But to discuss some of things with him, we may well want to remove him from the head of the Criminal Division and say, "That related to this case, you will have no relation." Give him some special assignment over here where he could sit down and say, "Yes, this is an obstruction, but it couldn't be proved," so on and so forth. We almost need him out of there to take his counsel. I don't think he would want that, but he is the most knowledgeable.

P. How could we get him out?

D. I think an appeal directly to Henry—

P. Why couldn't the President call him in as Special Counsel to the White House for the purpose of conducting an investigation. Rather than a Dean in office, having him the Special Counsel to represent us before the Grand Jury.

D. I have thought of that. That is one possibility.

H. On the basis that Dean has now become a principal, rather than a Counsel.

D. I could recommend that to you.

H. Petersen is planning to leave, anyway.

D. Is he?

P. You could recommend it and he could come over and I would say, "Now Petersen, we want you to get to the bottom of the damn thing. Call another Grand Jury or anything else. Correct? Well, now you gotta know whether Kleindienst can get Sirica to hold off. Right? Second, you have to get Mitchell down here. And you and Ehrlichman and Mitchell by tomorrow.

H. Why don't we do that tonight?

P. I don't think you can get Mitchell that soon, can you?

H. John?

P. It would be helpful if you could.

D. It would be better if he could come down this afternoon.

P. It would be very helpful to get going. Actually, I am perfectly willing to meet with the group. I don't know whether I should.

H. Do you think you want to?

P. Or maybe have Dean report to me at the end. See what conclusions you have reached. I think I need to stay away from the Mitchell subject at this point, do you agree?

D. Uh, huh.

D. Unless we see, you know, some sort of a reluctant dragon there.

H. You might meet with the rest of us, but I am not sure you would want to meet with John in this group at this time.

P. Alright. Fine. And my point is that I think it is good, frankly, to consider these various options. And then, once you decide on the right plan, you say, "John," you say, "No doubts about the right plan before the election. You handled it just right. You contained it. And now after the election we have to have another plan. Because we can't for four years have this thing eating away." We can't do it.

H. We should change that a little bit. John's point is exactly right. The erosion here now is going to you, and that is the thing that we have to turn off at whatever cost. We have to turn it off at the lowest cost we can, but at whatever cost it takes.

D. That's what we have to do.

P. Well, the erosion is inevitably going to come here, apart from anything and all the people saying well the Watergate isn't a major issue. It isn't. But it will be. It's bound to. (Unintelligible) has to go out. Delaying is the great danger to the White House area. We don't, I say that the White House can't do it. Right?

D. Yes, Sir.

Text of Nixon's April 29 Televised Watergate Speech

Following is the text, as delivered, of President Nixon's April 29 speech in which he disclosed that he would make public the voluminous transcripts of some Watergate tapes. The address was nationally televised from the White House.

Good evening.

I have asked for this time tonight in order to announce my answer to the House Judiciary Committee's subpoena for additional Watergate tapes, and to tell you something about the actions I shall be taking tomorrow—about what I hope they will mean to you, and about the very difficult choices that were presented to me.

These actions will at last, once and for all, show that what I knew and what I did with regard to the Watergate break-in and cover-up were just as I have described them to you from the very beginning.

I have spent many hours during the past few weeks thinking about what I would say to the American people if I were to reach the decision I shall announce tonight. And so, my words have not been lightly chosen; I can assure you they are deeply felt.

It was almost two years ago, in June 1972, that five men broke into the Democratic National Committee headquarters in Washington. It turned out that they were connected with my Re-election Committee, and the Watergate break-in became a major issue in the campaign.

The full resources of the FBI and the Justice Department were used to investigate the incident thoroughly. I instructed my staff and campaign aides to cooperate fully with the investigation. The FBI conducted nearly 1500 interviews. For nine months —until March 1973—I was assured by those charged with conducting and monitoring the investigations that no one in the White House was involved.

Nevertheless, for more than a year, there have been allegations and insinuations that I knew about the planning of the Watergate break-in and that I was involved in an extensive plot to cover it up. The House Judiciary Committee is now investigating these charges.

On March 6, I ordered all materials that I had previously furnished to the Special Prosecutor turned over to the committee. These included tape recordings of 19 presidential conversations and more than 700 documents from private White House files.

On April 11, the Judiciary Committee issued a subpoena for 42 additional tapes of conversations which it contended were necessary for its investigation. I agreed to respond to that subpoena by tomorrow.

In these folders that you see over here on my left, are more than 1,200 pages of transcripts of private conversations I participated in between September 15, 1972 and April 27 of 1973, with my principal aides and associates with regard to Watergate. They include all the relevant portions of all the subpoenaed conversations that were recorded—that is, all portions that relate to the question of what I knew about Watergate or the cover-up, and what I did about it.

They also include transcripts of other conversations which were not subpoenaed, but which have a significant bearing on the question of Presidential actions with regard to Watergate. These will be delivered to the committee tomorrow.

In these transcripts, portions not relevant to my knowledge or actions with regard to Watergate are not included, but everything that is relevant is included—the rough as well as the smooth, the strategy sessions, the exploration of alternatives, the weighing of human and political costs.

As far as what the President personally knew and did with regard to Watergate and the cover-up is concerned, these materials—together with those already made available—will tell it all.

I shall invite Chairman Rodino and the committee's ranking minority member, Congressman Hutchinson of Michigan, to come to the White House and listen to the actual, full tapes of these conversations, so that they can determine for themselves beyond question that the transcripts are accurate and that everything on the tapes relevant to my knowledge and my actions on Watergate is included. If there should be any disagreement over whether omitted material is relevant, I shall meet with them personally in an effort to settle the matter. I believe this arrangement is fair, and I think it is appropriate.

For many days now, I have spent many hours of my own time personally reviewing these materials, and personally deciding questions of relevancy. I believe it is appropriate that the committee's review should also be made by its own senior elected officials, and not by staff employees.

The task of Chairman Rodino and Congressman Hutchinson will be made simpler than was mine by the fact that the work of preparing the transcripts has been completed. All they will need to do is satisfy themselves of their authenticity and their completeness.

Ever since the existence of the White House taping system was first made known last summer, I have tried vigorously to guard the privacy of the tapes. I have been well aware that my effort to protect the confidentiality of Presidential conversations has heightened the sense of mystery about Watergate and in fact, has caused increased suspicions of the President. Many people assume that the tapes must incriminate the President, or that otherwise, he would not insist on their privacy.

But the problem I confronted was this: Unless a President can protect the privacy of the advice he gets, he cannot get the advice he needs.

This principle is recognized in the constitutional doctrine of Executive privilege, which has been defended and maintained by every President since Washington and which has been recognized by the courts whenever tested as inherent in the Presidency. I consider it to be my constitutional responsibility to defend this principle.

EXCEPTION TO EXECUTIVE PRIVILEGE

Three factors have now combined to persuade me that a major unprecedented exception to that principle is now necessary.

First, in the present circumstances, the House of Representatives must be able to reach an informed judgment about the President's role in Watergate.

Second, I am making a major exception to the principle of confidentiality because I believe such action is now necessary in order to restore the principle itself, by clearing the air of the central question that has brought such pressures upon it—and also to provide the evidence which will allow this matter to be brought to a prompt conclusion.

Third, in the context of the current impeachment climate, I believe all the American people, as well as their Representatives in Congress, are entitled to have not only the facts, but also the evidence that demonstrates those facts.

I want there to be no question remaining about the fact that the President has nothing to hide in this matter.

The impeachment of a President is a remedy of last resort, it is the most solemn act of our entire constitutional process. Now, regardless of whether or not it succeeded, the action of the House in voting a formal accusation requiring trial by the Senate would put the Nation through a wrenching ordeal it has endured only once in its lifetime, a century ago, and never since America has become a world power with global responsibilities.

The impact of such an ordeal would be felt throughout the world, and it would have its effect on the lives of all Americans for many years to come.

Because this is an issue that profoundly affects all the American people, in addition to turning over these transcripts to the House Judiciary Committee, I have directed that they should all be made public—all of these that you see here.

TRANSCRIPTS OF TAPES

To complete the record, I shall also release to the public transcripts of all those portions of the tapes already turned over to the Special Prosecutor and to the committee that relate to Presidential actions or knowledge of the Watergate affair.

During the past year, the wildest accusations have been given banner headlines and ready credence, as well. Rumor, gossip, innuendo, accounts from unnamed sources of what a prospective witness might testify to have filled the morning newspapers and then are repeated on the evening newscasts day after day.

Time and again, a familiar pattern repeated itself, a charge would be reported the first day as what it was—just an allegation. But it would then be referred back to the next day and thereafter as if it were true.

The distinction between fact and speculation grew blurred. Eventually, all seeped into the public consciousness as a vague general impression of massive wrongdoing, implicating everybody, gaining credibility by its endless repetition.

The basic question at issue today is whether the President personally acted improperly in the Watergate matter. Month after month of rumor, insinuation and charges by just one Watergate witness—John Dean—suggested that the President did act improperly.

This sparked the demands for an impeachment inquiry. This is the question that must be answered and this is the question that will be answered by these transcripts that I have ordered published tomorrow.

These transcripts cover hour upon hour of discussions that I held with Mr. Haldeman, John Ehrlichman, John Dean, John Mitchell, former Attorney General Kleindienst, Assistant Attorney General Petersen and others with regard to Watergate.

They were discussions in which I was probing to find out what had happened, who was responsible, what were the various degrees of responsibilities, what were the legal culpabilities, what were the political ramifications and what actions were necessary and appropriate on the part of the President.

I realize these transcripts will provide grist for many sensational stories in the press. Parts will seem to be contradictory with one another, and parts will be in conflict with some of the testimony given in the Senate Watergate committee hearings.

REASONS FOR DELAY

I have been reluctant to release these tapes not just because they will embarrass me and those with whom I have talked, which they will—not just because they will become the subject of speculation and even ridicule—which they will—and not just because certain parts of them will be seized upon by political and journalistic opponents—which they will.

I have been reluctant because in these and in all the other conversations in this office, people have spoken their minds freely, never dreaming that specific sentences or even parts of sentences would be picked out as the subjects of national attention and controversy.

I have been reluctant because the principle of confidentiality is absolutely essential to the conduct of the Presidency. In reading the raw transcripts of these conversations, I believe it will be more readily apparent why that principle is essential and must be maintained in the future. These conversations are unusual in their subject matter, but the same kind of uninhibited discussion—and it is that—the same brutal candor, is necessary in discussing how to bring warring factions to the peace table, or how to move necessary legislation through the Congress.

Names are named in these transcripts. Therefore, it is important to remember that much that appears in them is no more than hearsay or speculation, exchanged as I was trying to find out what really had happened; while my principal aides were reporting to me on rumors and reports that they had heard; while we discussed the various, often conflicting stories that different persons were telling.

As the transcripts will demonstrate, my concerns during this period cover a wide range. The first and obvious one was to find out just exactly what had happened and who was involved.

A second concern was for the people who had been, or might become, involved in Watergate. Some were close advisers, valued friends, others whom I had trusted. And I was also concerned about the human impact on others, especially some of the young people and their families who had come to Washington to work in my Administration, whose lives might be suddenly ruined by something they had done in an excess of loyalty or in a mistaken belief that it would serve the interests of the President.

And then I was quite frankly concerned about the political implications. This represented potentially a devastating blow to the Administration and to its programs, one which I knew would be exploited for all it was worth by hostile elements in the Congress as well as in the media. I wanted to do what was right, but I wanted to do it in a way that would cause the least unnecessary damage in a highly charged political atmosphere to the Administration.

And fourth, as a lawyer, I felt very strongly that I had to conduct myself in a way that would not prejudice the rights of potential defendants.

And fifth, I was striving to sort out a complex tangle, not only of facts, but also questions of legal and moral responsibilities. I wanted, above all, to be fair. I wanted to draw distinctions, where those were appropriate, between persons who were active and willing participants on the one hand, and on the other, those who might have gotten inadvertently caught up in the web and be technically indictable but morally innocent.

THE COVER-UP

Despite the confusions and contradictions, what does come through clearly is this:

John Dean charged in sworn Senate testimony that I was "fully aware of the cover-up" at the time of our first meeting on September 15, 1972. These transcripts show clearly that I first learned of it when Mr. Dean, himself, told me about it in this office on March 21—some six months later.

Incidentally, these transcripts—covering hours upon hours of conversations—should place in somewhat better perspective the controversy over the 18½ minute gap in the tape of a conversation I had with Mr. Haldeman back in June of 1972.

Now, how it was caused is still a mystery to me and I think to many of the experts, as well. But I am absolutely certain, however, of one thing: That it was not caused intentionally by my secretary, Rose Mary Woods, or any of my White House assistants. And certainly, if the theory were true that during those 18½ minutes Mr. Haldeman and I cooked up some sort of a Watergate cover-up scheme, as so many have been quick to surmise, it hardly seems likely that in all of our subsequent conversations—many of them are here—which neither of us ever expected would see the light of day, there is nothing remotely indicating such a scheme; indeed, quite the contrary.

From the beginning, I have said that in many places on the tapes there were ambiguities—statements and comments that different people with different perspectives—might interpret in drastically different ways. But although the words may be ambiguous—though the discussions may have explored many alternatives—the record of my actions is totally clear now and I still believe it was totally correct then.

A prime example is one of the most controversial discussions, that with Mr. Dean on March 21st—the one in which he first told me of the cover-up, with Mr. Haldeman joining us midway through the conversation.

His revelations to me on March 21st were a sharp surprise, even though the report he gave to me was far from complete, especially since he did not reveal at that time the extent of his own criminal involvement.

HUSH MONEY

I was particularly concerned by his report that one of the Watergate defendants, Howard Hunt, was threatening blackmail unless he and his lawyer were immediately given $120,000 for legal fees and family support, and that he was attempting to blackmail the White House, not by threatening exposure on the Watergate matter, but by threatening to reveal activities that would expose extremely sensitive, highly secret national security matters that he had worked on before Watergate.

I probed, questioned, tried to learn all Mr. Dean knew about who was involved, what was involved. I asked more than 150 questions of Mr. Dean in the course of that conversation.

He said to me, and I quote from the transcripts directly: "I can just tell from our conversation that these are things that you have no knowledge of."

It was only considerably later that I learned how much there was that he did not tell me then—for example, that he himself had authorized promises of clemency, that he had personally handled money for the Watergate defendants, and that he had suborned perjury of a witness.

I knew that I needed more facts. I knew that I needed the judgments of more people. I knew the facts about the Watergate cover-up would have to be made public, but I had to find out more about what they were before I could decide how they could best be made public.

I returned several times to the immediate problem posed by Mr. Hunt's blackmail threat, which to me was not a Watergate problem, but one which I regarded, rightly or wrongly, as a potential national security problem of very serious proportions. I considered long and hard whether it might in fact be better to let the payment go forward, at least temporarily, in the hope that this national security matter would not be exposed in the course of uncovering the Watergate cover-up.

I believed then, and I believe today, that I had a responsibility as President to consider every option—including this one —where production of sensitive national security matters was at issue, protection of such matters. In the course of considering it and of "just thinking out loud," as I put it at one point, I several times suggested that meeting Hunt's demands might be necessary.

But then I also traced through where that would lead. The money could be raised. But money demands would lead inescapably to clemency demands and clemency could not be granted. I said, and I quote directly from the tape: "It is wrong, that's for sure." I pointed out, and I quote again from the tape: "But in the end we are going to be bled to death. And in the end, it is all going to come out anyway. Then you get the worst of both worlds. We are going to lose, and people are going to—''

Then Mr. Haldeman interrupts me and says: "And look like dopes!"

And I responded, "And in effect look like a cover-up. So that we can't do."

Now I recognize that this tape of March 21 is one which different meanings could be read in by different people. But by the end of the meeting, as the tape shows, my decision was to convene a new Grand Jury and to send everyone before the Grand Jury with instructions to testify.

Whatever the potential for misinterpretation there may be as a result of the different options that were discussed at different times during the meeting, my conclusion at the end of the meeting was clear. And my actions and reactions as demonstrated on the tapes that follow that date show clearly that I did not intend the further payment to Hunt or anyone else be made. These are some of the actions that I took in the weeks that followed in my effort to find the truth, to carry out my responsibilities to enforce the law.

As the tape of our meeting on March 22, the next day, indicates, I directed Mr. Dean to go to Camp David with instructions to put together a written report. I learned five days later, on March 26, that he was unable to complete it. And so on March 27 I assigned John Ehrlichman to try to find out what had happened, who was at fault, and in what ways and to what degree.

DATA FROM TRANSCRIPTS

One of the transcripts I am making public is a call that Mr. Ehrlichman made to the Attorney General on March 28, in which he asked the Attorney General to report to me, the President, directly, any information he might find indicating possible involvement of John Mitchell or by anyone in the White House. I had Mr. Haldeman separately pursue other, independent lines of inquiry.

Throughout, I was trying to reach determinations on matters of both substance and procedure—on what the facts were, and what was the best way to move the case forward. I concluded that I wanted everyone to go before the Grand Jury and testify freely and fully. This decision, as you will recall, was publicly announced on March 30, 1973. I waived Executive privilege in order to permit everybody to testify. I specifically waived Executive privilege with regard to conversations with the President and I waived the attorney-client privilege with John Dean in order to permit him to testify fully, and I hope, truthfully.

Finally, on April 14—three weeks after I learned of the cover-up from Mr. Dean—Mr. Ehrlichman reported to me on the results of his investigation. As he acknowledged, much of what he had gathered was hearsay—but he had gathered enough to make it clear that the next step was to make his findings completely available to the Attorney General, which I instructed him to do.

And the next day, Sunday, April 15, Attorney General Kleindienst asked to see me, and he reported new information which had come to his attention on this matter. And although he was in no way whatever involved in Watergate, because of his close personal ties, not only to John Mitchell, but to other potential people who might be involved, he quite properly removed himself from the case.

We agreed that Assistant Attorney General Henry Petersen, the head of the Criminal Division, a Democrat and career prosecutor, should be placed in complete charge of the investigation.

Later that day I met with Mr. Petersen. I continued to meet with him, to talk with him, to consult with him, to offer him the full cooperation of the White House, as you will see from these transcripts, even to the point of retaining John Dean on the White House staff for an extra two weeks after he admitted his criminal involvement because Mr. Petersen thought that would make it easier for the prosecutor to get his cooperation in breaking the case if it should become necessary to grant Mr. Dean's demand for immunity.

On April 15, when I heard that one of the obstacles to breaking the case was Gordon Liddy's refusal to talk, I telephoned Mr. Petersen and directed that he should make clear not only to Mr. Liddy, but to everyone that—and now I quote directly from the tape of that telephone call—"As far as the President is concerned, everybody in this case is to talk and to tell the truth." I told him if necessary I would personally meet with Mr. Liddy's lawyer to assure him that I wanted Liddy to talk and to tell the truth.

From the time Mr. Petersen took charge, the case was solidly within the criminal justice system, pursued personally by the Nation's top professional prosecutor with the active, personal assistance of the President of the United States.

I made clear there was to be no cover-up.

Let me quote just a few lines from the transcripts—you can read them to verify them—so that you can hear for yourself the orders I was giving in this period.

Speaking to Haldeman and Ehrlichman, I said: "...It is ridiculous to talk about clemency. They all knew that."

Speaking to Ehrlichman, I said: "We all have to do the right thing.... We just cannot have this kind of a business...."

Speaking to Haldeman and Ehrlichman, I said: "The boil had to be pricked.... We have to prick the boil and take the heat. Now that's what we are doing here."

Speaking to Henry Petersen, I said: "I want you to be sure to understand that you know we are going to get to the bottom of this thing."

Speaking to John Dean, I said: "Tell the truth. That is the thing I have told everybody around here."

And then speaking to Haldeman: "And you tell Magruder, now Jeb, this evidence is coming in, you ought to go to the Grand Jury. Purge yourself if you've perjured and tell this whole story."

TAPES AS FRAGMENTARY RECORDS

I am confident that the American people will see these transcripts for what they are, fragmentary records from a time more than a year ago that now seems very distant, the records of a President and of a man suddenly being confronted and having to cope with information which, if true, would have a most far reaching consequence, not only for his personal reputation, but more important, for his hopes, his plans, his goals for the people who had elected him as their leader.

If read with an open and a fair mind, and if read together with the record of the actions I took, these transcripts will show that what I have stated from the beginning to be the truth has been the truth: That I personally had no knowledge of the break-in before it occurred, that I had no knowledge of the cover-up until I was informed of it by John Dean on March 21, that I never offered clemency for the defendants, and that after March 21 my actions were directed toward finding the facts and seeing that justice was done fairly and according to the law.

The facts are there. The conversations are there. The record of actions is there.

To anyone who reads his way through this mass of materials I have provided, it will be totally abundantly clear that as far as the President's role with regard to Watergate is concerned, the entire story is there.

As you will see, now that you also will have this mass of evidence I have provided, I have tried to cooperate with the House Judiciary Committee, and I repeat tonight the offer that I have made previously: To answer written interrogatories under oath and if there are then issues still unresolved to meet personally with the Chairman of the committee and with Congressman Hutchinson to answer their questions under oath.

As the committee conducts its inquiry, I also consider it only essential and fair that my Counsel, Mr. St. Clair, should be present to cross-examine witnesses and introduce evidence in an effort to establish the truth.

I am confident that for the overwhelming majority of those who study the evidence I shall release tomorrow—those who are willing to look at it fully, fairly and objectively—the evidence will be persuasive and I hope conclusive.

CHALLENGE AND OPPORTUNITY

We live in a time of very great challenge and great opportunity for America.

We live at a time when peace may become possible in the Middle East, for the first time in a generation.

We are at last in the process of fulfilling the hope of mankind, for a limitation on nuclear arms—a process that will continue when I meet with the Soviet leaders in Moscow in a few weeks.

We are well on the way toward building a peace that can last, not just for this, but for other generations as well.

And here at home, there is vital work to be done in moving to control inflation, to develop our energy resources, to strengthen our economy so that Americans can enjoy what they have not had since 1956: full prosperity without war and without inflation.

Every day absorbed by Watergate is a day lost from the work that must be done—by your President and by your Congress—work that must be done in dealing with the great problems that affect your prosperity, affect your security, that could affect your lives.

The materials I make public tomorrow will provide all the additional evidence needed to get Watergate behind us, and to get it behind us now.

Never before in the history of the Presidency have records that are so private been made so public.

In giving you these records—blemishes and all—I am placing my trust in the basic fairness of the American people.

I know in my own heart that through the long, painful and difficult process revealed in these transcripts, I was trying in that period to discover what was right and to do what was right.

I hope and I trust that when you have seen the evidence in its entirety, you will see the truth of that statement.

As for myself, I intend to go forward, to the best of my ability with the work that you elected me to do. I shall do so in a spirit perhaps best summed up a century ago by another President when he was being subjected to unmerciful attack. Abraham Lincoln said:

"I do the very best I know how—the very best I can; and I mean to keep doing so until the end. If the end brings me out all right, what is said against me won't amount to anything. If the end brings me out wrong, ten angels swearing I was right would make no difference."

Thank you, and good evening. √

April 30 Summary of Taped Presidential Conversations

Following is the text of the April 30 White House summary of taped presidential conversations, the edited transcripts of which were given to the House Judiciary Committee the same day:

On April 11, 1974, the Committee on the Judiciary of the House of Representatives of the Congress caused a subpoena to be issued to the President of the United States, returnable on April 25, 1974. The subpoena called for the production of tapes and other materials relating to forty-two Presidential conversations. With respect to all but three of these conversations, the subpoena called for the production of the tapes and related materials without regard to the subject matter, or matters, dealt with in these conversations. In the President's view, such a broad scale subpoena is unwarranted. As the U.S. Court of Appeals in *Nixon* vs. *Sirica* has stated, "wholesale public access to Executive deliberations and documents would cripple the Executive as a co-equal branch," and as the President has repeatedly stated, he will not participate in the destruction of the office of the Presidency of the United States by permitting unlimited access to Presidential conversations and documents.

The President, on the other hand, does recognize that the House Committee on the Judiciary has constitutional responsibilities to examine fully into his conduct and therefore the President has provided the annexed transcripts of all or portions of the subpoenaed conversations that were recorded and of a number of additional nonsubpoenaed conversations that clearly show what knowledge the President had of an alleged cover-up of the Watergate break-in and what actions he took when he was informed of the coverup. The President believes that these are the matters that primarily concern the Congress and the American people.

In order that the Committee may be satisfied that he has in fact disclosed this pertinent material to the Committee, the President has invited the Chairman and ranking minority member to review the subpoenaed tapes to satisfy themselves that a full and complete disclosure of the pertinent contents of these tapes has, indeed, been made. If, after such review they have any questions regarding his conduct, the President has stated that he stands ready to respond under oath to written interrogatories and to meet with the Chairman and ranking minority member of the Committee at the White House to discuss these matters if they so desire.

The President is making this response, which exceeds the material called for in the subpoena, in order that the Committee will be able to carry out its responsibilities and bring this matter to an expeditious conclusion.

The attached transcripts represent the best efforts accurately to transcribe the material contained on the recording tapes. Expletives have been omitted in the interest of good taste, except where necessary to depict accurately the context of the conversation. Characterization of third persons, in fairness to them, and other material not relating to the President's conduct has been omitted, except where inclusion is relevant and material as bearing on the President's conduct.

In order that the material submitted in this response to the Committee's subpoena can be viewed in the context of the events surrounding the Watergate incident and thereafter, the following summary is provided.

The Break-in at the Watergate—June 17, 1972

When the break-in at Watergate occurred and the participants were arrested, the President was in Florida. As he has stated many times, he had no prior knowledge of this activity and had nothing whatsoever to do with it. No one has stated otherwise, not even Mr. Dean, former Counsel to the President, who is the only one who has made any charges against the President. During the course of Dean's conversation with the President on February 28, 1973, the President stated to Dean:

P. Of course I am not dumb and I will never forget when I heard about this—forced entry and bugging. I thought "what is this? What is the matter with these people, are they crazy?" I thought they were nuts.

During the conversation between the President and Dean on the morning of March 21, 1973, the tape of which has also previously been provided the Committee, Dean strongly disclaimed

---

"But the way you have handled all this seems to me has been very skillful putting your fingers in the leaks that have sprung here and sprung there."

—President Nixon to John W. Dean III,
Sept. 15, 1972

---

to the President that anyone at the White House know of the break-in in advance.

D. I honestly believe that no one over here knew that. I know that as God is my maker I had no knowledge that they were going to do this.

In the conversation of the President with Mr. Haldeman and Mr. Ehrlichman on the 27th of March 1973, the following exchange, which conclusively demonstrates the President's lack of foreknowledge, took place:

H. O'Brien raised the question whether Dean actually had no knowledge of what was going on in the intelligence area between the time of the meetings in Mitchell's office, when he said don't do anything, and the time of the Watergate discovery. And I put that very question to Dean, and he said, "Absolutely nothing."

P. I would—the reason I would totally agree—that I would believe Dean there (unintelligible) he would be lying to us about that. But I would believe for another reason—that he thought it was a stupid damn idea.

E. There just isn't a scintilla of hint that Dean knew about this. Dean was pretty good all through that period of time in sharing things, and he was tracking with a number of us on—

P. Well, you know the thing the reason that (unintelligible) thought—and this incidentally covers Colson—and I don't know whether—. I know that most everybody except Bob, and perhaps you, think Colson knew all about it. But I was talking to Colson, remember exclusively about—and maybe that was the point— exclusively about issues...

             * * *

P. Right. That was what it is. But in all those talks he had plenty of opportunity. He was always coming to me with ideas, but Colson in that entire period, John, didn't mention it. I think he would have said, "Look we've gotten some information," but he never said they were. Haldeman, in this whole period, Haldeman I am sure—Bob and you, he talked to both of you about the campaign. Never a word. I mean maybe all of you knew but didn't tell me, but I can't believe that Colson—well—

Allegations of a Cover-up Prior to March 21, 1973

Of all the witnesses who have testified publicly with respect to allegations of an illegal cover-up of the Watergate break-in prior to March 21, 1973, only Mr. Dean has accused the President of participation in such a cover-up. In his testimony before the Senate Select Committee Dean stated *(Bk. 4, p. 1435)*[1] that he was "certain after the September 15 meeting that the President was fully aware of the cover-up." However, in answering questions of Senator Baker, he modified this by stating it "is an inference of mine." *(Bk. 4, p. 1475)* Later he admitted he had no personal knowledge that the President knew on September 15th about a cover-up of Watergate. *(Bk. 4, p. 1482)*

The tape of the conversation between the President and Dean on September 15, 1972, does not in any way support Dean's testimony that the President was "fully aware of the cover-up." The tape of September 15, 1972, does indeed contain a passage

---

"We have a cancer within close to the Presidency, that is growing."

—John W. Dean III, March 21, 1973

---

in which the President does congratulate Dean for doing a good job:

P. Oh well, this is a can of worms as you know a lot of this stuff that went on. And the people who worked this way are awfully embarrassed.

P. But the way you have handled all this seems to me has been very skillful putting your fingers in the leaks that have sprung here and sprung there.

This was said in the context not of a criminal plot to obstruct justice as Dean alleges, but rather in the context of the politics of the matter, such as civil suits, counter-suits, Democratic efforts to exploit Watergate as a political issue and the like. The reference to "putting your finger in the leaks" was clearly related to the handling of the political and public relations aspect of the matter. At no point was the word "contained" used as Dean insisted had been the case in his testimony. *(Bk. 4, pp. 1476, 1477)*

This is an example of the possible ambiguities that the President says exists in these tapes that someone with a motive to discredit the President could take out of context and distort to suit his own purposes.

If Dean did in fact believe that the President was aware of efforts illegally to conceal the break-in prior to March 21, 1973, it is strange that Dean on that date felt compelled to disclose to the President for the first time what he later testified the President already knew.

Further questions of Dean's credibility concerning the President's conduct are raised by his testimony before the Senate Select Committee that it was on March 13, 1973, that he told the President about money demands and threats of blackmail *(Bk. 3, pp. 995, 996)*. He said he was "very clear" about this date. *(Bk. 4, p. 1567)* It now develops that the conversation with the President, on the date of which Dean was so clear, did not in fact take place until the morning of March 21, 1973, as the President has always contended. At no point in the tape of the March 13, 1973, conference between the President and Dean is there any reference to threats of blackmail or raising a million dollars. These references are contained in the tape of the March 21, 1973, A.M. meeting between the President and Dean.

This discrepancy in Dean's testimony from the tapes of these two meetings is surprising in the light of Dean's self-professed excellent memory *(Bk. 4, p. 1433)* and the certainty with which he fixed the date of the blackmail disclosure as March 13, 1973, rather than March 21, 1973. Curiously, on April 16, 1973, as evidenced by the recording of his meeting on that morning with the

President, Dean recalled very specifically that his revelation to the President was on the Wednesday preceding the Friday (March 23) that the Watergate defendants were sentenced.

Dean's testimony to the Senate may have been simply an error, of course, or it may have been an effort to have his disclosures to the President predate what was then at least thought to be the date of the last payment to Hunt's attorney for his fees, namely March 20, 1973, *(Bk. 9, p. 3799)*. As far as the President is concerned, however, it makes no difference when this payment was made; he not only opposed the payment, but never even knew that it had been made until mid-April when the facts were finally disclosed to him.

In this connection it is interesting to note that Dean testified that on March 30, 1973, he told his attorneys "everything that I could remember." *(Bk. 3, p. 1009)* Yet Dean's list of April 14 of persons whom he believed were indictable did not include the President. *(Ex. 34-37)* Attorney General Kleindienst testified that Mr. Silbert, who had been interviewing Mr. Dean and conferring at length with his counsel, reported on the night of April 14, 1973, that "Nothing was said to me that night that would implicate the President of the United States." *(Bk. 9, p. 3586)* This same thing was confirmed by Mr. Petersen who testified that as of April 27 they had no information implicating the President. *(Bk. 9, pp. 3635, 3636)* In fact it was not until April 30, 1973, when Dean was discharged that he for the first time charged the President with knowledge of a cover-up as early as September 15, 1972.

The Meeting of March 21, 1973, A.M. Between the President and Dean and later Haldeman

On or about February 27, 1973, Dean had been instructed to report directly to the President regarding the Executive Privilege issues raised in the context of the Gray nomination hearings and the prospective Ervin Committee hearings, rather than to Ehrlichman as it was taking up too much of Mr. Ehrlichman's time from his regular duties. *(Bk. 7, p. 2739)* Previous to this Dean had been keeping himself informed as to the progress of the FBI and Department of Justice investigation on Watergate so that he could keep Ehrlichman and Haldeman informed. Both Attorney General Kleindienst and Mr. Petersen confirmed that Dean had represented to them that he was "responsible to keep the President informed." *(Bk. 9, p. 3618)*; that he "had been delegated by the President to be posted and kept informed throughout the course of the investigation." *(Bk. 9, pp. 3575, 3576, 3652)* It is equally clear from the recorded conversations between Dean and the President that he did not keep the President fully informed until March 21, 1973.[2] Indeed, on April 16, 1973, Dean so acknowledged that fact to the President, when he said:

D. I have tried all along to make sure that anything that I passed to you didn't cause you any personal problem.

An analysis of the March 21, 1973, A.M. conversation thus becomes important in assessing the conduct of the President. On the previous evening the President and Dean talked by telephone and Dean requested a meeting with the President. They met the next morning, alone, at first, and later Mr. Haldeman joined them about half way through the meeting, rather than for only the last few minutes, as Dean testified. *(Bk. 4, p. 1383)* After some preliminary remarks concerning the Gray confirmation hearings, Dean stated the real purpose for the meeting:

D. The reason that I thought we ought to talk this morning is because in our conversations *I have the impression that you don't know everything I know* and it makes it very difficult for you to make judgments that only you can make on some of these things and I thought that— (Emphasis supplied in original transcript)

He then proceeded to detail for the President what he believed the President should be made aware of, first in the "overall."

Dean stated, "We have a cancer within, close to the Presidency, that is growing" and that "people are going to start perjuring themselves..." He described the genesis of the DNC break-in; the employment of Liddy; the formulation of a series of plans by Liddy which Dean disavowed, as did Mr. Haldeman; the belief that the CREP had a lawful intelligence gathering operation and the receipt of information from this source; and the arrest at the DNC on June 17, 1972. He then informed the President of a call to Liddy shortly thereafter inquiring "...whether anybody in the White House was involved in this" and the response "No, they weren't."

Dean then advised the President of the allegation that Magruder and Porter had committed perjury before the grand jury in denying knowledge that the DNC was to be bugged. He did not tell the President he had helped "prepare" Magruder's testimony as he later admitted before the Senate Committee. *(Bk. 3, p. 1206)* Dean said he did not know what Mitchell had testified to before the grand jury.

Dean next laid out for the President what happened after June 17. He informed the President "I was under pretty clear

---

"I know, sir, I can just tell from our conversation that these are things you have no knowledge of."

—John W. Dean III to President Nixon
March 21, 1973

---

instructions not to investigate this...I worked on a theory of containment—to try to hold it right where it was," and he admitted that he was "totally aware" of what the FBI and grand jury was doing. Throughout these disclosures the President asked Dean a number of questions such as:

P. Tell me this: did Mitchell go along?
P. Did Colson know what they (Liddy and Hunt) were talking about?
P. Did he (Colson) talk with Haldeman?
P. Did he (Haldeman) know where it (the information) was coming from?

All together, the President asked Dean more than 150 questions in the course of this meeting.

Dean then described to the President the commencement of what he alleges was a cover-up involving himself and others. Implicit in these revelations, of course, is that the President was not involved but rather he was learning of these allegations for the first time. In fact, later in the conversation, Dean said:

D. I know, sir, I can just tell from our conversation that these are things *you have no knowledge of.* (Emphasis supplied in original transcript)

Dean next recited receiving a demand "from Hunt to me" through an intermediary for "$120,000 for personal expenses and attorney's fees."

D. "...he wanted it as of the close of business yesterday" (March 20).

Dean told how he rejected the demand

D. "If you want money, you came to the wrong man, fellow. I am not involved in the money. I don't know a thing about it. I can't help you. You better scramble about elsewhere."

Dean also claimed that Hunt has threatened Ehrlichman if he wasn't paid the money he demanded. Dean analyzed the situation as he saw it, pointing out that a number of people knew about these events, including Mrs. Hunt who had died in a plane crash. At the mention of Mrs. Hunt, the President interjected that this

was a "great sadness" and that he "recalled a conversation with someone about Hunt's problem on account of his wife and the President said that "of course commutation could be considered on the basis of his wife's death, and that was the only conversation I ever had in that light." During their conversations, the President repeatedly and categorically rejected the idea of clemency.

Following this lengthy description of what had transpired, the conversation dealt with what should be done about the situation presented by Hunt's demands. A number of alternatives were considered. Dean pointed out that the blackmail would continue, that it would cost a million dollars and it would be difficult to handle.

D. What really bothers me is this growing situation. As I say, it is growing because of the continued need to provide support for the Watergate people who are going to hold us up for everything we've got, and the need for some people to perjure themselves as they go down the road here. If this thing ever blows, then we are in a cover-up situation. I think it would be extremely damaging to you and the—
P. Sure. The whole concept of administration (of) justice which we cannot have.

Dean then made a recommendation: Dean was unsure of the best course to follow, but stated the approach he preferred.

D. That's right. I am coming down to what I really think, is that Bob and John and John Mitchell and I can sit down and spend a day, or however long, to figure out, one, how this can be carved away from you, so that it does not damage you or the Presidency. It just can't. You are not involved in it and it is something you shouldn't.
P. That is true!

The President then began to press Dean for his advice as to what should be done.

P. So what you really come to is what we do.... Complete disclosure isn't that the best way to do it?
D. —Well, one way to do it is—
P. —That would be my view.

Dean then suggested that another grand jury be convened but Dean points out that "some people are going to have to go to jail. That is the long and the short of it also."

Among the alternatives considered were the payment of the money generally and the payment of the amount demanded by Hunt, specifically. The mechanics of these al-

---

"I was under pretty clear instructions not to investigate this...I worked on a theory of containment—to try to hold it right where it was."

—John W. Dean III, March 21, 1973

---

ternatives, such as how the money could be raised and delivered, were explored.

The President expressed the belief that the money could be raised, and perhaps, even, a way could be found to deliver it. However, he recognized and pointed out that blackmail would continue endlessly, and in the final analysis would not be successful unless the Watergate defendants were given executive clemency, which he said adamantly, could not be done. The President stated:

P. No, it is wrong that's for sure.

After the alternatives were explored, the President's conclusion regarding the demands for money were clearly stated:

P. ...But in the end, we are going to be bled to death. And in the end, it is all going to come out anyway. Then you get the worst of both words. We are going to lose and the people are going to—

H. And look like dopes.

P. And in effect look like a cover-up. So that we can't do....

Restating it, the President said:

P. But my point is, do you ever have any choice on Hunt? That is the point. No matter what we do here now, John, whatever he wants if he doesn't get it—immunity, etc., he is going to blow the whistle.

"So what you really come to is what we do... Complete disclosure isn't that the best way to do it?...That would be my view."

—President Nixon, March 21, 1973

Finally the discussion as to what should be done was concluded by the President, at least tentatively deciding to have another grand jury investigation at which members of the White House staff would appear and testify:

P. I hate to leave with differences in view of all this stripped land. I could understand this, but I think I want another grand jury proceeding and we will have the White House appear before them. Is that right John?

D. Uh huh.

Further discussion ensued concerning the benefits of calling for a grand jury investigation—political as well as substantive—and the meeting ended with an agreement to have Dean, Mitchell, Haldeman and Ehrlichman meet the next day to consider what they would recommend. The conclusion of the meeting, however, was not ambiguous:

H. We should change that a little bit. John's point is exactly right. The erosion here now is going to you, and that is the thing that we have to run off at whatever cost. We have to turn it off at the lowest cost we can, but at whatever cost it takes.

D. That's what we have to do.

P. Well, the erosion is inevitably going to come here, apart from anything and all the people saying well the Watergate isn't a major issue. It isnt. But it will be. It's bound to. (Unintelligible) has to go out. Delaying is the great danger to the White House area. We don't, I say that the White House can't do it. Right?

D. Yes, Sir.

As the President has stated, the transcript of the meeting on the morning of March 21, 1973, contains ambiguities and statements which taken out of context could be construed to have a variety of meanings. The conversation was wide ranging, consideration was given to a number of different possibilities, but several things clearly stand out:

1. The President had not previously been aware of any payments made allegedly to purchase silence on the part of the Watergate defendants.
2. The President rejected the payment of $120,000 or any other sum to Hunt or other Watergate defendants.
3. The President determined that the best way to proceed was to have White House people appear before a grand jury even though it meant that some people might have to go to jail.

Tapes of recorded conversations following the meeting in the morning of March 21, 1973, further establish that the President not only did not approve of any payment to Hunt, but he did not even know a payment had been made to Hunt's lawyer in the amount of $75,000.

In the afternoon of the same day, March 21, 1973, the President met again with Dean, Haldeman and now Ehrlichman. This conversation makes it even more clear that the President did not suggest that blackmail should be paid to Hunt. Ehrlichman pointed out:

E. The problem of the Hunt thing or some of these other people, there is just no sign off on them. That problem goes on and on.

The President again reiterated his view:

P. Maybe we face the situation. We can't do a thing about the participants. If it is going to be that way eventually why not now? That is what you are sort of resigned to, isn't it?

And later near the end of the meeting:

P. You see, if we go your route of cutting the cancer out—if we cut it out now. Take a Hunt, well wouldn't that knock the hell out from under him?

D. That's right.

Shortly after this the President terminated the meeting, apparently rather abruptly, inquiring as to the time for the meeting the next day among Mitchell, Dean, Haldeman and Ehrlichman.

Again the recorded conversation clearly discloses that not only did the President not approve or even know of a payment made or to be made to Hunt. It is in fact quite clear that, subject to some other solution being suggested at a meeting scheduled for the next day at which Mr. Mitchell would attend, he favored "cutting the cancer out...now."

The President next met with his principal aides and now Mitchell on the afternoon of March 22, 1973. This was the first meeting of the President with John Mitchell following the disclosures of March 21, 1973. Mitchell and the others had met that morning as the President has requested. If the allegations of the grand jury as stated in pending indictments are correct as to when the arrangements for the payment of Hunt's legal fees were made, they would have had to have been made prior to this meeting on the afternoon of March 22nd. The tape recording of this meeting establishes that no one at the meeting disclosed to the President that such an arrangement had been made. In fact, the President was not informed about these arrangements until mid-April when Ehrlichman was reporting the results of his investigation to the President. In attempting to pin down what had happened, the President was given two versions, one by Ehrlichman and Haldeman on April 14 and another by John Dean on April 16.

"...But in the end, we are going to be bled to death. And in the end, it is all going to come out anyway...."

—President Nixon, March 21, 1973

Ehrlichman and Haldeman explained to the President what had transpired:

P. What happened?

E. And he just said, "It's taken care of."

H. Mitchell raised the problem to Dean and said, "What have you done about that other problem?" Dean said, he kind of looked at us, and then said, "Well, you know, I don't know." And Mitchell said, "Oh, I guess that's been taken care of." Apparently through LaRue.

P. Apparently who?

H. LaRue. Dean told us, LaRue.

On April 16 Dean described how it happened that Hunt's legal fees were paid. After repeating Hunt's threat against Ehrlichman he said:

D. ...Alright I took that to John Ehrlichman. Ehrlichman said "Have you talked to Mitchell about it?" I said "No I have not." He said Well, will you talk to Mitchell?" I said "Yes I will." I talked to Mitchell. I just passed it along to him. And then we were meeting down here a few days later in Bob's office with Bob, and Ehrlichman and Mitchell and myself, and Ehrlichman said at that time, "Well, is that problem with Hunt straightened out?" He said it to me and I said "Well, ask the man who may know; Mitchell." Mitchell said "I think that problem is solved."

P. That's all?

D. That's all he said.

If Dean's disclosure to the President on April 16, 1973, about the payment of Hunt's legal fees is to be believed, then it is clear that this fact was concealed from the President when he met with Mitchell and the others on the afternoon of March 22. The explanation for this concealment perhaps is contained in a significant statement made by Dean to the President at their meeting on the morning of April 16, 1973:

D. I have tried all along to make sure that anything I passed to you myself didn't cause you any personal problems.

This explanation for not making a full disclosure to the President may have been well intentioned at the time but in the last analysis only served to prolong the investigation.

The Conduct of the President Following the Disclosures Made on March 21, 1973

Dean disclosed for the first time on March 21, 1973, that he had been engaged in conduct that might have amounted to obstruction of justice and allegations that other high officials and former officials were also involved. These matters were thoroughly probed by the President in his talk with Dean, with the President often taking the role of devil's advocate; sometimes merely thinking out loud.

Having received this information of possible obstruction of justice having taken place following the break-in at the DNC the President promptly undertook an investigation into the facts. The record discloses that the President started his investigation the night of his meeting with Dean on March 21st, as confirmed by Dean in his conversation with the President on April 16, 1973.

P. Then it was that night that I started my investigation.

D. That's right...

P. ...That is when I frankly became interested in the case and I said, "Now I want to find out the score" and set in motion Ehrlichman, Mitchell and—not Mitchell but a few others.

At the meeting with Mitchell and the others on the afternoon of March 22nd, the President instructed Dean to prepare a written report of his earlier oral disclosures:

H. I think you (Dean) ought to hole up for the weekend and do that and get it done.

P. Sure.

H. Give it your full attention and get it done.

P. I think you need - why don't you do this? Why don't you go up to Camp David?

D. I might do it, I might do it.

D. Completely away from the phone. Just go up there and

P. (inaudible). *I want a written report.* (Emphasis supplied in original transcript)

Later during this same conversation the President said:

P. I feel that at a very minimum we've got to have this statement. Let's look at it. I don't know what it— where is it—If it opens up doors, it opens up doors—you know.

The recording of this conversation in which the President instructed Dean to go to Camp David to write a report should be compared with Dean's testimony in which he stated:

"He (the President) *never at any time* asked me to write a report, and it wasn't until after I had arrived at Camp David that I received a call from Haldeman asking me to write the report up." *(Bk. 4, p. 1385)* (Emphasis supplied in original transcript)

Dean in fact did go to Camp David and apparently did some work on such a report but he never completed the task. The President then assigned Ehrlichman to investigate these allegations.

"As the President has stated, the transcript of the meeting on the morning of March 21, 1973, contains ambiguities and statements which taken out of context could be construed to have a variety of meanings."

—White House summary, April 30, 1974

By as early as March 27, the President met with Ehrlichman and Haldeman to discuss the evidence thus far developed and how it would be best to proceed.

Again the President stated his resolve that White House officials should appear before the grand jury:

P. ...Actually if called, we are not going to refuse for anybody called before the grand jury to go, are we, John?

The President then reviewed with Haldeman and Ehrlichman the evidence developed to that time. They stated that they had not yet talked to Mitchell and indicated this would have to be done. They reviewed what they had been advised was Magruder's current position as to what had happened and compared that with what Dean had told them. They reported that Hunt was before the grand jury that same day. It is interesting to note that neither the President, Haldeman nor Ehrlichman say anything that indicate surprise in Hunt's testifying before the grand jury. If in fact he had been paid to keep quiet, it might have been expected that someone would have expressed at least disappointment that he was testifying before the grand jury less than a week later.

They confirmed to the President, as Dean had, that no one at the White House had prior knowledge of the Watergate breakin. Ehrlichman said, "There just isn't a scintilla of a hint that Dean knew about this." The President asked about the possibility of Colson having prior knowledge and Ehrlichman said, "His response was one of total surprise.... He was totally non-plussed, as the rest of us." Ehrlichman then reviewed with the President the earlier concern that they had for national security leaks and the steps taken to find out about how they occurred.

It was decided to ask Mitchell to come to Washington to receive a report of the facts developed so far and a call was placed to him for that purpose. It was also decided that Ehrlichman should also call the Attorney General and review the information on hand with him. It was during this meeting that the possibility of having a commission or a special prosecutor appointed in order to avoid the appearance of the Administration investigating itself and a call was placed to former Attorney General

Rogers to ask him to meet with the President to discuss the situation.

The next day Ehrlichman, pursuant to the President's direction given the previous day, called Attorney General Kleindienst and among other things advised him that he was to report directly to the President if any evidence turns up of any wrongdoing on the part of anyone in the White House or about Mitchell. Kleindienst raised the question of a possibility of a conflict of interest and suggests that thought be given to appointing a special prosecutor.

"We have to prick the boil and take the heat. Now that's what we're doing here...."

—President Nixon, April 14, 1973

On March 30, 1973, consideration was given to the content of a press briefing with respect to White House officials appearing before the grand jury. As a result thereof, Mr. Ziegler stated at the Press briefing that day:

> "With regard to the grand jury, the President reiterates his instructions that any member of the White House staff who is called by the grand jury will appear before the grand jury to answer questions regarding that individual's alleged knowledge or possible involvement in the Watergate matter." [3]

Even prior to the completion of Ehrlichman's investigation, the President was taking steps to get the additional facts before the grand jury. On April 8, 1973, on the airplane returning to Washington from California, the President met with Haldeman and Ehrlichman and directed they meet with Dean that day and urge him to go to the grand jury—"I am not going to wait, he is going to go." (Bk. 7, p. 2757) Haldeman and Ehrlichman met with Dean that afternoon from 5 to 7. At 7:33 Ehrlichman reported the results of that meeting to the President by telephone:

P. Oh, John, Hi.

E. I just wanted to post you on the Dean meeting. It went fine. He is going to wait until after he'd had a chance to talk with Mitchell and to pass the word to Magruder through his lawyers that he is going to appear at the grand jury. His feeling is that Liddy has pulled the plug on Magruder and that (unintelligible) he thinks he knows it now. And he says there's no love lost there, and that that was Liddy's motive in communicating informally.

Indeed, Dean did, in fact, communicate his intentions to Mitchell and Magruder not to support Magruder's previous testimony to the grand jury. (Bk. 6, p. 1006) This no doubt was the push, initially stimulated by the President, which got Magruder to go to the U.S. Attorneys on the following Saturday, April 14, and change his testimony.

On the morning of April 14, 1974, the President met again with Haldeman and Ehrlichman to discuss the Watergate matter. This was an in-depth discussion lasting more than two and one-half hours. The obvious purpose was to review the results of three week's investigation on the part of Ehrlichman and Haldeman and determine what course of action they would recommend.

Several conclusions were reached at that meeting by the President. From Ehrlichman's report on what Ehrlichman called "hearsay" facts, the President concluded, with regard to Mitchell:

P. I'm not convinced he's guilty but I am convinced that he ought to go before a grand jury.

There was a discussion as to who would be the appropriate person to talk to Mitchell and tell him that continued silence did not well serve the President. Ultimately, it was decided that Haldeman should call Mitchell to come to Washington and that Ehrlichman should talk to him.

With respect to Magruder, the President said:

P. We've come full circle on the Mitchell thing. The Mitchell thing must come first. That is something today. We've got to make this move today. If it fails, just to get back our position I think you ought to talk to Magruder.

H. I agree.

P. And you tell Magruder, now Jeb, this evidence is coming in, you ought to go to the grand jury. Purge yourself if you're perjured and tell this whole story.

H. I think we have to.

P. Then, well Bob, you don't agree with that?

H. No, I do.

The President instructed Ehrlichman to see Magruder, also, and tell him that he did not serve the President by remaining silent.

The President's decision to urge Mitchell and Magruder to go to the grand jury was based on his recognition of his duty to act on the body of information Ehrlichman had reported to him:

E. Here's the situation. Look again at the big picture. You now are possessed of a body of fact.

P. That's right.

E. And you've got to—you can't just sit there.

P. That's right.

E. You've got to act on it. You've got to make some decisions you have to make....

At another point in the discussion, the same point was reiterated:

E. Well, you see, that isn't that kind of knowledge that we had was not action knowledge like the kind of knowledge that I put together last night. I hadn't known really what had been bothering me this week.

P. Yeah.

E. But what's been bothering me is—

P. That with knowledge we're still not doing anything.

E. Right.

P. That's exactly right. The law and order—That's the way I am. You know it's a pain for me to do it—the Mitchell thing is damn painful.

A decision was reached to speak to both Mitchell and Magruder before turning such information as they had developed over to the Department of Justice in order to afford them "an opportunity to come forward." The President told Ehrlichman that when he met with Mitchell to advise him that "the President has said let the chips fall where they may. He will not furnish cover for anybody."

The President summed up the situation by stating:

P. No seriously, as I have told both of you, the boil had to be pricked. In a very different sense—that's what December 18th was about. We have to prick the boil and take the heat. Now that's what we're doing here. We're going to prick this boil and take the heat. I—am I overstating?

E. No, I think that's right. The idea is this will prick the boil. It may not. The history of this thing has to be though that you did not tuck this under the rug yesterday or today, and hope it would go away.

The decision was also made by the President that Ehrlichman should provide the information which he had collected to the Attorney General. Ehrlichman called the Attorney General, but did not reach him.

Mitchell came to Washington that afternoon and met with Ehrlichman. Immediately following that meeting, Ehrlichman reported to the President, stating Mitchell protested his innocence, stating:

"You know, these characters pulled this thing off without my knowledge...I never saw Liddy for months at a time... I didn't know what they were up to and nobody was more surprised than I was...I can't let people get away with this kind of thing...I am just going to have to defend myself every way I can."

Ehrlichman said he explained to Mitchell that the President did not want anyone to stand mute on his account; that everyone had a right to stand mute for his own reasons but that the "interests of the President...were not served by a person standing mute for that reason alone."

Ehrlichman said that he advised Mitchell that the information that had been collected would be turned over to the Attorney General and that Mitchell agreed this would be appropriate.

Even later on April 14, Ehrlichman finally was able to reach Magruder and met with Magruder and his lawyers for the purpose of informing him that he should not remain silent out of any misplaced loyalty to the President. Ehrlichman found, however, that Magruder had just come from a meeting with the U.S. Attorneys where he had told the full story as he knew it. He, Magruder, told Ehrlichman what he had told the U.S. Attorney, which Ehrlichman duly reported to the President.

During this meeting with the President, Ehrlichman's earlier call to the Attorney General was completed, and Ehrlichman spoke to the Attorney General from the President's office. Ehrlichman told the Attorney General that he had been conducting an investigation for about the past three weeks for the President as a substitute for Dean on White House and broader involvement. He also told him that he had reported his findings to the President the day before and that he had advised people not to be reticent on the President's behalf about coming forward. He informed the Attorney General that he had talked to Mitchell and had tried to reach Magruder, but that he had not been able to meet with Magruder until after Magruder had conferred with the U.S. Attorneys. He offered to make all of his information available if it would be in any way useful.

Following the telephone call Ehrlichman said that the Attorney General wanted him to meet with Henry Petersen the next day regarding the information he had obtained. During the course of the conversation relating to Magruder changing his testimony the President stated:

> **P.** It's the right thing. We all have to do the right thing. Damn it! We just cannot have this kind of business, John. Just cannot be.

Late on the evening of April 14th, after the correspondents' dinner, the President spoke by telephone first with Haldeman and then with Ehrlichman. The President told each that he now thought all persons involved should testify in public before the Ervin Committee.

On the morning of Sunday, April 15th, the President talked with Ehrlichman and told him that he had received a call from the Attorney General who had advised him that he had been up most of the night with the U.S. Attorney, and with Assistant Attorney General Petersen. The Attorney General had requested to see the President, personally, the President told Ehrlichman, and the President had agreed to see him after Church. The President and Ehrlichman again reviewed the available evidence developed during Ehrlichman's investigation and the status of relations with the media.

In the early afternoon of April 15, the President met with Attorney General Kleindienst. Kleindienst confirmed to the President that the U.S. Attorneys had broken the case and knew largely the whole story as a result of Magruder's discussions with them and from disclosures made by Dean's attorneys, who were also talking to the U.S. Attorney. The Attorney General anticipated indictments of Mitchell, Dean and Magruder and others, possibly including Haldeman and Ehrlichman. Kleindienst indicated that he felt that he could not have anything to do with these cases especially because of his association with Mitchell, Mardian and LaRue. The President expressed reservations about having a special prosecutor:

> **P.** First it's a reflection—it's sort of an admitting mea culpa for our whole system of justice. I don't want to do that...

The President then suggested that Kleindienst step aside and that the Deputy Attorney General, Dean Sneed, be placed in charge of the matter. The President expressed confidence in Silbert doing a thorough job.

Kleindienst pointed out that even if he were to withdraw, his deputy is still the President's appointee and that he would be "in a tough situation..." Kleindienst recommended that a Special Prosecutor be appointed and a number of names were suggested. The President's reaction to the idea of a Special Prosecutor was negative.

> **P.** "...I want to get some other judgments because I—I'm open on this. I lean against it and I think it's too much of a reflection on our system of justice and everything else."

Following a further review of the evidence, Kleindienst raised the question about what the President should do in the event charges are made against White House officials. The President resisted the suggestion that they be asked to step aside on the basis of charges alone.

> **P.** ...the question really is basically whether an individual, you know, can be totally, totally - I mean, the point is if a guy isn't guilty, you shouldn't let him go.
> **K.** That's right, you shouldn't.
> **P.** It's like me - wait now - let's stand up for people if there - even though they are under attack.

Further discussion on this subject included the suggestion that Assistant Attorney General Henry Petersen might be placed in charge rather than the Deputy Attorney General. Kleindienst pointed out, "He's the first career Assistant Attorney General I think in the history of the Department."

Shortly after this the tape at the President's office in the Executive Office Building ran out. It is clear, however, from a recorded telephone conversation between the President and Kleindienst that he and Henry Petersen met later in the afternoon with the President. This was verified by Mr. Petersen's testimony before the Senate Committee. It was during this meeting that the President assigned the responsibility for the on-going investigation to Mr. Petersen.

At his meeting with the President, Assistant Attorney General Petersen presented to the President a summary of the allegations which related to Haldeman, Ehrlichman and Strachan, and that the summary indicated no case of criminal conduct by Haldeman and Ehrlichman at that time. *(Bk. 9, p. 3875)*

The President, on the afternoon of April 15, 1973, had every reason to believe that the judicial process was moving rapidly to complete the case. He continued to attempt to assist. He had four telephone conversations with Petersen after their meeting. In the afternoon, having been told that Liddy would not talk unless authorized by "higher authority," who all assumed was Mitchell, the President directed Petersen to pass the word to Liddy through his counsel that the President wanted him to cooperate. Subsequently, the President told Petersen that Dean doubted Liddy would accept the word of Petersen, so Petersen was directed to tell Liddy's counsel that the President personally would confirm his urging of Liddy to cooperate. The President stated:

> **P.** I just want him (Liddy) to be sure to understand that as far as the President is concerned, everybody in this case is to talk and to tell the truth. You are to tell everybody, and you don't even have to call me on that with anybody. You just say those are your orders.

The President continued to seek additional facts and details about the whole matter. Petersen could not reveal the details of the further disclosures by Dean's attorneys, so the President sought Petersen's advice about getting further information from Dean.

P. Right. Let me ask you this - why don't I get him in now if I can find him and have a talk with him?

HP. I don't see any objection to that, Mr. President.

P. Is that all right with you?

HP. Yes, sir.

P. All right - I am going to get him over because I am not going to screw around with this thing. As I told you.

HP. All right.

P. But I want to be sure you understand, that you know we are going to get to the bottom of this thing.

HP. I think the thing that -

P. What do you want me to say to him? Ask him to tell me the whole truth?

After talking with Dean and reviewing Dean's further information, the President raised the question about when Dean and perhaps Haldeman and Ehrlichman should resign and Petersen responded, "We would like to wait, Mr. President."

On the morning of April 16, the President began a long series of meetings on the entire subject. Being uncertain of when the case would become public, the President decided he wanted resignations or requests for leave in hand from those against whom there were allegations. He had Ehrlichman draft such letters, and discussed them with Haldeman and Ehrlichman.

The President then met with Dean and discussed with him the manner in which his possible resignation would be handled. Dean resisted the idea of his resigning without Haldeman and Ehrlichman resigning as well. The President reviewed with Dean the disclosures Dean made to the President on March 21st, and on the evening of April 15th.

The President had some more advice for John Dean on this occasion:

P. Thank God. Don't ever do it, John. Tell the truth. That is the thing I have told everybody around here - tell the truth! All they do, John, is compound it. That Hiss would be free today if he hadn't lied. If he had said, "Yes I knew Chambers and as a young man I was involved with some Communist activities but I broke it off a number of years ago." And Chambers would have dropped it. If you are going to lie, you go to jail for the lie rather than the crime. So believe me, don't ever lie."

As to the President's actions, he told Dean:

P. No, I don't want, understand when I say don't lie. Don't lie about me either.

D. No, I won't sir - you -

The President met with Haldeman at noon on April 16th to discuss at length how and when Haldeman should make a public disclosure of his actions in the Segretti and Watergate matters. Haldeman reported that Mr. Garment recommended that he and Ehrlichman resign. Garment had been assigned by the President on April 9 to work on the matter. The President stated that he would discuss that problem with William Rogers that afternoon and asked Haldeman to get with Ehrlichman and fill in Rogers on the facts.

The President met in the early afternoon alone with Henry Petersen for nearly two hours in the Executive Office Building. They discussed the effect the Senate Committee hearings would have on the trials in the event indictments are returned.

The President then asked Petersen what he should do about Dean's resignation.

HP. Yes. As Prosecutor I would do something different but from your point of view I don't think you can sit on it. I think we have the information under control but that's a dangerous thing to say in this City.

P. Ah

HP. And if this information comes out I think you should have his resignation and it should be effective...

Petersen, however, urged the President not to announce the resignation if the information did not get out, as that would be "counter-productive" in their negotiations with Dean's counsel.

Petersen reviewed the status of the evidence at length with the President with a view toward making a press release before an indictment or information was filed in open Court.

During the course of the conversation Petersen informed the President that they were considering giving Dean immunity. As for Haldeman and Ehrlichman, Petersen recommended that they resign. The status of the situation was reviewed as follows:

P. Okay. All right come to the Haldeman/Ehrlichman thing. You see you said yesterday they should resign. Let me tell you they should resign in my view if they get splashed with this. Now the point is, is the timing. I think that it's, I want to get your advice on it, I think it would be really hanging the guy before something comes in if I say look, you guys resign because I understand that Mr. Dean in the one instance, and Magruder in another instance, made some charges against you. And I got their oral resignations last night and they volunteered it. They said, look, we want to go any time. So I just want your advice on it. I don't know what to do, frankly. (Inaudible) so I guess there's nothing in a hurry about that is there? I mean I—Dean's resignation. I have talked, to him about it this morning and told him to write it out.

HP. (Inaudible).

P. It's under way—I asked for it. How about Haldeman and Ehrlichman? I just wonder if you have them walk the plank before Magruder splashes and what have you or what not. I mean I have information, true, as to what Magruder's going to do. (Inaudible) nothing like this (inaudible).

HP. Or for that matter, Mr. President.

P. Yeah.

HP. Its confidence in the Office of the Presidency.

P. Right. You wouldn't want—do you think they ought to resign right now?

HP. Mr. President, I am sorry to say it. I think that mindful of the need for confidence in your office—yes.

P. (Inaudible) basis?

HP. That has nothing to do—that has nothing to do with guilt or innocence.

At the end of the meeting with Petersen, the President had every reason to believe that a public disclosure of the entire case in court would be made within forty-eight hours and perhaps

---

"Thank God. Don't ever do it, John. Tell the truth. That is the thing I have told everybody around here— tell the truth!"

—President Nixon to John Dean, April 16, 1973

---

sooner. The remaining questions for Presidential decision were: (1) What action he should take on the resignation, suspension or leave of Haldeman, Ehrlichman and Dean and whether it should be before or after they were formally charged; (2) what position he should take on immunity for Dean; and (3) what statement he should issue prior to the public disclosure in court.

On the afternoon of April 17, the President discussed the problem of granting immunity to White House officials with Henry Petersen. Petersen pointed out that he was opposed to immunity but he pointed out that they might need Dean's testimony in order to get Haldeman and Ehrlichman. The President agreed that under those circumstances he might have to move on

Haldeman and Ehrlichman, provided Dean's testimony was corroborated. The President told Petersen:

> P. That's the point. Well, I feel it strongly - I mean - just understand - I am not trying to protect anybody - I just want the damn facts if you can get the facts from Dean and I don't care whether -
> HP. Mr. President, if I thought you were trying to protect somebody, I would have walked out.

As for Dean, the President told Petersen:

> P. "...No I am not going to condemn Dean until he has a chance to present himself. No he is in exactly the same position they are in."

The President remained convinced, however, that a grant of immunity to a senior aide would appear as a cover-up.

> P. What you say - Look we are having you here as a witness and we want you to talk.
> HP. That is described as immunity by estoppel.
> P. I see, I see - that's fair enough.
> HP. That is really the prosecutor's bargain.
> P. That is much better basically than immunity - let me say I am not, I guess my point on Dean is a matter of principle - it is a question of the fact that I am not trying to do Dean in - I would like to see him save himself but

---

"In all of the thousands of words spoken, even though they often are unclear and ambiguous, not once does it appear that the President of the United States was engaged in a criminal plot to obstruct justice."

—White House summary, April 30, 1974

I think find a way to do it without—if you go the immunity route I think we are going to catch holy hell for it.

> HP. Scares hell out of me.

The President went over the draft of his proposed statement with Petersen. Petersen further counseled the President that no discussion of the facts of the case could be made without prejudicing the case and the rights of the defendants.

Later on the afternoon of April 17, the President issued his statement, revealing that he had new facts and had begun his own investigation on March 21; that White House staff members who were indicted would be suspended, and if they were convicted, they would be discharged. He announced that all members of the White House staff would appear and testify before the Senate Committee. The President further stated that:

> I have expressed to the appropriate authorities my view that no individual holding, in the past or present, a position of major importance in the Administration should be given immunity from prosecution.

In addition he stated that all White House staff employees were expected fully to cooperate in this matter.

After making his public statement, the President met with Secretary of State Rogers, and they were joined later by Haldeman and Ehrlichman. Secretary Rogers reiterated his advice that the President could not permit any senior official to be given immunity. He also reiterated his advice that for the President to discharge his senior aides before they were formally charged with a crime would highly prejudice their legal rights and convict them without a trial.

The President had concluded that he should treat Dean, Haldeman and Ehrlichman in the same manner. Petersen had advised the President that action on Dean would prejudice the

negotiations of the U.S. Attorneys with Dean's lawyers, and that Dean's testimony might be needed for the case.

On the evening of April 19, the President met with Messrs. Wilson and Strickler, counsel retained by Haldeman and Ehrlichman upon recommendation of Secretary Rogers. Wilson and Strickler made strong arguments that Haldeman and Ehrlichman had no criminal liability and should not be discharged.

The President continued to struggle with the question of administrative action against his aides.

On April 27, Petersen reported to the President that Dean's lawyer was threatening that unless Dean got immunity, "We will bring the President in - not in this case but in other things."

On the question of immunity in the face of these threats, the President told Petersen:

> P. All right. We have got the immunity problem resolved. Do it, Dean if you need to, but boy I am telling you - there ain't going to be any blackmail.

On April 27, the President was also advised by Petersen that the negotiations with Dean's attorneys had bogged down, and action by the President against Dean, Haldeman and Ehrlichman would now be helpful to the U.S. Attorney.

Three days later, on April 30, the President gave a nationwide address. He announced that he accepted the resignations of Haldeman, Ehrlichman, Attorney General Kleindienst and Dean. The President then announced the nomination of Elliot Richardson as the new Attorney General.

Conclusion

Throughout the period of the Watergate affair the raw material of these recorded confidential conversations establishes that the President had no prior knowledge of the break-in and that he had no knowledge of any cover-up prior to March 21, 1973. In all of the thousands of words spoken, even though they often are unclear and ambiguous, not once does it appear that the President of the United States was engaged in a criminal plot to obstruct justice.

On March 21, 1973, when the President learned for the first time of allegations of such a plot and an alleged attempt to blackmail the White House, he sought to find out the facts first from John Dean then others. When it appeared as a result of these investigations that there was reason to believe that there may have been some wrongdoing he conferred with the Attorney General and with the Assistant in charge of the criminal division of the Department of Justice and cooperated fully to bring the matter expeditiously before the grand jury.

Ultimately Dean has plead guilty to a felony and seven former White House officials stand indicted. Their innocence or guilt will be determined in a court of law.

This is as it should be.

The recent acquittals of former Secretary Stans and former Attorney General Mitchell in the Vesco case demonstrate the wisdom of the President's actions in insisting that the orderly process of the judicial system be utilized to determine the guilt or innocence of individuals charged with crime, rather than participating in trials in the public media.

---

1 *References to testimony before the Senate Select Committee are indicated. "(Bk.—, p.—)."*

2 *Apparently Dean even on March 21, 1973, concealed other matters from the President as well. In U.S. v. Stans, et al., he testified that despite the fact that he had made calls to the SEC, he told the President "no one at the White House has done anything for Vesco." Of course the statement to the President was not true if Dean did make such calls for he certainly was at the White House.*

Among the other significant matters which Dean did not report to the President, even on March 21, 1973, were (1) that Dean had assisted Magruder in preparing his perjured Grand Jury testimony; (2) that Dean had authorized promises of executive clemency to be made to Watergate defendants; (3) that he had personally handled money which went to the Watergate defendants; (4) that he had delivered documents from Hunt's safe to F.B.I. Director Gray; (5) that Dean had personally destroyed documents from Hunt's safe; or (6) that Dean had ordered Hunt out of the country, and then retracted the order.

Directory of Persons Mentioned in Transcripts

Allen, Robert H.
President, Gulf Resources & Chemical Corp., Houston

Bailey, F. Lee
Law partner of McCord's attorney Gerald Alch

Baker, Sen. Howard H. Jr. (R Tenn.)
Ranking Republican, Senate Watergate committee

Barker, Bernard L.
Convicted Watergate break-in conspirator

Baroody, William J. Jr.
Special assistant to President

Bayh, Sen. Birch (D Ind.)

Bennett, Robert G.
President of Robert R. Mullen & Co., political consulting firm that employed E. Howard Hunt briefly after he resigned from the C.I.A. in 1970; Washington representative of billionaire Howard Hughes; son of Sen. Wallace F. Bennett (R Utah)

Bennett, Sen. Wallace F. (R Utah)

Berrigan, Rev. Daniel J. and Rev. Philip F.
Antiwar activists.

Bittman, William D.
Hunt's attorney

Buchanan, Patrick J.
Special consultant to the President; White House speechwriter.

Byrd, Sen. Robert C. (D W.Va.)

Campbell, Donald E.
Assistant U.S. Attorney for the District of Columbia; a prosecutor at Watergate break-in trial.

Caulfield, John J.
Retired New York police detective; former White House aide who did undercover work for Ehrlichman and Dean; former Committee for the Re-election of the President employee; former consultant at the Treasury Department's Bureau of Alcohol, Tobacco & Firearms

Chapin, Dwight L.
Former Nixon appointments secretary (1969 - Feb. 1973)

Colson, Charles W.
Former special counsel to the President (Nov. 1969 - March 1973)

Connally, John B. Jr.
Former Texas Governor (1962-68); former Nixon Treasury Secretary (1971 - May 1972); former special Nixon adviser on domestic and foreign matters (May - June 1973)

Cook, Richard K.
Former White House lobbyist (1969 - 1973)

DeLoach, Cartha D.
Former assistant FBI director under Hoover

De Marco, Frank Jr.
Kalmbach's law partner; Nixon's tax lawyer

Duncan, Walter T.
Texas businessman whose 1972 contribution to Nixon was returned for Duncan's private financial reasons

Eastland, James O. (D Miss.)
Chairman, Senate Judiciary Committee

Ellsberg, Daniel
Pentagon Papers defendant

Ervin, Sam J. Jr. (D N.C.)
Chairman, Senate Watergate Committee

Felt, W. Mark
Former deputy associate FBI director under Hoover and Gray

Fielding, Fred F.
Former Dean assistant

Ford, Gerald R.
Former House Minority Leader (1965-1973); Vice-President

Fortas, Abe
Former U.S. Supreme Court justice (1965 - 1969)

Glanzer, Seymour
Assistant U.S. Attorney for the District of Columbia; a prosecutor at Watergate break-in trial

Goldblatt, ——
Probably a mistake for Rothblatt, Henry B. *(see below)*

Goldwater, Sen. Barry (R Ariz.)

Gray, L. Patrick III
Former acting FBI director (Feb. - April, 1973)

Greenspun, Hank
Publisher, *Las Vegas Sun*

Gurney, Sen. Edward J. (R Fla.)
Member, Senate Watergate Committee

Harlow, Bryce
Former White House congressional liaison chief 1973-April 1974); Washington representative for Proctor and Gamble Corp.

Harris, Patricia Roberts
Attorney, member of 1972 Democratic Convention credentials committee

Heckler, Rep. Margaret A. (R Mass.)

Hersh, Seymour M.
New York Times reporter

Higby, Lawrence M.
Former Haldeman assistant

Hoback, Mrs. Judy
Former secretary to Hugh Sloan at Committee for the Re-election of the President

Hoover, J. Edgar
Former FBI Director (1924 - 1972)

Hruska, Sen. Roman L. (R Neb.)

Hughes, Howard R.
Billionaire industrialist

Humphrey, Sen. Hubert H. (D Minn.)
Nixon's opponent in 1968 presidential election

Hunt, E. Howard Jr.
Former CIA agent; former White House consultant; convicted Watergate conspirator

Hunt, Mrs. Dorothy
E. Howard's deceased wife

Huston, Tom Charles
Former White House aide who drafted 1970 intelligence-gathering plan

Jackson, Sen. Henry M. (D Wash.)

Jenkins, Walter W.
Aide to former President Lyndon B. Johnson, who resigned after being arrested on a morals charge

Johnson, Haynes
Washington Post reporter

Kalmbach, Herbert W.
Nixon's former personal attorney

Kleindienst, Richard G.
Former Attorney General (1972-1973)

Krogh, Egil (Bud) Jr.
Former Ehrlichman assistant

LaRue, Frederick C.
Former White House aide; former assistant to Mitchell at Committee for the Re-election of the President

Liddy, G. Gordon
Former White House aide; former counsel to Committee for the Re-election of the President; former staff member of 1972 Nixon Finance Committee; convicted Watergate conspirator

MacGregor, Clark
Former Minnesota Republican Representative who became chairman of the Committee for the Re-election of the President when Mitchell resigned the post on July 1, 1972

Magruder, Jeb Stuart
Former deputy director of the Committee for the Re-election of the President

Manson, Charles M.
Convicted mass murderer

Mardian, Robert C.
Former assistant Attorney General under Mitchell, former deputy manager of Committee for the Re-election of the President.

McCord, James W. Jr.
Former security director for Committee for the Re-election of the President; convicted Watergate conspirator

McPhee, Henry Roemer
Former general counsel, Republican National Finance Committee

Mitchell, John N.
Former Attorney General (1969 - 1972); former Committee for the Re-election of the President director (March 1 - July 1, 1972)

Mollenhoff, Clark
Former White House aide (1969 - 1970); Washington bureau chief for the *Des Moines Register & Tribune*

Moore, Richard A.
Special counsel to the President

Muskie, Sen. Edmund S. (D Maine)
1972 presidential contender

Nixon, Donald Jr.
Nixon's nephew, aide to Vesco

O'Brien, Lawrence F.
Democratic National Committee chairman during 1972 election.

O'Brien, Paul L.
Former Committee for the Re-election of the President attorney

Packwood, Sen. Robert W. (R Ore.)

Pappas, Thomas A.
Massachusetts millionaire

Patman, Rep. Wright (D Texas)
Chairman, House Banking and Currency Committee

Petersen, Henry E.
Assistant Attorney General; head of original Justice Department Watergate inquiry

Porter, Herbert L. (Bart)
Former scheduling director, Committee for the Re-election of the President

Richey, Judge Charles R.
U.S. District Court judge for the District of Columbia

Rietz, Kenneth S.
Head of 1972 Nixon youth campaign

Rogers, William P.
Former Secretary of State (1969 - 1973)

Rothblatt, Henry B.
Attorney for convicted Watergate conspirators Barker, Sturgis, Gonzalez, Martinez

Ruckelshaus, William D.
Former Environmental Protection Agency administrator; former deputy Attorney General

Segretti, Donald H.
Former Treasury Department attorney; convicted of political sabotage against Democrats in 1972 election

Shaffer, Charles N.
Dean's attorney

Shapiro, David
Colson's law partner

Silbert, Earl J.
Principal Assistant U.S. Attorney for the District of Columbia; chief prosecutor at original Watergate trial

Stennis, Sen. John C. (D Miss.)

Strachan, Gordon C.
Former assistant to Haldeman

Sirica, Judge John J.
Former chief judge, U.S. District Court for the District of Columbia; U.S. District judge

Sloan, Hugh W. Jr.
Former treasurer, 1972 Nixon finance committee

Stans, Maurice H.
Former Secretary of Commerce (1969 - Jan. 1973); former chairman of 1972 Nixon finance committee

Sullivan, William C.
Former FBI associate director under Hoover

Titus, Harold H. Jr.
Former U.S. attorney, District of Columbia

Tuck, Richard (Dick)
Democratic political consultant

Ulasewicz, Anthony T. (Tony)
Former aide to John J. Caulfield

Vesco, Robert L.
Fugitive financier residing in Costa Rica; indicted along with Mitchell and Stans for attempting to influence a Security and Exchange Commission investigation

Wallace, Gov. George C. (D)
Alabama Governor

Walters, Johnnie M.
Former I.R.S. commissioner (1971 - 1973)

Weicker, Sen. Lowell P. (R Conn.)
Member, Senate Watergate committee

Widnall, Rep. William B. (R N.J.)

Williams, Edward Bennett
Attorney who represented Democratic National Committee in Watergate break-in civil suit

Wilson, Jerry V.
D.C. chief of police

Wilson, John J.
Attorney for Haldeman and Ehrlichman during 1973 Senate Watergate hearings

Woodward, Bob
Washington Post reporter

Ziegler, Ronald L.
White House press secretary

INDEX

CQ

INDEX